ARKANSAS WATERFALLS

THIRD EDITION

BY TIM ERNST

WATERFALL INDEX IS ON PAGE 480

.

There are thousands of waterfalls in Arkansas—no one will ever see them all. I've included more than 400 here for you to explore and enjoy, including a couple hundred new ones not in my previous guidebooks.

THANK YOU for using this guidebook!

TIM ERNST PHOTOGRAPHY AND PUBLISHING

JASPER, ARKANSAS

www.TimErnst.com

The photo on the front cover is of Balanced Rock Falls (see page 69 for info).

First edition, 2002; Color edition, 2003, 2006, 2008
Second edition, 2011, 2014, 2019
Third edition, 2025

Printed in the USA!

ISBN: 9781882906741

Book designed by Tim Ernst, maps drawn by Pam Ernst

Other publications by Tim Ernst
Arkansas Nature Lover's guidebook
Arkansas Hiking Trails guidebook
Buffalo River Hiking Trails guidebook
Ozark Highlands Trail guidebook
Ouachita Trail guidebook
Arkansas Dayhikes For Kids guidebook
Arkansas Greatest Hits picture book (2020)
Arkansas Splendor picture book (2019)
Arkansas Beauty picture book (2017)
Arkansas In My Own Backyard picture book (2016)
A Rare Quality Of Light picture book (2015)
Arkansas Nightscapes picture book (2014)
Buffalo River Beauty picture book (2013)
Arkansas Landscapes II picture book (2012)
Arkansas Portfolio III picture book (2011)
Arkansas Autumn picture book (2010)
Arkansas Wildlife picture book (2009)
Arkansas Landscapes picture book (2008)
Arkansas Waterfalls picture book (2007)
Buffalo River Dreams picture book (2006)
Arkansas Portfolio II picture book (2004)
Arkansas Wilderness picture book (2002)
Arkansas Spring picture book (2000)
Buffalo River Wilderness picture book (1998)
Wilderness Reflections picture book (1996)
Arkansas Portfolio picture book (1994)

The Search For Haley
Cloudland Journal ~ Book One

www.TimErnst.com

WARNING:

Visiting waterfalls may be hazardous to your health!

By their very nature and location, waterfalls can be dangerous to be around. There are many hazards that can cause accidents, resulting in serious injury or death. It is not the intent of this guidebook—nor any of the directions or recommendations presented here—that when followed will assure safe passage to or from any waterfall. Many of the descriptions suggest backcountry routes over rugged and dangerous terrain, where there are no trails—significant experience with travel under these conditions is suggested.

It is understood that if you pick up and read this guidebook and use the information contained within to venture out into the wilderness to visit these waterfalls, that you do so at your own risk, with full knowledge of your own limitations, and that no matter what you do, there is a possibility of serious injury or death, and that you accept and are responsible for your own actions and safety. The author, publisher, and any re-seller cannot and do not accept any liability resulting from the material in this book. If you do not agree with any of the above, please return this book to the shelf and stay home!

If you want to take your KIDS with you to visit these waterfalls, please choose which ones you visit wisely—the high bluffs around waterfalls require that you *pay close attention to your children at all times* and *hold onto them*. It is up to the parents to decide which waterfalls are suitable. Some waterfalls may be more kid-friendly than others—but it is recommended that parents visit each waterfall first to decide for themselves. We want our youth to experience the great natural beauty that is around us, but we also want to keep them alive—they are the future of the world!

Introduction

WATERFALL RESOURCES Social media is the best place to find volumes of info about waterfalls these days (except, of course, in THIS guidebook!). Web pages and groups come and go but a simple internet search should yield lots of current info. I'm not affiliated with any sites other than my own, BUT I do have a web page where you can find the most current and up-to-date info about the *this* guidebook, and I plan to add additional info as needed, including corrections, closures, and news. You are welcome to report any changes or updates you find, and those will be added. Visit:

www.TimErnst.com/guidebookupdates.html

• **Rick Henry's blog** with descriptive hikes and data for hundreds of waterfalls may still be online: **henry411.blogspot.com**
• **Danny Hale** has many guidebooks with tons of waterfalls included: **TAKAHIK.com**
• **ArkansasWaterfalls.com** is a new-age waterfall resource worth checking out.
• **Richland Waterfalls Welcome Center**, Witts Springs, with displays and info for 30 waterfalls in the surrounding Searcy County area. Located a few miles east of the Falling Water Road area on Hwy. 16.

DIFFICULTY RATINGS are RELATIVE to your personal fitness level, the weather, your mood (happy or sad), trail conditions, other people with you, and especially how FAST you are trying to go. An easy trail can be difficult for some, a difficult trail easy for others. It just all depends. If it's difficult, slow down.

Easy Hike—short distance over generally level terrain following an established trail or road that most everyone should be able to do. **Easy+** means it's a little harder or longer than usual.

Medium Hike—longer distances of two or three miles up to eight or ten miles over varying terrain on established trails or roads. Most folks with hiking experience should be able to make these trips, although weaker hikers may have a tougher time.

Difficult Hike—longer distances of eight to ten miles or more over rough terrain but still following an established trail or road. Best suited for more physically fit folks.

Easy Bushwhack—short distance through the woods over easy terrain, no trail or road to follow. Most hikers should be able to make these trips as long as you are careful and watch where you are going, and how to get back!

Medium Bushwhack—longer distances of several miles or more over moderate terrain with some steep sections here and there, no trail or roads to follow. Experienced hikers who want a challenge can make these trips, but you need to be in good physical condition and have plenty of time, also be able to read a map well and/or use your GPS.

Difficult Bushwhack—longer distances of several miles or more over varying terrain that includes steep slopes, boulder scrambling, and fighting through thick brush. Only those with a great deal of experience in backcountry travel off trails, who are in top physical condition and prepared for the rigors of serious bushwhacking should attempt these trips. A GPS/APP is highly recommended, as well as a thorough knowledge of how to use it and read maps. You should also probably leave an updated will at home just in case.

Black Diamond Slope ♦—this is an extremely steep slope that often times you are unable to stand up on without hanging onto something—almost a vertical bluff, but still terra firma (dirt) to dig your heels into. I much prefer to claw my way UP these slopes rather than slide down them—which I frequently do on my behind for safety. Most people will find a ♦ slope too difficult to manage, so only the most experienced and able hikers should attempt these. Unfortunately, there are a lot of hikes in this guidebook that area generally only medium difficulty with just one or two sections of ♦ slopes.

WATERFALL NAMES Most waterfalls do not have official names—literally only a handful in all of Arkansas are "officially" recognized by the U.S. Geological Survey. Any other waterfalls on public property that have names listed are simply reference markers we use to help identity one from another. I try to use names that are historical, geographical, educational, honoring a particular person, or maybe just plain FUN. Feel free to name any waterfall you like—there are still thousands out there with no reference names at all.

WATERFALL HEIGHT Almost all of the waterfalls in this guidebook have been measured by myself, or by my able assistant, Fireman Jeff Davis (Norma Senyard measured a couple we were unable to reach without ropes). The first few hundred of them we used a 250' rolled measuring tape. In recent years I've been using a special digital laser rangefinder that uses trigonometry to calculate a very accurate height measurement (wish I had this last century when I started all this!!!). Note that heights will vary with water flow amounts, where the measurement is taken, and a lot of other variables.

GPS units and phone APPS have gotten a lot better and I've included more data points then in the past. All are listed in digital decimal degrees (these can be read by most any device and automatically translated into whatever spec you prefer). NOTE that traveling distance is also quite accurate, but *NOT when you STOP*, even for a moment—the GPS signal will keep going and adding distance even though you may have just stopped for a few minutes to water the flowers.

RECORDED HIKE DISTANCES will vary greatly depending on many factors, but I have included my personal data as a general reference—as they say, your mileage may vary! (and it will *always take you longer* than you think)

PARKING AREAS Many of the new waterfalls in this guidebook do not have trails to follow or trailheads for parking. I have included GPS coordinates as a reference where to PARK—until and unless an open spot eventually develops many of these will just be "park along the road where you can." I drive a soccer-mom Toyota van with low clearance. so my parking spots should be OK for most normal vehicles. If you have an SUV/jeep/etc. in many cases you will be able to drive a lot closer to the waterfalls.

ROADS Many roads have multiple names and numbers, and those often change. (one road I know now has SIX different numbers!!!) I've tried to list the current info that's available, but as always, it is best to ZERO your odometer and follow the mileage distances provided.

DOGS Well-behaved dogs on leashes are welcome on many hiking trails and other outdoor areas. The main exception is that currently the Buffalo National River park only allows dogs along the river corridor, in campgrounds, and on just a couple of hiking trails, and only one of those has waterfalls (page 74). Fortunately, there are LOTS of great waterfall trips on trails near the park, mostly in the Ozark National Forest, where dogs are generally welcome. Each waterfall map lists the agency who owns the land and you need to know where you are if you plan to hike with your pup. See emergency contact info.

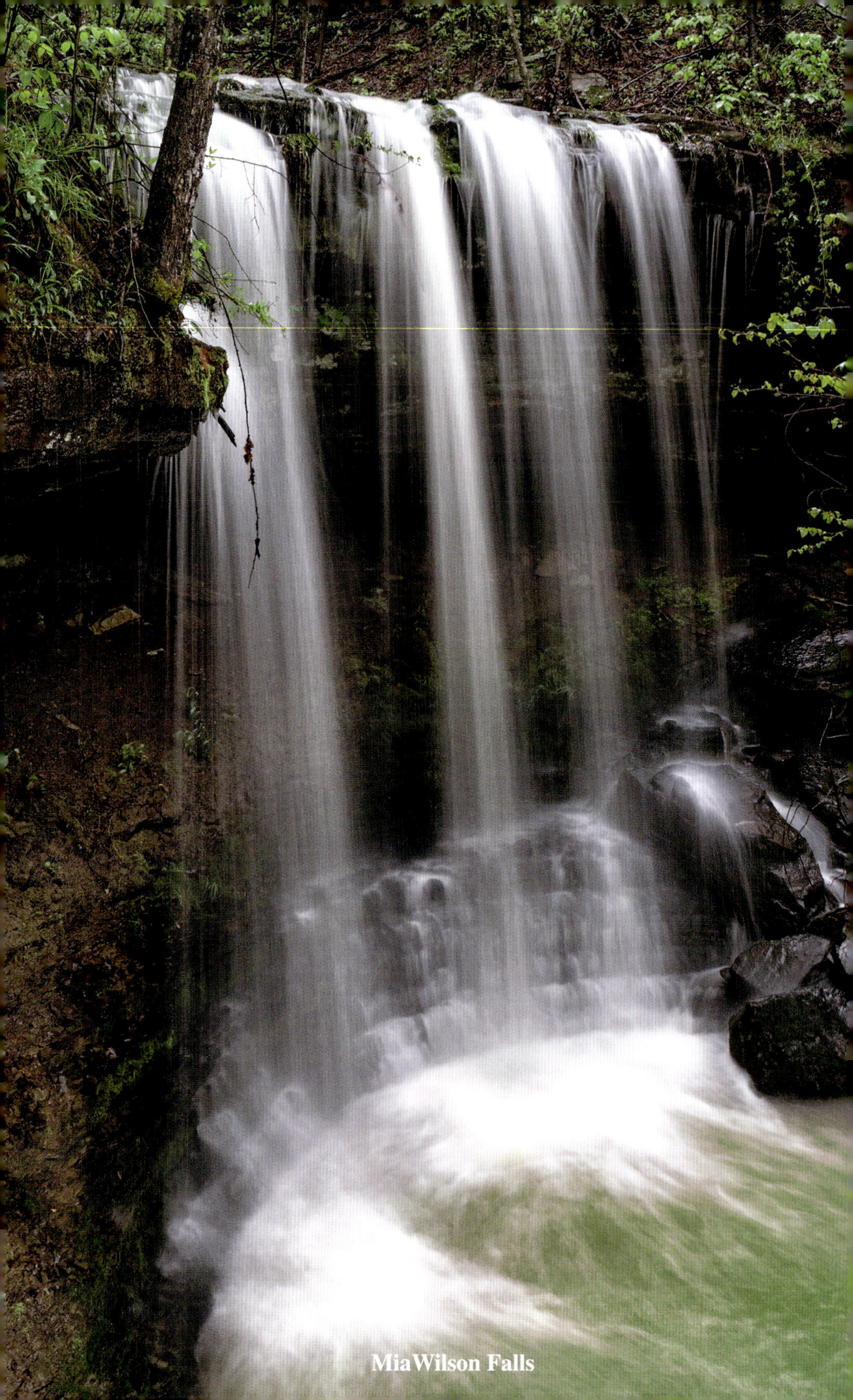

Mia Wilson Falls

About The Author

When I was a kid growing up at the edge of Fayetteville, Arkansas I used to run out into the rain and spend hours building little mud and rock dams on the tiny streams around our house, which created miniature waterfalls. Since those early days of bliss I always get a twinkle in my eye when it rains, and seek out real waterfalls whenever I can.

Along the way I started building hiking trails and taking pictures, lots of pictures (I've photographed thousands of waterfalls all across the United States in my 50+-year career as a wilderness photographer). I enjoy telling others about the many special places that we have here in Arkansas, and showing them how to get there through our many guidebooks.

My lovely bride (Pam of Pam's Grotto, page 249) and I have lived in Newton County, Arkansas for 25 years. Our daughter, Amber (that's her and I at Amber Falls below) returns home now and then and continues to enjoy the wild places she grew up in. And we have a very nice 25' tall waterfall in the back yard, named after our pups, Mia and Wilson.

The first edition of this guidebook was published in 2002. I explored and photographed several of the more difficult and most beautiful new waterfall areas included in this edition after my 70th birthday. So when folks ask me how long it took me to put this guidebook together, I'll have to just say—about 70 years!

My hope is that you will fill up your joy bucket while visiting some of our many great Arkansas waterfalls. And I hope to see ya in the woods next to one some day!

Tim Ernst

October 2025

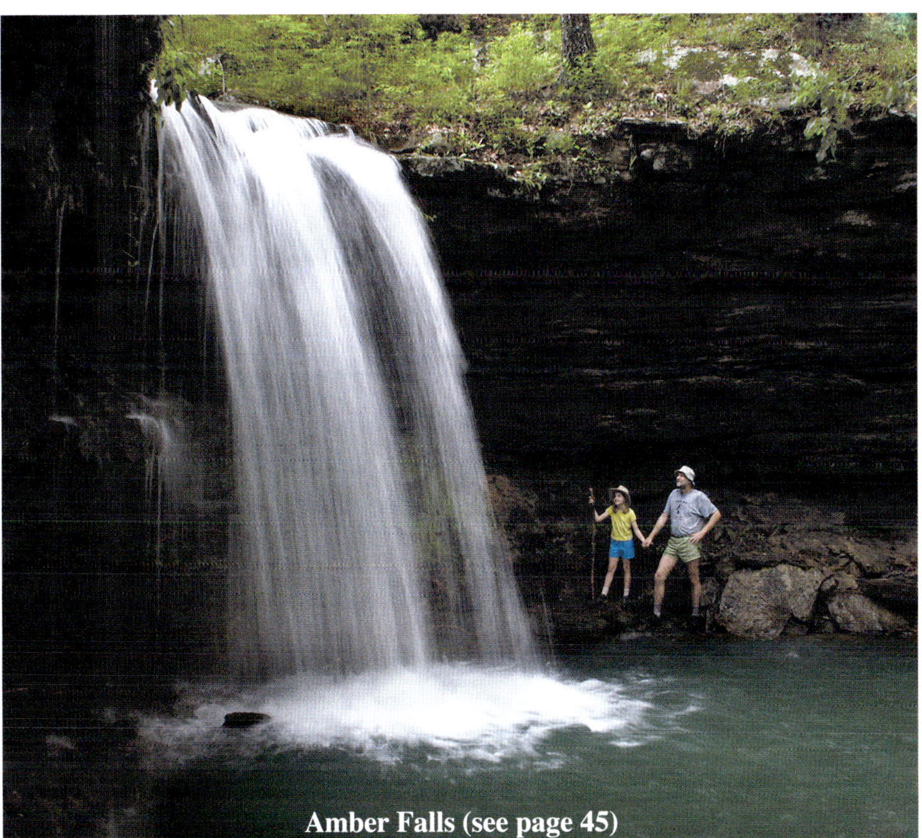

Amber Falls (see page 45)

Buffalo River Region Waterfalls

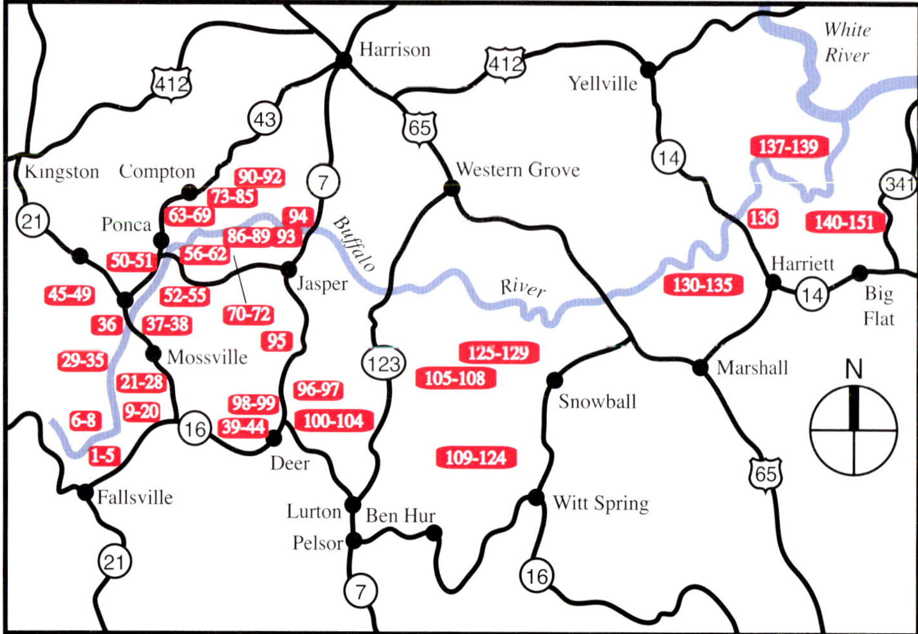

The Buffalo River region in northwest Arkansas is a land of towering limestone and sandstone bluffs, caves, springs, rivers, and countless waterfalls. This section contains the waterfalls that are located in the actual watershed of the Buffalo River, which is one of the last free-flowing rivers in the United States. It has long been one of the premiere floating streams in the country, but once was threatened to be dammed up. The result of the long fight to save the Buffalo was the creation of America's first national river, Buffalo National River. Many of the waterfalls in this section are named after those individuals who led that fight. All of the waterfalls in this section are located in either the Buffalo National River or in the Ozark National Forest. There are still many great waterfalls out there that are not listed here—available for you to "discover" on your own! **NOTE:** dogs are not allowed on most of the trails within Buffalo National River (they are OK in the surrounding Ozark National Forest though). Best to look at each map and see what agency owns the land you will be using.

Emergency Contact info line at the bottom of each waterfall listing will usually say if dogs are allowed or not.

Fall #	Name	Height	Hike Difficulty	Page #
1	*Buffalo River Falls	6	Easy	**11**
2	Leaning Log Falls	27	Diff.	**12**
3	Adkins Canyon Falls	42	Diff.	**12**
4	*Lovell Hollow Falls	36	Diff.	**12**
5	*Don Kitts Falls	22	Diff.	**12**
6	Bowers Hollow Falls	56	Diff.	**17**
7	Smith Falls (2)	54/71	Diff.	**19**
8	McClure Falls (2)	24/33	Diff.	**19**
9	*Fort Falls	24	Med.	**23**
10	*Leonardo Falls	12	Diff.	**23**
11	*Rafael Falls	17	Diff.	**23**
12	*Michelangelo Falls	29	♦	**23**
13	*Donatello Falls	31	♦	**23**
14	*Curtis Falls	58	♦	**23**
15	*Mossy Falls	33	♦	**23**
16	*Tilted Rock Falls	15	♦	**23**
17	*Three-Toed Falls	20	♦	**23**
18	*Lazy Boulder Falls	24	♦	**23**
19	*Square Boulder Falls	16	♦	**23**
20	*Terrapin Branch	45	♦	**23**
21	Magnolia Falls	26	Med.	**32**
22	Woods Boys Falls	33	Med.	**32**
23	Stahle Falls	63	Med.	**32**
24	Hadlock Cascade	27	Med.	**32**
25	Paradise Falls	32	Diff.	**37**
26	*Courageous Light	27	Easy	**39**
27	*Boulder City Falls	56	Med.	**39**
28	*Bathroom Falls	36	Med.	**39**
29	Beagle Point Falls	76	Diff.	**42**
30	Wild Burro Falls	21	Diff.	**42**
31	Compton's Double	39	Med.	**45**
32	Amber Falls	18	Med.	**45**
33	Haley Falls (2)	17/45	Med.	**47**
34	Mule Trail Falls	31	Med.	**47**
35	Thousand Kisses	48	Med.	**47**
36	Hedges Pouroff	113	Easy	**51**
37	QuiVaLa Elise Falls	21	Med.	**53**
38	*Martin Falls	18	Easy	**53**
39	*Dismal Divide Falls	37	Diff.	**56**
40	*Dismal Four Drop	35	Diff.	**56**
41	*Dismal Shelter Falls	63	Diff.	**56**
42	*Dismal Dbl. Drop	63	Diff.	**56**
43	*Dismal South Falls	75	Diff.	**56**
44	Stepp Cr. Falls (2)	12/25	Med.	**60**
45	*Hole In Rock Falls	66	Easy	**62**
46	*Sunshine Falls	15	Easy	**62**
47	*Johnny B Goode Falls	26	Easy	**62**
48	*Panther Pool Falls	7	Easy	**62**
49	*Leprechaun Falls	34	Med.	**62**
50	Eden Falls	31-53	Easy	**66**
51	Armadillo Falls (2)	18/24	Med.	**66**
52	*Balanced Rock Falls	17	Easy	**69**
53	*Leatherwood Grotto	15	Med.	**69**
54	*Top of the Slots Falls	<10	Med.	**69**
55	*Recluse Falls	59	Med.	**69**
56	*Rum Hole Falls	36	Easy	**74**
57	*Hidden Falls Ponca	37	Easy	**74**
58	*Clemmer Falls	33	Med.	**74**
59	*Half Moon Falls	61	Med.	**74**
60	*Ponca Polyfoss	9-39	Easy	**74**
61	*Roark Bluff Falls	195	Easy	**81**
62	*Firehose Falls	126	Easy	**81**
63	*Chimney Rock Mine	35	Easy	**83**
64	*Cat Man Falls	47	Diff.	**83**
65	*Cliff Hollow Grotto	30	Med.	**83**
66	*Cliff Hollow Falls	35	Med.	**83**
67	*Green Goddess Falls	44	Med.	**83**
68	*Cliff Twin Cascades	100+	♦	**83**
69	*Jackie Hollow Falls	54	Diff.	**90**
70	*Bigfoot Falls	69	Diff.	**92**
71	*Littlefoot Falls	33	Diff.	**92**
72	*Shark Fin Falls	21	Diff.	**92**
73	Hemmed-In Hollow	209	Diff.	**96**
74	Diamond Falls	148	Diff.	**96**
75	Fishtrap Hollow Falls	83	Diff.	**99**
76	*Bear Cave Cascades	20	Easy	**101**
77	*Bear Slide Falls	17	Easy	**101**
78	*Bear Cave Hol. Falls	29	Easy	**101**
79	*Antenna Pine Falls	39	Diff.	**103**
80	*Antenna Twin Falls	13	Diff.	**103**
81	*Smokey Joe Falls	105	♦	**105**
82	*Cecil Hollow Falls	108	♦	**105**
83	*Big Boulder Falls	36	♦	**105**
84	*Cecil Middle Step	51	♦	**105**
85	Hideout Hollow Falls	37	Easy	**109**
86	Hammerschmidt Falls	43	Easy	**111**
87	*Indian Creek Twin	21	Diff.	**111**
88	*Evalengine Falls	44	♦	**111**

* New waterfalls in this edition

* New waterfalls in this edition

Buffalo River Falls – 6′

4.1 roundtrip, easy old road, GPS **35.83563, -93.51555**

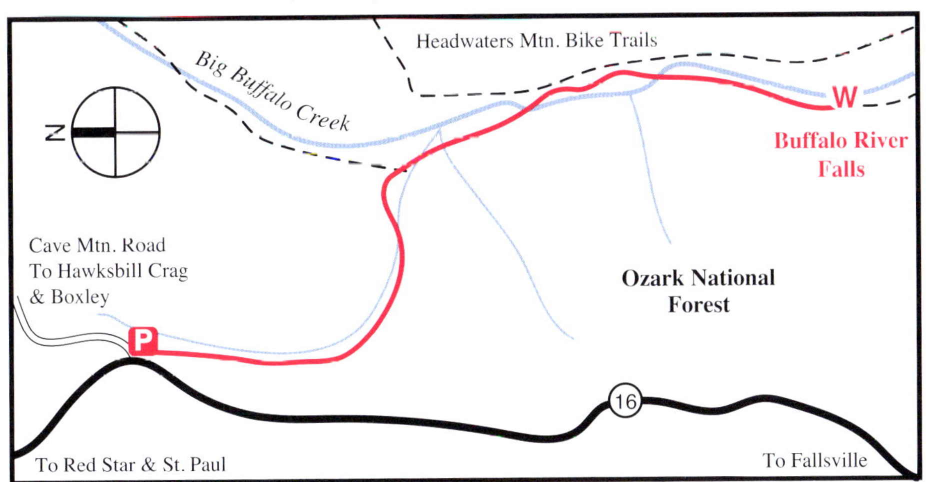

BUFFALO RIVER FALLS. This is not a tall or powerful waterfall, but I consider it significant since it's the only waterfall that spans the Buffalo River. The hike follows an old roadbed the entire way, alongside what begins as a tiny creek but joins with others and becomes the Buffalo River. Beautiful SSS wildflower area in the spring!

PARK at the intersection of Cave Mountain Road and Hwy. 16 just east of Red Star, about ten miles west of Fallsville. **(35.85867, -93.52537)** From your parking spot head down the old road—(this is part of the Buffalo Headwaters Mountain Bike Trail System, with 40+ miles of biking and hiking trails), and follow the road downhill (crossing the creek once). At 1.0 a larger creek and another road will join from the left—STAY RIGHT, cross the creek you have been following, and continue along the old road heading downstream. (FYI, the actual beginning of the Buffalo River is on a ridge about 2.5 miles upstream from this point, just above Roberts Gap.) You will cross what is now the main Buffalo River twice (still small unless it's flooded), and will soon arrive at **Buffalo River Falls** on the LEFT at 2.06.

Emergency contact: Newton County Sheriff, 870–446–5124 Dogs are OK.

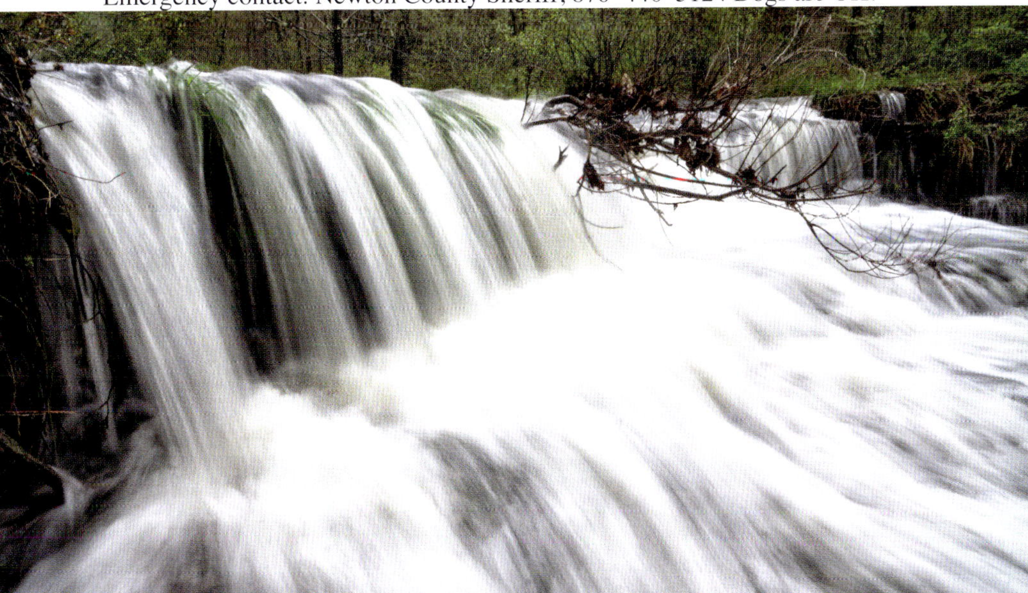

Leaning Log Falls – 27′

3.4 miles roundtrip, difficult bushwhack, GPS recommended

GPS **35.82219, -9653.42696**

Adkins Canyon Falls – 42′

Add .6 to above (4.0 total), difficult bushwhack, GPS recommended

GPS **35.82321, -93.42302**

Lovell Hollow Falls – 36′

Add 2.5 to above (6.5 total), difficult bushwhack, GPS recommended

Lat/Lon **35.83556, -93.42620**

Don Kitts Falls – 22′

Add .5 to above (7.0 total), difficult bushwhack, GPS recommended

35.83501, -93.42269

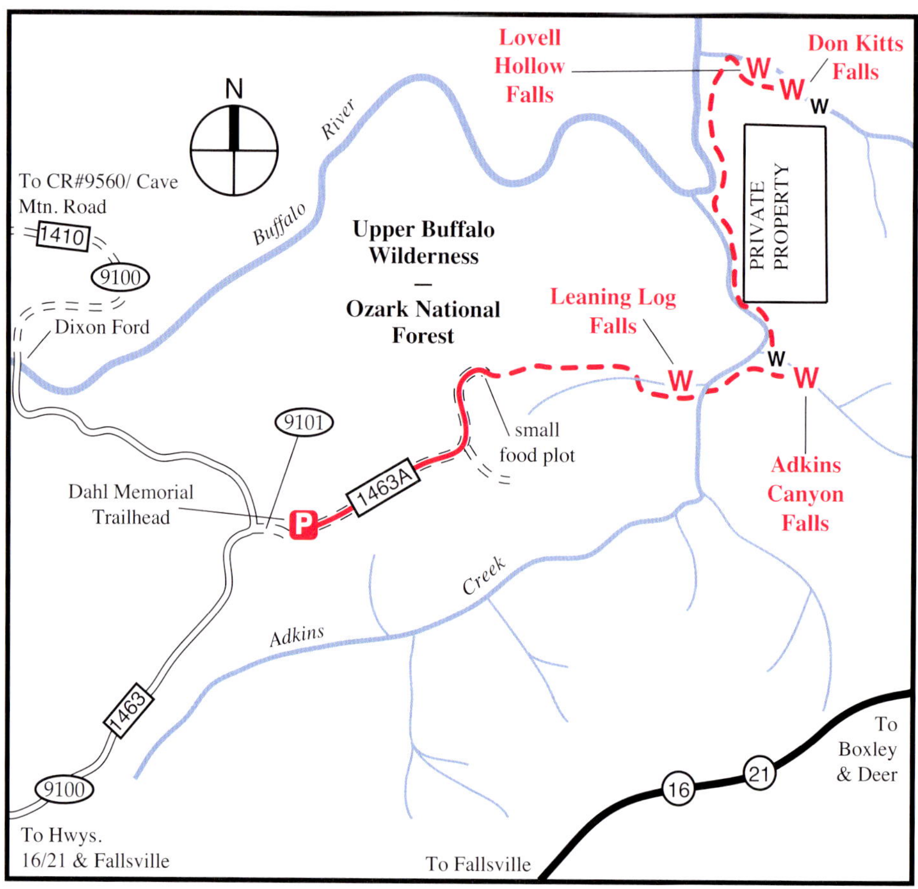

LEANING LOG FALLS/ADKINS CANYON FALLS. My first trip into this area was in 1979, right after a 10-inch snowfall had blanketed the area. I remember two things most about that trip: the fact that I did not carry a sleeping pad and had to sleep on a bed of snow; and these beautiful waterfalls that were covered with ice. I did not return to them until recently, and found them to be even more spectacular. The first part of the trip down

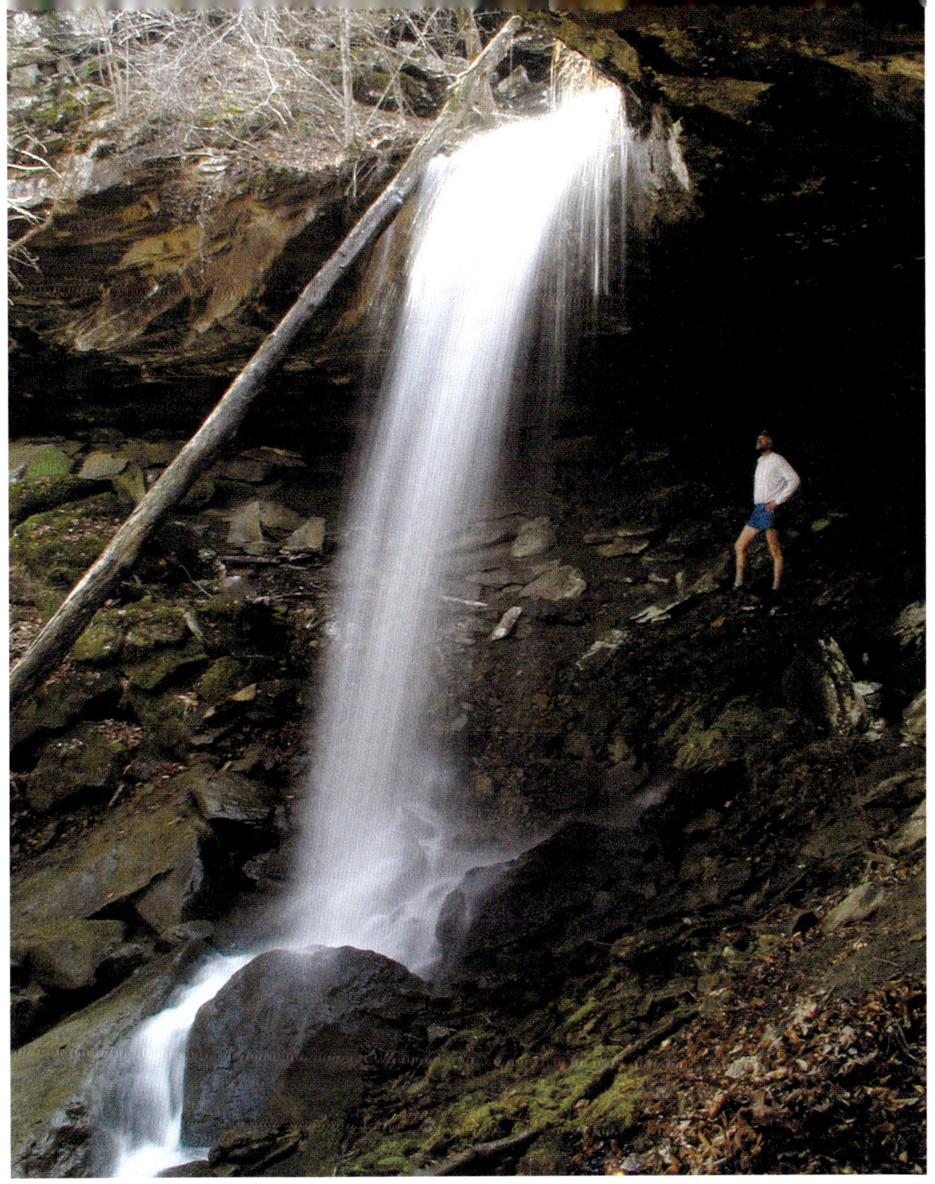

Leaning Log Falls

into the canyon is an easy hike along a jeep road, but the second half of the trip involves some pretty serious bushwhacking, and the hike out is tough on a weary body.

From Fallsville take Hwy. 16/21 east for 1.4 miles and TURN LEFT onto CR#9100/FR#1463. Go 2.0 miles and TURN RIGHT onto CR#9101/FR#1463A and PARK at the Dahl Memorial Trailhead.

From the parking area head out to the east and hike along the jeep road there. It runs along the top of the ridge, dips down just a little bit, then back up again and levels off where it comes to a "T" intersection at .8. TURN LEFT and continue to follow the jeep road as it makes its way on around the head of the hollow to the right and to a small food plot at 1.1. (This will be as far as you can go with a jeep—the wilderness boundary is just beyond.) I recommend that you begin to head down into the hollow to the right at this point, on an angle. When you come to the creek below TURN LEFT and follow the creek downstream. You

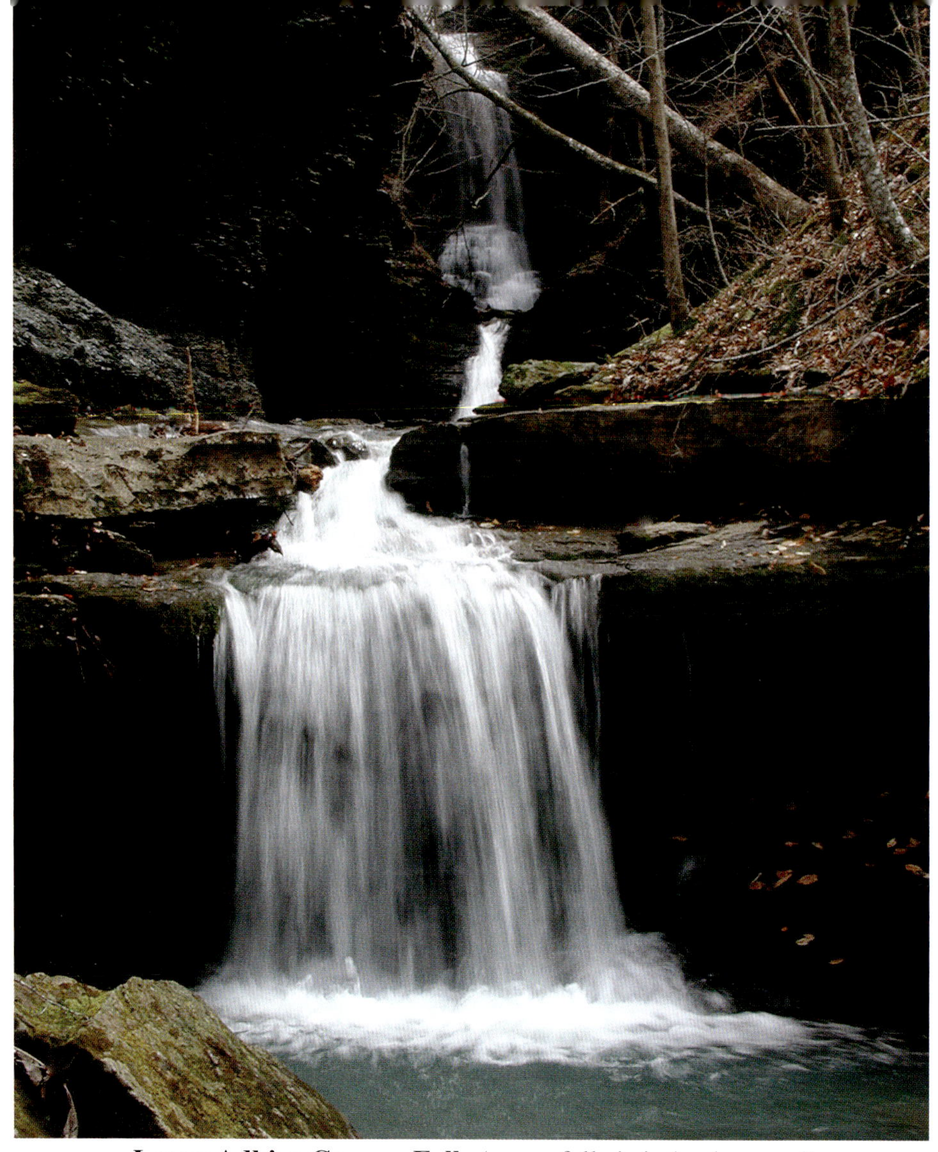

Lower Adkins Canyon Falls (upper falls is in background)

will come to **Leaning Log Falls** at 1.7 (the log has been washed away). There is a safe way to get down to the bottom of the falls after you cross the creek and go around to the right.

To get to Adkins Canyon from **Leaning Log Falls** go down to the river just below the falls—that is Adkins Creek. Find a way across it and follow it downstream to your LEFT. After a short distance you will come to a side drainage coming in from the RIGHT—that is the canyon, and you will see the lower waterfall right there. In fact it is a nice view from there looking up into the canyon because you can see all three waterfalls at the same time (see photo above). The lower two falls are not all that tall, but the entire little canyon area is really nice. You can find a route up the hill on the right side of the canyon and get to the upper **Adkins Canyon Falls** at 2.0.

LOVELL HOLLOW FALLS/DON KITTS FALLS. If you want to extend your waterfall adventure (adds about 3.0 miles roundtrip) continue from **Adkins Falls** downstream on Atkins

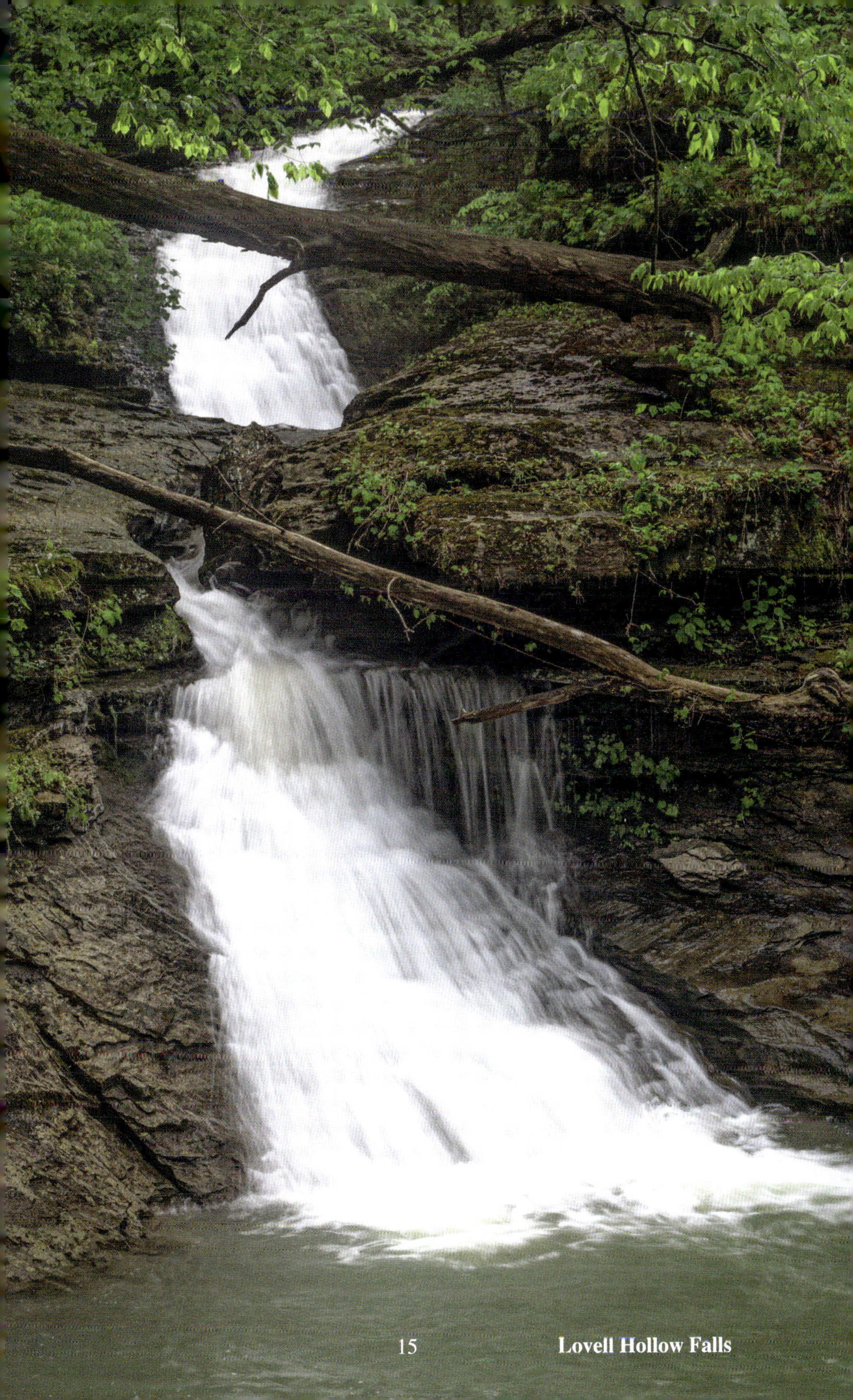

Lovell Hollow Falls

Creek until you reach the Buffalo River. TURN RIGHT and follow the river downstream to the next drainage on the right, which is Lovell Hollow (you may have to climb up and around part of the bluffline to stay out of the river). TURN RIGHT and follow the creek up to the two-tiered **Lovell Hollow Falls** that is just upstream, and it's a beauty!

Continue upstream in Lovell Hollow another quarter mile or so to **Don Kitts Falls** (total hike from **Adkins Falls** is about 1.5 miles each way). Don was an incredible artist and person who lived nearby at the Heartsong Retreat Center, an interfaith center that he founded in the 1970's. I especially enjoyed his egg tempera painting technique, a traditional method using egg yolk as a binder for pigments.

BE AWARE of private property beyond the wilderness boundaries above this area, and stay BELOW the big bluffline to be sure.

Emergency contact: Newton County Sheriff, 870–446–5124 Dogs are OK.

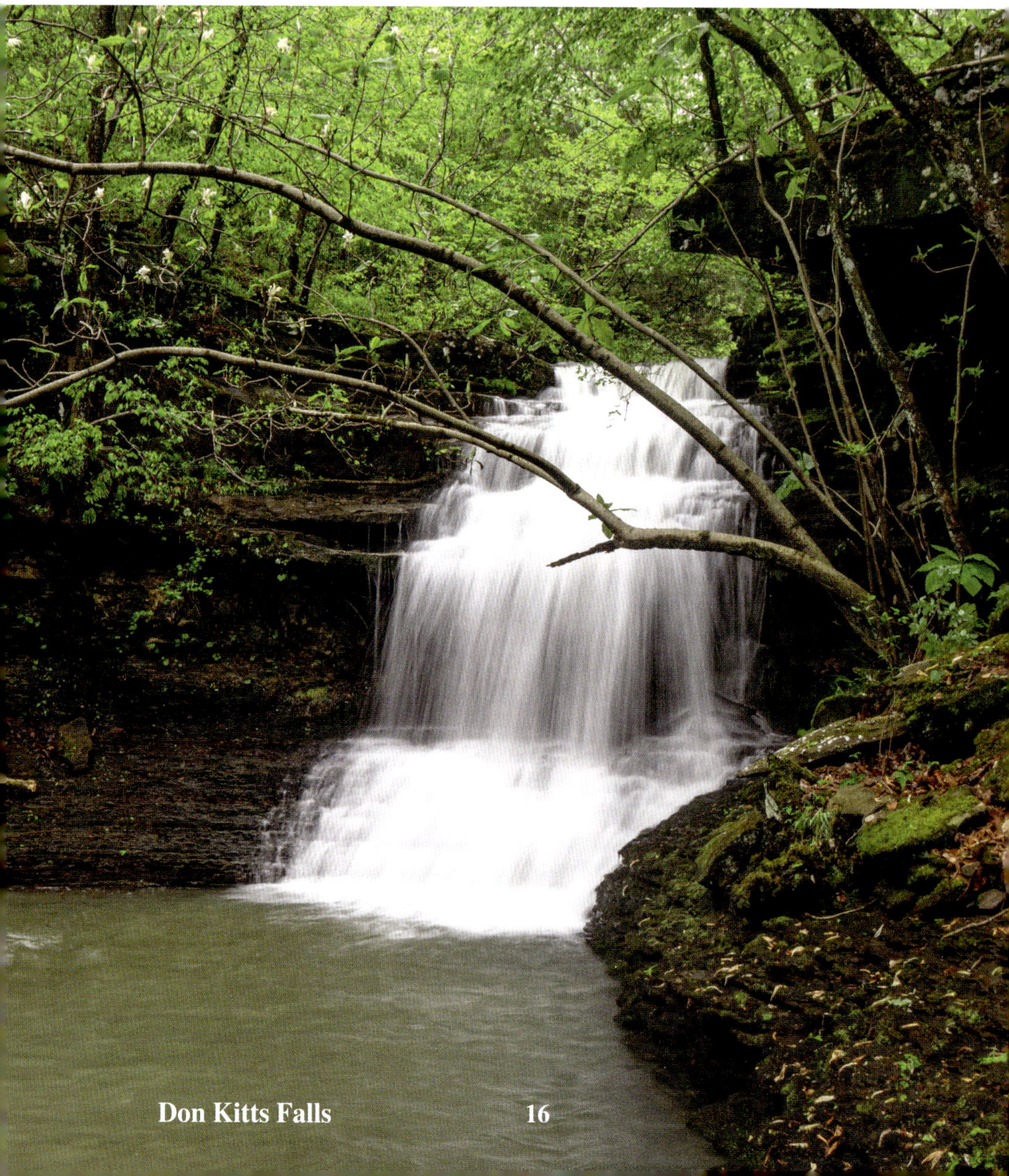

Don Kitts Falls

Bowers Hollow Falls – 56′

4.0 miles roundtrip, difficult bushwhack, GPS highly recommended

GPS 35.85428, -93.43159

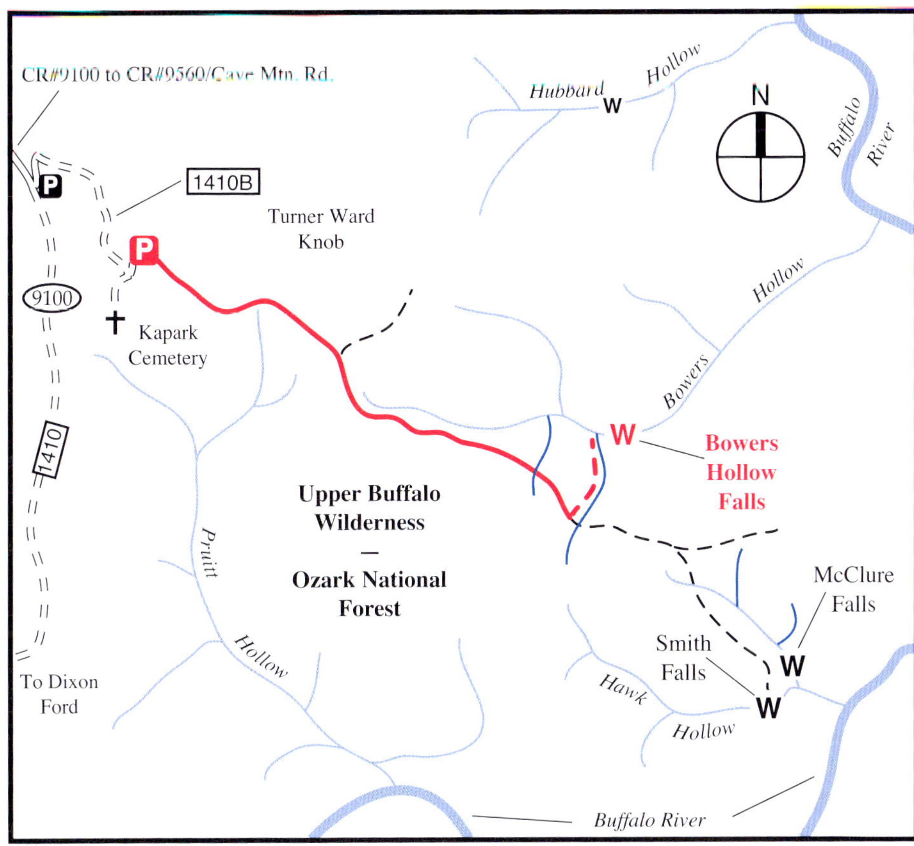

BOWERS HOLLOW FALLS. This is one of the most powerful and scenic waterfalls in Arkansas. The old road/trail into the area is used a lot by hikers so the path most of the way is easy to follow. The trail is not maintained, so there may be downed trees blocking the way. The last part is a steep bushwhack, and the falls will be easier to find with a GPS.

From Ponca, take Hwy. 43 south through Boxley to the intersection with Hwy. 21. TURN LEFT and follow Hwy. 21 for 1.2 miles (across two bridges) and TURN RIGHT just before you cross the bridge across the Buffalo River. This gravel road is CR#9560/Cave Mountain Road, and it takes off *steeply* up the hillside. Go past Cave Mtn. Church (at 5.5), Hawksbill Crag Trailhead (at 6.0), and TURN LEFT onto CR#9100/FR#1410 at 8.6. Go 1.6 miles and TURN LEFT onto FR#1410B. If you have a normal car, PARK here (add 1.0 to your hike). If you have a 4wd you can continue on to the trailhead. The jeep road does continue on through a really bad mud hole for another .5 mile, then comes to a "T" intersection—TURN LEFT and PARK a few feet ahead where the road is blocked. (The other road goes to Kapark Cemetery.)

Begin hiking along the road past the hump. It is mostly level with a little bit of up and downing. At .8 you will come to a fork in the road, and may not even see it, but you want to TURN RIGHT and continue along the jeep road (be sure to make this turn on the way back out!). The road will now begin to drop on down the hill. At 1.2 you will come alongside a creek

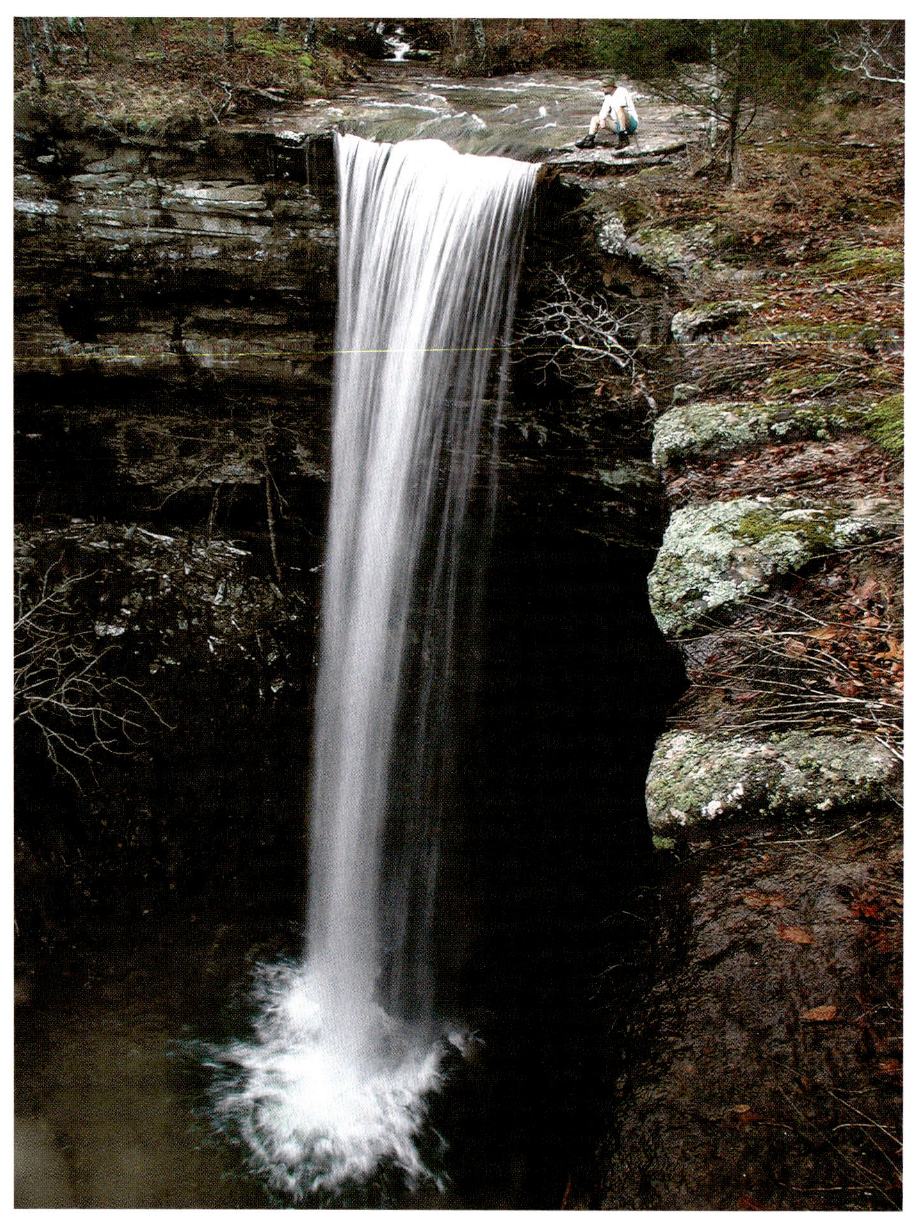

Bowers Hollow Falls

on the left—it should be running well. This is the creek that runs through Bowers Hollow. You can simply follow that creek downstream until you come to the falls, or I recommend staying on the jeep road a little while longer and bushwhacking down the hill to the top of the falls. To do that, continue on the old jeep road as it remains fairly level but does a little up and downing as it crosses a couple of small creeks. At 1.7 you will come to a creek that is mostly filled up with wild rose bushes—look for a rock cairn (pile of rocks) on the left side of the road. TURN LEFT at the creek and follow it down the hill and you will come out right at the top of **Bowers Hollow Falls** at 2.0. It is indeed a magical spot—enjoy!

Emergency contact: Newton County Sheriff, 870–446–5124 Dogs are OK.

Smith Falls (2) – 54′/71′

5.4 miles roundtrip, difficult hike/bushwhack, GPS highly recommended

GPS 35.84375, -93.42615

McClure Falls (2) – 24′/33′

Same area as above, difficult hike/bushwhack, GPS highly recommended

GPS 35.84550, -93.42568

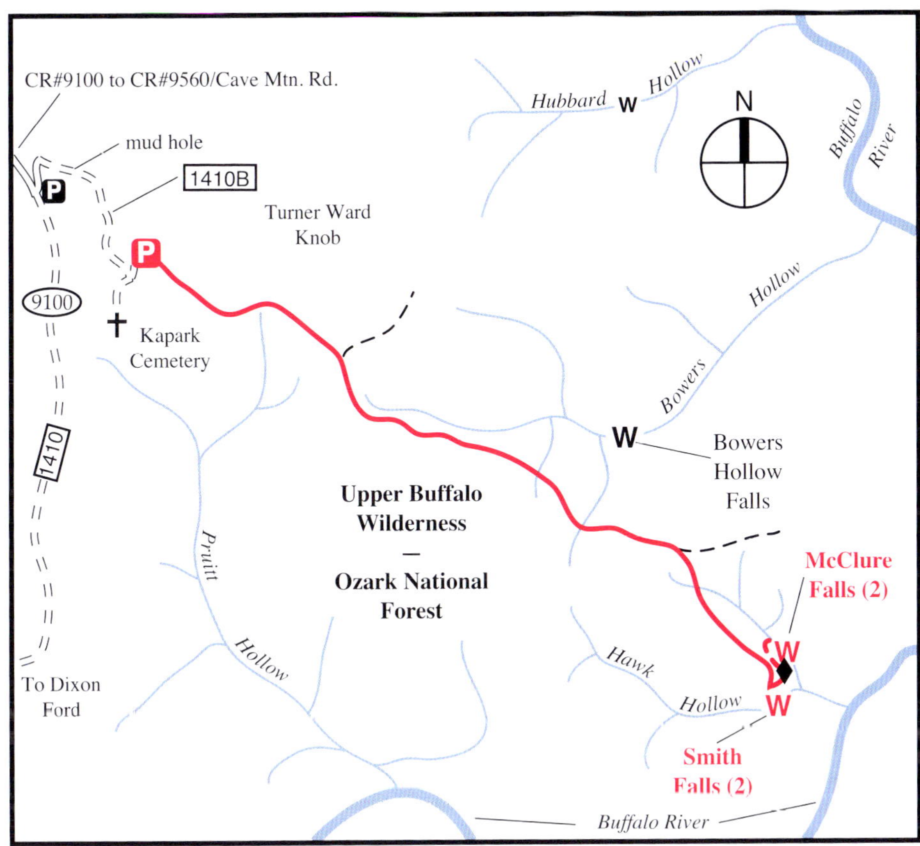

SMITH FALLS/McCLURE FALLS. I first found out about this little scenic area that contains these four waterfalls from Ken Smith, who had spent a great deal of time exploring these hills in the early 1960's. The forest service had originally wanted to protect only 625 acres of this "scenic area." The wilderness is now more than 13,000 acres. Ken worked tirelessly for many years with Neil Compton and the Ozark Society to get the Buffalo River area protected. It is fitting that two of the most beautiful waterfalls now bear his name.

Two others that were inspired by Ken Smith in the years to come were Tom McClure and Ellen Neaville. Tom led the fight for the Arkansas Wilderness Coalition in the early 1980's that resulted in the creation of most of the wilderness areas we have in Arkansas. When a group of us traveled to Washington, D.C. to testify before Congress about wilderness, Tom and I bunked together. I found it funny when he came knocking on my door in the middle of the night wanting to know if I had a spare toothbrush—he is a *dentist*, but had forgotten his! Ellen worked on the wilderness campaign, and was also instrumental

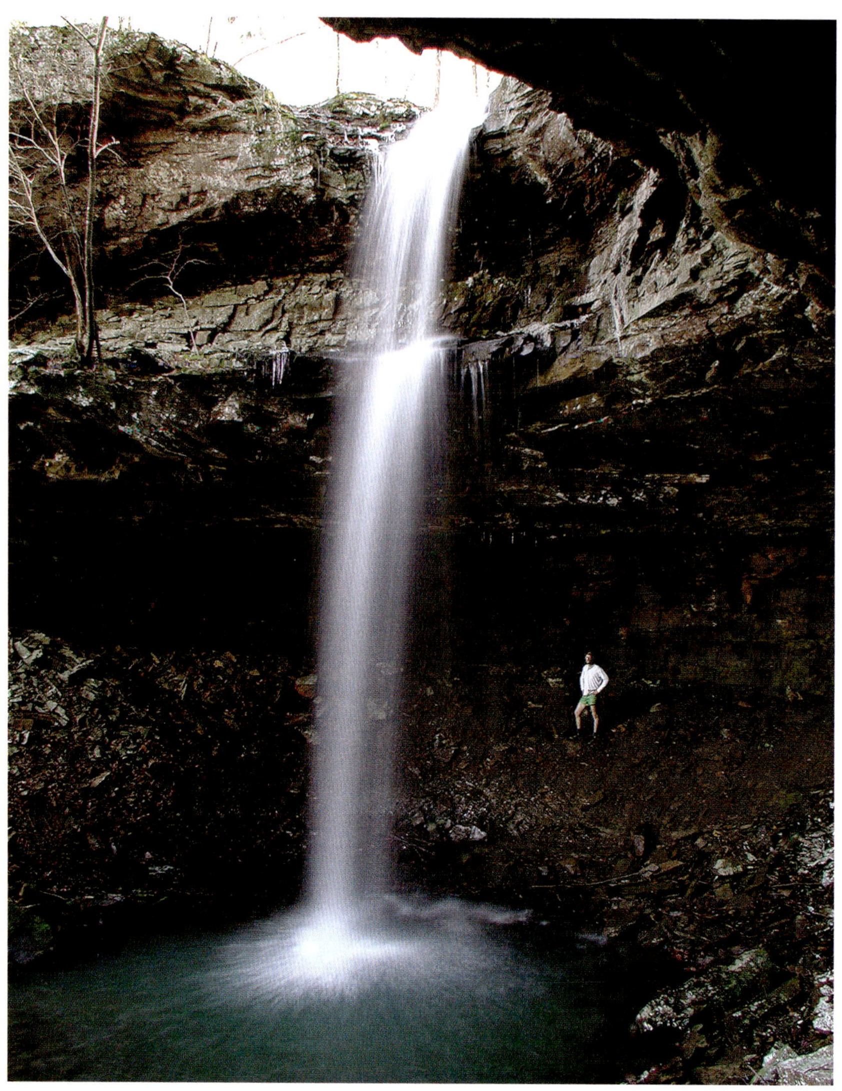

Upper Ken Smith Falls

in creating many of the "Natural Areas" that we have in Arkansas through the Natural Heritage Commission. Most importantly though, she has devoted her life to educating our young people about the natural world, and the creatures and plants that call it home. In a wonderful twist of fate these two people so dedicated to the environment got married. The waters of the pair of **McClure Falls** flow together as one.

The access for these waterfalls is the same as for **Bowers Hollow Falls**, and the first 1.7 miles of the route into them is the same as well. See the previous two pages for the directions to the trailhead, and for the first 1.7 miles of trail.

Once you get to the 1.7 mile point on the hike into **Bowers Hollow Falls**—at the point where you leave the road and bushwhack down to the falls—CONTINUE STRAIGHT AHEAD to get to **Smith/McClure Falls**. Stay on the road trace as it levels out and passes through an area with lots of giant trees around. Many of the trees were knocked down by a tornado that swept through the area in the late 1990's. At 2.0 the road will make a

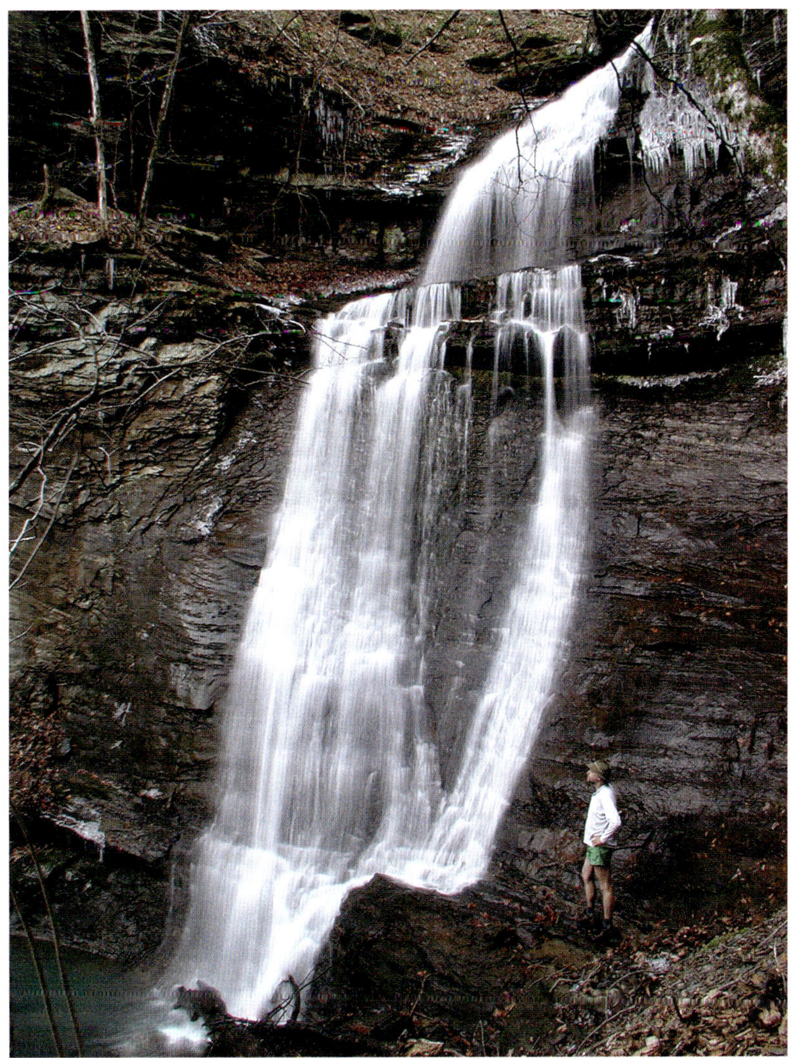

Lower Ken Smith Falls

turn to the left—look for a rock cairn on the RIGHT, where a smaller old road trace takes off—TURN TO THE RIGHT (straight ahead) and go down the hill on the smaller road.

Follow this little road down the hill and across a small stream, then along a level bench just up above the stream, which will be down on your left. The road remains basically level as it curves on around the nose of a ridge to the right. As you come around the hill and straighten out look for a trail that leaves the road and goes down the hill TO THE LEFT. This little trail will take you right on down to the top of the **Upper Smith Falls**, which will be on the left at 2.7. The unofficial name for this area is Hawk Hollow.

To get to **McClure Falls** from the top of **Smith Falls**, follow the top of the bluff to the left, past the overhang *(careful!)*, and on around the mountain and you will come to **McClure Falls** on the right. It is possible to get down below the bluffline to both **Lower McClure** and **Lower Smith Falls** by going around the bluff beyond **McClure Falls** 100 yards or so, but the trip down into that area is *very steep and hazardous* ♦, only for experts.

Emergency contact: Newton County Sheriff, 870–446–5124 Dogs are OK.

Upper McClure Falls

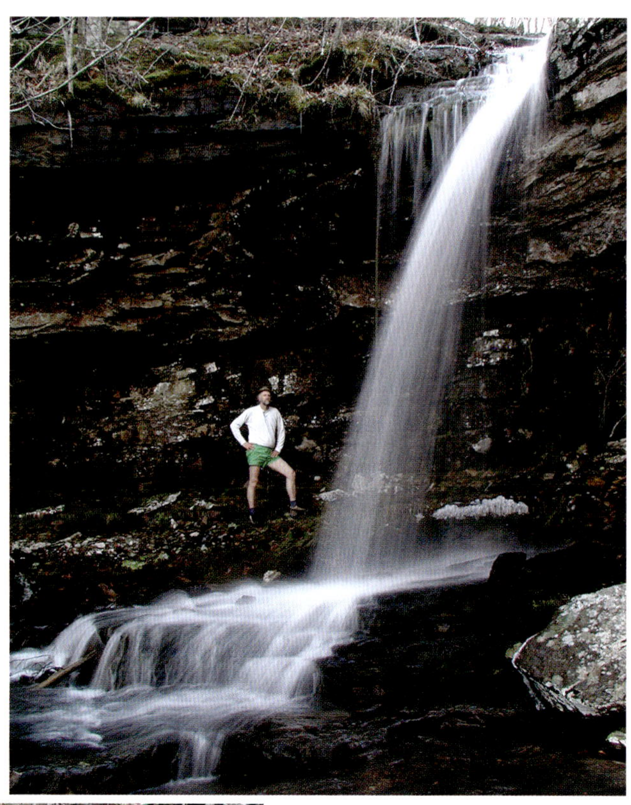

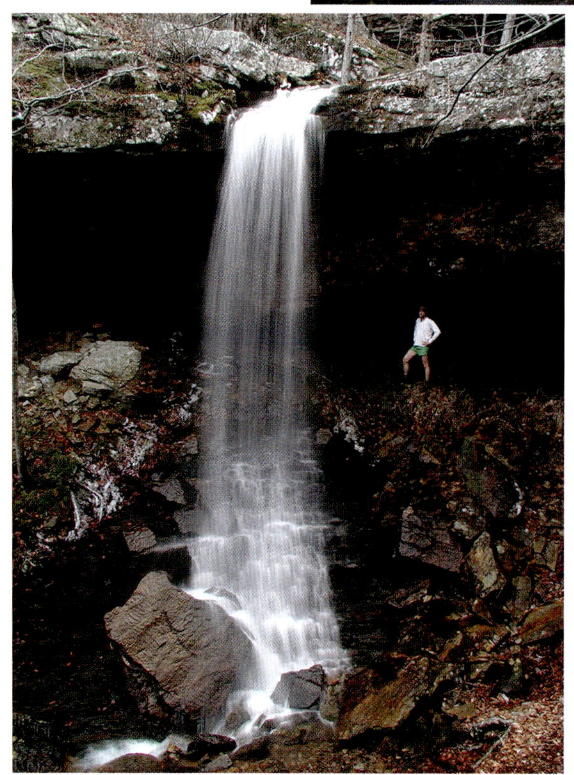

Lower McClure Falls

Fort Falls – 24′

.8 mile, medium bushwhack GPS **35.84599, -93.39044**

Leonardo Falls – 12′

1.4, medium/difficult bushwhack GPS **35.84529, -93.39900**

Rafael Falls – 17′

1.5, medium/difficult bushwhack GPS **35.84409, -93.40011**

Michelangelo Falls – 29′

1.6 difficult bushwhack ♦ GPS **35.84345, -93.40044**

Donatello Falls – 31′

1.7, difficult bushwhack ♦ GPS **35.84343, -93.40048**

Curtis Falls (double drop) – 58′

2.0, difficult bushwhack ♦ GPS **35.84102, -93.40474**

Mossy Falls – 33′

2.1, difficult bushwhack ♦ GPS **35.84003, -93.40494**

Tilted Rock Falls – 15′

2.2, difficult bushwhack ♦ GPS **35.83937, -93.40481**

Three-Toed Falls – 20′

2.2, difficult bushwhack ♦ GPS **35.83918, -93.40475**

Lazy Boulder Falls – 24′

2.8, difficult bushwhack ♦ GPS **35.84015, -93.39677**

Square Boulder Falls – 16′

2.8, difficult bushwhack ♦ GPS **35.84022, -93.39638**

Terrapin Branch Falls – 45′

3.2, difficult bushwhack ♦ GPS **35.84305, -93.39231**

TOTAL LOOP distance is 4.3 miles

TERRAPIN BRANCH WATERFALLS. When the water is flowing great this difficult loop is one of the most beautiful waterfall loops in Arkansas. It's all bushwhack, with several Black Diamond slopes ♦ and a lot of downright steep and rocky terrain—not for the faint of heart. You can just hike to the main waterfall, do the entire loop, or pick and choose as your day progresses. It's a wild and beautiful corner of the Upper Buffalo Wilderness.

From the intersection of Hwy. 21 and 16 at Edwards Junction (south of Boxley Valley), go west 1.2 miles and TURN RIGHT onto CR9008. OR from Fallsville, go east on Hwy. 21/16 6.8 miles (past the Glory Hole Trailhead) and TURN LEFT onto CR9008. Go .2 and PARK on the RIGHT (**35.84012, -93.38009**).

The small parking spot is an old forest service trailhead, and the bushwhack down to

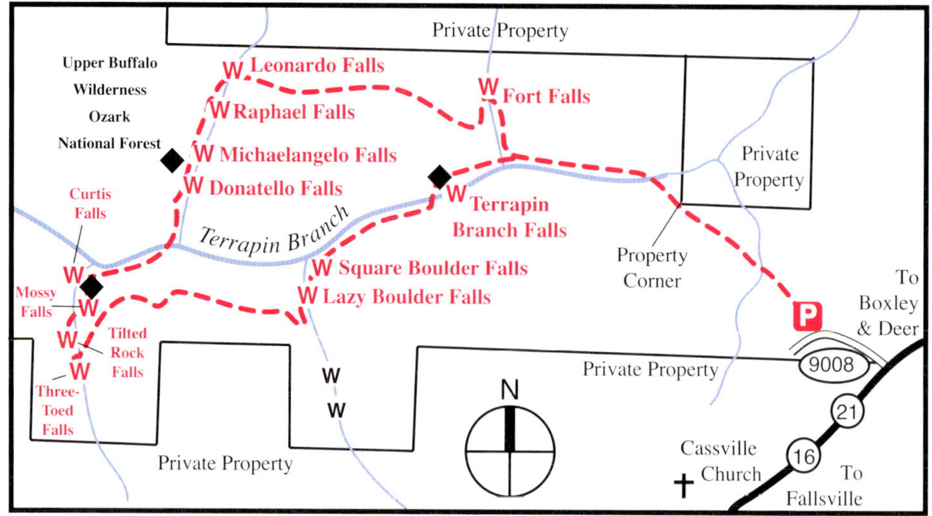

Terrapin Branch is across a part of forest service property between two parcels of private land—be sure to AVOID any private property and stay in the national forest. If you have GPS or a map APP. I recommend you put in the coordinates for this private property corner (**35.84282, -93.38410**) and simply make a beeline down the hillside, across a creek, and directly to this property corner at .35 (basically northwest from the parking spot to the corner). OR simply head northwest down the hillside, across the creek, and continue that direction until you run into a fence line or Terrapin Branch. Or just follow the social trails.

From the property corner continue northwest downhill and to the left a little until you hit Terrapin Branch and then head LEFT/DOWNSTREAM. If the water is high you may have trouble finding a safe spot to cross Terrapin Branch—GREAT for waterfalls, not so good for a safe crossing! Once across the creek head downstream to the first drainage—TURN RIGHT and head up into this drainage and follow it on up to **Fort Falls** at .8.

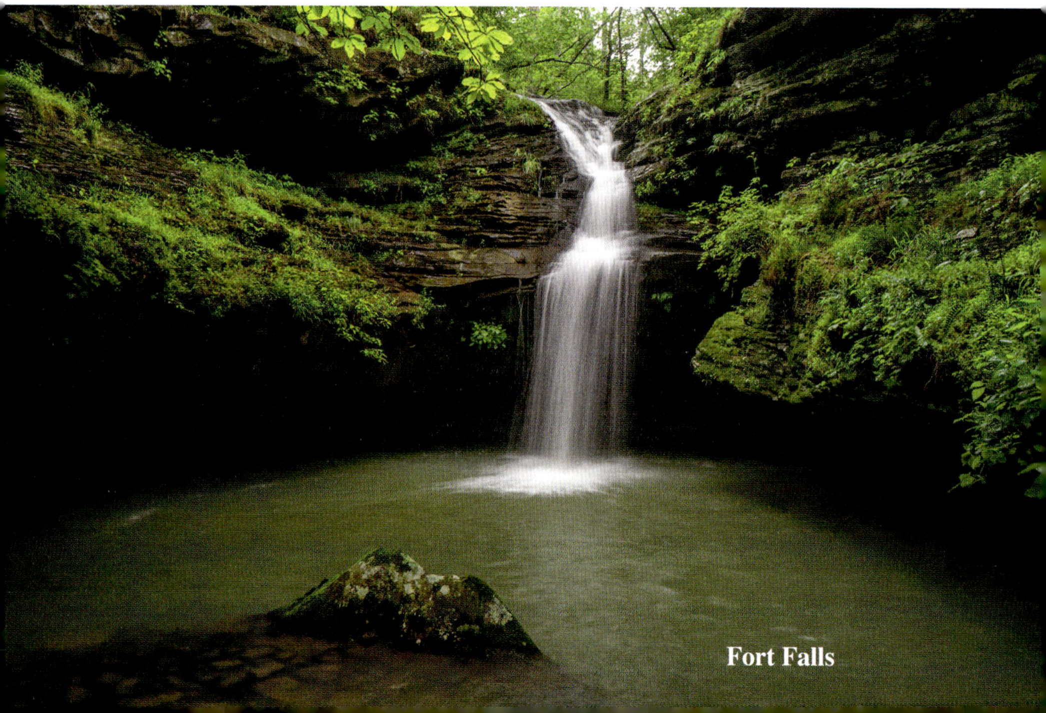

Fort Falls

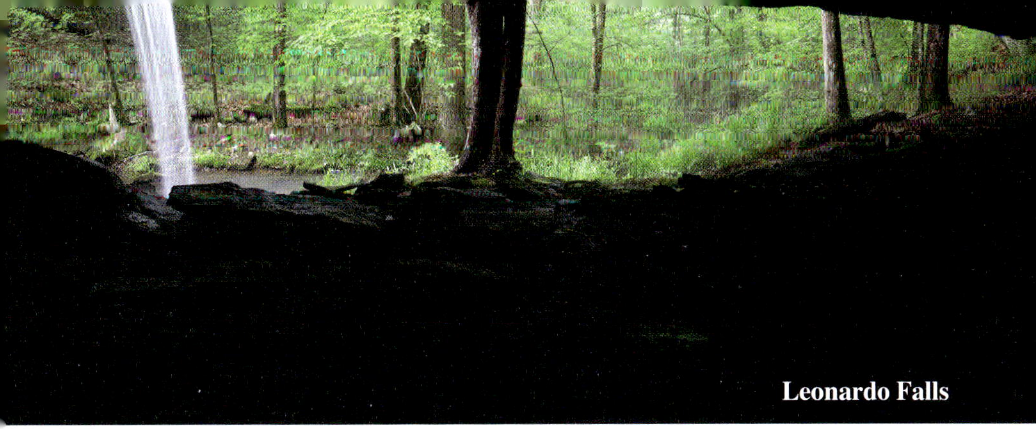

Leonardo Falls

To continue the loop from the falls, cross the creek, go back downstream and climb up to get above the bluff on the right (very steep). Climb up until you come to an open forest that is much less steep, then work your way around to the left and follow this flat-ish "bench" as it curves around to the right, dipping down into and out of a couple of small drainages, easy hiking. Stay below the private property that's above and to the right.

At 1.4 you will drop down into a small creek—TURN RIGHT and find a very short but quite unique SSS **Leonardo Falls** just upstream, the first of four waterfalls named after the Teenage Mutant Ninja Turtles (by waterfall explorers Kristen and Harrison). This low triple falls overhang goes back 50 feet, with the wide shelf being about 60' wide.

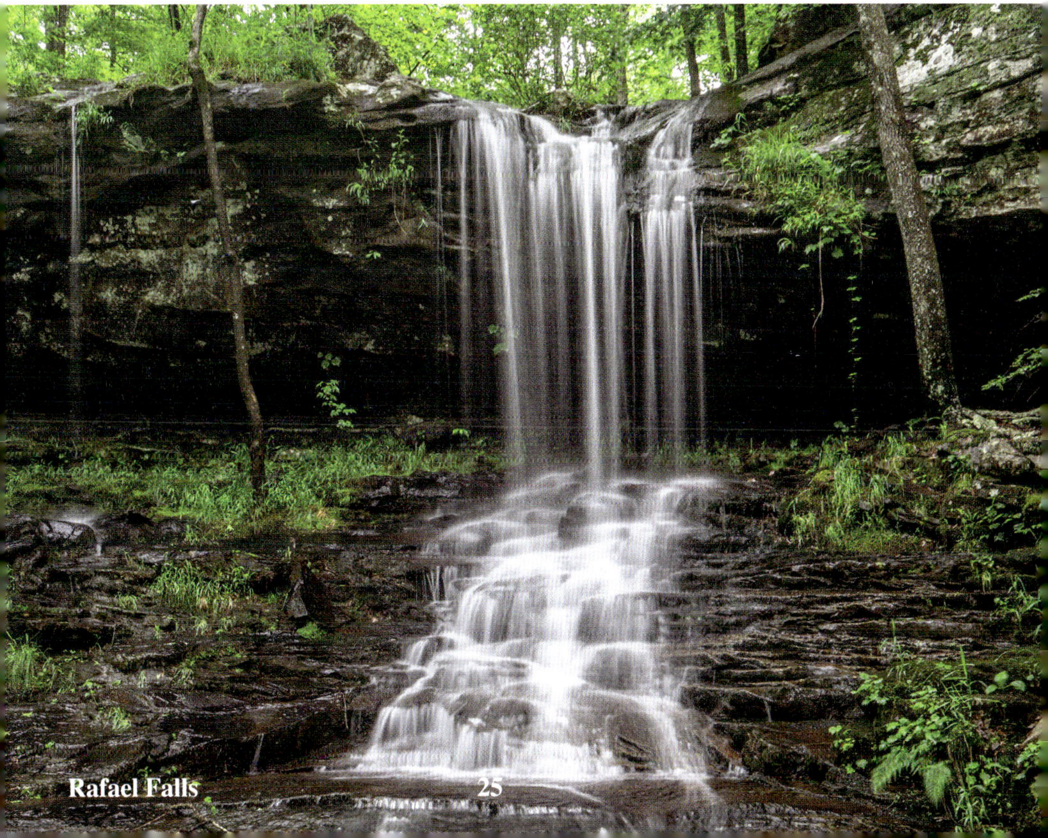

Rafael Falls

The next three waterfalls are downstream—simply follow the creek and you will come to bluff lines, and of course the waterfalls. **Rafael Falls**, then **Michelangelo Falls**, and finally **Donatello Falls**—each one an SSS for sure! CAUTION—you will need to scramble down Black Diamond slopes ♦ to access the bottom of each waterfall (I stay on the right side of the canyon going down—there is no easy or obvious safe route).

Once below **Donatello Falls** continue carefully down the drainage until you come to

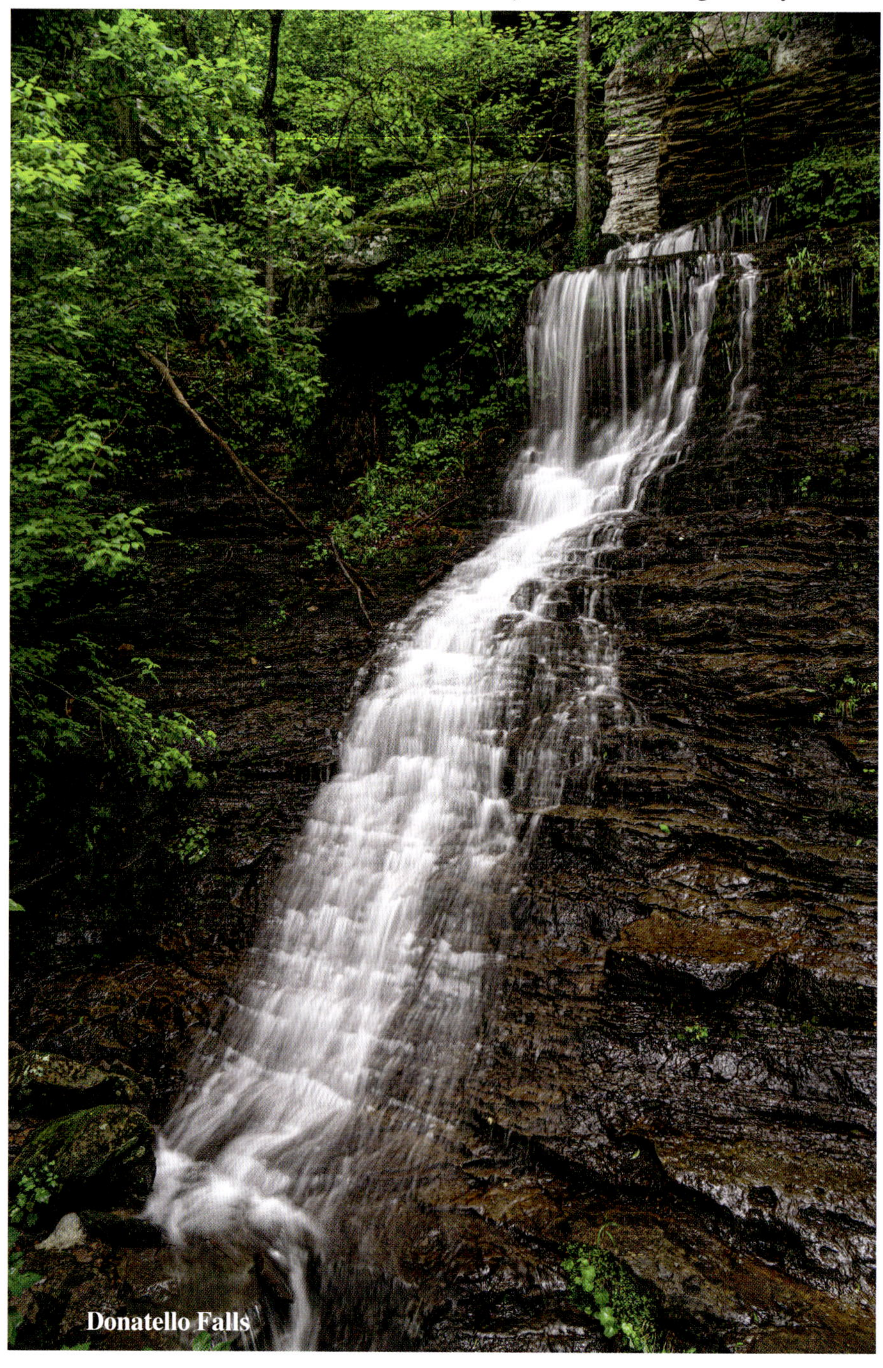

Donatello Falls

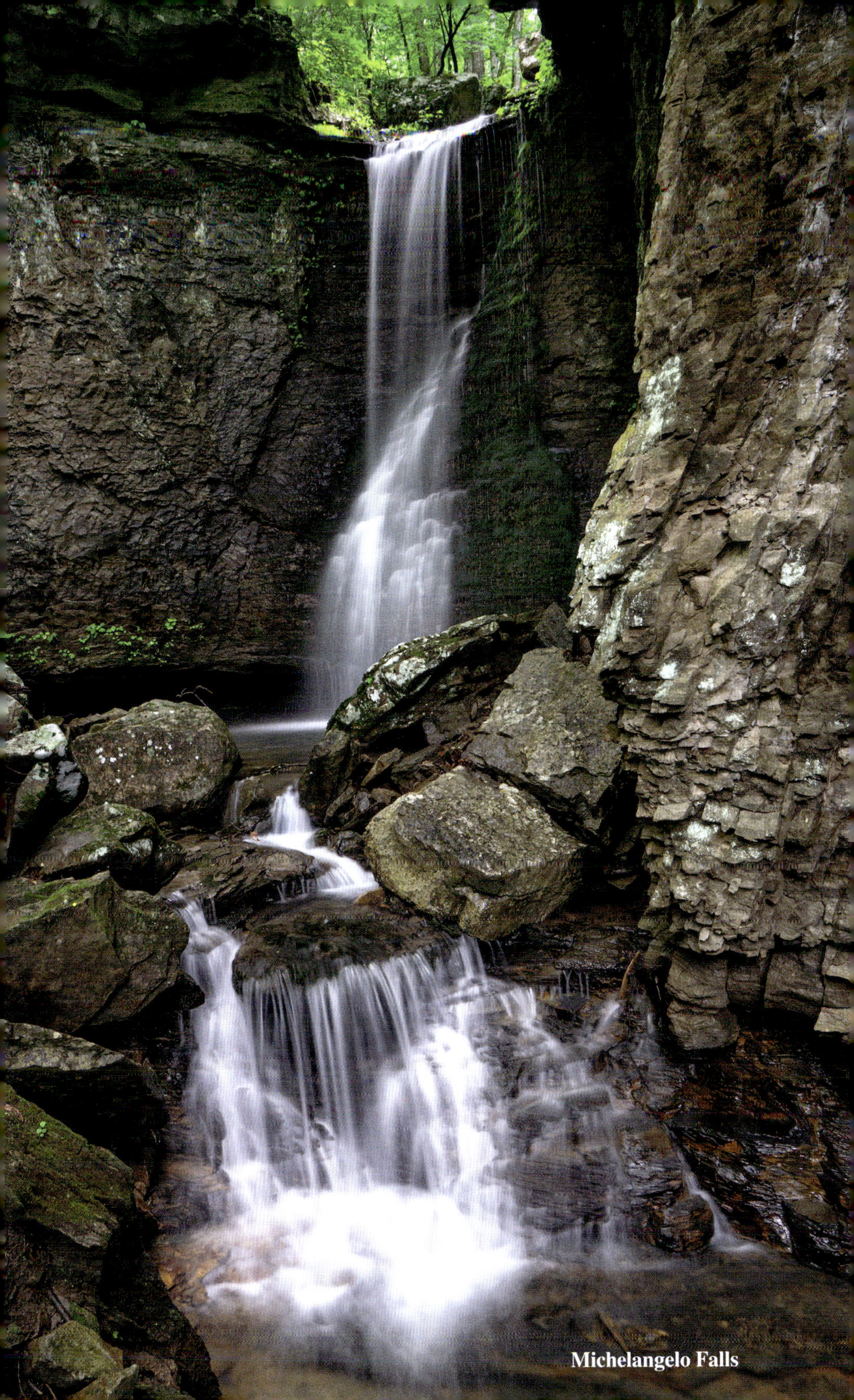

Michelangelo Falls

Terrapin Branch at 1.8. (At this point if you have had enough, simply follow the creek back upstream to **Terrapin Branch Falls** and back out to the trailhead.) OR CONTINUE your adventure and TURN RIGHT and follow Terrapin Branch downstream until you come to the first drainage coming in from the left, then TURN LEFT and hike up the stream to the amazing double-decker SSS **Curtis Falls** at 2.0.

From **Curtis Falls** scramble up a Black Diamond hillside ♦ on the left, then across to the right (above upper Curtis Falls) and then down a short Black Diamond slope ♦ and upstream to an almost hidden **Mossy Falls**, another SSS.

From there climb out of the steep canyon up to the right to the base of a bluff line, and follow it to the LEFT upstream. At the far end of this bluff is **Three-Toed Falls** at 2.25 with a pool, then below it is **Tilted Rock Falls**.

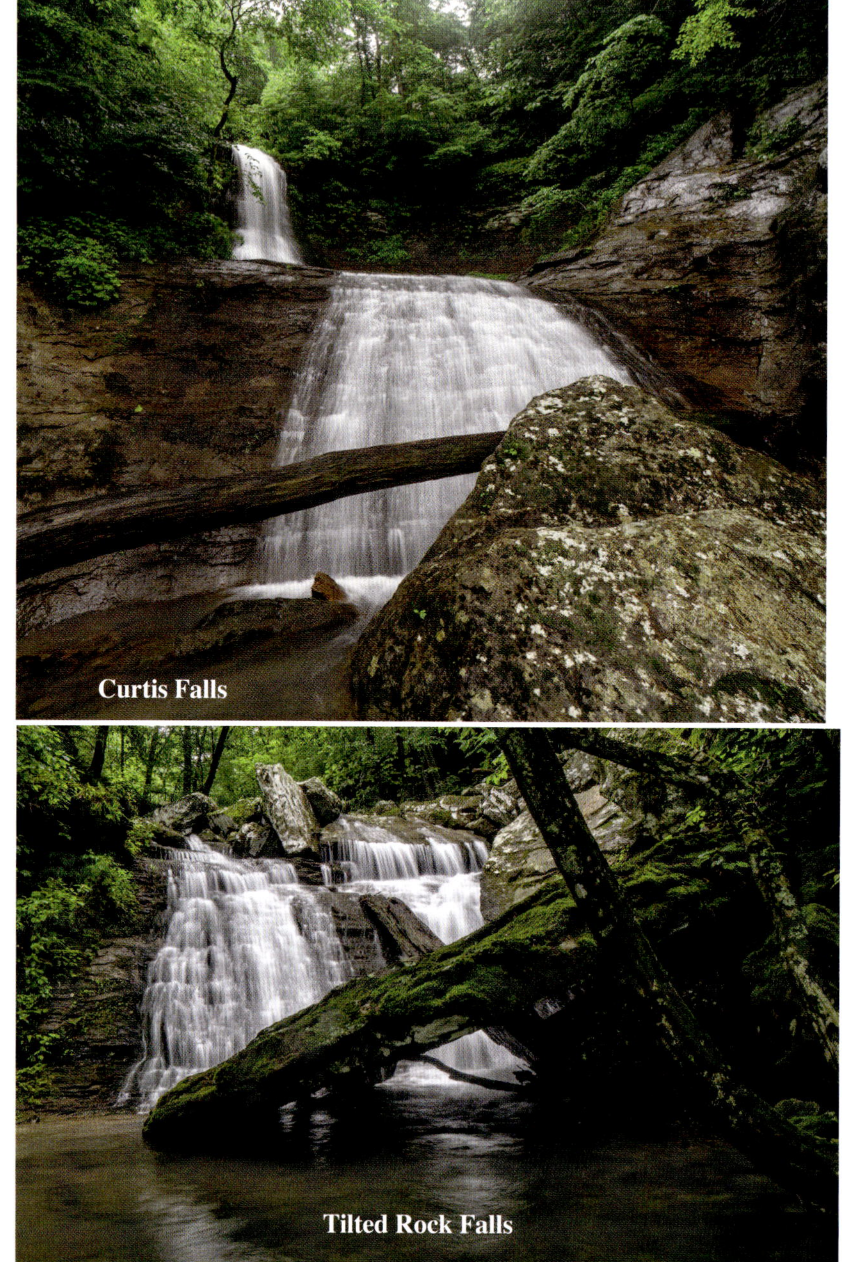

Curtis Falls

Tilted Rock Falls

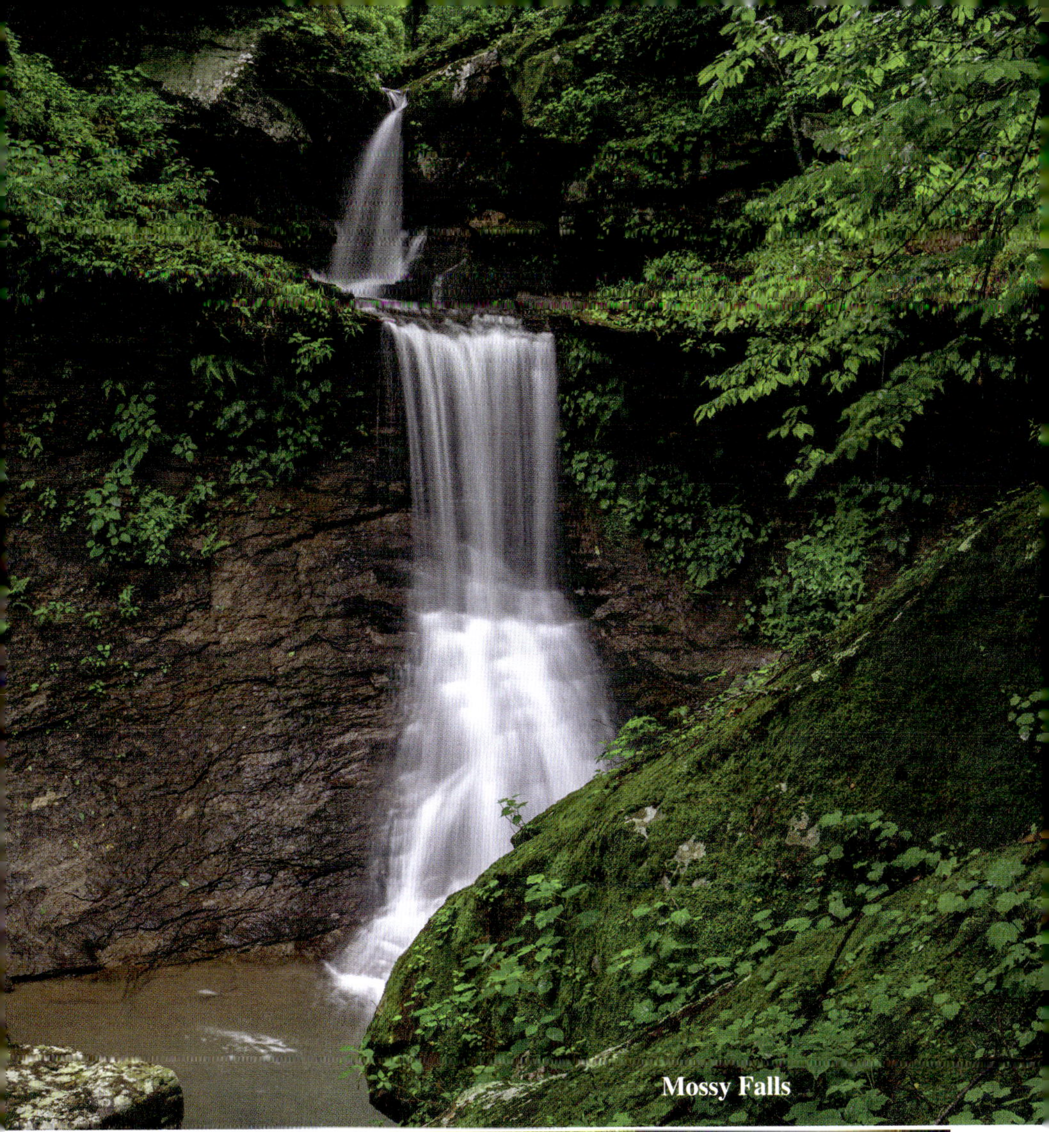

Mossy Falls

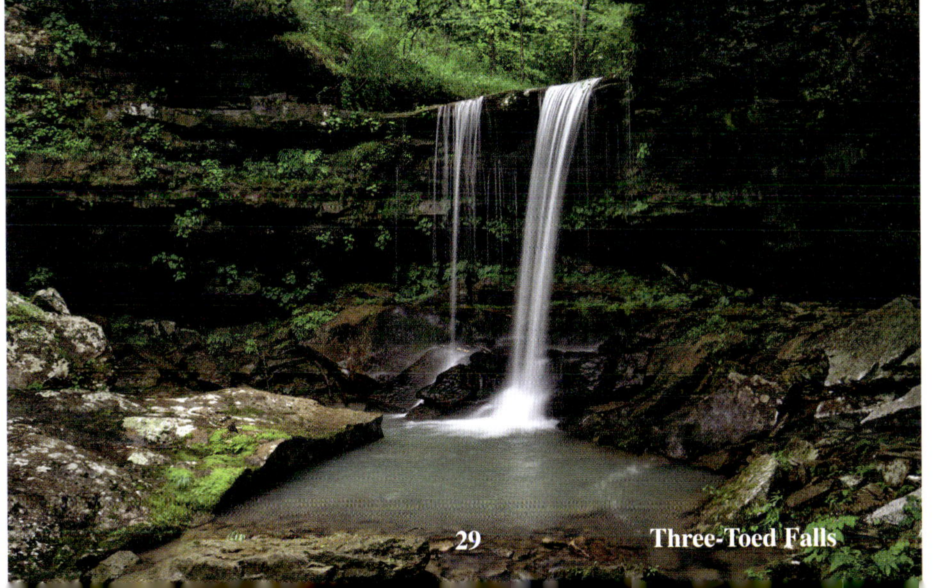

Three-Toed Falls

OK, that is enough waterfalls for a while—time for some flat-out hiking! Looking at **Tilted Rock Falls** from below, climb up and out to the LEFT and follow the base of the big bluff line up there—you will be heading back towards the parking area, and below private property that is above the bluffs. You want to stay at the base of the bluff and follow along as best you can. Eventually the bluff will curve to the right and away from Terrapin Branch (which is below you on the left) and up into a side creek. There are some cascades up the side creek but unless you have a lot of time I would recommend that you TURN LEFT away from the bluff and drop down to the side creek below—an SSS area down there!

Once in the creek—which should be filled with boulders—follow the creek downstream to the top of **Lazy Boulder Falls** at 2.8. CAUTION HERE!!! I scrambled down to the left of the falls to the bottom—another amazing SSS. And just downstream is another unique waterfall, **Square Boulder Falls**.

A little more downstream and you will come back to Terrapin Branch. TURN RIGHT and head upstream until you come to the MAIN waterfall complex, **Terrapin Branch Falls** at 3.2. There's a giant boulder blocking the stream there, with an emerald pool just on the other side and waterfalls upstream. Sometimes I'm able to climb up and over the boulder, other times I've backtracked downstream and climbed up some bluffs and around to the middle section of the waterfall complex—it's all an SSS and also all steep and questionable terrain. It's one of the great waterfall locations in the state.

Enjoy it while you can because it will be pretty tough going getting out of this spot! There are a couple of different ways to continue upstream and around the waterfall wall—I usually climb up to the base of the tall bluff—through a thick jungle jumble of boulders and vines ♦. Then once you reach the bluff TURN RIGHT and follow the base of the bluff as best you can upstream until the bluff eventually disappears—then follow Terrapin Branch upstream and back out past the private property corner and up to the parking spot, a total loop hike of 4.3 miles. CONGRATS if you made it!!!

Emergency contact: Newton County Sheriff, 870–446–5124 Dogs are OK.

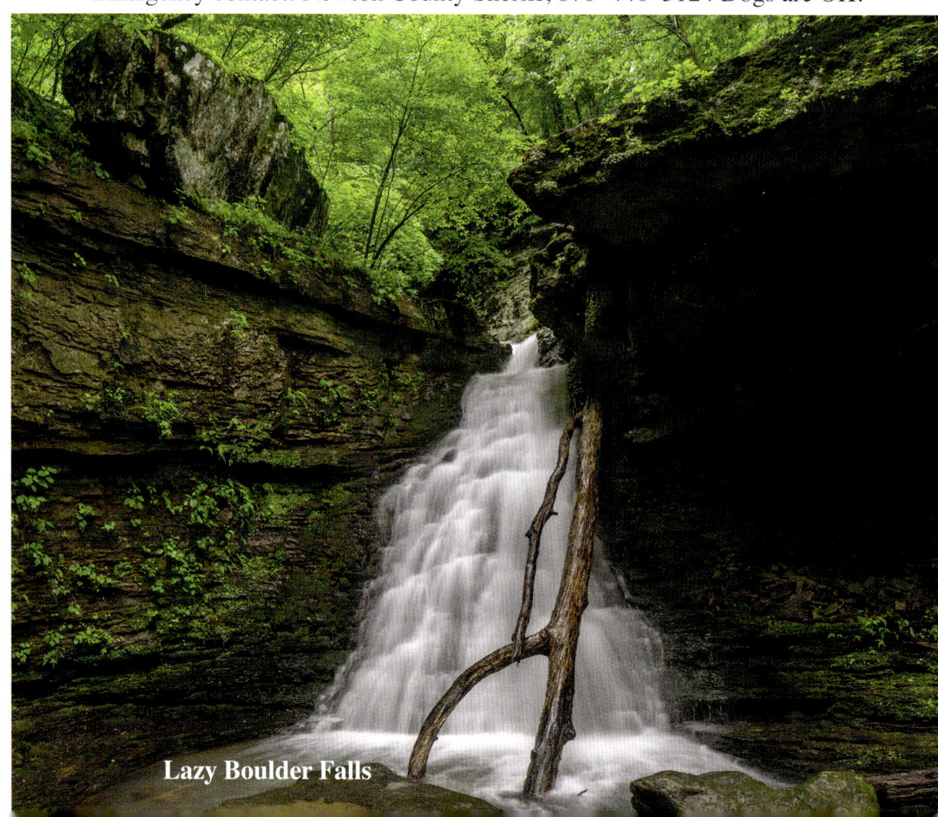

Lazy Boulder Falls

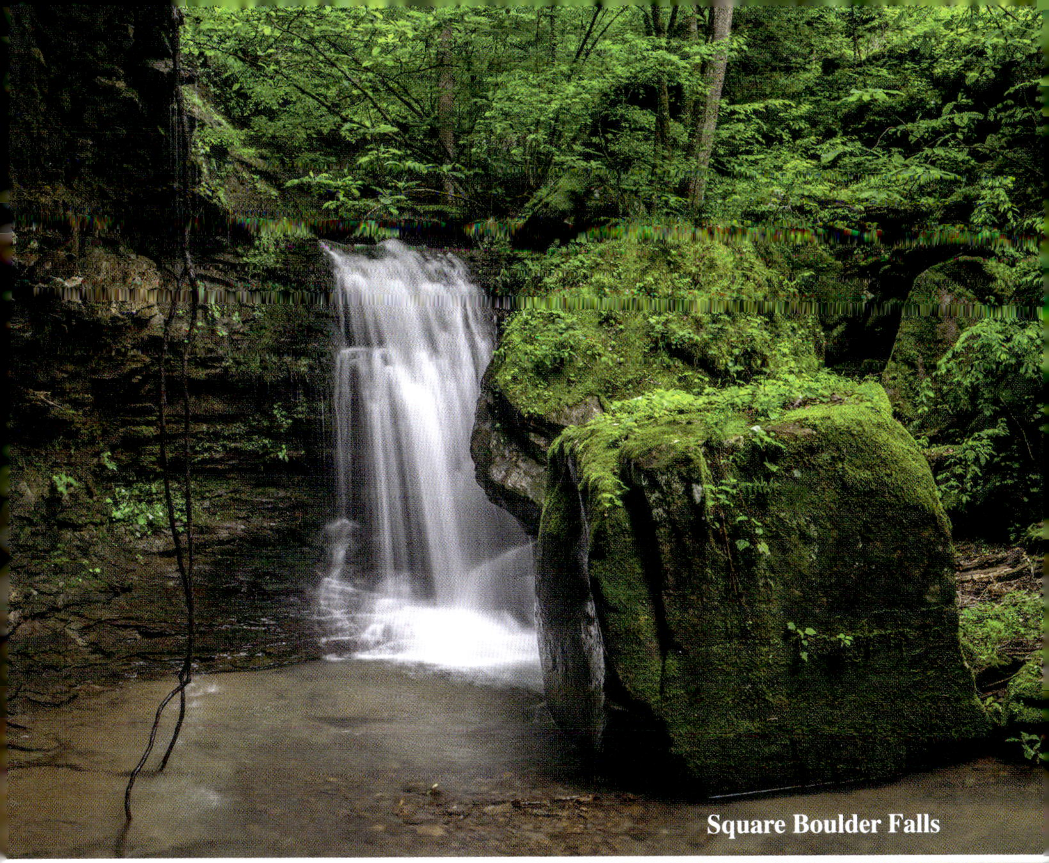

Square Boulder Falls

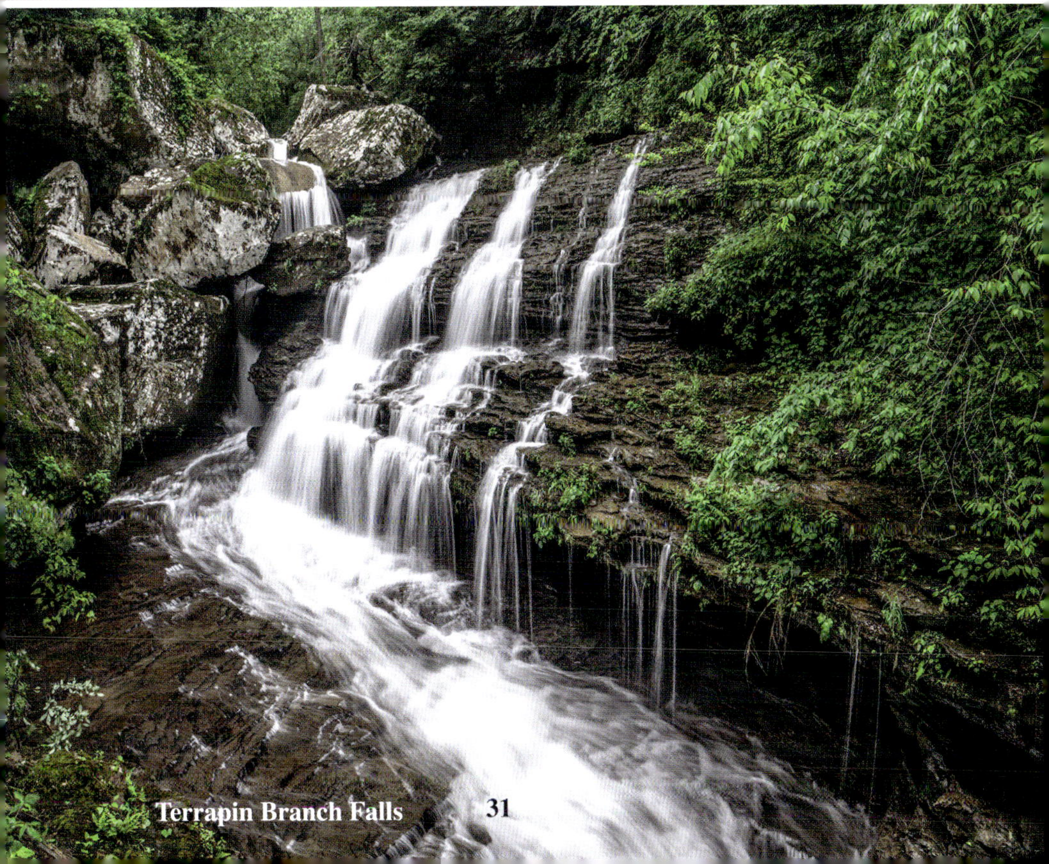

Terrapin Branch Falls

Magnolia Falls – 26′

2.1 miles roundtrip, medium hike/bushwhack, GPS recommended

GPS **35.86538, -93.39840**

Woods Boys Falls – 33′

Same location as above, medium hike/bushwhack, GPS recommended

GPS **35.86560, -93.39903**

Stahle Falls – 63′

Add .6 mile to above , medium hike/bushwhack, GPS recommended

GPS **35.86532, -93.40190**

Hadlock Cascade – 27′

Add .1 mile to above , medium hike/bushwhack, GPS recommended

GPS **35.86595, -93.40022**

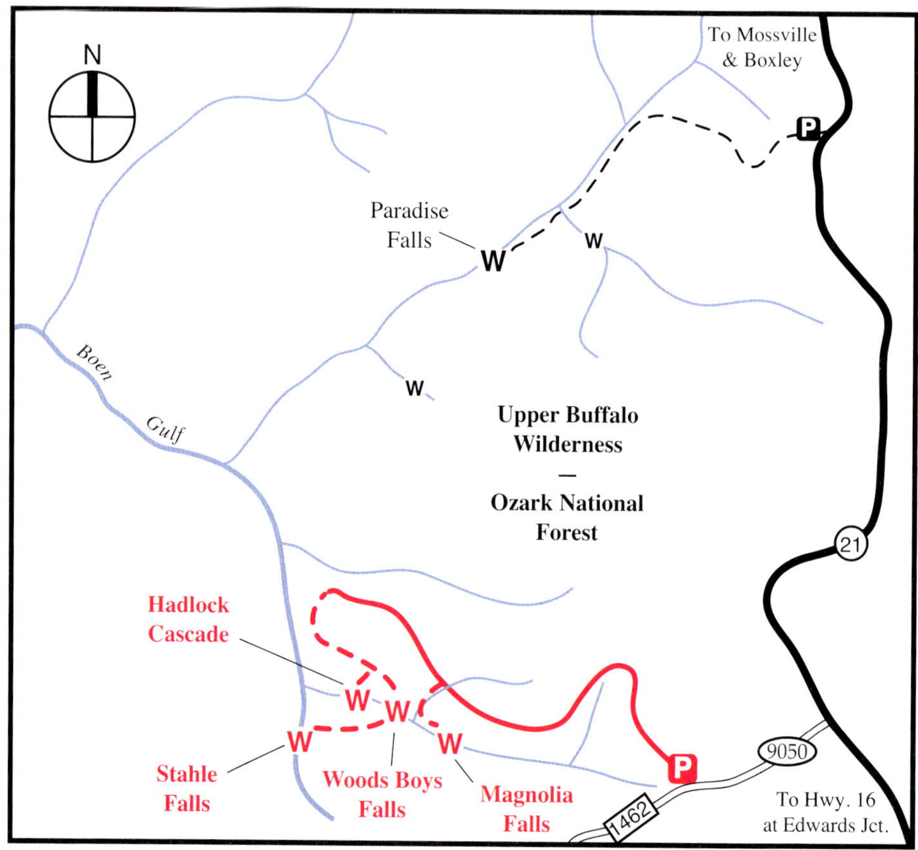

MAGNOLIA/WOODS BOYS/STAHLE FALLS. For the amount of effort involved to reach these waterfalls, getting to see four in the same trip is a pretty good bang for your buck (a polyfoss!). The hike is mostly on an old jeep road, and the scenery is first rate.

The turnoff for the trailhead is located between Mossville and Edwards Junction on Hwy. 21. From the Mossville Church go south on Hwy. 21 for 2.5 miles and TURN RIGHT onto CR#9050/FR#1462 (gravel); OR go north on Hwy. 21 from Edwards Junction for 1.8

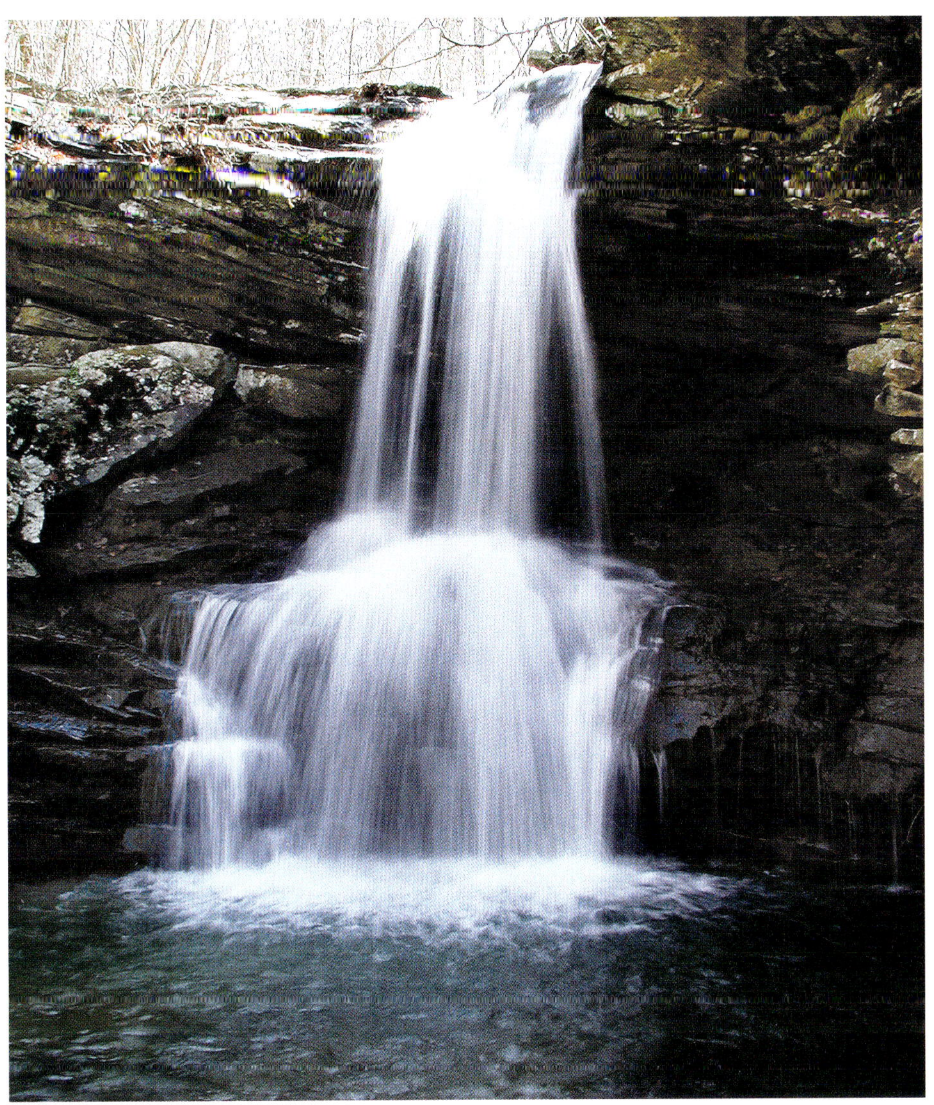

Magnolia Falls

miles and TURN LEFT onto CR#9050/FR#1462. Go just .3 mile and PARK on the right at the "Wilderness Access" sign (**35.86287, -93.38501**).

From the main gravel road hike on the jeep road past some mud holes, to the trailhead register just down the road. CONTINUE STRAIGHT AHEAD here along the road trace. You'll cross a small creek and then come to an intersection of sorts about 100 yards beyond—TURN LEFT onto a jeep road as you enter the wilderness boundary (painted blue blazes on the trees).

This little road drops on down the hill past some interesting stone walls and rock formations up on the right. After you have gone just about 1.0 mile, the road will dip down and come to a little creek, then the road heads uphill just a little bit. You want to TURN LEFT at the creek and follow it downstream, leaving the road. This creek will take you on down just a couple hundred yards to a larger creek below. **Magnolia Falls** will be just upstream on the larger creek, and **Woods Boys Falls** will be just downstream.

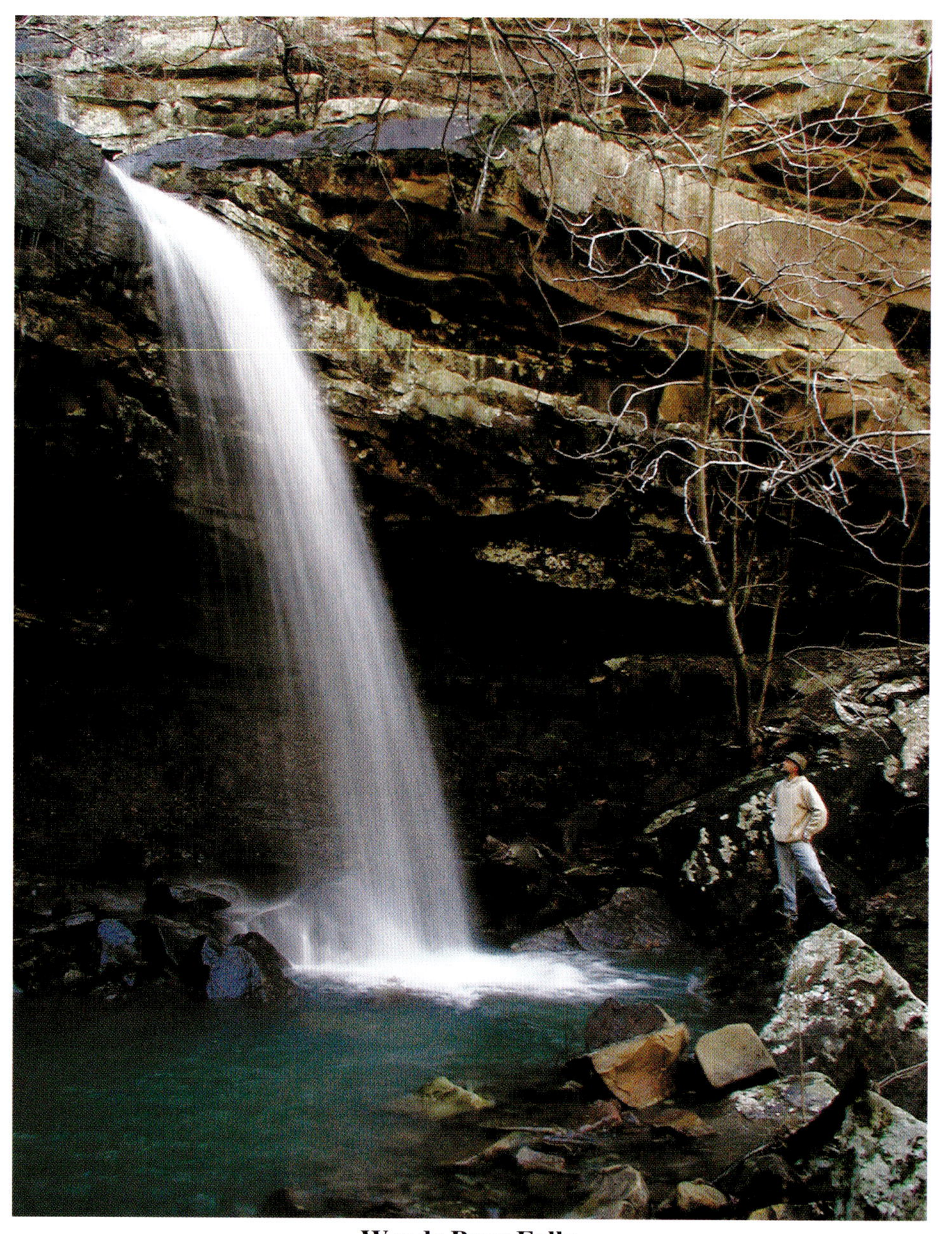

Woods Boys Falls

From here you will have a couple of options. If you simply want to make an easy hike on over to see **Stahle Falls** from the top, make your way on around and up to the top of **Magnolia Falls** and cross the creek up there, then follow the top of the bluffline on around to the right until you come to the falls. This area is thick with huckleberry underfoot.

If you want a longer (add 2.0 miles to the roundtrip total), more scenic hike, then back up and return to the jeep road at the point where you left it. CONTINUE hiking along the road. It will bump up just a little, then drop on down the hill at a pretty good clip, coming underneath some overhanging bluffs. At the bottom of those bluffs TURN LEFT and bushwhack along the base of that bluffline to the bottom of **Woods Boys Falls**.

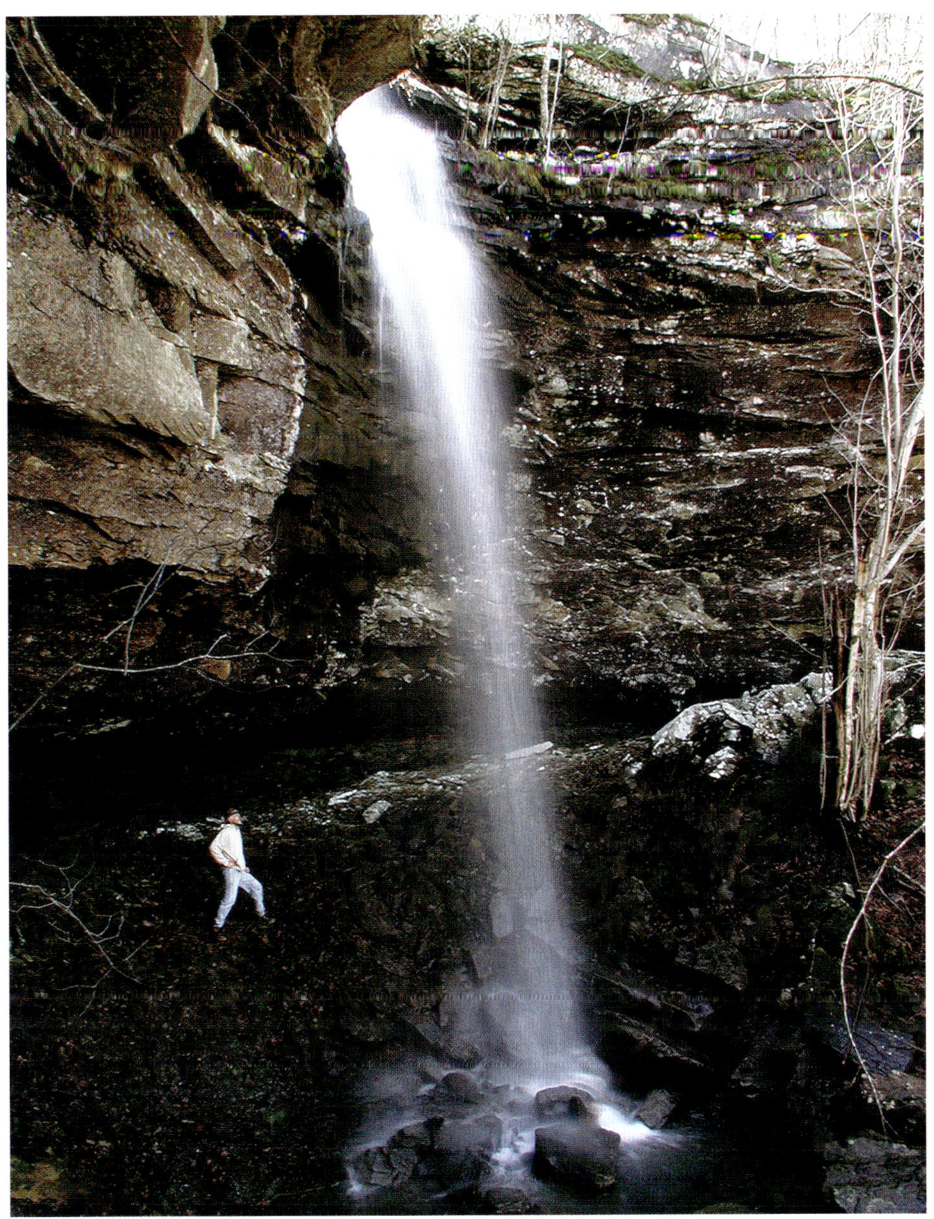

Dave Stahle Falls (the top of the falls is out of sight)

The Woods Boys are Danny, Billy, Spanky, Kenny, and Landon Woods, all friends of mine who grew up in the area and probably know this country better than anyone. They logged the forest by hand, and took very good care of it in the process.

From **Woods Boys Falls** continue following the base of the bluff to the right and you will eventually come to the bottom of **Stahle Falls**. Professor Dave Stahle is another friend of mine, and owns a cabin at the head of this drainage. He is one of the world's leading authorities on determining the age of trees. There are some in this area many hundreds of years old. He can bore into a tree and show you evidence of great floods, fires and drought.

So far the route you have just taken from the trailhead to all these falls is the same route

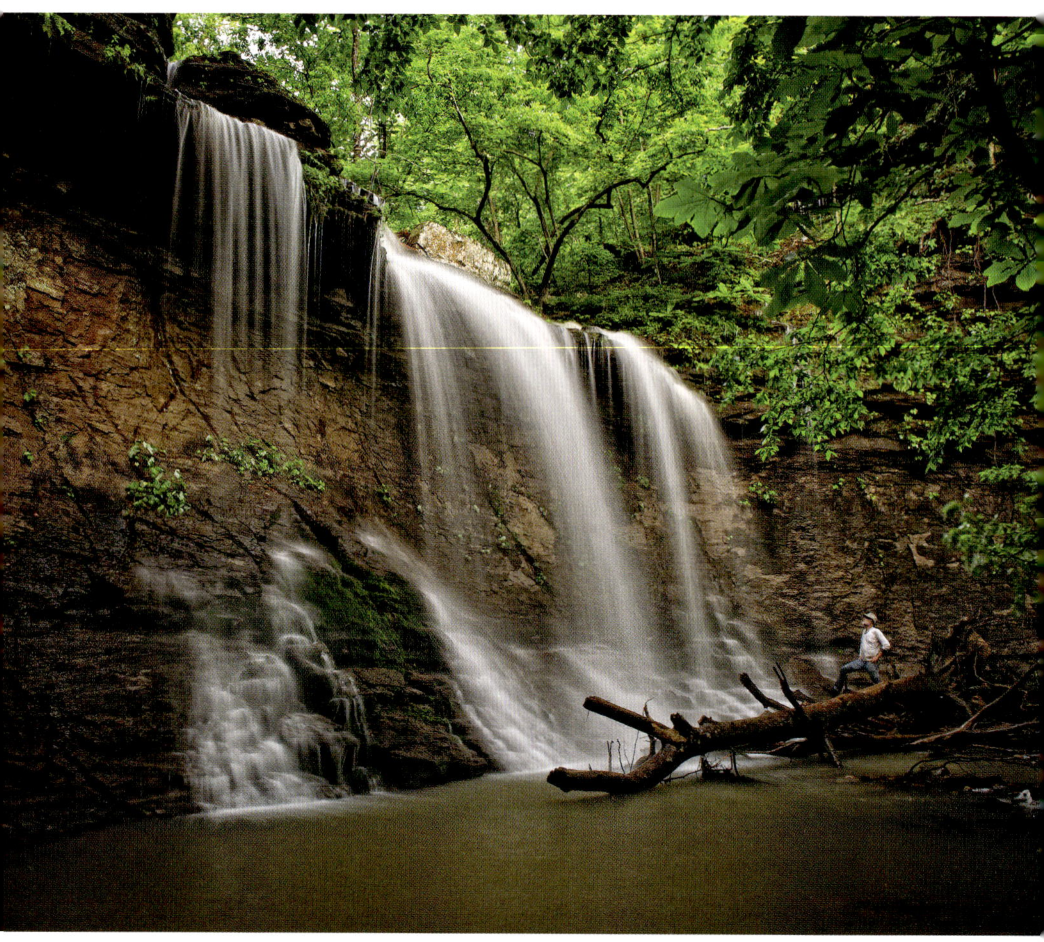

David Hadlock Cascade

David Hadlock followed when he hiked into this area on an icy day, February 20, 2010. David was a surveyor by trade but loved to get out and explore the wilderness with camera in hand, and he photographed each of these waterfalls that day (his photos included a lot of ice formations—the southern side of this canyon was covered with ice from recent cold weather). On his way back from **Stahle Falls**, David noticed a waterfall in the bottom of the canyon that was below Woods Boys Falls. In his quest to scramble down to this new waterfall he slipped and fell to his death on the steep icy slope. David was one of the really good guys in the world, and this was a tragic accident. But now the waterfall he found will forever bear his name, and his family hopes it will bring joy to generations of waterfall hunters and photographers who visit. A week after David's accident his camera was recovered from the bottom of a pool downstream, and his family was able to view the great sights he saw.

To reach **Hadlock Cascade** begin at the base of **Woods Boys Falls** and follow the north side of the bluff downstream a short distance (100 yards or so), then bushwhack down the steep slope to the creek and falls—best to end up below the falls. During high water the left side of the falls is actually 38' tall. The steep-walled canyon below the cascade is filled with boulders and white water—David's spirit dancing and having a grand old time!

Emergency contact: Newton County Sheriff, 870–446–5124 Dogs are OK.

Paradise Falls – 32′

2.4 miles roundtrip, difficult bushwhack, GPS recommended

GPS **35.88118, -93.39310**

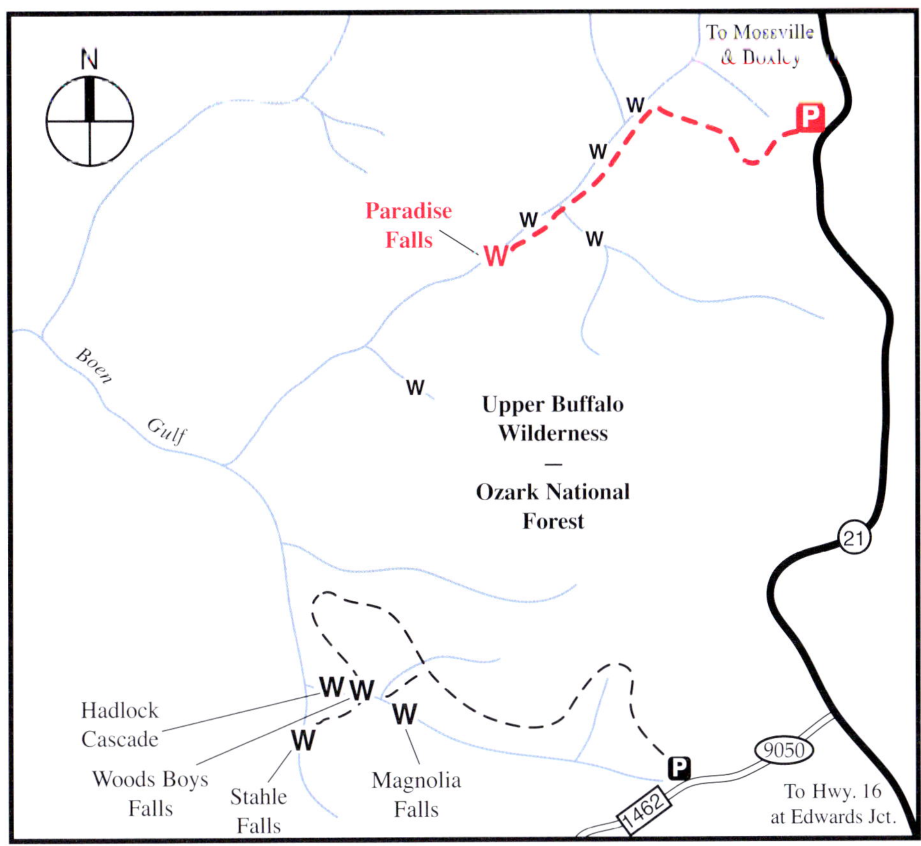

PARADISE FALLS. Something about this falls made me think of a tropical paradise the minute I saw it. It's a wide cascade that plunges down into a large emerald pool. I happened upon it one day while simply out exploring some drainages to see what I could find. Seems like a perfect skinny-dipping hole to me!

There is a social trail and part of the hike is along an old logging road, and there are several smaller waterfalls along the way. To get to the parking spot, take Hwy. 21 south from the Mossville Church (between Boxley and Edwards Junction). Go just .8 mile and PARK on the right at a pulloff area. (OR 3.4 miles north on Hwy. 21 from Edwards Junction). The old road that is closed and blocked that takes off to the west from this spot.

Hike along the old road as it heads down a hill. It will soon level out some and come to an intersection—there are a number of logging roads in this area—all of them growing up—and things will be rather confusing, but as long as you keep going downhill you will eventually get to the waterfall. A GPS will help. At the first intersection stay STRAIGHT AHEAD and curve a little to the left. Soon you will come to an area where there are several old roads that take off—TURN RIGHT and head straight down the hill on one of the road traces. Continue on down the hill past a couple of more intersections, and eventually you will curve around to the right and enter the wilderness boundary (blue blazes on the

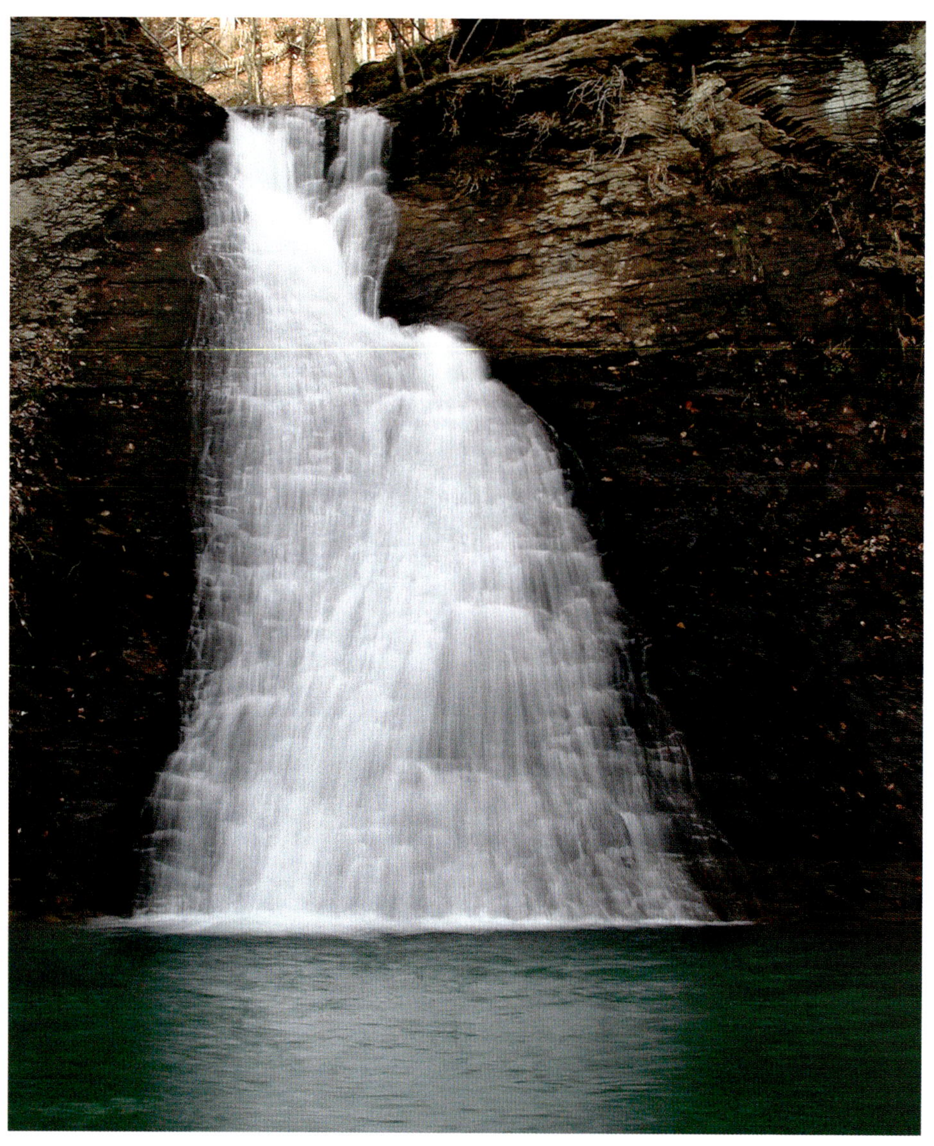

Paradise Falls

trees). If you are at the right spot, the old road will cross a creek not too far beyond the boundary paint at about .6. There is a small waterfall on the creek just below where the old road crosses the creek. TURN LEFT and bushwhack down alongside the creek.

You will pass another waterfall and then a good-sized creek coming in from the left at 1.0 (there is a nice waterfall just upstream to the left on that creek). CONTINUE STRAIGHT AHEAD and downstream. If the water is running high you will probably have to be up on the hillside looking down on the creek instead of right alongside it. You will pass another waterfall and cascade area, and then you will come to the top of **Paradise Falls** at 1.2.

If you are a tough woodsman and have lots of time and energy, it is possible to find your way downstream and then back up a different fork of Boen Gulf to the trio of waterfalls noted on the bottom of this map and described on the following pages.

Emergency contact: Newton County Sheriff, 870–446–5124 Dogs are OK.

Courageous Light Falls – 27′

.5, mile, 1.0 mile easy+ roundtrip GPS **35.89735, -93.40720**

Boulder City Falls – 56′

1.4, 2.8 mile medium roundtrip GPS 35.89392, -93.41895

Bathroom Falls – 36′

1.6 **(3.2 miles medium roundtrip to all)** GPS **35.89122, -93.41843**

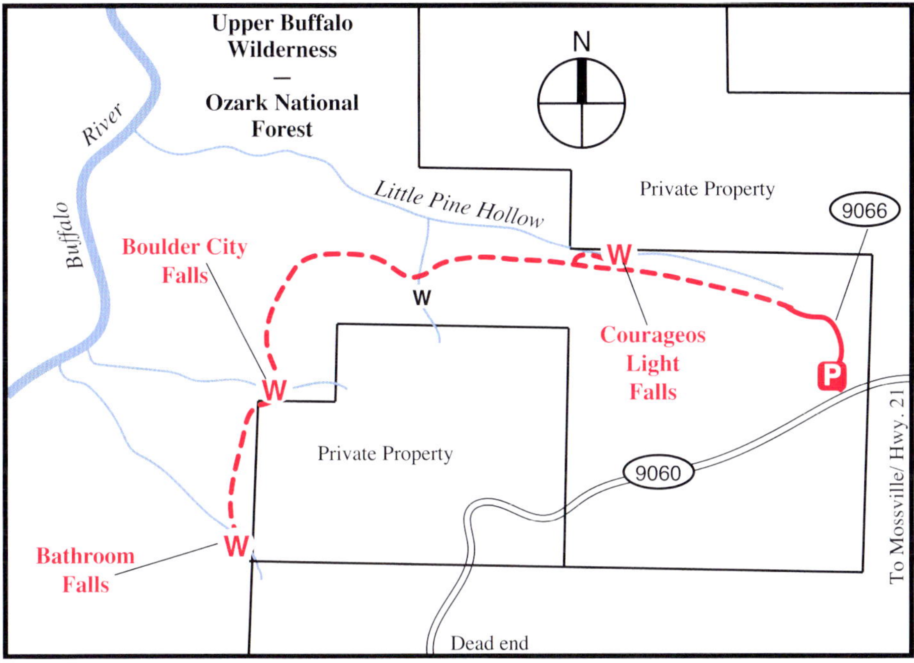

COURAGEOUS LIGHT FALLS/BOULDER CITY FALLS/BATHROOM FALLS. From the church at Mossville (on Hwy. 21 south of Boxley), take Newton County Road 9060 (it's across the highway from the church) 1.0 and TURN RIGHT onto Road 9066 then PARK on the LEFT at the power line (**35.89521, -93.40119**).

Hike down the road a couple hundred yards and TURN LEFT onto an old road trace just before a creek. Follow this trace gradually downhill into Little Pine Hollow to a break in the bluff line and TURN RIGHT and back upstream will be **Courageous Light Falls** at .5, an SSS. This was named in honor of Andrea Eileen Norton, a young lady from South Dakota who tragically perished nearby in the wilderness in 2019. By all accounts she was indeed a "Courageous Light" that shone brightly on those around her and the lives she touched.

Return to the road trace and continue a bit more down into the hollow and then level and you'll pass a series of waterfalls up on the left at .9—cross the creek there and soon after the road trace curves around to the left, following a tall bluff line to and through several house-size boulders, and SSS all around! You are now overlooking the main Buffalo River Canyon as Little Pine Hollow drops steeply away down to the river.

Make your way along the big bluff to **Boulder City Falls** at 1.4. Then continue along the bluff to **Bathroom Falls** at 1.6. OK, since you asked, this one is named so because it could be seen through a window while sitting on the throne from the upstairs bathroom in a log cabin that is located on the other side of the Buffalo River Canyon. During really high water both of these waterfalls plunge 700 feet in a continuous cascade all the way down to the Buffalo River. It's quite a sight from that bathroom! You can't quite see it from this area, but the distant canyon across the river to the west that you can see during leaf-off is Whitaker Creek, home to Hawksbill Crag and many great waterfalls.

Emergency contact: Newton County Sheriff, 870–446–5124 Dogs are OK.

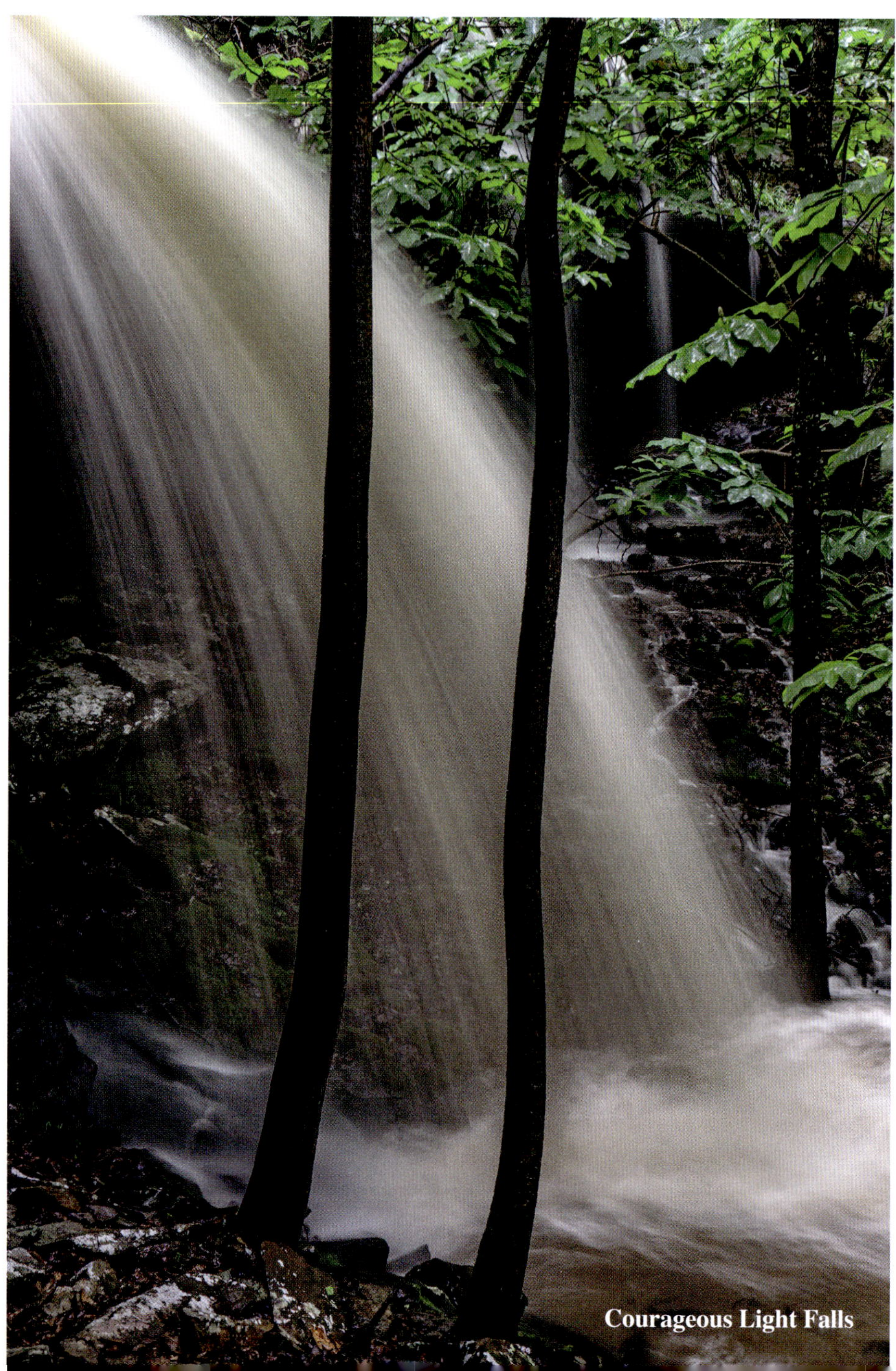

Courageous Light Falls

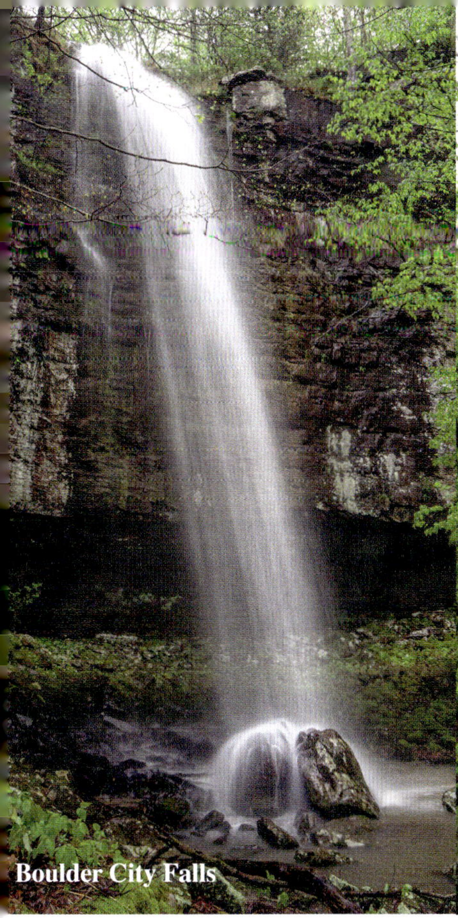

Boulder City Falls

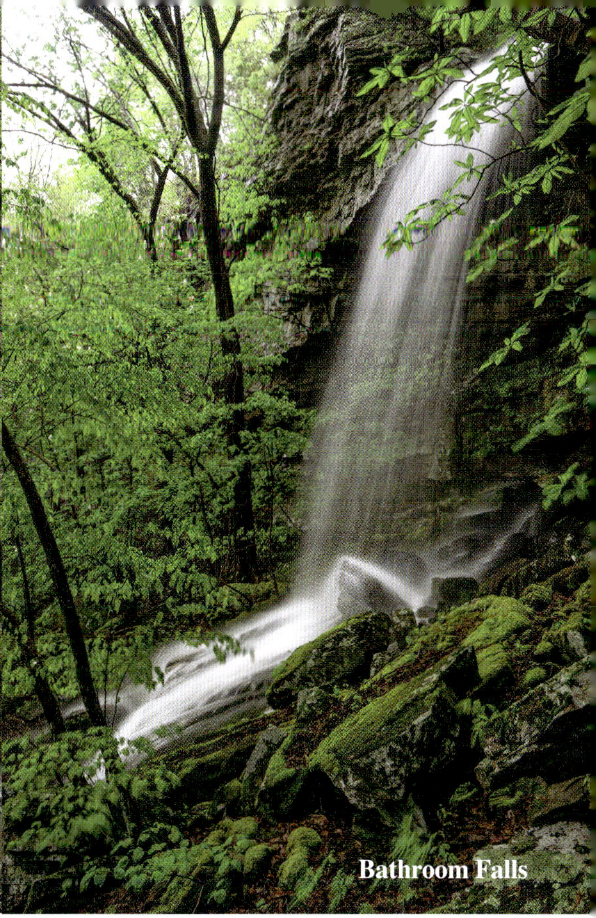

Bathroom Falls

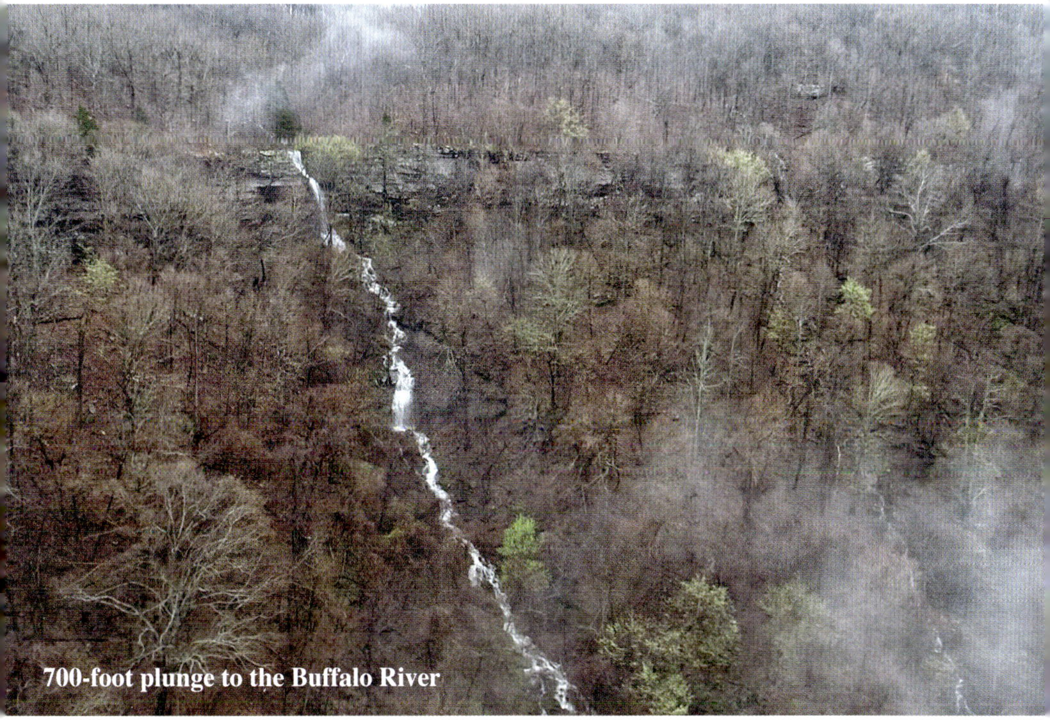

700-foot plunge to the Buffalo River

Beagle Point Falls – 76′

4.4 miles roundtrip, difficult bushwhack, GPS helpful

GPS **35.87768, -93.44922**

Wild Burro Falls –21′

4.2 miles roundtrip, difficult bushwhack, GPS helpful

GPS **35.87667, -93.45140**

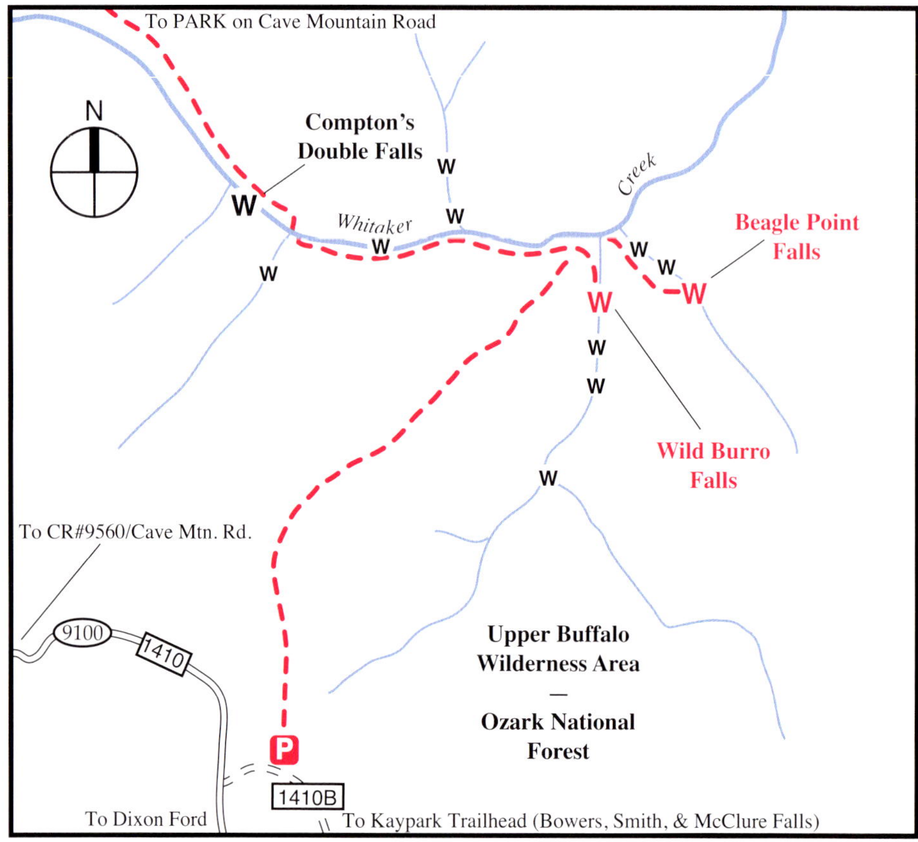

BEAGLE POINT FALLS/WILD BURRO FALLS. Beagle Point Falls is the second tallest waterfall in the Buffalo River headwaters area (after Hedges Pouroff), with a lush forest of towering umbrella magnolia trees around its base. Nearby, Wild Burro Falls (named after a band of wild burros I found living nearby) is tucked into a small grotto and protected by a large boulder in front, and by a hanging valley of waterfalls upstream.

There are a couple of different ways to access these waterfalls that are located deep in the Upper Buffalo Wilderness Area. If you are already visiting Compton Double Falls, then simply continue downstream .75 miles to a creek and TURN RIGHT and follow the creek about 200 yards to **Wild Burro Falls**. To reach **Beagle Point Falls** go back to Whitaker Creek and continue downstream 200 yards and TURN RIGHT up a smaller creek—it is a *steep climb* past several scenic waterfalls to the big one above!

Direct route: From the parking spot for **Compton Double Falls**, continue driving on CR#9560 for 1.5 miles and TURN LEFT onto CR#9100/FR#1410. Go 1.6 miles and TURN LEFT onto FR#1410B (the road to **Bowers Hollow Falls**). Go a couple hundred yards and PARK on the LEFT (**35.86528, -93.46178).** You can either just scramble down into the

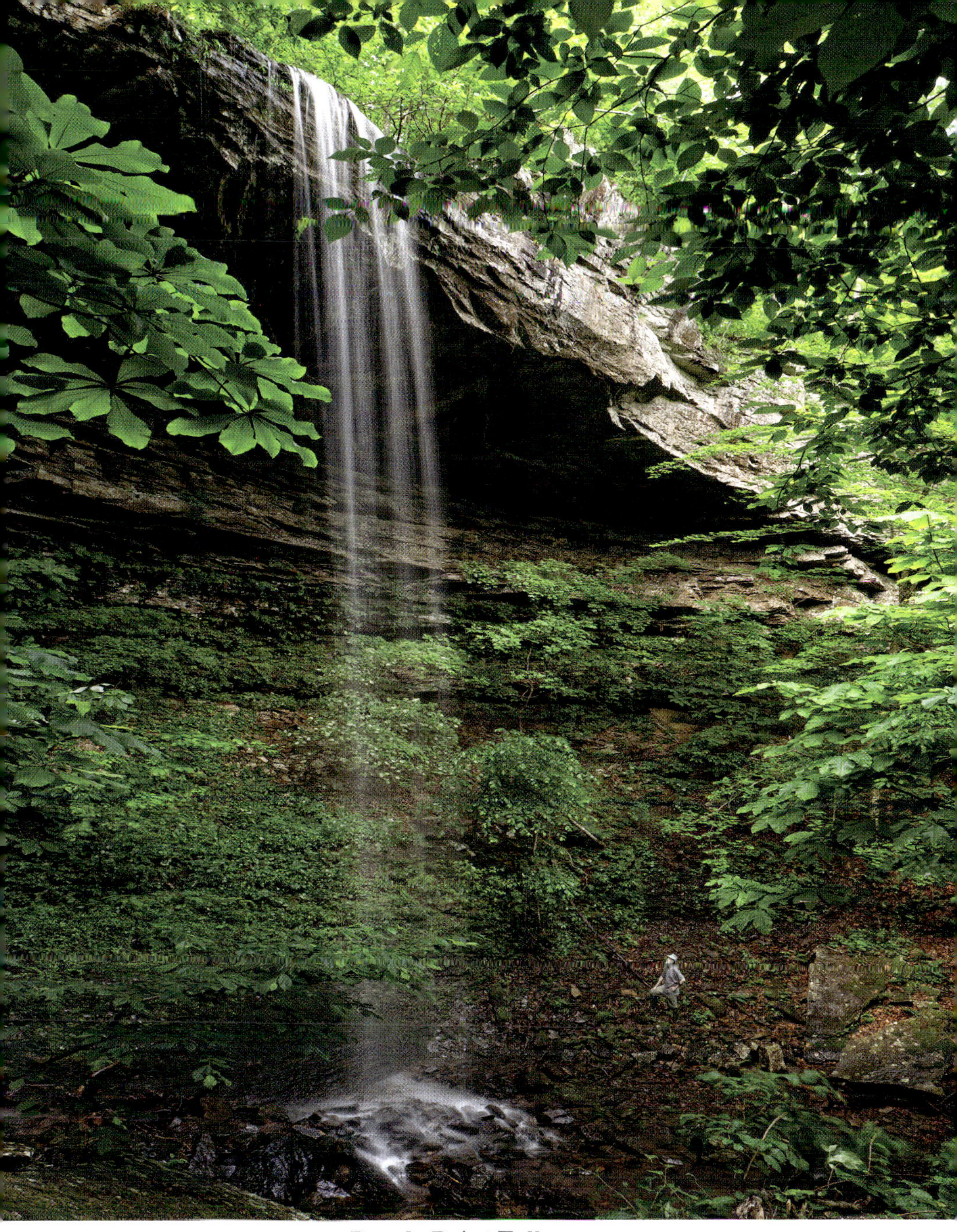

Beagle Point Falls

drainage and follow the creek all the way to **Wild Burro Falls** (past several small falls and a hanging canyon near the end—difficult); OR head out to the northwest on the level (shown on map), then swing to the northeast and follow the ridgetop as it drops gradually to Whitaker Creek. Once in the bottom, TURN RIGHT on Whitaker Creek, then TURN RIGHT and follow the first creek upstream to **Wild Burro**; and/or follow the second creek to your right *UP* to **Beagle Point Falls**. Either route is a very rugged 3–4 mile roundtrip bushwhack total.

Emergency contact: Newton County Sheriff, 870–446–5124 Dogs are OK

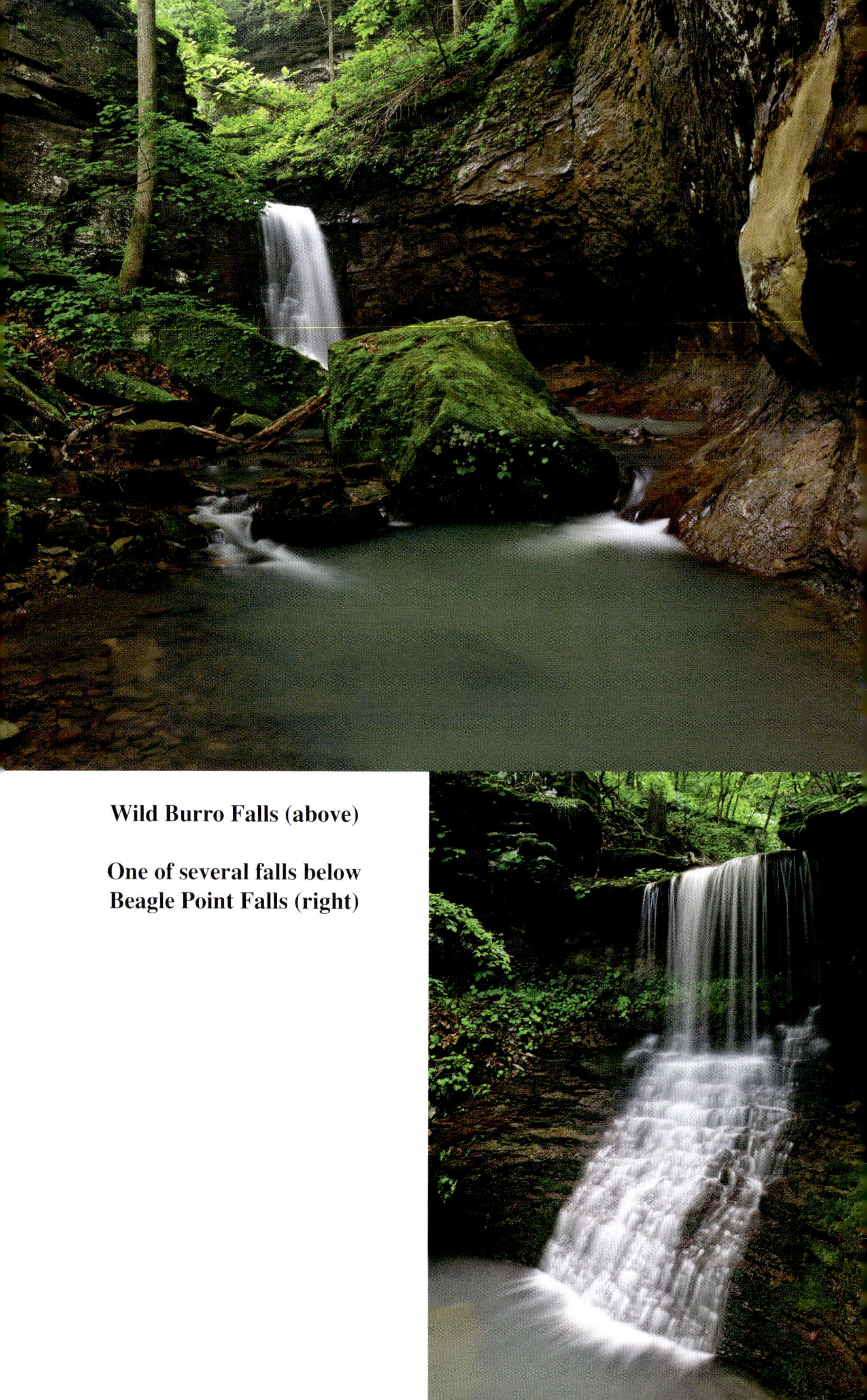

Wild Burro Falls (above)

One of several falls below Beagle Point Falls (right)

Amber Falls – 18′ (photo is on page 7)

.7 miles roundtrip, medium bushwhack, GPS helpful

GPS **35.88395, -93.47017**

Compton's Double Falls – 39′

2.1 miles roundtrip, medium bushwhack, GPS helpful

GPS **35.87930, -93.46257**

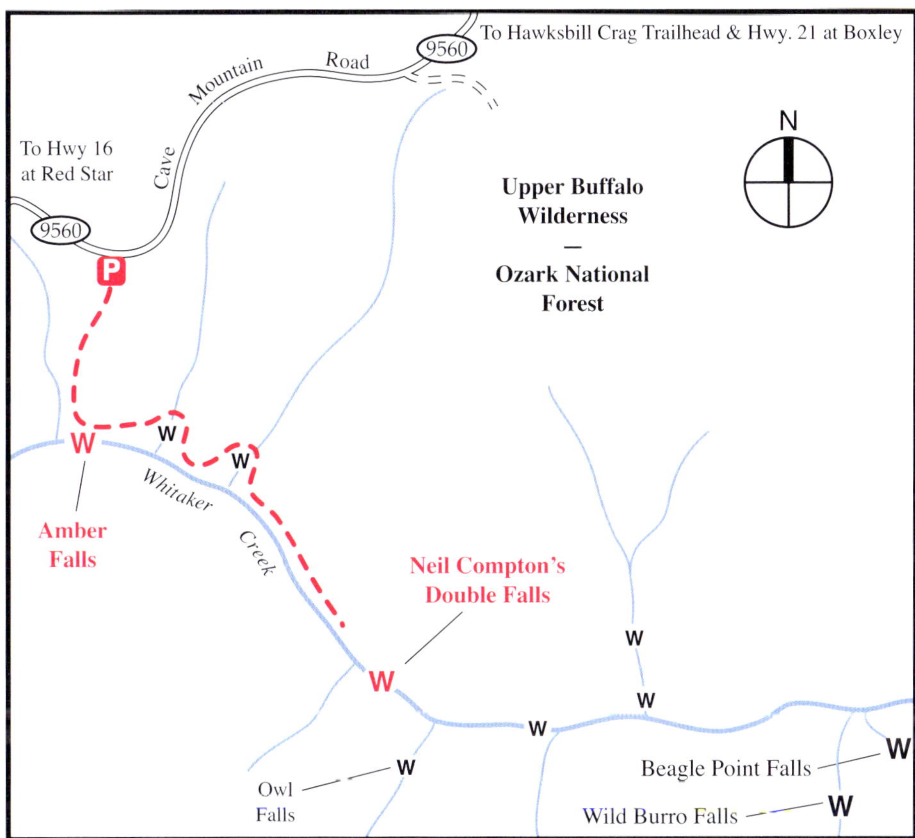

AMBER FALLS/ NEIL COMPTON'S DOUBLE FALLS. Neil Compton sat on our deck at Cloudland one morning and told about the cougar scat he had found just above this waterfall many years before. No one could tell a story like Neil Compton, and he made the simple act of finding a pile of scat seem extraordinary. No one has done more for the natural beauty of Arkansas than he. The day he died I decided to name this beautiful double waterfall in his honor—no single falls would do. His vision is what saved the Buffalo River, and is why so many of us attempt to follow his path and keep the torch lit to protect our wild places. That cougar is out there somewhere, keeping Neil's spirit alive. On the way down you will pass a waterfall that I named after our daughter, Amber. She is a special young lady and loves the outdoors. The photo of her waterfall is on page 7.

There is no official trail to these falls, but a medium social trail has developed down to them. The parking spot is located on CR#9560/Cave Mountain Road near the Hawksbill Crag Trailhead. From Ponca take Hwy. 43 south through Boxley Valley to the intersection with Hwy. 21. TURN LEFT and go south on Hwy. 21 for 1.2 miles (over two bridges) and

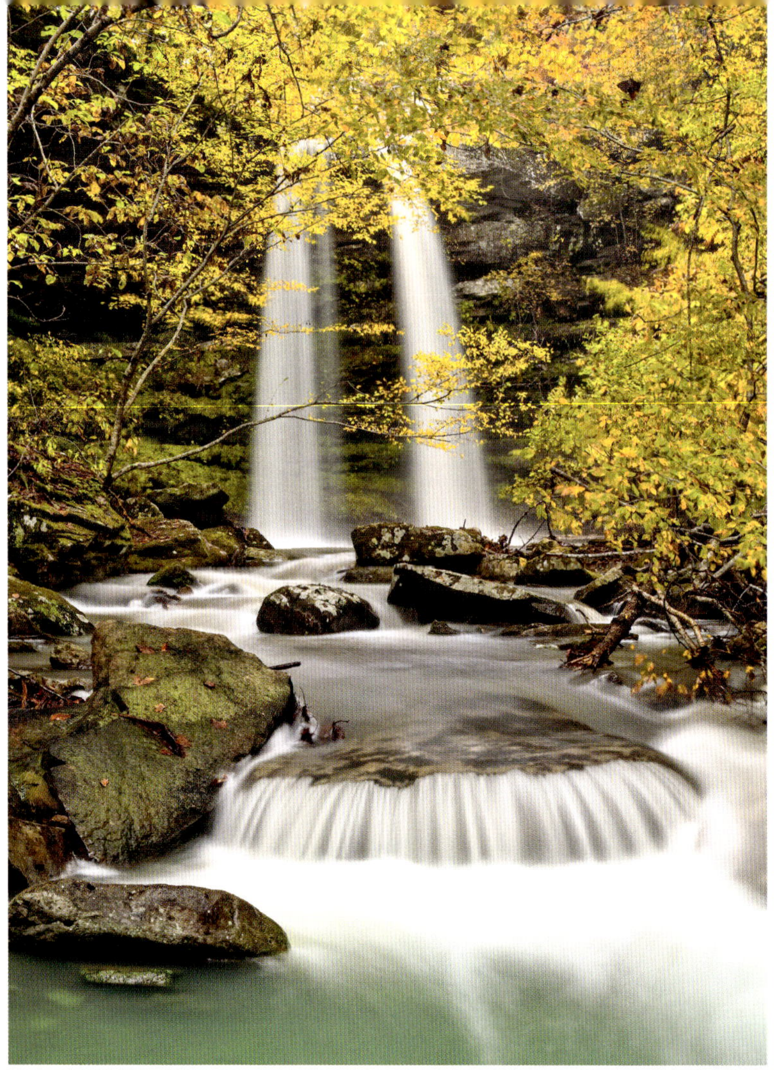

Neil Compton's Double Falls (high water)

TURN RIGHT onto CR#9560/Cave Mtn. Road (gravel) just before the bridge over the Buffalo River (zero your odometer). This road is *steep!* You will pass Cave Mtn. Church at 5.4, then the Hawksbill Crag Trailhead at 6.0. Continue PAST the trailhead for another 1.1 miles until you come to a wooden sign on the left that says "Upper Buffalo Wilderness" and PARK along the road near there.

Head into the woods behind the sign and follow the social trail *straight down* the hill. There is a small drainage on the right—follow this all the way to the bottom of the hill where you will hit Whitaker Creek. Once you get to the bottom, TURN LEFT and follow Whitaker Creek downstream and you will come to **Amber Falls** (beloved daughter of ours!).

To get to **Compton's Double Falls** from there continue heading downstream—stay up on the bench overlooking the creek, keeping Whitaker Creek just off to your right. You will pass a couple of other nice waterfalls that come in on side drainages along the way. You will know Neil's waterfall when you come to it—the creek will drop away sharply below, and you will hear a big roar. It takes a good bit of water to get this waterfall running as a double, so save it for a rainy day! Hike back out the same way that you came in.

Emergency contact: Newton County Sheriff, 870–446–5124 Dogs are OK

Haley Falls (2) – 17′/45′

2.2 miles roundtrip, medium hike, GPS not needed

GPS **35.89350, -93.44688**

Mule Trail Falls – 31′

2.2 miles roundtrip (inc. above), medium hike/bushwhack, GPS helpful

GPS **35.89363, -93.44988**

Thousand Kisses Falls – 48′

Add .2 to above, medium hike/bushwhack, GPS helpful

GPS **35.89242, -93.45053**

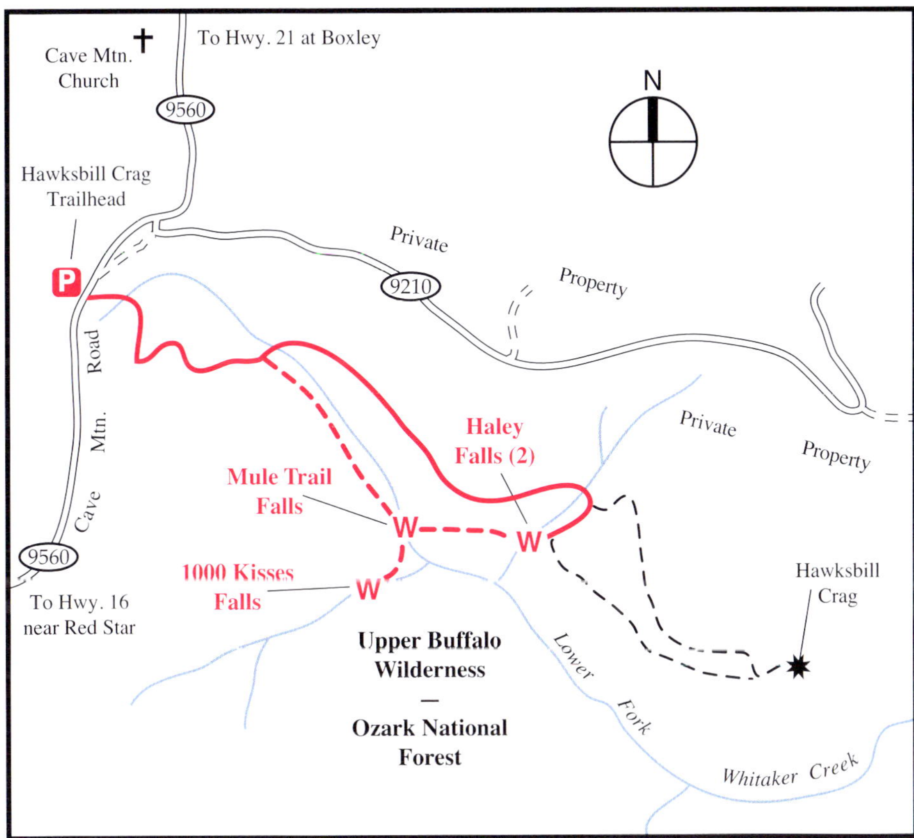

HALEY/MULE TRAIL/THOUSAND KISSES FALLS. The largest search and rescue mission in Arkansas history centered around Haley Falls, and was the subject of a ***Dateline NBC*** story, my book ***The Search For Haley***, and countless other media reports. Six-year-old Haley Zega got separated from her group and was on her own in the wilderness for three days and two nights—all she wanted was to go have a closer look at the waterfall that would later bear her name. Haley Falls is located along the trail to the famous Hawksbill Crag. The other two falls are in the same area, but require a bit of bushwhacking to find.

The trailhead is located on CR#9560/Cave Mtn. Road (the Hawksbill Crag Trailhead). From Ponca take Hwy. 43 south through Boxley Valley to the intersection with Hwy. 21.

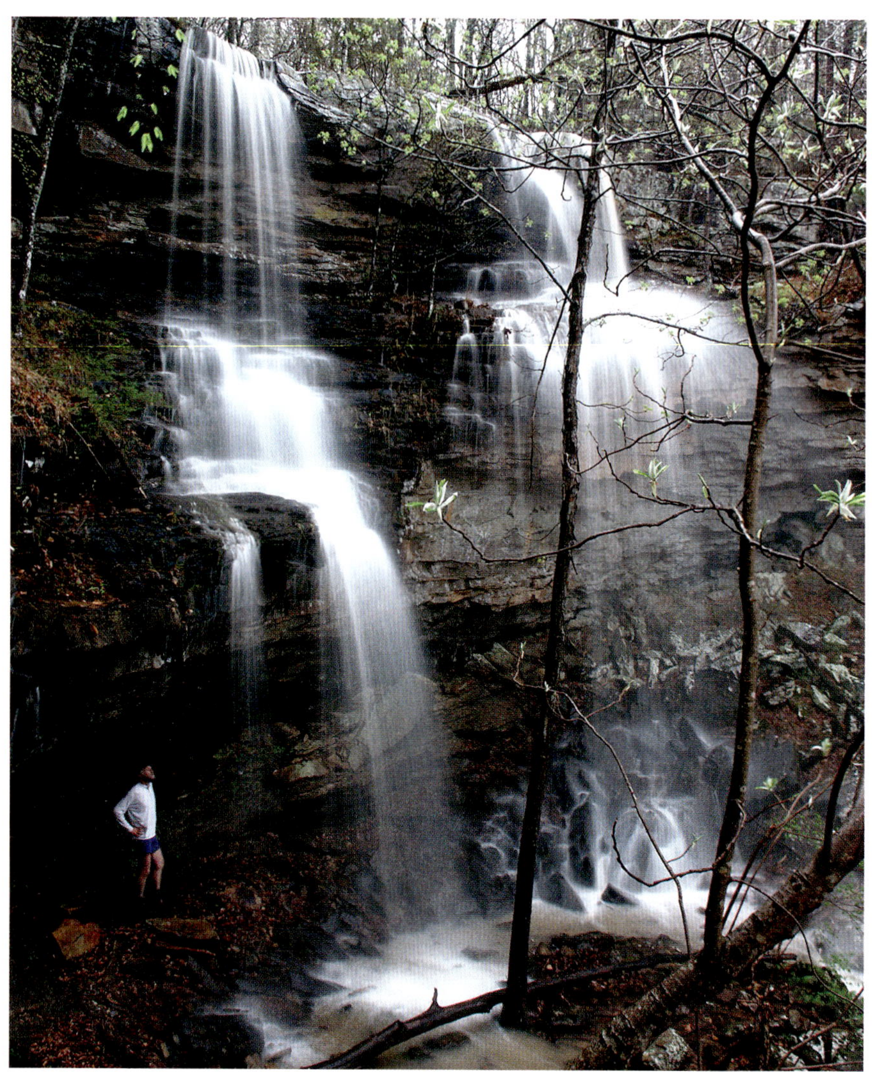

Lower Haley Falls (during high water)

TURN LEFT and go south on Hwy. 21 for 1.2 miles (over two bridges) and TURN RIGHT onto CR#9560/Cave Mtn. Road (gravel) just before the bridge over the Buffalo River (zero your odometer). The road goes *steeply* up Cave Mountain. Go past Cave Mountain Church at 5.4, then past CR#9210 (dead end road), and come to the Hawksbill Crag Trailhead at 6.0—PARK there.

We are going to do a loop to visit all three waterfalls, but you could cut the trip short and only see two of them if you wanted, or just see Haley Falls and come back. The trail begins across the road from the billboard and drops down a rocky slope, across a tiny stream (if it is running, there will be water in Mule Trail Falls!), and up a rise to the trailhead register. The trail switchbacks down the hill and comes to the creek again at .4. (If you only wanted to visit **Mule Trail** and **Thousand Kisses**, turn right and follow this creek downstream .4 to **Mule Trail**, then follow the bluff to the right to **Thousand Kisses**.)

From the creek crossing, the main trail remains level for a while, then drops on down a bench and comes to a larger creek at 1.0 and a trail intersection. The trail to the left is the

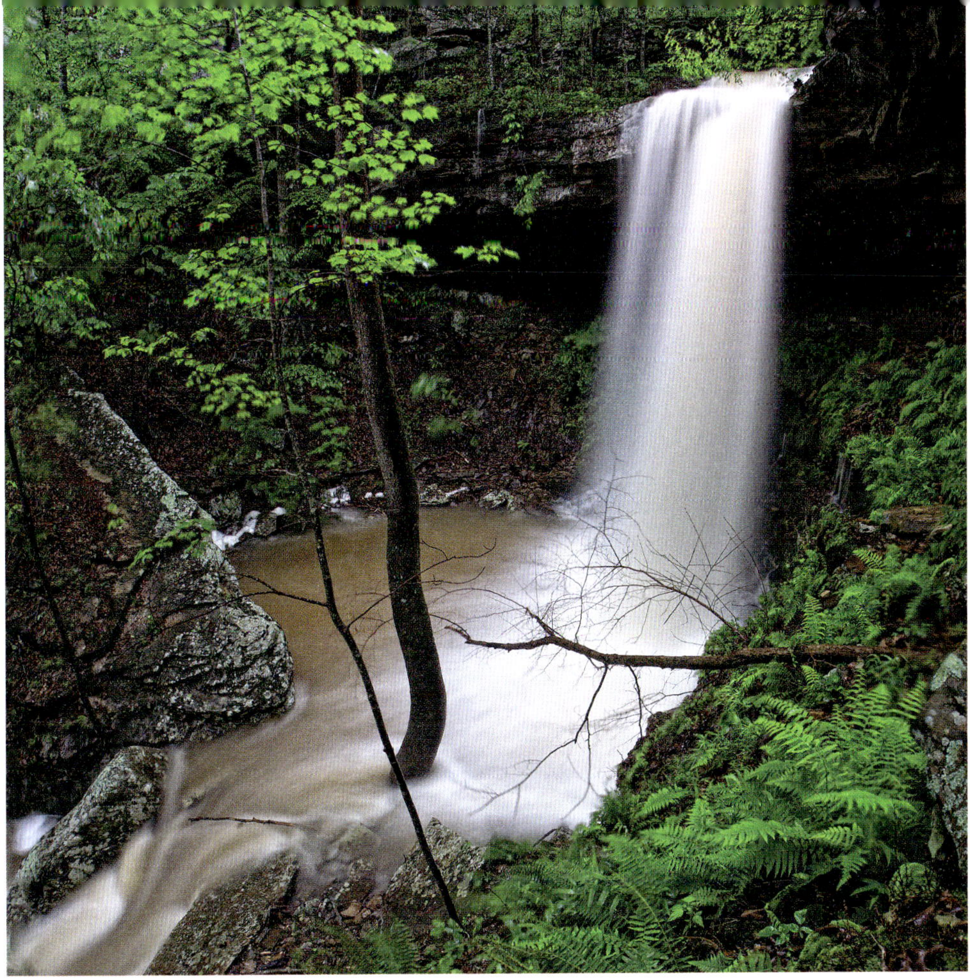

Mule Trail Falls (above), **Upper Haley Falls** (below—with Haley Zega)

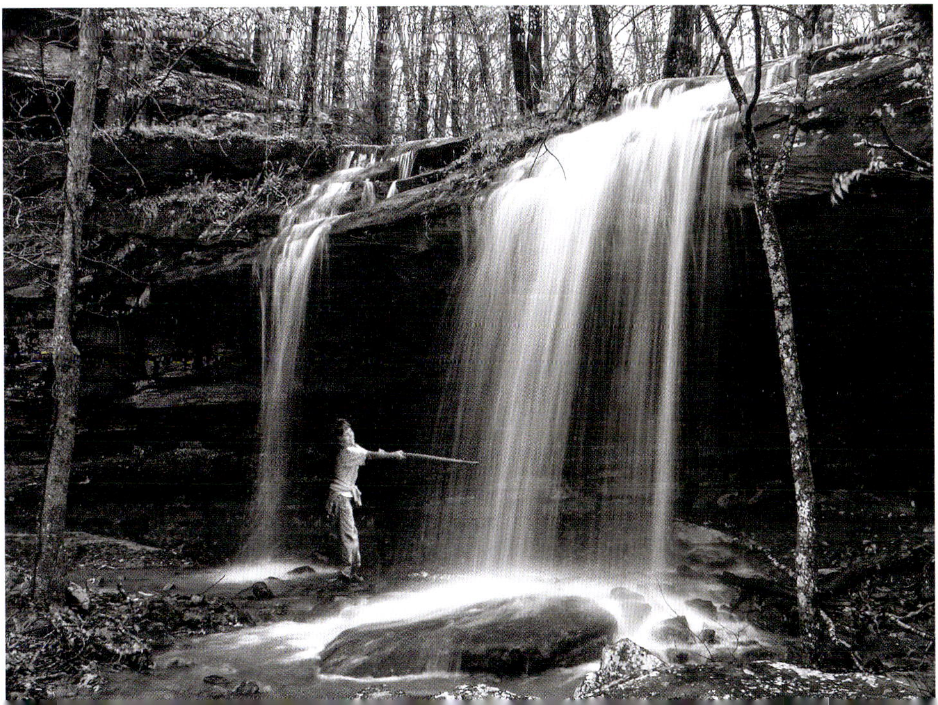

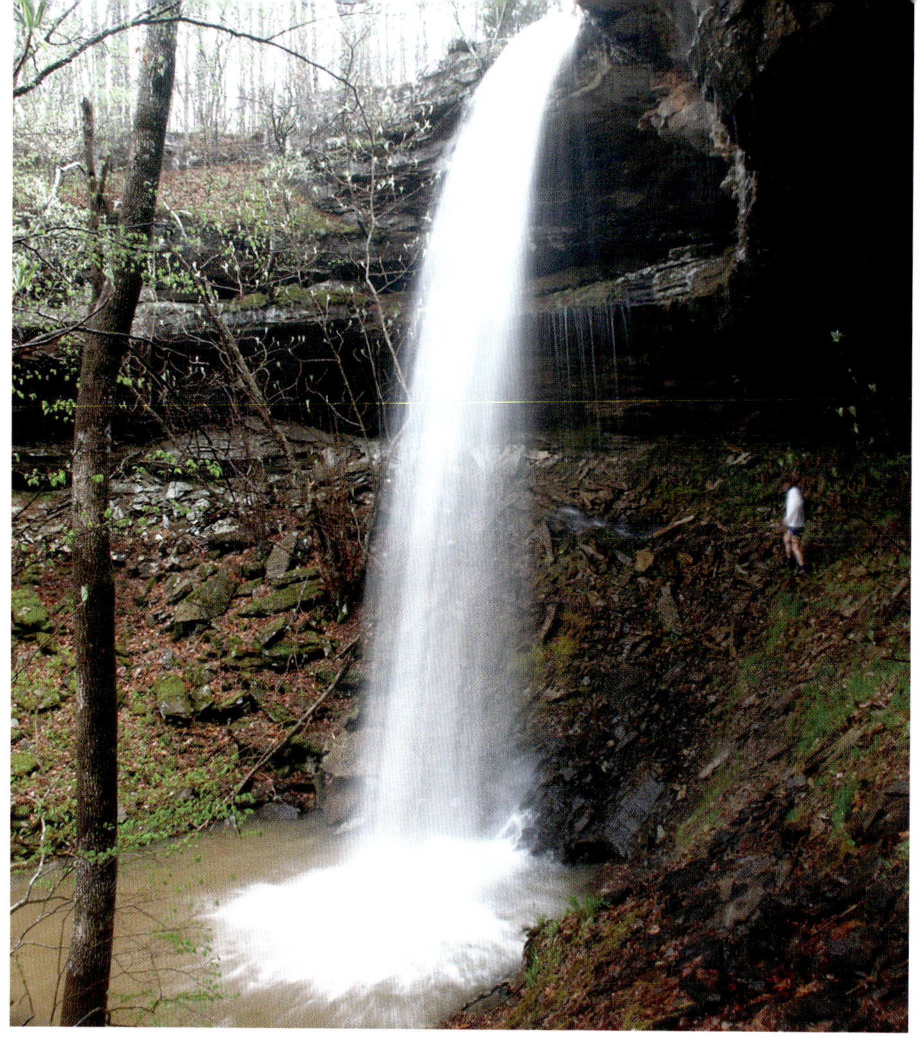

Thousand Kisses Falls (during high water)

upper route to Hawksbill Crag. You want to TURN RIGHT and follow the creek downstream 100 yards and you will come to the **Upper Haley Falls** (this is where Haley got lost).

If you are careful it is possible to find a way down this upper bluffline over on the left side, and get to the base of the upper falls. From there go behind the upper falls and you can get down to the base of the lower falls from over on the right side of them.

To continue with the hike follow along the base of the bluffline to the northwest (to your LEFT as you are looking up at the falls) and you will come to **Mule Trail Falls** at 1.4. There is an old mule trail there that once ran all the way up from the mouth of Whitaker Creek on the Buffalo River to Cave Mountain Road (much of this route has disappeared).

From this falls continue along the bluffline (either above or below) and you will come to **Thousand Kisses Falls** at 1.5. When I first took my bride-to-be Pam here I promised that I would kiss her under 1,000 more waterfalls in our lifetime together. I've got a long ways to go, but look forward to each and every one of them!

To get back to the trailhead return to Mule Trail Falls and follow the creek there upstream until you intersect with the main trail—TURN LEFT and follow the trail back to the trailhead. This creek is the Lower Fork of Whitaker Creek.

Emergency contact: Newton County Sheriff, 870–446–5124 Dogs are OK

Hedges Pouroff –113′

400 yards roundtrip, easy bushwhack, GPS not needed

GPS **35.94495, -93.41705**

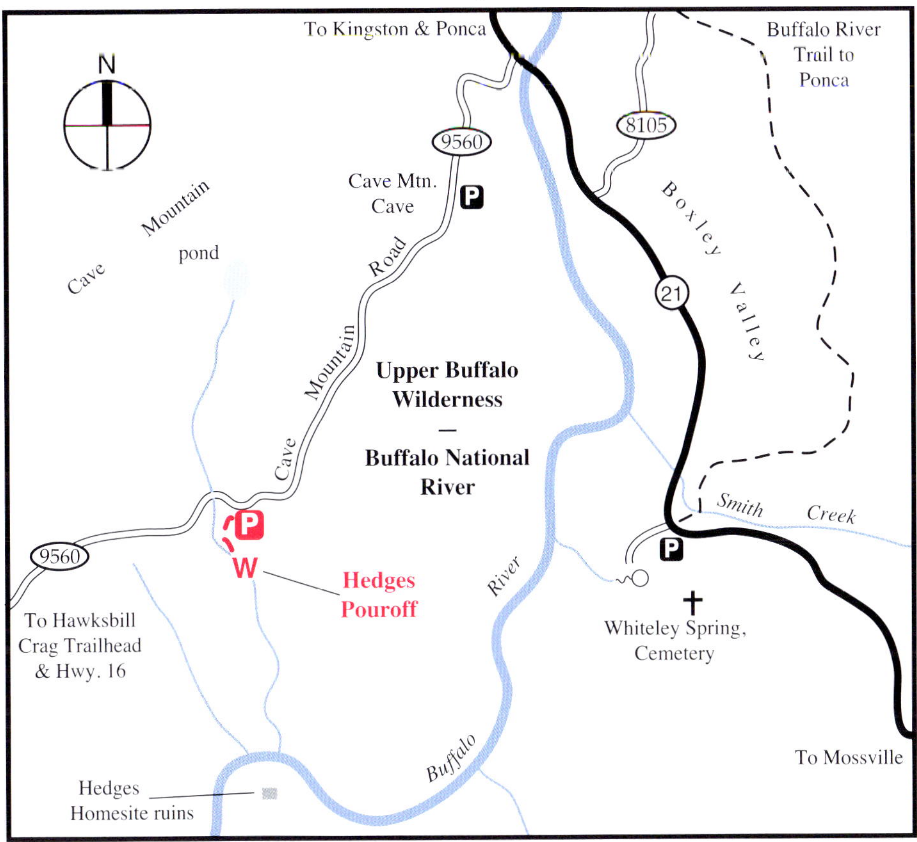

HEDGES POUROFF. I drove past the little creek that forms this waterfall hundreds of times, always thinking, "There must be a waterfall down there somewhere!" One day I finally stopped and took a look. Not only did I find one of the tallest waterfalls in Arkansas, but also one incredible view as well—one of the best in all the Buffalo region. This pouroff is named after Harold and Margaret Hedges who had a beautiful home down in the valley along the river. They could look up and marvel at this falls from their front porch. Harold once told me he had seen as many as *nine* waterfalls coming off this spot at the same time! (It wasn't moonshine he had been drinking, but rather the fact that the creek splits up as it gets to the top of the bluff, and the more water there is, the more waterfalls it creates.) They were instrumental in helping to get the Buffalo saved as a National River, and we all owe them a great deal. Their lovely home was burned to the ground one year while they were away for Christmas, and it is widely believed it was an act of arson by people opposed to the river being protected. The home was never rebuilt.

To get to the parking area take Hwy. 43 south from Ponca through Boxley Valley to the intersection with Hwy. 21. TURN LEFT onto Hwy. 21 there and go 1.2 miles (over two bridges) and TURN RIGHT onto CR#9560/Cave Mountain Road (just before you cross over the Buffalo River bridge). Follow this road as it climbs *steeply up* Cave Mountain. Go 1.4 miles (almost 1.5) and PARK on the LEFT (there's room for one or two cars). This

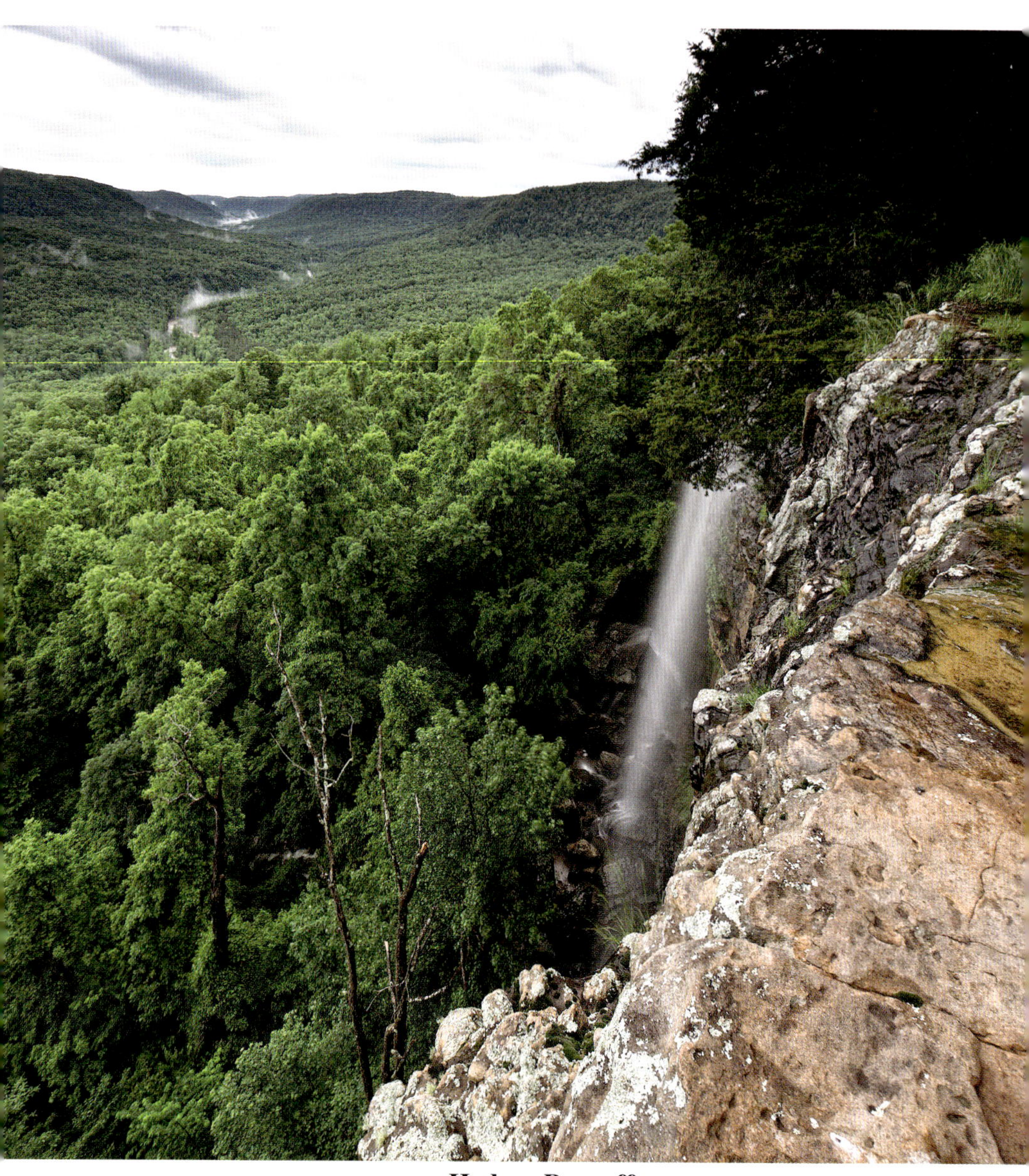

Hedges Pouroff

will be a couple of hundred yards after you climb up through the bluffline and level out on top. You will be able to look out to your left and see that you are up high. If you come to the little creek at a hairpin turn, go back 100 yards and park.

There is a little primitive path from the parking spot that drops down the hill to the top of **Hedges Pouroff**—it is only 200 yards or less and everything is close by (creek, bluff, falls). The main falls pours out from under an ancient cedar tree that is growing over the edge, and then the water crashes onto the jagged rocks far below. It is a difficult falls to photograph. This is a 100 foot tall bluff so ***extreme caution is advised!!!***

Emergency contact: Newton County Sheriff, 870–446–5124 No dogs on trail.

QuiVaLa Elise Falls – 21′

1.7 mile roundtrip, medium hike, GPS helpful

GPS **35.93808, -93.38302**

Martin Falls – 18′

.3 mile roundtrip, easy hike, GPS helpful

Lat/Lon **35.92443, -93.38625**

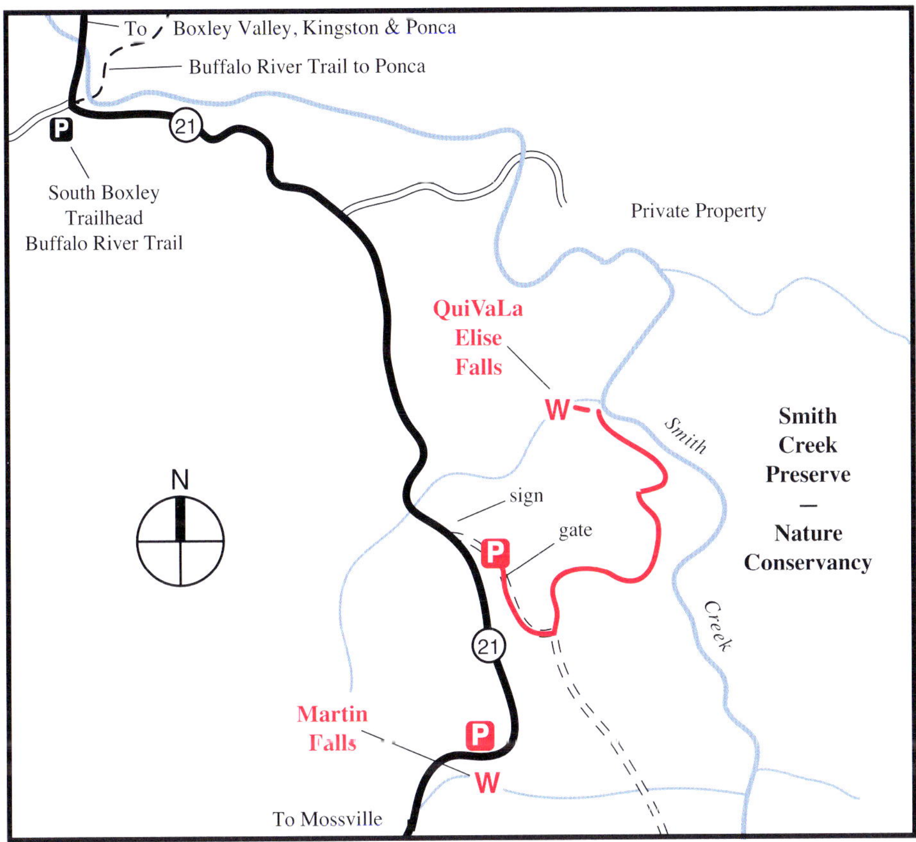

QUIVALA ELISE FALLS/MARTIN FALLS. Pronounced "Ke-v[a'] -l[a']" and is a French-Indian word meaning "who goes there?" Elise and Marty Roenigk bought 1100 acres of prime Buffalo River Headwaters country and made the tract available to the Nature Conservancy in January 2005, who has now preserved the land. One day while out exploring on her own, Elise discovered this waterfall that now bears her name. **"Who Goes There Elise?" Falls** is part of this new nature preserve that is open to the public to explore and enjoy.

The scenic area is located south of Boxley Valley, along Smith Creek. The parking area is right next to the highway and easy to get to (watch for the sign). The hike in to the falls is downhill most of the way along an old jeep road, and is easy to follow. It is a 500 foot drop in elevation going in, and the very same 500 feet UP on the way out! The very last part of the hike to the falls is a slippery scramble up into a side canyon of Smith Creek.

To reach the parking area **(35.93458, -93.38584)**, go south on Hwy. 21 from the South Boxley Trailhead for 1.2 miles and turn left onto a jeep road, then park at the gate just beyond (don't block the gate). Or go 3.2 miles north from the Mossville Church and turn right.

Begin your hike going past the gate and down the steep hill on the jeep road, then just as you get to the bottom of the first hill at .2, the main road will go to the right but you will TURN LEFT onto an old logging road/trail. Follow this well-used trail on down the hill. It will eventually get to the very bottom of the drainage and come alongside Smith Creek—the road will end there at .7. You will need to go downstream a little bit, but the left side is blocked by a small bluff, so you will have to get out into Smith Creek, which is normally dry. (If Smith Creek is up and running and you cannot see the bottom, do not enter it!) Just downstream you will see a little creek coming in from your left at the far end of the small bluff—follow this watercourse UPSTREAM about 100 yards until you come to the base of the falls.

Martin Falls is easy to reach, with a nice flow during high water that pours over a deep shelter. Named for Elise's husband, Martin Roenigk. From the main Preserve parking area TURN LEFT/uphill on the highway, drive past the nearby Smith Creek Overlook area on the left, then around the curve to the right. There's room to PARK on the right side of the highway where a driveway used to be (**35.92558, -93.38568**). Cross the highway and climb over the guard rail, then hike .15 into the woods and a little to the right to a creek and **Martin Falls** is just downstream. OR hike straight into the woods until you reach the top of a bluff then TURN RIGHT and follow the bluff to the falls. Only room for one or two vehicles, but you can also park back at the overlook and hike up beside the highway.

The stream continues below the falls as a series of smaller falls and beautiful cascades, dropping down the mountain to the small picnic area/bridge at the bottom of the scenic area. THANK YOU MARTIN AND ELISE!

Emergency contact: Newton County Sheriff, 870–446–5124 Dogs are OK.

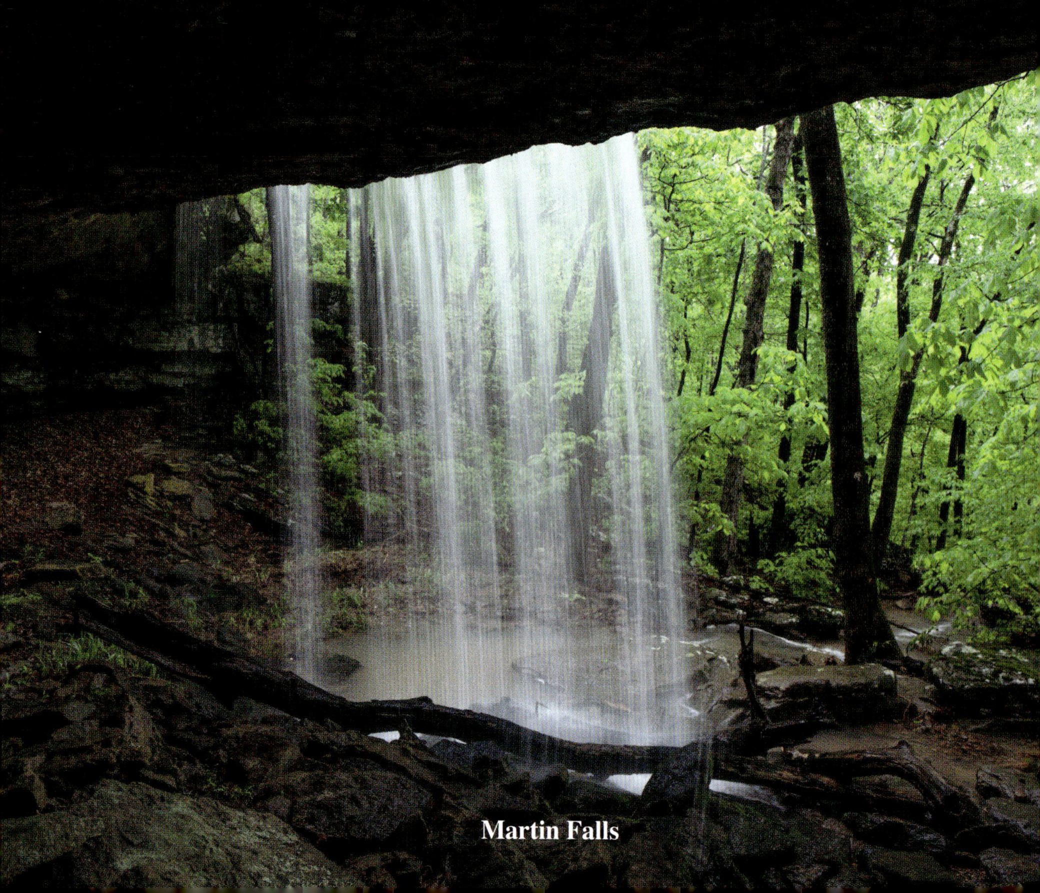

Martin Falls

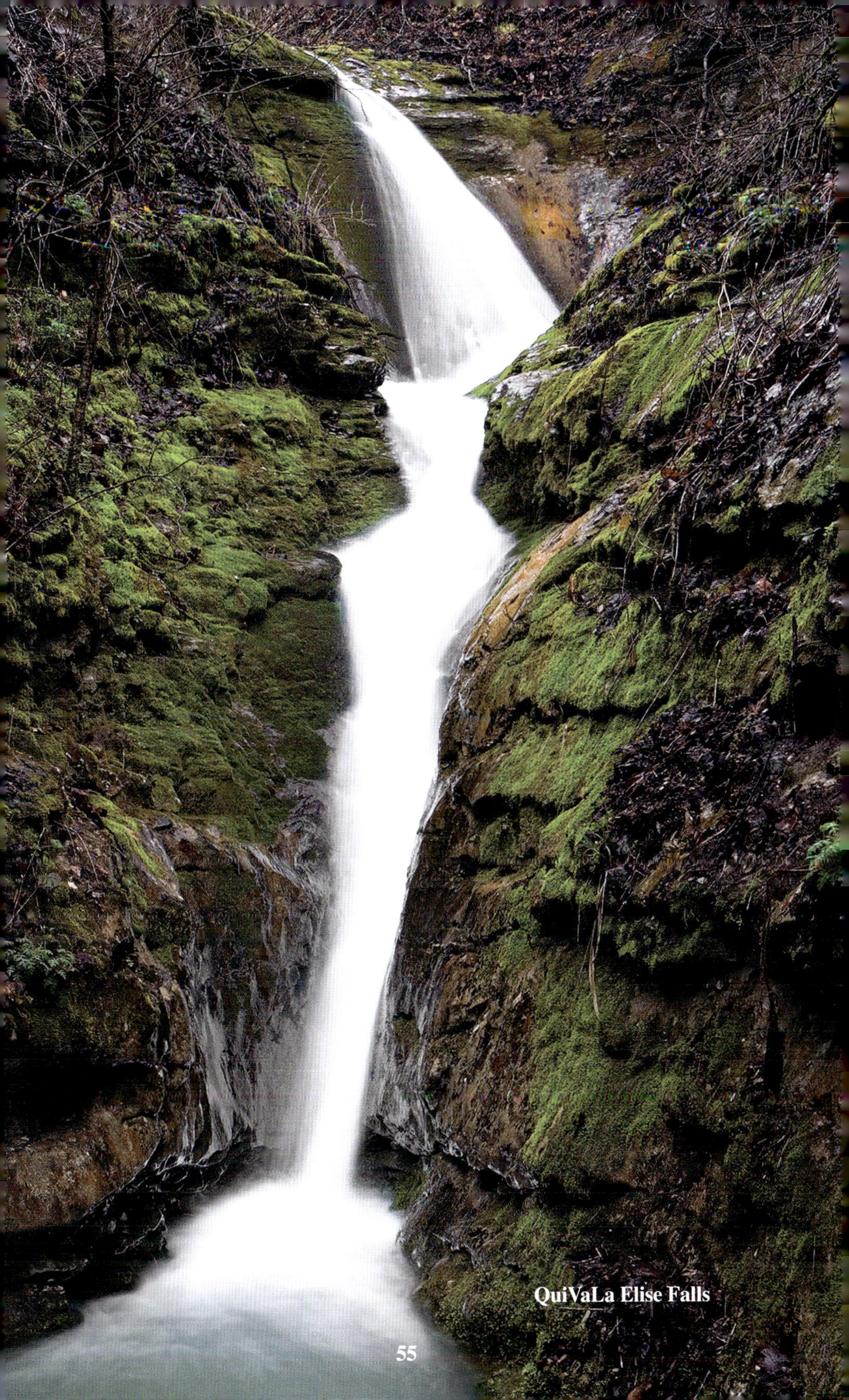

QuiVaLa Elise Falls

Dismal Divide Falls – 37′

GPS **35.84739, -93.29171**

3.7 mile round trip to all falls, medium to difficult bushwhack

Dismal Four Drop Falls – 35′

GPS **35.84682, -93.29360**

Dismal Shelter Falls – 63′

GPS **35.84790, -93.28790**

Dismal Double Drop Falls – 63′

GPS **35.84977, -93.28312**

Dismal South Falls – 75′

GPS **35.84702, -93.29075**

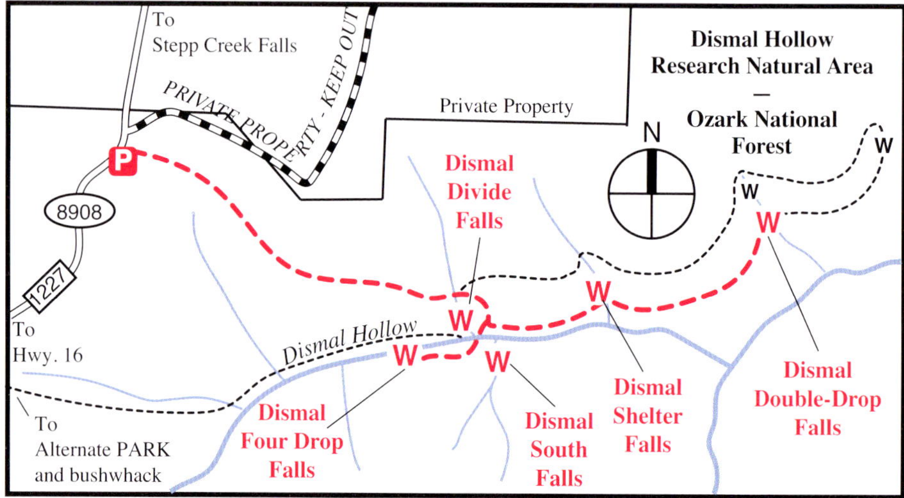

Dismal Hollow Research Natural Area waterfalls. It's an area set aside in the Ozark National Forest with no trails or other improvements, so it's all bushwhacking. SO many wonderful things to see and explore, including many great waterfalls. Plan to spend MORE time than you expect. There is private property to avoid around the ridgetops.

From the little store/gas/cemetery in Nail on Hwy. 16 between Deer and Fallsville, go west on Hwy. 16 for 1.5 miles and TURN RIGHT onto CR8908/FR1227. Go .8 and PARK on the RIGHT side of the road (**35.85128, -93.30111**) just BEFORE THE ROAD SPLITS off to the left towards Stepp Creek Falls (If you go towards the right on road 92160A you will be on private property, so AVOID THIS!).

I'm going to keep the meter running and visit five waterfalls, but your mileage will probably be longer since there is so much to see, and multiple options to get to and fro. From the parking spot head into the woods to the right and downhill, staying to the left of a small drainage. Curve around the hill to the left along a pretty level and wide open bench—it's a lovely walk through a mature forest. As the bench curves around to the left into steeper terrain, bear towards the right and downhill and work your way down to a creek below. TURN RIGHT and follow this creek downstream until you come to the top

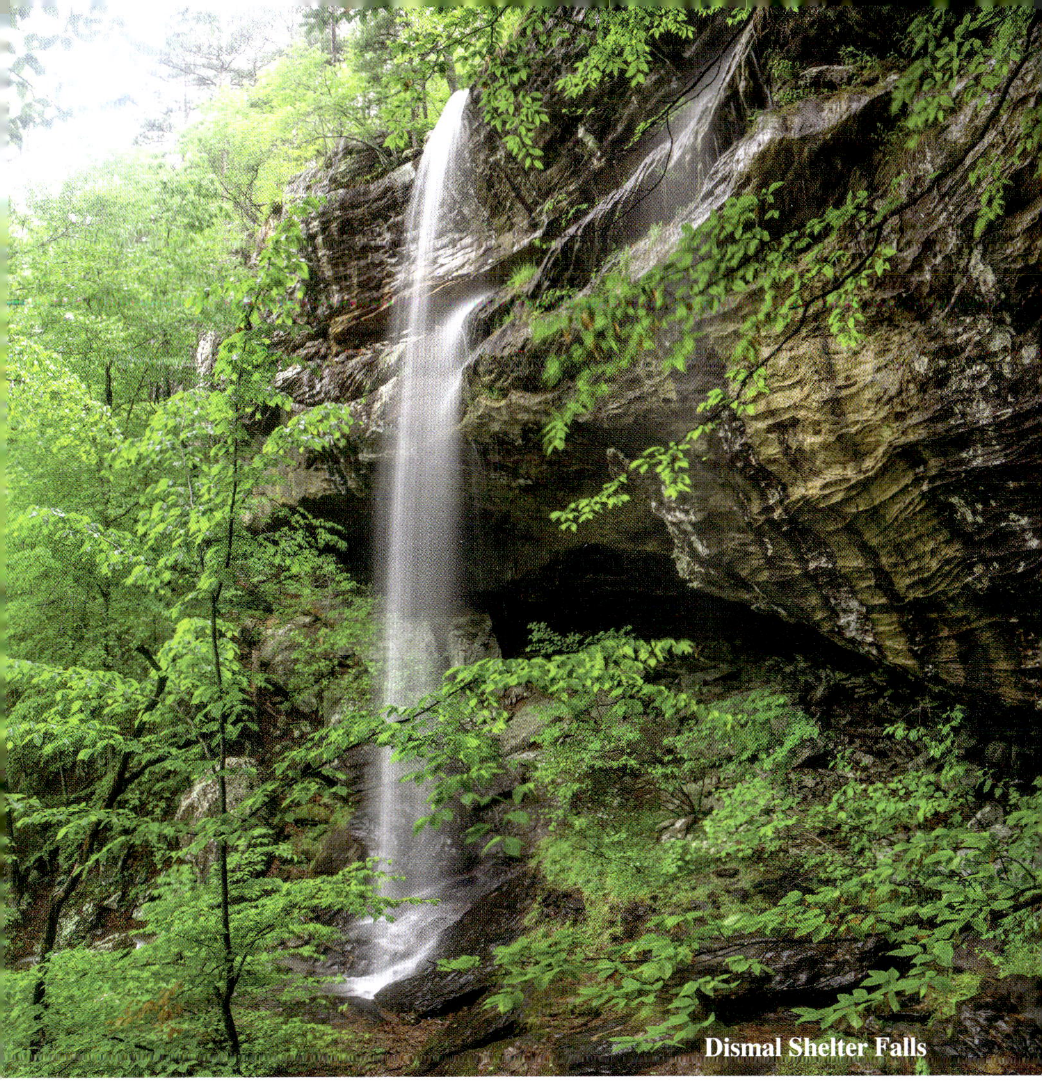
Dismal Shelter Falls

of **Dismal Divide Falls** at .8. This is the edge of the Dismal Hollow Canyon where you will find many wonderful things below the bluff!

To get below the bluff I cross the creek above the falls and find a spot a couple hundred feet or so along the bluff to the left, then work down back towards the bottom of the falls. This multi-tiered falls marks the divide between the upper and lower canyon. Go UPstream and you will come to **Four Drop Falls** at the end of the box canyon at .9, guarded by wonderful towering bluffs on both sides.

Return to **Dismal Divide Falls** and head downstream along the base of the massive bluff, with the creek below at first, but it will soon drop away out of sight (there's a really tall waterfall pouring off the bluff on the other side if water levels are high and you can get across the creek). Soon you will come to a giant shelter and find **Dismal Shelter Falls** at 1.3. Continue along the bluff line until you reach **Dismal Double Drop Falls** at 1.9.

If you continue along the bluff you can climb up above the top and take that route back to the parking spot. Or turn around and enjoy the bluff again heading back the way you came—if so and the water is high you might want to drop down and cross the creek over to **Dismal South Falls** at 2.6. Total hike of about 3.7 miles.

Emergency contact: Newton County Sheriff, 870–446–5124 Dogs are OK.

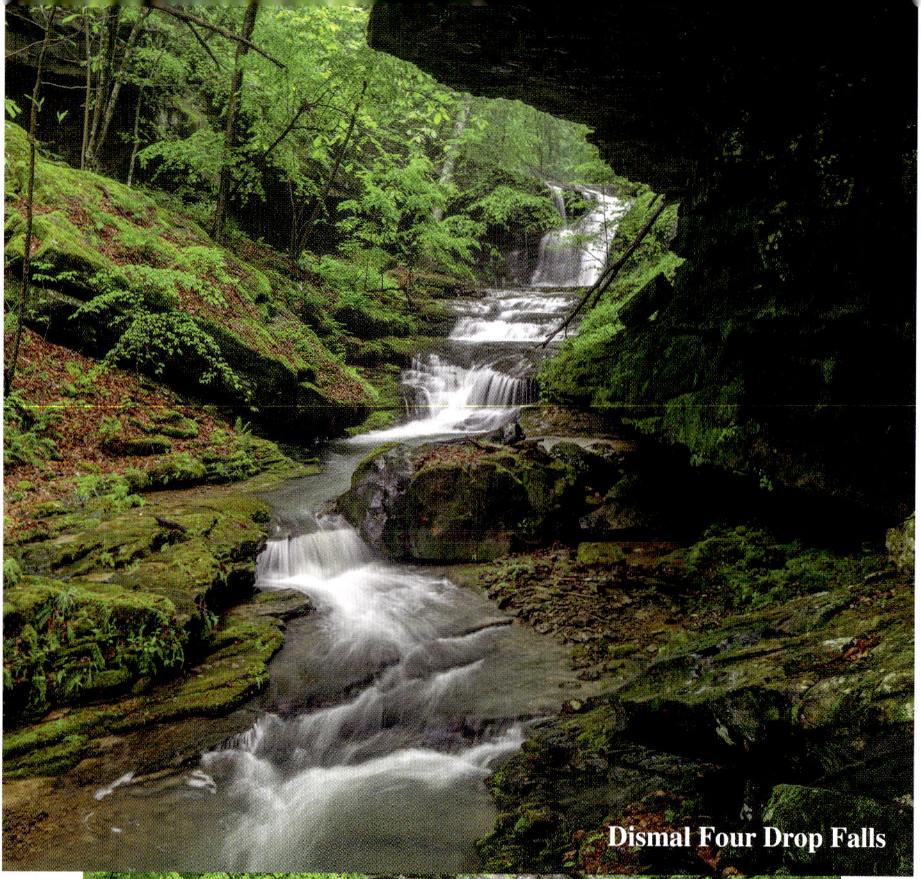

Dismal Four Drop Falls

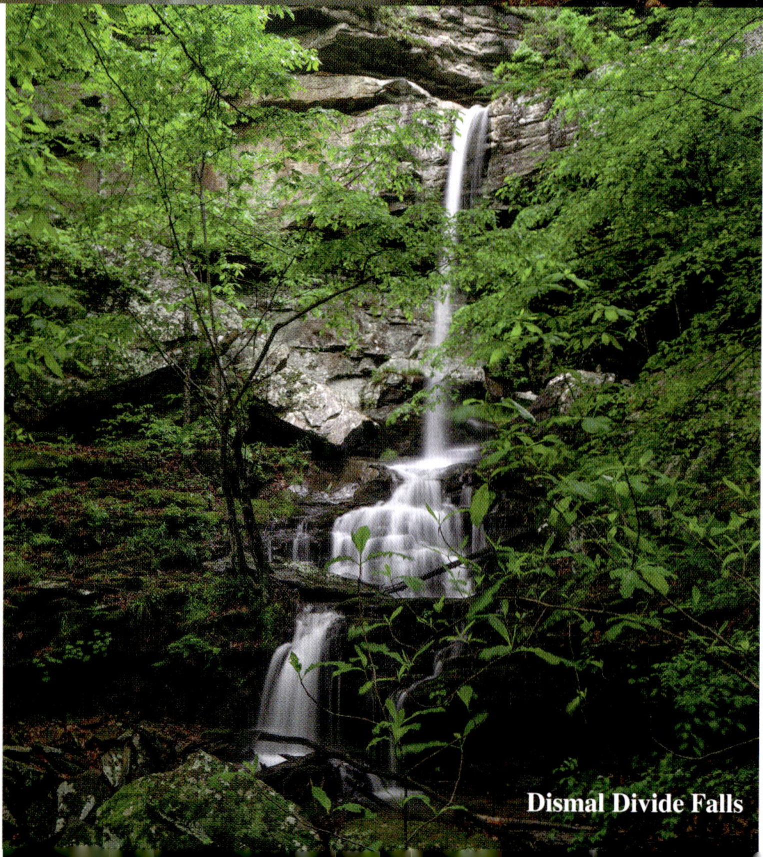

Dismal Divide Falls

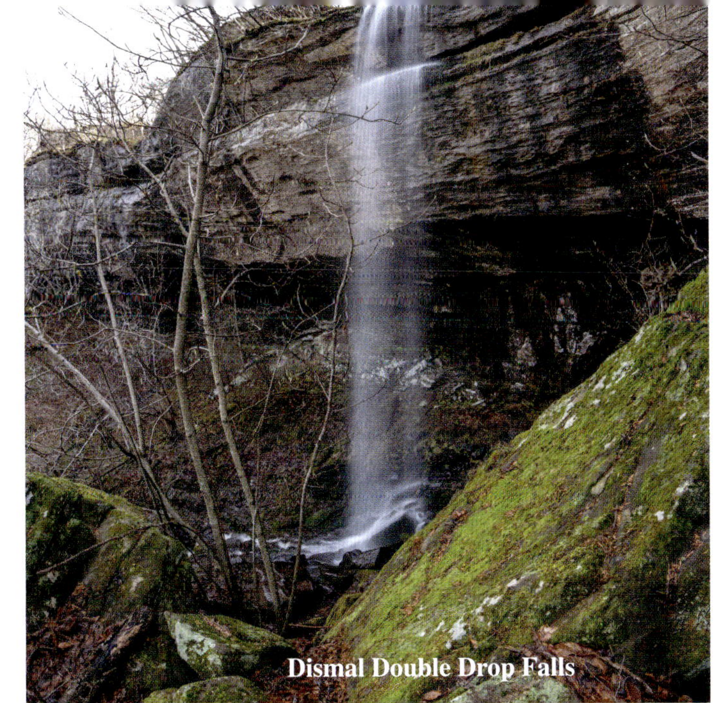

Dismal Double Drop Falls

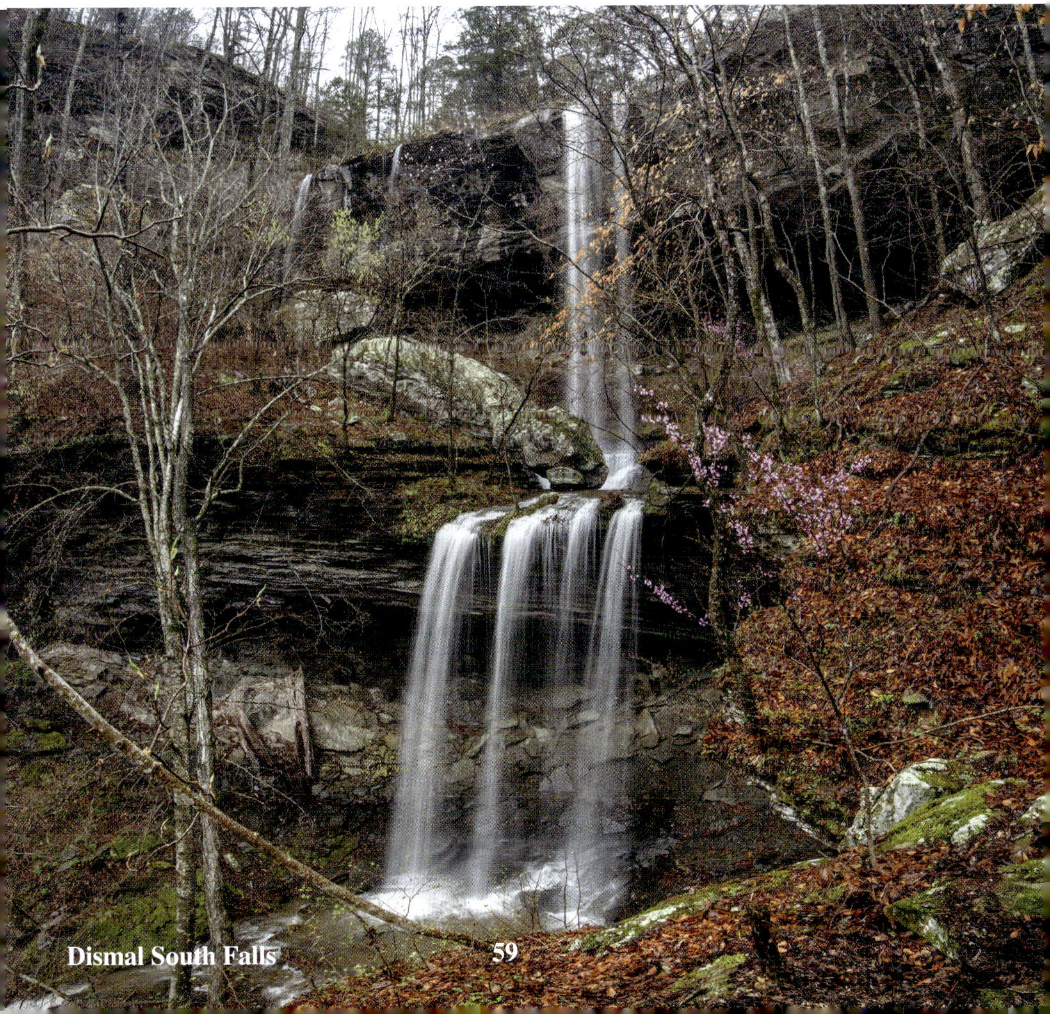

Dismal South Falls

Stepp Creek Falls (2) –12′/25′

2.1 mile roundtrip, medium bushwhack, GPS helpful

GPS **35.85775, -93.30943**

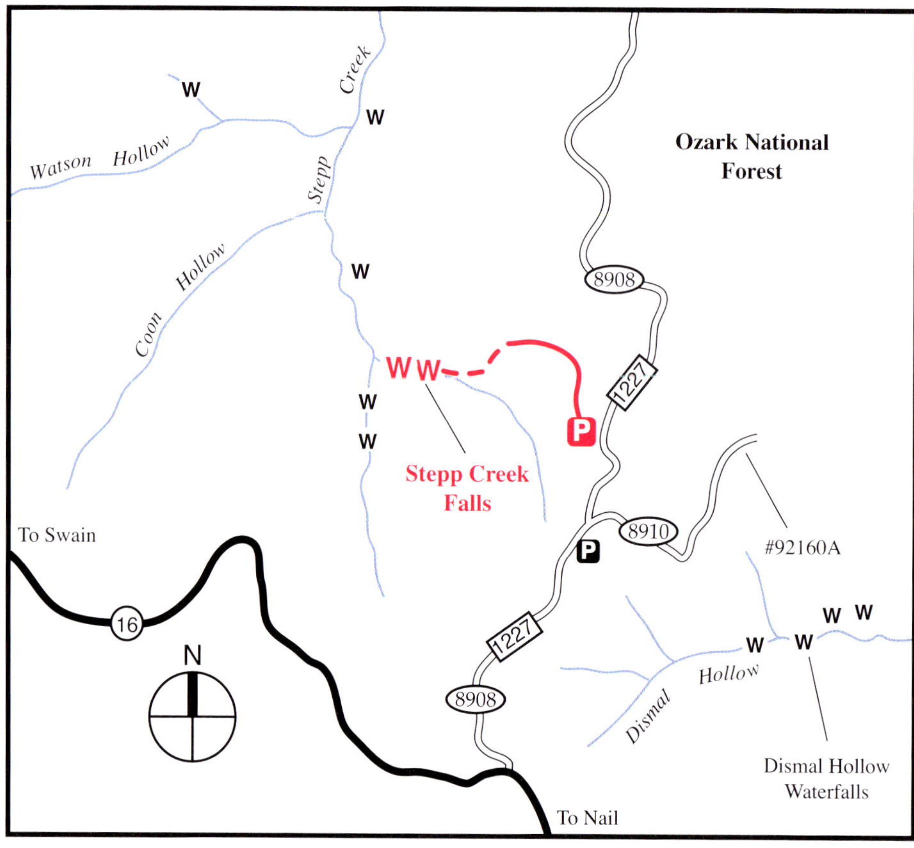

STEPP CREEK FALLS. There are several nice waterfalls in the upper reaches of this drainage near Nail, that eventually flows into the Little Buffalo River. To reach the parking spot from Nail (between Deer and Edwards Junction on Hwy. 16), go west on Hwy. 16 from the Nail store for 1.5 miles and TURN RIGHT (north) onto CR#8908/FR#1227. Go .8 and TURN LEFT onto Union Grove Road (still CR#8908/FR#1227)—road #92160A goes straight ahead/right at this intersection. Go .25 mile (just past a cattle corral on both sides of the road) and TURN LEFT onto a logging road and PARK (**35.85505, -93.30051).**

From the parking spot, I like to follow the logging road ahead about a quarter mile until it curves back to the left, then I leave the road and simply head downhill into the hollow. Keep going downhill until you hit the creek below, then follow the creek downstream until you come to the top of the first **Stepp Creek Falls**. The second waterfall is just downstream and you can see the upper one from there.

There are more waterfalls in the little side drainage that comes in from the south just below the main waterfalls; more falls on the main Stepp Creek downstream; also more falls and some very neat areas farther downstream (see the small w's on the map above). Explore and have fun, but just remember you still have to climb back out to the car!

Emergency contact: Newton County Sheriff, 870–446–5124 Dogs are OK.

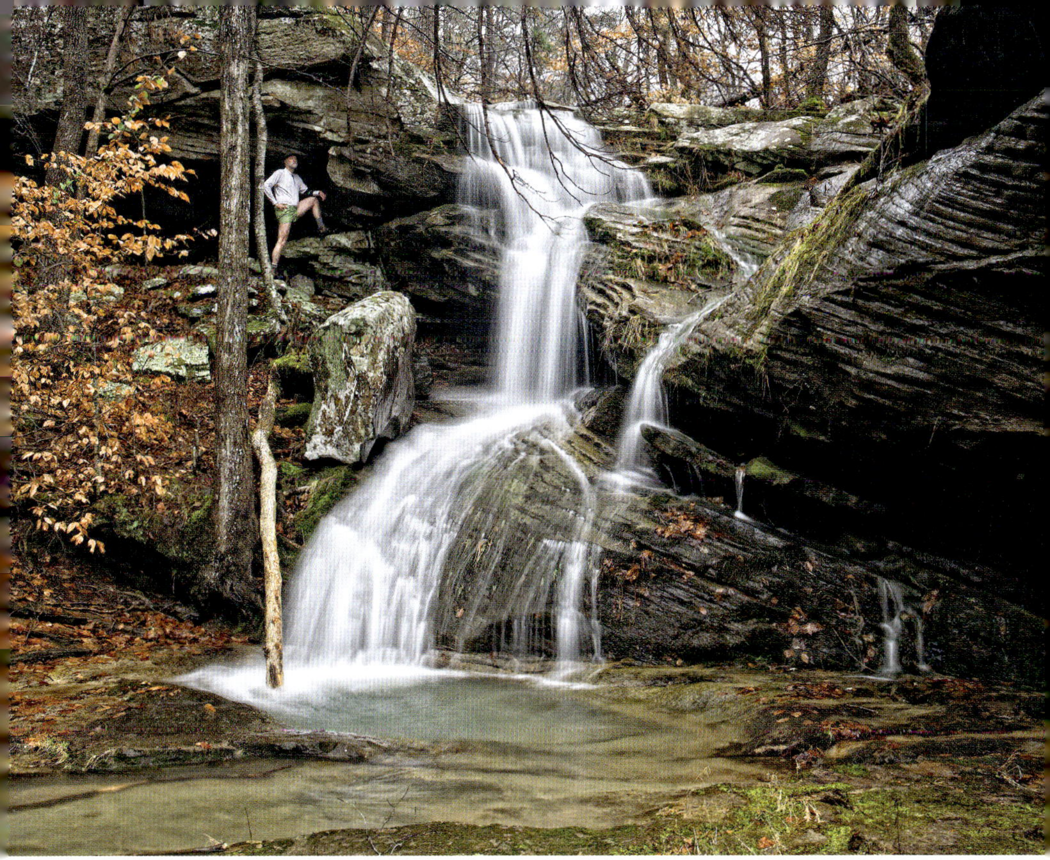

Stepp Creek Falls (main falls above, and below showing both falls)

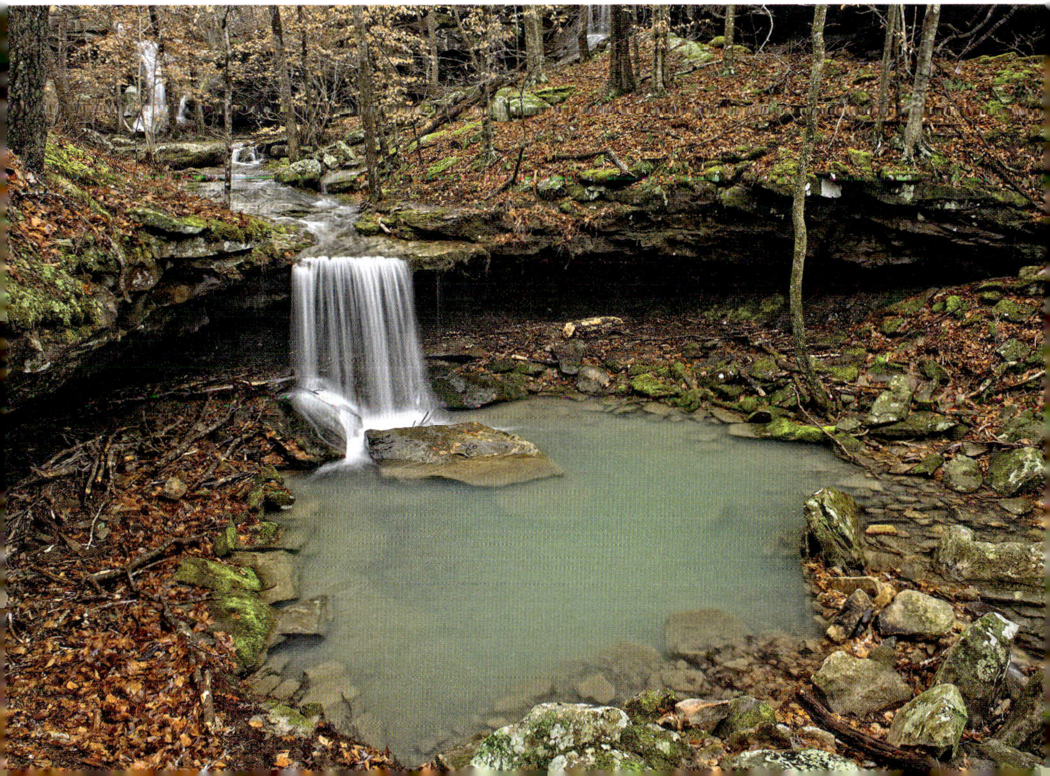

Hole In Rock Falls–66′

GPS **35.96621, -93.44381**

Sunshine Falls–15′

GPS **35.96575, -93.44345**

Johnny B Goode Falls–26′

GPS **35.95365, -93.46734**

Panther Pool Falls–7′

GPS **35.95403, -93.47034**

Leprechaun Falls–34′

GPS **35.94537, -93.45120**

WILDERNESS RIDER RANCH WATERFALLS. Wilderness Rider Ranch (WildernessRider.com) is a unique 3,500+ acre private outdoor playground with beautiful landscapes of open mountain top meadows, giant oak trees standing alone along the skyline, ***primitive*** campsites overlooking the surrounding wild areas (including Boxley Valley—a VERY unique camping experience), miles and miles of jeep/ATV/hiking trails throughout the property—AND WATERFALLS, they have LOTS of waterfalls ranging from 6' to 66' tall! Oh, and also a Buffalo herd!

There are jeep trails to most of the waterfalls, including many that you can literally drive right up to; others are just a short hike away. The distance and difficulty will depend on if you are on foot, or have a jeep or ATV—those can get you up really close to the falls. There are three parking spots available to non-jeepers, although note some of the roads are pretty rough and kind of mucky during wet weather. If you simply parked at the office and hiked a big loop to all of the falls the total distance would be 7-8 miles, all of that on jeep roads or trails. There is a nominal daily access fee (currently $10 per person, more if you bring a jeep or ATV), but I highly recommend this special place if only for the waterfalls, but my goodness there is so much more to explore and enjoy here!

The ranch has a great map of the property to give you that shows all of the waterfalls (updated from time to time), trails, and campsites so I won't include a map here. You will need to check into their office to sign in, pickup a map, and find out all the info you need to have a splendid day! I've included a few of my favorite waterfalls here, but there are so many more. At a minimum be sure to visit **Hole-In-Rock-Falls** (**Sunshine and Honeymoon Falls** are at the same spot), **Panther Branch Falls**, **Johnny B Goode Falls**, and **Leprechaun Falls**.

The well-marked turnoff to the Ranch is located between Boxley and Kingston on Hwy. 21, then four miles of sometimes rough county road to the entrance (**35.96047, -93.45582**). You drive right past the Sweden Creek Trailhead, so I recommend you do both areas while you are there!) Visit www.WildernessRider.com to get started.

Emergency contact: Newton County Sheriff, 870–446–5124 Dogs are OK.

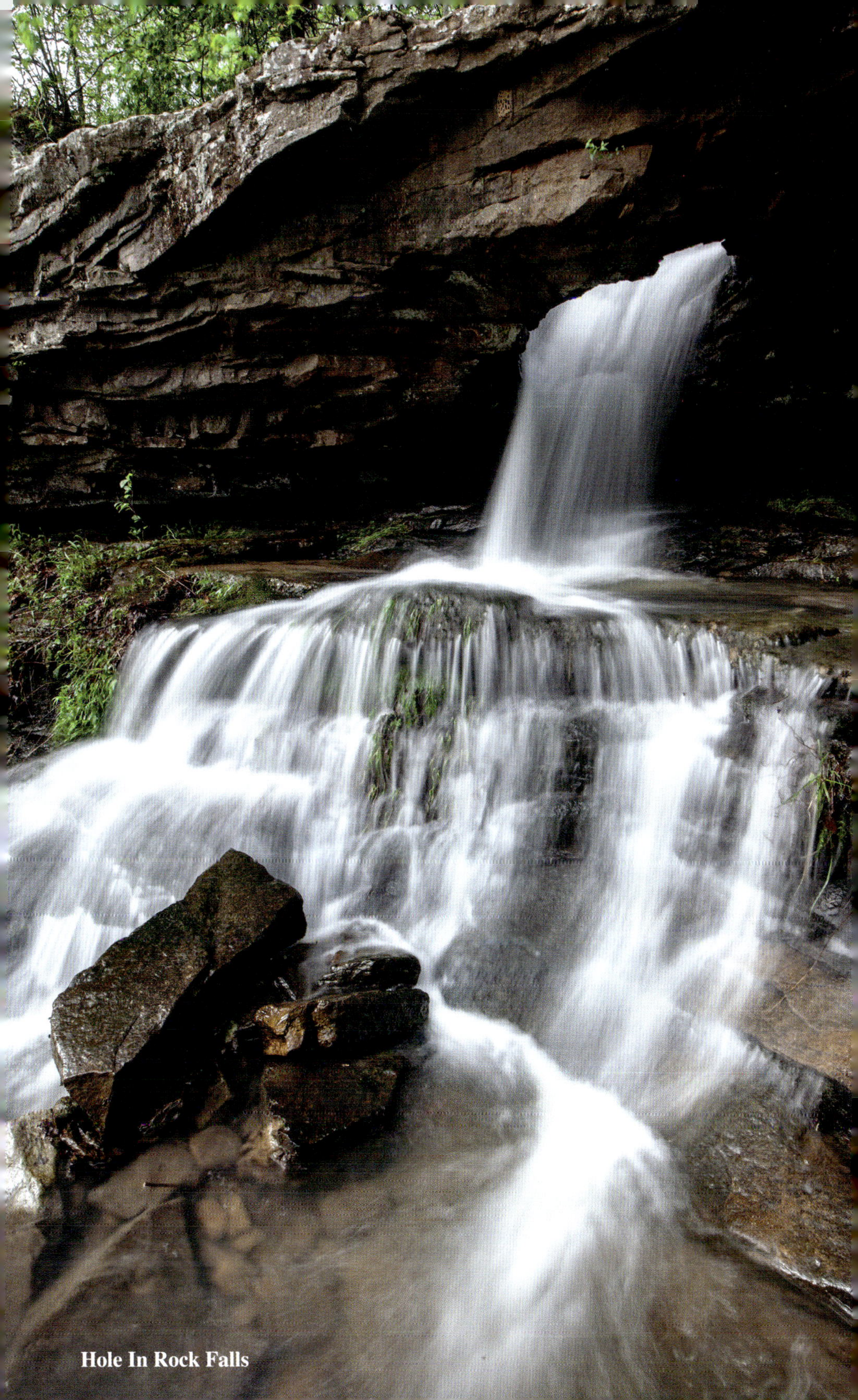
Hole In Rock Falls

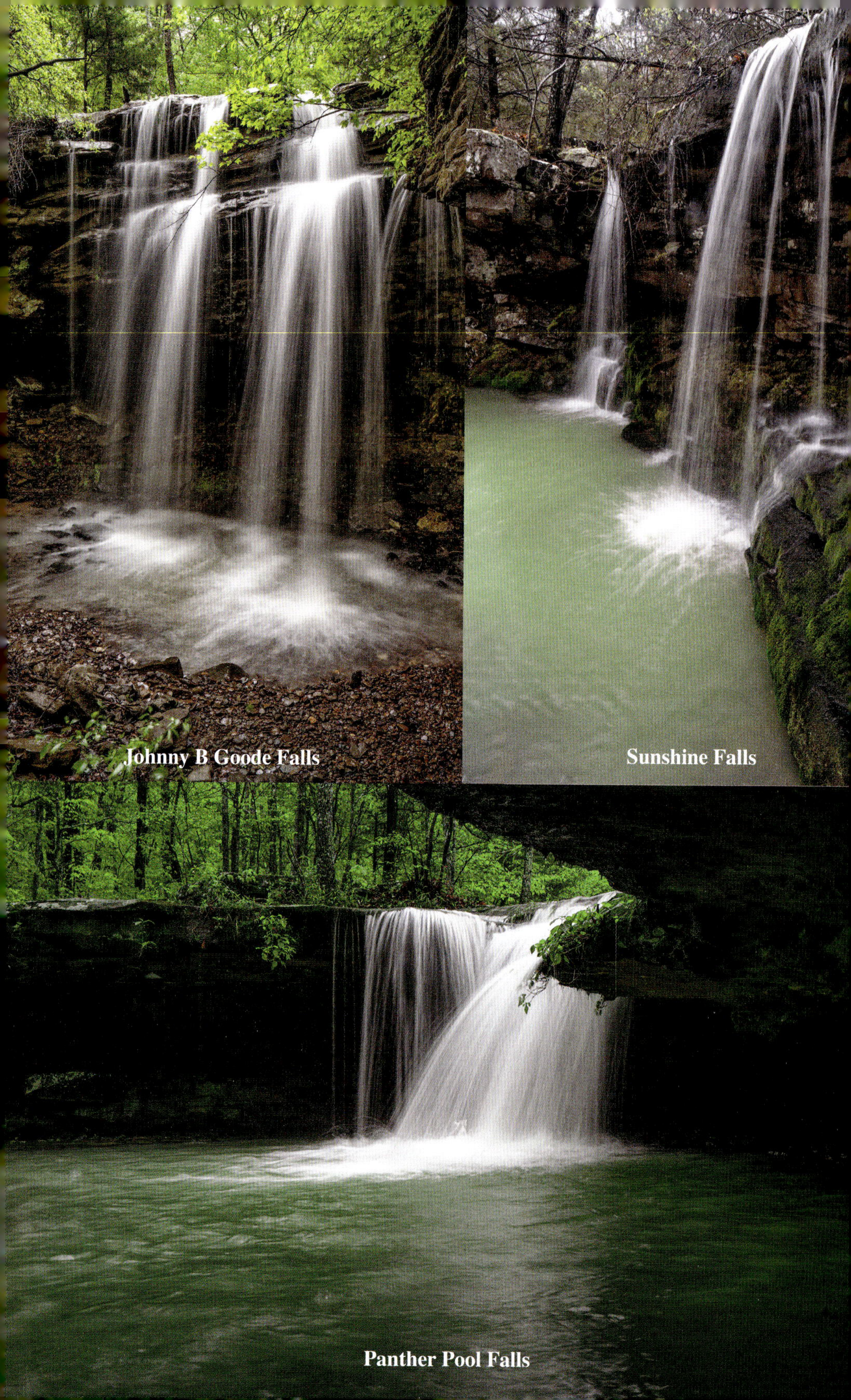

Johnny B Goode Falls

Sunshine Falls

Panther Pool Falls

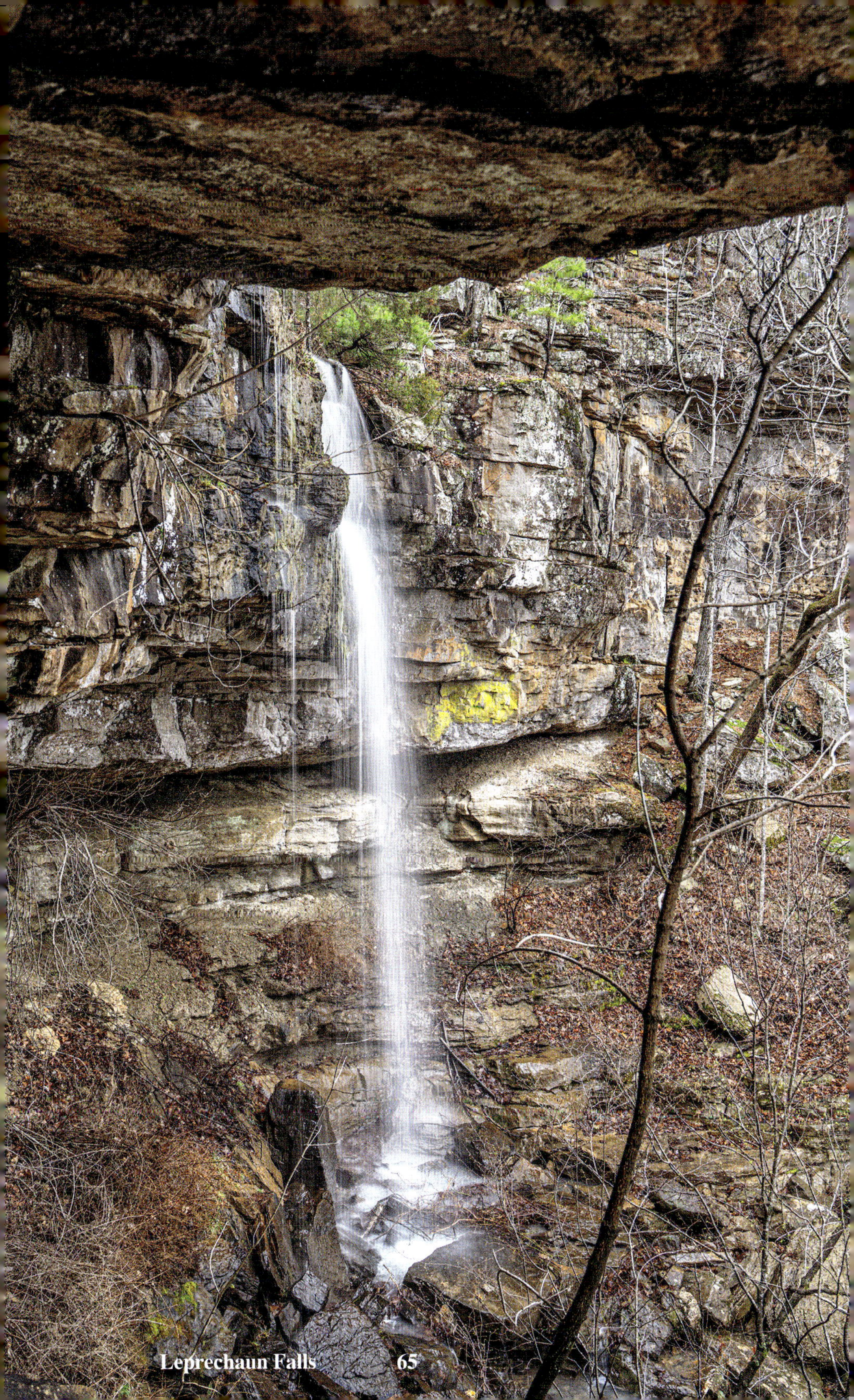

Leprechaun Falls

Eden Falls – 31′-53′

2.4 miles roundtrip, easy hike, GPS not needed

GPS **36.01752, -93.38730**

Armadillo Falls (2) –18′/24′

Add .4 to above, medium bushwhack, GPS helpful

GPS **36.01515, -93.38088**

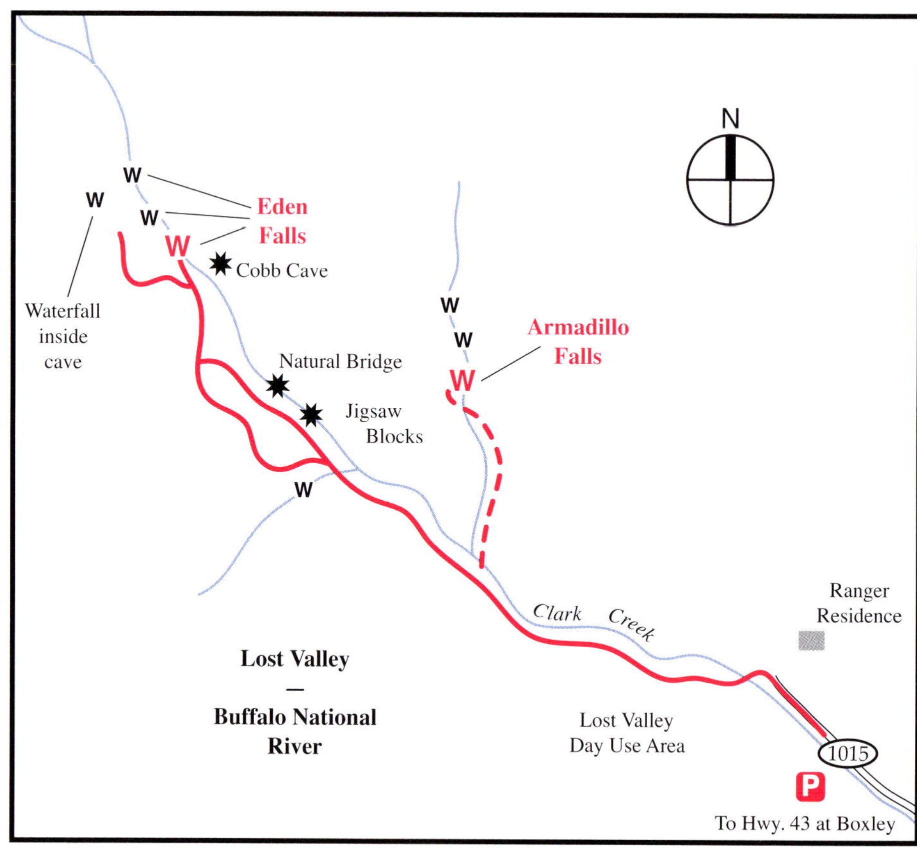

EDEN FALLS/ARMADILLO FALLS. Lost Valley is one of the crown jewels of the Ozarks, and Eden Falls one of the most beautiful, and most visited waterfalls in the region. It's easy to get to, even for kids and older folks. There are actually four separate waterfalls there, including one back inside a cave (take a flashlight). And if you are in the mood for a bit of bushwhacking, there are several more falls off in a side canyon that we'll visit.

Lost Valley is easy to find—the turnoff is just south of Ponca on Hwy. 43. Turn at the big sign (paved, then gravel) and PARK **(36.00896, -93.37169)**. The trail heads off across Clark Creek (someday a new bridge may be here). While more water makes it better, you *may* still see a good waterfall even if Clark Creek is dry at the bridge (the water often goes underground). Follow the trail upstream to .8 and take the RIGHT fork—past the Jigsaw Blocks and the Natural Bridge (a small waterfall exits this tunnel). The trail climbs up next to the creek and rejoins the main trail—TURN RIGHT and follow it on over to Cobb Cave and to the base of **Lower Eden Falls** at 1.2. This is the falls that most people see. Continue

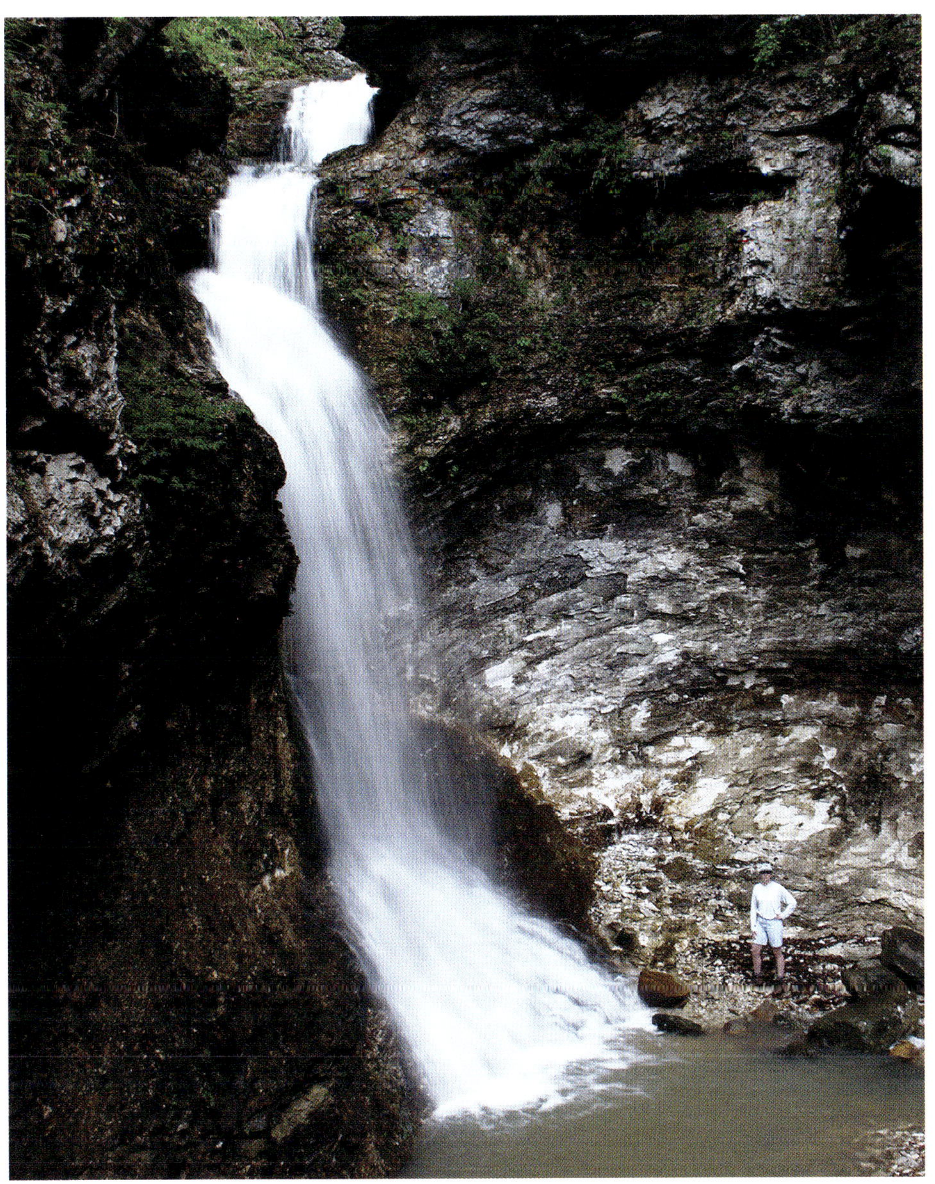

Lower Eden Falls

on up the trail (steep) and it will end at the mouth of **Eden Falls** Cave. Middle Eden Falls just below is created by the stream that exits the cave. You can get a glimpse of Upper Eden Falls in the gorge upstream. The waterfall in the cave is located a couple hundred feet inside—it pours out of the ceiling 30 feet above.

On the way back out, locate the stream coming in from the opposite side of the valley on the left, go across Clark Creek, and follow this side creek upstream a couple of hundred yards to the base of Armadillo Falls (not suitable for small kids). At one point you can see three different waterfalls at the same time—the upper one is the tallest, but out of reach.

Emergency contact: Newton County Sheriff, 870–446–5124 *No dogs allowed on trail.*

Middle
Armadillo Falls

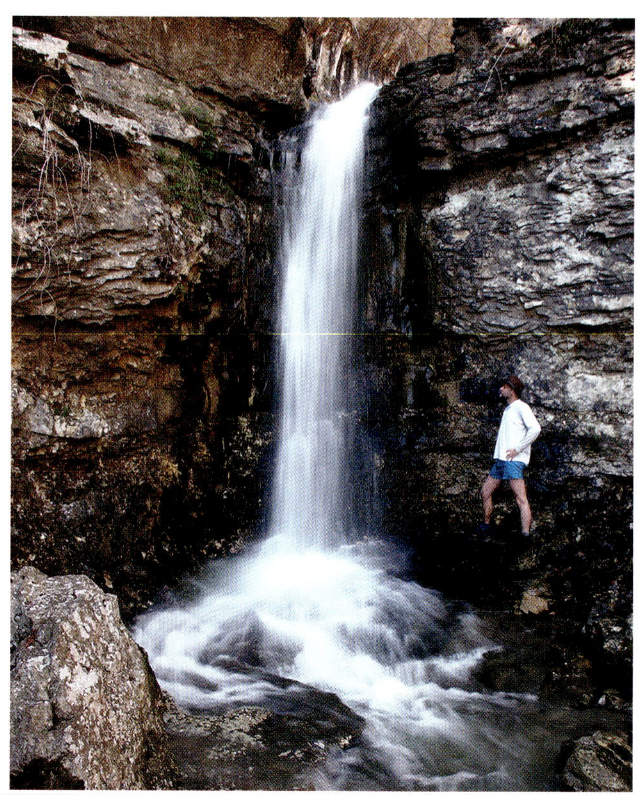

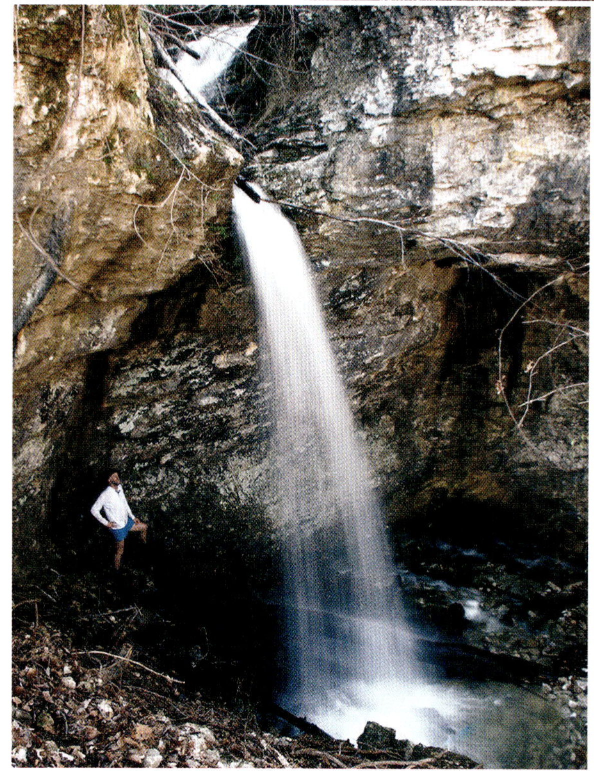

Lower
Armadillo Falls

Balanced Rock Falls – 17′

.7 (1.4 miles roundtrip, easy+, steep social trail, GPS **36.01673, -93.34805**

Leatherwood Grotto – 15′

1.6 mile, moderate social trails, GPS **36.01082, -93.34432**

Top Of The Slots Falls – <10′

1.9 mile, moderate social trails, GPS **36.01243, -93.34667**

Recluse Falls – 59′

2.2 miles, moderate social trails, GPS **36.01331, -93.34859**

Total loop hike to all falls 3.2 miles

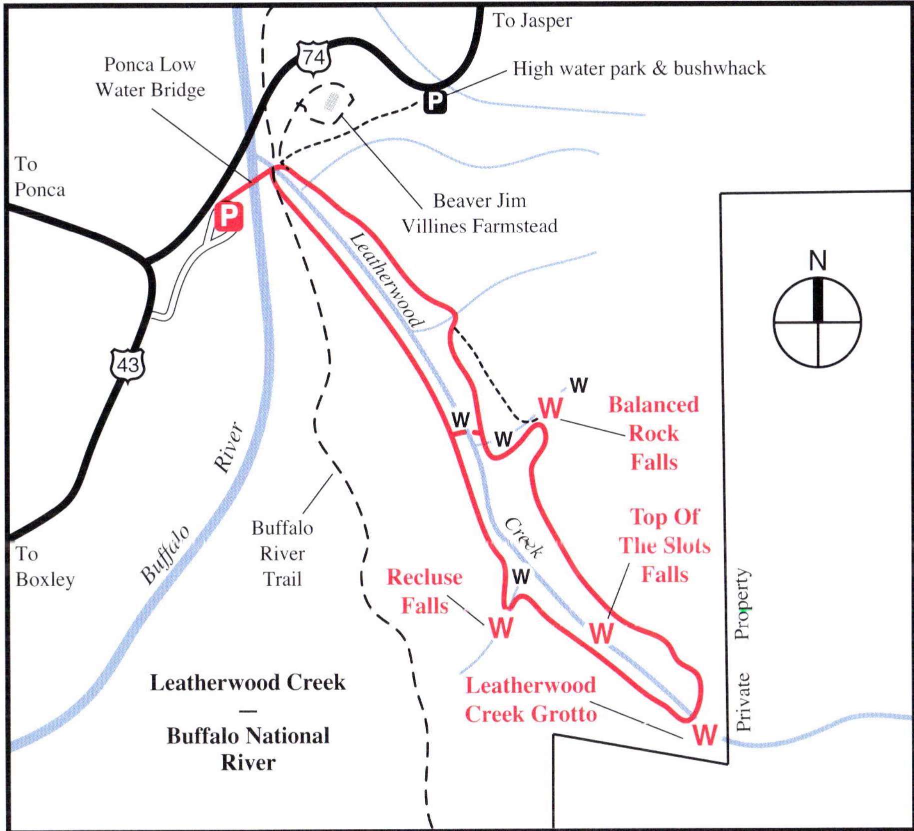

LEATHERWOOD CREEK WATERFALLS. Balanced Rock Falls is the signature waterfall in this drainage and is easy to get to, except for a steep climb up to the falls at the end. There are several other nice waterfalls that we'll visit while doing a loop to the back of the canyon (most folks will stop at Balanced Rock though).

PARK at the Ponca Low Water bridge (**36.02075, -93.35551**), one of the main canoe access points on the upper river, and it can get crowded. (*See note at the end for High Water Access.) Hike across the bridge and then CONTINUE STRAIGHT another couple hundred feet until you cross Leatherwood Creek on a much shorter concrete bridge. *There is a main social trail that takes off to the right just before crossing Leatherwood Creek, but if you go on that trail you will have to cross the creek at least twice.

So GO ACROSS Leatherwood Creek on the short bridge then TURN RIGHT immediately on the other side and follow a social trail upstream, which passes below a power line. It's a beautiful easy hike along the creek, past a couple of cascades and lots of springtime wildflowers. Eventually there's a small bluff that comes down to the creek and you will have to leave the creek and hike a short distance up and around that bluff. The social trail then goes back down alongside the creek and comes to Beaver Jim Cascade that spans the entire creek, a wonderful SSS.

Continue upstream until you come to a creek coming in from the left (you will probably have to get your feet wet here)—there's a small waterfall there, and just on the other side is a very STEEP climb to the LEFT, straight UP the hillside (social trail), and past Villines Falls, which is on the left. Once you reach the top of that climb continue to follow the stream and soon **Balanced Rock Falls** will come into view at .7. It's one of the most unique waterfalls in all of Arkansas. To reach the base of the falls you have to climb up and over or around a rock feature (or just view the falls from your first view spot). And there are waterfalls above the Balanced Rock also that you'll have to climb out, up, and around to get to—best if the water is really flowing good.

To continue your hike go back down below **Balanced Rock** and TURN LEFT and head upstream—you will be above the main Leatherwood Creek and there should be some sort of social trail to follow. Stay pretty much up above the creek—there are some nice waterfalls and cascades down on the creek but it's easier to visit them on the return loop from the other side of the creek. Eventually the creek will come up to meet you and there you will find an amazing box canyon/grotto that is **Leatherwood Grotto**, a marvelous SSS at 1.6. Oh my! There is PRIVATE PROPERTY beyond this area so please don't explore upstream any further.

Once you've soaked it all in, cross the creek and head back downstream (on the opposite side), first along the base of the bluff, then just follow the stream/social trail—you will be closer to the creek on this side and will be able to see several short falls and cascades, including **Top Of The Slots Falls**. As the name suggests this begins kind of a slot canyon downstream for a while—tough to access from above, but beautiful all the way.

Continue downstream to a side drainage and nice waterfall that comes from the left and pours almost directly into Leatherwood Creek. TURN LEFT and hike UP this side drainage (steep) and you will come to the base of the tallest waterfall we visit, **Recluse Falls** at—2.3. This was named after an elderly recluse that lived nearby during the early 20th century (you will pass the remains of her cabin's chimney on the way back).

Return to the creek and follow the social trail all the way back to the bridge and parking area for a total hike of around 3.2.

*High water access. If the river is flooded and the Ponca low water bridge is under water (which means the waterfalls should be GREAT!), there is another small parking area you can use to access the far side of Leatherwood Creek and get to **Balanced Rock Falls**. Drive across the Hwy. 74 bridge towards Jasper, go around the first corner, and at the next corner PARK ON THE RIGHT (**36.02293, -93.35026**)—only room for one or two cars—there is a power line overhead. Then hike the powerline downhill (past the Beaver Jim Villines Homestead area) until you get to Leatherwood Creek and the social trail there—TURN LEFT and hike upstream.

Emergency contact: Newton County Sheriff, 870–446–5124 No dogs on trails.

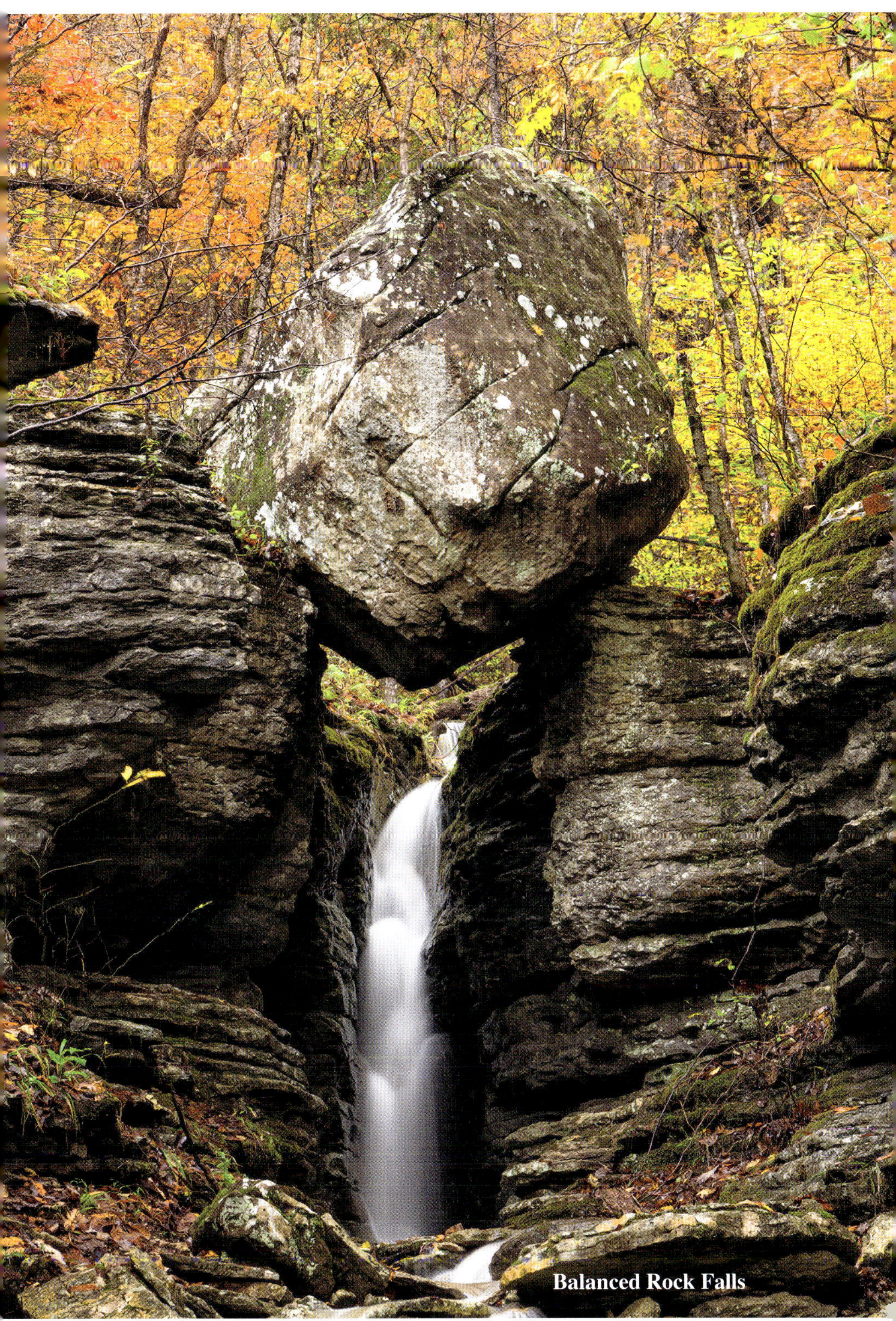
Balanced Rock Falls

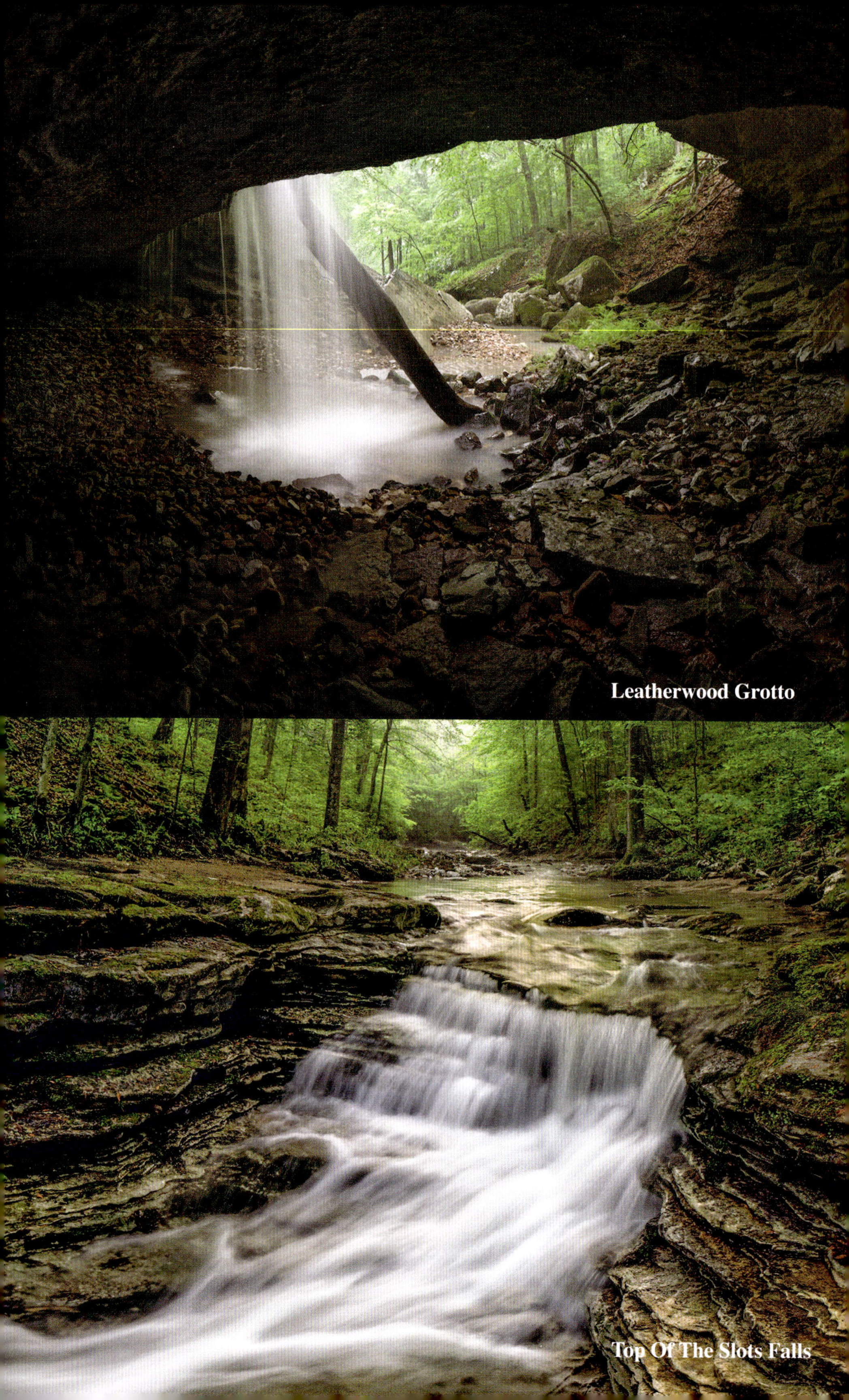

Leatherwood Grotto

Top Of The Slots Falls

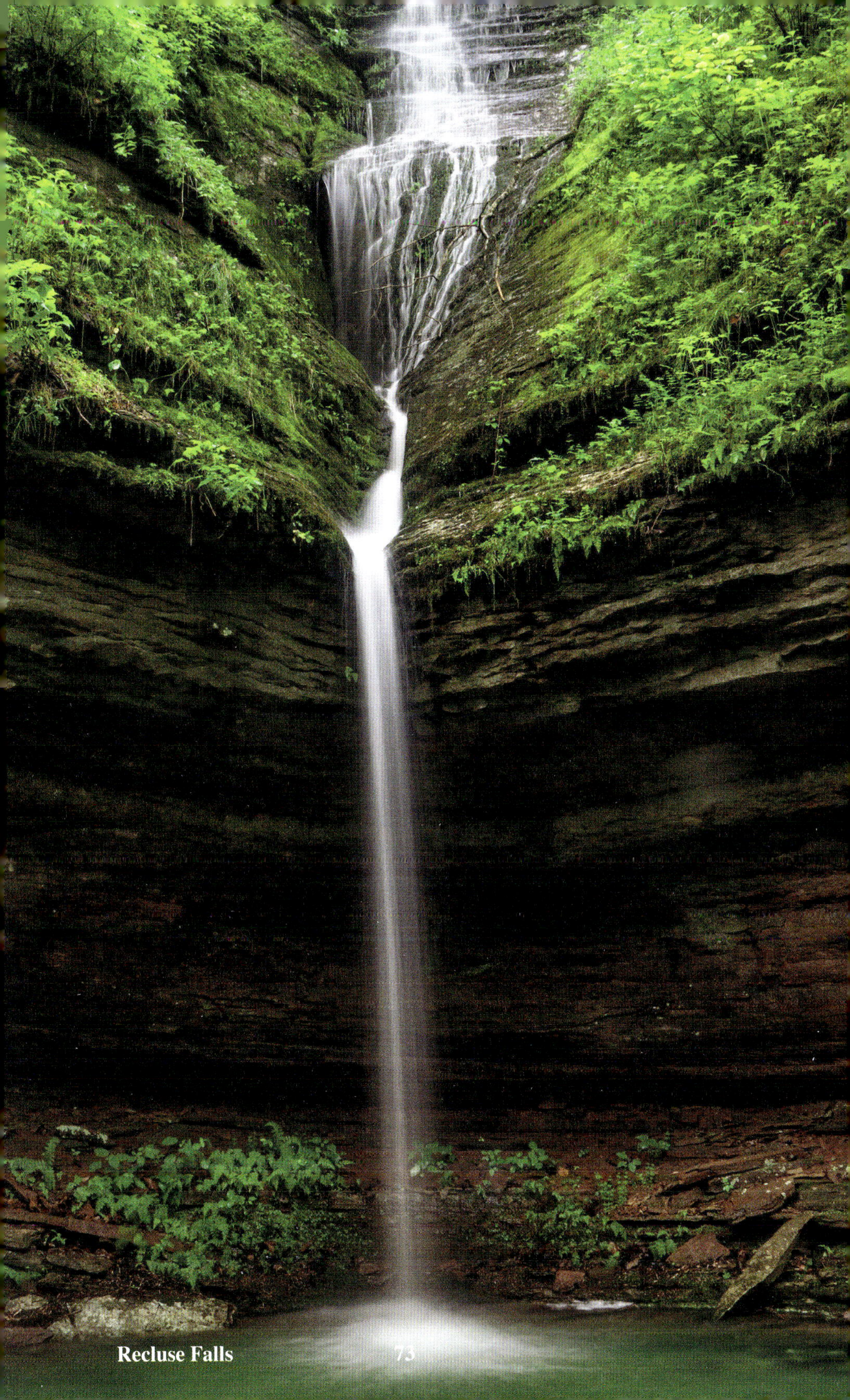

Recluse Falls

Rum Hole Falls – 36′

.6, easy trail/bushwhack, GPS **36.02582, -93.35262**

Hidden Falls (Ponca) – 37′

.7 easy trail/bushwhack, GPS **36.02734, -93.34974**

Clemmer Falls – 33′

.85, easy trail/moderate bushwhack, GPS **36.02835, -93.34770**

Half Moon Falls – 61′

1.0, easy trail/moderate bushwhack, GPS **36.02967, -93.34603**

Ponca Polyfoss – 9-39′

.9 easy trail, GPS **36.02778, -93.34684**

Total roundtrip hike to all falls 2.4 miles

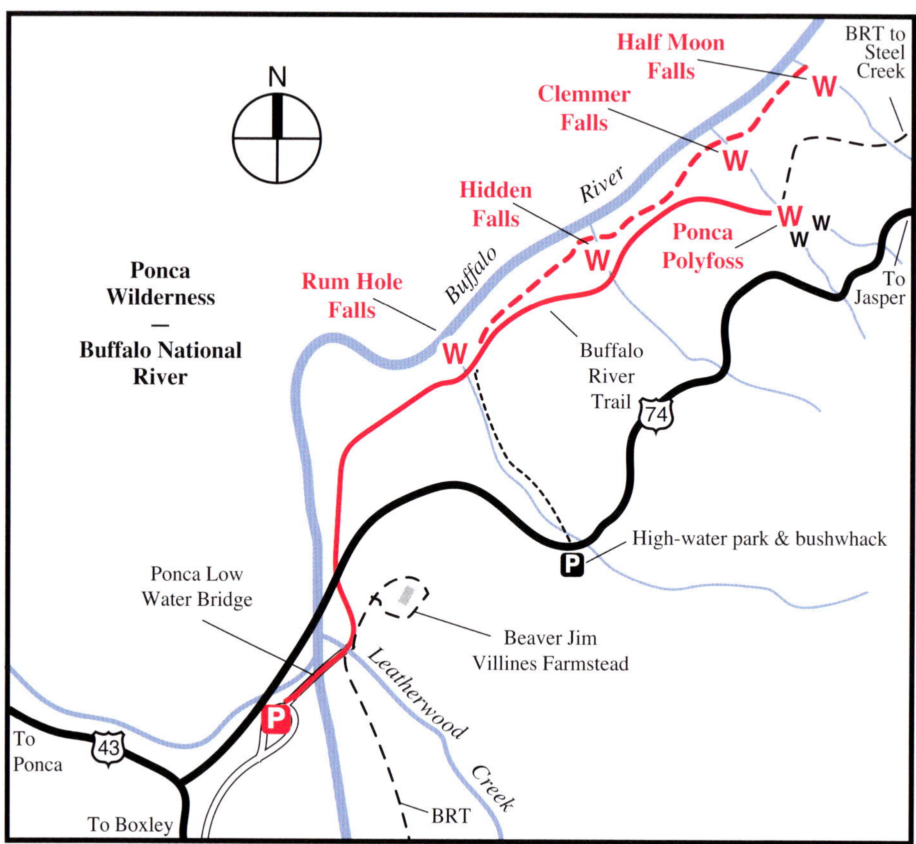

PONCA BRIDGE DOWNSTREAM WATERFALLS. Here are MORE great waterfalls within easy hiking of the popular Ponca Low Water Bridge access. These are great to visit for times when the river is too high to float and there are waterfalls everywhere—you can check to see if they are flowing by driving Hwy. 74 from Ponca up to the Steele Creek turnoff —each switchback should have water flowing down the bluff beside the road (if not, the waterfalls may still be flowing, just not as well).

PARK at the Ponca Low Water Bridge (**36.02075, -93.35551**) and hike across the bridge and a couple hundred feet farther and TURN LEFT onto the Buffalo River Trail (BRT). (See note at the end of this section for High Water Access.) Follow this trail downstream alongside the Buffalo River, then away from the river a bit, then back alongside the river and across a small creek at .6. This creek pours over a bluff to your left as **Rum Hole Falls**, named after a local teenage party spot on the river. To reach the bottom of the falls continue on the trail a little ways and past an overlook spot—until you see a split in the bluff line with a ramp of sorts where you can get down to the bottom of the bluff, then follow the bluff base back to the LEFT to the falls.

Instead of climbing back up to the top of the bluff, stay BELOW the bluff and hike downstream along the base of the bluff. Not only is the bluff itself quite scenic, but there

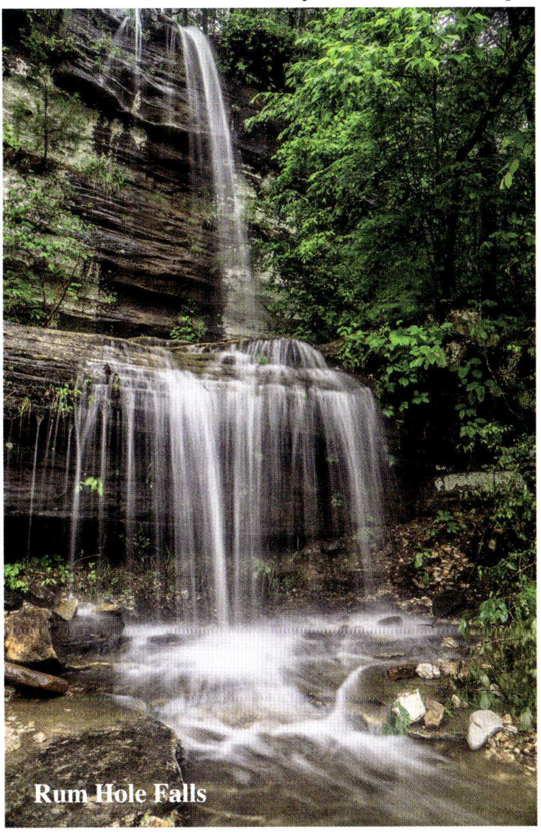
Rum Hole Falls

are three really terrific waterfalls ahead! First is **Hidden Falls**. The trail above it literally comes within a few feet of the top of this waterfall, but few people ever see it. Stunning how it is hidden by a fold in the bluff.

Next along the bluff is **Clemmer Falls**, named after the Clemmer family who used to live and farm the fields across the river. Of course it's an SSS!

The terrain is a little more steep and tricky but still continue along the base of the same bluff to **Half Moon Falls** at 1.0, the tallest of them in this area and another SSS (I'm sort of a lunatic and see a large half-moon-shaped opening in the bluff.) Due to its height it takes a lot more water to be impressive than the rest, but even at lower water levels the bluff and rocks are just amazing to visit.

If you want to visit the **Ponca Polyfoss** area, turn around and head back upstream along the base of the bluff and climb back up on top of the bluff. Then TURN LEFT on

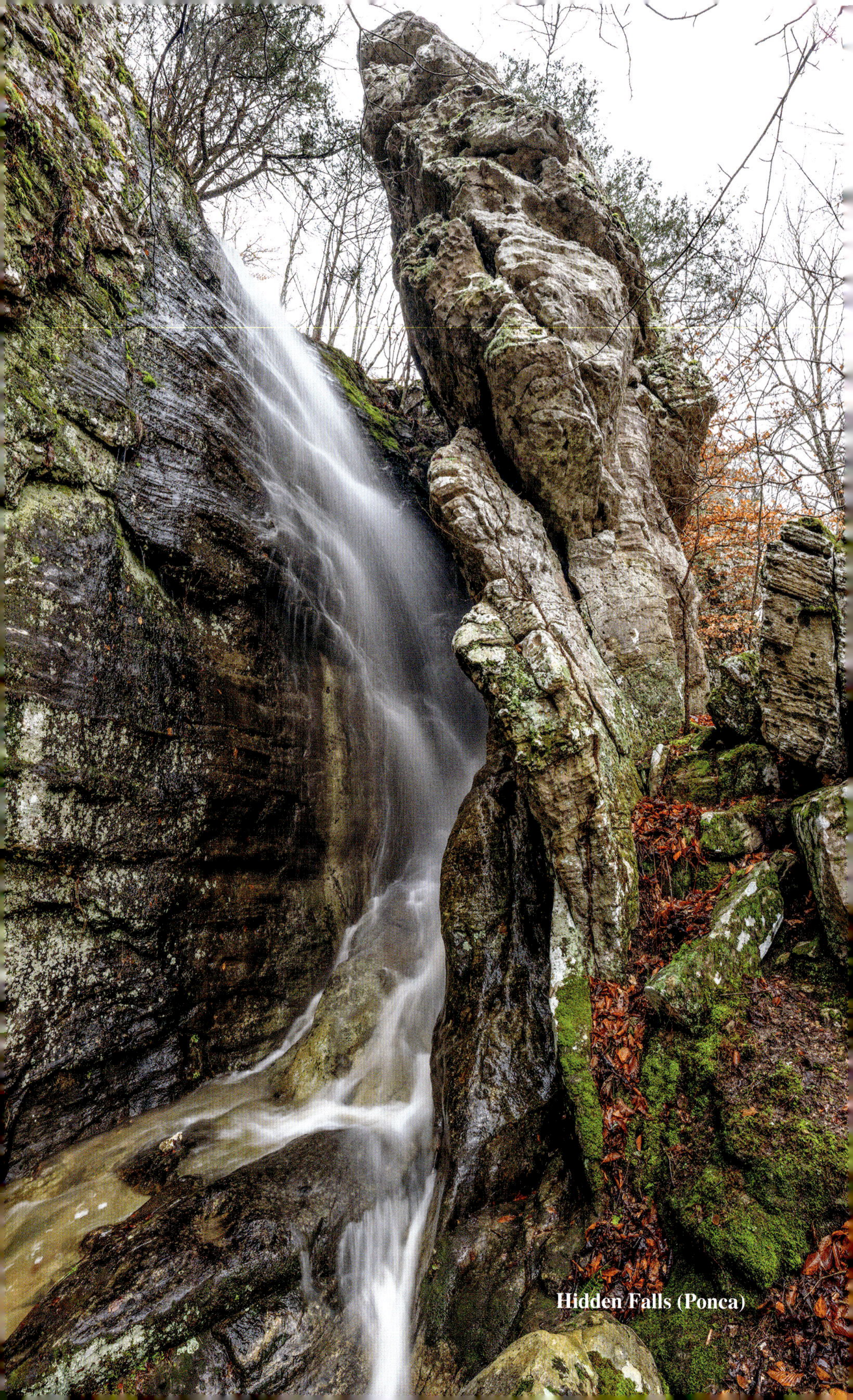
Hidden Falls (Ponca)

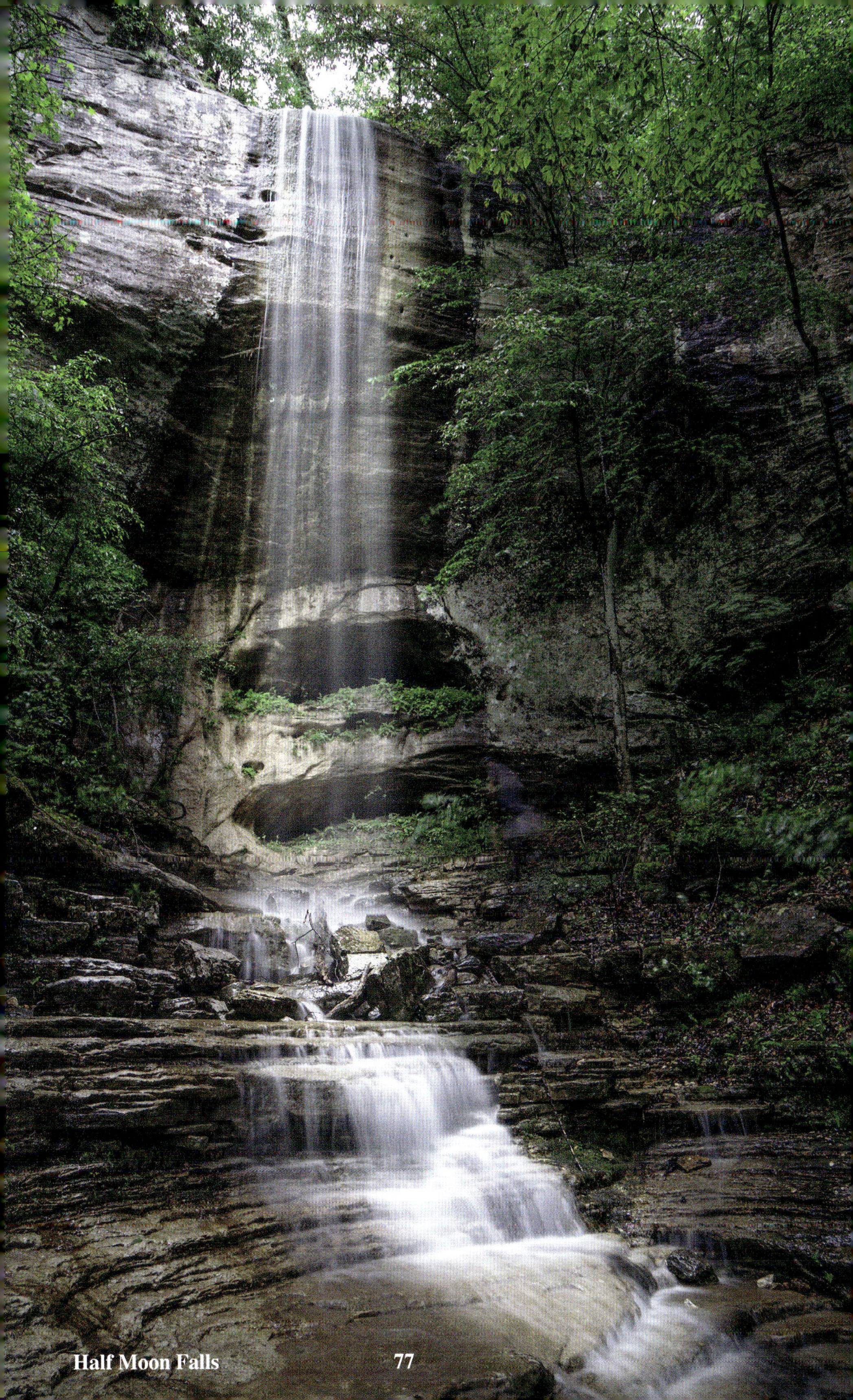
Half Moon Falls

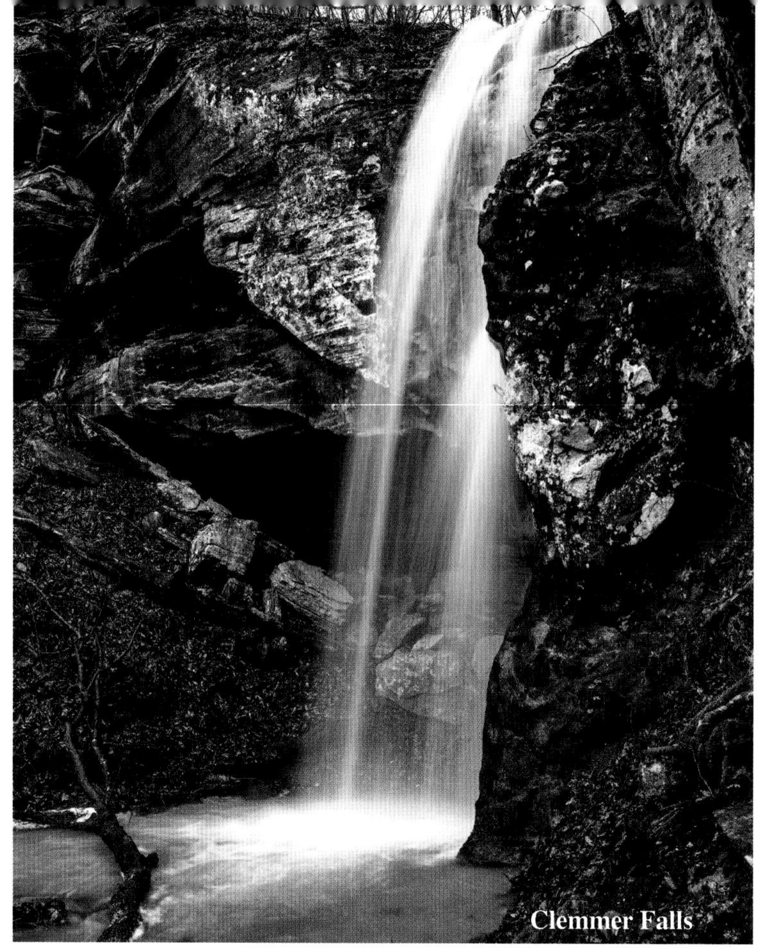
Clemmer Falls

the BRT and follow it across the top of **Hidden Falls** and uphill a little bit, then the trail curves right into a drainage until you come to the **Ponca Polyfoss,** a large cascade area on the RIGHT (you'd have to get your feet wet on the trail if the cascades are flowing). This is an AMAZING spot during high water (POLYFOSS means "many waterfalls" in Icelandic—or actually I just made that term up after spending a week in Iceland.). You can see several different cascades and at least six or seven waterfalls above you from the trail. Each one of course looks even better up close, but I must warn you the steep hillsides can get pretty SLICK so be extra careful!

It's less than a mile back to the parking lot, for a total distance to visit all these waterfalls being about 2.5 miles.

HIGH WATER ACCESS. If the river is flooded and the Ponca low water bridge is under water (which means the waterfalls should be GREAT!), there is another parking area you can use to access the Buffalo River Trail. Drive across the Hwy. 74 bridge towards Jasper, go around the first corner, and at the next corner PARK ON THE RIGHT—only room for one or two cars—there is a power line overhead. Then CROSS the highway to a culvert and follow that creek downhill until you hit the Buffalo River Trail, then turn right.

Emergency contact: Newton County Sheriff, 870–446–5124

Dogs are allowed on this short section of the BRT (2025 update)

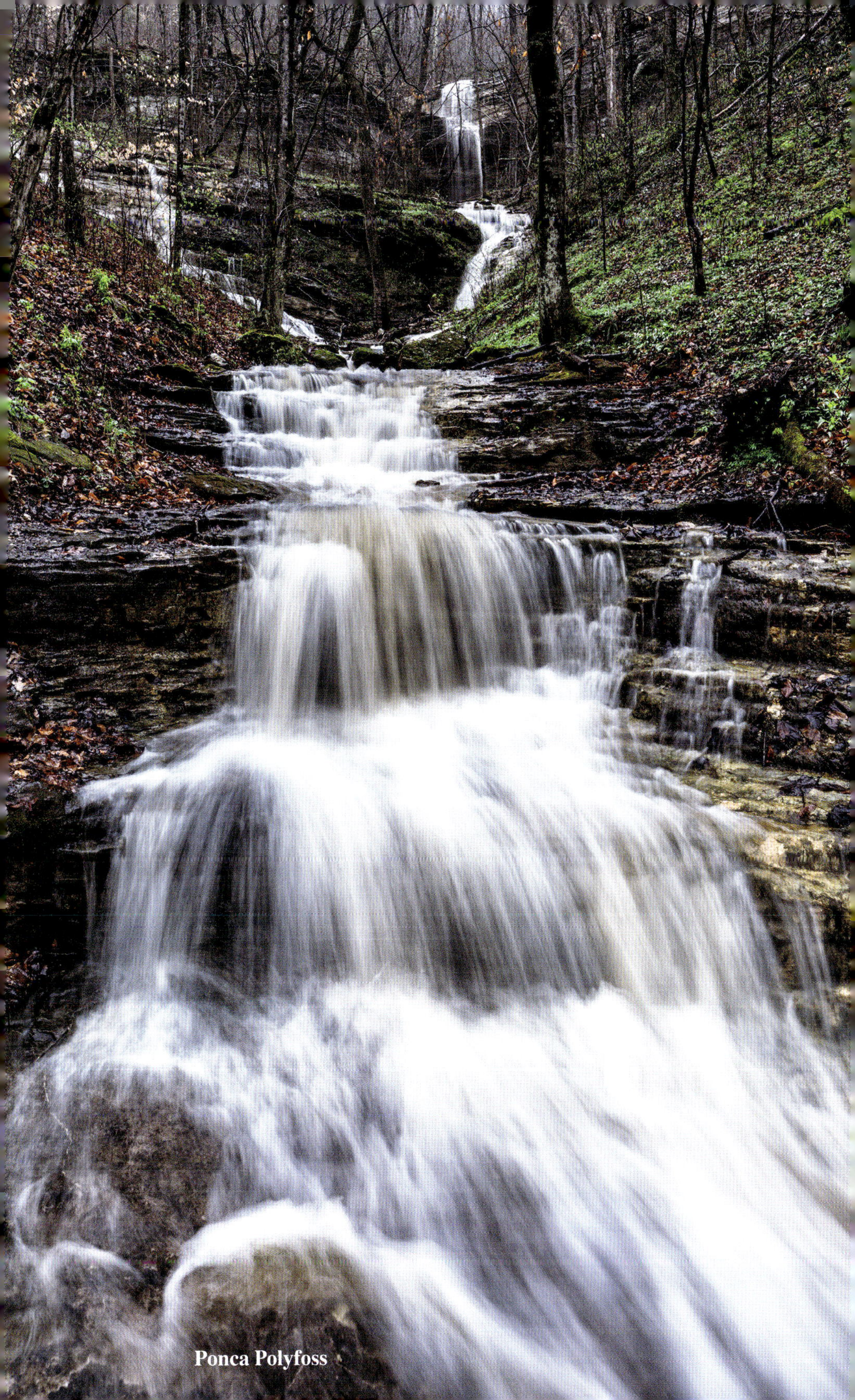

Ponca Polyfoss

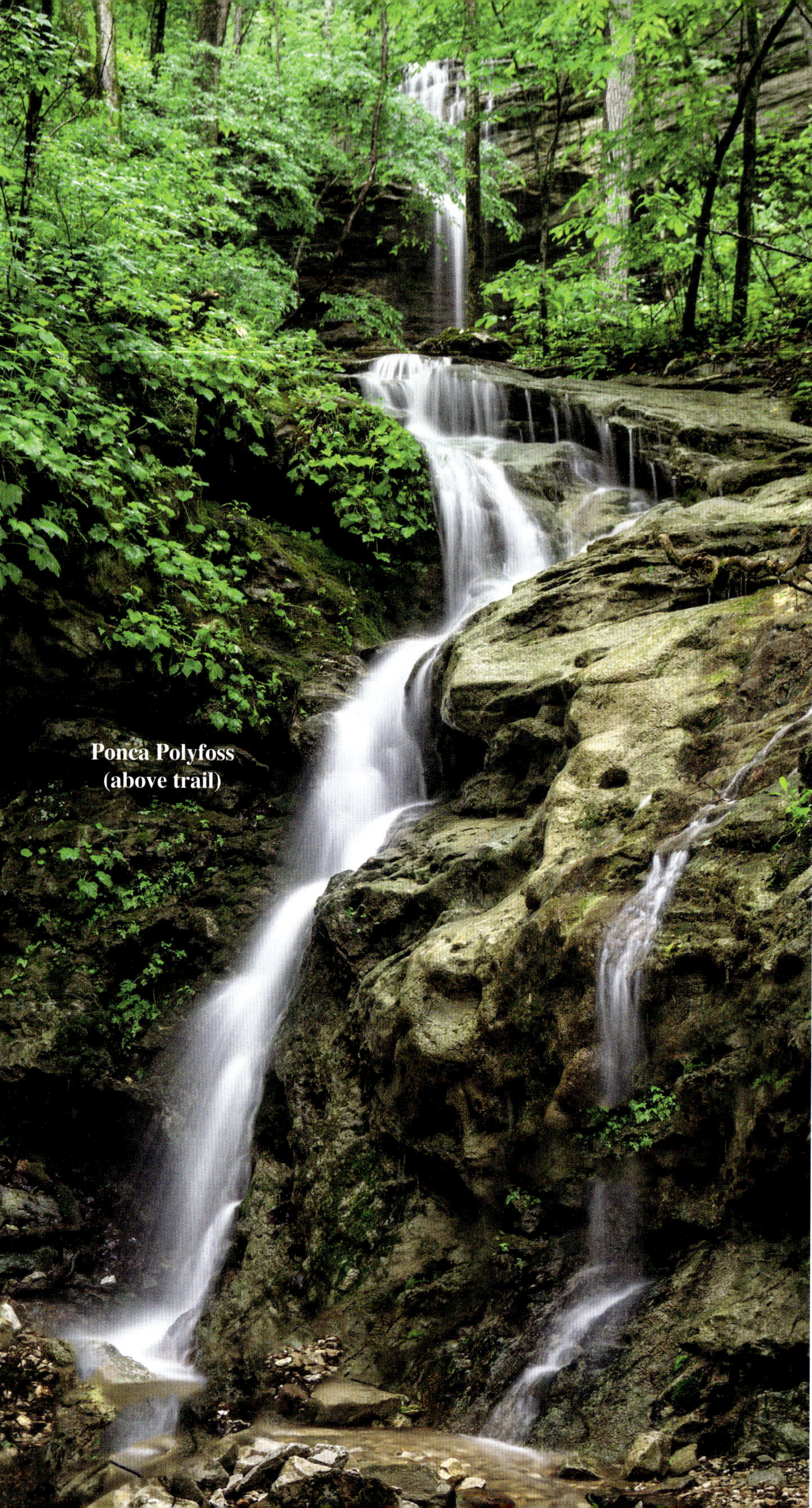
Ponca Polyfoss
(above trail)

Roark Bluff Falls – 195′

view from car or short hike to edge of river, GPS **36.04382, -93.34430**

Firehose Falls – 126′

short hike to edge of river, GPS **36.04137, -93.34725**

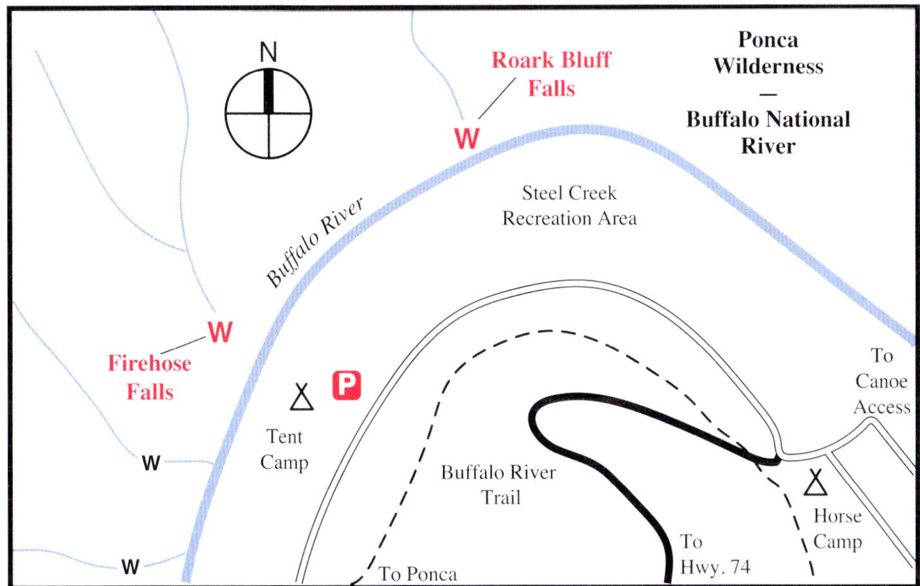

ROARK BLUFF FALLS/FIREHOSE FALLS. Roark Bluff Falls is the second tallest waterfall in Arkansas at 195' when it is flowing. ***It's normally dry though***, and usually takes a pretty good flood to get it rolling. But it seems like it has been running a lot more lately, and when that happens there's not much else to do but go after big waterfalls (since the river will be flooded)—and you can see this one right from your car! FYI, the mineral-stained Roark Bluff is a stunning SSS at any time of the year, wet or dry.

Drive to the Steel Creek Campground—turnoff is located between Ponca and Low Gap. (turn LEFT at the bottom of the hill). You will see the majestic Roark Bluff off to the right, and **Roark Bluff Falls** will be near the upstream end of it. View from your car, or continue to the campground and park there (**36.04072, -93.34546**), then hike into the large field for a closer view. You can bushwhack through the canebrake and get to the edge of the river—but stay away from the edge since high water tends to collapse river banks.

Return to the campground and find a social trail out the back of campsite #4 or #8 (ask politely if you can barge in on any campers), and this will take you a couple hundred feet to the river's edge to see **Firehose Falls**. Redbud trees crowd around the base in March to soak up the spray.

Emergency contact: Newton County Sheriff, 870–446–5124 No dogs on trails.

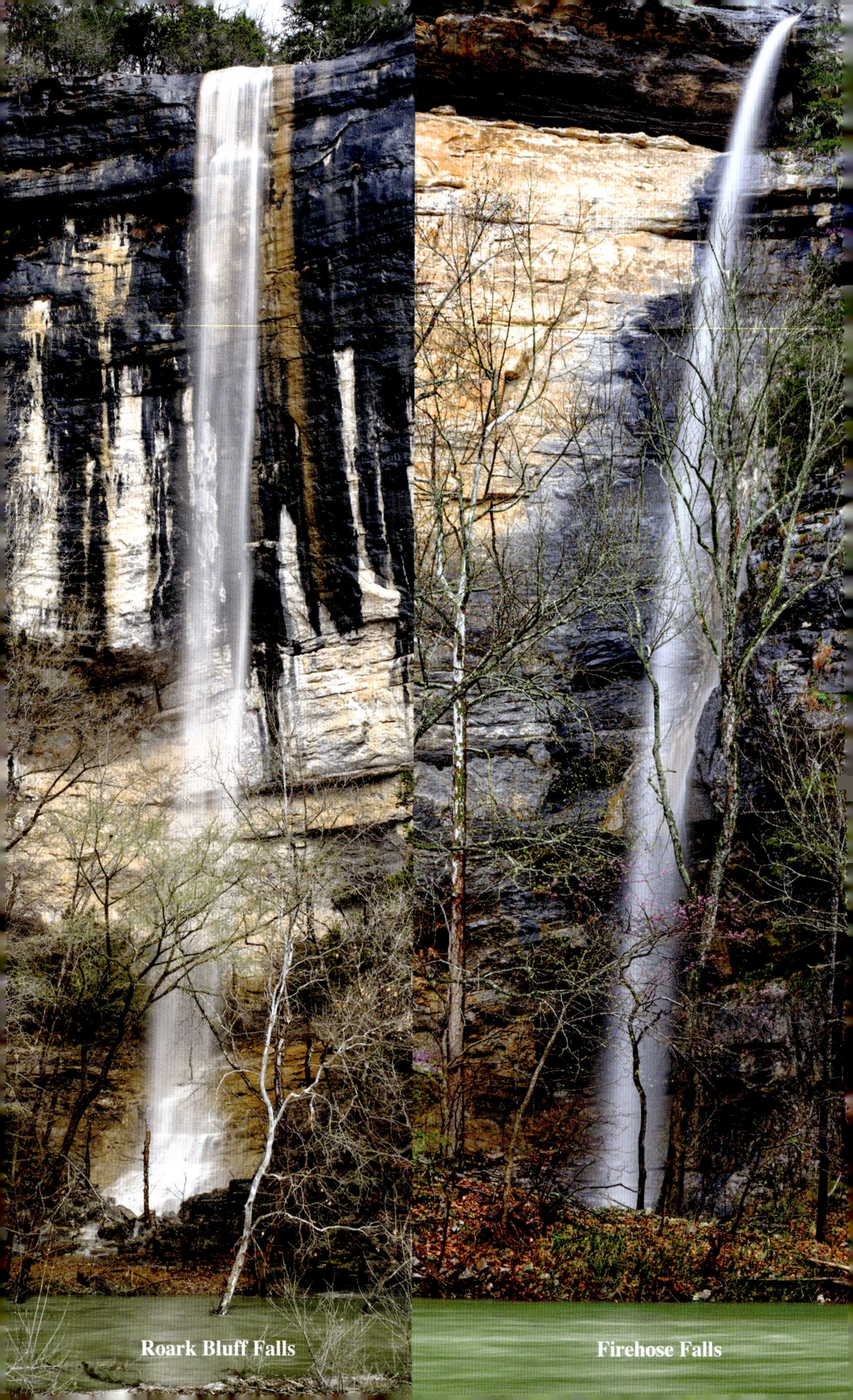

Roark Bluff Falls

Firehose Falls

Chimney Rock Mine Falls – 35′

.5 to 1.4 mi, easy bushwhack GPS **36.05445, -93.34299**

Cat Man Falls – 47′

1.6 mi, moderate/difficult ending GPS **36.05672, -93.34322**

Cliff Hollow Grotto – 30′

2.2 mi, moderate bushwhack GPS **36.05967, -93.34935**

Cliff Hollow Falls – 35′

2.4 mi.moderate bushwhack GPS **36.05877, -93.35103**

Green Goddess Falls – 44′

2.6 mi, moderate bushwhack GPS **36.05947, -93.35283**

Cliff Twin Cascades – 100′+

.5 (from the top down), difficult bushwhack ♦ GPS **36.06271, -93.35706**

CLIFF HOLLOW WATERFALLS. Here's a waterfall mecca that's been hiding in plain sight all this time. It is the first drainage downstream from the canoe launch at Steel Creek, Cliff Hollow. You can wade across the river and hike the Old River Horse Trail from the canoe launch to this creek (there's a spectacular bluff line along the way), or float to it and stop for a quick trip upstream. It's easy to spend an entire day exploring many waterfalls in this drainage. If you follow this creek (all located within the Ponca Wilderness Area) all the way UP to the top, it will come out at the Centerpoint Trailhead on Hwy. 43 (3.4 miles from Ponca, it's the trailhead for hikes to Big Bluff and Hemmed-In-Hollow). Between the river and the trailhead I've found a couple dozen pretty nice falls, with many others along the way. Most of them remain unnamed. There are no trails, and only one old mining road that I know of, though it's mostly so grown up you can't follow it. Most of the waterfalls are located in side drainages, with sometimes two or three layers of bluffs with waterfalls above. No doubt social trails will develop to some of the most popular. FYI, top to bottom of this drainage is 1,229' elevation change.

Historical note about the name "Chimney Rock Mine." While there was a large zinc mining operation in the late 1800's named Chimney Rock Mine just off the Chimney Rock Horse Trail near Hwy. 43 (**36.04949, -93.34769**), there is no actual "chimney rock" to be found anywhere. The mine's name comes from the type of mining operation and not a particular rock formation. (There are dozens of "Chimney Rocks" in the country, notably one at Owl Creek Pass in the San Juan Mountains of southwest Colorado—famous for being in the background of the shoot out scene with John Wayne in the original True Grit movie!).

COMING FROM THE BOTTOM, PARK at the canoe access at Steel Creek Recreation Area (**36.03839, -93.33572**)—the turnoff is between Ponca and Low Gap on Hwy. 74. Wade across the Buffalo River on The Old River Horse Trail and follow it downstream to .6 where the trail crosses the river to the right, BUT you continue STRAIGHT ahead bushwhacking along the river bank to the first drainage at .9, then TURN LEFT at the entrance to Cliff Hollow (**36.05026, -93.33725**)—**OR float to this point and park your canoe at the mouth of Cliff Hollow.** There is room along the river on the left bank to

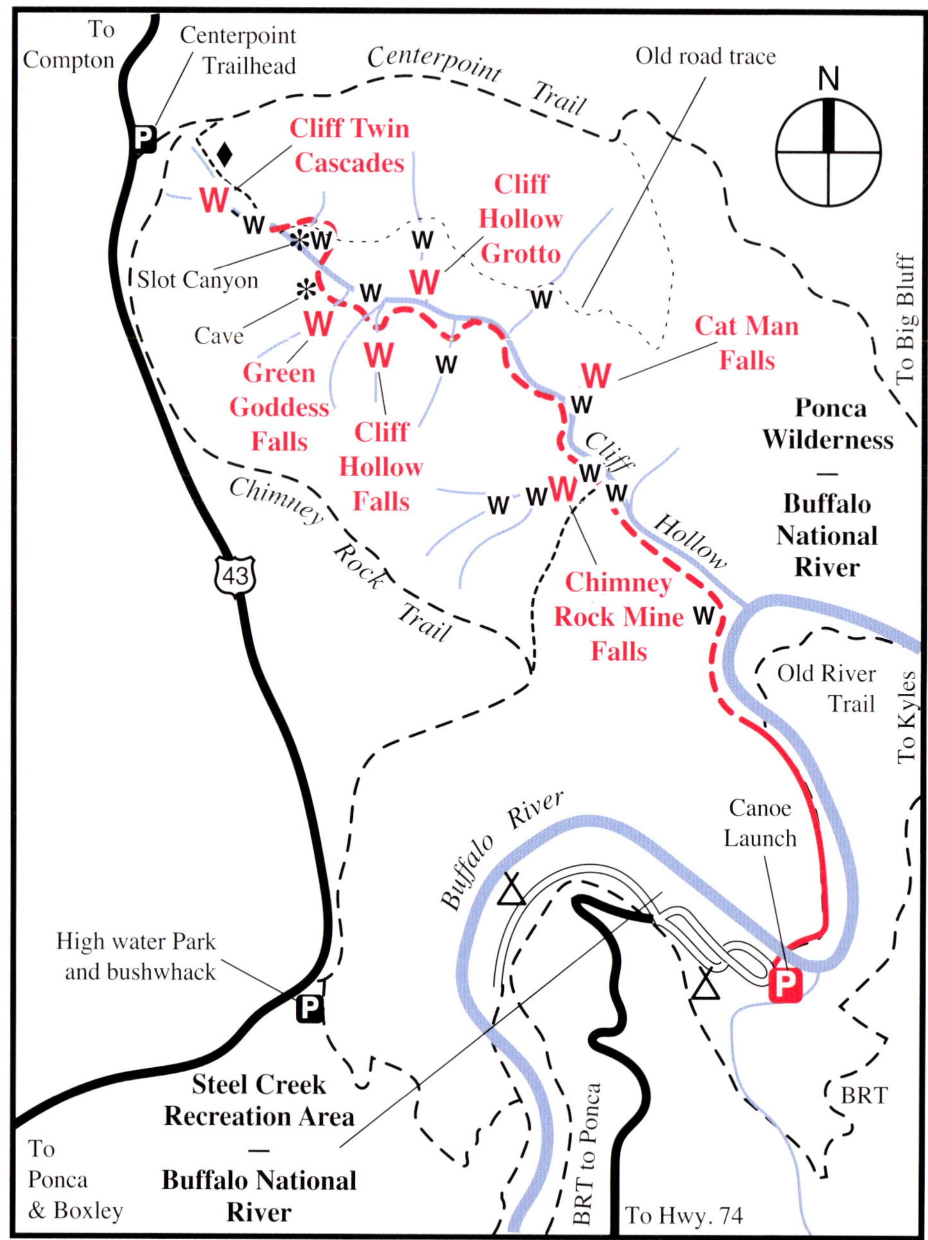

hike unless the river is at historic flood levels. If it's merely high, there might be a 91' tall waterfall pouring off the big bluff on the left just before Cliff Hollow. The bushwhack hike from the mouth up to the Centerpoint Trailhead is about 3.0 miles (plus side trips), 1,229' total CLIMB! SSS all the way, but the last section is brutal. Most folks just hike upstream and visit two or three falls and return.

From the mouth of Cliff Hollow at the Buffalo River it's an easy stroll upstream to a nice cascade that spans the creek. Just upstream from this cascade TURN LEFT into a side drainage that has a couple of smaller falls, then a larger falls, and then the big, wonderful **Chimney Rock Mine Falls** at 1.4, an SSS of course! Even if this is all you want to see,

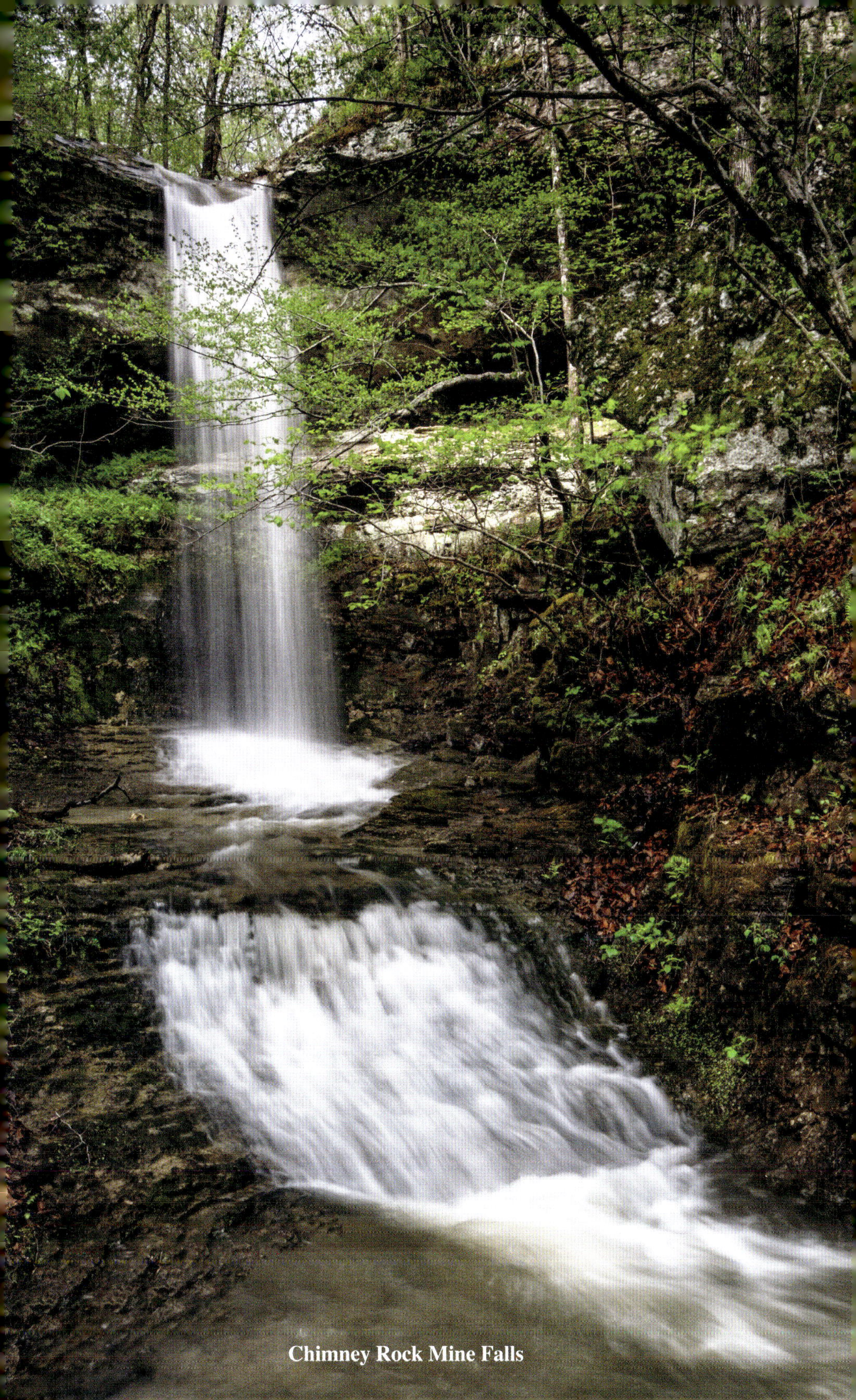

Chimney Rock Mine Falls

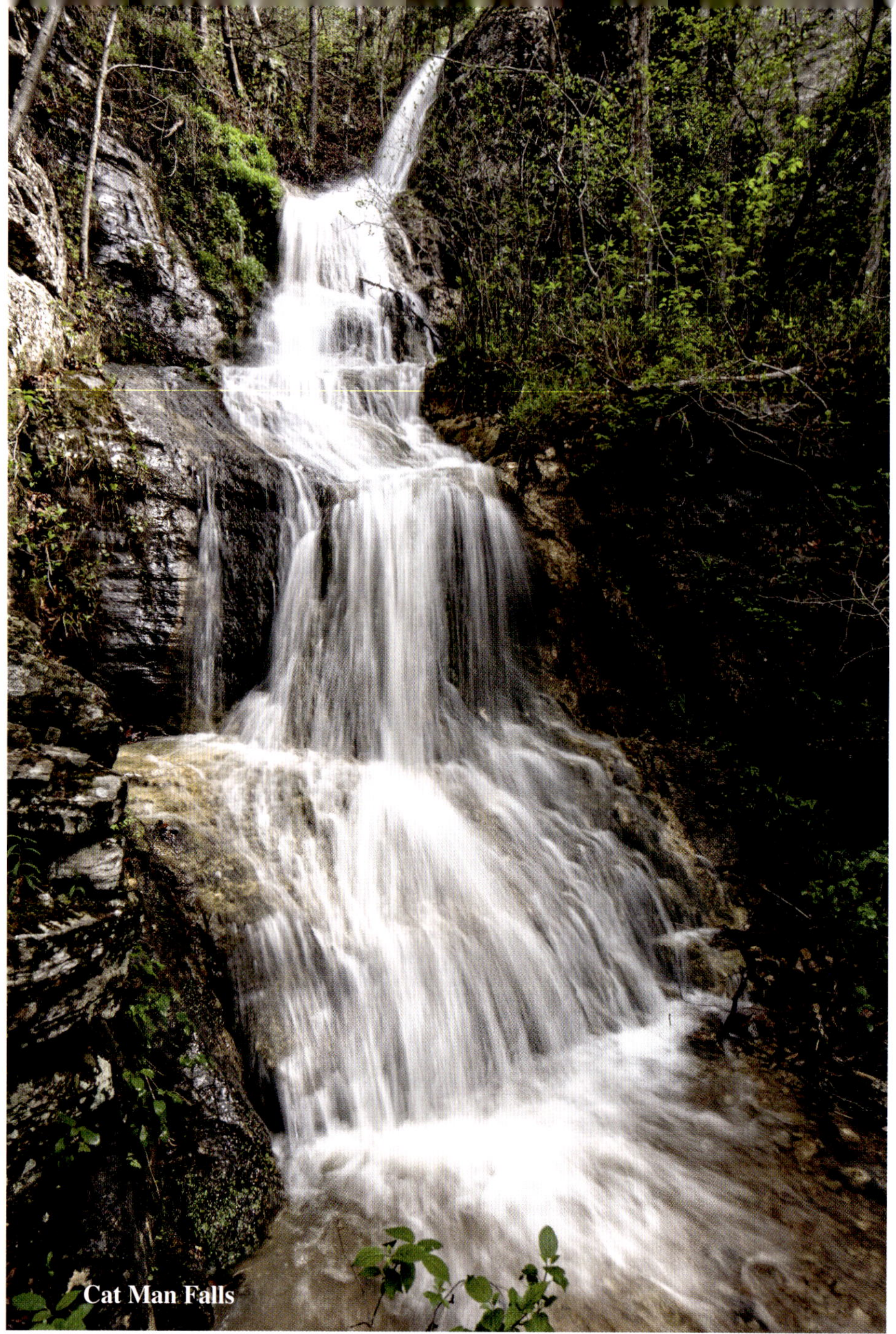
Cat Man Falls

it's a nice spot to visit and then return to your canoe, or hike back to Steel Creek. There are more falls above in this side drainage, but you have to back out a little bit and climb up and around to the LEFT of the main falls, then follow the stream uphill for at least a couple more falls—maybe more.

To explore more, return to the main creek and continue upstream as it curves around right then left through a really nice SSS area along the creek with lots of boulders (climb up on the left side to get through). Just as the creek straightens out there is a side creek

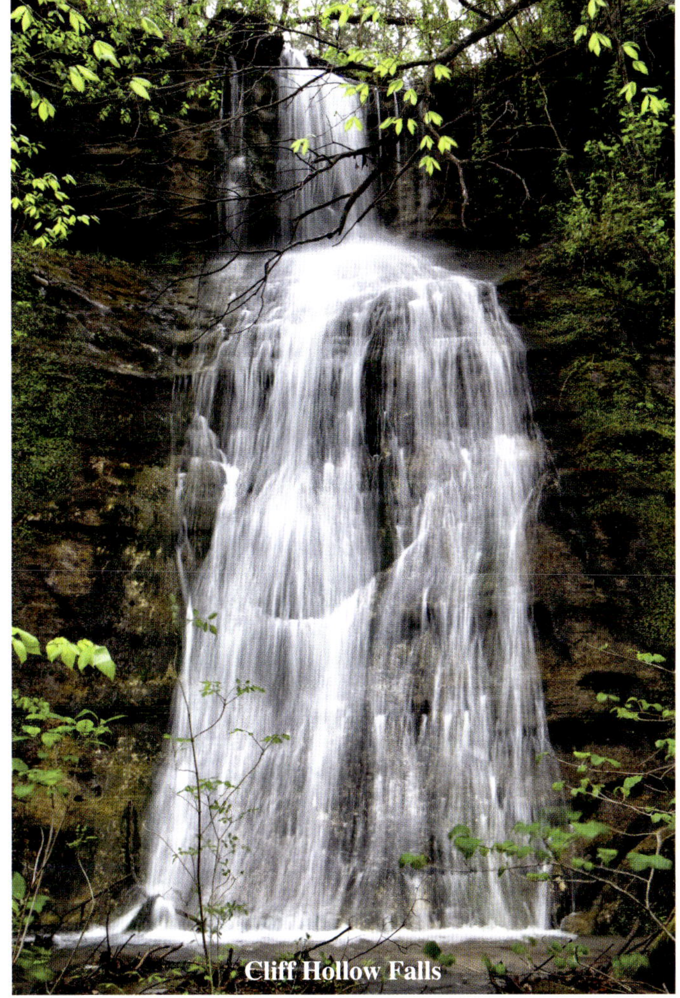

coming in from the RIGHT with a nice multi-level waterfall. That one is great, but there is a really tall 47' falls above what you can see, although it is a STEEP scramble to get up to the base of **Cat Man Falls** at 1.6 (named for Frank Little, who lived on the ridgetop above, usually with 15-30 cats).

Back on the main creek continue upstream to the next side drainage on the LEFT. A short steep climb brings you to an interesting 33' tall **Sinkhole Falls** (no photo provided)—to the right of the falls on the same bluff you walk into the bottom of what was once a sinkhole and can gaze up to the sky. Another SSS, right?

Back on the main creek continue upstream and on the RIGHT at 2.2 to **Cliff Hollow Grotto**, SSS. Like many of the other side drainages there is a tall falls and maybe more above this, farther up the hillside on a main bluff up there—tough climbing to reach from below though.

Back on the main creek upstream TURN LEFT and hike up to **Cliff Hollow Falls** at 2.4 (THIS one is my favorite! Oops, until the next one, and the one before this...).

Back on the main creek upstream is the first of three waterfalls on the main creek itself. It's not a giant one but pours into an emerald pool with an interesting root wrapped around the base of a giant tree. SSS (no photo provided).

Next upstream on the LEFT is **Green Goddess Falls**, SSS—the entire wall seems to be covered with lush green moss. And beyond this one upstream there's a neat cave

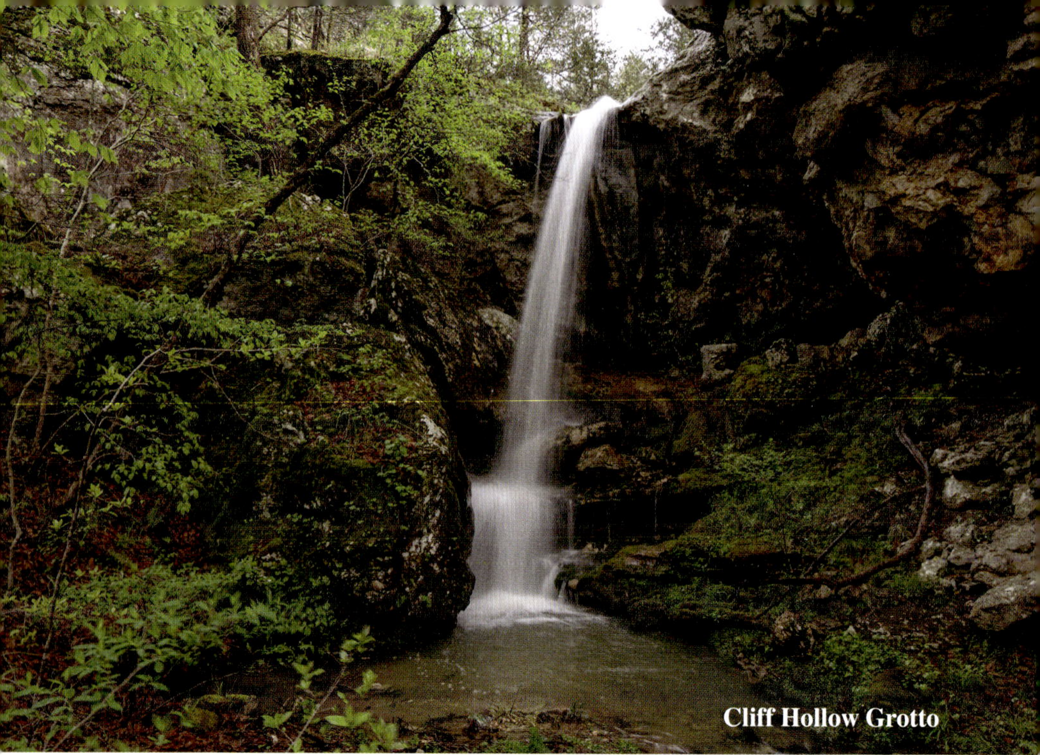
Cliff Hollow Grotto

opening up on the LEFT. I may have slept in there a time or two.

Next upstream you will come to a narrow slot canyon at about 2.8. I've never been able to work my way up into it very far—there might be a waterfall half way up. I've always backed out and then found a place to climb out of the main canyon on the right—and in fact there is a side creek with spectacular waterfalls there, just SSS after SSS! (no photos provided) If you can make it up and out of the main creek canyon there is an old road trace just up on top—TURN LEFT on that road and follow it upstream and it will come back to and cross the creek ABOVE the slot canyon at about 3.0.

Just upstream from this is a really nice falls on the main creek, **Four Drop Falls**, 23' (no photo provided—I bet you can figure it out though.) And then upstream from that you will enter the interesting SSS upper box canyon with a falls and cascades—then at the very top end is **Cliff Twin Cascades**.

Most sane folks would turn around here and return to the river and/or Steel Creek Trailhead, for a total hike of about six miles. This spot is almost to the very top, and if you can climb out of the canyon (I usually go back downstream until I can climb up and out to the northeast) and continue up a BLACK DIAMOND ♦ slope you can end up at the Centerpoint Trailhead, almost four miles from the mouth of Cliff Hollow down on the Buffalo River, 1,229' below.

COMING DOWN FROM THE TOP of the drainage (recommended only for extreme adventures—BLACK DIAMOND ♦ terrain), PARK at the Centerpoint Trailhead (**36.06399, -93.36046**). Start down the trail towards Big Bluff, then TURN RIGHT onto the Chimney Rock Horse Trail. Follow it a couple hundred yards to a low point in the terrain, then TURN LEFT and head straight DOWNHILL. This will become a BLACK DIAMOND slope ♦, especially farther down where it will connect with a second drainage joining from the right. Where these two meet is the top of an SSS canyon. At that point I measured what I could see of both twin cascades at 100'+ each.

To continue will depend on your skill level, but I will note that if you get below this upper canyon area the terrain gets easier, and there are three waterfalls along the main creek. Then you come to a short slot canyon that is probably only suitable for those with ropes and hard hats—others can make your way around to the left downstream along an old road trace until you can find a way to get back down to the creek through the bluff line that forms the slot canyon. This slot canyon and bluff marks the end of the upper section and the beginning of the lower, more friendly section of the Cliff Hollow drainage. (FYI, that old road trace goes all the way up and out of the canyon to the Centerpoint Trail, 1.7 miles from the creek, part of it running along the top of the big bluff where more waterfalls live. It's badly grown up and hard to follow in places.)

Downstream of the slot canyon all the waterfalls but one are in side drainages, a few of them shown here—simply explore as you like. You can hike up and out of the canyon in many places—and either top out on the trail to Big Bluff or along Hwy. 43—but no matter which route you choose it will be pretty steep BLACK DIAMOND ♦ slopes much of the way, and at least a couple of blufflines to get around.

Either way, from the top or bottom, WOW, what an adventure!

Emergency contact: Newton County Sheriff, 870–446–5124 No dogs on trails.

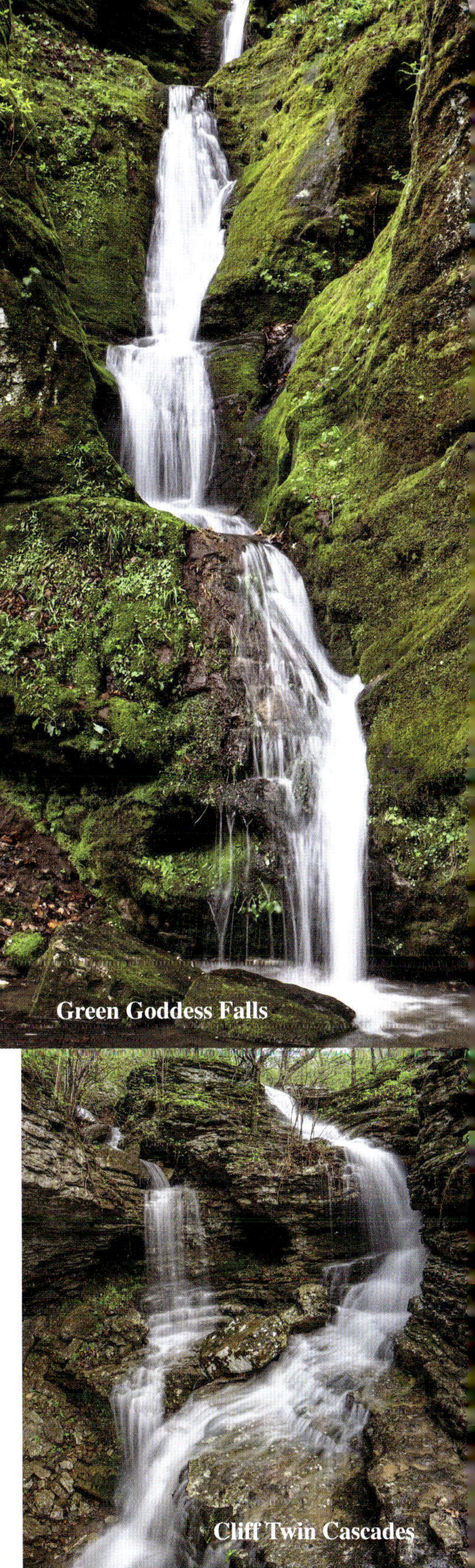

Green Goddess Falls

Cliff Twin Cascades

Jackie Hollow Falls – 54′

1.1 mile roundtrip, difficult bushwhack

GPS **36.07851, -93.34542**

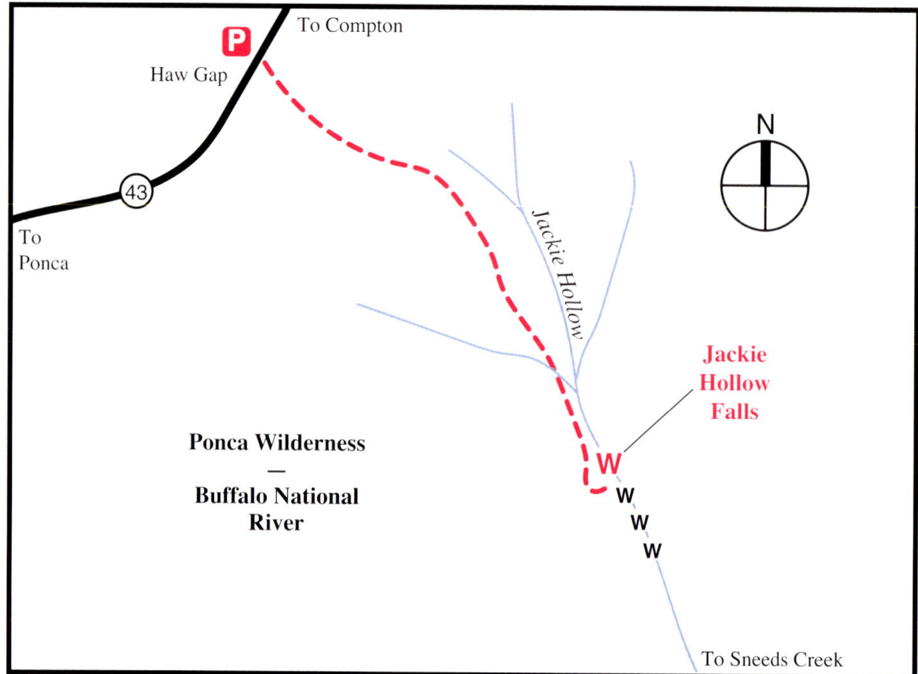

JACKIE HOLLOW FALLS. Park at Haw Gap on Hwy. 43 (**36.08342, -93.35039**), 2.8 miles from Compton, or 5.1 miles from Ponca. 1.1 mile round trip.

Jackie Hollow Falls is pretty easy to get DOWN TO, but it's a 700' climb back UP to get back to the car. Basically you simply PARK at Haw Gap, cross the highway, head into the woods, and hike straight DOWNHILL. There are several little drainages but they all come together below—the main thing is to continue DOWN the steep HILL as best you can. At .5 you should arrive at the top of a big bluff and **Jackie Hollow Falls**. There is a ramp of sorts a little off to the right of the falls that will lead you down to the bottom of the falls—not a bad climb down. SSS of course!

Below the big falls there is a smaller "step" falls—you may need to hike out into the woods and scramble down to get to the base, and you can see the big falls from below. There is at least one more step falls below that one, maybe two or more. Stunning! Head back UP the same way you came in—just keep climbing uphill until you reach the highway—stop and rest a time or two! Total roundtrip is 1.1, but it may feel like several, haha...

Emergency contact: Newton County Sheriff, 870–446–5124 No dogs on trails.

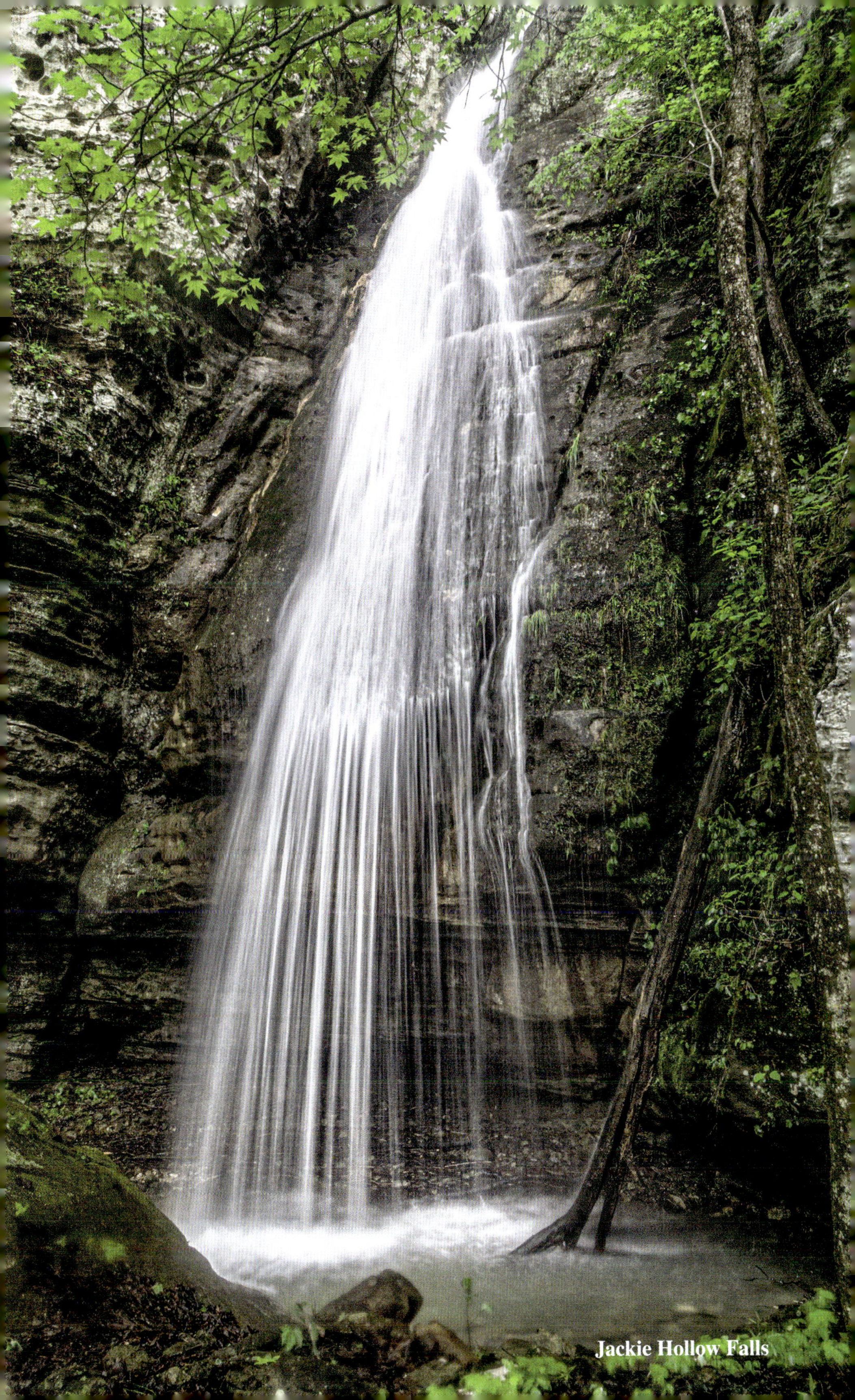

Jackie Hollow Falls

Bigfoot Falls – 69′

2.0, medium/difficult trail, then short bushwhack, GPS **36.03971, -93.32045**

Littlefoot Falls – 33′

2.05, medium/difficult trail, steep bushwhack, GPS **36.03997, -93.32044**

Shark Fin Falls – 21′

1.6, medium/difficult trail, steep bushwhack GPS **36.03683, -93.31959**

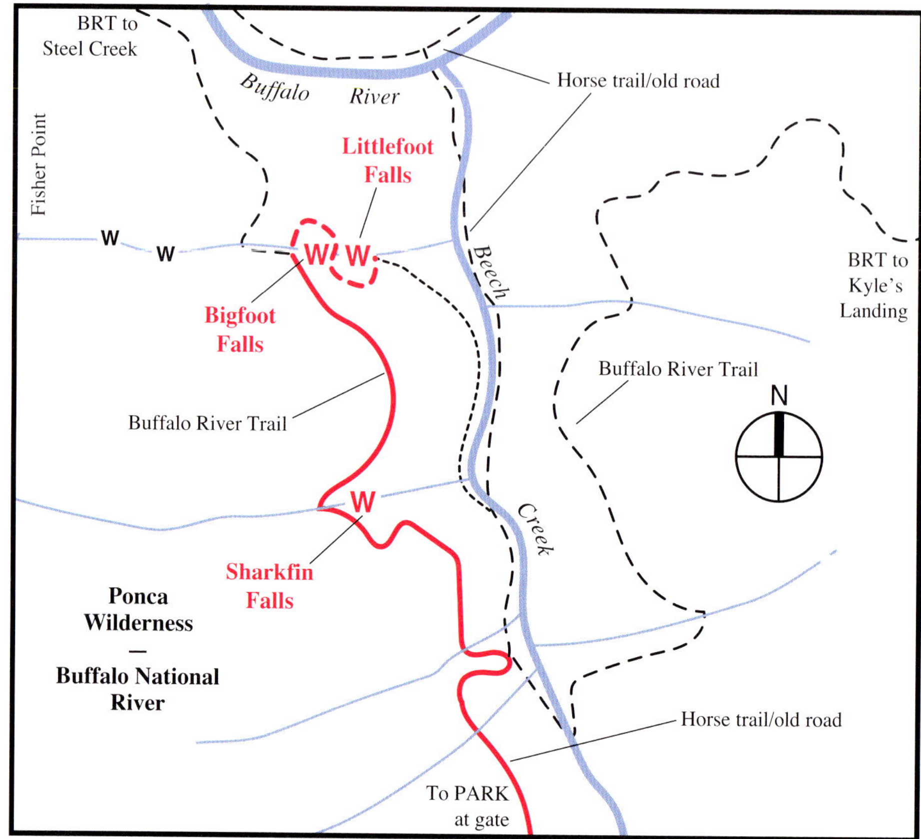

BIGFOOT/LITTLEFOOT/SHARK FIN FALLS. To reach the parking spot take county road #2200 next to the church at Low Gap (on Hwy. 74 between Ponca and Mt. Sherman), and go 1.4 miles to the end of the road (**36.02047, -93.31289**). There is no "trailhead" here, just the end of the road with room for one or two cars to park on the side—DO NOT BLOCK THE GATE or GET ONTO ANY PRIVATE PROPERTY (it's ALL private property before the gate). With multiple cars you may need to park at Low Gap and carpool.

Hike past the gate on a rough road (closed) until you come to the top of a small rise at .45 and TURN RIGHT onto a seldom-used horse trail (this turn may or may not be blazed with a yellow blaze). You are now inside the Ponca Wilderness Area of Buffalo National River park. Follow this trail STEEPLY down the hill and it will become an old road trace.

Continue down and eventually you may hear the rushing waters of Beech Creek down below on the right, also criss cross a couple of small streams with cascades, until you come to a trail intersection at 1.3. TURN LEFT onto the Buffalo River Trail (BRT).

Follow it to a creek crossing at 1.6. If you can find a way down below the trail to your right and scramble down below the bluff you will find **Shark Fin Falls**, a small SSS tucked into the hillside. When I first found this falls I came up from below and the first thing I saw was a thin "fin" of stone rising up and the waterfall behind—in my mind I saw a giant shark fin! Climb back up to the trail and continue (OR bushwhack on over to **Bigfoot Falls**—it's a lot easier back up on the trail though.)

OK, back up on the BRT, continue along the trail to 1.9 where it makes a sharp turn to the left to avoid a creek ahead. You want to LEAVE THE TRAIL there and go STRAIGHT AHEAD and cross that creek (this creek forms Bigfoot Falls). There will be a bluff line on the right, and you will pick up an old road trace past the creek that runs along near the top of the bluff—follow the road trace for a couple hundred yards until you can find an obvious break in the bluff and an easy route down to the bottom—then TURN RIGHT and you will come to **Bigfoot Falls** at 2.0—a major SSS area!

It takes a LOT of water to get this fall going, but it's pretty darn amazing when it does, and very nice even at lower flow. You can crawl back under the bluff on the right and look back out and see the waterfall—this just might be a summer hideout for the elusive Mrs. Bigfoot.

Littlefoot Falls is on the bluff just below—make your way carefully around to the right ABOVE the bluff and around down to the base. From this point simply turn around and hike back to the trail the way you came to get back to the parking spot.

You can make a loop out of your trip—from **Littlefoot Falls** follow the creek downstream (passing the creek that goes up to **Shark Fin Falls**) until it intersects with the old road/horse trail, then follow this on up the hill to the RIGHT back to the BRT (the horse trail is across Beech Creek at one point and you have to cut across the side of the hill).

The total distance for this hike either way is about 4.0 miles roundtrip.You can also get to **Bigfoot Falls** if hiking the BRT from Steel Creek, about five miles.

Emergency contact: Newton County Sheriff, 870–446–5124 No dogs on trails.

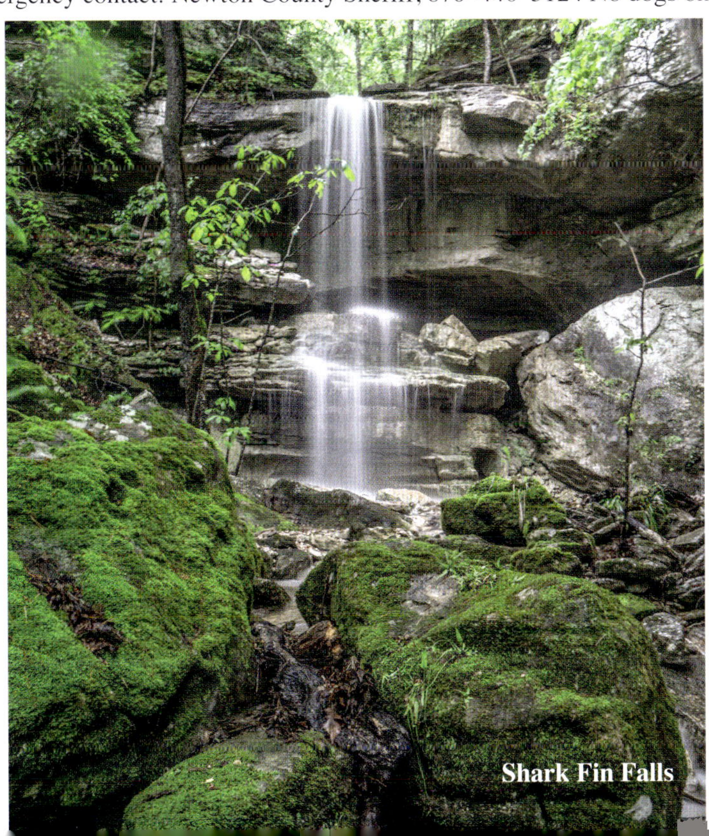

Shark Fin Falls

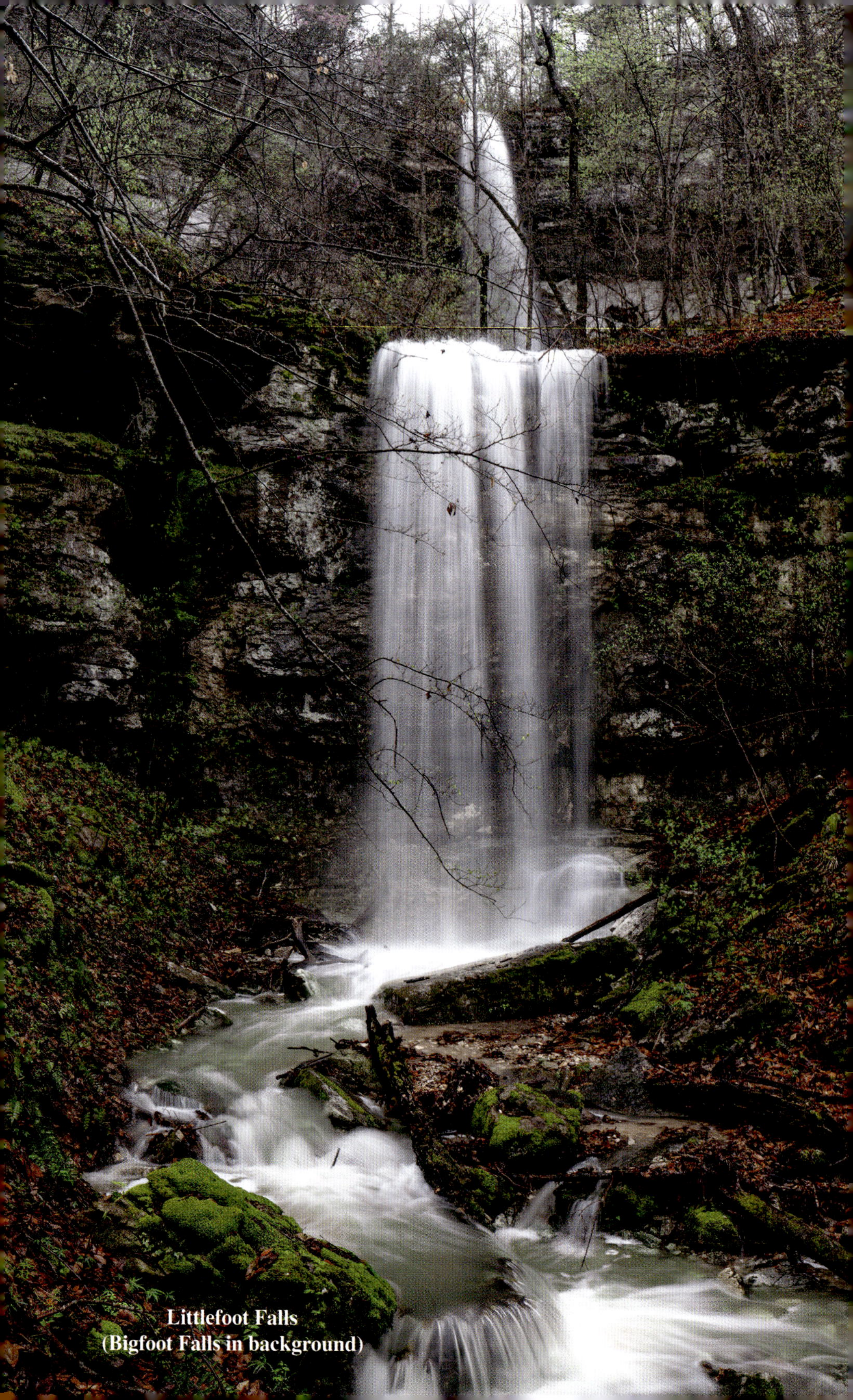

Littlefoot Falls
(Bigfoot Falls in background)

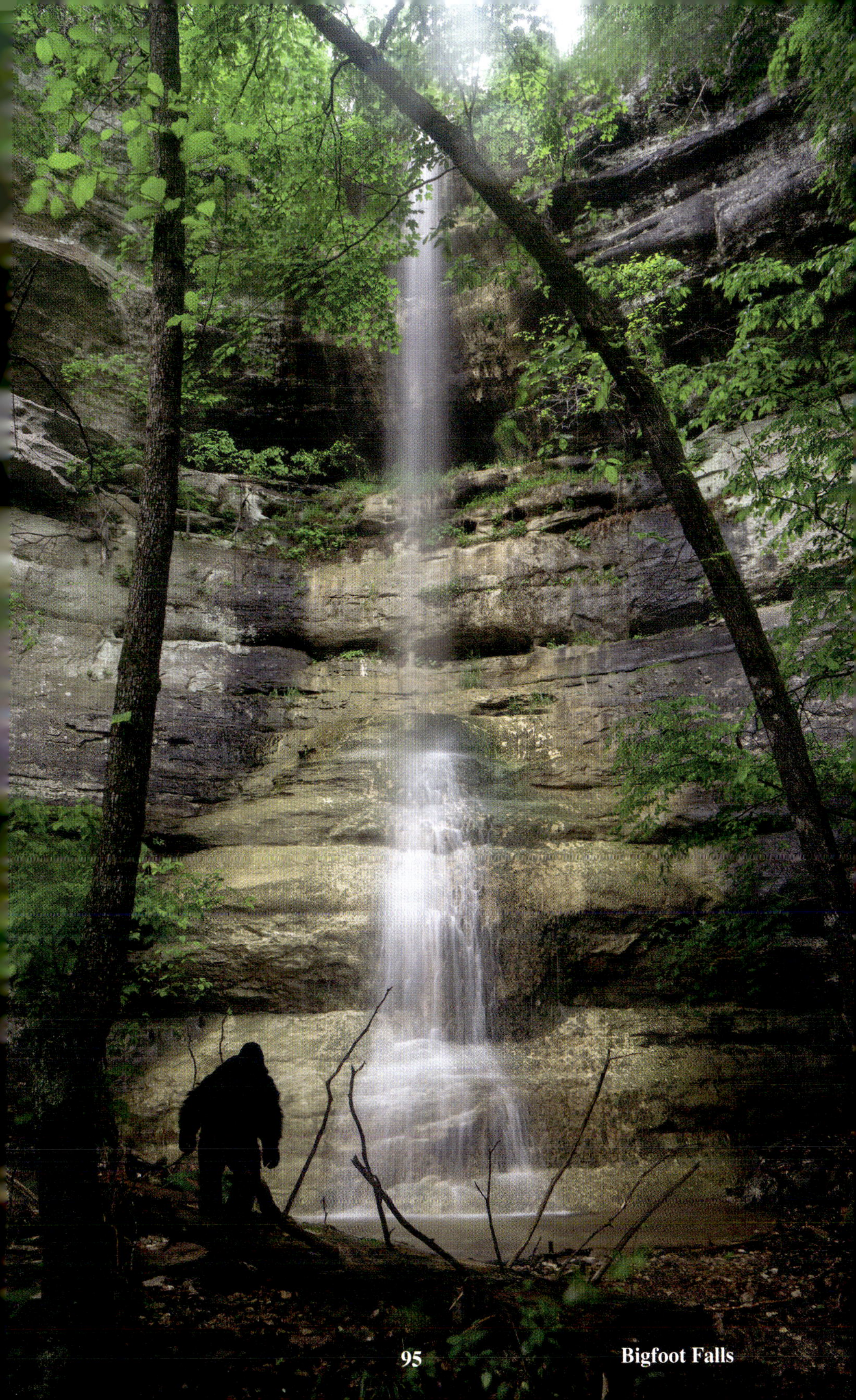

Bigfoot Falls

Hemmed-In Hollow Falls – 209′

5.0 miles roundtrip, difficult hike, GPS not needed

GPS **36.07213, -93.30753**

Diamond Falls –148′

Add .5 to above, difficult bushwhack, GPS not needed

GPS **36.07167, -93.30946**

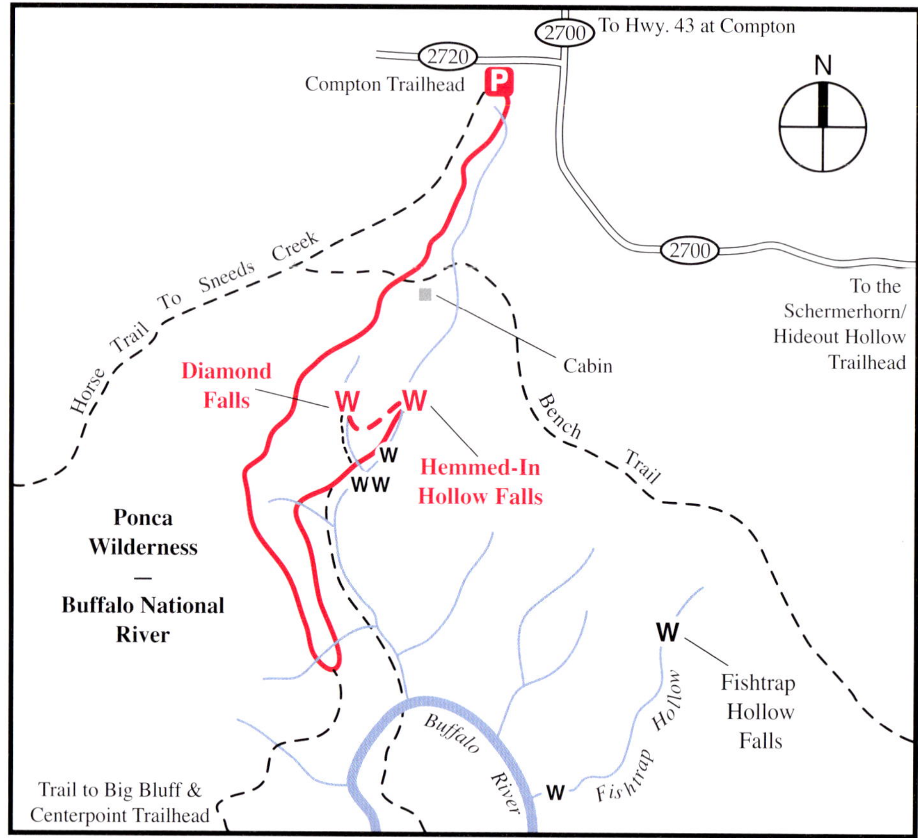

HEMMED-IN HOLLOW FALLS/DIAMOND FALLS. Hemmed-In Hollow Falls is the tallest waterfall between the Appalachians and the Rockies. Many thousands of folks have seen it, and it continues to be one of the most popular destinations in the Ozarks. What a lot of folks don't realize is that the second tallest waterfall in Arkansas—Diamond Falls— is literally just right around the corner. You can get to both falls by making the short hike up from the river if you are floating the Buffalo from Steele Creek to Kyles. You can also hike the trail down from Center Point (past Big Bluff and Granny Henderson's Cabin). But a quicker way to the falls is from the Compton Trailhead, and that is what we are going to do. NOTE that while the total hike miles may seem short on paper, the trail is *steep and rugged,* and the climb out is *more than a thousand feet **up***—you should be in great shape for this one, and plan an entire day for the hike!

The turnoff for the trailhead is located at Compton, between Harrison and Ponca on Hwy. 43. Take the gravel road across from the post office in Compton (CR#2700), TURN RIGHT at the first intersection (stay on CR#2700), and go just less than a mile and TURN RIGHT at CR#2720 into the trailhead parking lot (**36.08121, -93.30310**). There are two

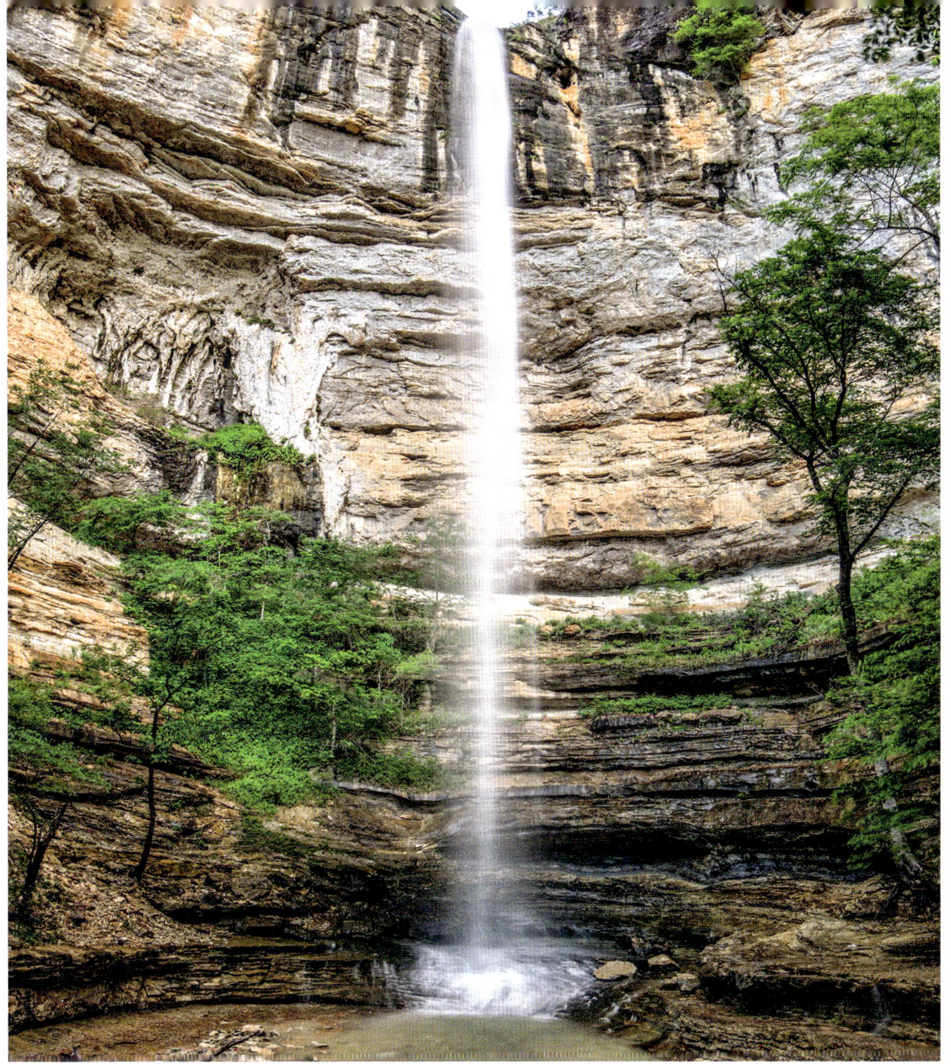

Hemmed-In Hollow Falls

trails that leave this lot—the one on the right is a horse trail that goes down to Sneeds Creek and beyond. For a longer hike you can return on this trail and make a 7.2 mile loop.

Hike down the trail on the left, and follow it across a small stream and then on down the rocky hillside. You will come to a trail intersection at .7—GO STRAIGHT. (The trail to the left is the Bench Trail that you take to get to Fishtrap Hollow and Antenna Pine Falls—and the trail to the right connects with the horse trail to Sneeds Creek.)

From the trail intersection our trail continues heading down the hillside, and it gets pretty steep at times. There is a terrific viewpoint at 1.5—you can look over to your left and see **Hemmed-In Hollow Falls**, and out to the right is the Buffalo River and the wilderness beyond. Continue down the steep trail until you come to another intersection at 1.8. TURN LEFT there. The trail to the right goes out to Granny's Cabin, Big Bluff and to the Center Point Trailhead, and connects with the horse trail that runs up Sneeds Creek and on back out to our trailhead.

OK, so turn left at that intersection. You are now heading up into Hemmed-In Hollow proper, hiking through a wonderful beech forest. You will drop down and cross a creek at 2.2, and just beyond intersect with the trail that goes down the hollow to the Buffalo

River—continue STRAIGHT AHEAD there. Hemmed-In Hollow Creek is now down to your right, and soon you will come to and cross another creek that flows right into it. (nice Twin Falls at the junction of the two creeks.)

The trail continues up the main creek, past another waterfall down on your right. Then the trail intersects with the creek itself, and you will have to cross it. Once you do, you will be standing at the base of **Hemmed-In Hollow Falls** at 2.5. If it is a windy day, the falls will be tossed back and forth by the wind. It is truly one of the greatest natural spots in mid-America.

Diamond Falls is located to the left of **Hemmed-In Hollow Falls**, and around the corner, but to get to it you have to first climb up to the right of the big falls, and go behind them. Continue making your way across the bluffline behind the falls and out the other end—there are several ancient, twisted and weathered cedar trees there. Just keep going on around at the base of this bluffline to the left, and you will come to Diamond Falls within a quarter mile. Neil Compton named it Diamond Falls because the big plunge often hits a rock shelf part way down, sending spray all over the place. When backlit by the sun high above it looks like a million diamonds falling from the sky. Alternate bushwhack route shown on map—scramble up the creek from the main trail to the falls.

Emergency contact: Newton County Sheriff, 870–446–5124 No dogs on trails.

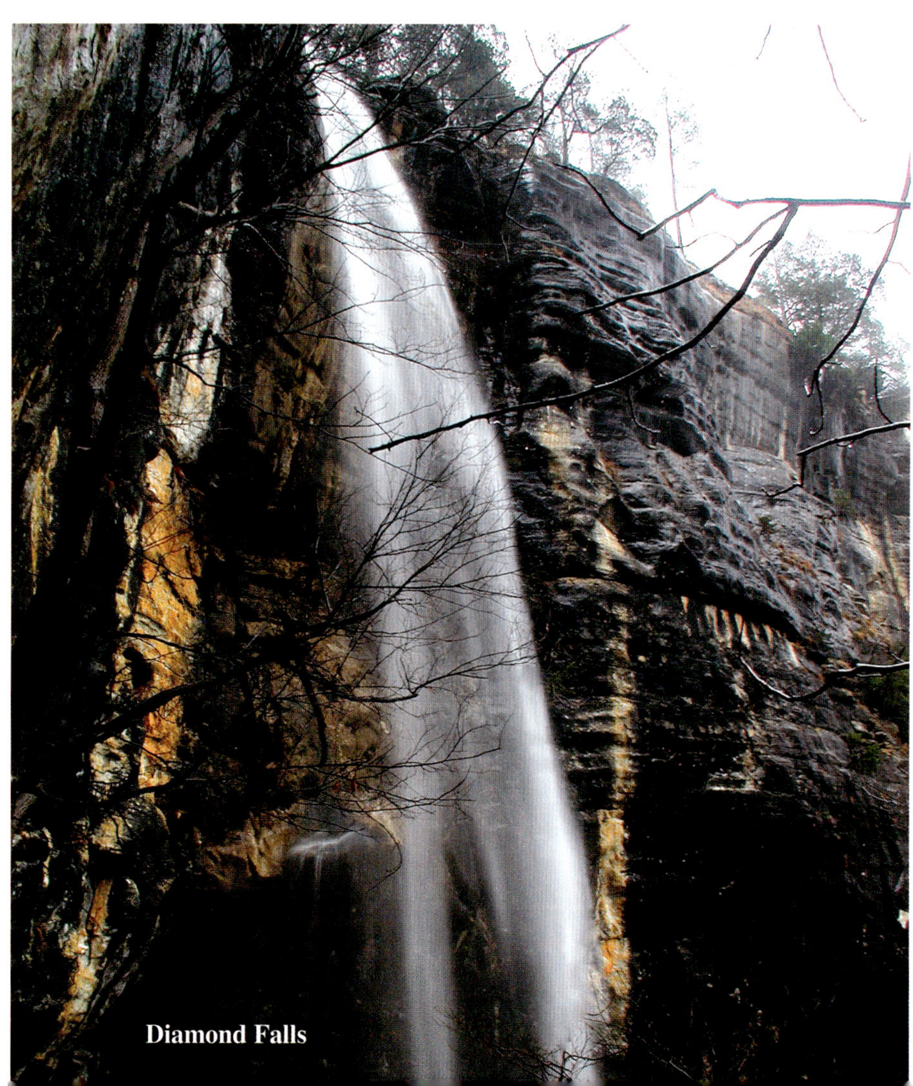

Diamond Falls

Fishtrap Hollow Falls – 83′

5.2 miles roundtrip, difficult bushwhack ♦, GPS highly recommended

GPS **36.06495, -93.29887**

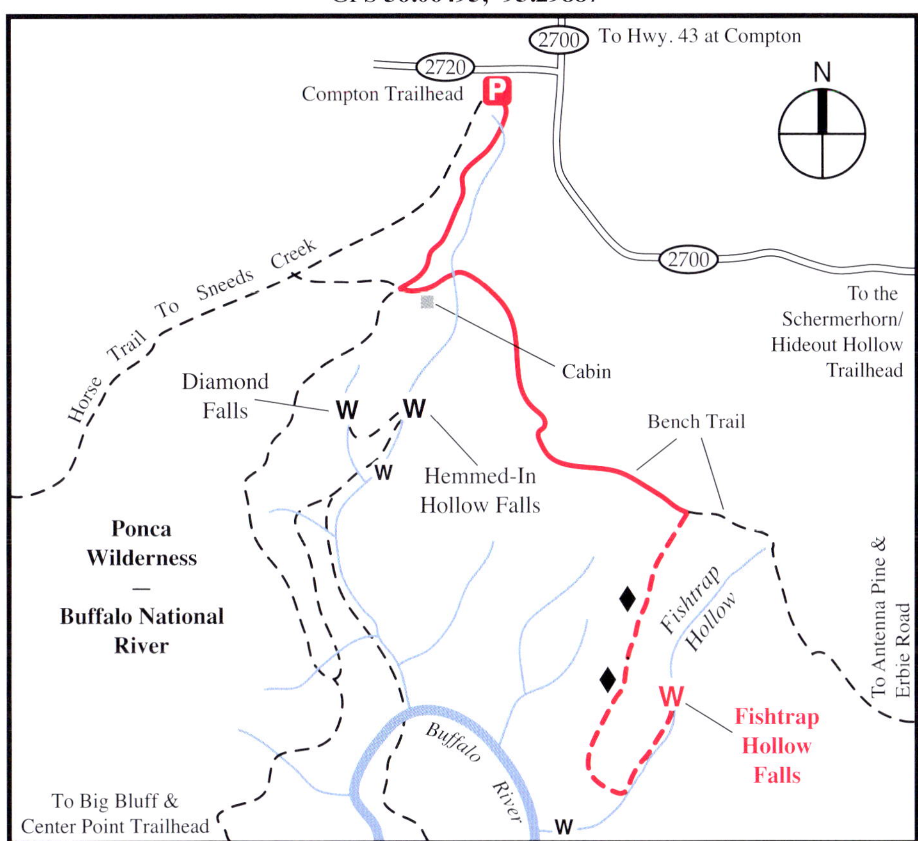

FISHTRAP HOLLOW FALLS. This is a tough waterfall to get in to and out of, but if you visit during high water, it's a real treat. The first part of the trek is on trails/roads, but then you bushwhack down a really steep hillside, and it takes a great deal of *umph* to get back out. You could find the falls without it, but a GPS will make life a lot easier on you.

The turnoff for the trailhead is located at Compton, between Harrison and Ponca on Hwy. 43. Take the gravel road across from the post office in Compton (CR#2700), TURN RIGHT at the first intersection (stay on CR#2700), and go just less than a mile and TURN RIGHT at CR#2720 into the trailhead parking lot (**36.08121, -93.30310**). There are two trails that leave this lot—the right is a horse trail that goes down to Sneeds Creek.

Hike down the trail on the LEFT, follow it across a small stream and then on down the rocky hillside. You will come to a trail intersection at .7—this is the Bench Trail and you TURN LEFT onto it. (The trail straight ahead goes down to Hemmed-In Hollow, and the trail to the right goes over to the horse trail to Sneeds Creek). You will pass a rustic little cabin on the right after several hundred yards on the Bench Trail—what a view!

The Bench Trail is one of the main horse trails in the area (can get muddy at times), and gives us better access to a lot of areas above and below along the way. It follows along a mostly-level bench through what used to be an obvious homestead—look at the large stones that form rock walls along the trail. The trail drops on down the hill, crosses

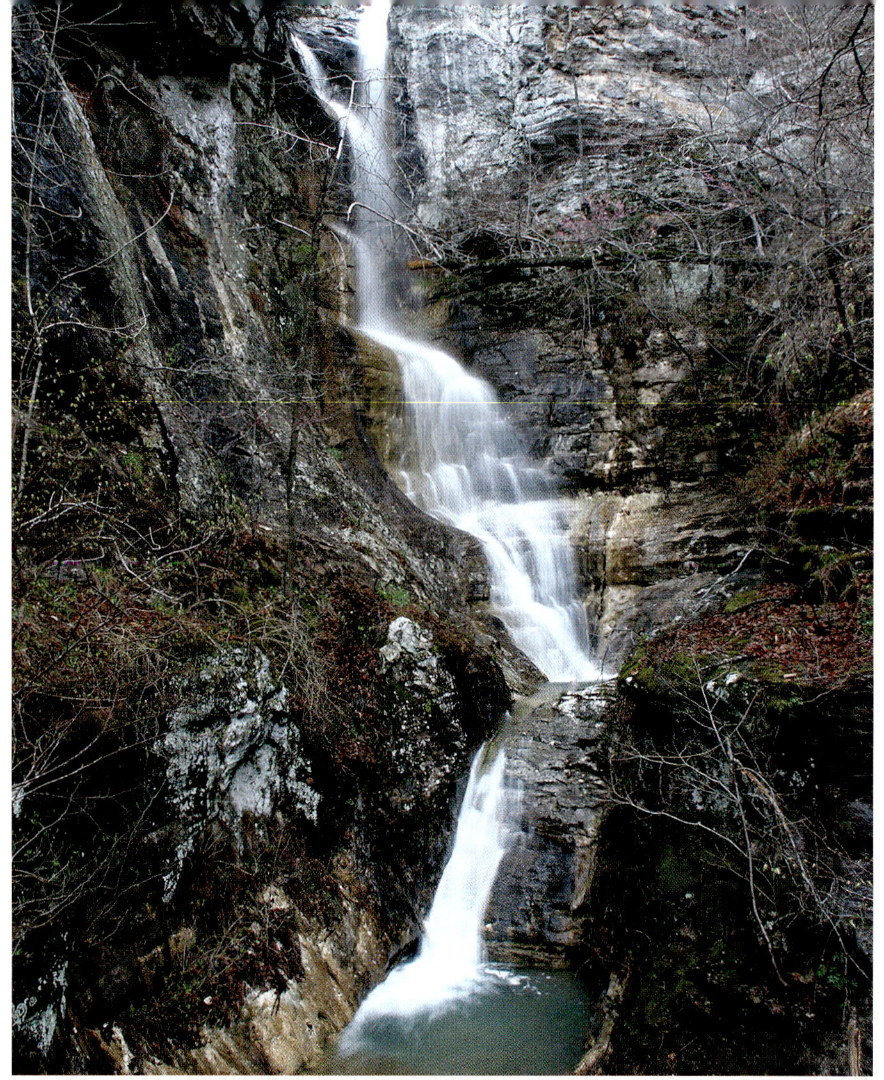

Fishtrap Hollow Falls (during high water)

several small drainages, and then somewhere around 1.85 **(36.06953, -93.29833)** LEAVE THE ROAD TO THE RIGHT and begin to bushwhack straight DOWN the steep hillside. Continue down as it gets a lot steeper, a BLACK DIAMOND slope ♦. There is a narrow ridgetop you can follow that is less steep in the middle—that's where you want to be—with the canyon off to your left. Just keep going down.

Once you get to the bottom follow the base of the bluffs back to the LEFT and upstream to the bottom of **Fishtrap Hollow Falls** at about 2.6. It is quite slickery in the canyon.

ANTENNA PINE FALLS AND OVERLOOK. If you are headed on to Antenna Pine go back up to the Bench Trail and continue right for another mile to Cecil Creek at 3.0 (from Compton TH). Find your way across the creek and then TURN LEFT onto a trail that heads steeply uphill. This trail will intersect with another trail coming up from the right—it goes back down to the Bench Trail—See page 103 for this trail description and map (shortest route), and to continue with your hike up to **Antenna Pine Falls** and overlook.

Emergency contact: Newton County Sheriff, 870–446–5124 No dogs on trails.

Bear Cave Cascades – 20′

.05, easy access from river, GPS **36.05690, -93.29876**

Bear Slide Falls -17′

.15, easy access from river GPS **36.05750, -93.29855**

Bear Cave Hollow Falls – 29′

.3, easy access from river, GPS **36.05870, -93.29687**

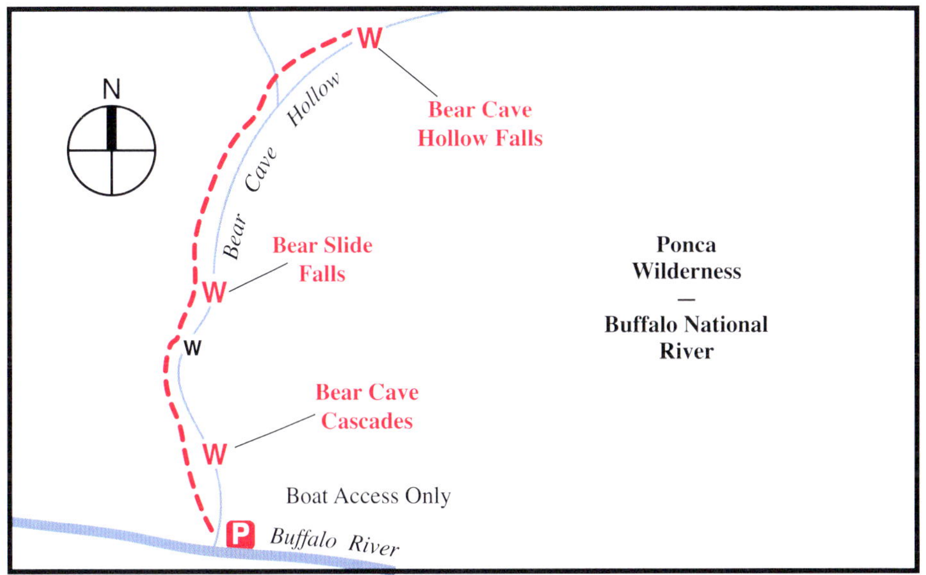

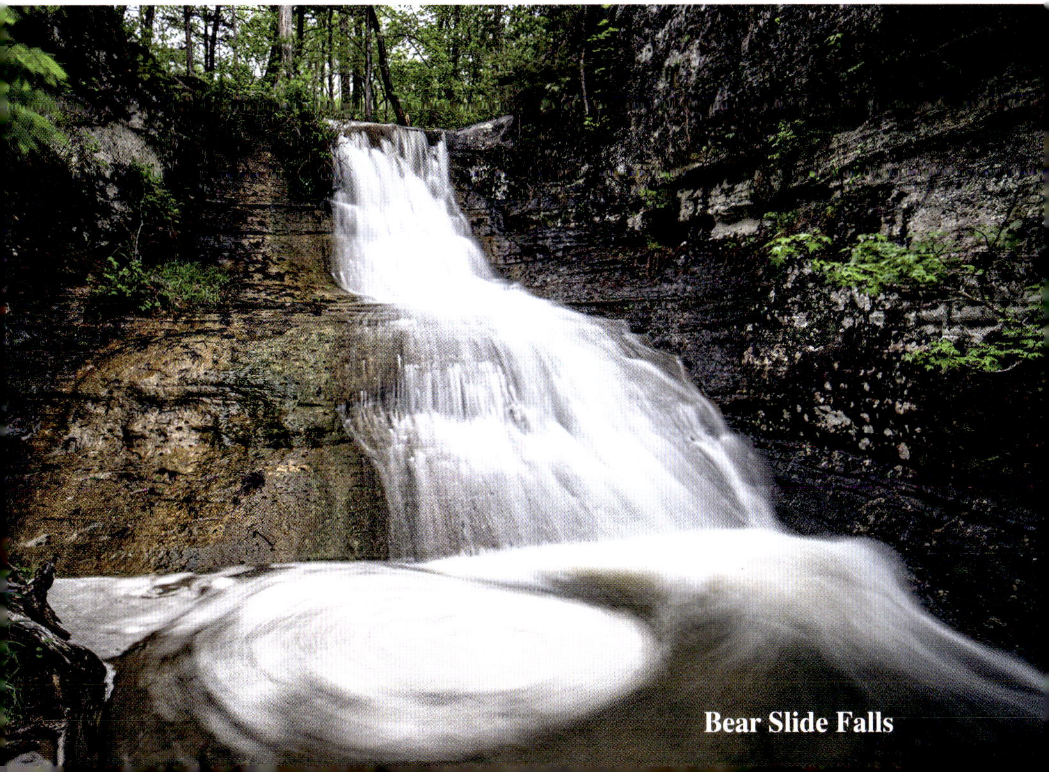

Bear Slide Falls

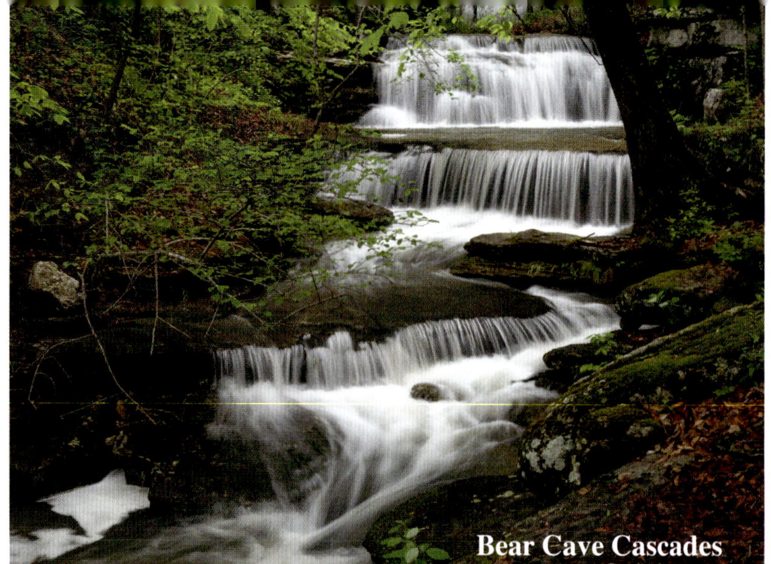
Bear Cave Cascades

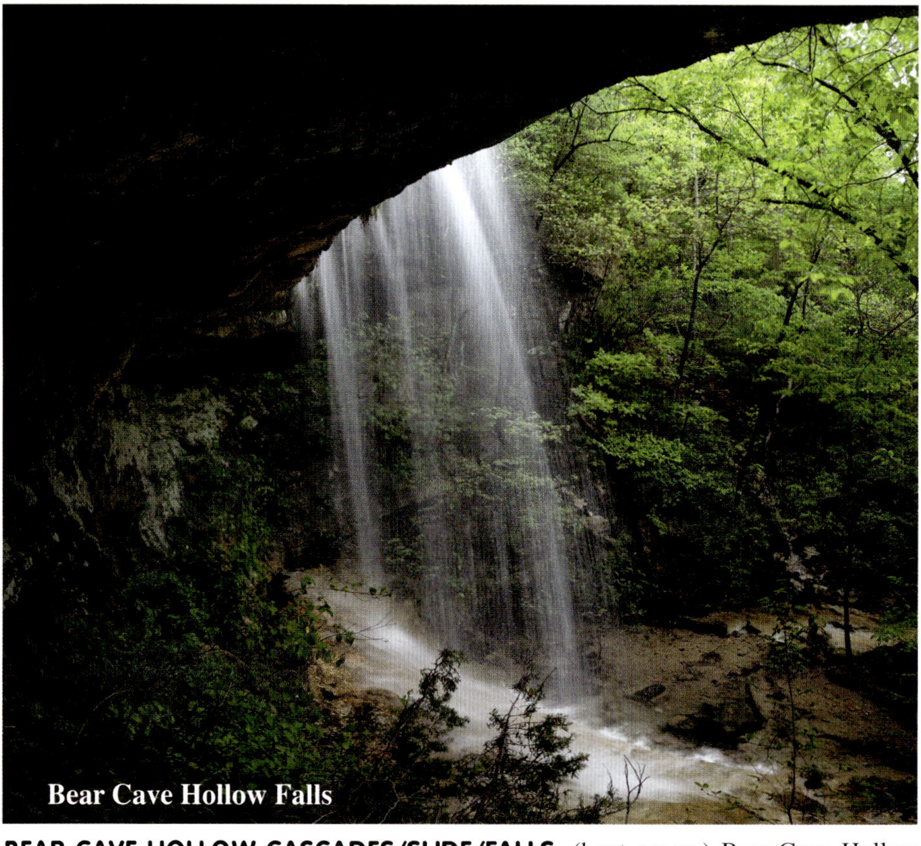

Bear Cave Hollow Falls

BEAR CAVE HOLLOW CASCADES/SLIDE/FALLS. (boat access) Bear Cave Hollow meets the Buffalo River a couple of drainages downstream on the LEFT from Hemmed-In-Hollow—pull over at this SSS and enjoy **Bear Cave Cascades** just up the creek (**36.05674, -93.29858**). There are also waterfalls upstream—pretty easy hiking and less than a half mile up past **Bear Slide Falls** (my favorite photo), to the largest one, **Bear Cave Hollow Falls**. (stay to the RIGHT where the creek forks). .6 mile total roundtrip for all three.

Emergency contact: Newton County Sheriff, 870–446–5124 No dogs on trails.

Antenna Pine Falls – 39′

4.6 miles roundtrip, moderate/difficult trail GPS **36.06901, -93.28731**

Antenna Twin Falls – 13′

5.2 miles roundtrip, moderate/difficult trail GPS **36.06976, -93.28744**

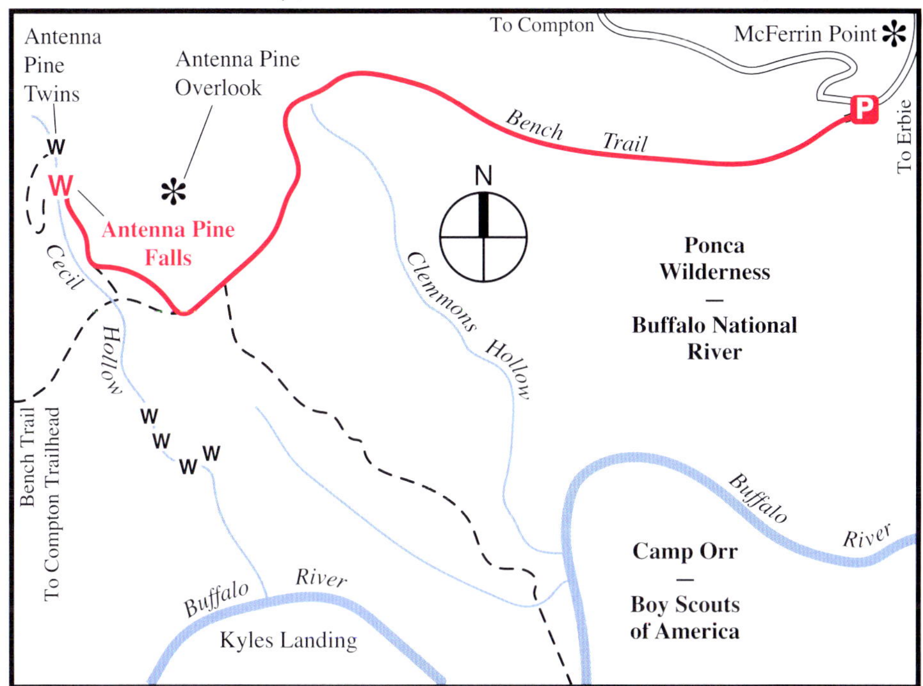

ANTENNA PINE FALLS. This is the most direct route to reach Antenna Pine Falls and overlook, and also the shortest (the hike from Compton Trailhead is 6.8 miles roundtrip).

The turnoff for the trailhead is located at Compton, between Harrison and Ponca on Hwy. 43. Take the gravel road across from J.B. Trading/post office in Compton (CR#2700), TURN RIGHT at the first intersection (stay on CR#2700/Compton-To-Erbie Road), go past the Compton Trailhead for Hemmed-In Hollow, past Hideout Hollow trailhead, and past McFerrin Point parking spot. Continue down a couple of switchbacks to a powerline and PARK on the right, 4.1 miles from Hwy. 43.

From the parking spot go down into an opening and across beneath a power line and into the woods, entering the Ponca Wilderness Area. This is the Bench Ttrail you will follow for a couple of miles. It runs level some of the way, going up and down as needed, and it can get muddy in spots and rocky much of the way. Just stay on the road and enjoy the mostly easy hiking. There is an intersection at 1.75—CONTINUE STRAIGHT on the Bench Trail. (the trail that goes to the left drops all the way down into private property at Camp Orr Boy Scout Camp.)

Just past this intersection there is a large rock on the left beside the trail, and just past that rock at 1.85 TURN RIGHT onto a narrow trail and head UP the hill away from the Bench Trail. (the Bench Trail goes on another 3.1 miles to Compton Trailhead). You will follow this trail all the way up to Antenna Pines Falls. It is STEEP and rocky much of the way. Part way up another trail joins from the left (it goes back down to the Bench Trail)—just CONTINUE straight and then right with more STEEP UPHILL and you will soon see a giant bluff above. The trail will eventually swing to the left and along the base of an apartment-size chunk of that bluff—fror this point on for a while is a major SSS! Th trail then follows along the base of the bi bluff and then to **Antenna Pine Falls** at 2.3

For an extra treat, follow the base of th bluff past the falls and you'll hike through magical hall of giant bluffs on both sides. A the far end of this the trail switchbacks up t the RIGHT and continues on top of the bluf on the level and goes to **Antenna Twin Fall** at 2.6. Not very tall but an interesting littl spot that pours into a short canyon.

Not done yet? Follow a social trail alon the top of the bluff line and out to the left yo will come to one of the most spectacular ope bluff views in mid-America—this is Antenn Pine, known for the ritual of scout troop raising their troop flag up on a giant pine tre that could be seen from Camp Orr far below

Emergency contact: Newton County Sheriff 870–446–5124 No dogs on trails.

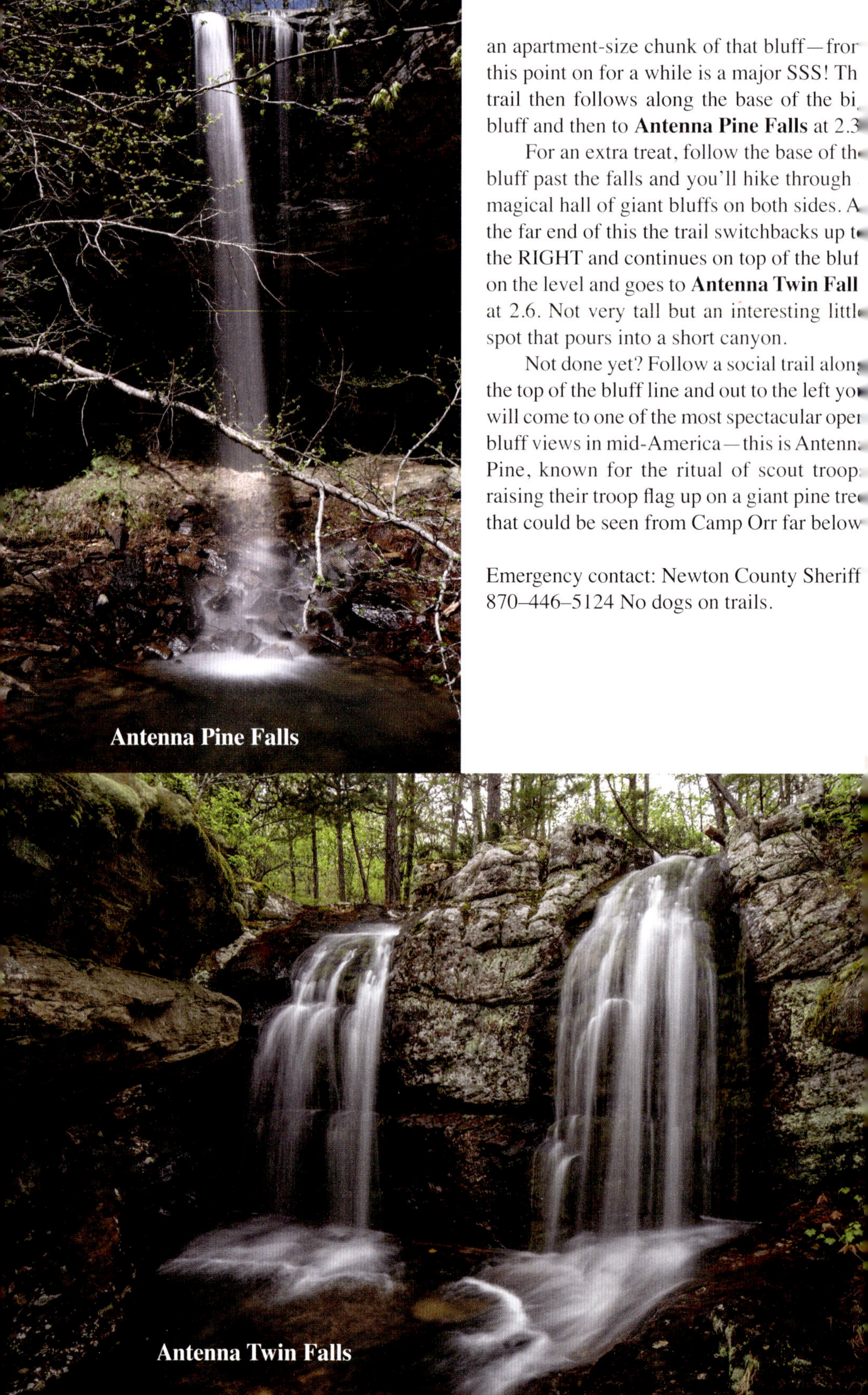

Antenna Pine Falls

Antenna Twin Falls

Smokey Joe Falls – 105′

.4 easy to 2.5 miles difficult ♦ GPS **36.06105, -93.28181**

Cecil Hollow Falls – 108′

.4 easy to 2.5 miles difficult ♦ GPS **36.06085, -93.28208**

Big Boulder Falls – 36′

2.1 miles difficult ♦ GPS **36.06169, -93.28379**

Cecil Middle Step Falls – 51′

2.1 miles difficult ♦ GPS **36.06175, -93.28371**

Total roundtrip hike from the top to all falls 5.0 miles

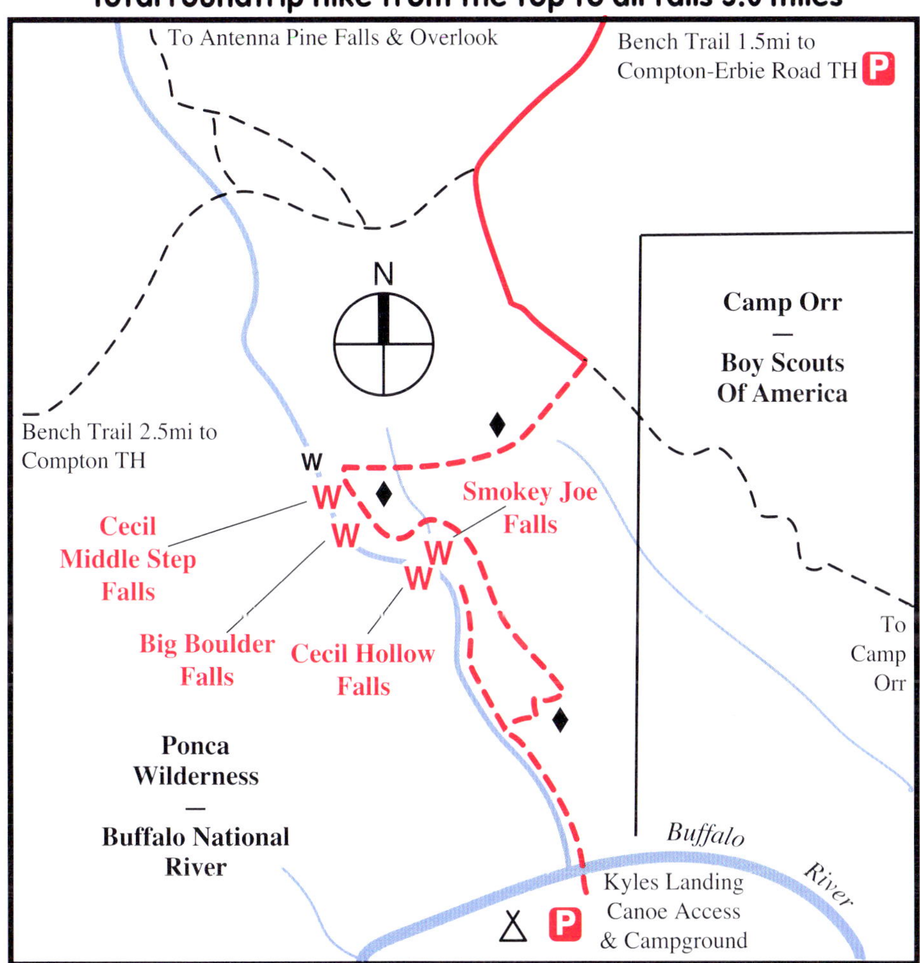

CECIL CREEK WATERFALLS. There are a series of spectacular waterfalls in the lower Cecil Creek drainage that are best viewed during very high water levels. I'll describe two different routes—one is longer and along the Bench Trail, then a difficult bushwhack across BLACK DIAMOND ♦ slopes—this route does not require crossing the Buffalo River. The second, much shorter hike from Kyles Landing campground requires crossing the Buffalo, which may not be possible or safe during the flooded conditions these waterfalls require.

To reach the upper parking spot on the Compton—Erbie Road for the Bench Trail, see directions for Antenna Pine Falls on page 103.

From the parking spot go down into an opening and across beneath a power line and into the woods, entering the Ponca Wilderness Area. This is the Bench Trail you will follow for a couple of miles. It runs level some of the way, going up and down as needed, and it can get muddy in spots and rocky much of the way. Just stay on the road and enjoy the mostly easy hiking. There is an intersection at 1.75 with the trail that drops all the way down the hill to the Boy Scouts Camp Orr Private Property. TURN LEFT and follow that trail/old road DOWNHILL.

There is no specific route from this trail over to the Cecil Creek waterfalls, but what I do is generally go down the trail a couple hundred yards to lose some altitude, then leave the trail to the RIGHT and either head down at a 45 degree angle, OR plug in GPS for the **Cecil Middle Step Falls** and head to a point just a bit below it. You will find the slope along the way turns into a VERY steep BLACK DIAMOND ♦ slope. Arrive at the falls at 2.1.

There are at least three "step" falls—a nice waterfall and then a flat area 100' long or so and the creek pours over the next step. The top of the three is unnamed, **Cecil Middle Step Falls** you will know since there is a big rock slab or two sitting on the flat area, and the lowest and most AMAZING one has a giant boulder right at the base.

There is a big cascade coming out the bottom of **Big Boulder Falls** that runs downhill past another rock slab, then around the corner and plunges 108' in three drops—this is **Cecil Hollow Falls**, one of the tallest waterfalls in Arkansas. There is another waterfall over to the left on the same bluff that drops 104' into the same pool—**Smokey Joe Falls**.

The Legend of Smokey Joe (Troop 1 Scoutmaster Joe Kelly) comes from a 1950's account involving a scout master from Camp Orr, told around the campfire during summer camp for scouts. Most of the versions I've heard include the reason for the name, Smokey Joe. It's because each time the man/beast gets cornered he disappears into the smoke or mist along a bluff. This waterfall kind of does the same thing—it runs best during a major downpour, and almost always disappears soon after in a cloud of mist. The Legend of Smokey Joe lives on with this waterfall that bears his name.

To get to the bottom and pool below—and for the best view of both falls—you need to carefully cross over to the opposite side of the canyon—I would do so BACK uphill a ways to stay AWAY from the bluff edge (it is very steep). Work your way downstream across an open glade and there is a route down the bluff to the creek below (**♦ 36.05912, -93.28032**)—then just TURN RIGHT and follow the creek up to the falls at 2.5. SSSSSSSSS! TWO of the tallest waterfalls in Arkansas…

OK, that was the long version. Here is the short version—with obviously only one minor sticking point—you can't/shouldn't attempt this route if the Buffalo River is flooded. The turnoff to get to Kyles Landing is located between Jasper and Ponca. From Jasper, go west on Hwy. 74 to Mt. Sherman and TURN RIGHT on CR#2300 (gravel) at the sign for Kyles Landing (OR go east from Low Gap on Hwy. 74 for 5.2 miles to Mt. Sherman and TURN LEFT on CR#2300 at the sign). Go 1.0 mile and TURN LEFT at the fork (still on CR#2300), then go 1.6 miles down a steep hill to the Kyles Landing Campground and PARK at the canoe access (**36.05681, -93.27966**). From the canoe access at Kyles Landing go directly ACROSS the river to the mouth of Cecil Creek. Follow the creek upstream and at .4 you will arrive at the base of the two towering waterfalls! To reach the upper waterfalls you can go back downstream and scramble up the bluff at the point noted above (**♦ 36.05912, -93.28032**), then hike around the top of the bluff to the upper creek area and claw your way upstream to the three step falls, total roundtrip for all about 2.0 miles.

Emergency contact: Newton County Sheriff, 870–446–5124 No dogs on trails.

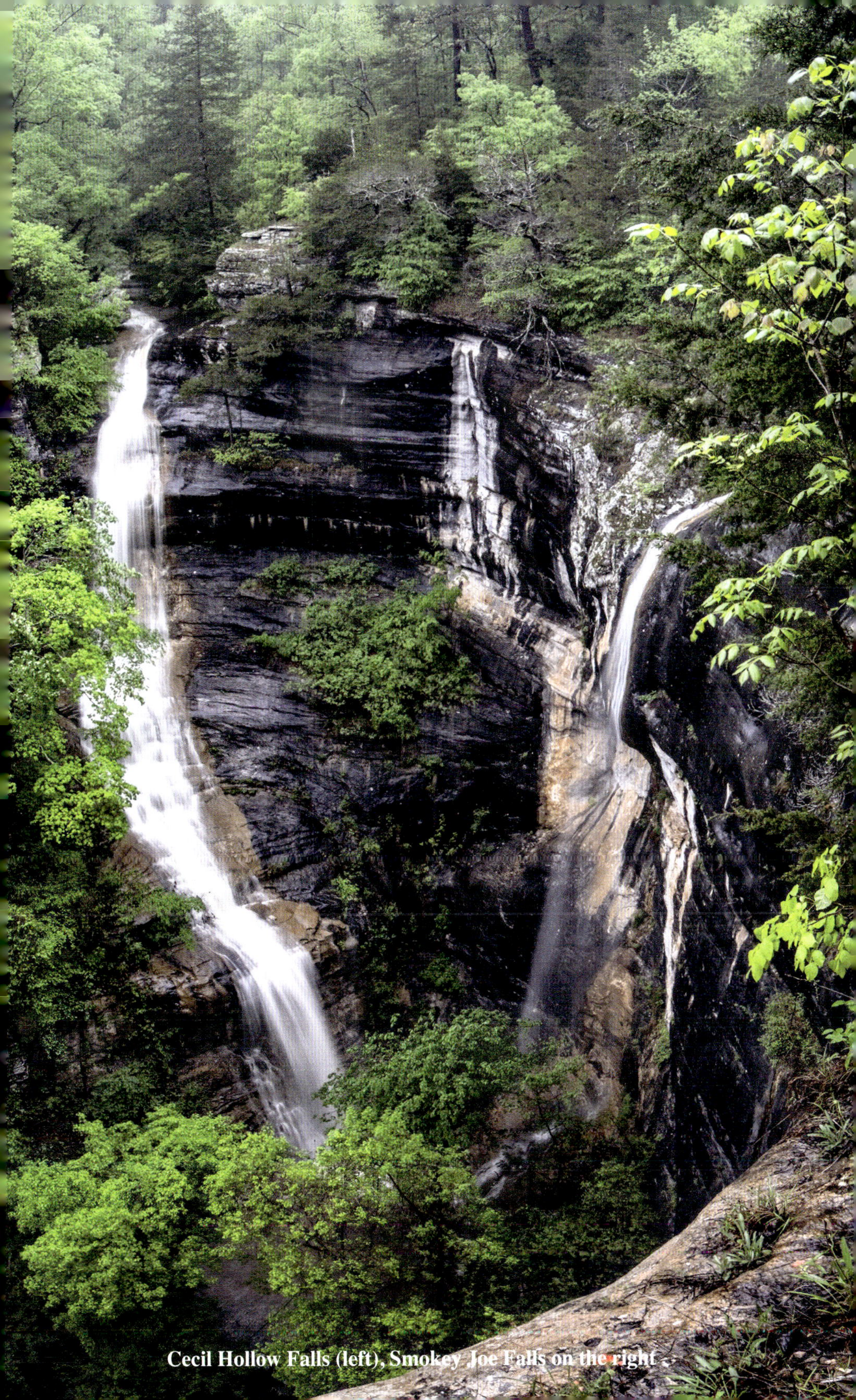

Cecil Hollow Falls (left), Smokey Joe Falls on the right

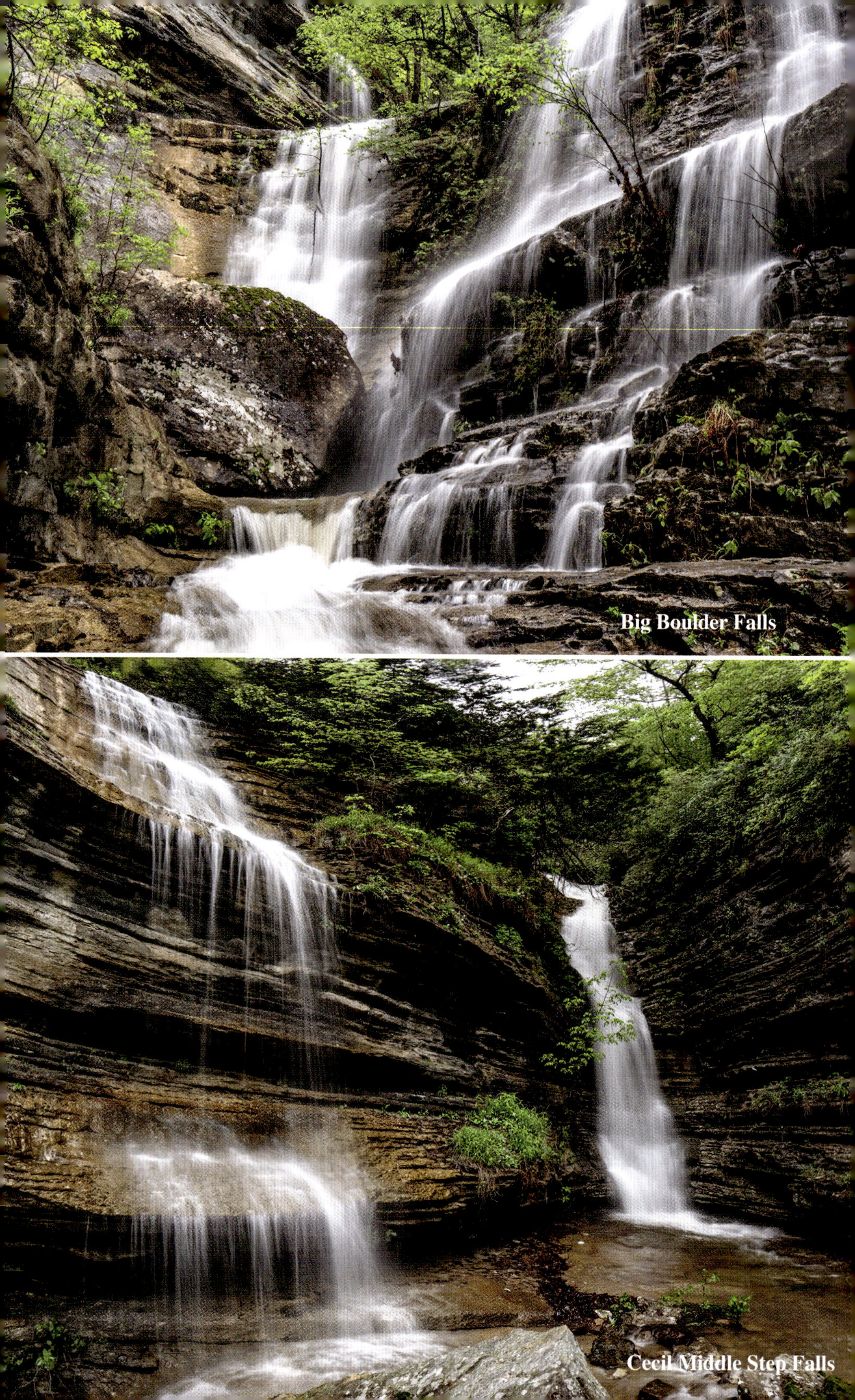

Big Boulder Falls

Cecil Middle Step Falls

Hideout Hollow Falls – 37′

2.0 miles roundtrip, easy hike, GPS not needed

GPS **36.08080, -93.26977**

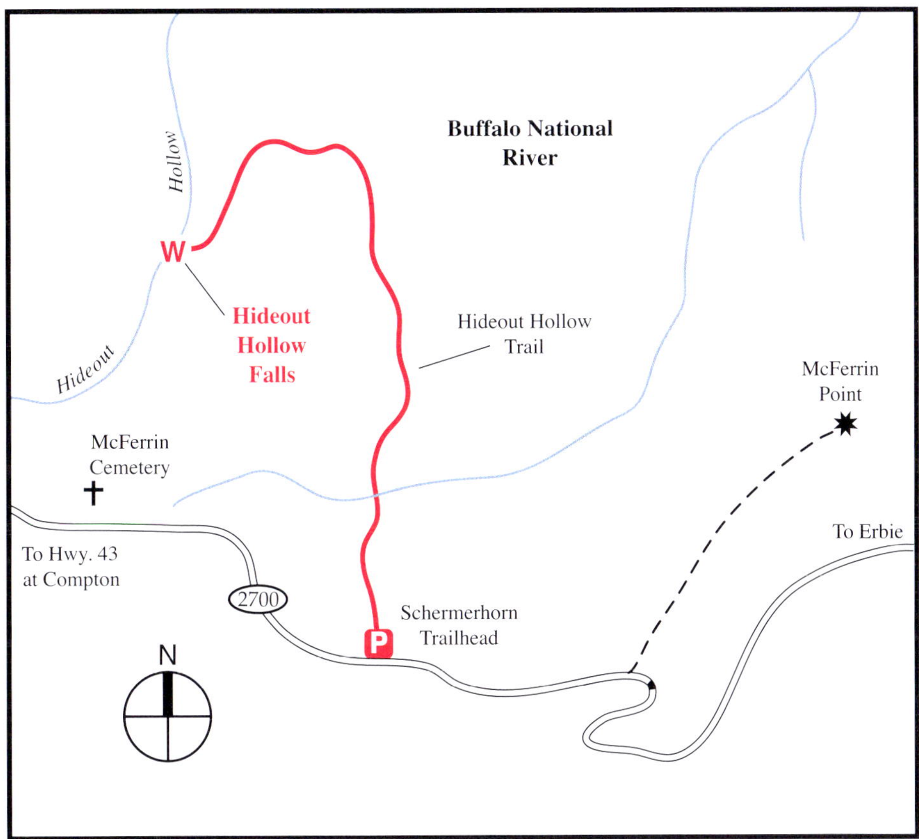

HIDEOUT HOLLOW FALLS. The shelter at the end of this trail (below the bluff) was once inhabited by a group of draft dodgers called The Slacker Gang during World War I. There are numerous tall bluffs and giant slabs of stone in this area, plus the wonderful falls at the head of the canyon. The hike in is pretty easy, but if you have young folks with you hang on to them because the trail runs along the top of the bluffs and can be really dangerous (for adults too!).

The turnoff for the trailhead is located at Compton, between Harrison and Ponca on Hwy. 43. Take the gravel road across from the post office in Compton (CR#2700), TURN RIGHT at the first intersection (stay on CR#2700/Compton-Erbie Road), go past the Compton Trailhead for Hemmed-In Hollow, then TURN LEFT into the Schermerhorn Trailhead and PARK (3.5 miles from Hwy. 43 (**36.07310, -93.26505)** named after renowned caver, Jim Schermerhorn)

Follow the Hideout Hollow Trail down a little hill and across a stream, then up the other side and under a powerline. It levels out and comes to the edge of the bluffs that form the canyon wall, then curves around to the left. You'll have some nice views down into the canyon as the trail follows the top of the bluff all the way to the creek at the head of the canyon at 1.0. The falls is just downstream a few feet—the rocks are super slick there!

Emergency contact: Newton County Sheriff, 870–446–5124 No dogs on trails.

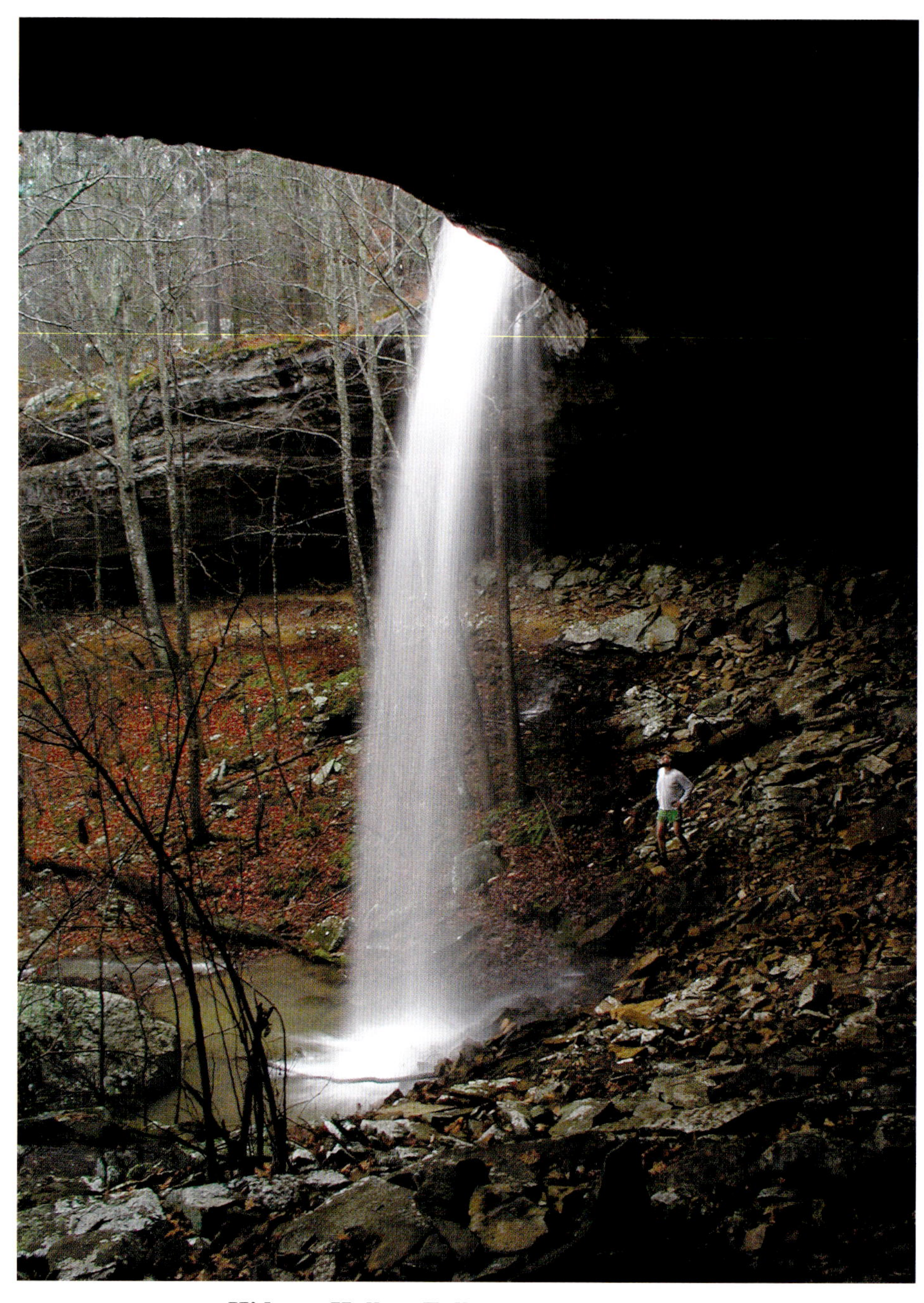

Hideout Hollow Falls (during high water)

Hammerschmidt Falls – 43′

1.0 mile roundtrip, easy+ road/social trail, GPS not needed

GPS **36.02208, -93.28803**

Indian Creek Twin – 21′

.3 difficult bushwhack GPS **36.02443, -93.29085**

Evangeline Falls – 44′

1.4 mile roundtrip, difficult ♦ GPS **36.02579, -93.28784**

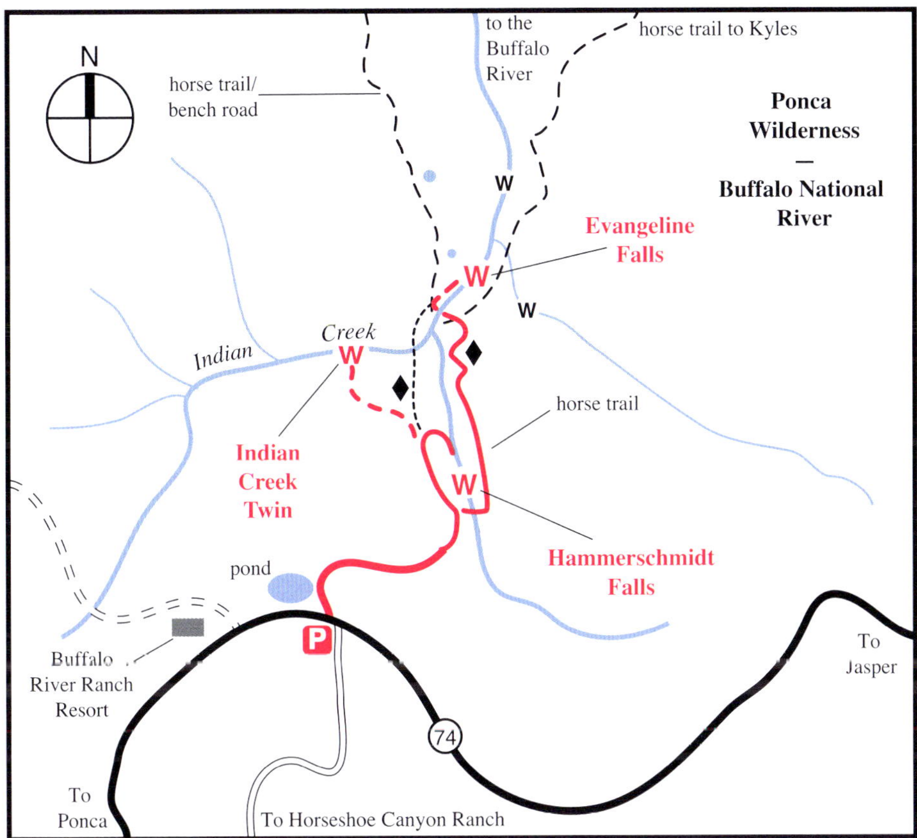

HAMMERSCHMIDT FALLS/INDIAN CREEK TWIN/ EVANGELINE FALLS. These are the uppermost waterfalls in what is one of the great canyons in the Ozarks. Indian Creek is filled with steep, rocky, sometimes nearly impassable terrain, caves, and lots of waterfalls.

The unofficial parking spot is located between Jasper and Low Gap on Hwy. 74. To get there take Hwy. 74 east from Low Gap 2.4 miles (or 2.8 miles west of the turnoff to Kyles Landing) and TURN RIGHT at the entrance to Horseshoe Canyon Ranch (private). PARK where you can but don't block the road (**36.01822, -93.28979**)—if crowded you may have to park along the highway. CROSS the highway to begin your hike.

Hammerschmidt Falls is named after longtime Arkansas Congressman John Paul Hammerschmidt from Harrison who helped get the legislation through Congress that created America's first National River. THANKS JPH!

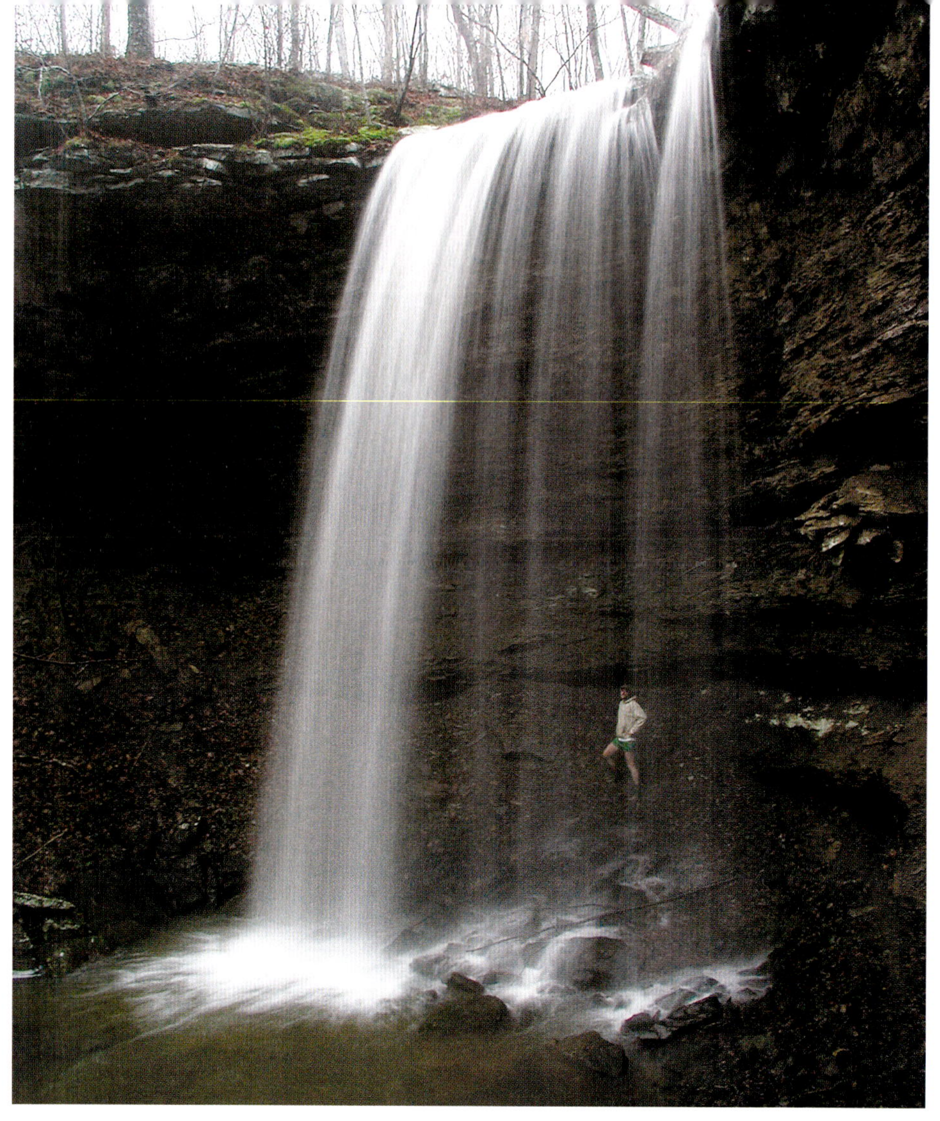

Hammerschmidt Falls (high water)

From the parking spot on Hwy. 74, cross the highway and hike down the old road past the pond about a quarter mile to a power line opening to a creek—this is one branch of Indian Creek. TURN LEFT before you cross the creek and follow a social trail along the creek 100 yards or so to the top of the big waterfall. Follow the trail to the LEFT along the top of the bluffline, then TURN RIGHT and scramble down back to the base of **Hammerschmidt Falls**. What a beautiful spot!

Indian Creek Twin. If you like a challenge and are already at **Hammerschmidt Falls** and it's roaring, you might take a little side trip over to **Indian Creek Twin**. From **Hammerschmidt Falls** climb back out to the top of the bluff and head into the woods to the left/west and contour around the hillside (dotted red line on the map), dropping down a bit where you can. Stay clear of the black diamond ♦ slope down on the right—you want to be heading away from that slope and working your way up into the drainage to the left, eventually dropping down to the bluff and to **Indian Creek Twin** at .3.

Evangeline Falls. Evangeline Pratt Archer grew up on Markham Hill in Fayetteville and was a staunch supporter of women's rights. She became involved in the battle to protect the Buffalo River in the 1950's, and later joined up with Dr. Neil Compton as a founding member of the Ozark Society. There's a famous photo of her welcoming U.S. Supreme Court Chief Justice William O. Douglas at the Harrison airport for his two day canoe trip down the Buffalo that led to the creation of Buffalo National River. She had friends in high places and we owe her a great deal for her efforts!

Make your way back up (or down to) the top of **Hammerschmidt Falls** and STEP OVER the creek that feeds it—there's an old horse trail on the other side—TURN LEFT and follow the trail along the top of the bluff downstream, past **Hammerschmidt Falls**.

Continue along the horse trail and it will soon leave the top of the bluff and begin to switchback STEEPLY DOWN the hill ♦ and a little to the right (away from the canyon). This trail will eventually level out and intersect with an old Bench Road/horse trail. (This road used to go all the way down to Kyles Landing, but it's mostly grown up and hard to follow—last time I looked there were a couple of massive oak trees blocking this intersection area. Horses no longer use the Bench Road due to a landslide across Indian Creek)

TURN LEFT on this old road and/or go over to and CROSS Indian Creek just below the landslide. Once across, follow Indian Creek downstream to the RIGHT and you will soon come to the top of **Evangeline Falls** at .7.

Emergency contact: Newton County Sheriff, 870–446–5124 No dogs on trails.

(● 36.02794, -93.28906)

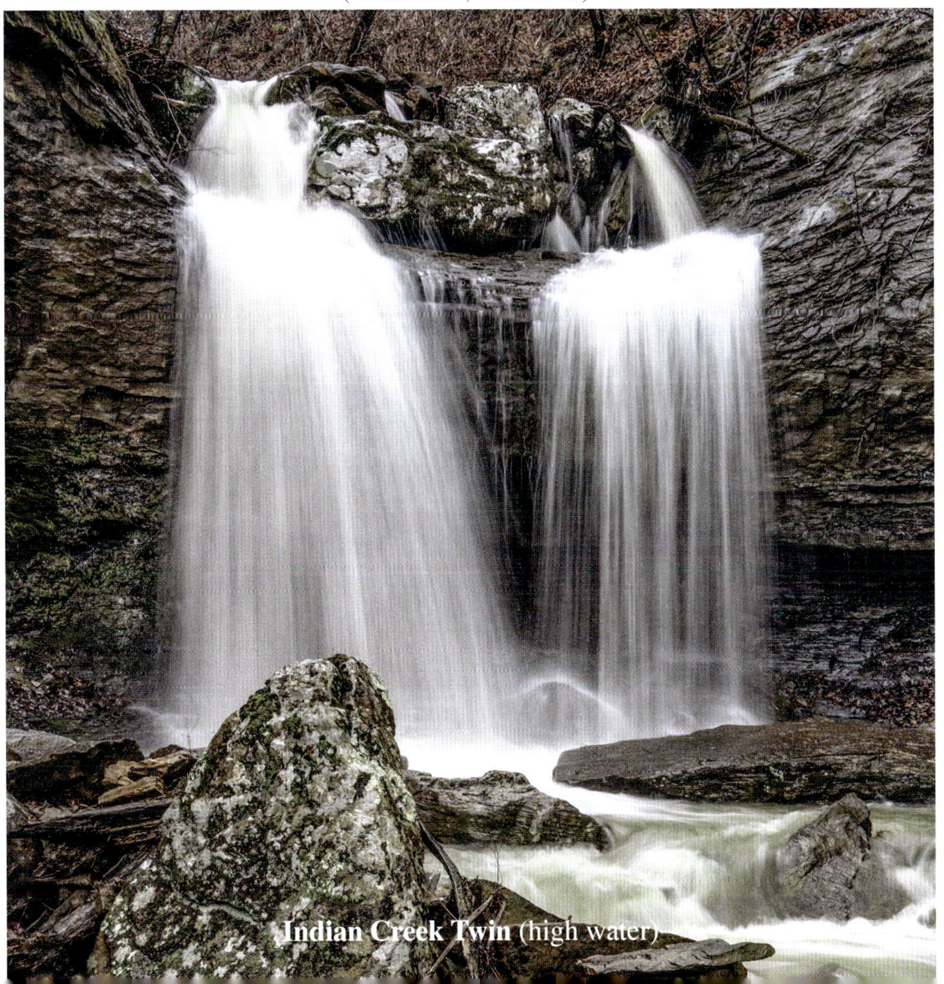

Indian Creek Twin (high water)

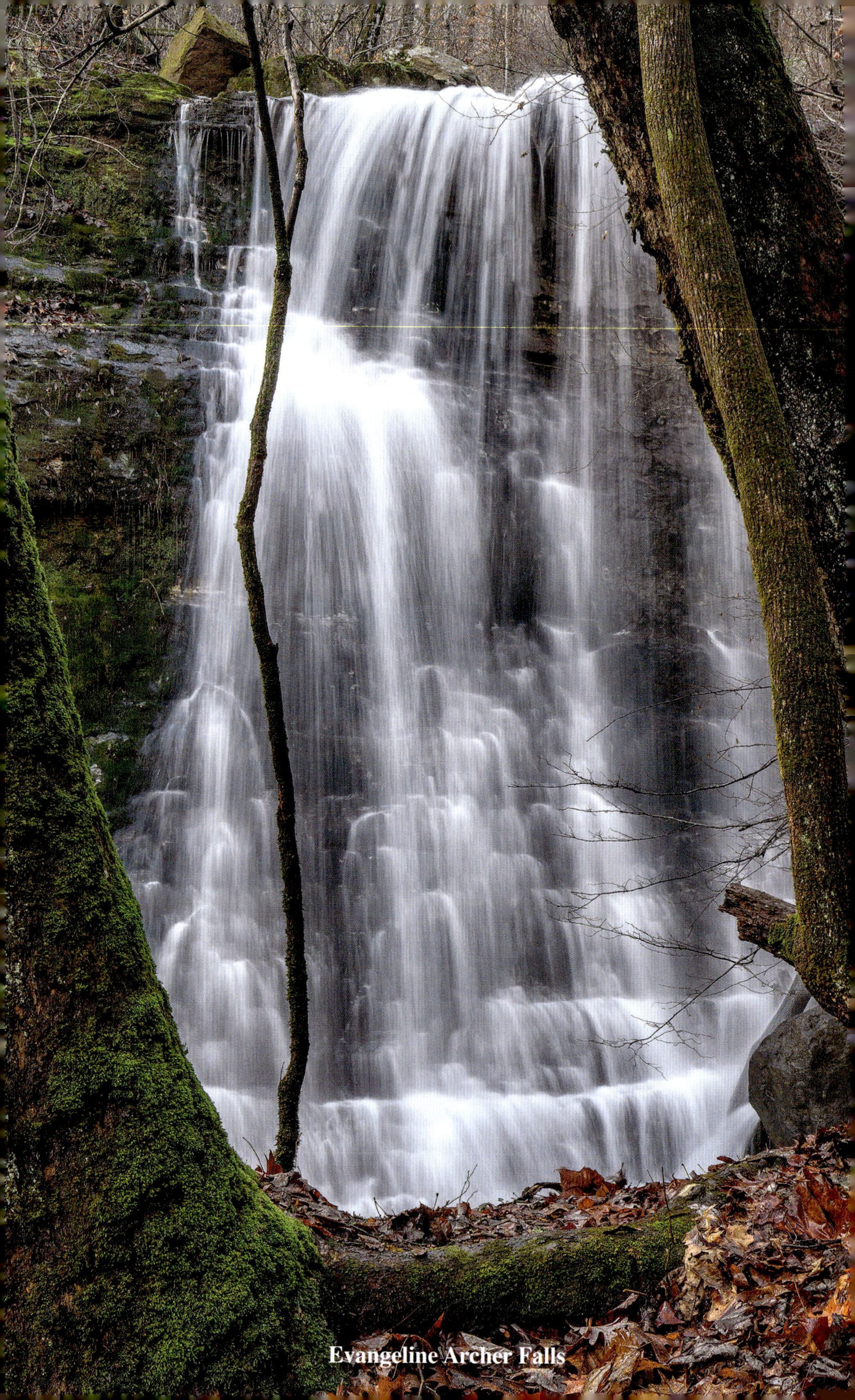

Evangeline Archer Falls

Twin Falls at Camp Orr – 48′

.1 mile roundtrip, easy hike, GPS not needed

GPS **36.05470, -93.25830**

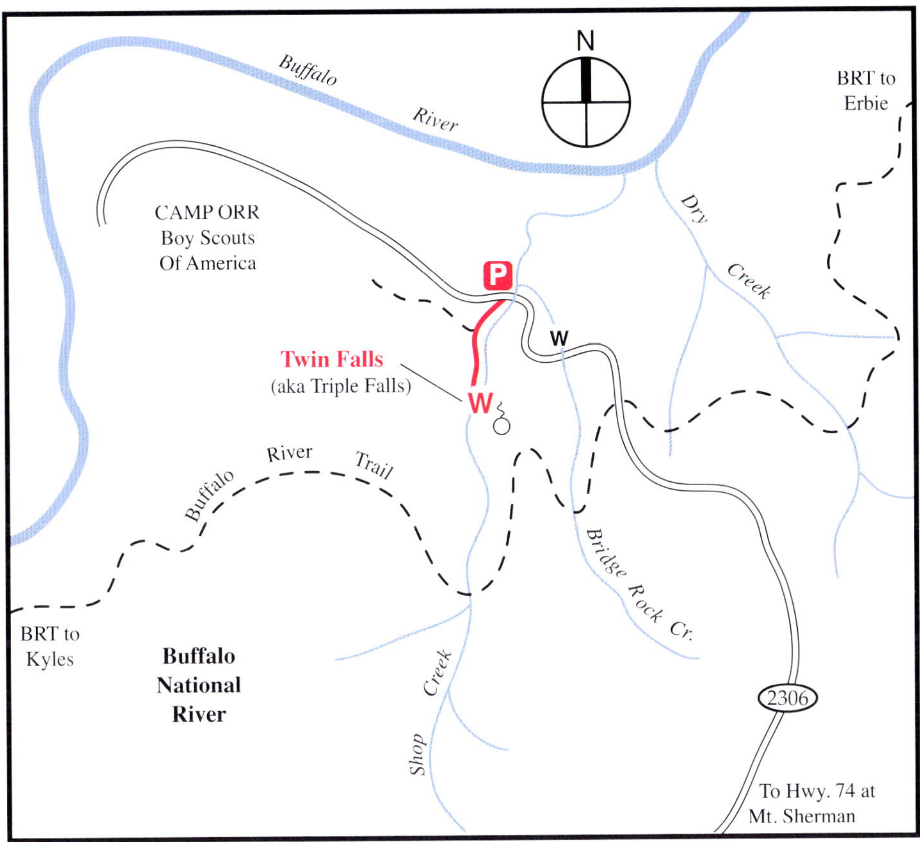

TWIN FALLS (aka Triple Falls) at Camp Orr. This is one of the most scenic easy waterfalls to get to—even kids can walk right up to the edge of the creek near the base for a perfect view. It has long been called Twin Falls, but there is enough water flowing during waterfall season to make it a triple.

The turnoff to get to the parking area is located between Jasper and Ponca. From Jasper, go west on Hwy. 74 to Mt. Sherman and TURN RIGHT on CR#2300 (gravel) at the sign for Kyles Landing (OR go east from Low Gap on Hwy. 74 for 5.2 miles to Mt. Sherman and TURN LEFT on CR#2300 at the sign). Go 1.0 mile and BEAR RIGHT at the fork onto CR#2306 (the left fork goes down into Kyles Landing). Continue heading down the hill for another 1.8 miles until you hit bottom right after crossing a creek and PARK on the RIGHT (**36.05654, -93.25763** there is a sign for Twin Falls there). NOTE that the last mile of this road is *really steep* and may be slick and muddy!

From the parking area, cross the road and hike on a trail that follows Shop Creek upstream into the woods—a level hike of a couple hundred yards. There will be another trail that comes in from your right, but just keep going STRAIGHT AHEAD and you will come to the falls (you might be able to hear the falls from the parking spot).

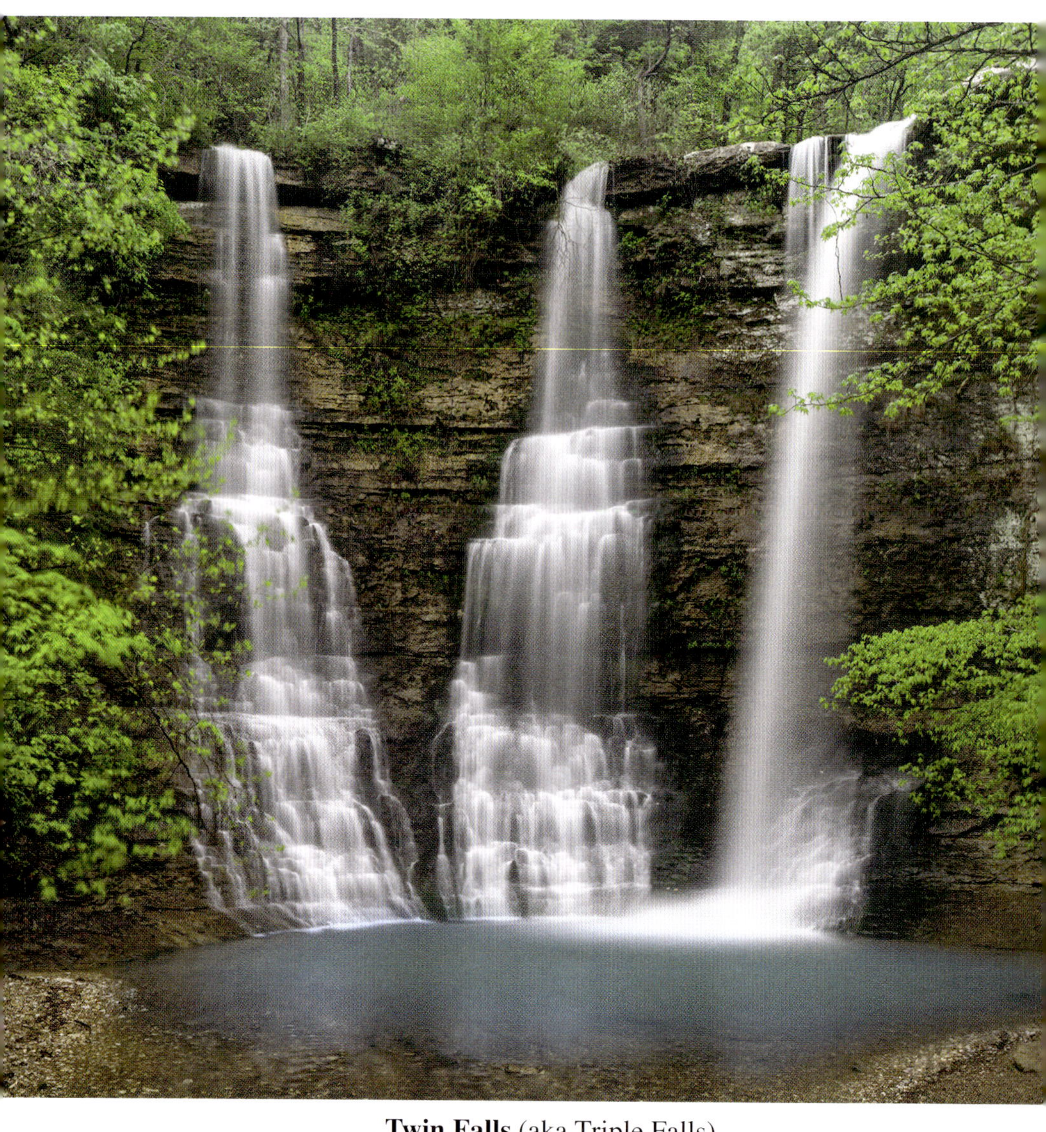

Twin Falls (aka Triple Falls)

NOTE that the land beyond the parking area is the Boy Scout facility Camp Orr, and generally off limits to the public. Scouts from all over the region come there to learn outdoor skills each summer—I was one of them when I was a "tenderfoot" scout in the 1960's. One of the things I remember most about my trip was hearing about the Legend of Smokey Joe. This is a tale that I believe was created to help explain the existence of the Buffalo Bigfoot, a creature that has been reported up and down the Buffalo drainage for many generations, going all the way back to the mid 1800's, and perhaps even before. Is it possible he is still out there today? Well at least we finally have a waterfall named after him—see page 105.

Emergency contact: Newton County Sheriff, 870–446–5124

Thunder Canyon Falls – 71′

4.0 miles roundtrip, medium hike/bushwhack, GPS recommended

GPS **36.08460, -93.25428**

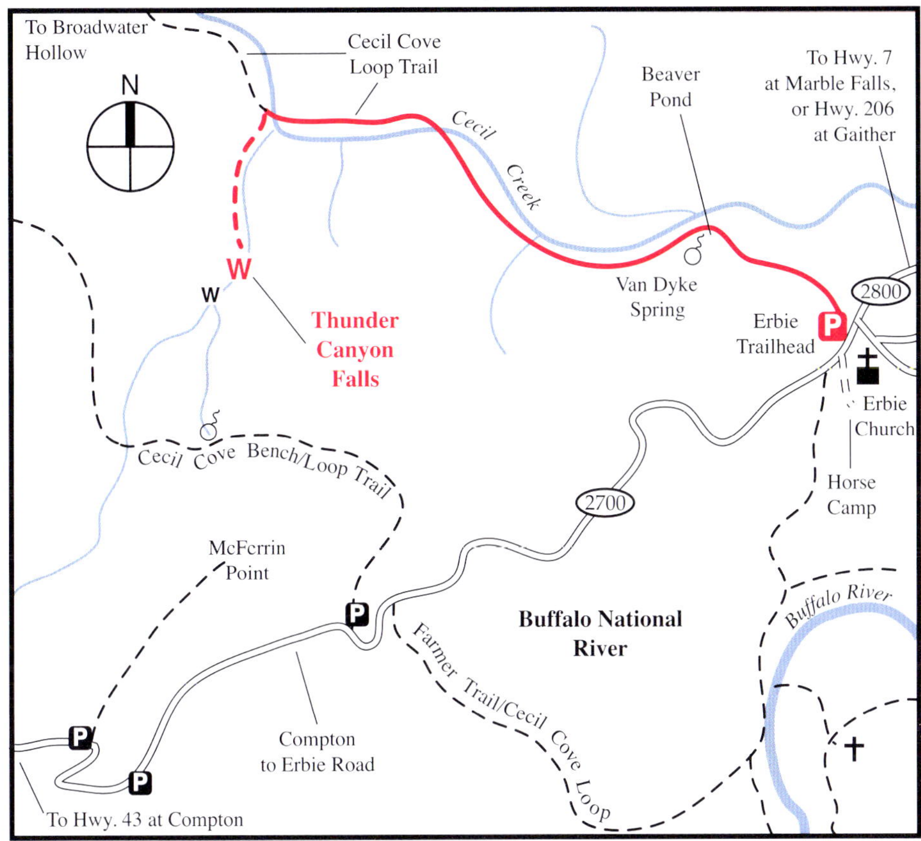

THUNDER CANYON FALLS. When I first approached this falls I could hear a distant roar, or the sound of thunder, coming from the waterfall. When I rounded the corner and stepped into this incredible little canyon I was stunned at the sight of the falls. I consider it one of the most scenic waterfalls in Arkansas,.

The trailhead (Cecil Cove Loop Trail, (**36.08359, -93.23344**) is located on the other side of the Buffalo River from Erbie Campground, and just across the road from the old Erbie Church. There are several ways to get to this area, but the traditional route is from Compton via the Compton-Erbie road, 6.2 miles—but ***THIS road may be in bad condition*** (if in doubt, check with J.B. Trading at Compton or social media). Other routes—#1) From Hwy. 206 at Gaither, take CR#2825/Erbie Cutoff Road south (next to the water tower, paved, then gravel) for 2.2 miles then TURN RIGHT onto CR#2800 (gravel) for 5.6 miles to Erbie. #2) From Hwy. 7 at Marble Falls take CR#2800 (gravel) west 7.4 miles to Erbie. #3) You can also get here by crossing the river at Erbie, but during good waterfall flow periods the river will be much too high to ford. See Broadwater Hollow for alternate trail route.

From the trailhead the trail heads down the hill towards Cecil Creek. At .3 it comes to a beaver pond and dam, which is actually the water from Van Dyke Spring that emerges from the base of a bluff just upstream. You can cross the top of the dam, or cross the small stream below it. The trail heads upstream to the LEFT along the spring pool (you don't cross Cecil Creek yet), past Van Dyke Spring. It is a level hike to the first crossing of Cecil

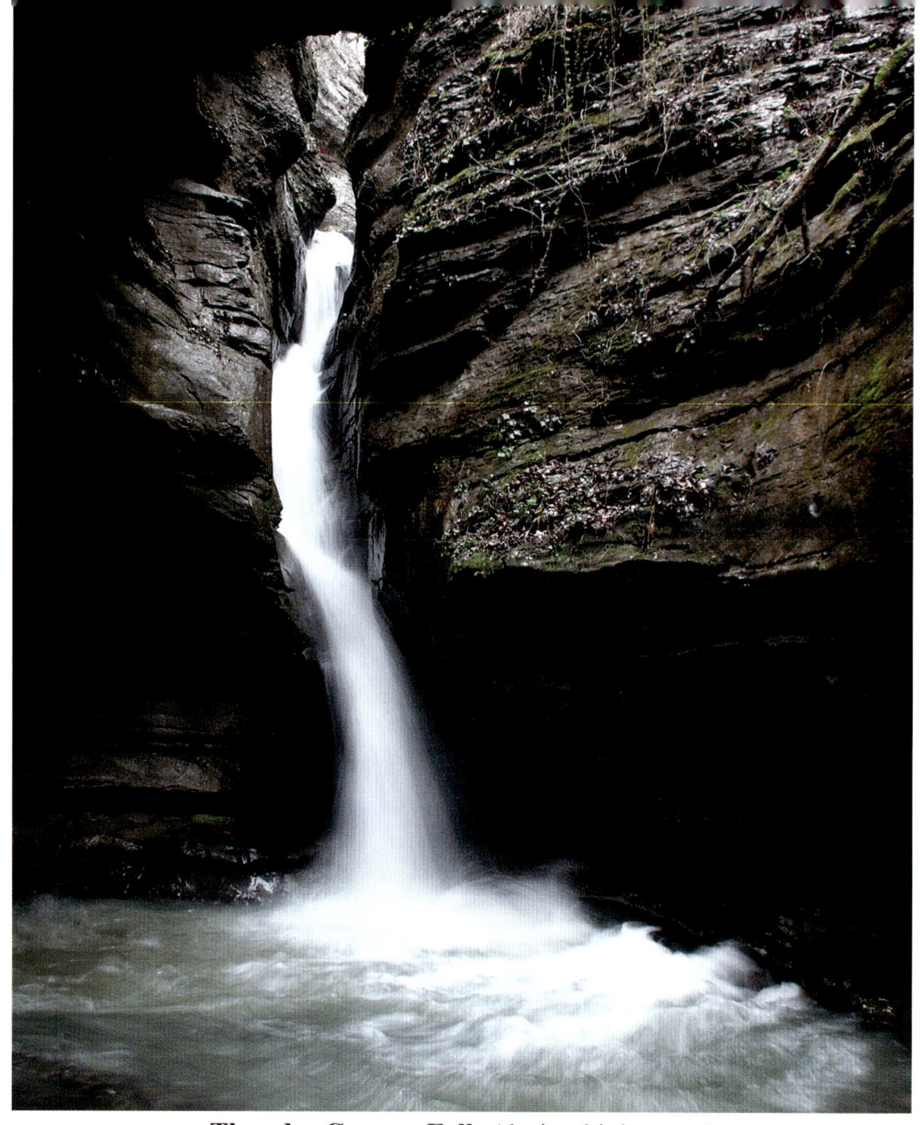

Thunder Canyon Falls (during high water)

Creek at 1.0, then more easy hiking. Just after you cross the creek for a second time at 1.4, LEAVE THE TRAIL and hike BACK TO THE LEFT and over to a stream that flows into Cecil Creek. TURN RIGHT and follow this creek upstream.

There are many places where the creekbed is solid rock carved out by the rushing waters, and you will have to climb up onto and hike across the steep hillside above—pick your way the best you can. After about a half mile of this at 2.0 you will enter Thunder Canyon and will hear the falls. The waterfall is at the end of the short box canyon. You cannot actually see the top of the falls—it continues on up and out of sight. (We had to rappel down from above to measure this one.) CAUTION—SLICK FOOTING!!! The falls drilled a hole in the bottom of the canyon about 20 feet in diameter and 14 feet deep. The canyon wall on one side arches completely over your head. It is a remarkable SSS. See a popular alternate route (more creek crossings) from Broadwater Hollow on page 120.

Emergency contact: Newton County Sheriff, 870–446–5124 No dogs on trails.

Paige Falls 8′, Broadwater Hollow 21′

.6 mile roundtrip, easy bushwhack, GPS not needed

GPS **36.10500, -93.26707**

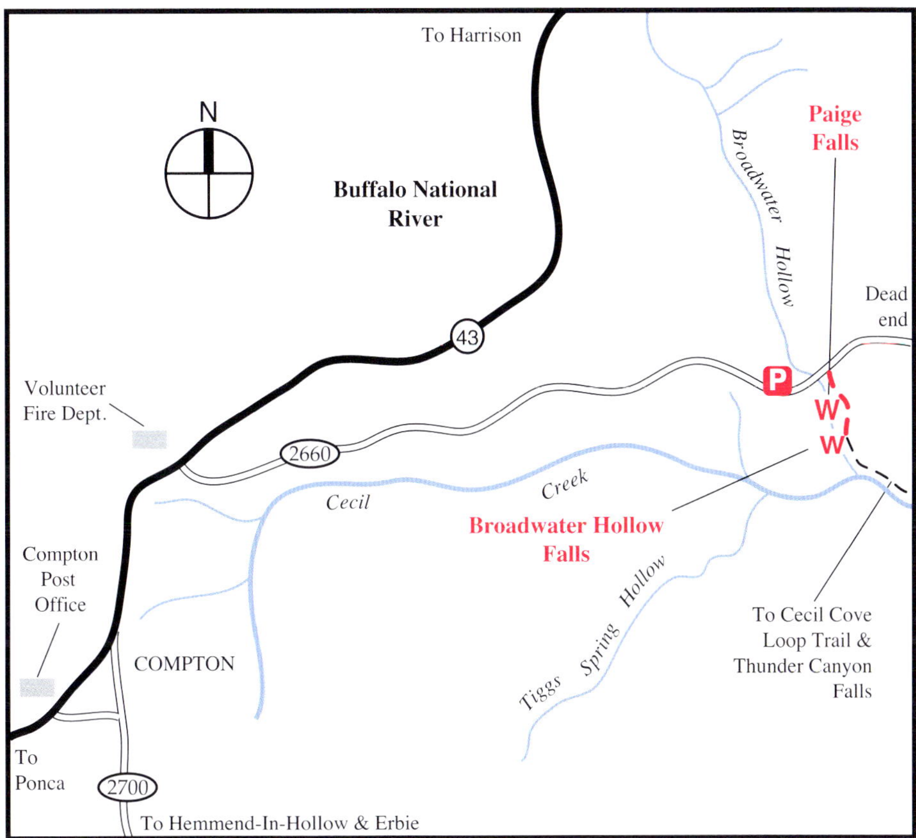

PAIGE FALLS/ BROADWATER HOLLOW FALLS. There are a couple of scenic waterfalls in this hollow, plus other tumbling cascades all within an easy hiking distance. Also this is a back-door route to Thunder Canyon Falls (longer, with more creek crossings, but better road—see the next page for that info).

From the Compton post office go north on Hwy. 43 for .8 miles and TURN RIGHT onto CR#2660 (gravel, right across from the Volunteer Fire Station). Follow this rough road 2.0 miles until you come to the crossing of Broadwater Hollow—PARK in a small lot up the hill just before you get to the creek (**36.10516, -93.26792**). The property upstream from the road crossing is private, so stay below the road while hiking.

There is a good social trail on the east side of the creek that heads down the hill alongside the stream—follow this trail a couple hundred yards past a pair of giant boulders on the right and you will see **Paige Falls** just beyond, which spills into a beautiful emerald pool. Paige Slape was killed in a car accident at age 17 on the morning of her first day of summer vacation. She lived, and died, within a few miles of this waterfall.

The next waterfall downstream is **Broadwater Hollow Falls**. It is much taller, and can get rolling pretty good after a large rainstorm. It's all an SSS, and so easy to get to!

For the route to Thunder Canyon Falls see the next page.

Emergency contact: Newton County Sheriff, 870–446–5124 No dogs on trails.

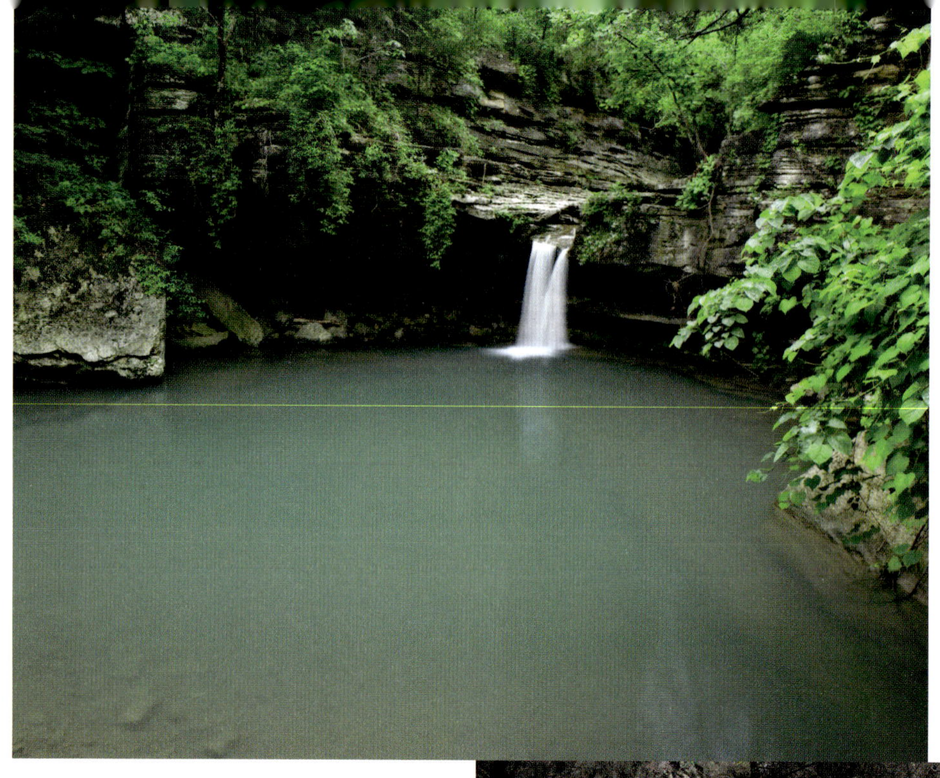

Paige Falls (above)
Broadwater Hollow Falls
(at right)

Alternate route to **Thunder Canyon Falls**. This route is longer (4.8 miles roundtrip vs. 4.0), with two more creek crossings, but the trailhead is easier to get to and you skip the Compton–To–Erbie Road (which can be in bad shape).

From Broadwater Hollow Falls on the previous page, CONTINUE downstream on that trail and it soon turns left and follows Cecil Creek for a little bit, and then crosses Cecil Creek to the RIGHT at .75. Follow the trail to Cecil Cove Loop Trail intersection at 1.0. If you turn LEFT there and go downstream, there are two more crossings of Cecil Creek, then you come to the route to Thunder Canyon Falls just before the third crossing at 1.8 (*JOIN the trail on previous page to get to Thunder Canyon.)

Liles Falls – 41′

.2 mile roundtrip, easy bushwhack, GPS not needed

GPS **36.05713, -93.19548**

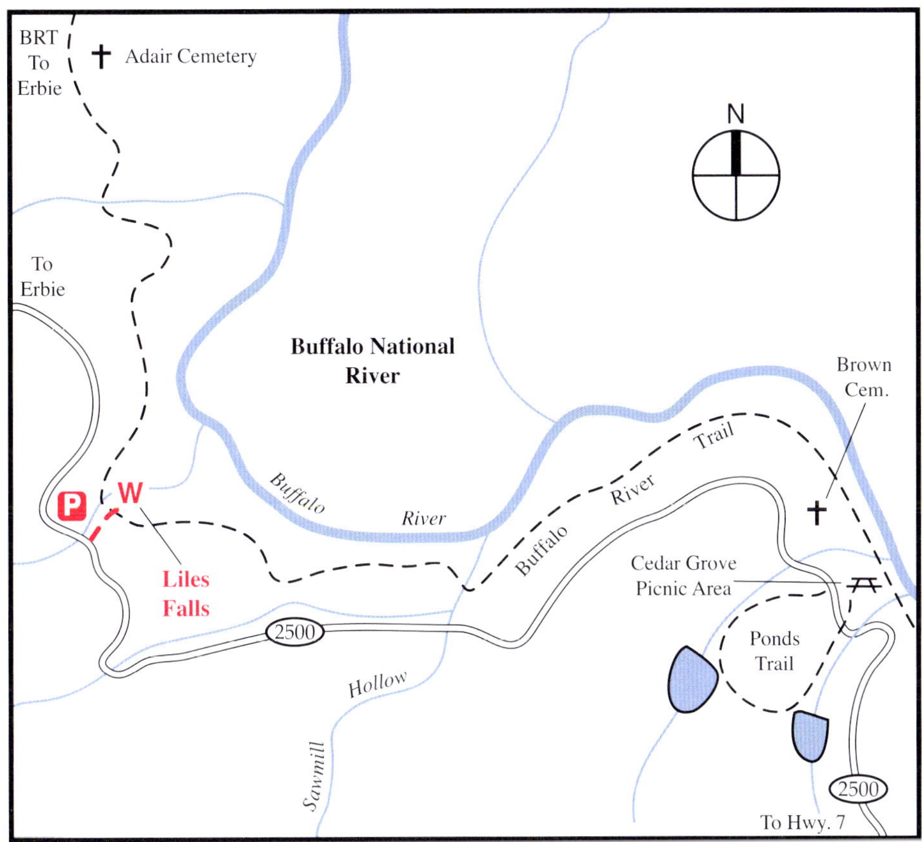

LILES FALLS. This waterfall is really beautiful when the water is high, and it is so simple to get to! The falls is named after Jim Liles, former Assistant Superintendent with Buffalo National River. He was in charge of developing the trail systems in the early days of the Park, and had a great deal to do with their design, layout and construction (he even spent a lot of time building trails himself, on his days off). We have a great trail system at the Park thanks to Jim!

The turnoff is located between Jasper and Pruitt on Hwy. 7. TURN WEST onto CR#2500 (gravel)—it is marked as the turnoff to Erbie Campground. Go 3.5 miles (1.5 miles past the Cedar Grove Picnic Area—there is a short, easy loop trail there that is great for kids), and PARK just after you cross the small creek that runs across the road **(36.05633, -93.19685)**. This creek is the one that feeds the waterfall, so it should be running well.

To get to the falls, go back and cross the creek next to the parking area, and then head downhill into the woods. There is no trail and you simply follow the creek for a couple hundred yards—you will come to and cross the Buffalo River Trail near the top of the falls. The creek runs into the Buffalo River a little ways below the falls.

Emergency contact: Newton County Sheriff, 870–446–5124 No dogs on trails.

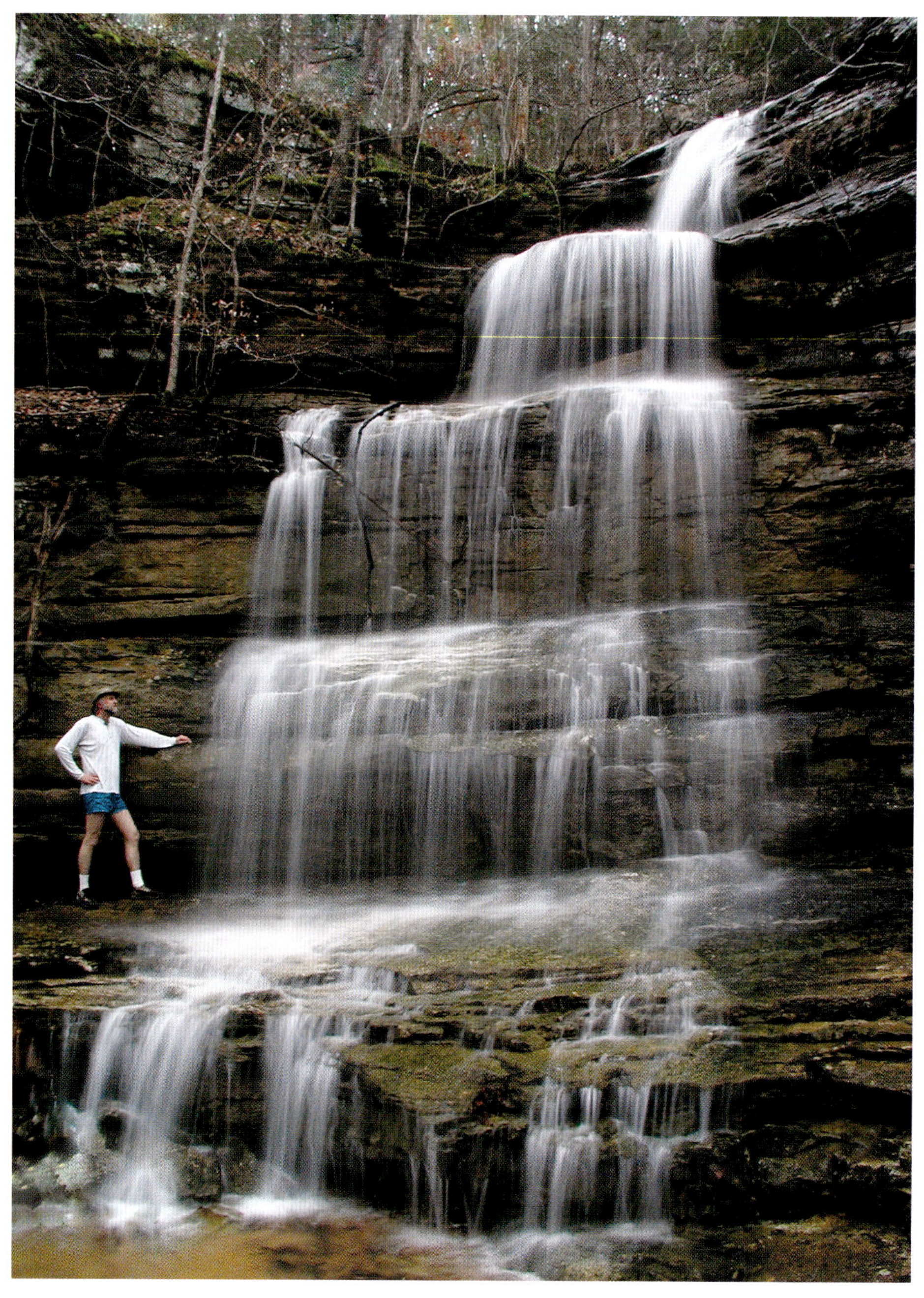

Jim Liles Falls

Kevin Falls – 27′

Roadside

GPS **36.06919, -93.15995**

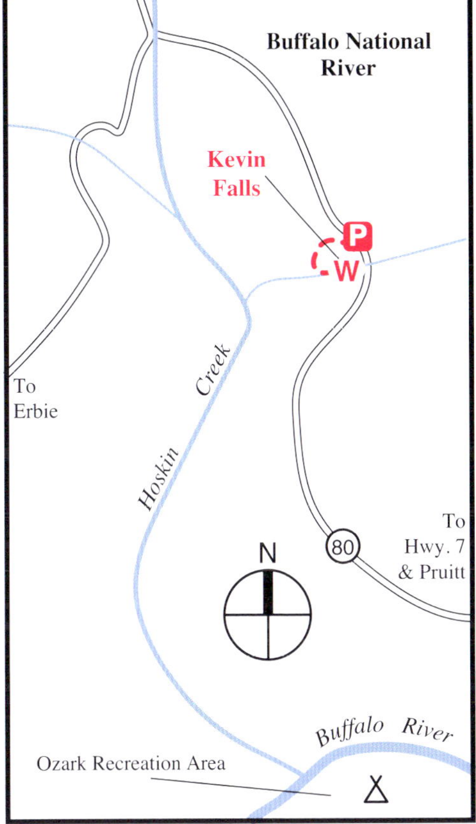

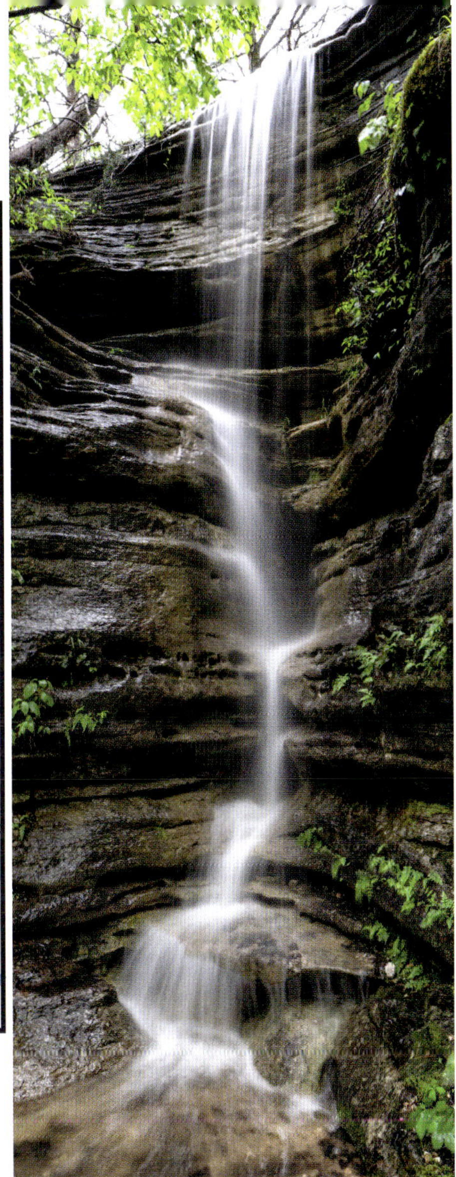

KEVIN FALLS. From Hwy. 7 across from the turnoff to the Lower Erbie Access, take NC Road #80 2.3 miles and park on the left (**36.06947, -93.15984**). Very rough road.

Kevin Middleton has been a fixture in the Newton County and Buffalo River area for decades, working with "Eco Tours," as a National Park Service Ranger, and especially as a social media personality. He often describes his daily rambles through the forest and streams to share online his unique outlook on the landscape, critters, and people who live and visit the area. He discovered this beautiful waterfall decades ago.

The waterfall pours over the bluff just a few feet from the road. Go into the woods and to the right just a little bit to the bluff then get down below the bluff and follow it back to the LEFT to the falls. I highly recommend you take the time to visit Hoskin Creek just below the falls and follow it downstream to the Buffalo River. It's a beautiful clearwater limestone creek SSS (maybe a couple of graves along the way on the right.

Emergency contact: Newton County Sheriff, 870–446–5124 No dogs on trails.

Fern Falls – 42′

1.5 miles roundtrip, medium hike/bushwhack, GPS helpful

GPS **35.89748N, -93.19250W**

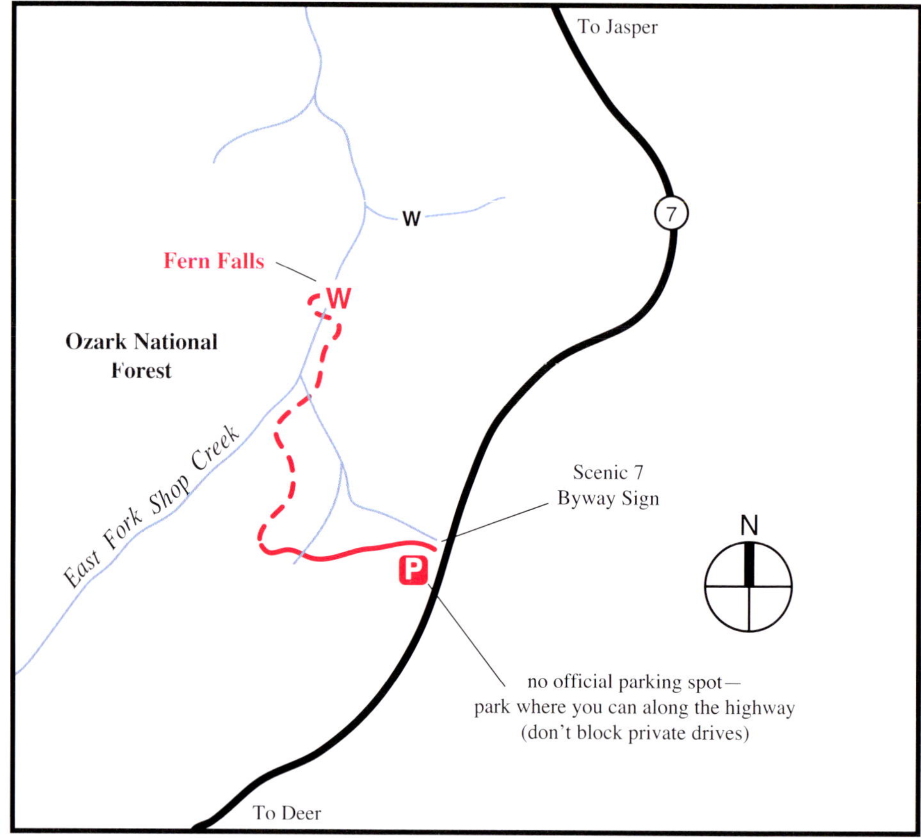

FERN FALLS. This is a beautiful waterfall that takes its name from hundreds of lush ferns that spring to life in April and May. There are some nice dogwoods too!

The parking area is located between Jasper and the turn off to Deer along Hwy. 7— look for the "Scenic 7 National Scenic Byway" highway sign (**35.89284N, -93.18995W**—11.4 miles south of the Jasper square, or 3.4 miles north of the Hwy. 16 & 7 intersection near Deer). There is no actual parking spot so you just have to find some place to pull off of the highway, but be careful not to block a driveway or get onto private property.

Start from the big sign and hike back into the woods and past a powerline where you should see a four-wheeler trail straight ahead. Follow this trail on the level until it begins to curve back to the left, then VEER RIGHT onto a very faint road trace that heads downhill. The original road trace leads right down to the waterfall, but it was mostly covered up with debris by the big ice storm in 2009 and so you may have to crawl around a bit to make it down the hill. The old road trace drops down to and runs alongside the creek—keep going downstream until you come to the top of **Fern Fall**s. If you can cross the creek, there is an easy way down through the bluffline a couple hundred feet beyond.

Emergency contact: Newton County Sheriff, 870–446–5124 Dogs are OK.

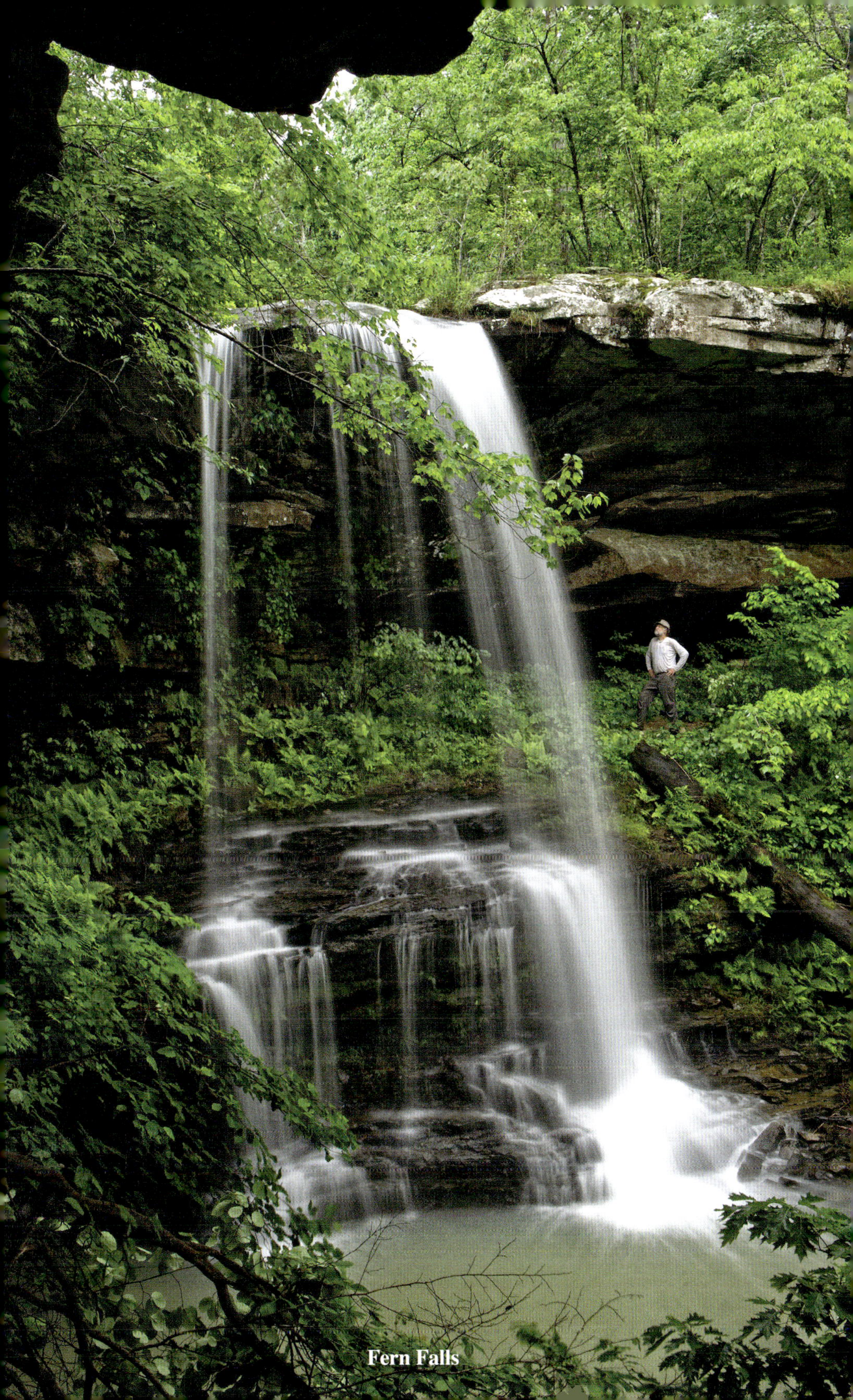

Fern Falls

Big Creek Cave Falls – 29′

3.2 miles roundtrip for both falls, medium social trail, GPS helpful

GPS **35.86318, -93.15447**

Wolf Creek Cave Falls – 18′

GPS **35.86063, -93.15243**

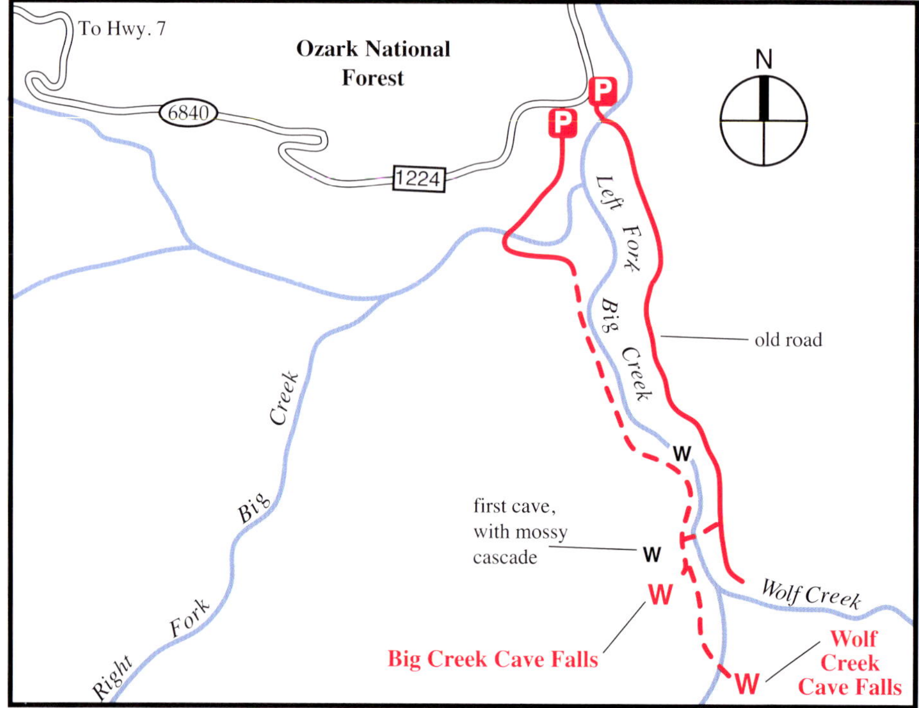

BIG CREEK CAVE FALLS/WOLF CREEK CAVE FALLS. There are three unique waterfalls that pour out of caves in this beautiful wild area, and lots to see and explore along the creeks.

From the intersection of Hwys. 7 and 16 near Deer, head north on Hwy. 7 for 1.3 miles and TURN RIGHT onto CR#6840/FR#1224 (**35.87088, -93.19208**). Go 2.8 miles (several switchbacks) until you have almost reached the very bottom of the hill and PARK* on the RIGHT (**35.87685, -93.15878**)—there is a gate across an old driveway there. Hike south along the old driveway down to the Right Fork of Big Creek then wade the creek. Follow an old field back to the left and then up the hill and then back to the right—you will now be headed up into the Left Fork of Big Creek drainage.

Follow a social trail above the creek in the woods upstream and you will eventually curve around to the right and come to a spring that flows into Big Creek from the right—follow this spring up to the first cave entrance that will have a really neat mossy cascade coming out of it—very unique SSS.

To reach **Big Creek Cave Falls** continue along the bluffline to your left. WOW!!! **Wolf Creek Cave Falls** is another gem of a waterfall pouring out of a cave, is 1/4 mile upstream (take the right fork) then across the creek and up the hill.

**NOTE alternate parking spot and route shown in solid red on the map—follows an old road all the way, crosses the creek twice. Lots more to explore in the area...*

Emergency contact: Newton County Sheriff, 870–446–5124 Dogs are OK.

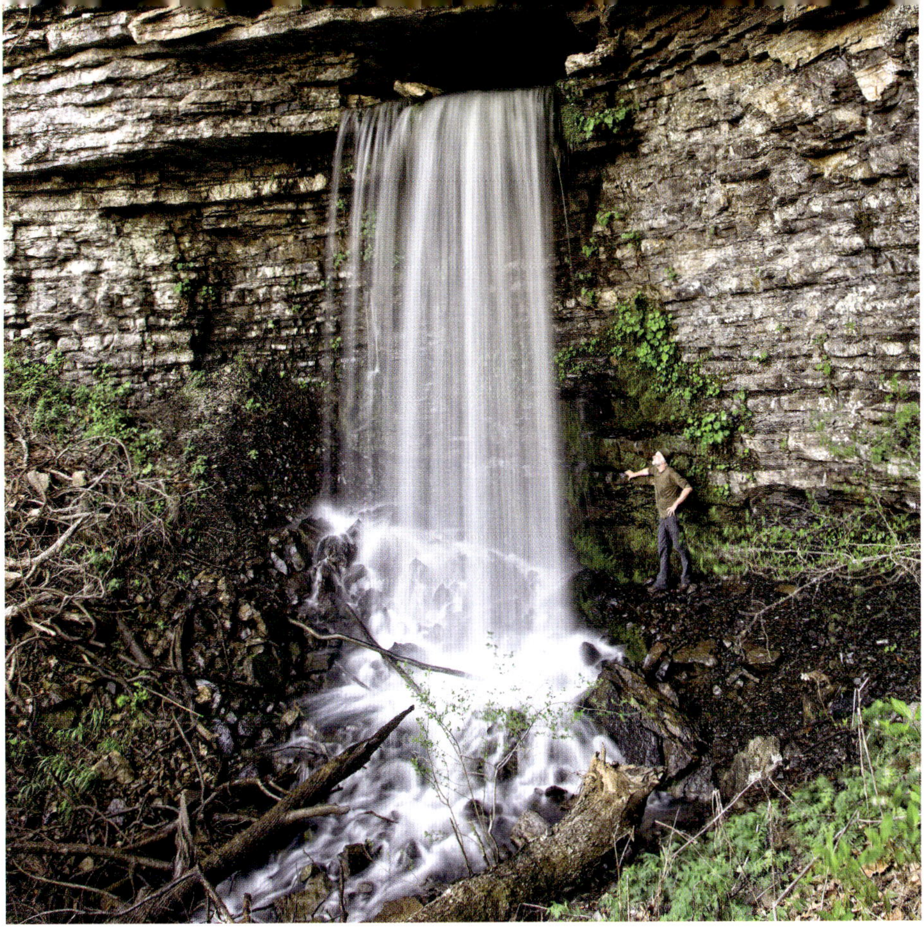

Big Creek Cave Falls (above), Wolf Creek Cave Falls (below)

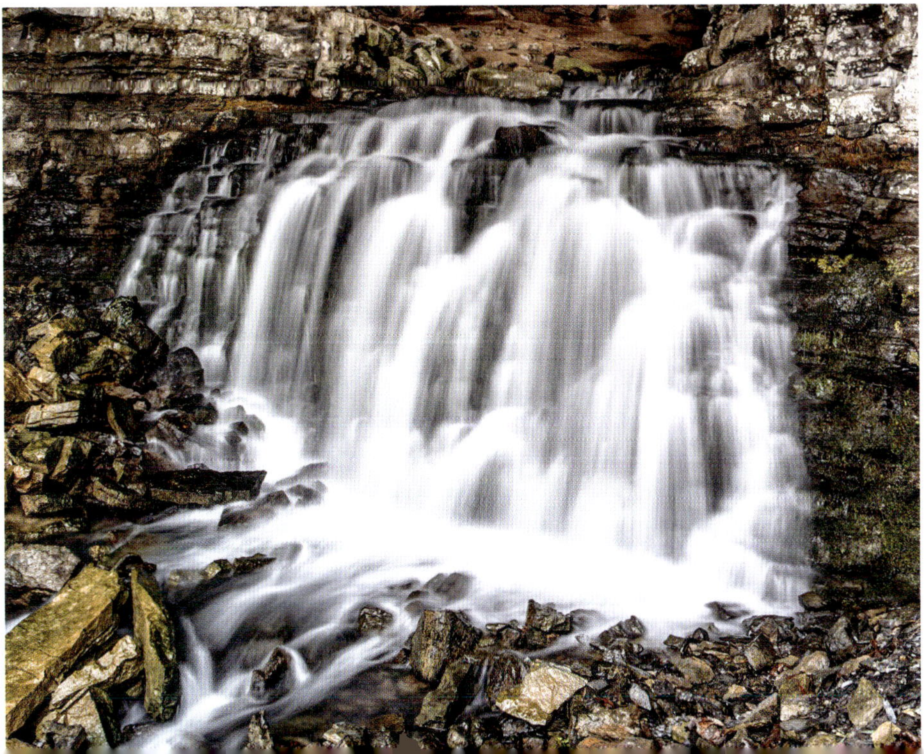

Alum Cove Natural Bridge Falls – 21′

1.1 miles loop to both falls, easy+ trail GPS **35.86206, -93.23404**

Alum Cove Loop Falls – 31′

GPS **35.86238, -93.23596**

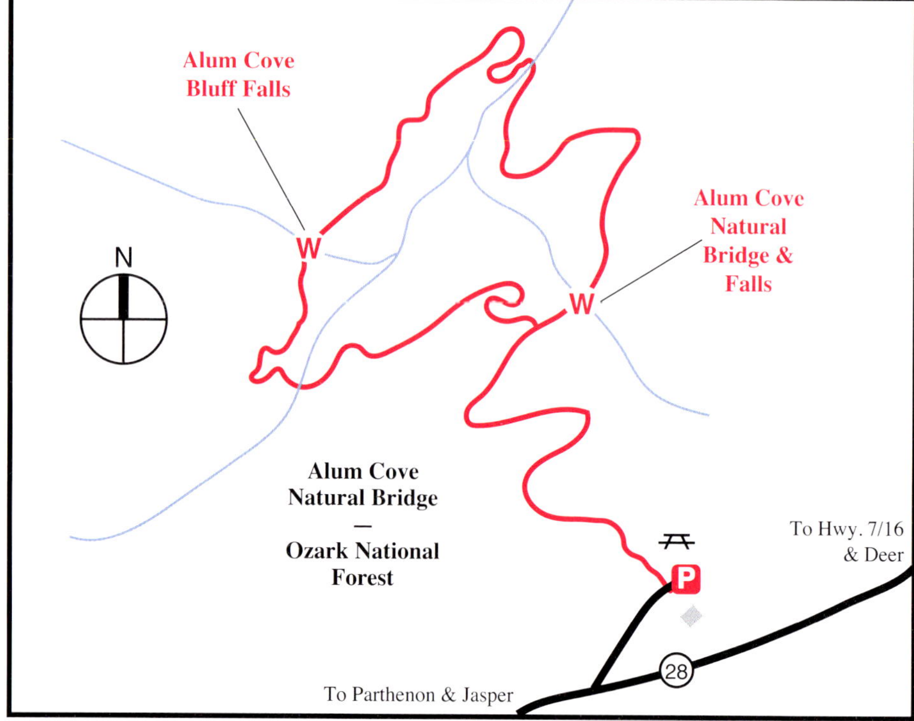

ALUM COVE NATURAL BRIDGE & BLUFF FALLS. This is not your average waterfall location! From the square in Jasper go south on Hwy. 7 14.5 miles and turn RIGHT onto Hwy. 16 towards Deer. Go 1.2 miles and turn RIGHT onto county road 28 (paved). (or from Deer go 1.0 miles east on Hwy. 16 and turn LEFT) Go 3.2 miles and turn RIGHT at the sign for Alum Cove Natural Bridge and PARK (**35.85996, -93.23296**).

A wide trail heads through the picnic area and down the hillside, swinging back to the right, left, then right again and goes right on out onto the Natural Bridge, a major SSS in itself! Turn LEFT just before the bridge and scramble down below it for one of the most magical spots in Arkansas. When it's flooding there's a creek that pours in-between the bridge and the bluff line, creating quite a SPECTACULAR sight of **Alum Cove Natural Bridge Falls!** The Bridge and bluff line on the opposite side of the canyon are worth the trip and hike even if it's dry when you arrive.

Continue on the trail to the left before the Bridge, or across the top of the Bridge and the trail either direction will drop down to the creek below and then climb up to the base of a beautiful bluff line. Follow the trail along the bluff to **Alum Cove Loop Falls**. Lots to explore wet or dry along this bluff. Follow the trail either way back past the bridge (bit of a climb, especially after the bridge) for a total loop hike of 1.1 miles.

Emergency contact: Newton County Sheriff, 870–446–5124 Dogs are OK.

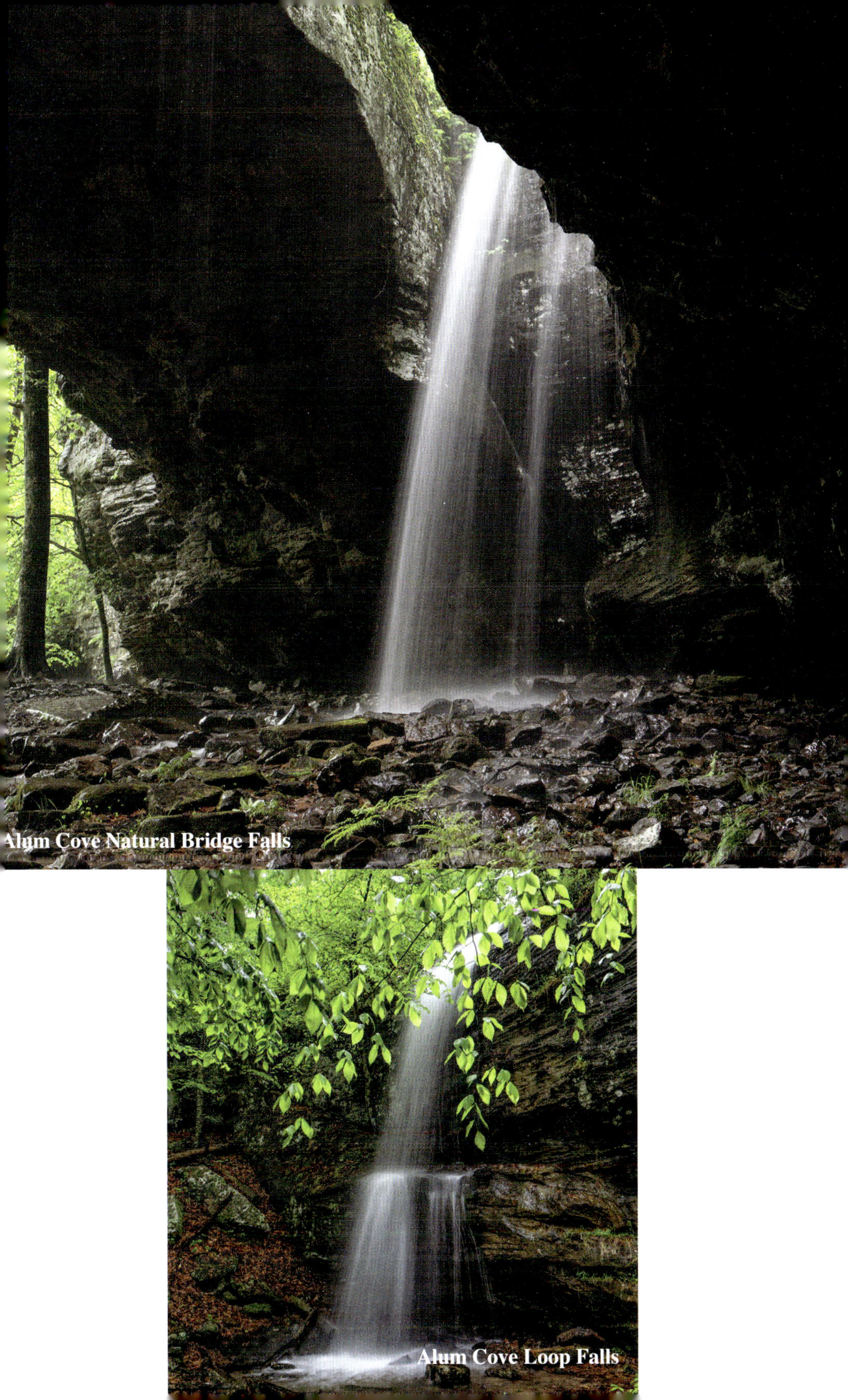

Alum Cove Natural Bridge Falls

Alum Cove Loop Falls

Hudson Shelter Falls – 24′

.8 miles roundtrip, easy bushwhack, GPS helpful

GPS **35.85148, -93.12411**

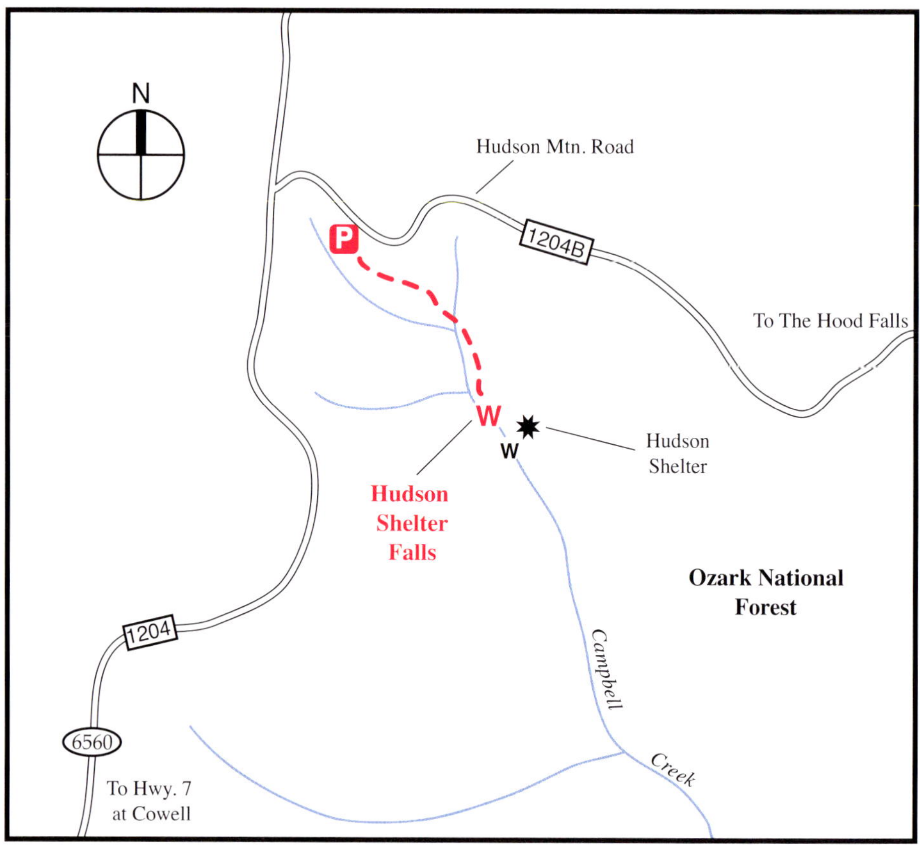

HUDSON SHELTER FALLS. When I first went to this falls it was nearly dark and I just barely had time to snap a photo and hike back out to the truck. When I returned later to measure the height of the waterfall I found there was a second falls just below the upper one, and it too was over 20 feet tall. These falls are named for the bluff shelter that they pour over, which is one of the deepest shelters in the Ozarks—it goes back under the bluff more than 75 feet, and provides a nice level spot for a picnic lunch. (*Please note* that there is no digging or collecting of artifacts allowed in our national forests!) While there is no trail down to this waterfall, it is a short, easy bushwhack to get down to it.

To get to the parking area go south from Jasper on Hwy. 7 about 14 miles to the intersection with Hwy. 16. Continue south on Hwy. 7/16 another 2.9 miles to Cowell and TURN LEFT onto CR#6560/FR#1204 (gravel). Go 4.2 miles and TURN RIGHT onto FR#1204B, Hudson Mtn. Road. Go just a 100 yards or so and pull over and PARK ON THE RIGHT where an old log road takes off to the right (**35.85416, -93.12622**).

Head down the old log road for about 100 yards and when it begins to swing back to the left, LEAVE the road trace to the LEFT and begin to bushwhack straight down the hillside. There is a small creek on the right and one on the left that will come together down in front of you—keep following the water downhill and you will get to the upper falls in

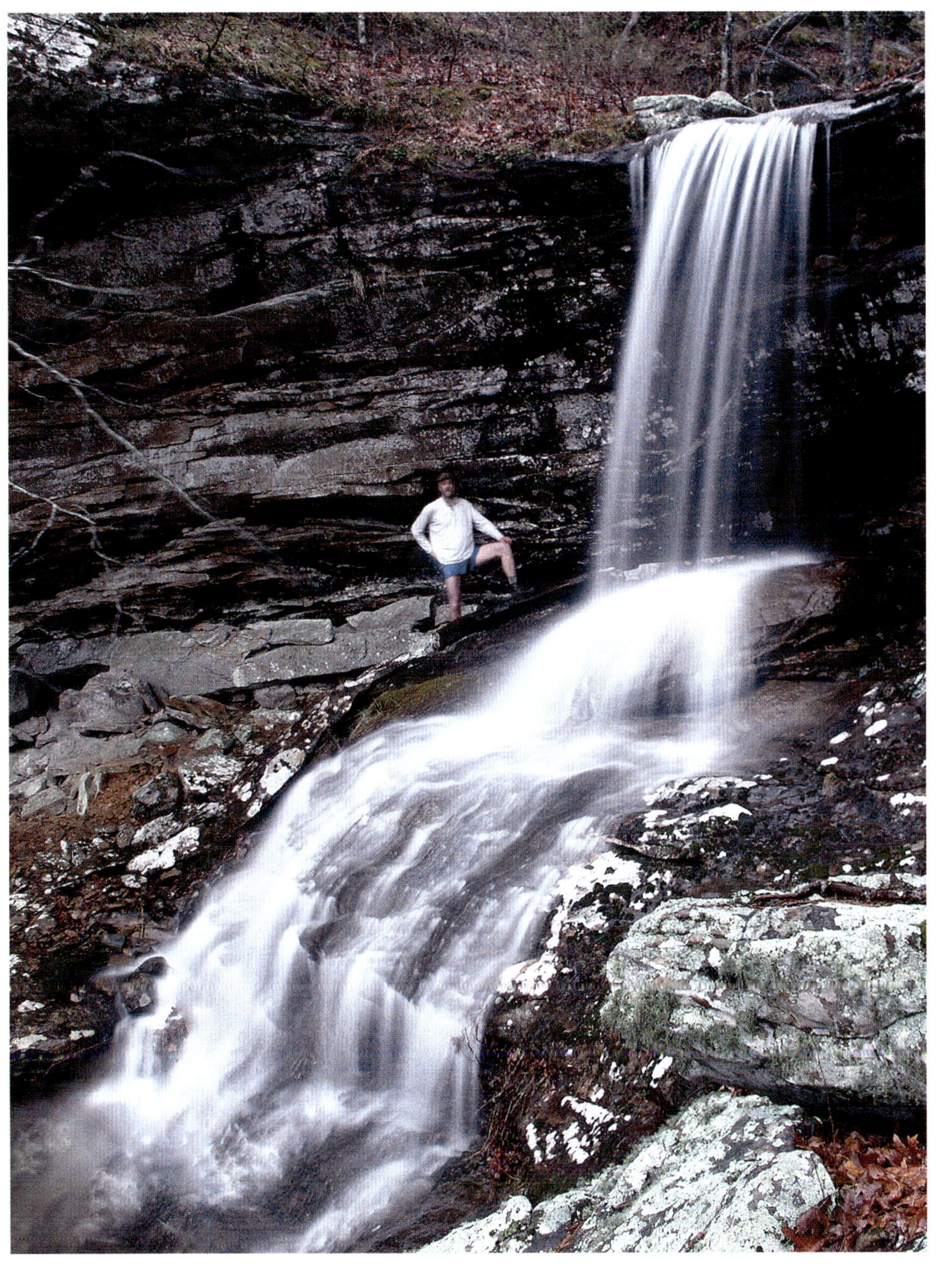

Upper Hudson Shelter Falls

another couple hundred yards. As always, be very careful if you decide to get down to the lower falls and the shelter below.

Emergency contact: Newton County Sheriff, 870–446–5124 Dogs are OK.

The Hood Falls – 45′

.6 roundtrip easy social trail to all falls

GPS **35.85874, -93.10949**

The Hood Pouroff – 49′

GPS **35.85894, -93.10953**

Hudson Mtn. Falls – 45′

GPS **35.86192, -93.10971**

Macedonia School Falls – 43′

GPS **35.85796, -93.11044**

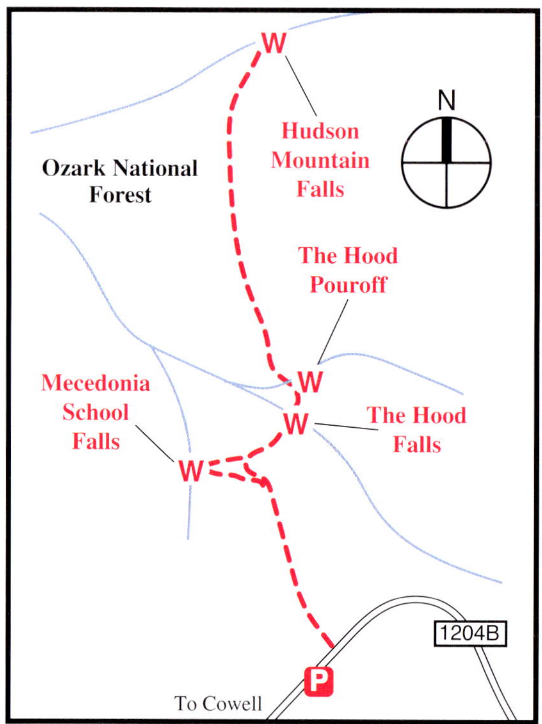

HOOD FALLS AREA. To get to the parking area go south from Jasper on Hwy. 7 about 14 miles to the intersection with Hwy. 16. Continue south on Hwy. 7/16 another 2.9 miles to Cowell and TURN LEFT onto CR#6560/FR#1204 (gravel). Go 4.2 miles and TURN RIGHT onto FR#1204B, Hudson Mtn. Road. Go 1.2 miles and PARK on the right **(35.85623, -93.10882)**.

A social trail leaves the road and heads into the woods, dropping down to the top of the bluff line at .2, then carefully climb down to the base of the bluff. You can see three waterfalls from this spot—first one is back to the left, and will be the last one we visit. But first, **The Hood Falls** is just ahead, dropping off the bluff you just came down through.

Continue along the base of the bluff to the left to **The Hood Pouroff**. Keep following the bluff beyond to **Hudson Mountain Falls** at .5—an SSS bluff walk. Return by the same route. BUT when you get back to the beginning, instead of climbing out, continue on through a jumble of boulders to **Macedonia School Falls**. To return, follow the bluff to the left and up a ramp to the top and back to the road for a total hike of about .6.

Emergency contact: Newton County Sheriff, 870–446–5124 Dogs are OK.

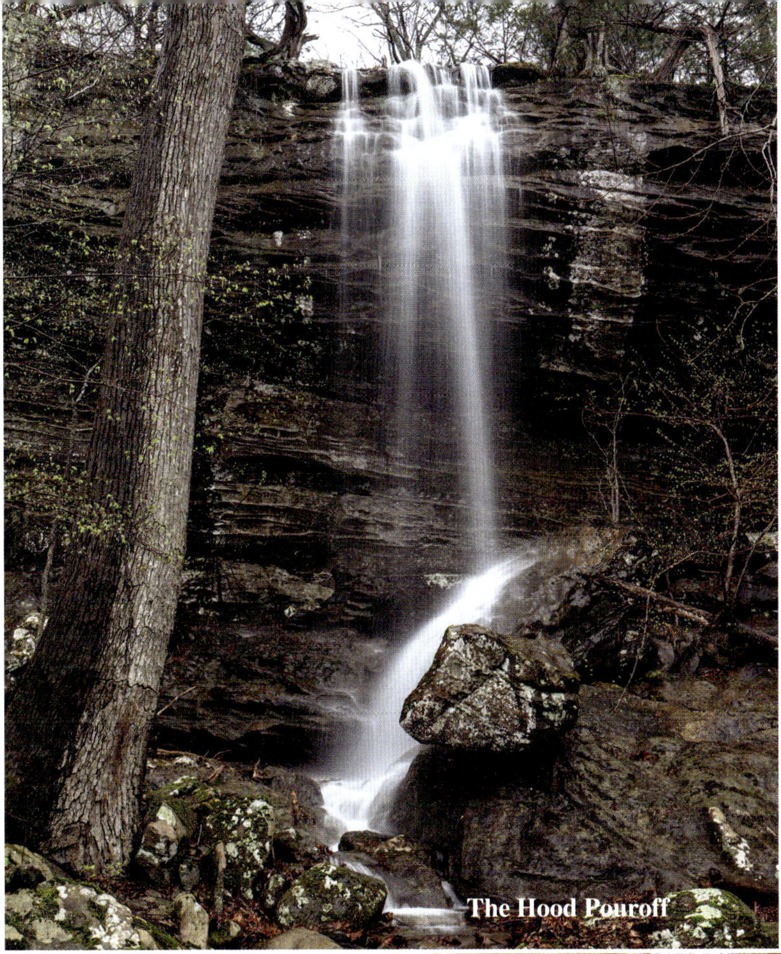

The Hood Pouroff

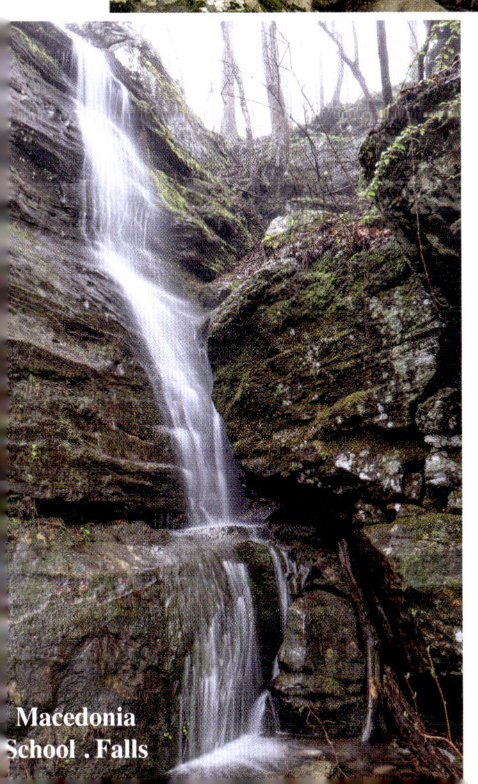

Macedonia School . Falls

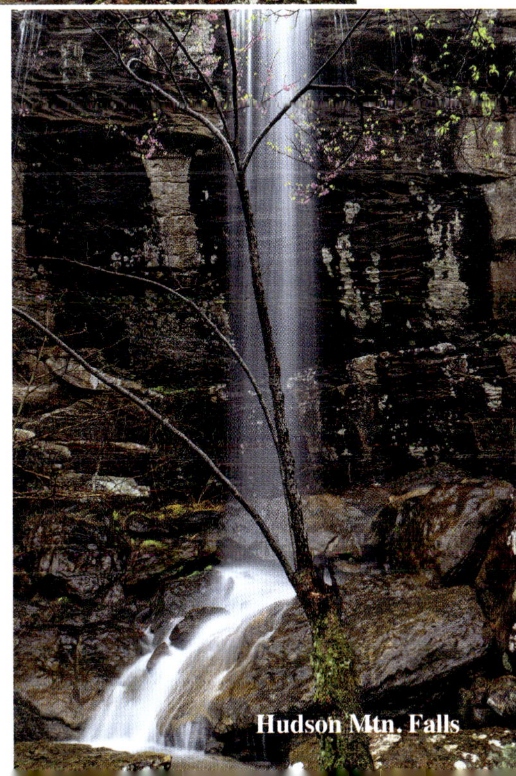

Hudson Mtn. Falls

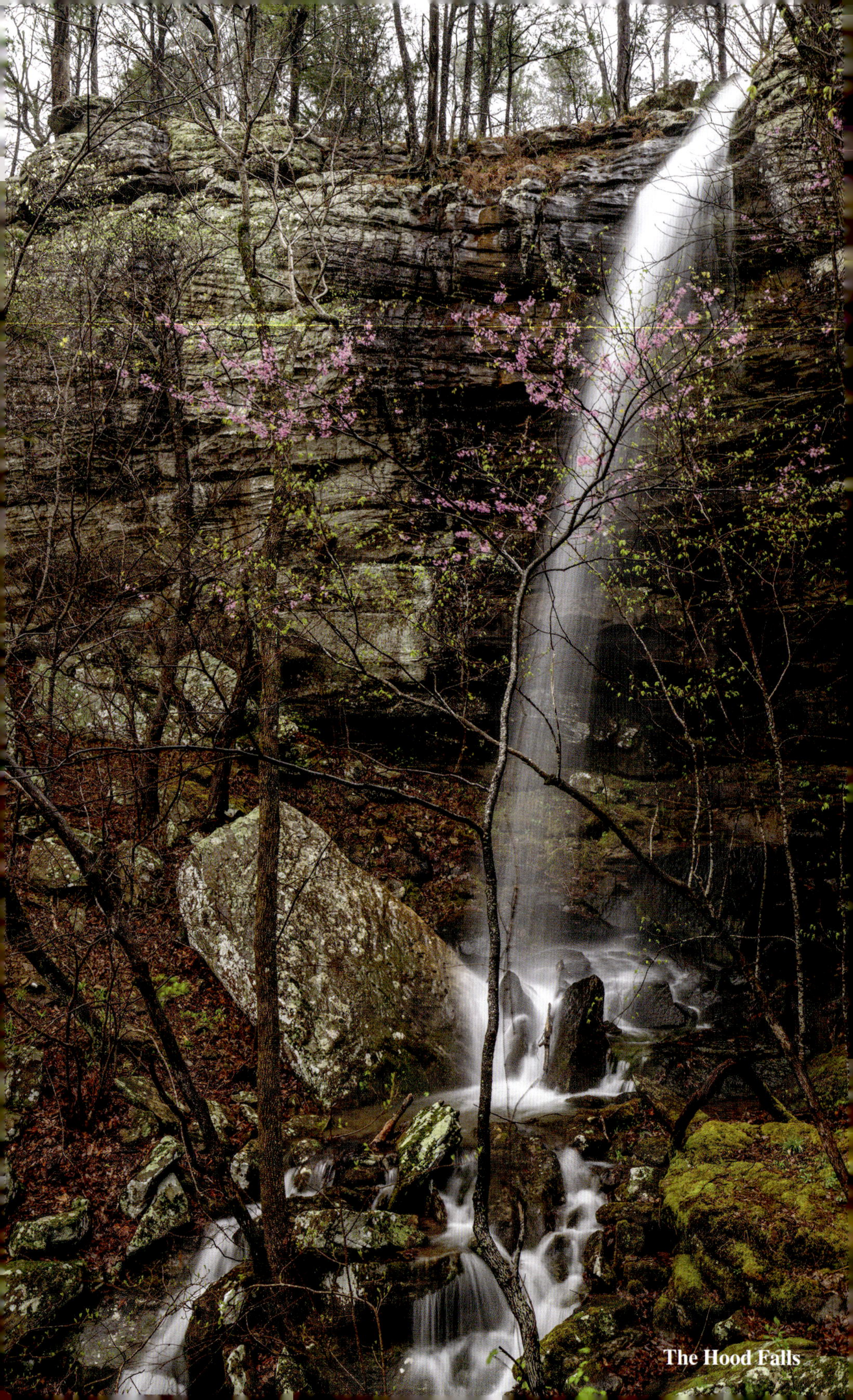

The Hood Falls

Dogwood Falls – 37′

1.2 miles roundtrip, medium bushwhack, GPS recommended

GPS **35.84978, -92.98455**

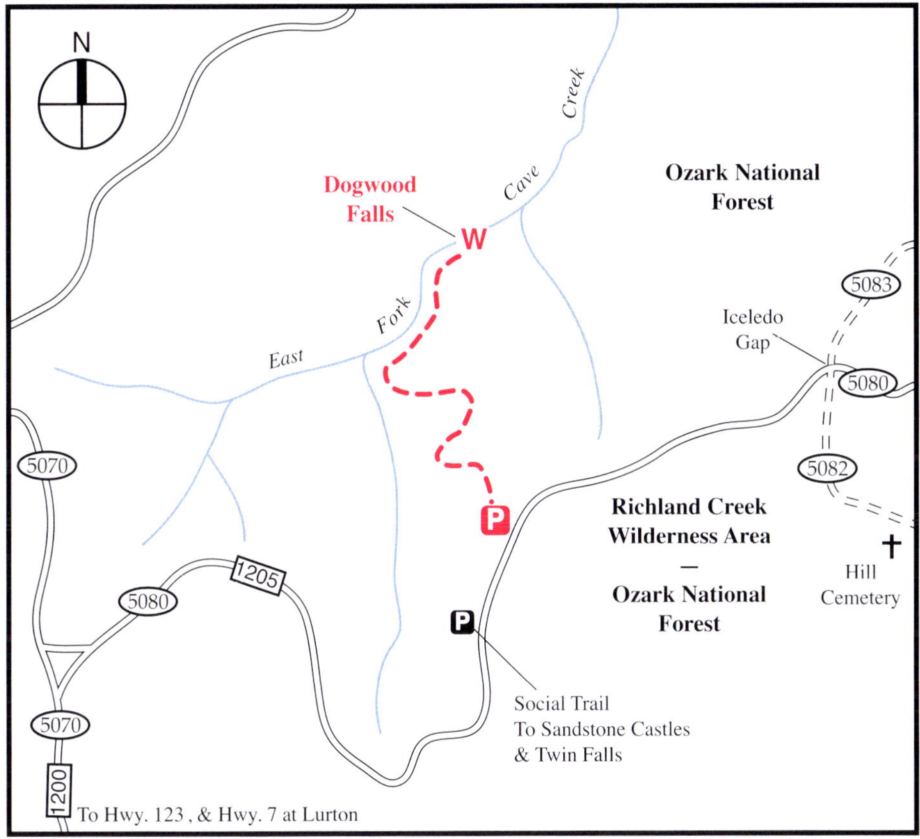

DOGWOOD FALLS. There are many dogwood trees growing at the base of waterfalls in the Ozarks, but for some reason this one is especially pleasing. I'm not sure if dogwood trees enjoy looking at waterfalls, or they simply want a constant drink!

Take Hwy. 123 east out of Lurton (located on Hwy. 7 north of Pelsor and south of Cowell). Go 1.5 miles and TURN RIGHT onto CR#5070/FR#1200 (paved, then gravel). Go 6.8 miles and TURN RIGHT onto CR#5080/FR#1205. Go 1.1 and PARK on the left side of the road, under a powerline (**35.84547, -92.98319**). If coming from the other direction, take CR#5080/FR#1205 north from Richland Creek Campground and go .4 mile past Iceledo Gap and PARK on the right.

Head off into the woods to your left, under the powerline, and then DOWN the hill. There is no trail, just a steep hill between you and the waterfall. Once you get to the creek at the bottom of this hill TURN RIGHT and follow the creek downhill. That will lead you to the top of **Dogwood Falls** at .6.

Emergency contact: Newton County Sheriff, 870–446–5124 Dogs are OK.

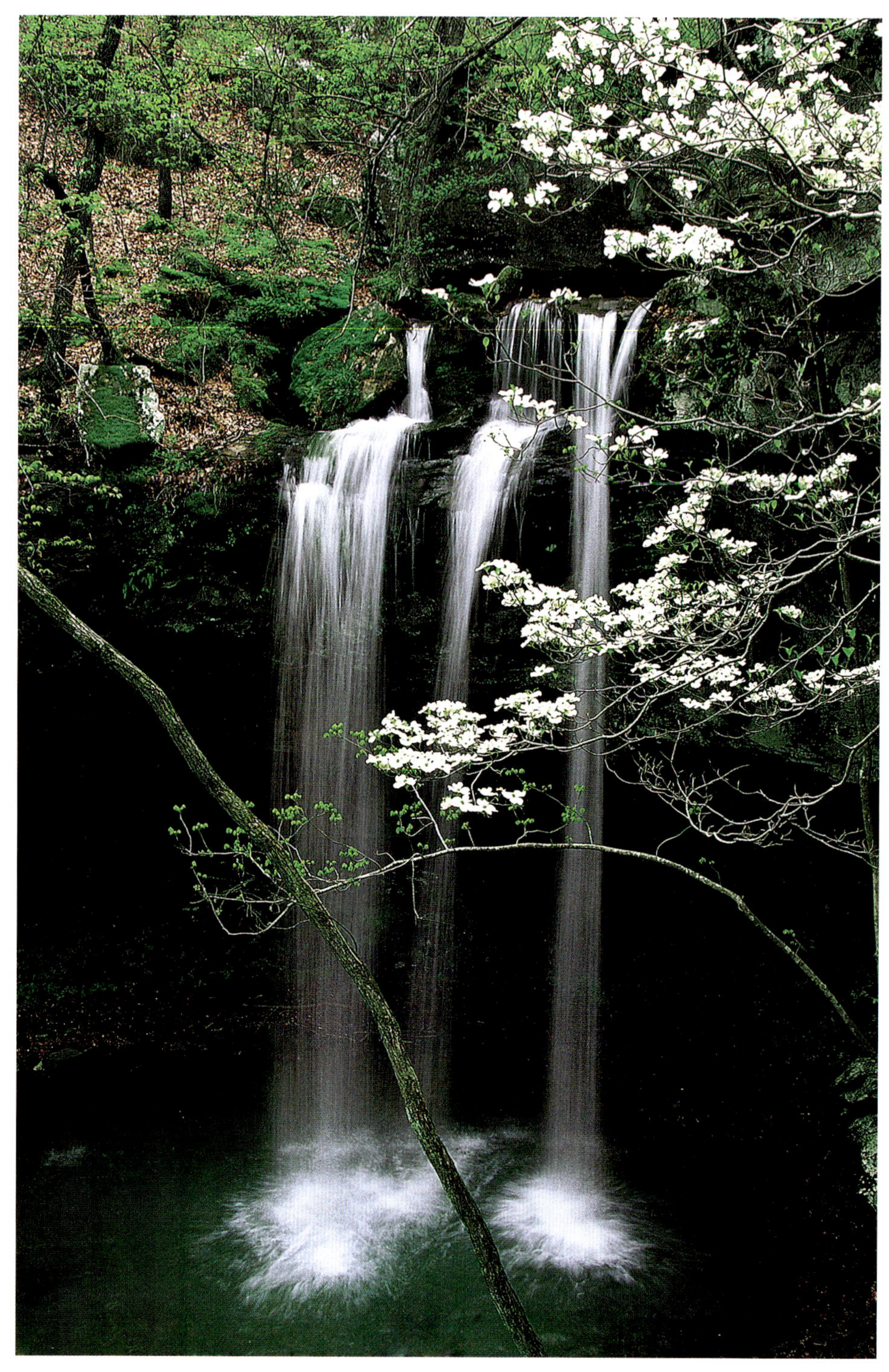

Dogwood Falls

Twin Falls of Richland – 17′/19′

3.8 miles roundtrip, difficult bushwhack, GPS recommended
GPS **35.80582, -92.96407**

Richland Falls – 8′

4.8 roundtrip total, difficult bushwhack, GPS recommended
GPS **35.80085, -92.96015**

Hamilton Falls – 12′

4.8 miles roundtrip, difficult bushwhack, GPS recommended
GPS **35.81188, -92.96397**

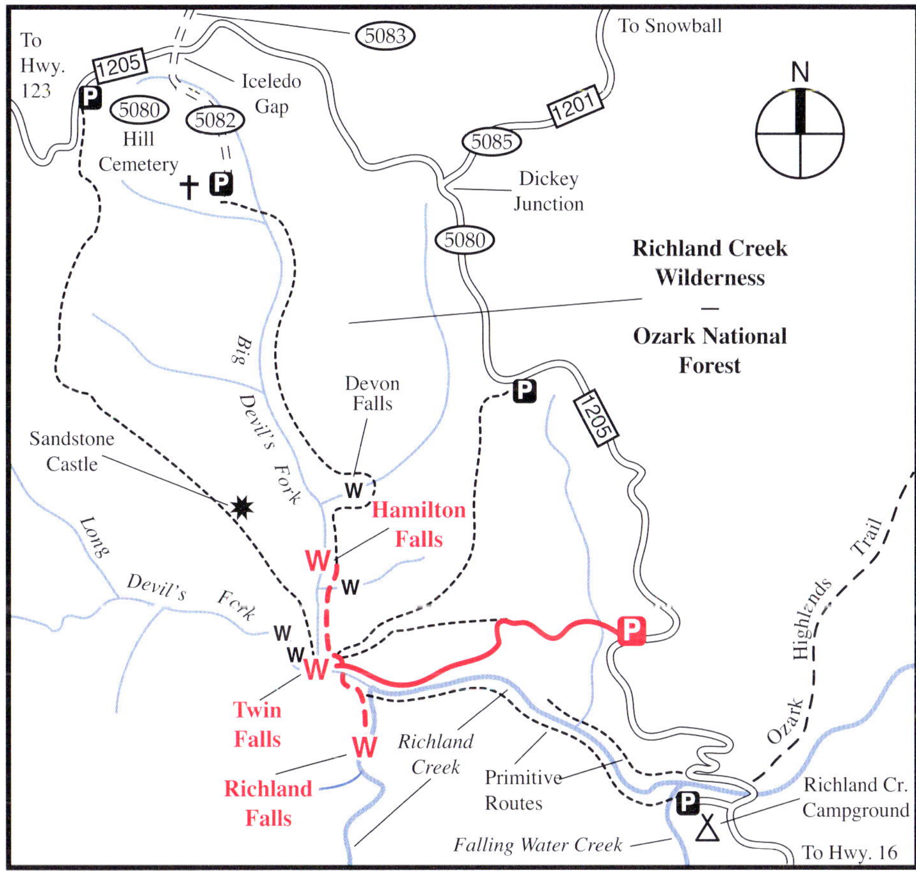

TWIN FALLS/RICHLAND FALLS/HAMILTON FALLS. The Richland Creek Wilderness area is rich with waterfalls and tumbling cascades—you will find them in nearly every drainage no matter how small. **Twin Falls of Richland** (aka Twin Falls of Devil's Fork) is one of the most classic and beautiful of all Ozark waterfalls. There are no official trails in this wilderness area, but there are several different bushwhack routes and social trails to get to it—some of those are marked on the map above.

Here's my favorite shortest and most direct route to **Twin Falls** (3.8 miles roundtrip, moderate to difficult social trail). Take Hwy. 123 east out of Lurton (located on Hwy. 7 north of Pelsor and south of Cowell). Go 1.5 miles and TURN RIGHT onto CR#5070/FR#1200 (paved, then gravel). Go 6.8 miles and TURN RIGHT onto CR#5080/FR#1205 at the "Road Triangle Intersection.*" Go 6.5 miles (past Iceledo Gap and Dickey Junction) and PARK on the RIGHT at **(35.80759, -92.93937)**, the RED park symbol.

A well-used social trail heads into the woods and drops down the hill at a pretty good clip, down to and across a creek, and then heads straight UP the hill on the other side. It eventually levels out on an old road, curves around to the right and then back to the left.

At about .6 be on the lookout for a trail intersection (old road trace/social trail). IF the rivers are flooded (or you want to go visit **Hamilton Falls** first), then you probably should follow this upper trail (small black dotted line on the map) as it stays up high before eventually dropping down into the Big Devil's Fork drainage just above Twin Falls—you don't have to cross any big flooded creeks this route, although it may be less traveled and therefore more difficult to follow.

The main trail at that intersection turns LEFT and heads downhill into the Richland Creek Valley—some really great leaf-off views overlooking the wilderness along the way. The trail eventually continues on down to the bottom of the hill where it lands on Devil's Fork just upstream from the point where it joins Richland Creek. TURN RIGHT and follow Devil's Fork upstream to **Twin Falls** at 1.9.

Hamilton Falls is a beautiful little waterfall that empties into an emerald pool. It's located about .5 mile up Big Devils Fork (the creek on the right) from Twin Falls. You can follow the creek or climb out of the little canyon and hike along the upper edge (probably a social trail both routes), and pass another waterfall along the way. Don Hamilton was one of the leaders of the Arkansas Wilderness Coalition in the early 1980's when we were fighting to establish wilderness areas. His influence and expertise helped us secure protection for many wilderness areas in Arkansas, including Richland Creek.

To get to **Richland Falls** (from Twin Falls) hike back downstream to where Devil's Fork meets Richland Creek. TURN RIGHT and continue to follow a trail upstream on Richland Creek. Just keep on going and you will come to Richland Falls before too long at 3.3. This falls is not too tall, but it spans the entire creek. It is tough to get a good photo of this falls because it is so wide. I like to isolate one section of it with a long lens instead of trying to get the entire thing in the picture.

If you are at Richland Falls when the water is low there will be many different waterfalls instead of just one wide one. When the weather is warm each of the individual falls can have a different water temperature, depending on how deep the pool is upstream that is feeding it. The sun will heat the shallow pools more than the deep ones. Also, there are some terrific exposed fossil beds to look for in low water upstream.

*To reach the other parking areas shown on the map (black park symbols) from the "Road Triangle Intersection"—continue .8 miles and PARK on the RIGHT at (**35.84185, -92.98433**) for the trail to Sandstone Castles (3.7 miles one way to Twin Falls). OR go 1.6 miles and TURN RIGHT (**35.84728, -92.97606**) to reach Hill Cemetery (bad road). OR go 4.5 miles and PARK on the right (**35.82568, -92.94734**) for a pretty good ridgetop social trail down to the Falls. OR go 8.3 miles to Richland Creek Campground (**35.79648, -92.93044**) and hike upstream to the falls (quite scenic and a wonderful summer route, but don't attempt if the rivers are flooded since it requires two river crossings!).

Emergency contact: Newton County Sheriff, 870–446–5124 Dogs are OK.

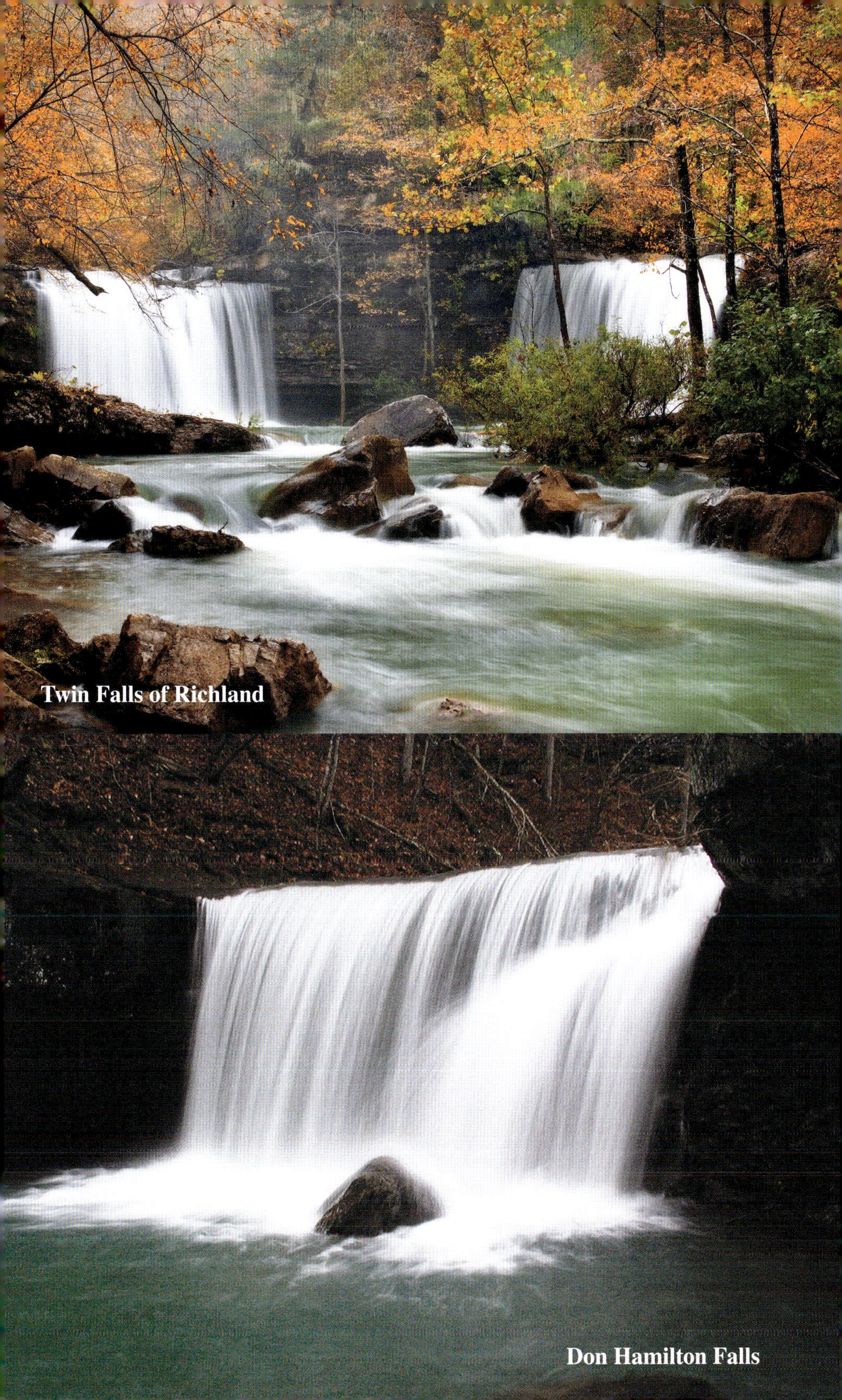
Twin Falls of Richland

Don Hamilton Falls

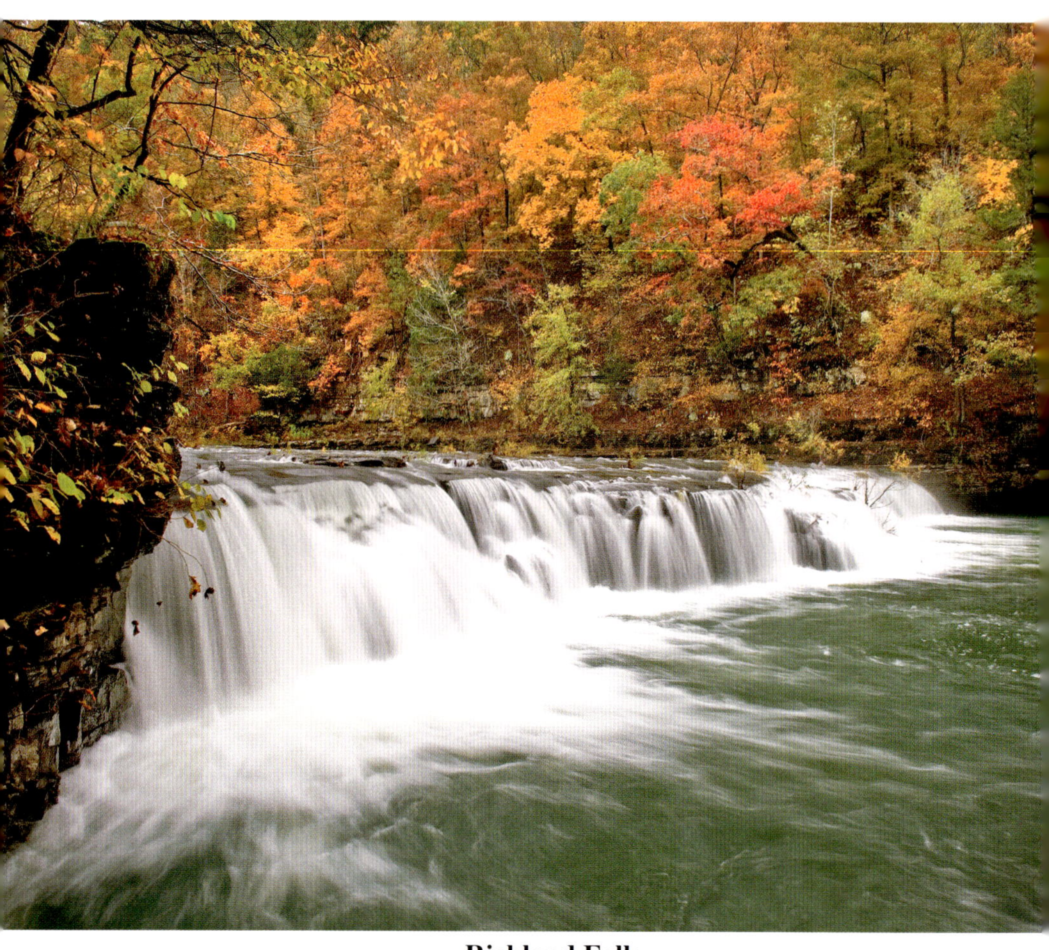

Richland Falls

Falling Water Falls – 10′

View from car, GPS not needed

GPS **35.72195, -92.94940**

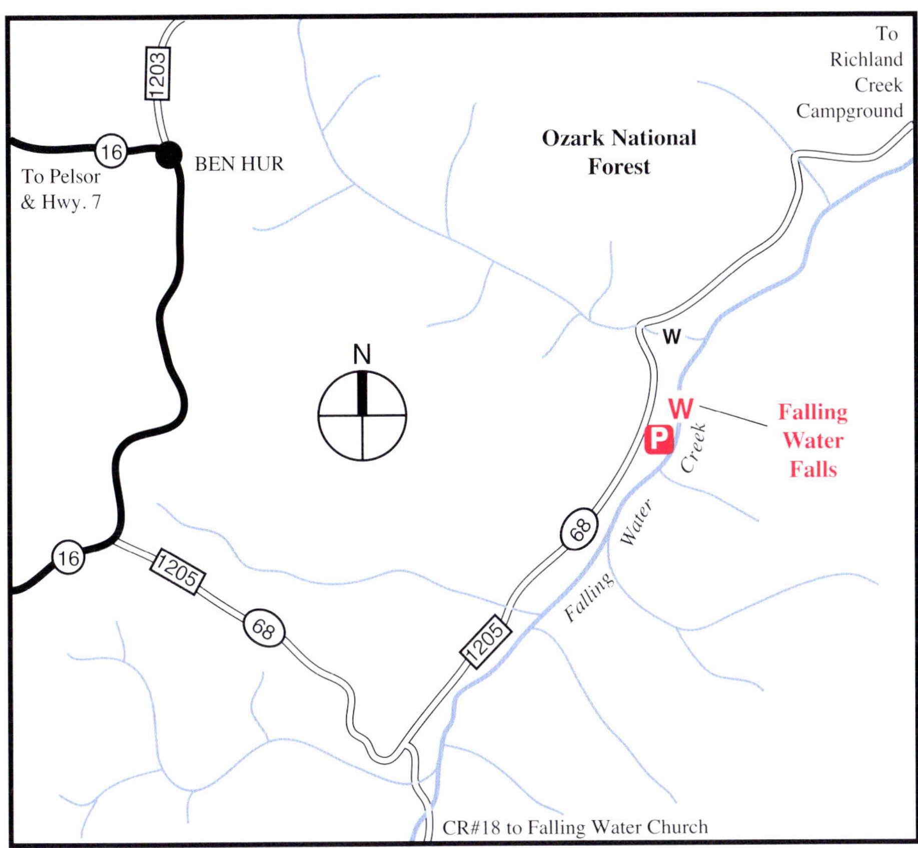

FALLING WATER FALLS. Here is a scenic waterfall right next to the road that is also a terrific swimming hole. I've even seen a baptism take place there. And to see what else goes on there see page 104 in my ***Arkansas Spring*** picture book.

To get to the falls, take Hwy. 16 east from Pelsor (on Hwy. 7 between Russellville and Jasper). Go about nine miles to Ben Hur (past the parking area for Kings Bluff Falls), then continue past Ben Hur about a mile and TURN LEFT onto FR#1205/CR#68 (gravel). Go 2.3 miles and PARK **(35.72151, -92.94960)**. To get to Falling Water Falls from Richland Creek Campground, head south on FR#1205 and follow it for about 7 miles and the falls will be on the left.

You may also want to visit the other waterfalls that are downstream—see the next few pages for photos and descriptions.

Emergency contact: Pope County Sheriff, 479–967–9300. Dogs are OK.

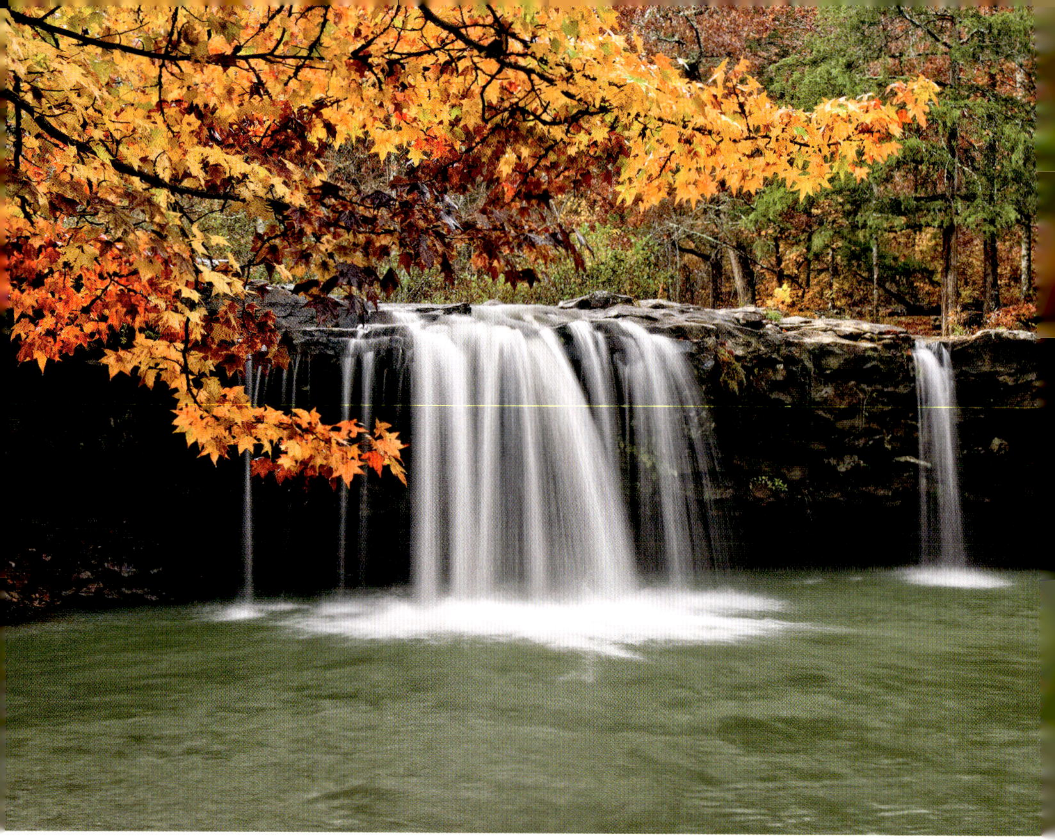

Falling Water Falls (typical flow above, and during high water below)

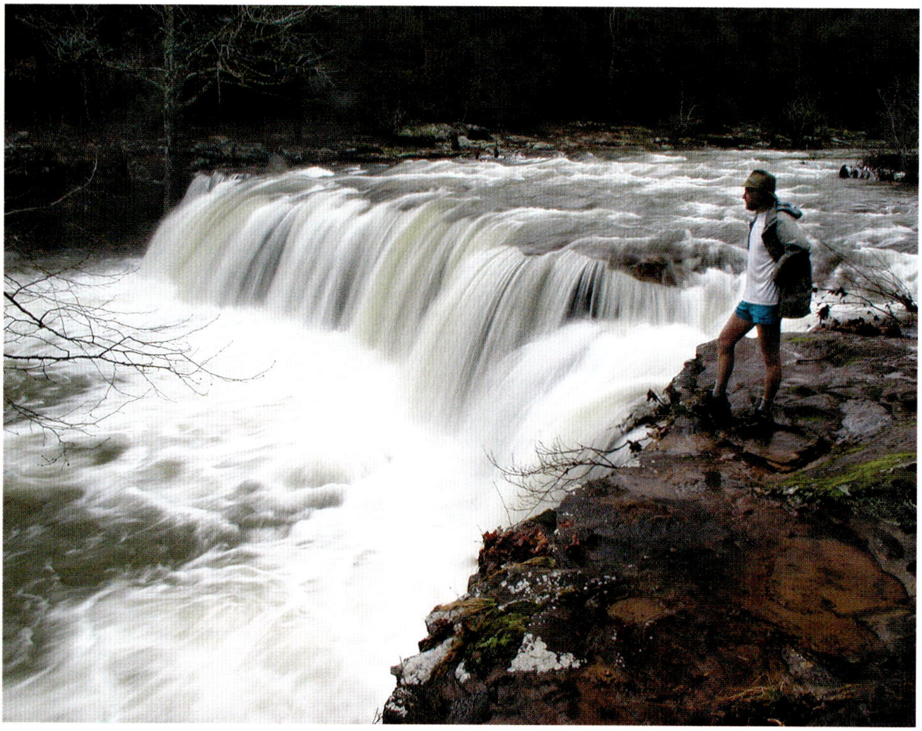

Horsetail Falls (2) – 31′/70′

1.1 mile roundtrip, medium social trail, GPS helpful GPS **35.75662, -92.94120**

Intersection Falls –31′

.1 mile roundtrip, easy GPS **35.75821,92.93647**

Six Finger Falls – 6′

100 feet from road GPS **35.76193, -92.93753**

Fuzzybutt Falls –16′

2.0 mile roundtrip, easy hike, GPS helpful GPS **35.76368, -92.93839**

Keefe Falls – 78′

1.0 mile roundtrip, easy social trail, GPS helpful GPS **35.76548, -92.92609**

Splashdown Falls – 37′

1.3 mile, roundtrip, medium bushwhack GPS **35.76247, -92.92499**

Calypso Falls – 11′

1.25 mile roundtrip, medium bushwhack GPS **35.76303, -92.92599**

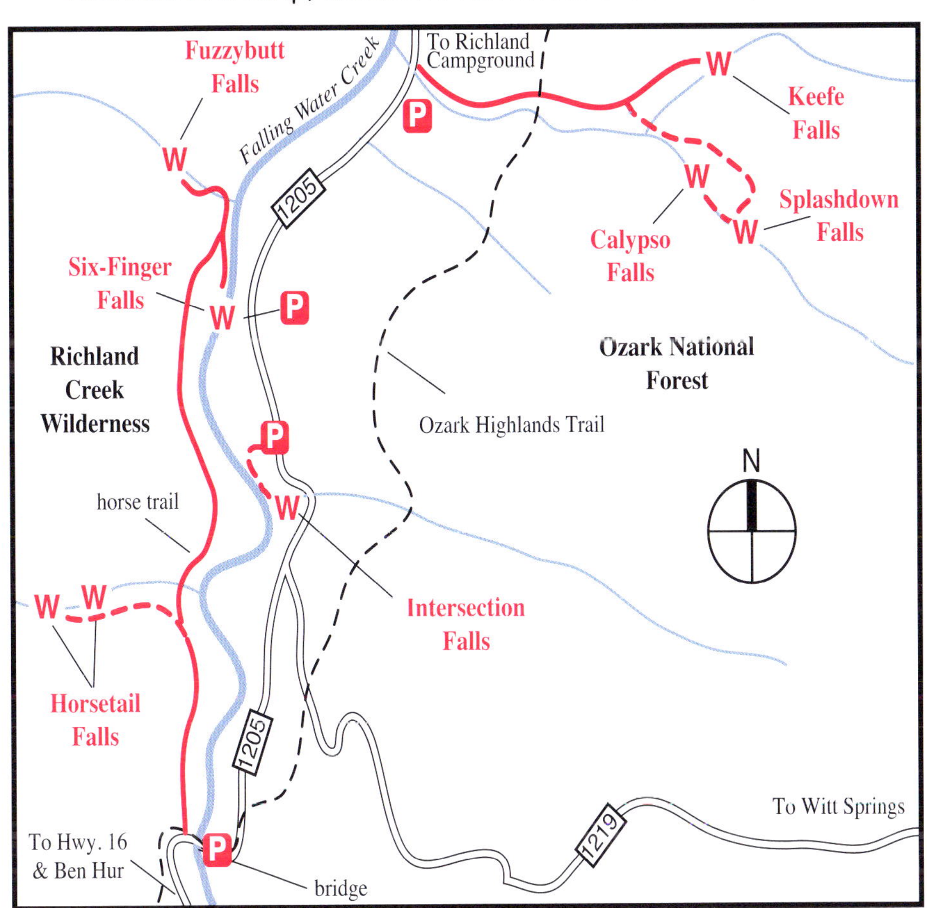

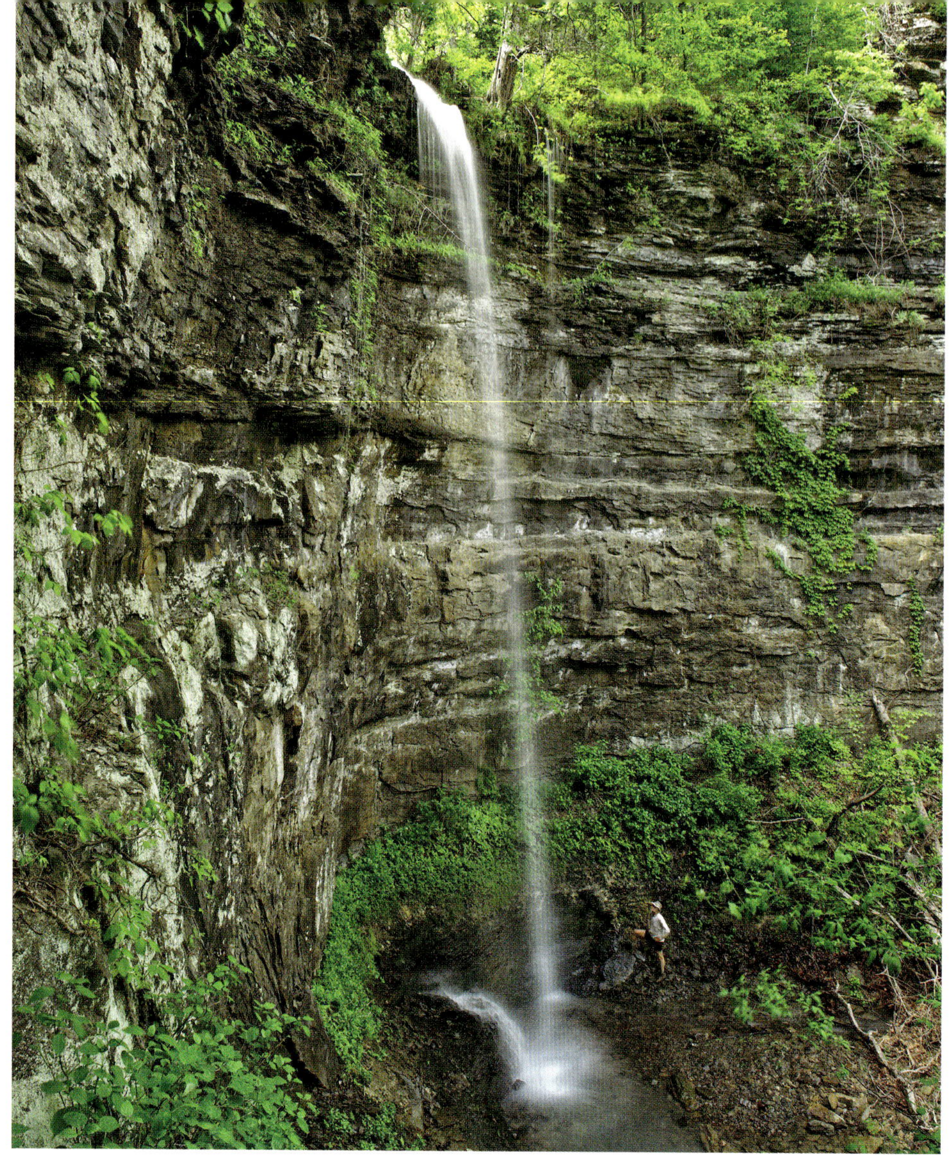

Horsetail Falls

FALLING WATER ROAD AREA WATERFALLS. You can get to eight different waterfalls along a short stretch of road next to Falling Water Creek (plus MORE after these!). This river runs along the edge of the Richland Creek Wilderness area, which contains many great waterfalls and other scenic areas. Further exploration on your part may reveal lots of neat stuff, including more waterfalls!

HORSETAIL FALLS. To get to the first falls (Horsetail), take Hwy. 16 east from Pelsor (on Hwy. 7 between Russellville and Jasper). Go about nine miles to Ben Hur (past the parking area for Kings Bluff Falls), then continue past Ben Hur about a mile and TURN LEFT onto FR#1205/CR#68 (gravel—Richland Campground sign). Follow this road 5.2 miles (from the highway) and park at the bridge that crosses Falling Water Creek **(35.75254, -92.93815)**—this bridge is **2.9 miles past Falling Water Falls.** Find the horse trail on the west side of the bridge and follow it downstream to the first creek crossing (easy hike, small waterfall there). Leave the horse trail to the LEFT and bushwhack up

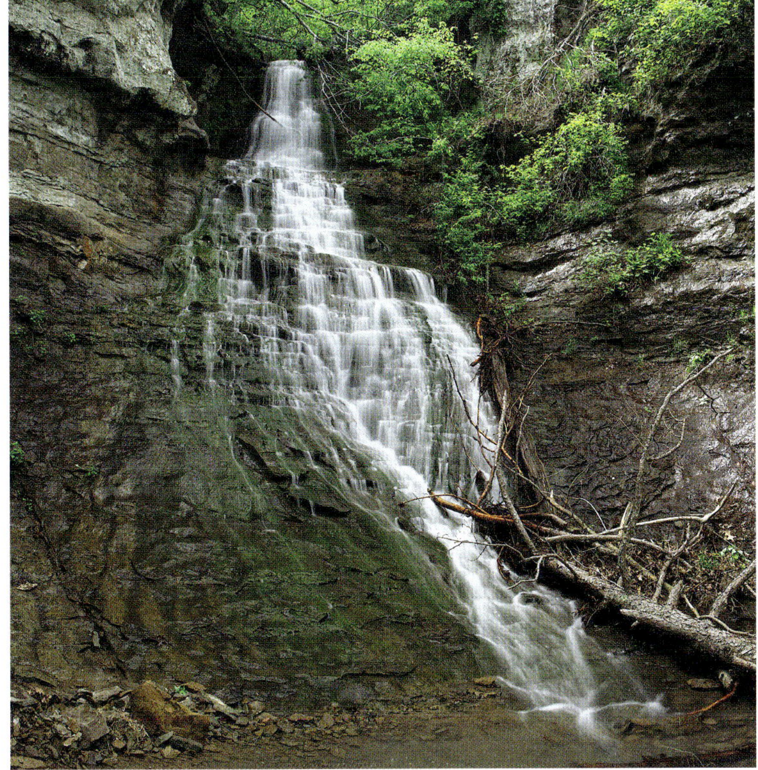

Upper Horsetail Falls

the small stream until you come to **Horsetail Falls**. Continue *UP* the left side of the falls (difficult, steep scramble), and you will come to Upper Horsetail Falls.

FUZZYBUTT FALLS. The same horse trail provides access to the famous Fuzzybutt Falls (instead of having to wade the river). Simply continue on the horse trail from the bridge and it will come right to the mouth of a small box canyon at 1.0—TURN LEFT and follow the canyon 200' to Fuzzybutt. 'Tis a magical, narrow canyon only a couple hundred feet long that is cut into layers of shale rock and ends at **Fuzzybutt Falls**. Known to locals as Box Canyon Falls, but feel free to make up your own name —what would you call it? You can also park along the road at Six Finger Falls and wade the creek to reach this waterfall, but this can be dangerous if the river is high.

INTERSECTION FALLS. From the bridge, continue on the forest road .4 mile to the intersection with FR#1219, then go STRAIGHT another couple of hundred yards on the forest road past the sharp curve and PARK on the left side of the road **(35.75888, -92.93632)**. Bushwhack straight out through the woods on the left and to Falling Water Creek, then hike upstream 100 yards to the base of the falls—this is a really neat area but the rocks are slick!

SIX FINGER FALLS. Continue on FR#1205 for another couple of hundred yards to a pulloff and sign board on the LEFT and PARK **(35.76172, -92.93703)**. **Six Finger Falls** will be down in front of you on the creek through the trees—it's a beautiful cascade with lots of character!

KEEFE FALLS. Drive down the road another quarter mile (.6 from the intersection with FR#1219) to where a creek comes in from the right and goes under the road—PARK where you can **(35.76538, -92.93341)**. You can also get to this spot from Richland Creek Campground—go south on FR#1205 for 2.8 miles and PARK at the stream crossing.

There is a well-worn social trail from the road that follows the creek upstream, across

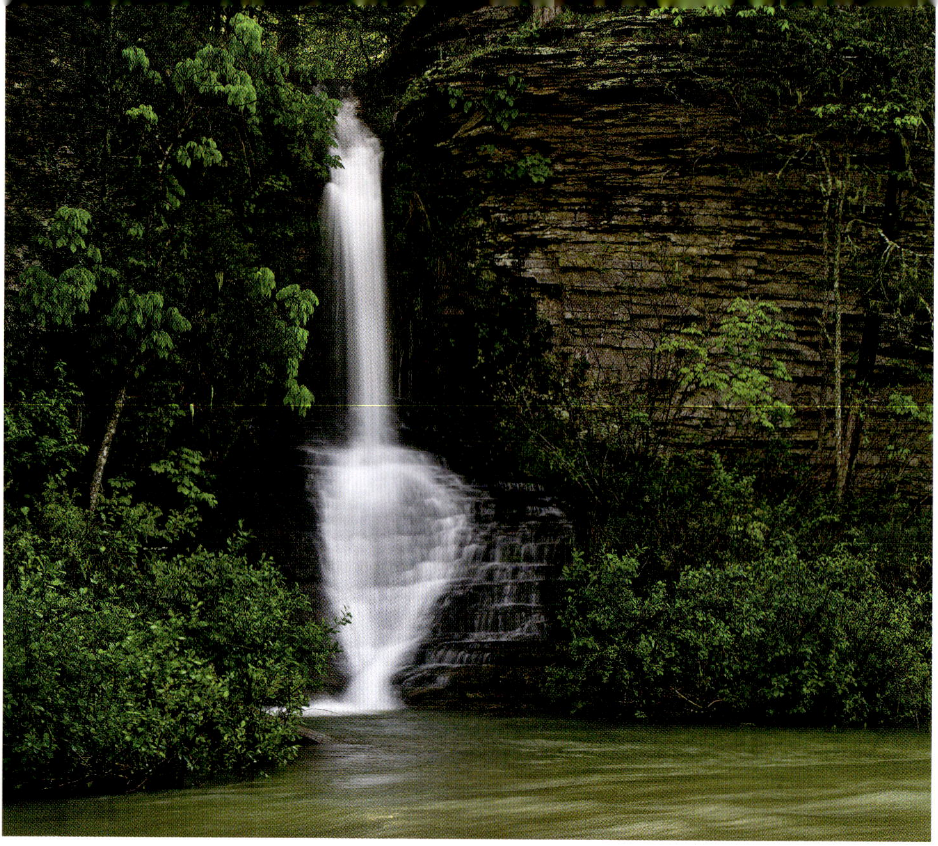

Intersection Falls (above), **Six Finger Falls** (below)

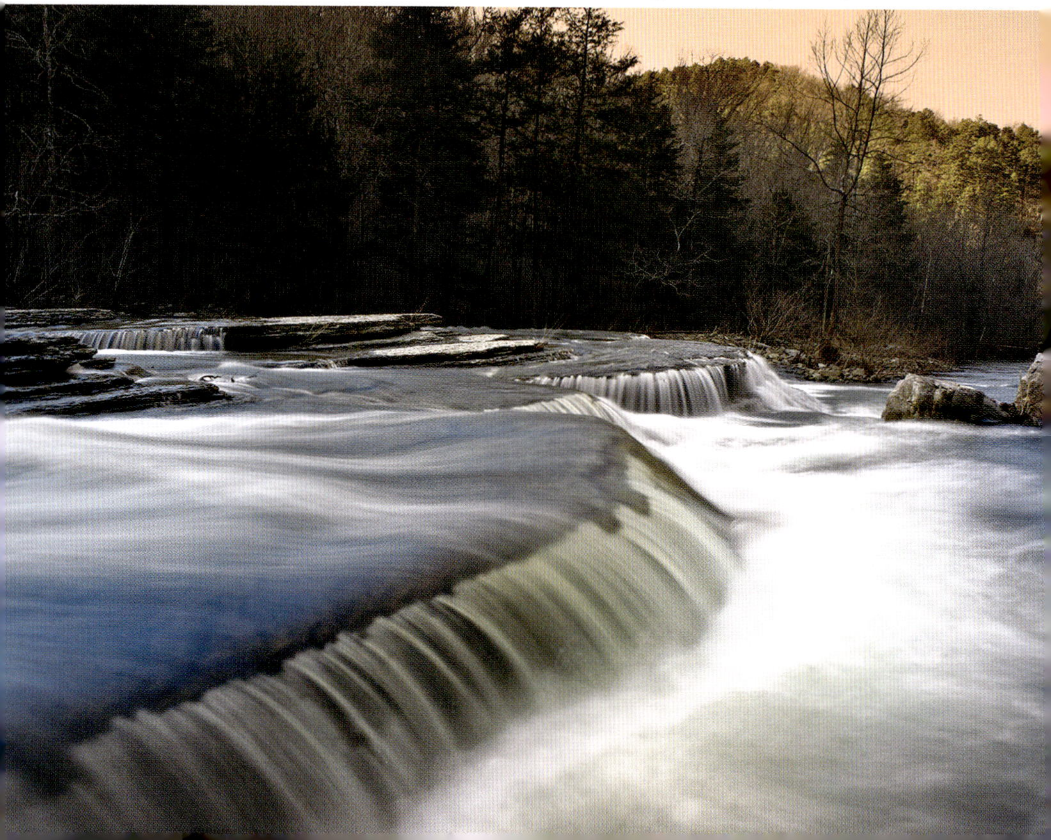

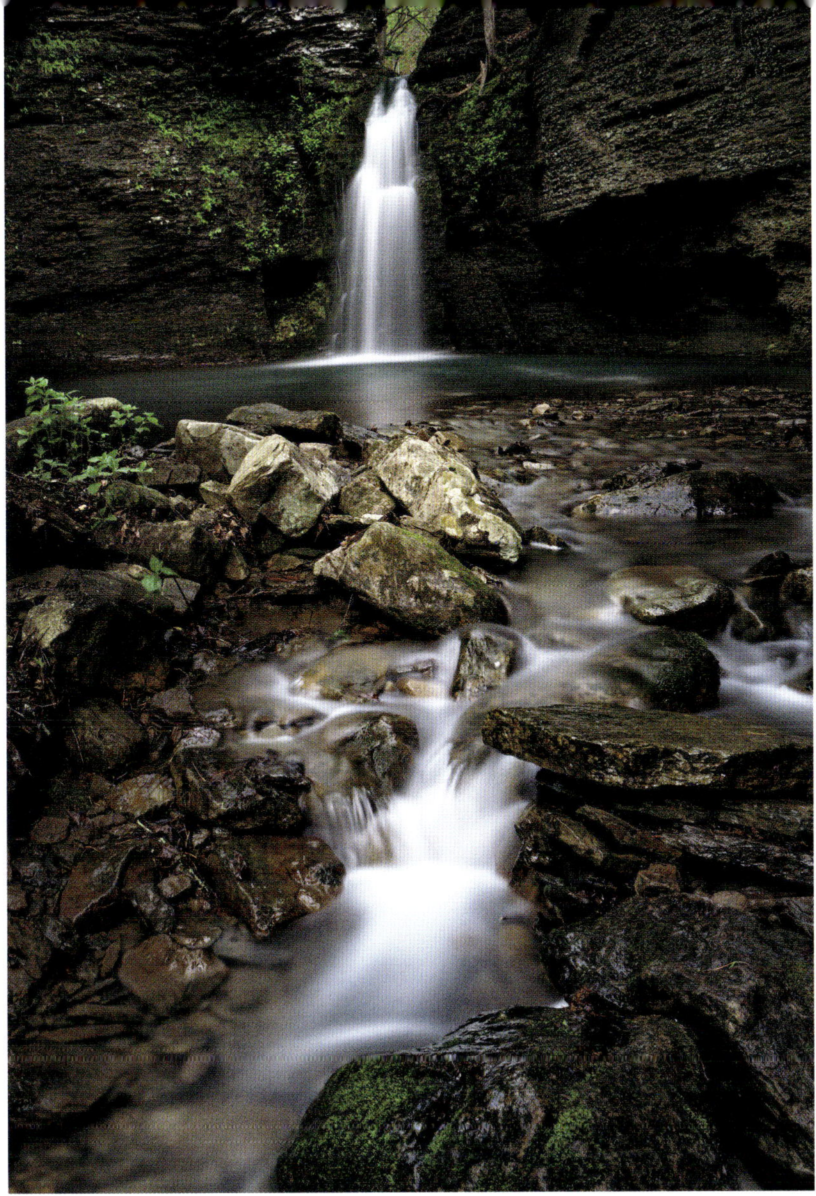

Fuzzybutt Falls

the Ozark Highlands Trail (past a fork that goes to the left), and then on up to **Keefe Falls** at .5. The lower areas of this bluff are made up of many layers of shale rock, but the upper layers are more traditional solid layers.

SPLASHDOWN & CALYPSO FALLS. From **Keefe Falls** head back downstream and take the left fork of the creek, following a trail UP out of the creekbed to the left, up to the base of the big bluff (a bit of a climb but worth it). Follow the bluff up into the hollow and then drop down to **Splashdown Falls**—a delightful SSS! From there you can either follow the canyon back downstream at creek level (pretty tough going), or climb back up to the base of the bluff and head back down until you can drop down to **Calypso Falls**, another magical spot (named by Amy White and Brennen Nicole). You may need to return to the bluff for the hike out, or explore as you can downstream to the main creek.

Emergency contact: Searcy County Sheriff, 870–448–2340 Dogs are OK.

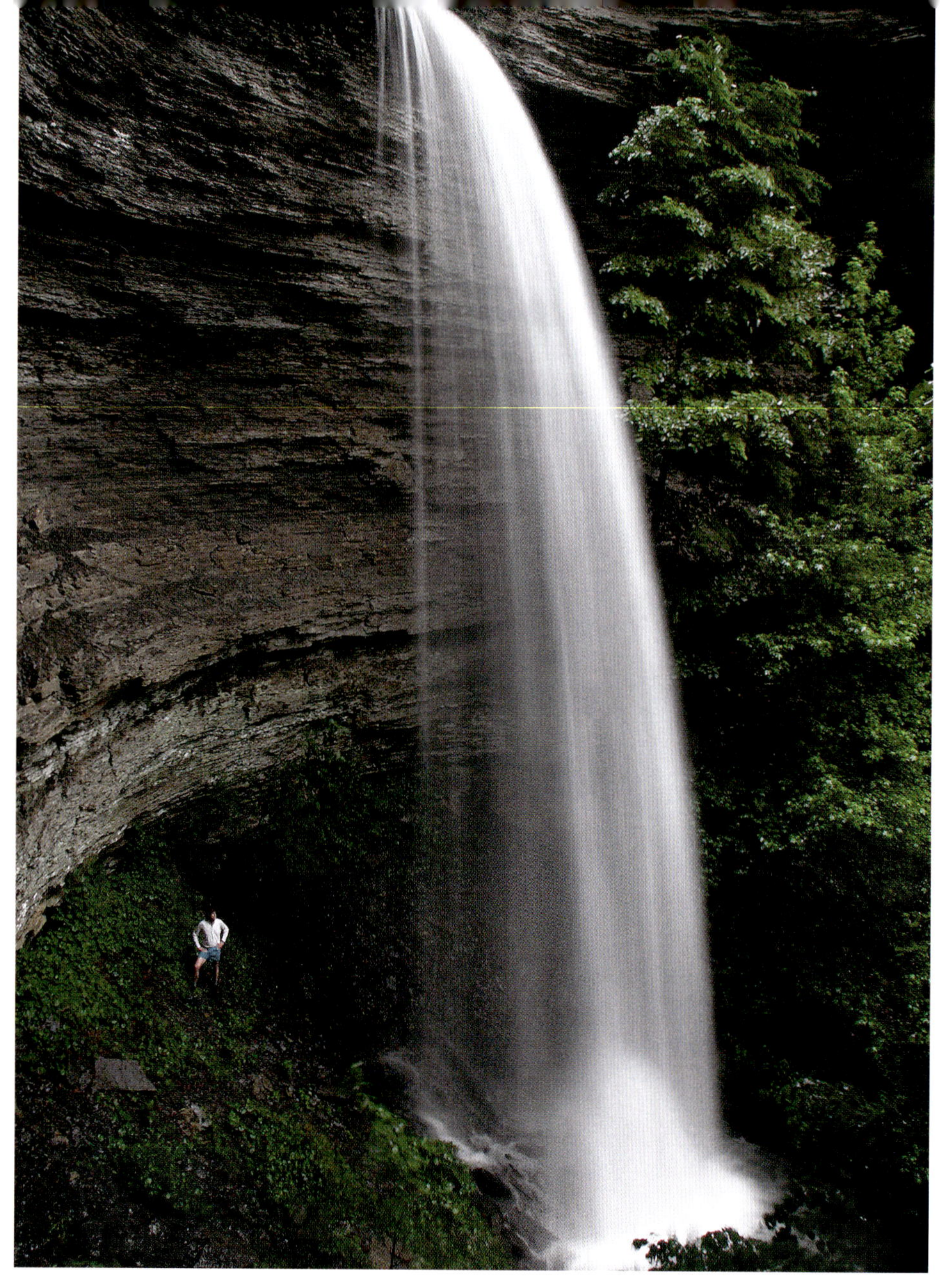

Terry Keefe Falls

Keefe Falls is named after one of the great waterfall hunters and outdoorsmen in Arkansas, in the Ozarks, Terry Keefe (R.I.P.). He took me to countless unknown waterfalls and other scenic places in the early years, and has always done so at a pretty good clip I might add. I can keep up a fast pace myself, but he has run off and left me a time or two. See also **Keefe Grotto** on page 396.

Emergency contact: Searcy County Sheriff, 870–448–2340 Dogs are OK.

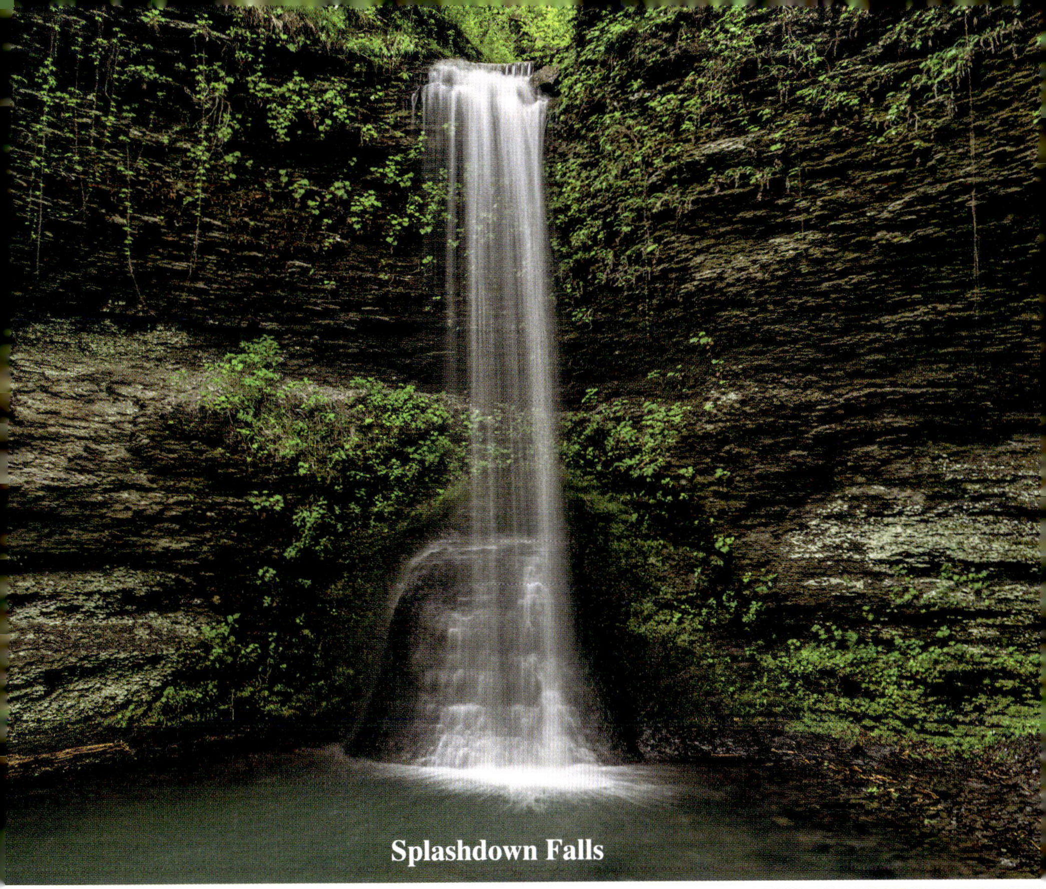

Splashdown Falls

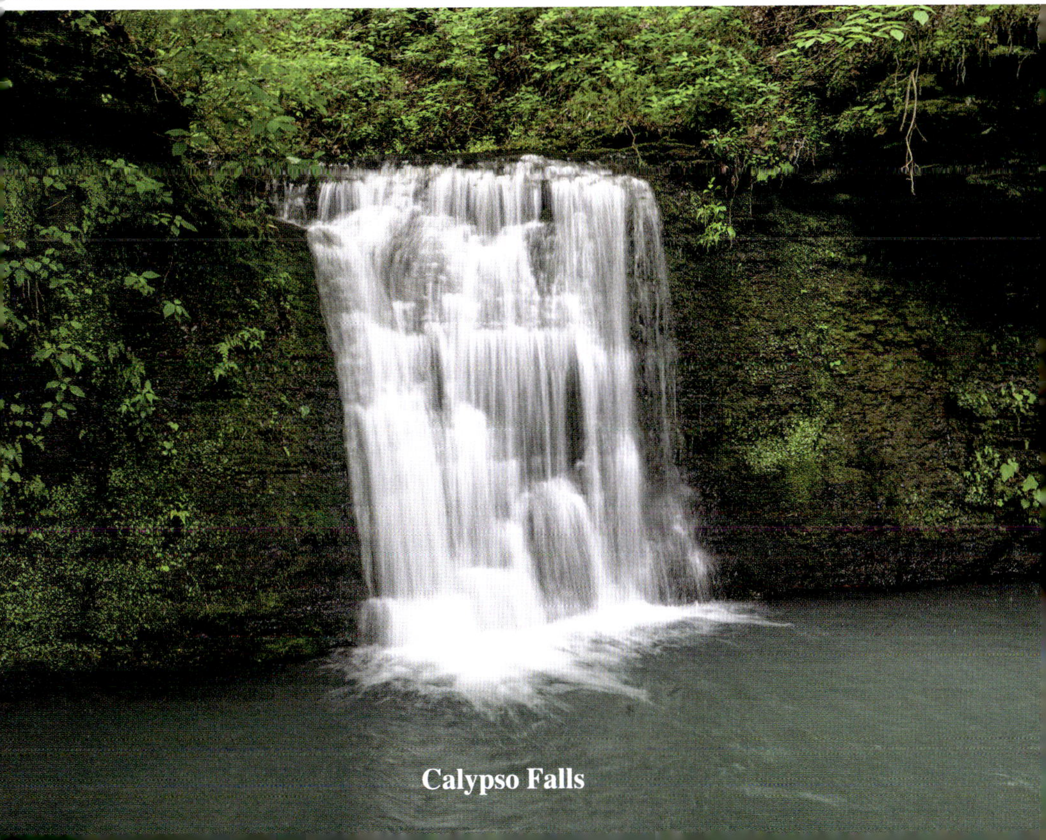

Calypso Falls

Hidden Falls Falling Water – 37′

.25 medium bushwhack GPS **35.77294, -92.92851**

Ripple Slide Falls – 45′

.4 medium bushwhack GPS **35.77579, -92.9292**

Lilly Falls (2) – 23-25′

.3 medium bushwhack GPS **35.77652, -92.92966**

Landslide Falls – 27′

.4 roundtrip, easy^{+} GPS **35.78139, -92.93173**

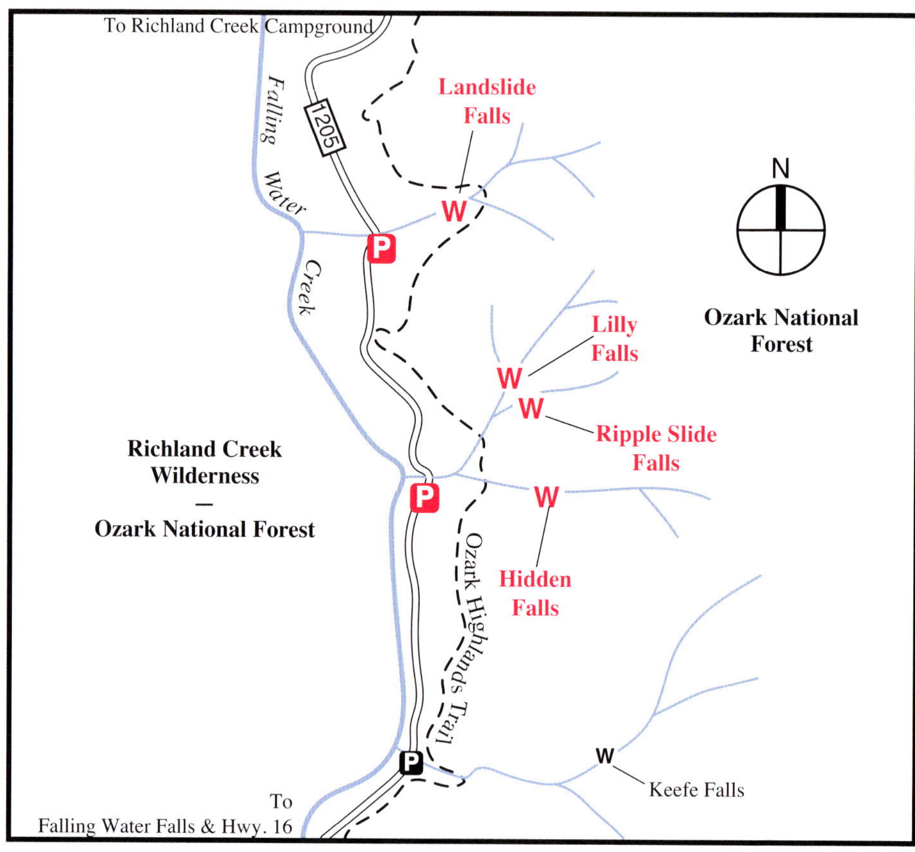

MORE FALLING WATER ROAD WATERFALLS. Here are still more waterfalls in side drainages along Falling Water Road past the popular Keefe Falls. There are no official trails to these but social trails probably have developed. All are pretty easy to reach from the road—although you might encounter some classic OZARK JUNGLE if visiting during the summertime!

From **Keefe Falls** continue on the road downstream .6 and park along the road near a creek crossing **(35.77348, -92.93273)**. Hike up the creek, take the right hand fork, cross the Ozark Highlands Trail, then continue up the creek to **Hidden Falls Falling Water**.

From there follow the terrain around to the LEFT and on up into the next drainage to **Ripple Slide Falls**.

Continue around to the left and up into the next drainage to **Lower Lily Falls**, then **Upper Lily Falls** just above—nice SSS.

Turn around and follow the creek downstream across the OHT and down to your car—total hike of about 1.0 mile.

To get to **Landslide Falls** drive another .6 and park at the edge of the big landslide **(35.78120, -92.93451)**. Follow a road on the right side of the slide next to the creek on up to **Landslide Falls** at .2.

Emergency contact: Searcy County Sheriff, 870–448–2340 Dogs are OK

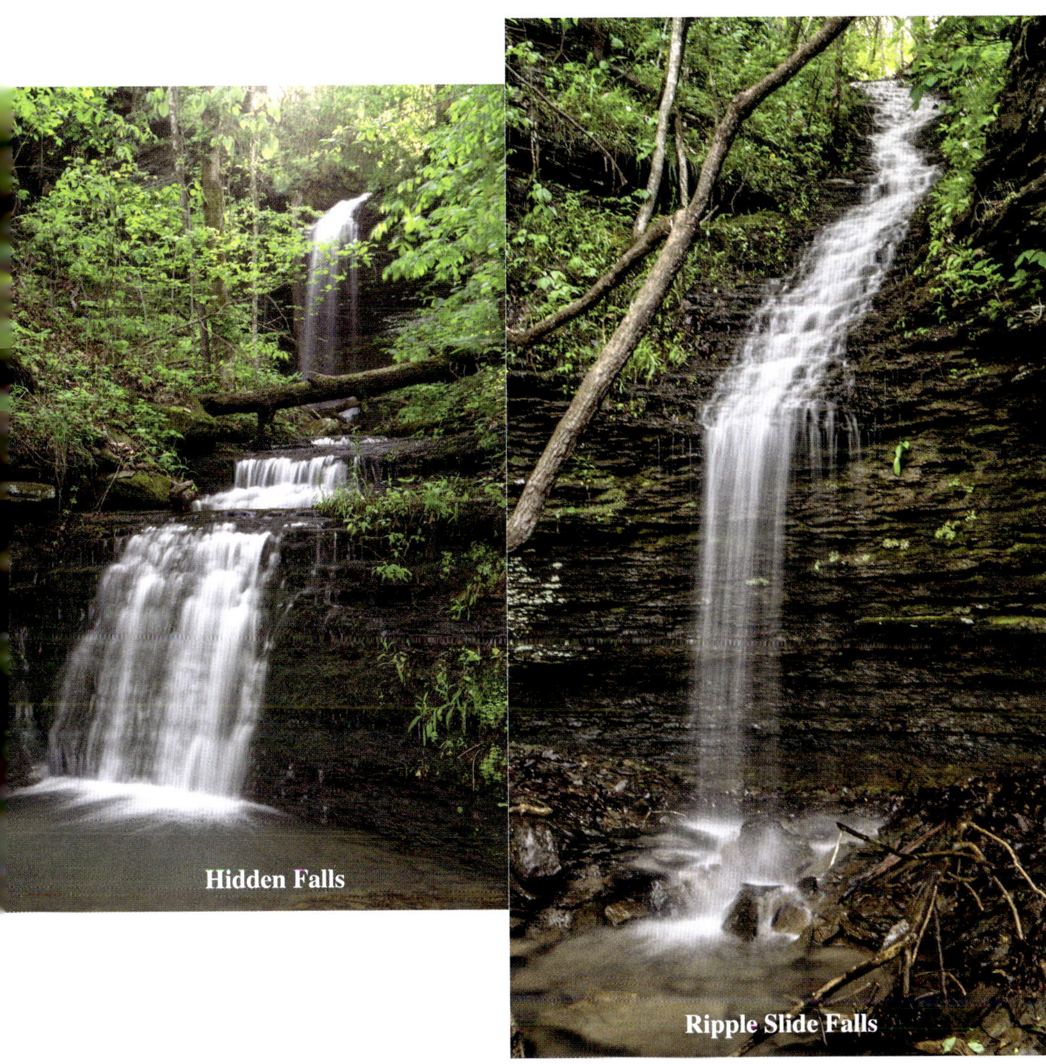

Hidden Falls

Ripple Slide Falls

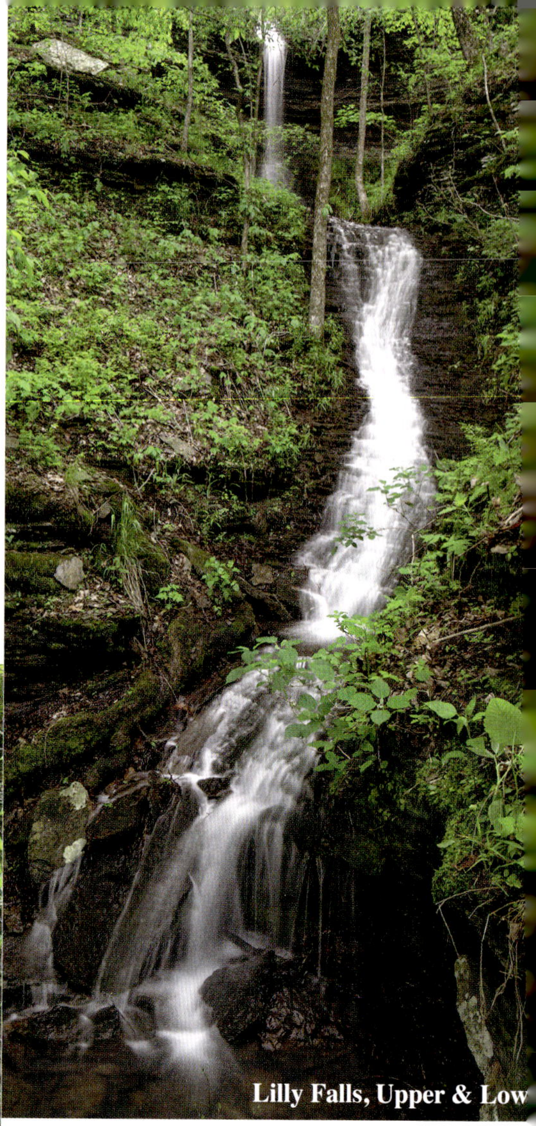

Lilly Falls, Upper & Low

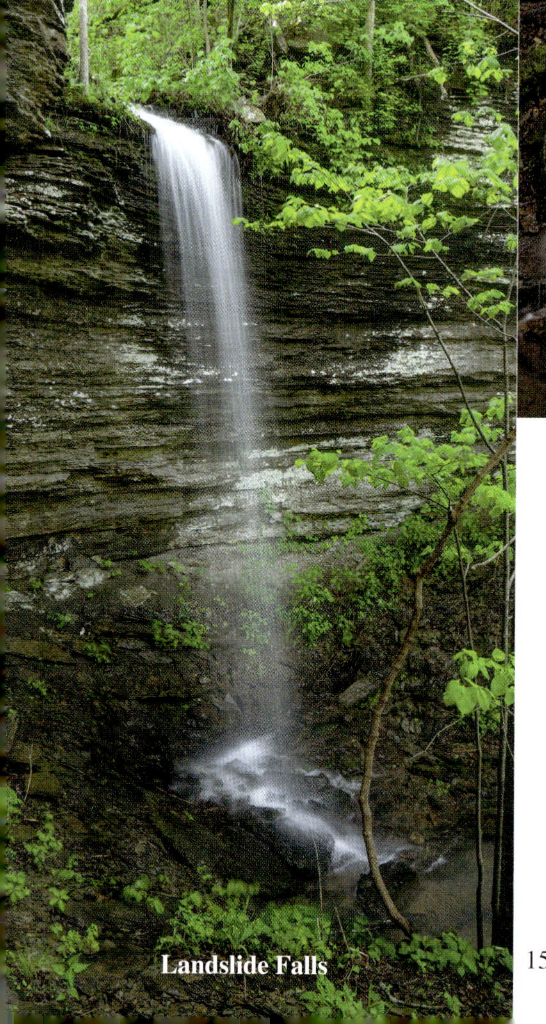

Landslide Falls

Rick Henry Falls (2) 21' & 32'+

1.0 mile roundtrip, GPS **35.78960, -92.92589**

Wild Hollow Falls – 47'+

1.6 miles medium, easy road/med bushwhack GPS **35.79813, -92.91338**

Wild & Scenic Grotto – 17'

1.6 miles, easy road/medium bushwhack GPS **35.79774, -92.91292**

Diehard Falls –

1.8 miles easy road, med/diff ♦ bushwhack GPS **35.79730, -92.91266**

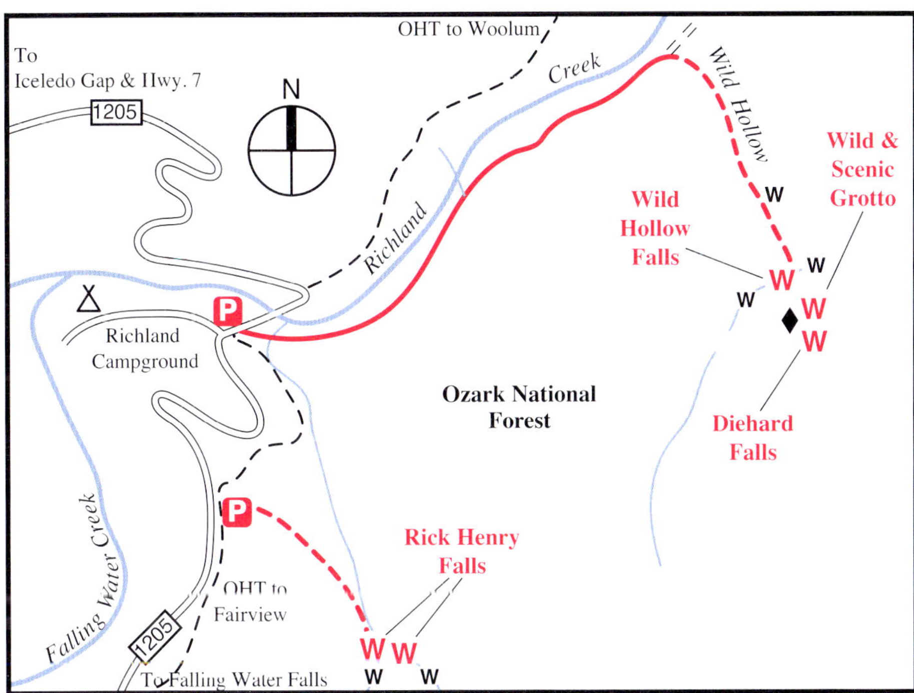

RICK HENRY FALLS. In 2014 Rick Henry was one of the first to explore, discover, and post pictures and directions to waterfalls and other places on his personal blog that was free for all to enjoy. Rick covered many of the waterfalls in this guidebook, then continued to expand his range and ended up finding and naming many hundreds more waterfalls—hundreds and ***hundreds*** more. When Rick died of cancer in 2022, one of his best hiking buddies (and probably a guy who has found more waterfalls than anyone, Daniel Few), named this pair of waterfalls after Rick, a fitting tribute to the man who created so many crazy waterfall hunters! (Rick's blog was still available online as of 2025 henry411.blogspot.com.) The last waterfall area he explored and documented was in 2020—Rick Henry Falls #804, on page 235).

Directions from **Landslide Falls** (previous pages), drive another 1.1 miles and PARK on the right **(35.79323, -92.93057)**, or 6.2 miles from Falling Water Falls, or .5 miles from Richland Campground. There's a bluff right in front of you—hike to the LEFT side of that bluff, and just follow the base of the bluff as it works into a drainage around to the right, to

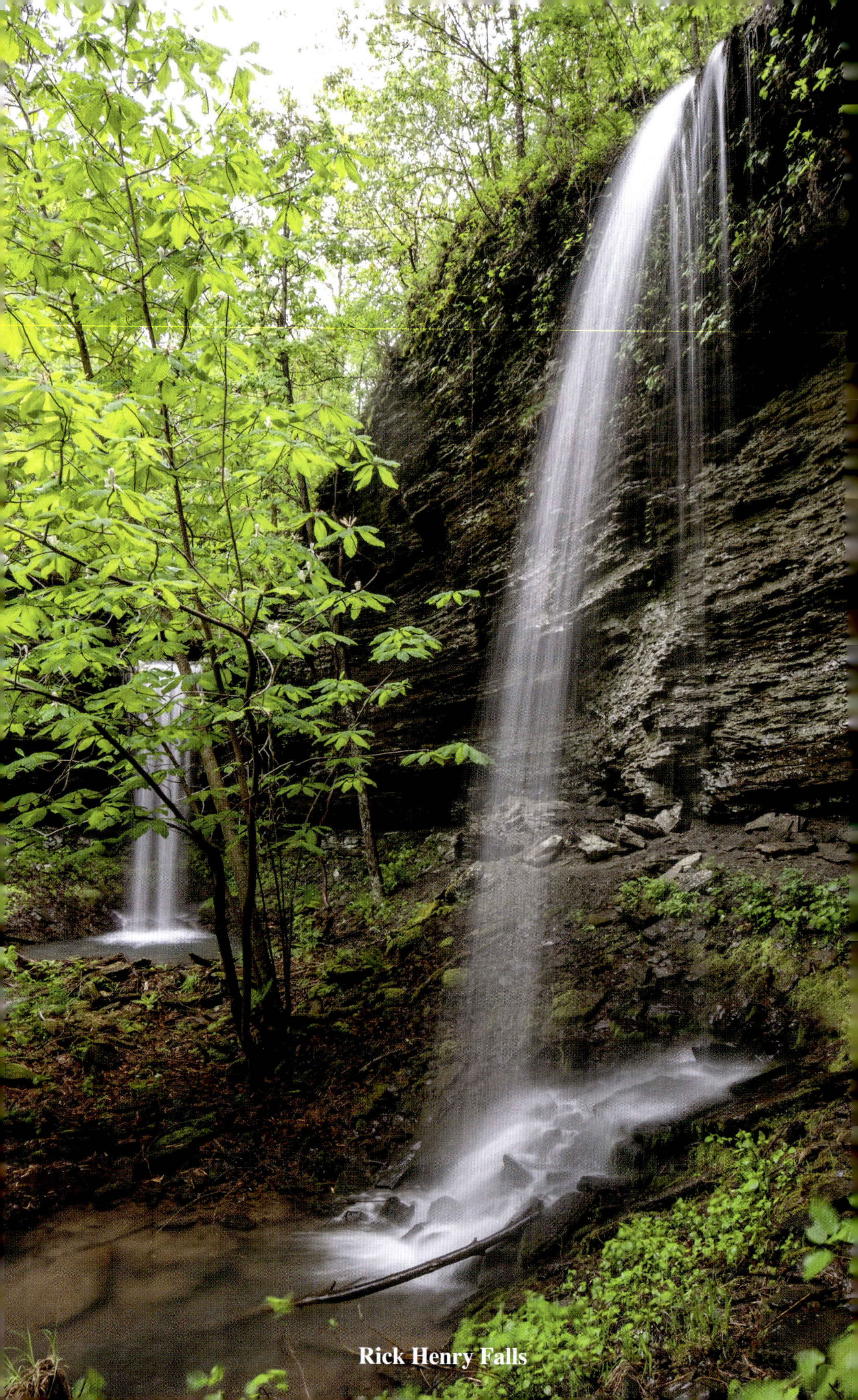

Rick Henry Falls

Rick Henry Falls 5. It's mostly level but kind of rocky too. Eazy Peazy! There's a forest of umbrella magnolia trees living at the base of these waterfalls that bloom in springtime. Feeding each of Rick's falls are cascades that go up a ways.

WILD HOLLOW WATERFALLS. From Rick's waterfall continue another .5 miles and PARK at the entrance to Richland Creek Campground (**35.79656, -92.92990**). Hike down towards the bridge and TURN RIGHT onto a jeep road before the bridge. Follow this lovely trace downstream along Richland Creek for about a mile and TURN RIGHT up into a side drainage (**35.80425, -92.91687** Rick named this Wild Hollow). It's very rocky all the way up and you will pass several nice cascades and small waterfalls, and come to a side creek on the RIGHT at 1.6—this is **Wild Hollow Falls**, an SSS for sure (that's Rick Henry himself in the photo). There's a long tall cascade above feeding this that goes on up the hillside a ways.

From the base of **Wild Hollow Falls** hike along the base of the bluff to the LEFT upstream until you come to **Wild & Scenic Grotto**, another SSS that forms a nice grotto.

Diehard Falls is another waterfall above this one but it's kind of difficult to get to. If you want to climb a little and explore, return to Wild Hollow Falls, and climb UP the bluff on the right side of the waterfall, up to a narrow and very steep SSS cascade canyon that feeds the falls. Cross to the other side of this canyon and then make your way across a BLACK DIAMOND ♦ slope, passing above the Grotto below, and you will come out to **Diehard Falls** in the main creek upstream. Return the way you came for a 4.0 mile roundtrip.

Emergency contact: Searcy County Sheriff, 870–448–2340 Dogs are OK

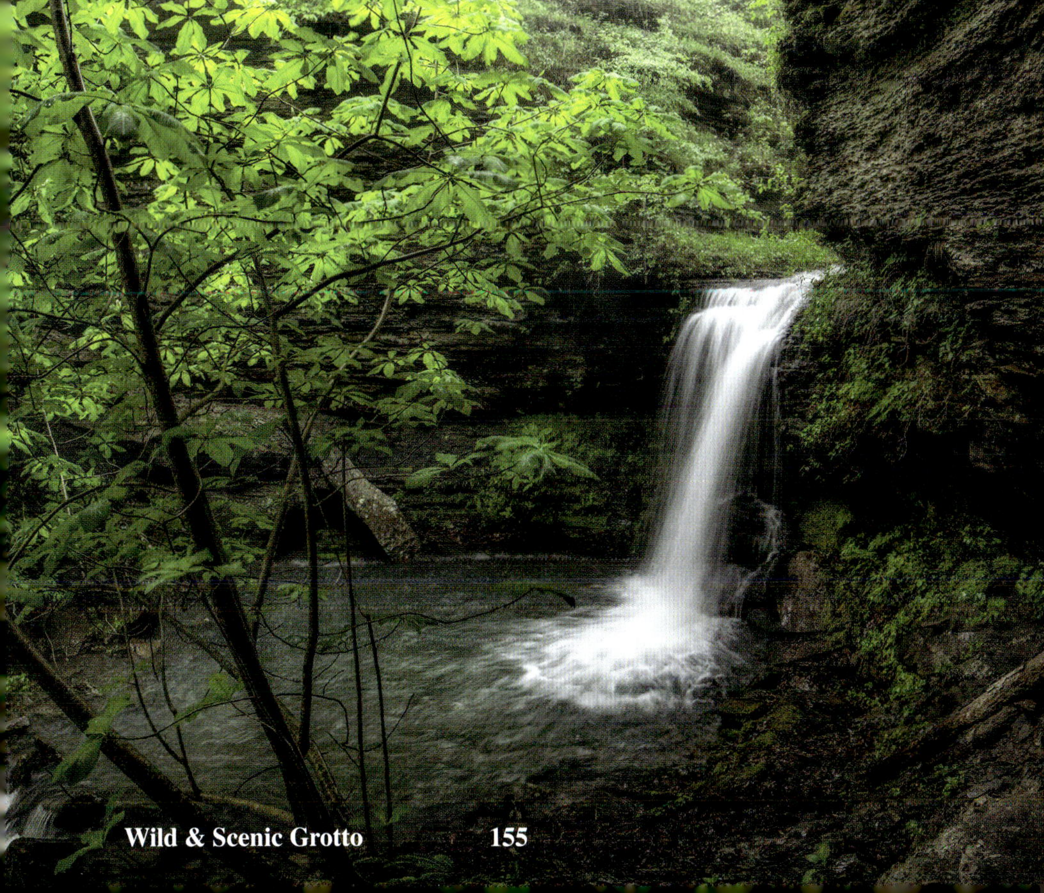

Wild & Scenic Grotto

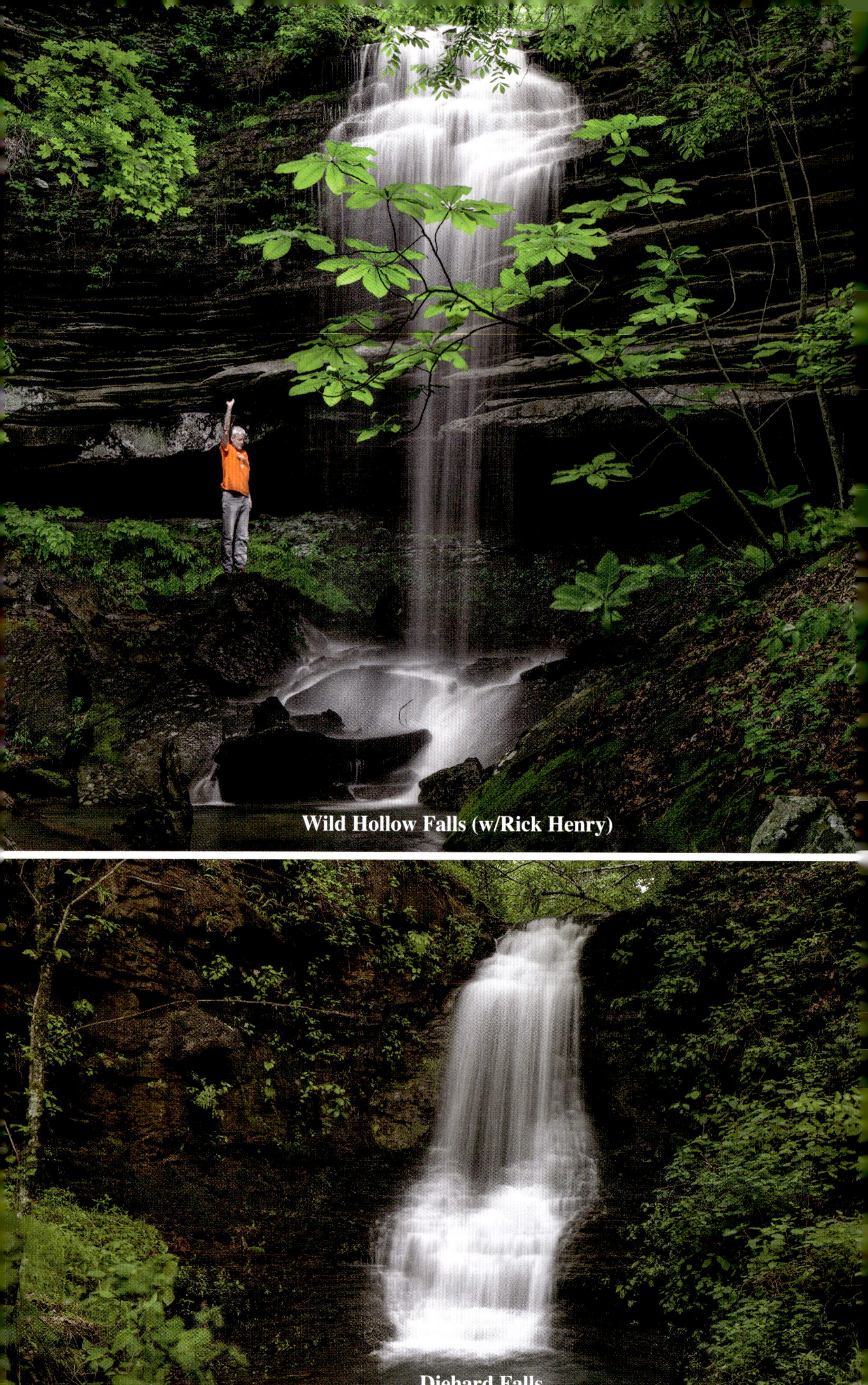
Wild Hollow Falls (w/Rick Henry)

Diehard Falls

Bearcat Hollow Falls – 35′

2.0 miles medium bushwhack GPS **35.86316, -92.90605**

Prohibition Falls – 27′

1.7 miles medium bushwhack, GPS **35.86308, -92.90185**

Bear Stair Falls – 39′

2.2 miles medium bushwhack GPS **35.86167, -92.90394**

Total roundtrip to all falls is about 4.5—miles or so

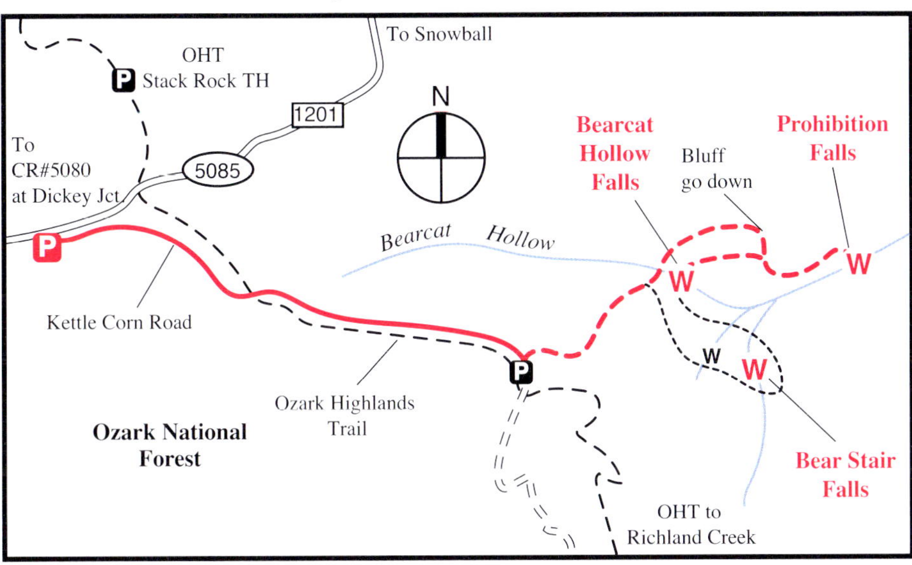

BEARCAT HOLLOW WATERFALLS. Take Hwy. 123 east out of Lurton (located on Hwy. 7 north of Pelsor and south of Cowell). Go 1.5 miles and TURN RIGHT onto CR#5070FR#1200 (paved, then gravel). Go 6.8 miles and TURN RIGHT onto CR#5080/FR#1205. Go 3.4 miles to Dickey Junction and TURN LEFT onto CR#5085/FR#1201. Go 2.8 miles and PARK along the road **(35.86456, -92.92686)**.

Hike down Kettle Corn Road (usually closed to vehicles, but if the gate is open you can drive the first mile) to 1.0 and TURN/PARK on the LEFT **(35.86110, -92.91110)**. There's probably a social trail from this point on down the hill to near the top of the bluff—follow this trail across the creek and up and over a hill to a break in the main bluff line at 1.5 **(35.86424, -92.90428)**.

Drop below the bluff, TURN RIGHT and follow the base of the bluff to where it heads back into the main hollow, then TURN LEFT and drop down the hill to **Prohibition Falls** at 1.7. There are more falls and cascades below, but it gets pretty steep! I usually hike back up to the big bluff, then TURN LEFT and follow the bluff to the back of the canyon to **Bearcat Hollow Falls** at about 2.0—the bluff and waterfall area are SSS of course!

If the water is really high I recommend one other waterfall (if not, then just return the way you came). Continue along the bluff past the falls and then past another falls to what I call **Bear Stair Falls**. No social trail there, but you might be able to climb up the rock formation just to the left of this falls to the top of the bluff—but watch out for bears! Once on top I would hike the top of the bluff to the right and back to the main creek, then follow the social trail back up to Kettle Corn Road and the parking spot.

Emergency contact: Searcy County Sheriff, 870–448–2340 Dogs are OK

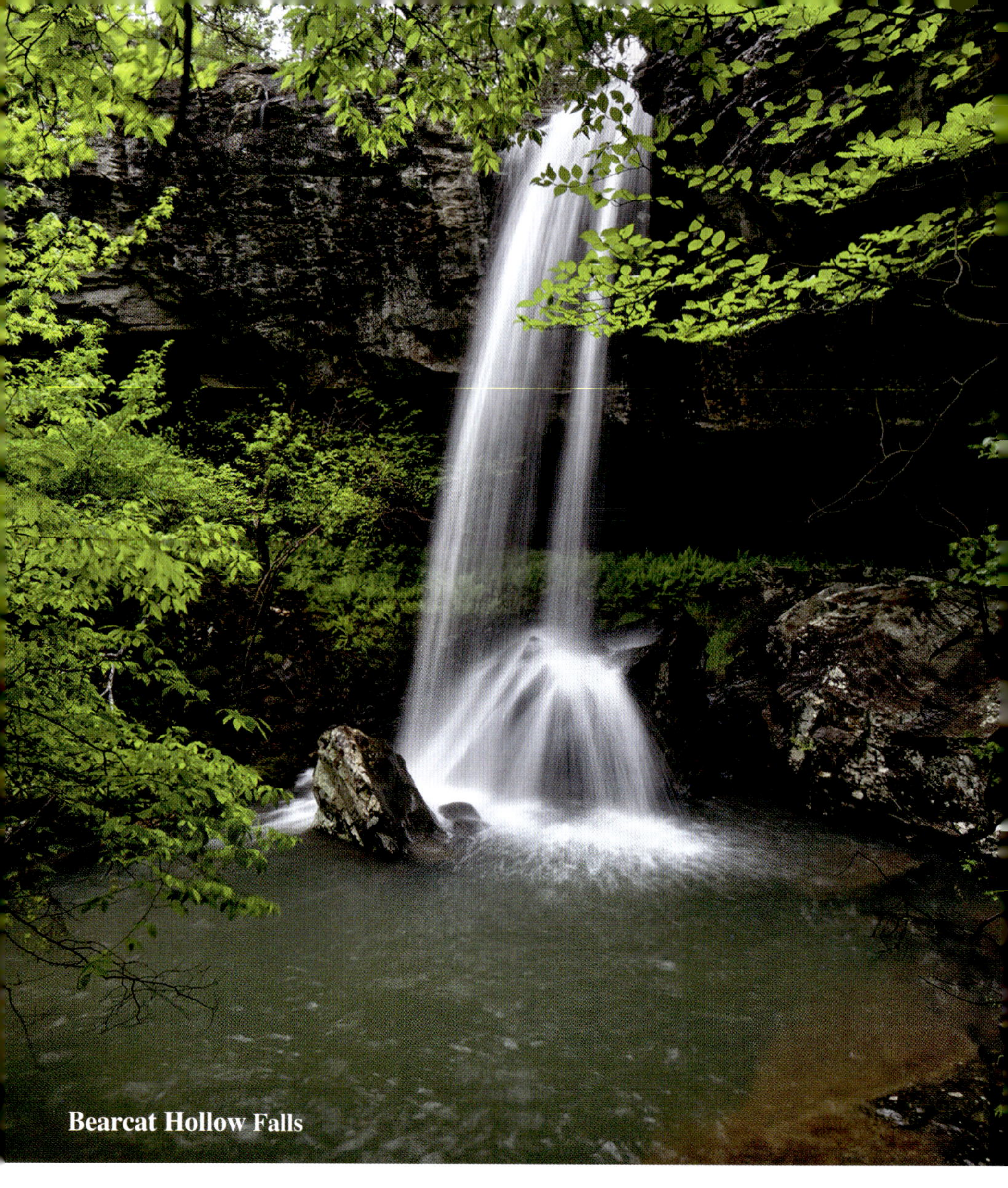
Bearcat Hollow Falls

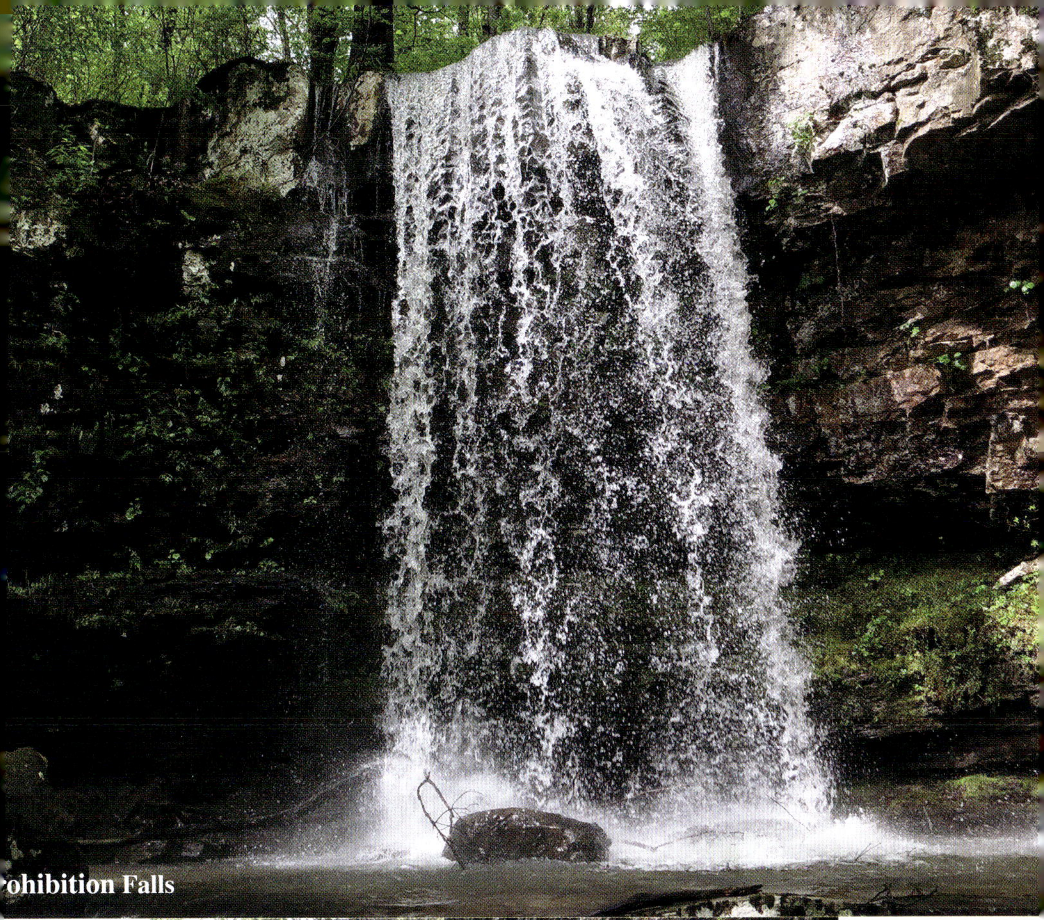

ohibition Falls

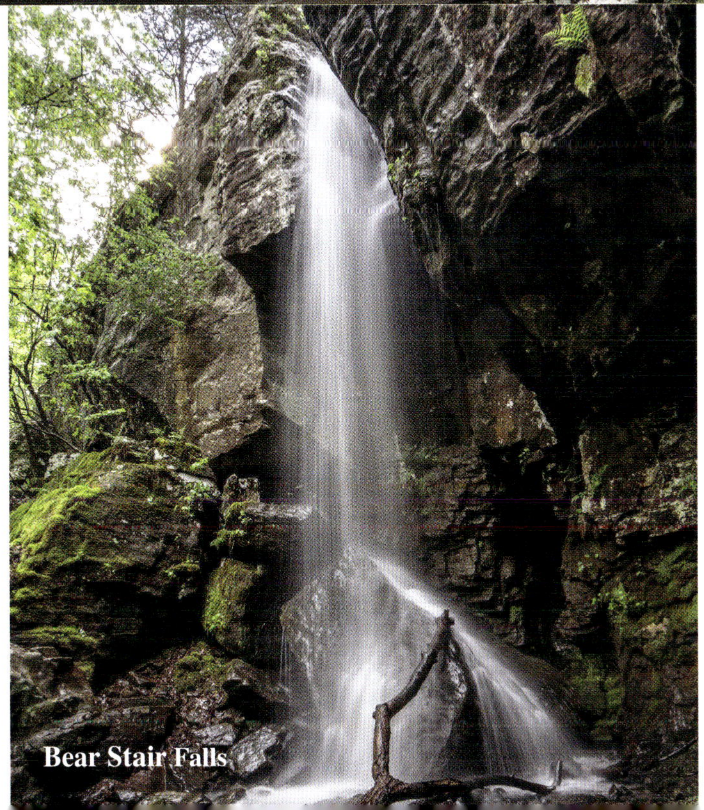

Bear Stair Falls

Stack Rock Homestead Falls – 35′

2.0 miles roundtrip, easy+ hike, GPS helpful

GPS **35.87452, -92.93038**

Punchbowl Falls – 20′

5.2 roundtrip, moderate trail w/tough bushwhack at the end, GPS helpful

GPS **35.87578, -92.94057**

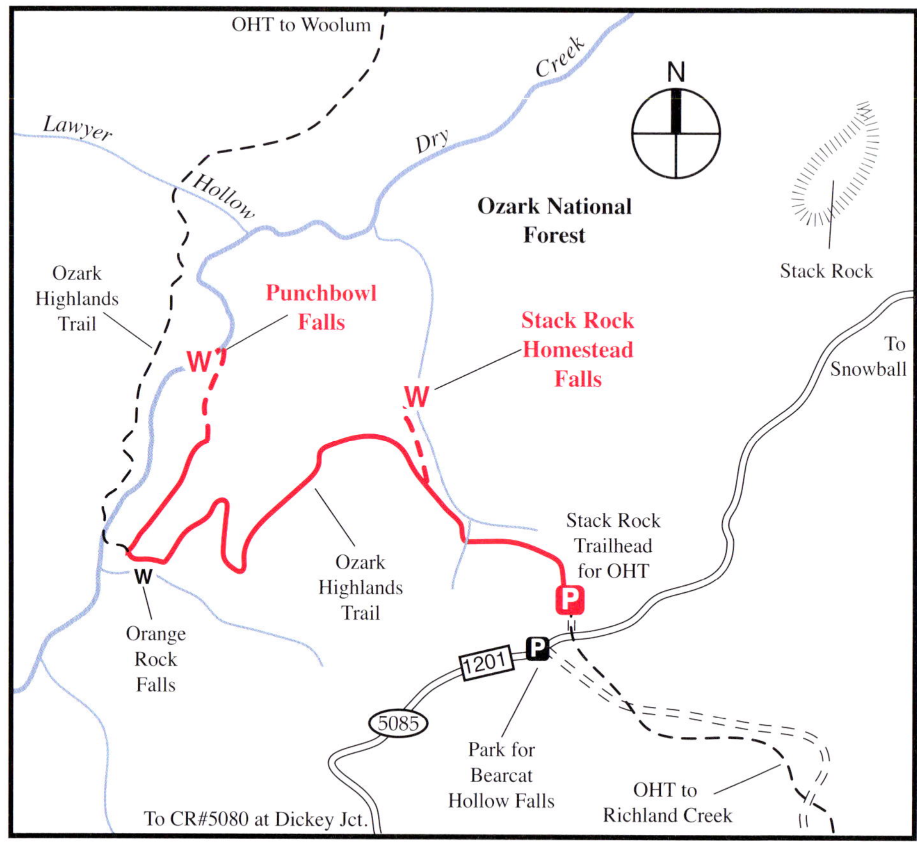

STACK ROCK HOMESTEAD/PUNCHBOWL FALLS. Both of these falls are accessible from the Ozark Highlands Trail (OHT)—one is a short hike off the main trail and the other is a longer trek down into Dry Creek Canyon.

Take Hwy. 123 east out of Lurton (located on Hwy. 7 north of Pelsor and south of Cowell). Go 1.5 miles and TURN RIGHT onto CR#5070FR#1200 (paved, then gravel). Go 6.8 miles and TURN RIGHT onto CR#5080/FR#1205. Go 3.4 miles to Dickey Junction and TURN LEFT onto CR#5085/FR#1201. Go 3.0 miles and TURN LEFT into the trailhead and PARK.

The trail heads out of the parking area to the north on an old jeep road, then soon leaves the road TO THE LEFT. It drops down the hill, past OHT milepost #151, across a creek—TURN RIGHT onto a blue-blazed spur trail, then level out at 1.0 near a pioneer homesite. A stone chimney is off the trail to the left. **Stack Rock Homestead Falls** is just below the trail TO THE RIGHT—go down to the creek and follow it to the falls.

To get to **Punchbowl Falls**, backtrack up to the OHT, and TURN RIGHT. It will run level for a while, past OHT milepost #152, then begin to switchback down the hillside,

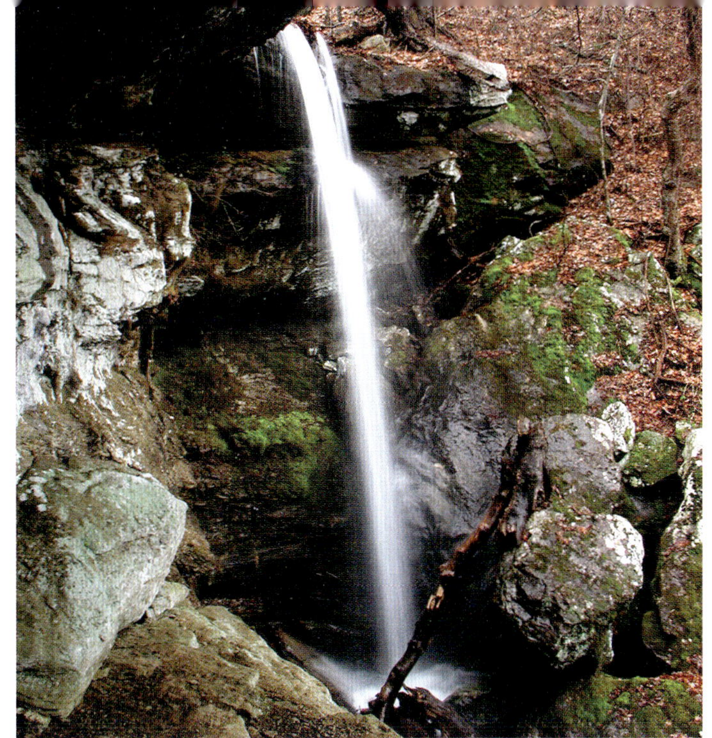

Stack Rock Homestead Falls (above), **Punchbowl Falls** (below)

coming to Dry Creek at 2.0. But JUST BEFORE you get to Dry Creek, TURN RIGHT onto a jeep/ATV trail and follow it along mostly level to 2.3 (**35.87299, -92.94034**). Then LEAVE the road to the LEFT and head downhill and slightly to the right until you reach the creek and **Punchbowl Falls** at 2.6. CAUTION—it's better to go past the falls, scramble down to the creek and come up to the falls from downstream.

Emergency contact: Searcy County Sheriff, 870–448–2340

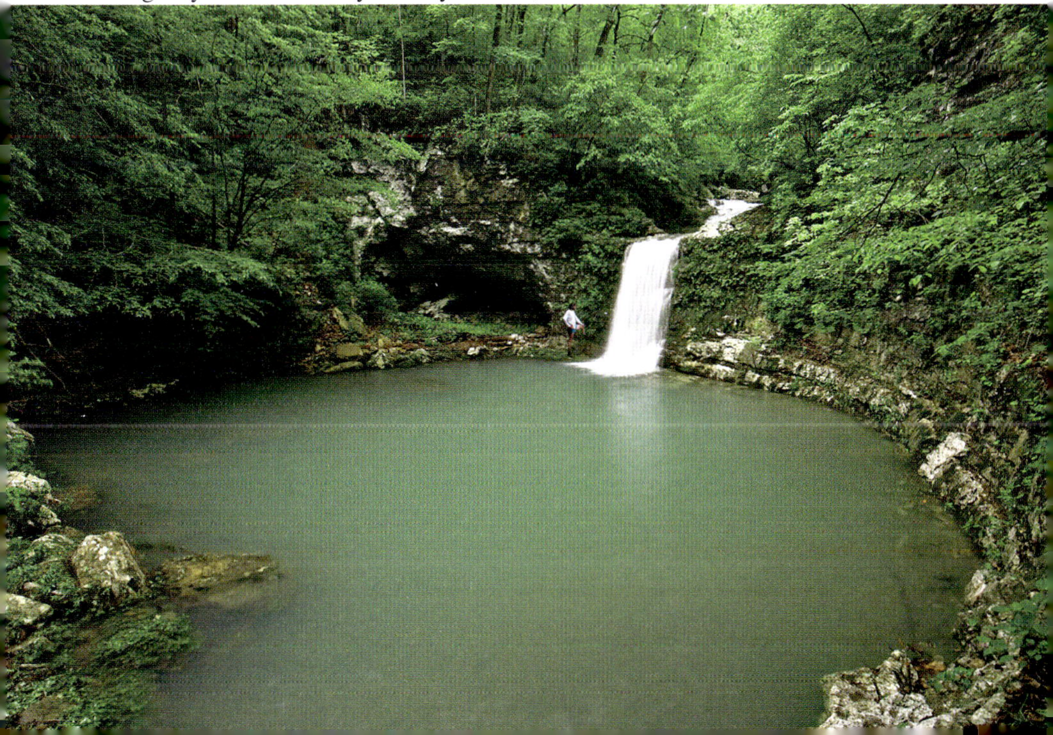

Amphitheater Falls – 47′

1.6 miles roundtrip, easy+ trail GPS **35.98354, -92.72607**

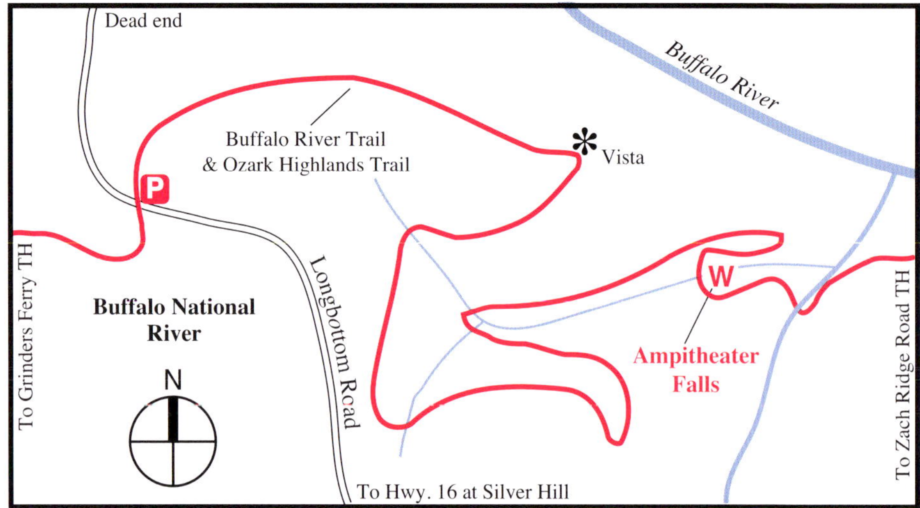

AMPHITHEATER FALLS. At Silver Hill on Hwy. 65 near Tyler Bend, turn onto Blue Ribbon Road and go 1.25 miles then TURN LEFT onto Longbottom Road and PARK where the BRT/OHT crosses the road at .8 (**35.98405, -92.73171**).

Take the trail to the RIGHT as it runs level along the edge of the hill to an overlook where the trail TURNS RIGHT and heads downhill away from the river. The trail will drop down across a small creek, then switchback and cross the creek again, then drop down more and finally switchback to the RIGHT and come to the bottom of **Amphitheater Falls** at .8 (OHT mile 180.9).

This is a short drainage and needs a lot of water, but I just LOVE the look of the towering bluff edge above! Lots of trout lily wildflowers in the spring, an SSS.

Emergency contact: Searcy County Sheriff, 870–448–2340 No dogs on trail.

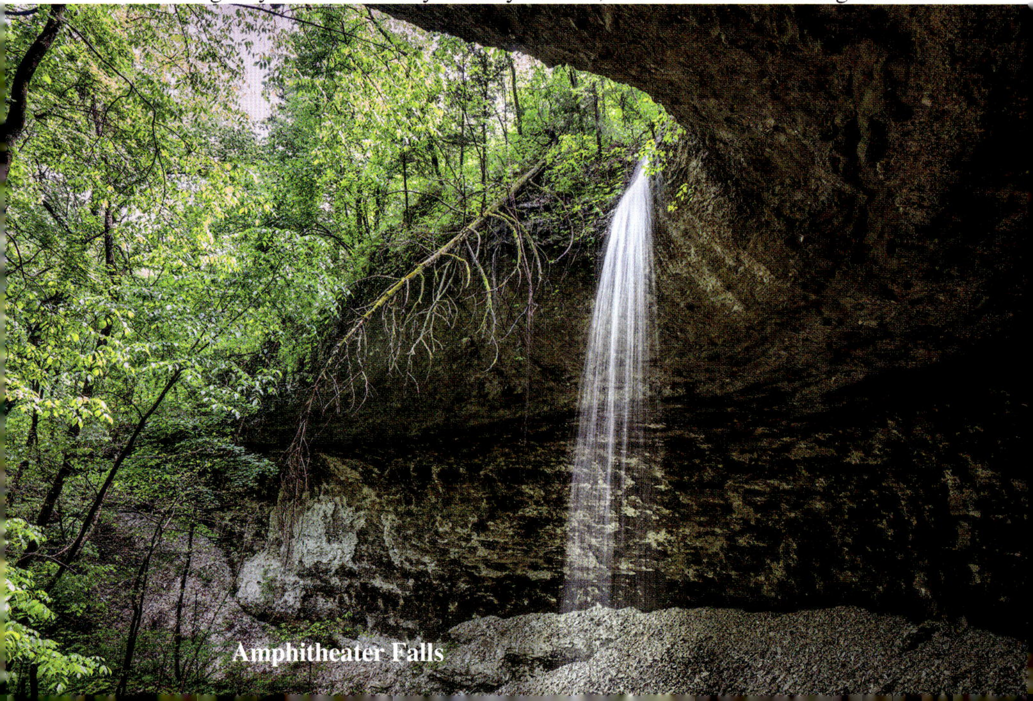

Amphitheater Falls

Stalagmite Falls – 31′

4.0 miles roundtrip, medium trail

GPS **36.00553, -92.67527**

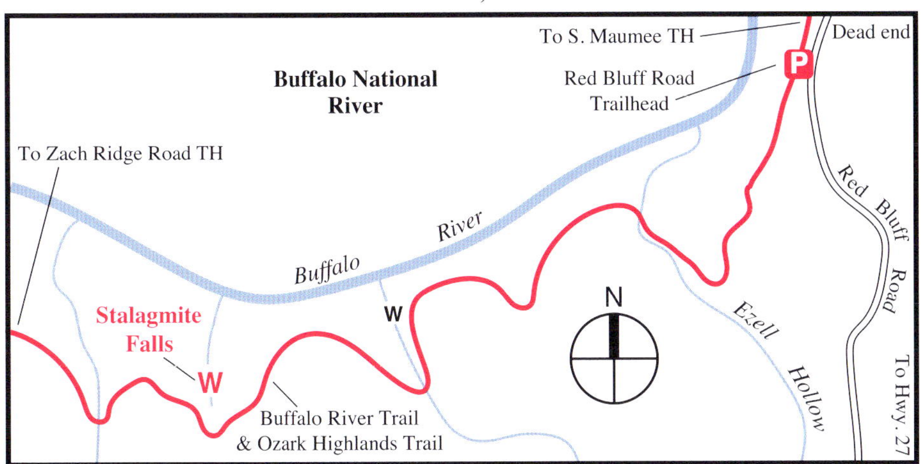

STALAGMITE FALLS. From Marshall—go north on Hwy. 27 for 4.0 miles then TURN LEFT onto paved Trout Farm Road (Howard Hensley WMA sign), go 3.0 miles and TURN RIGHT onto Red Bluff Road (gravel), then go 2.3 miles and TURN RIGHT onto Red Bluff Road/CR#49, go 1.5 miles and park on the left. **(36.01624, -92.65714)**

From the trailhead TURN LEFT on the BRT/OHT, hike on the level then down to a crossing of Ezell Hollow at .9. The trail climbs up and around into and out of a small hollow, then to a second hollow and past a small falls at 1.4. Then back out towards the river and around into another hollow to 2.0 (OHT mile 187.1), then leave the trail TO THE RIGHT **(36.00478, -92.67534)** and drop down to the bluff line to **Stalagmite Falls**. There is a giant stalagmite growing up from the base of the falls—a cave formation made of calcium carbonate (calcite, being delivered by the waterfall), just like those inside caves. An amazing SSS! (Cindy & Shane Jetton found this jewell while doing volunteer trail work.) Emergency contact: Searcy County Sheriff, 870–448–2340 No dogs on trail.

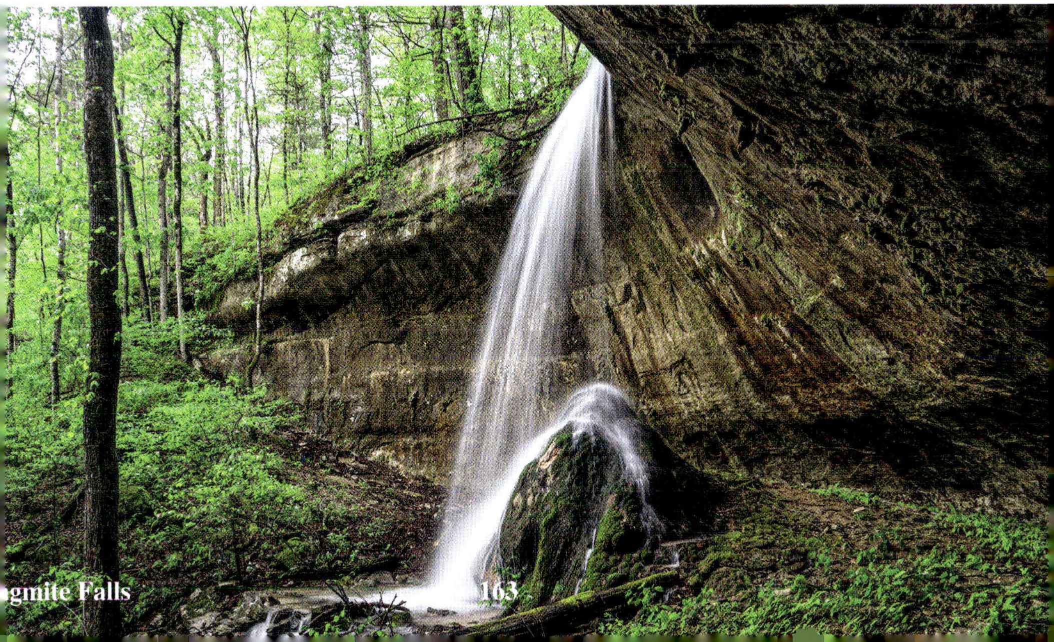

gmite Falls

Saw-Whet Owl Falls – 43′

2.6 miles roundtrip, medium trail GPS **36.01507, -92.62033**

Christmas Falls – 45′

3.4 miles roundtrip, (both falls) medium trail GPS **36.01076, -92.62223**

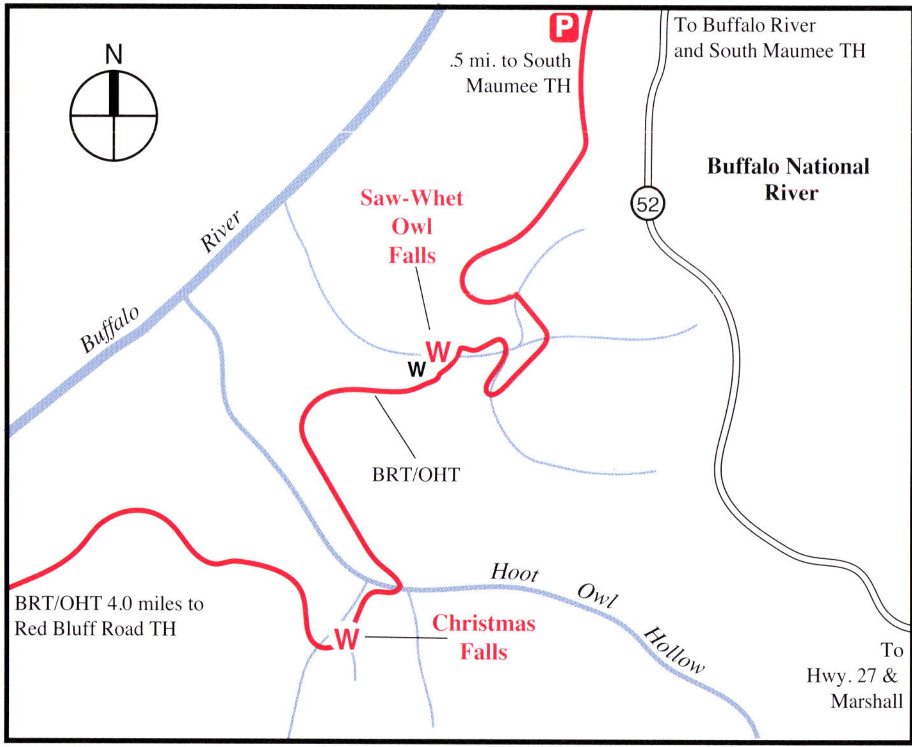

SAW-WHET OWL FALLS/ CHRISTMAS FALLS. Both of these waterfalls are located along the BRT/OHT between Red Bluff Road and S. Maumee Road. We'll hike to them from the South Maumee Trailhead.

To reach the South Maumee Trailhead, from Hwy. 27 at Morning Star (between Marshall and Harriet), turn onto CR#52/South Maumee Road (signed, road paved for the first few miles), and go 5.0 miles and park where the BRT/OHT crosses the road (this is about 1/2 mile past the Buffalo River boundary sign). **(36.02344, -92.61695)**.

From the South Maumee parking spot head west/left/upstream on the trail into the woods and follow as it winds around the hillside down to a couple of hollows up to a wonderful SSS viewpoint at .4 —nice leaf-off views of the Buffalo River both upstream and downstream. Continue along the trail where it will switchback down to the right, then across a small stream to the left, then follow that little stream and cross it again at 1.1. THIS is the top of **Saw-Whet-Owl Falls**. CAUTION if you try to get a good look—don't get too close to the edge of the big bluff the falls pours over! (OHT mile 194)

Continue past this a couple hundred yards (crossing another small creek) until you can find a way to the RIGHT down the bluff line, then follow it back to the base of the falls. Sit for a spell and see if you can see or hear one of the smallest owls in the USA (would almost fit in the palm of your hand). They migrate through the Ozarks in the fall, and some stop and spend the winter in this forest.

Back up on the trail it continues level for a little bit then switchbacks RIGHT down to the same bluff line, then immediately back to the LEFT, and continues easing down and around to the left and across Hoot Owl Hollow at 1.5. Turn RIGHT and head downstream, then across an old logging road and uphill to a cascade across the trail at 1.5—THIS is **Christmas Falls** up to the left. It takes quite a bit of water to flow well, but it's an amazing place when it does! (OHT mile 193.5)

A special thanks to Jim Liles who retired from the park service and built much of this trail that you've been walking on as a volunteer—see page 121 for **Liles Falls**. It was Christmas Day when Jim completed work on this particular section of trail, hence the name. He also spotted and listened to Saw-Whet-Owls on several of those late fall and winter trail work trips. Emergency contact: Searcy County Sheriff, 870–448–2340 No dogs on trail.

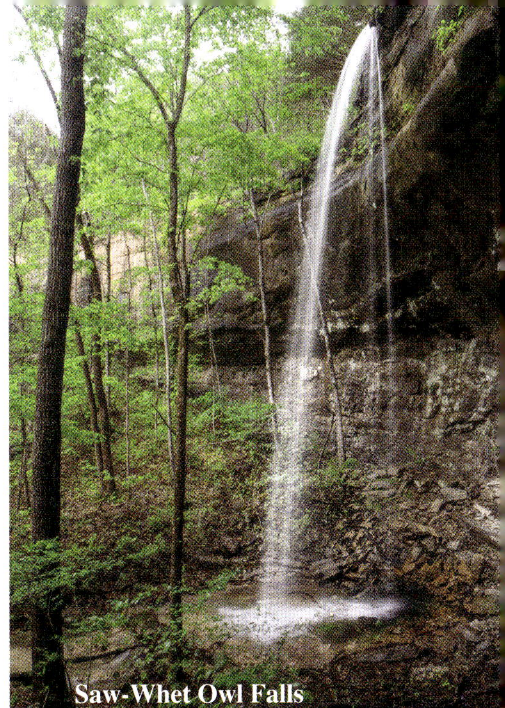

Saw-Whet Owl Falls

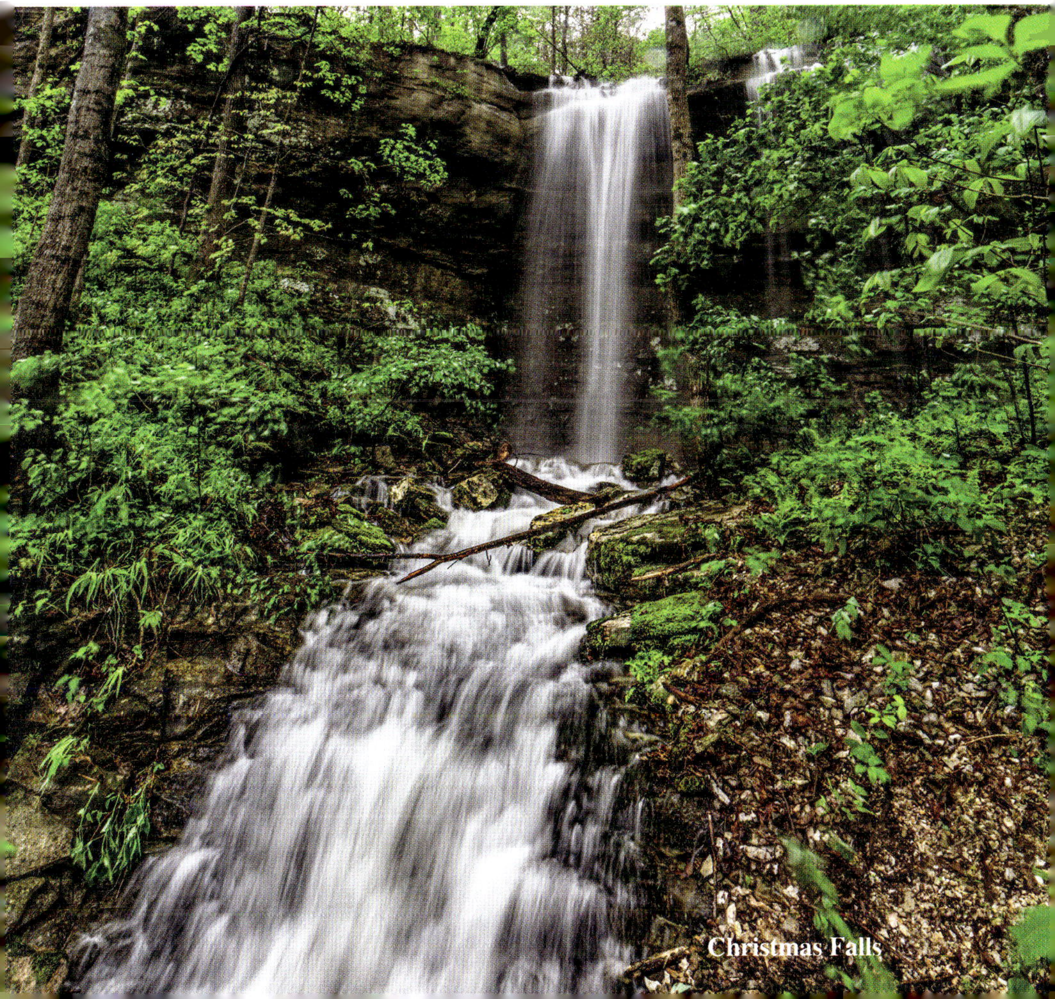

Christmas Falls

Maumee Falls East – 67′

1.8 miles roundtrip, easy hike, GPS helpful

GPS **36.01651, -92.61032**

Maumee Falls West – 53′

1.5 miles roundtrip (included in above hike), easy hike, GPS helpful

GPS **36.01602, -92.61237**

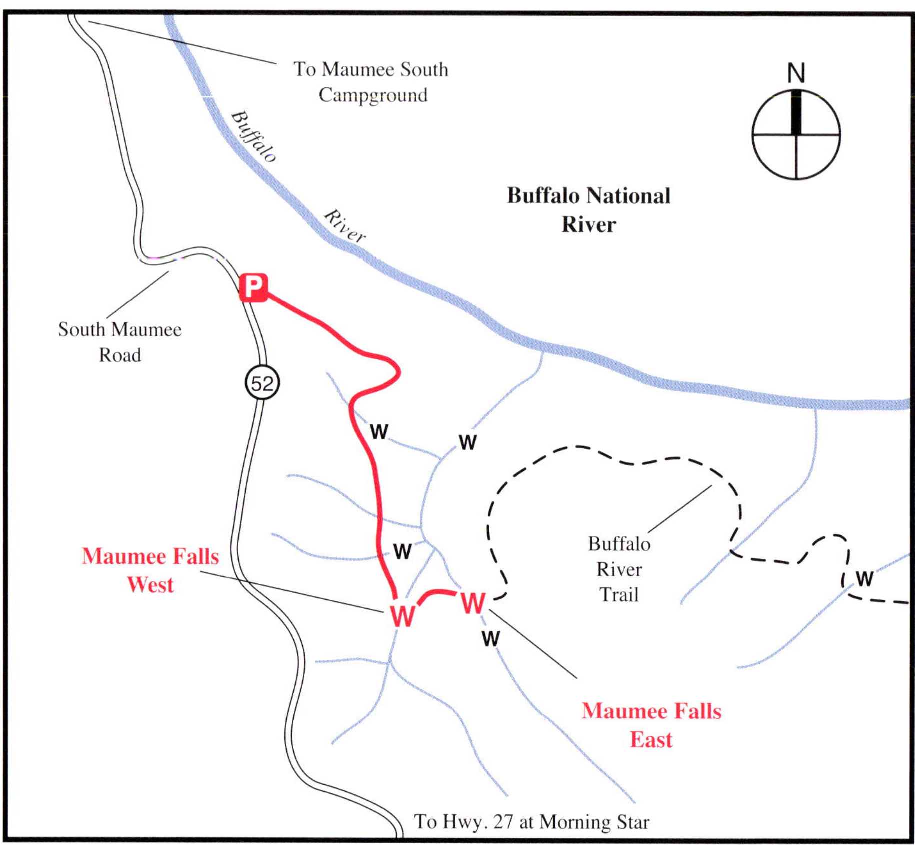

MAUMEE FALLS. Here are a couple more waterfalls along this lower stretch of the Buffalo River Trail that you can see right from the trail. If you are the adventurous sort you might be able to find a way to scramble down through the bluffline for the views like you see here. There are lots of great views along this 11.3 mile stretch of trail from South Maumee to Hwy. 14, but you don't have to hike nearly that far to see the waterfalls.

To reach the trail from Hwy. 27 at Morning Star (between Marshall and Harriet), turn onto CR#52/South Maumee Road (signed) and go 5.0 miles and PARK on the right side of the road (this is about .5 miles past the Buffalo River boundary sign). The trail begins on the RIGHT. CR#52 dead-ends at the Maumee South campground and river access.

From the parking area the trail runs level and then curves away from the river to the right, then swings around to the left and drops down to the top of a bluffline (past a couple of smaller waterfalls). You come to **Maumee Falls West** at .75, and it is right on the trail. Continue along the trail until you reach **Maumee Falls East** at .9. You have good views of both waterfalls as you approach, but be careful getting close to the edge for a view! During high water there may be several other neat waterfalls just upstream along the trail.

Emergency contact: Searcy County Sheriff, 870–448–2340 No dogs on trail.

Maumee Falls East
(right)

Maumee Falls West
(below)

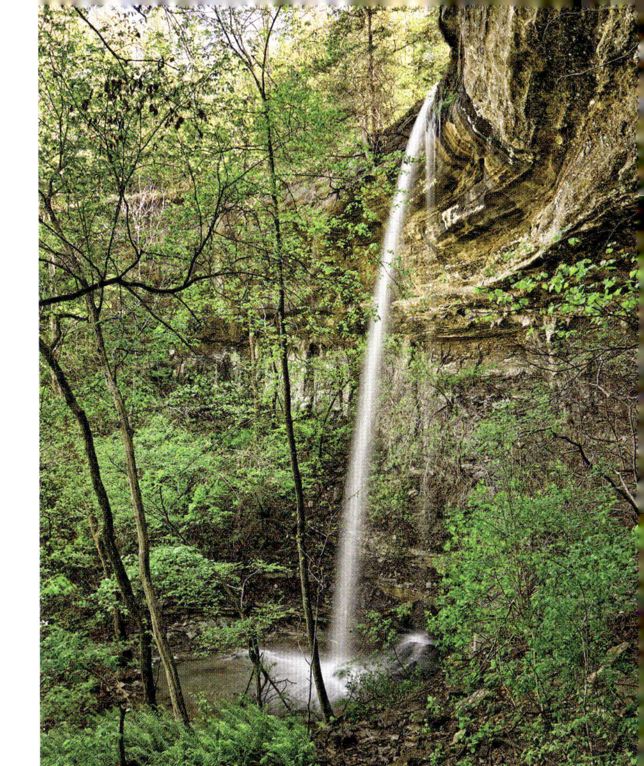

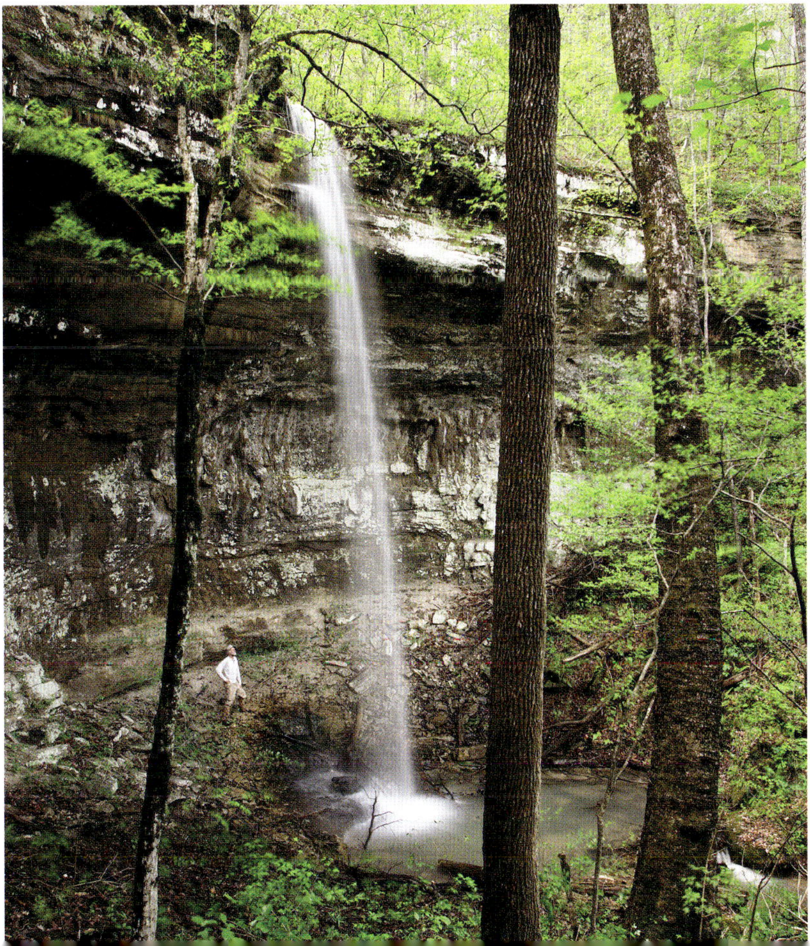

Gray Fox Falls – 58′

1.6 mile roundtrip, easy+ bushwhack

GPS **36.06688, -92.56929**

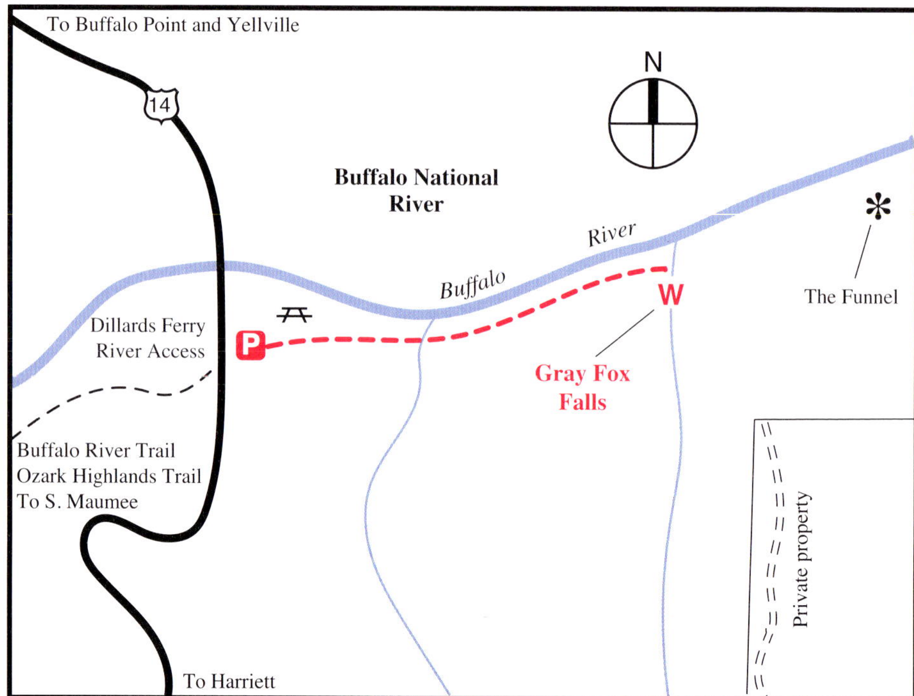

GRAY FOX FALLS. The first time I saw this waterfall I was wearing snowshoes in a foot of snow. The waterfall and much of the bluff were a solid ice castle. It had been below zero the day before, and I'd found a gray fox frozen on top of the snow a few miles back. I could not find any marks of trauma on her, in fact she looked perfectly beautiful with a full fur coat and so colorful! This waterfall is a small nod to such a magnificent wild creature. (Turns out the old road above this is also named after a fox.)

PARK at the river access below the big Hwy. 14 bridge over the Buffalo River at Dillards Ferry. Hike downstream following the river and along the base of a bluff (or next to the river) to **Gray Fox Falls** at .8. Not only is this a terrific towering waterfall with lush cascades below, but there are many interesting things to see along the way up close to the bluff too—in fact I think I'd rate most of this entire hike an SSS!

If you continue to explore the bluff downstream near the end of it at 1.0, you will find a scenic tall "funnel" that's been drilled in the bluff from top to bottom—you can walk right into the bottom of this funnel and stare UP **(36.06817, -92.56592)**.

Emergency contact: Marion County Sheriff, 870-449-4236 No dogs on trail..

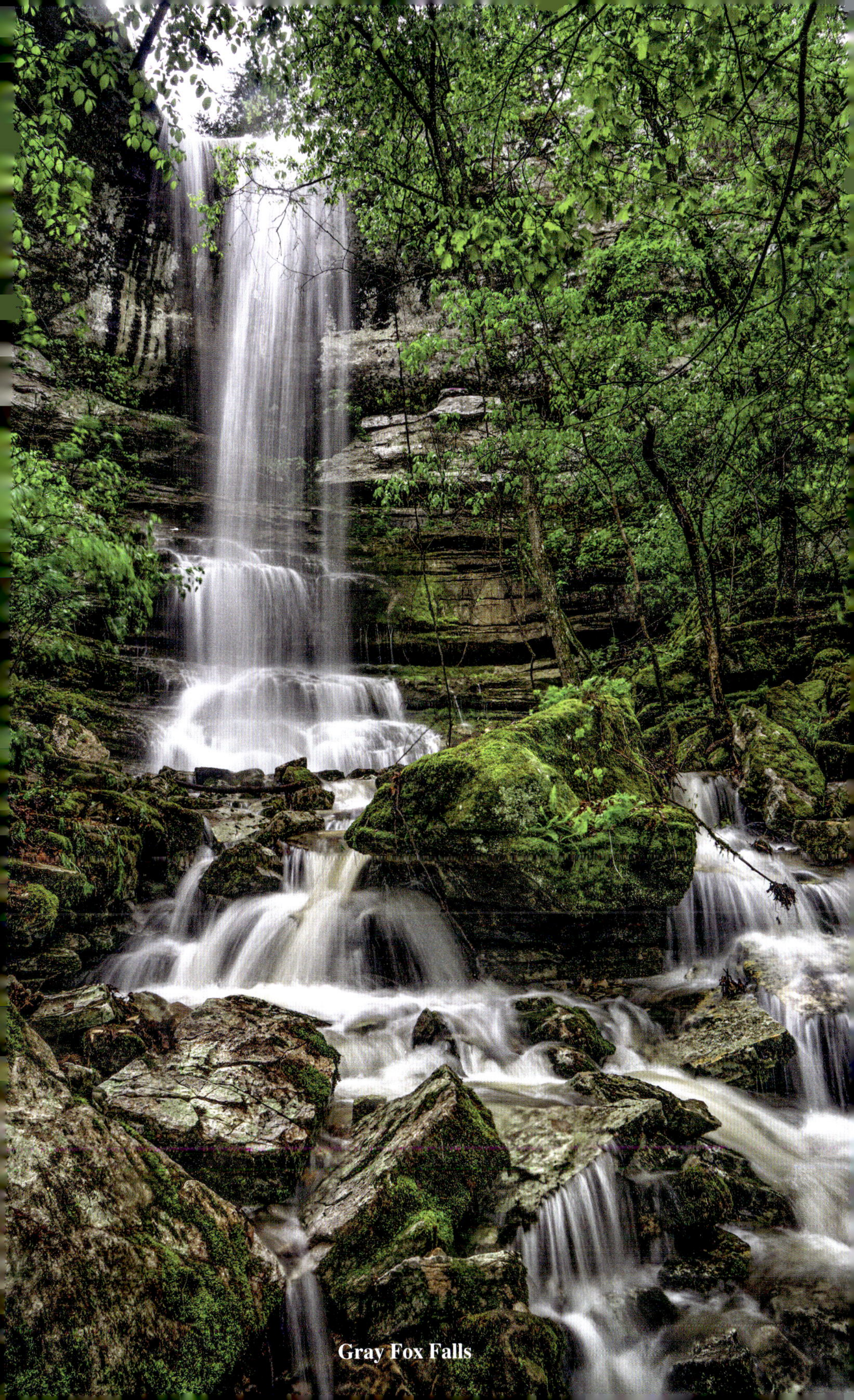
Gray Fox Falls

Dark Hollow Falls – 65′

11.0 miles roundtrip, medium-difficult long hike GPS **36.10796, -92.46762**

Cinnamon Bear Falls – 32′

medium-difficult long hike GPS **36.11058, -92.45713**

Grapevine Escape Falls – 21′

medium-difficult long hike GPS **36.11054, -92.45718**

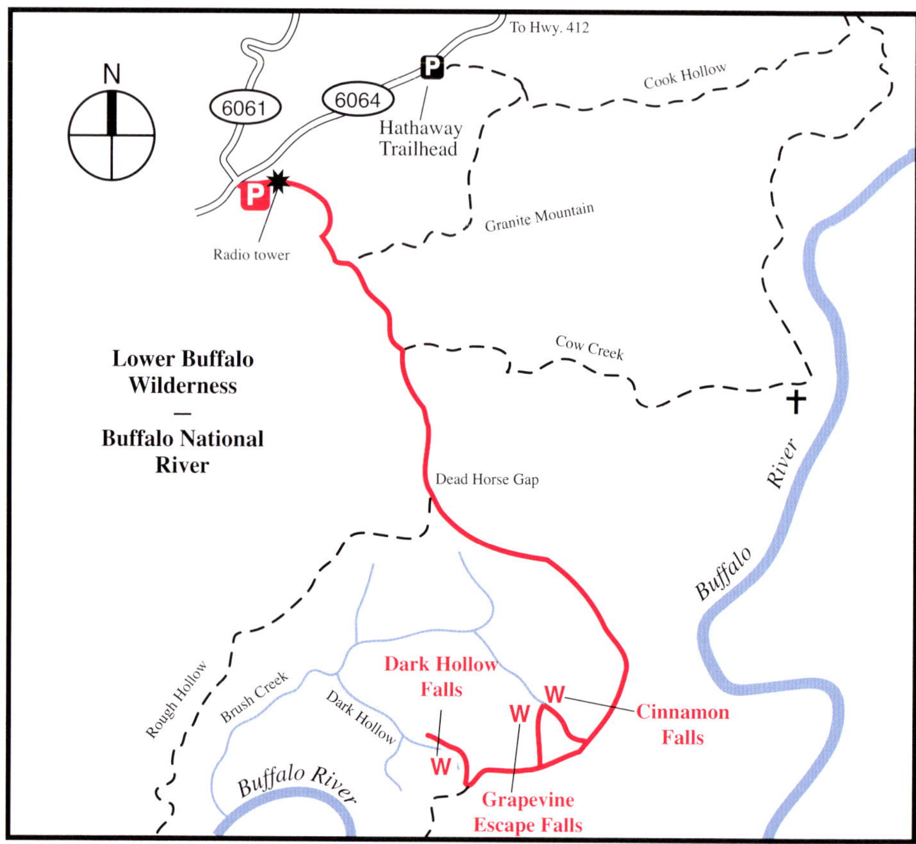

DARK HOLLOW FALLS. Directions from Hwy. 412 between Flippen and Cotter—turn south onto AR 101S for 3.6 mi, then left onto Marion County 6064 for 8.3 miles to the Hathaway Trailhead (on the left).

CONTINUE PAST the trailhead 1.2 miles to the top of the hill and TURN LEFT on MC 6061, then take the center road past a building on left, and go up the hill to the NPS boundary and PARK just beyond **(36.15022, -92.48790)**—not much room.

Hike along this old road up the hill, past a gate to a radio tower site at the top. Continue on the road down the other side and into the Lower Buffalo Wilderness. You will be on old roads inside the wilderness the entire hike except for a short trail near the end, and short bushwhack below the bluff to the base of the waterfall.

At 1.0 the trail from the Hathaway Trailhead joins the road from the left—continue STRAIGHT. At 1.5 there's another trail intersection from the left that goes down into Cow Creek, to a mining area, and to Cow Creek Cemetery—continue STRAIGHT.

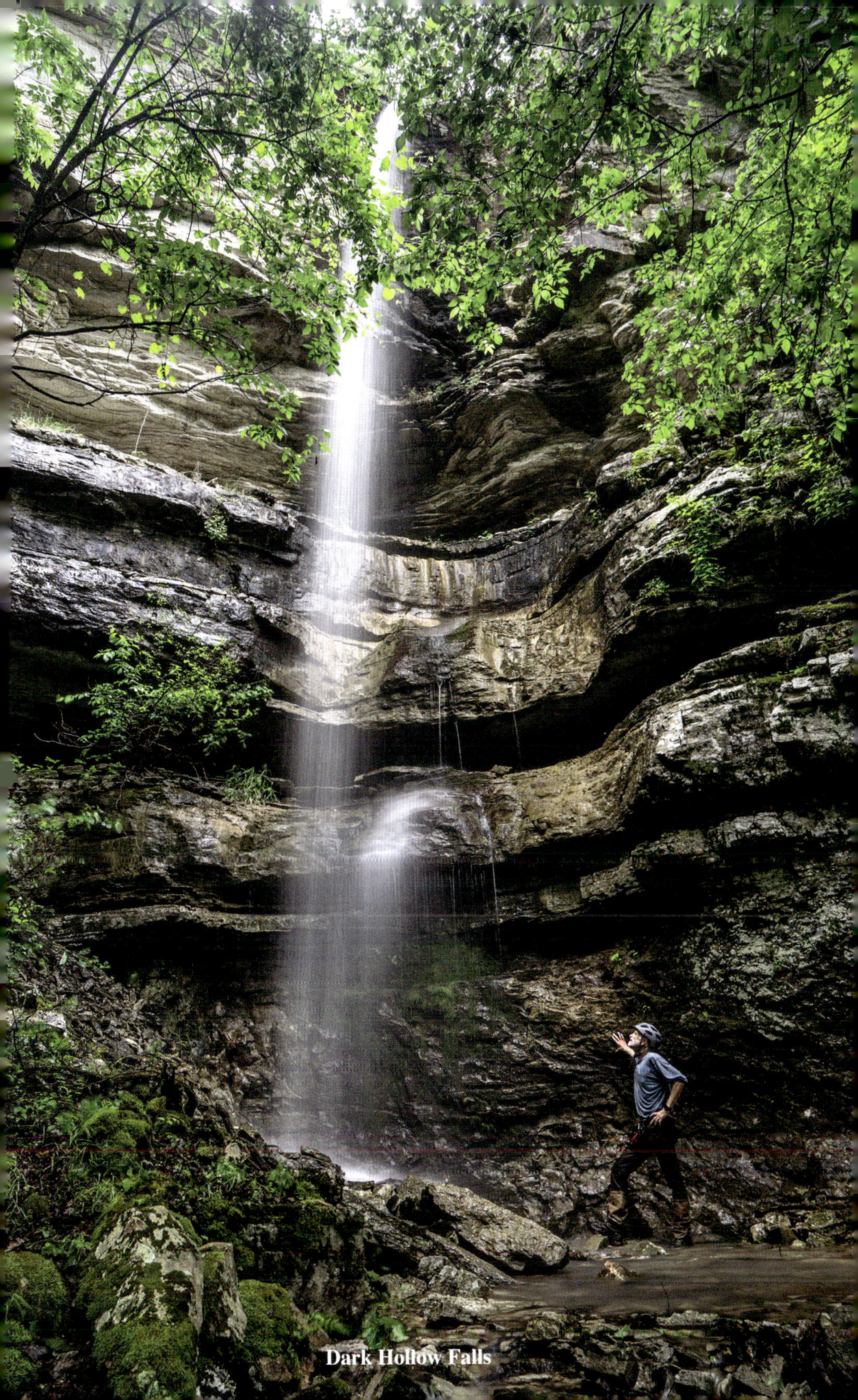
Dark Hollow Falls

Then the trail forks—go RIGHT at the fork, up and around a steep hill, then it will rejoin the road and continue STRAIGHT. You will be up mostly on top now for a while. The next intersection is at 2.4—be sure to TURN LEFT. This will take you around the tops of Brush Creek and Dark Hollow drainages (which are down off to the right).

Continue along the old road as it works around the hilltops to the right and into a saddle at 5.1 **(36.10469, -92.46567)**—this is where you LEAVE THE ROAD and TURN RIGHT to head into Dark Hollow. You basically just head downhill on an old road/trail next to the creek until you come to the top of **Dark Hollow Falls**—there's a nice wildflower glade on top, and this begins an epic SSS area.

Continue on top to the right of the falls and above the bluff until about 5.4 where there is a way down the bluff. Did I mention you might should bring a 20' section of rope? What I do is tie the rope off to a tree that I can use to help myself back up on top. Otherwise, find your way to the base of the bluff and head on over to the bottom of **Dark Hollow Falls** at 5.5. (I'm sure there are other ways to the bottom if you look around.)

FYI, the old road continues past the turnoff to Dark Hollow Falls another 2.4 miles down to the Buffalo River, just downstream from the mouth of Big Creek. You could begin your hike to the falls from the river, but the river would probably be at flood stage when the Falls was running well enough to justify the trip.

To get to the pair of smaller waterfalls, go back out to the main road and turn LEFT, go .4 into a saddle and TURN LEFT off the road and follow the creek downhill about .4 until you come to **Grapevine Escape Falls**—find a way down to the base, and then **Cinnamon Bear Falls** is just across the holler. Return to the road and continue home!

In case you were wondering, one time when I was at these smaller waterfalls taking pictures, a "cinnamon" colored black bear wandered in for a visit (about 30% of black bears in Arkansas are cinnamon color). I slowly packed up, backed away and used a giant grapevine growing next to the waterfall to make my escape.

Emergency contact: Marion County Sheriff, 870-449-4236 No dogs on trail.

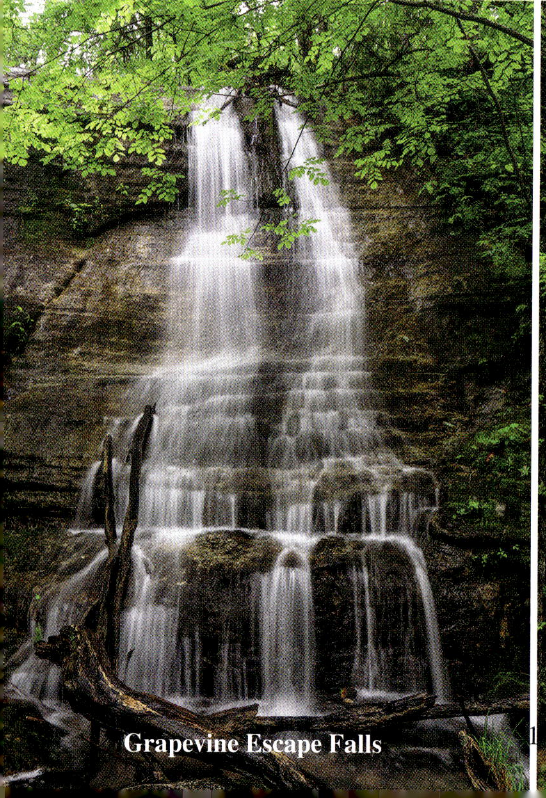

Grapevine Escape Falls

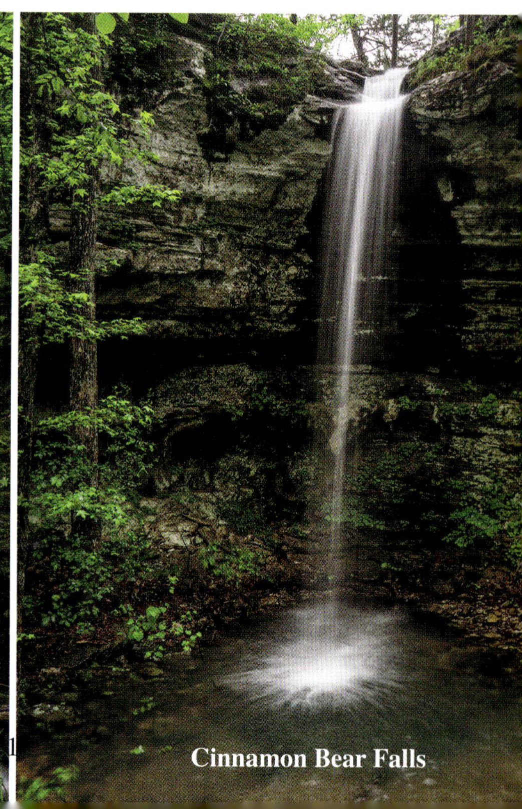

Cinnamon Bear Falls

Cougar Falls – 77′

.6 mile roundtrip, easy bushwhack, GPS helpful

GPS **36.04055, -92.37685**

China Falls – 68′

.5 mile roundtrip, easy bushwhack, GPS recommended

GPS **36.04380, -92.38364**

Little Glory Hole –18′

.6 mile roundtrip, easy bushwhack, GPS recommended

GPS **36.04842, -92.38603**

Crosscut Falls – 53′

.6 mile roundtrip, easy bushwhack, GPS recommended

GPS **36.05048, -92.39205**

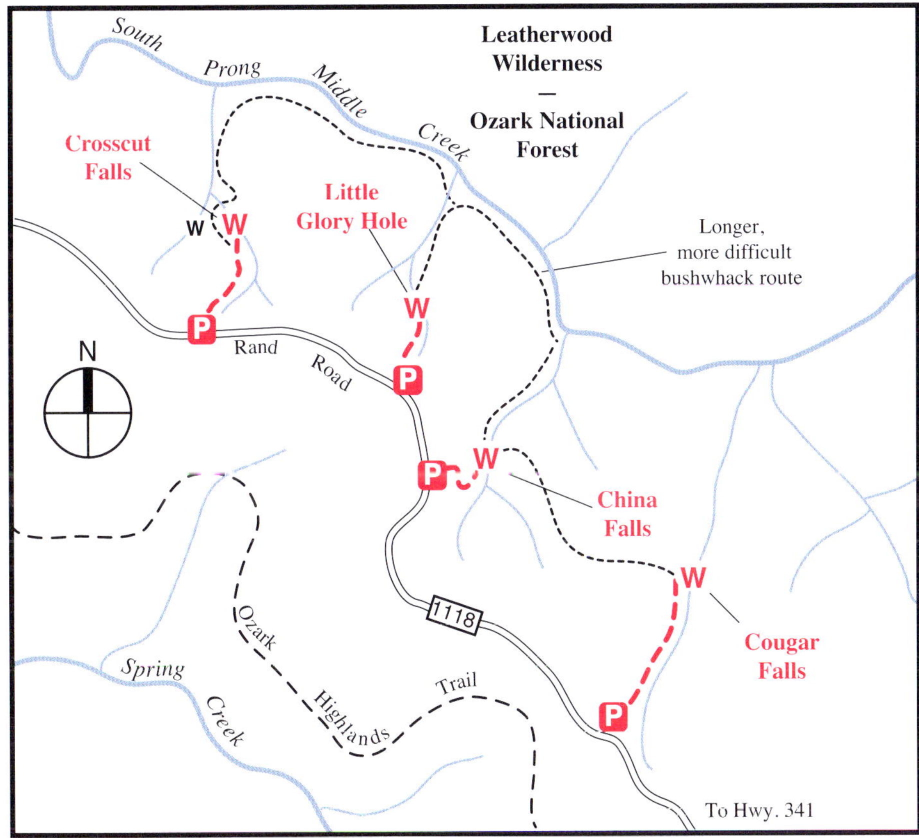

COUGAR/CHINA/LITTLE GLORY HOLE/CROSSCUT FALLS. Here are four beautiful waterfalls all in a line just inside the Leatherwood Wilderness. It is possible to do one longer and more difficult bushwhack loop from Cougar Falls to visit all of them and come in from the bottom of each (4.5 miles roundtrip—bushwhack 3.2, plus 1.3 along road), but we are going to take the easiest route to each one, requiring short drives along the road. Save these for the monsoon season—they look best with a *lot* of water.

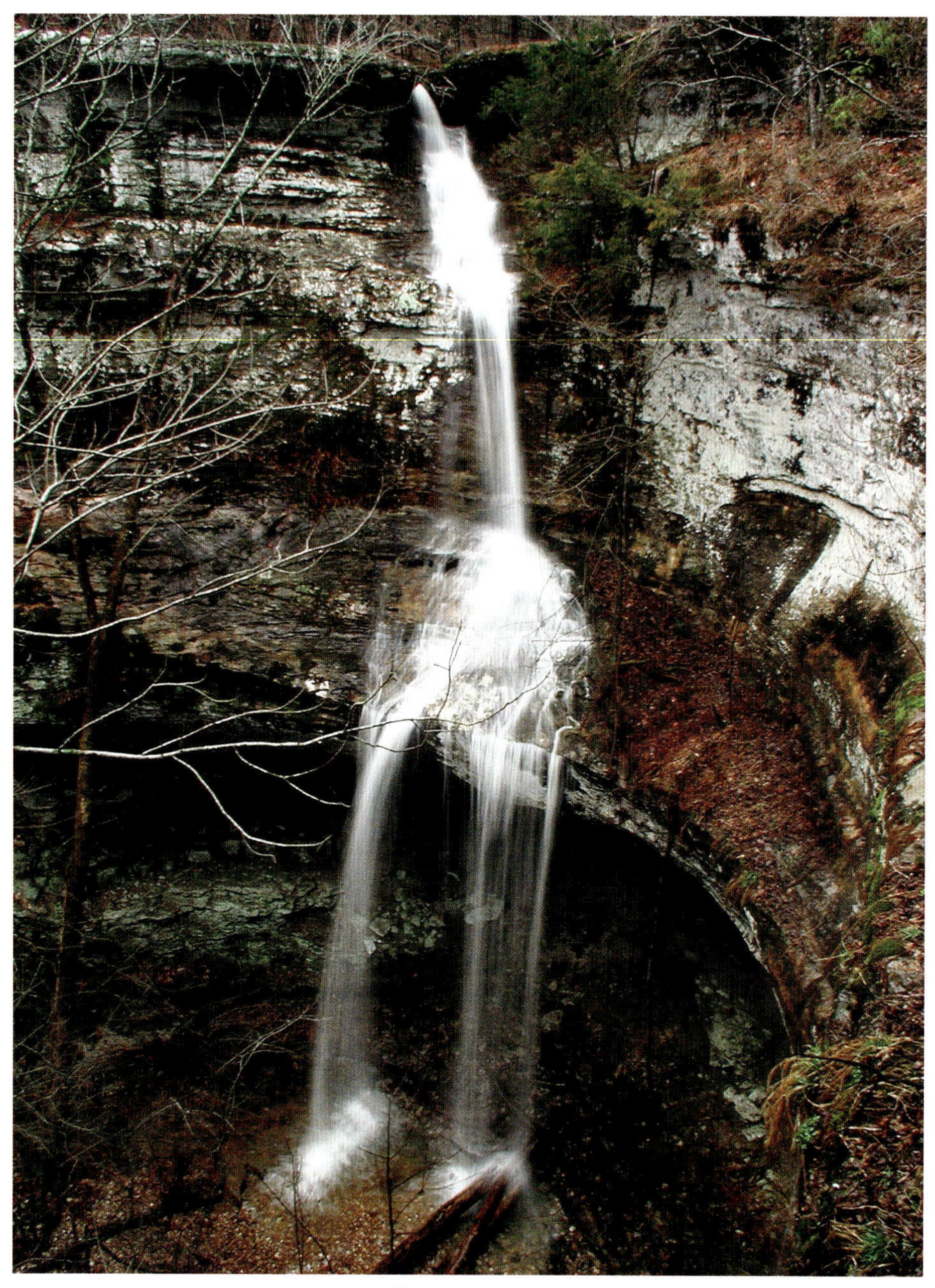

Cougar Falls

From Big Flat, go 3.8 miles east on Hwy. 14 and TURN LEFT onto Hwy. 341 (paved). Go 2.3 miles and TURN LEFT onto Rand Road/FR#1118 (gravel). Go 1.2 miles and PARK on the RIGHT for Cougar Falls **(36.03651, -92.37940)**. PARK at 1.9 for China, 2.1 for Little Glory Hole, and 2.5 for Crosscut.

To get to **Cougar Falls**, simply head down the hill from the road into the drainage and follow the little creek. You will come to the top of **Cougar Falls** at .3. There is a spot on the left that you can drop down to in order to get the same view as pictured above.

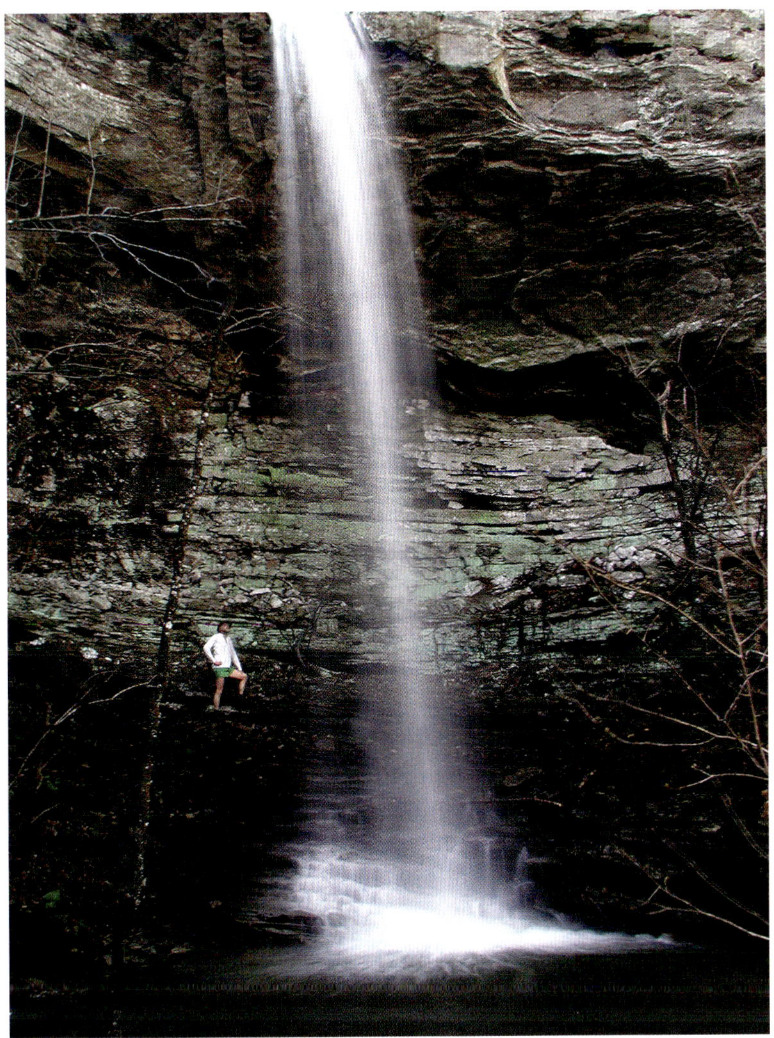

China Falls

To get to **China Falls**, drive on the road another .7 and PARK. Bushwhack down the hill to your right—it gets steep, so take it easy and zig-zag on the way back up. If you hit the bluffline going in, TURN RIGHT to get to the falls, if you hit the creek, TURN LEFT and follow it to the top of the falls. This falls was named after a favorite horse that Helen Elsner was riding when she first found these falls.

To get to **Little Glory Hole,** drive on the road another .2 and PARK. Drop down into the drainage and follow the creek down to the falls. This one isn't too tall but is interesting because the creek has drilled a hole into the roof of the bluff, creating a miniature waterfall in the same vein as the famous Glory Hole, described elsewhere in this book.

To get to **Crosscut Falls,** drive on the road another .4 and PARK. Work your way down into the drainage and follow the creek downstream to the top of the falls. There is another neat falls off on the left, and also a place where you can get down below the bluff. This falls gets its name from an old crosscut saw that was found nearby.

Emergency contact: Baxter County Sheriff, 870–425–6222 Dogs are OK.

Little Glory Hole

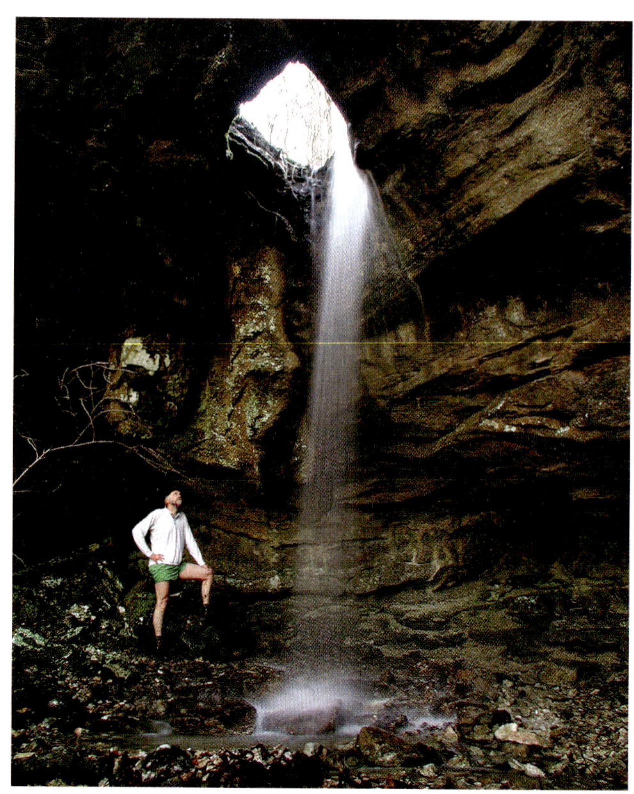

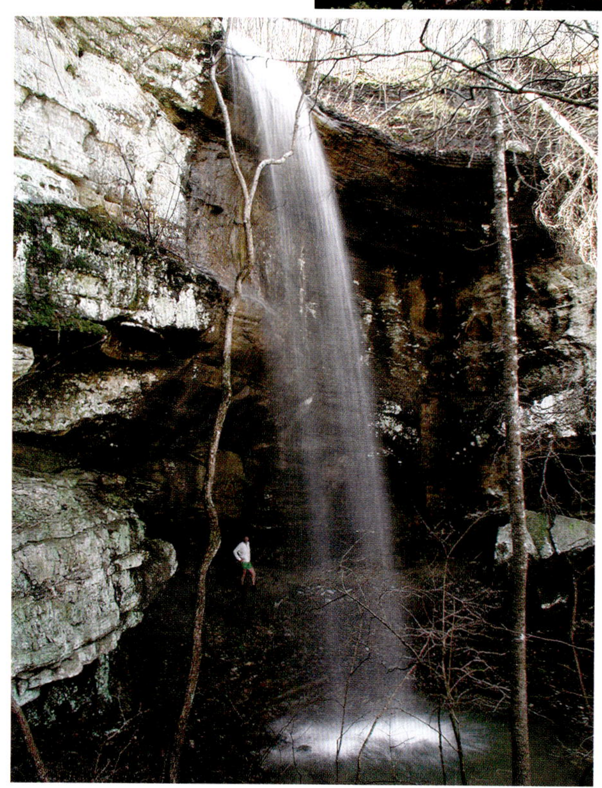

Crosscut Falls

Funnel Falls (2) – 41′/52′

1.0 mile roundtrip, medium bushwhack, GPS helpful

GPS **36.06975, -92.43840**

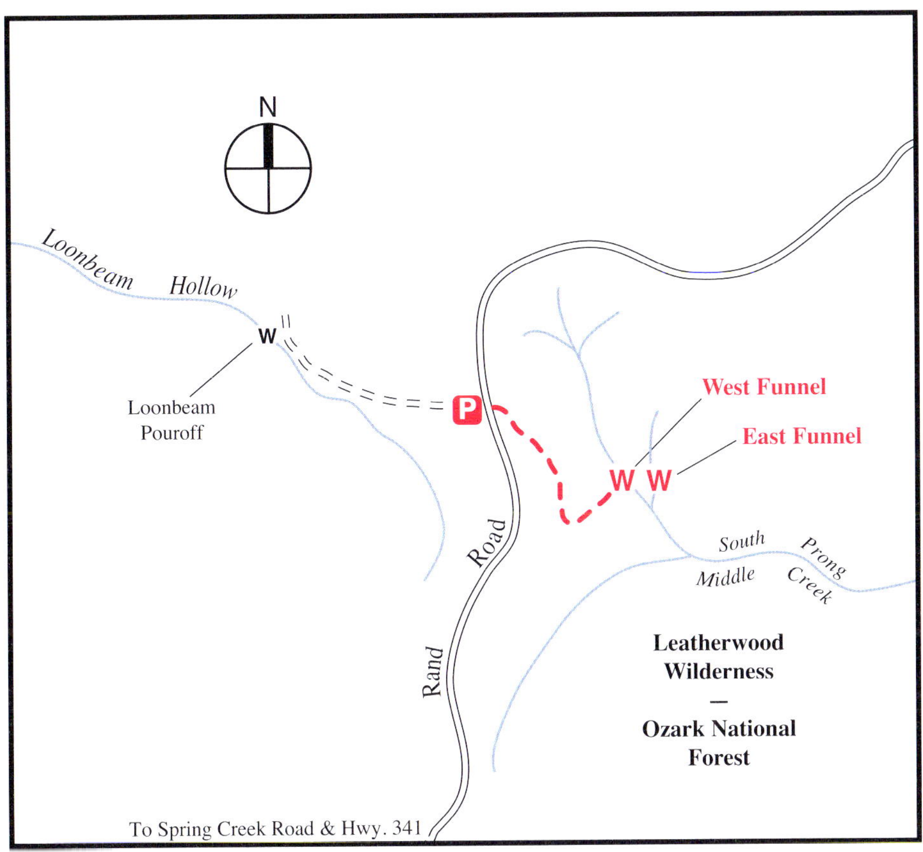

FUNNEL FALLS, East and West. *Wow*—this is one terrific spot, and pretty easy to get to! If you are a photographer, be sure to take plenty of film because you will need it. It is known as "the Funnel" because the rock formation at the East Falls funnels water down into it. The water action has created a natural stone arch.

From Big Flat, go 3.8 miles east on Hwy. 14 and TURN LEFT onto Hwy. 341 (paved). Go 2.3 miles and TURN LEFT onto Rand Road/FR#1118 (gravel). Go 6.5 miles to the intersection with Spring Creek Road and TURN RIGHT (still on Rand Road). Go .8 mile and PARK on the left where a little jeep road takes off **(36.06942, -92.44153)**.

Cross the road and head straight down into the woods. You will soon come to an old road trace—TURN RIGHT and follow this road until it begins to swing sharply back to the right—there are many rock outcrops here so it will be easy to find. LEAVE THE ROAD there, TURN LEFT and head steeply down the hill on a faint trail. This will take you on down to the falls area (additional photos on the next pages). Be *extra careful* there because the rock formations could also "funnel" you into a fatal fall.

If you have the time, take the short, easy hike down the jeep road on the opposite side of the road from The Funnel (where you parked). It drops on down less than a half mile to an incredible viewpoint that looks out over the lower Buffalo River area. There is also

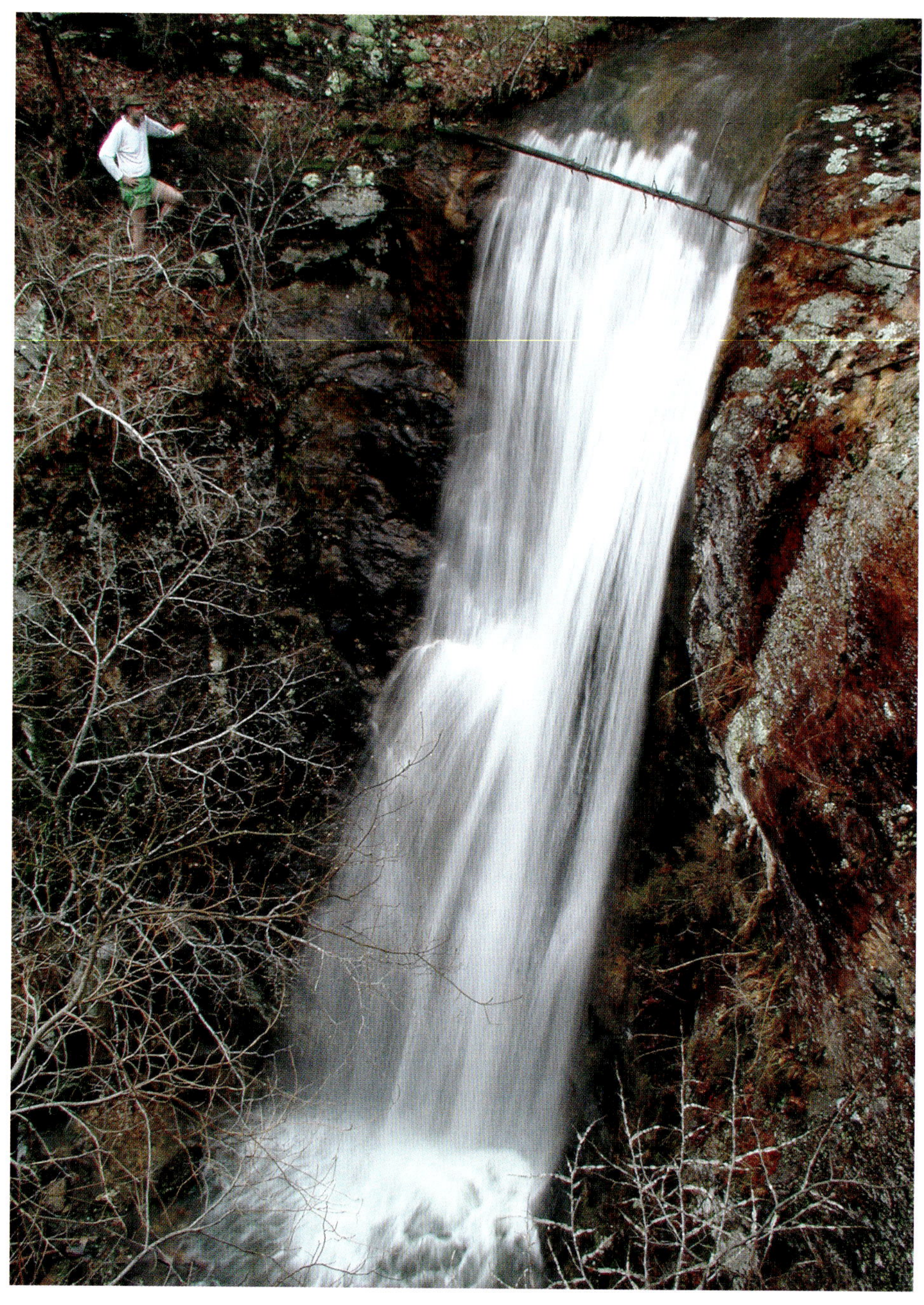

West Funnel Falls

a pouroff there. The flow is seldom enough to create a big waterfall, but the sheer height of the drop makes it impressive (more than 80 feet). The first time I visited it the wind was blowing so hard and coming in from out in front of the falls that the entire volume of water was blown back up and over the bluff! It was below freezing, and the bushes and trees above the falls were all coated with layers of ice—it was quite a sight.

Emergency contact: Marion County Sheriff, 870-449-4236 Dogs are OK.

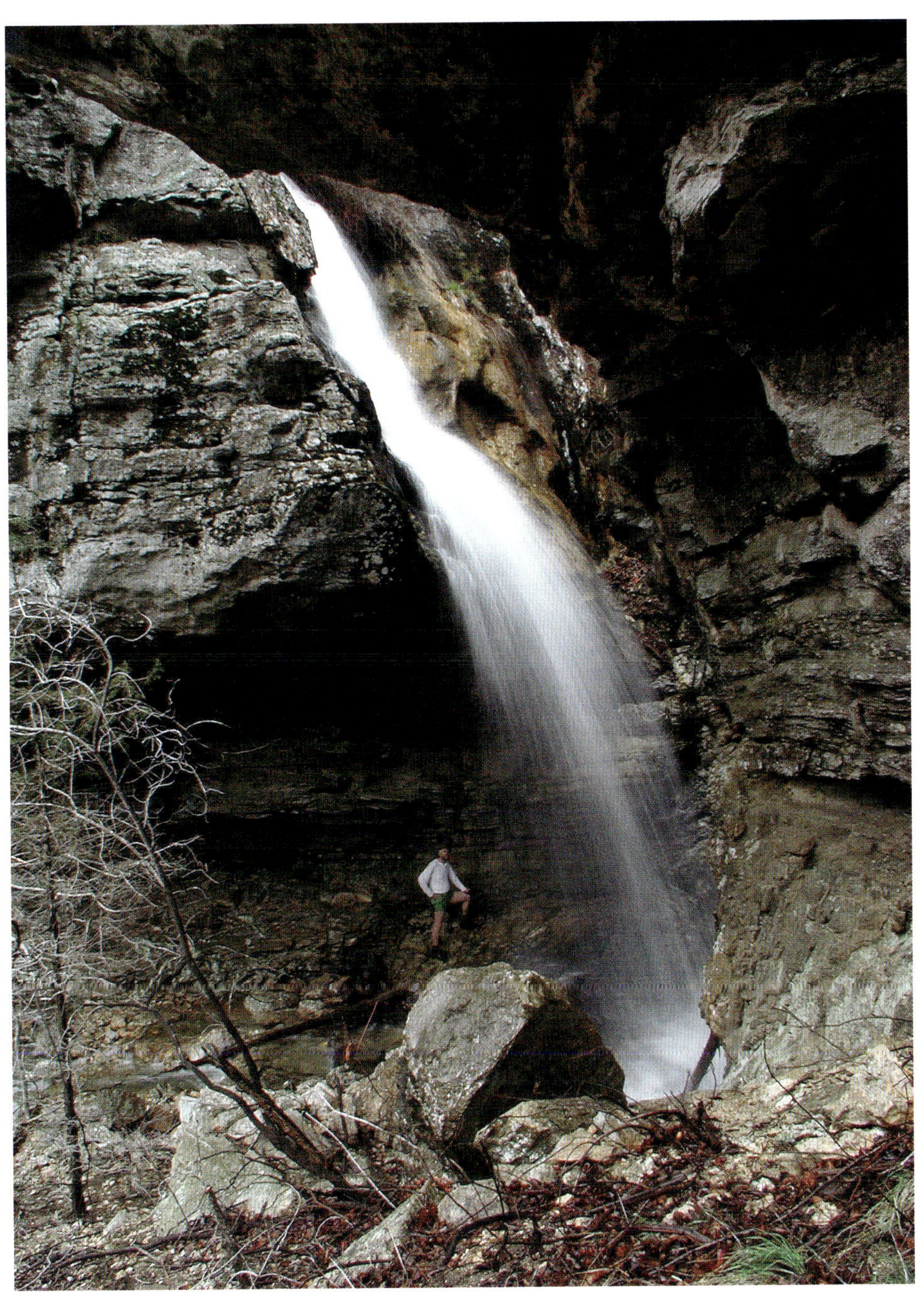

East Funnel Falls (the bottom part)

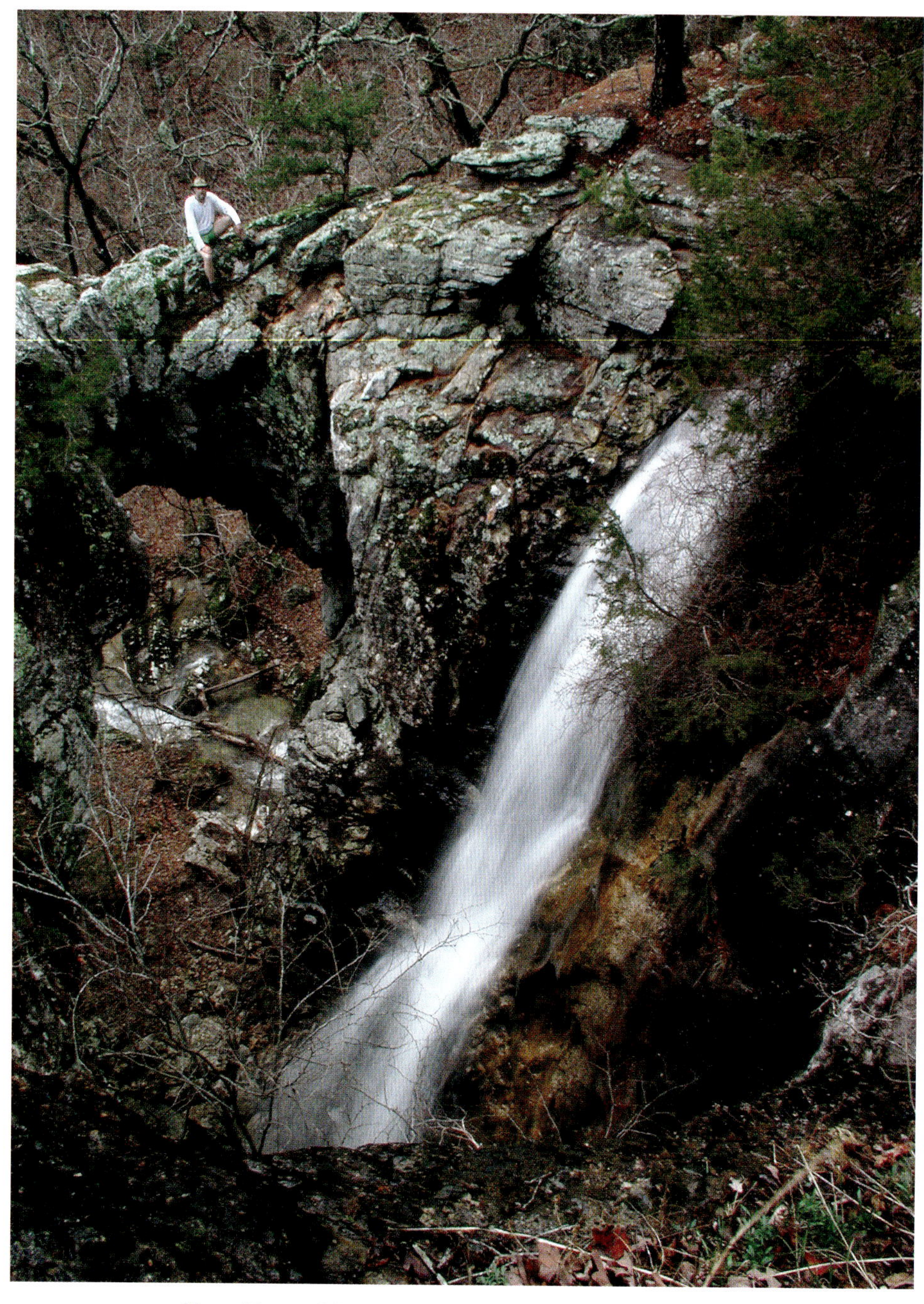

East Funnel Falls (the top part w/natural bridge)

Tassel Spring Falls – 44′

.5 mile roundtrip, easy bushwhack, GPS helpful

GPS **36.07558, -92.36747**

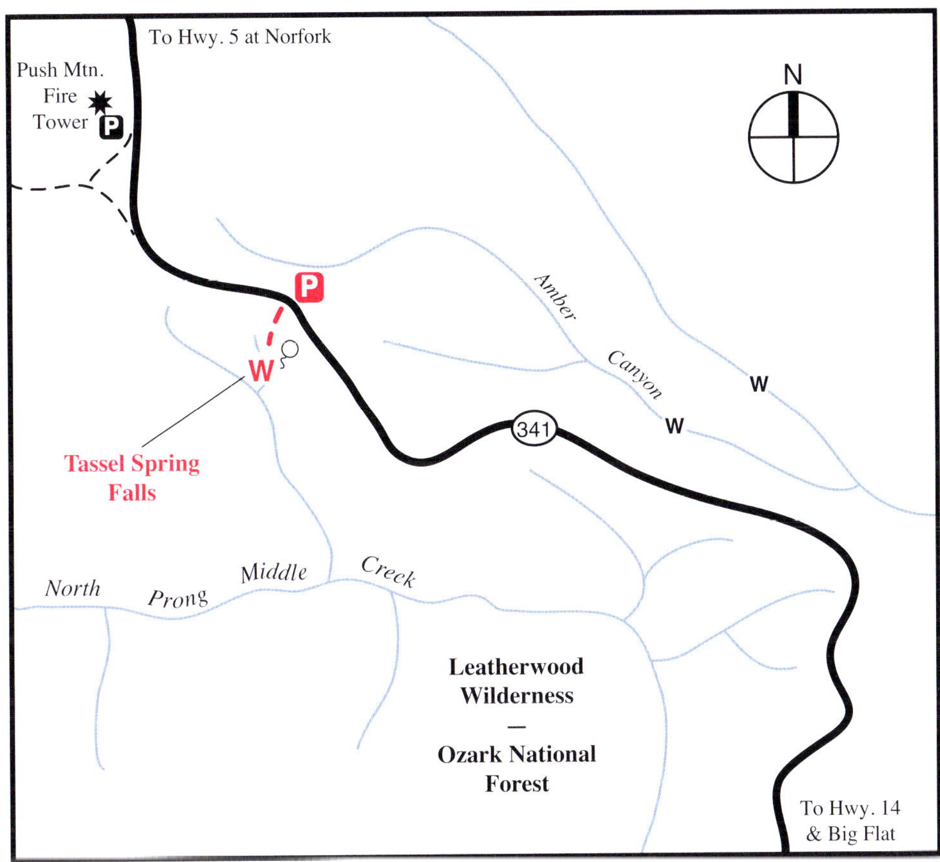

TASSEL SPRING FALLS. This is one of the more unusual waterfalls we have. The falls is not really all that great, but the moss "tassel" that grows there is very interesting. They say this tassel, which is actually a tangle of moss, roots, vines, and probably some dirt, used to grow nearly all the way to the ground. But vandals shot off the lower half of it, and now only about half of it remains. There is no trail, but the bushwhack down to the falls is short, although the climb back out is pretty steep. It's a quick stop on the way to or from the other waterfalls further up the road.

From Big Flat, go 3.8 miles east on Hwy. 14 and TURN LEFT onto Hwy. 341 (paved). Go 6.4 miles and PARK on the side of the road—look for a pulloff on the right **(36.07612, -92.36645)**.

Go across the highway and head steeply down the hill. You will come to the edge of the bluff soon. Look for the concrete basin that sits at the very top of the bluff—the tassel is attached to the base of a tree next to this basin, and the waterfall flows over the bluff and down the tassel. No swinging!

Emergency contact: Baxter County Sheriff, 870–425–6222 Dogs are OK.

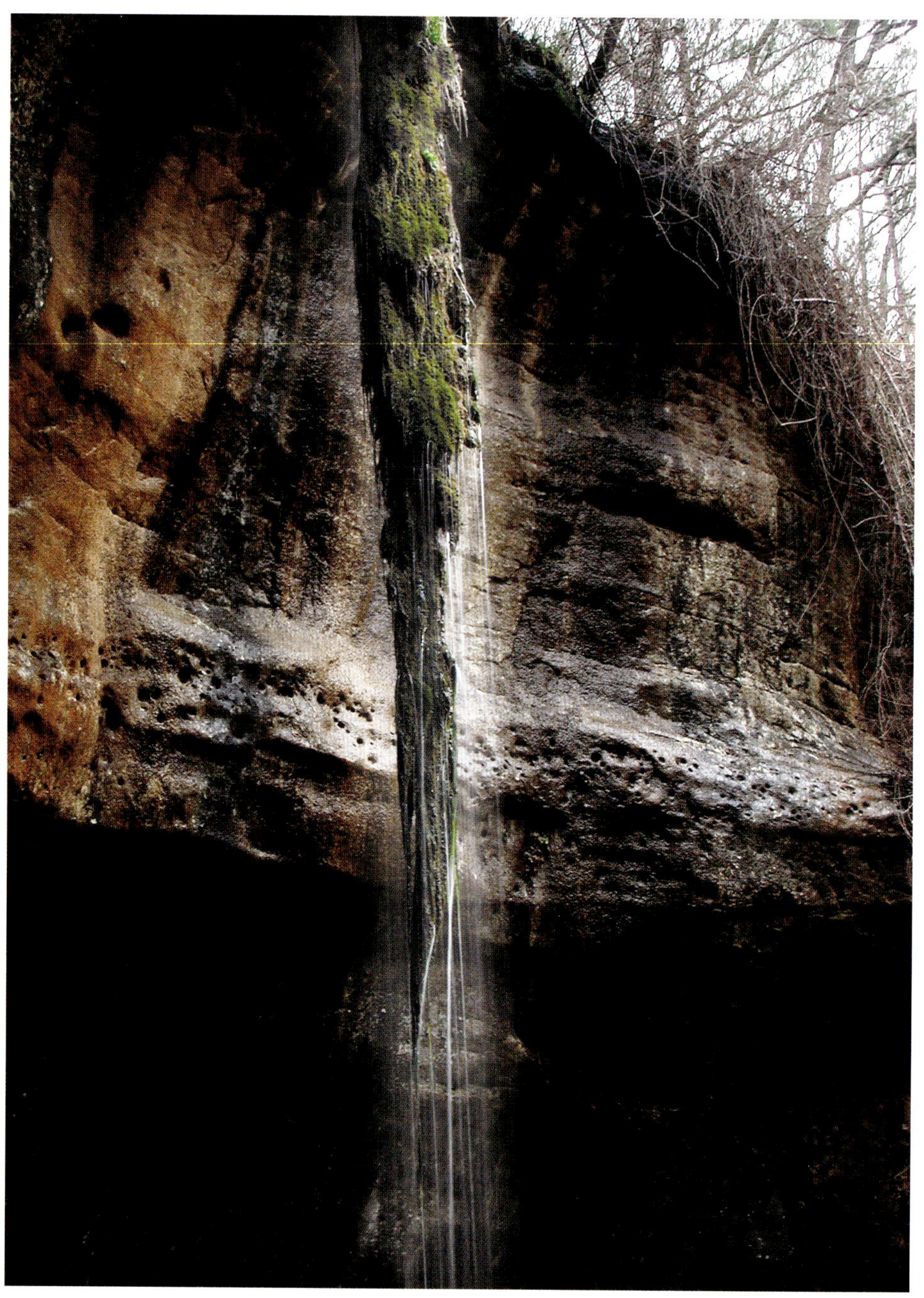

Tassel Spring Falls

(This is the top 25 feet of the moss "tassel" that used to hang all the way to near the ground—it's trying to grow back a little bit every day. 2025 update—I've heard it's looking much better and back to full height again!)

Helen's Pouroff – 71′

5.4 miles roundtrip, medium hike/bushwhack, GPS required

GPS **36.09688, -92.39310**

Woodsman Pouroff – 66′

Add 1.2 to above (6.6 total), medium hike/bushwhack, GPS required

GPS **36.09770, -92.40280**

Cathedral Falls – 87′

Add .7 to above (7.3 total for all), medium-difficult hike/bushwhack

GPS required

GPS **36.10332, -92.40360**

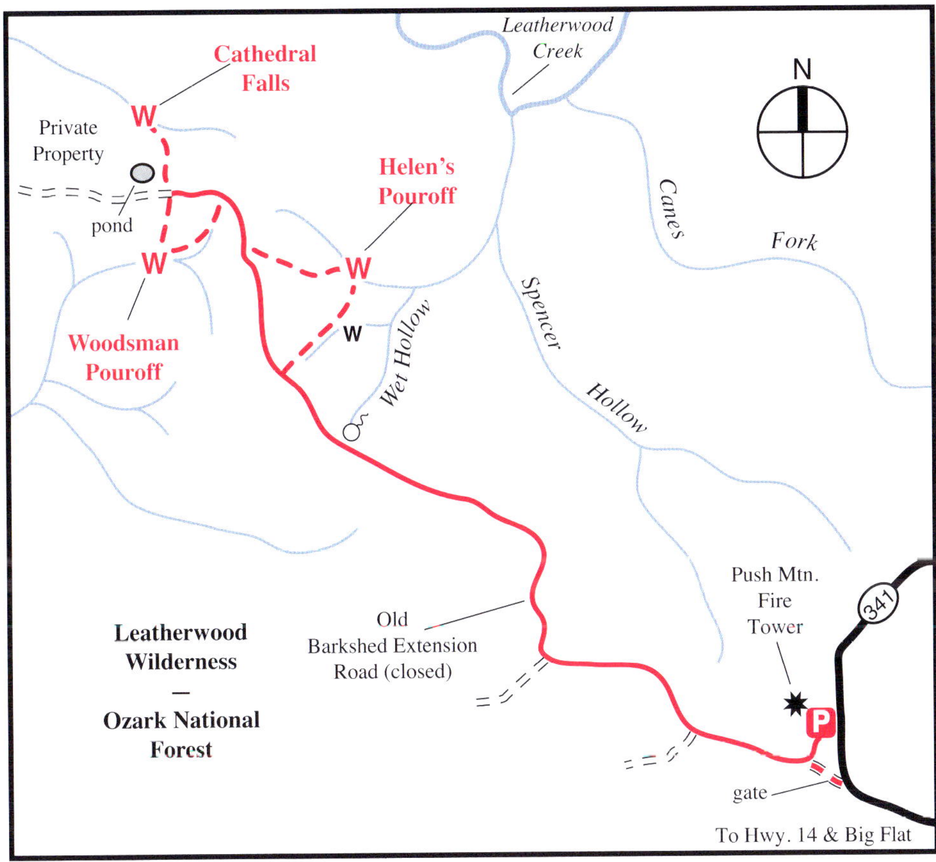

HELEN'S POUROFF/WOODSMAN POUROFF/CATHEDRAL FALLS. All three of these falls pour over tall bluffs and are well worth the extra effort to get to. The hike is along the old Barkshed Extension Road (closed to vehicles, except for property owners). It is easy hiking, but there are short bushwhacks required to each falls. A GPS is really a must here.

From Big Flat, go 3.8 miles east on Hwy. 14 and TURN LEFT onto Hwy. 341 (paved). Go 6.9 miles, TURN LEFT and PARK next to the base of Push Mountain Tower (**36.08029, -92.37126**). You can also park at gated Barkshed Extension Road on the left just before the tower, but there's not much room to park without blocking the gate.

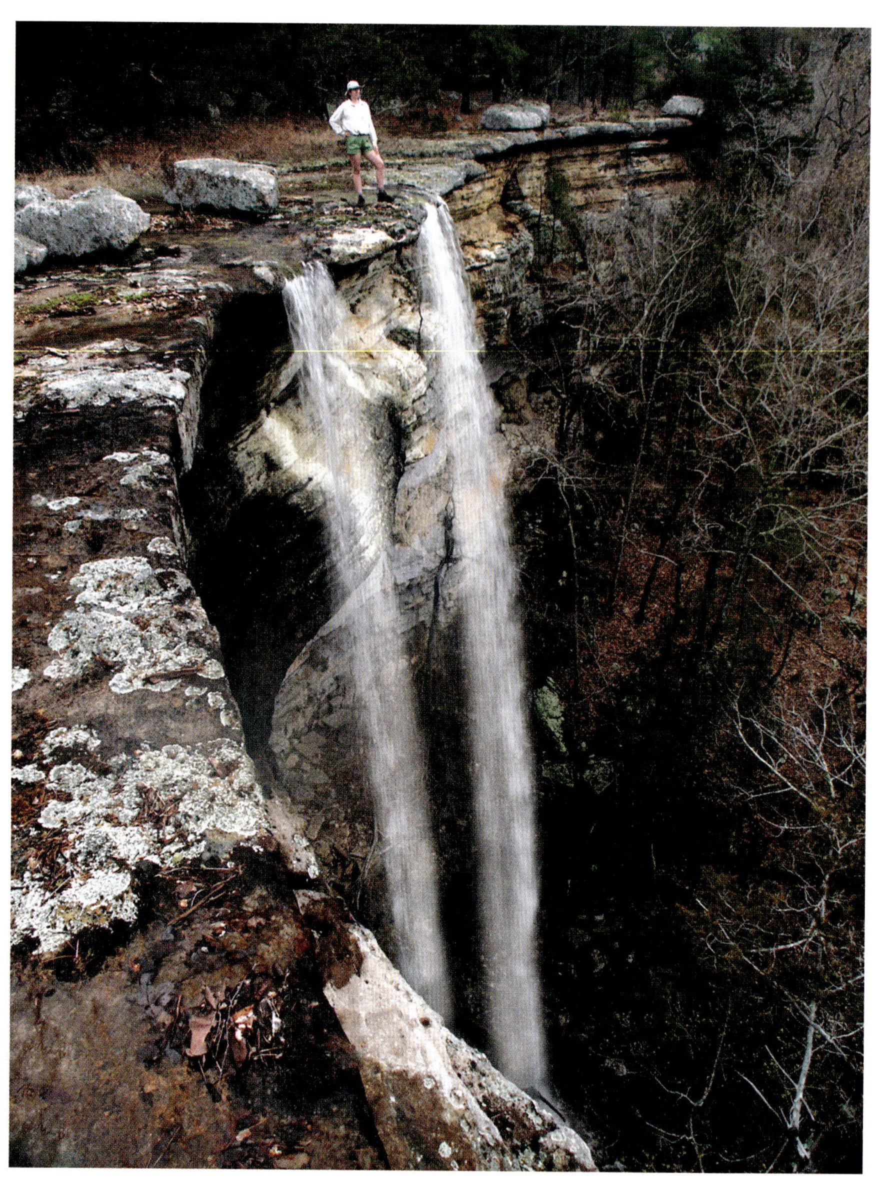

Helen's Pouroff

Head down the hill on the little horse trail that is next to the hitching post—TURN RIGHT once you get to the jeep road just below. Follow the road (stay RIGHT at the first fork) for 2.3 miles, then LEAVE THE ROAD to the RIGHT and drop down into a small drainage. This will take you down to a bluffline—TURN LEFT and follow the bluff. You may come to a nice 40 foot falls first, or arrive at **Helen's Pouroff** at 2.7 depending on where you hit the bluff. There are several large chunks of rock sitting on top of the bluff near the big falls, plus a little hole in the bluff that you can see down through. Some of the rocks are in the shape of a slice of pizza! This is named after Helen Elsner, who directed me to many of the waterfalls in "The Leatherwoods"—it is one of her favorites. Her book ***The Buffalo River and Surrounding Watershed*** is a great resource for many places up and down the Buffalo River area (research was all from horseback, with L.R. Alexander).

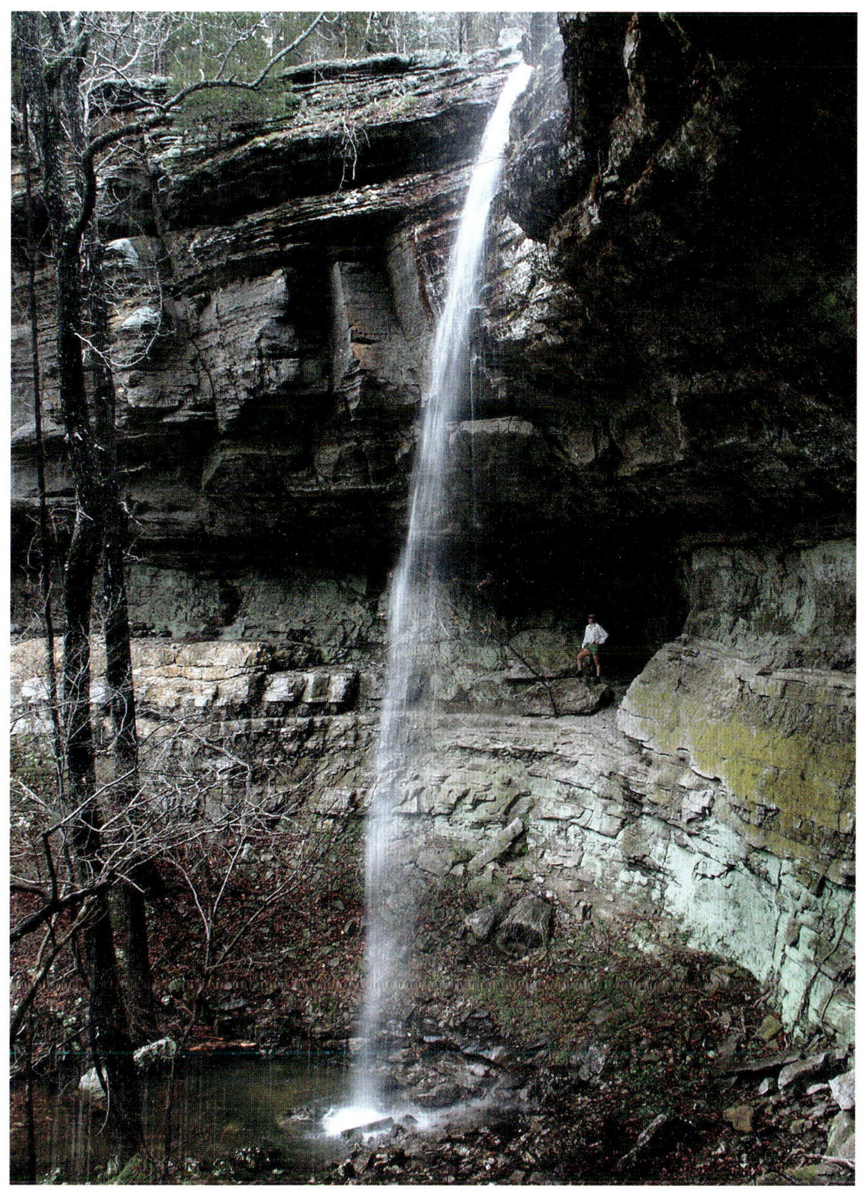

Woodsman Pouroff

From **Helen's Pouroff** hike back up to the jeep road and TURN RIGHT. Stay on the road a little bit, then LEAVE THE ROAD to the LEFT and bushwhack down into the drainage that will take you to **Woodsman Pouroff** at 3.4. It was named for Gene "Jake the Woodsman" Boyd who has spent a lifetime exploring The Leatherwoods. There is a neat little cove of sorts in behind the waterfall that my wife, Pam, is standing in above. Every time she sees this picture she reminds me that there was a "critter of some sort" back in it!

From the top of this falls you can head up around to the left of the hill and follow an old road trace most of the way back up to the jeep road. TURN LEFT at the road and you will come to an opening which is private property. TURN RIGHT and follow the property line straight down the hillside, past a pond over on the left. Go all the way down to the

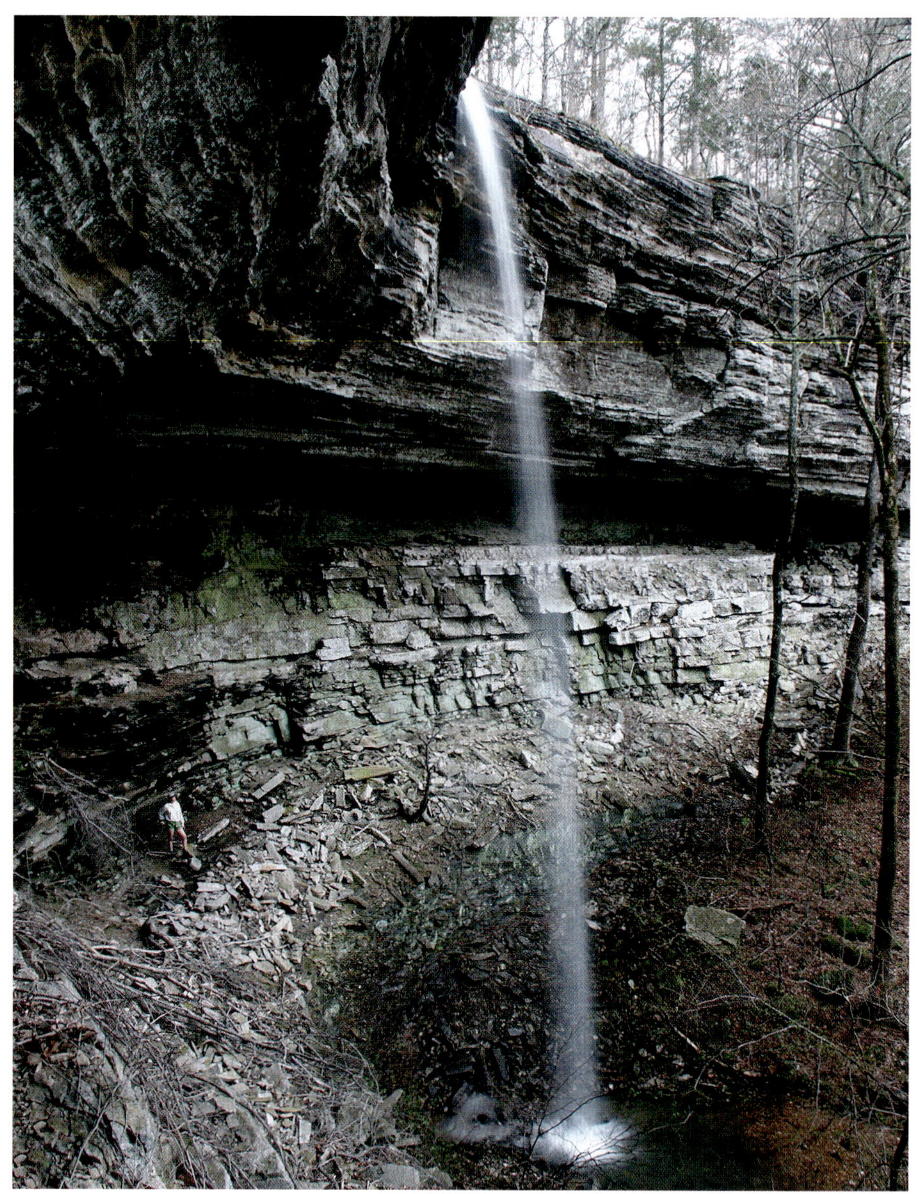

Cathedral Falls

creek (which is below the private property) and TURN LEFT and follow the creek just a little way to the top of **Cathedral Falls** at 3.9. To get to the bottom of the falls, cross the creek and follow the bluffline to the right for .25 mile or so (some great views down into the Leatherwood Creek Valley) until you can find a way down through it, then hike along the base of the bluff back to the falls. There are some giant pine trees in here, and the bluffline is quite spectacular—reminded me of a great wilderness cathedral.

To return to the parking area, simply make your way back up to the jeep road, TURN LEFT and follow it all the way back to the parking area—a hike of just over 3.0 miles. None of the hiking is all that difficult, but it does make for a very long day.

Emergency contact: Baxter County Sheriff, 870–425–6222 Dogs are OK.

Dewey Canyon Falls – 88′

.4 miles roundtrip, easy bushwhack, GPS not needed

GPS **36.09058, -92.34738**

Bumpers Falls (2) – 27′/71′

Same as above, easy bushwhack, GPS not needed

GPS **36.09028, -92.34765**

Heuston Falls – 54′

Add .4 to above, easy bushwhack, GPS not needed

GPS **36.09107, -92.35032**

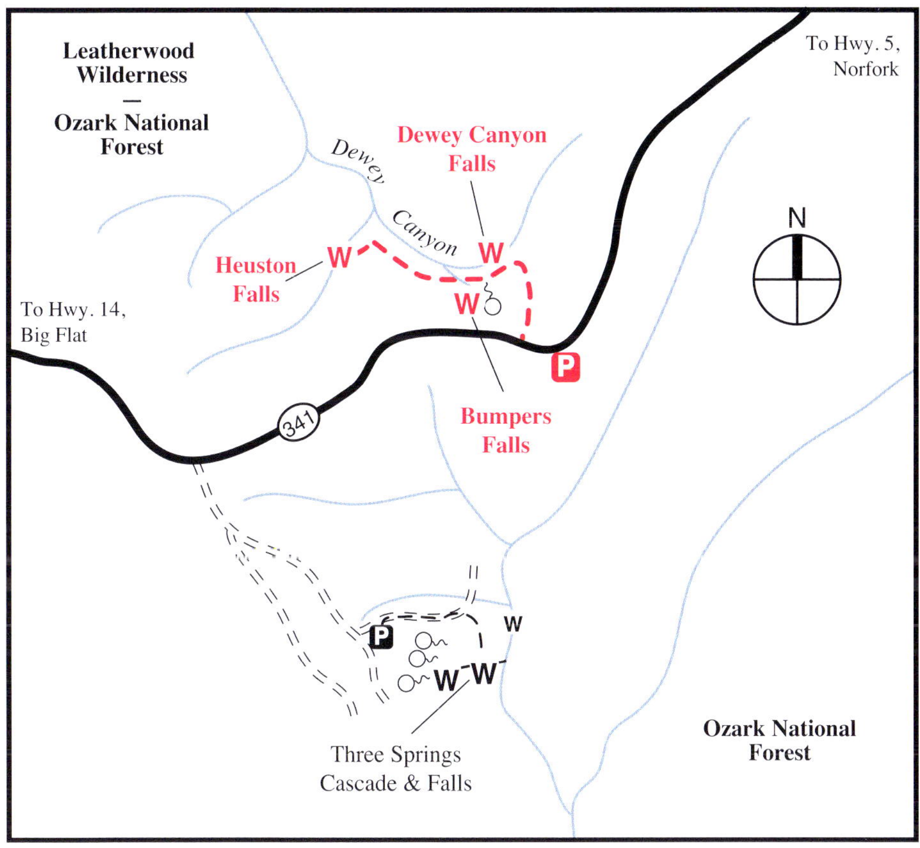

DEWEY CANYON/BUMPERS/HEUSTON FALLS. Here are four great waterfalls just a stone's throw off the highway. Like many of the falls in this area they look best when the water is really high.

From Big Flat, go 3.8 miles east on Hwy. 14 and TURN LEFT onto Hwy. 341 (paved). Go 8.9 miles and PARK on the right at the big curve **(36.08684, -92.35428)**.

CROSS the road and go back to the left to the beginning of a guard rail. You will find a faint trail there that heads down into the drainage to a little creek. TURN LEFT and follow the creek just a short distance to the top of **Dewey Canyon Falls**.

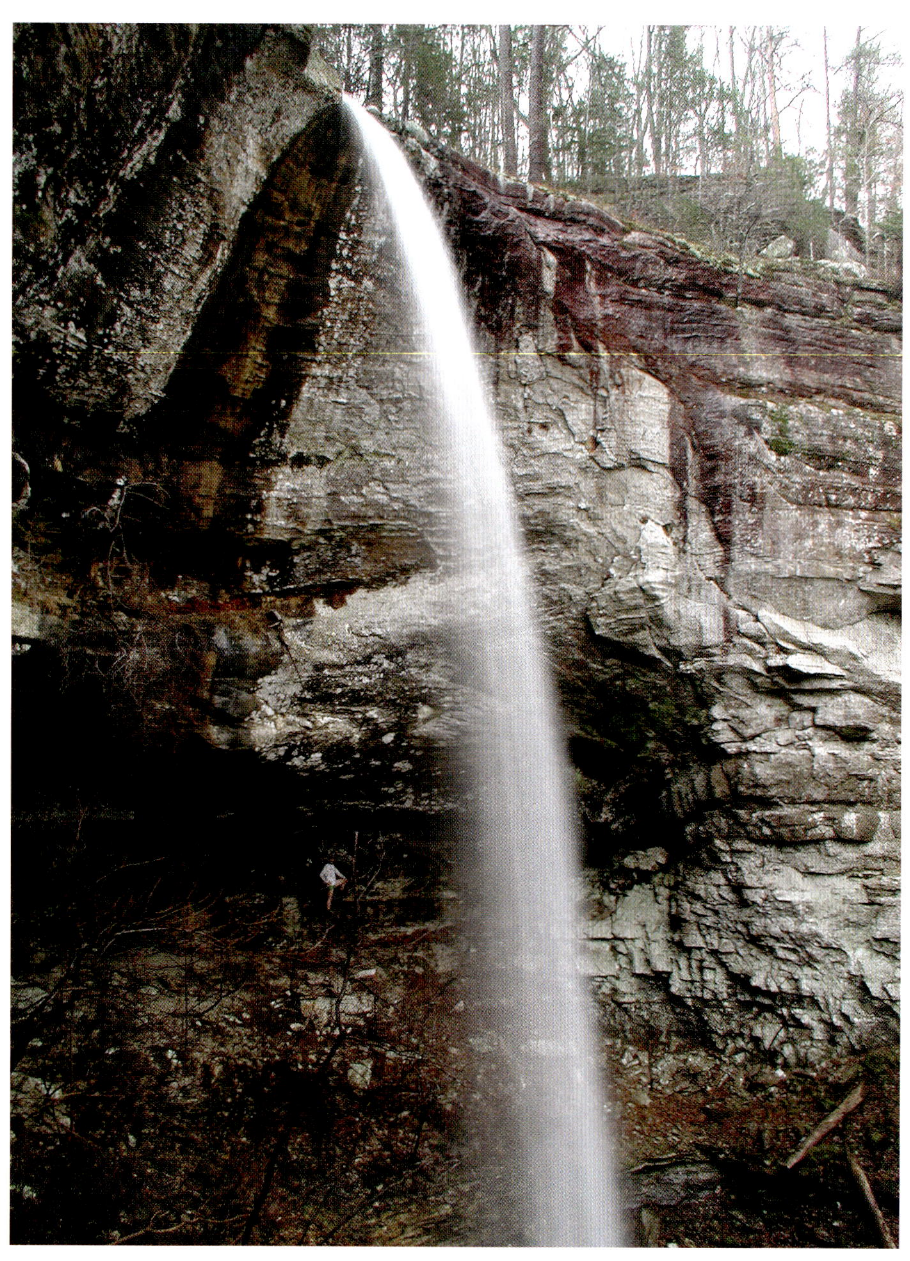

Dewey Canyon Falls

From the top of **Dewey Canyon Falls** TURN LEFT and follow the bluffline and you will come to the **Upper Bumpers Falls** (turn page for photo). The bluffline actually splits, or should I say a second bluffline rises up above. There is a spring up there that pours off the upper bluffline and creates this upper falls, then the water continues over the lower, taller bluff creating the lower falls. This is all close together and easy to see. You can get behind the upper falls and look back and see both **Bumpers Falls** and **Dewey Canyon Falls** at the same time. Bumpers Falls is named after our former governor and United States Senator from Arkansas, Dale Bumpers. He wrote the forward to the very first guidebook that I ever

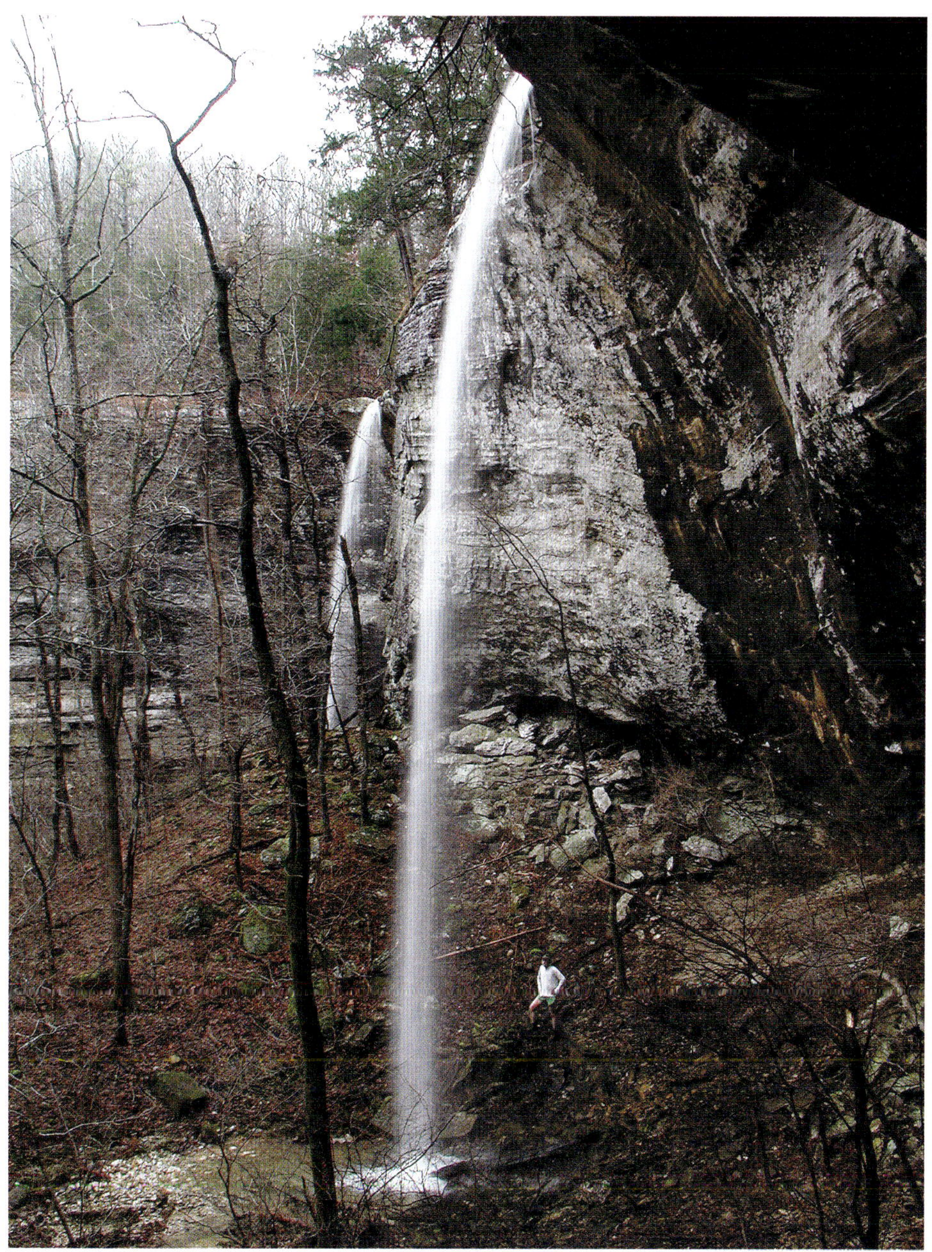

Lower Dale Bumpers Falls (Dewey Canyon Falls visible in background)

did (Ozark Highlands Trail Guide). Besides doing a great deal for the state of Arkansas, he was a tireless supporter of wilderness and other conservation issues his entire career.

To get to **Heuston Falls** CONTINUE along the top of the bluffline and it will curve back to the left and come to the top of the falls. John Heuston has been one of the driving forces behind the Ozark Society for several decades. He fought in those early years to save the Buffalo River and to establish our wilderness areas. He is an eloquent outdoor writer and a great story teller.

Emergency contact: Baxter County Sheriff, 870-425-6222 Dogs are OK.

Upper
Dale Bumpers Falls

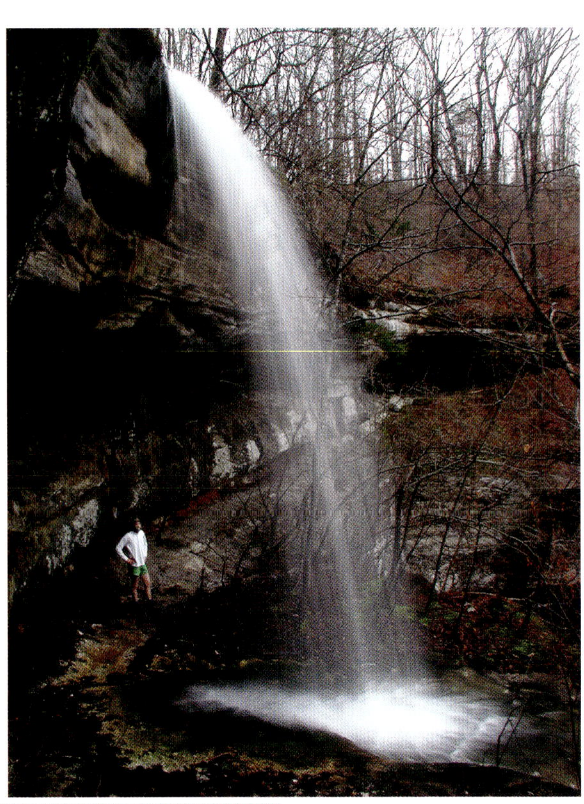

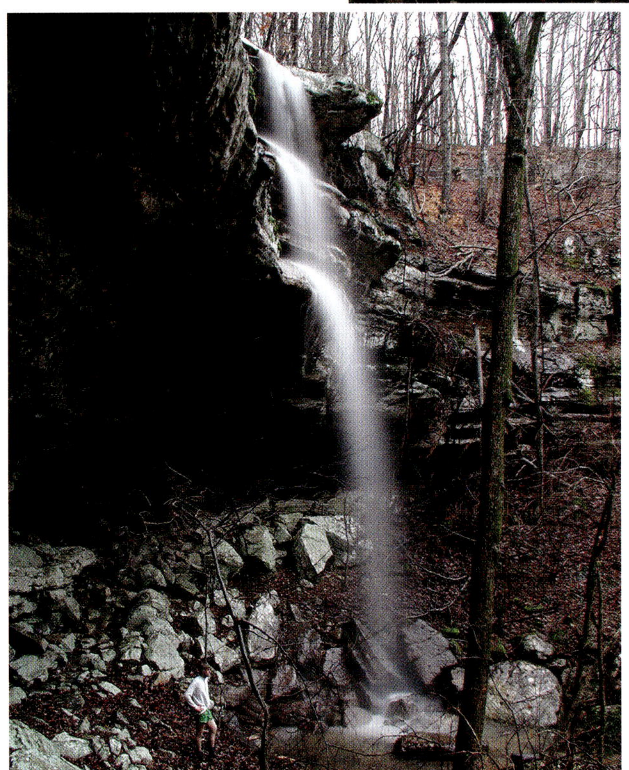

John Heuston Falls

Ozarks Region Waterfalls
(outside the Buffalo River drainage)

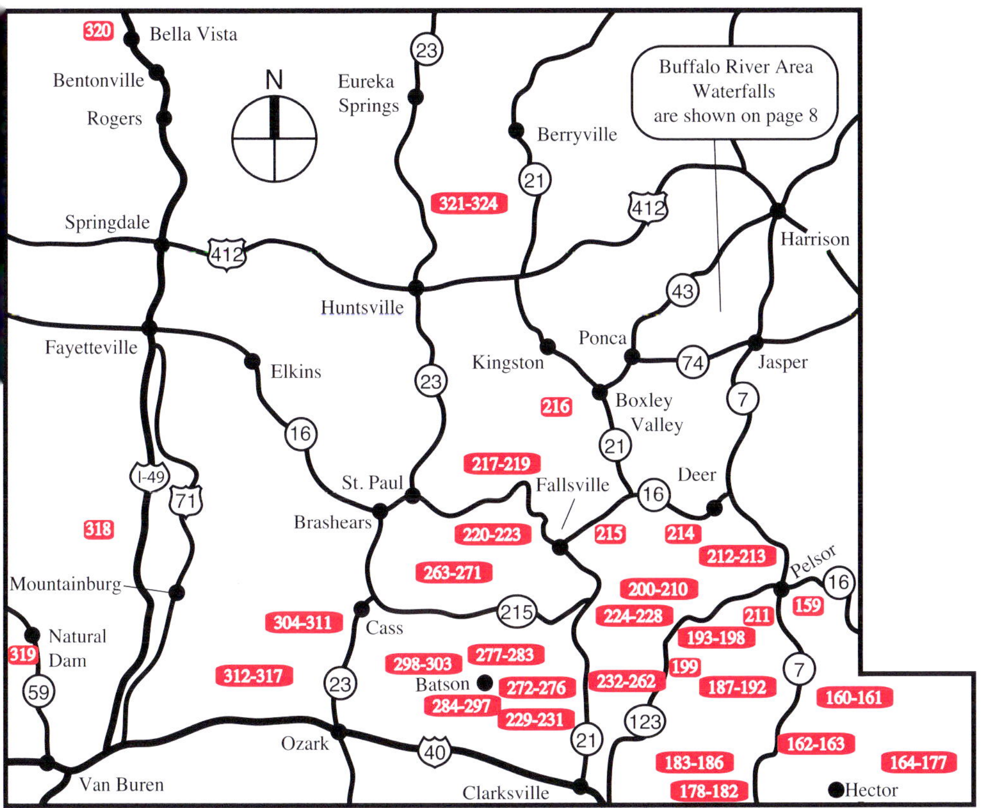

Not shown above since they are off the map: Blanchard Springs, Mirror Lake Falls, Steele Falls, or Three Springs Falls near Fifty-Six; nor Collins Creek Cascade, Bridal Veil Falls, or Cornelius Falls at Heber Springs.

"Ozark" is the word for "waterfall" used by some of the wandering Nomad tribes in the Sahara Desert. Just kidding, but it does seem like there are more waterfalls in the Ozarks than just about anyplace else in the central United States. We have two raw materials here in great abundance—water and bluffs—and when combined the two produce, what else—*waterfalls*. During the rainy season you can probably hike up just about any drainage in the Ozarks and find a waterfall of some sort. I have picked out some of the best that I know of—and that others have told me about—to include in this section. Some of them are located in the middle of nowhere and require a serious and often difficult trek to get to, while others are right next to the road and offer easy access. And just in case you have not read the first part of this guidebook yet and were wondering where the famous Buffalo River waterfalls are listed—they have their own section (see page 8).

Fall #	Name	Height	Hike Difficulty	Page #
152	Three Springs Cas.	14/45	Easy	**194**
153	Blanchard Springs	10	Easy	**196**
154	*Mirror Lake Falls	29+	Easy	**196**
155	Steele Falls	66	Med.	**198**
156	Collins Creek Cascade		Easy	**200**
157	Cornelius Falls	49	Easy	**202**
158	Bridal Veil Falls	33	Med.	**202**
159	Kings Bluff Falls	114	Easy	**204**
160	N. Fork Rd. Falls S.	33	Easy	**206**
161	N. Fork Rd. Falls N.	53	Easy	**206**
162	Cabin Falls	36	Med.	**208**
163	Maidenhair Falls	30	Med.	**208**
164	Penhook Falls	41	Med.	**210**
165	*Fiddlehead Falls	19	Easy	**212**
166	Blue Hole Cascades		Diff.	**212**
167	Green Grotto Falls	21	Diff.	**212**
168	*Grapevine Shelter	63	Med.	**215**
169	*Sand Cave Quint.	13-33	♦	**215**
170	*Jacob's Stairway	23+	Med.	**219**
171	Schoolhouse Falls	30	Med.	**221**
172	Lizard Log Falls	47	Diff.	**221**
173	Iris Falls	64	Diff.	**221**
174	Voices Falls	44	Diff.	**221**
175	Whiskey Chute Falls	83	Diff.	**221**
176	Ladderbucket Falls	36	Diff.	**226**
177	John Mountain Falls	84	Diff.	**226**
178	*Rough Hollow Falls	34	Easy	**229**
179	*Giant Rocks Falls	13	Easy	**229**
180	*Trigg Falls	37	Easy	**229**
181	*Balcony Falls	28	Med.	**229**
182	Longpool Falls	44	Easy	**233**
183	*Waldo Mtn. Falls	23	Med.	**235**
184	*Rick Henry #805	19	Med.	**235**
185	Forever Falls	47	Diff.	**238**
186	Graves Canyon	31/35	Diff.	**238**
187	*Teapot Hollow	29	Med.	**242**
188	*Teapot Cascade	23+	Med.	**242**
189	*Earl Grey Falls	23	Med.	**242**
190	*Littishie Falls	39	Med.	**242**
191	*Waterman Falls	36	Med.	**242**
192	*Calendar Falls	25	Med.	**242**
193	Sidewinder Falls	21	Diff.	**246**
194	Swamp Falls	19	Diff.	**246**
195	V Slot Falls	10	Diff.	**246**
196	Pam's Grotto	37	Med.	**249**
197	Haw Creek Falls	6	Easy	**251**

Fall #	Name	Height	Hike Difficulty	Page
198	Pack Rat Falls	24	Med.	**25**
199	Highway 123 Falls	47	Easy	**25**
200	Car Wash Falls	21	Easy	**25**
201	Rock Cr. Bluff Falls	47	Med.	**25**
202	Deer Trail Falls	55	Med.	**25**
203	Big Buck Falls	62	Med.	**25**
204	Piney Bowl Falls	64	Diff.	**26**
205	*Mrs. O'Leary's Falls	57	Med.	**26**
206	*Bull Falls	63	Med.	**26**
207	*Sprinkler Falls	94	Med.	**26**
208	*Cincinnati Freedom	27	Med.	**26**
209	*Little Cow Grotto	18-22	Med.	**26**
210	*Norman Falls	19	Med.	**26**
211	Native American	41	Med.	**26**
212	Cub Hol. Falls	39/47/48	Diff.	**27**
213	Lonesome Hol. Falls	47	Easy	**27**
214	*Eliana Falls	71	Med.	**27**
215	Glory Hole, The	31	Med.	**27**
216	Sweden Creek Falls	81	Med.	**27**
217	Kings River Falls	10	Easy	**28**
218	*Tenderfoot Falls	21	Easy	**28**
219	*Thong Tree Falls	29	Easy	**28**
220	Lichen Falls	28	Easy	**28**
221	*Accord Hollow (4)	41-66	Med.	**28**
222	Estep Creek Falls	16	Med.	**28**
223	Waterfall Hollow (3)	17-23	Med.	**28**
224	Hobo Falls (2)	23/27	Med.	**29**
225	Bear Skull Falls	22	Med.	**29**
226	Slot Rock	8	Med.	**29**
227	Sunset Falls	70	Diff.	**29**
228	Discovery Falls	43	Diff.	**29**
229	Spainhour Falls	16	Med.	**29**
230	Lucy Falls	17	Med.	**29**
231	Aspen Falls	37	Med.	**29**
232	*January Falls	10	Easy	**30**
233	*Anniversary Falls	17	Easy	**30**
234	*Three Tier Falls	29	♦	**30**
235	*Bigger Rock Falls	15	Med.	**30**
237	*Redbud Falls	36	Med.	**30**
238	*Ledge Snake Falls	54	Diff.	**30**
239	*Rock Layer Falls	17	Diff.	**30**
240	*Silverbell Falls	27	Easy	**30**
241	*Sally Ann Quads	81/27	♦	**30**
242	*Sally Ann Quads	85/23	♦	**30**
243	*Sally Ann Mystic	69/30	♦	**30**

* New waterfalls in this edition

Fall #	Name	Height	Hike Difficulty	Page #
244	*Sweet Magnolia	35	♦	**311**
245	*Beechnut Falls	57	♦	**311**
246	*Hickory Falls	24	♦	**311**
247	*Tombstone Falls	63	♦	**314**
248	*Danny's Hideout	35	♦	**314**
249	*High In Dry Falls	53	♦	**314**
250	*Carolyn Falls	45	Diff.	**318**
251	*Z Falls	67	♦	**318**
252	*Four Step Falls	58	♦	**320**
253	*Feeder Falls	42	♦	**320**
254	*Leeds Falls	91	♦	**320**
255	*Paw Paw Falls	23	♦	**320**
256	*Calcite Falls	43	Diff.	**326**
257	*Caleb Falls	61	Med.	**327**
258	*Hundred Foot Falls	57	Med.	**327**
259	*Cecil Falls	57	Med.	**330**
260	*McKay Twin Falls	30	Diff.	**330**
261	*McKay Two Step	31	Diff.	**330**
262	*Footprint Hol.	39/42	♦	**330**
263	Black Bear Falls	31	Med.	**336**
264	Monkey Falls	33	Med.	**336**
265	Murray Falls	37	Med.	**338**
266	Senyard Falls	29	Med.	**338**
267	Spirit Mt. Falls	15	Diff.	**341**
268	Mt. Fork Cr. Falls	13	Diff.	**341**
269	Sixty Foot Falls	56	Diff.	**341**
270	Spy Rock Falls	19	Easy	**345**
271	High Bank Twins	71	Easy	**347**
272	*Curve Ball Falls	33	Diff.	**349**
273	*Log In Way Falls	30	Diff.	**349**
274	*Cove Creek Cascade	21	Diff.	**349**
275	*Never Again Falls	39	Diff.	**349**
276	*Never Ever Again	31	Diff.	**349**
277	Doppelgänger Falls	19	Med.	**352**
278	*Boars Head Falls	49	Med.	**354**
279	*Two Tier Falls	37	Med.	**354**
280	*Fallen Timber Falls	21	Med.	**354**
281	*Whiskey Fall Upper	24	Med.	**354**
282	*Amy Falls	29	Med.	**354**
283	*Short Grotto Falls	<10	Med.	**354**
284	*Briandjen Twin	33/31	♦	**358**
285	*JenLynn Br. Falls	10	♦	**358**
286	*Marilyn/Cinn. Falls	61	♦	**358**
287	*Lucky Falls	23	♦	**358**
288	Brian's Polyfoss(4)	15-35	♦	**362**
289	*Secretariat Falls	51	Diff.	**366**
290	*Wildfire Falls	33	♦	**366**
291	*Snowman Falls	54	♦	**366**
292	*Seabiscuit Falls	44	♦	**366**
293	*Mr. Ed Falls	23	♦	**366**
294	*Trigger Falls	35	♦	**366**
295	*Silver Falls	27	♦	**366**
296	*Scout Falls	30	♦	**366**
297	*White Horse Falls	24	♦	**366**
298	Shower Chair Falls	41	Med.	**375**
299	Legos Falls	40	Med.	**375**
300	Bingham Hol. Falls	51	Easy	**377**
301	Sentinel Rock Falls	52	Med.	**377**
302	White Oak Cr. Falls	37	Med.	**380**
303	Mineral Springs Falls	43	Med.	**380**
304	Pig Trail Falls	18	Easy	**383**
305	Train Trestle Falls	31	Med.	**385**
306	Spirits Creek Falls	8	Med.	**387**
307	Robinson Falls	17/21	Med.	**387**
308	White Rock Cr. Fall	31	Med.	**391**
309	White Rock Cr. Cas	10	Med.	**391**
310	Jack White Falls	41	Med.	**393**
311	Phipps Branch Falls	23	Easy	**393**
312	*Tom Kennon Falls	42	Med.	**396**
313	*Keefe Grotto	21	Med.	**396**
314	Devils Canyon Falls	63	Diff.	**399**
315	Devils Can. Jr. Falls	18	Med.	**399**
316	Rattlesnake Falls	29	Easy	**402**
317	Dockery Gap Falls	36	Diff.	**404**
318	Twin Falls D. Den	47/56	Easy	**406**
319	Natural Dam	8x187	Easy	**408**
320	Tanyard Creek Falls	12	Easy	**409**
321	Eagle's Nest Falls	41	Easy	**411**
322	Tea Kettle Falls	46	Med.	**413**
323	Road 299 Falls	21	Easy	**415**
324	Glory B Falls	16	Easy	**415**

* New waterfalls in this edition

Three Springs Cascade/Falls – 14′/45′

.6 mile roundtrip, easy hike, GPS helpful

GPS **36.08317, -92.34692**

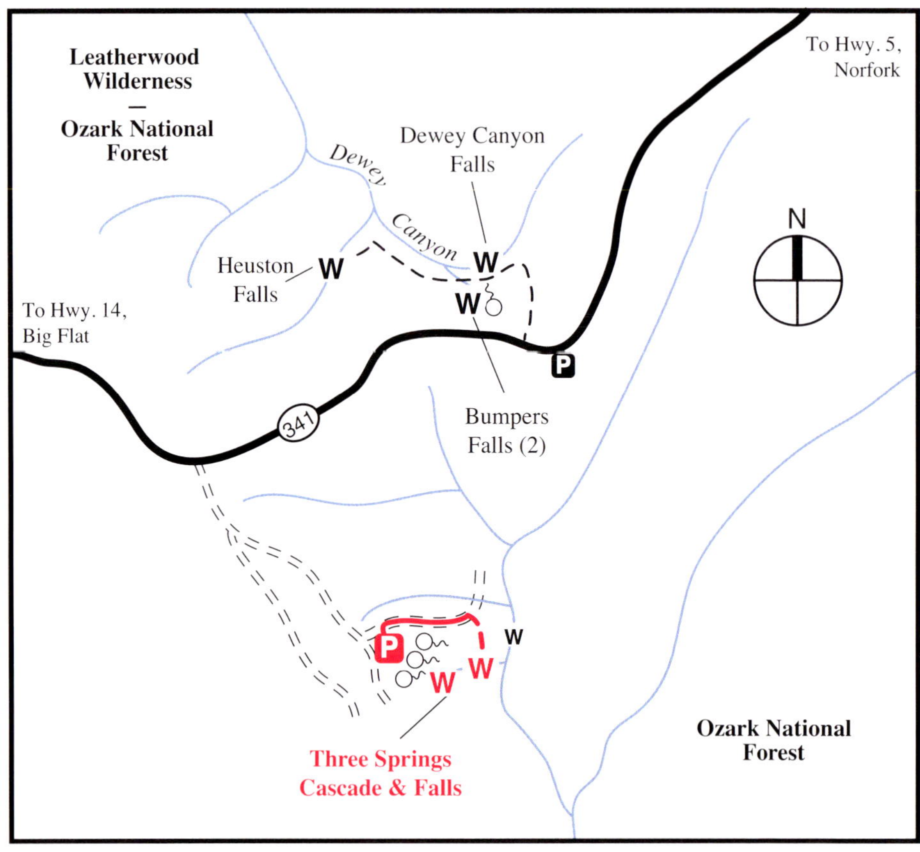

THREE SPRINGS CASCADE & FALLS. There are two little springs and one large spring that all run together to form a waterfall. And there is a nice cascade that is just below the big spring that is worth a look too. Both are easy to get to right off the highway.

From Big Flat, go 3.8 miles east on Hwy. 14 and TURN LEFT onto Hwy. 341 (paved). Go 8.3 miles and TURN RIGHT onto a jeep road (used to be Cook Road). Bear LEFT at the first fork, and then TURN LEFT at the bottom of the next hill and PARK in a clearing (this is a wildlife food plot), about .4 from the highway. The last run down to the food plot may be rough, but most vehicles should be able to make it.

Follow the jeep road that goes down the hill on the LEFT side of the food plot, and where it levels out a bit and curves back to the left TURN RIGHT onto a four-wheeler trail. This will take you over above the waterfall, which is just down on your LEFT, and to the base of the cascade, which will be up on your right. All of this only .3 from the food plot. If you follow the bluffline at the top of the falls back to the left you will come to another waterfall (23 feet tall), which has some interesting rock formations around it. OR you could follow the bluffline around to the right from the top of the falls and you will eventually find a way down into the canyon to see both falls.

Emergency contact: Baxter County Sheriff, 870–425–6222

Three Springs Cascade

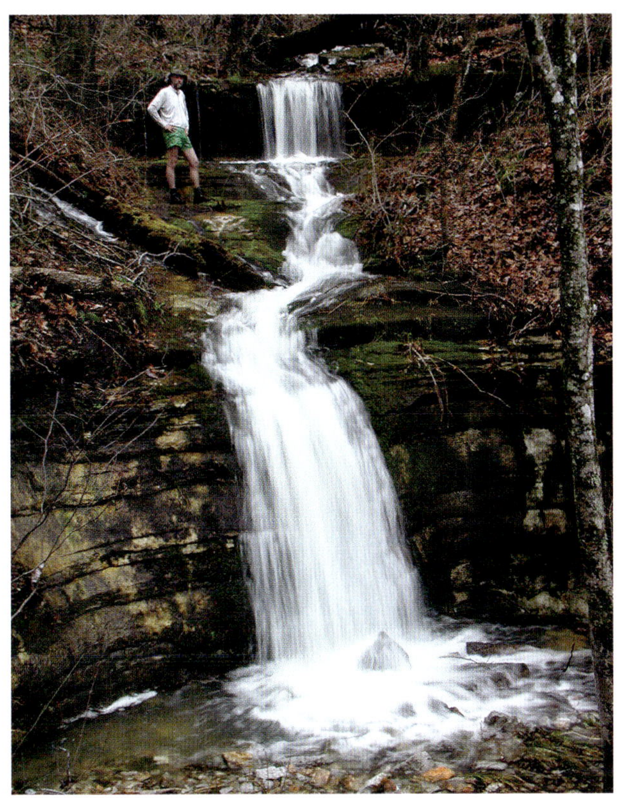

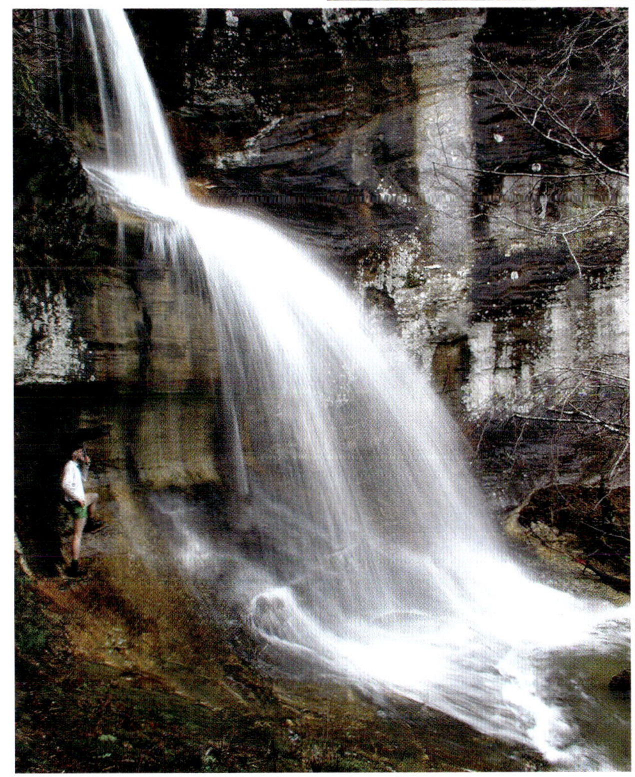

Three Springs Falls

Blanchard Springs –10′

.25 mile roundtrip, easy stroll, GPS not needed

GPS **35.95915, -92.17574**

Mirror Lake Falls –29′+

.25 mile roundtrip, easy stroll, GPS not needed

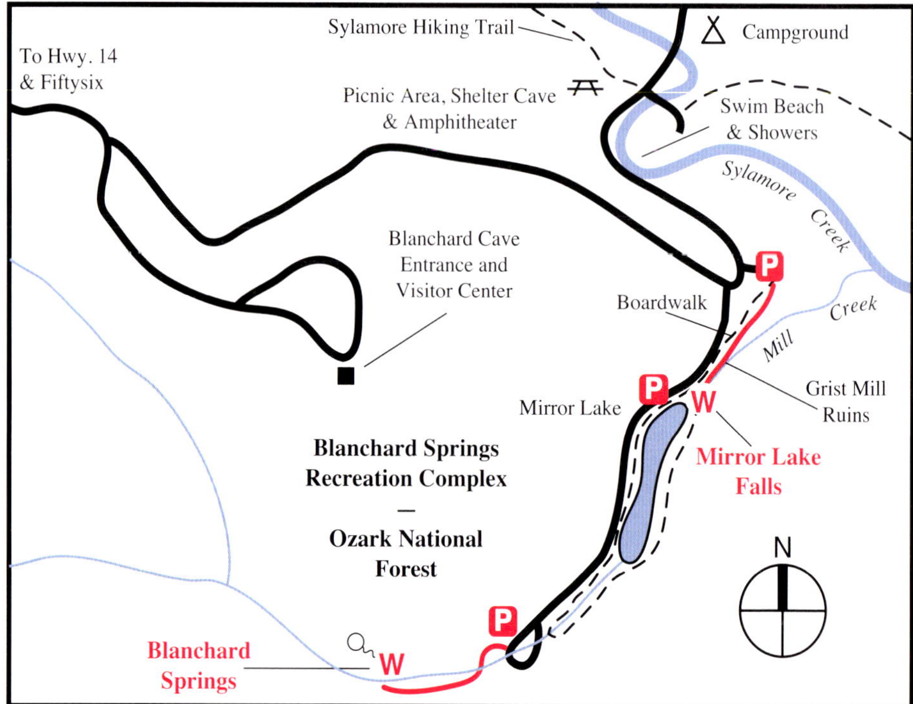

BLANCHARD SPRINGS/MIRROR LAKE FALLS. This is a delightful spot that has attracted visitors for many generations. The spring and falls run all summer long, so you can always go there for a refreshing moment on a hot day.

The turnoff to Blanchard Springs is located just east of the community of Fiftysix (between Big Flat and Sylamore on Hwy. 14). There are many thousands of visitors a year to this place so everything is well marked. Just follow the signs to the parking area for the spring **(35.95895, -92.17551)**, then take the boardwalk along the creek to the mouth of the spring. This is one waterfall where you can bring your baby along in a stroller! My recommendation is that you plan to visit during the winter when you will have the place to yourself. Tour the cave and spend the night in the campground, then go see the spring early the next morning—when it is cold you can see mist coming from the spring.

Mirror Lake Falls is a neat double-decker waterfall that is actually multiple dams that were constructed to power an historic grist mill just below. Hike the accessible boardwalk to read about the history—there's a trail below it that runs next to the creek to the base of the falls, and SSS for sure! (park here for lower trail access **35.96583, -92.16942**)

Emergency contact: Stone County Sheriff, 870–269–2700 Dogs are OK.

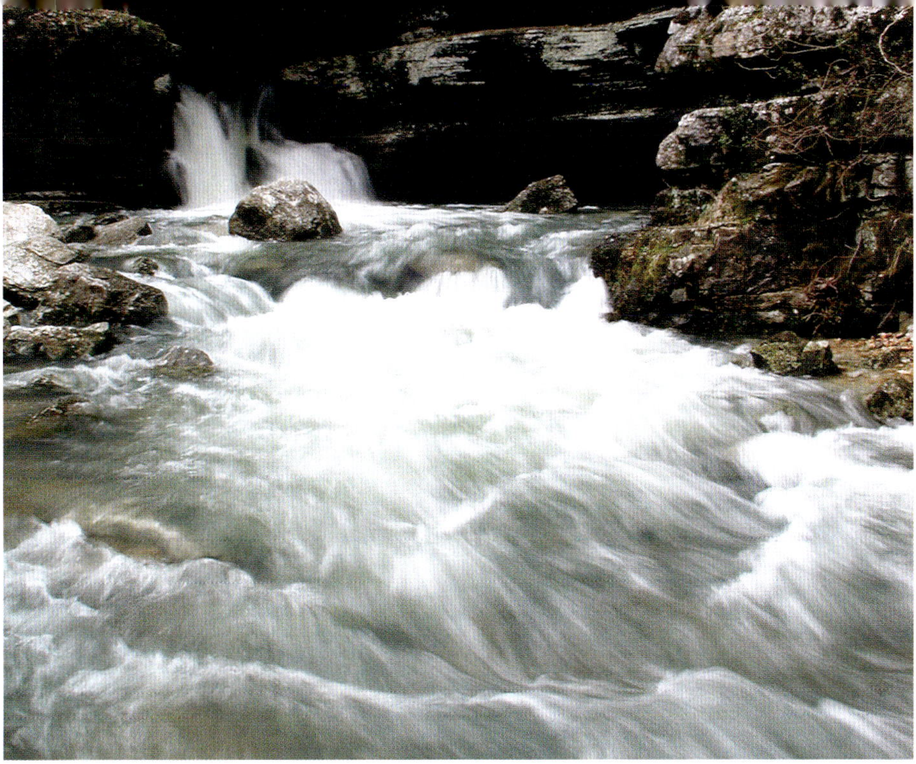

Blanchard Springs (above), Mirror Lake Falls (below)

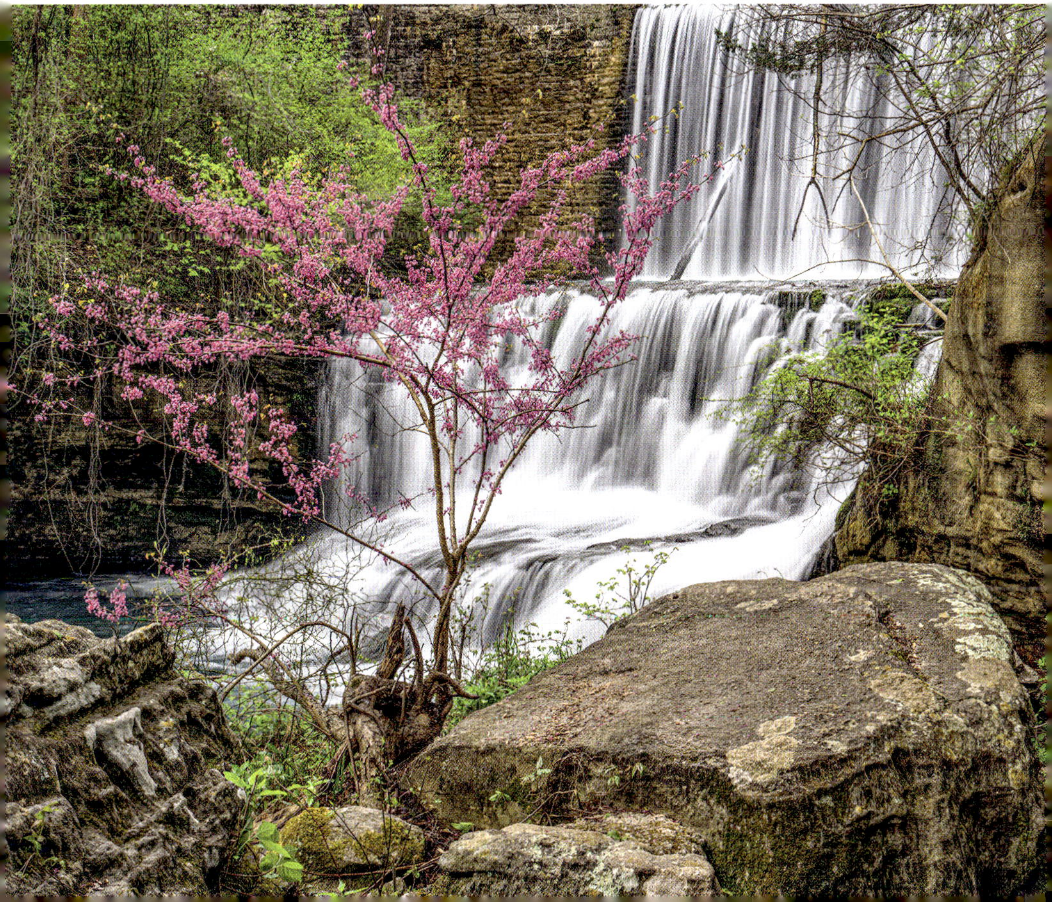

Steele Falls – 66′

3.2 miles roundtrip, easy-medium hike, GPS not needed

GPS **36.01728, -92.17963**

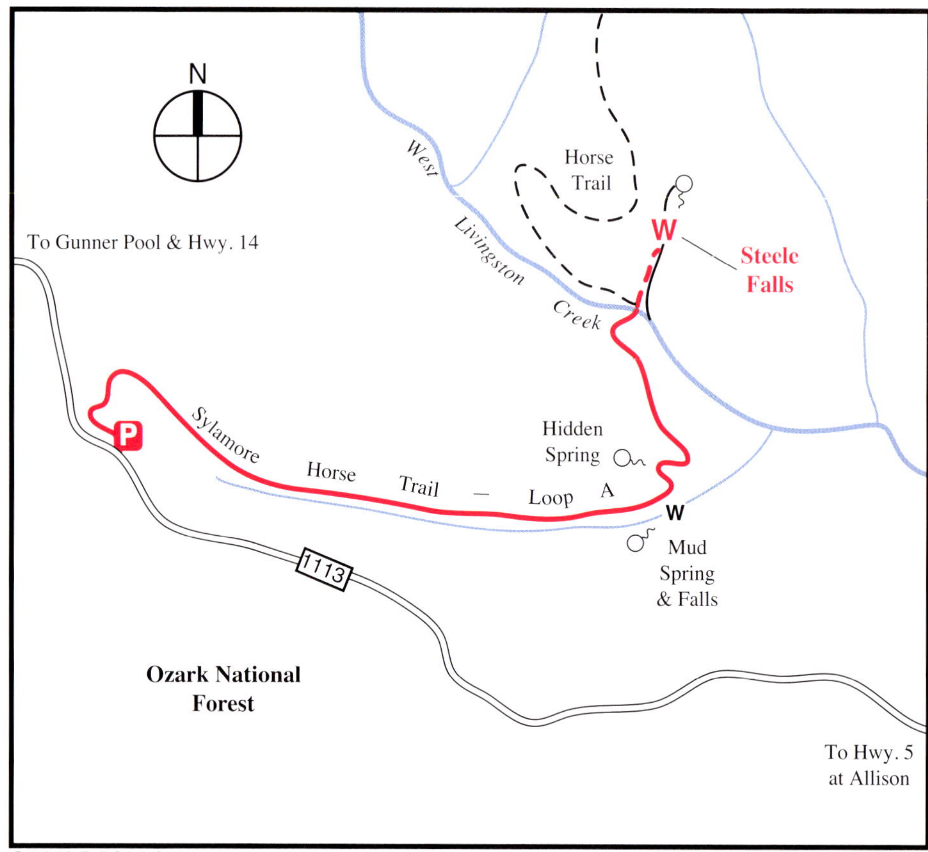

STEELE FALLS. The Sylamore District of the Ozark National Forest is known for its many springs. One of them produces this wonderful waterfall that is located along part of the main horse trail in the area. It is an easy hike to get down to, but is a bit of a climb coming out.

To get to the parking area, first go to the town of Fiftysix (located between Big Flat and Sylamore on Hwy. 14), then go west on Hwy. 14 about a mile and TURN RIGHT onto FR#1102 (gravel). This is the road to Gunner Pool Campground and will be well marked. Go 5.8 miles (past Gunner Pool Campground) and TURN RIGHT onto FR#1113. Go 1.0 and PARK on the left **(36.01393, -92.19302)**.

The horse trail (Sylamore Horse Trail, Hidden Springs/Loop A) follows an old forest service road from this point on and is no longer open to vehicle traffic—get on the horse trail and follow it down the hill. It is a lovely gentle hike through open forest. Soon you will pass a nice waterfall off the trail to the right—it is just out of sight but if the water is running you will be able to hear it. It's called Mud Spring Falls, and is 39 feet tall.

Just beyond this point the trail swings to the left and switchbacks down the hill a couple of times. Near the bottom of the hill it curves to the right and comes to West Livingston Creek. WADE THE CREEK and then LEAVE THE ROAD to the RIGHT and head up into the woods on a narrow volunteer trail. This little trail follows a smaller stream right on up to the base of **Steele Falls** at 1.6.

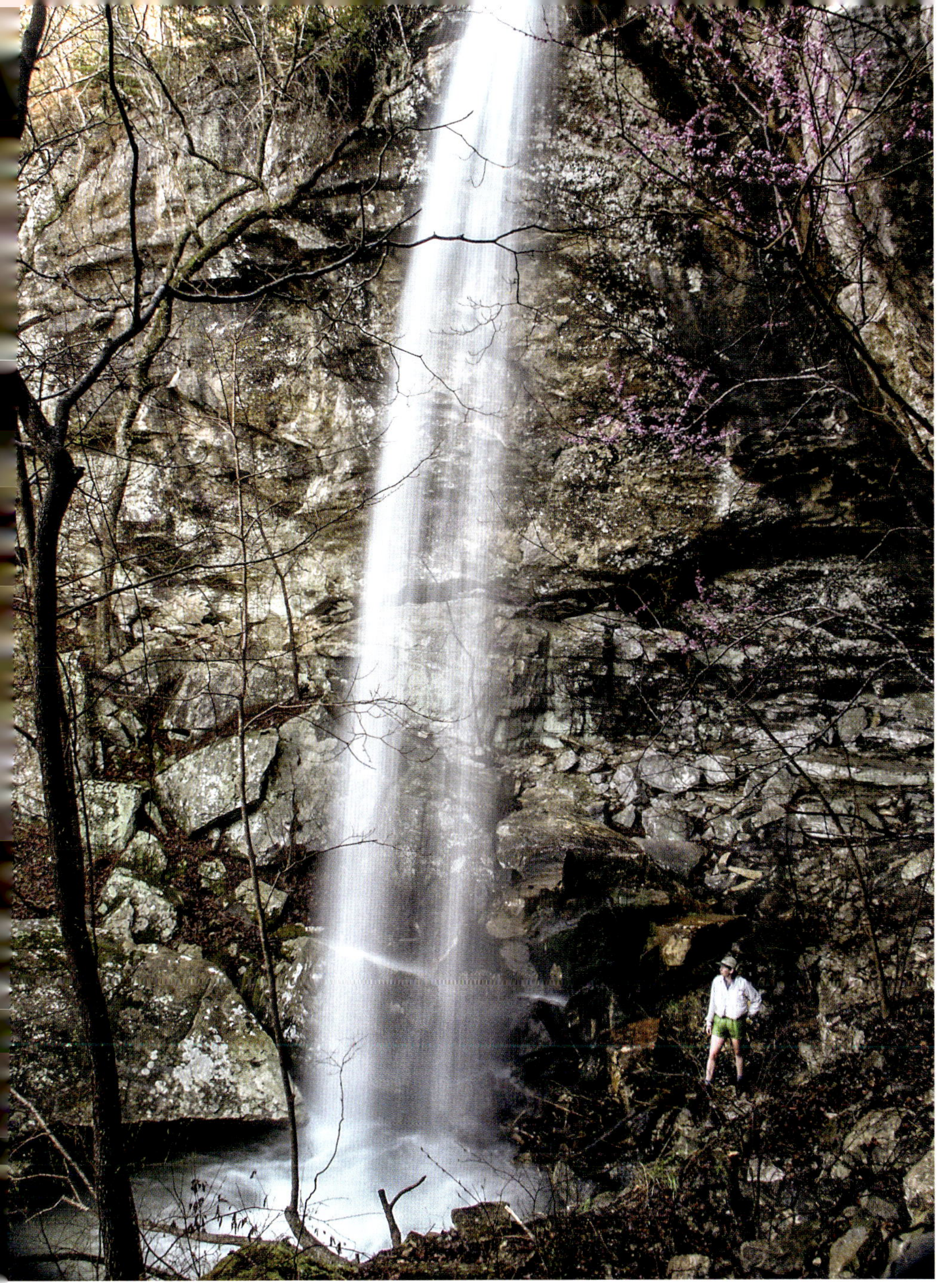

Jim Steele Falls

This falls is named after Jim Steele, a forest service guy I worked with 30 years ago on this ranger district. He has been responsible for trail development in the district, and for the management of Leatherwood Wilderness. One time he rode way back into the wilderness on horseback, cut up an old car body that was an eyesore, and carried it out piece by piece on pack horses. I guess he was sticking to the letter of the law that says no vehicles are allowed in wilderness areas!

Emergency contact: Stone County Sheriff, 870–269–2700 Dogs are OK.

Collins Creek Cascade

.5 mile roundtrip, easy hike, GPS not needed

GPS **35.51449, 91.98963**

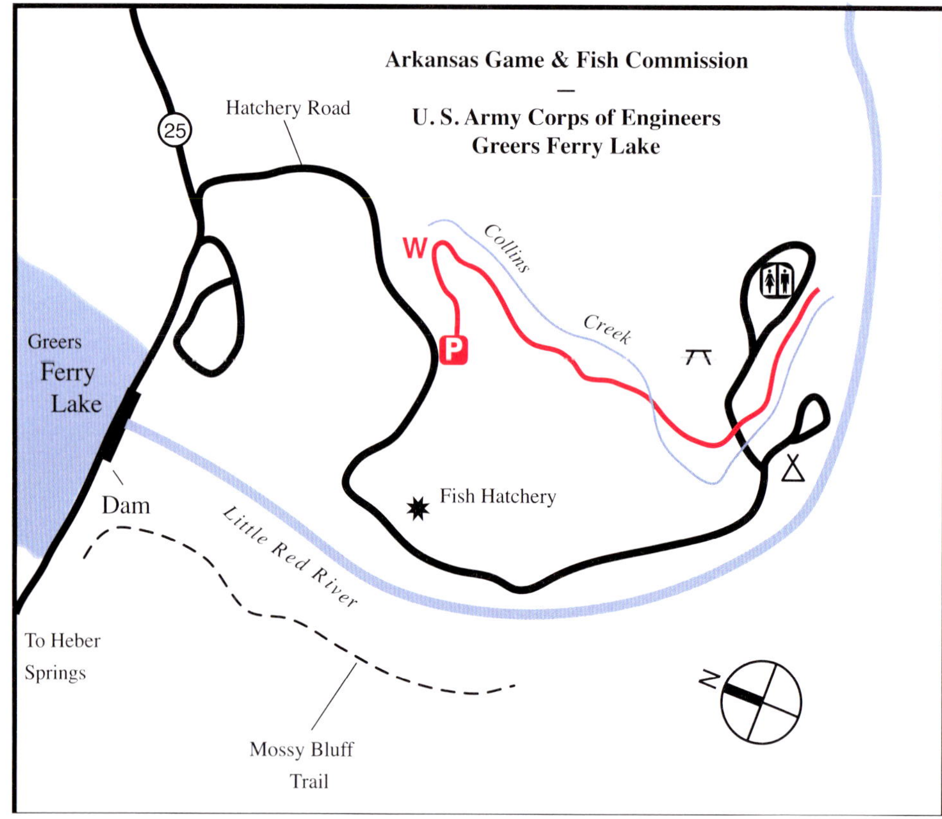

COLLINS CREEK CASCADE. This is one of the few water features in Arkansas that flows well all year, and is a great place to spend a few hours on a hot, sultry summer day! The water actually comes from the bottom of the lake and has been rerouted to an outlet that you can just barely see in the upper right of the photo. The water is always cold, and often produces mist. This easy hiking trail is great for kids, and there is some great trout fishing at the far end of the trail where it comes out to the Little Red River.

To get to the trailhead, take Hwy. 25 north from Heber Springs out to and across Greers Ferry Dam, past JFK Park, then TURN RIGHT onto Hatchery Road—the trailhead is .4 mile on the left (**35.51407, 91.99124**).

The trail heads out into the woods and drops down to the cascade after only a couple hundreds yards. If you hike the entire trail it is only 1.0 mile roundtrip. Take your kids, splash in the cool water, catch a trout, and enjoy!

Emergency contact: Cleburne County Sheriff, 501–362–8143 Dogs are OK.

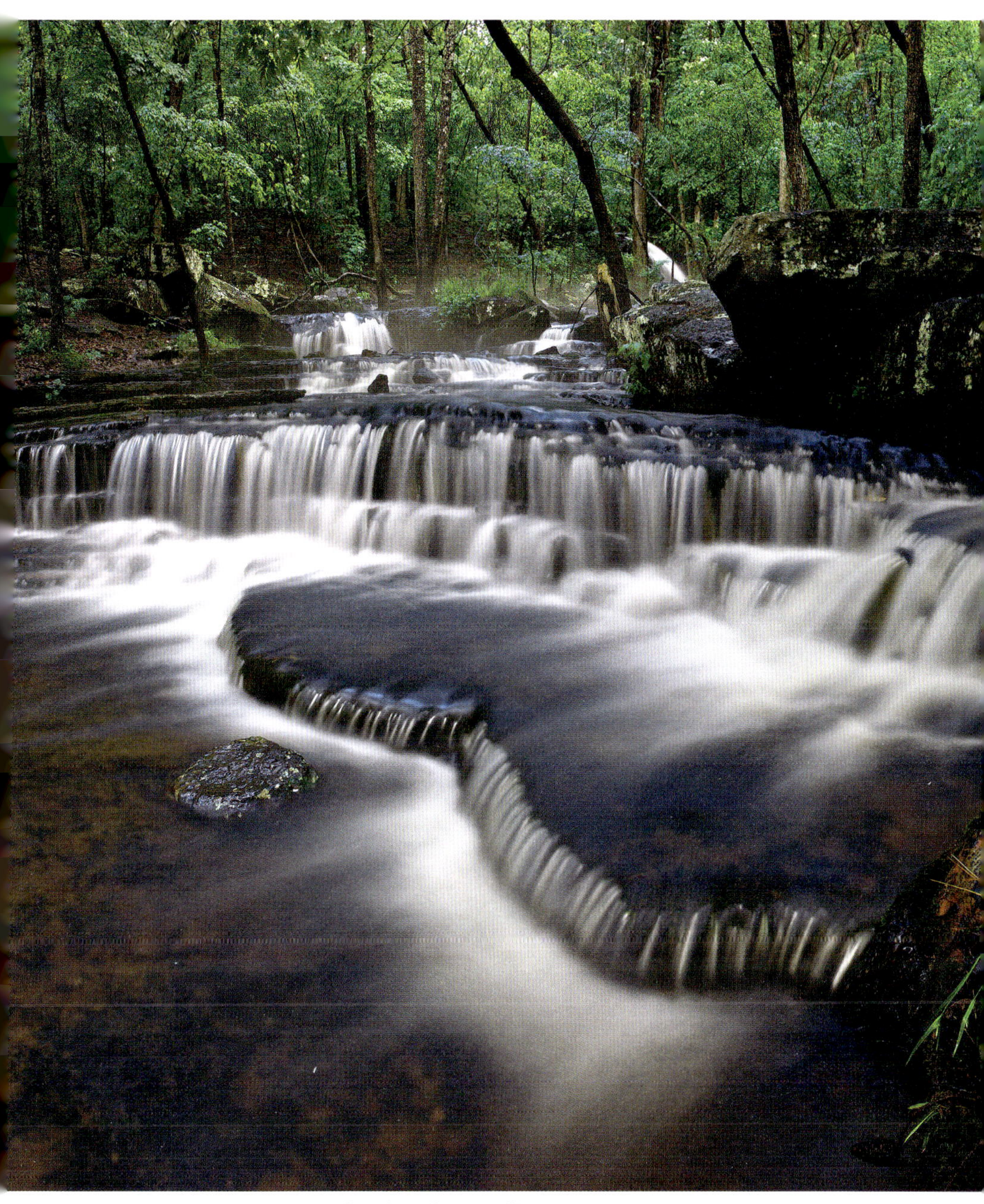

Collins Creek Cascade

Bridal Veil Falls (aka Cornelius) – 49′

200 yards roundtrip to overlook, easy hike, GPS not needed

GPS **35.46915, -92.03862**

Bridal Veil Falls (historic location) – 33′

.6 mile roundtrip, easy/medium bushwhack to bottom, GPS not needed

GPS **35.47020, -92.03977**

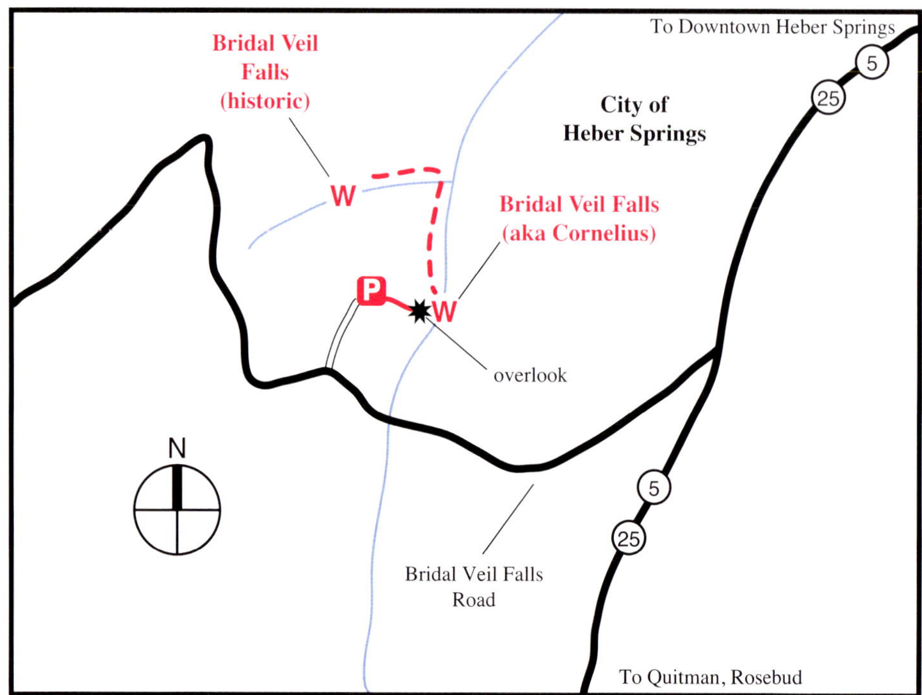

BRIDAL VEIL FALLS. We actually have two Bridal Veil Falls, and they are located right next to each other at the edge of Heber Springs. The original Bridal Veil is tucked back into a side canyon and not many folks have seen it in decades. The "new" Bridal Veil is taller and much easier to get to, and this is the one most folks in modern times know as Bridal Veil Falls—its original name was Cornelius Falls. Both falls are located on private property, but the city of Heber Springs has recently obtained an easement that allows public access, and they have improved the parking area and built a nice viewing platform too. *Yippie!*

To reach the parking area from Hwys. 25/5/16 intersection south of Heber Springs, go north on Hwy. 25/5 towards town .7 mile and turn LEFT onto Bridal Veil Falls Road, go .3 mile and TURN RIGHT into the parking area (**35.46924, -92.03970**). There is a trail to the RIGHT that leads to the overlook of the big waterfall. There are also some trails on both sides of the creek that make their way to the bottom of the falls, but can be slick so be careful if you try them, especially during high water!

The original **Bridal Veil Falls** is located in the drainage back to the left—from the base of the big waterfall head downstream for 100 yards and then turn left at the next creek and follow it upstream to the original waterfall..

Emergency contact: Cleburne County Sheriff, 501–362–8143

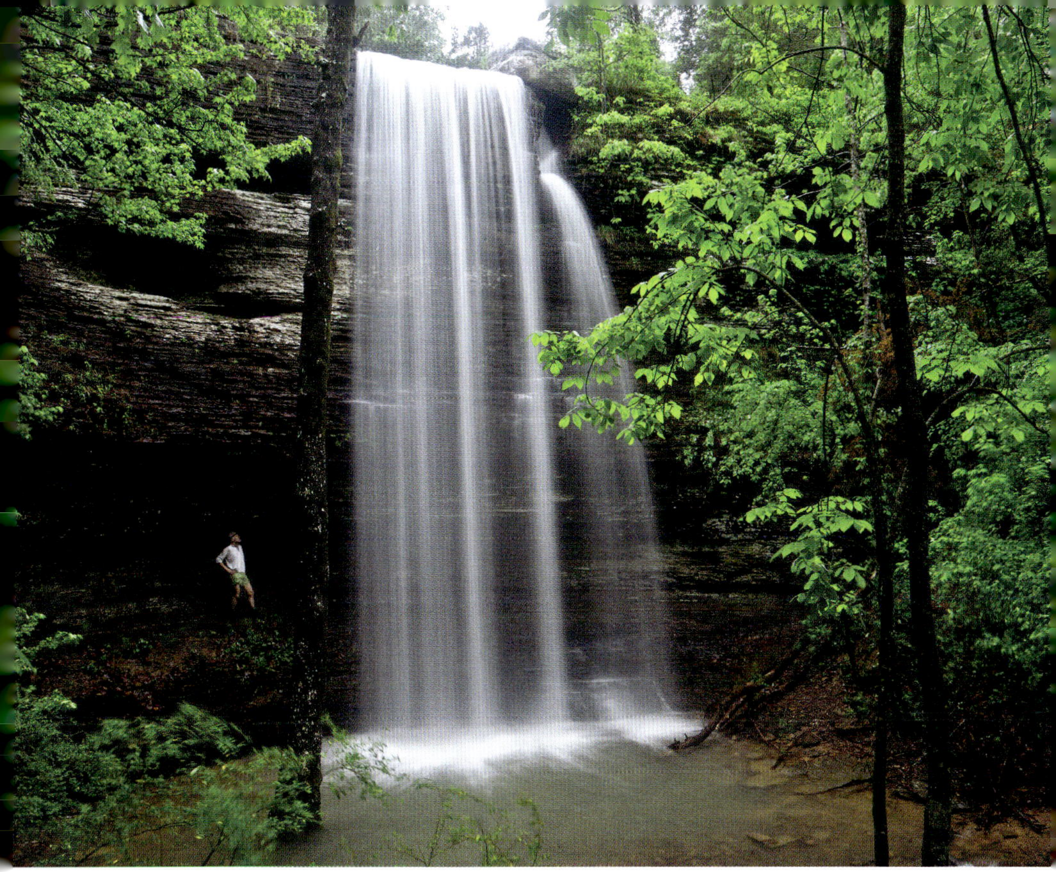

Bridal Veil Falls (above, aka Cornelius), **Bridal Veil Falls** (historic location, below)

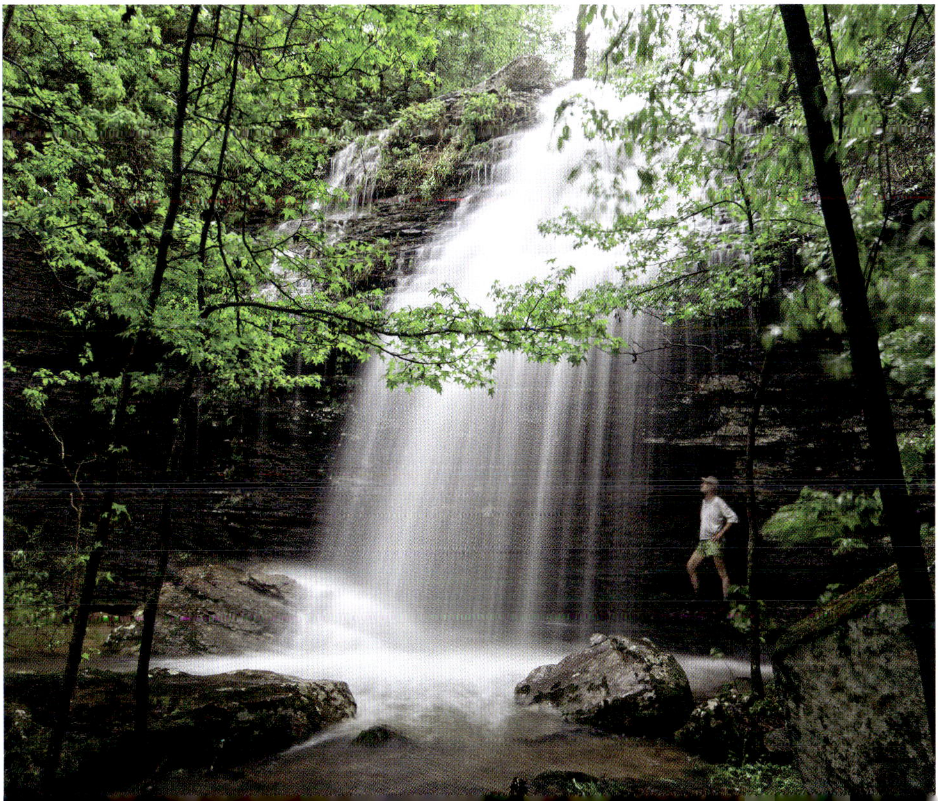

Kings Bluff Falls – 114′

1.9 mile loop, easy hike, GPS not needed

GPS **35.72480, -93.02512**

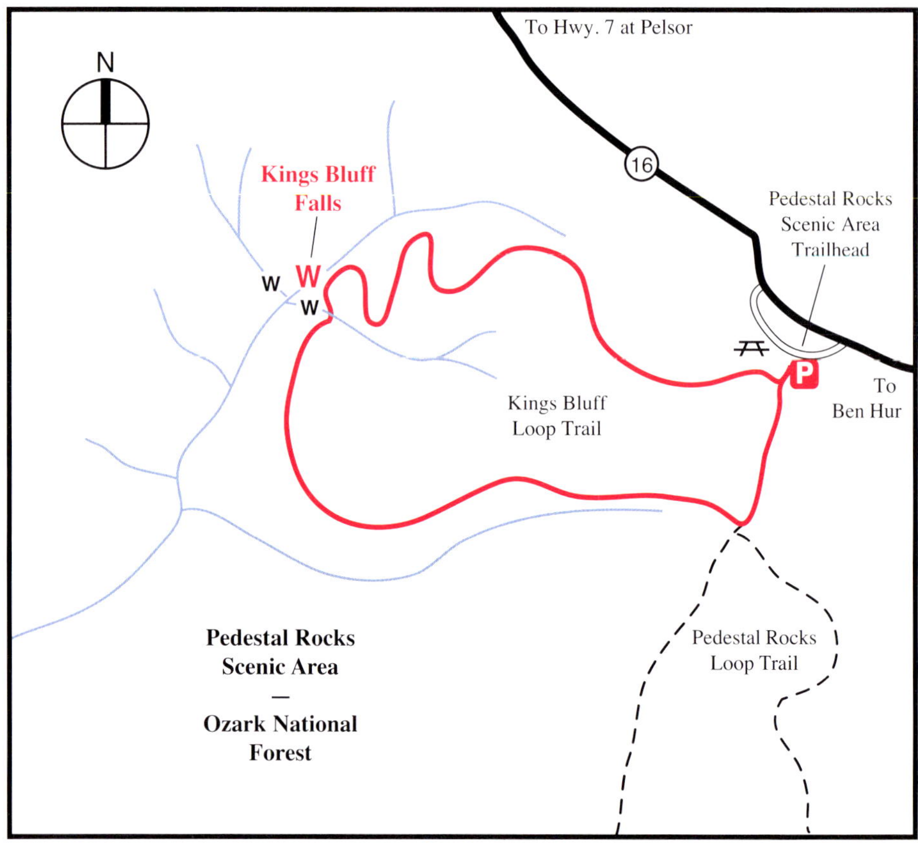

KINGS BLUFF FALLS. This is one of the tallest waterfalls in Arkansas, and it is a beauty! It is located in the Pedestal Rocks Scenic Area, and the trail to it is one of two loops that visit the area. The bluffline there is quite grand, with many interesting geological formations, including stone features sculpted over time by wind and rocks. The big bluffs make for a dangerous situation, especially for younger folks, so be sure to keep a hand on them if you take them along. There is a railing along the top of the tallest bluff at the waterfall, but it would be easy for someone to get over it so ***be careful!***

To get to the trailhead, take Hwy. 16 east from Pelsor on Hwy. 7 (Pelsor is located between Russellville and Jasper). Go about 6.0 miles and look for the sign to the RIGHT **(35.72379, -93.01566)**. If you get to Ben Hur, you've gone too far, so just turn around and go back about 2.5 miles. There is a picnic table and restroom, but camping is not allowed.

As soon as you head out on the trail and go across the stone bridge TURN RIGHT and head out on the Kings Bluff Trail (the trail straight ahead goes out to Pedestal Rocks—we will join it on the way back). This first part of the trail is actually an old road that heads up the hill just a little bit, then levels out and swings to the left. It begins to drop on down the hillside and becomes just a plain hiking trail. After several switchbacks you will come right out onto the top of Kings Bluff at the 1.0 point. This is one spectacular spot, so plan to stick around a while.

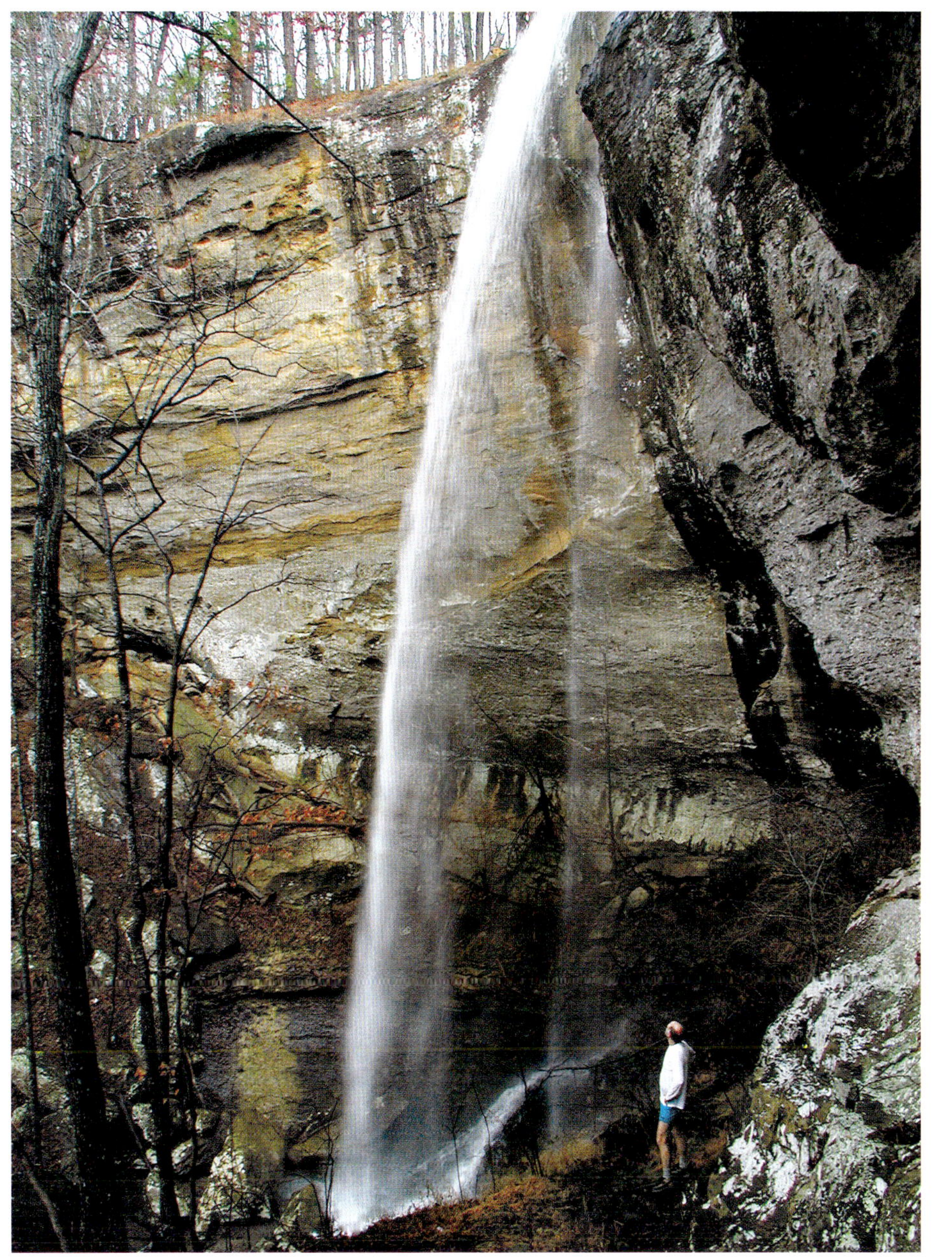

Kings Bluff Falls

This waterfall will run much of the wet season, but for a real treat try to get here after a big rain. You may see other waterfalls in the valley below too. A very nice area! Be sure to save some film though, because the next section of bluffline is quite scenic. The trail continues along the top of the bluff to the LEFT, past deep crevices and scenic views. It eventually comes to the end of the bluff, then makes its way gradually up through the forest and intersects with the Pedestal Rocks Loop at 1.8—TURN LEFT and follow the trail back to the trailhead. (Turn right for the 2.6 mile loop out to Pedestal Rocks.)

Emergency contact: Pope County Sheriff, 479–967–9300 Dogs are OK.

North Fork Road Falls South – 33′

100 yards roundtrip, easy-next to road, GPS not needed

GPS **35.57046,93.01993**

North Fork Road Falls North – 53′

100 yards roundtrip, easy-next to road, GPS not needed

GPS **35.57612, -93.01894**

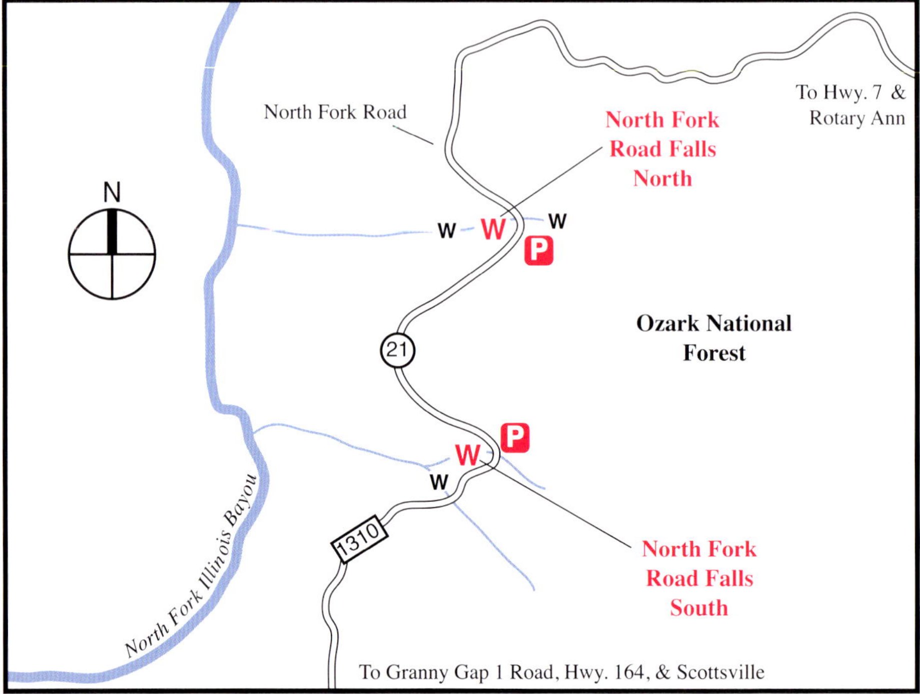

NORTH FORK ROAD FALLS. This pair of nice waterfalls are located within sight of a forest road and are easy to get to the top of, and with a little extra effort you might be able to scramble down to the base of each—pretty steep though so be careful! There are many other waterfalls in the area as well if you are into exploring.

To reach the falls from the south, start at Scottsville on Hwy. 27 between Dover and Hector and head north on Hwy. 164. Go 5.1 miles (becomes Granny Gap 1 road, gravel) and TURN LEFT onto FR#1310/North Fork Road/CR#21. Go 8.7 miles and PARK at the curve—the south falls will be just down to your left. Continue on the forest road another .6 mile and PARK at the curve—the north falls will be just down to your left. There are ways to scramble down to the base of both waterfalls but it is steep and dangerous so watch your step. There are also other waterfalls down there, including a really nice cascade/falls just a little ways below the North falls.

If coming from the north via Hwy. 7, begin at Rotary Ann picnic area south of Pelsor and go 2.5 miles then TURN LEFT onto FR#1000/Victor Road/CR#17. Continue for 7.7 miles and TURN RIGHT onto FR#1310/North Fork Road/CR#21. Go 8.2 miles and park for the north falls, continue another .6 mile and park for the south falls. (Or from the Cabin Falls park, go south on Hwy. 7 and turn left onto Granny Gap Road 2, go 5.1 miles and turn left onto FR#1310/North Fork Road/CR#21.)

Emergency contact: Pope County Sheriff, 479–967–9300 Dogs are OK.

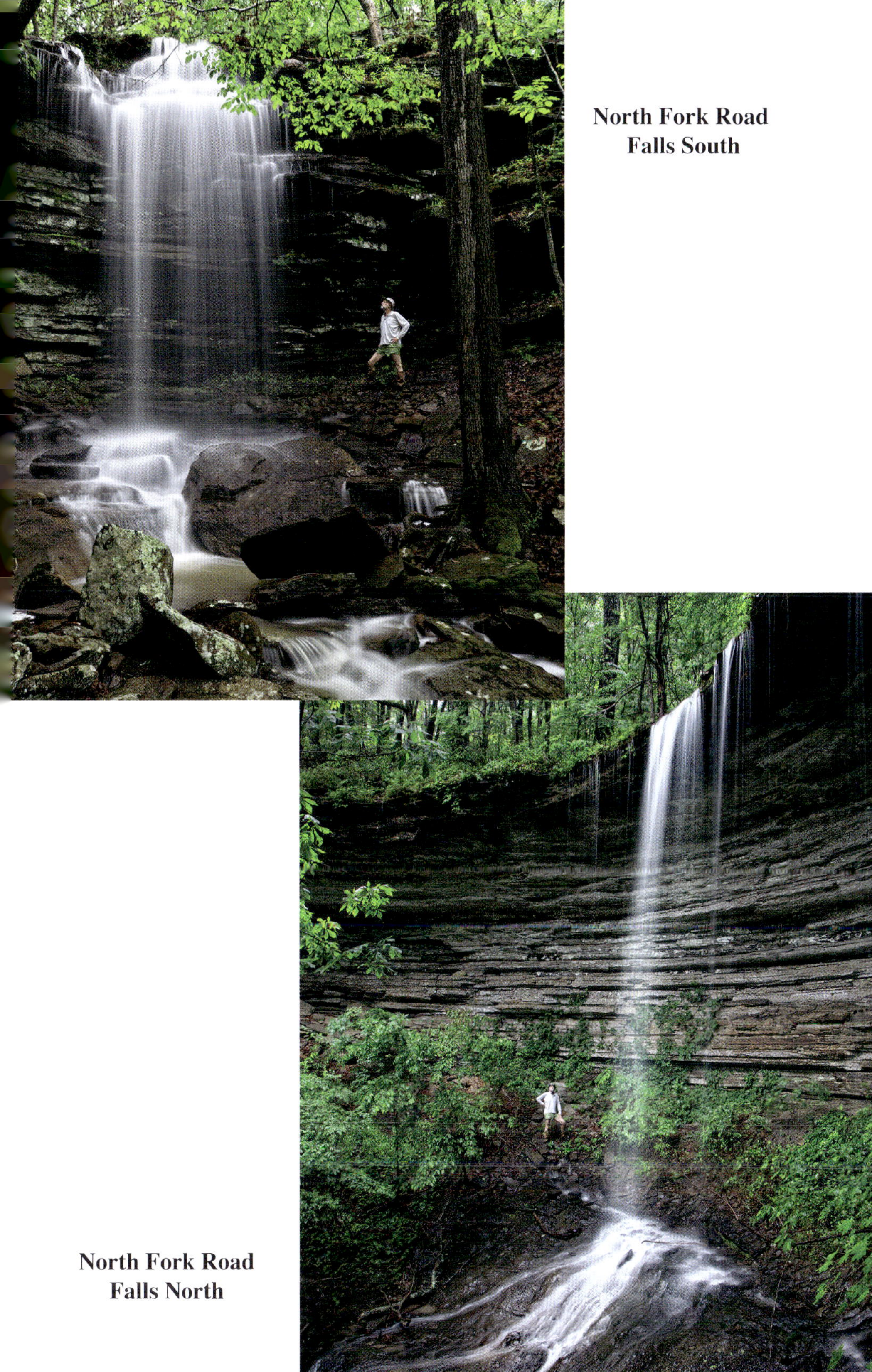

North Fork Road
Falls South

North Fork Road
Falls North

Cabin Falls – 36′

1.3 miles roundtrip (to both falls), medium bushwhack, GPS helpful

GPS **35.56936, -93.06311**

Maidenhair Falls – 30′

1.3 miles roundtrip (to both falls), medium bushwhack, GPS helpful

GPS **35.56613, -93.06165**

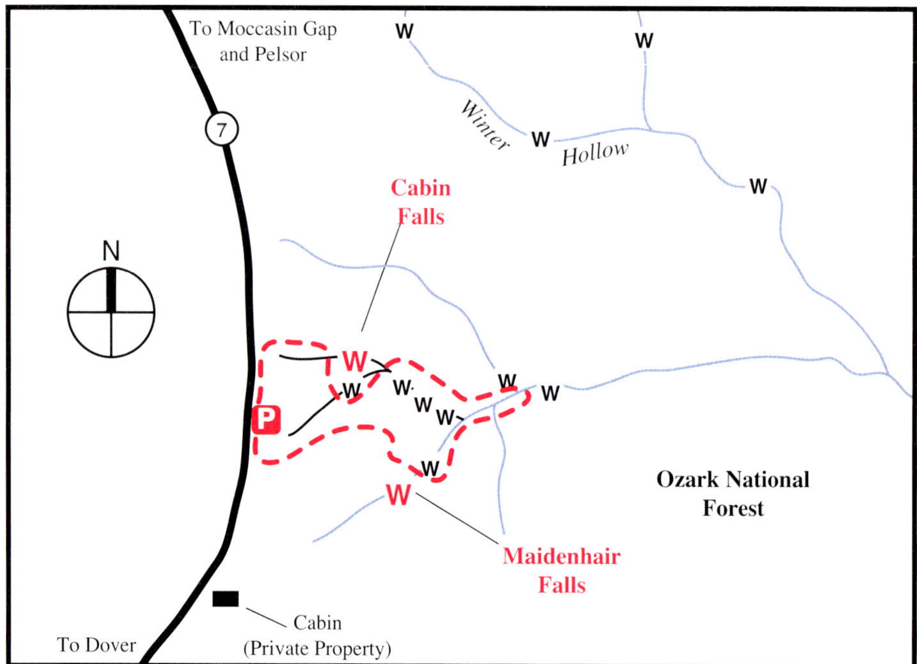

CABIN FALLS/MAIDENHAIR FALLS. There are several nice waterfalls in this neat little polyfoss area right off of Hwy. 7 north of Dover. One waterfall leads to another to another and to another! None of them are towering waterfalls, but they are scenic.

To access the area go .6 mile south of the turnoff to the Moccasin Gap Trailhead on Hwy. 7 (1.1 miles north of Mac Pines) and PARK along the side of the road in the power line right-of-way (**35.56781, -93.06618).**

Hike north along the powerline right-of-way about 100 yards down to a dip and then turn RIGHT and head into the woods going downhill. There is a faint road trace that follows along the little creek—just keep going downhill and you will eventually come to the top of **Cabin Falls**.

From that point you have a couple of options. There is another neat waterfall along the same bluffline—just follow it around to the right/south until you reach it. OR continue to follow the stream below **Cabin Falls** and you will come to one waterfall after another after another (OR do both!). See the small w's on the map for more waterfalls. Where the creek levels out a bit there is another creek that joins there—follow this back upstream to the right and you will come to one nice waterfall, and then beyond it is **Maidenhair Falls**. The route shown on the map is the one I normally do and it gets me to most of the waterfalls in the immediate area, although as you can see there are more just to the north!

Emergency contact: Pope County Sheriff, 479–967–9300 Dogs are OK.

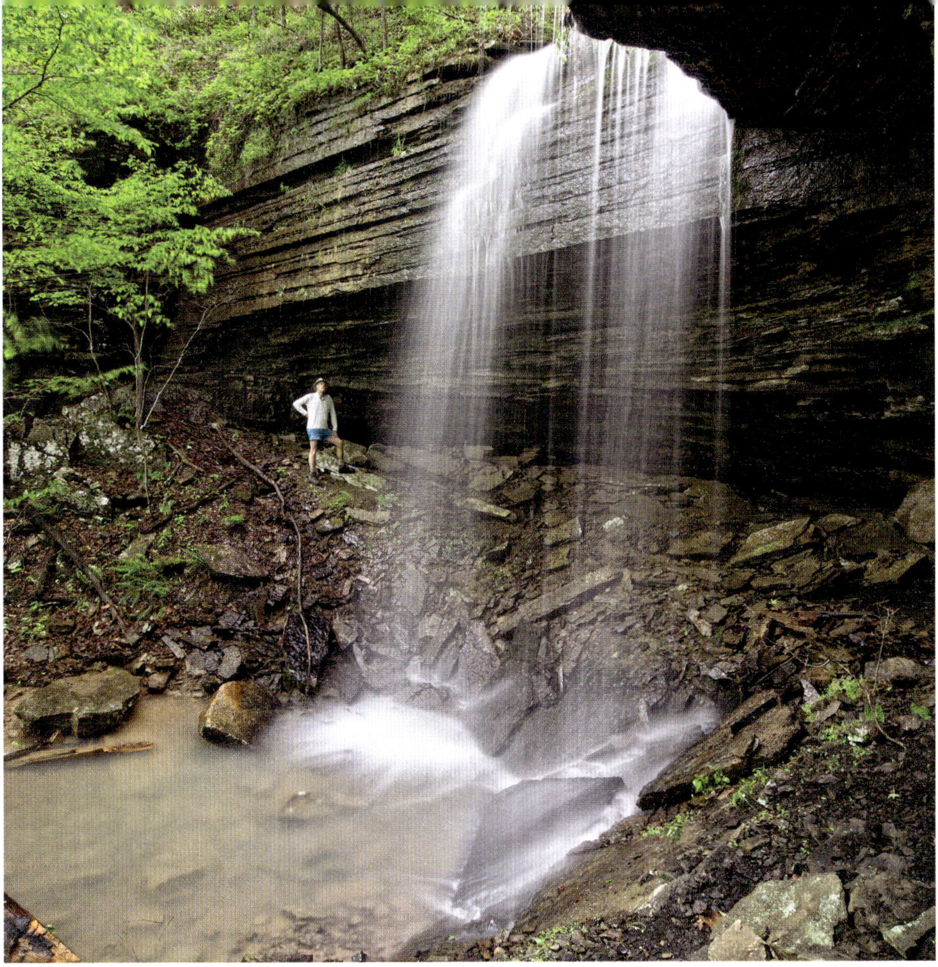

Cabin Falls (above), **Maidenhair Falls** (below)

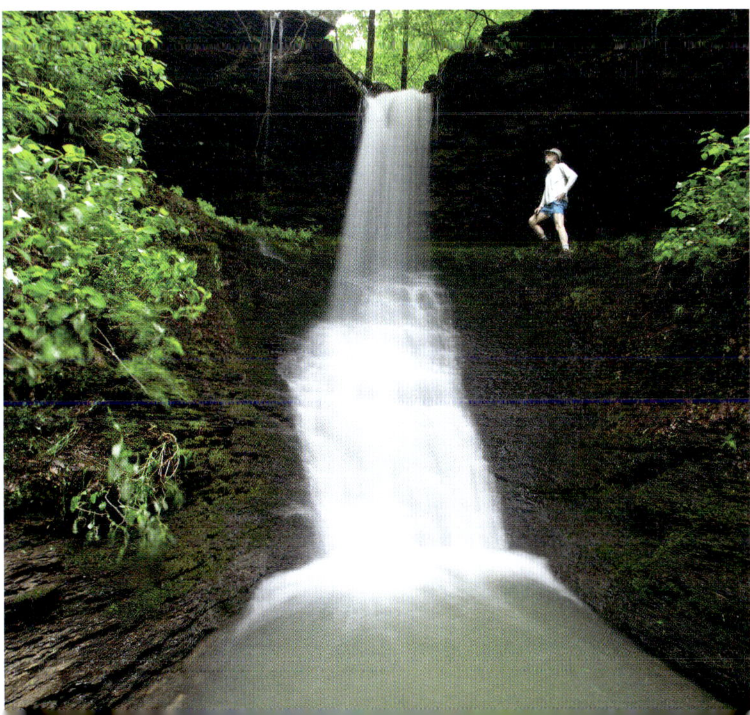

Penhook Falls – 41′

2.3 miles roundtrip, medium hike/bushwhack, GPS helpful

GPS **35.56745, -92.95155**

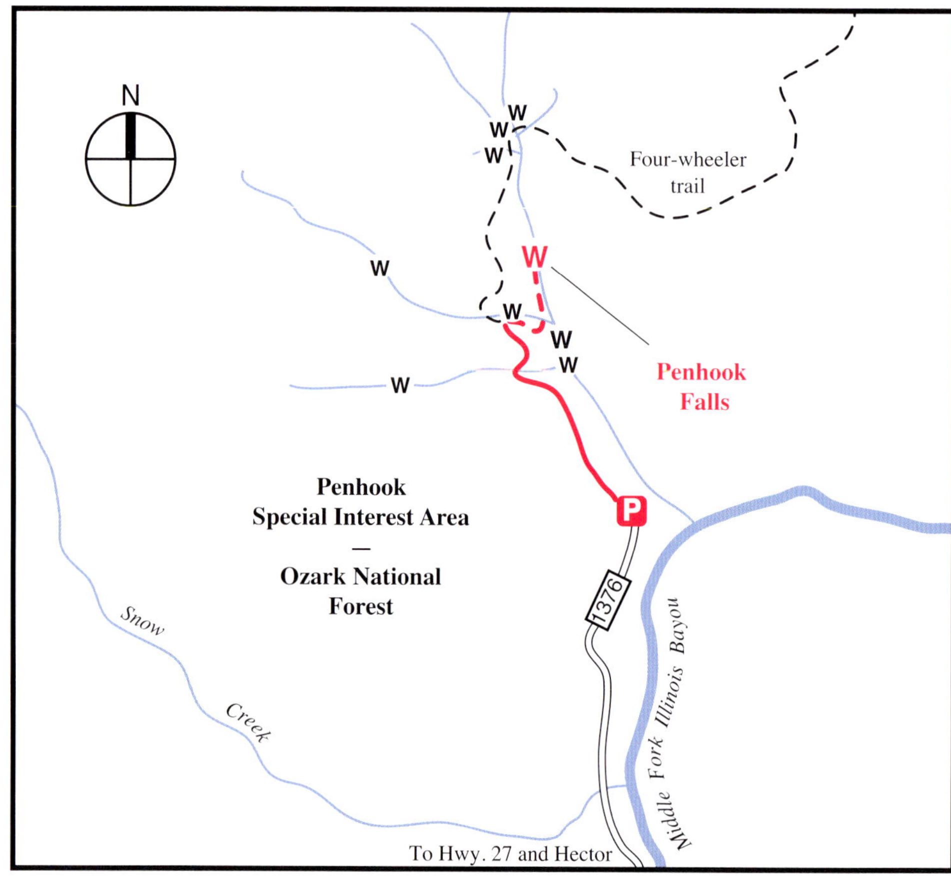

PENHOOK FALLS. Here is another great polyfoss area that includes a couple of major waterfalls plus many smaller but still scenic ones. All but the biggest one are pretty easy to reach and are in a small area. This hollow was once considered for wilderness area status in the 1980's but got cut out—it is kind of a mini wilderness area and I like it a lot!

From Hector go north on Hwy. 27 .3 miles past the Bayou Bluff Campground and TURN LEFT onto FR#1376 (about 5.5 miles from town). Follow this road all the way to the end and park at 2.2 (**35.56015, -92.94792).** During high water you may not be able to ford Snow Creek at 2.1. Look for waterfalls in side drainages along the road.

From the parking spot follow a four-wheeler trail into the woods and stay mostly on the level as it works along the contour into Penhook Hollow (don't turn uphill). Drop down into and out of one drainage, and then when you drop down into a second drainage, leave the four-wheeler trail and follow the little creek downhill to the RIGHT to a nice waterfall. Continue downstream below the falls and you will soon come to the main Penhook Hollow creek. Just downstream from there to the right are two really nice waterfalls. And just upstream from there to the left a little ways is the main **Penhook Falls**.

The tallest waterfall is in the upper reaches of that second drainage back where you left the four-wheeler trail—it requires a difficult and steep bushwhack to reach the upper

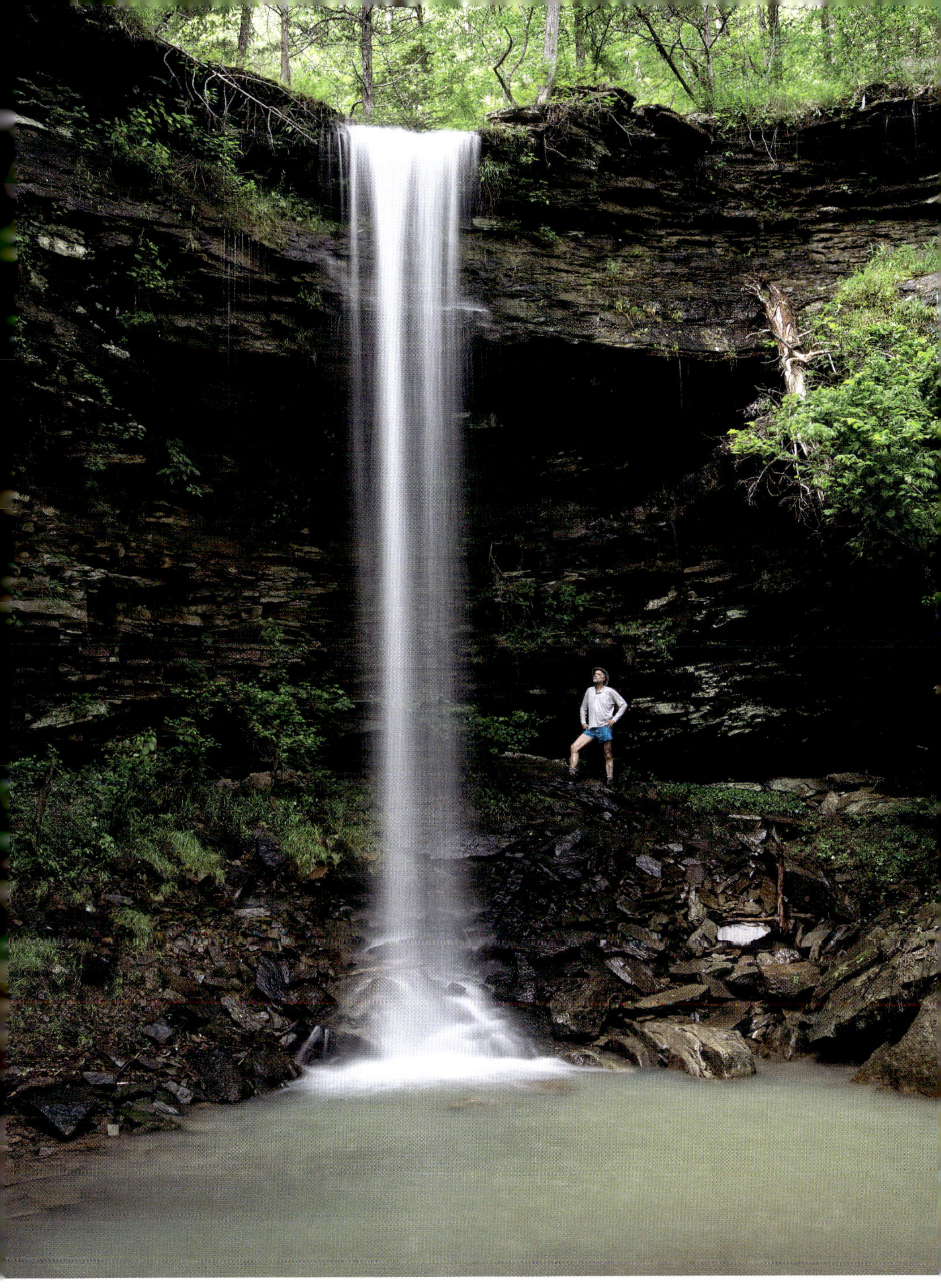

Penhook Falls

bluffline where it lives. During high water there are even more waterfalls along that high bluffline, and you could easily spend an entire day exploring.

Emergency contact: Pope County Sheriff, 479–967–9300 Dogs are OK.

Fiddlehead Falls – 19′

.5 roundtrip, easy social trail GPS **35.53681, -92.86131**

Blue Hole Cascades (several)

4.0 miles roundtrip (includes grotto), difficult bushwhack, GPS helpful
GPS **35.52098, -92.88063**

Green Grotto Falls – 21′

4.0 miles roundtrip (includes cascades), difficult bushwhack, GPS helpful
GPS **35.52586, -92.86998**

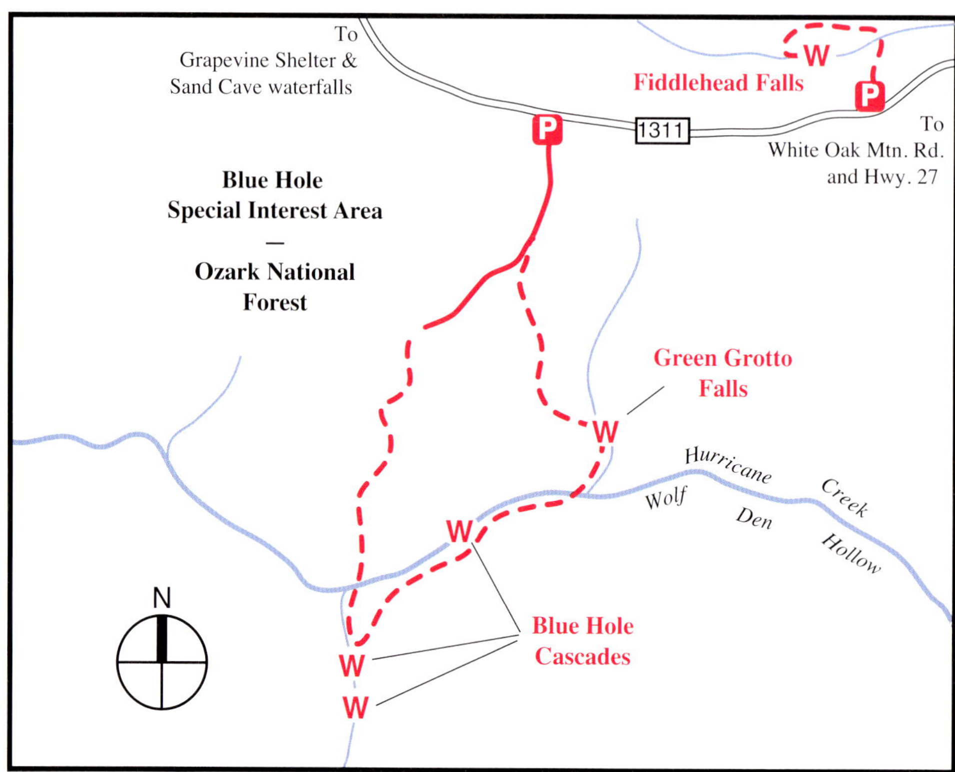

FIDDLEHEAD FALLS. From Hector go north on Hwy. 27 and TURN RIGHT onto White Oak Mtn. Road/FR#1301. Go 11.3 miles (bear left at 6.9) and TURN LEFT onto FR#1311. Directions to Blue Hole Special Interest Area—TURN LEFT onto 1311 jeep road, go .75 and PARK on the right **(35.53555, -92.86031)**.

Follow a social trail down the hill to and cross Mill Creek, TURN LEFT and follow the creek downstream to near the top of the falls, then find your way down the bluff to the base of the falls at .25. This is such a peaceful, beautiful, emerald pool SSS.

BLUE HOLE CASCADES/GREEN GROTTO FALLS. The water is not really blue, but there are often beautiful emerald pools and many cascades that make it well worth the steep climb in and out. And the grotto is a very special spot indeed.

From **Fiddlehead** CONTINUE another .6 miles on the same road and TURN LEFT onto a jeep road and PARK **(35.53507, -92.87201).**

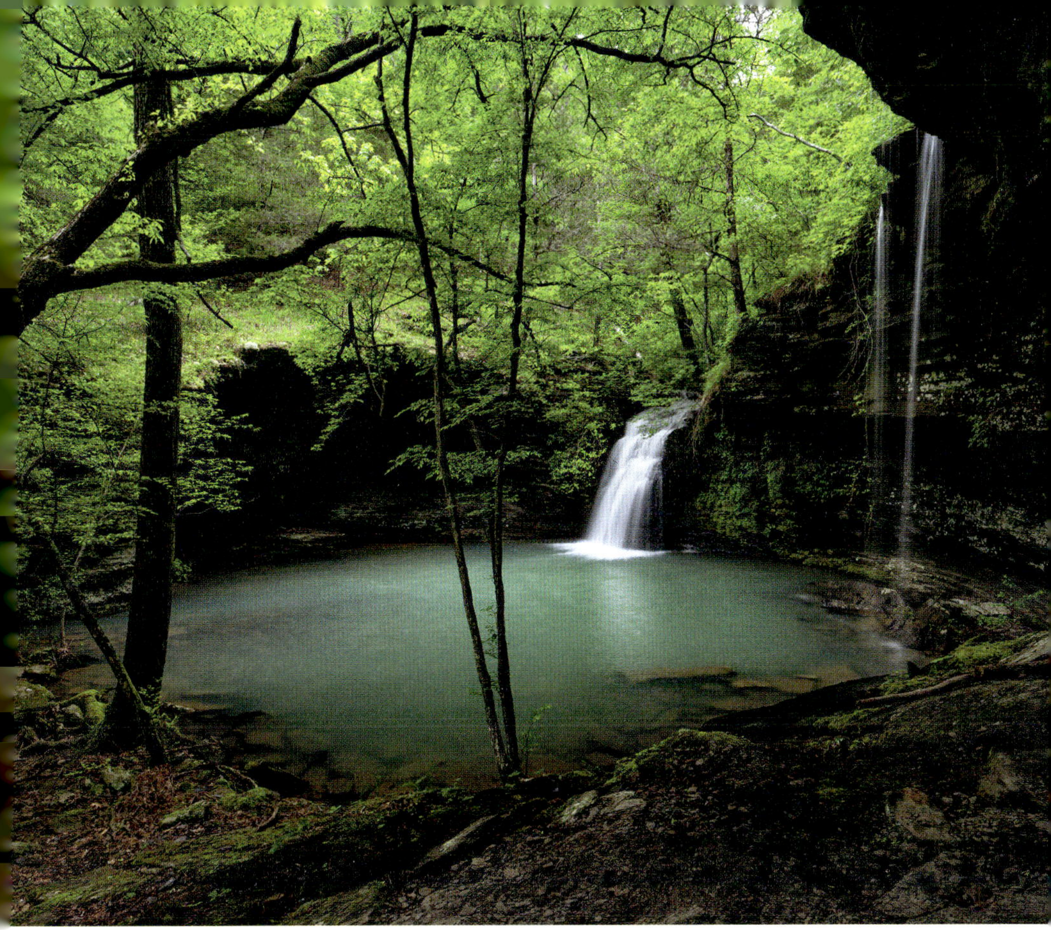

Fiddlehead Falls

Follow the jeep road (mostly level) for about a half mile as it curves around to the right and it will end in a clearing/deer camp area. TURN LEFT and head down into the woods and bushwhack down, down, down the hill until you land in the bottom at Hurricane Creek/Wolf Den Hollow. Locate the creek that joins the main creek from the south. From that intersection there are nice cascades up Hurricane Creek to the left and two nice ones up the stream a couple hundred yards that enters from the south on the other side of Hurricane Creek.

To get to **Green Grotto Falls** hike up Hurricane Creek about a half mile to a creek that comes in from the LEFT and follow the creek a couple hundred yards into the grotto. From that point I normally head UP the hill and make my way back to the parking spot, making a big loop.

Emergency contact: Pope County Sheriff, 479–967–9300 Dogs are OK.

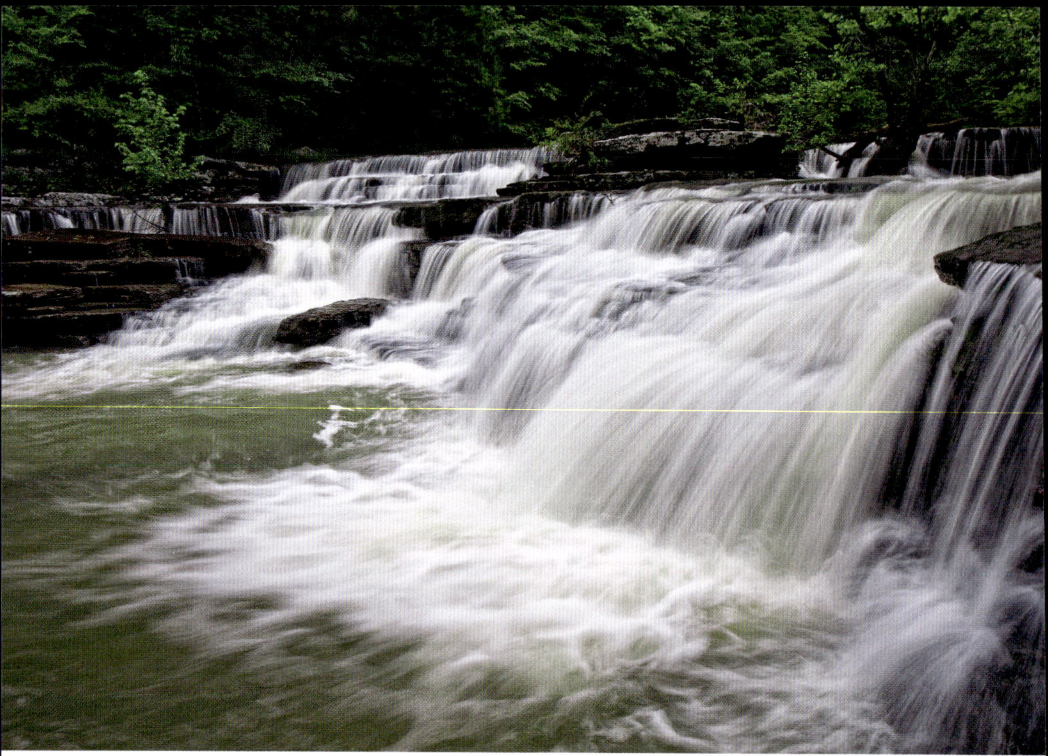

Blue Hole Cascades (above), Green Grotto Falls (below)

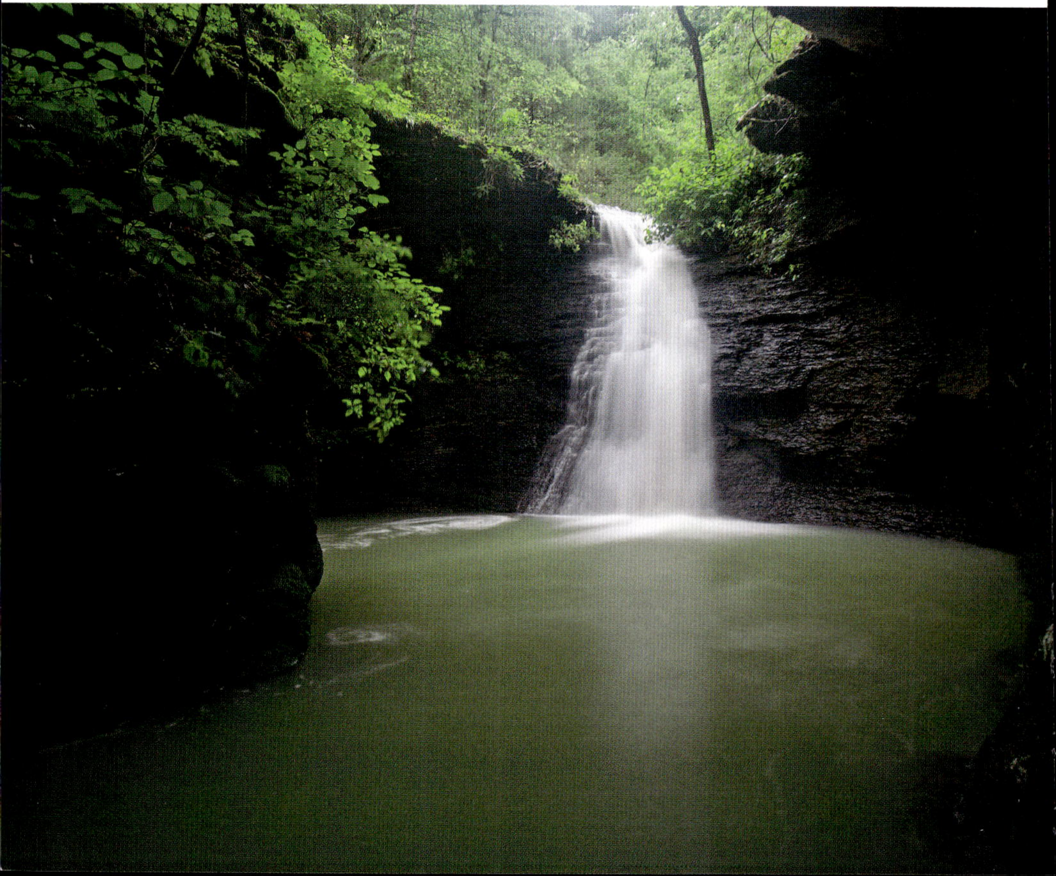

Grapevine Shelter Falls–63′

1.4 miles roundtrip, easy to moderate, some steep bushwhack

GPS **35.53193, -92.88495**

Sand Cave Quintuple–13-33′

1.4 miles roundtrip, ♦ bushwhack

GPS helpful **35.54104, -92.89217**

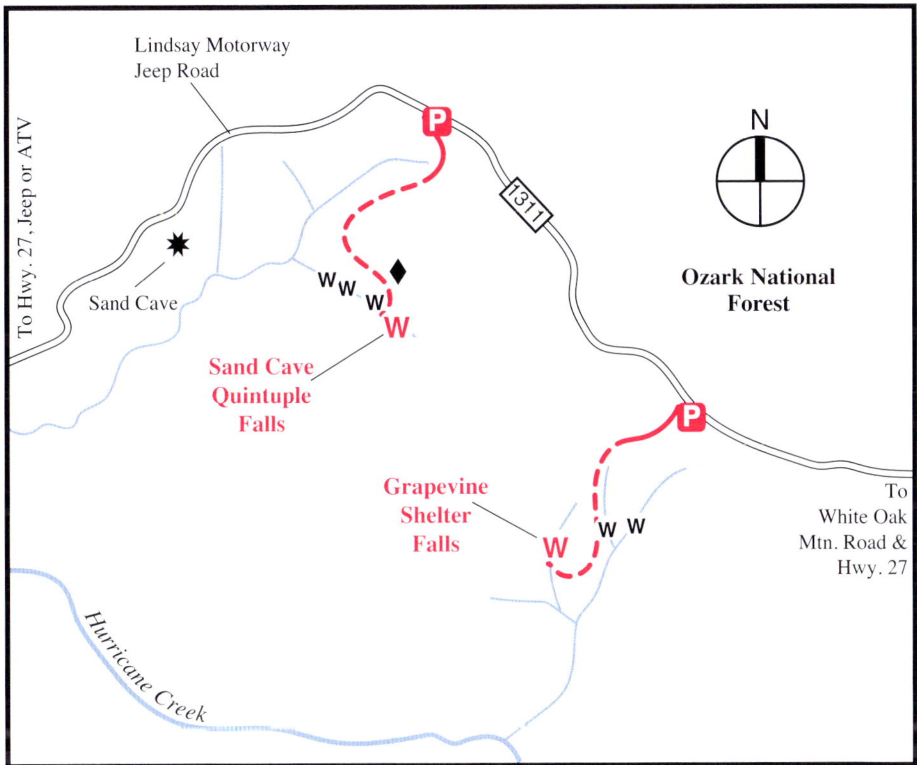

GRAPEVINE SHELTER FALLS. From Hector go north on Hwy. 27 about a mile and TURN RIGHT onto White Oak Mtn. Road/FR#1301. Go 11.3 miles (bear left at 6.9) and TURN LEFT onto FR#1311 (jeep road), go 1.8 miles and TURN LEFT into a parking spot **(35.53755, -92.87875)**. Sometimes this road gets in pretty bad shape...

Follow the jeep road ahead as it curves around to the right for about .3, then veer off to the LEFT and head downhill. It gets steep and you want to try and find your way between two small drainages—or just keep going down until you reach a bluff line, then find a way down through the bluff. There's a nice waterfall where each of those creeks pours over the bluff—in fact this little area with some giant sandstone block is an SSS all by itself.

Once below the bluff TURN RIGHT and follow the bluff along through a magical SSS of house-size sandstone blocks and the beautiful bluff until you reach the base of **Grapevine Shelter Falls** at .7. This is really a powerful place, not only from the waterfall and deep shelter behind it, but it just has some sort of positive energy to it—plan to spend a while.

Emergency contact: Pope County Sheriff, 479–967–9300 Dogs are OK.

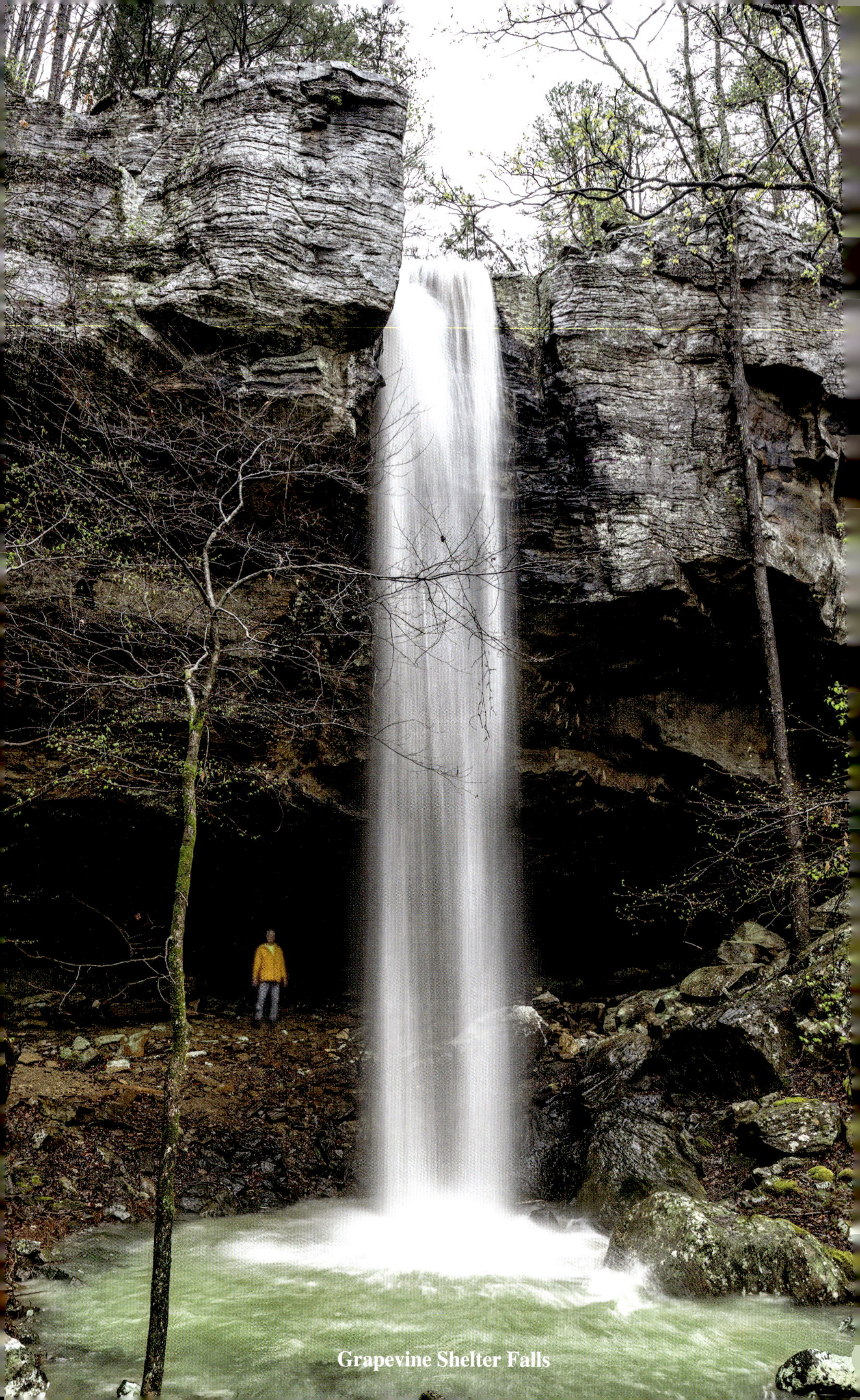
Grapevine Shelter Falls

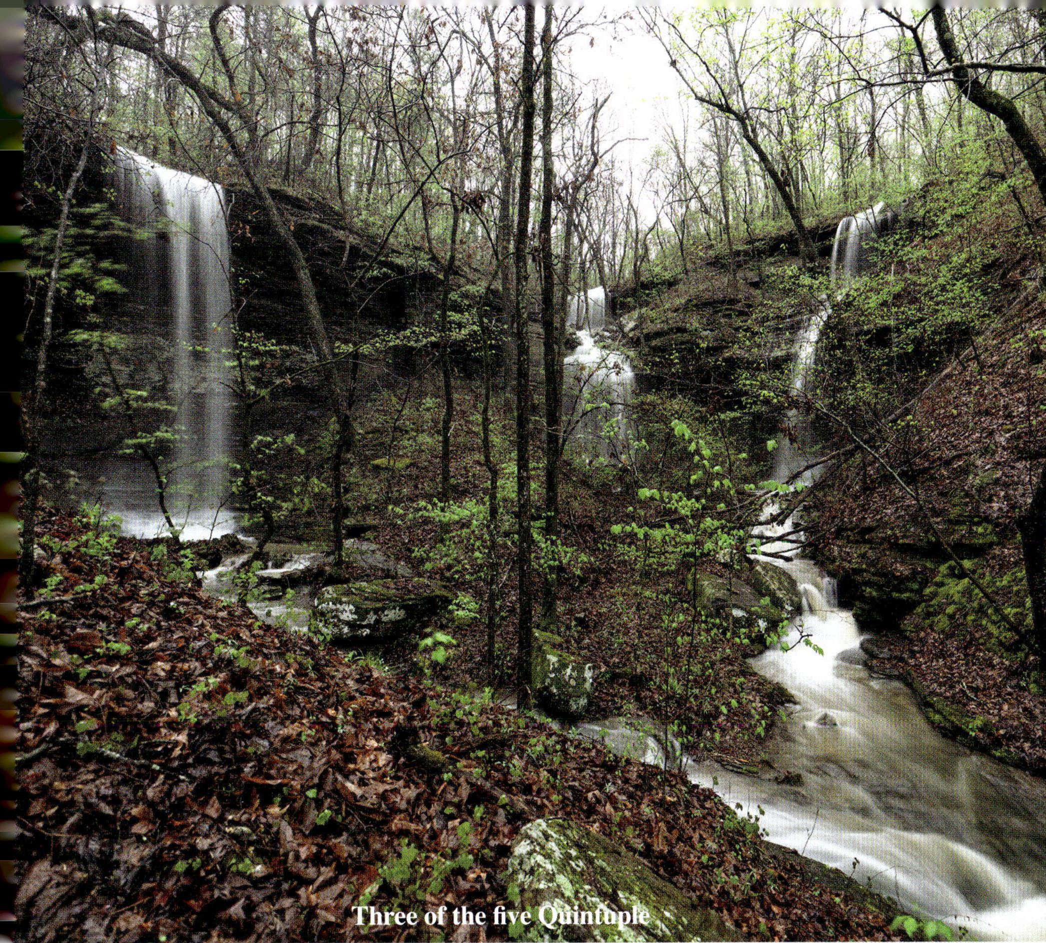

Three of the five Quintuple

SAND CAVE WATERFALLS. From the **Grapevine** parking spot continue along FR#1311 another .7 miles and PARK on the left **(35.54444, -92.88507)**, which is 2.5 miles from White Oak Mtn. Road.

I've seen different descriptions of how to get to these waterfalls but this is the way I go. Head out on the old road ahead of your vehicle on the level past a couple of dirt mounds and a small pond, the road will curve back to the left. When you come to a small drainage that's flowing a little LEAVE the road to the RIGHT at .4 and head straight downhill. (It's OK to keep going on the road a ways—you will still likely end up down at the falls unless you go way too far. Or take a social trail if you find one.) Continue downhill and curve back towards the left into the drainage a little and you should soon hear falling water. When you come to a BLACK DIAMOND ♦ slope you are almost there! Just keep going down until you land on the creek at the bottom at .7. There are several waterfalls (8-10) within a couple hundred yards of each other, including three on a side creek.

It's possible to get multiple waterfalls in the same photo—getting four or even five (or more) means you've got the official **Sand Cave Quintuple Falls** group—CONGRATS!

OK, on the way down in the middle of the Black Diamond ♦ slope there is an old road trace, waterfall above and below it—this side drainage has a third falls that's down on the main creek just to the left of the main Sand Cave Hollow Falls when looking upstream. Everything is an SSS.

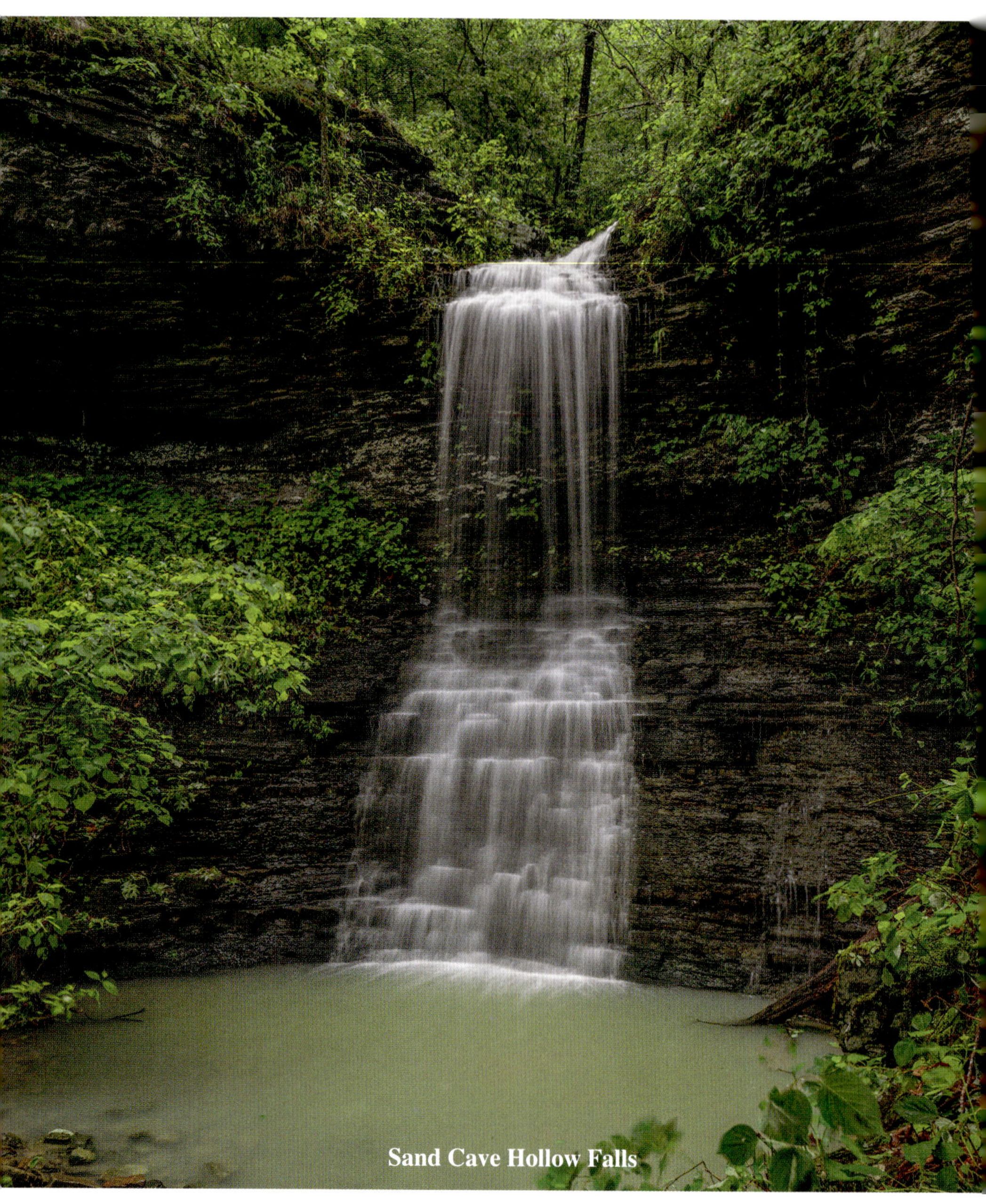
Sand Cave Hollow Falls

Three waterfalls from different drainages all come together just above a 13' footer, not pictured (that's four waterfalls), then **Sand Cave Hollow Falls** is just downstream for the fifth of the Quintuple. There is one nice falls just to the left of the photo above, plus three more waterfalls up that side drainage on the left.

Emergency contact: Pope County Sheriff, 479–967–9300 Dogs are OK.

Jacob's Stairway – 23'+

1.1 roundtrip, moderate social trail, GPS **35.53403, -92.77090**

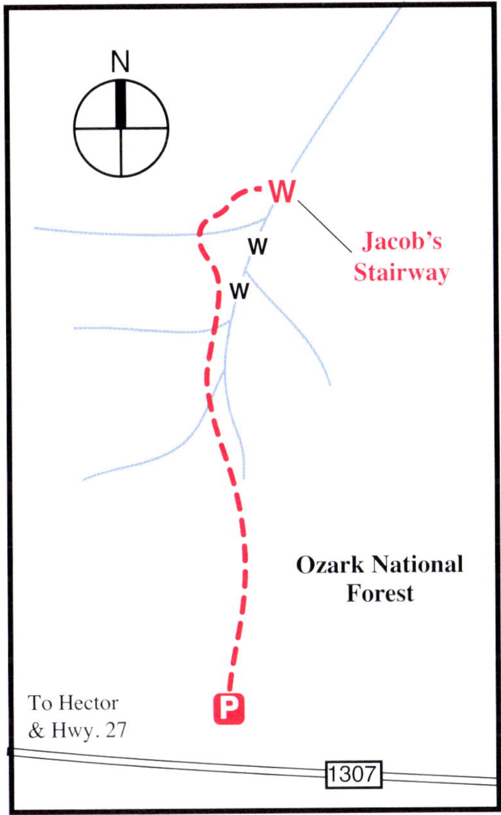

JACOB'S STAIRWAY. From Hector go north on Hwy. 27 and turn RIGHT onto White Oak Mtn. Road/FR#1301. Go 11.8 miles (stay LEFT at 6.9) and turn RIGHT onto FR#1307/CR#2/Wilderness Trail. Go 5.1 miles and turn LEFT onto an old road and PARK **(35.52936, -92.77158)**.

From the parking area hike along the jeep road and head down into the hollow. Once you get to the creek continue downstream along the left side past some small falls and nice cascades. Close to the creek there tends to be a lot of thorns but if you stay a little away from the creek uphill there may be less. This is a really nice long and tall cascade, and you'll reach the bottom about .5. It looks best with someone standing in the water about half way up the creek for scale! (I know a photographer who carries a blow-up doll to include in photos for perspective and scale—some of the landscape photos she has taken are really amazing—you would never know!)

Emergency contact: Pope County Sheriff, 479-967-9300 Dogs are OK

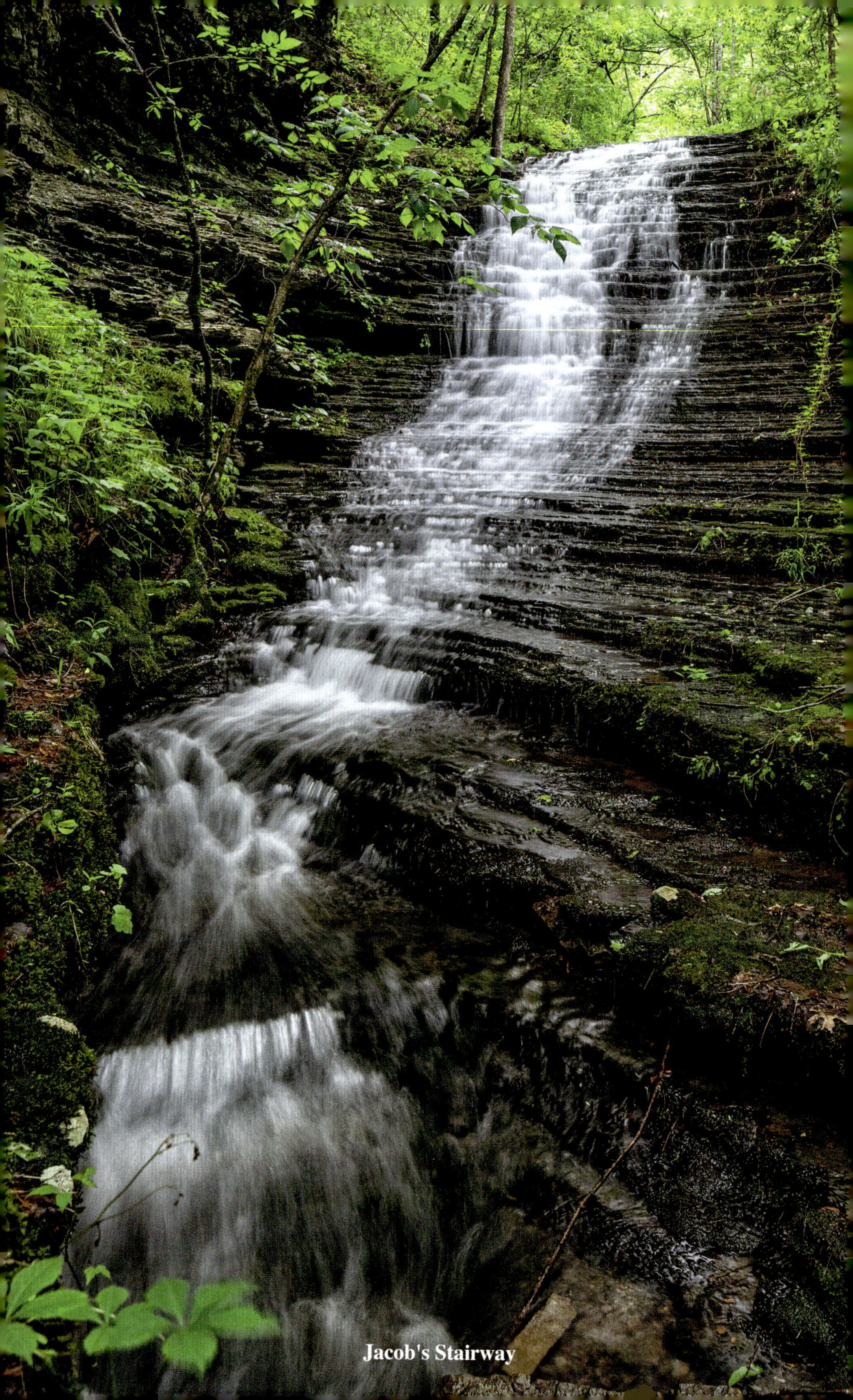
Jacob's Stairway

Schoolhouse Falls – 30′

.6 mile roundtrip, medium bushwhack, GPS helpful

GPS **35.53019, -92.79877**

Lizard Log Falls – 47′

7.0 miles roundtrip (w/3 falls below), difficult bushwhack, GPS recommended

GPS **35.53297, -92.81144**;

Iris Falls – 64′

7.0 miles roundtrip, difficult bushwhack, GPS recommended

GPS **35.54018, -92.81531**

Voices Falls – 44′

7.0 miles roundtrip, difficult bushwhack, GPS recommended

GPS **35.53660, -92.82390**

Whiskey Chute Falls – 83′

7.0 miles roundtrip, difficult bushwhack, GPS recommended

GPS **35.53084, -92.83022**

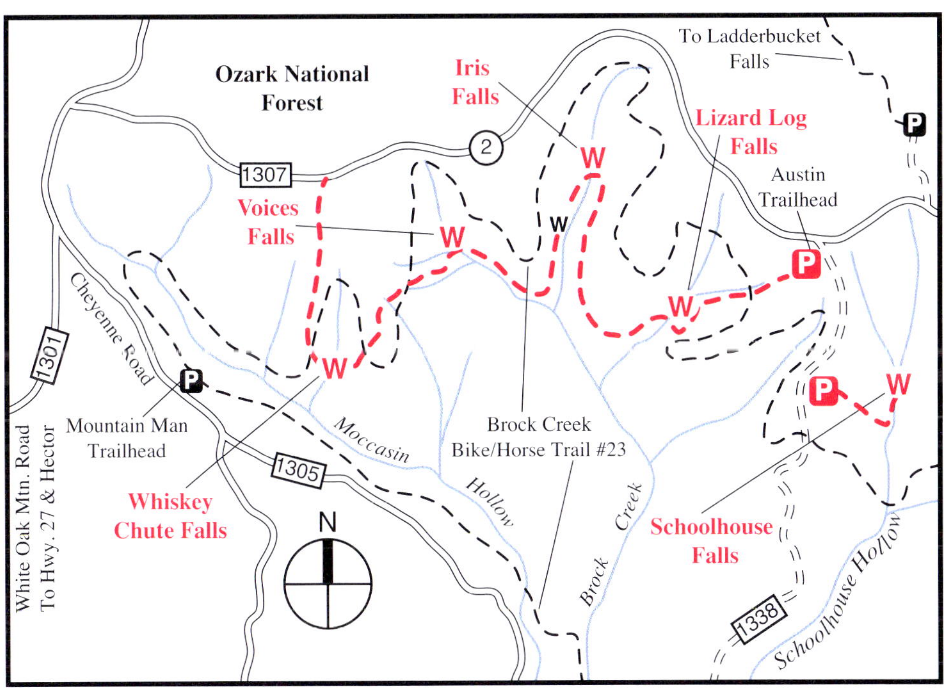

SCHOOLHOUSE/LIZARD LOG/IRIS/VOICES/WHISKEY CHUTE FALLS. This is a really nice polyfoss area with at least five significant waterfalls in adjoining hollows. The route to see them all can be complicated or easy, using a maze of horse/bike trails that run through the area (longer—only one of the bike trails is shown on the map); or simply bushwhacking below the bluffline to them all (shorter, my preferred route); or a combination. There is a road just above them all so you could also visit just one or two quickly. The area is part of the Brock Creek Recreation Area that is a mecca for ATVs, horses, and mountain bikes.

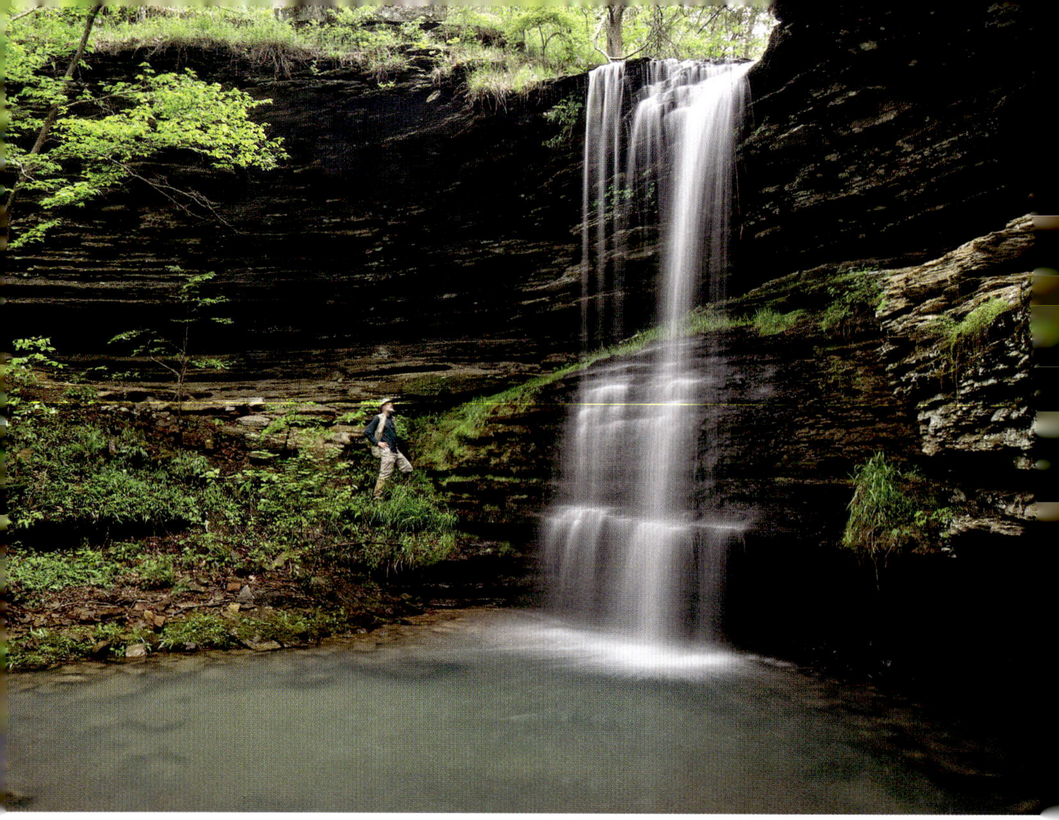

Schoolhouse Falls (above), **Lizard Log Falls** (below)

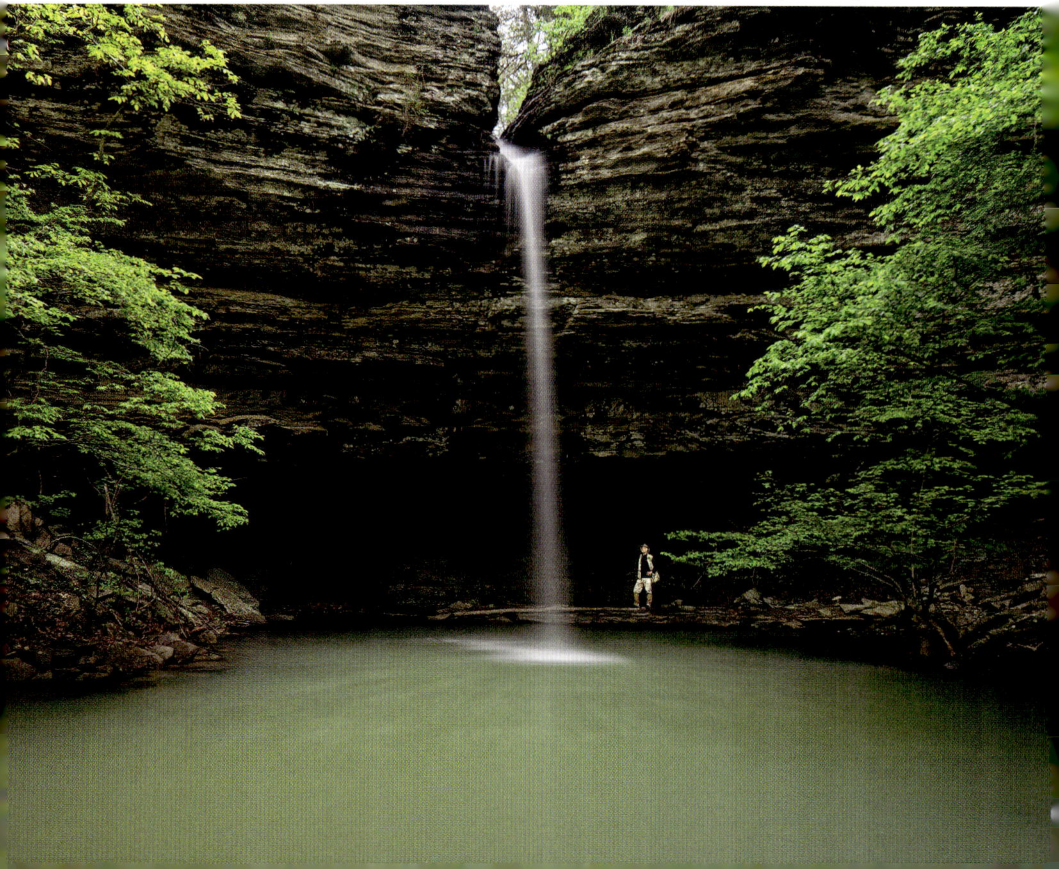

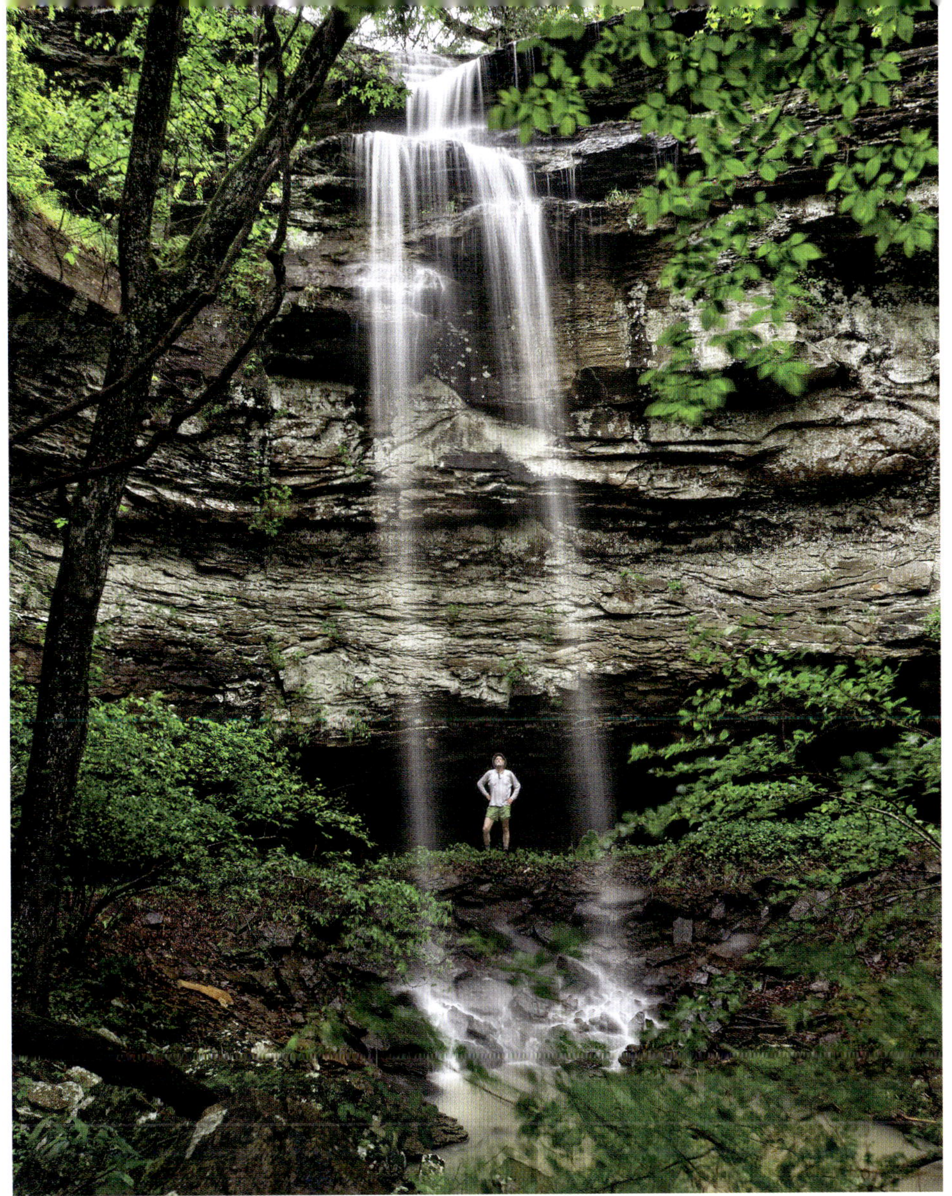

Iris Falls

And now for waterfall hunters! New Age waterfall guru Zack Andrews documented the seven waterfalls in this area, and named all but one (I heard *Voices*).

From Hector go north on Hwy. 27 and TURN RIGHT onto White Oak Mtn. Road/ FR#1301. Go 11.8 miles (bear left at 6.9) and TURN RIGHT onto FR#1307/CR#2. Go 2.9 miles and TURN RIGHT onto FR#1338 (a jeep trail). This is the Austin Trailhead (**35.53615, -92.80377**), where we'll come back to in a minute for the rest of the waterfalls. But first, stay on the jeep trail and drive .5 mile then TURN LEFT into a clearing/deer camp area and PARK (**35.52963, -92.80266**). Bushwhack out into the woods to the east and drop all the way down the hill to the creek below, then TURN LEFT and follow the creek upstream to **Schoolhouse Falls**.

Hike back out to your car and either bushwhack over to **Lizard Log Falls** or drive back out to and PARK at the Austin Trailhead (my preferred route). From the trailhead,

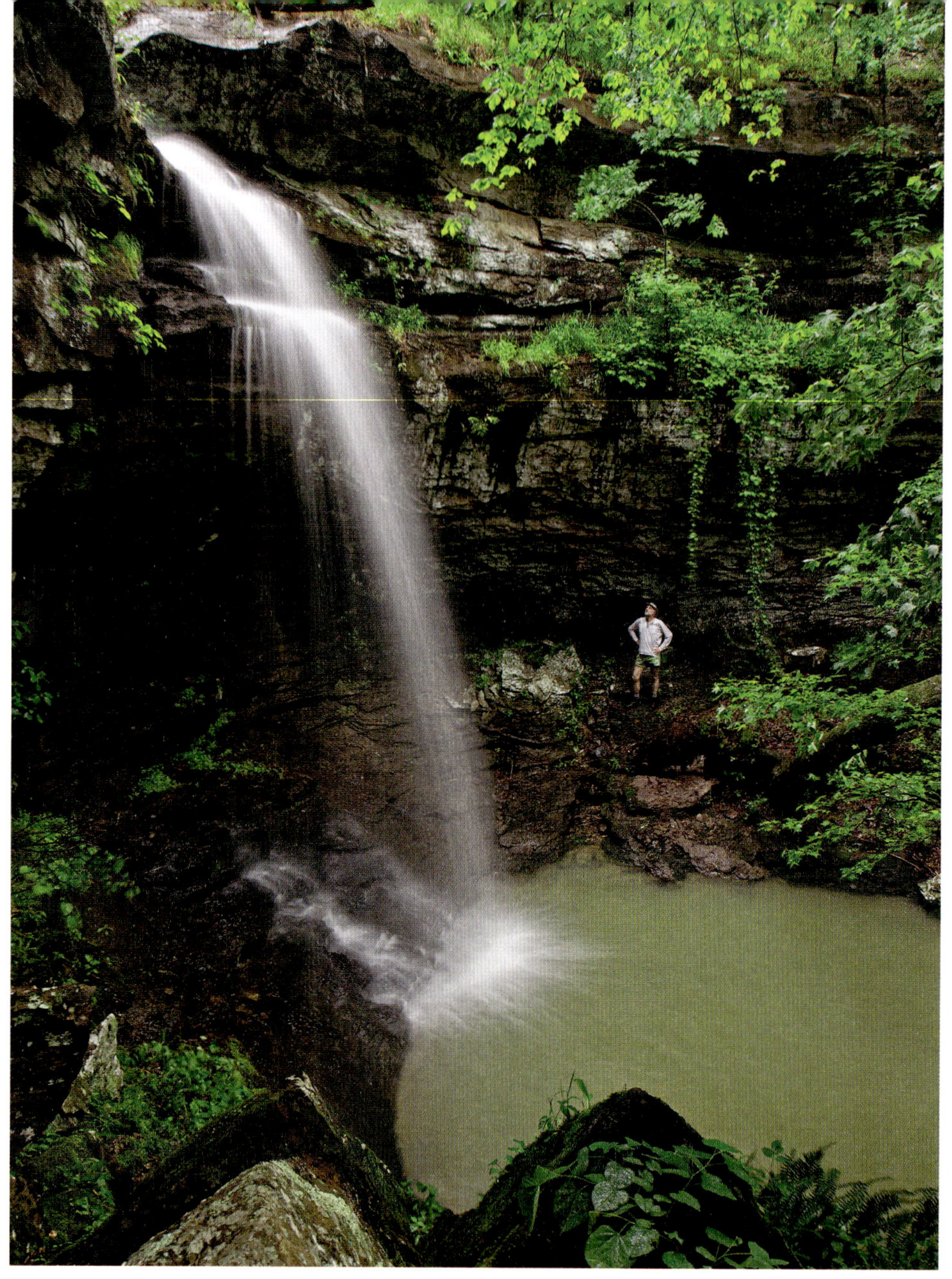

Voices Falls

bushwhack down into the woods (you will cross the bike trail) and follow the drainage until you come to the top of **Lizard Log Falls** (steep, difficult). To get to the bottom of the falls, follow the top of the bluffline around to the left until you can find a way down, then back upstream to the base of the falls. (OR, from the Austin Trailhead drop down the hill and TURN LEFT on the bike trail, follow it around until you get near the top of the falls—using your GPS—then leave the trail and bushwhack down to the falls.)

Once below the bluffline my preference is to simply follow along near the base of the bluffline (difficult but scenic) and visit the next two waterfalls—**Iris** (there is a carpet of wild iris near the base, everything guarded by some giant boulders); then **Voices** (I've

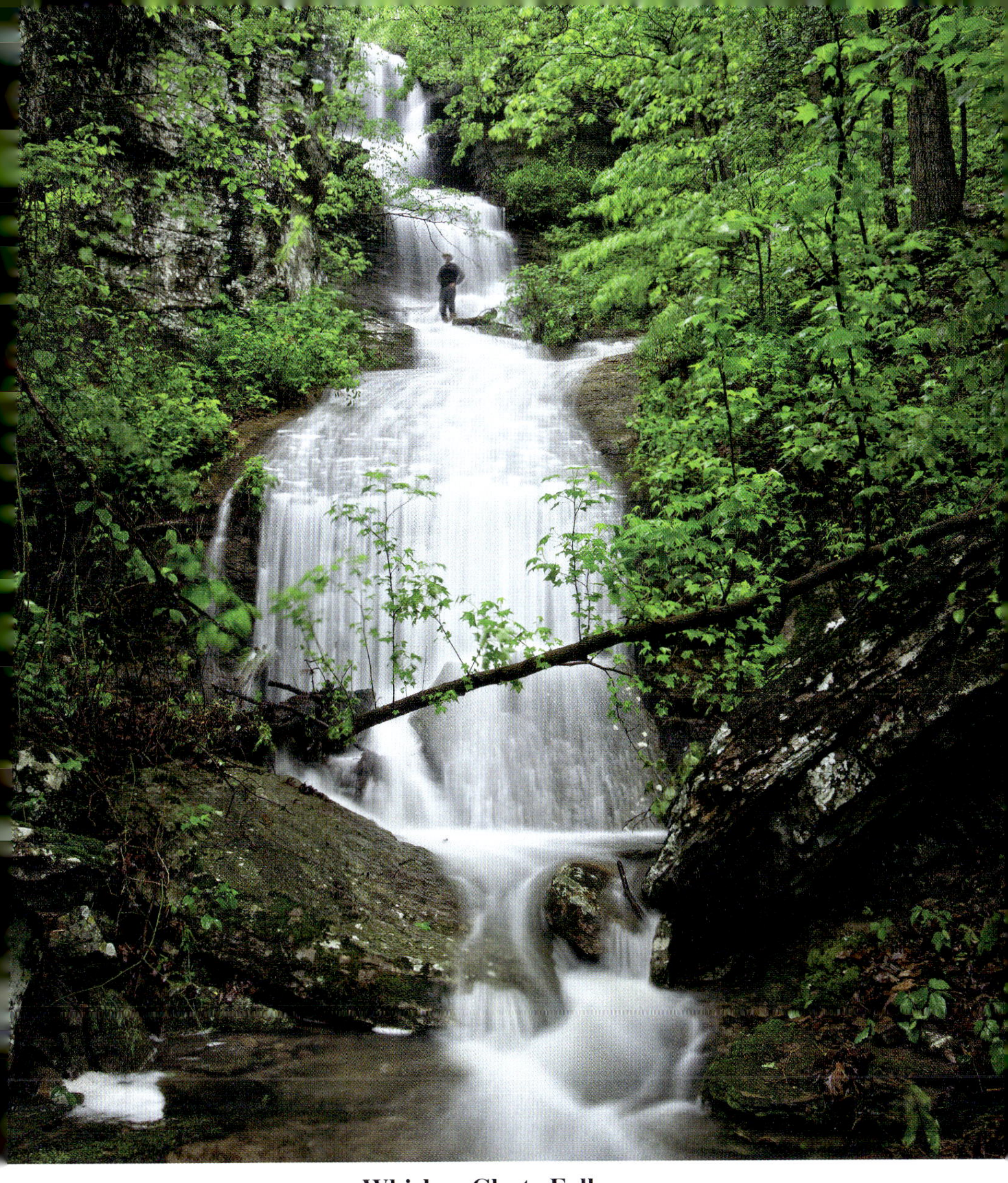

Whiskey Chute Falls

always heard voices coming from somewhere when I've been there).

From **Voices Falls**, I follow the bluffline downstream a bit and then work my way up through the bluff—past several nice smaller waterfalls, including three in a row—then cut across the top of the ridge and drop down into **Whiskey Chute Falls** (it is a *very long* way around if you stay below the bluff). From there, I climb back up and out to the main road and just follow it back to the trailhead to complete a big loop. You could also use the horse/bike trail to access the tops of all of these waterfalls—longer and easier going but less scenic. And if you have two cars you could spot one of them at the Mountain Man Trailhead (**35.52995, -92.83918**) and save a lot of hiking.

Emergency contact: Van Buren County Sheriff, 479–495–4881 Dogs are OK.

Ladderbucket Falls – 36′

4.0 miles roundtrip (both falls), difficult bushwhack, GPS recommended

GPS **35.54868, -92.79469**

John Mountain Falls – 84′

4.0 miles roundtrip (both falls), difficult bushwhack, GPS recommended

GPS **35.55112, -92.79336**

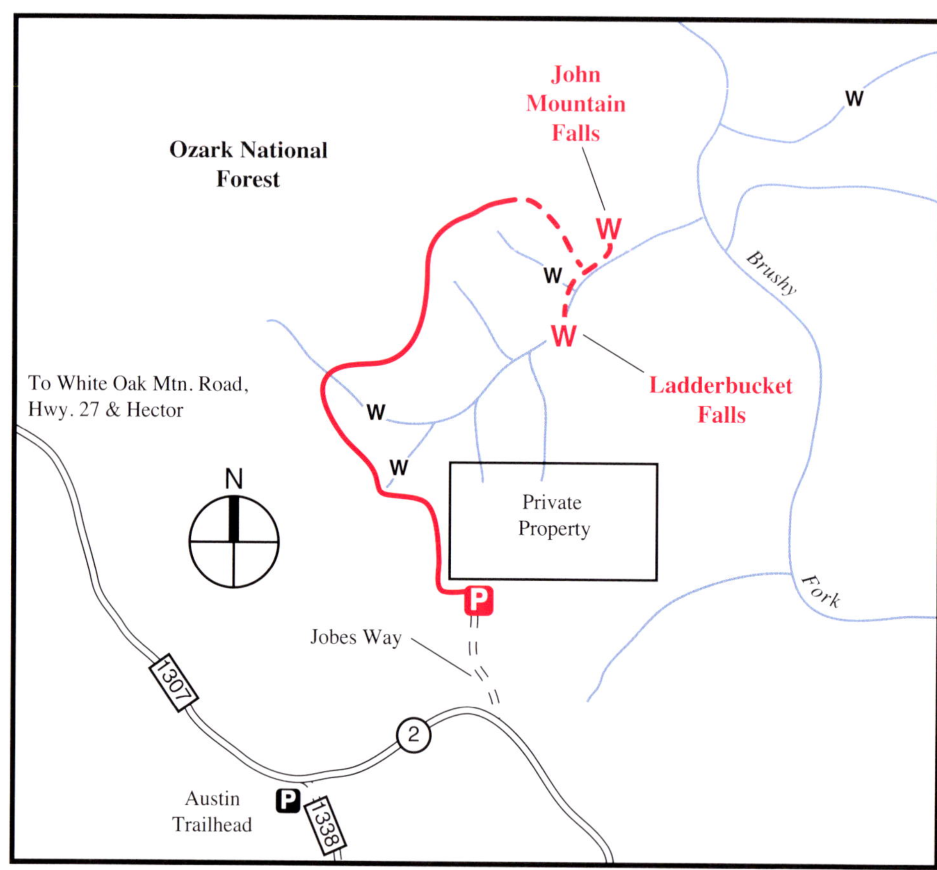

LADDERBUCKET FALLS/JOHN MOUNTAIN FALLS. (photos are on the following pages) One of the tallest waterfalls and one of the most unique grottos in the state will make the steep terrain worth the trip, especially if you visit during high water. The parking spot is located near the Austin Trailhead (previous five waterfalls)—extreme bushwhackers can visit them all and you'll have a world-class day of waterfall hunting!

From Hector go north on Hwy. 27 and TURN RIGHT onto White Oak Mtn. Road/ FR#1301. Go 11.8 miles (bear left at 6.9) and TURN RIGHT onto FR#1307/CR#2. Go 3.5 miles and TURN LEFT onto a jeep road (Jobes Way) and go .2 and PARK near the private property gate (**35.54143, -92.79749**). Please don't block the gate..

Make your way to the left around the private property, then curve back down to the right until you come to a four-wheeler trail and TURN LEFT. Follow this trail as it wraps around the head of the big hollow to the right (OR you can simply head downhill until you come to the waterfalls). After about a mile you can leave the trail and head downhill into the hollow. There is a spot in between the two waterfalls where you can get down through the big bluff.

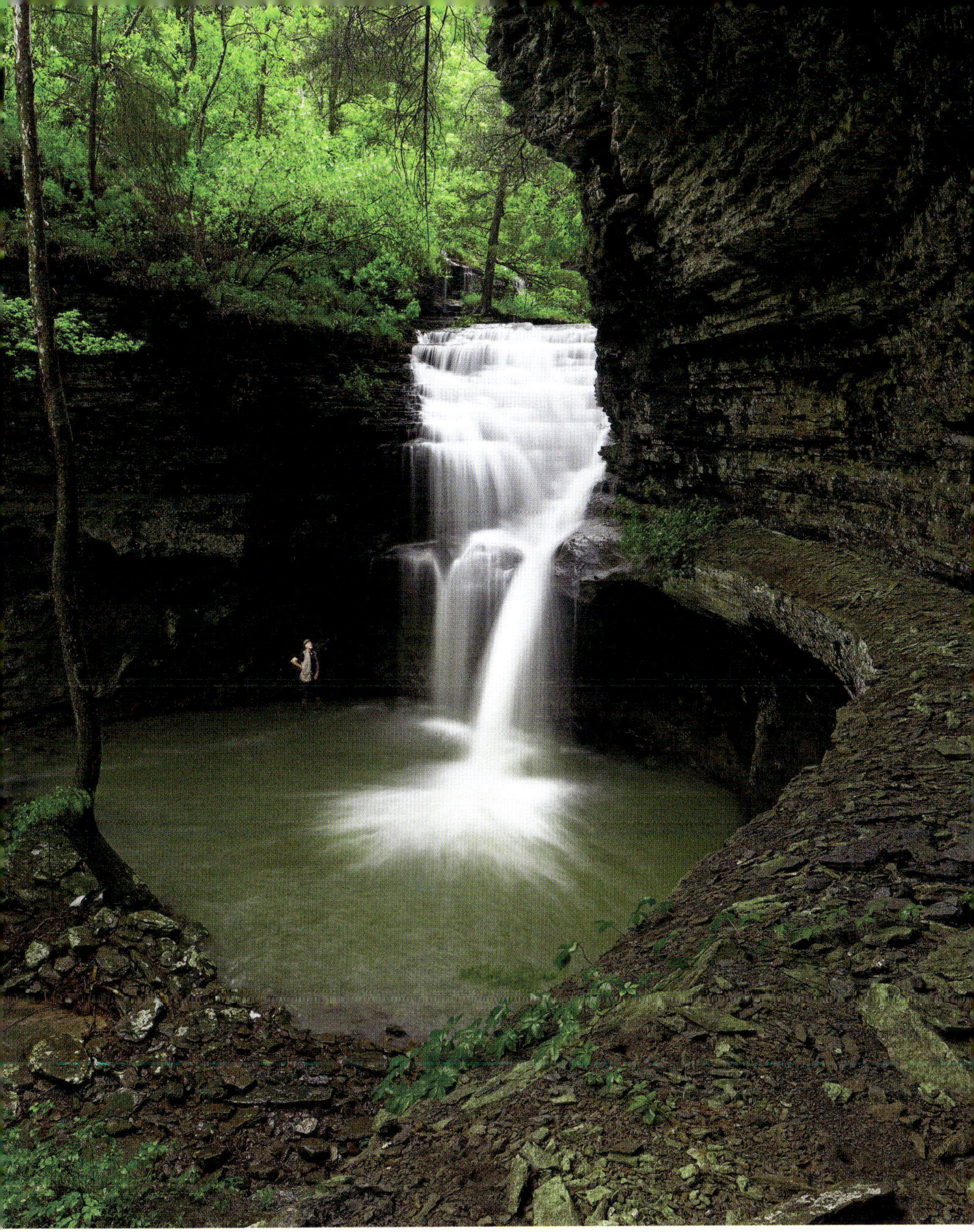

Ladderbucket Falls

TURN LEFT and follow the bluff to **John Mountain Falls**. Then come back and follow the bluff or creek upstream (past another tall waterfall) to **Ladderbucket Falls**.

Emergency contact: Van Buren County Sheriff, 479–495–4881 Dogs are OK.

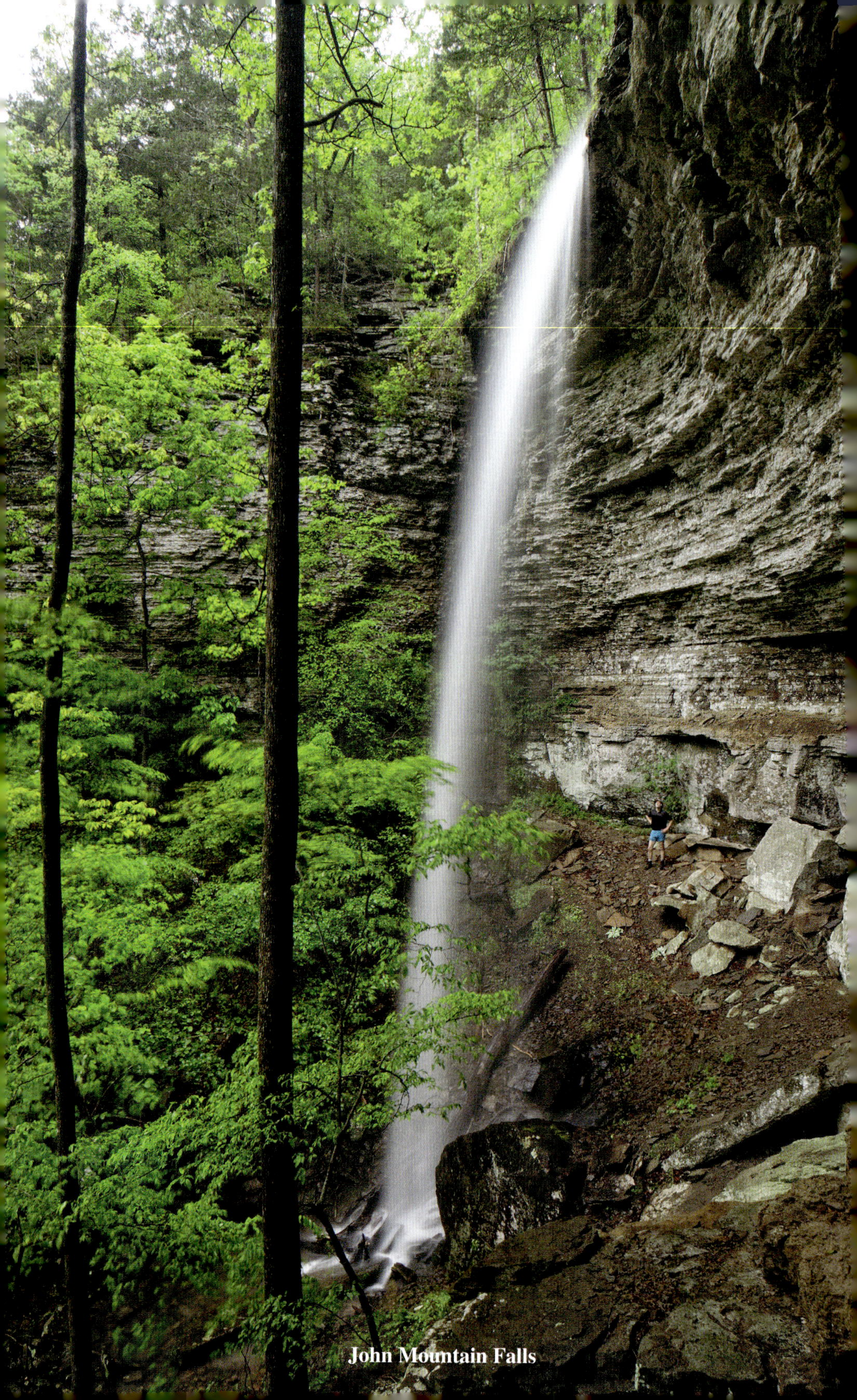

John Mountain Falls

Rough Hollow Falls – 34′

.4, easy GPS **35.53338, -93.14472**

Giant Rocks Falls – 13′

1.0 easy+ GPS **35.53347, -93.14112**

Trigg Falls – 37′

1.1 easy+ GPS **35.53447, -93.14065**

Balcony Falls – 28′

.8 roundtrip, moderate bushwhack GPS **35.53730, -93.12192**

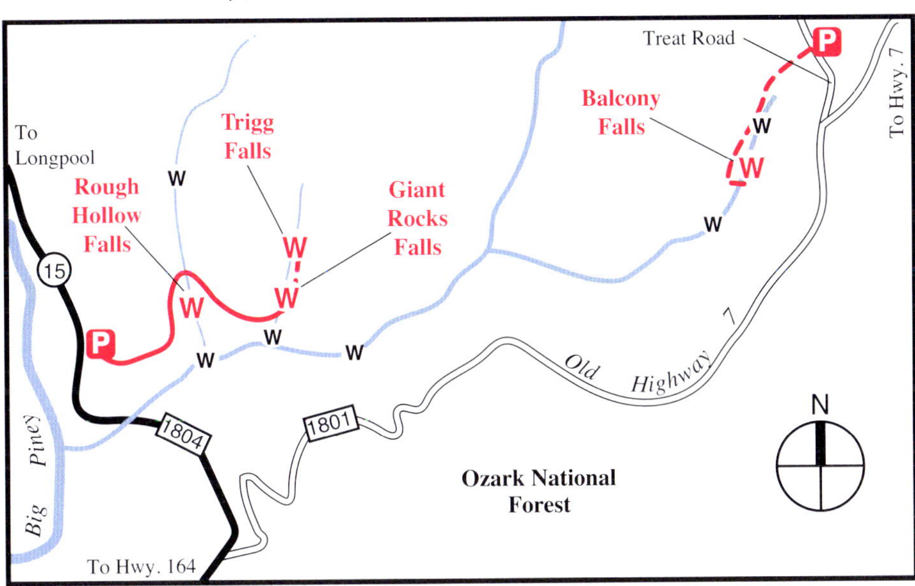

ROUGH HOLLOW WATERFALLS. Directions from Dover to the lower parking area—head north on Hwy. 7 and go five miles then TURN LEFT onto Hwy. 164. Go 3.5 miles and TURN RIGHT onto old Hwy. 7 (paved). Go 2.7 miles and keep straight on the pavement (old Hwy. 7 turns RIGHT here and is gravel—you will return to this intersection for the upper parking area.) The paved road becomes CR#15/FR1804/Longpool Road. Continue straight on pavement .8 mile and TURN RIGHT onto a gravel road and PARK **(35.53127, -93.14713)**.

There are a lot of waterfalls and cascades in the Rough Hollow drainage—several are on the main creek and others are in side hollows. Here are three of my favorites from the lower end of the drainage (all in side hollows), plus one from the very top on the main creek, which has a different/upper parking area.

From the lower parking area follow the road that you parked on and go upstream and it will curve to the left into a side hollow. There will be a social trail to access to the RIGHT, down through a bluff and below to **Rough Hollow Falls** at .4. (the old road continues above the bluff, across the creek, and on towards the next hollow)

(If you stayed above the bluff on the old road it curves around the head of this side hollow and cross the creek—upstream there's a low but nice "Ten Tier Falls" to visit—we will use this road again.)

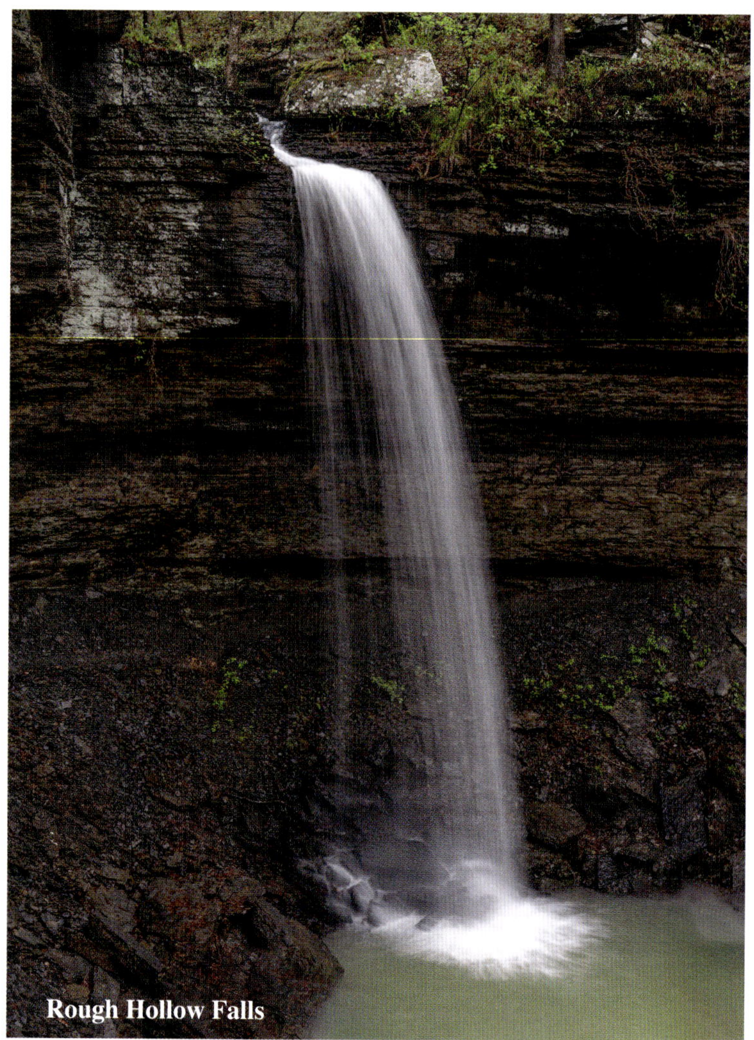
Rough Hollow Falls

From **Rough Hollow** climb up through the bluff on the right side and rejoin the old road trace and TURN RIGHT. Follow this around as it curves to the left into the next side hollow. Where it crosses the creek TURN LEFT and follow the creek upstream. (Rat Snake Falls, 27' (no photo provided), is just below the bluff on the right, downstream. It's an OK falls and you can get down below it—but it's been my experience most folks don't like anything with "snake" in the name or description so I've not added a photo, but it's worth a look, especially if the water levels are high.)

BUT UPSTREAM on the creek you come to a lovely SSS area, **Giant Rocks Falls** at 1.0. Continue on further upstream for another great SSS spot, **Trigg Falls** at 1.1.

It's possible to follow the main Rough Hollow Creek all the way to the top (it gets pretty "rough"), but to get to the best waterfall in that upper section I recommend you return to your car and drive up and park near at the upper parking area.

To get to the upper parking location for **Balcony Falls**—go back .8 miles to the Old Highway 7 intersection and TURN LEFT (gravel). Go up the hill 2.6 miles, TURN LEFT onto Treat Road/Maupin Flat Road (this is 1.4 miles from the current Hwy. 7), then go .2 and PARK (**35.54181, -93.11963**).

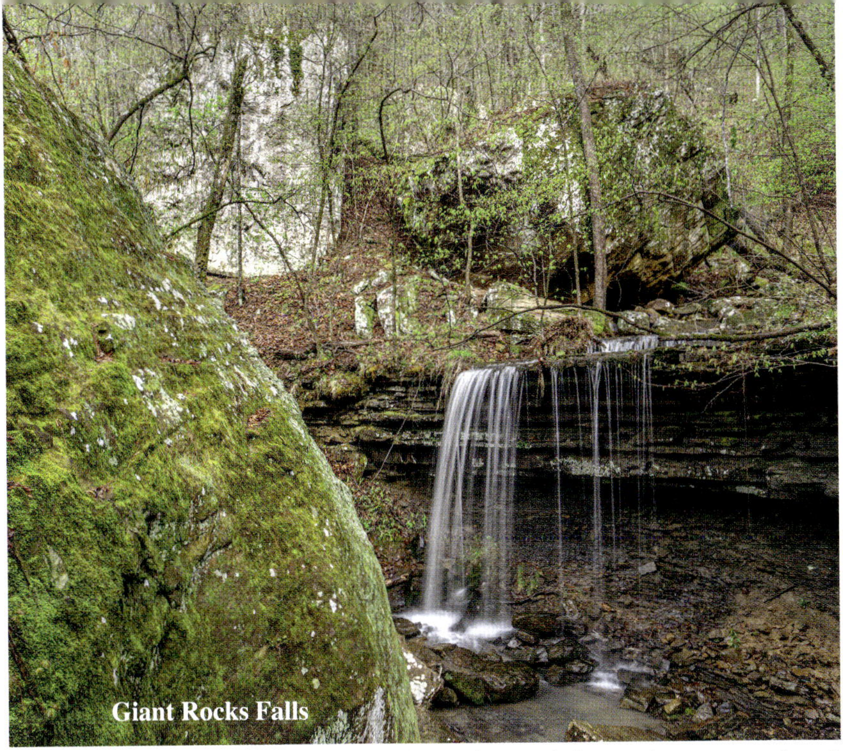

Giant Rocks Falls

Balcony Falls is just a short distance down the creek from where you park—either follow the creek (past a nice smaller waterfall) to **Balcony Falls** at .4, or follow a timber road down the right side of the drainage until you come beside the falls at .55 (use GPS).

There is a true "balcony" behind the falls with easy access—I love these areas and often spend more time behind waterfalls than in front of them!

Emergency contact: Pope County Sheriff, 479–967–9300 Dogs are OK

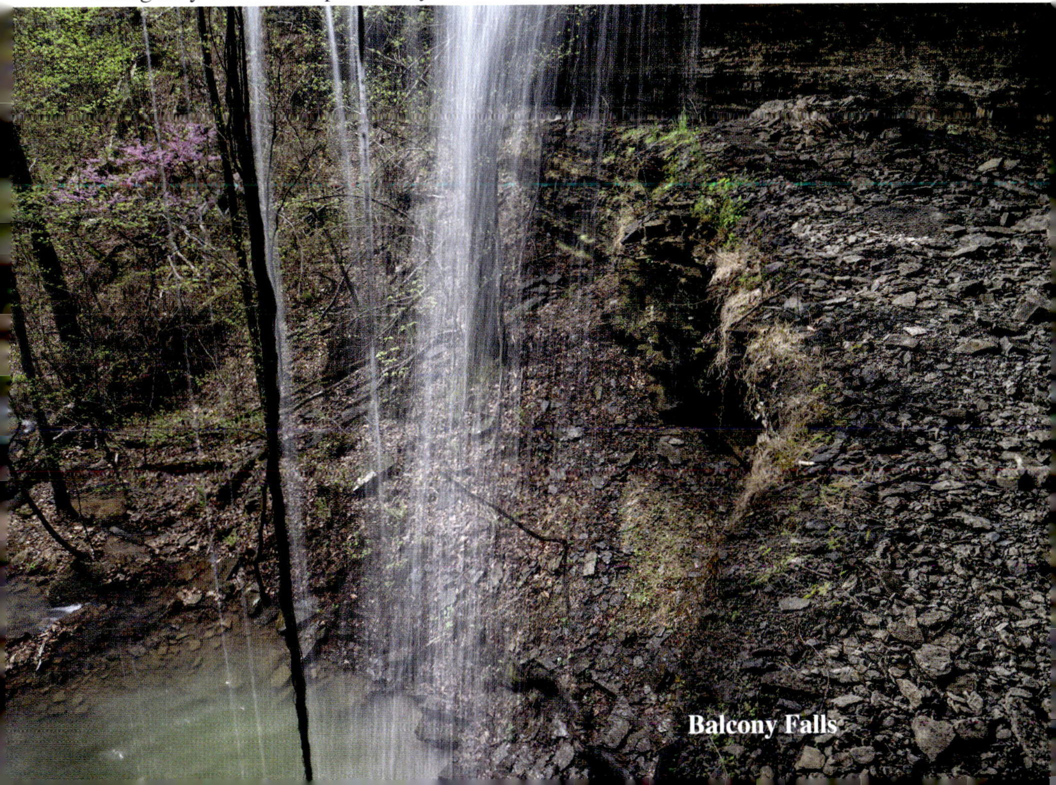

Balcony Falls

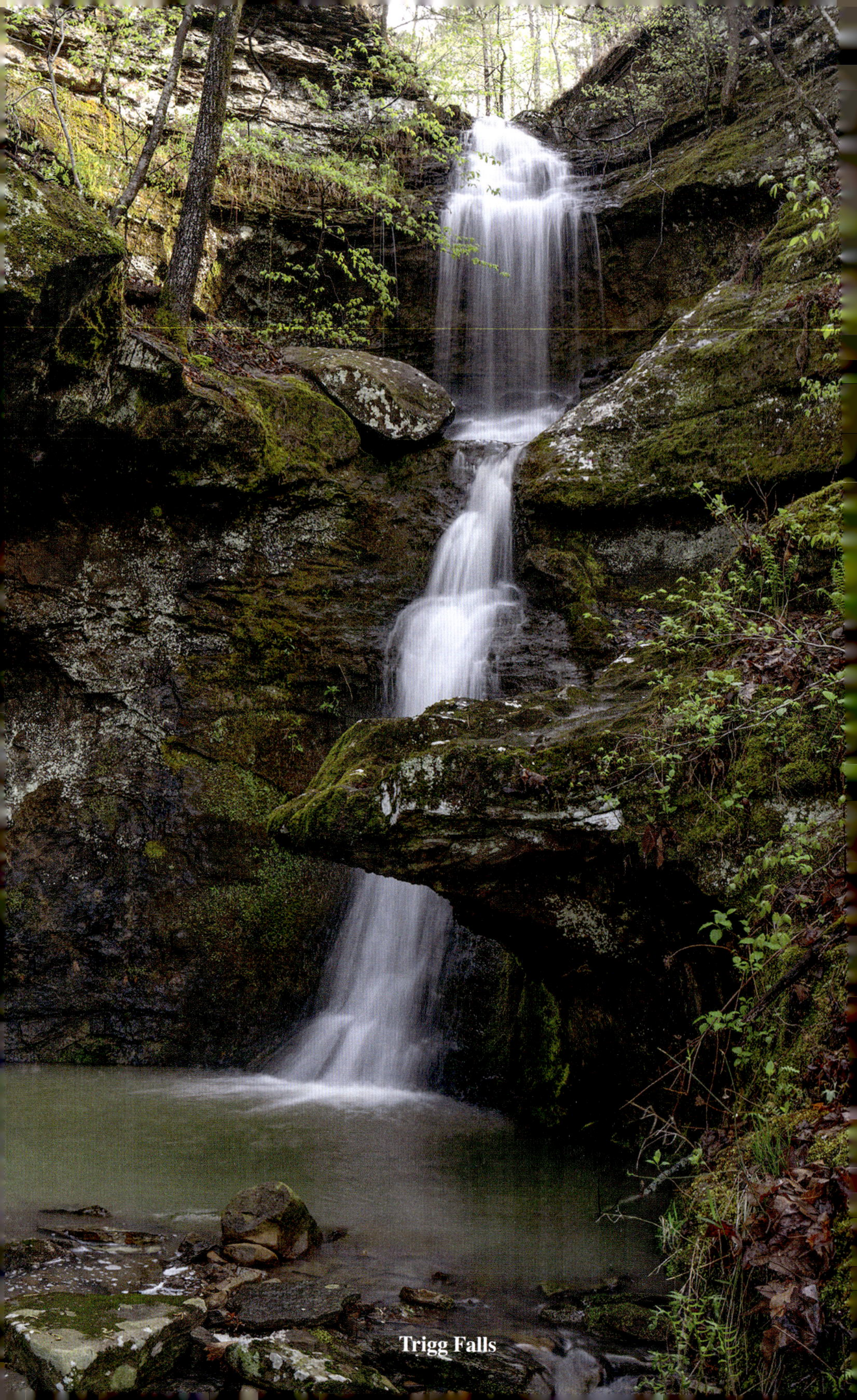

Trigg Falls

Longpool Falls – 44′

1.5 miles roundtrip, easy hike, GPS not needed

GPS **35.54930, -93.15210**

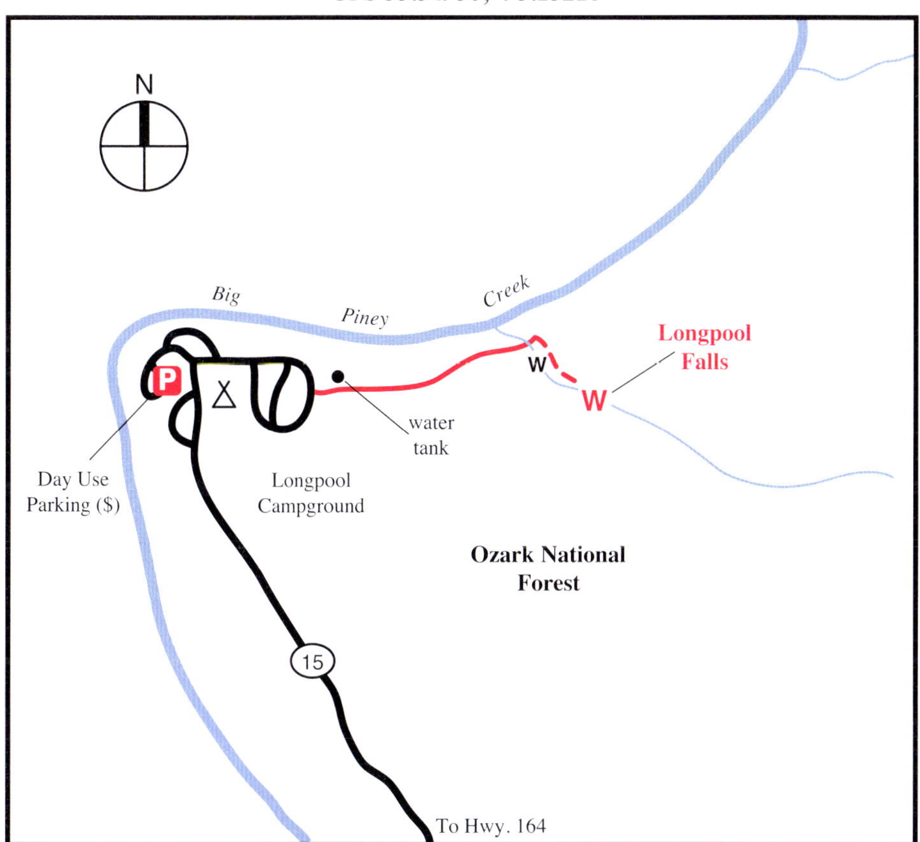

LONGPOOL FALLS. This waterfall is located right next to a very popular recreation area, but few folks ever go see it. The hike to the falls is easy, and the water coming over the bluff is quite powerful, especially since it comes from a very small drainage above. There is a big swimming hole at the recreation area, a picnic area, quite a few campsites, and nice restrooms. The place will be crowded on spring weekends and the river filled with canoeists as this is also one of the main access points for the river. Waterfall season is the same as floating season, and we all want high water! There is a day use fee charged to park here, and the parking area is on the opposite side of the area from where we begin our hike.

To get to Longpool Recreation Area, head north on Hwy. 7 from Dover (north of Russellville). TURN LEFT onto Hwy. 164, and then TURN RIGHT onto CR#14 (old Hwy. 7) at the sign. This road becomes CR#15, which ends at Longpool, 4.8 miles from Hwy. 164 (it is all paved). To get to the PARKING AREA, go past the pay station and follow the main road around to the LEFT, then PARK in the big lot.

From the parking area, head on over to the Loop B Camp Area, and go all the way to the back. There is an old road trace that takes off from the main road in between campsites #14 & #9. Take this roadbed up past an old water tank, then continue uphill just a little bit. The roadbed soon tops out and begins to head downhill. You are hiking upstream along Big Piney Creek which you can see down on your left. Big Piney is one of the most

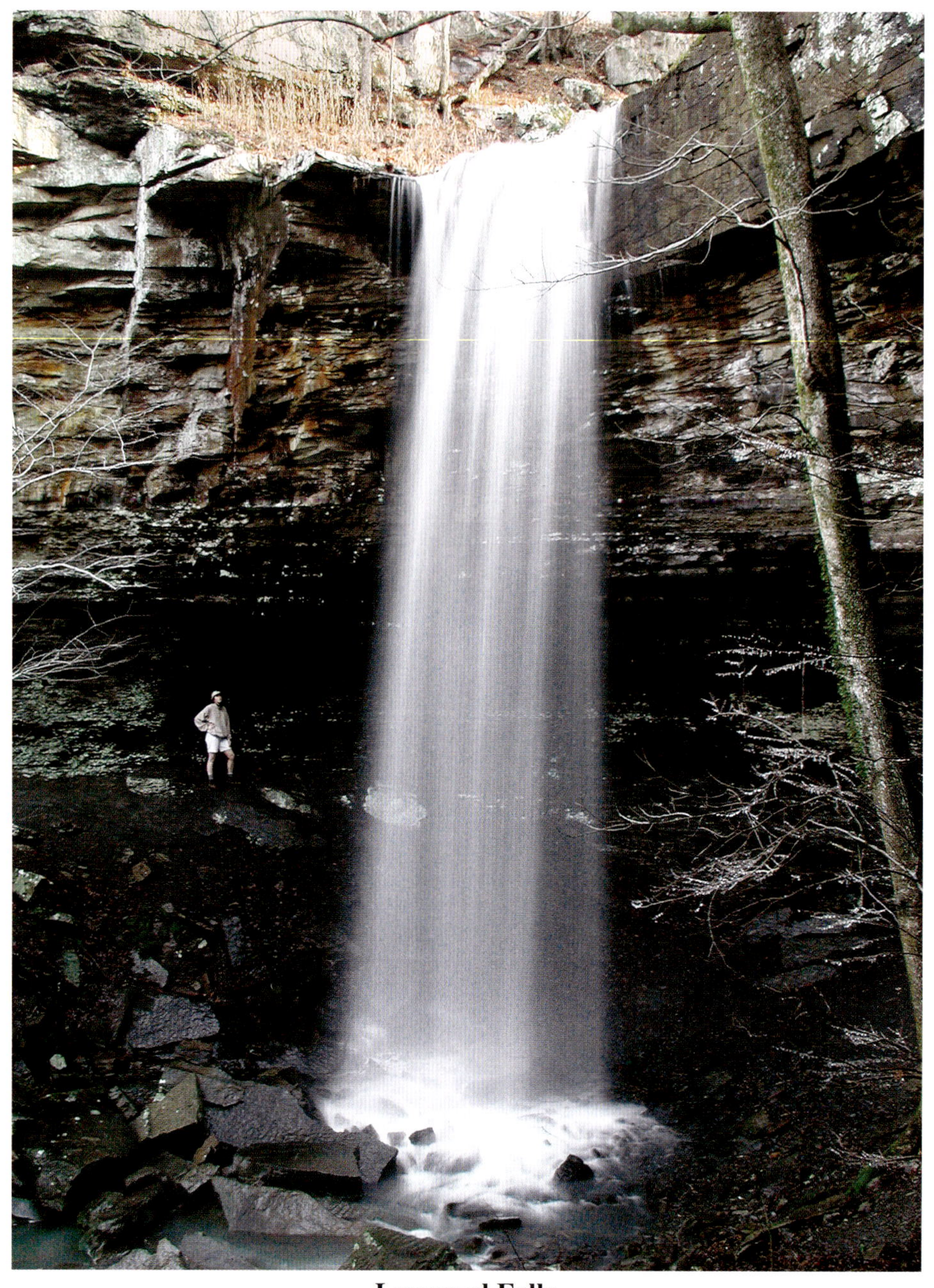

Longpool Falls

beautiful and popular floating streams in the Ozarks. The roadbed comes on down to river level where you come to a creek—there is a nice little waterfall just up to your right here that should be running well. The big falls is up behind that one—cross the stream, TURN RIGHT, and head up past the little falls. You'll have to do a bit of boulder scrambling so be careful, but you will soon hear the thunder and see this hidden beauty.

Emergency contact: Pope County Sheriff, 479–967–9300 Dogs are OK.

Waldo Mtn. Falls – 23′

2.4 miles roundtrip, moderate bushwhack to both falls

GPS **35.54465, -93.18165**

Rick Henry Falls #805 –19′

GPS **35.54456, -93.18160**

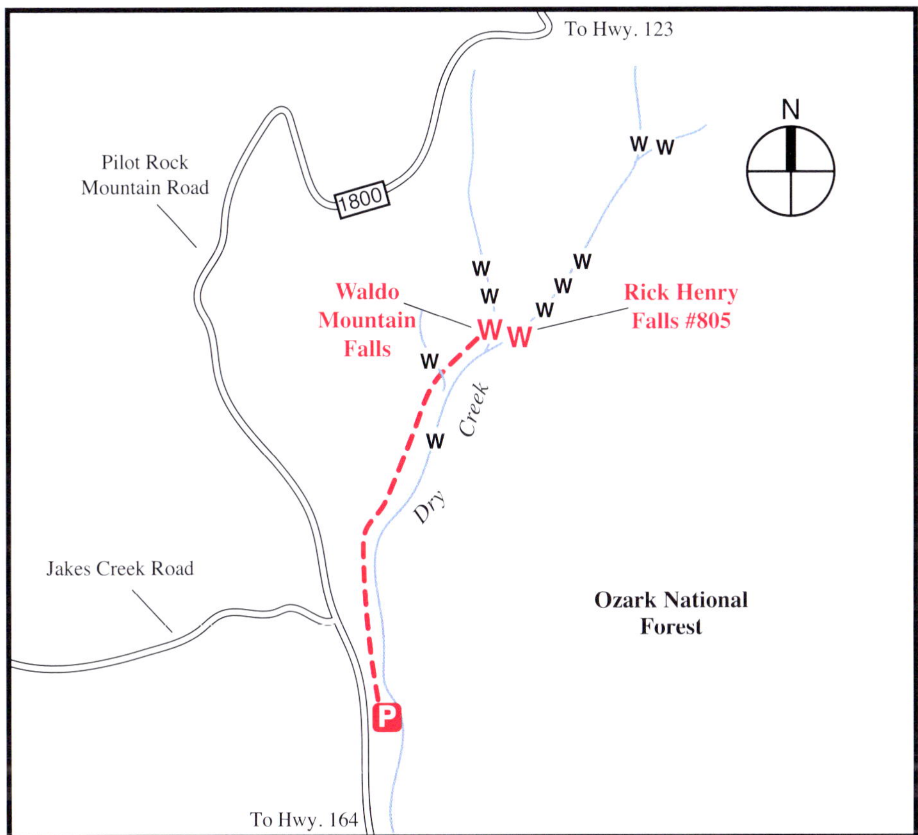

WALDO MTN. FALLS/RICK HENRY FALLS #805. Waldo Mountain is just west of the Big Piney River near Longpool, and there are several nice waterfalls along one of its creeks, Dry Branch. This is an especially important area as it's the last set of waterfalls that legendary waterfall guru, Rick Henry, documented and shared on his public blog before he died of cancer. I just went through all of his waterfall posts from January 2014 to his last post on January 13th, 2020. He documented so many waterfalls that he could not keep up with giving each one a special name, so he ended up numbering a lot of them—one hollow alone having more than 67 waterfalls. I wanted to name a waterfall after Rick, and so I picked the last one he visited and left without a name—to correspond with the total number of waterfalls he documented online—it is called RICK HENRY FALLS #805! (also see Rick Henry Falls on page 153)

Directions from Dover—head north on Hwy. 7 and go five miles, then TURN LEFT onto Hwy. 164. Go 4.7 miles and TURN RIGHT onto Pilot Rock Mtn. Road/FR1800. Go 1.6 miles and PARK on the right by the creek **(35.53506, -93.18561)**.

From the parking spot follow Dry Creek upstream, passing a couple of smaller falls

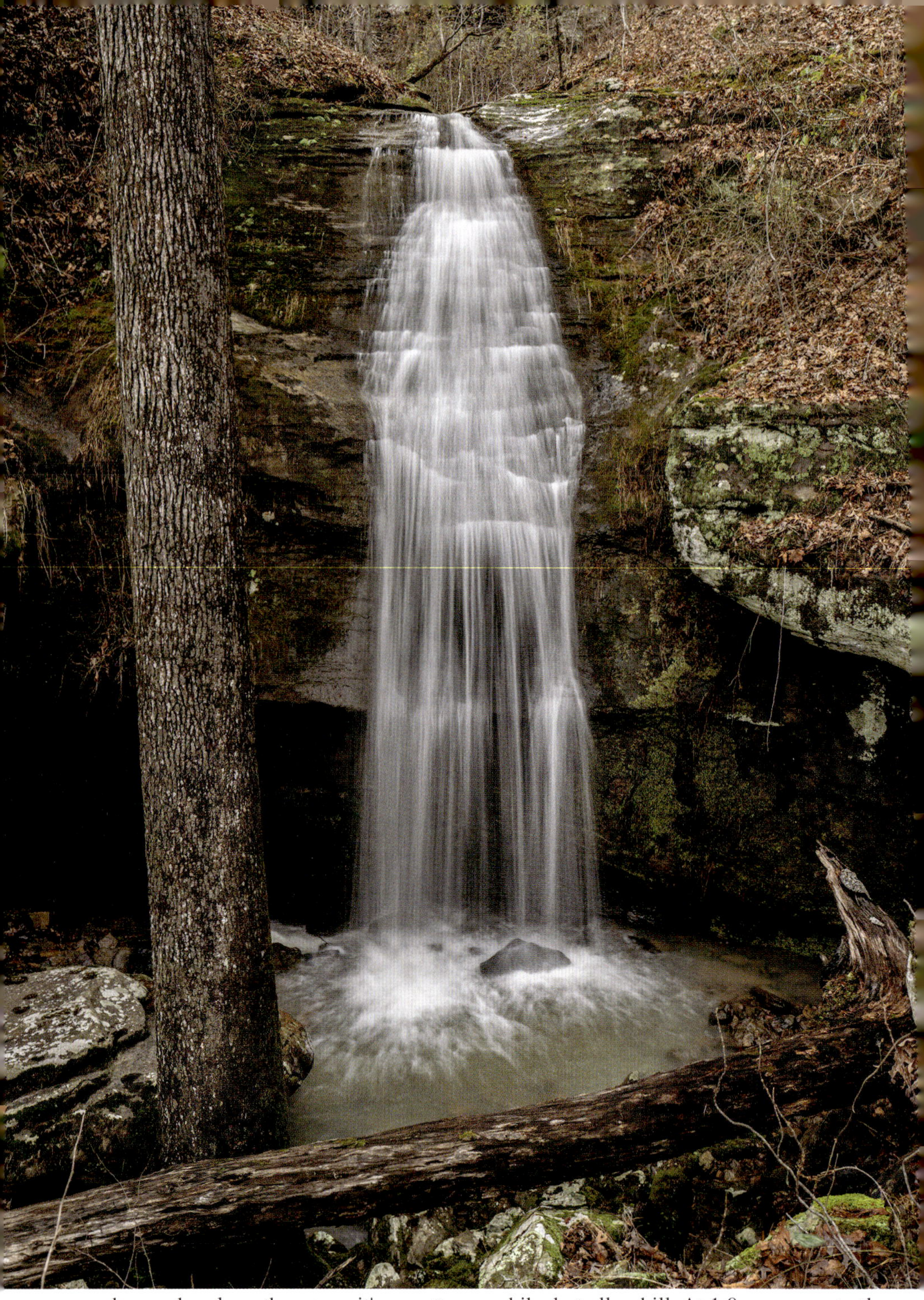

and cascades along the way—it's a pretty easy hike but all uphill. At 1.0 you come to the main attraction area—there is a side creek coming in from the left, and a quite beautiful **Waldo Mountain Falls** pouring over the bluff there. If you stand in front of the falls and wave your right hand from your left to right and all the way around you, that's all a pretty darn terrific and wonderful SSS!

There is a nice waterfall above Waldo—you have to claw your way up a very steep hillside on the right side of the falls to get up to it. And also a smaller one above that (Rick would be thrilled if you named them.). Otherwise, back down on the main creek to the right of **Waldo Falls** and upstream is **Rick Henry Falls #805**, where the creek pours between moss-covered boulders into a swirling emerald pool. This was the last area that Rick documented and posted on his public blog. On that blog he commented about crawling through a bear cave to get from one level of the rugged terrain to the other—that's over on the right beneath the giant slabs of sandstone—'tis an amazing place.

Further upstream another .1 is one of my favorite waterfalls here, like many others was left unnamed by Rick. There are several more waterfalls upstream of this area and eventually you can climb up and out to another parking area up high off of the main road **(35.55076, -93.17578)**, but it's a pretty steep climb and most folks will rather simply enjoy the main group of falls and return downstream to the parking area, a round trip of about 2.4 miles. THANKS RICK!

Emergency contact: Pope County Sheriff, 479–967–9300 Dogs are OK.

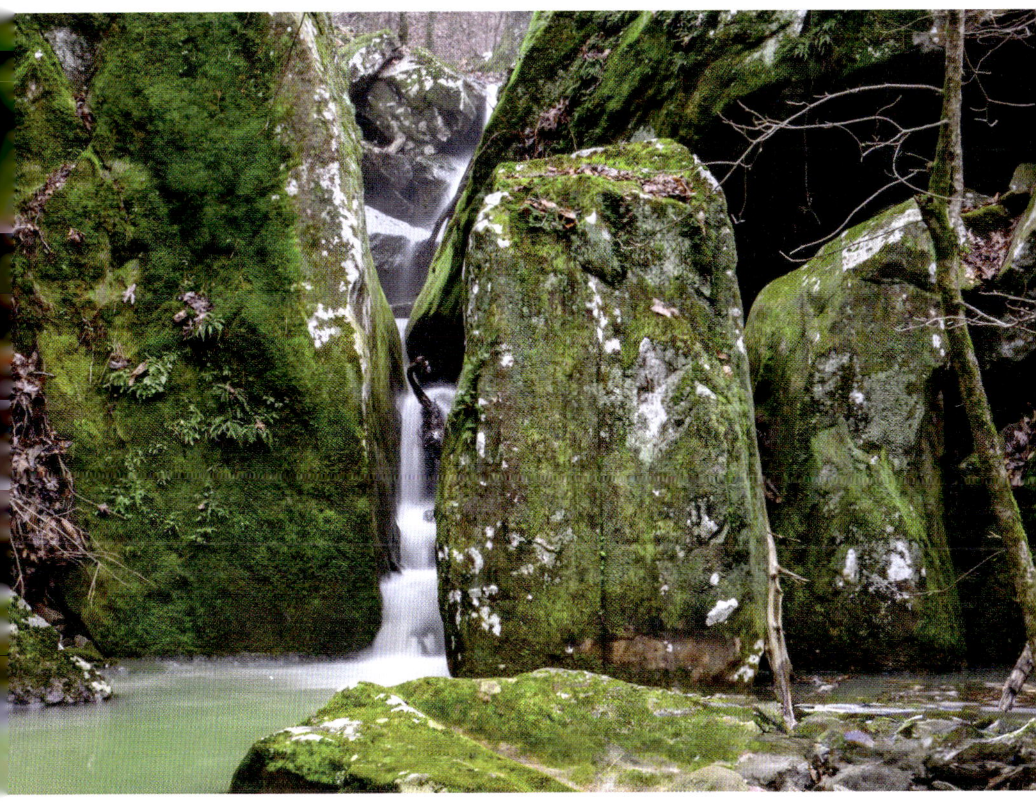

Rick Henry Falls #805 (photo by Rick Henry)

Forever Falls – 47′

2.0 miles roundtrip, difficult bushwhack, GPS recommended

GPS **35.59188, -93.18915**

Graves Canyon Falls (2) – 31′/35′

Same area as above, difficult bushwhack, GPS recommended

GPS **35.59503, -93.18653**

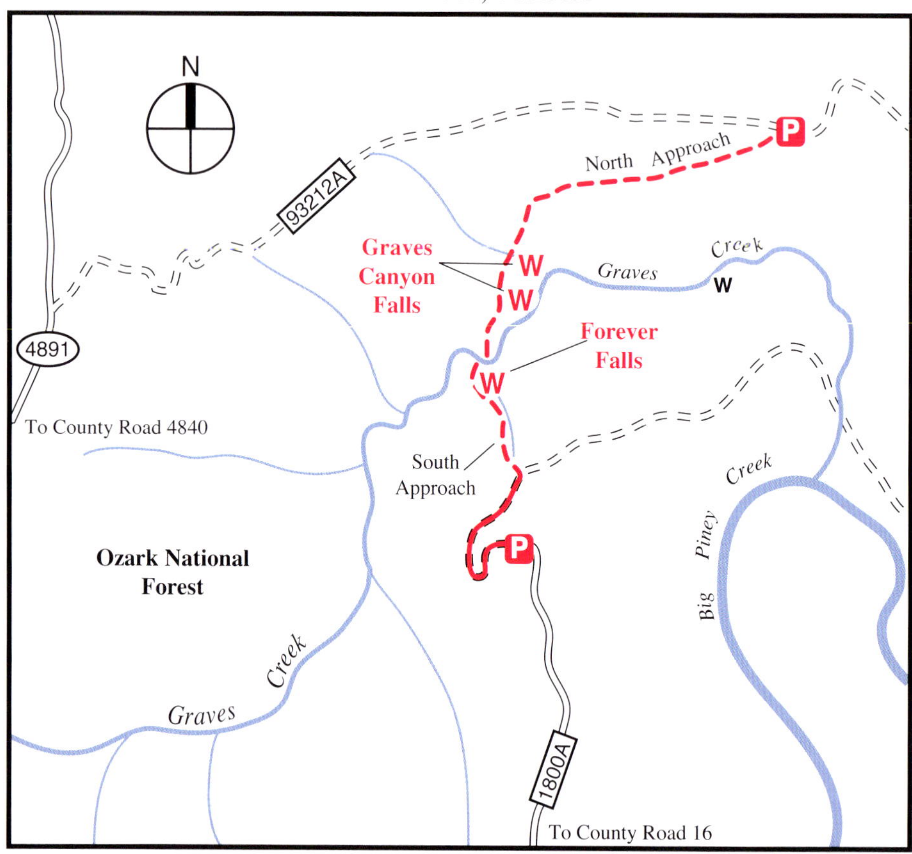

FOREVER FALLS/GRAVES CANYON FALLS. Here is a wonderful canyon tucked into a side pocket of the Big Piney River. These falls are difficult to get to (easier with a *serious* 4wd), but well worth the trip if you can make it. You will want to stay here forever! One kayaker that I know calls this the most scenic wild run in the Ozarks.

North Approach. From Hwy. 123, go 3.9 miles south of Haw Creek Campground (.6 south of FR#1003 turn) and TURN LEFT onto CR#4840 (gravel). Go 9.8 miles (past Pilot Knob) and TURN LEFT onto CR#4891 (or *turn right* for the south approach to get to FR#1800-A). Go 1.7 miles (the road # may change) and TURN RIGHT onto log road #93212A. This is a *rough* 4wd road with pending timber sales. You can PARK anytime after 1.8 miles (**35.60045, -93.17718** ish...)—the road runs along the top edge of the ridge, with the canyon being down on the right, way down. (If you have a *serious* 4wd you may be able to drive all the way to the bottom.) Park and head south (downhill) into the woods. If you have a GPS, simply make a beeline towards the falls. If not, make your way down the hillside any way that you choose to the creek below. Either way the going will be tough,

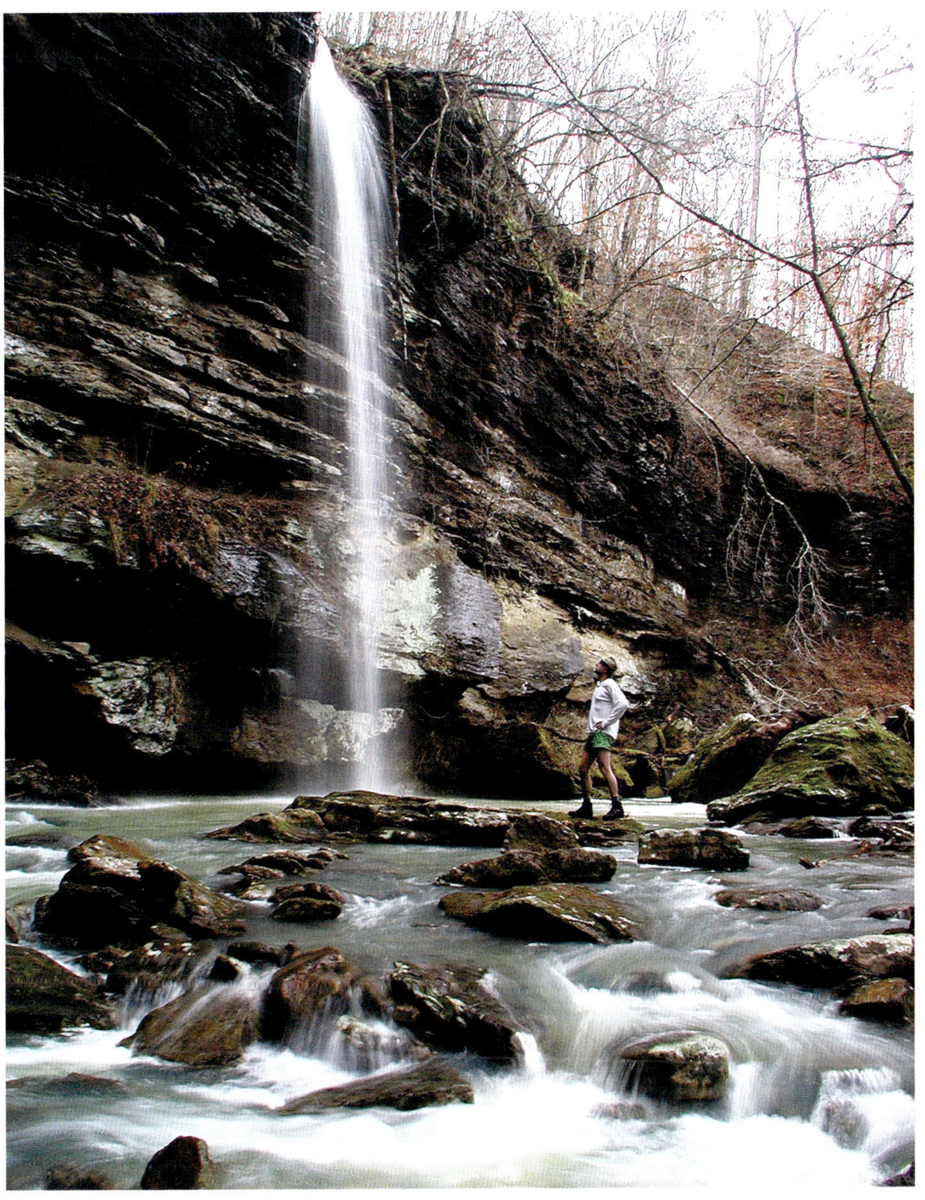

Forever Falls

down a *very steep* hillside. Once you get to the creek you will need to look around a bit in order to find the falls. It's a mile hike or less from the road to the creek, give or take.

The lower two falls are on the north side of the creek (turn page for photos), right next to each other in the middle of a narrow canyon that is flanked by 20–30 foot tall bluffs—if you get down into this winding canyon you may not be able to get back out for a while! **Forever Falls** is on the south side of the creek at the upper end of the canyon, several hundred yards upstream from the other falls, located in a hairpin curve.

South Approach. This parking spot will get you closer (especially if you have a 4wd), but if the water is really high you will end up on the wrong side of the river to view the waterfalls and may not be able to cross the creek. From Dover take Hwy. 7 north and TURN

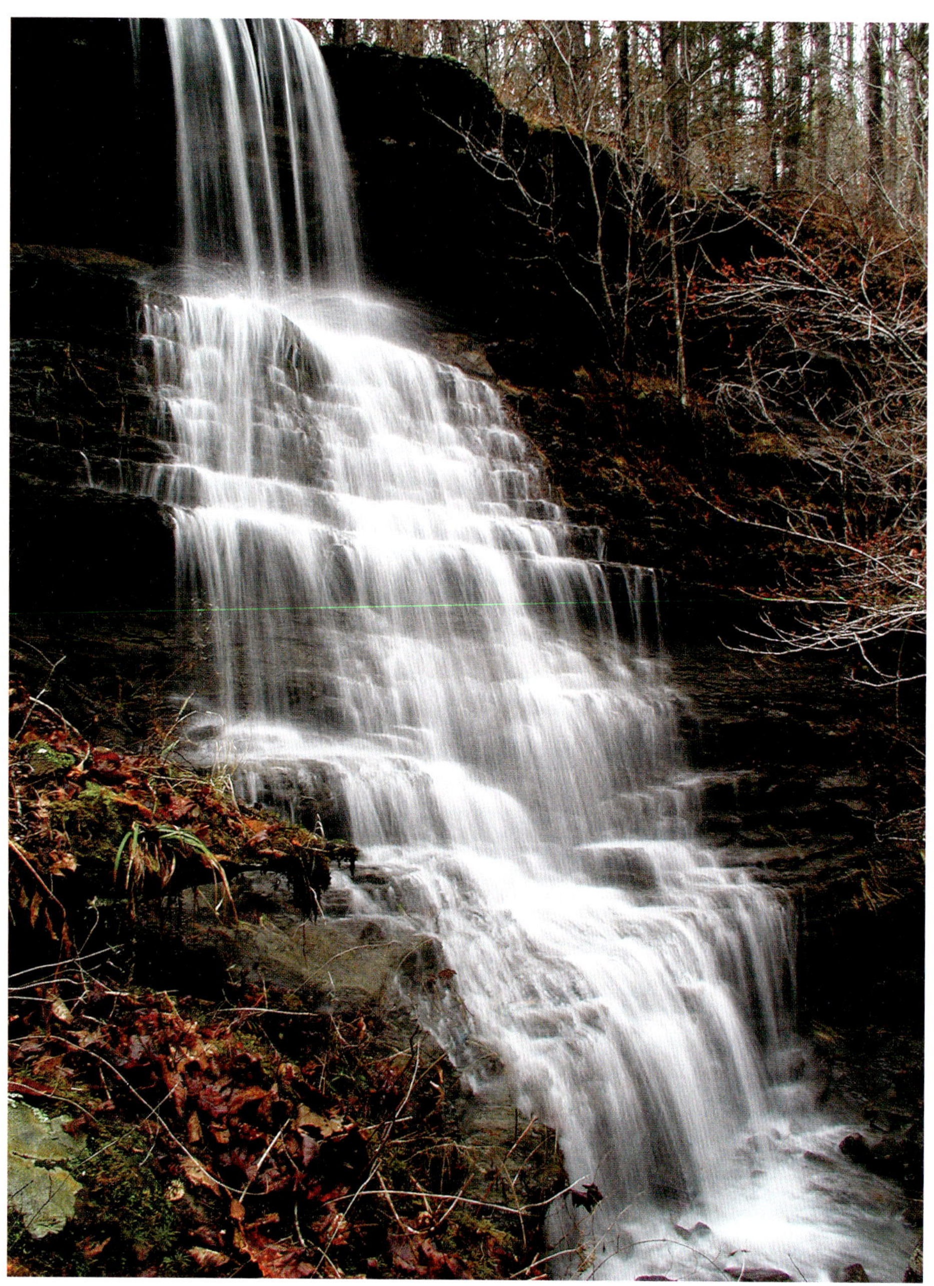

Graves Canyon Falls (upstream falls)

LEFT onto Hwy. 164. Go past the turn to Longpool and cross the Big Piney River, then TURN RIGHT onto CR#16/Pilot Knob Road (gravel). Go 4.5 miles and TURN RIGHT onto FR#1800–A. (You can also reach 1800–A from Hwy. 123—go 9.8 miles on CR#4840 and TURN RIGHT onto CR#4891/CR#16, go about 3.3 miles, then TURN LEFT onto FR#1800–A.) This is a good road for the first 1.6 miles—park there if you have a normal vehicle **(35.58566, -93.18615)**. (A *serious* 4wd can continue on down the jeep trail, even all the way to the river if you are adventurous.) Continue down the jeep road on foot as it swings to the left downhill and makes a big switchback to the right. Eventually the jeep

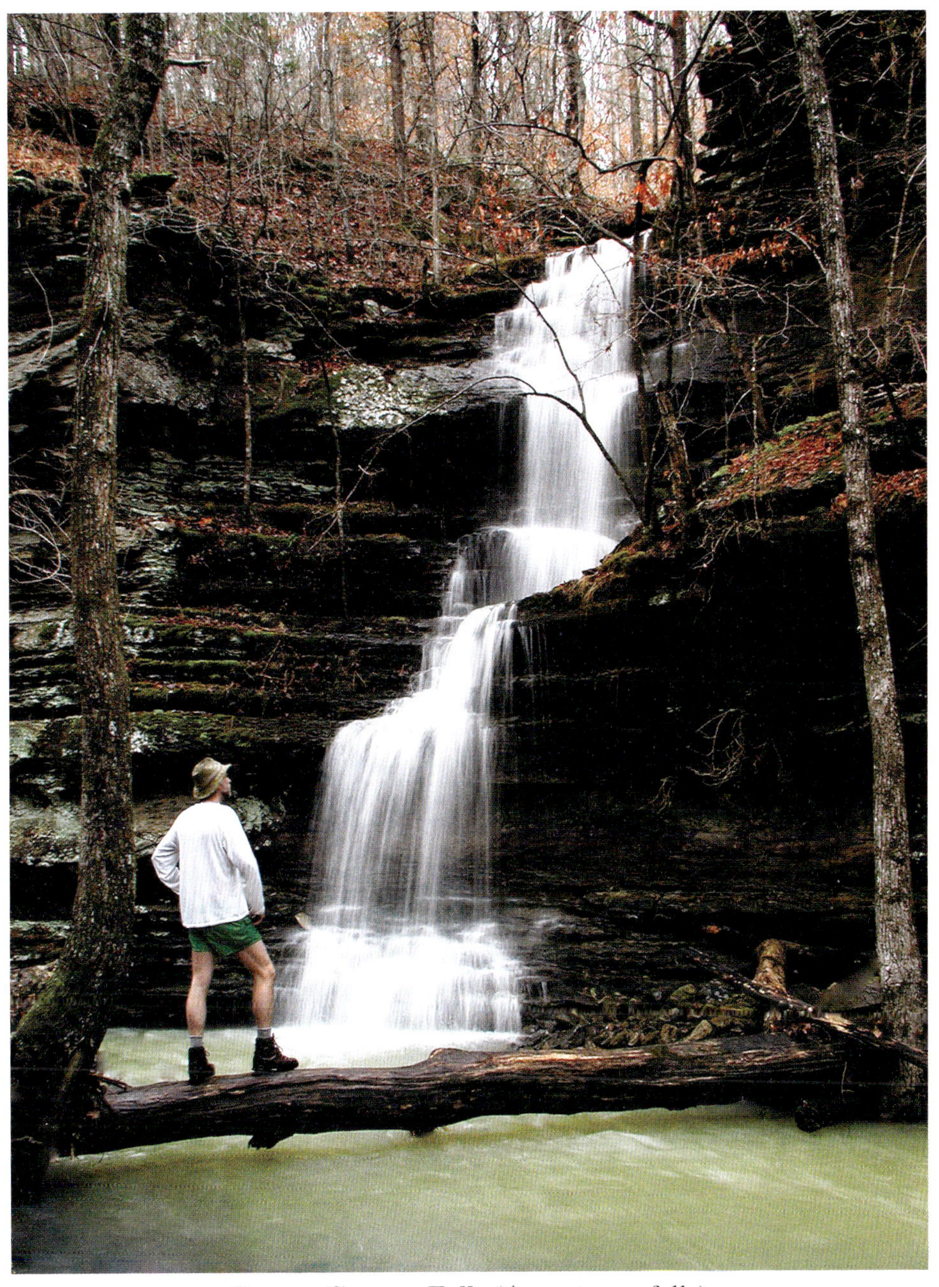

Graves Canyon Falls (downstream falls)

road will level out some (watch out for a pending timber sale in the area). Somewhere in here leave the road TO THE LEFT and strike off through the woods downhill. It will be a lot easier to navigate with a GPS. This hillside is not as difficult as the North Approach, but it does get steep as you get close to the creek. Once you find the creek you will simply have to explore around to find the falls. The hike down to the creek is a little less than a mile.

Emergency contact: Pope County Sheriff, 479–967–9300 Dogs are OK

Teapot Hollow Falls – 29′

1.5 mile medium+ bushwhack loop to visit all

GPS **35.65101, -93.22903**

Teapot Cascade – 23′+

GPS **35.65103, -93.229823**

Earl Grey Falls – 23′

GPS **35.65114, -93.23076**

Littishie Falls – 39′

GPS **35.64836, -93.23349**

Waterman Falls – 36′

GPS **35.64850, -93.23168**

Calendar Falls – 25′

GPS **35.64856, -93.23123**

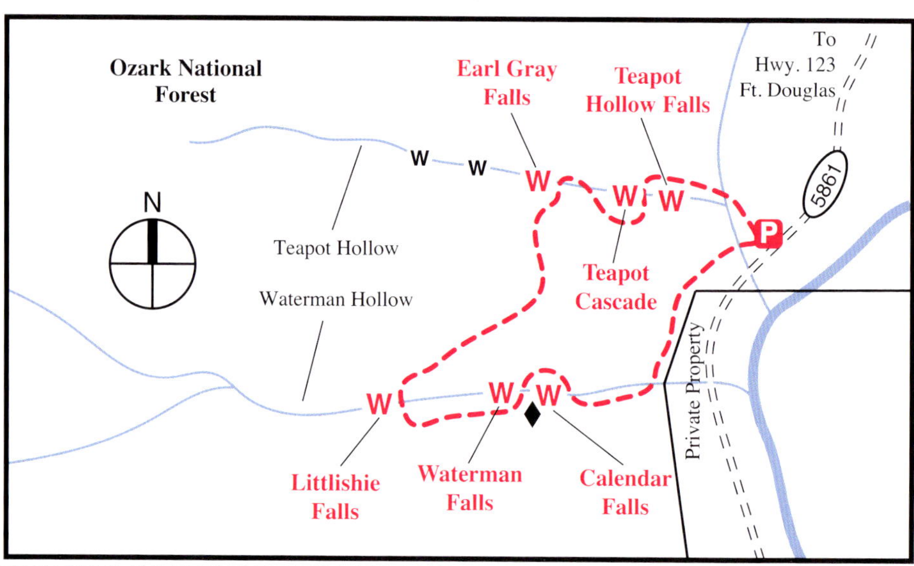

TEAPOT & WATERMAN HOLLOWS WATERFALLS. From the Big Piney Bridge on Hwy. 123 at Ft. Douglas, go .4 mile and TURN LEFT onto FR1002/CR5861. It's a rough road. (15.3 miles from Hagarville, 11.3 miles from Hwy. 7 at Pelsor, or 1.2 miles from Haw Creek Falls Campground.)

When you get to about 2.0 CAUTION—this is weird—unless they have fixed this you cannot cross a side creek there, and have to cross a small bridge on the right, but then have to make a sharp turn LEFT back to the forest road—all without falling into a hole, or getting onto private property. (very tight space).

Continue on the main road until you come to the end of an open pasture at 2.5 and PARK at the edge of the road on the RIGHT **(35.64989, -93.22870)**. This pasture is forest service land that is leased to a private individual—please do not drive out into the field and mess it up! The Big Piney River is just on the left, and when flooded it may cover the road ahead.

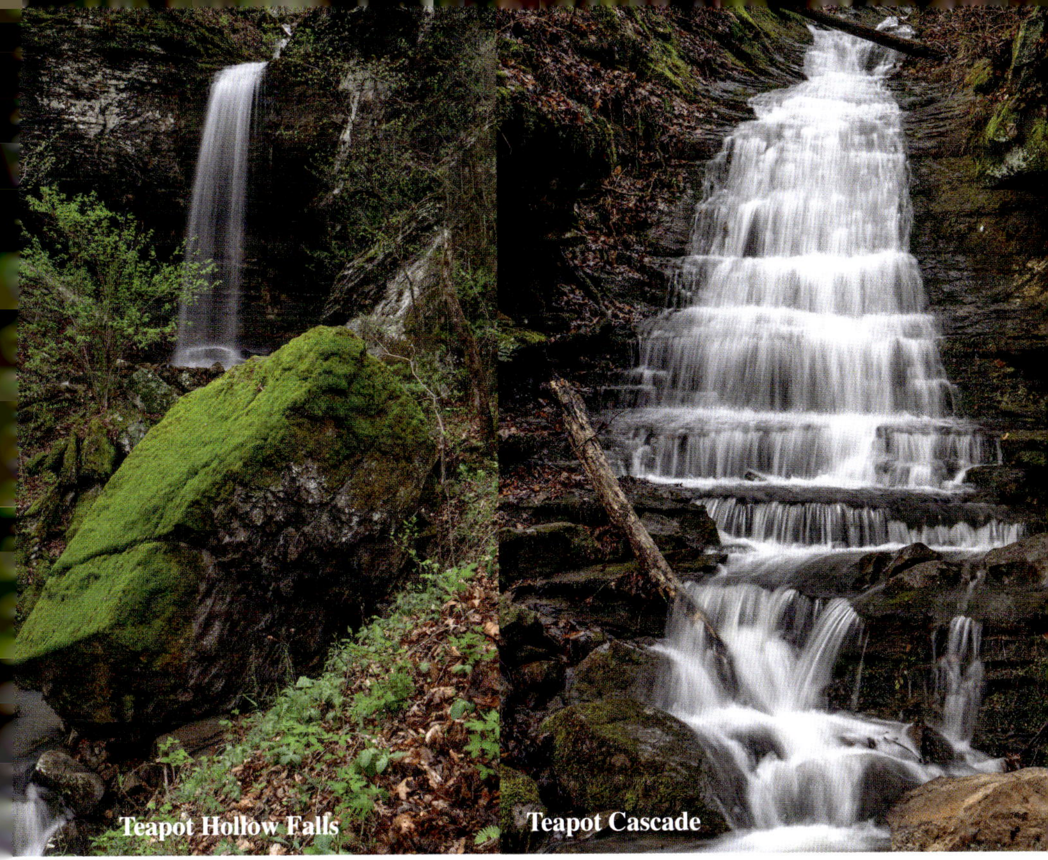

Teapot Hollow Falls

Teapot Cascade

During leaf-off you can probably look up the hill from your car and see/hear the first waterfall. That's where you want to head—cross the end of the pasture and follow the creek uphill to **Teapot Hollow Falls**, a delightful SSS that is guarded by a giant moss-covered boulder. The terrain gets really steep from that point—and let's just label the entire creek and falls up this drainage and down the second drainage a terrific SSS! Go UP and around this bluff on the right and back to the creek to the really nice **Teapot Hollow Cascade** upstream. Then continue more upstream to **Earl Grey Falls** at .3.

There are more waterfalls above in this drainage, but I usually leave the creek at this point, TURN LEFT and follow the base of the bluff out of the hollow, around the hill to the right and into the next hollow, which is Waterman Hollow, to **Littishie Falls** at .6. This is a wonderful SSS with multiple side-by-side waterfalls pouring over the moss-covered bluff. This is named for Sarah Littishie Waterman. She and her family (with eight siblings) lived in the valley below. She died in 1898 at age seven, and is the only grave in the Waterman Cemetery that is located at the top of the mountain. I felt that she and her family needed to be remembered in some way, and so this is her falls, and their Hollow! The area above this falls is especially rocky with lots of interesting places to explore.

The area below her waterfall is quite STEEP, especially as you try to make your way downstream and into the creek canyon to **Waterman Falls** ♦. And finally, just below is another nice waterfall. When I first found this one I immediately took a series of photos from the front side, and then crawled behind it and shot outward, all the while there was lots and lots of mist being kicked up by the waterfall. I had settled on Misty Falls for the name, but as I was leaving I turned around and realized a photo looking upstream right into the face of it would be perfect for a calendar I was working on, and so this is **Calendar**

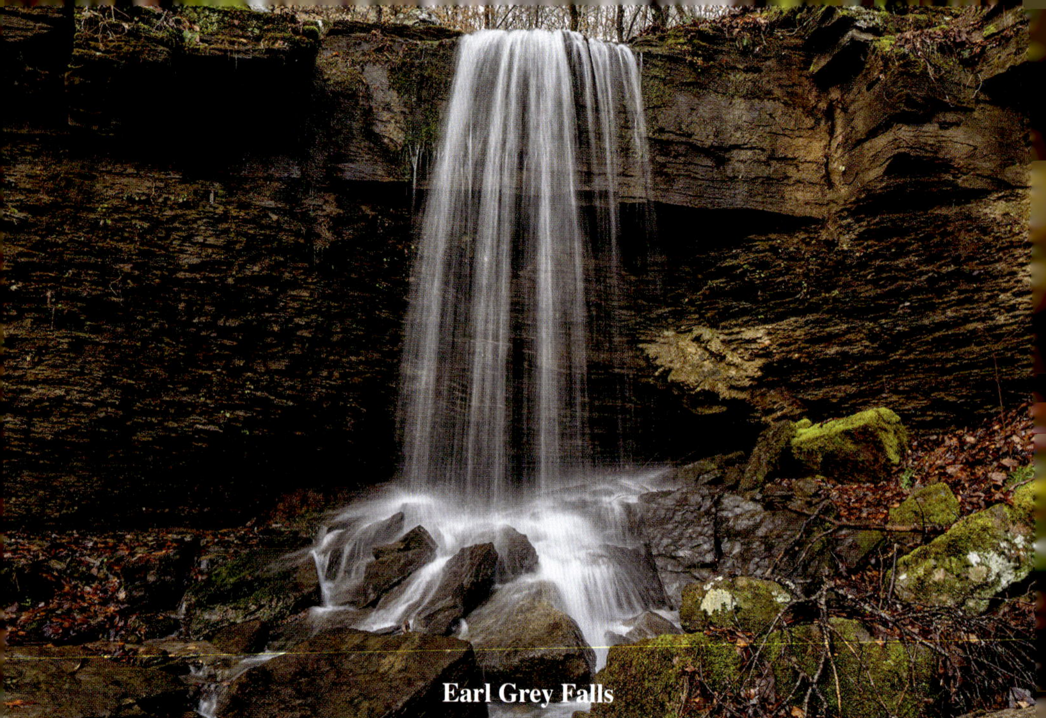
Earl Grey Falls

Falls, and it was the March photo in my 2026 Arkansas Wall Calendar. You should put all of these waterfalls on your calendar to come explore and enjoy one day!

It's a difficult, boulder-clogged drop to the bottom of the hill along the creek, and once you hit bottom you need to TURN LEFT and hike away from the creek to avoid PRIVATE PROPERTY below. Follow the base of the hill to the LEFT past a property corner **(35.64979, -93.22869)** and then on back through the canebrake to your car, a total of 1.5 miles.

Emergency contact: Johnson County Sheriff, 479–754–2200 Dogs are OK

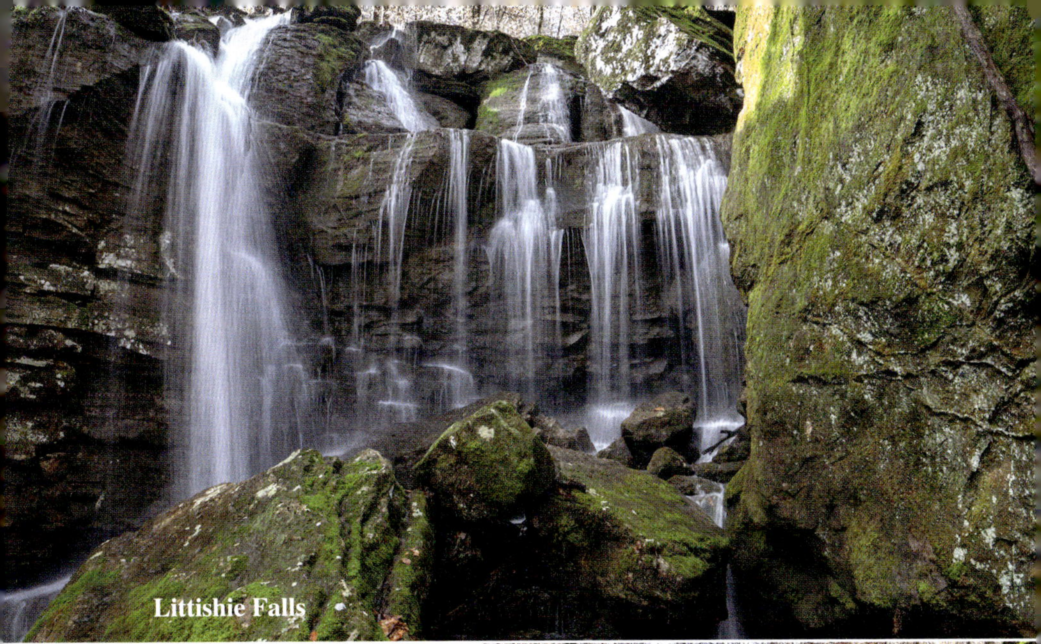

Littishie Falls

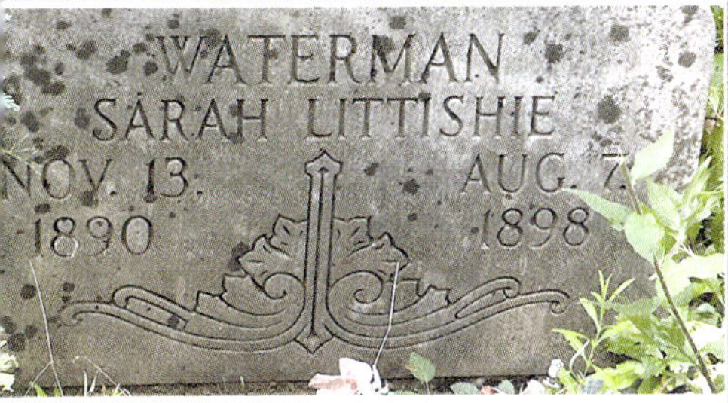

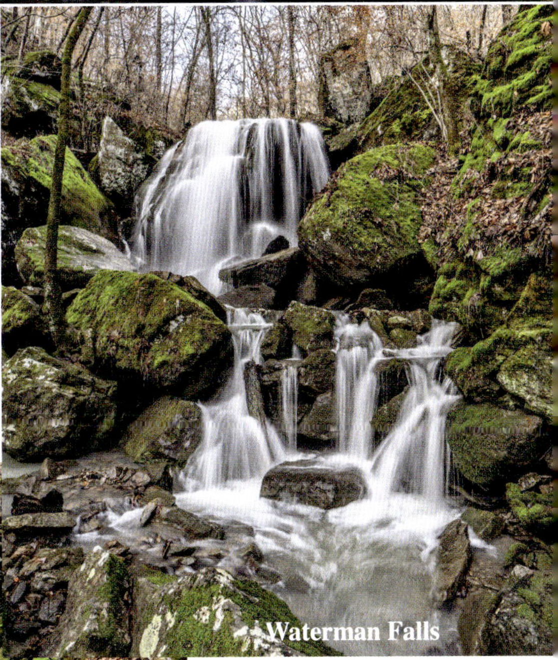

WATERMAN
SARAH LITTISHIE
NOV. 13. AUG. 7.
1890 1898

Waterman Falls

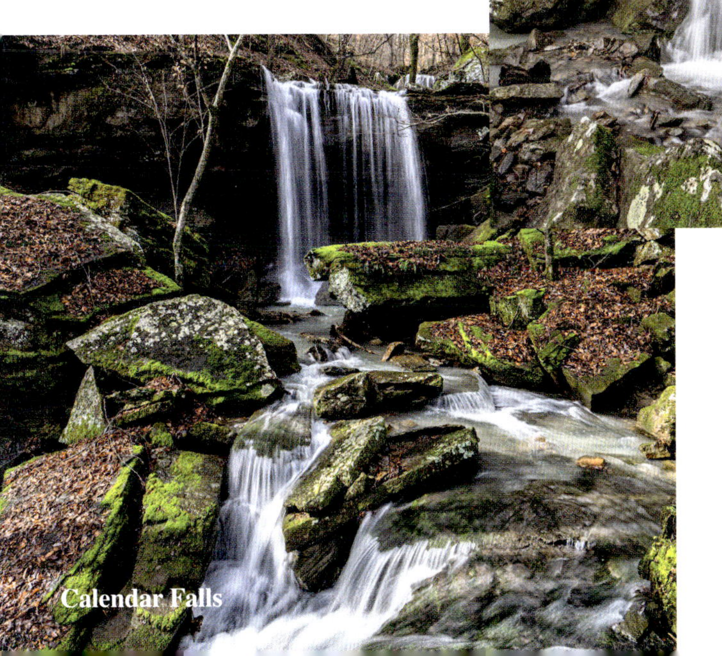

Calendar Falls

Sidewinder Falls – 21′
Swamp Falls – 19′
V Slot Falls – 10′

3.0 miles roundtrip (includes all falls), STEEP social trail,
GPS recommended GPS **35.68930, -93.18470**

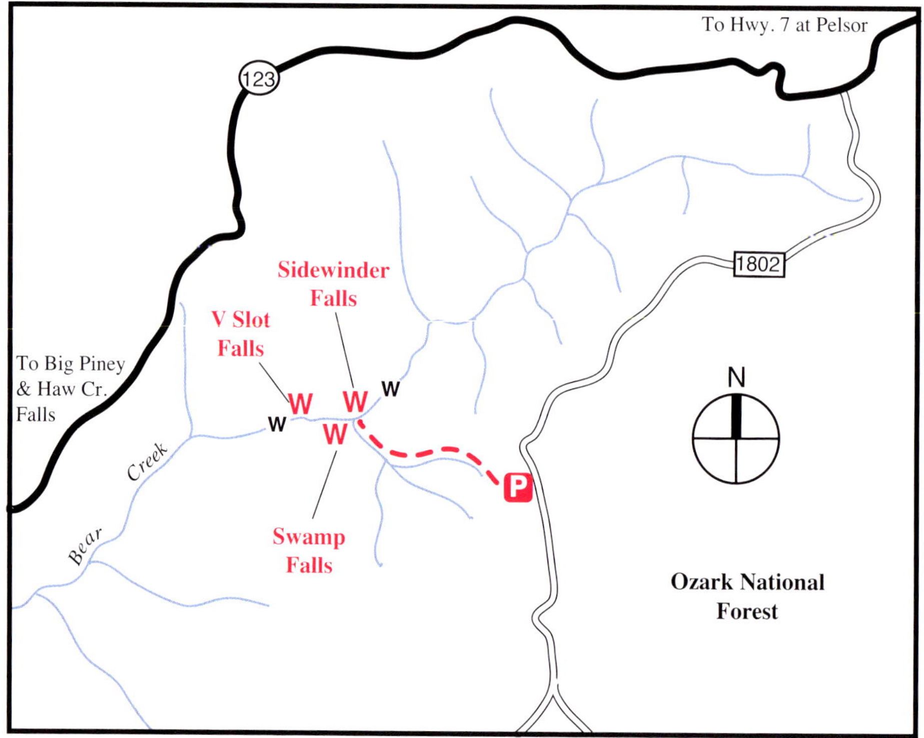

SIDEWINDER/SWAMP/V SLOT FALLS. This was perhaps the largest and most scenic unknown tracts of waterfalls I've seen in Arkansas in a good long while. A few others explored before me—my first trip into this really neat area was in the spring of 2008. This one 1/4 mile long stretch of the creek contains five beautiful waterfalls and is the highlight of a spectacular Bear Creek drainage that empties into the Big Piney River. Even though the area is bordered by a paved highway and major forest road, it has seen little use in many decades—no road or trails penetrate the area so it is all bushwhacking, a difficult hike at best, and not for the faint of heart. But if you visit when the waters are flowing you will be amply rewarded for your efforts. Tons of wildflowers too in the early spring!

From Pelsor/Sand Gap on Hwy. 7 (between Jasper and Dover) take Hwy. 123 west for 4.7 miles and TURN LEFT onto FR#1802/1805, CR#14/61 (gravel road—it has five names, and is also called Treat Road—this is the turn off to Buzzard Roost Special Interest Area as well). Go 2.2 miles and pull into a little jeep road on THE RIGHT and park where you can (it is marked as road #93179A **(35.68646, -93.17382)**.

Follow the jeep road back into a small food plot, then locate an upland swamp in the back of it, to the right, just inside the woods. This is one of only two upland swamps I know

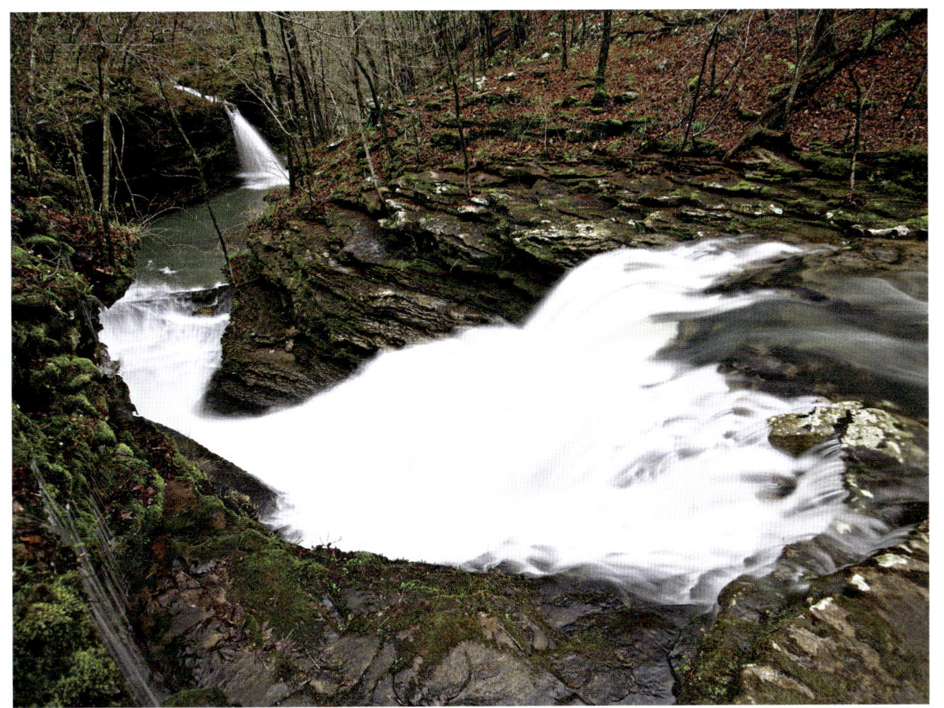

Sidewinder Falls

(looking downstream—that is Swamp Falls in the distance—see the view from below looking upstream on the next page)

in the Ozarks. There is a small outlet on the left side of this swamp—you want to follow this drainage all the way to the bottom of the hill—easier said than done though! There is no easy way, but as long as you keep going downhill and following close by this little creek you will be OK. If the water is running high there will be some terrific cascades (over beautiful moss-covered rocks all the way) and a couple of very nice waterfalls along this route. Keep going down, down, down (and try not to think about the fact that you have to climb back UP this very steep hill!). In about a mile from the road this creek will join the main Bear Creek at the very bottom—the little creek pours over a bluff directly into Bear Creek, creating **Swamp Falls**. Look upstream to your right and you will find **Sidewinder Falls**, which is the main Bear Creek feeding directly into a little canyon.

Upstream from these two waterfalls there is the upper of two "punchbowl" falls that pours into a gorgeous emerald pool. But don't spend all of your time up there—continue downstream (**below Swamp Falls** a couple hundred yards) and you will soon come to **V Slot Falls** on the main creek. This falls is created by a boulder that lodged into the stream and forced the creek to pour around both sides of it. This is at the head of a small and very scenic "slot" canyon, one of only three genuine ones I know of in Arkansas. The lower part of this giant water slide pours off as another "punchbowl" falls into a beautiful pool of green. This entire area is SLICK AND HAZARDOUS though, so admire the view from a safe distance!

There are other waterfalls in this Bear Creek drainage as well—in fact many of the side creeks have very nice ones. Most of this area sees very little traffic, so explore, enjoy, and be careful!

Emergency contact: Johnson County Sheriff, 479–754–2200 Dogs are OK.

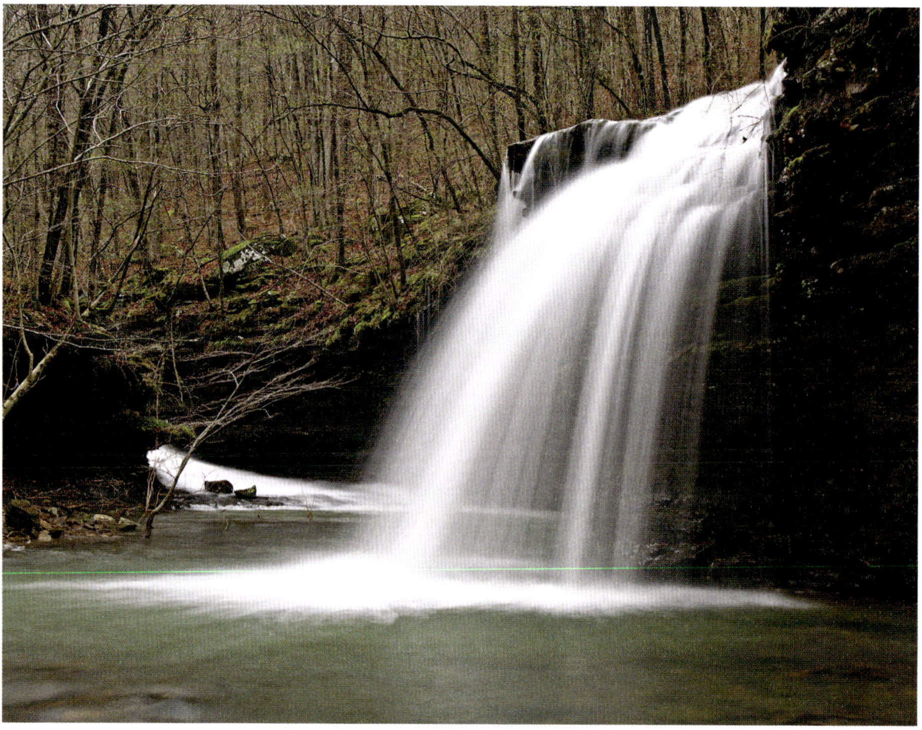

Swamp Falls (above, this view is looking up towards the base of Sidewinder Falls)

V Slot Falls (below, looking upstream)

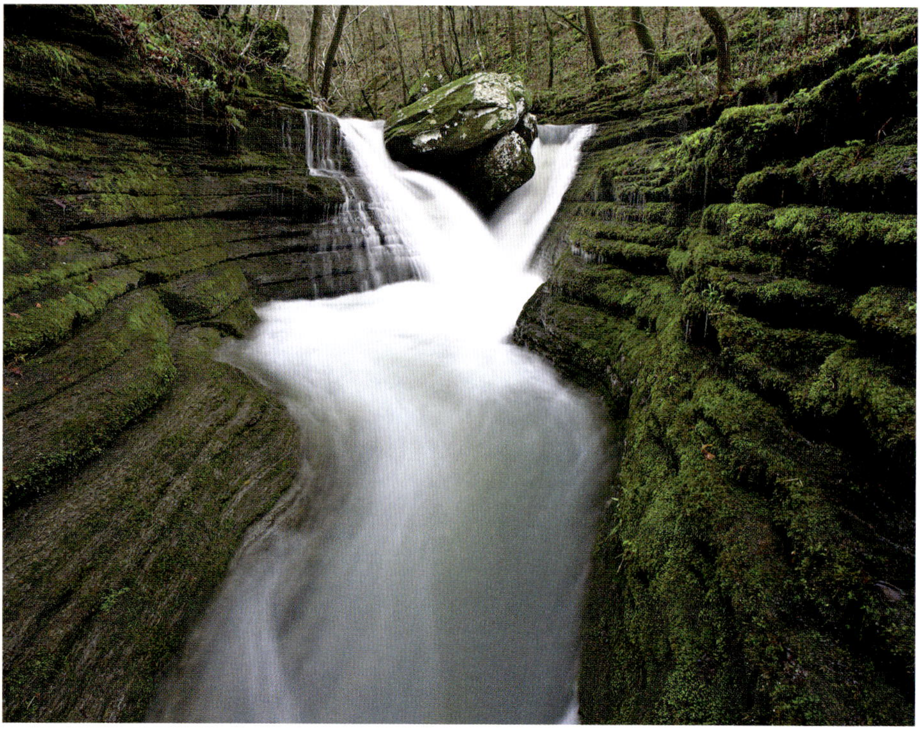

Pam's Grotto – 37′

1.0 mile roundtrip, medium hike/bushwhack, GPS not needed

GPS **35.68330, -93.25539**

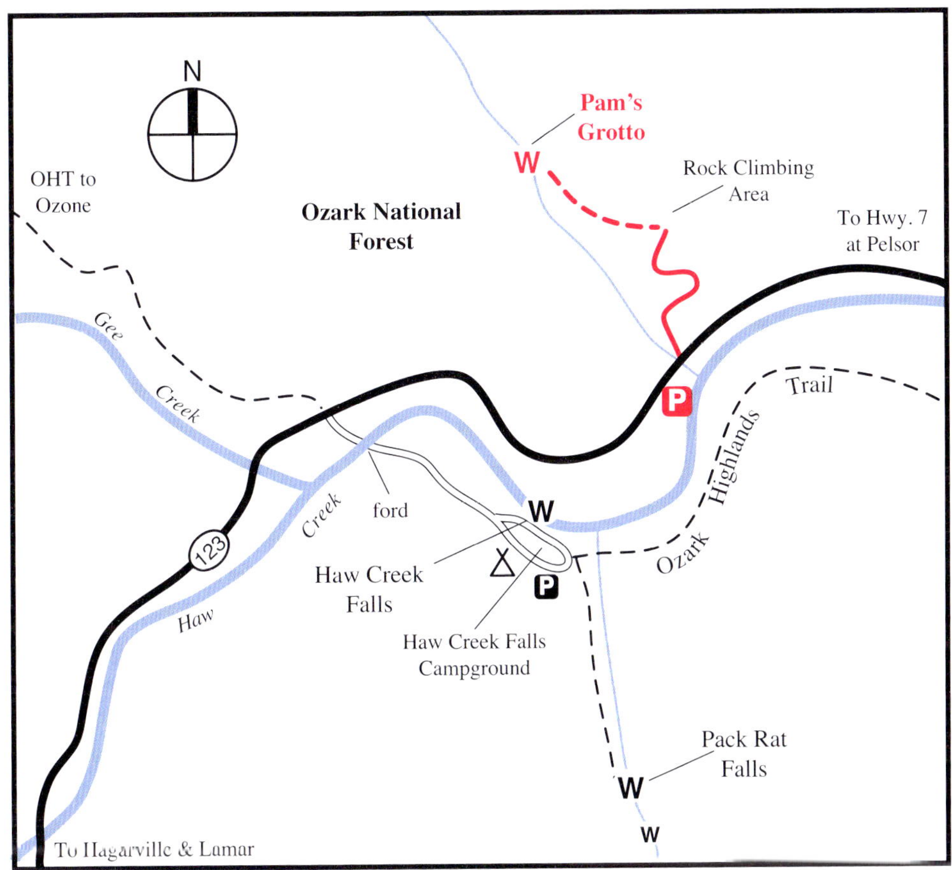

PAM'S GROTTO. I first stumbled onto this beautiful spot in 1982 while looking for a possible route of the Ozark Highlands Trail through the area. I knew it was a very special place then. The next time I saw the falls I was with my future bride, Pam, who the falls is named after. We were working with a group of 60 volunteers from the Petra Rock Climbing Gym in Springfield, MO, and helped them build the short, but steep trail up to a rock climbing area. You will see those towering bluffs as you make your way to Pam's Grotto.

Take Hwy. 123 to Haw Creek Campground (located between Lamar and Pelsor near the Big Piney River), then go .5 mile east on Hwy. 123 from the turnoff to the campground. There is a pulloff that drops down to a small parking area on the RIGHT—park there **(35.68012, -93.25202)**, next to Haw Creek). The trail begins ***across*** the road and to the right of the small creek that comes out of the forest and goes under the highway.

Follow the trail up the hill about .25 mile to the base of the big bluffs. TURN LEFT and follow along the base of the bluffs and you will come right into the Grotto after about .5 mile total. You will be hiking along admiring the bluff and all of a sudden there it will be! The waterfall itself is guarded by a house-sized boulder. It is a small area with a giant personality, and really looks good with a lot of water.

Emergency contact: Johnson County Sheriff, 479–754–2200 Dogs are OK.

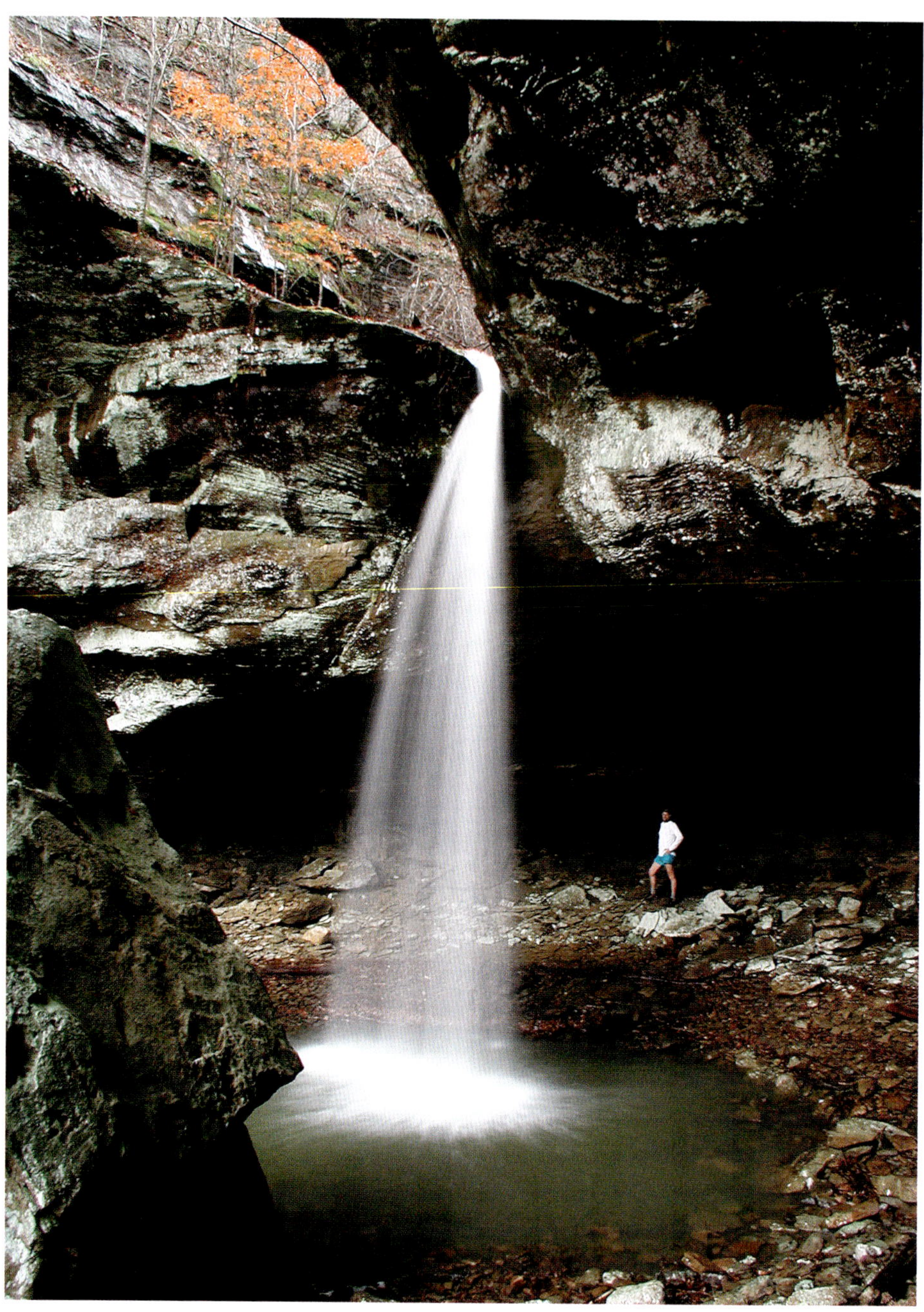

Pam's Grotto

(This waterfall was featured in an October, 2008 *National Geographic* article about the nearby Ozark Highlands Trail. It has become a favorite spot for photographers and is quite an unusual and indeed magical location.)

Haw Creek Falls – 6′

Drive to within 100 feet of the falls, GPS not needed

GPS **35.67782, -93.25520**

Pack Rat Falls – 24′

.5 mile roundtrip, easy-medium bushwhack, GPS not needed

GPS **35.67267, -93.25335**

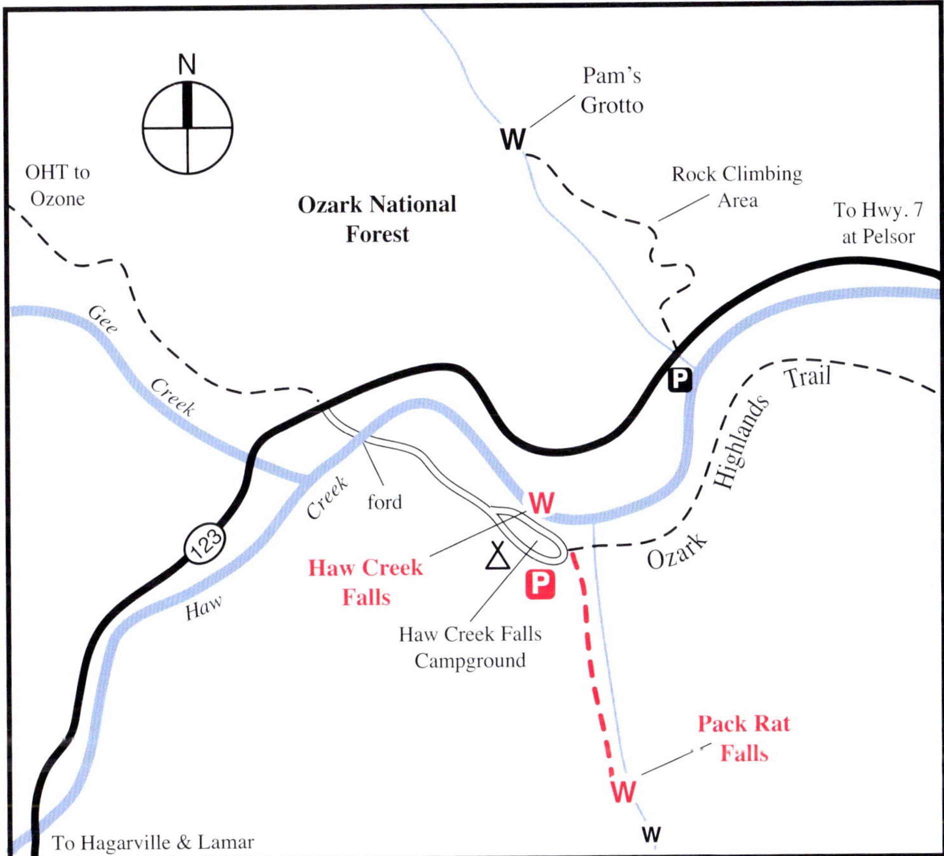

HAW CREEK FALLS. You can drive to within 100 feet of this falls, which is located at the edge of one of my favorite campsites in the Ozarks (picnic tables, toilets, water). The falls aren't very tall or impressive, but make a refreshing stop if you are touring in the area. I like to lie out on the rock slab at night and count falling stars. Haw Creek Falls Campground is located on Hwy. 123 between Lamar (near Clarksville) and Pelsor (on Hwy. 7)—watch for the sign on the highway **(35.67942, -93.25998)**. The gravel road into the campground fords Haw Creek. Look out for high water and don't drive or hike across if there is flooding.
PACK RAT FALLS. There is a hidden canyon that comes out next to the campground where you will find this falls. It is a magical little place, filled with moss-covered rocks, tumbling water, and wildflowers. Simply go to the back of the campground and follow the little creek upstream to the RIGHT. Watch out for slippery rocks! You will come to the falls within .25 mile. There is a second nice falls just upstream, but it requires a bit more scrambling up and over steep hillsides to get to.

Emergency contact: Johnson County Sheriff, 479–754–2200 Dogs are OK.

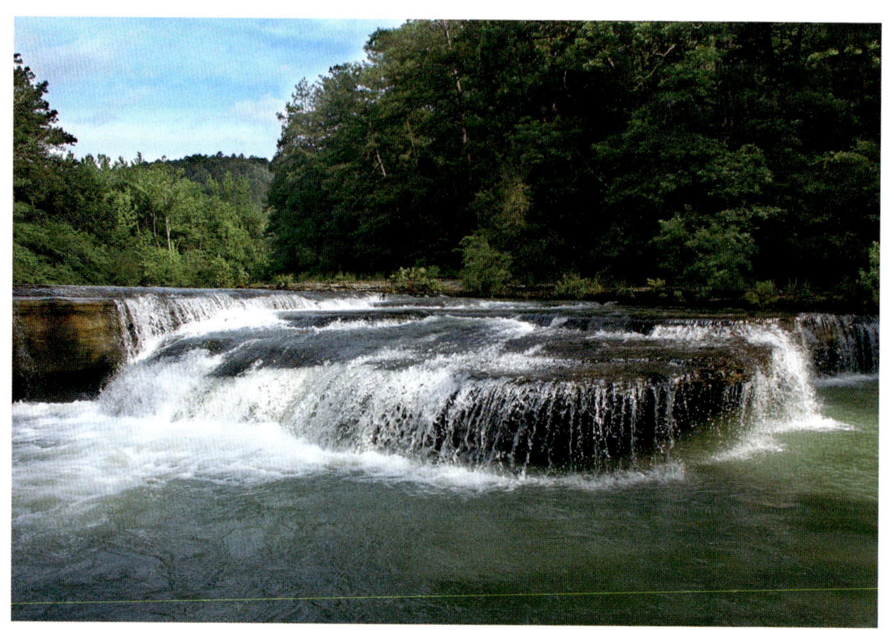

Haw Creek Falls (above), **Pack Rat Falls** (below)

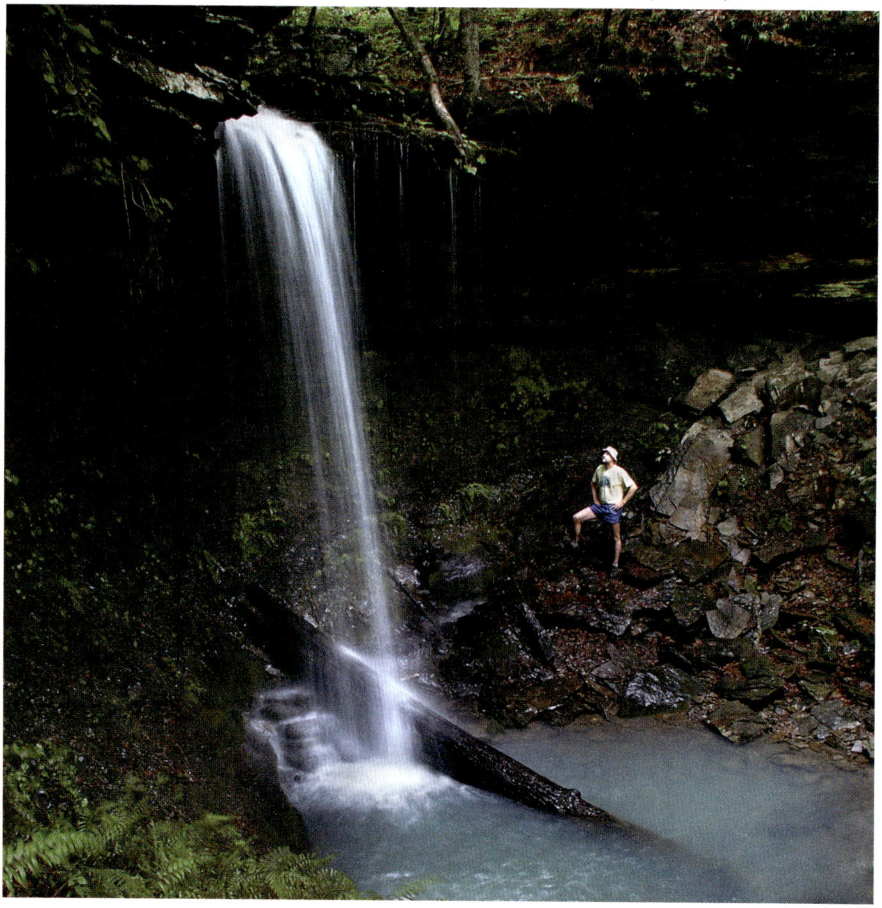

Highway 123 Falls – 47′

200 yard roundtrip, easy social trail, GPS not needed

GPS **35.61908, -93.29014**

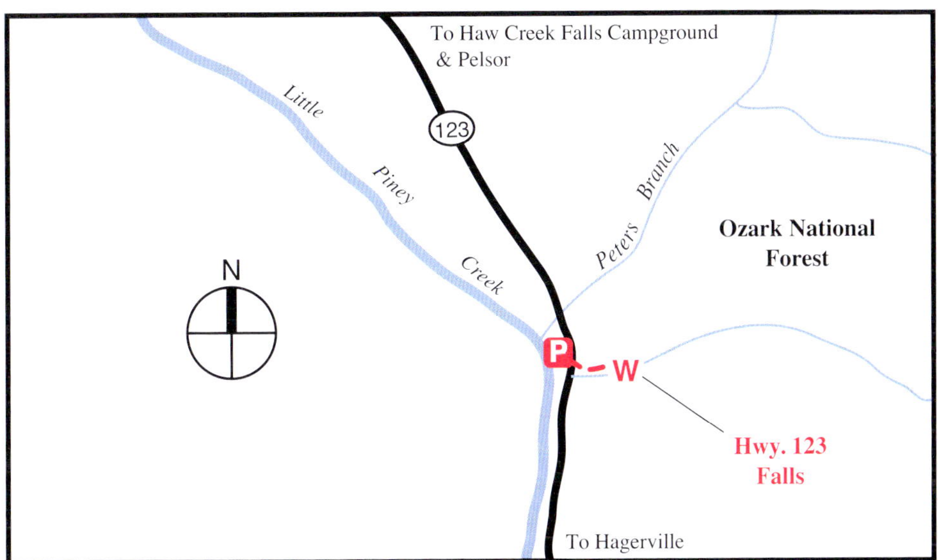

HIGHWAY 123 FALLS. This one is easy! Park next to the highway, make the short scramble to the base of the falls and you have a refreshing delight within minutes of your car!

This waterfall is located along Hwy. 123 between Hagarville and Haw Creek Falls Campground and only takes minutes to explore. From Hagarville go north on Hwy. 123 9.0 miles (2.8 miles north of the bridge across Little Piney Creek) and PARK in the big area on the LEFT next to Little Piney Creek (**35.61949, -93.29146**). OR go south on Hwy. 123 from Haw Creek Falls Campground 6.0 miles and PARK. Go across the highway and make the short scramble up the little canyon to the base of the falls—you can even see the waterfall from the highway when the leaves are off.

Emergency contact: Johnson County Sheriff, 479–754–2200 Dogs are OK.

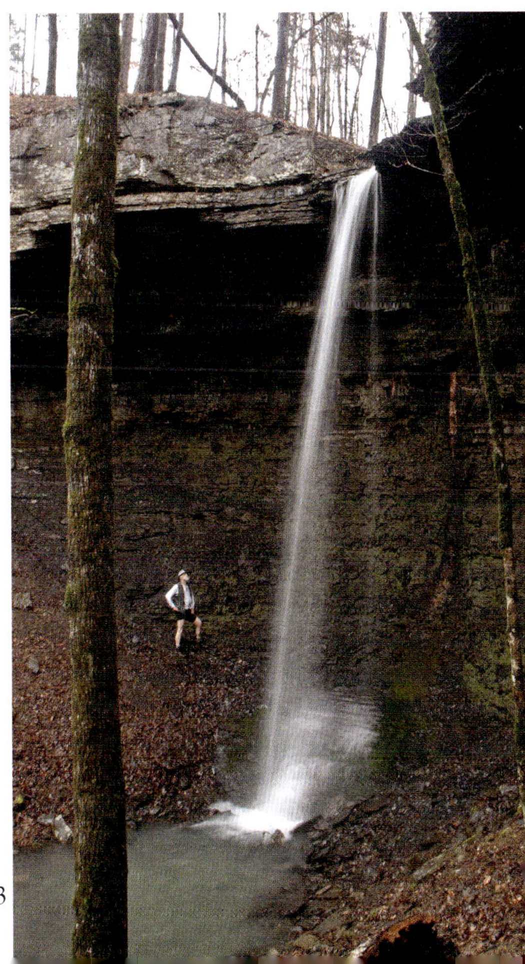

Car Wash Falls – 21′

View from car, GPS not required

GPS **35.70529, -93.25474**

CAR WASH FALLS. This is one of the most unique waterfalls in the country, and you don't even have to get out of your car to enjoy it—in fact it is a drive-thru waterfall! The waterfall pours off of a bluff and right onto the middle of a county road that runs along the Big Piney Creek—instant car wash!

From Deer go south on CR#7410/FR#1202/Parker Ridge Road 11.7 miles and TURN LEFT onto CR#5881/FR#1002. Go 2.5 miles to the waterfall. OR from Hwy. 123 at the Big Piney Bridge go north on CR#5881/FR#1002 for 2.8 miles to the waterfall **(35.70542, -93.25455)** Note: this route may be inaccessible during high water since you have to ford Hurricane Creek.

Emergency contact: Johnson County Sheriff, 479–754–2200 Dogs are OK.

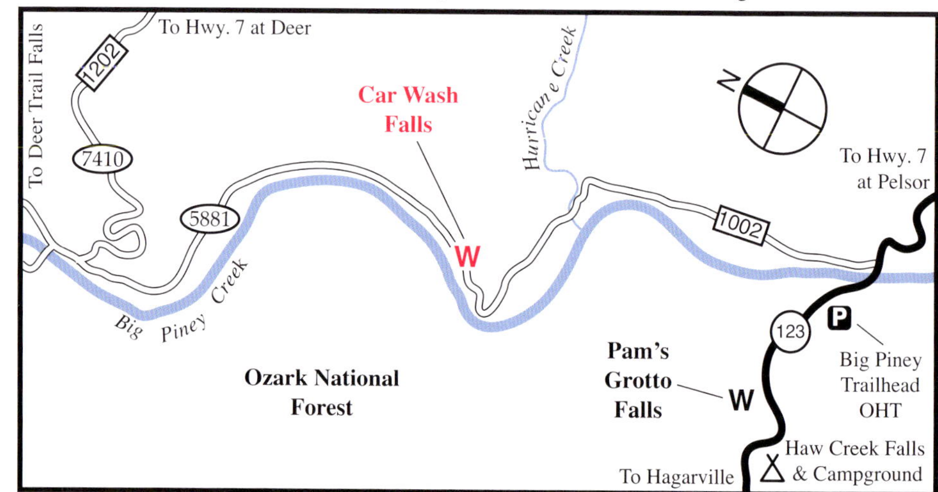

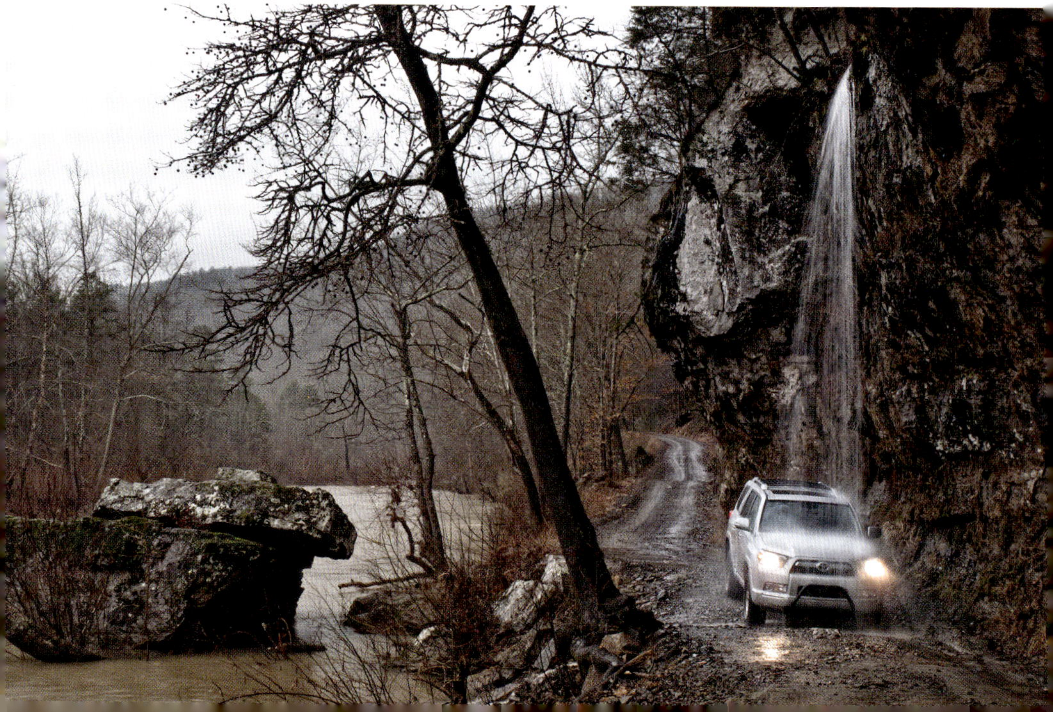

Rock Creek Bluff Falls – 47′

1.2 miles roundtrip, medium bushwhack, GPS helpful

GPS **35.74699, -93.26805**

Deer Trail Falls – 55′

3.6 miles roundtrip (includes falls above), med. bushwhack, GPS helpful

GPS **35.75530, -93.27187**

Big Buck Falls – 62′

4.6 miles roundtrip (all falls above), medium bushwhack, GPS helpful

GPS **35.75717, -93.26870**

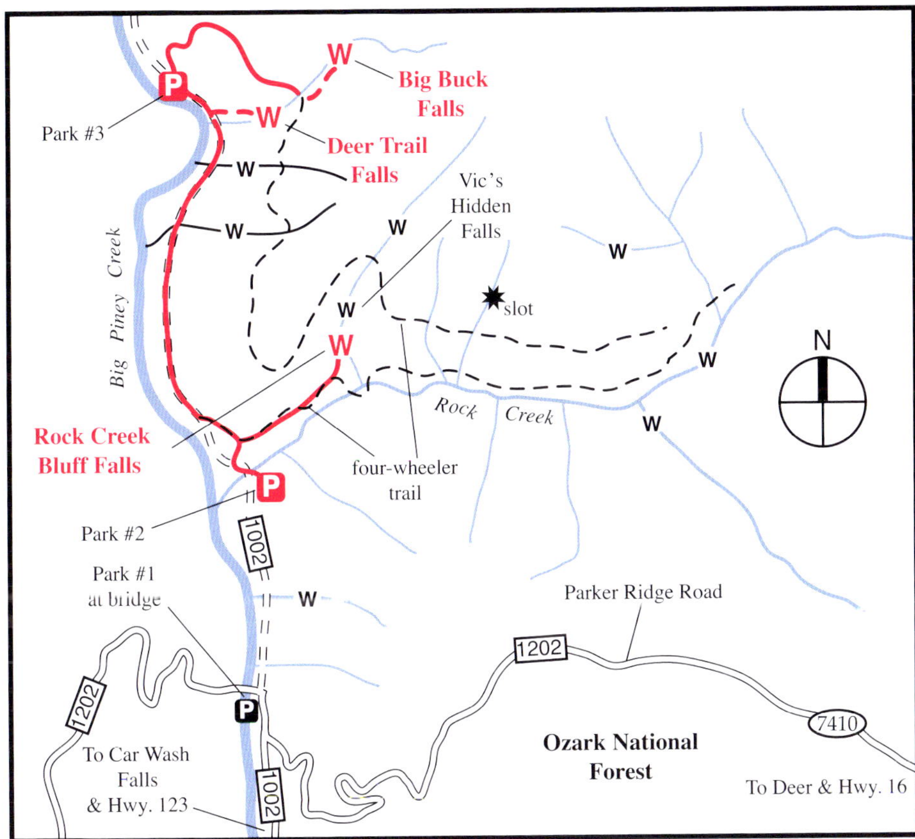

ROCK CREEK BLUFF/DEER TRAIL/BIG BUCK FALLS. This is a beautiful large area with towering bluffs, boulder-strewn creeks, and plenty of spectacular waterfalls! Access can be tough with rough roads and/or high water blocking your way, but if you can make it there are many great things to see and do. Bear with me through the discussion as I try and cover the options.

First off, I should tell you that there are at least two major sandstone blufflines that run through this area—you could easily spend an entire day just looking at the beautiful bluff faces. One of the blufflines is just above the road. The second bluffline is farther up the hillside and is every bit as spectacular as the lower one, but more difficult to get to. I found several nice waterfalls along both blufflines. There are many house-sized boulders

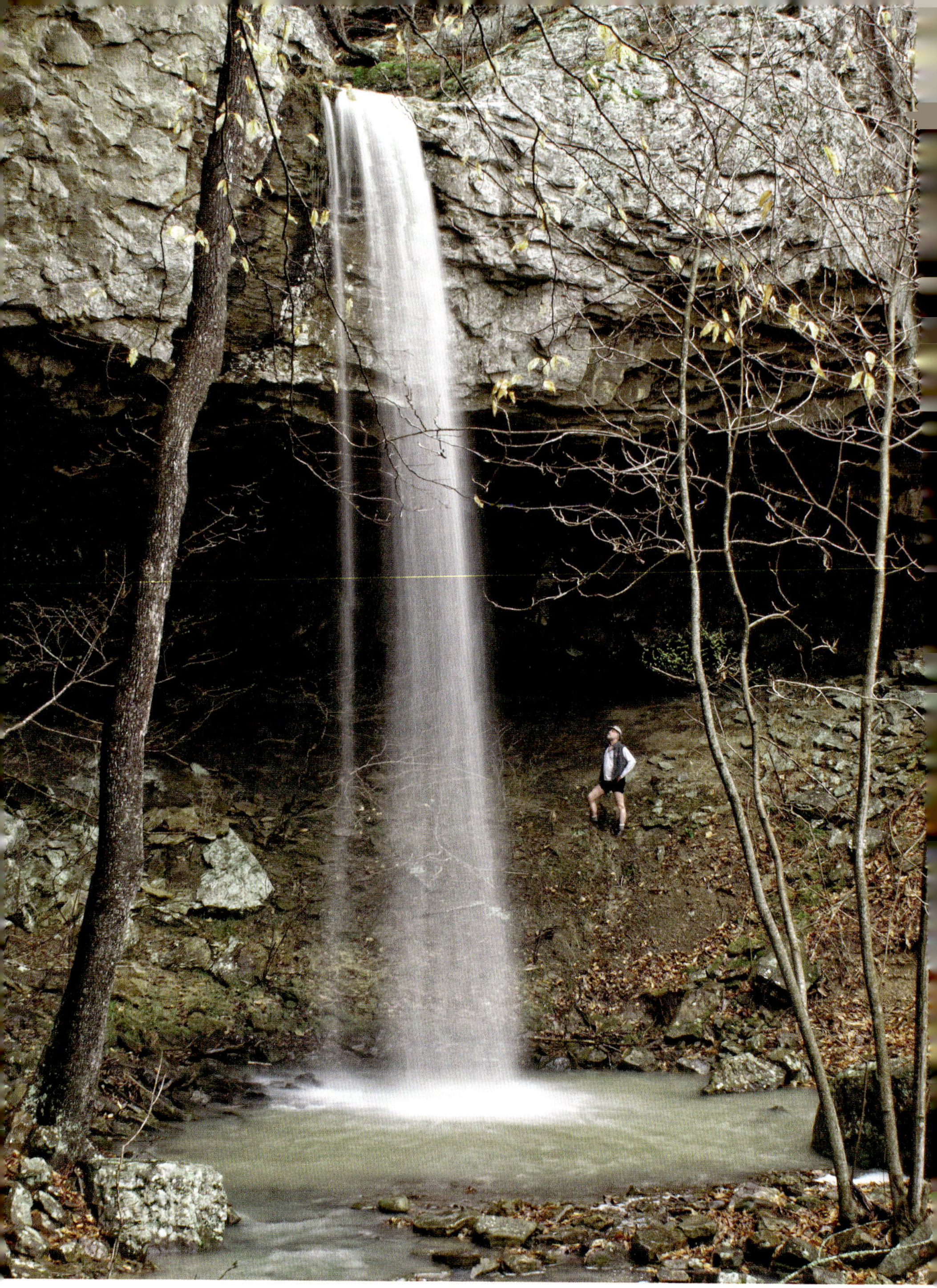

Rock Creek Bluff Falls

strewn about—some covered with green mosses, a slot canyon, and even a small sandstone arch. An ATV trail runs along below the lower bluff and also in between both bluffs. It does not go directly to any waterfalls, but we will use some of it—part of the ATV trail is shown on the map (I have not included the part that goes farther upstream).

There are three different parking spots for this group of waterfalls—which one you use will depend on your type of vehicle, how high the creeks are, and the road conditions, which have not been consistent. From Deer, on Hwy. 16 go south on CR#7410/FR#1202/ Parker Ridge Road 11.7 miles and TURN RIGHT onto FR#1002/CR#5881—normal cars may need to PARK at the bridge across the Big Piney (Park #1, black "P" on the map). You can also reach this spot during low water times from Hwy. 123—see page 254 for directions to Car Wash Falls and just continue north to this intersection on FR#1002—during high water you won't be able to ford Hurricane Creek. From the bridge, if you have an SUV or high-clearance 4WD you can proceed up the hill to the right on FR#1002 for .6 miles to PARK #2 on the right (**35.74200, -93.27243**), just before the road crosses Rock Creek. With an SUV and low water conditions you might be able to drive across Rock Creek and get closer to all three falls—and possibly make it all the way to the north parking spot, #3—but please be careful crossing the creek with vehicle or your own body and never try either during high water. I'm going to begin the description from Park #2 and make my way to all three waterfalls—take your vehicle wherever you can and hike from there.

To get to **Rock Creek Bluff Falls**, hike down to where the road crosses Rock Creek and wade across—if the water is high you will not be able to make it to any of the waterfalls, sorry. Once on the other side hike along the road for a couple hundred yards and TURN RIGHT onto an ATV trail that heads up the hill. Follow it first to the right and then as it curves around to the left and heads up the Rock Creek drainage—you can look down and see the creek in some places. Just before the trail heads down the hill to cross the creek, leave the trail TO THE LEFT and bushwhack up the creek to the base of Rock Creek Bluff Falls. This entire bluffline is wonderful and you could spend a lot of time just exploring it in either direction.

To reach **Deer Trail Falls**, head BACK to the forest road and continue to hike/drive to the north for 1.0 mile (great views of Big Piney Creek), then leave the road (**35.75528, -93.27386**) and follow a tumbling creek uphill to **Deer Trail Falls**. If driving you could also drive to Park #3, then hike the short distance back to the creek. Be sure to look behind the waterfall and see all the deer tracks—they LOVE it back under there!

To reach **Big Buck Falls**, hike or drive another .2 miles to PARK #3 (**35.75659, -93.27581**). There is large flat area on the left to camp. A four-wheeler trail leaves the road to the RIGHT—follow this uphill first to the left, and then it will curve around to the right and eventually end up above the lower bluffline that runs through the area—continue STRAIGHT at a fork with another ATV trail once it all levels out.

Continue along the trail to the next major drainage, then leave the trail TO THE LEFT and follow the steep ravine up to **Big Buck Falls**, which is located on the upper bluffline (I like the right side of the ravine best, but any way you go will be tough).

The ATV trail runs on the benches in between the two blufflines for at least a couple of miles. Whenever it crosses a creek that is flowing, hike either up or down the ravine (or both!) until you come to a waterfall. I prefer to visit in the wintertime when you can see so much more—and there is a lot to see along both blufflines, and also back down on the main Rock Creek itself—the waterfalls shown on the map there are smaller but still scenic. There is a spot on the upper bluffline where the bluff has split open and now a creek runs through it, all guarded by a giant boulder. And another neat spot is Vic's Hidden Falls, a 33' tall waterfall in a short hanging canyon above Rock Creek Bluff Falls (can't see it from below though). I named it after intrepid explorer Vic Trolio, who first told me about this area many years ago.

FYI, the forest road along Big Piney Creek (#1002) goes out to Limestone and to Hwy. 16—it is marked as CR#7460 on the highway. Parts of this road may be impassable.

Emergency contact: Newton County Sheriff, 870–446–5124 Dogs are OK.

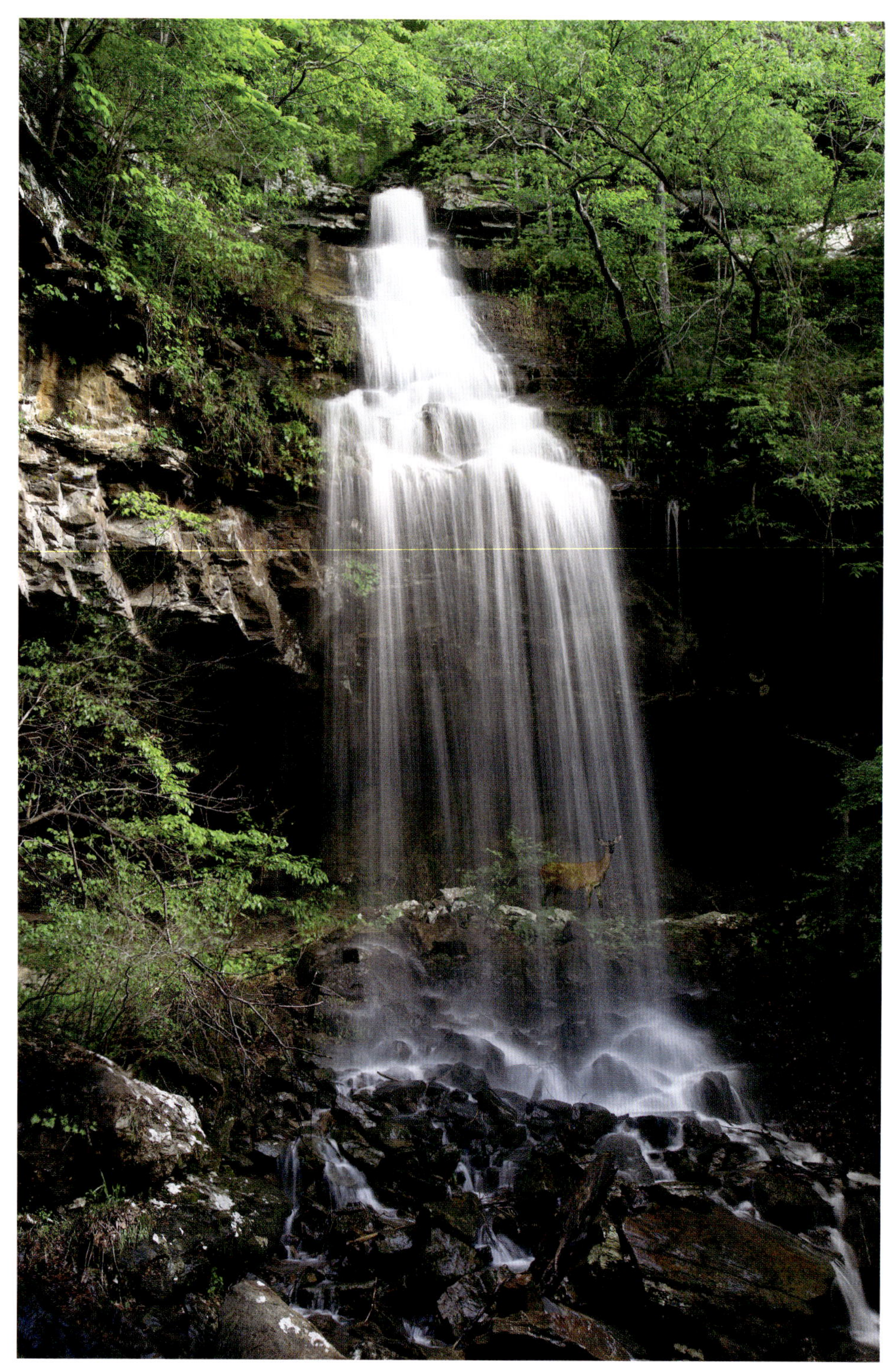

Deer Trail Falls

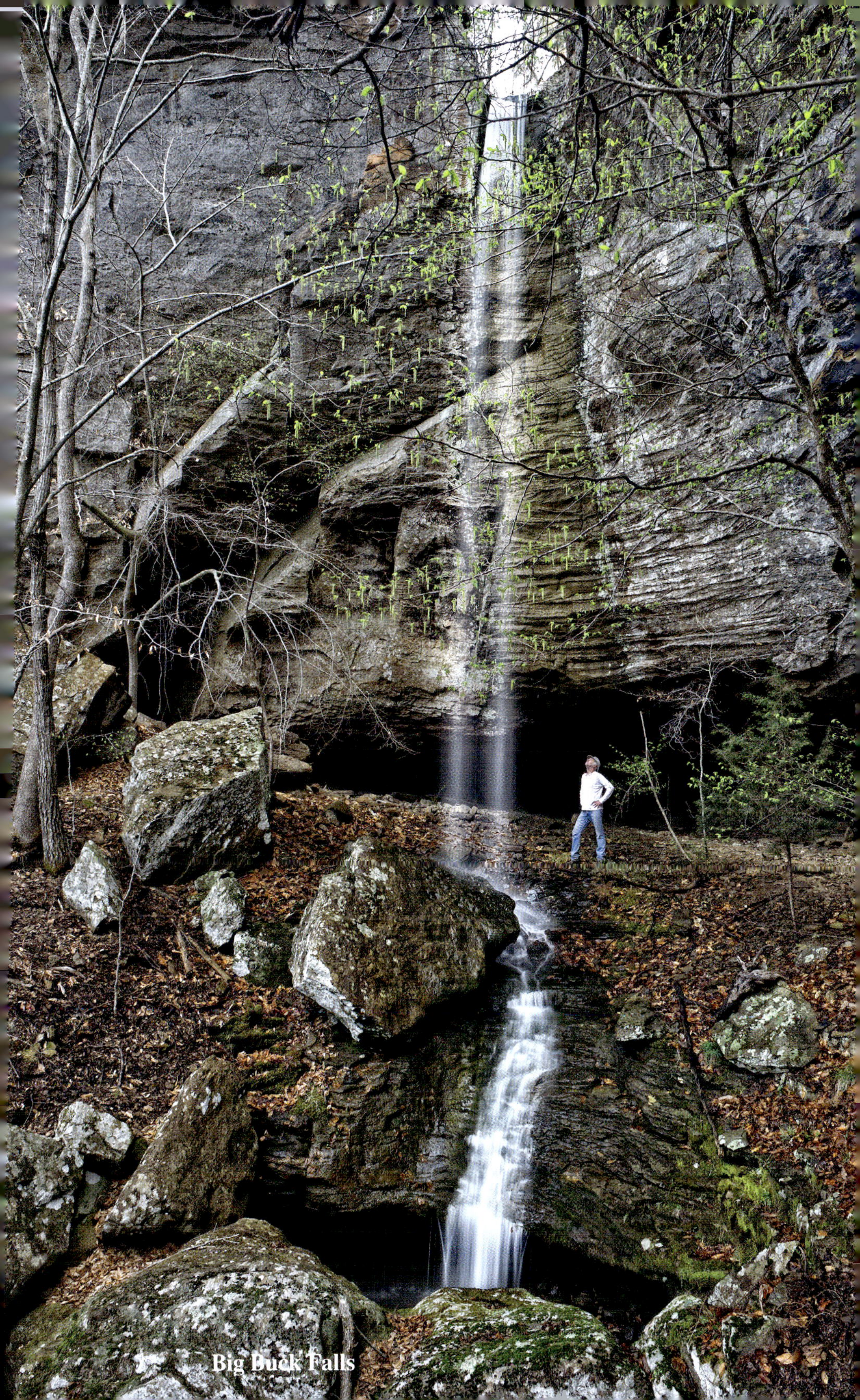
Big Buck Falls

Pineey Bowl Falls – 64′

2.4 miles roundtrip, difficult bushwhack, GPS recommended

GPS **35.75190, -93.27895**

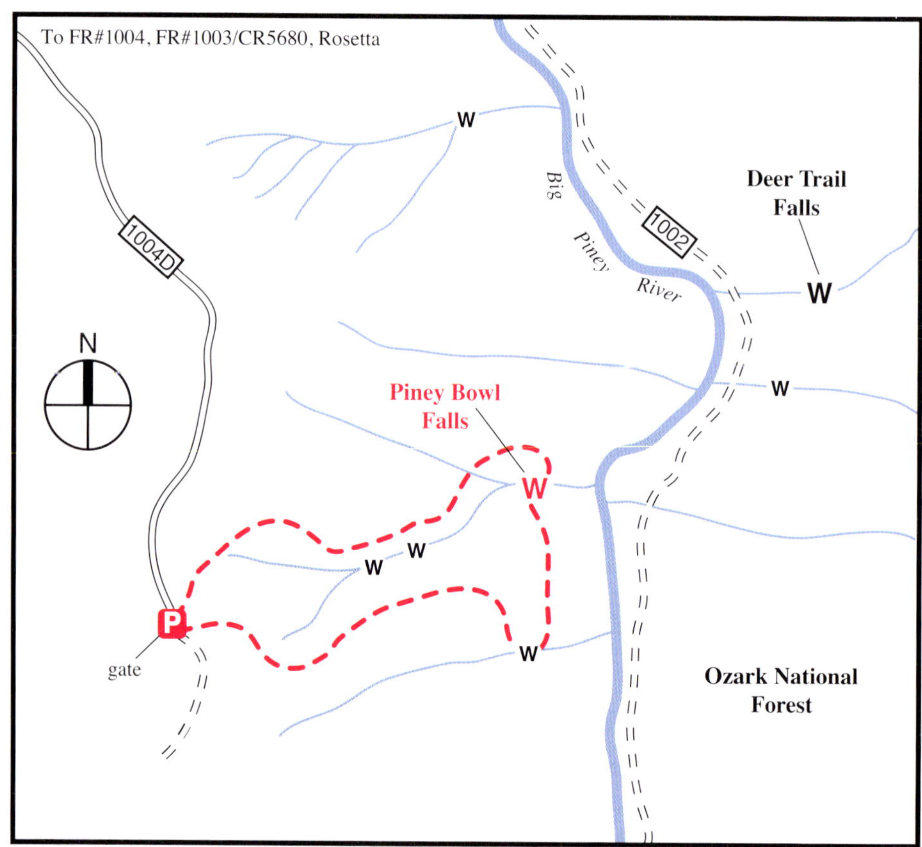

PINEY BOWL FALLS. This is one of my most favorite waterfalls, and is one that I first discovered from a great distance away while I was high on a bluff exploring the Rock Creek drainage on the other side of the Big Piney River. There are lots of waterfalls on this hillside and along the big bluff, but this is the tallest and most powerful. There is something so peaceful about it—perhaps it is the pool—and I could sit there all day long.

From Hwy. 21 just south of Salus (north of Ozone), take FR#1003/CR#5680 to the east for 6.8 miles (just past the Rosetta Cemetery) and TURN LEFT/NORTH onto FR#1004/CR#5661. Go 5.6 miles and TURN RIGHT onto FR#1004D (may be unmarked) and go 1.7 miles to the end/gate and PARK (**35.74915, -93.28691).** OR from Haw Creek Campground go south on Hwy. 123 for 3.3 miles and TURN RIGHT onto FR#1003, then go 7.7 miles and TURN RIGHT onto FR#1004/CR#5661, go 5.6 miles to FR#1004D, then 1.7 miles and park at the gate.

The map shows the loop that I take and it visits several of the waterfalls along the way. From the car, I bushwhack straight down into the woods and try to stay on top of a narrow ridge towards the right as it goes down, down, down. Continue down through an upper bluffline and then farther down until you come to the top of the big bluff. Make your way along the top of the bluffline and you will find an easy way down right next to

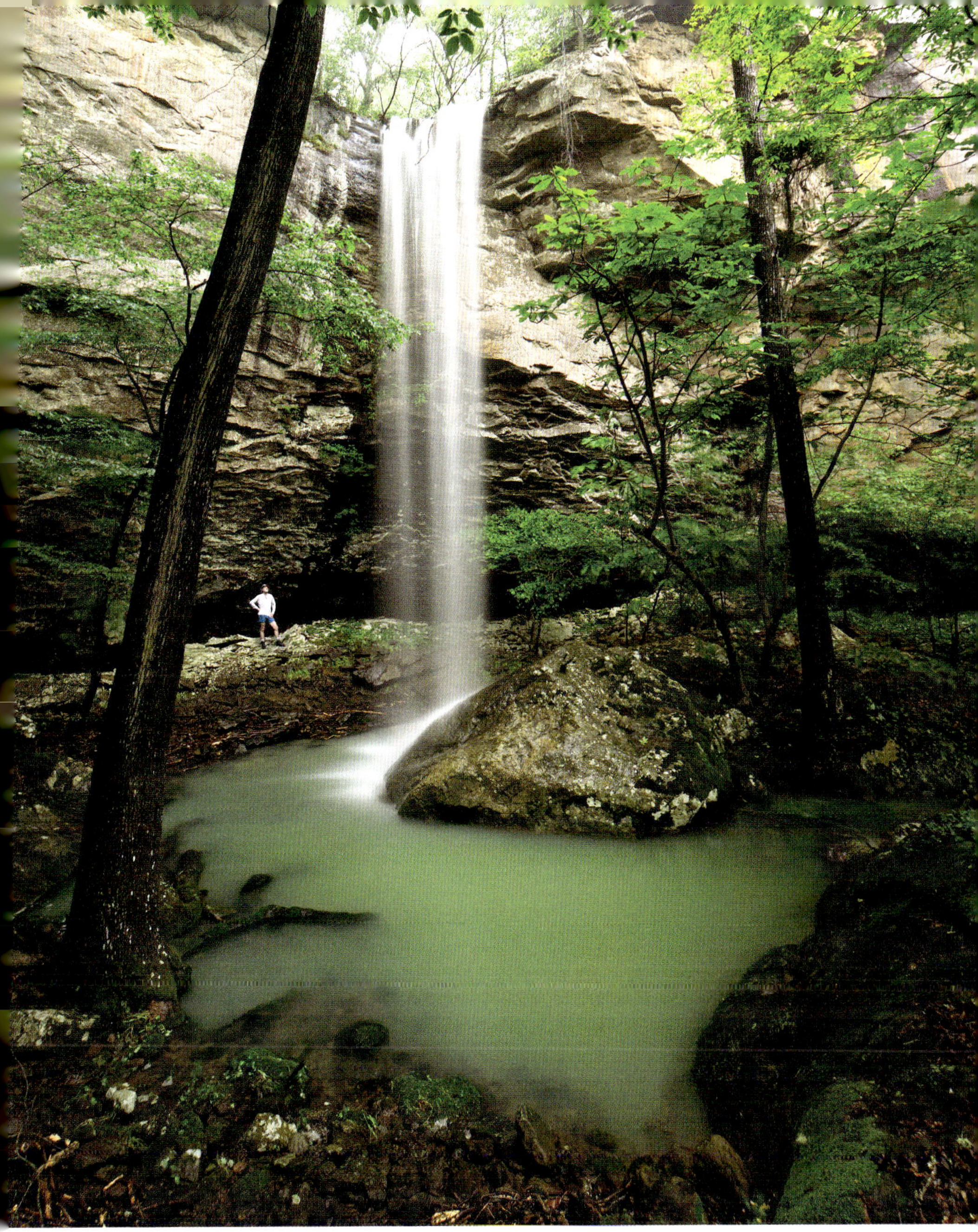

Piney Bowl Falls

a neat 37' tall falls (**35.74894, -93.27913).** Once below the bluff simply follow it back to the north to the big falls shown above. You are not far above the Big Piney River.

To return via a different route, from the base of the big falls continue along the bluffline just a hundred yards and you will find a crack that leads to the top of the bluff (quite steep). Follow the creek that feeds the big falls back uphill to a couple of other nice waterfalls—you'll have to stop and catch your breath anyway so you might as well admire them! Continue on up and up back out to your car.

Emergency contact: Newton County Sheriff, 870–446–5124 Dogs are OK

Mrs. O'Leary's Falls – 57′

1.8 miles, medium bushwhack GPS **35.74799, -93.31919**

Bull Falls – 63′

2.0 miles, medium bushwhack GPS **35.74722, -93.31625**

Sprinkler Falls – 94′

2.3 miles, medium bushwhack GPS **35.74552, -93.32022**

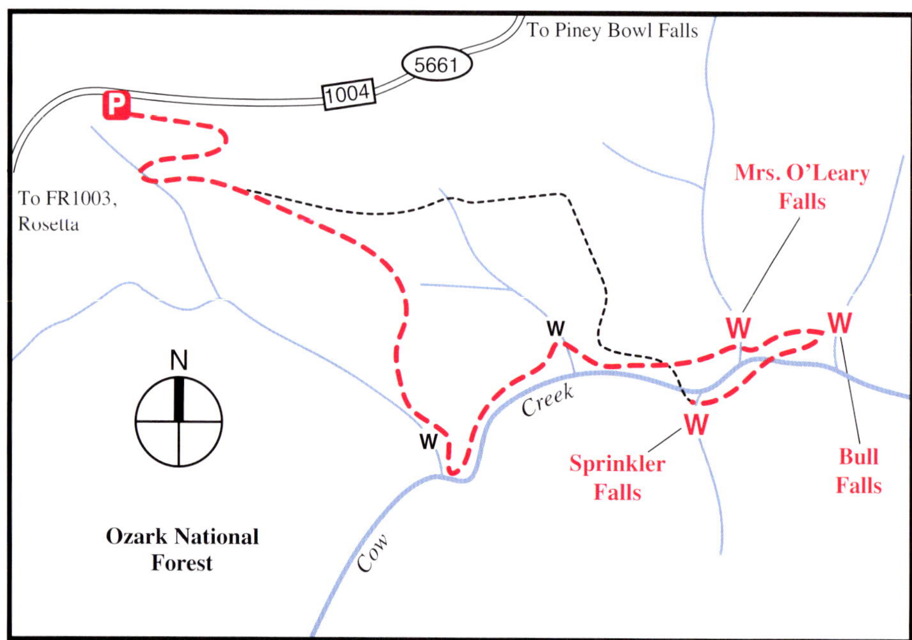

BULL FALLS/MRS. O'LEARY'S FALLS/SPRINKLER FALLS. The greater Cow Creek Waterfall Plex—Cow Creek, Middle Cow Creek, and Little Cow Creek (next pages)—with many side drainages—has a reported 70+ named waterfalls. I first learned of this area from my firemen friends, Jason Weaver and Jeff Davis (Russellville Fire Department) in 2011. Both had worked with me to locate and measure waterfalls. Since then Rick Henry and company, Danny Hale, John Moore, and a host of other waterfall Documentarians have amassed quite a collection of waterfalls. I've visited several times but only have room for a few to share here.).

From Hwy. 21 just south of Salus (north of Ozone), take FR#1003/CR#5680 to the east for 6.8 miles (just past the Rosetta Cemetery) and TURN LEFT/NORTH onto FR#1004/CR#5661. Go 3.6 miles and PARK on the right. **(35.75219, -93.33644)** You can also access from the south with a serious 4WD.

The goal here is to hike DOWN the mountain about 600' and get to the main Cow Creek level. There are no official trails, but there is one old road I've used that helps quite a bit—although unless it gets a lot of traffic it may be tough to find. Mostly you just want to hike DOWNHILL. (I seem to go a little different route each time, but always end up at the same point—down on the creek.)

From the parking spot follow an old logging road that's headed downhill to the south-east. It will switchback on itself a couple of times and continue dropping down, then will mostly level off a bit. You can then leave the road to the RIGHT at any point (somewhere around this point at .5 would be good—**35.74954, -93.33023**), and head straight down to a side drainage below, then follow it downstream (past a couple of waterfalls) to the main creek at 1.0, a 600' drop from the trailhead. That was easy! (you gotta climb back up later…)

TURN LEFT and follow the bluff line and/or creek downstream, past another side drainage (with a nice waterfall) until you come to **Mrs. O'Leary's Falls** at 1.8, a wonderful SSS! Continue along the bluff to **Bull Falls** at 2.0—all of it an SSS of course!

What I do next is go down to the creek and work my way back upstream until I find a good spot to cross Cow Creek, then up to the bluffline and **Sprinkler Falls** (aka Fireman's Falls) at 2.3—at 94' it's the tallest I know of in this drainage—named in honor of brave firemen and women everywhere! From there I usually cross the creek again and hike up through the bluffline (here's a good spot—**35.74659, -93.32278**), straight up to the old logging road we started on, then TURN LEFT and follow it all the way back up to the trailhead. Total roundtrip about 4.1

Emergency contact: Newton County Sheriff, 870–446–5124 Dogs are OK

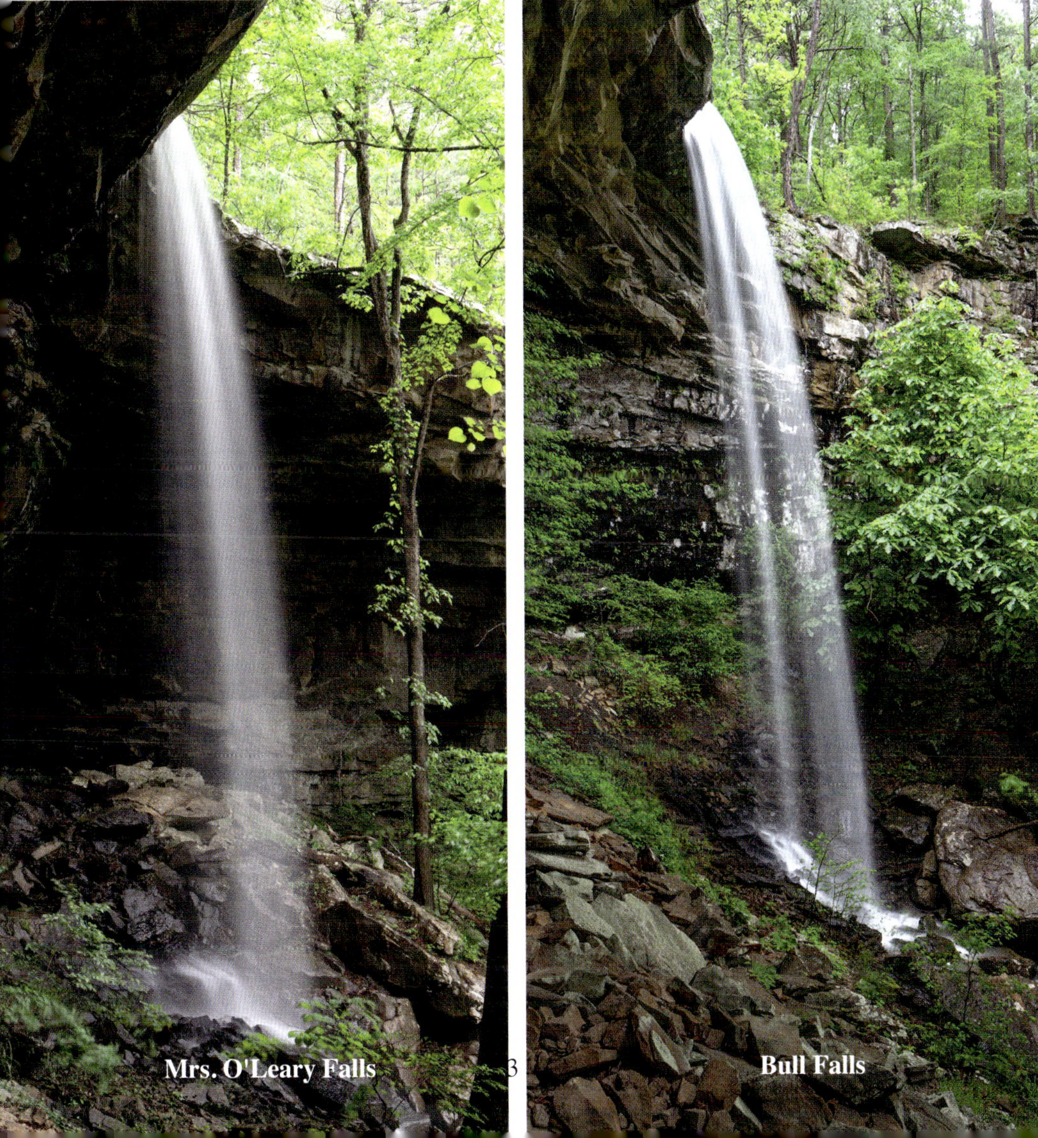

Mrs. O'Leary Falls

Bull Falls

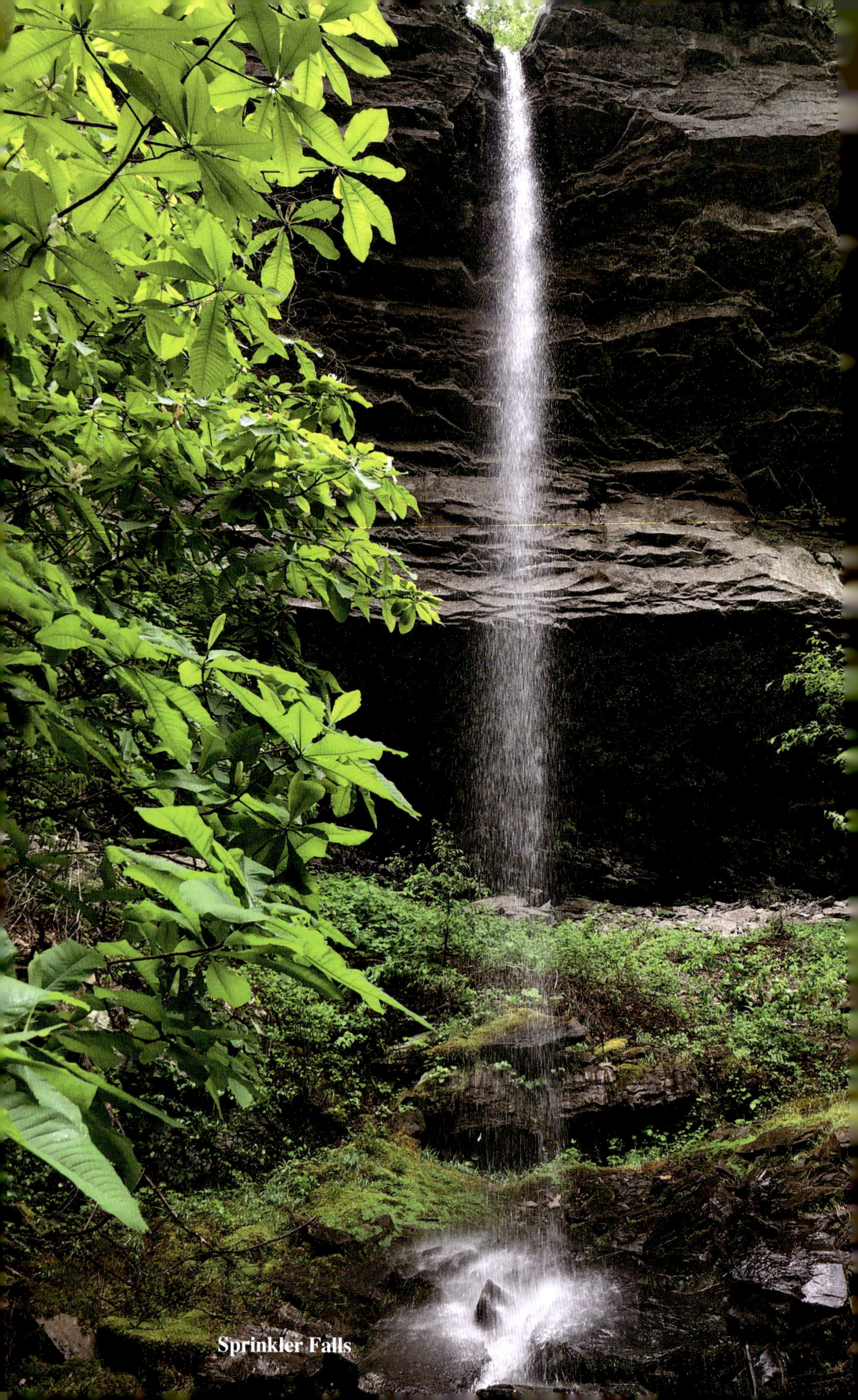

Sprinkler Falls

Cincinnati Freedom Falls – 27′

GPS **35.72695, -93.28999**

2.5 miles roundtrip medium social trail for all three falls

Little Cow Creek Grotto (3) – 18-22′

GPS **35.72979, -93.28969**

Norman Falls – 19′

GPS **35.72987, -93.29087**

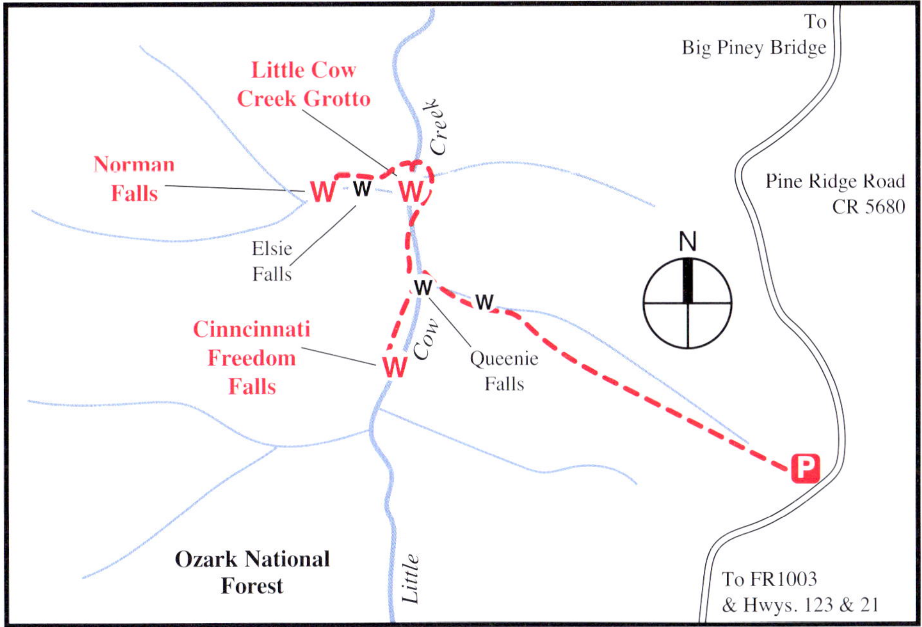

CINCINNATI FREEDOM FALLS/LITTLE COW CREEK GROTTO/NORMAN FALLS.

From the community of Pelsor (Sand Gap), go 16.2 miles south on Highway 123, then turn right onto FR-1003, aka Johnson County CR-5741. This is 3.3 miles past the Haw Creek Campground. If you are coming from the other direction on Highway 123, this junction is 10.5 miles north of Hagarville. Go north on CR-5741 for 5.7 miles, then turn right on CR-5680, also known as Pine Ridge Road. Go 3.5 miles on Pine Ridge Road, and turn left (west) onto a Jeep road and park. **(35.72582, -93.28086)**

We have Turtles, Horses, and now COWS to think about! There should be a social trail for most of this hike, which is pretty simple to begin with, although you do lose almost 400 feet in elevation. While there are three really outstanding waterfalls at the bottom of the hill you are about to go on, there are many other beautiful waterfalls in this Little Cow Creek drainage, and of course many dozens more throughout the other linked drainages of Cow Creek for you to explore.

From the parking area head downhill into the drainage on a social trail that follows the creek on down, past a nice little falls. When you get to the top of the bluff at the bottom there is Queenie Falls (34') pouring into the canyon. You can go around to the RIGHT and get below the bluff to Little Cow Creek Below. TURN LEFT and make your way to and past Queenie Falls (no photo provided) and on up to **Cincinnati Freedom Falls** at .6—a wonderful SSS that pours into an emerald pool.

Return downstream until you come to the top of a waterfall, then make your way around on the RIGHT and down the bluff to the creek and upstream into the spectacular **Little Cow Creek Grotto** with *three waterfalls* pouring into it. Oh My!!

OK, back up just a little bit downstream and work your way up the bluffline on the left and to the creek on the left (that's feeding one of the falls in the grotto), and follow that creek upstream to Elsie Falls (33'), then continue up a little bit farther to **Norman Falls**.

And that's just a taste of the more than 75 waterfalls in the Main, Middle, and Little Cow Creek drainages. See Rick Henry, Danny Hale, and other's resources and ENJOY!

Emergency contact: Johnson County Sheriff, 479–754–2200 Dogs are OK

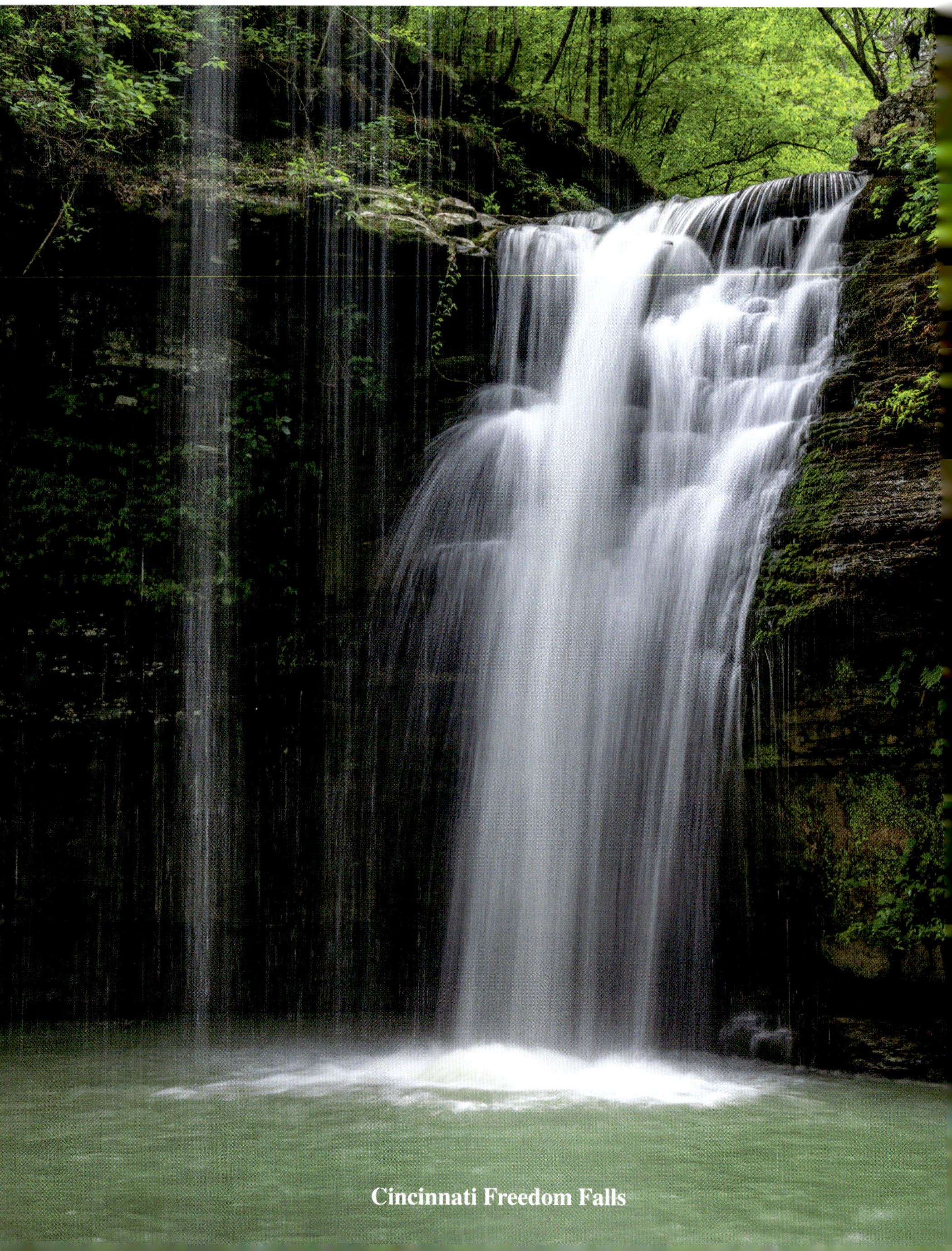

Cincinnati Freedom Falls

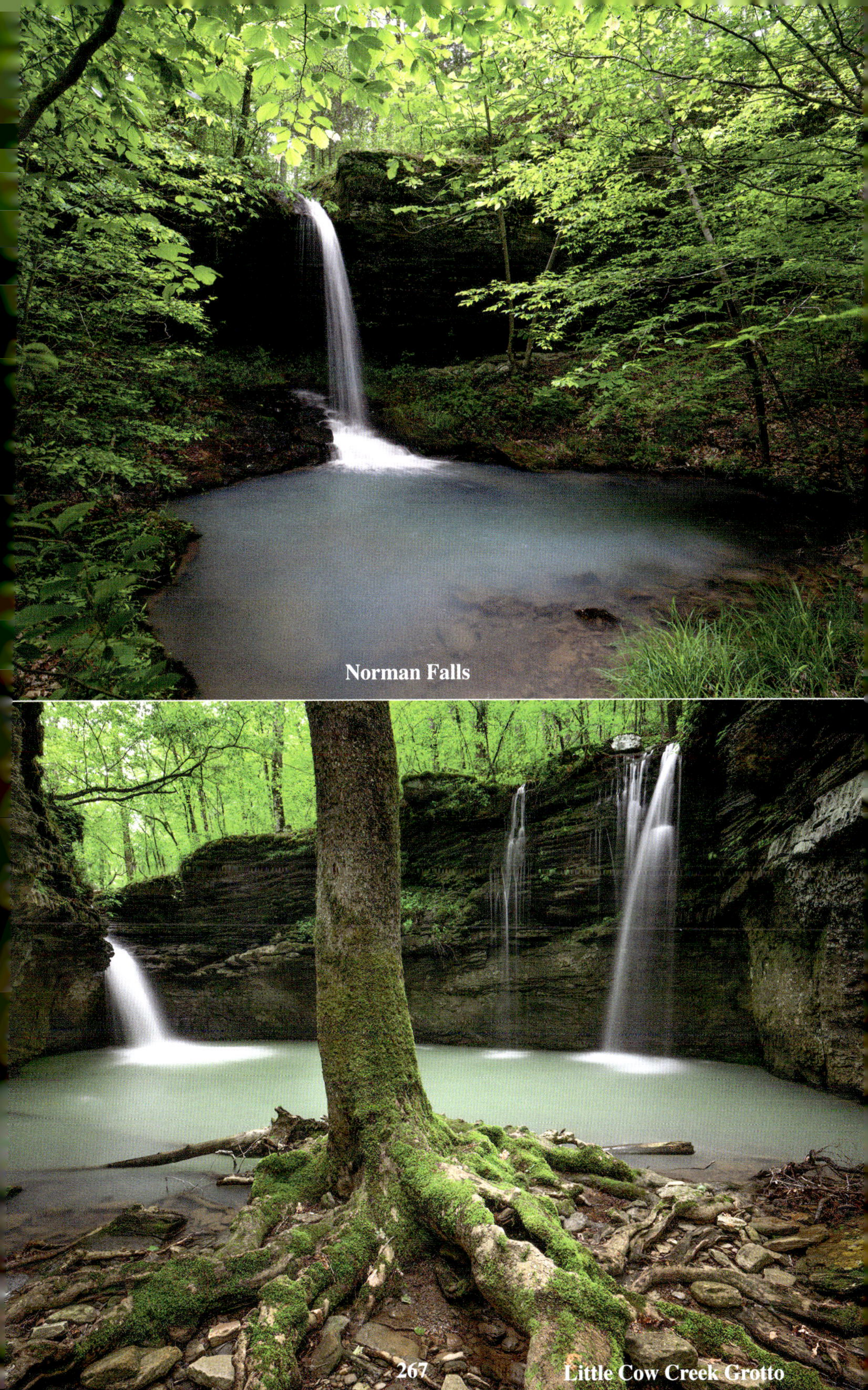
Norman Falls

Little Cow Creek Grotto

Native American Falls – 41′

1.5 miles roundtrip, medium bushwhack, GPS helpful

GPS **35.71345, -93.10533**

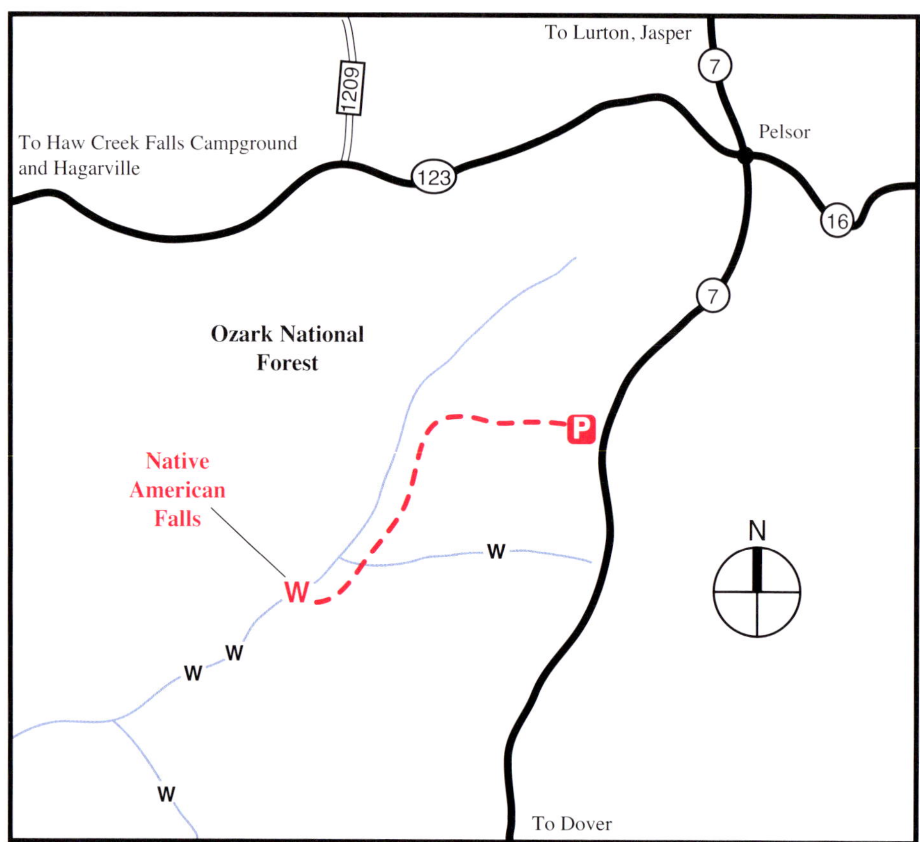

NATIVE AMERICAN FALLS. I *love* this waterfall, and named it in honor of those who explored the land before us. From Pelsor (between Jasper and Dover on Hwy. 7), go south on Hwy. 7 only .4 mile and PARK on the right where the big Wildlife Management Area sign is (**35.71632, -93.09876).**

From the sign head out into the woods to the west and bushwhack down to the creek below, then TURN LEFT and follow the creek downstream to the top of the falls. It is steep and rugged past the falls, you might be able to find a way down to the base. There is a neat overhanging rock on one side.

A little farther downstream there is a short slot canyon with a small waterfall at both ends! And a little farther downstream yet there is a side creek that comes in from the left with a nice taller waterfall just a little ways up. There is also a neat little grotto waterfall on the hillside back up towards the parking area (all of these are shown on the map above).

Emergency contact: Pope County Sheriff, 479–967–9300 Dogs are OK.

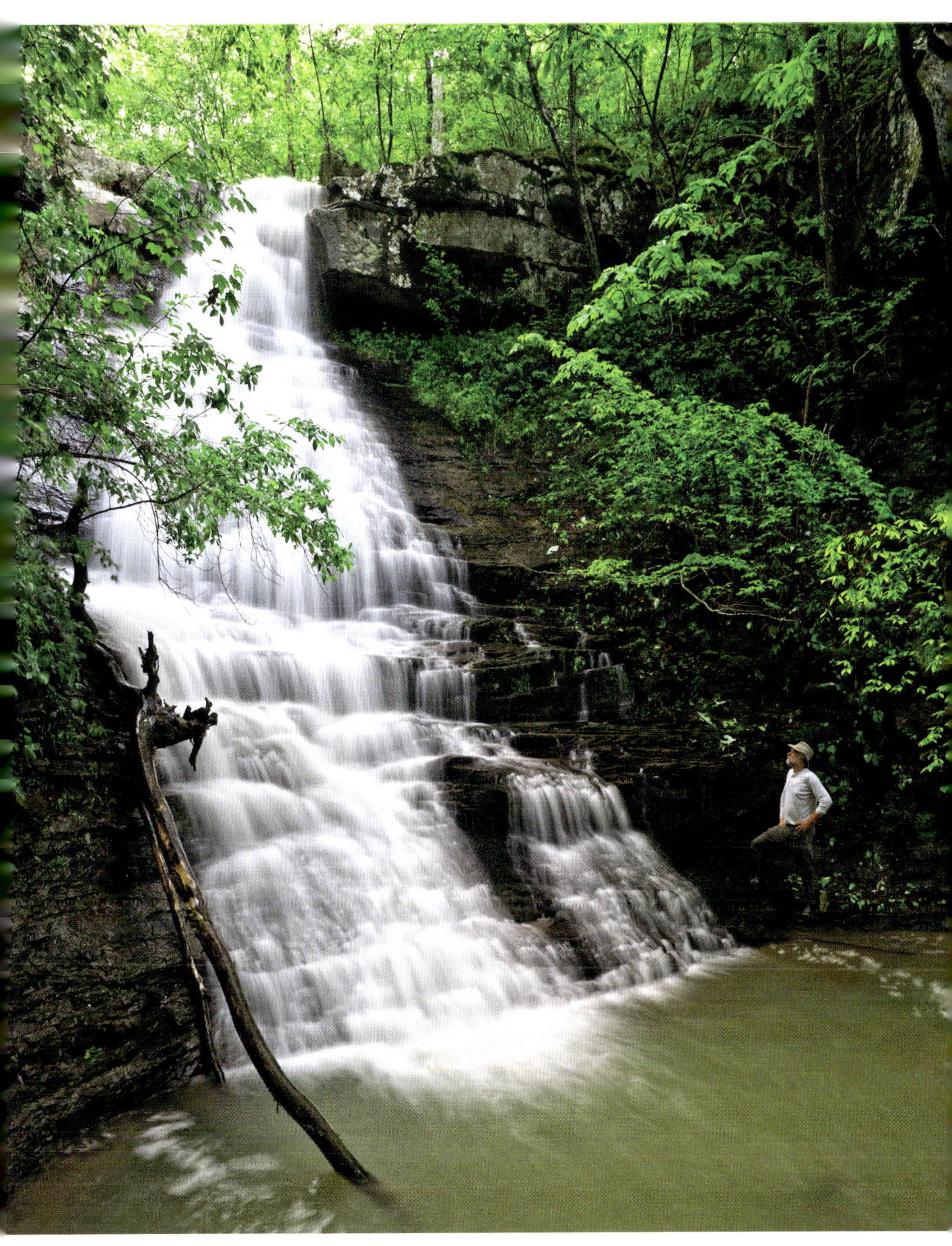

Native American Falls

Cub Hollow Falls (3) – 39′/47′/48′

3.8 miles roundtrip, medium-difficult bushwhack, GPS recommended

GPS park at **35.80237, -93.12692**

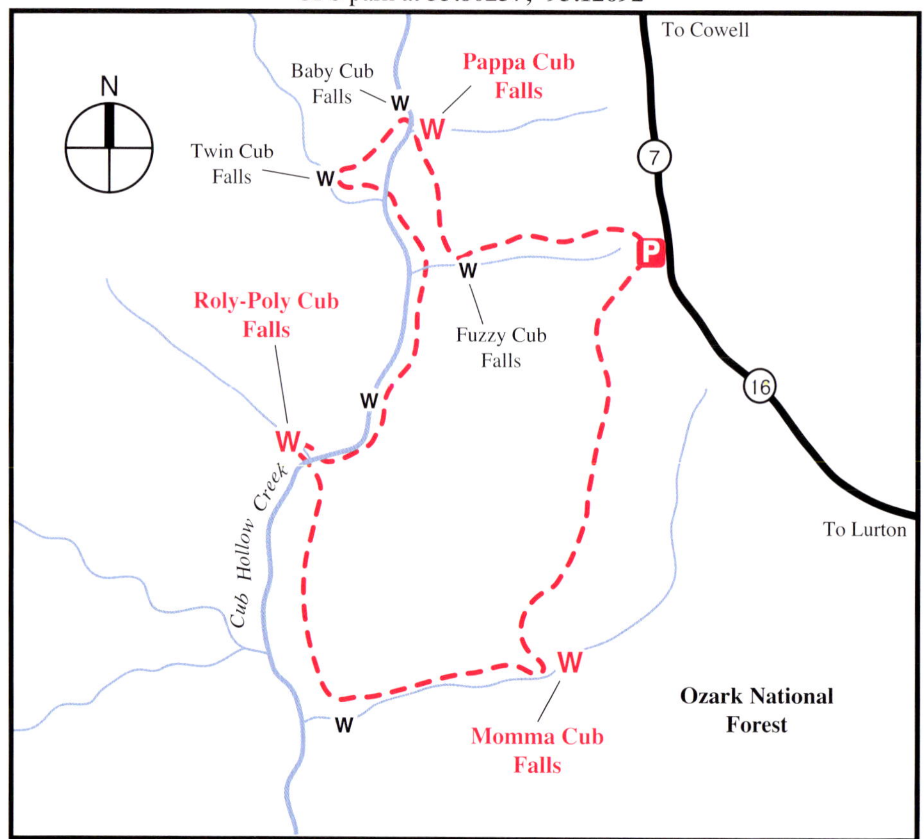

CUB HOLLOW FALLS. This is a really neat and rugged wild area right next to busy Hwy. 7 (between Cowell and Lurton), with a beautiful creek that tumbles over boulders and many waterfalls—in fact an entire family of "cub" falls—three of them are detailed here.

To reach the pulloff along the highway go south from Cowell 3.1 miles (1.7 miles north of the Who-Da-Thought-It store) and PARK on the west side of the road (**35.80237, -93.12692).** Here is the circuit that I make. From the parking spot bushwhack down the little drainage to the west until you come to the nice 31' Fuzzy Cub Falls. Get below the bluff there and follow the bluff back upstream/north until you come to a big overhang and the spectacular 48' **Pappa Cub Falls** (**35.80504, -93.13348**). At the far end of the bluffline there is the short Baby Cub Falls on the main creek that spills into an emerald pool.

Next I follow the bluffline on the other side of the creek up to a small twin falls, then back down to the main creek and then head downstream—lots of really neat boulder and cascade areas and some pretty tough hiking. At the next side creek coming in from the west/right—the 47' **Roly-Poly Cub Falls** is just above (**35.79825, -93.13655**). From there head downstream to the next creek (comes in from the east), and follow it all the way up to the big bluffline where you will find the 39' **Momma Cub Falls** (**35.79364, -93.13010**). From there find a way to the top of the bluff and bushwhack your way back.

Emergency contact: Newton County Sheriff, 870–446–5124 Dogs are OK.

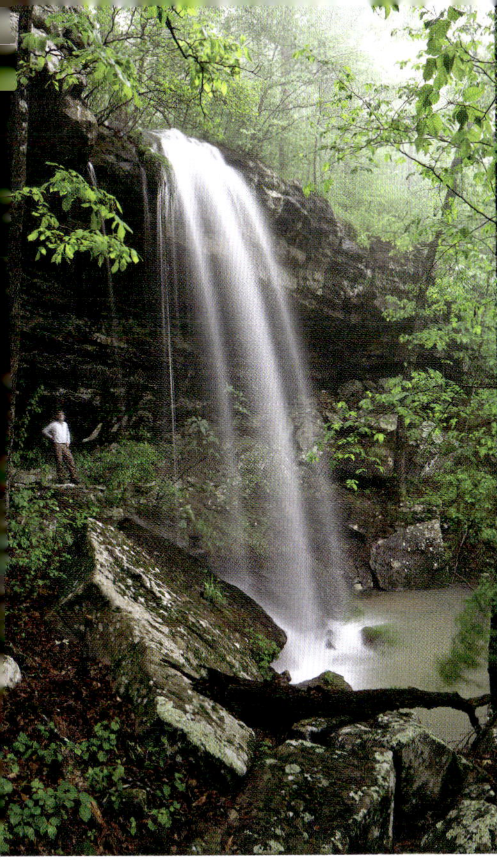

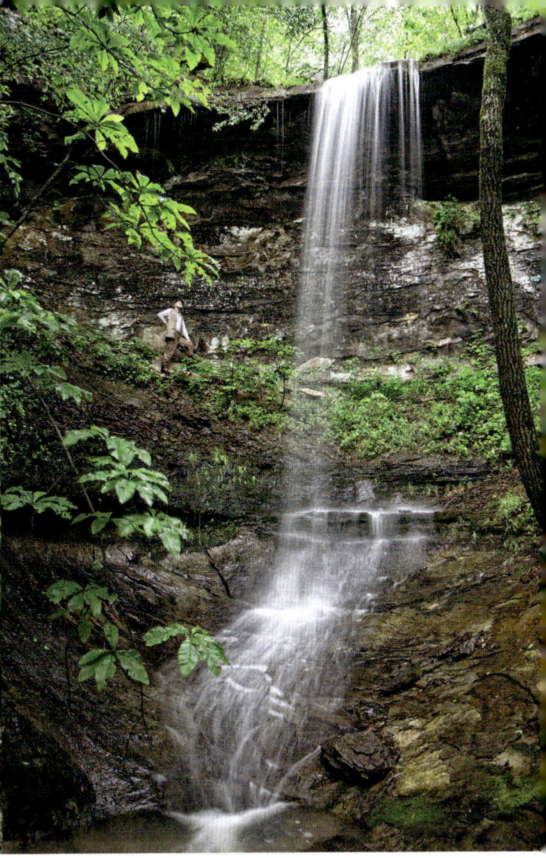

Momma Cub Falls (39', above left), **Roly-Poly Cub Falls** (47', above right)
Pappa Cub Falls (48', below)

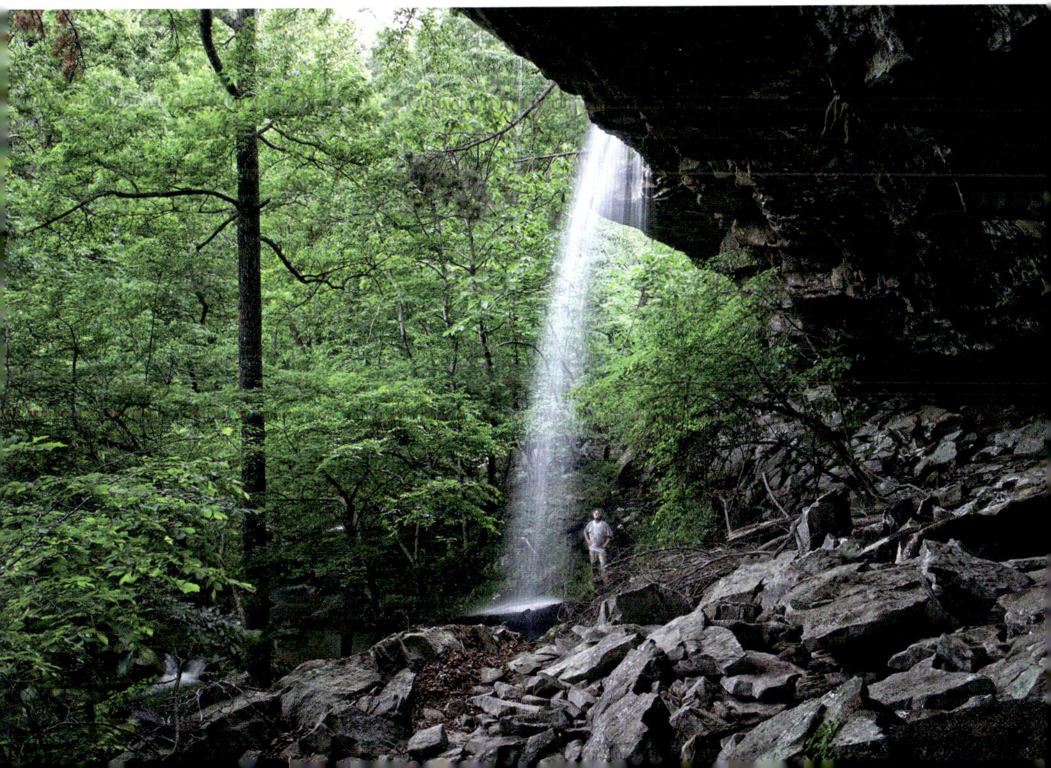

Lonesome Hollow Falls – 47′

1.1 miles roundtrip, easy social trail, GPS helpful

GPS **35.80487, -93.16006**

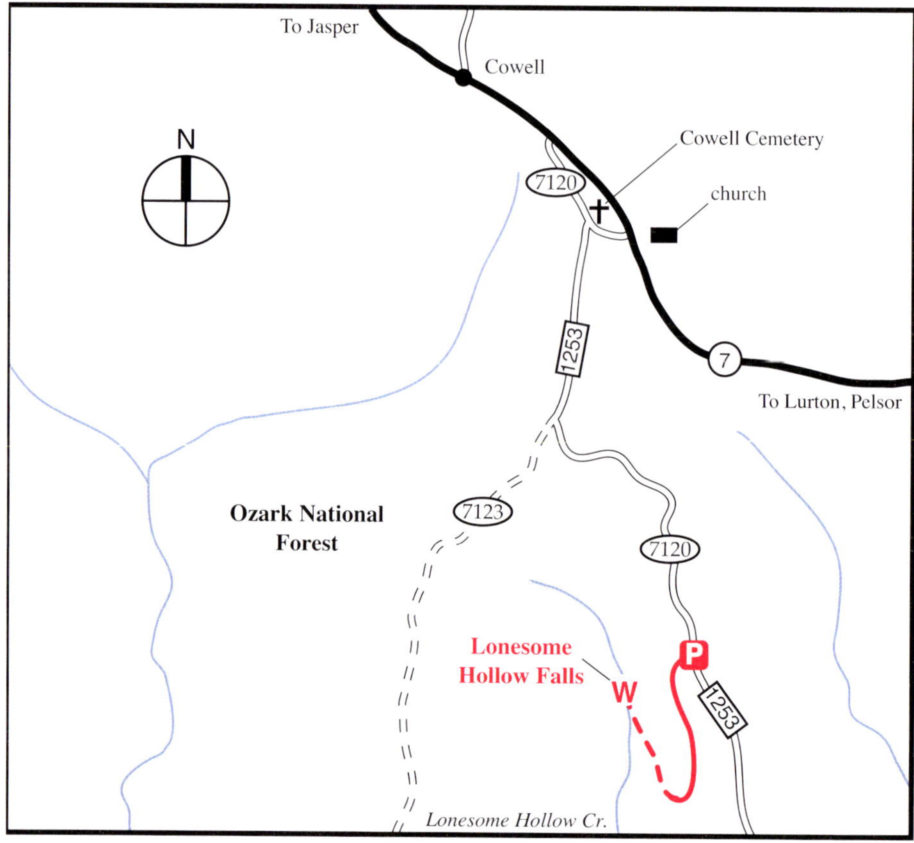

LONESOME HOLLOW FALLS. This is a neat waterfall under a big overhang that is pretty easy to get to—and after visiting it you won't feel quite so lonesome! It was the first of many new waterfalls that Randy Wilson found and told me about. He explores the wilderness with his camera and faithful canine companion, with a creative eye and joyous spirit. The access is near the little community of Cowell, which is between Deer and Lurton on Scenic Hwy. 7.

From Cowell, take Hwy. 7 south just .2 mile and TURN RIGHT onto CR#7120 towards the Cowell Cemetery. About half way around the cemetery TURN RIGHT onto CR#7120/FR#1253 (marked as "dead end"). Go .9 miles and PARK on the RIGHT at a dirt barricade where an old four-wheeler road takes off (**35.80638, -93.15760).** The main road may be shown as Taylor Ridge Road.

Begin your hike along the four-wheeler trail as it heads away from the main road and drops downhill and back to the left. Where it descends through the bluffline leave the trail and TURN RIGHT and follow a social trail along the base of the bluff until you come to the waterfall—lots of loose rock so be careful!

Emergency contact: Newton County Sheriff, 870–446–5124 Dogs are OK.

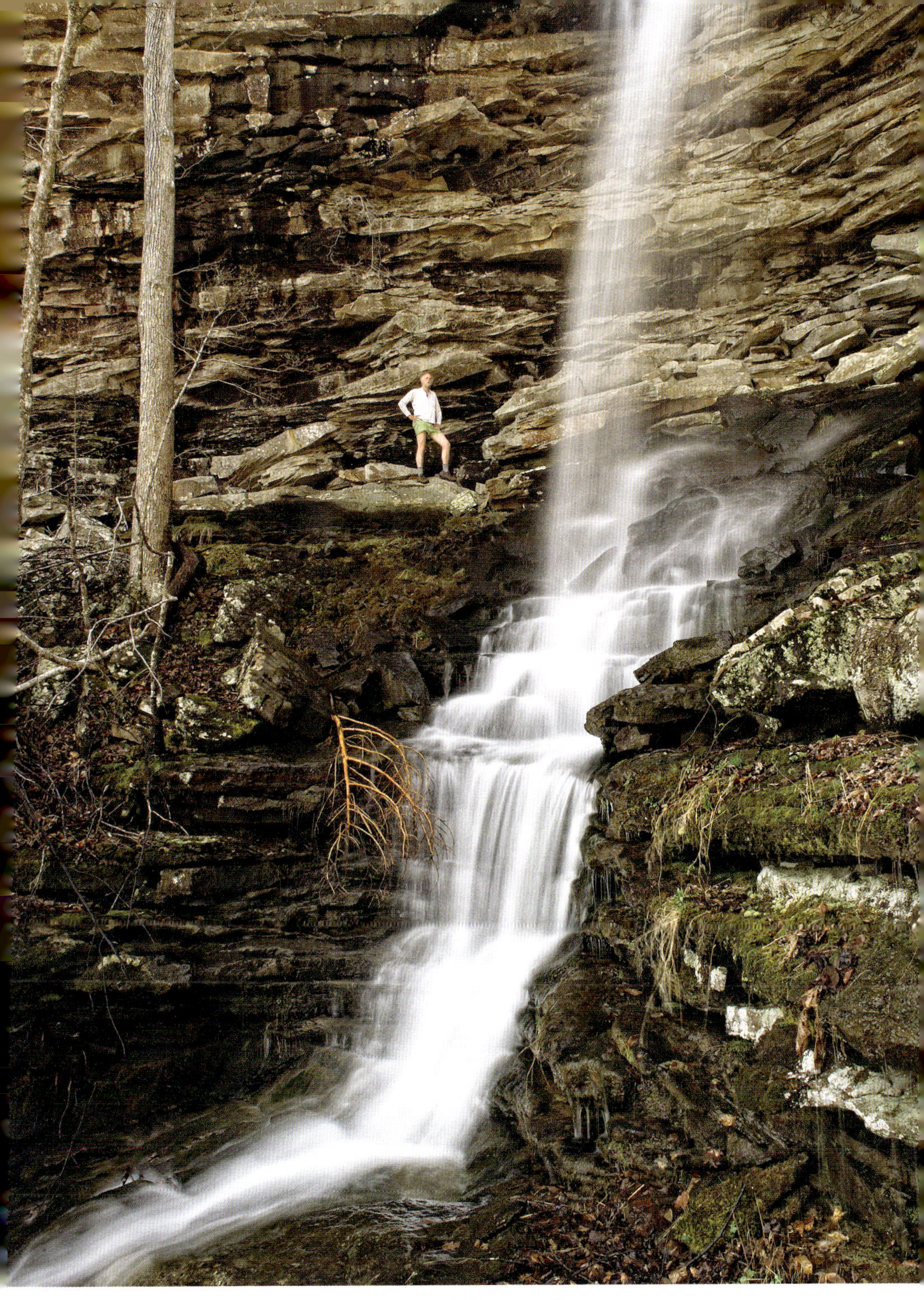

Lonesome Hollow Falls

Eliana Falls – 71′

1.2 roundtrip easy social trail then steep bushwhack

GPS **35.80854, -93.24976**

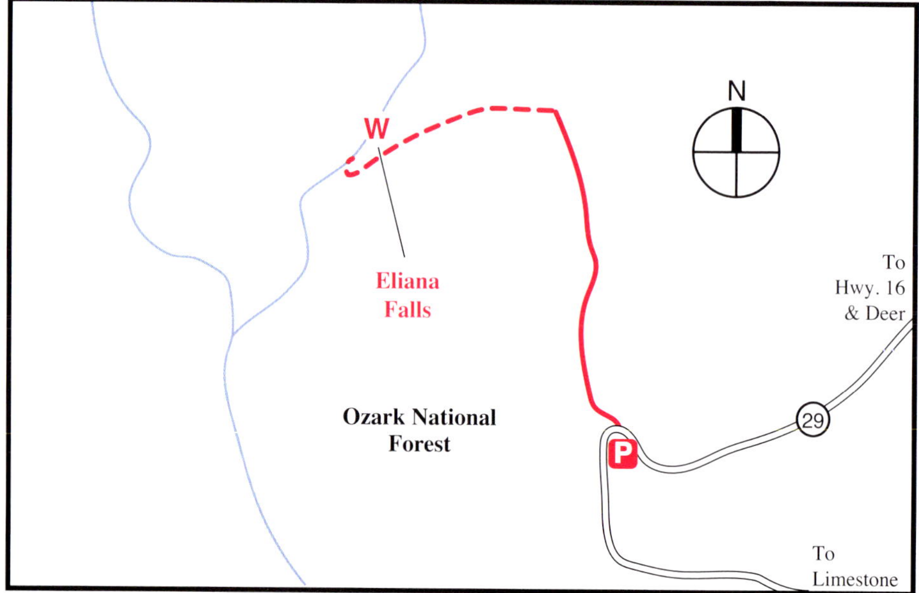

ELIANA FALLS. This is named by her dad for a special young lady—the daughter of the great "Bushwhacker of the Ozarks," Jorge Garcia. He finds the most AMAZING wild places off the beaten path, and THIS waterfall is one of them! Unlike most of Jorge's adventure finds, this one is very easy to get to, yet still an incredible SSS.

From the country store at Deer, take Hwy. 16 west for 1.8 miles TURN LEFT onto CR29, the road to Limestone (may not be marked, or may have a different number). Go 1.3 miles (down a couple of steep switchbacks) and park on the LEFT at the third switchback **(35.80498, -93.24624)**.

Cross the road and follow an old logging road straight ahead mostly level through a thick forest. If you lose the road just keep hiking along a level bench—it's a jungle out there! After crossing a couple of small streams it's time to TURN LEFT at .4 and work your way down a steep hillside, veering a little to the right as you go down. (If you just kept going on the old road you would come to a larger creek at .5 and could just follow it downstream to the falls, although it is very steep and not recommended).

Once at the bottom of this steep grade TURN RIGHT and follow the hillside back into the base of **Eliana Falls**, a really terrific moss-covered boulder, multi-tiered falls SSS! It's always scenic, but if you come on a dreary day with mist and thundering water, it will be so magical you may just need to spend the rest of the day!

Emergency contact: Newton County Sheriff, 870–446–5124 Dogs are OK.

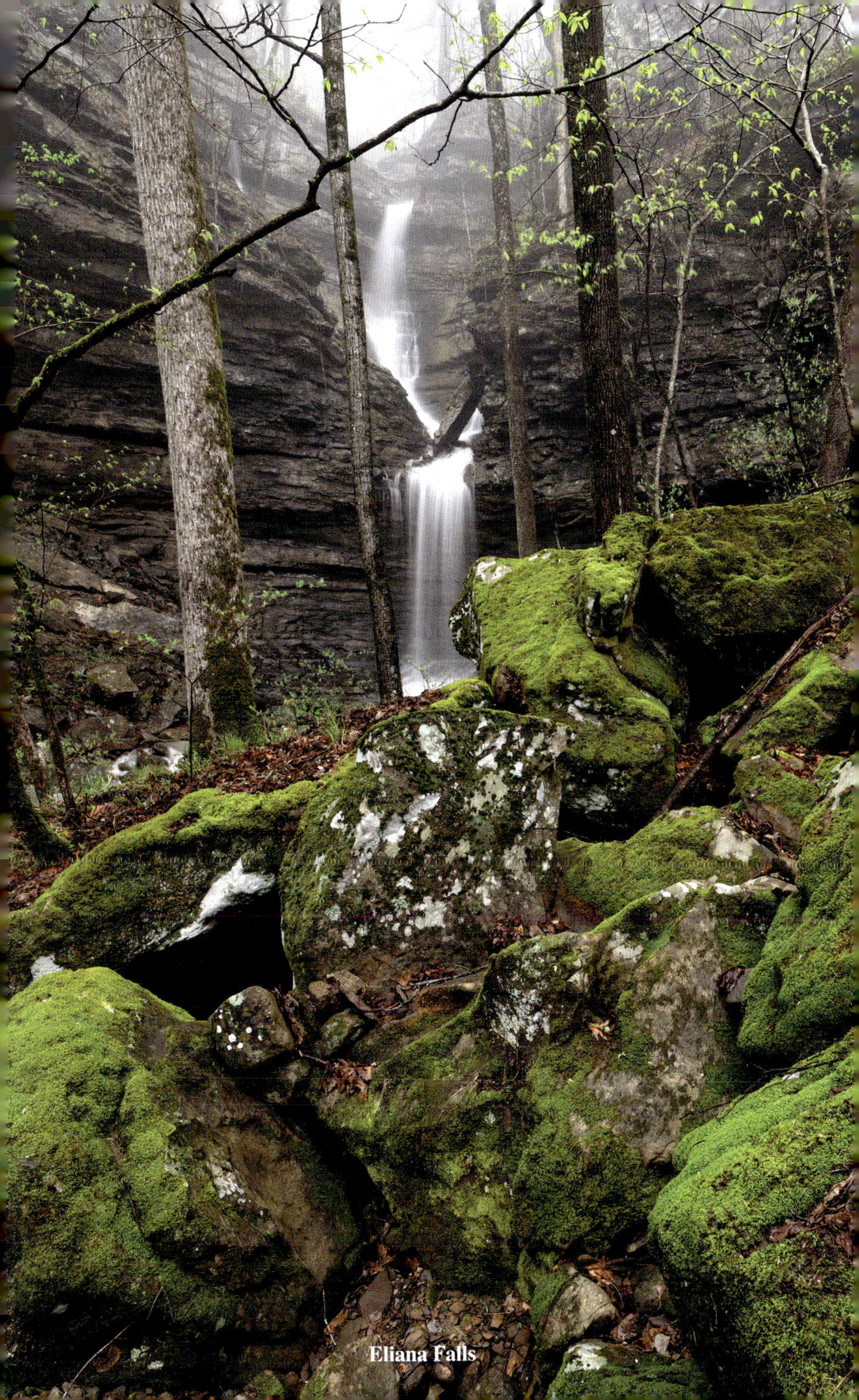
Eliana Falls

The Glory Hole – 31′

2.0 miles roundtrip, medium hike, GPS not required

GPS **35.82210, -93.39352**

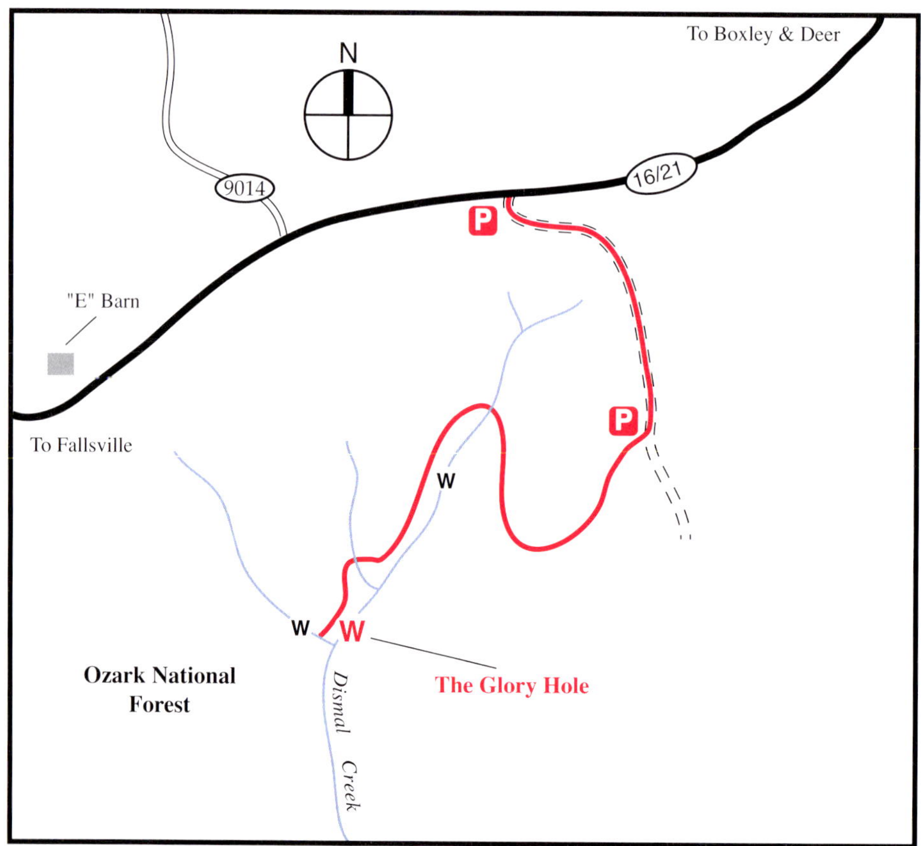

THE GLORY HOLE. This is perhaps the most interesting waterfall of them all. The creek has drilled a large hole right down through the roof of an overhanging bluff, and the resulting waterfall pours out below. The height is measured from the very top of the falls, and includes the thickness of the bluff. It's about a mile hike each way.

To get to the spot to begin this hike, take Hwy. 16/21 east out of Fallsville for 5.7 miles. Here you will pass a red barn on the left that has a large, white "E" on the side of it. Go .5 miles past this barn, and pull off to a large parking area on the right side of the highway—easy to see **(35.80498, -93.24624)** . This is 2.3 miles west of Edwards Junction.

From the highway hike along the well-used jeep road about .25 mile, then TURN RIGHT and head on down the hill. It gets a bit steep as the wide trail curves back to the right, and crosses the main stream at the bottom. Stay on this old roadbed as it curves back to the left and heads down the hill, eventually turning into plain trail before landing on top of the bluffline—go carefully around to the right to get below the bluff to the base of the falls. Be *extremely careful* if you make your way to the bottom! FYI, the Glory Hole is not normally frozen—I just love this photo from 2008.

Emergency contact: Newton County Sheriff, 870–446–5124 Dogs are OK.

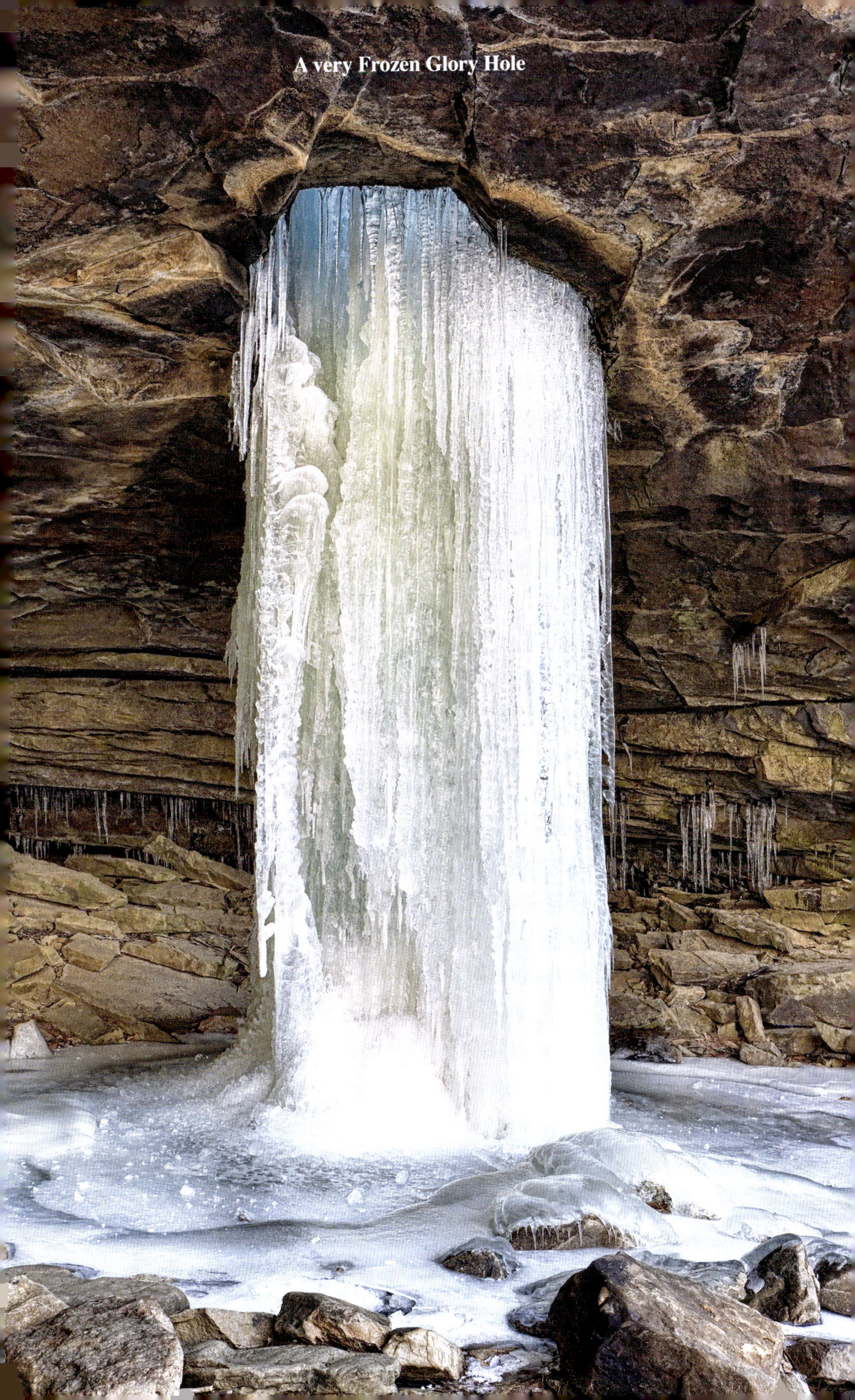

A very Frozen Glory Hole

Sweden Creek Falls – 81′

1.8 miles roundtrip, easy-medium trail

GPS **35.97145, -93.45915**

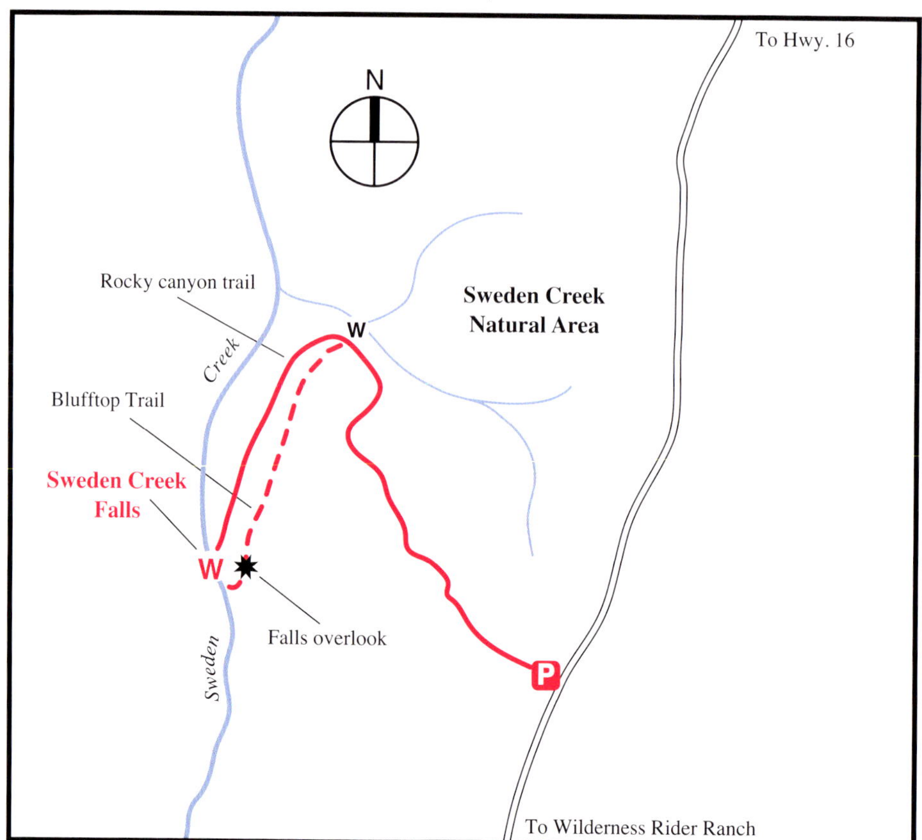

SWEDEN CREEK FALLS. The turnoff to get to the Natural Area is located on Hwy. 21 between Boxley and Kingston—from Kingston go 5.2 miles south on Hwy. 21 and TURN RIGHT onto a well-marked gravel road, or from Boxley go 3.9 miles north on Hwy. 21 and TURN LEFT onto the gravel road. This turnoff is just opposite the turn for Elkhorn Church. Stay on the gravel road for 3.3 miles, then PARK on the right **(35.96946, -93.45281)**.

Hike past the big sign on a good trail that drops down the hill and winds around through the woods to a three-way intersection at .5—this is the top of the bluff. There's a nice waterfall on the right, and a Blufftop Trail to the LEFT that follows the top of the bluffline and ends at the falls overlook .75. (FYI, you are not going crazy—there used to be a really nice house with detached garage near the intersection up to the right—those have been removed by the state.)

To reach the bottom of the big waterfall from the intersection, go STRAIGHT AHEAD down through the bluffline and TURN LEFT at the bottom of the bluff and follow along the base of the bluff. This bluff will curve back to the left and forms the eastern wall of the canyon. It will lead you right to Sweden Creek Falls at .75. It is one incredible place to say the least, and no wonder the state of Arkansas has protected it as one of its Natural Areas. There are dozens of "Natural Areas" all over the state—go to the Arkansas Natural Heritage Commission's web site for a complete list (Arkansasheritage.com). I also recom-

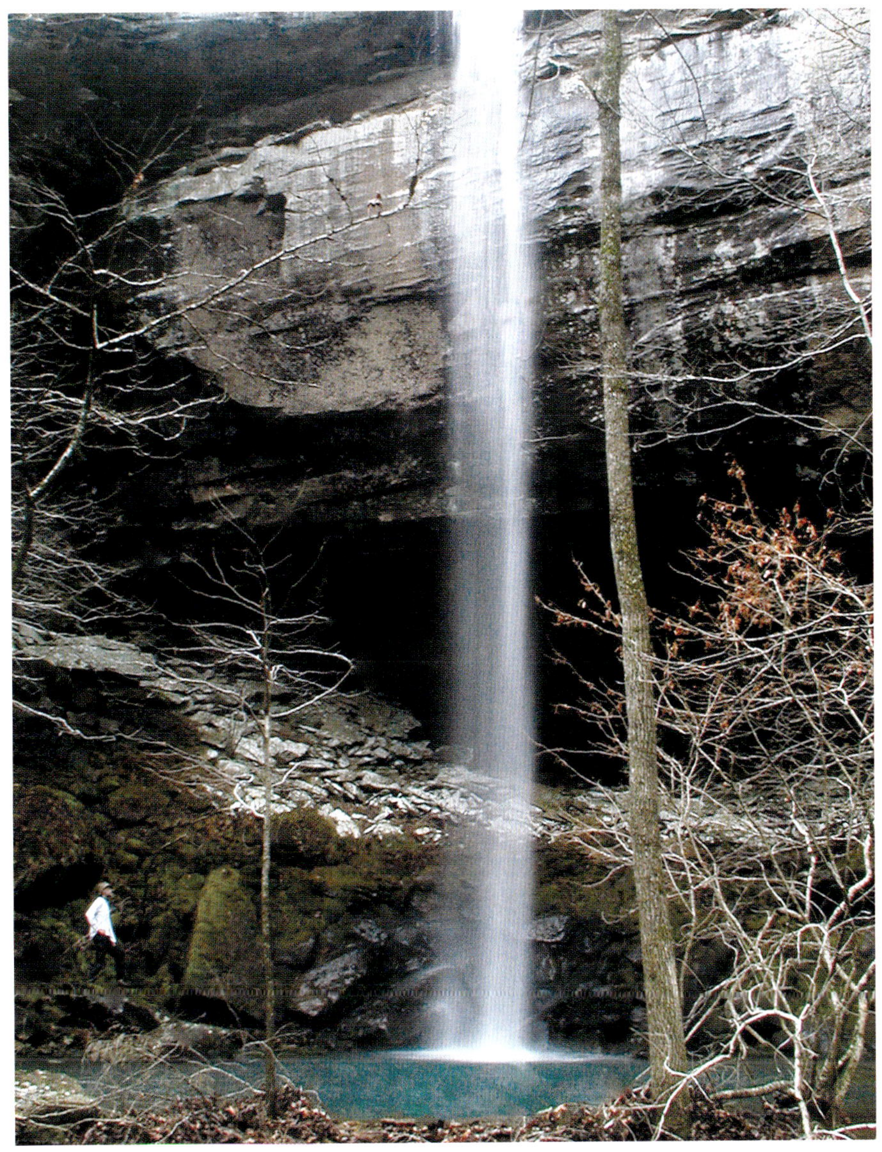

Sweden Creek Falls

mend the Danny Hale/TAKAHIK Natural Areas guidebook. Like all really tall waterfalls in the Ozarks, it looks best when the water levels are high, but it does run most of the wet season.

Emergency contact: Madison County Sheriff, 479–738–2320 Dogs are OK.

Kings River Falls –10′

1.2 miles roundtrip, easy hike, GPS not needed

GPS **35.90190, -93.57443**

Tenderfoot Falls–21′ add .2, social trail

GPS **35.90261, -93.57604**

Thong Tree Falls – 29′ add.4, social trail

GPS **35.90376, -93.57765**

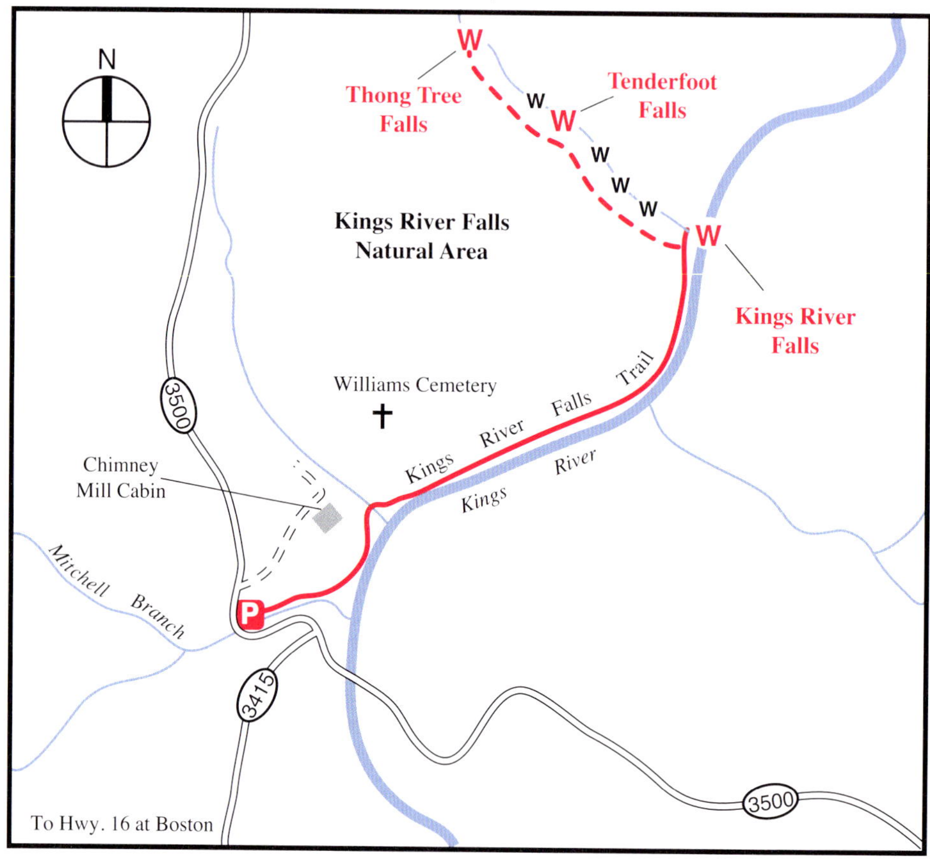

KINGS RIVER FALLS/TENDERFOOT FALLS/THONG TREE FALLS. Easy level trail, and the pool below the falls a wonderful SSS! (may be dry in summer) Spring brings out many wildflowers along the trail, plus there are lots of wild azaleas and dogwoods blooming.

To get to the trailhead from the old community of Boston—located on Hwy. 16 between Pettigrew and Red Star, and is actually the place where the mighty White River begins. From Boston head north on CR#3175 (gravel) for 2.0 miles and TURN RIGHT at the fork onto CR#3415. Stay on this road 2.3 miles until you come to a "T" intersection—TURN LEFT onto CR#3500. Go a couple of hundred yards and park at the trailhead on the RIGHT (**35.89459, -93.58491**).

The trail begins at the parking area and heads downstream along the top of a small levy, and follows in between the creek (on the right) and hay field/fenceline (on the left—the Chimney Mill rental cabin is across the field). The trail comes alongside the Kings

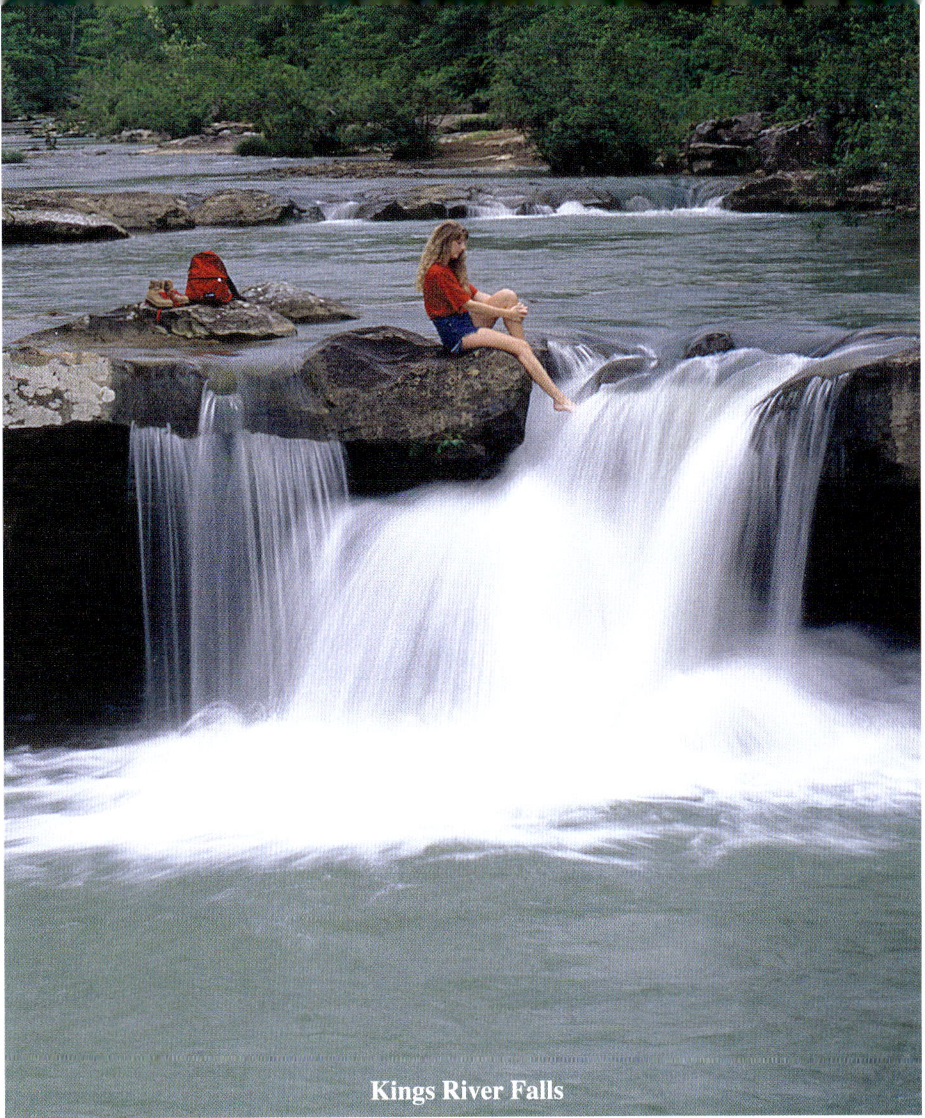
Kings River Falls

River and follows the field to and across a small stream. Parts of the old trail were washed away by the river so the trail was moved up onto the edge of the field here and continues downstream. There is an old rock wall part of the way that defines the hay field. Besides tons of wildflowers that carpet the area in the spring, there are lots of wild azaleas around too. Stay next to the river, and you'll eventually come to **Kings River Falls** at .6.

The immediate area of the big falls was once used as a grist mill site—can you spot the marks carved into the stone? The mill had a fireplace and chimney and thus was known as the Chimney Mill. The mill was washed out by a flood in 1914. The Chimney Mill Cabin (rental) is located upstream near the trailhead.

You can also explore up the side creek just before the main falls—there are several waterfalls, including **Tenderfoot Falls** (named for noted waterfall chasers Marianne Bassinger and her pup, Shadow), and **Thong Tree Falls** —"Thong Trees" were young trees bent over by Native Americans to mark a feature or turn. These tree shapes are also created during storms when a larger tree falls and bends over a smaller tree, which eventually corrects it's growth and grows straight again—I call these "N" trees due to the shape.

Emergency contact: Madison County Sheriff, 479–738–2320 Dogs are OK.

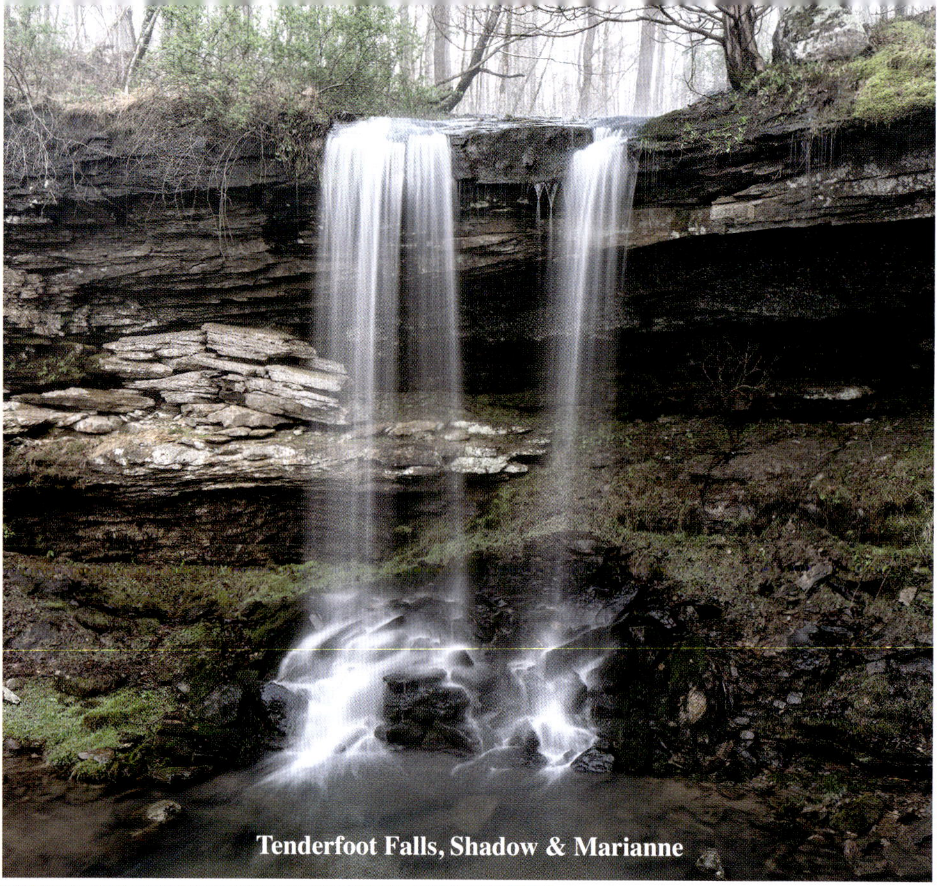

Tenderfoot Falls, Shadow & Marianne

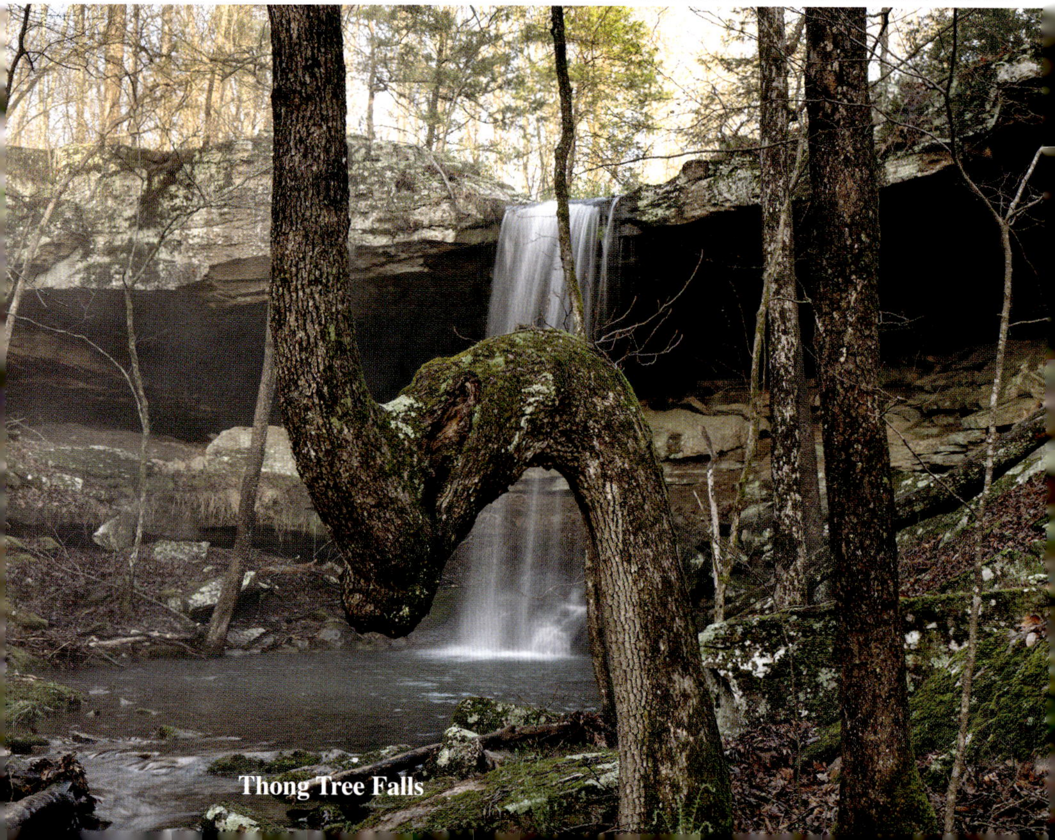

Thong Tree Falls

Lichen Falls – 28′

.5 mile roundtrip, easy hike, GPS not needed

GPS **35.75677, -93.53128**

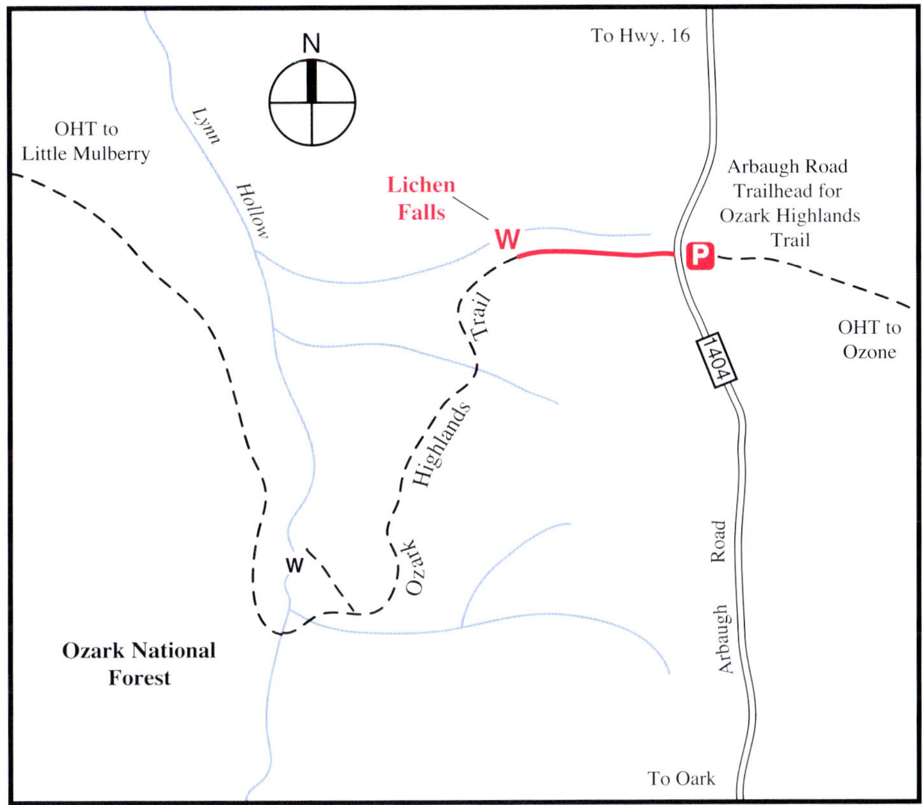

LICHEN FALLS. This is a pretty little double-decked cascade located right next to the Ozark Highlands Trail. It's only a .25 mile hike from the trailhead over level terrain, so most anyone will be able to visit it.

To get to the trailhead, from Fallsville take Hwy. 16 west 2.6 miles and TURN LEFT onto CR#9180/FR#1404/Arbaugh Road (gravel). OR take Hwy. 16 east from Red Star 7.9 miles and TURN RIGHT onto CR#9180/FR#1404/Arbaugh Road. Stay on this road 3.2 miles (bear right at the fork) until you come to the trailhead on the LEFT **(35.75754, -93.52801)**—it is marked quite well. This road continues on to the community of Oark.

Take the trail across the road to the west. It is level trail and follows a small stream on your right—this is the stream that forms the waterfall. Soon the trail begins to head down the hill just a little bit, and the stream begins to tumble over lichen-covered rocks. The waterfall is located just a little way farther down the stream. If you leave the trail to get a closer look be careful because the hillside is very steep!

If you continued on down the trail past the falls, you would come to a really neat area known as Lynn Hollow (.8 from the trailhead). There is a spur trail to the right that goes to an emerald pool at the base of a series of small waterfalls. Very nice!

Emergency contact: Johnson County Sheriff, 479–754–2200 Dogs are OK.

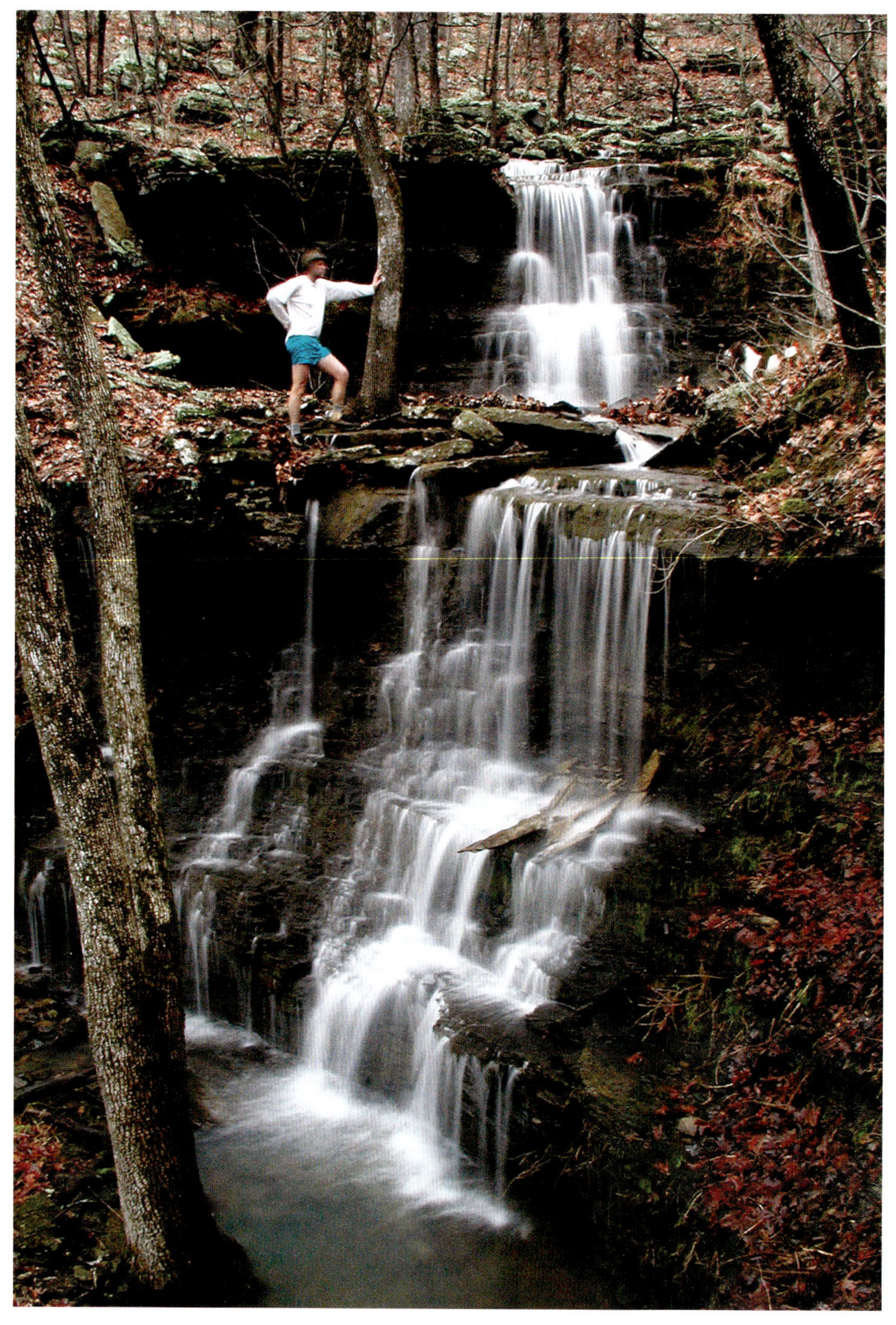

Lichen Falls

Accord Hollow Falls – 66′, 58′, 51′, 41′

2.0 miles roundtrip to all 4, medium bushwhack, GPS helpful
GPS **35.73477, -93.57667**

Estep Creek Falls – 16′

2.1 miles roundtrip, medium bushwhack, GPS helpful
GPS **35.72030, -93.57376**

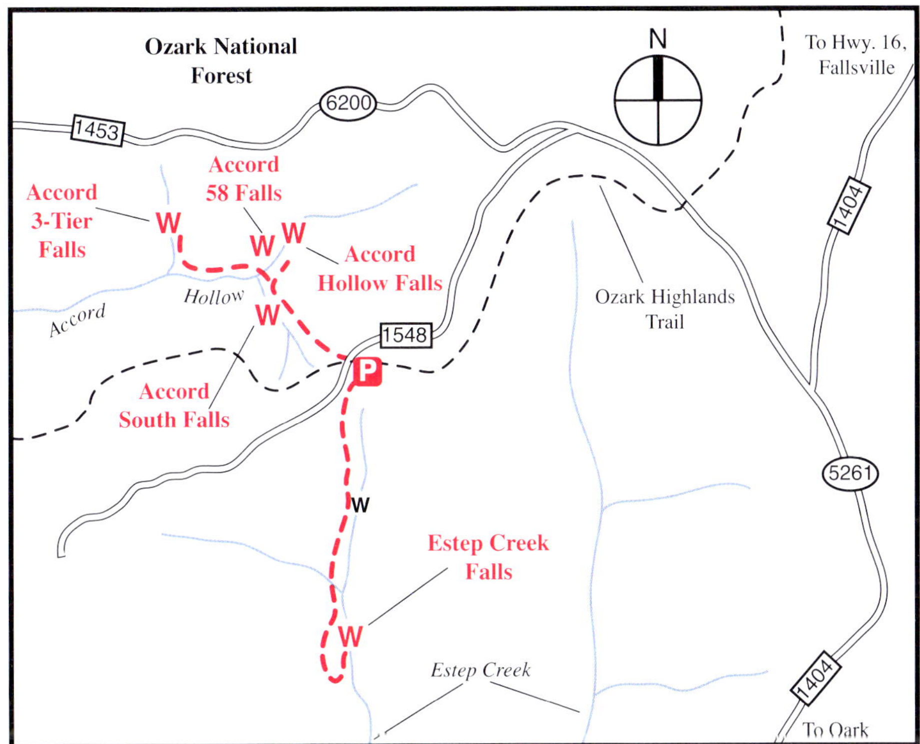

ACCORD HOLLOW FALLS. There are three beautiful waterfalls and a great bluffline to explore that is not too far off of the Ozark Highlands Trail at mile 64.1. There is another nice waterfall along the way too. Another short bushwhack from the same parking spot will take you down to more waterfalls on the other side of the road.

From Hwy. 16 (2.6 west of Fallsville) go south on CR#9180/FR#1404/Arbaugh Road for 6.3 miles and TURN RIGHT/WEST onto FR#1453/CR#6200. Go .9 miles and TURN LEFT onto FR#1548. Go .9 miles and PARK on the left **(35.73016, -93.57360)** just past where the Ozark Highlands Trail crosses the road. OR from Oark go north on FR#1404/CR#5261 for 3.6 miles and TURN LEFT/WEST onto FR#1453/CR#6200, then as above.

Get on the OHT and hike to your left/west for just a hundred yards or so and then leave the trail and bushwhack downhill to your right. Follow the little stream there to **Accord South Falls**, 41' (**35.73236, -93.57724,** photo unavailable). Continue downstream until you reach a larger creek (Accord Hollow), then TURN RIGHT and follow it upstream a little ways to the big waterfall, **Accord Hollow Falls**, 66' (**35.73477, -93.57667**). WOW! There is another tall falls (when running) that pours off of the same bluffline to the west/left, **Accord 58** (58', **35.73448, -93.57760**).

CONTINUE to follow the base of that bluffline downstream, then work your way into a side drainage back to the RIGHT to **Accord 3-Tier Falls** (51'), another SSS! (**35.73439, -93.57760**) There's an upper tier (total of 3) that is not shown in the photo.

ESTEP CREEK FALLS. From your car, bushwhack south/downhill and follow the creek to a lovely spot where four different waterfalls all come together (**35.72478, -93.57324**), then continue downstream to **Estep Falls** that pours into an emerald pool.

Emergency contact: Johnson County Sheriff, 479–754–2200 Dogs are OK.

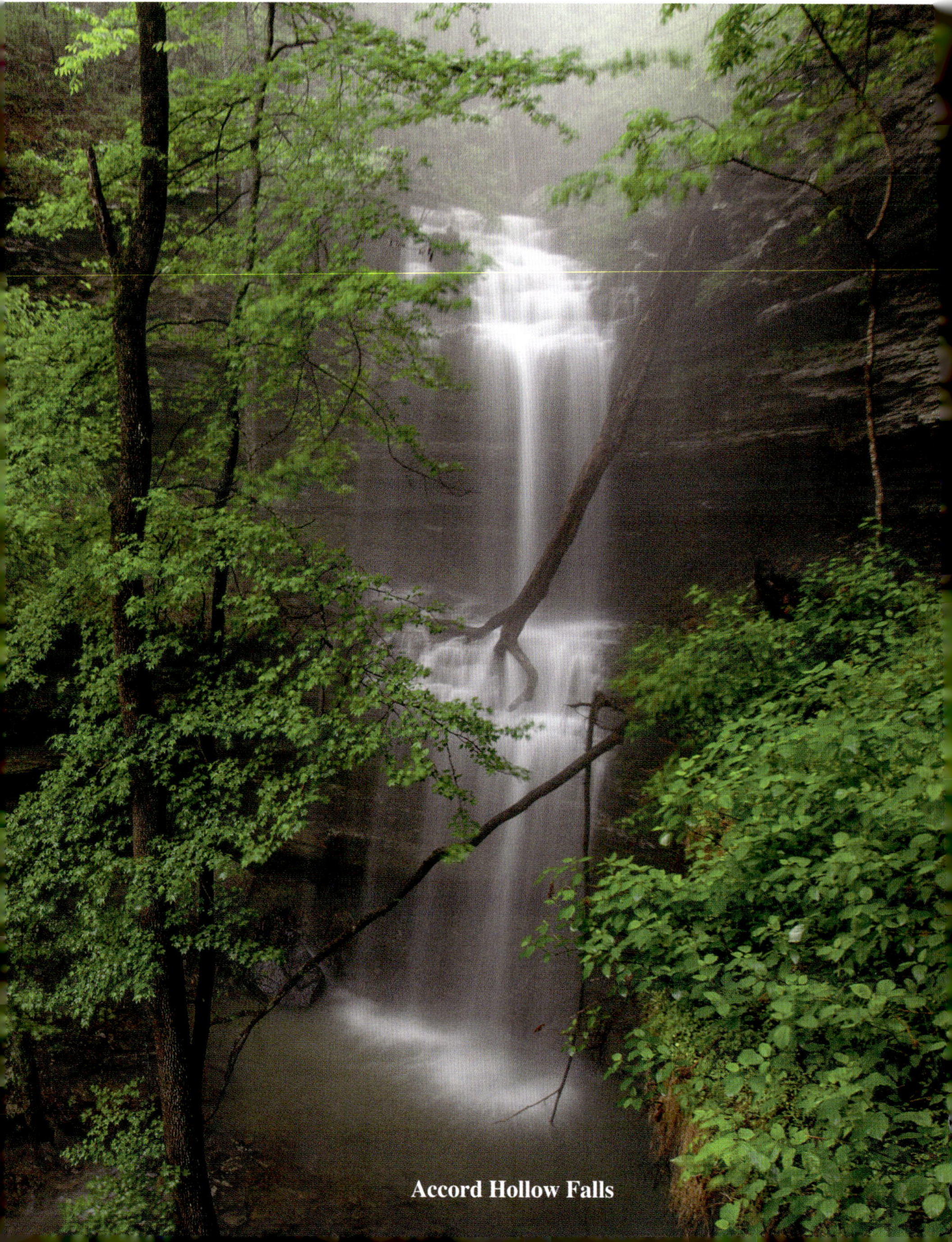

Accord Hollow Falls

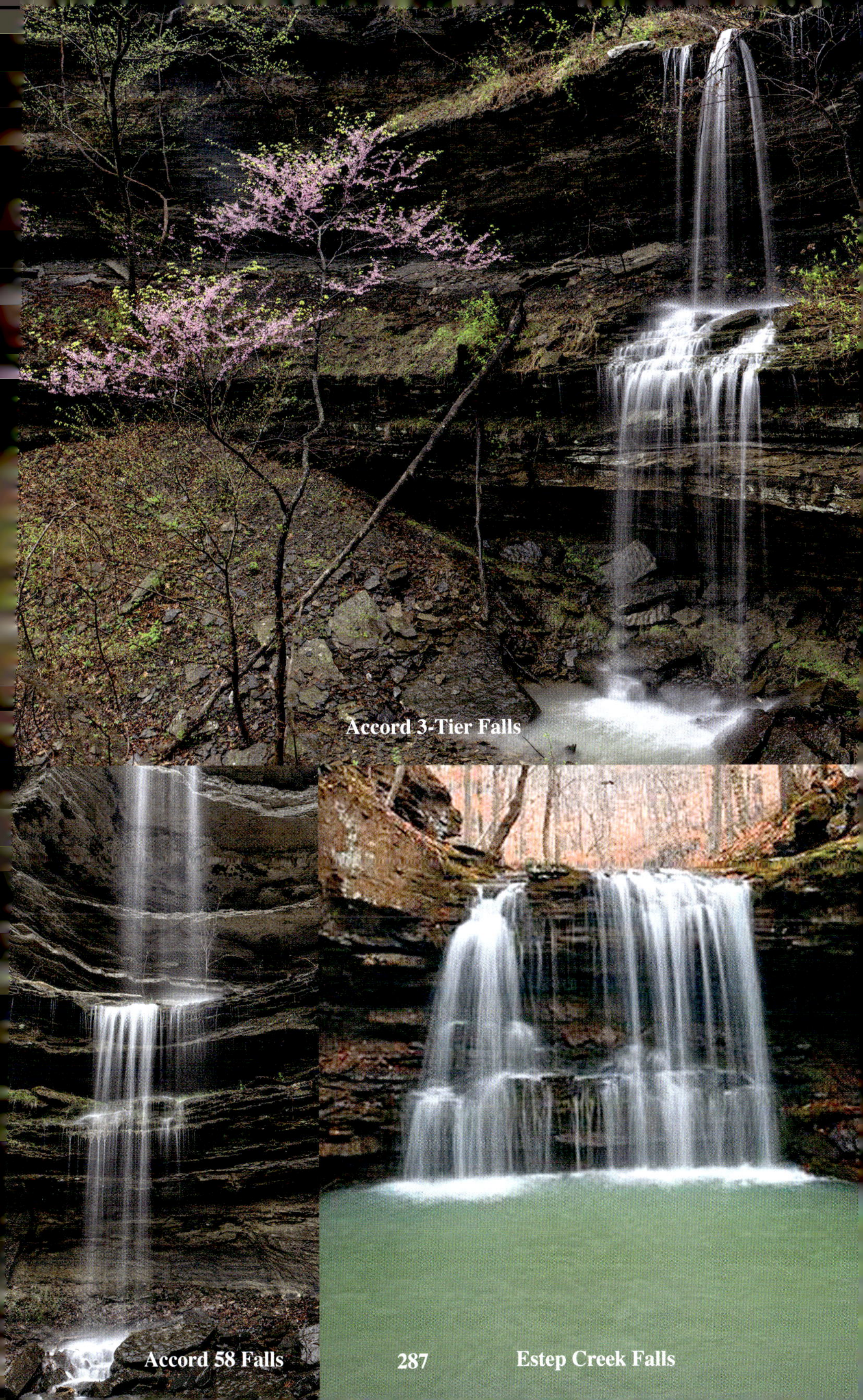

Accord 3-Tier Falls

Accord 58 Falls

Estep Creek Falls

Waterfall Hollow Falls (3) – 17-23′

1.5 miles roundtrip (all), easy/medium hike, GPS helpful

GPS #1—**35.74475, -93.45934; #2—35.74573, -93.45912; #3—35.74736, -93.46147**

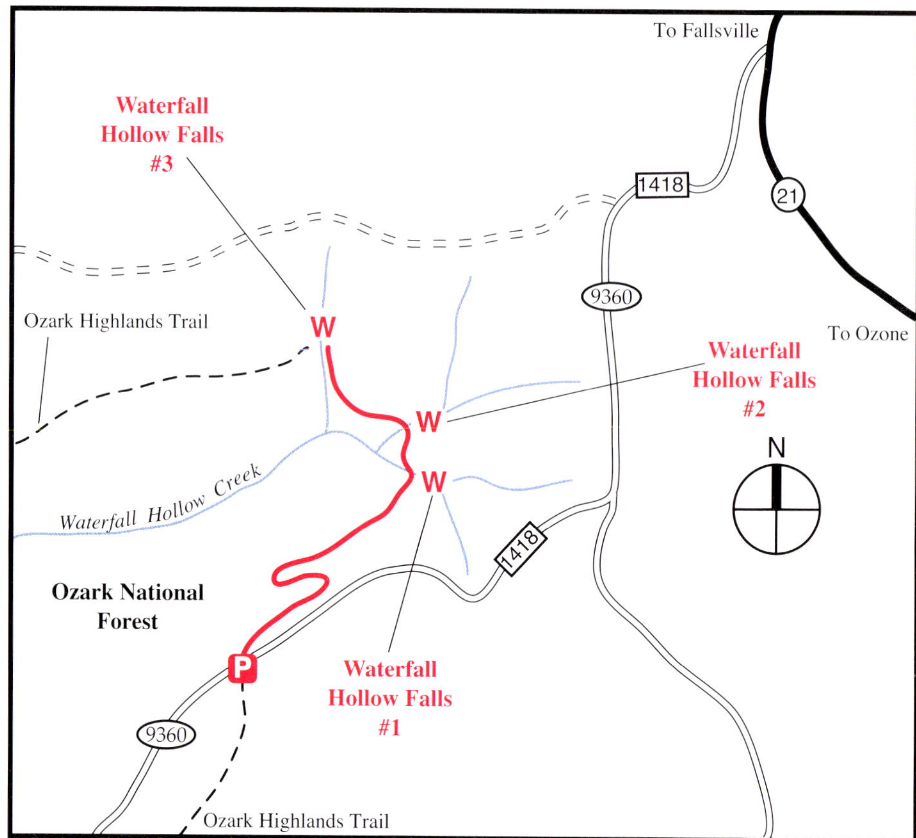

WATERFALL HOLLOW FALLS. These are three nice falls right along the Ozark Highlands Trail (between miles 77–78) near, where else—Fallsville! You can see from the photos that the area was hit hard by the big ice storm in 2009, but the debris will rot away and the waterfalls will continue to flow.

To reach the parking spot from Fallsville, head south on Hwy. 21 for 2.3 miles and TURN RIGHT onto CR#9360/FR#1418 (head towards the Moonhull Full Gospel Church). Go 1.3 miles (bear right at .7) and PARK on the road where the Ozark Highlands Trail crosses (**35.74090, -93.46386**).

Hike down the Ozark Highlands Trail to your right/north and you will come to the first waterfall at the bottom of the hill at the first creek crossing (upstream to your right). Continue on the trail another several hundred yards to the next creek and waterfall #2. Continue on the trail one more time until you reach the third creek and waterfall #3.

Emergency contact: Newton County Sheriff, 870–446–5124 Dogs are OK.

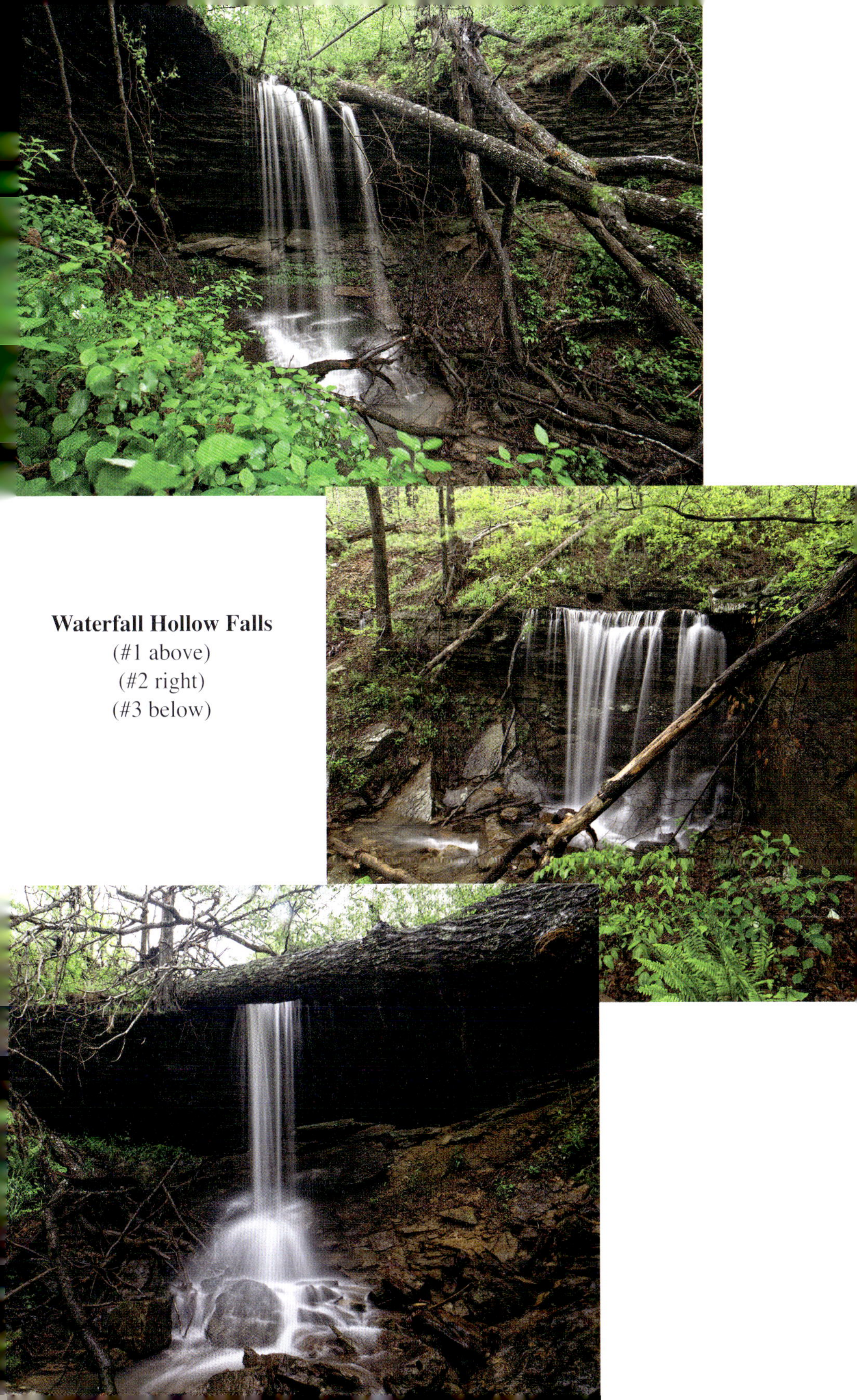

Waterfall Hollow Falls
(#1 above)
(#2 right)
(#3 below)

Hobo Falls (2) – 23′/27′

3.0 miles roundtrip, medium hike, GPS not required

GPS **35.68090, -93.33400**

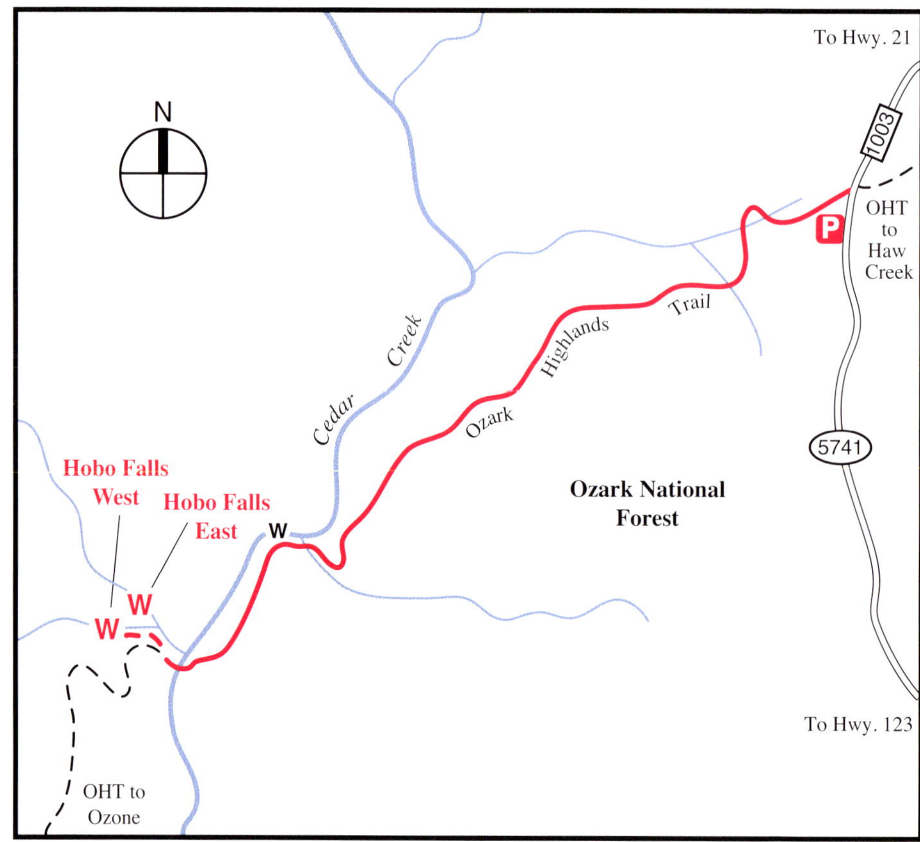

HOBO FALLS. Most folks walk right on past the neat little canyon that holds these two waterfalls. They are definitely worth a look, especially when there is lots of water. Over the years we have found the remnants of a hobo camp several different times in the area, even one right under the bluffline next to these waterfalls—hence the name.

To get to the parking area from the community of Ozone, take Hwy. 21 north 6.7 miles & TURN RIGHT onto CR#5570/FR#1003 (becomes CR#5680 & then CR#5741). Go 10.1 miles & park where the Ozark Highlands Trail (OHT) crosses the road **(35.68968, -93.31700)**. **OR** from Haw Creek Falls Campground, take Hwy. 123 south 3.3 miles & TURN RIGHT onto CR#5741/FR#1003 & go 4.7 miles.

The OHT takes off to the west, drops down the hill, crossing a couple of small streams, and eventually makes its way down to and alongside Cedar Creek. There is a wonderful slough area at 1.1 that ends with a small pouroff into an emerald pool (too shallow to dive into!). This is a very fragile area, and if you camp here, be sure to camp *away* from the pool area. The trail continues downstream, and crosses Cedar Creek at 1.4.

As you continue on the trail you will see a side canyon just ahead and on the RIGHT—leave the trail and follow the canyon just a couple hundred feet upstream. **The East Falls** will be visible on your right in a second side canyon, and the **West Falls** will be straight ahead another 100 yards or so. Be sure to save some energy for the climb out!

Emergency contact: Johnson County Sheriff, 479–754–2200 Dogs are OK.

Hobo Falls East

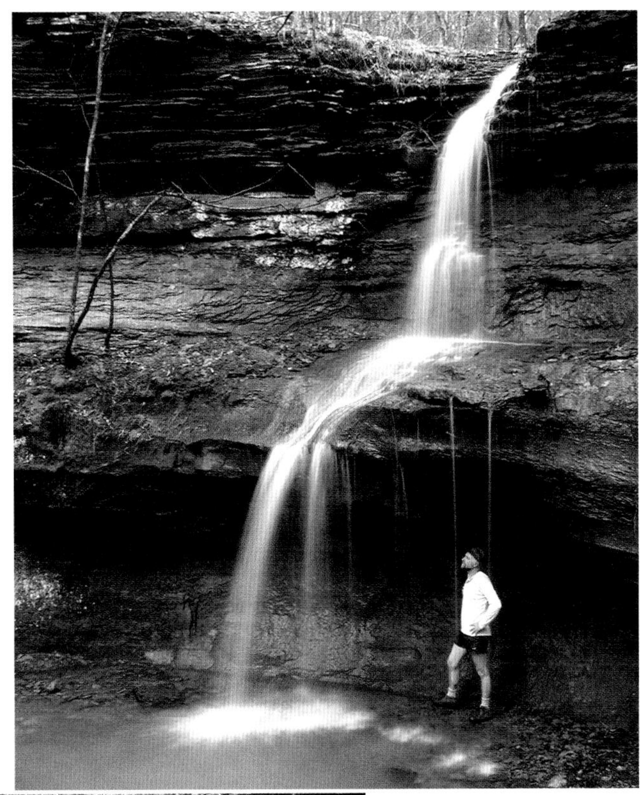

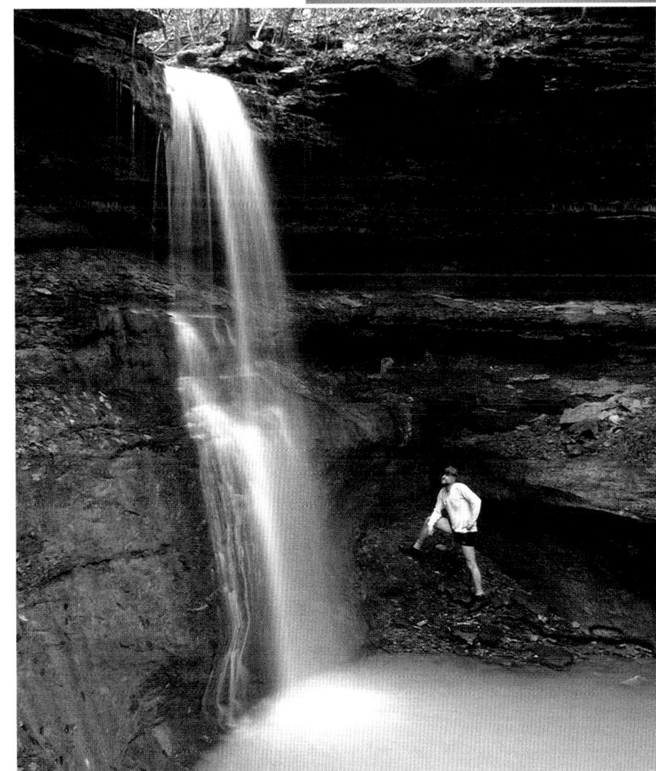

Hobo Falls West

Bear Skull Falls – 22′

3.0 miles roundtrip, medium hike, GPS helpful
GPS **35.66987, -93.36220**

Slot Rock – 8′

4.4 miles roundtrip (includes above), medium hike, GPS helpful
GPS **35.67600, -93.36318**

Sunset Falls – 70′

5.8 miles roundtrip (includes above), difficult bushwhack, GPS recommended
GPS **35.67652, -93.35357**

Discovery Falls – 43′

6.4 miles roundtrip (includes all of the above), difficult bushwhack, GPS recommended GPS **35.67703, -93.35291**

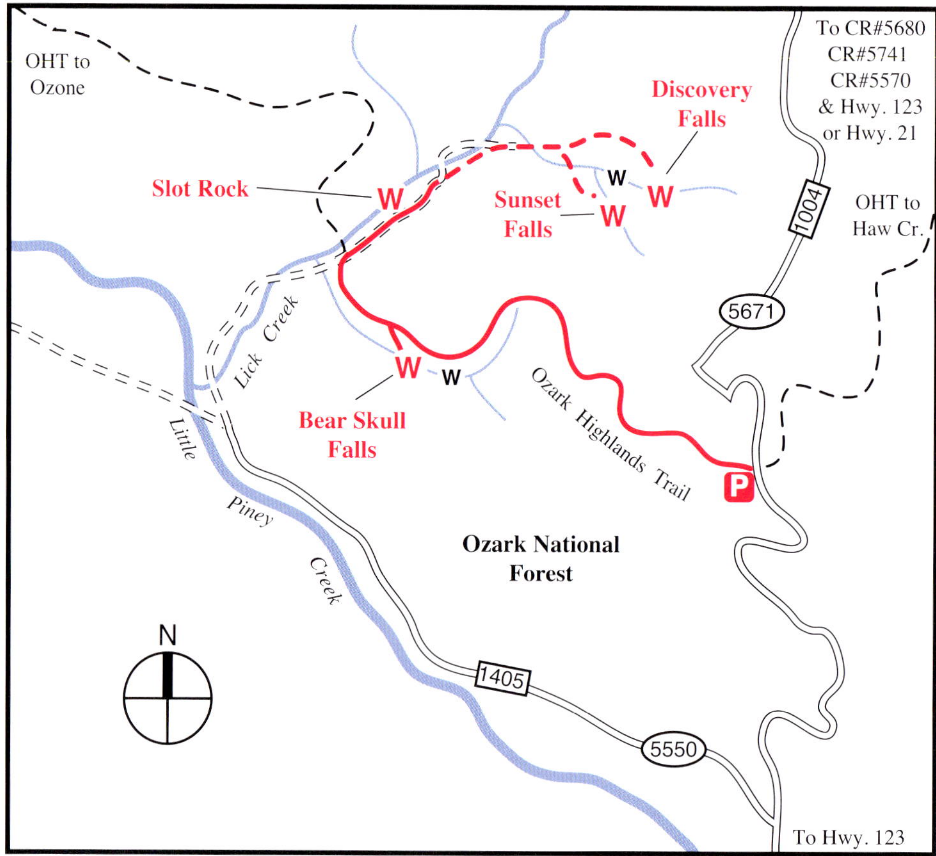

BEAR SKULL/SLOT ROCK/SUNSET/DISCOVERY FALLS. Spend a day in this area and visit four waterfalls with very different personalities. One is tall and skinny, another barely a waterfall at all but a wonderful swimming hole, a third is a typical Ozark waterfall along the Ozark Highlands Trail (OHT), and finally a surprise—a beautiful waterfall high up in a hanging valley that I discovered one day while frantically looking for a direct way back

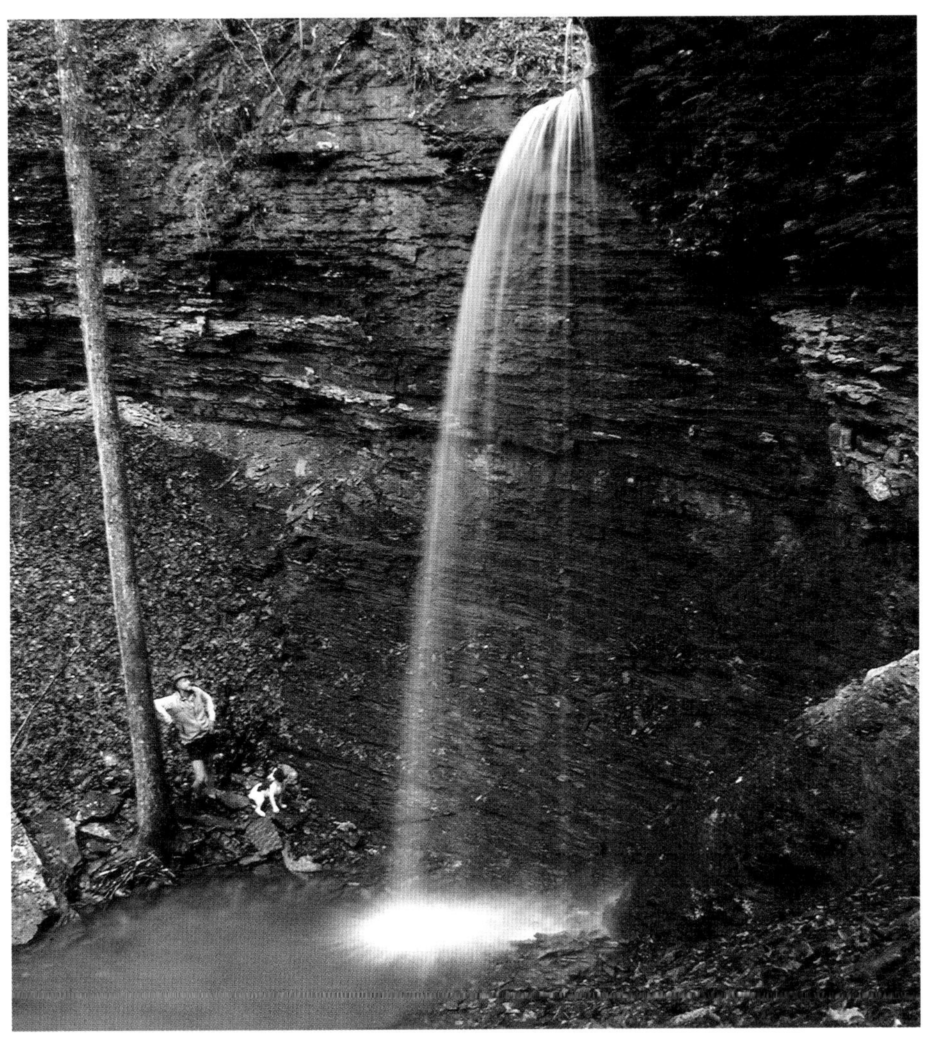

Bear Skull Falls

to my car as darkness overtook me.

To get to the parking area from the community of Ozone, take Hwy. 21 north 6.7 miles and TURN RIGHT onto CR#5570/FR#1003 (it becomes CR#5680). Go 6.9 miles and TURN RIGHT onto CR#5671/FR#1004. Go 5.1 miles and PARK where the OHT crosses the road **(35.66644, -93.34691)**. **OR** from Haw Creek Campground, take Hwy. 123 south 3.3 miles and TURN RIGHT onto CR#5741/FR#1003 (becomes CR#5680) and go about 7.7 miles and TURN LEFT onto CR#5671/FR#1004. Go 5.1 miles and PARK where the OHT crosses the road.

Get on the OHT and take it to the west from the parking area. It will work around a hillside and down into a big drainage, eventually coming to **Bear Skull Falls** at 1.5 (there is a short blue-blazed spur trail that goes over to the base of it). From there the trail continues down the hill on an old road all the way to the bottom of the hill and hits a jeep road. The OHT continues straight across the road at this point, but you want to TURN RIGHT and hike along the jeep road about .2 and you will come to **Slot Rock** down on the LEFT.

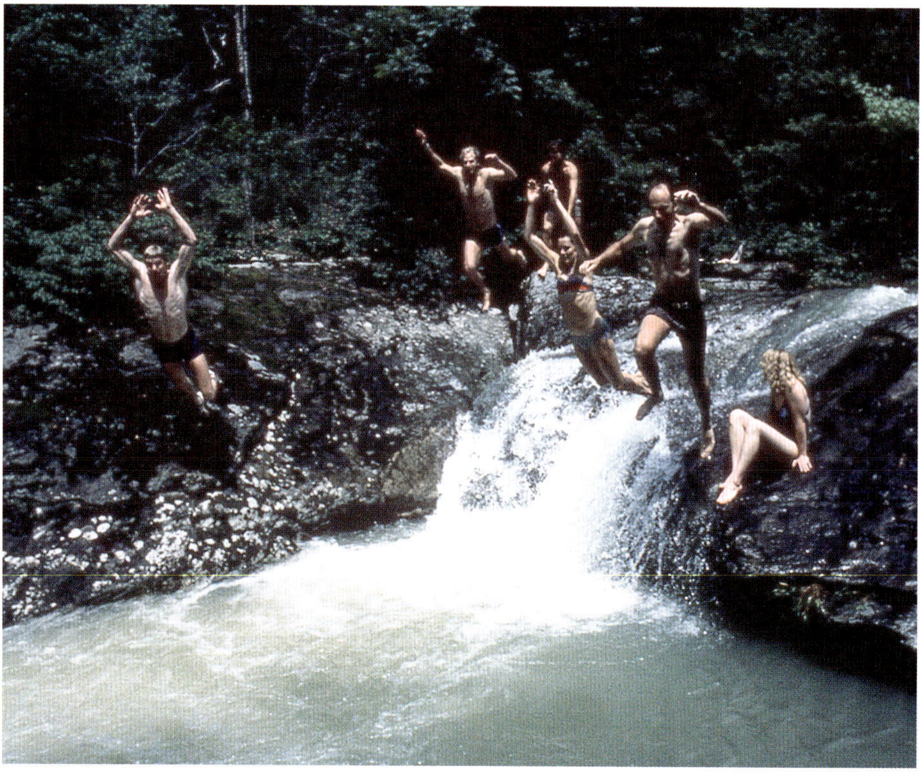

Slot Rock (above), **Sunset Falls** (below)

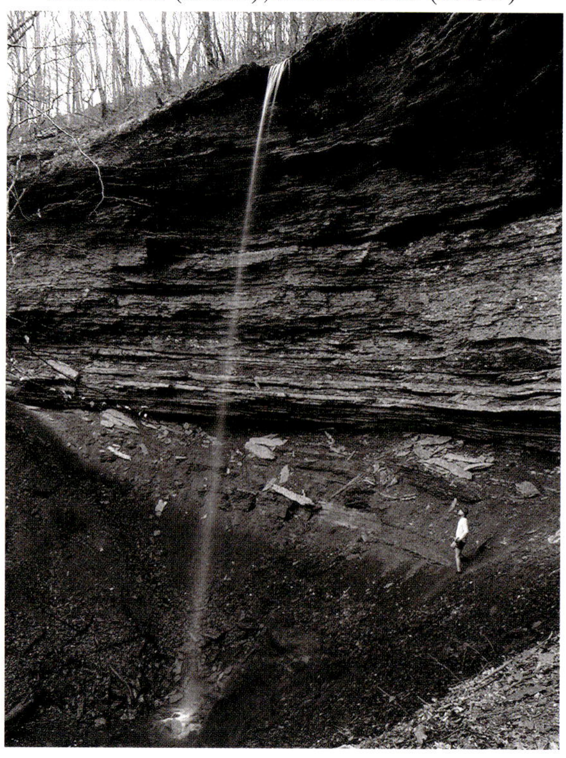

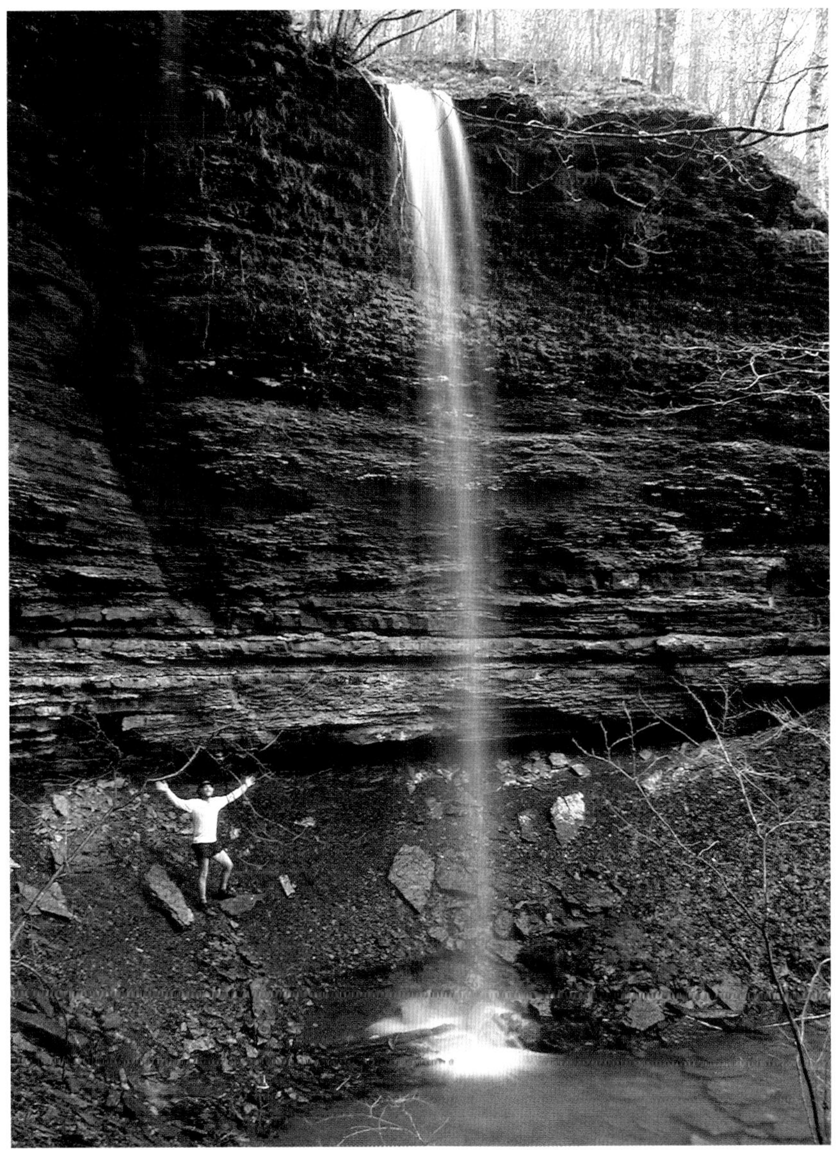

Discovery Falls

From **Slot Rock** continue along the jeep road upstream, then begin to bushwhack upstream when the road crosses the creek (you don't cross the creek). Follow the main creek until you come to a side creek coming in from the right (the jeep road has rejoined you now). TURN RIGHT and head up this side creek—it will take you to **Sunset Falls** if you bear right at the fork (the last part is *really* steep). The left fork goes up to another nice falls that is not pictured (19' tall). Above that falls is **Discovery Falls**, but you have to get up on top of the bluff to get to it.

From the 19' falls, follow the bluffline back to the LEFT a couple of hundred yards and find a way up to the top of the bluff. Then TURN RIGHT and make your way *carefully* around to **Discovery Falls**. It's a 3.1 mile trip back out, a tough uphill hike.

Emergency contact: Johnson County Sheriff, 479–754–2200 Dogs are OK.

Spainhour Falls –16′

7.2 miles roundtrip (if you hike), medium hike, GPS helpful

GPS **35.62165, -93.46502**

Lucy Falls –17′

Add .6 to above, medium bushwhack, GPS recommended

GPS **35.61227, -93.45959**

Aspen Falls – 37′

Add .4 to above, medium bushwhack, GPS recommended

GPS **35.61329, -93.45720**

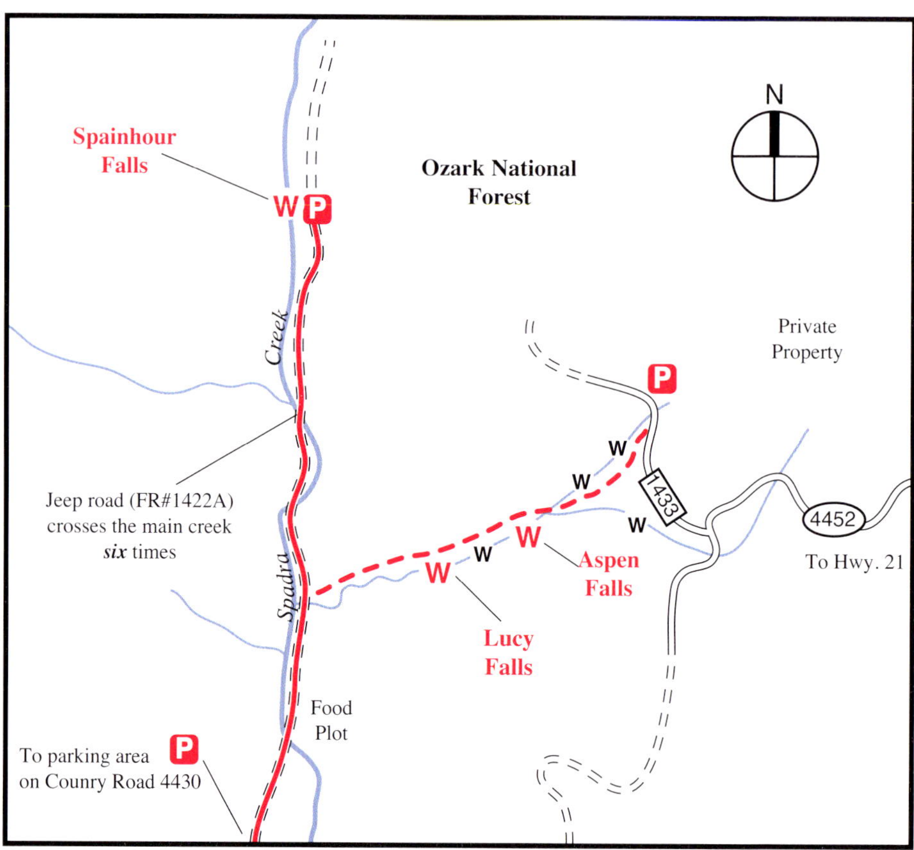

SPAINHOUR/LUCY/ASPEN FALLS. When we went to visit the locals' favorite Spainhour Falls, we took a little detour on the way back and discovered a narrow gorge filled with waterfalls. Our pups, Aspen and Lucy, had a big trip that day, and they are the ones that led us up into the gorge, so I have named a couple of the falls after them. The normal way into this area is to drive/hike along a jeep road. The road is pretty rough, and crosses the creek six times, so when the water is high this route isn't a real possibility for driving. During normal water flow you can probably get all the way to the falls if you have a *serious* 4wd and don't mind the abuse, thus saving you the 7.2-mile hike. Most folks that I know simply park at the county road and hike in, making a day of it. If the water is really high, or you want an extreme challenge, there is another way in, which requires a *steep and difficult* bushwhack. There are

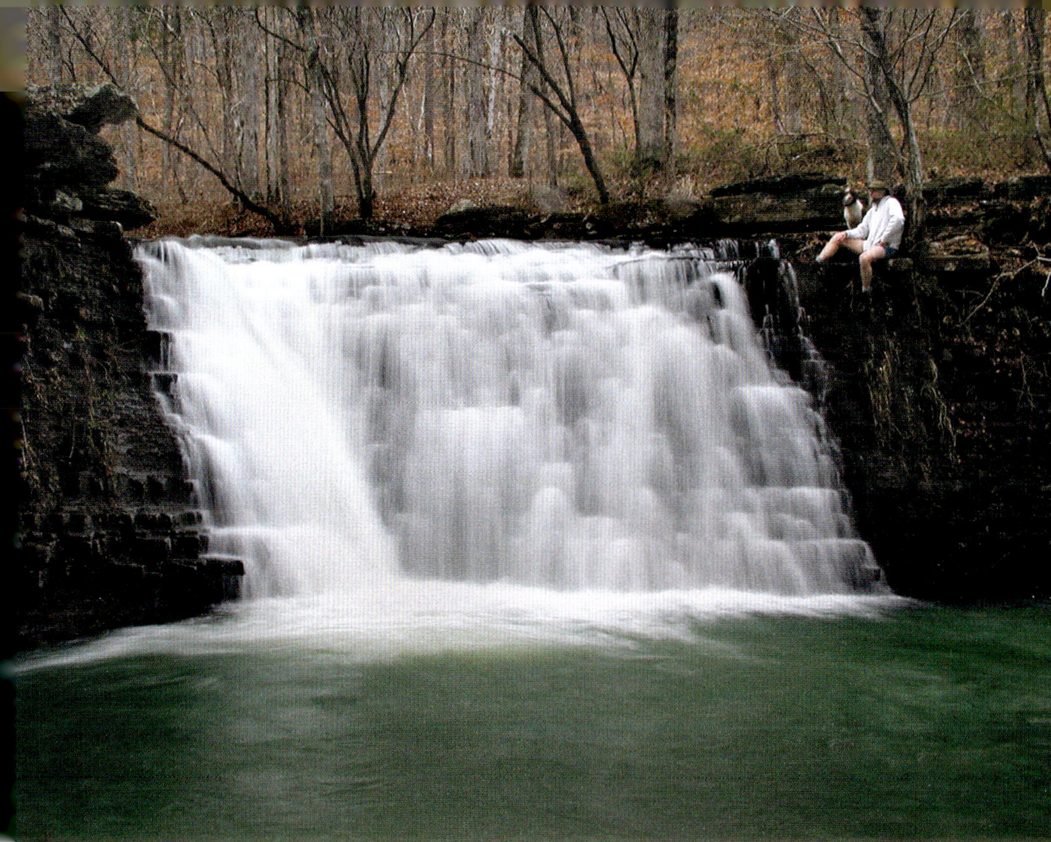

additional waterfalls along the way, but it is a really tough trip, and only recommended for the seasoned bushwhacker who doesn't mind a broken ankle or two.

To get to the main route take Hwy. 21 north from Clarksville 6.3 miles and TURN LEFT onto CR#4400 (paved). (7.7 miles south of the Ozone Post Office.) This is the road to Zion Church, and the turn is just north of a little store on Hwy. 21. Go 2.0 miles and TURN RIGHT onto FR#1430 (paved, then gravel). Go .6 miles and TURN LEFT onto CR#4418 (this turn is right after the road becomes CR#4451). Go 1.0 miles and TURN RIGHT onto CR#4420/FR#1422. Go .6 miles and TURN RIGHT onto CR#4430, then go .2 miles and TURN LEFT onto FR#1422A (jeep road) and PARK (or continue in your 4wd).

Hike/drive on this road for a total of 3.6 miles as it follows Spadra Creek upstream, crossing it six times, and you will find the falls down on the left. At the second crossing of the creek around 1.2 there may be a neat waterfall pouring off the bluff on the other side. After the fourth crossing at 2.4 there is a wildlife food plot on the right. The next side creek that you come to after this (it comes in from the right or east) is the creek that leads up into the gorge that is filled with waterfalls—TURN RIGHT and bushwhack up the creek to **Lucy and Aspen Falls** (about .5 up to Aspen—turn the page for photos). This is also the creek that you would come down if bushwhacking in from the difficult route.

To reach the parking spot for the alternate bushwhack into the falls, CONTINUE on Hwy. 21 north from the Hwy. 76 turnoff another 5.0 miles (2.7 miles south of Ozone) and TURN LEFT onto CR#4452. Go 1.3 miles and TURN RIGHT onto FR#1433 at the fork in the road. Go .3 and PARK just past a little creek crossing **(35.61682, -93.45305)**. You may be able to look out from the road on that last little bit of the drive and see big bluffs way down in there—that is where you are headed, and those bluffs are above Aspen Falls.

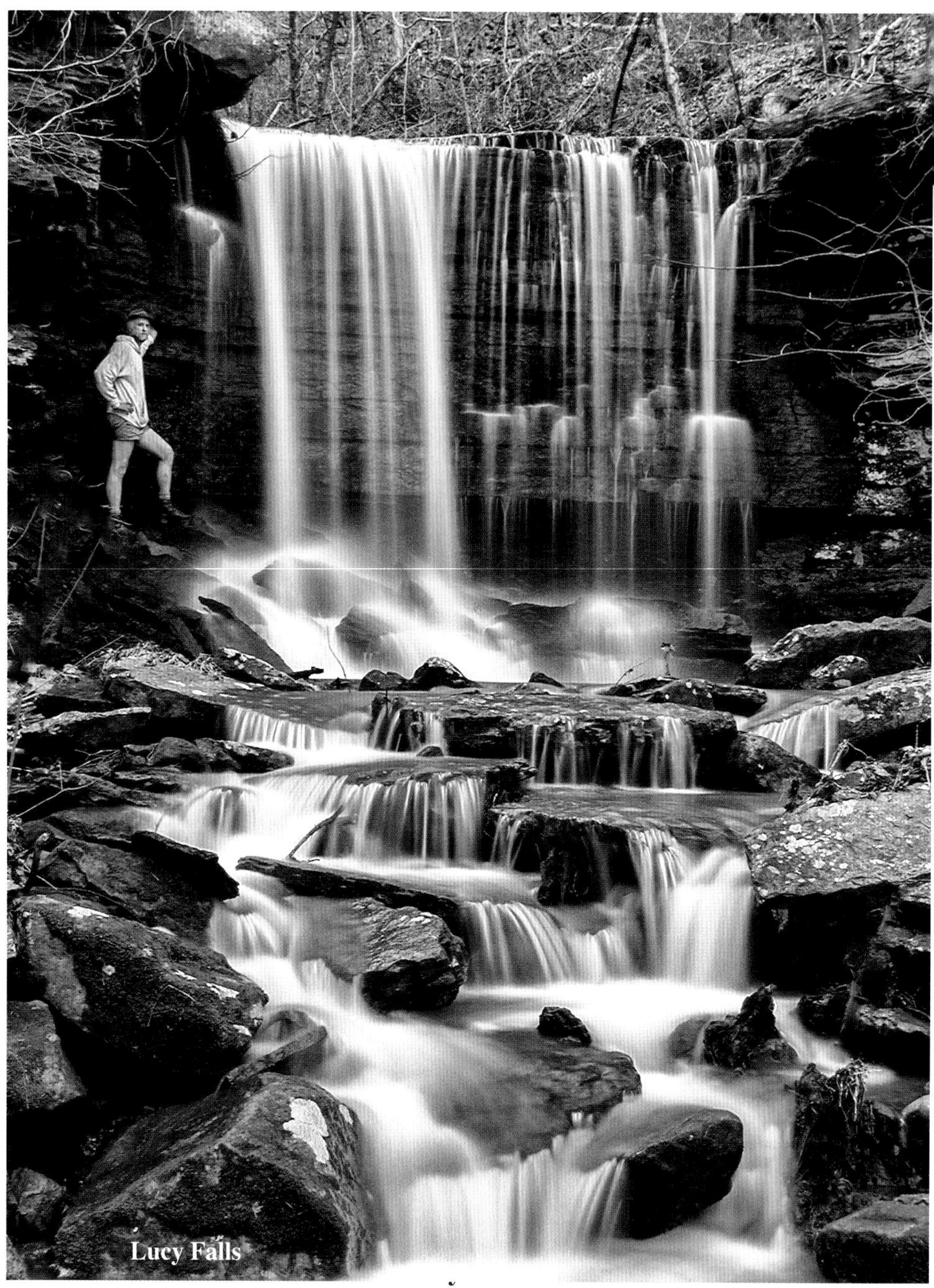

Lucy Falls

From the parking spot you will want to hike down that little creek you just crossed—it drops off in a big hurry, and is an *extremely* steep and difficult bushwhack and not for the inexperienced or faint of heart. But when the water is running it is a spectacular gorge filled with boulders and lots of whitewater. You will pass a couple of waterfalls—one a pretty good-sized one—cross a four-wheeler trail, then intersect with a second creek coming down from your left (on the way back out you may want to take this fork—it comes out up on top on the road that you came in on, near where the road forks).

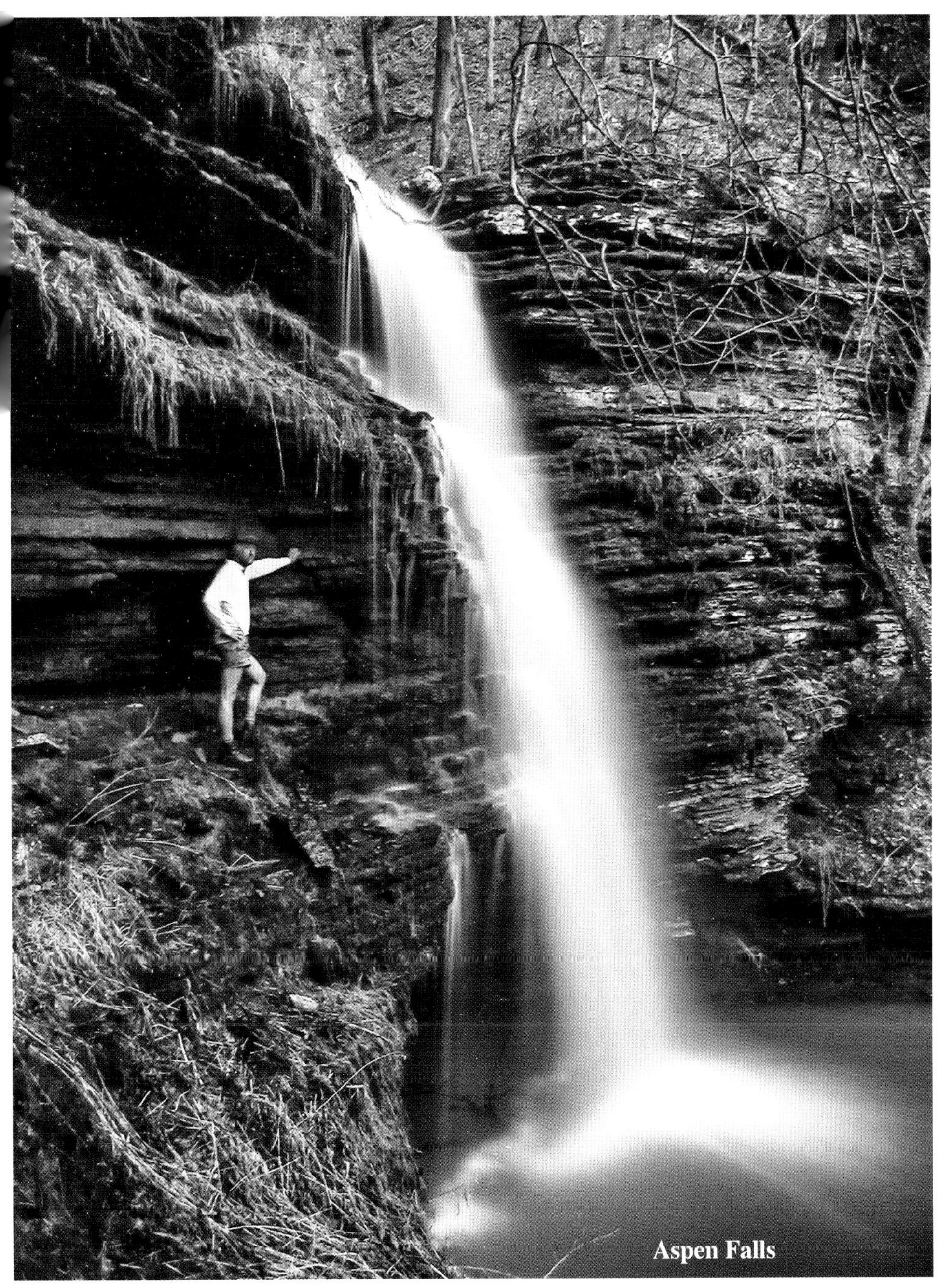
Aspen Falls

From the intersection of the two creeks, just keep on heading down the gorge, and soon you will come to the top of **Aspen Falls** at .5, and the big bluffline that is up on the right. Keep on going past another waterfall, and then **Lucy Falls**. It is all fabulous scenery! You will finally hit bottom around the .9 mark and land on the jeep road—TURN RIGHT and follow the jeep road, crossing Spadra Creek twice, and **Spainhour Falls** will be on your left at 1.8. Good luck on the bushwhack out!

Emergency contact: Johnson County Sheriff, 479–754–2200 Dogs are OK.

January Falls –10′

.2 easy GPS **35.59008, -93.32615**

Anniversary Falls –17′

.7 easy+ bushwhack GPS **35.58751, -93.33214**

Three Tier Falls – 29′

1.0 moderate bushwhack GPS **35.58740, -93.33453**

Bigger Rock Falls –15′

1.2 moderate+ bushwhack **GPS 35.58774, -93.33585**

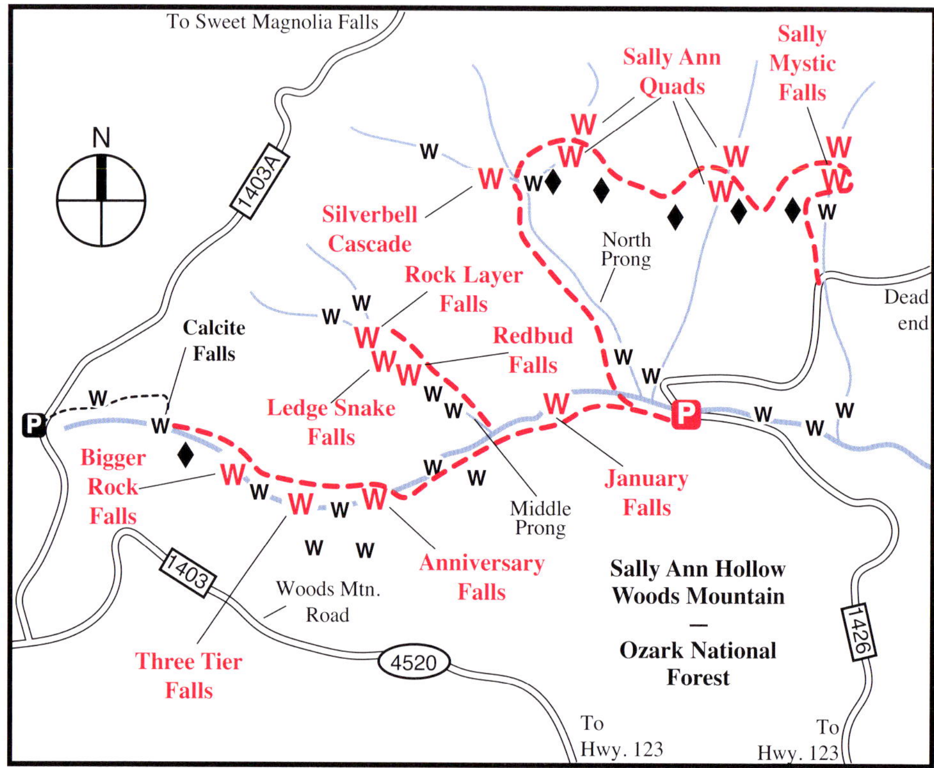

SALLY ANN HOLLOW WATERFALLS. Originally documented and shared on his personal blog by Brent Robinson (long before social media), Sally Ann Hollow is one of MANY drainages on the greater Woods Mountain area that he and others found and named. Names of the falls that Brent shared will remain the same, along with a few new waterfalls and names that have been found since. I will include waterfalls from several of these areas in the following pages. Danny Hale/TAKAHIK guidebooks and others on social media and elsewhere have lots and ***lots*** of additional waterfalls and info available for you to explore. As always, if you find a waterfall that speaks to you, feel free to name it anything you like!

From Hwy. 7 at Pelsor take Hwy. 123 west 21.9 miles and TURN RIGHT onto FR1426. OR from Hagarville take Hwy. 123 north 4.7 miles and TURN LEFT onto FR1426. Go 1.6 miles and PARK (**35.59020, -93.32299**) just before crossing the creek (if you are like me), or cross the creek and park on the other side if you dare to.

EASY to BLACK DIAMOND ♦, all bushwhacking, but social trails will develop to many.

SO MANY WATERFALLS in this one drainage, with lots of EASY ones—some right next to the road—many medium ones, and a few pretty difficult BLACK DIAMOND ♦ slopes for the extreme adventure seekers. And unlike a lot of drainages, you begin at the bottom and hike uphill, which means the return trip is always going to be downhill, yippie! There's not enough room to include specifics or photos for even half of these, but I'll share some of my favorites and you can pick and choose from all the rest.

There are several cascades and waterfalls located right next to the forest road that you drive in on and park along—just pull over out of the way and ENJOY them! I usually park just before the road crosses the creek, so my directions will begin there.

I'm going to visit three different prongs/forks/hollows—the MAIN/SOUTH Sally Ann Hollow, MIDDLE PRONG, and NORTH PRONG, all from the main parking spot.

MAIN/SOUTH PRONG FALLS. Follow the main Sally Ann Hollow creek on the LEFT side upstream from the forest road crossing—you will pass the entrance to the North Prong on your right, on the other side of the creek—we'll get to that later.

Heading up the main creek there's a road trace some of the way up, and probably social trails will develop, but mostly you just stay near the creek. The first couple of waterfalls are easy to get to, but as the old road trace disappears the terrain will get steeper and the hiking more difficult. Just keep going from one waterfall to the next until you've had enough—then turn around and head back downstream.

January Falls is really close at .2—there's kind of a little grotto on the right side of it. There are several waterfalls as you continue upstream—are beautiful and interesting and worth some time to stop and enjoy. At .4 you will pass the Middle Prong creek that joins from the right—we'll get back to it later.

Continue up the main creek as the hillsides on either side of the creek get closer in and steeper, and soon you will come to **Anniversary Falls** at .7. Things start to get more interesting (aka—more rugged and beautiful!) as you reach Sadie Falls and others.. During high water there are also a couple of really nice waterfalls in short side canyons on the left (one of them is 32' tall!).

At 1.0 is **Three Tier Falls**, a wonderful SSS with 3x the visual pleasure! Continue on up if you can past what is called Big Rock Falls (no photo provided), up to what I labeled as **Bigger Rock Falls** at 1.2 (aka Sally Ann Hollow Falls). This is where most folks turn around and go back—save plenty of time to see what you missed on the way up!

BONUS. I've got one more waterfall for anyone who wants to stretch themselves just a little bit more. Continue up the creek—BLACK DIAMOND SLOPE ♦ past a waterslide to 43' **Calcite Falls** at 1.35 (**35.58880, -93.33728).** See page 326 for photo and alternate route and parking location at the top). The big bluff up to the right has a lot of calcite formations on it.

Emergency contact: Johnson County Sheriff, 479–754–2200 Dogs are OK

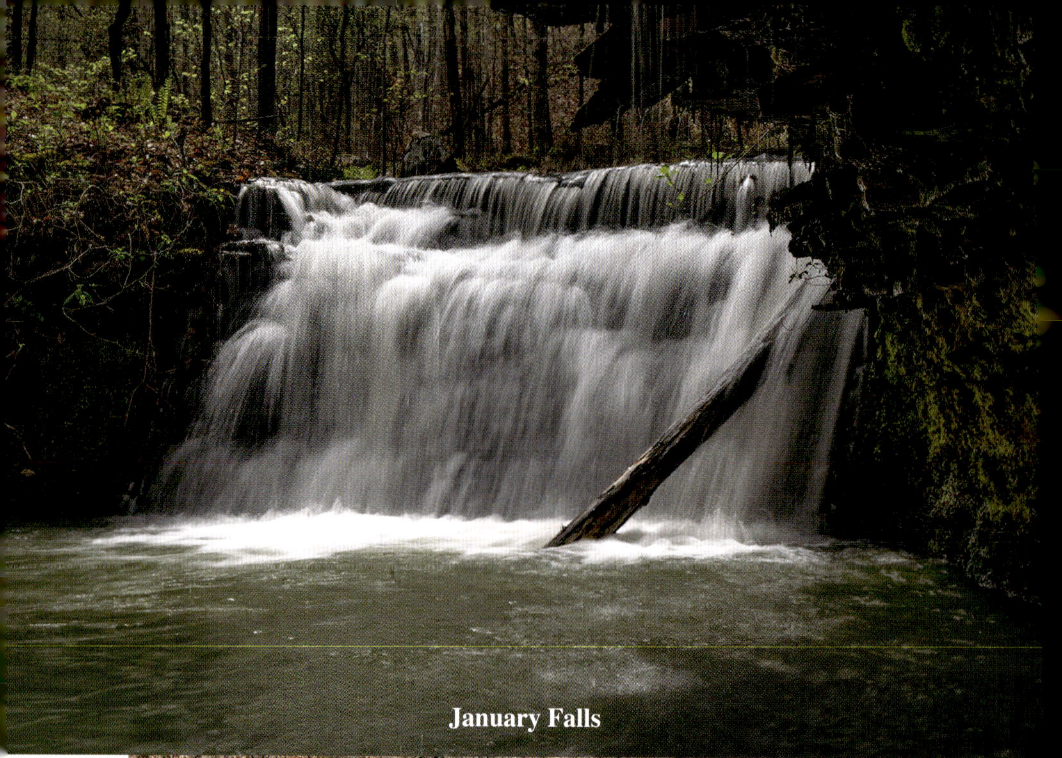

January Falls

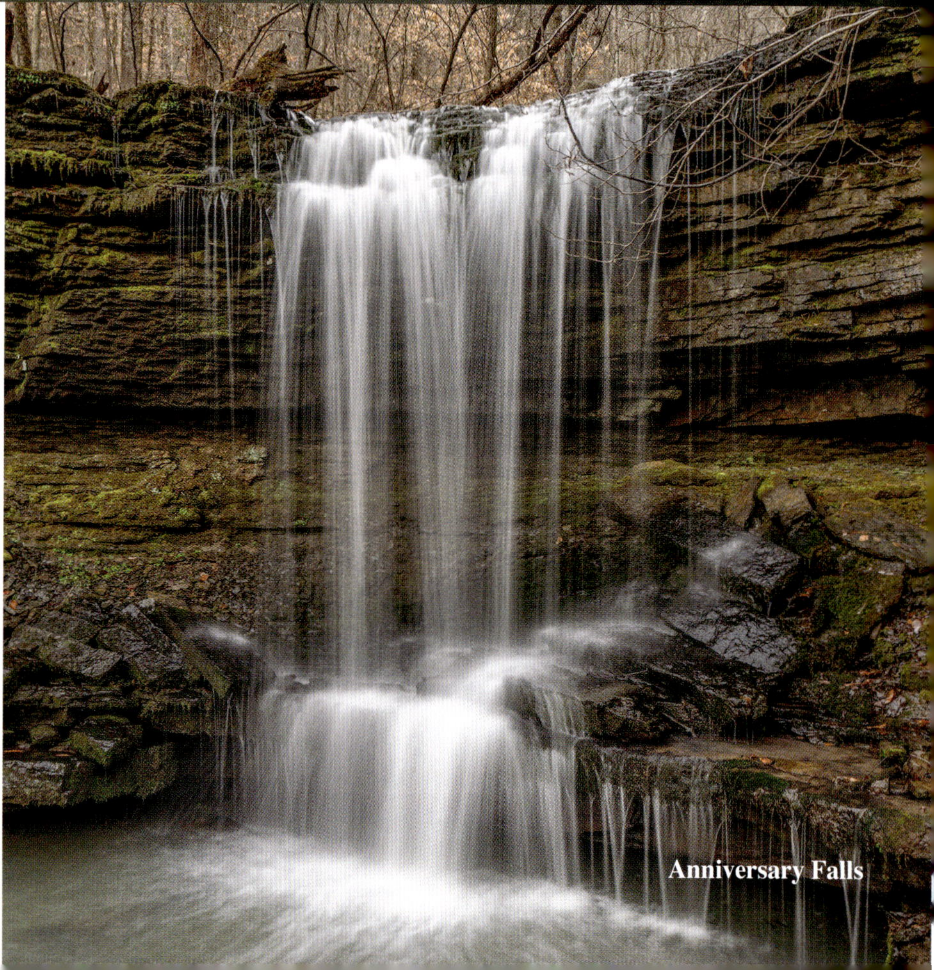

Anniversary Falls

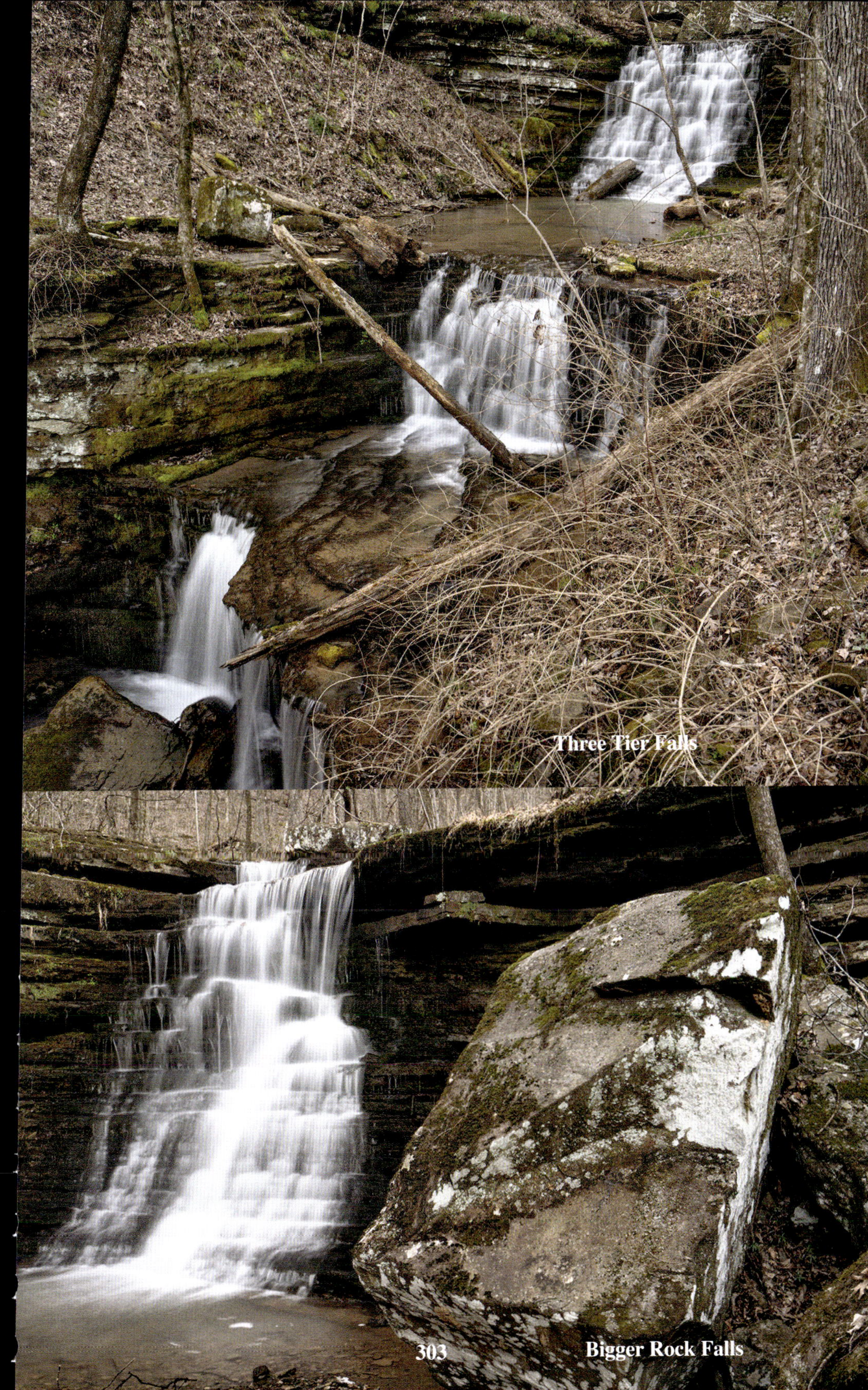

Three Tier Falls

Bigger Rock Falls

Redbud Falls – 36′

.6 medium+ bushwhack GPS **35.59075, -93.33155**

Ledge Snake Falls – 54′

.7 difficult bushwhack GPS **35.59094, -93.33174**

Rock Layer Falls – 17′

.8 difficult bushwhack GPS **35.59104, -93.3318**

1.6 mile roundtrip for all three falls

See map on page 300

MIDDLE PRONG FALLS. The MIDDLE PRONG is much shorter with fewer waterfalls but there are some really nice ones—rated more difficult due to the STEEP terrain.

From the main parking spot head up the main creek past January Falls, cross the creek when you can, and continue upstream to the middle prong intersection at .38—TURN RIGHT and follow this creek upstream. You will pass a couple of nice falls as the terrain gets steeper, up to **Redbud Falls** at .6. In spring you can hardly see the waterfall for the redbud TREES—it's amazing! This begins a three-falls SSS area, especially when the redbuds are blooming.

From **Redbud** climb UP and around on the RIGHT, then to the left below a ledge/bluff to the base of **Ledge Snake Falls**. Yes there WAS a snake tucked away along the ledge and someone I know (me) put his hand right on top of Mr. Snake—YIKES!

From there I had to climb up to the LEFT and back around to the creek for the final waterfall in this trio, **Rock Layer Falls** at .8. Maybe more falls above to explore!

Emergency contact: Newton County Sheriff, 870–446–5124 Dogs are OK.

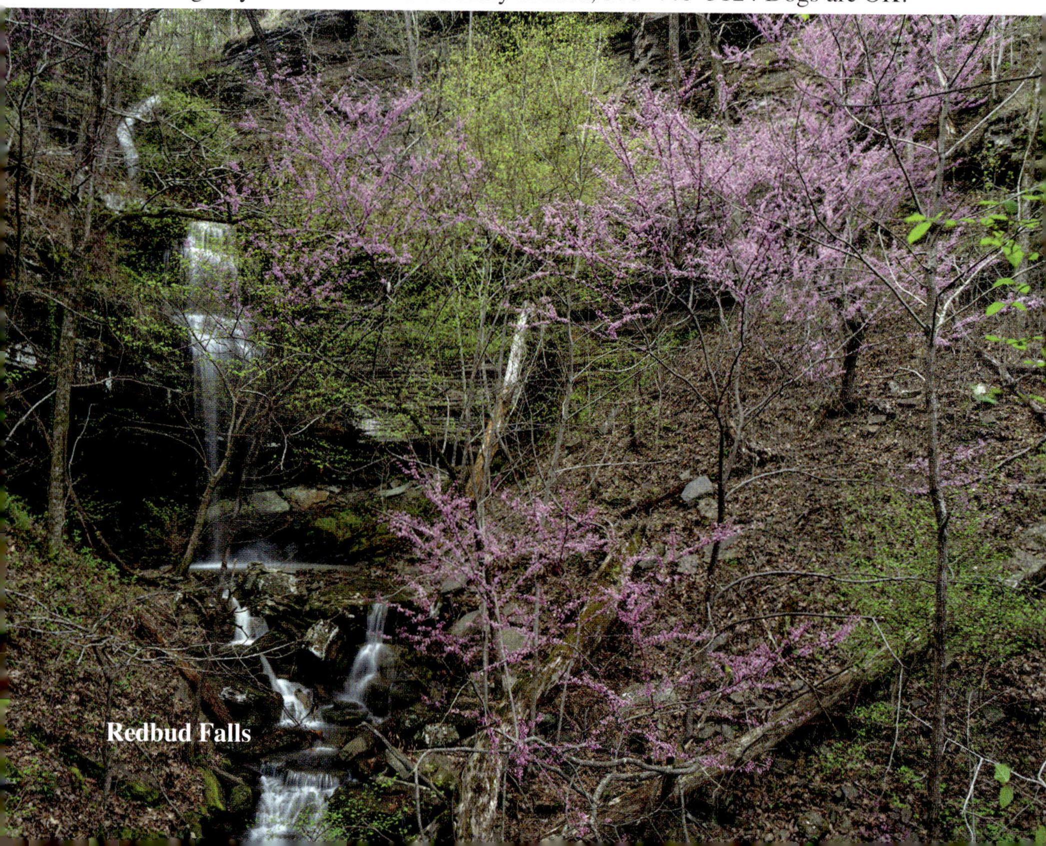

Redbud Falls

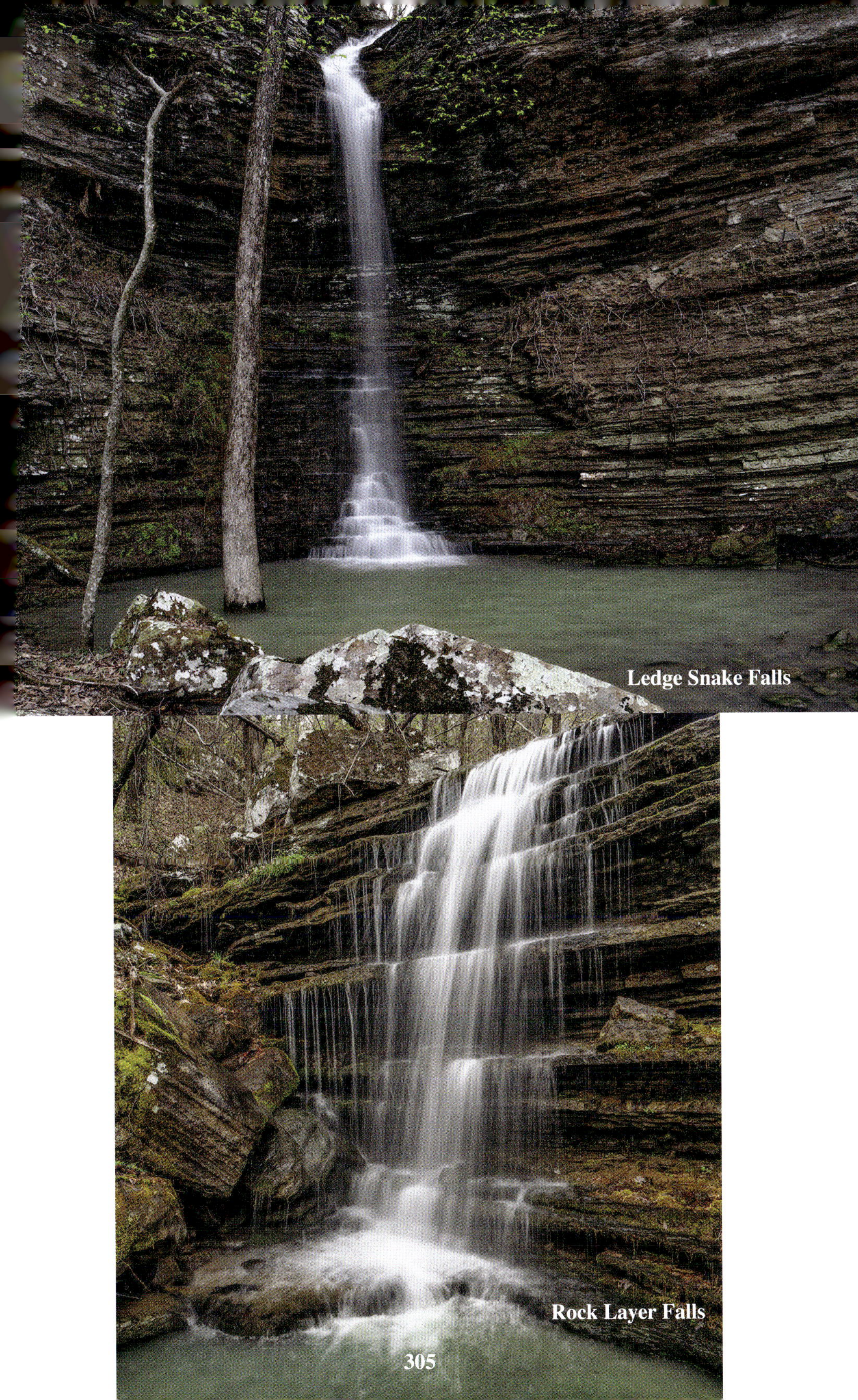
Ledge Snake Falls
Rock Layer Falls

Silverbell Falls – 27′

.6 mile easy+ bushwhack GPS **35.59534, -93.32782**

Sally Ann Quads West – 81′ & 27′

.7 mile medium bushwhack black diamond ♦ GPS **35.59616, -93.32602**

Sally Ann Quads East – 85′ & 23′

1.1 mile difficult bushwhack black diamond ♦ GPS **35.59503, -93.32169**

Sally Ann Mystic – 69′ & 30′

1.4 mile difficult bushwhack black diamond ♦ GPS **35.59540, -93.31794**

2.1 mi roundtrip for all falls, black diamond slope ♦

See map on page 300.

NORTH PRONG FALLS. OK, back to the main parking spot, head upstream past the first drainage coming in from the right, then TURN RIGHT and go up the second drainage—this is the North Prong of Sally Ann Hollow. Bathtub Falls is just ahead (no photo). Continue upstream pretty easy hiking to .6 where you can see three different drainages come together at almost the same spot, and of course it's all an SSS!

First, just upstream on the LEFT is **Silver Bell Falls** that cascades from a side drainage (named after silver bell trees that I found blooming in this area—they are quite beautiful and unexpected!) Secondly, the main stream continues straight ahead in a series of boiling cascades that seem to go on upstream forever. And finally, on the RIGHT is a pretty darn nice waterfall that joins the main creek—we're going to TURN RIGHT and follow that creek on up to the big bluff line above it.

The hillside above the falls is partly a BLACK DIAMOND ♦ slope so take your time—you can see the thundering waterfalls above almost immediately. At the top of the climb at .7 is the first set of **Sally Ann Quads West**—81' tall top waterfall and 27' tall lower. (there's more above but it's quite a climb to get up there) The falls and the amazing BLUFF of course are an SSS!

To reach the second set of the Quads TURN RIGHT and follow the base of the bluff as best you can (it breaks down and opens up along the way)—much of this is BLACK DIAMOND ♦ slopes and thick thorn bushes for company. Follow as the bluff line curves around to the LEFT into another drainage, and you will come to **Sally Ann Quads West** at 1.1.—85' tall top waterfall and 23' tall lower. Every time I visit this one the wind is blowing the waterfall back and forth, a lot like Hemmed-In-Hollow Falls does.

OK, now you've been to the Sally Ann Quads! How about a BONUS set of waterfalls? This one is tough to get to and also pretty rough to get back down from. Continue along the base of the bluff and follow as it curves out and then back LEFT into the hillside and finally to **Sally Ann Mystic** at 1.4.—69' tall top falls, 30' tall lower falls, PLUS another three falls below. Scramble down the steep hillside ♦ to a point where you can look up and see FIVE waterfalls to the top!

Continue down the steep slope through a thorny mess to the road below at 1.6—TURN RIGHT and follow the road down to the parking spot at the bottom of the hill at 2.1. YEA, YOU MADE IT!

Emergency contact: Johnson County Sheriff, 479–754–2200 Dogs are OK

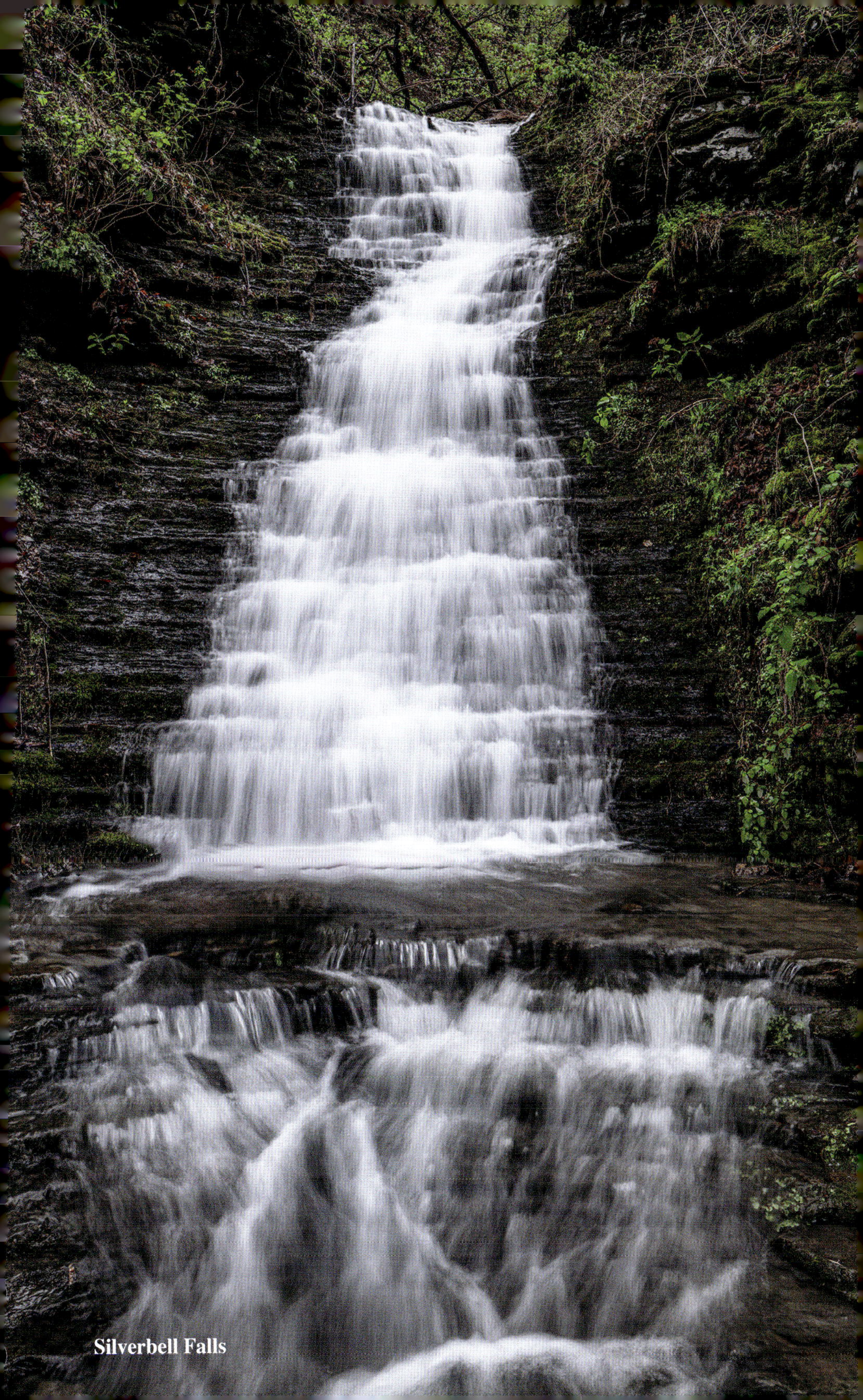
Silverbell Falls

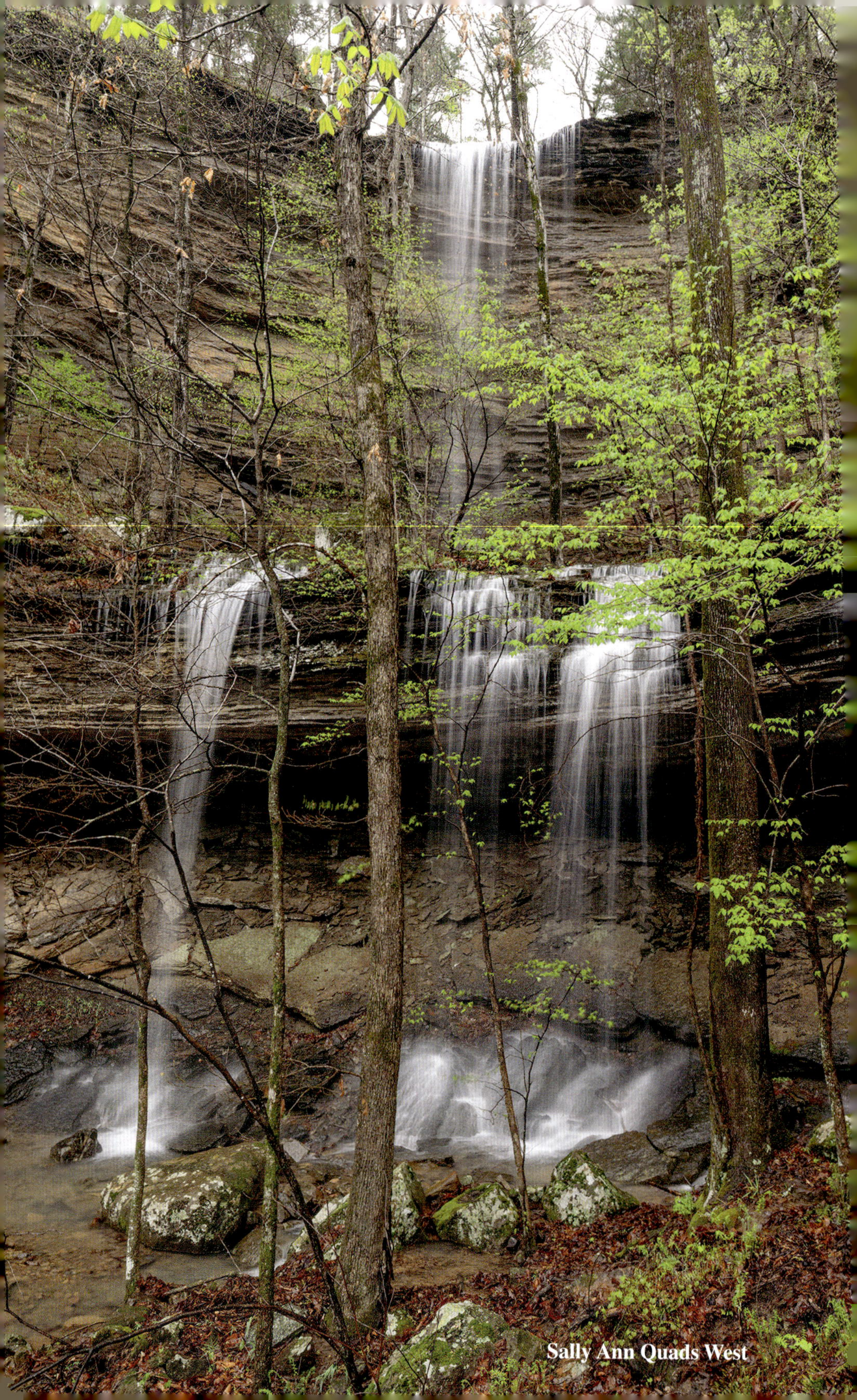
Sally Ann Quads West

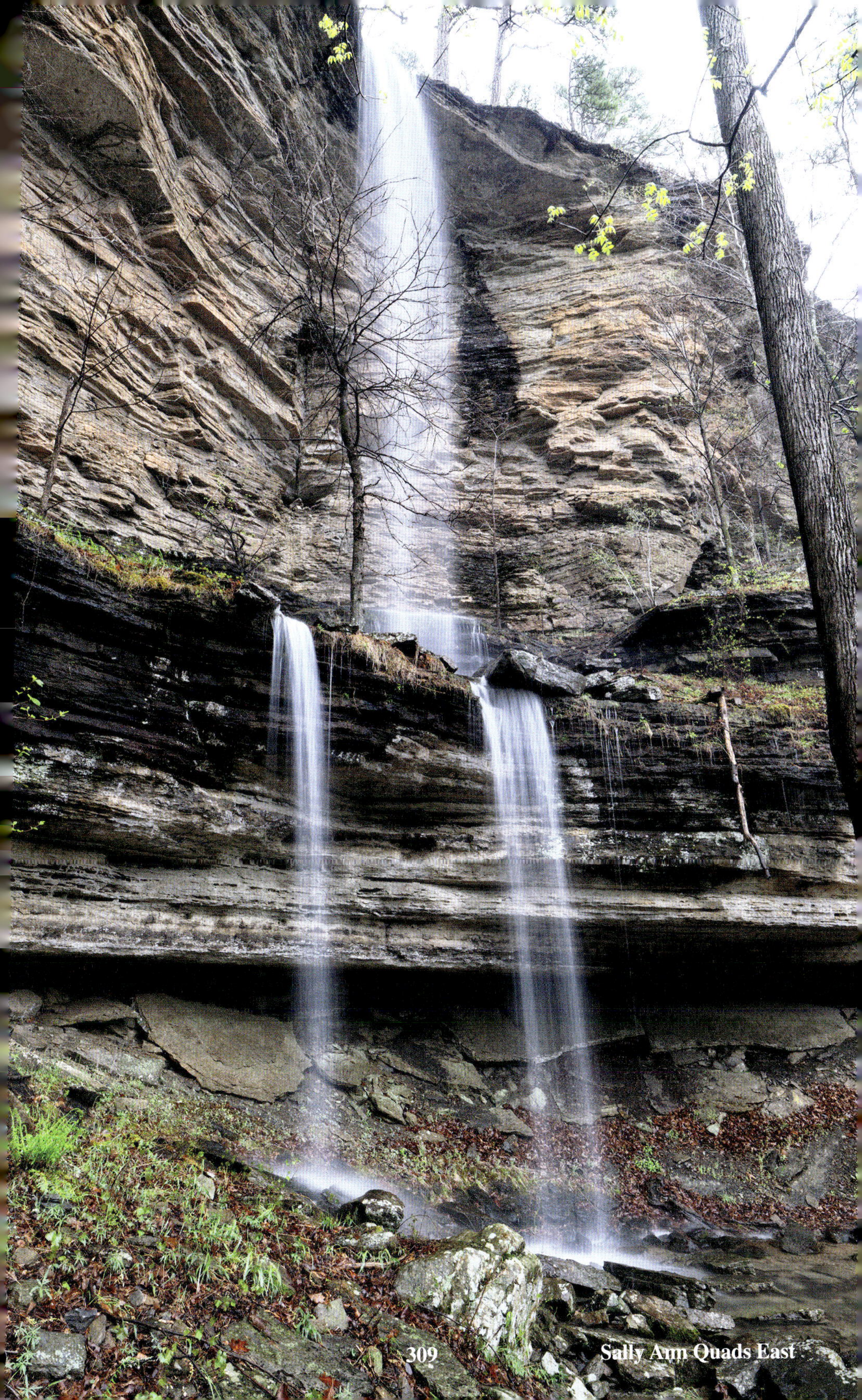

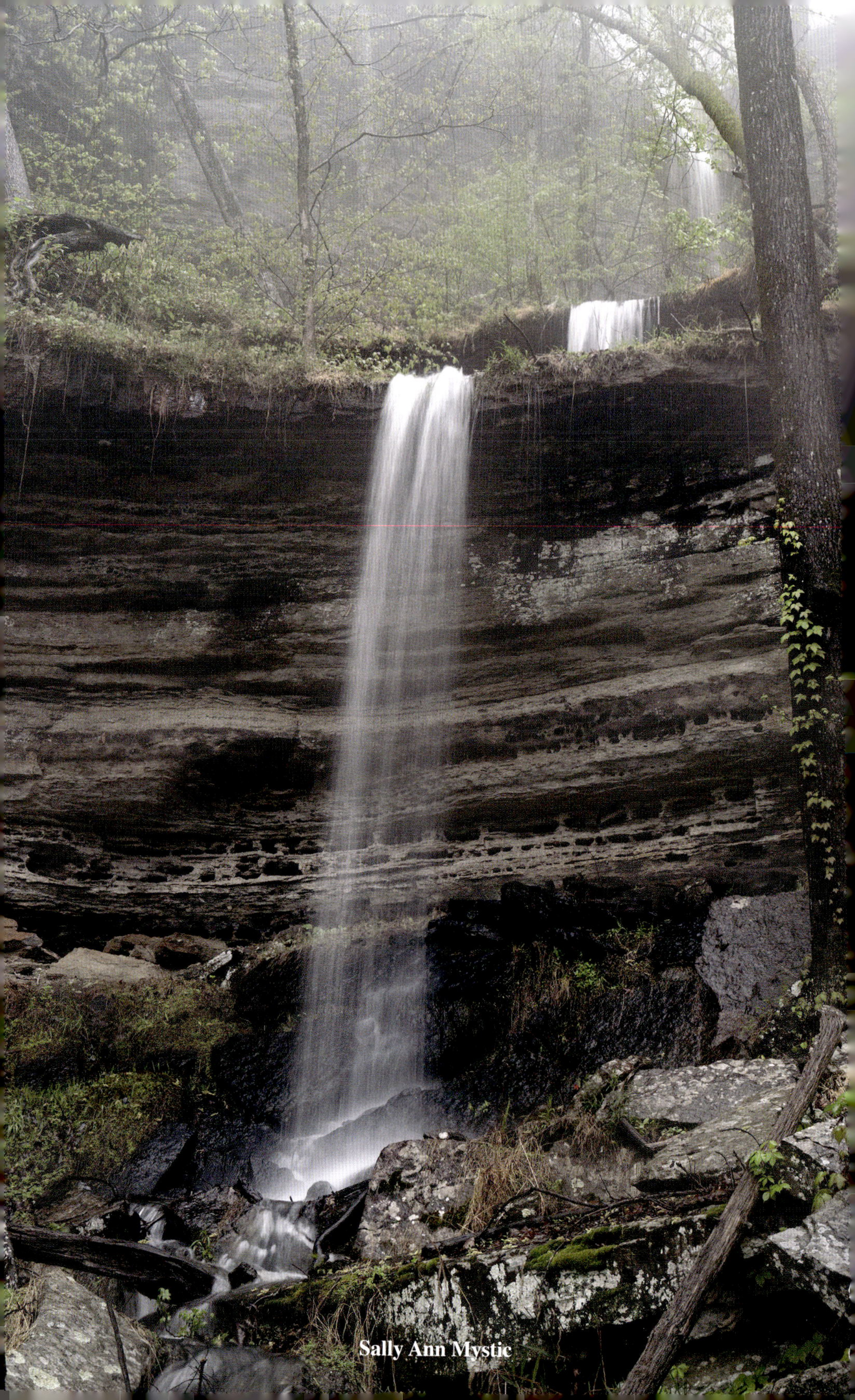
Sally Ann Mystic

Sweet Magnolia Falls – 35′

.7 mi roundtrip for all three falls, black diamond slope ♦

GPS **35.61825, -93.32888**

Beechnut Falls – 57′

GPS **35.61873, -93.32926**

Hickory Falls – 24′

GPS **35.61876, -93.32920**

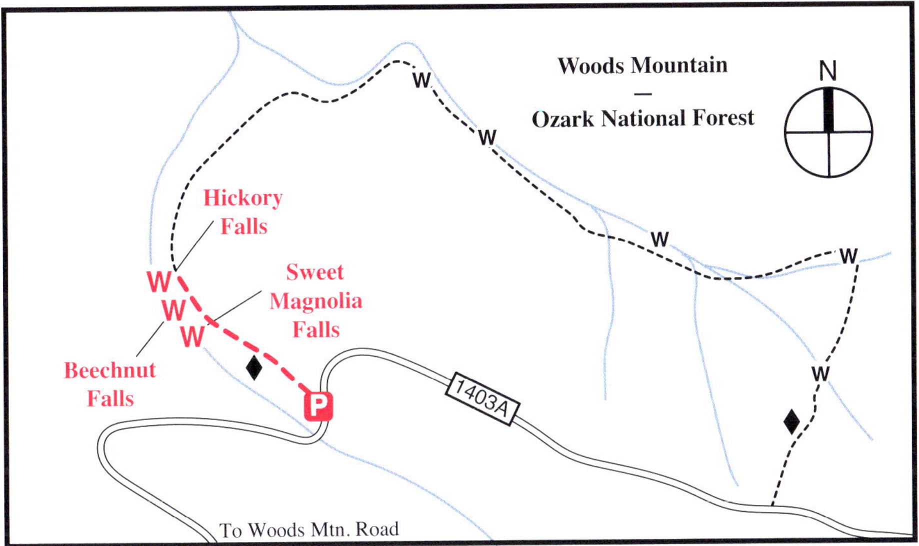

SWEET MAGNOLIA FALLS/BEECHNUT FALLS/HICKORY FALLS. From Hagarville, take Hwy. 123 north 4.1 miles (or from Pelsor 22.5 miles), to JC4540/FR1403/Woods Mtn. Road. Take 4540 west, 3.5 miles to FR 1403A and TURN RIGHT/NORTH. Go 3.9 miles and park (this is just after you cross the creek in a tight left turn).

From the parking spot just head into the woods on your left/north and follow the creek STEEPLY DOWNHILL—it's a BLACK DIAMOND slope ♦. You will soon come to **Sweet Magnolia Falls** at .2. Continue downstream to the big one, **Beechnut Falls**. Then one more nice falls below, **Hickory Falls** at .35.

IF you want a workout and adventure to visit some BONUS waterfalls (HIGH water would be best), continue downstream to a creek intersection at the bottom and TURN RIGHT. This is a beautiful stroll upstream to several 16'+ waterfalls on the creek, and towards the end of the low part of the drainage, on the left fork is a 37' one. Much of this an SSS, but you will have to gut it out CLIMBING up 700' on a BLACK DIAMOND slope ♦ to get back to your car (this detour adds about 2.0 miles for a total roundtrip of about 2.6).

Emergency contact: Johnson County Sheriff, 479–754–2200 Dogs are OK

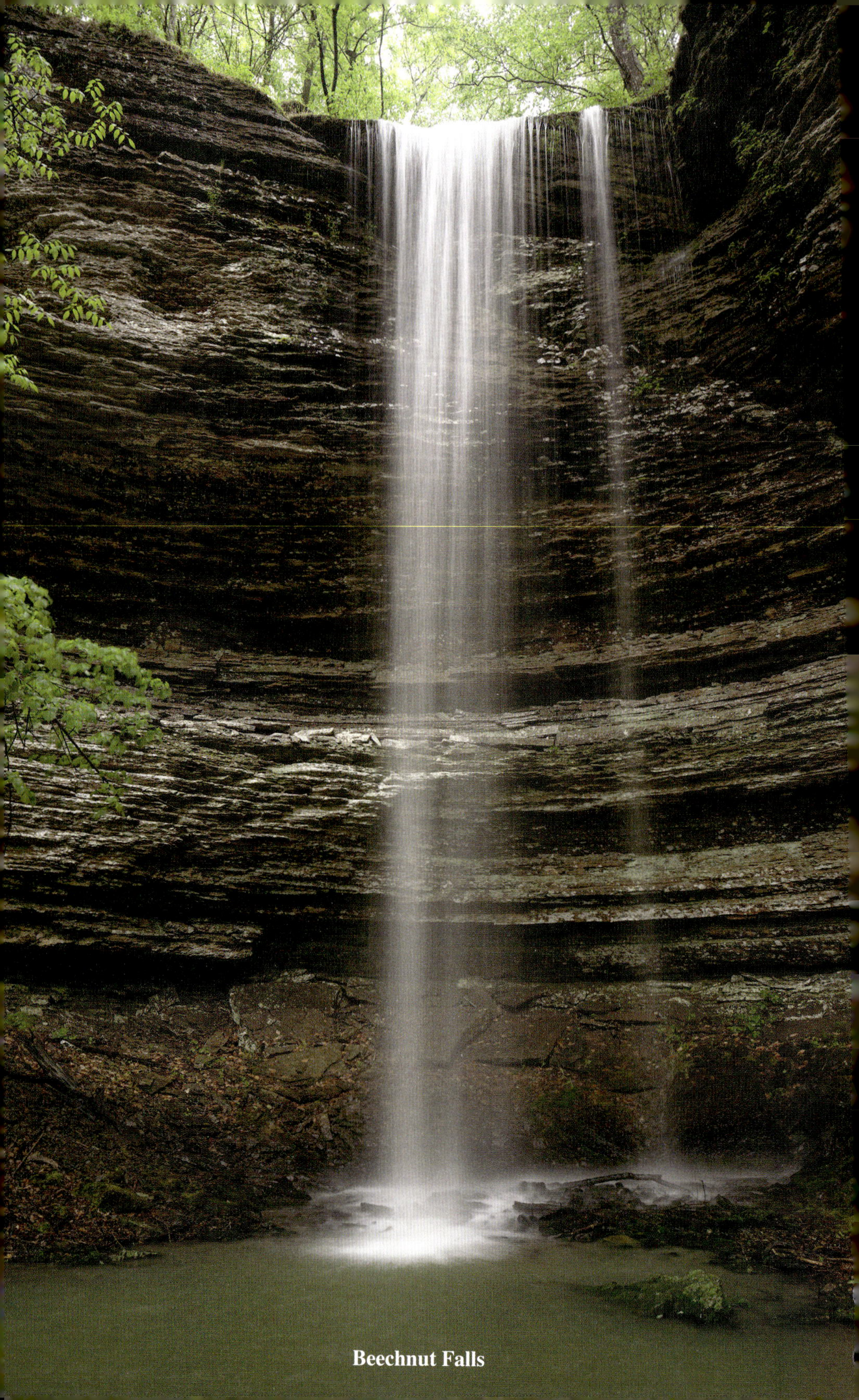

Beechnut Falls

Sweet Magnolia Falls

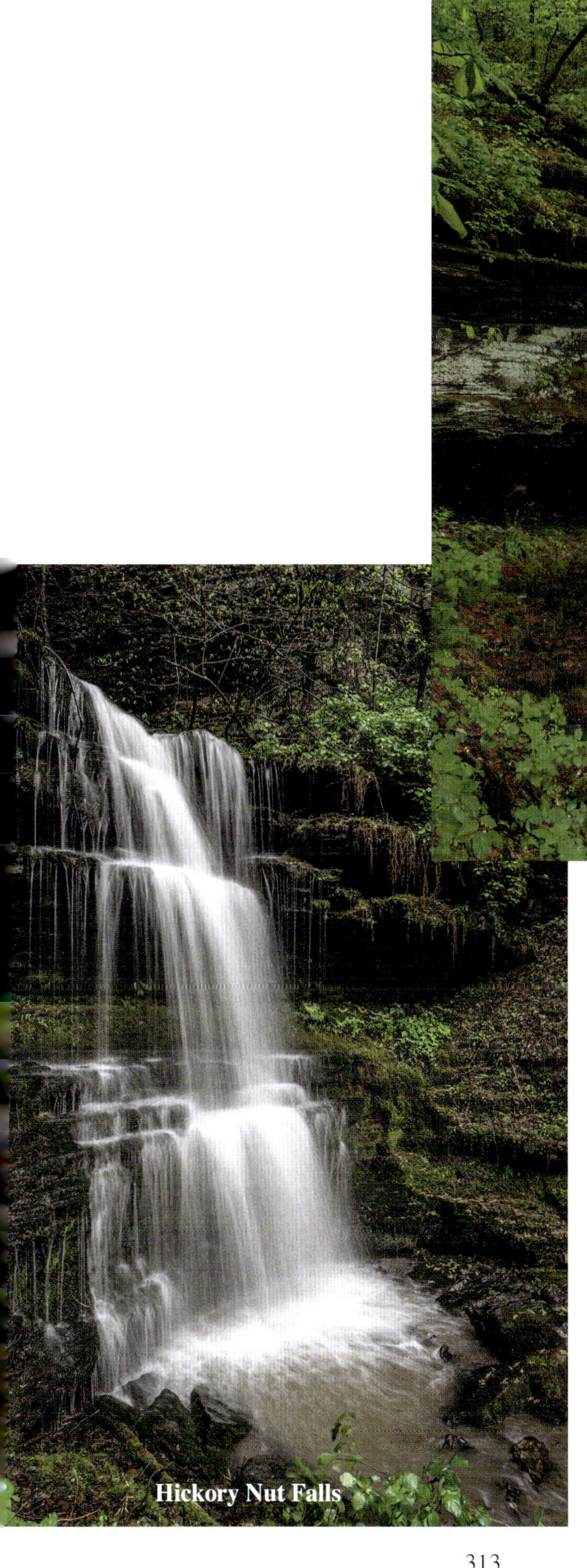
Hickory Nut Falls

Tombstone Falls –63′

.25 difficult bushwhack black diamond ♦ GPS **35.57903, -93.32857**

Danny's Hideout–35′

.26 difficult bushwhack black diamond ♦ GPS **35.57869, -93.32867**

High In Dry Falls – 53′

1.0 mile difficult bushwhack black diamond ♦ GPS **35.57985, -93.33452**

2.0 miles roundtrip for all three falls

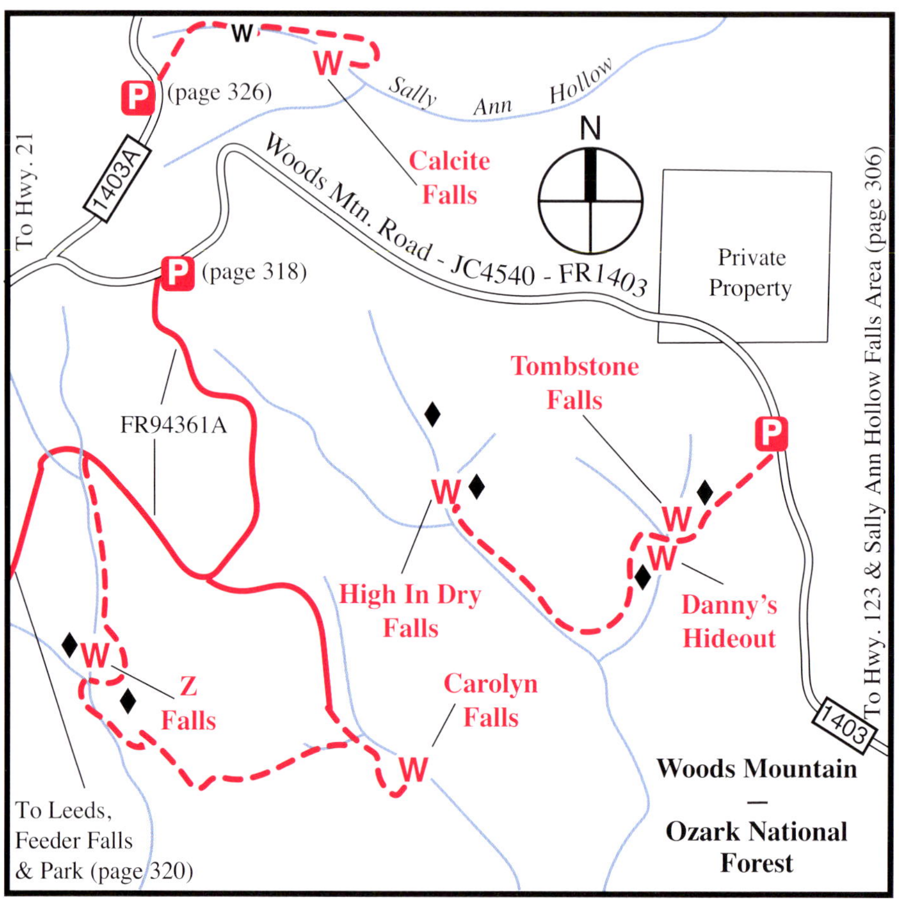

TOMBSTONE/DANNY'S HIDEOUT/AND HIGH IN DRY FALLS. This is the third set of waterfalls on Woods Mountain, with more to come! Tombstone Falls was the last new waterfall I found and named for this guidebook. It is tucked away high in a small drainage that pours over a really big bluff. It's so high it does need a lot of water to look good, so save this trip for when all the creeks and ditches are flooding.

Directions from Hagarville, take Hwy. 123 north 4.1 miles and TURN LEFT on JC4540/FR1403/Woods Mtn. Road (or from Pelsor 22.5 miles and TURN RIGHT). Take 4540 west for 2.2 miles and PARK where you can **(35.58055, -93.32575)**.

From the parking spot head directly into the woods (to the left/SW if you came from Hwy. 123). Thick woods at first but mostly level, then soon the hill turns into a BLACK

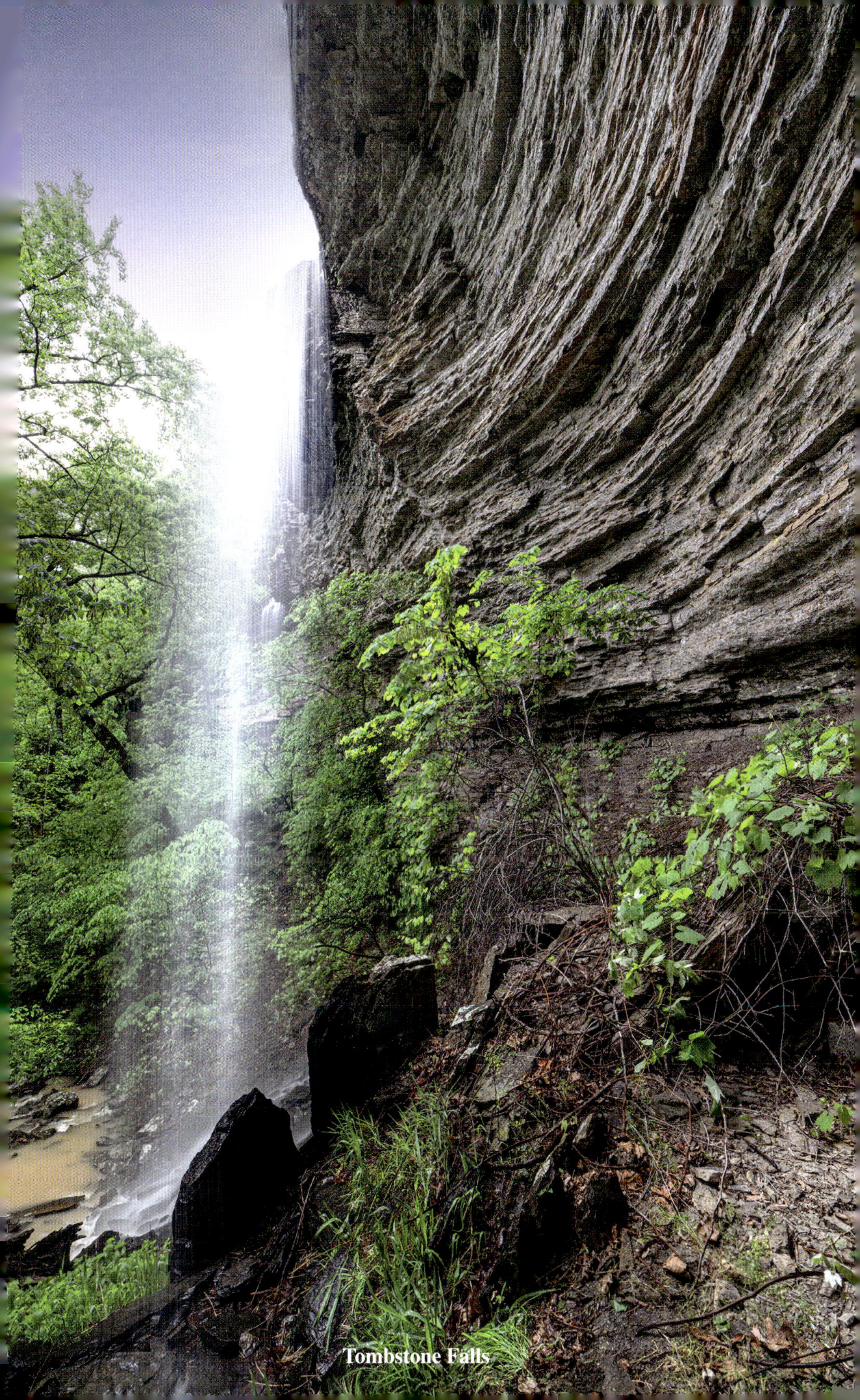
Tombstone Falls

DIAMOND slope ♦ and quickly drops a couple hundred feet. As you encounter a broken bluff and get below it TURN RIGHT and follow the base of the bluff over to **Tombstone Falls** at .25, an SSS for sure! Standing behind this falls taking pictures I realized I was as much in love with the layers of rocks in the bluff above as anything—oh my it's beautiful there! Can you see the tombstones?

Directly below **Tombstone** is **Danny's Hideout Falls**—I go to the RIGHT to get around the top and then down a steep bluff and into the shelter behind the falls—someone built a rock wall in the far corner, was it Danny?

Continue downstream past some smaller but quite wonderful waterfalls (including one up a side creek on the left) until you hit bottom—then TURN RIGHT and follow the creek upstream. There are a couple more nice waterfalls, including one in a moss-covered mini canyon. TURN RIGHT when the creek forks and continue upstream to **High in Dry Falls** at 1.0.

If you are headed back to the car then just continue UP the drainage as best you can (OR go back the same way you came). There are many small falls, water slides, and cascades—some are quite long and all are VERY slick! It's really one long SSS—but it's all so STEEP ♦ and slick you are better off keeping away from the creek and just scrambling up the BLACK DIAMOND slope ♦ to the top. Once you get up there just keep going out to the road at 1.3, then TURN RIGHT to get back to your car at about 2.0.

Emergency contact: Johnson County Sheriff, 479–754–2200 Dogs are OK

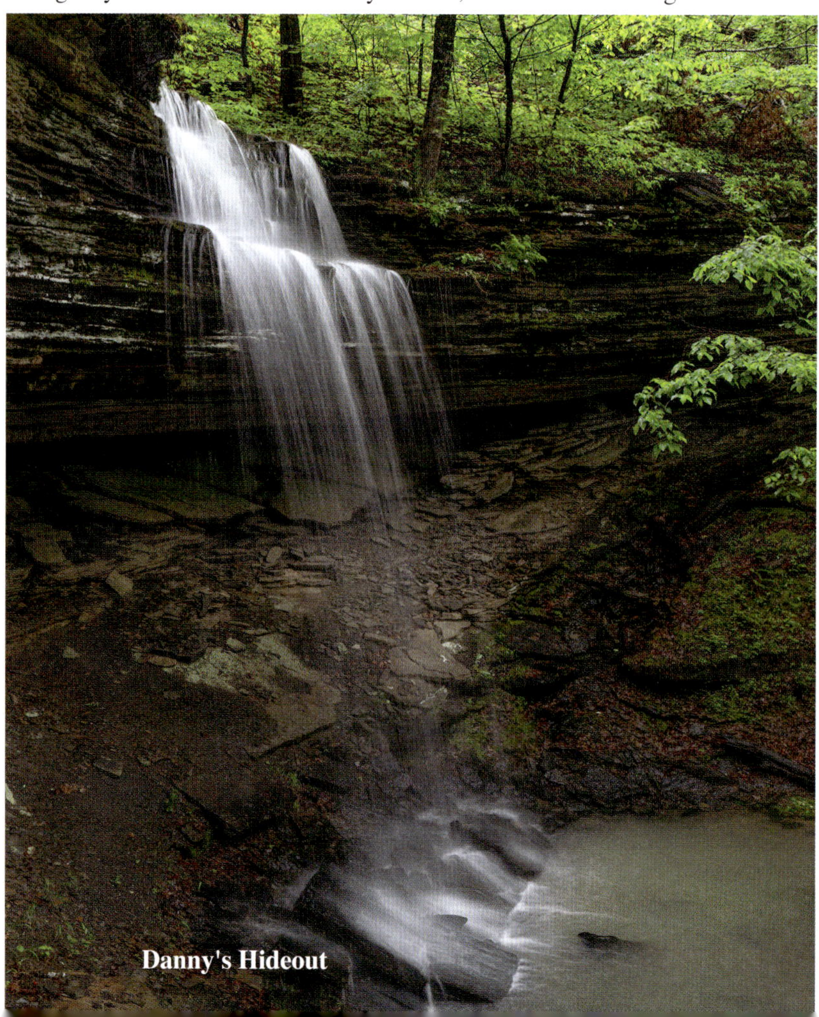
Danny's Hideout

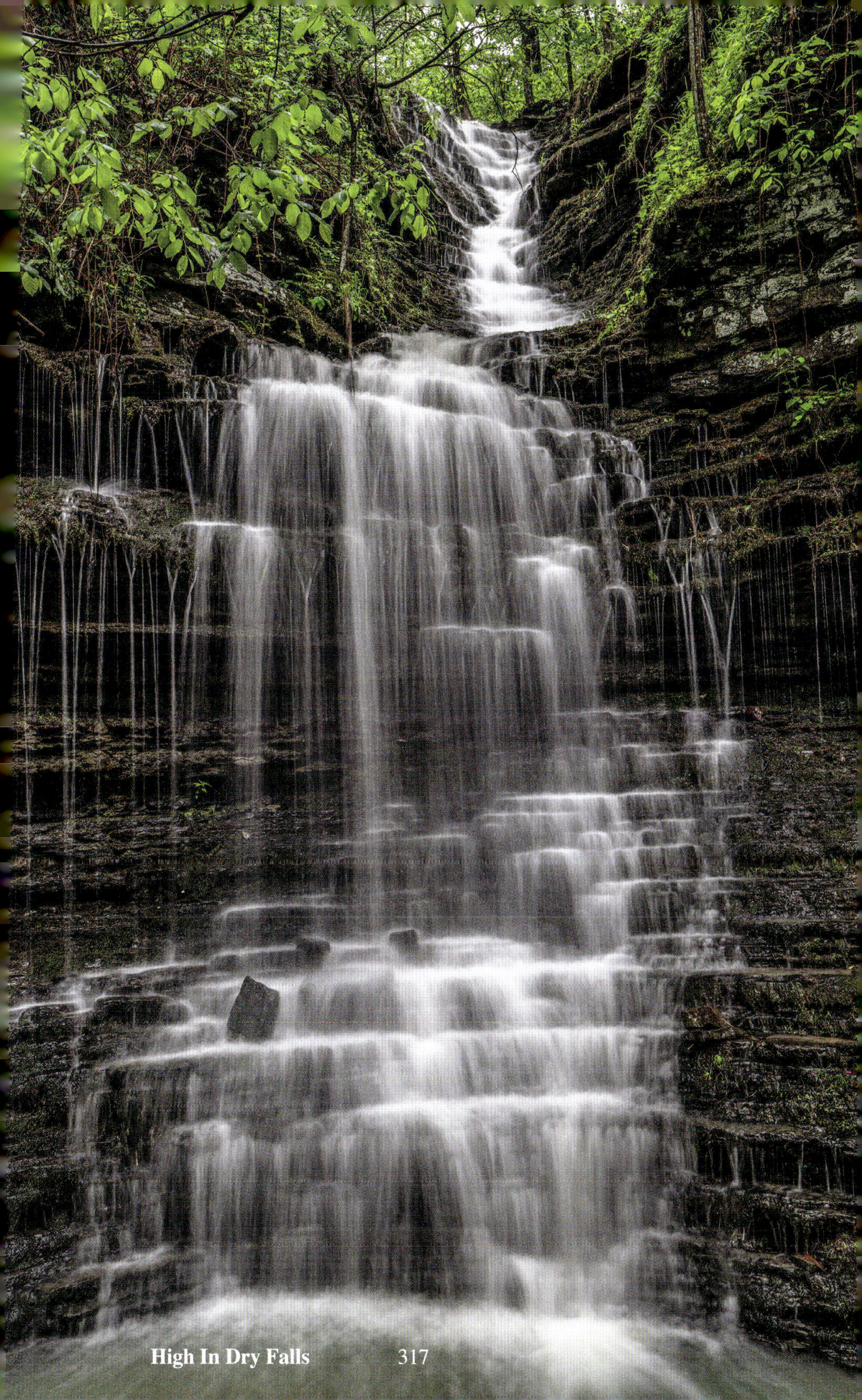

Carolyn Falls – 45′

2.2 miles roundtrip, difficult bushwhack at end GPS **35.57382, -93.33529**

Z Falls –67 ′

Add 1.0 miles to above, difficult bushwhack ♦ GPS **35.57631, -93.34338**

See map on page 314 for both falls

CAROLYN FALLS. From Hagarville: take Hwy. 123 north 4.1 miles and TURN LEFT on JC4540/FR1403/Woods Mtn. Road (or from Pelsor 22.5 miles and TURN RIGHT). Take 4540 west for 3.4 miles and PARK **(35.58419, -93.34161)**.

Head down the logging road as it heads steeply DOWN the hill (FR94361A—it connects to the parking area for Leeds Falls in 2.4 miles). Stay on the road to an intersection with the main logging road that joins from the right at .6, then continue to follow the original road as it goes TO THE LEFT and levels out. Go past one logging road on the right (it ends up in an old field), and then TURN RIGHT onto a second logging road/old trace at .9 (the main road curves away to the left). Stay on this road trace over a couple of dirt berms as it curves to the right and the straightens out.

There will be a creek down to the LEFT that the road follows—this is the creek that goes to the waterfall. You can drop down to the creek and follow it downstream to the falls, or stay on the road a while until it begins to curve around to the right into a drainage—then TURN LEFT and head steeply down the hill to the creek. Follow the creek past a nice waterfall to the top off the big falls, then TURN RIGHT along the top of the bluff until you can find a spot to scamper down, then back LEFT to the base of **Carolyn Falls** at 1.1. (Carolyn is Fireman Jeff's wife, special thanks to her for allowing Jeff to cart me all over the woods in search of waterfalls—they found this one while hiking together.)

Z FALLS. From **Carolyn Falls** go back up to the road trace you were following and head west away from the road and across the top of the flat ridge, then work your way down into the next drainage, very steep ♦ slope and large bluff (go-down near **35.57423, -93.34181**). Once you land on the creek below turn RIGHT and follow the creek upstream to **Z Falls,**

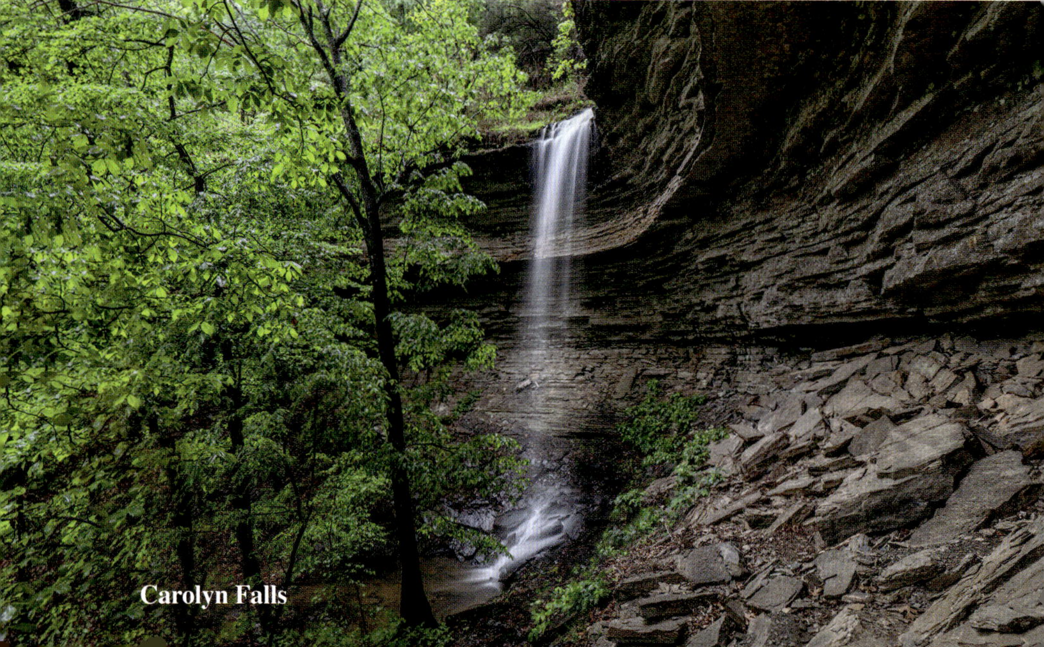

Carolyn Falls

about a mile bushwhack from **Carolyn Falls**. All of this canyon is an SSS! From the base of **Z Falls** I have made one trip clawing my way up a near-vertical ♦ slope just downstream on the right side of the falls and out to the top, then followed the creek upstream to the old forest road and back to the parking area. EXPERT ONLY. (or climb out of the canyon the same route you took to get down into it)

Emergency contact: Johnson County Sheriff, 479–754–2200 Dogs are OK

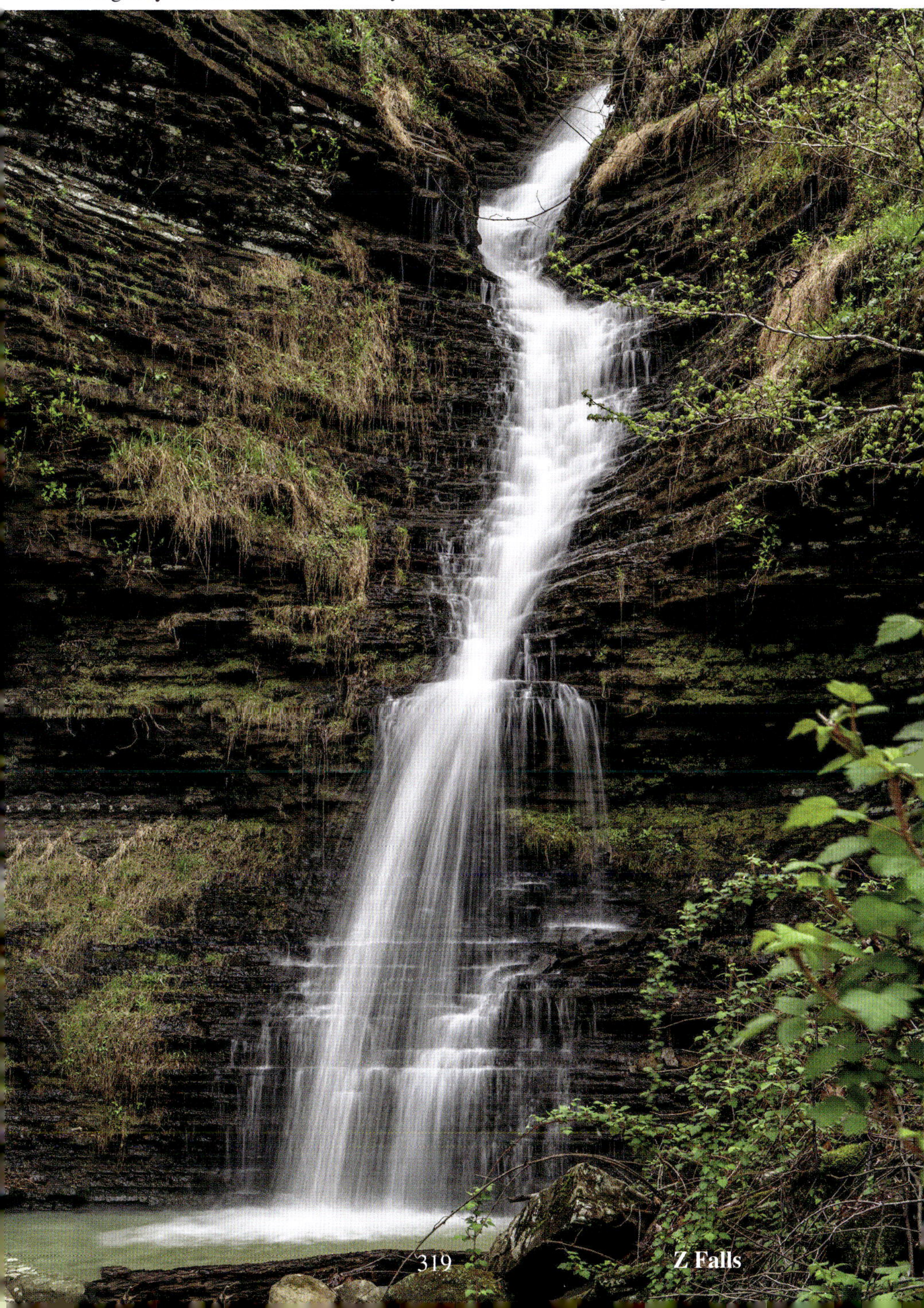

Z Falls

Four Step Falls/Feeder Falls –58′/42′

1.3 miles roundtrip, difficult ♦ bushwhack GPS **35.57622, -93.35566**

Leeds Falls & Paw Paw Falls –91′ & 23′

2.6 miles roundtrip, difficult ♦ bushwhack **GPS 35.57479, -93.34920**

Z Falls –67′

4.0 miles roundtrip (to top), difficult ♦ bushwhack GPS **35.57631, -93.34338**

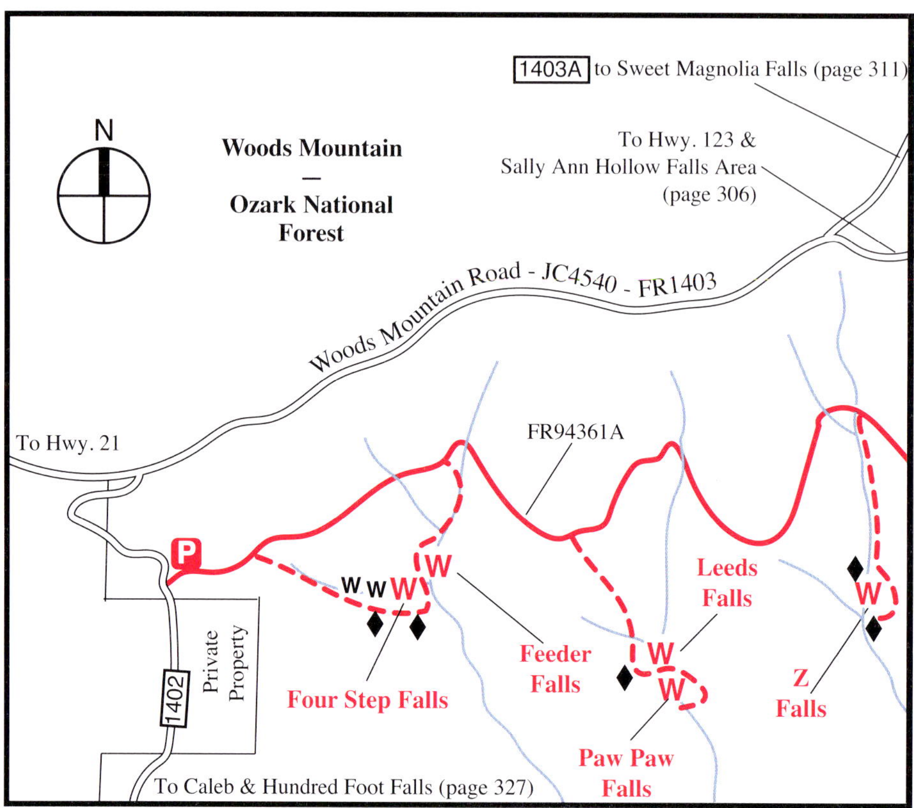

FOUR STEP FALLS/FEEDER FALLS/LEEDS FALLS/PAW PAW FALLS/Z FALLS

Directions from Hagarville: take Hwy. 123 north 4.1 miles and TURN LEFT on JC4540/FR1403/Woods Mtn. Road (or from Pelsor 22.5 miles and TURN RIGHT). Take 4540 west for 4.8 miles and TURN LEFT onto FR1402 (This is 1.2 miles beyond Carolyn Falls.), then go .4 miles and turn left onto jeep road FR94361A and PARK **(35.57628, -93.36307)**. This same jeep road connects to the parking spot for Carolyn Falls in 2.4 miles.

We'll be hiking this old forest road 94361A that runs along the top of the greater Dry Creek West and Dry Creek East areas providing access to the higher bluff line series of waterfalls by foot, bike and ATV (?). We'll visit a couple of spectacular falls in the Dry Creek West area, then visit one of the tallest waterfalls in Arkansas, Leeds Falls, and finally drop down to the top of Z Falls. The jeep road may be gated. It connects with the parking area for **Carolyn Falls** (see previous pages), which is an alternate route to get into this area from Woods Mountain Road..

From the parking area head along the road on the LEFT, down and around to the right, then back to the left, then TURN RIGHT and leave the road at **(35.57685, -93.36056)**, and head down into a little drainage. It will get STEEP in a hurry as you follow the creek, and in fact turns into a BLACK DIAMOND slope ♦, then comes to the top of a double-decker water slide falls that pours into a bathtub (**w**), then another slide, then another. And this begins an SSS area all the way down (in this case it also stands for "super slick as snot!").

Next is the top of a 54' falls (**w**), but you'll have to stay on the RIGHT side of the creek and veer away from the creek a bit until you can find a safe route down over the bluff, then back to the creek to view this beauty (no photo provided—my only one is all ICE!). Then cross the creek and make your away around on the left side and down to the base of really terrific **Four Step Falls** at .5, a beauty! (One of the two photos of these I flipped backwards for editorial reasons—can you figure out which one?)

Just below is the main creek (Dry Creek West), TURN LEFT and head upstream to another ***really nice*** waterfall, **Feeder Falls**.

To return to the road above, continue up and around to the left of **Feeder Falls** and on upstream all the way back UP a steep slope to the road at .8. Either return to the car (.5 back along the road) or TURN RIGHT and continue this hike.

To get to **Leeds** and **Paw Paw Falls**, continue about .3 to .75, then TURN RIGHT and leave the road **(35.57798, -93.35292)**. Go kind of level through the woods and then continue downhill along the top of a narrow ridge. As it begins to get steeper veer off to the left and head downhill to the top of a bluff, follow it to the LEFT until you can get below the bluff and to the bottom of **Leeds Falls** at 1.3. It's an AMAZING SSS, WOW!

Paw Paw Falls is just below. The creek leads to a narrow canyon and several waterfalls below, but pretty difficult hiking, eventually joining Dry Creek. There's a lower parking area and access to all of these upper areas from below.

RETURN back UP to the road at 1.8 and it's about .8 back to the trailhead, or TURN RIGHT and continue on the road to Z Falls.

BONUS: There is no good way to get to **Z Falls**—it's surrounded by BLACK DIAMOND slopes and bluffs—but if you can ever make it to the bottom, it is a magical spot. The straightforward way is to continue on the old forest service road another .8 to 1.6 (from parking spot) and TURN RIGHT, then follow the creek down the hillside to the top of Z FALLS at 2.0 (past small falls, cascades, water slides)—you'll know when you arrive!

From the top of the falls it is possible to work your way around the left side of the falls via an XTREME BLACK DIAMOND ♦ slope, and see if you can find a safe way down through the bluff to the creek below. (there may be access on the right side of the canyon also but I've never tried) I've only done this move once, and it was quite difficult, and I was wearing a hard hat. Just saying...

See page 318 for another route to **Z Falls** from **Carolyn Falls** next door (map is on page 314).

Emergency contact: Johnson County Sheriff, 479–754–2200 Dogs are OK

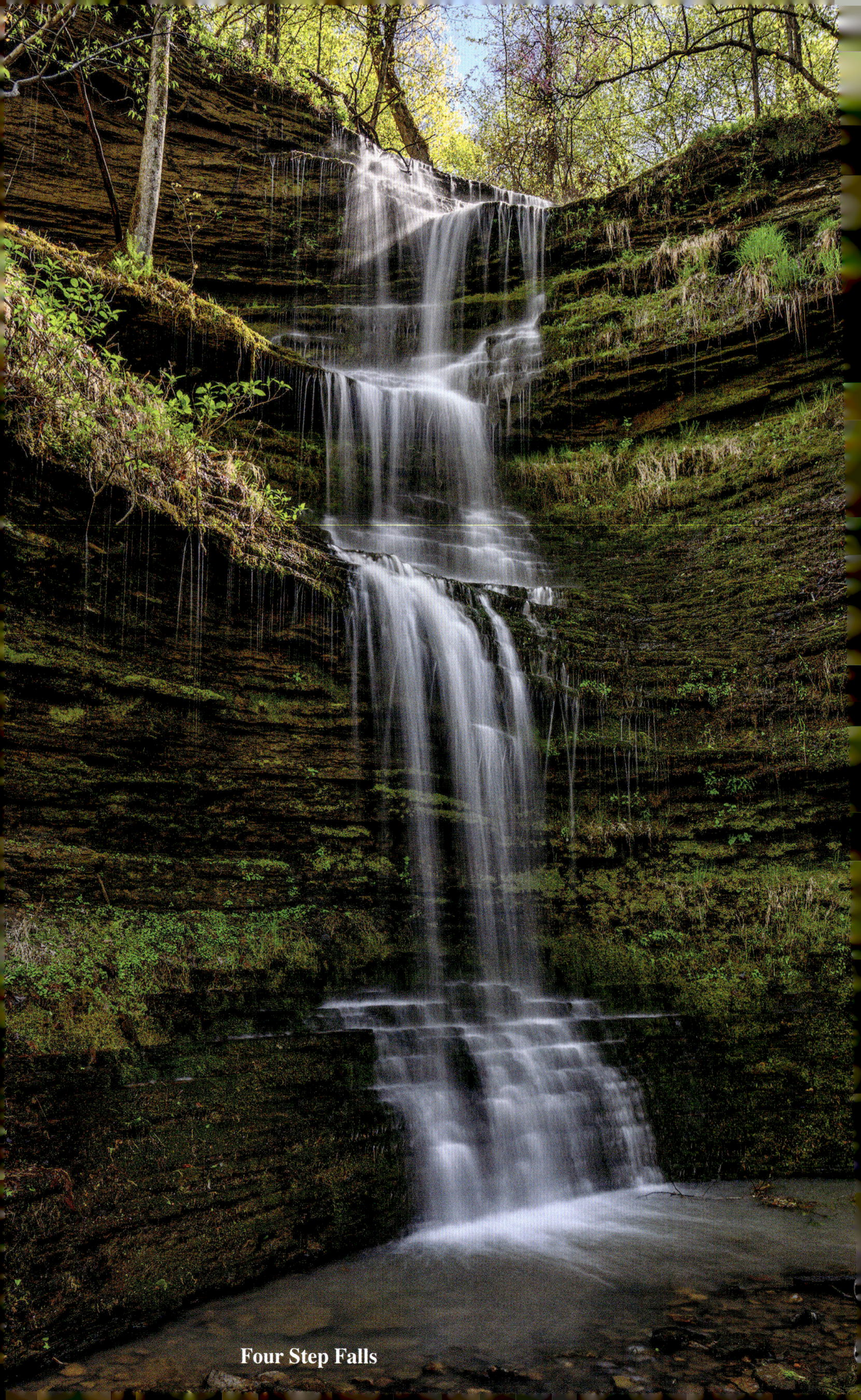

Four Step Falls

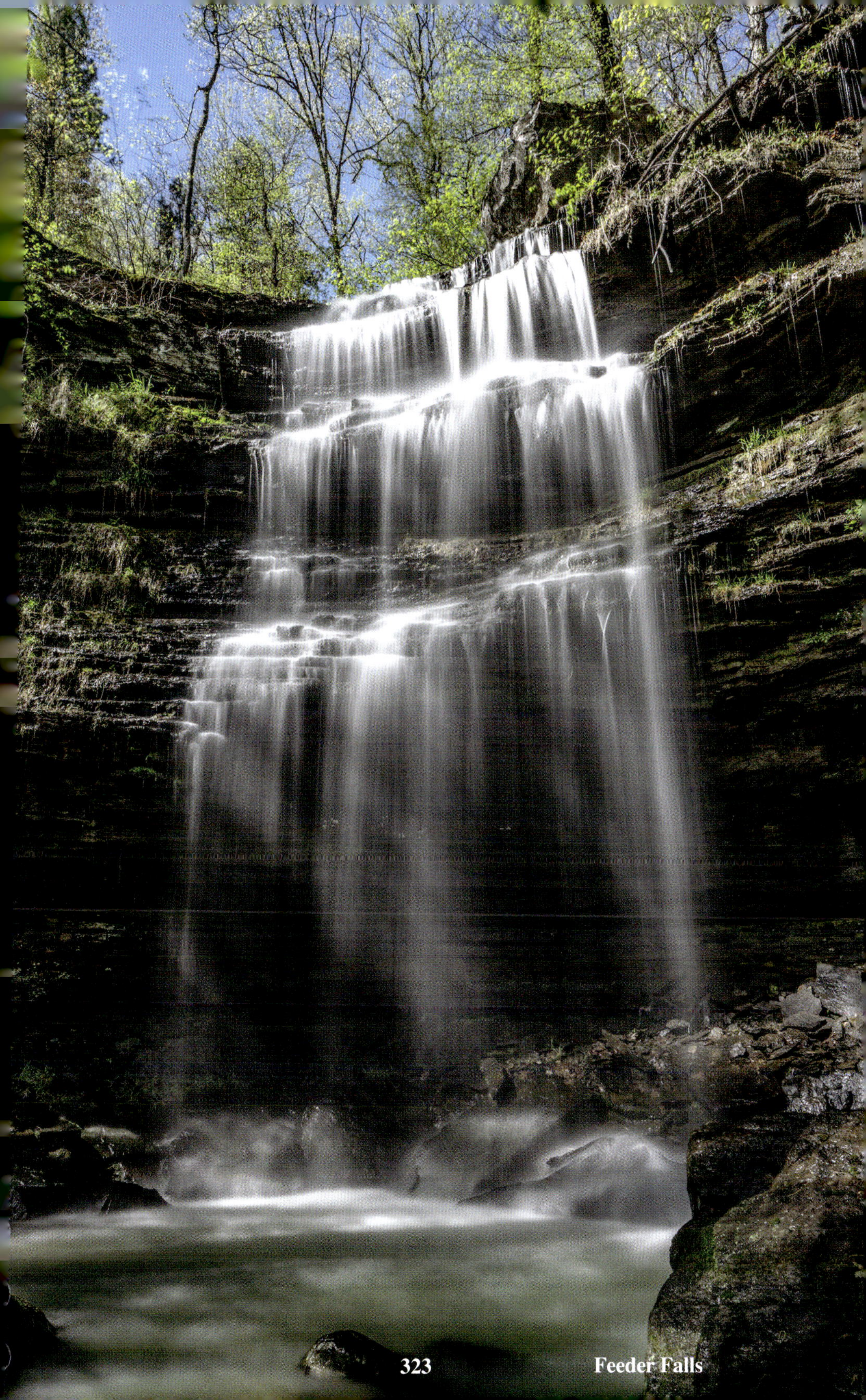

Feeder Falls

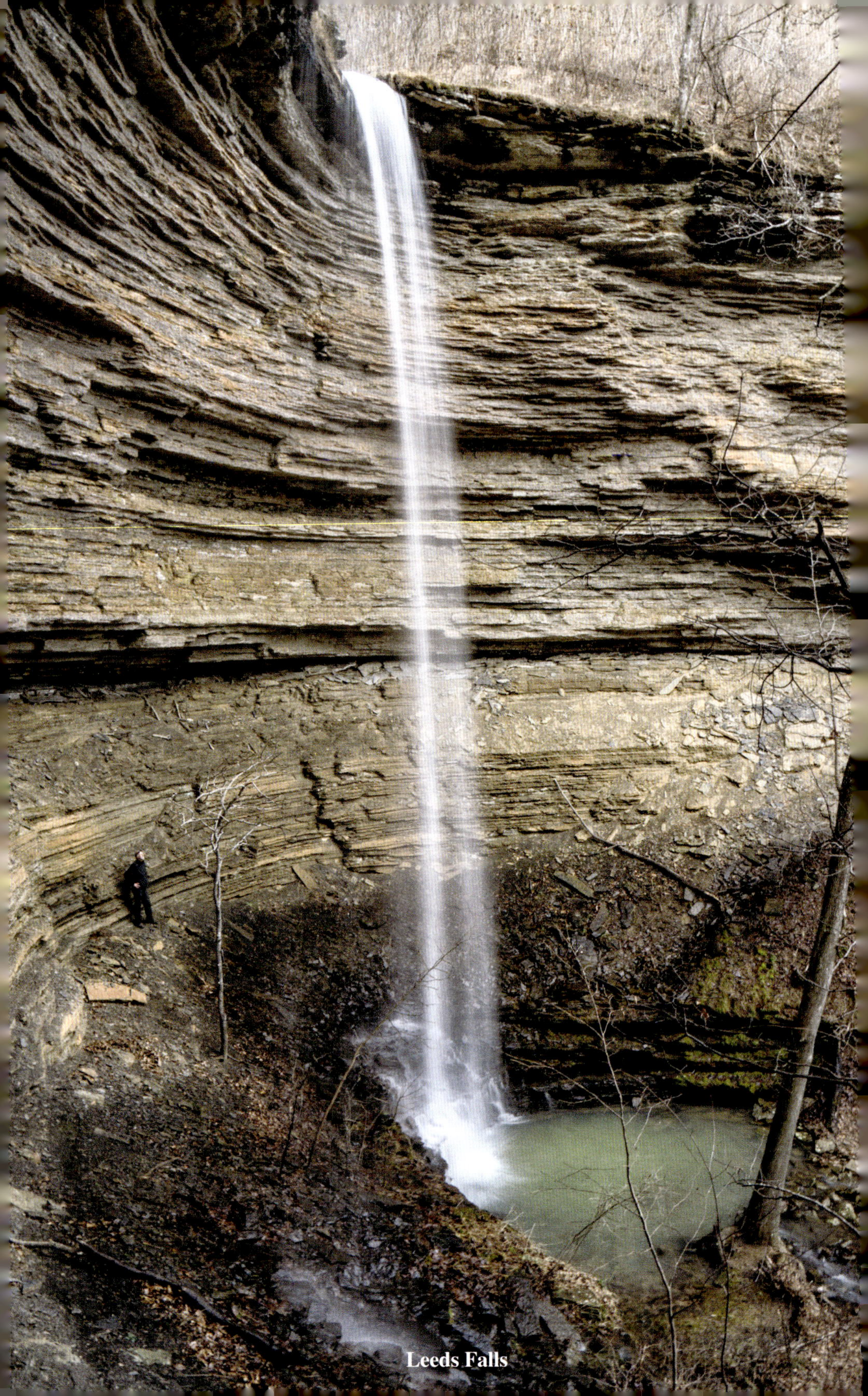
Leeds Falls

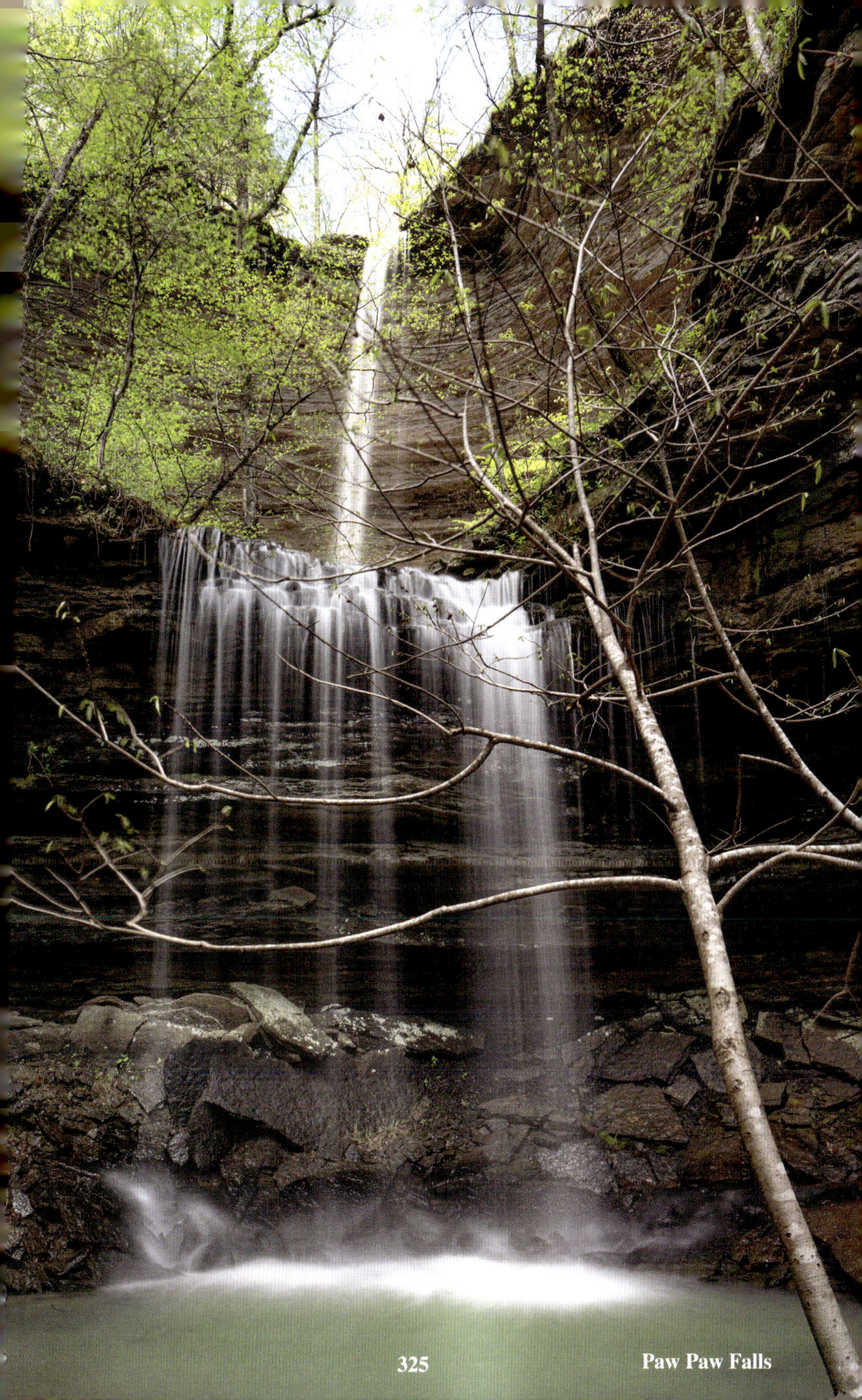

Paw Paw Falls

Calcite Falls – 43′

1.0 miles roundtrip, difficult bushwhack GPS **35.58880, -93.33728**

***See top of map on page 314**

CALCITE FALLS. From Hagarville take Hwy. 123 north 4.1 miles (or from Pelsor 22.5 miles), to JC4540/FR1403/Woods Mtn. Road. Take 4540 west, 3.5 miles to FR 1403A and turn RIGHT/NORTH. Go .3 miles and PARK (**35.58775, -93.34167**).

There's a concrete spring/well house near an old home site on the left, and the water pours down the hillside below and forms a couple of nice waterfalls, including Calcite Falls. Oh yes, this also forms the main prong of Sally Ann Hollow.

Head down the steep hillside and to the left a little, following the water past a nice 30' falls. Continue down on the left side of the creek down to a bluffline, then below the bluff and back to the right to Calcite Falls at .5. There are calcite deposits on the bluff—the same stuff cave formations are made out of. A lot of waterfalls in the Ozarks have calcite deposits—see Stalagmite Falls on page 163 as another example.

You can loop back up to the road either side of the bluff, or continue on downstream past many waterfalls to the main Sally Ann Hollow parking spot below.

Emergency contact: Johnson County Sheriff, 479–754–2200 Dogs are OK

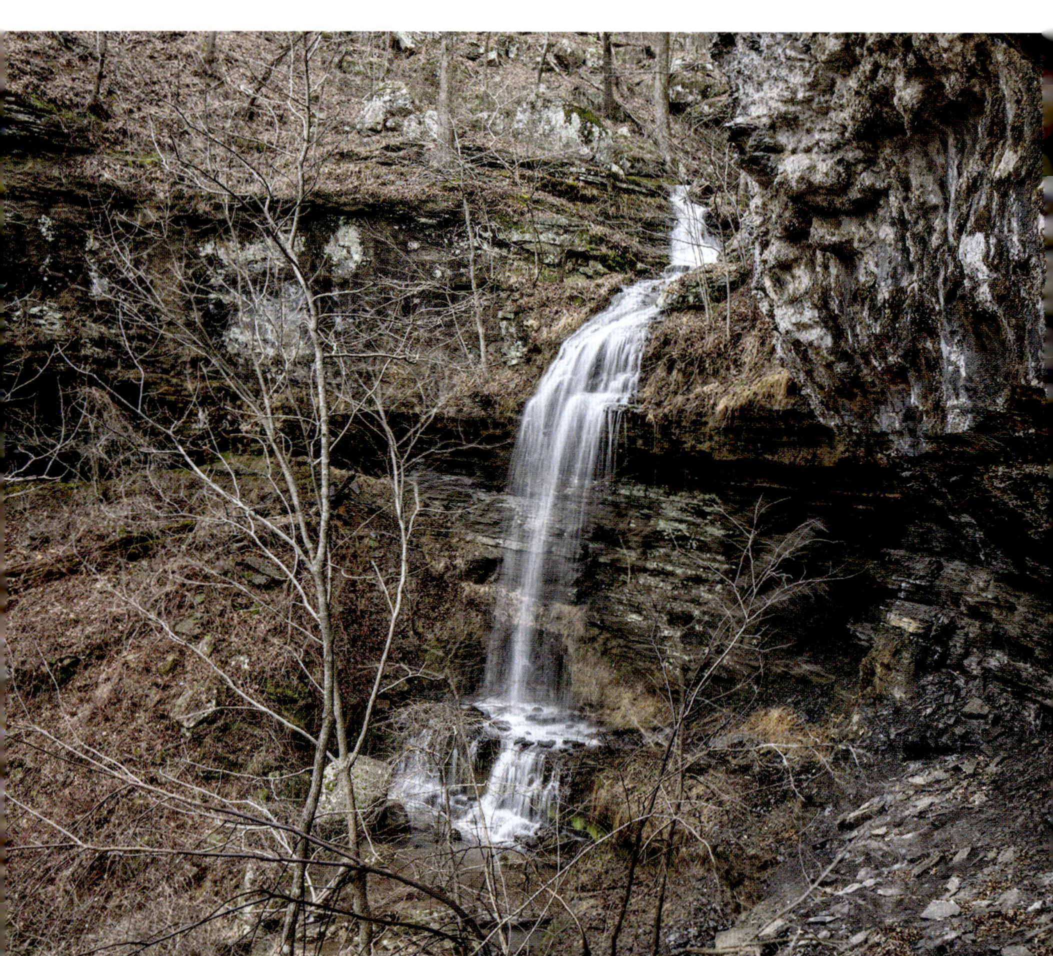

Caleb Falls –61′

.6 mi roundtrip, moderate steep bushwhack

GPS **35.57256, -93.37046**

Hundred Foot Falls –57′

2.2 mi roundtrip (both falls), moderate bushwhack

GPS **35.57589, -93.37569**

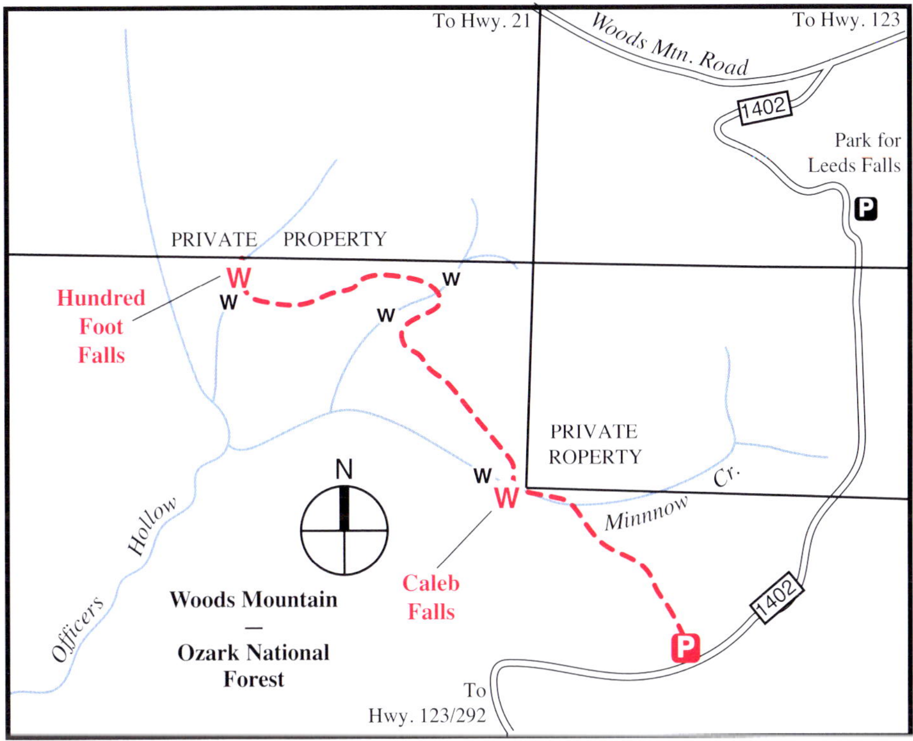

CALEB FALLS/HUNDRED FOOT FALLS. There are many waterfalls in the drainages below AND spectacular bluffs too, and as usual Danny Hale has them in his guidebooks (look for sections on Officers Hollow, and the BLUFFS of Officers Hollow). We're just going to visit two of the best waterfalls on the upper bluff line.

Directions from Hagarville: take Hwy. 123 north 4.1 miles and TURN LEFT on JC4540/FR1403/Woods Mtn. Road (or from Pelsor 22.5 miles and TURN RIGHT). Take 4540 west for 4.8 miles and TURN LEFT onto FR1402 (This is 1.2 miles beyond Carolyn Falls.), then go 1.0 mile and PARK on the right **(35.56933, -93.36685)**. This is .6 mile past the Leeds Falls park.

From PARK, head northwest into the woods downhill and angle to the left a little bit to the creek below, then TURN LEFT and follow the creek to the top of **Caleb Falls** at .3. (Brent Robinson's son) An SSS on its own, but we also have a super bluff line just across the creek that will magnify the pleasure of your trip! The waterfall just below is a beauty too! NOTE that there is PRIVATE PROPERTY upstream, and also above the big bluff we're about to follow—so always stay BELOW the big bluff please!

From the top of **Caleb Falls**, cross the creek over to the base of the big bluff—follow it to THE LEFT. There are many amazing things to see in the next half mile including towering painted bluffs, caves, giant stone pedestals, and rock arches—just follow the bluff and take time to explore.

As the bluffs begin to fade away follow them into a side canyon to the right where you'll find a giant "multi-slide" falls area that will go up and up and up the hillside. If there's lots of water you'll probably spend a good bit of time here—it's an SSS for sure! There is a bluff line and regular waterfall below with easy access over the bluff on the right side.

Continue along the upper bluff line until you come to another SSS at 1.1, **Hundred Foot Falls**. (I've measured it twice at 57', but who's counting...) There's also a smaller waterfall on the bluff line below. If you are like me you didn't get to spend enough time exploring the big bluffs, so now it's time to turn around and see them again on the way back! There are also many waterfalls below and beyond (in Danny's guidebooks)—but be aware there is a lot of PRIVATE PROPERTY in the area...

Emergency contact: Johnson County Sheriff, 479–754–2200 Dogs are OK

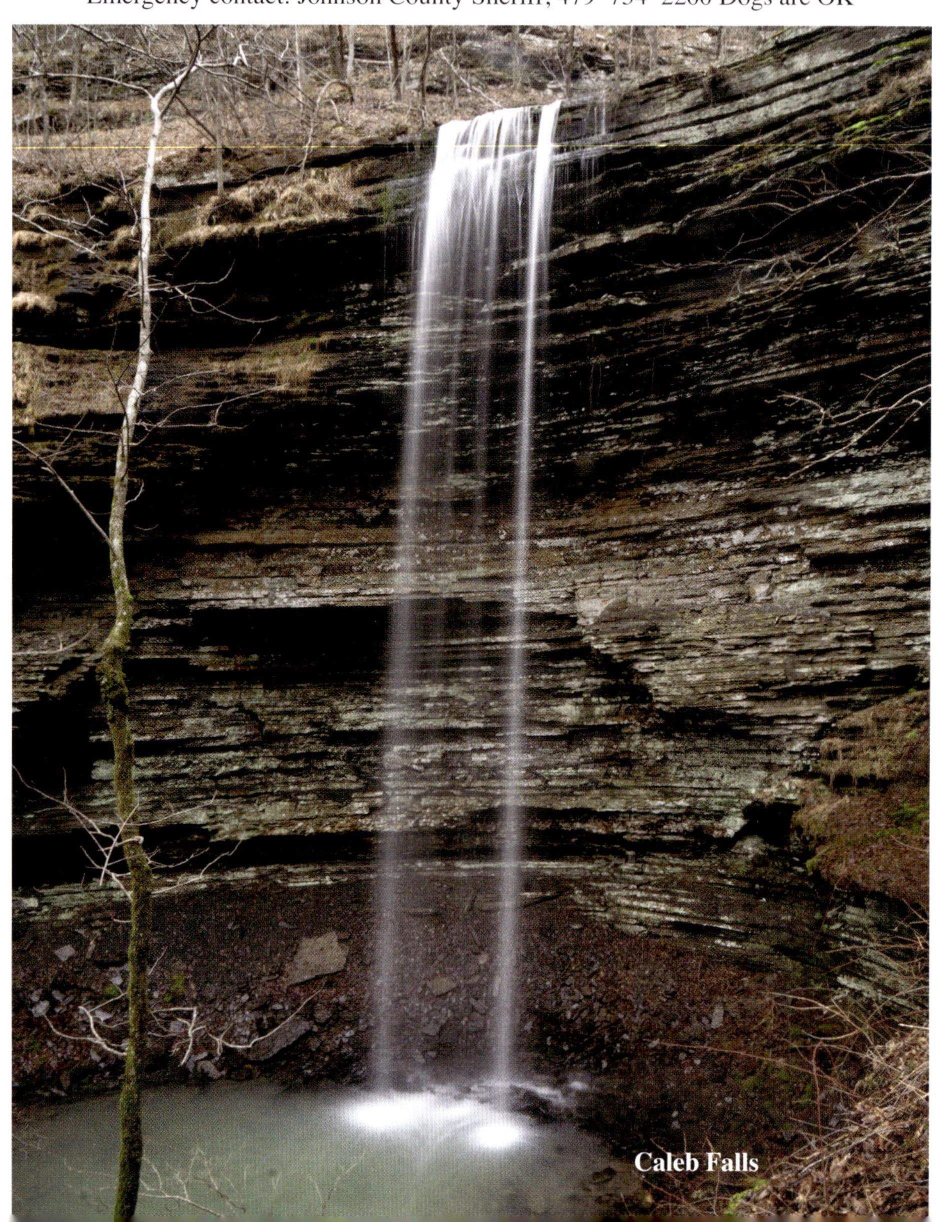

Caleb Falls

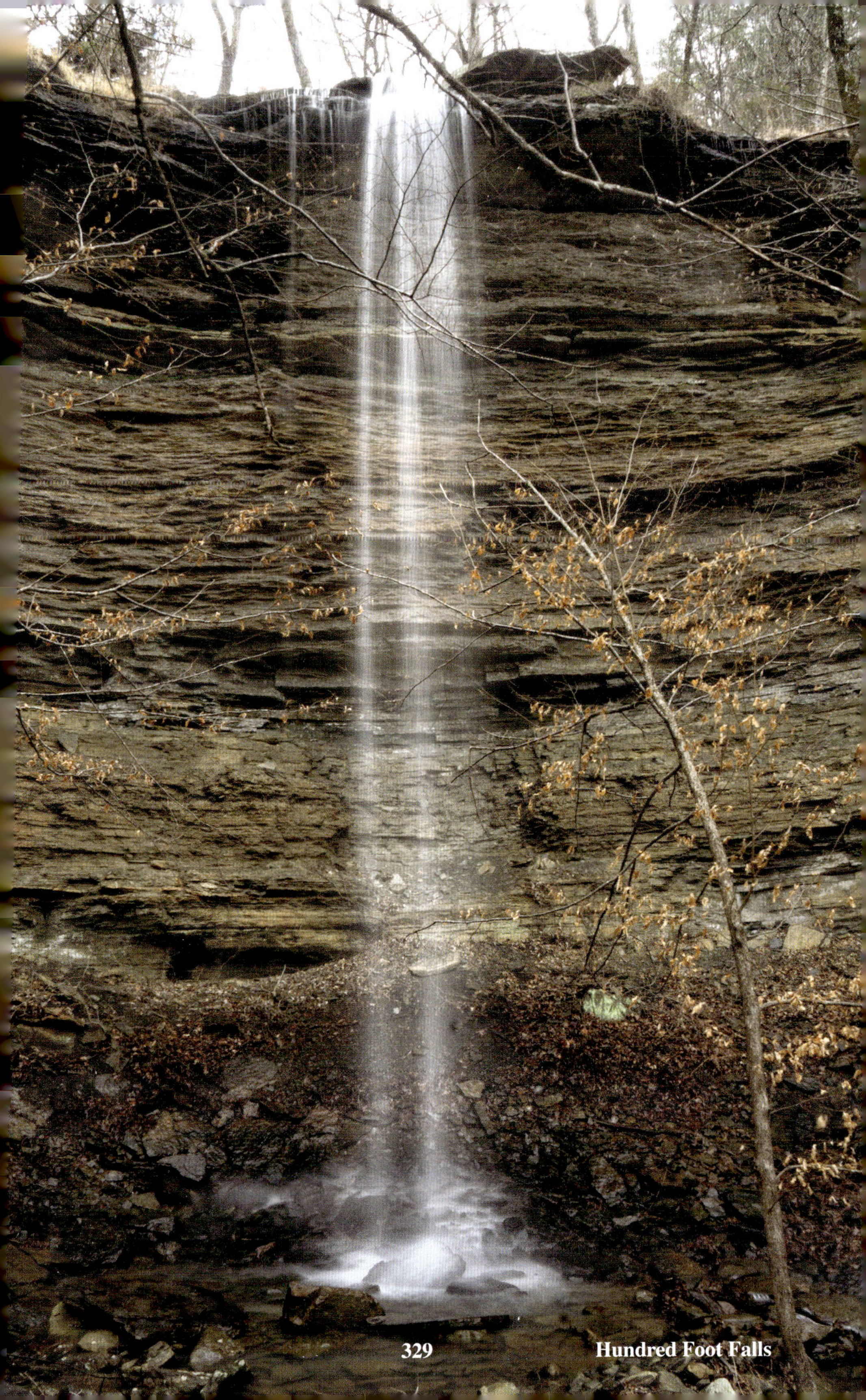

Hundred Foot Falls

Cecil Falls – 57′

.7 mi, easy trail then steep bushwhack GPS **35.57467, -93.38416**

McKay Twin Falls – 30′

1.25 mi moderate/difficult overall GPS **35.57483, -93.38945**

McKay Two Step Falls – 31′

same as above GPS **35.57498, -93.39019**

1.9 miles loop for all three falls above

Footprint Hollow Falls (2) – 39′ & 42′

.8 mi roundtrip to both, easy road then black diamond ♦ **GPS 35.58267, -93.39692**

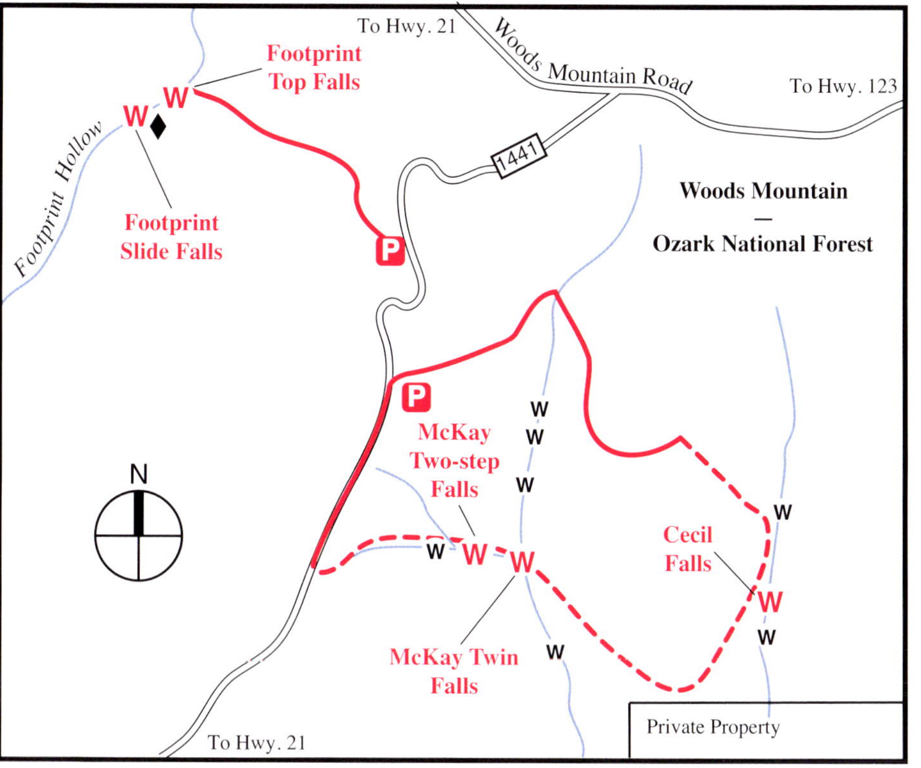

CECIL FALLS/McKAY FALLS/FOOTPRINT HOLLOW FALLS. Directions from Hagarville: take Hwy. 123 north 4.1 miles and TURN LEFT on JC4540/FR1403/Woods Mtn. Road (or from Pelsor 22.5 miles and TURN RIGHT). Take 4540 west for 6.3 miles and TURN LEFT onto FR1441. (if coming from Hwy. 21 it's 4.1 miles to this turn) Go .6 and PARK on the LEFT **(35.57803, -93.39209)**.

From the trailhead follow the old forest service road ahead mostly on the level to .5 and TURN RIGHT and head downhill away from the road (it's all bushwhacking from here on). Continue pretty much straight down the hillside until you reach the creek, then TURN RIGHT and follow it to the top of **Cecil Falls** at .7, a wonderful SSS! Go to the RIGHT to get down to the bottom. Cecil Jr. is just downstream.

OK, now we're going to continue the hike on over to the McKay Hollow waterfalls.

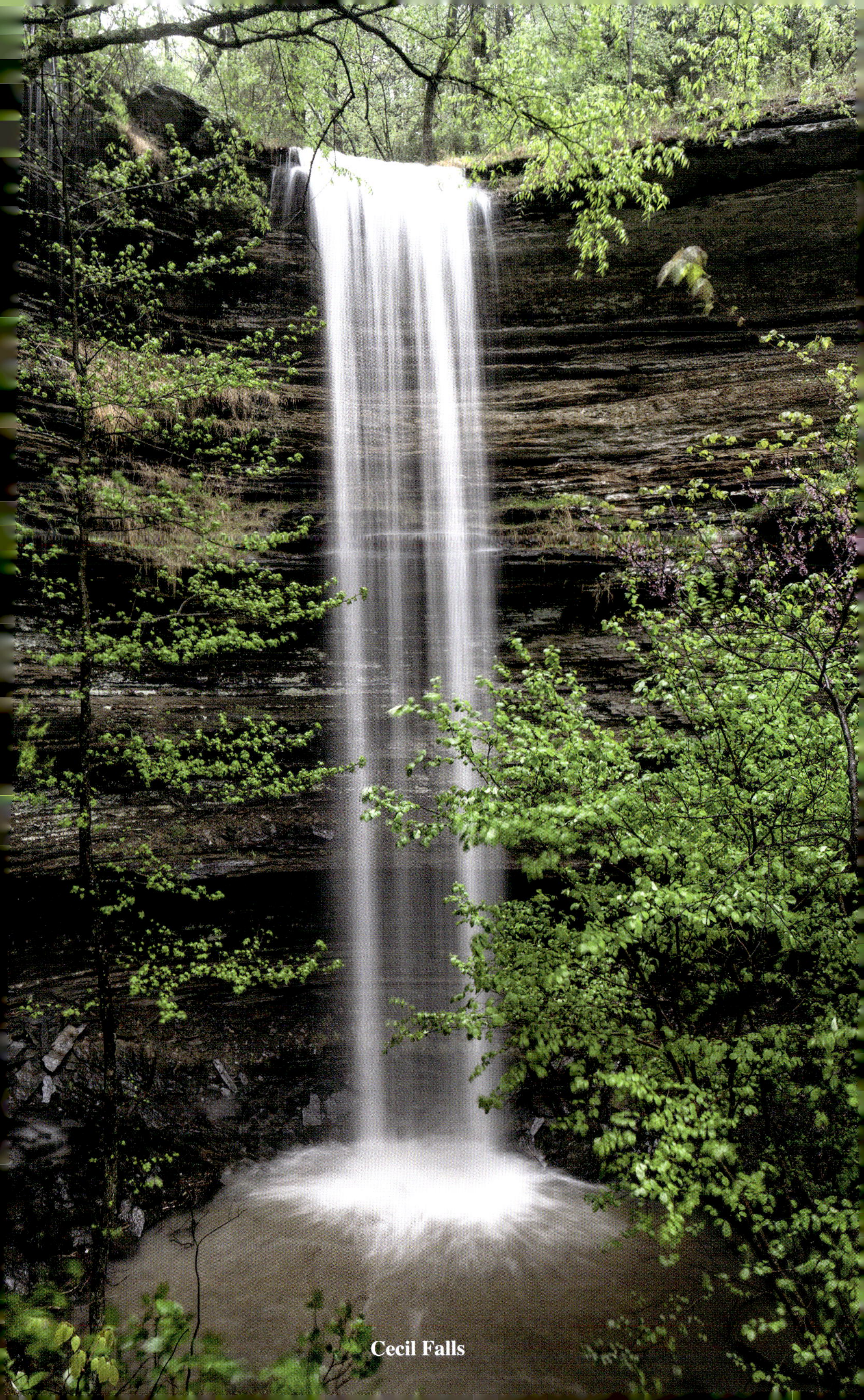

Cecil Falls

Looking downstream, climb on up the hillside on the RIGHT to the base of a small bluff line and follow that to the LEFT/DOWNSTREAM. It's a pretty easy and mostly level hike and will curve around to the LEFT and across the nose of a ridge—the small bluff will disappear and you just stay on the level and curve around to the RIGHT and into McKay Hollow.

As you hike upstream you should hear waterfalls down on the creek to the left—stay on the level and you will arrive at **McKay Twin Falls** at 1.25, another SSS! The falls on the right is the main creek, and there are more waterfalls upstream if you want to explore—you can actually hike all the way back out to the trailhead that way. I prefer to cross the creek and hike UP the side drainage, which is pretty much an SSS all the way up!

The first waterfall above the Twin is **McKay Two Step**, a great BEAUTY! There's another nice falls above that one. And climbing on up you will reach a land of giant boulder/rock slabs, SSS area, with a small falls coming from beneath. Oh my! Continue on up the steep creek and you will eventually emerge from the jungle at an old homesite and the road (FR 1441) on top at 1.6. TURN RIGHT and follow the road back to your vehicle at 1.9.

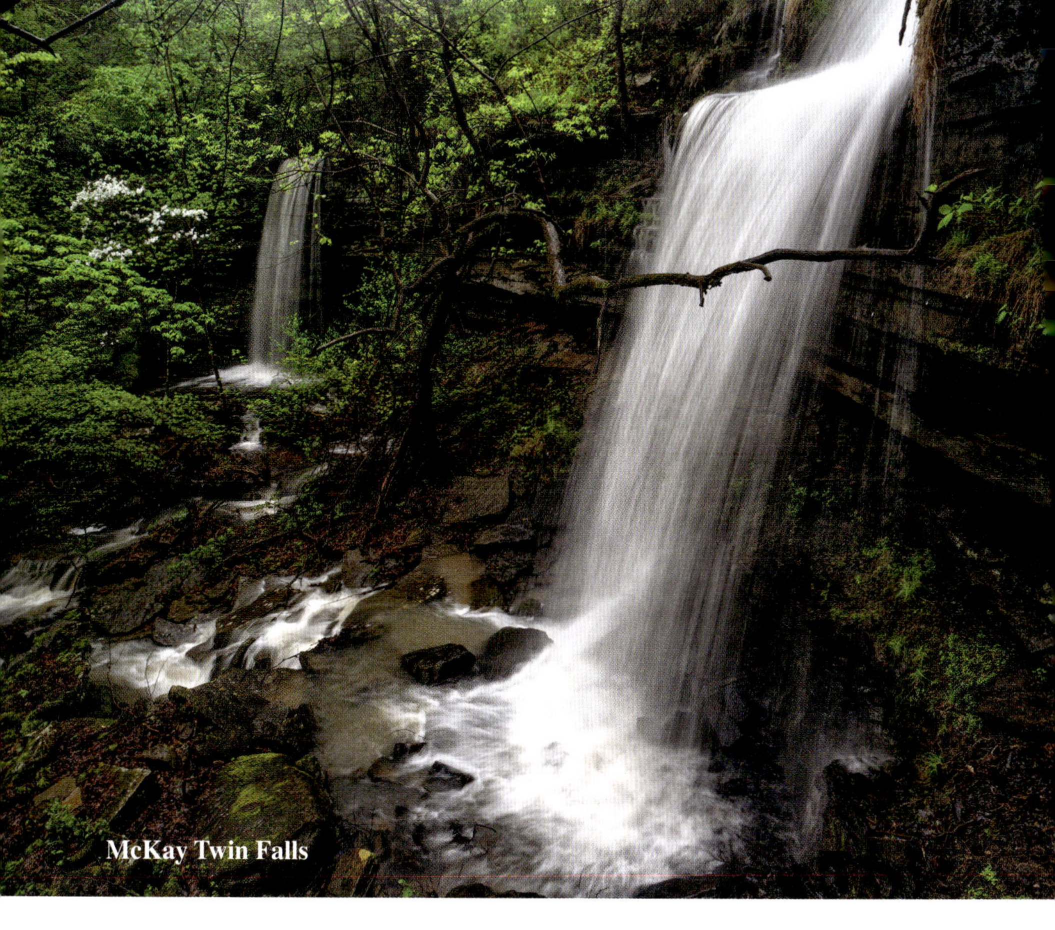
McKay Twin Falls

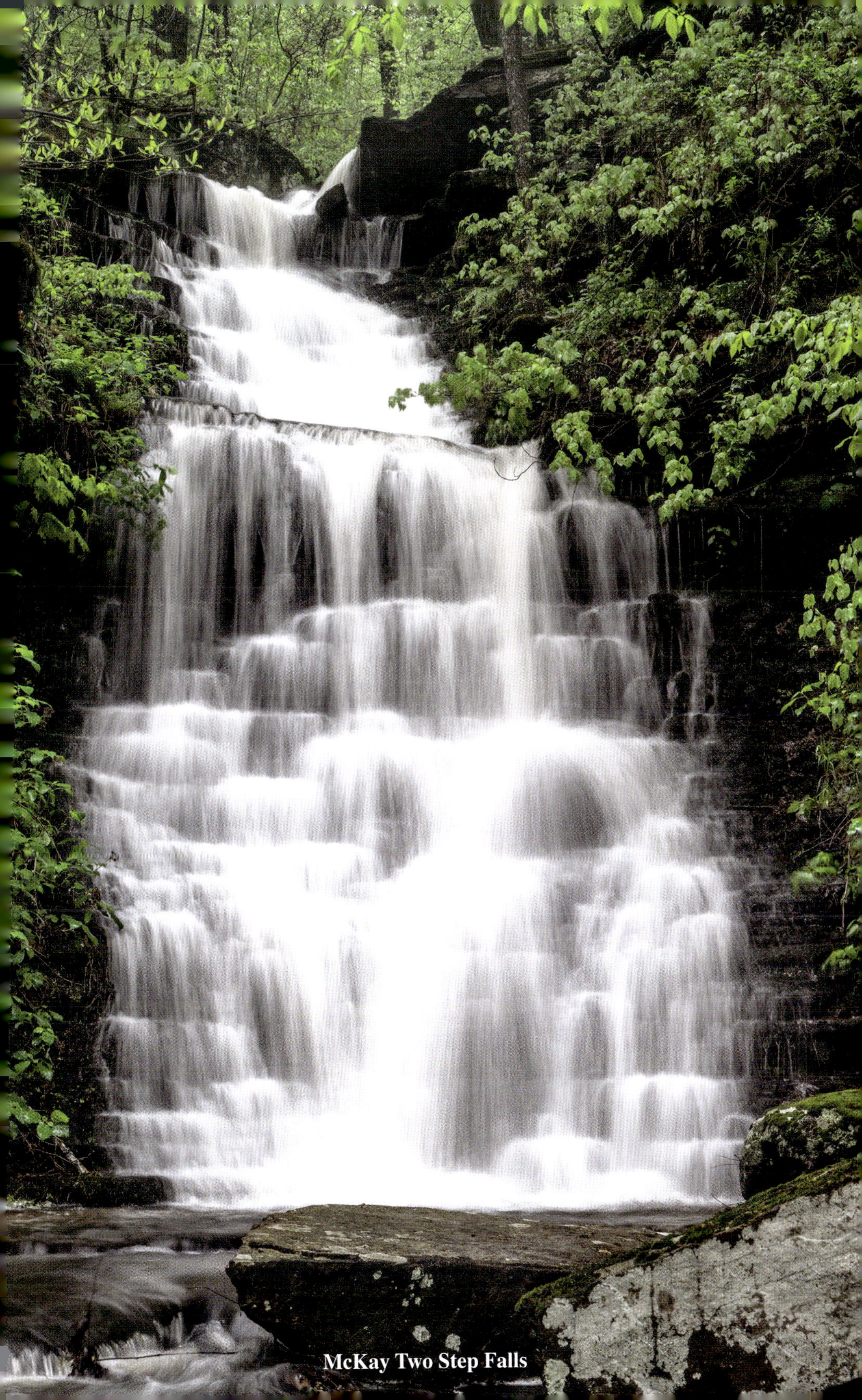

McKay Two Step Falls

FOOTPRINT HOLLOW FALLS. BONUS WATERFALLS: Footprint Hollow is next door to the **Cecil/McKay waterfalls**. Directions from Hagarville: take Hwy. 123 north 4.1 miles and TURN LEFT on JC4540/FR1403/Woods Mtn. Road (or from Pelsor 22.5 miles and TURN RIGHT). Take 4540 west for 6.3 miles and TURN LEFT onto FR1441. Go .4 and PARK on the RIGHT (**35.58019, -93.39197**).

From the road hike down a jeep road to the creek crossing at .35. If you look closely there are some "footprints" in the exposed rock just upstream at the very top, on the other

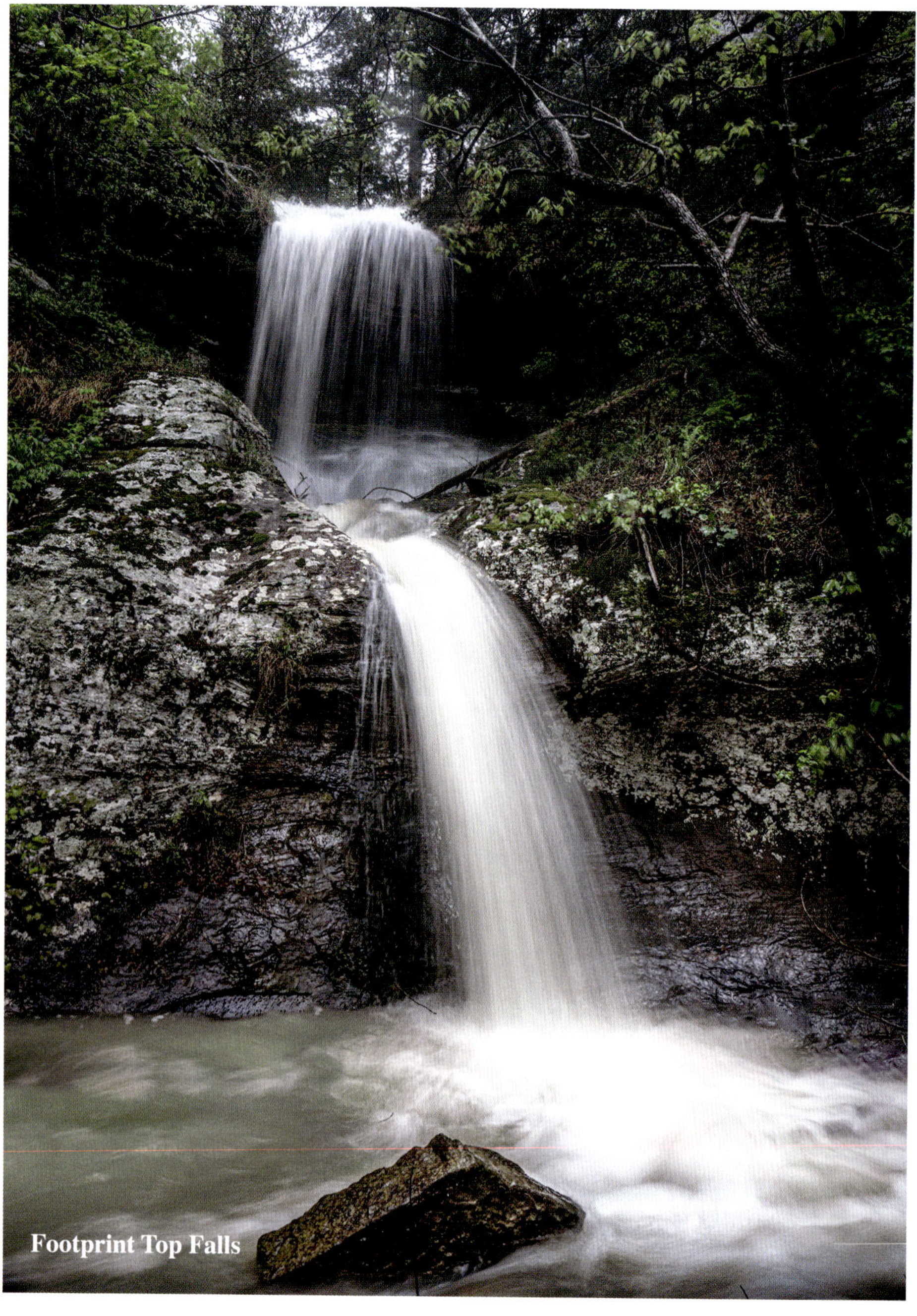

Footprint Top Falls

side of the creek (sometimes covered with the creek during high water). They really do look like footprints! While both of the waterfalls I show here are at the top of all this, it's pretty difficult to scramble down to get these views (I went down the left side.). Danny Hale documents 18 different waterfalls here in his waterfall guidebook, and his directions will bring you in from the bottom to access them all. ENJOY!

Footprints location **(35.58293, -93.39653)**

Emergency contact: Johnson County Sheriff, 479–754–2200 Dogs are OK

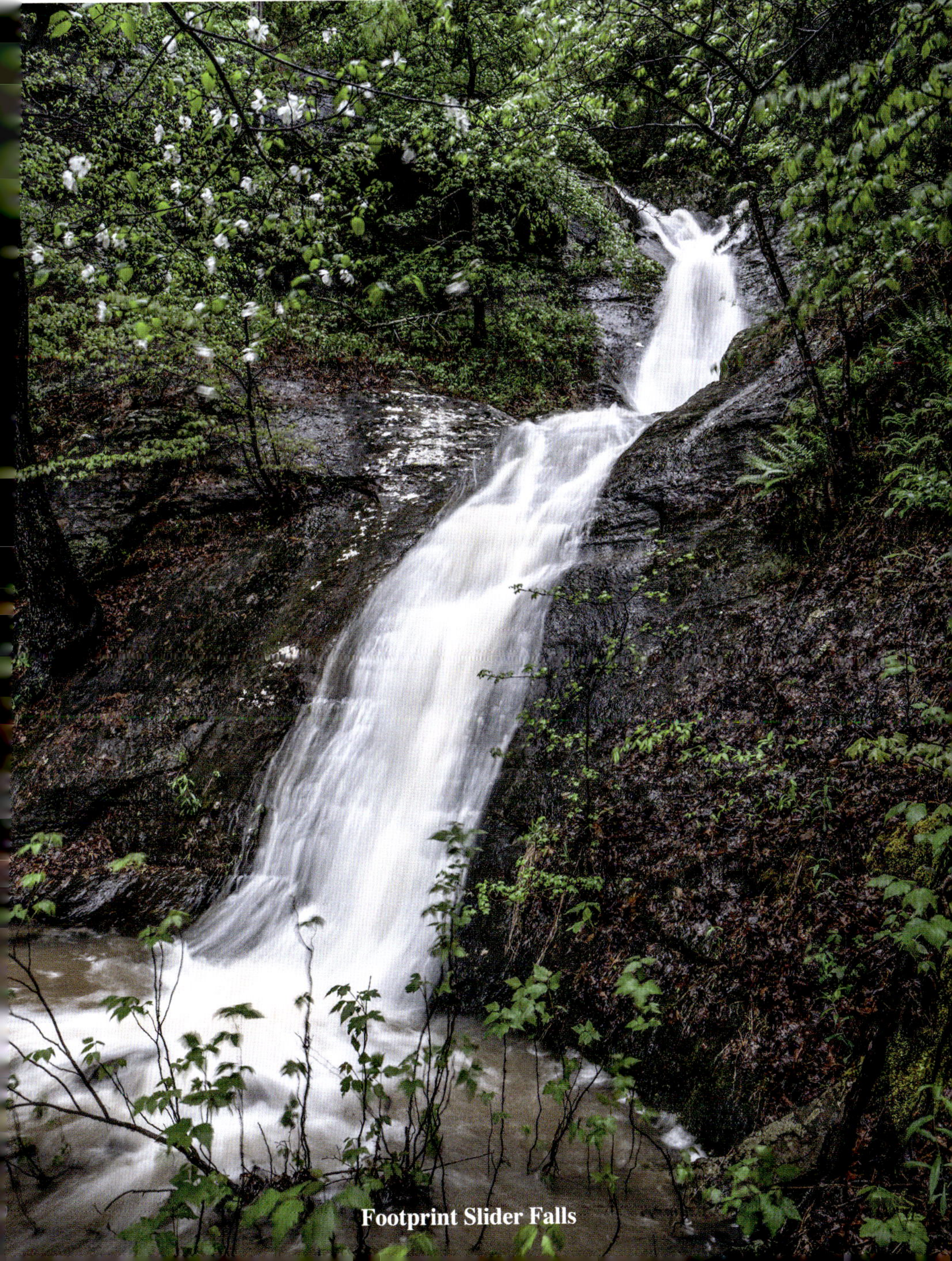

Footprint Slider Falls

Black Bear Falls – 31′

1.2 miles roundtrip (for both), medium/steep bushwhack, GPS helpful

GPS **35.75113, -93.68266**

Monkey Falls – 33′

1.2 miles roundtrip (for both), medium/steep bushwhack, GPS helpful

GPS **35.74978, -93.68219**

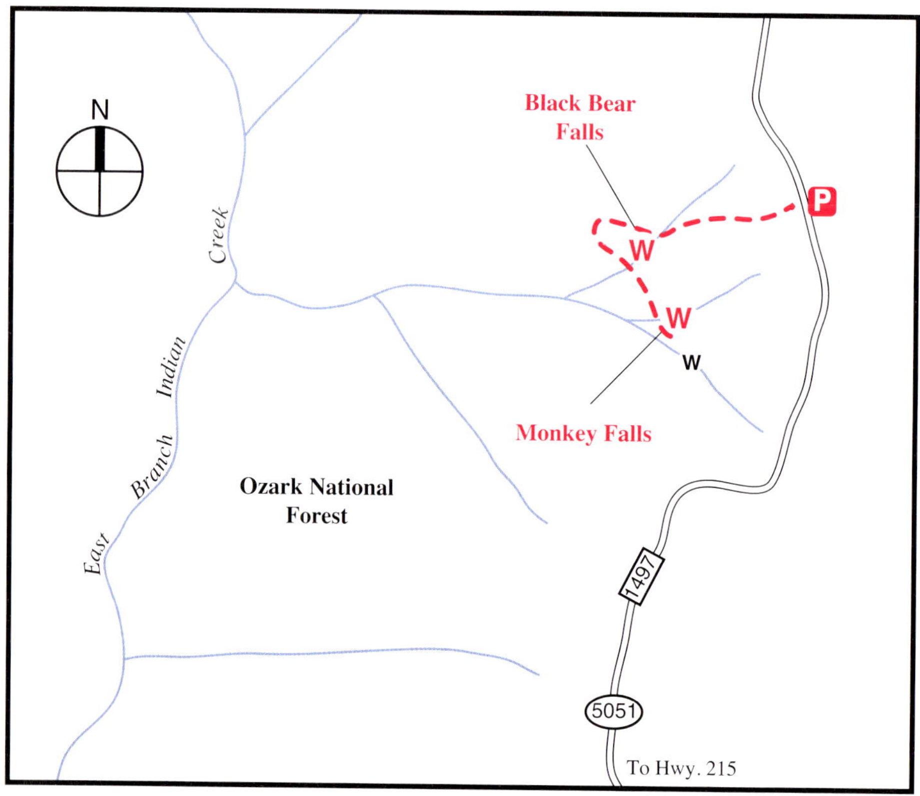

BLACK BEAR FALLS/MONKEY FALLS. Shhhhh—there might be bears in the area so don't make too much noise when you bushwhack the steep slope down to these nice waterfalls in the headwaters of Indian Creek near the Mulberry River. Waterfall guru John Moore and his kids found these waterfalls during one of their many "Moore Monkeys' Adventures" and so the waterfall is named after them.

From Hwy. 215 between Oark and Cass (just east of the bridge over the Little Mulberry river), go north on FR#1496/CR#5099 2.0 miles and TURN LEFT onto FR#1497/CR#5051. Go 5.2 miles (past the Lick Branch Trailhead for the OHT) and PARK (**35.75220, -93.67855**).

Head west down the steep hillside and follow the drainage to a nice cascade and then eventually to the top of a bluff and to **Black Bear Falls**. There is a spot to the right of the waterfall a ways where you can get down below the bluff. Then simply follow the base of the bluff back to **Black Bear Falls**, then continue along the bluff until you come to the twin fall area that is **Monkey Falls**. When I made the photo you see here that right-hand fork was running so muddy from a heavy rain that it looked just like hot chocolate!

Emergency contact: Johnson County Sheriff, 479–754–2200 Dogs are OK

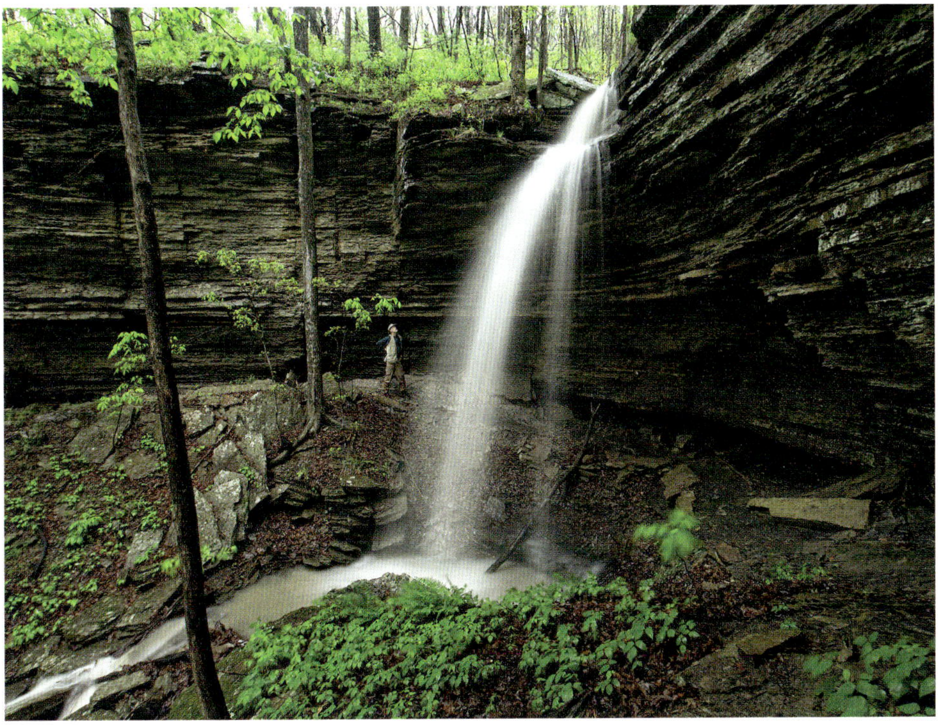

Black Bear Falls (above), **Monkey Falls** (below)

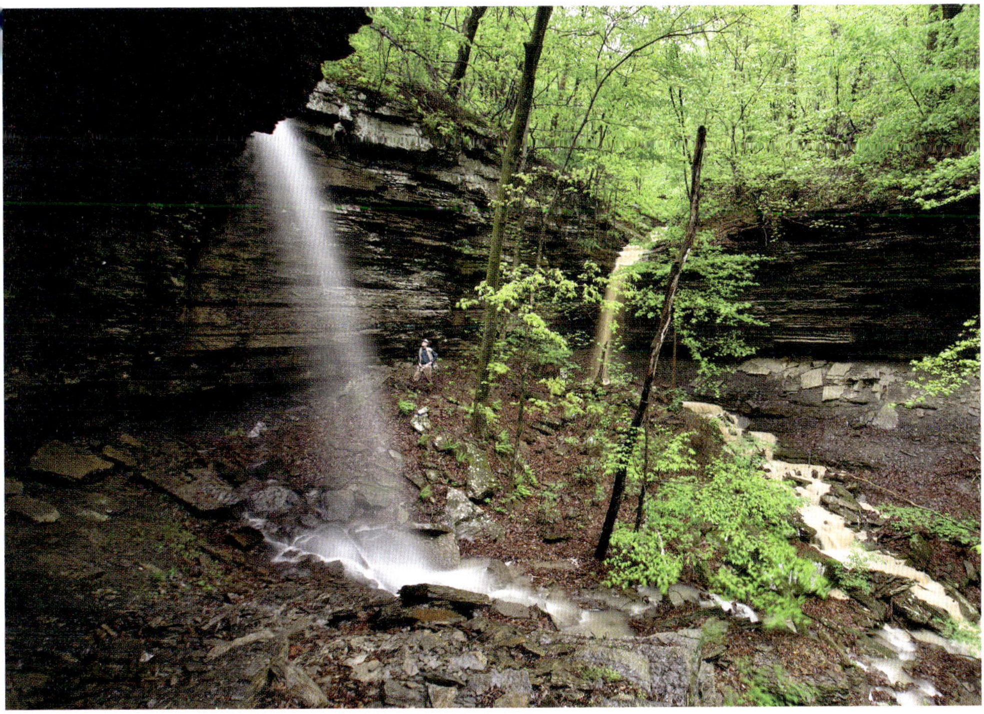

Murray Falls – 37′

1.0 mile roundtrip, medium bushwhack, GPS helpful

GPS **35.74328, -93.80773**

Senyard Falls – 29′

Same spot as above, medium bushwhack, GPS helpful

GPS Coordinates are the same as Murray Falls above

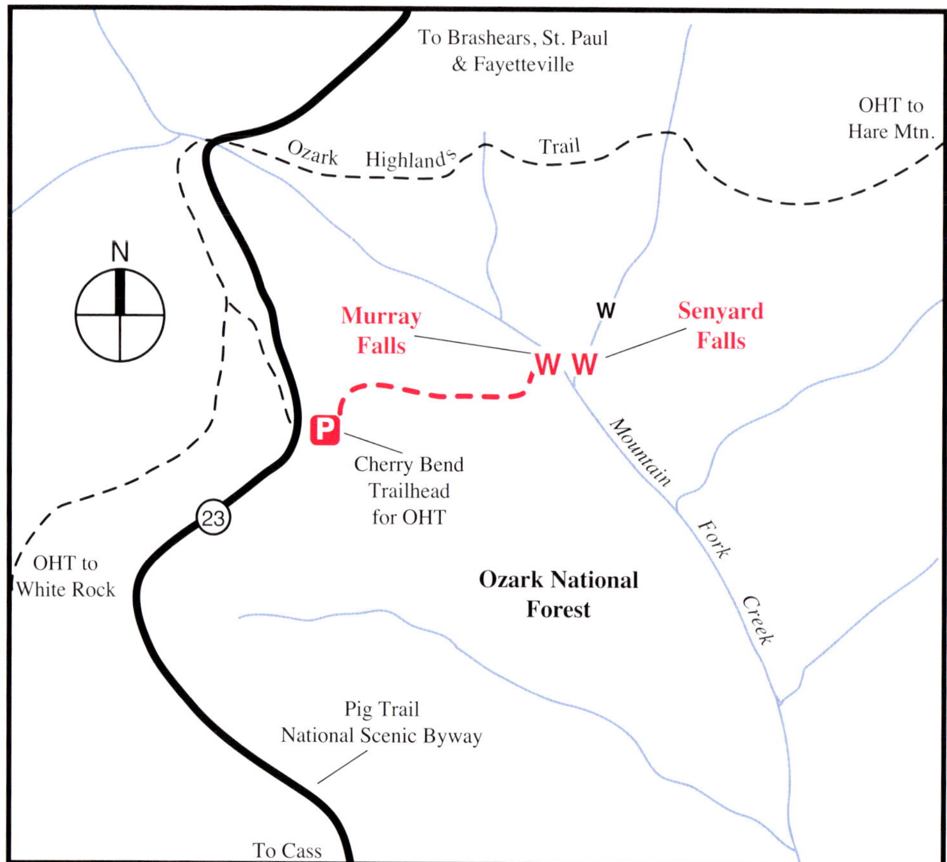

MURRAY FALLS/SENYARD FALLS. When the water is high I highly recommend the short bushwhack down to these waterfalls—most folks go screaming by on the highway above and never know what is below. Dick Murray was a pioneer in the hiking arena in Arkansas long before it became popular, and this falls bears his name. The other falls is named after Roy Senyard, who worked tirelessly for many years as volunteer maintenance coordinator for the Ozark Highlands Trail, and maintained the popular stretch of the OHT just above these falls for decades (R.I.P.). Some folks continue bushwhacking downstream from these falls to get to the Mountain Fork Falls area a couple of miles downstream, but it is a tough trip.

The Cherry Bend Trailhead is located between Cass and Brashears on the Pig Trail National Scenic Byway (Hwy. 23)—take exit 35 off I-40 and head north on Hwy. 23 about 5 miles past Cass, or head east on Hwy. 16 out of Fayetteville, then turn south on Hwy. 23 at Brashears for 5.5 miles **(35.74310, -93.81138)**.

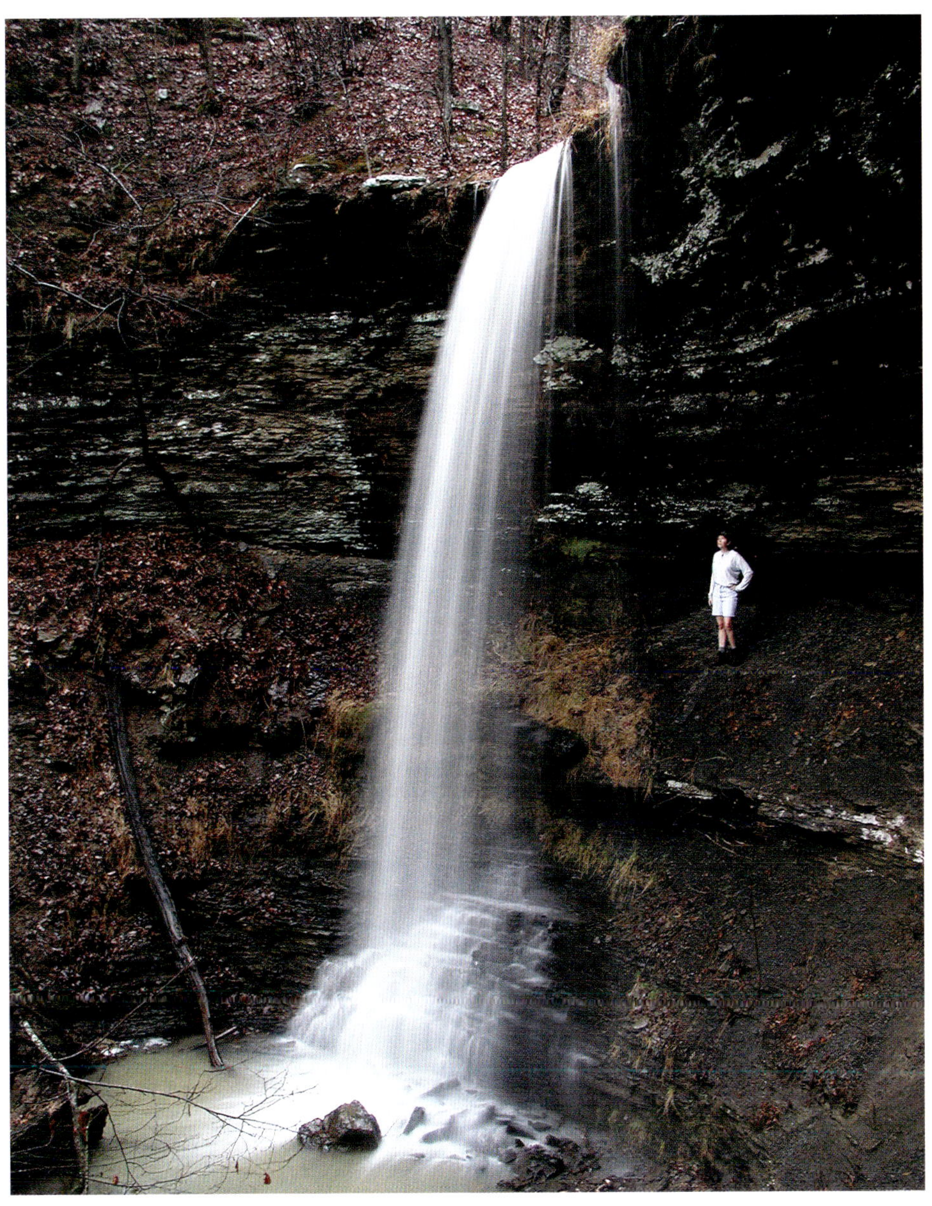

Dick Murray Falls (during high water)

To get to the falls, head off on a trail behind the bulletin board (the blue-blazed spur trail that connects to the OHT begins across the highway). It will go to the edge of a steep dropoff and lead you part way down the slope, then end. You want to CONTINUE downhill and generally follow the stream on your left until you come to **Murray Falls** less than .5 mile downstream (it may be easier to hike up above the creek a ways). If you can get across the creek, it is possible to make your way around to **Senyard Falls**, which comes in from the left just downstream (turn page for photos). There is a wonderful cascade up above Senyard Falls. Spend some time in this area and rest up for the *steep* climb back out!

Emergency contact: Franklin County Sheriff, 479–667–4127 Dogs are OK

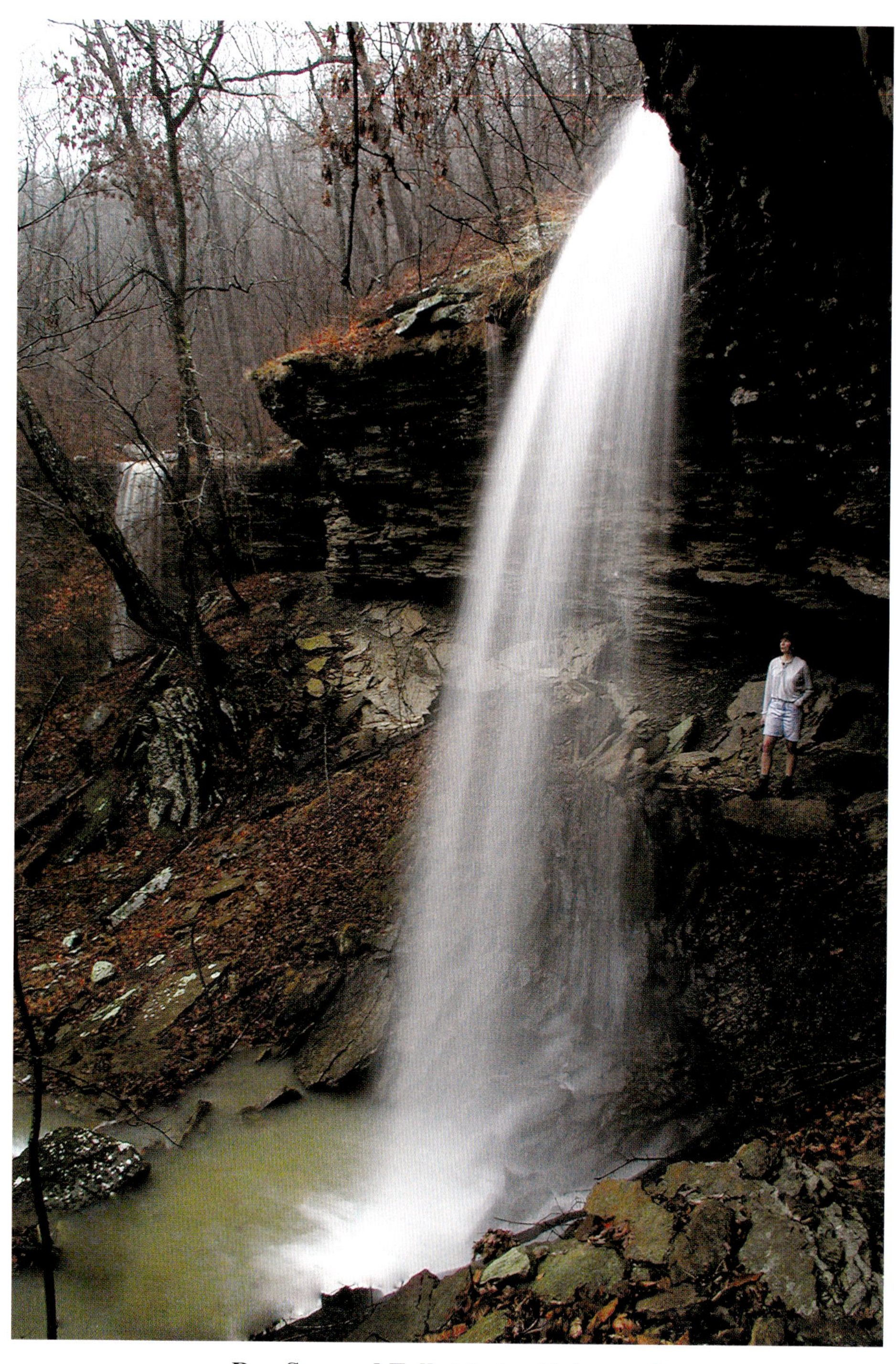

Roy Senyard Falls (during high water)
Murray Falls is visible in the background.

Spirit Mountain Falls –15′

3.0 miles roundtrip (all 3 falls), difficult bushwhack, GPS helpful

GPS **35.72080, -93.79031**

Mountain Fork Creek Falls –13′

Same trip as above, difficult bushwhack, GPS helpful

GPS **35.72343, -93.79195**

Sixty Foot Falls – 56′

Same trip as above, difficult bushwhack, GPS helpful

GPS **35.72120, -93.78648**

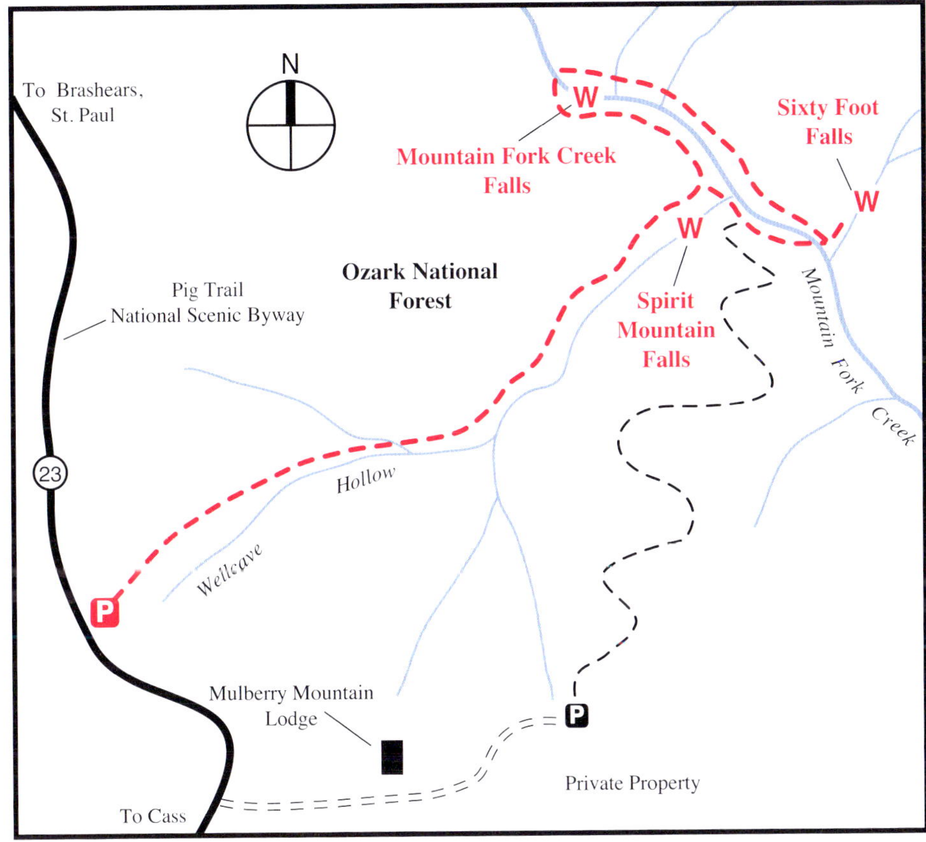

SPIRIT MTN. FALLS/MTN. FORK CREEK FALLS/SIXTY FOOT FALLS. There is a concentration of waterfalls in this one area along Mountain Fork Creek—some nice ones up in the headwaters too (Murray & Senyard Falls). The bushwhack down into the falls is not all that tough, but the nearly 700 foot climb back *up* is. If you want to stay in the area at least one night I recommend using Mulberry Mountain Lodge as a base camp—not only will you have a wonderful stay there, but you will have access to a four-wheeler trail that will make the hike a lot easier. Contact them for details at www.mulberrymountainlodge.com.

Take Hwy. 23 north out of Cass, go 2.6 miles past the Hwy. 215 intersection and

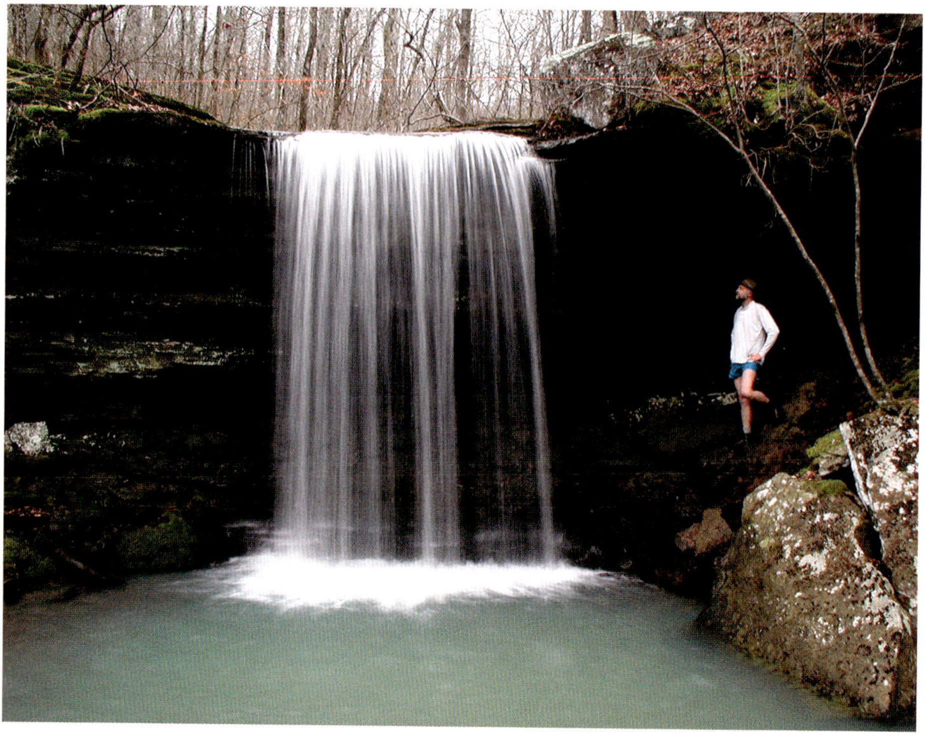

Spirit Mountain Falls (above), **Mountain Fork Creek Falls** (below)

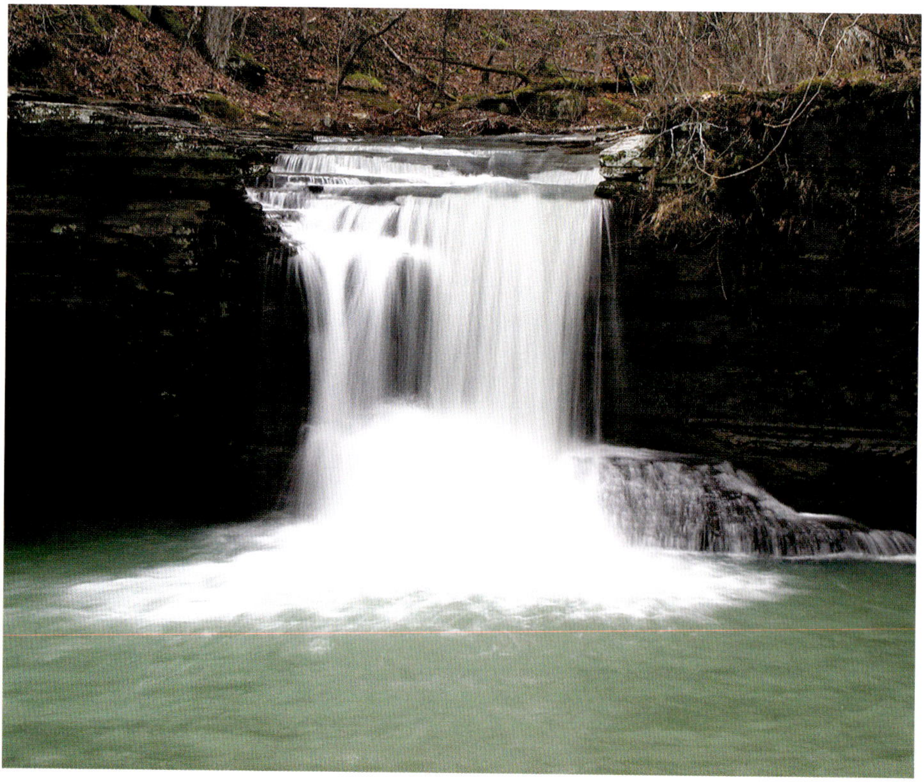

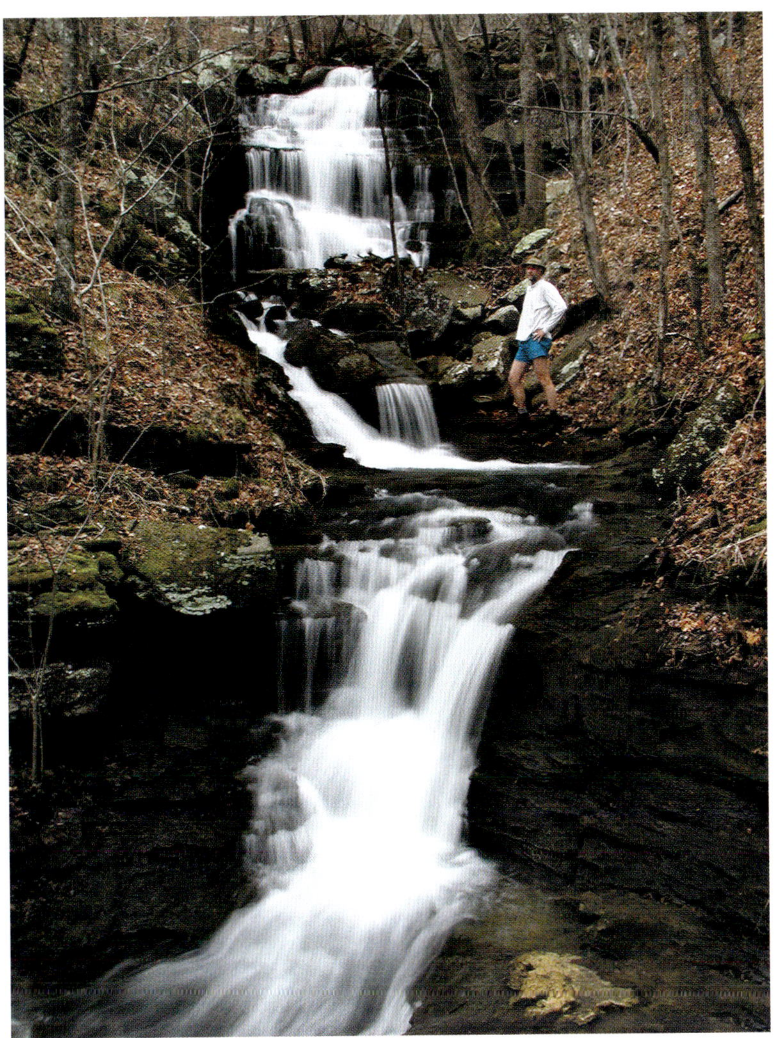

Cascade above Sixty Foot Falls

PARK on the right at the big pulloff area that is just across the highway from Whiting Mountain Road (**35.71441, -93.80262** about .2 past the turnoff for Mulberry Mtn. Lodge). OR head south on Hwy. 23 from the Cherry Bend Trailhead 2.4 miles to the parking area on the LEFT. There is no specific route to get to these falls—there are many four-wheeler and mountain bike trails in the area on the other side of the creek that you could use for possible access—but here is a general discussion of the way that I hike into them.

From the parking area head downhill into the woods (east) and just keep going. Down, down, down, any way that you can. There will be a creek on your right and one on your left that will eventually come together—just keep on following them downstream through Wellcave Hollow. You will eventually come to **Spirit Mountain Falls** at about 1.0. It's not a giant falls, but empties into an emerald pool that is beautiful.

To get to **Mountain Fork Creek Falls** continue on downstream and you will come to a jeep road just before you hit Mountain Fork Creek (the four-wheeler trail from the Lodge comes in off to your right here)—TURN LEFT and follow the jeep road about .25 mile to **Mountain Fork Creek Falls**. It's a perfect spot for a dip in the pool!

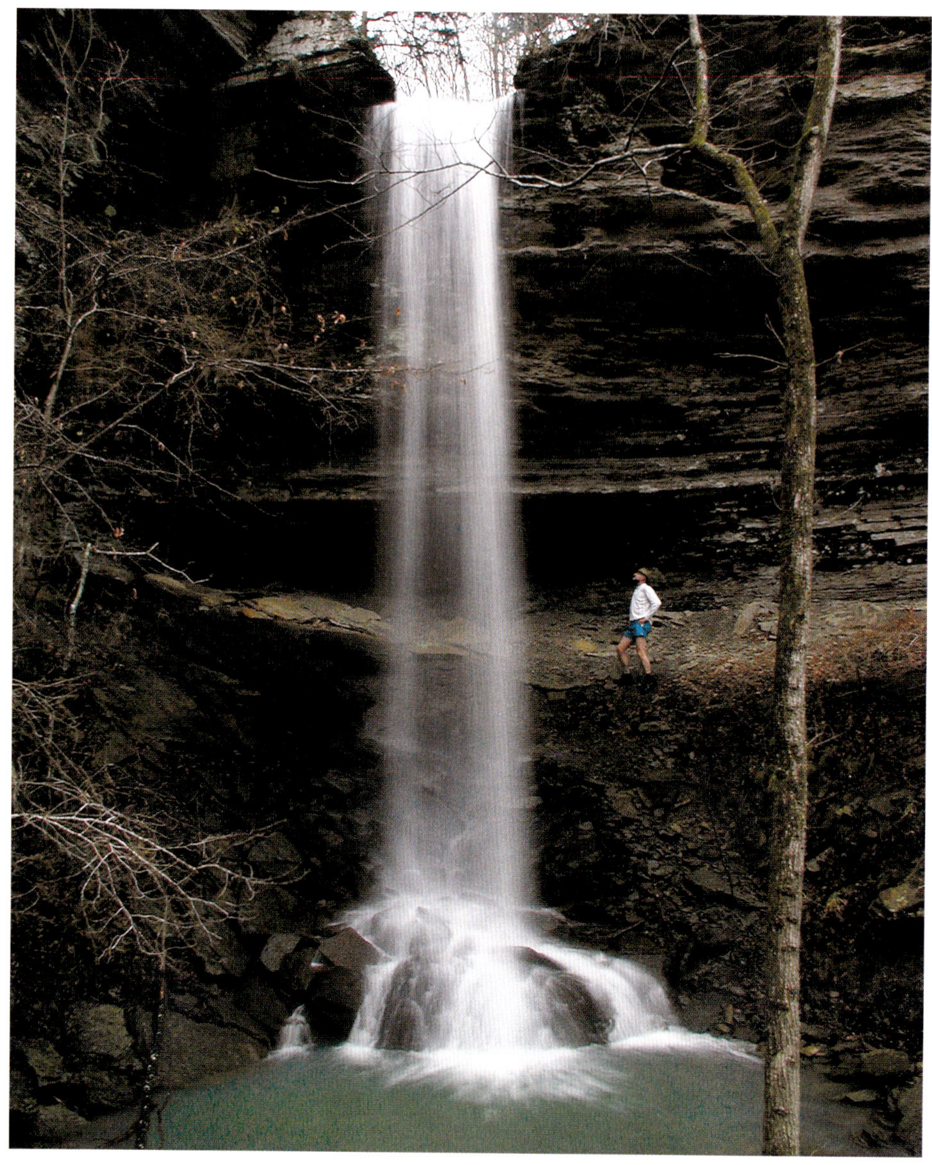

Sixty Foot Falls

To get to **Sixty Foot Falls** cross Mountain Fork Creek above the falls, TURN RIGHT and follow the creek back downstream—there is a jeep road you can follow part way. Continue for .4 (across a couple of small streams that may have little waterfalls of their own) until you come to a stream and you should hear the falls up on your left—follow the stream up to the base of the falls. The locals' guess at the height of this falls was pretty close ("Sixty" Foot Falls). If you can make your way up through the bluffline there is a really nice cascade above the falls, and a cave to explore.

To return to the parking area follow the stream below the falls down to Mountain Fork Creek, get across the creek and go upstream to Wellcave Hollow and make the 700 foot climb back out the same way you came in.

Emergency contact: Franklin County Sheriff, 479–667–4127 Dogs are OK

Spy Rock Falls – 19′

1.0 mile roundtrip, easy hike, GPS not needed

GPS **35.69373, -93.75690**

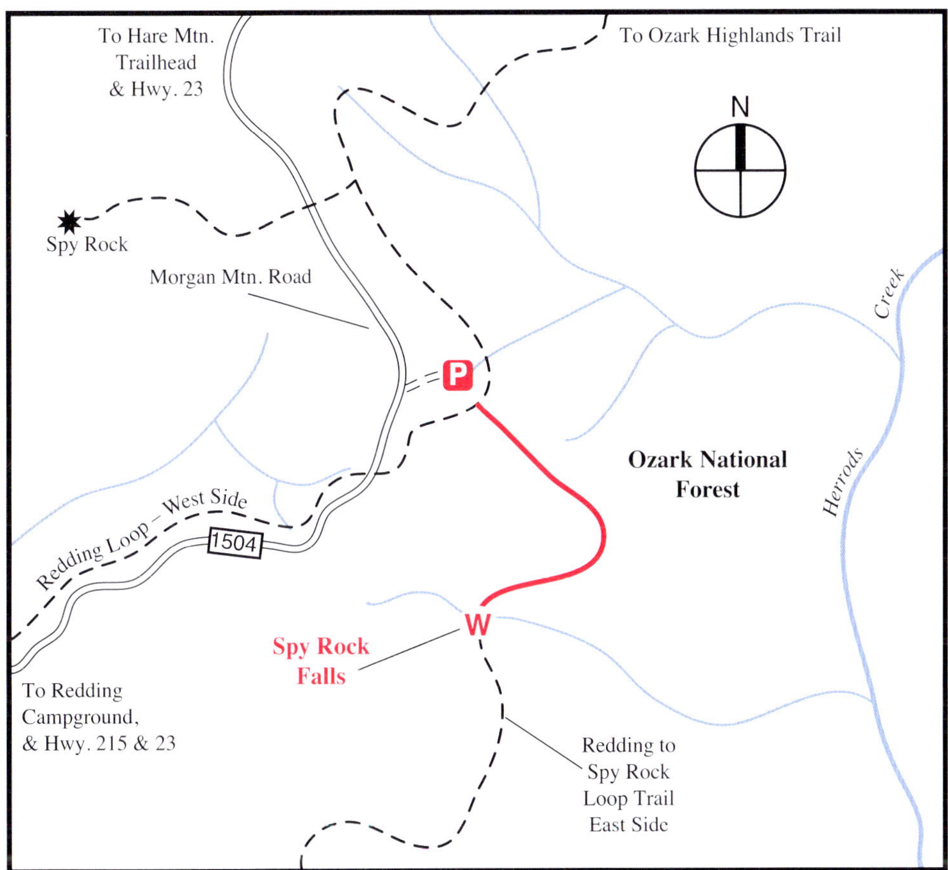

SPY ROCK FALLS. This waterfall takes its name from a nearby rock outcrop that was supposedly used as a lookout point while the Spanish hid hordes of gold nearby. No one has ever found the gold that we know of, but the legend lives on. The falls is located on a loop trail that comes up from Redding Campground, goes out to Spy Rock, and also connects with the Ozark Highlands Trail. We are going to take the easy way in and park near the falls, but you can also hike the 8.8 mile loop trail and make a day of it.

To get to the parking area from Cass, go north on Hwy. 23 and TURN RIGHT onto Hwy. 215 (just as you begin to climb the hill) and follow it about three miles to just past the turnoff to Redding Campground. TURN LEFT onto Morgan Mountain Road/FR#1504 (gravel), then go 1.8 miles up the hill and TURN RIGHT into an open area that is used for camping (**35.69808, -93.75907** ish...there is a small pond nearby).

Head off to the right into the woods along a jeep road where you will find a hiking trail intersection just a couple hundred feet or so ahead. The trail to the right is the West Loop and goes down to Redding Campground, the one on the left goes out to Spy Rock and the OHT—go STRAIGHT AHEAD at this intersection to head towards the falls (you will be on the East Side Loop Trail that also goes down to Redding Campground).

The trail is mostly level and goes downhill just a little bit along an old road trace,

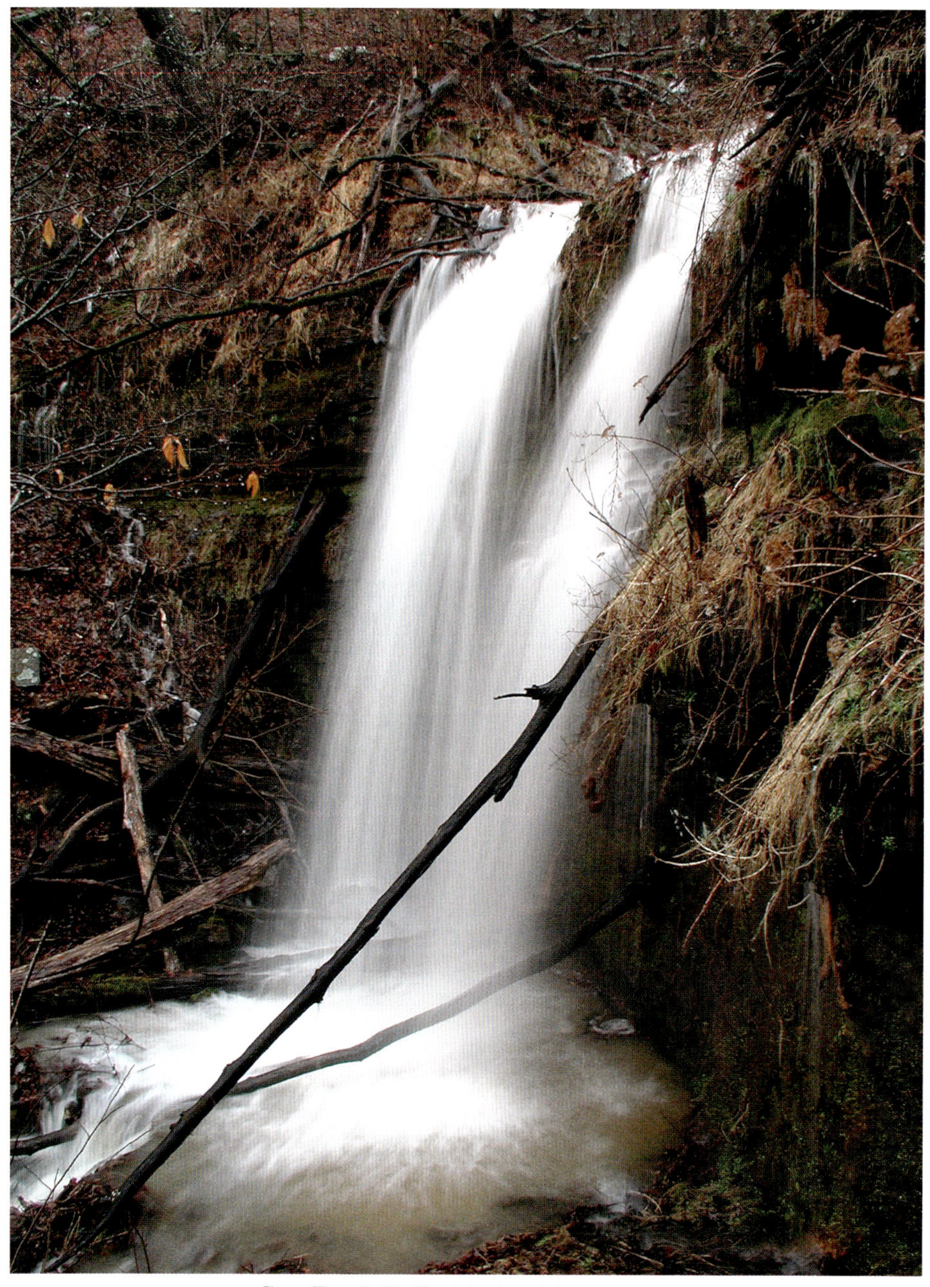

Spy Rock Falls (during high water)

swings around to the right, and comes to the small creek at .5. This is the creek that forms the waterfall, and you will see it just below the trail on your left. It was really pouring buckets when I took the photo above, and while the falls don't normally run that much, they are often a nice little falls worth a trip to go see.

If you want to hike the entire loop trail, start back down at a trailhead that is located just east of the Redding Campground turnoff, and hike the loop in either direction.

Emergency contact: Franklin County Sheriff, 479–667–4127 Dogs are OK

High Bank Twins – 71′

.5 mile roundtrip, easy bushwhack, GPS not needed

GPS **35.68077, -93.68694**

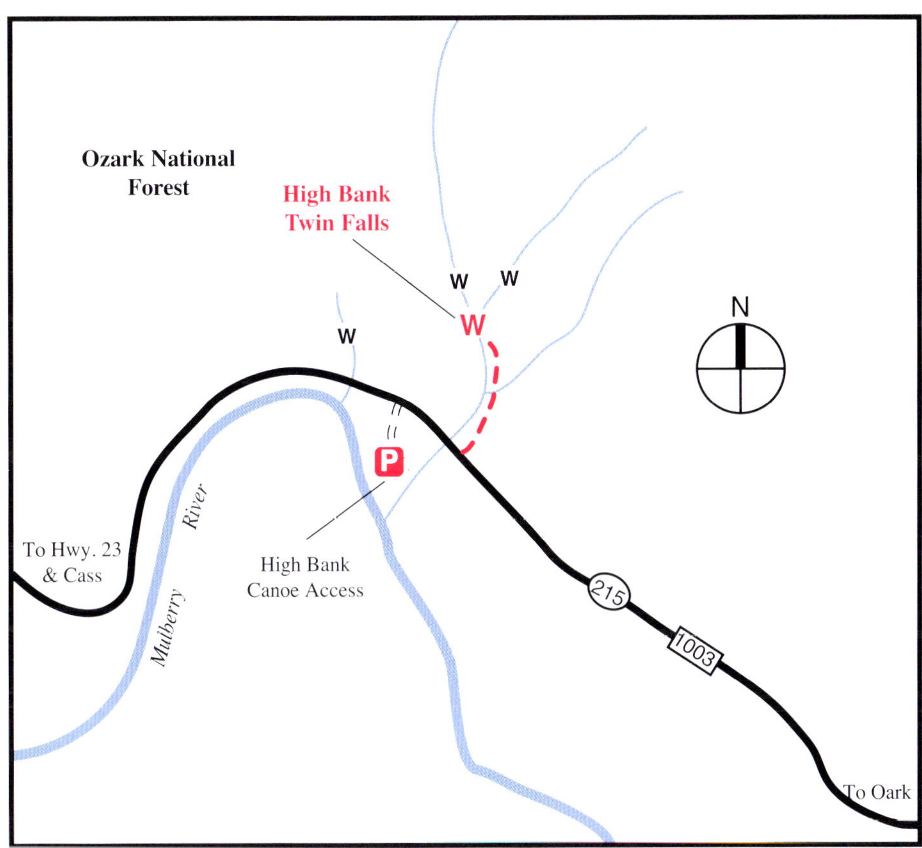

HIGH BANK TWINS. When the water is running high this is one of the most beautiful waterfalls in Arkansas! And it is located right next to a road so the access is quick and easy. You can't really see the falls from the road so few people have been to see it—let's just keep it our little secret.

To get to the High Bank Canoe Access area to park, take Hwy. 23 north from Cass and TURN RIGHT onto Hwy. 215 (just as you begin to climb the hill out of Cass), follow it 9.2 miles and TURN RIGHT into the High Bank Canoe Access parking area which is well signed **(35.67954, -93.68883)**. There is also a small paved pulloff right on the highway just past this turnoff). This is one of the major put-in points for the popular Mulberry River, a great Ozark floating stream.

From the parking area go out to the road, TURN RIGHT and cross over a stream that is coming in from the left, then leave the road TO THE LEFT and follow that creek upstream (no trail). The woods are level at first, but soon get a little rougher and rocky as you go along. Cross a small stream coming in from the right, and just another hundred yards farther and you will be looking right into the face of these magnificent falls.

Emergency contact: Franklin County Sheriff, 479-667-4127 Dogs are OK

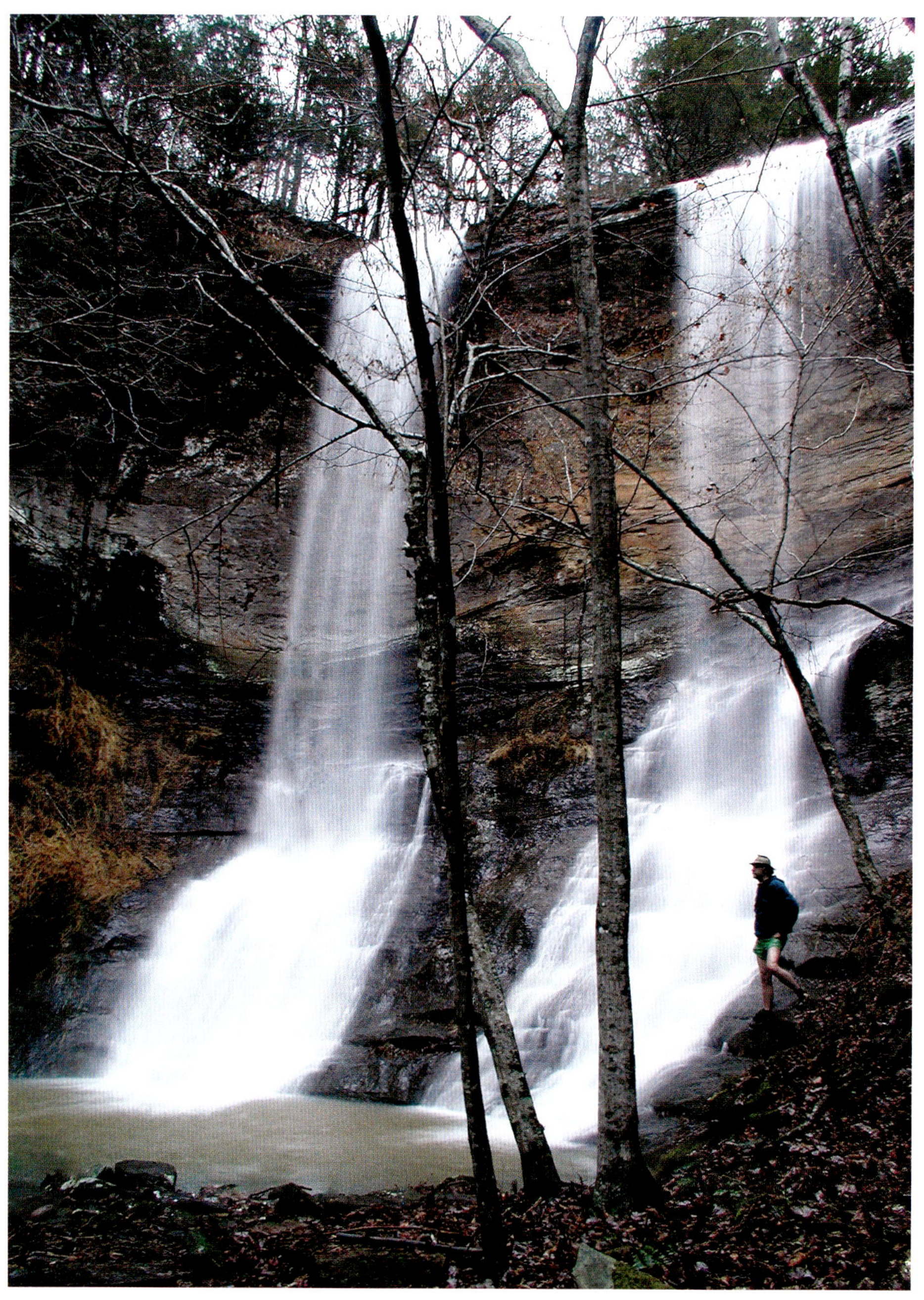

High Bank Twins (during high water)

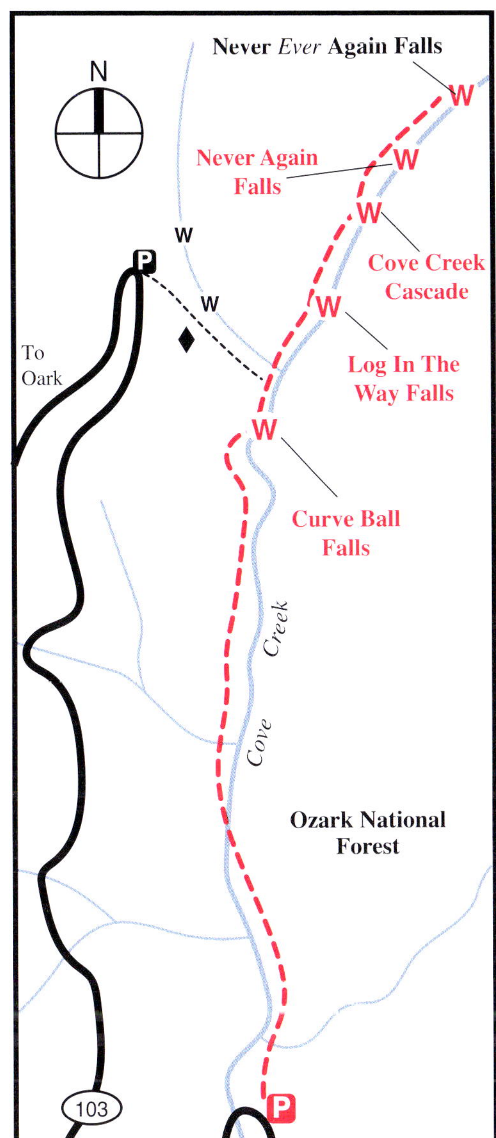

Curve Ball Falls–33′

.7 mi GPS **35.60990, -93.58324**

Log In The Way Falls–30′

GPS **35.61100, -93.58236**

Cove Creek Cascade–21′

GPS **35.61223, -93.58171**

Never Again Falls–39′

GPS **35.61281, -93.58109**

Never Ever Again Falls–31′

1.2 mi GPS **35.61351, -93.58038**

CURVE BALL AREA WATERFALLS. From the square in Clarksville take Hwy 103 north 12.3 miles and PARK on the right at the bridge across Cove Creek (**35.60082, -93.58328** sharp curve).

From this parking spot simply follow the Cove Creek upstream (bushwhacking—no trail, but probably a social trail), passing several cascades and short waterfalls, until you reach the signature waterfall in this drainage, **Curve Ball Falls** at .7. It's quite unique and looks different—changes personalities—with higher or lower water levels. The water was pretty high for my photos here.

Now the fun begins. The rest of the waterfalls are upstream, and the terrain gets difficult right away. For each you'll have to figure out a good way to get up and around the previous falls and to the base of the next—it's only a half mile to the farthest one up the creek, take your time.

The next falls above **Curve Ball** is **Log In The Way Falls**. Then it's up to **Cove Creek Cascade** (beautiful, and you can see Never Again Falls in the distance). **Never Again Falls** is next (I LOVE this one!). And then finally **Never *Ever* Again Falls** at about 1.2 from the parking spot.

TOUGH NUT NOTE. You can park on the highway very close to **Curve Ball Falls** (**35.61158, -93.58540** at the switchback 1.8 miles beyond the normal parking spot—only a tiny spot to park). It's a brutal BLACK DIAMOND ♦ slope down a side creek to Cove Creek, then **Curve Ball Falls** is just downstream, making the hike much shorter, but a LOT more difficult. There are some nice waterfalls in this side creek.

Emergency contact: Johnson County Sheriff, 479–754–2200 Dogs are OK

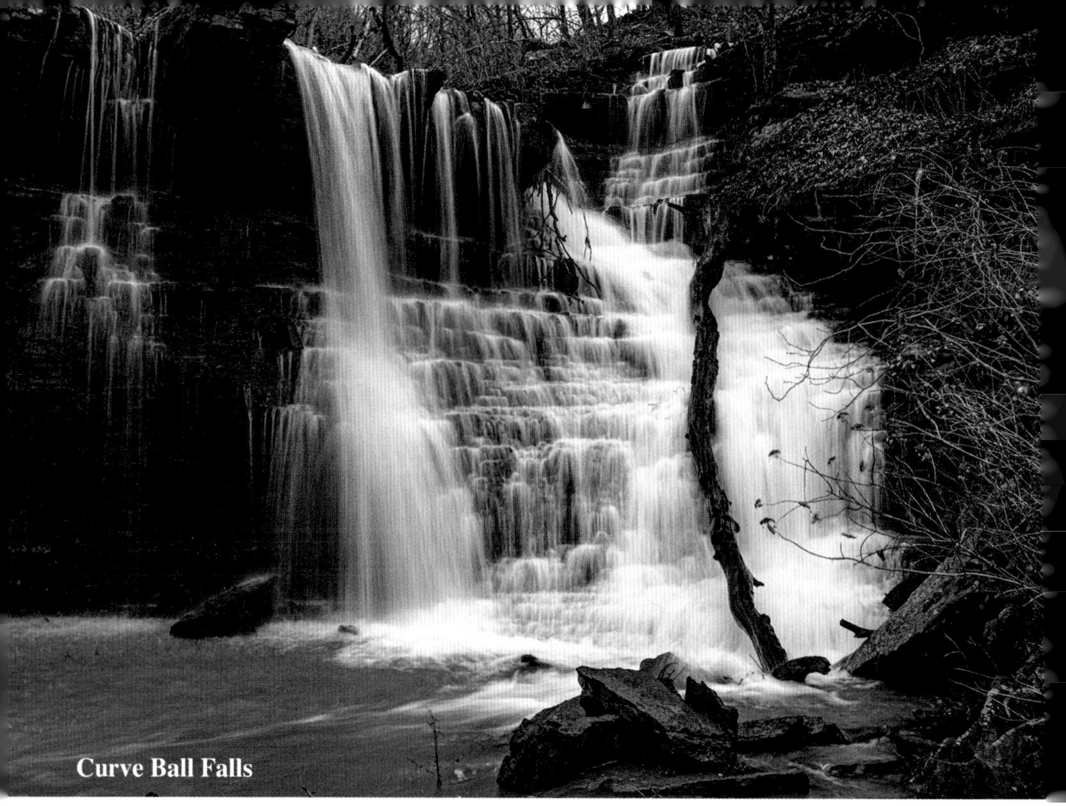

Curve Ball Falls

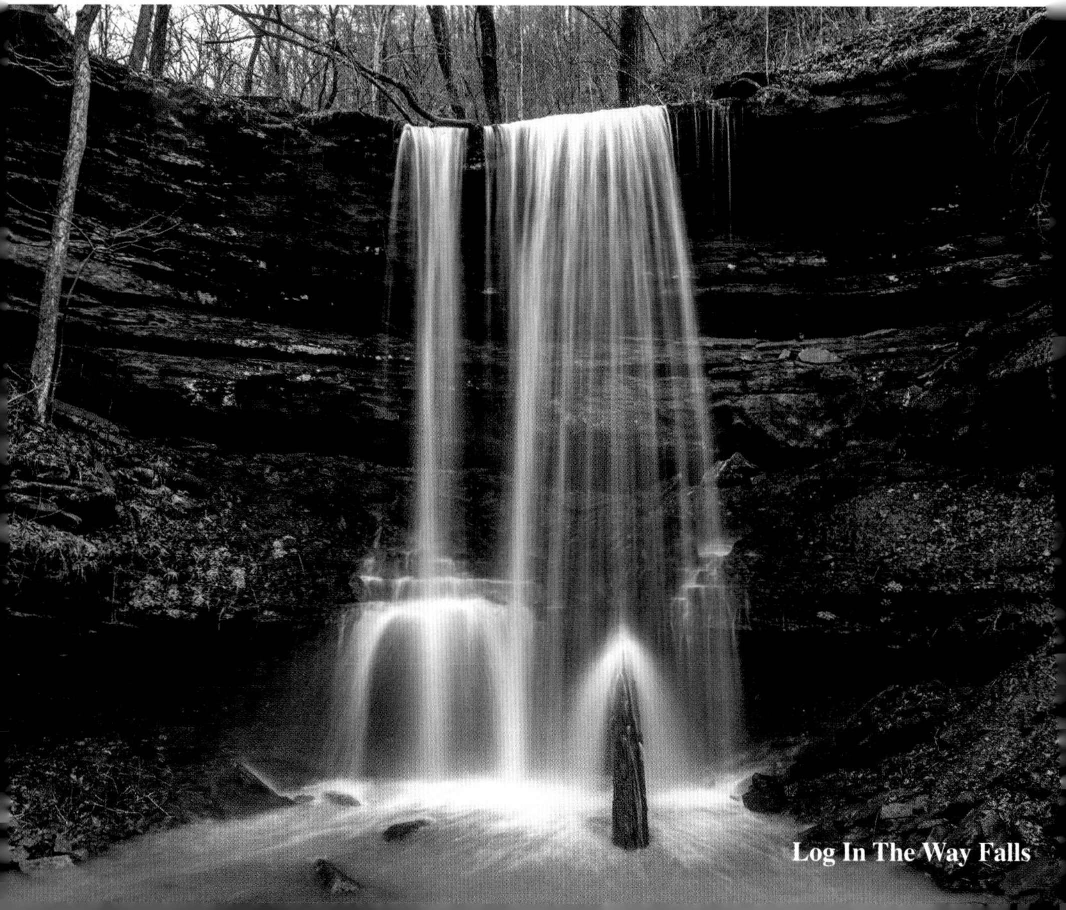

Log In The Way Falls

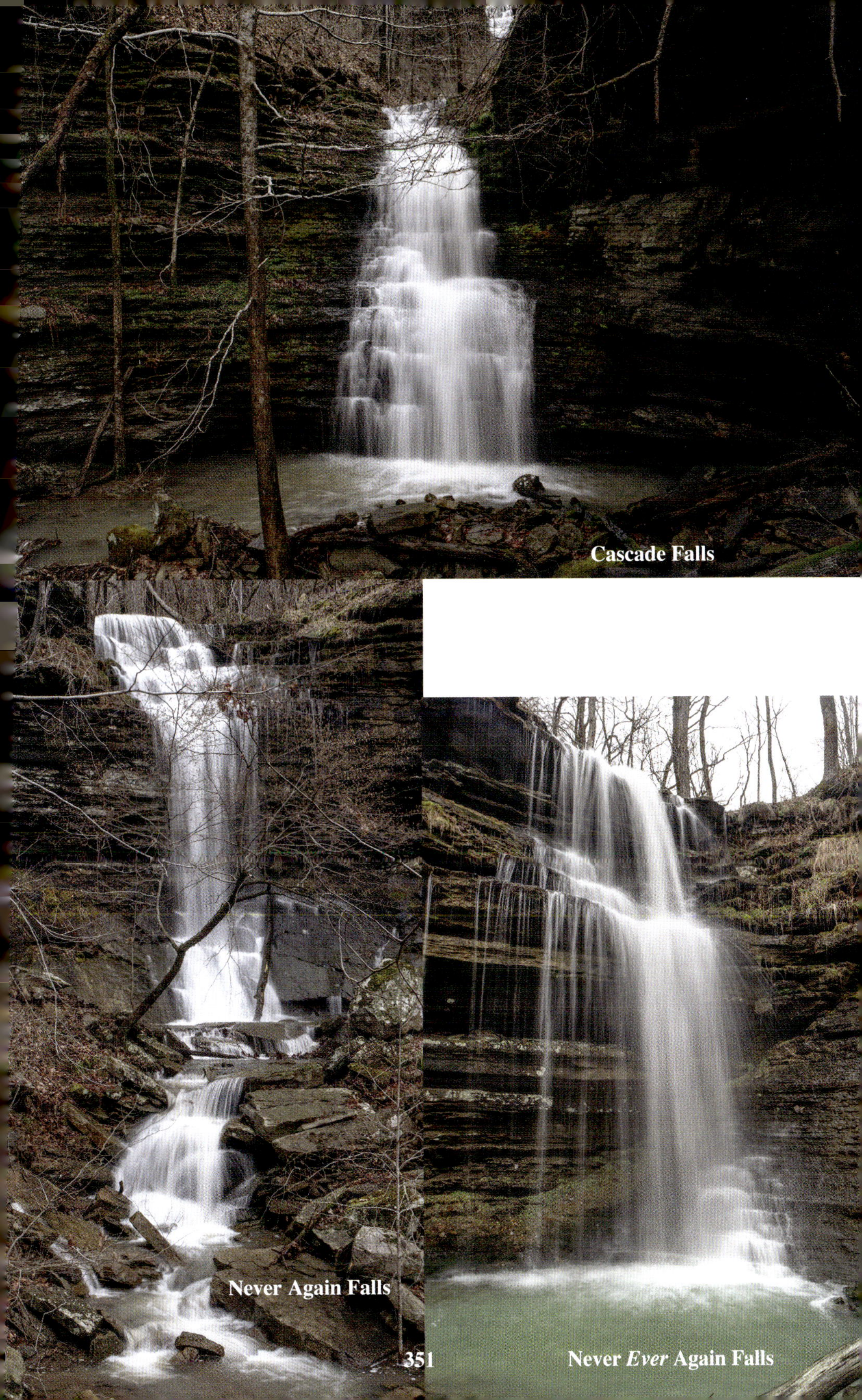

Cascade Falls

Never Again Falls

Never *Ever* Again Falls

Doppelgänger Falls –19'

1.5 mile roundtrip, medium bushwhack, GPS recommended

GPS **35.64950, -93.66066**

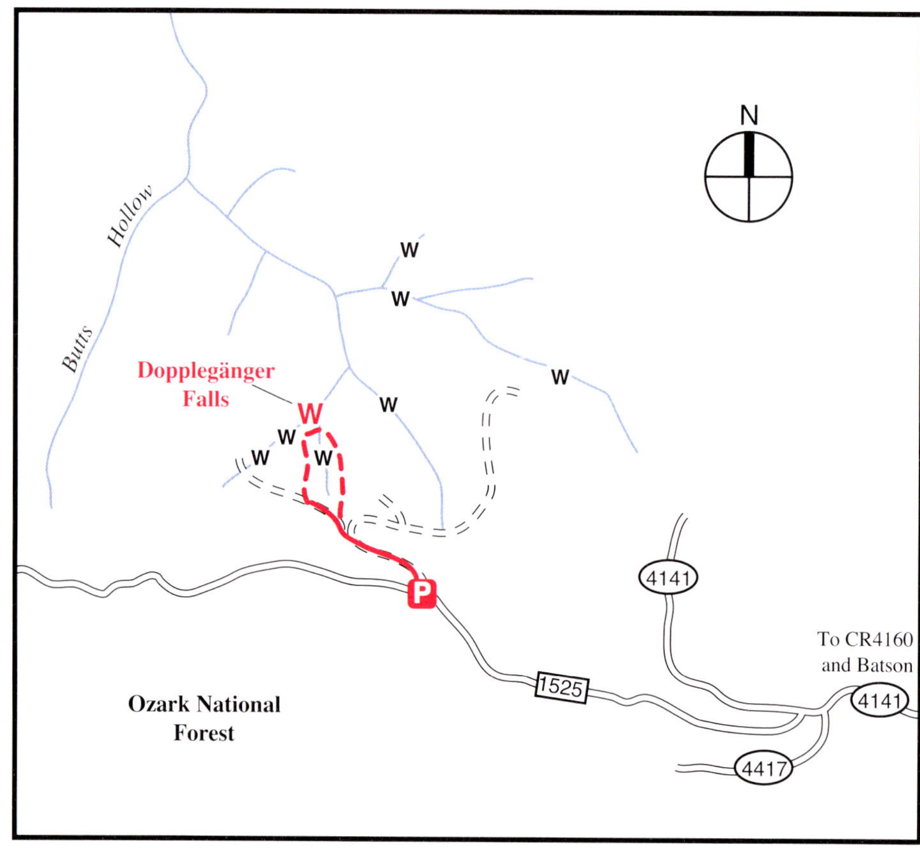

DOPPELGÄNGER FALLS. It means "twin." We have several great ones in Arkansas, and each one is unique and special (and one waterfall named "butt" in this guide was enough). There are other waterfalls in this polyfoss hollow to explore as well, including a 64' tall one. Some of them are noted on the map above.

From Hwy. 103 (between Oark and Clarksville) TURN WEST on CR#4160 towards Batson. Go 2.8 miles and TURN RIGHT onto FR#1525/CR#4141. Go 1.3 miles (just *past* CR#4417 on the left) and TURN LEFT as FR1525 continues (CR#4141 goes straight, up the hill). Go 1.0 on FR#1525 and PARK next to a jeep road that takes off down the hill to the right (**35.64384, -93.65612).**

Hike down the jeep road .2 to the bottom of the first hill and TURN LEFT onto a smaller jeep road. Follow this down to the first drainage and TURN RIGHT and start to bushwhack downhill. This will feed into a tall (64') waterfall. CONTINUE down the hill and you will run into the twin falls (easy access to the bottom). There are other waterfalls in the area too—see map.

Emergency contact: Johnson County Sheriff, 479–754–2200 Dogs are OK

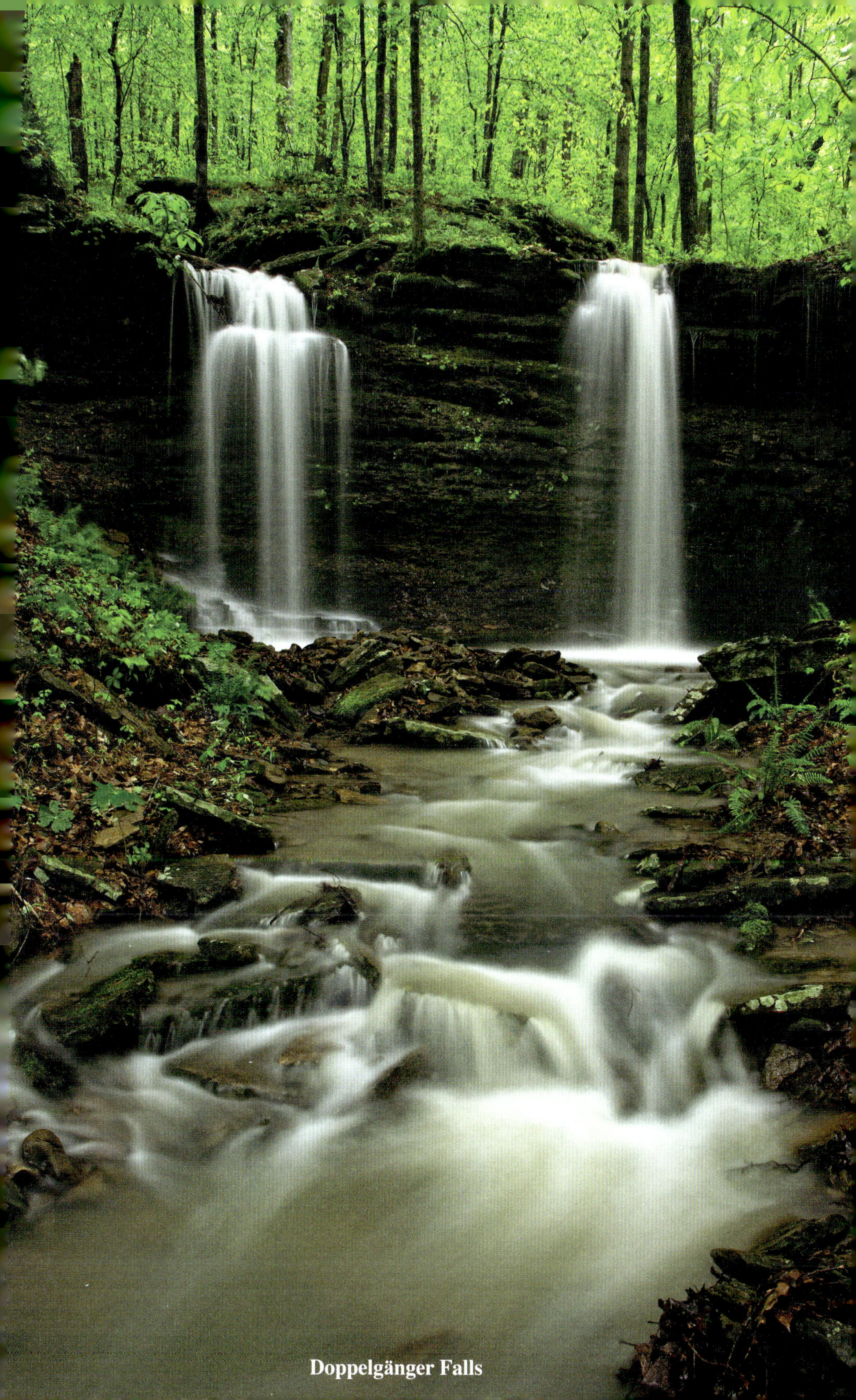

Doppelgänger Falls

Boars Head Falls – 49′

.1 mile GPS **35.66412, -93.62118**

Two Tier Falls – 37′

.2 mile GPS **35.66458, -93.62031**

Fallen Timber Falls – 21′

.3 mile GPS **35.66533, -93.62161**

Whiskey Falls Upper – 24′

.5 mile GPS **35.66747, -93.62112**

Amy Falls – 29′

.75 mile GPS **35.66680, -93.62425**

Short Grotto Falls – <10′

1.1 mile, moderate bushwhack GPS **35.66818, -93.62826**

2.6 mile medium bushwhack loop to all

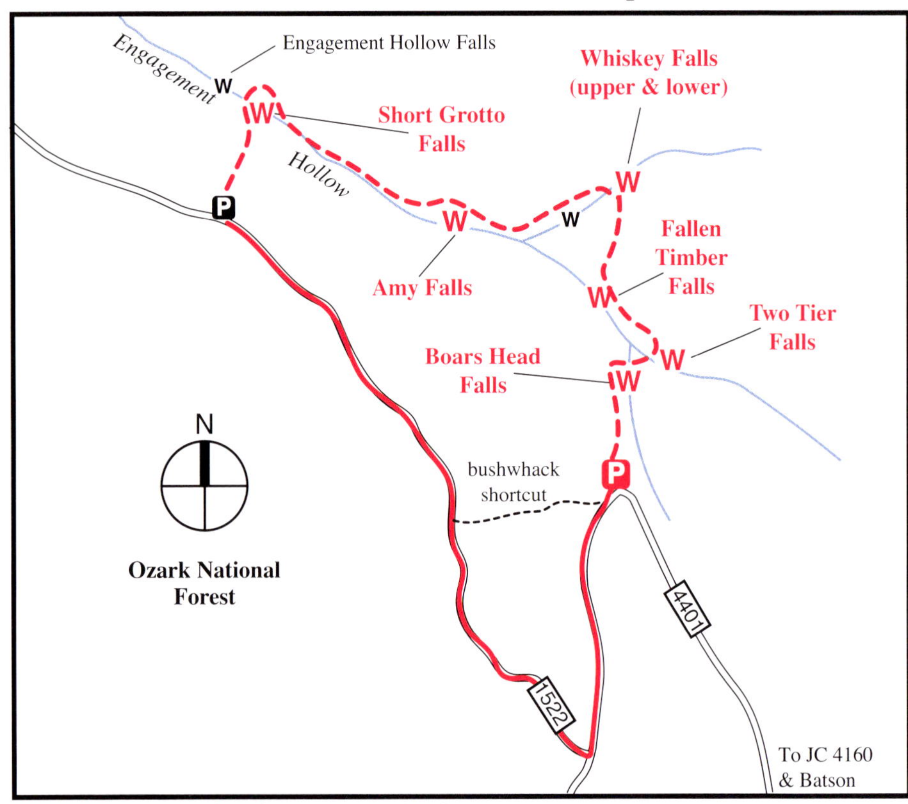

ENGAGEMENT HOLLOW WATERFALLS. Here's another Brian Emfinger group of waterfall finds—he named them to honor his friends who got engaged at one of the waterfalls (Amy Falls). All bushwhacking but there probably are social trails by now. Two parking areas—one at the top and one at the bottom, with an old forest road in between. If you just want to visit the signature waterfall here (Short Grotto Falls), you can drive to the lower parking spot and hike down to it. But there is so much more to see if you do the entire trip from top to bottom, and it's just a little more than a mile each way.

From Clarksville go north on Highway 103 for 14.3 miles and turn left (west) on CR4160 towards Batson. Go 2.8 miles and turn right (north) on CR4141. Go a half mile and turn right onto FR4401. Go 2.3 miles (bear left at the Y), and PARK **(35.66268, -93.62127)**—this is the main/upper parking area. To reach the lower parking area continue down FR4401 .3 mi and turn right onto FR1522 for .7 and PARK **(35.66666, -93.62910)**. The lower parking area is almost directly above **Short Grotto Falls**.

From the upper parking spot head into the woods and drop down into the drainage to the right. Follow this down to **Boars Head Falls**. From there work your way to the RIGHT across the hill or down to the creek and up to **Two Tier Falls**. Both of these are nice falls that look best with high water.

Follow the creek downstream to **Fallen Timber Falls** (I wonder if it is still clogged with lots of fallen timber?). From there continue downstream below the falls to a side creek on the RIGHT, and head up this drainage, past a nice 25' unnamed falls, to the next one above which is **Lower Whiskey Falls**. Continue to climb up to the next falls, **Upper Whiskey Falls**, an HSS (Historical Scenic Site). This was the site of an old still back in the prohibition days. (You could also take a short cut from Fallen Timber Falls across the steep hillside, curving around to Upper Whiskey Falls.)

Then turn around and follow the side creek back down to the main creek and TURN RIGHT. Just downstream is **Amy Falls**, the young lady who said YES! From Amy continue downstream until you come to the main attraction at about 1.1, **Short Grotto Falls**. This is a unique and quite beautiful SSS, and it helps if you don't mind getting your feet wet and going back into the grotto.

There's another waterfall downstream (Engagement Hollow Falls, I've not been to it). I usually just head on out of the canyon from Short Grotto and back to the car—when looking upstream at the falls go to the RIGHT/SW, straight UP the hillside to the old road (lower parking spot). Follow the road to the LEFT uphill for about a mile to the top parking spot at 2.6. (there's a shortcut through the woods up near the top that saves a little bit.) Emergency contact: Johnson County Sheriff, 479–754–2200 Dogs are OK

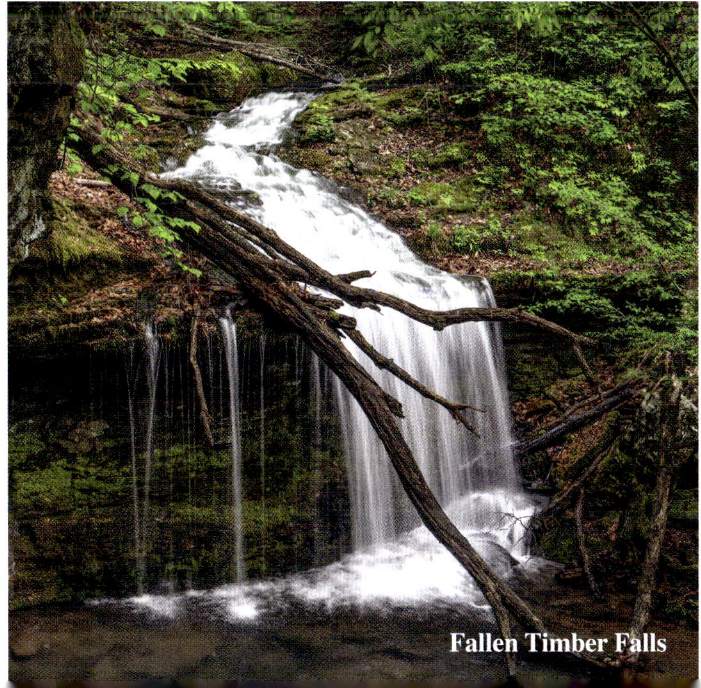

Fallen Timber Falls

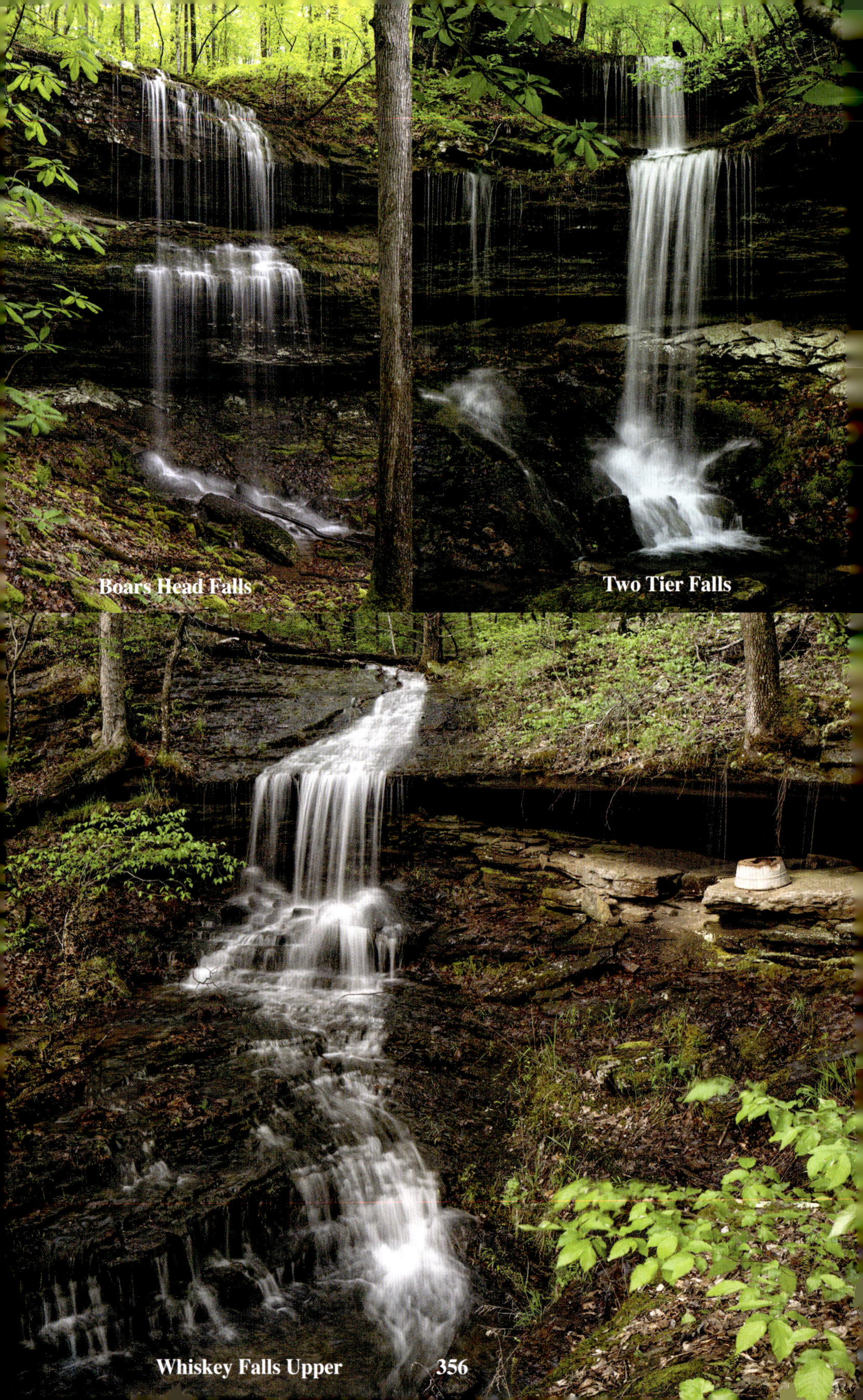
Boars Head Falls
Two Tier Falls
Whiskey Falls Upper

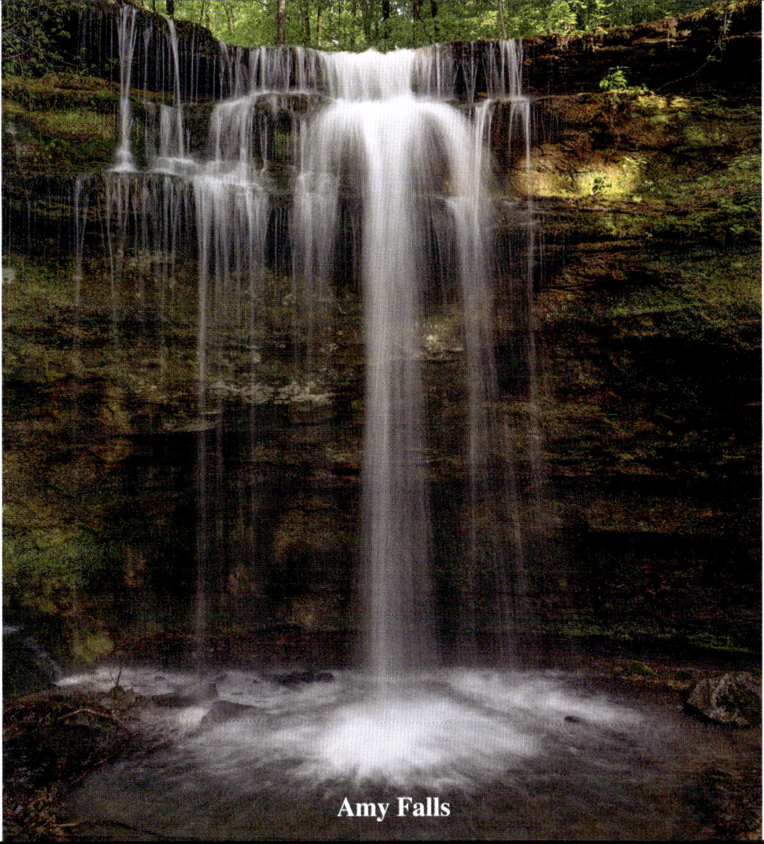

Amy Falls

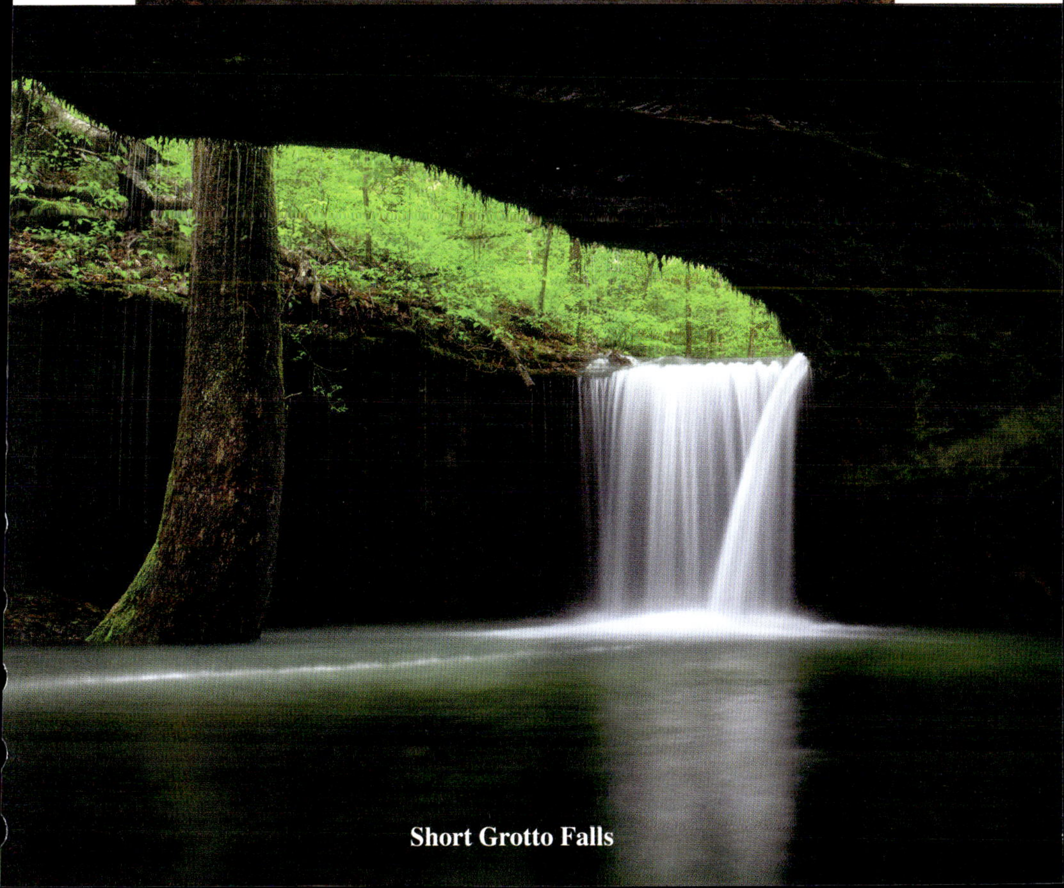

Short Grotto Falls

Briandjen Twin Falls – 33 & 31′

1.2 mi roundtrip, difficult bushwhack ♦ GPS **35.61691, -93.63286**

JenLynn Bridge Falls – 10′

difficult bushwhack ♦ GPS **35.61718, -93.63275**

Marilyn/Cinnamon Falls – 61′

difficult bushwhack ♦ GPS **35.61586, -93.63367**

Lucky Falls – 23′

difficult bushwhack ♦ GPS **35.61304, -93.63275**

3.5 miles roundtrip to all, difficult bushwhack ♦

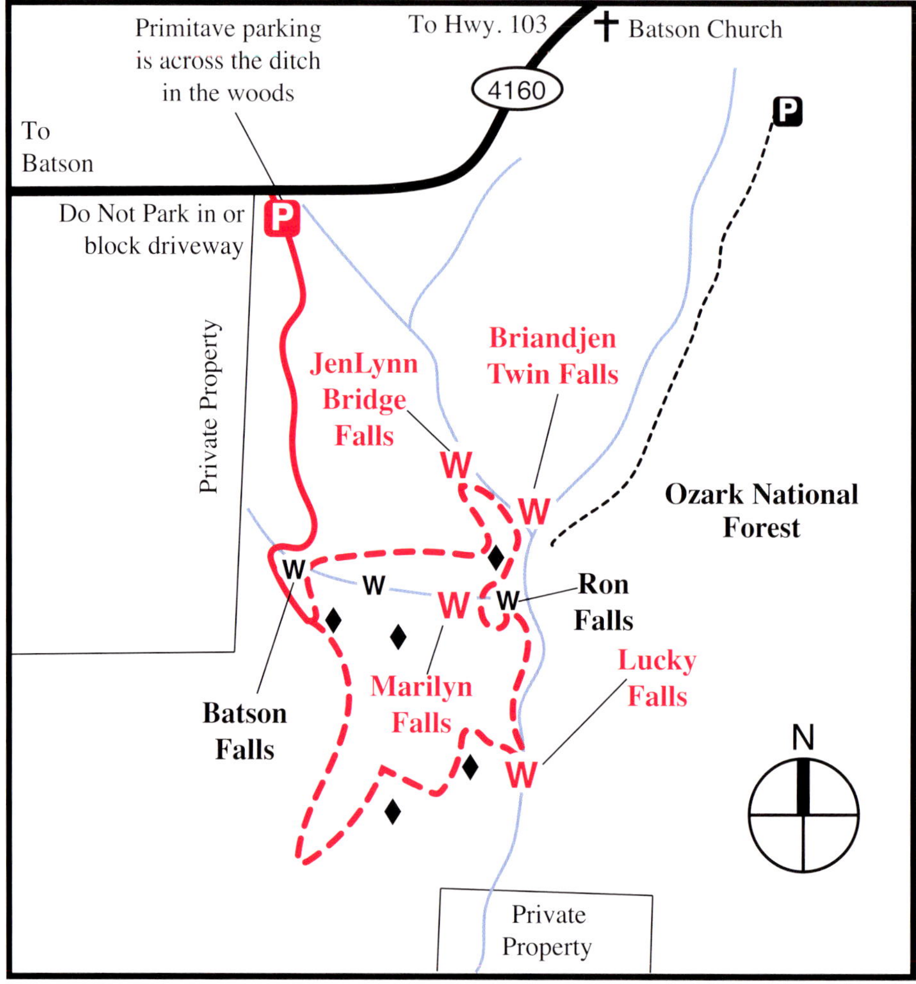

BATSON FALLS AREA. This is another outstanding area documented and named by Brian Emfinger. All but one of this group of falls is pretty close together, and not too long of a hike—BUT the terrain is mostly BLACK DIAMOND ♦ slopes and bushwhacking so it's quite a difficult hike, and there is not a good spot to park.

From Clarksville go north on Highway 103 for 14.3 miles and turn left (west) on CR-4160 towards Batson. Go 3.8 miles and PARK on the left alongside the highway or on the old logging road **(35.62273, -93.63790), just across a ditch and into the woods**. There is no designated parking spot so be sure you DO NOT PARK on private property.

Follow the old timber road into the woods and mostly on the level (there were a few giant trees blown down along the way my last visit in 2025) to .6 where you drop down to and across a stream, then a couple hundred yards past this make your way to the LEFT away from the road and down to the bluff hillside just below—find a way to the base of the bluff and TURN LEFT and follow the bluff back to the stream for **Baston Falls**, an SSS with a nice shelter behind (no photo provided).

Now the fun stuff begins. Follow that stream downhill as best you can—much of it is a BLACK DIAMOND slope ♦, with cascades and a couple of waterfalls along the way. Eventually you will end up at the top of the major bluff line in the area at 1.2. There's a way down through the bluff to the left of the stream, and once below the bluff TURN RIGHT and curve around into the hillside to the magnificent **Marilyn Falls**, a major SSS.

There's a balcony part way up behind the falls, and you will find giant cinnamon ferns along the shelf. This is a powerful, awe-inspiring place when the water is high, but even when almost dry it's a great place to spend some time and enjoy life.

OPTIONS NOW. Follow the stream down to the main creek (past **Ron Falls**, no photo provided), then TURN LEFT and hike upstream to the base of **Briandjen Twin Falls**.

OR what I do—from **Marilyn Falls** go back to the base of the bluff where you came down from and go UPSTREAM below the bluff and hike level across a very steep hillside ♦—don't get too close to the lower edge of the hillside above the main creek below. You are hiking into the head of the main canyon and will soon come to a view of **Briandjen Twin Falls** down on the right, another powerful SSS, especially when the waters are high.

At that point continue on across the steep slope you have been following, then up the small side creek to the left that feeds the first of the twins falls you just saw—drop down to this side creek to one of the most unusual waterfalls in Arkansas—a very flat and LOW Natural Bridge with the creek flowing beneath it, and waterfall just above—it's almost like it was AI generated! This is **JenLynn Bridge Falls**, of course an SSS!

If you want to get below twin falls, then work your way across both creeks to the other side and work your way above the bluff downstream until you can find a way to the bottom ♦—not for the faint of heart. Once down on the creek you can hike downstream to the side drainage of **Marilyn Falls** and there is a nice double-tiered cascade (**Ron Falls**).

Continue your hike downstream on the main creek until you come to a very wide **Lucky Falls** at about 2.0 that spans the entire creek—BEAUTIFUL! Be aware that PRIVATE PROPERTY is just downstream.

I've climbed the 700 vertical feet from this falls back to the highway two different ways, and I prefer a route #1 back to **Marilyn Falls** via the creek, then climb up through the bluff on the right and back out the same way I came in.

OR from **Lucky Falls** you can hike STRAIGHT UP the hillside to the big bluff above ♦, then turn LEFT and hike along it until you can find a wide break in the bluff—all of this is a BLACK DIAMOND slope ♦ and you may be down on all fours clawing!
When you reach a level bench above TURN LEFT and follow an old logging road over to the nose of the ridge, then up and it switchbacks to the right—continue on this road all the way back to the highway. This road may be totally grown up and difficult to follow—so just follow the level terrain if needed. Either route is about 3.5 miles roundtrip.

Emergency contact: Johnson County Sheriff, 479–754–2200 Dogs are OK.

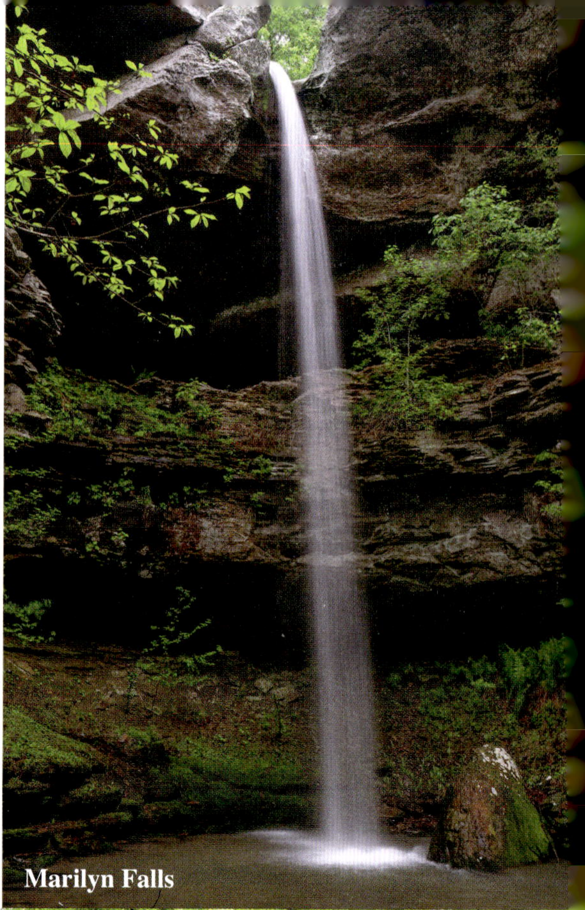

Marilyn Falls

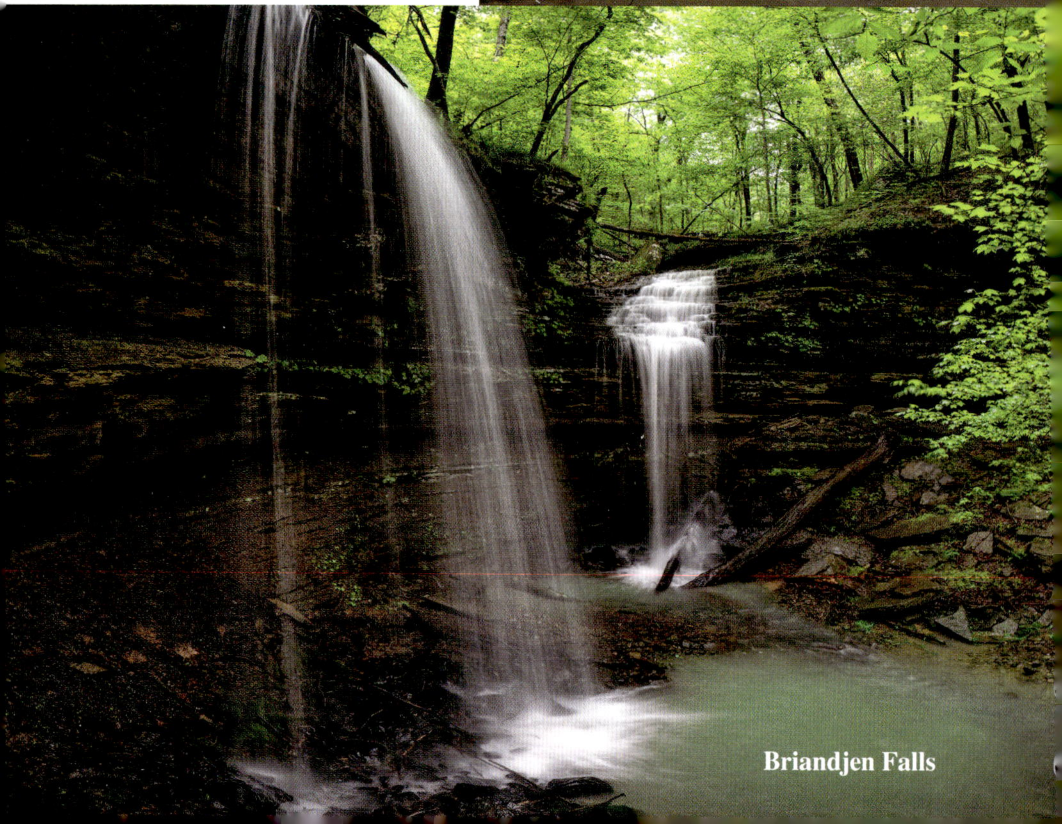

Briandjen Falls

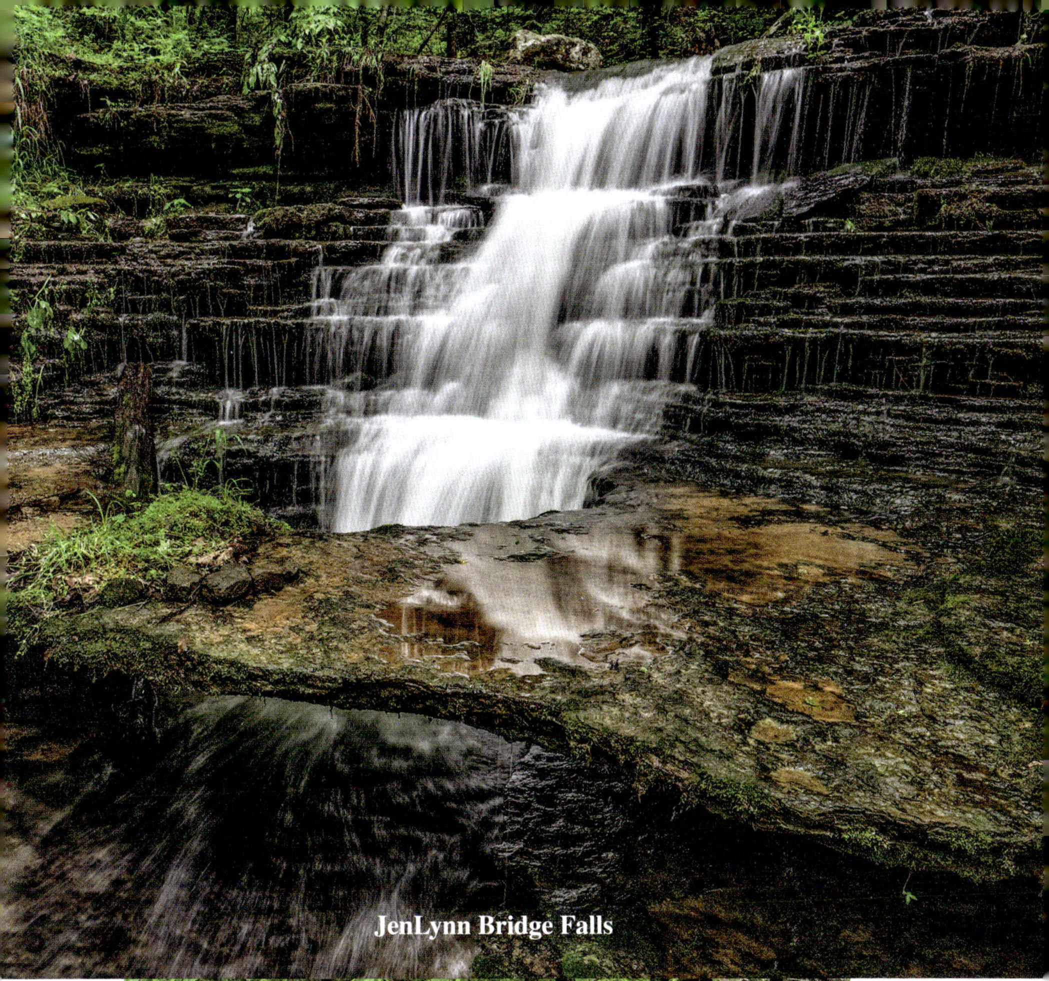

JenLynn Bridge Falls

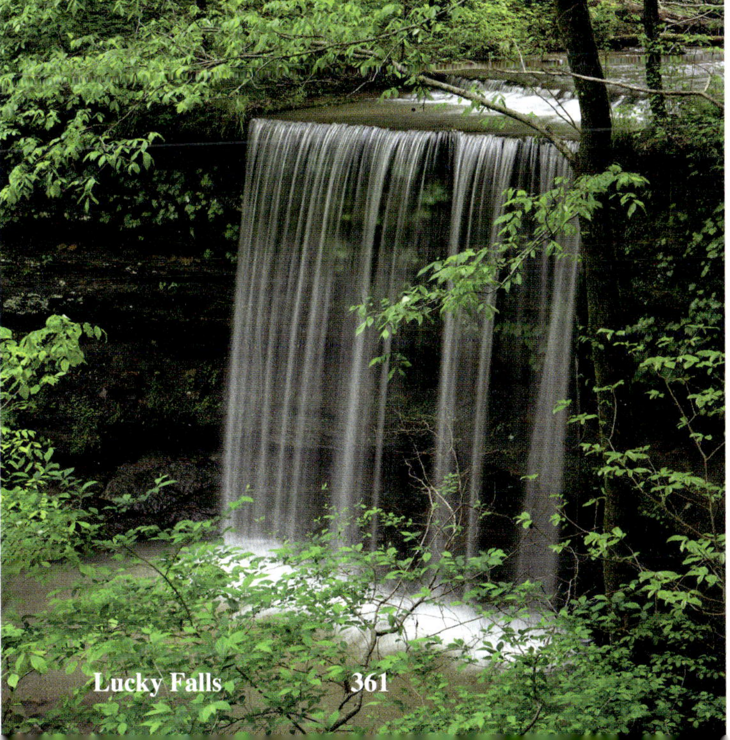

Lucky Falls

Brian's Polyfoss Area
Horsehead Creek Falls (4) –15′–35′

4.0 miles roundtrip (for all), difficult bushwhack, GPS recommended

GPS **35.60250, -93.65408**

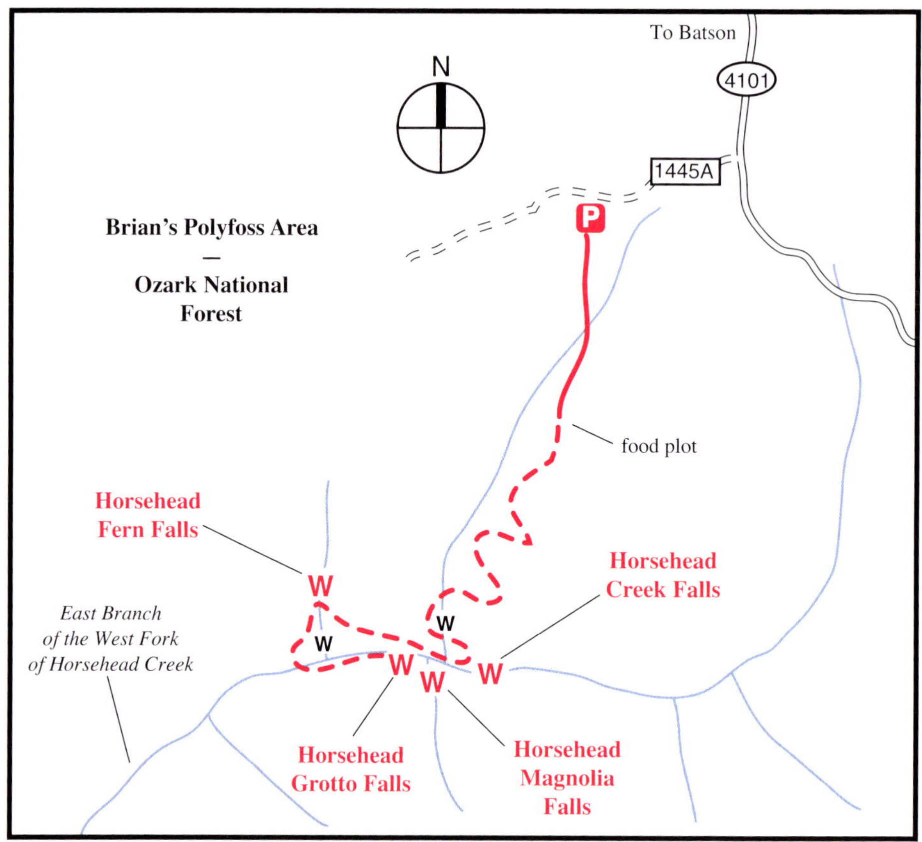

BRIAN'S POLYFOSS AREA, HORSEHEAD CREEK FALLS. Brian Emfinger started off just to explore a little creek—and discovered six waterfalls that day—then went on to discover 60 more waterfalls that same year in an area within a few miles of his home near Batson! (many more to come) So I thought it fitting to name this area after him—keep on hunting and finding more waterfalls Brian!

From Clarksville go north on Highway 103 for 14.3 miles and turn left (west) on CR-4160 towards Batson. Go 4.9 miles and TURN LEFT onto CR#4101. Go .7 and TURN RIGHT onto FR#1445A. Go .2 and TURN LEFT to PARK at the dirt barricade where a road was closed (**35.61052, -93.65133).**

This is a difficult spot to reach, but once you are down on the creek getting around is easy and it is just beautiful! From the parking area head out on an old roadbed that leads to a small field/food plot. Exit the far end of the field and bushwhack your way straight ahead through some very thick brush and make your way down through a bluffline. Then head STRAIGHT down the hillside until you land in the bottom on Horsehead Creek. There are four waterfalls within a couple hundred yards of each other where a side creek meets the Horsehead Creek, including the 35' waterfall pictured at right (upstream); one on the

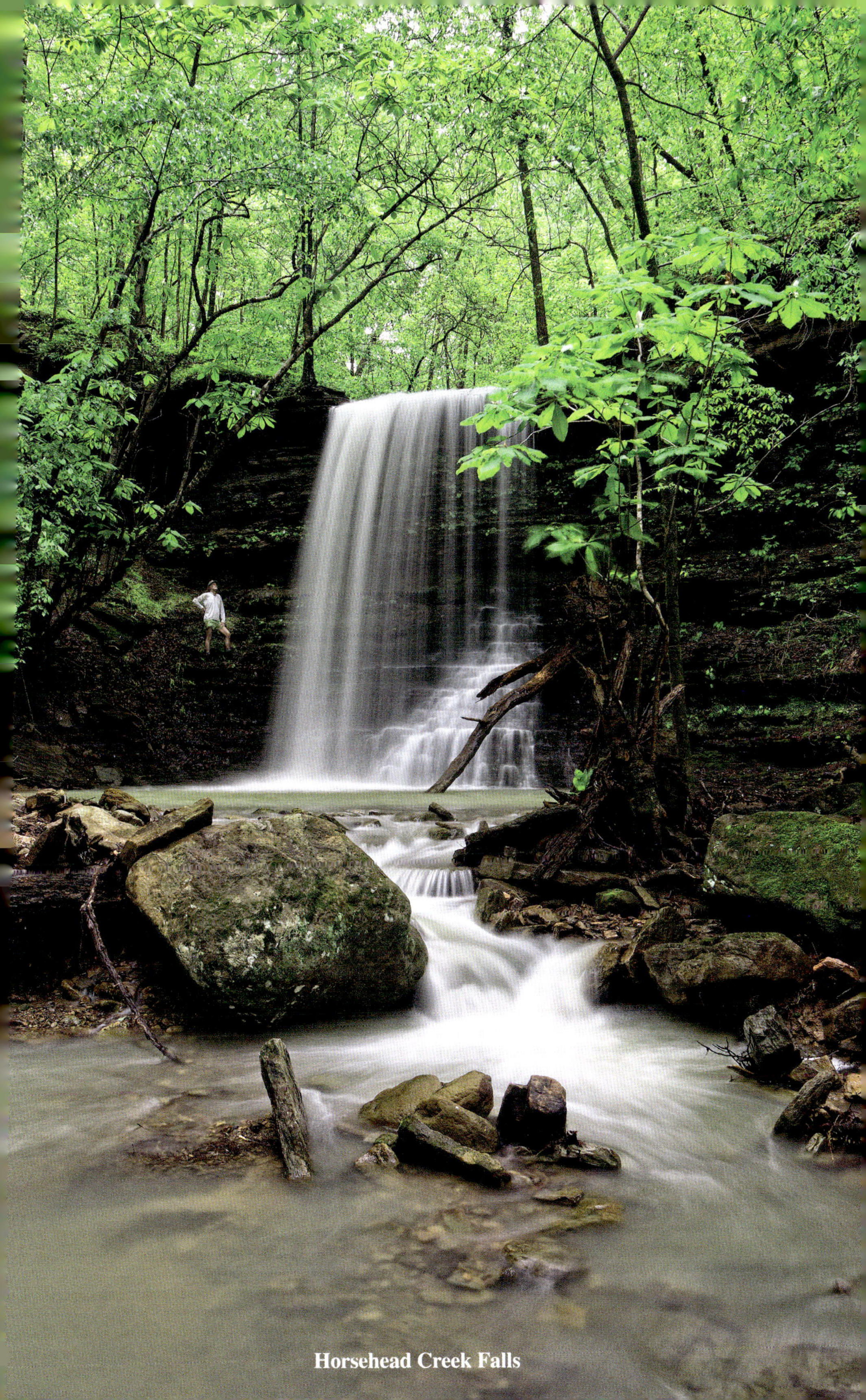

Horsehead Creek Falls

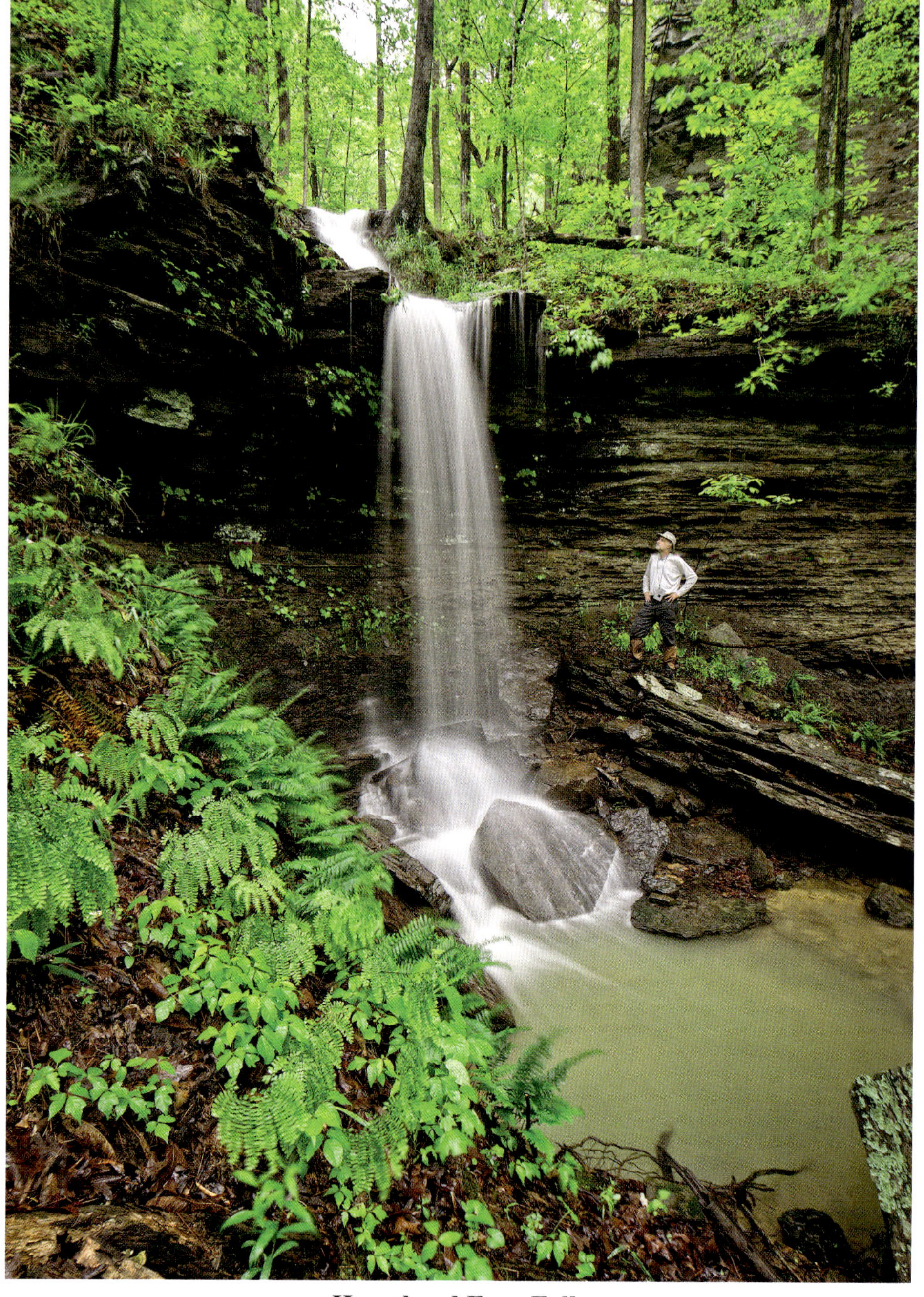

Horsehead Fern Falls

side creek; one that spills over a bluff into the main creek (**Magnolia**); and a nice cascade that ends with a 15' drop into a grotto on the main creek downstream (**Grotto**). Continue downstream on the right side and you will come to another side drainage with a waterfall down low and another one higher up (**Fern, 35.60295, -93.65762**). There are many more waterfalls in this area to explore and discover—just be sure to save enough energy for the climb out—it is one of the steepest hills in Arkansas!

Emergency contact: Johnson County Sheriff, 479–754–2200 Dogs are OK

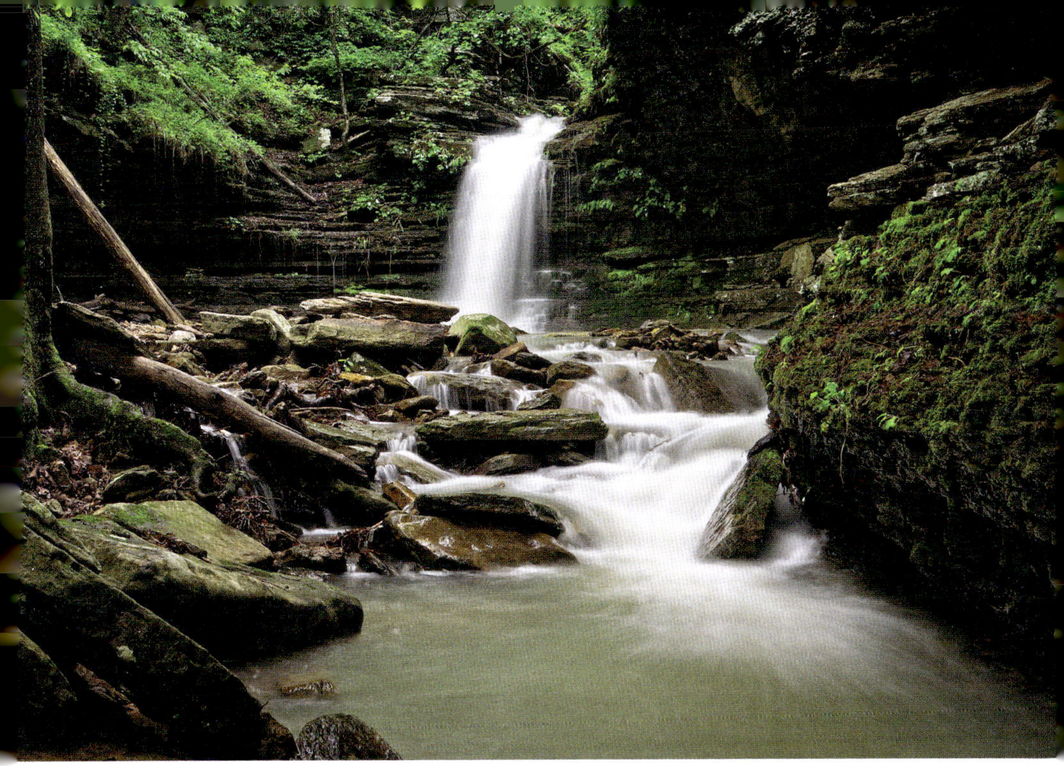

Horsehead Grotto Falls (above), **Horsehead Magnolia Falls** (below)

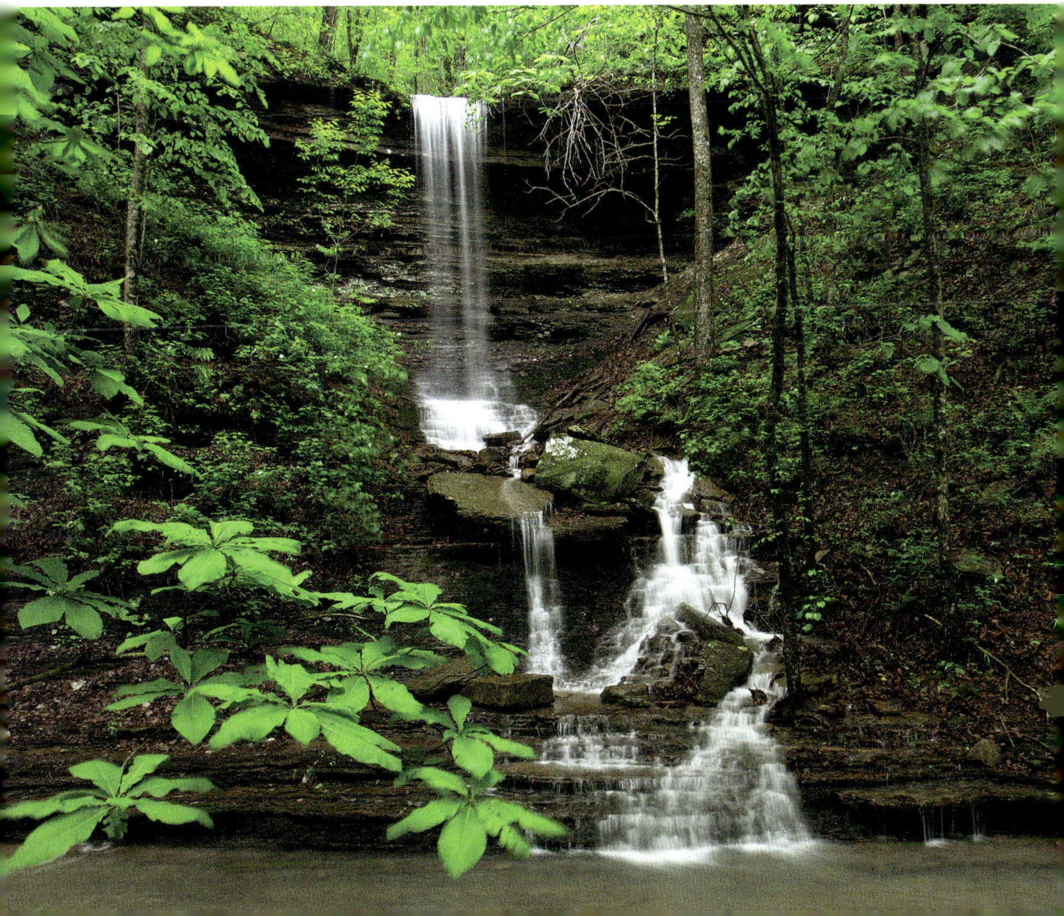

Secretariat Falls – 51′

2.0 mi, difficult bushwhack GPS **35.60035, -93.67920**

Wildfire Falls –33′

2.1 mi, difficult bushwhack ♦ GPS **35.59953, -93.67924**

Snowman Falls – 54′

2.25 mi, difficult bushwhack ♦ GPS **35.59802, -93.67985**

Seabiscuit Falls –44′

2.6 mi difficult bushwhack ♦ **GPS 35.60169, -93.68146**

Mr. Ed Falls – 23′

2.7 GPS **35.60227, -93.68243**

Trigger Falls – 35′

3.4 mi difficult bushwhack ♦ GPS **35.60578, -93.67796**

Silver Falls – 27′

3.5 mi difficult bushwhack ♦ GPS **35.60729, -93.67913**

Scout Falls – 30′

3.5 mi difficult bushwhack ♦ GPS **35.60743, -93.67890**

White Horse Falls – 24′

4.2 difficult bushwhack ♦ GPS **35.60566, -93.67317**

6.0 miles roundtrip loop to all, difficult bushwhack ♦

WEST HORSEHEAD CREEK WATERFALLS. HORSES WATERFALLS LOOP, 6.0 miles total, half road/half bushwhack, some BLACK DIAMOND ♦ slopes, many creek crossings.

From Clarksville go north on Highway 103 for 14.3 miles and turn left (west) on CR-4160 towards Batson. Go 4.9 miles and TURN LEFT onto CR#4101. Go .7 and TURN RIGHT onto FR#1445A. Go .3 and PARK (**35.61078, -93.65219**).

When the water is high, creeks are clear, and pools are emerald, THIS is one of the most beautiful waterfall loops in all of Arkansas. About half the loop is on old forest roads (easy hiking but also some very steep grades), with the rest of the loop being jungle bushwhacking—including several BLACK DIAMOND slopes ♦. Much of the bushwhacking is simply following creeks from one spot to another, and those creeks and surrounding landscapes are loaded with SSS areas. If you are comfortable in the wild woods with no trails it is possible to do this entire loop without a GPS or APP for guidance—by following the creeks—but I highly recommend some form of electronic location if you have it.

This area was originally documented by Brian Emfinger (one of many areas and dozens of waterfalls he has shared with everyone), though he did not name these. We have waterfall groups named after turtles (on Terrapin Branch) and cows (on Cow Creek), so I thought why not name these waterfalls on Horse Creek after famous HORSES? Being a geezer, many were well-known during my youth many moons ago (Silver and Trigger for instance), others were timeless epic horses from sport (Snowman, Secretariat), and others

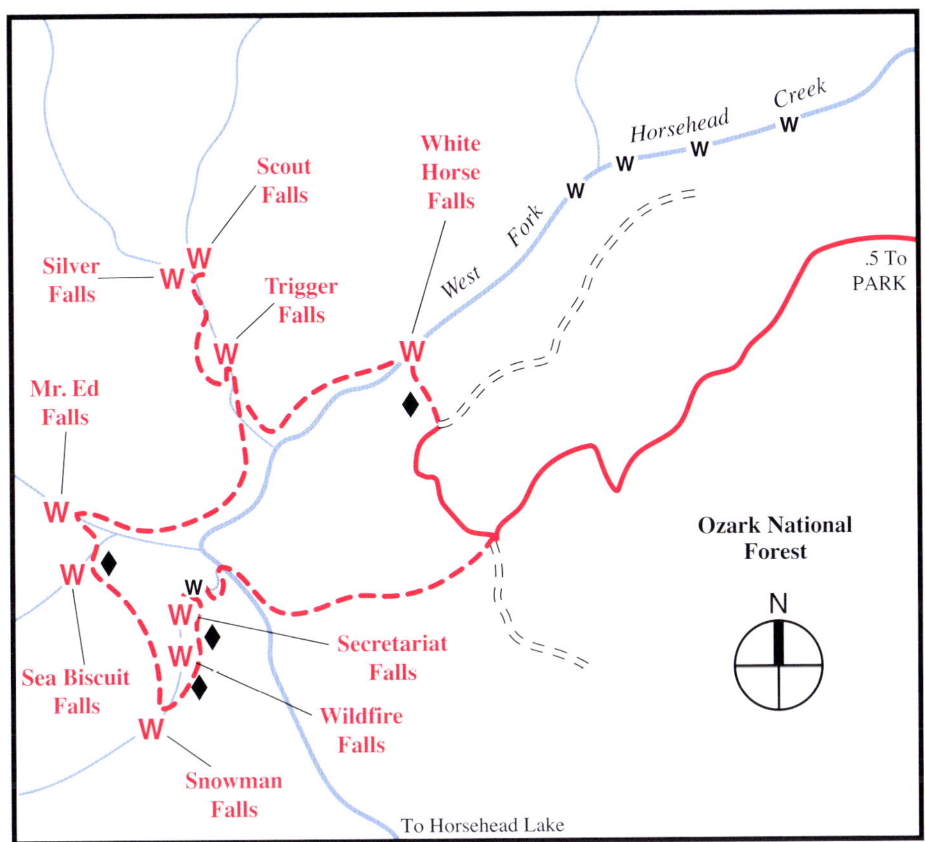

from popular culture (Mr. Ed the talking horse, Wildfire and White Horse from hit songs that I love). If you don't know some of these horses, I hope you will look them up and find some interesting info to go along with the amazing waterfalls these are.

The first mile or so of the old road may or may not be open to vehicles—it's got some really bad, nearly impassable areas—I always assume the road is no good and prefer to travel on foot. Your mileage may vary!

From the parking spot head out on the old forest road (southwest) which is mostly level, to a wildlife opening at 1.0. Continue on the road ahead down a STEEP grade to a T intersection of old roads at 1.5. This is the point where I leave the road and head into the woods and make a loop to visit all of the waterfalls. (you will return to this intersection from the road on the right on the way back out at 4.9.)

From the intersection LEAVE the road and head STRAIGHT DOWN INTO the woods. It's a 500' plunge down to the West Fork of Horsehead Creek at the bottom at 1.8, through mostly open woods, but you may have to negotiate a short bluff or two along the way. At the creek TURN RIGHT and head upstream. There is a nice cascade and pool that spans the creek at **(35.60013, -93.67700)**, so you should be somewhere near this.

Continue upstream to a creek that flows in from the LEFT at 1.9. It looks like there are actually three creeks that come together in this spot, if you look around a little bit you will realize there are two coming in from the left and the main creek from straight ahead. I love this spot—and SSS! You want to TURN LEFT and follow the first creek upstream and into a narrow, twisty canyon. It's beginning to get interesting.

Right away there is an unnamed waterfall that you probably will have to climb a little

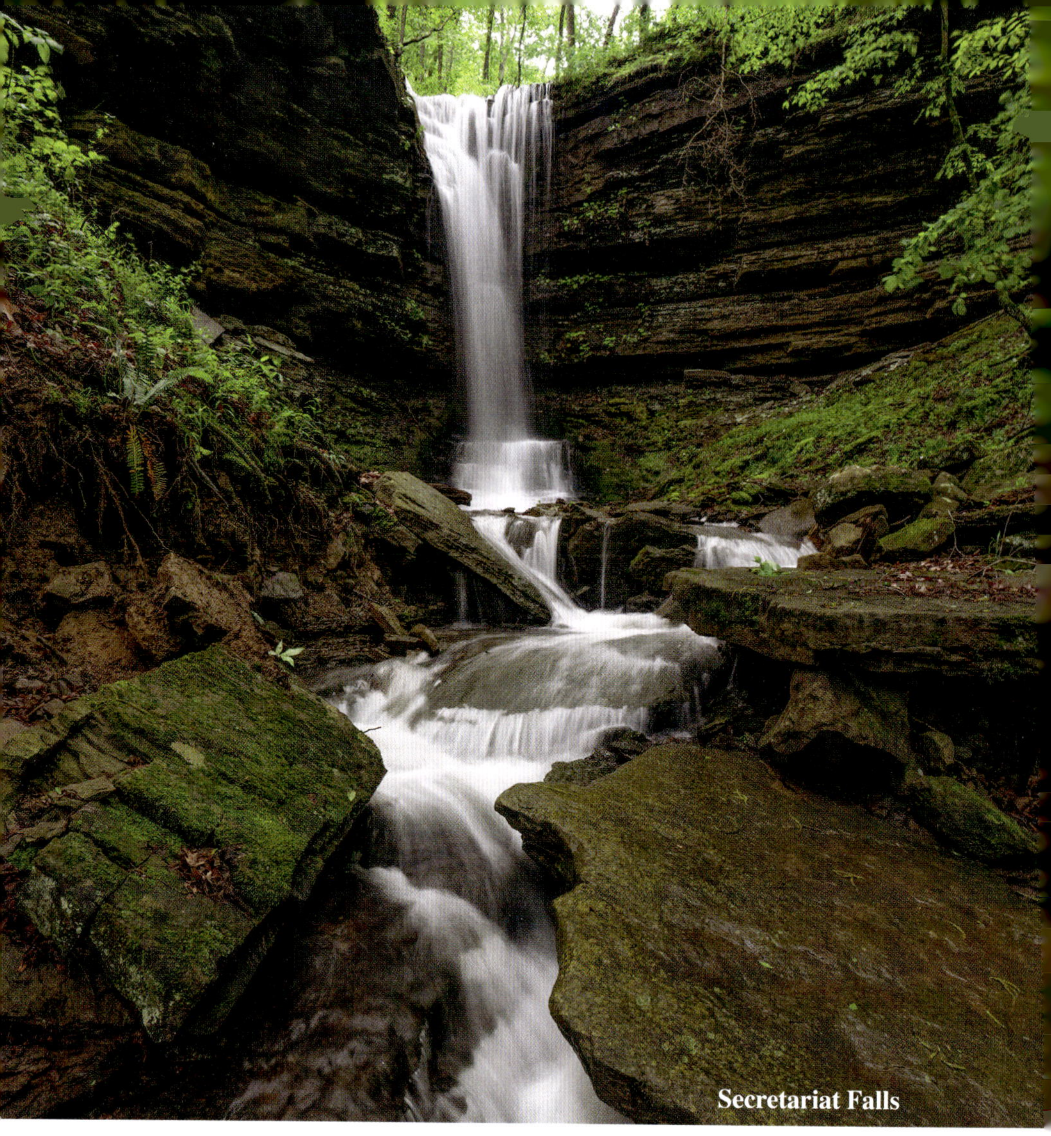
Secretariat Falls

bit out of the canyon to get past. Get used to this. I sometimes return to the creek after going around and continue upstream to the next waterfall, and sometimes I climb part way out of the canyon (on the left usually) to get around—your call—you will have a couple more, much larger spots like this upstream—everything to the top is an SSS, so enjoy! FYI, you probably will not be coming back down to these waterfalls, but rather will cut across the hillside from the waterfall on top and continue on to the next waterfalls.

The first named waterfall is next, **Secretariat Falls** at 2.0 (considered by many the greatest race horse of all time).

Climb UP and around it (I usually get up onto the next layer ♦) and continue upstream to **Wildfire Falls** at 2.1 (a great song by Michael Martin Murphey).

One last climb up and around but this time it will be a longer scramble upstream past lots of boulders and other interesting stuff (maybe an ancient tire wrapped around a tree?). At 2.25 you will come to the tallest waterfall in the drainage, **Snowman Falls** (not what you think—he was an $80 plow horse from Pennsylvania Dutch country, saved from the slaughter truck to become one of the greatest show jumping horses of all time, winning

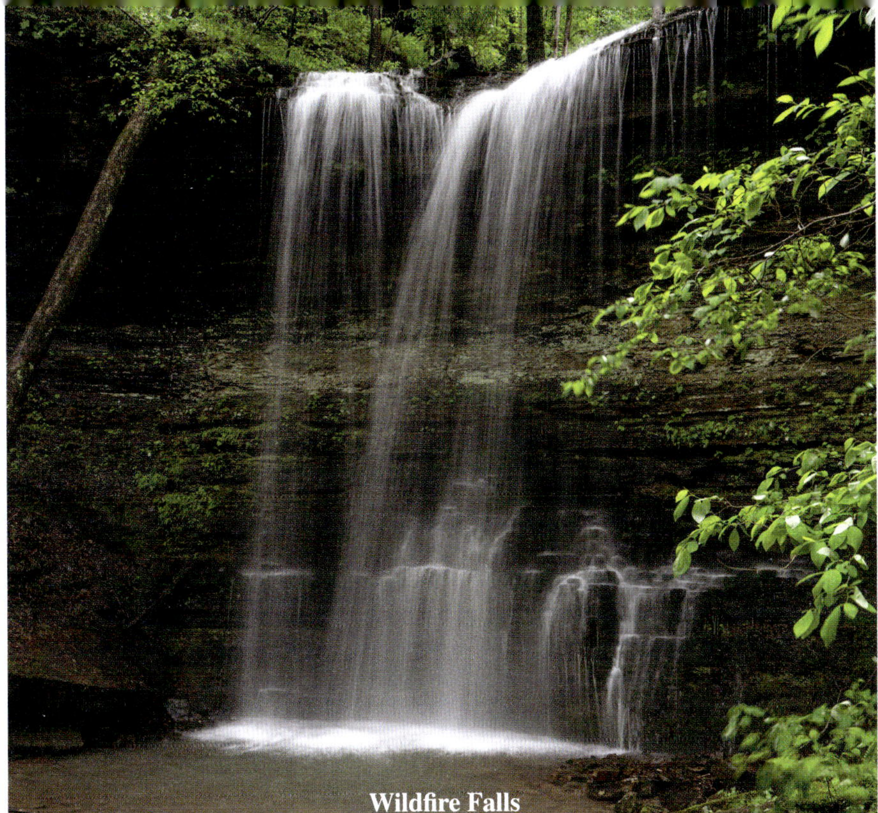
Wildfire Falls

their Triple Crown TWICE in a row! There's a great documentary about him...)

From **Snowman Falls** head out to the RIGHT about half way up and work your way around to a somewhat level bench that curves around to the left and into a little hollow. As the hillside curves more to the left into the hollow, straighten out and drop on down the hillside towards the bottom of that hollow ♦ at 2.6—that's where you will find a perfectly wonderful **Sea Biscuit Falls** (Undervalued, undesired, and underrated, but this racehorse redeemed himself and was one of the most successful horses in the 1930's—and I really like this name...)

There's a spot as you approach this falls part way down where you can see a shining blue pool in the bottom of the creek below where two hollows join. Carefully climb down a nice cascade between this falls and that pool—it's a wonderful SSS for sure!

Once at the bottom TURN LEFT to continue the SSS and follow this new creek up to **Mr. Ed Falls** at 2.7 (talking horse we used to watch every week on TV!)

Time to turn around and follow the creek downstream past **Sea Biscuit** (then maybe up above the creek a little) as the hillside curves around to the left and enters the main creek canyon at 2.9—this is the upstream part of where the three creeks come together we saw from downstream before.

Follow the main creek to the LEFT upstream but curve around more to the left as the hillside above you does and soon you will be in a new hollow—continue upstream as you can to 3.4 and **Trigger Falls** (Roy Roger's horse). This one seems to be extra scenic for some reason—like they all are!

Back up a little bit and then work your way UP onto a narrow bench going upstream on the left, past **Trigger Falls**. Keep going up to 3.5 where two creeks spill over the same bluff and join at your feet—on the left is **Silver Falls** (The Lone Ranger's horse), and on the right **Scout Falls** (Tonto's horse). The Lone Ranger and Tonto together again!

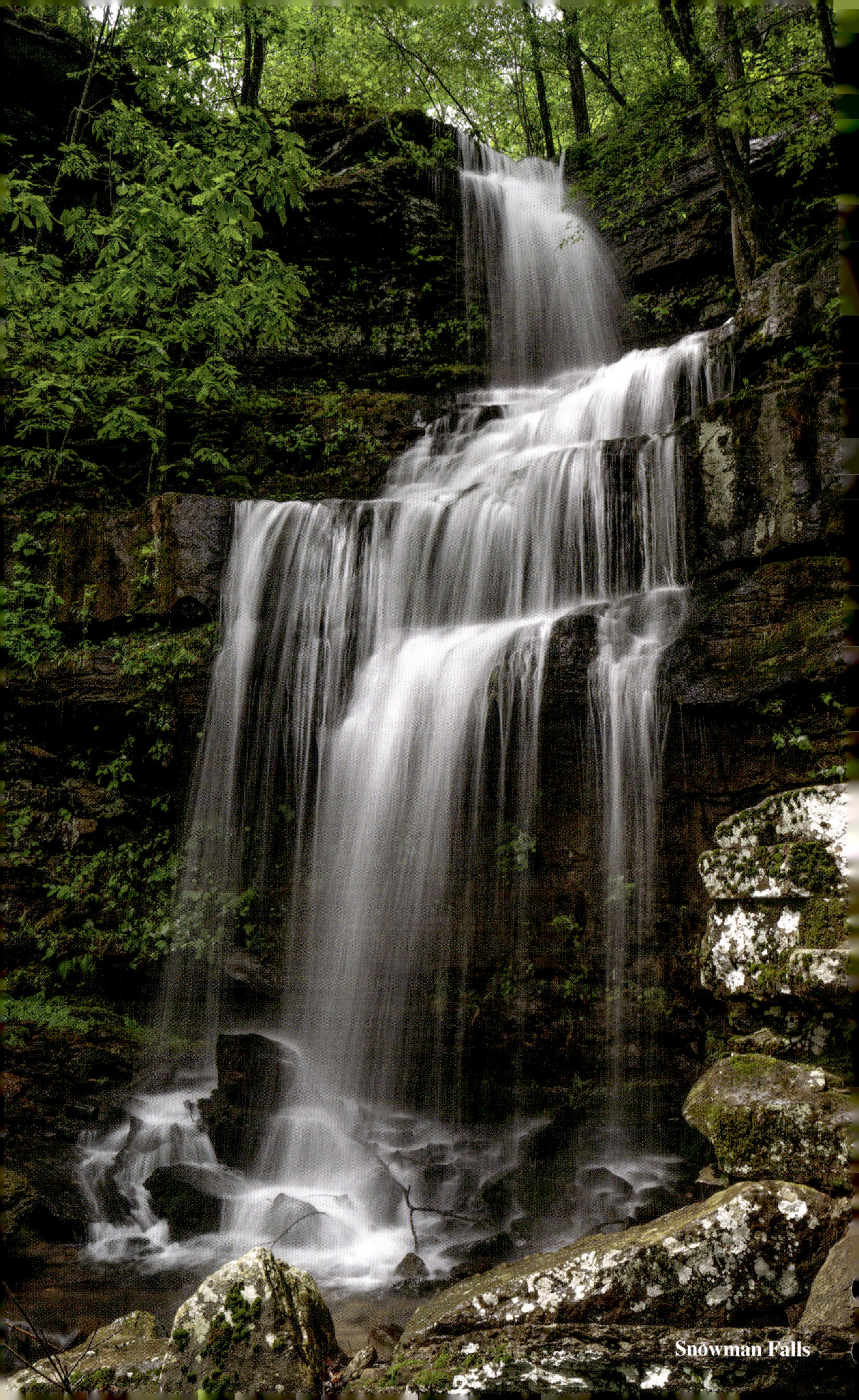
Snowman Falls

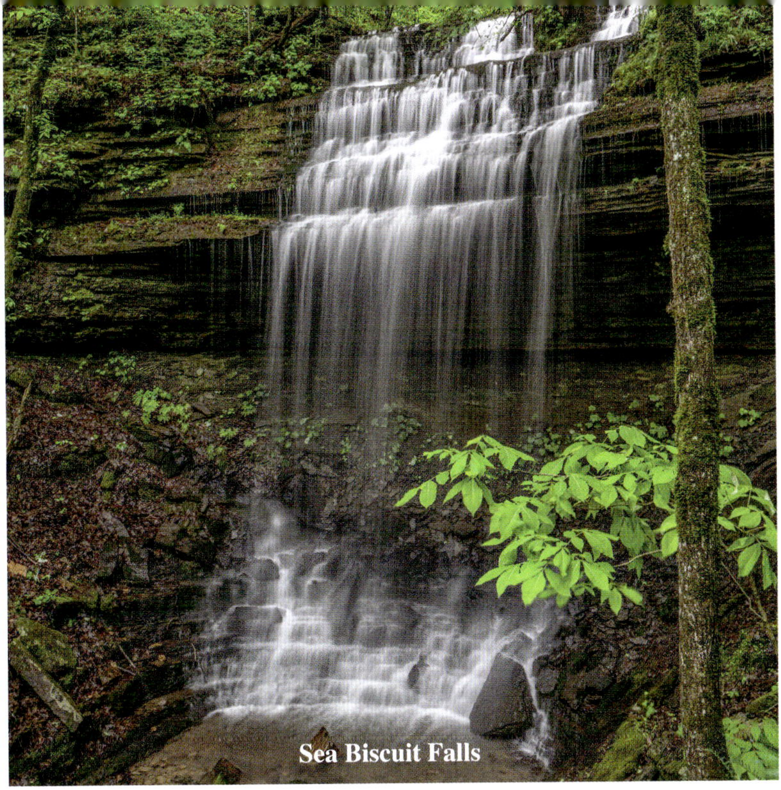

Sea Biscuit Falls

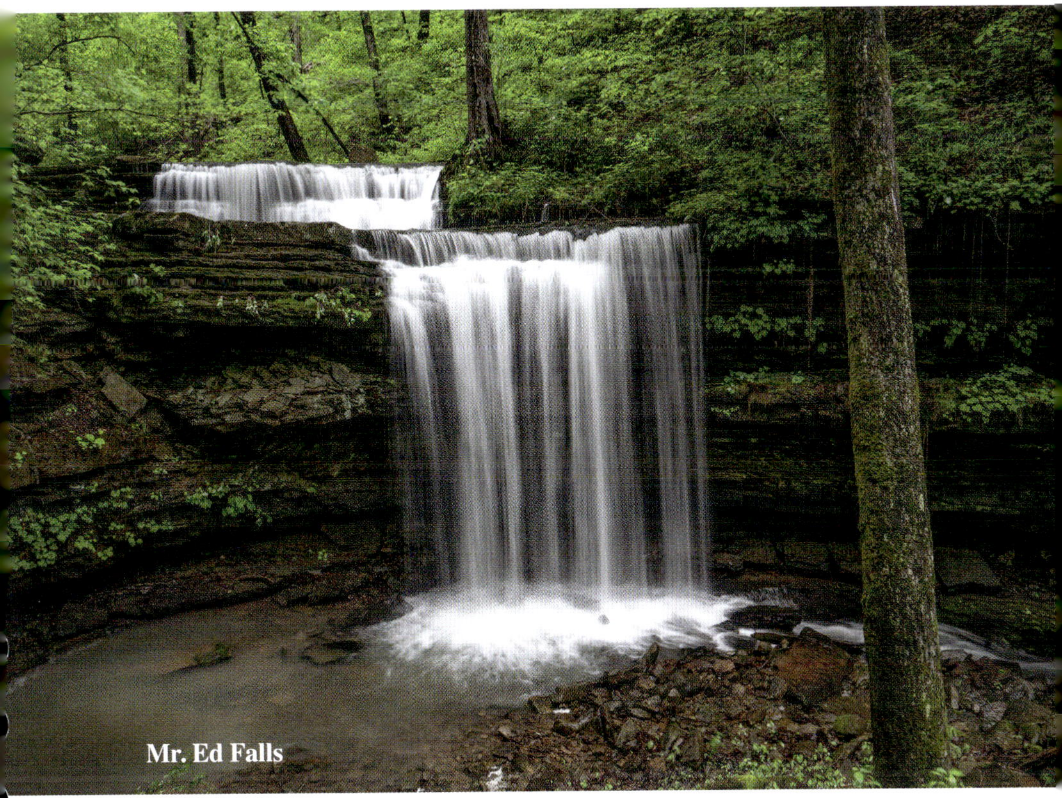

Mr. Ed Falls

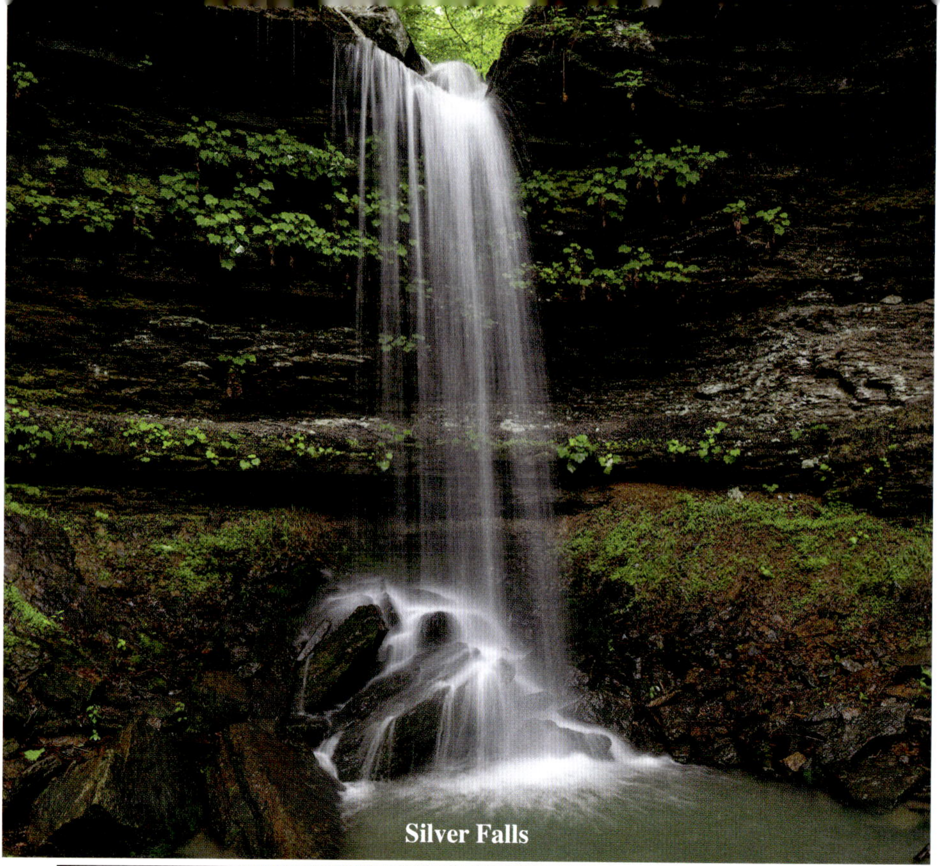

Silver Falls

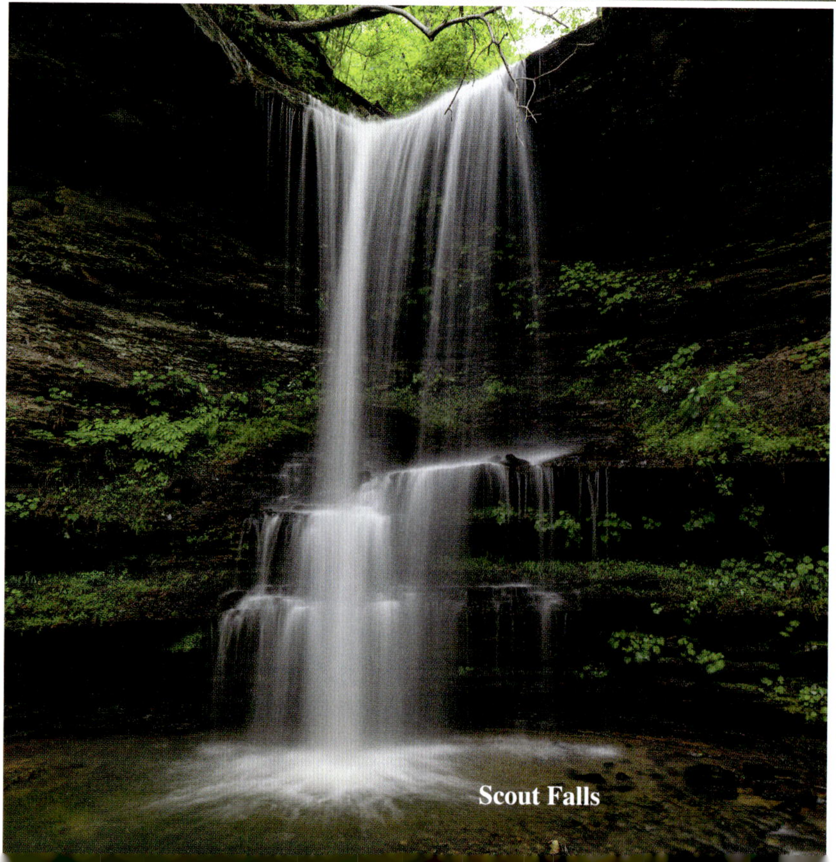

Scout Falls

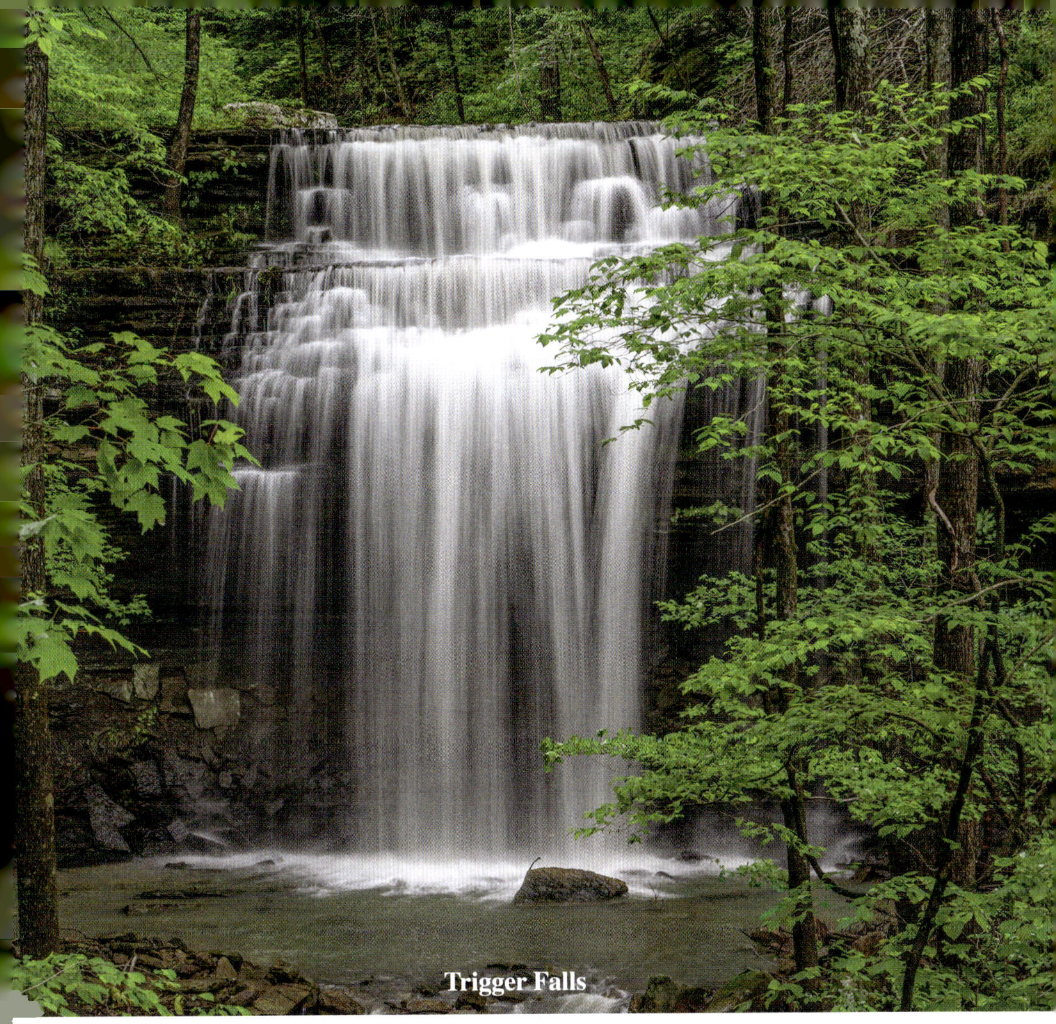
Trigger Falls

OK, only one more waterfall to go, turn around and follow the creek downstream back to the main creek canyon at 3.8 and TURN LEFT to go upstream. If the water is really high you should stay out of the creek and continue upstream until you reach the next waterfall. IF it is SAFE to do so (lower water levels) I like to get in the creek and wade upstream, up through a cascade canyon of sorts (the rocks are SLICK, but it's an SSS all the way!).

At 4.2 the canyon ends with a little whitewater at an emerald pool and **White Horse Falls** (Taylor's Version), the final SSS of this loop. Decision time. There are more waterfalls, cascades and water slides on the main creek upstream (especially during high water)—you can follow the main creek (stay RIGHT at the fork) for more than a mile, then whenever you've had enough, TURN RIGHT and climb straight UP and out of the canyon and back to your car.

BUT I'M TUCKERED OUT and ready to return to the trailhead (1.8 miles away). So from Taylor's falls I turn to the RIGHT and face the towering hillside before me, grit my teeth and head UP, UP, AND AWAY from the creek. Veer to the RIGHT as you go up to avoid a bluff line, then basically just gut it out straight up—it's a BLACK DIAMOND slope ♦ all the way up to the road. Sometimes the only way I can make it is to be down on all fours and claw my way up (I'm a 70 year old geezer though, haha) You can also angle to the right as you go up to make the steepness less—you will still land on the road above, maybe won't hurt as much.

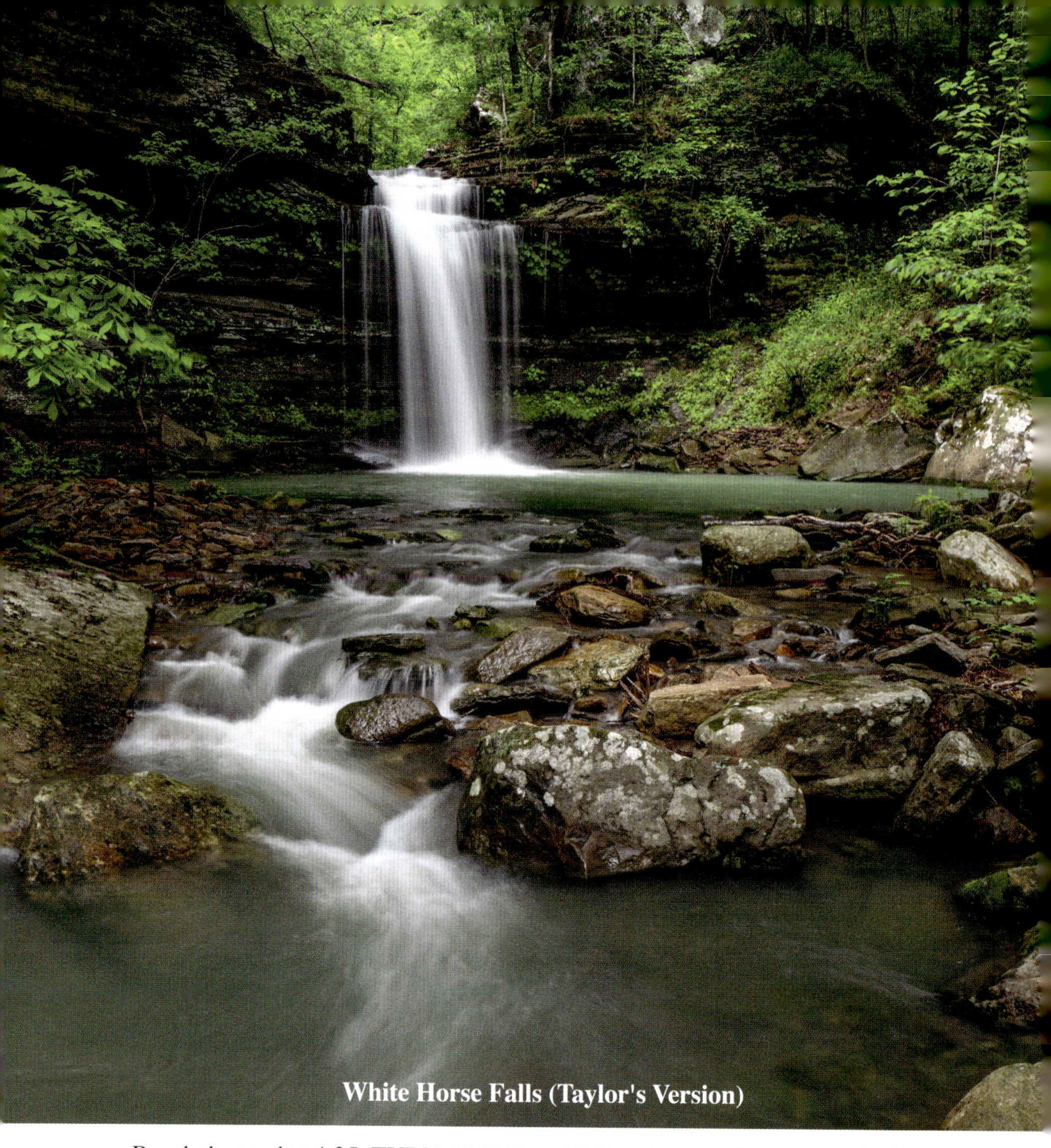

White Horse Falls (Taylor's Version)

Reach the road at 4.35, TURN RIGHT and follow the road back up to the T intersection at 4.5 (where you left the road coming in). TURN LEFT and head straight UP the hill, past the wildlife food plot, and then LEVEL all the way back to the trailhead at 6.0. CONGRATS—you made it!

Emergency contact: Johnson County Sheriff, 479–754–2200 Dogs are OK

Shower Chair Falls – 41′

1.5 mile roundtrip (below both falls), medium bushwhack, GPS helpful

GPS **35.62750, -93.69639**

Legos Falls – 40′

1.5 mile roundtrip (below both falls), medium bushwhack, GPS helpful

GPS **35.63084, -93.69154**

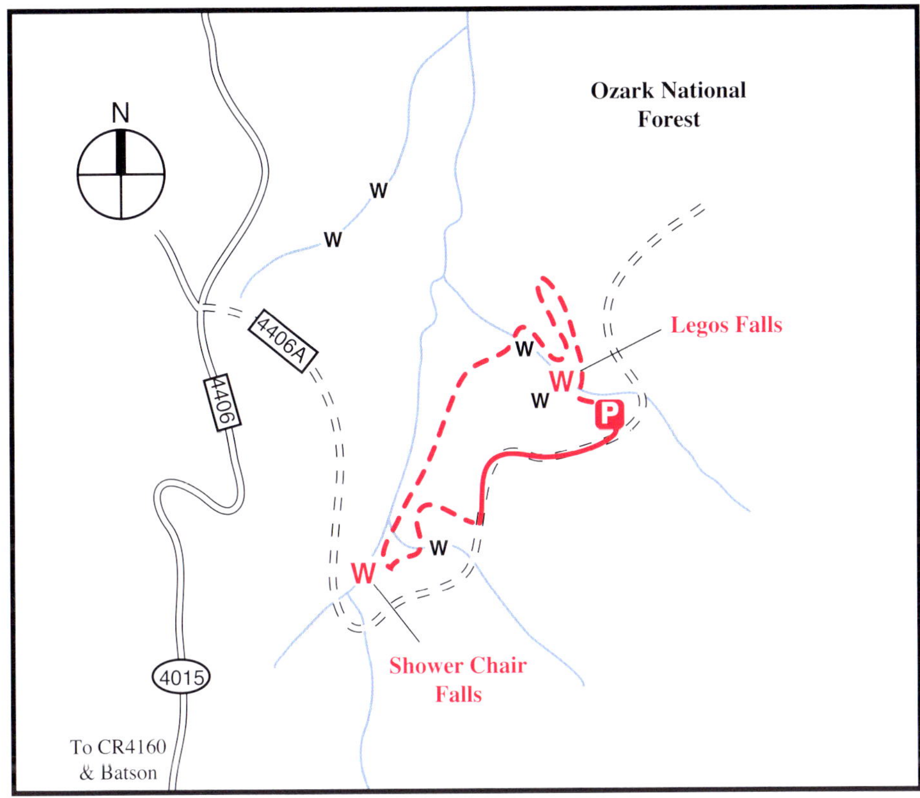

SHOWER CHAIR FALLS/LEGOS FALLS. A polyfoss area with waterfalls and cascades galore! The waterfall tops are easy to get to, but it is tougher to reach the bases of them.

From Hwy. 103 (between Oark and Clarksville) TURN WEST on CR#4160 towards Batson. Go 7.1 miles and TURN RIGHT onto FR#4406/CR#4015 (if you get to the rural fire station you have gone too far). Go 1.7 miles to the bottom of the hill and TURN RIGHT onto a jeep road FR#4406A. Go about 1.5 miles and PARK on the left just before a creek **(35.63054, -93.69046)**.

There is a big bluffline below the road all through this area—it is an easy bushwhack to reach the tops of Shower Chair and Legos Falls at the top of the bluff. I prefer to tour below the bluff and visit the base of the falls. From the parking spot, head down into the woods and follow the little creek to the top of **Legos Falls**. Follow the bluff to the right a ways and you will find an easy way down through it, then make your way back to the base of the falls and then down below for a beautiful cascade. Continue to work your way along the bluff until you reach **Shower Chair Falls**. Double-back to another cascade and upper waterfall, then continue along the bluff until you find a way up through the bluff back to the car.

Emergency contact: Johnson County Sheriff, 479–754–2200 Dogs are OK

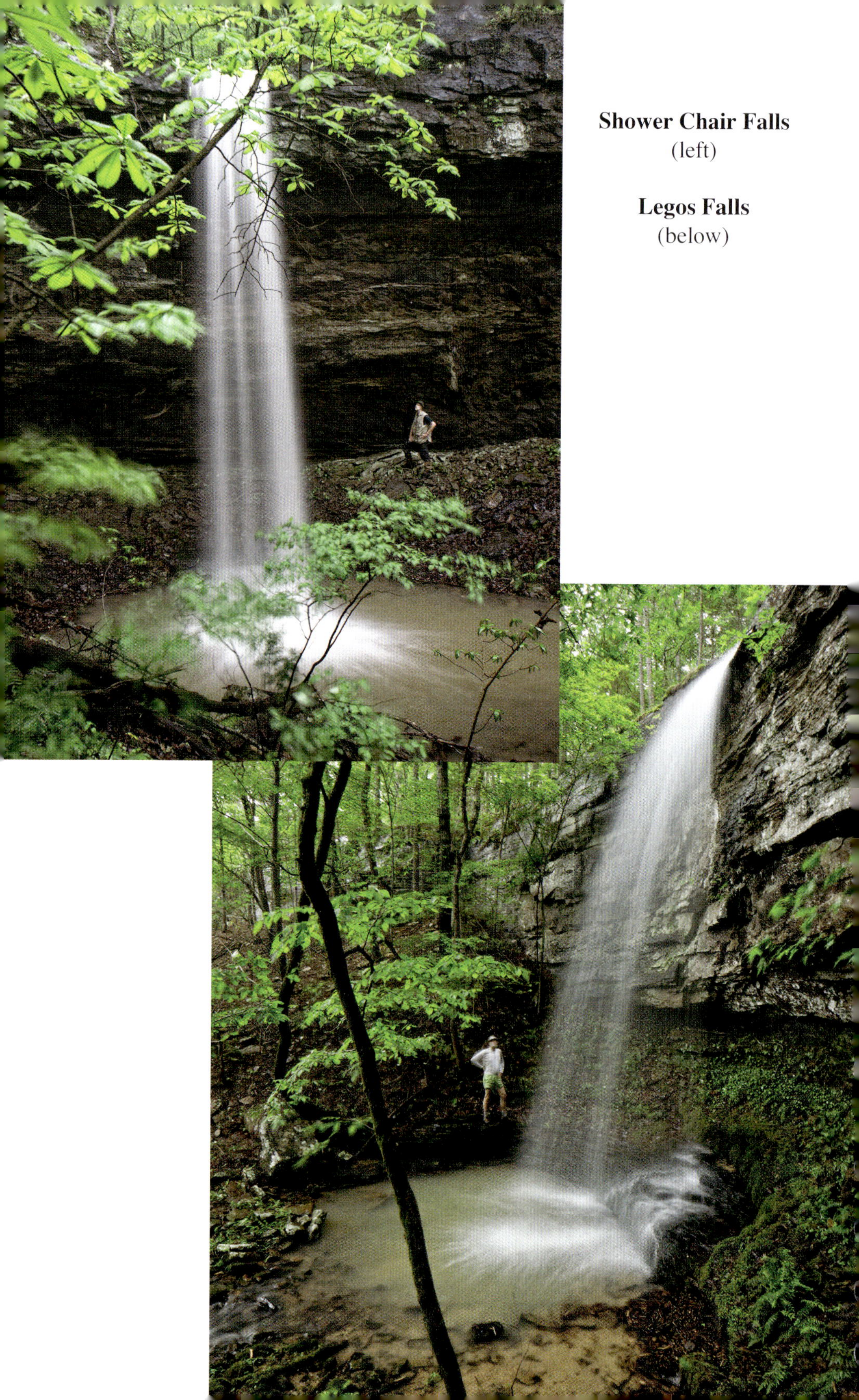

Shower Chair Falls
(left)

Legos Falls
(below)

Bingham Hollow Falls – 51′

.2 mile roundtrip, easy bushwhack, GPS not needed

GPS **35.66211, -93.74662**

Sentinel Rock Falls – 52′

2.2 mile roundtrip, medium bushwhack, GPS helpful

GPS **35.66155, -93.73088**

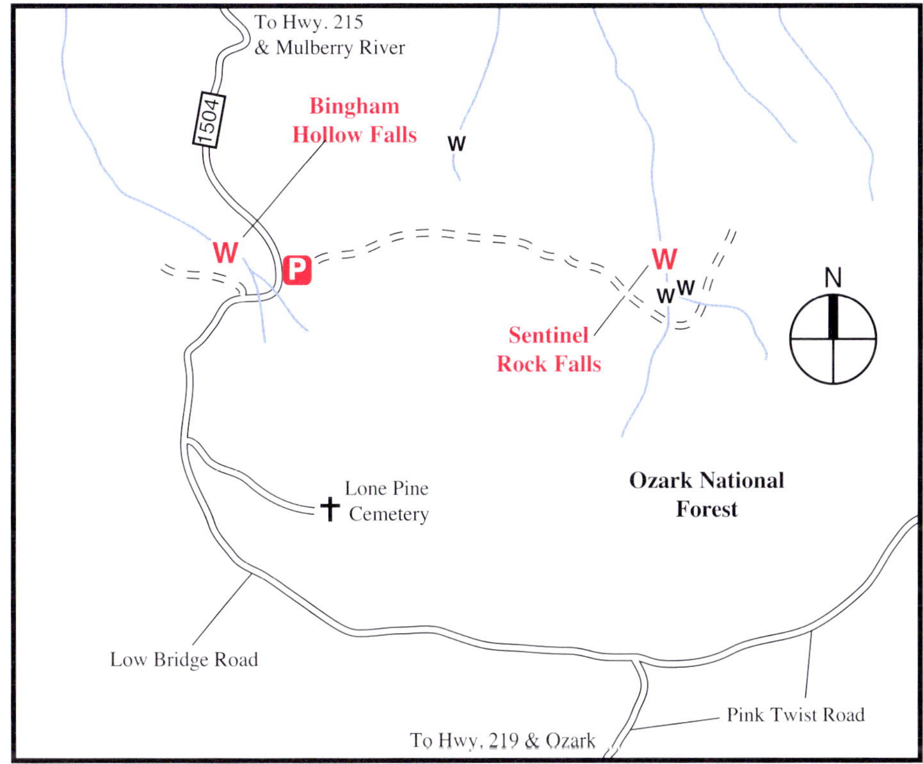

BINGHAM HOLLOW FALLS. It's going to take me longer to give directions to the parking spot than it will take you to bushwhack to this waterfall, but it will be worth the trip! It is a great location with a large bluff overhang that is within a couple hundred yards of the main road. Use the same parking spot for both waterfalls.

The easy way to get there is from Cass—go north on Hwy. 23 and TURN RIGHT onto Hwy. 215. Go past the Redding Campground turnoff about a mile and TURN RIGHT and drive across the Mulberry River on FR#1504/Low Bridge Road (impassable during high water). Go 2.4 miles and PARK (**35.66175 N, -93.74542**) at the corner where a jeep road takes off to the left. OR from Ozark head north on Hwy. 219 at I-40 and go 8.5 miles and TURN LEFT onto Pink Twist Road. Go 4.9 miles and TURN LEFT onto Low Bridge Road (this is Pittston Jct.). Go 1.6 miles to the parking spot/jeep road on the right. OR come across from Batson to the Hwy. 219/Pink Twist Road junction and turn north onto Pink Twist Road and then as above.

To get to the waterfall simply head downhill into the woods until you come to the falls. It is possible to get down through the bluff to the base of the falls—from the top of the falls follow the bluff around to the right a couple of hundred yards. The big bluff overhang is quite spectacular and worth the trouble!

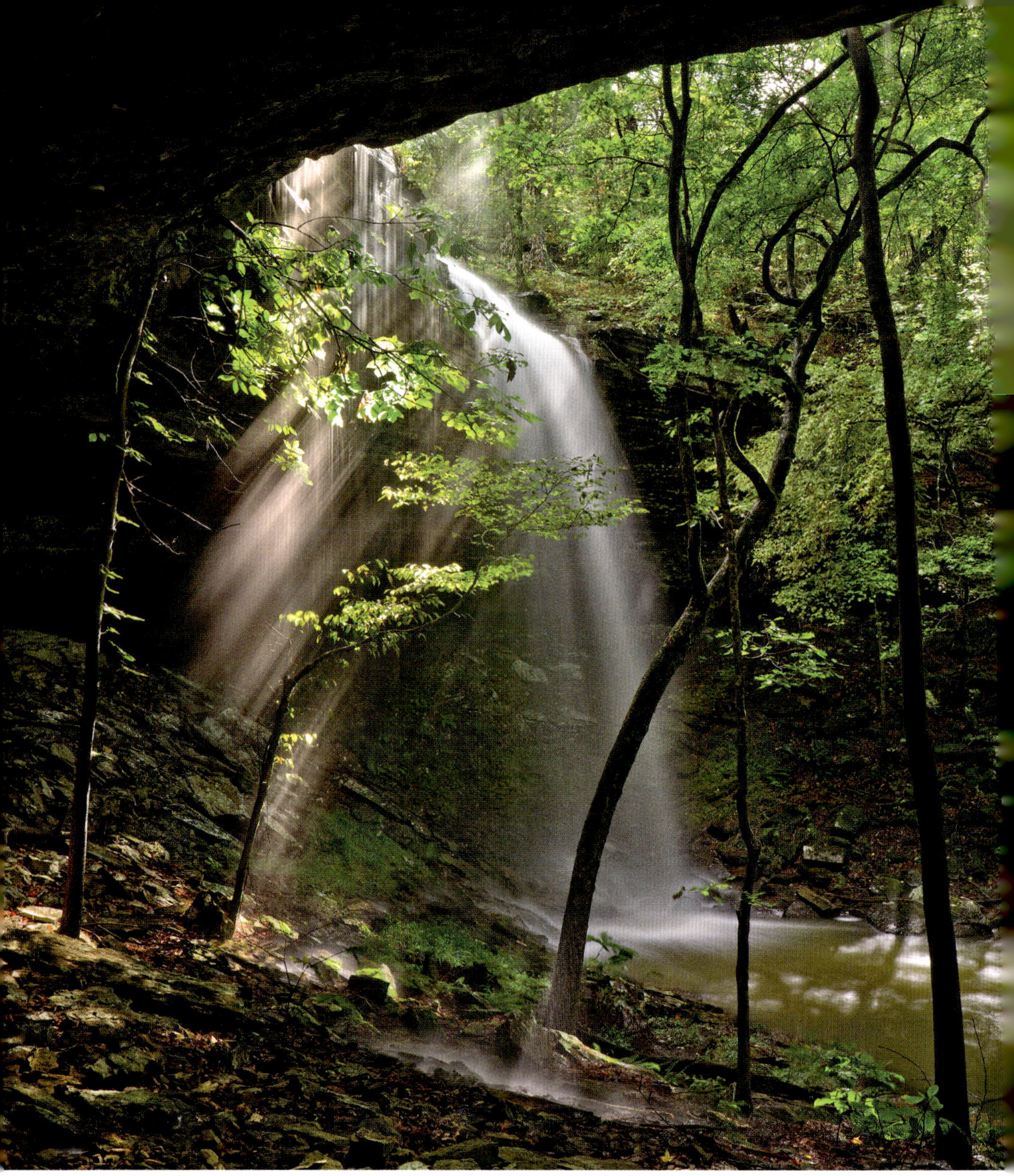

Bingham Hollow Falls

SENTINEL ROCK FALLS. Begin at the same parking lot as above. Hike east along the jeep road (or you could drive it if you have a serious 4WD). Go .9 mile and you will come to a creek across the road with a pair of waterfalls just downstream to your left (**35.65983, -93.73056**). Follow this creek downstream and you will come to the top of the big **Sentinel Rock Falls** (named after the lone rock in the pool below). There is another, taller, waterfall along the same bluffline to the right/northeast. There is a difficult way down through the bluffline a ways along the left side, and an easier one that is farther away along the right side (past the tall waterfall). All of this is quite steep so be careful!

Emergency contact: Franklin County Sheriff, 479–667–4127 Dogs are OK

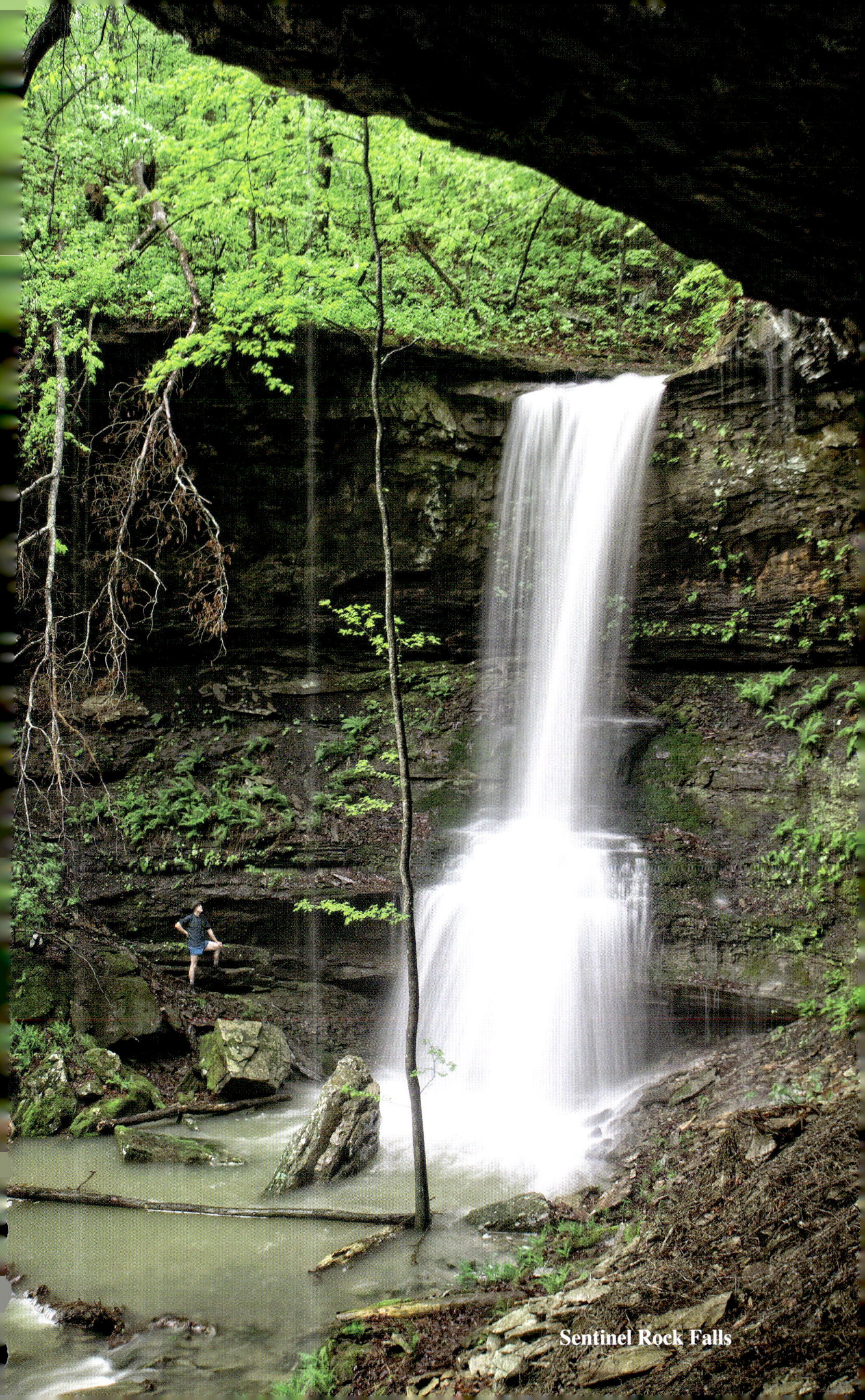
Sentinel Rock Falls

White Oak Creek Falls – 37′

1.5 miles roundtrip, medium hike, GPS helpful

GPS **35.62749, -93.75795**

Mineral Springs Falls – 43′

.8 mile roundtrip, medium/steep bushwhack, GPS helpful

GPS **35.64278, -93.72806**

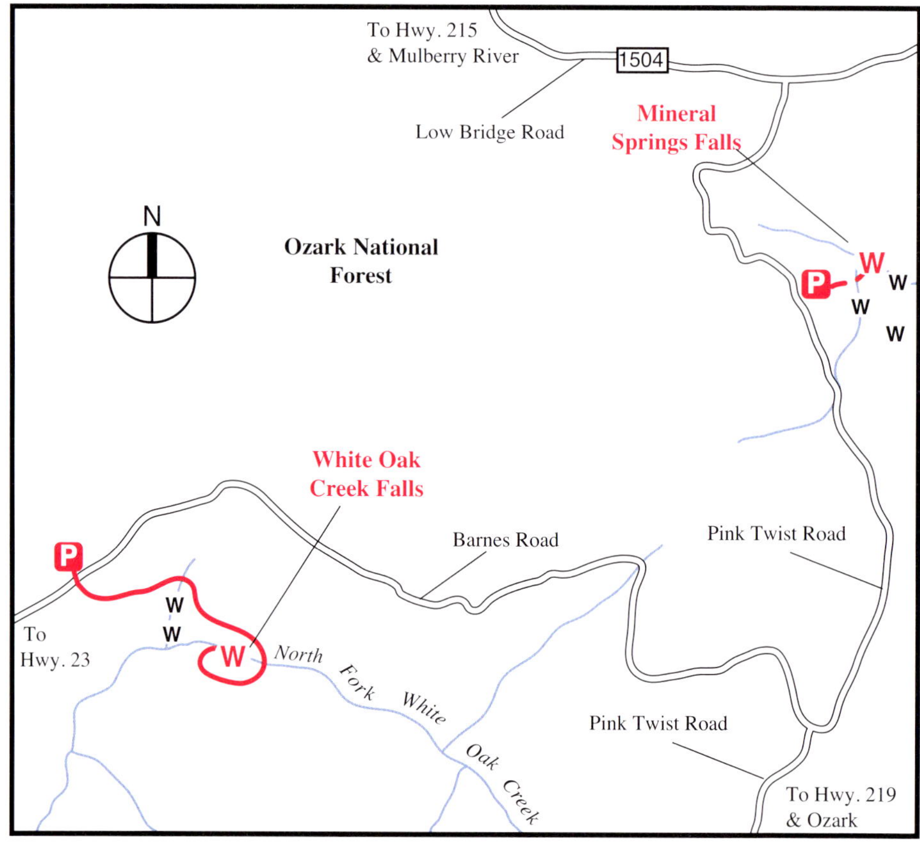

WHITE OAK CREEK FALLS. This is an unusual open waterfall that gets lots of sunshine. The hike to the top is an easy one along a jeep road.

To get to the parking spot from Ozark head north on Hwy. 219 at I-40 and go 8.5 miles and TURN LEFT onto Pink Twist Road. Go 2.7 miles and TURN LEFT onto Barnes Road, then go 2.8 miles and PARK on the right (**35.62991, -93.76665).**

Cross the road from your parking spot and follow the jeep road/4WD trail downhill as it swings back to the left past a couple of smaller waterfalls that are below the road. This will take you right to the very top of the waterfall. The best way to reach the bottom of the falls is to cross the creek and continue on the 4WD trail and follow it around to the right and it will eventually drop down to and cross White Oak Creek—splash upstream a couple hundred yards to the waterfall and enjoy! This is one of the tallest waterfalls I know of where you can linger at night and see a sky filled with stars, or perhaps get in some moondipping!

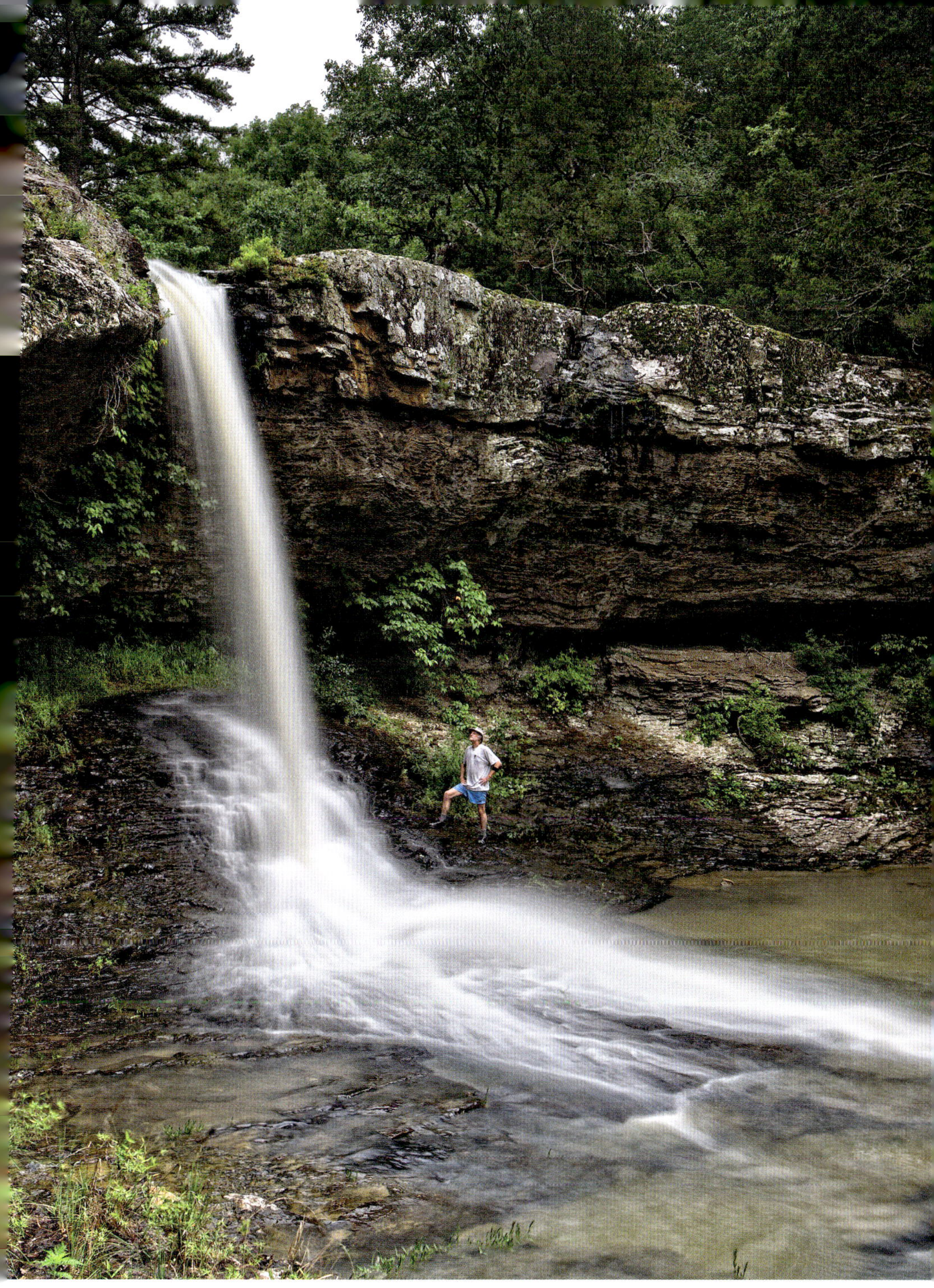

White Oak Creek Falls

MINERAL SPRINGS FALLS. A short, steep bushwhack takes you down to this polyfoss area that includes at least four waterfalls. From the parking spot above, head back out to the intersection of Barnes Road and Pink Twist Road and TURN LEFT onto Pink Twist

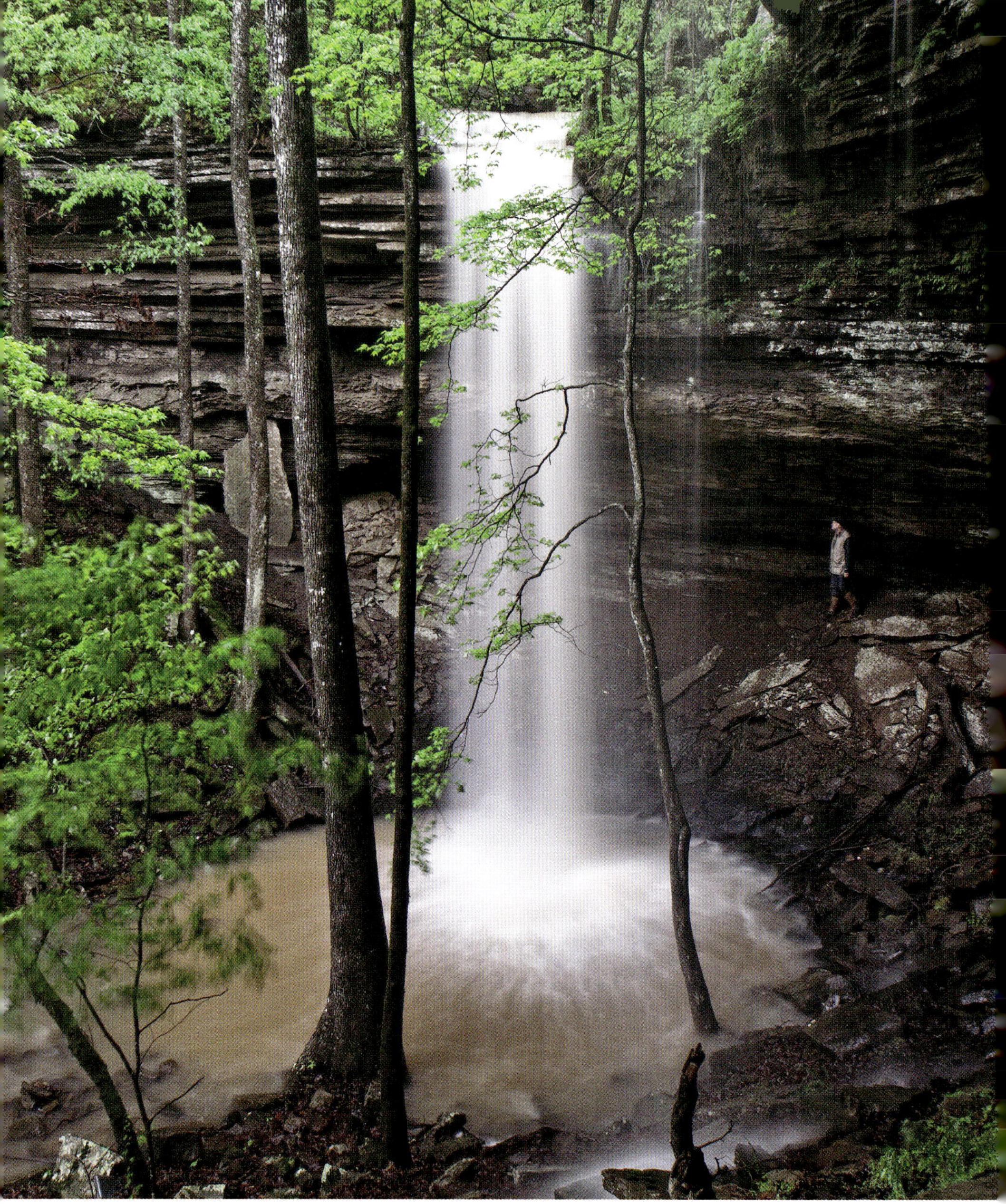

Mineral Springs Falls

Road. Go 1.3 miles and TURN RIGHT into an open area/gas well site and PARK (**35.64176, -93.73031)** If coming from the north/Bingham Hollow Falls this turnoff is .9 miles south of Pittson Junction. (Or 4 miles north of Hwy. 219 on Pink Twist Road.)

Hike down an old roadbed that leaves the back of the open area down to another open area, then head into the woods steeply downhill until you come to the falls or the creek. The main falls is upstream, a smaller one is downstream, plus there are nice waterfalls along the bluffline in each of the side drainages. Enjoy!

Emergency contact: Franklin County Sheriff, 479–667–4127 Dogs are OK

Pig Trail Falls – 18′

View from car, no hike involved, GPS not needed

GPS **35.64618, -93.83975**

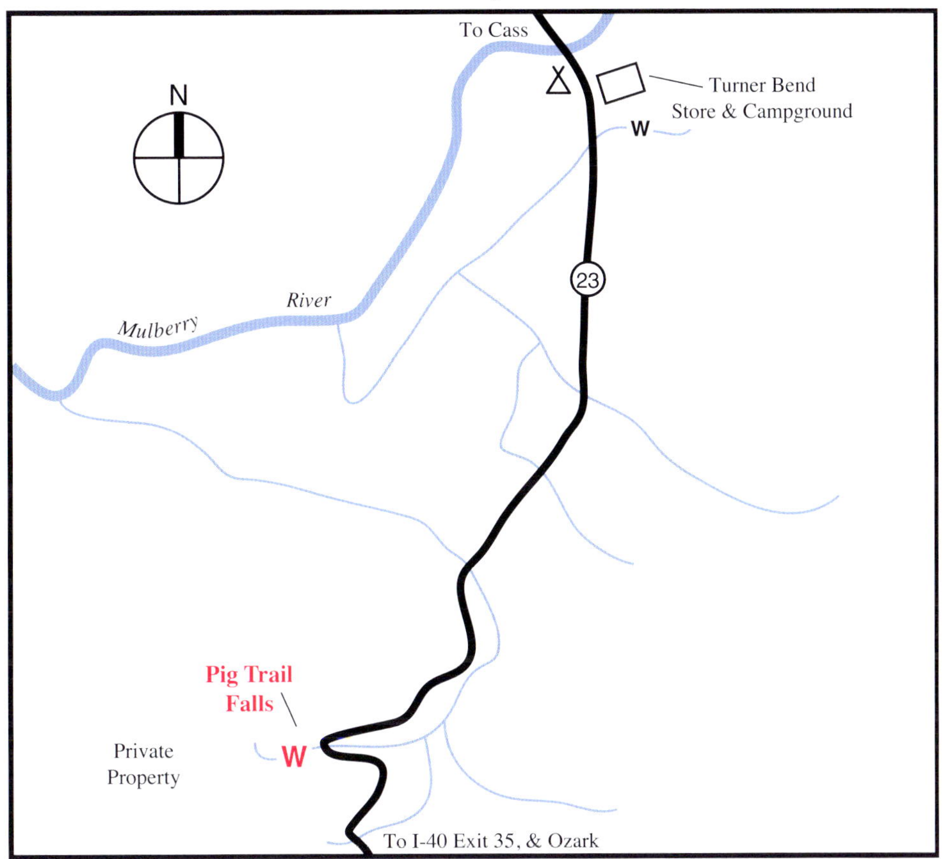

PIG TRAIL FALLS. Many generations of college students from the University of Arkansas going home for the weekend or back to school on Sunday passed by this waterfall. It is located right next to the famous "Pig Trail" highway, which is now a National Scenic Byway. You don't even need to get out of the car to see it!

To get to the falls take exit 35 off I–40 and head north on Hwy. 23. You will pass the falls on the left in a hairpin turn as you are dropping down into the Mulberry River Valley. (The property above the falls is private and not open to explore.) I suggest a lunch stop at the Turner Bend Store, just 1.8 miles north of the waterfall right on the highway—they make great sandwiches (campground and canoe floats too), and there is a nice little waterfall right next to the store that is worth a look when the water is high.

Emergency contact: Franklin County Sheriff, 479–667–4127 Dogs are OK

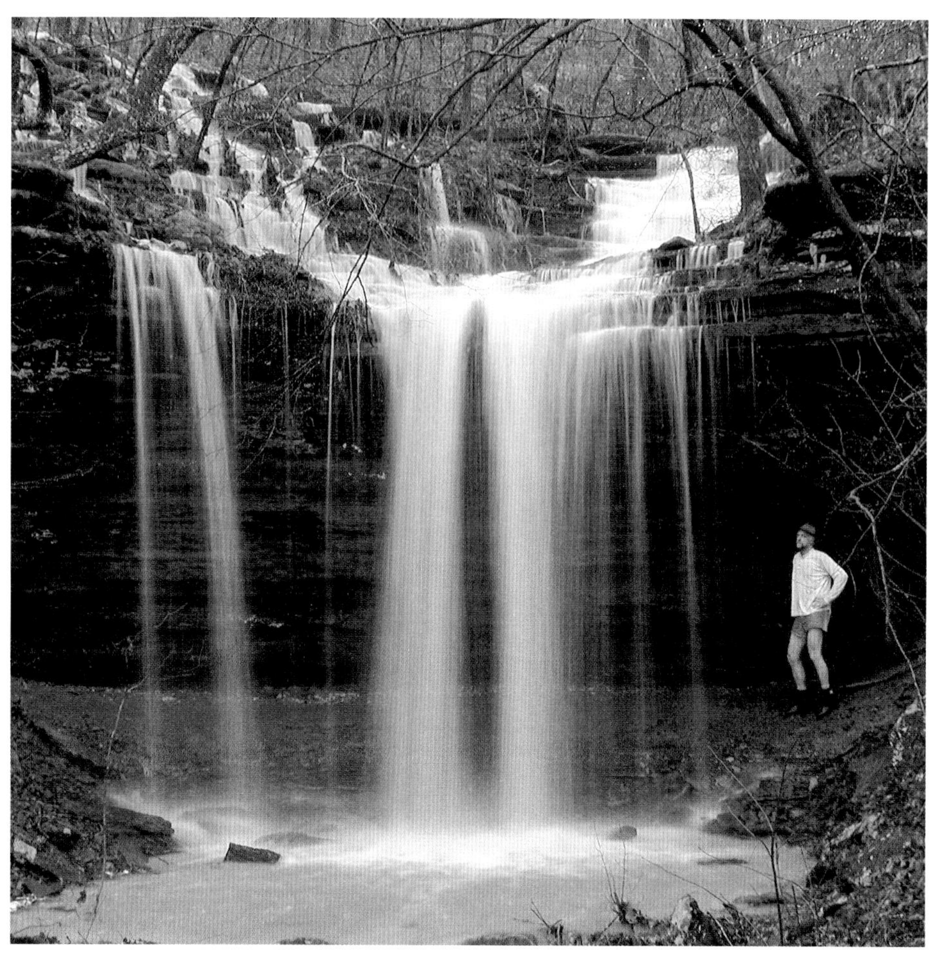

Pig Trail Falls (high water)

Train Trestle Falls – 31′

2.8 miles roundtrip, medium hike, GPS not needed

GPS **35.67758, -93.88565**

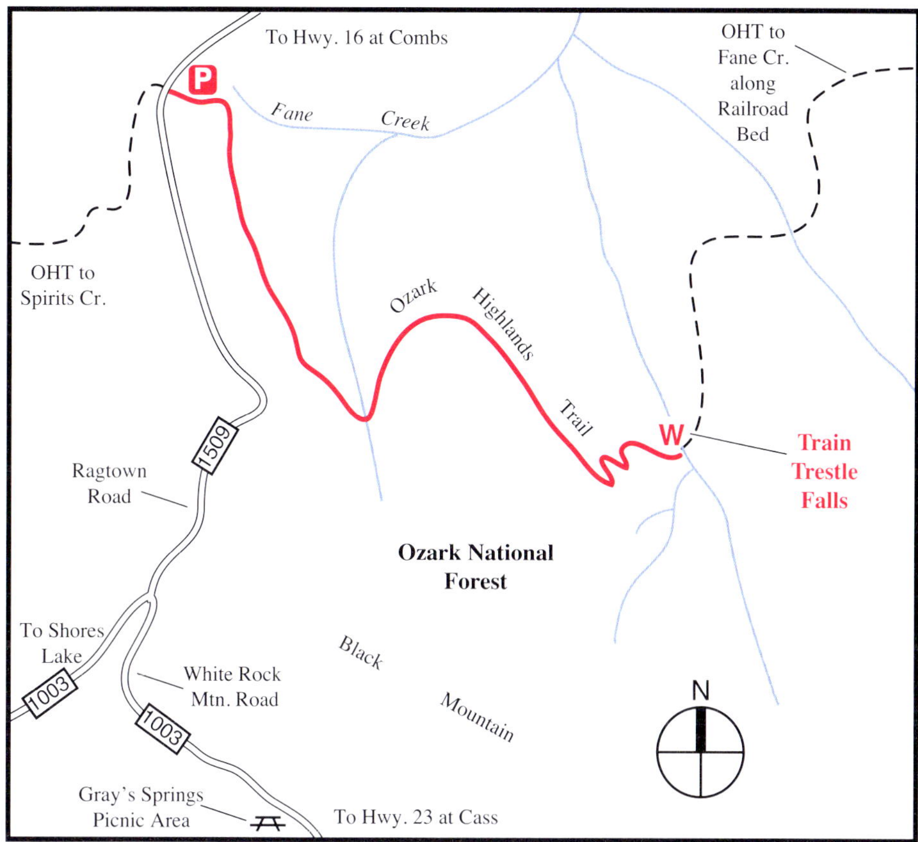

TRAIN TRESTLE FALLS. You can visit a piece of Ozark history at this wonderful waterfall. It is located at the base of what once was a towering wooden trestle where steam locomotives carrying giant white oak logs once roamed. All that remain today are the concrete pilings at the top of the falls, and dozens of rusting iron nuts and bolts that held the mighty timbers together. The Ozark Highlands Trail (OHT) runs along the top of the old railroad bed for several miles and passes this site on the north side of Black Mountain.

Access this area from Cass on Hwy. 23. Go south on Hwy. 23 and turn RIGHT onto White Rock Mountain Road (FR#1003). OR go north from the Turner Bend store on the Mulberry River to get to White Rock Mtn. Rd. This is a rough gravel road, but it is a scenic six-mile drive, and passes through a geological formation known as Bee Rocks (giant honey-combed boulders that are right next to the road—bees nest in them), and then past a unique picnic area called Gray's Spring. The picnic area was built of stone by the Civilian Conservation Corps in the 1930's (as were most of the roads in the area, and the cabins and lodge up on White Rock Mountain too). About a half mile past Gray's Spring TURN RIGHT onto Ragtown Road (FR#1509). Go .7 mile and PARK on the right just beyond where the OHT crosses the road (**35.68379, -93.89792**). This is the same parking spot as for Spirits Creek/Robinson Falls.

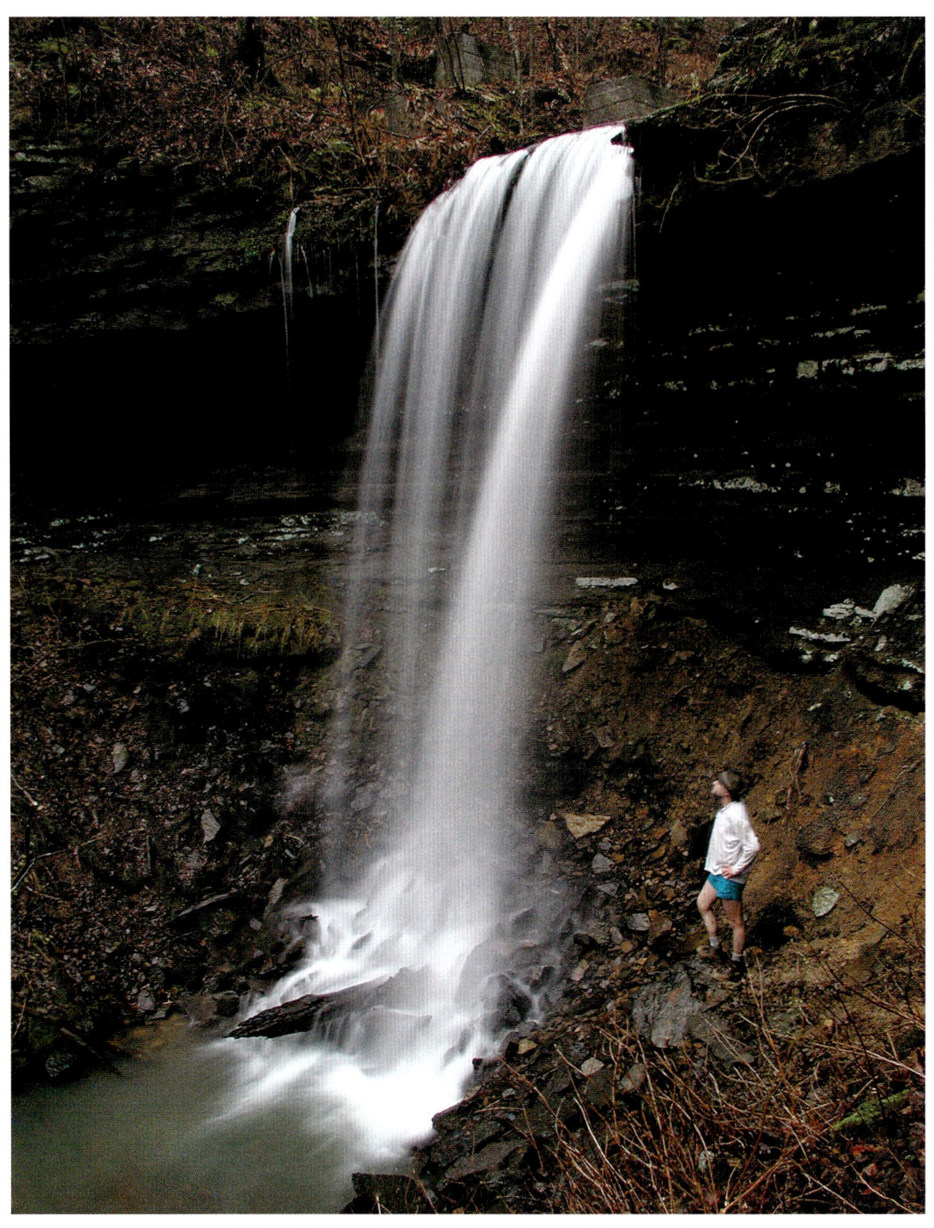

Train Trestle Falls (during high water)

From the road head east on the OHT (blazed white) as it drops down the hill—TURN RIGHT onto a logging road and follow it for a little ways, then TURN RIGHT again onto another old road trace that will take you uphill slightly, past OHT milepost #26, then TURN LEFT onto pure trail just after the mile marker. The trail swings around the hillside to the left past a beautiful moss-covered cascade, then intersects another log road that will take you through an old clearcut area. TURN LEFT off this road after a while onto regular trail, and drop on down the hill to a larger creek at 1.4—this is the gorge the old trestle spanned, and the waterfall is located just downstream.

Emergency contact: Franklin County Sheriff, 479–667–4127 Dogs are OK

Spirits Creek Falls – 8′

2.4 miles roundtrip, medium hike, GPS helpful

GPS **35.68712, -93.90804**

Robinson Falls (2) – 17′/21′

Add .2 mile to above distance, easy bushwhack from above, GPS helpful

GPS **35.68770, -93.91022**

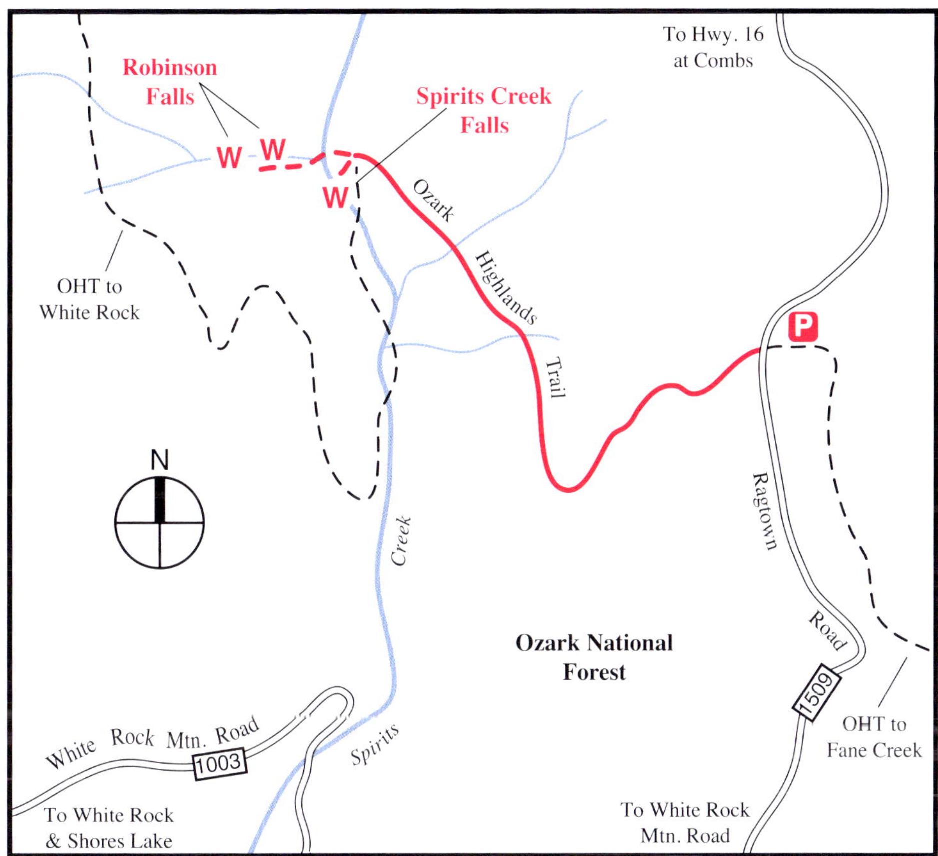

SPIRITS CREEK FALLS. Spirits Creek has long been an oasis along the Ozark Highlands Trail (OHT). The falls are not all that tall, but there is a certain magical feeling about the place—a very happy "spirit" must live there. The first time I ever camped beside this creek everyone in our group woke up around 3 in the morning. After a bit of discussion we realized that the creek had suddenly gone silent— it had frozen solid! The temperature was five below zero. It was a great hike the next morning through a winter wonderland.

Access this area from Cass on Hwy. 23. Go south on 23 (or north from the Turner Bend store on the Mulberry River) and turn RIGHT onto White Rock Mountain Road (FR#1003). This is a rough gravel road, but it is a scenic five or six mile drive, and passes through a geological formation known as Bee Rocks (giant honeycombed boulders that are right next to the road—bees nest in them), and then past a unique one-table picnic area called Gray's Spring. The picnic area was built of stone by the Civilian Conservation Corps in the 1930's (as were most of the roads in the area, and the cabins and lodge up on White

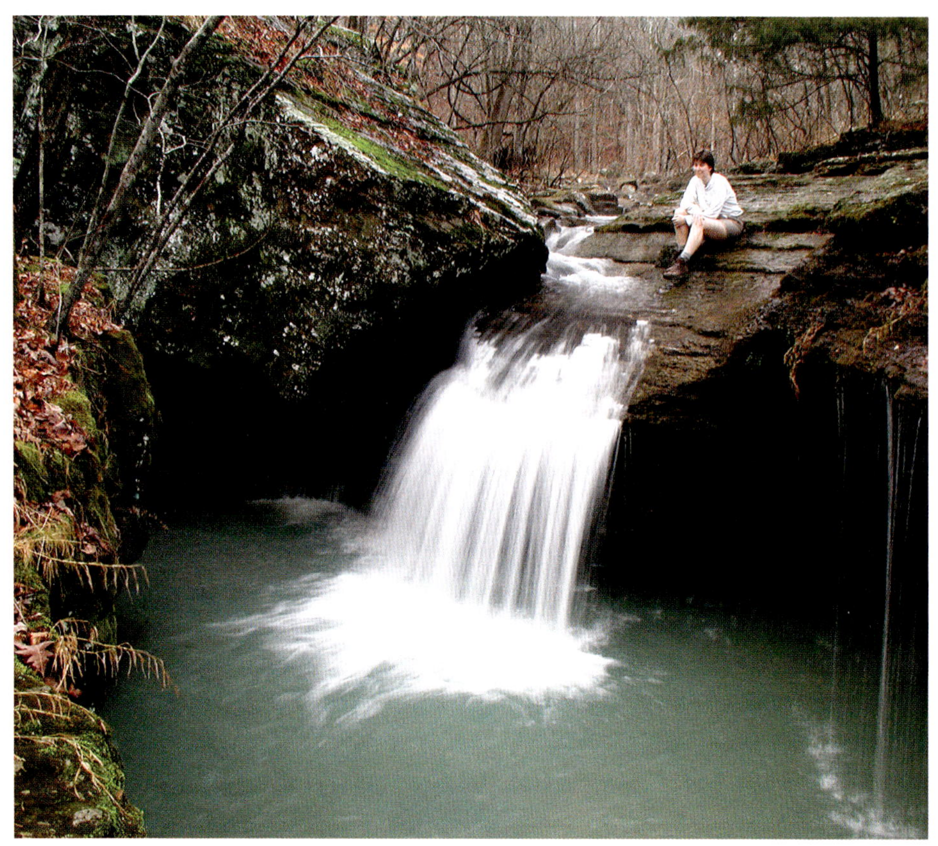

Spirits Creek Falls

Rock Mountain too). About a half mile past Gray's Spring TURN RIGHT onto Ragtown Road (FR#1509), go .7 mile and PARK on the right just beyond where the OHT crosses the road **(35.68379, -93.89792)**. This is the same parking spot as for Train Trestle Falls, but you hike in the opposite direction.

You can also get here from the other direction: Take the Mulberry exit off I-40 (exit #24) and head north on Hwy. 215 to Fern (past the turnoff to Devils Canyon), continue another three miles on the highway and TURN LEFT onto FR#1505/CR#75 (paved), continue past Shores Lake (pavement ends, road is called Bliss Ridge Road) another four miles up the hill and TURN RIGHT onto White Rock Mtn. Road (FR#1003) and take it down the mountain across Salt Fork Creek, up and over Potato Knob Mountain, down the mountain to Spirits Creek, and then up the hill to Ragtown Road where you will TURN LEFT and go .7 mile and park at the OHT parking spot. Whew, that was a mouthful!

To get to the falls take the OHT (blazed white) west from Ragtown Road. It will drop gradually down into the Spirits Creek drainage. When you get to the very bottom at 1.2 the trail will land on an old logging road and turn abruptly to the left—you want to actually TURN RIGHT here and go the opposite direction on the road trace for just 100 feet or so, then leave the road TO THE LEFT and head down the slope, across a primitive camping area to the creek below. This area is small and fragile, so handle with care.

ROBINSON FALLS. The first time I found this pair of waterfalls I was hiking with Bob and Dawna Robinson on a warm day in April. They had been in charge of organizing volunteers

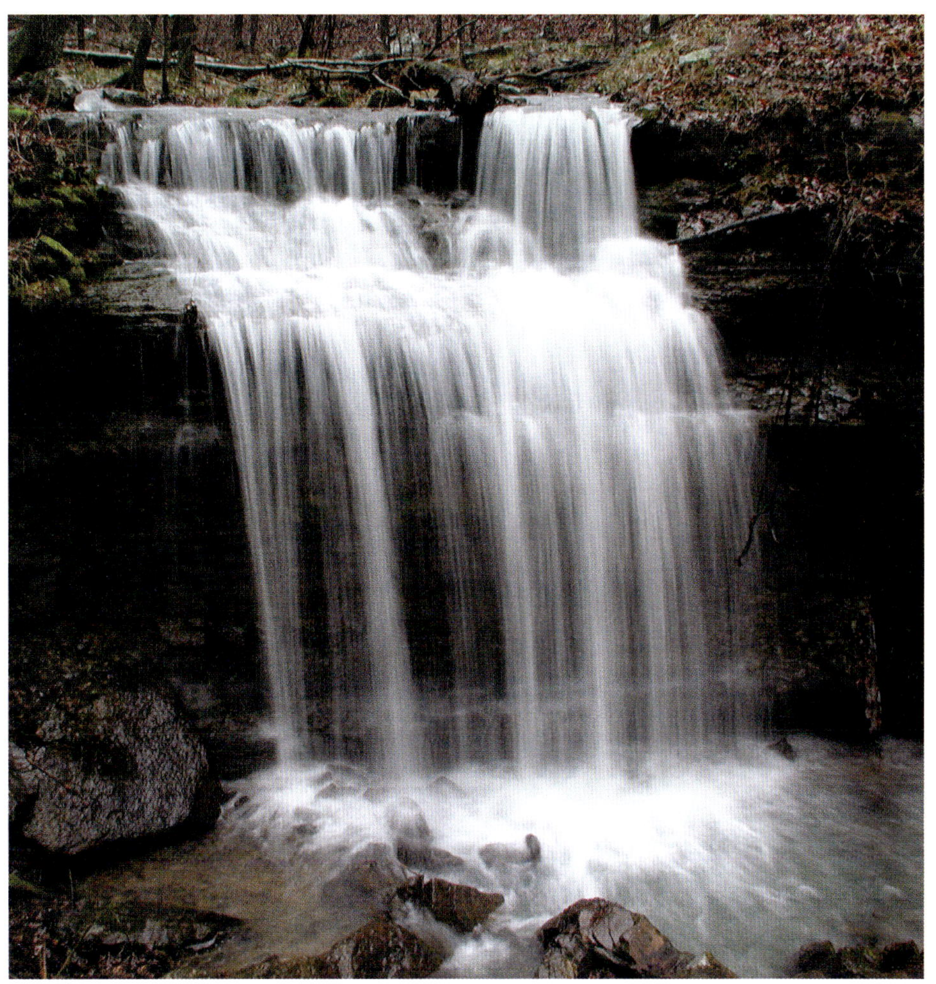

Lower Robinson Falls

from all over the United States to keep the OHT maintained for many years, and did quite a bit of trail work themselves too. We were on the hillside above Spirits Creek inspecting the trail when the sky got really black, opened up and began to pour buckets. The smart one in our group had rain gear, but Bob and I only had t-shirts and shorts to protect us from the blast. Anyway, we all survived just fine, and found these two beautiful waterfalls in the process. I have named them in honor of the great work these two fine folks did for the trail. We lost Dawna in 2010 to cancer and so these waterfalls have even more meaning to me. No doubt she will be smiling down each time you visit.

To reach the falls from Spirits Creek, simply go upstream from the waterfall on the creek a short distance, cross the creek where you can, and follow the side stream uphill that comes in from the west—you will get to the base of the lower falls after only 100 yards or so, and will be able to look up and see the upper falls from there.

Emergency contact: Franklin County Sheriff, 479–667–4127 Dogs are OK

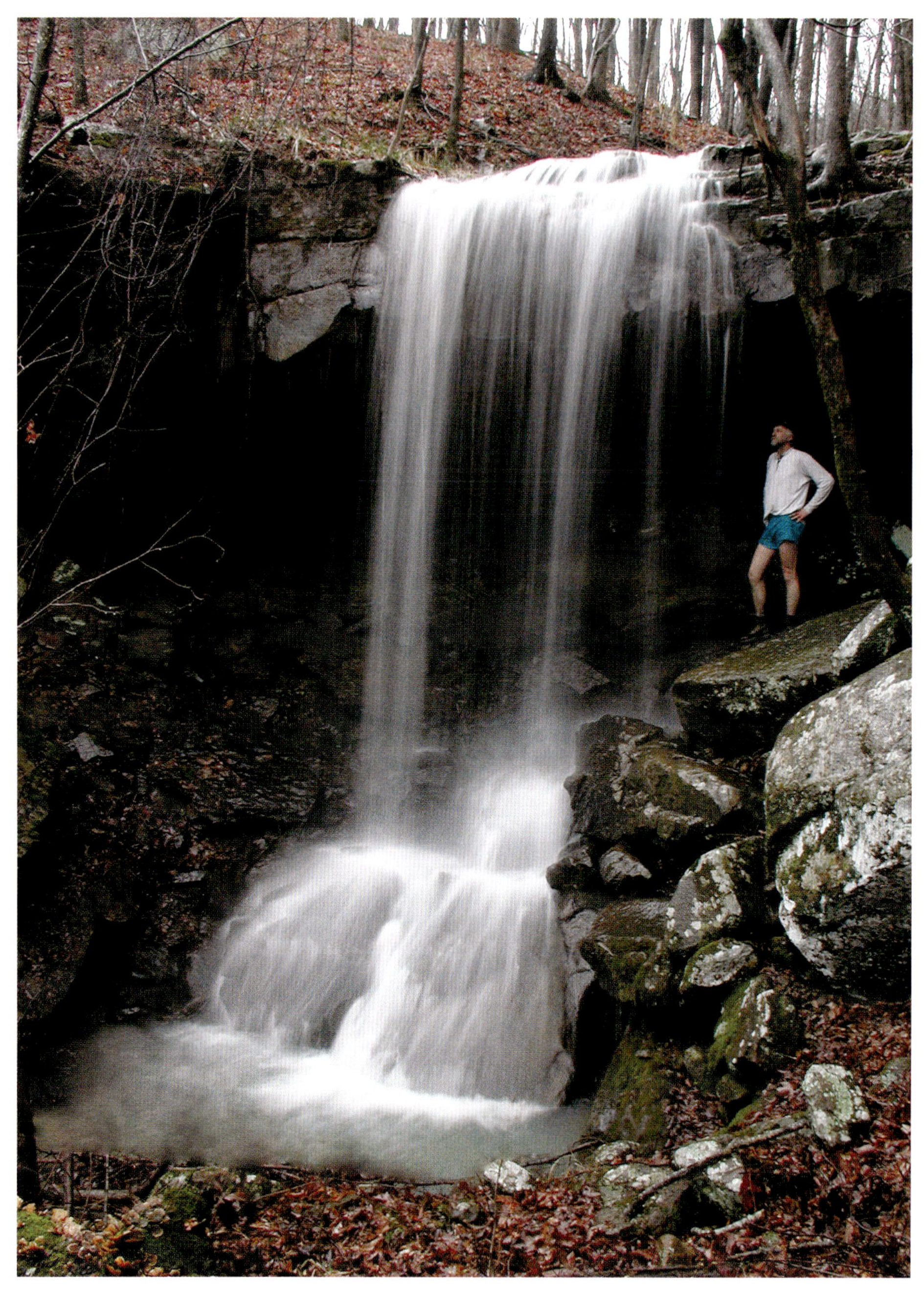

Upper Robinson Falls

White Rock Creek Falls – 31′

2.6 miles roundtrip, medium hike, GPS helpful

GPS **35.67328, -93.97112**

White Rock Creek Cascade –10′

Add .6 mile to above distance, medium hike, GPS not needed

GPS **35.67107, -93.96838**

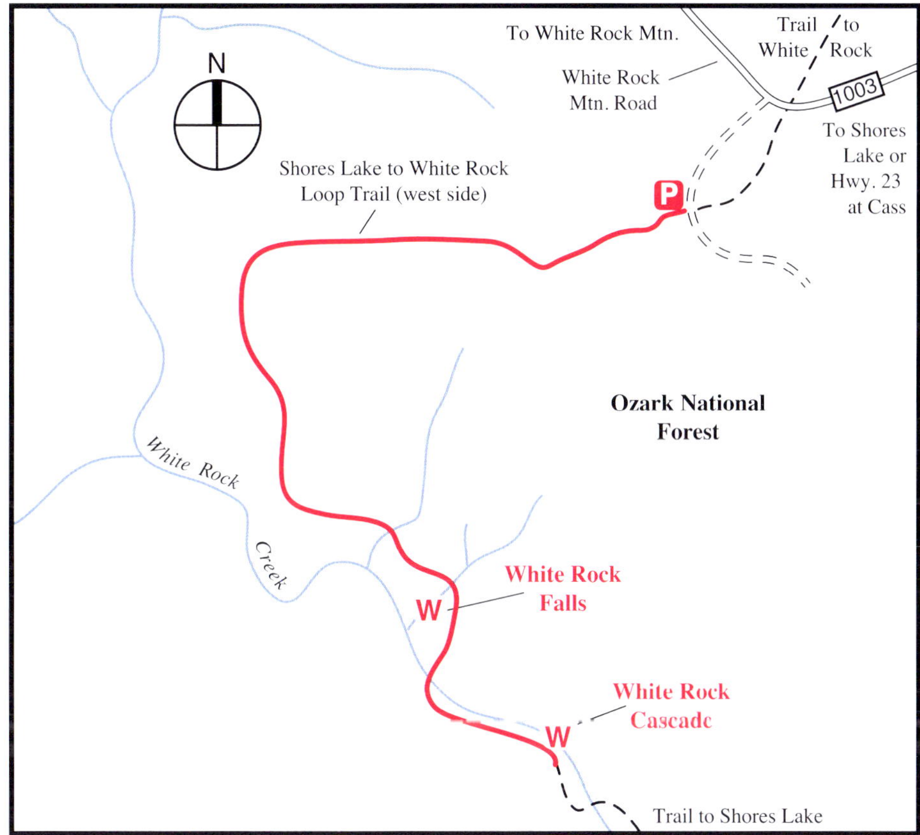

WHITE ROCK CREEK FALLS/CASCADE. My first picture ever published in a national magazine was of this waterfall—in the September, 1983 issue of ***Backpacker***. The falls are located along a popular loop trail, and near the best sunset spot in the Ozarks—White Rock Mountain.

Take the Mulberry exit off I-40 (exit #24) and head north on Hwy. 215 to Fern (past the turnoff to Devils Canyon). Continue another three miles on the highway and TURN LEFT onto FR#1505/CR#75 (paved). Go past Shores Lake (pavement ends, road is called Bliss Ridge Road) another four miles up the hill and TURN LEFT onto White Rock Mtn. Road (FR#1003). Go .6 mile and TURN LEFT onto a jeep road, then follow it a couple hundred yards and park where the Shores Lake to White Rock trail crosses it (**35.68071, -93.96527** — ish, blazed blue).

From the parking area get on the trail to the RIGHT and head off into the woods. The trail eases up a hill, then begins a *long* descent into the White Rock Creek drainage. It levels out some and curves around a couple of small streams. At 1.3 it crosses a stream that has

White Rock Creek Falls (right)

White Rock Creek Cascade (below)

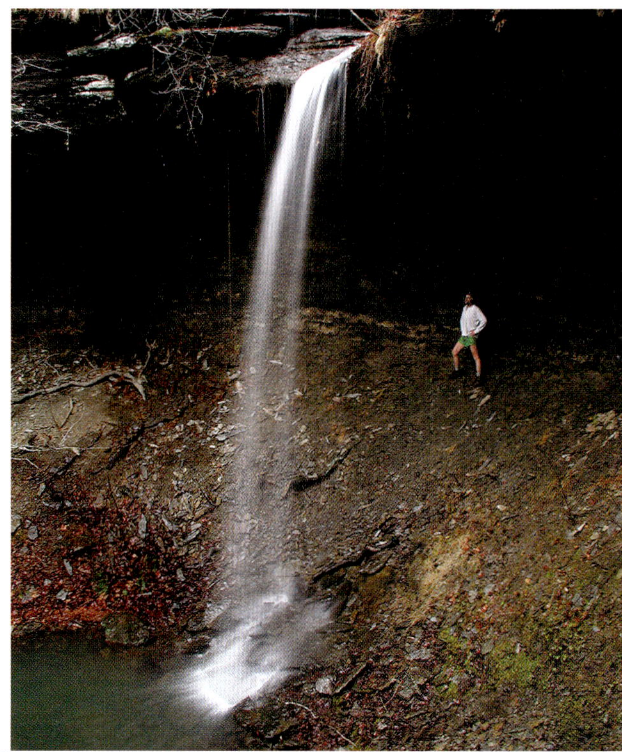

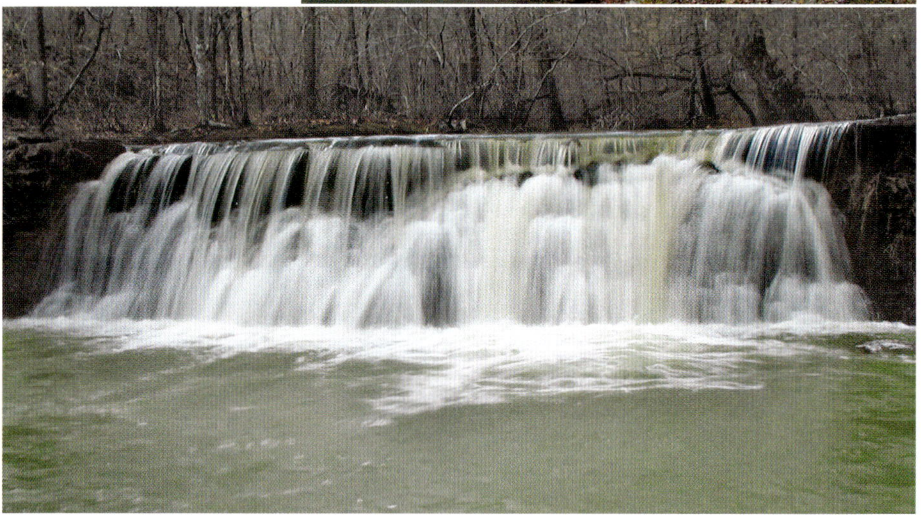

some cascades above and you can tell that the water goes over a dropoff down below—this is the falls. The best way to get to it is to continue on the main trail until it has landed in the flat bottoms, then bushwhack back to your right and up into the little grotto where the waterfall is. To get to the cascade, go back to the trail and continue hiking. Soon you will have to cross White Rock Creek, and then will follow it downstream just a little way further on the trail until you reach the cascade at 1.6. (You can also get to these waterfalls by hiking the Shores Lake to White Rock Loop Trail from Shores Lake—TURN RIGHT into the Shores Lake Campground to get to the trailhead, then take the West Side Loop to the cascade at 2.8, and on to the falls at 3.1.)

Emergency contact: Franklin County Sheriff, 479-667-4127 Dogs are OK

Jack White Falls – 41′

4.4 miles roundtrip, medium hike, GPS recommended

GPS **35.70711, -93.94729**

Phipps Branch Falls – 23′

Easy bushwhack, next to road, GPS not needed

GPS **35.70584, -93.88002**

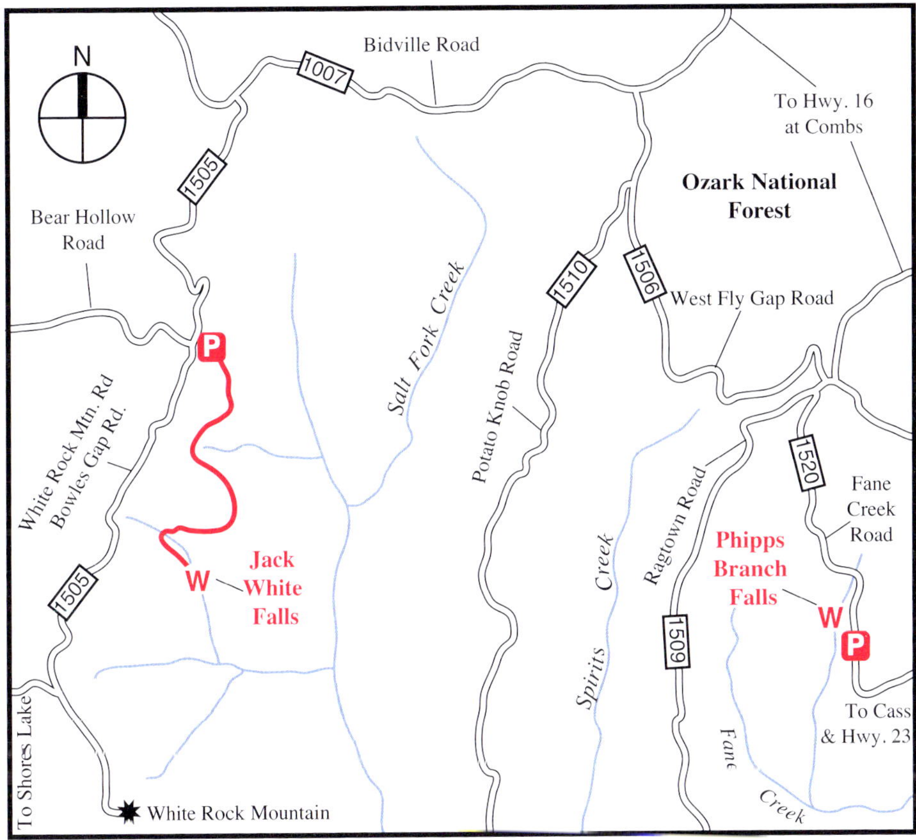

JACK WHITE FALLS. Jack was a friend of mine and good egg and used to manage the historic stone cabins at White Rock Mountain with his bride, Paula, before cancer got him. This is one of the largest waterfalls in the area and it is fitting to be named after a tower of a good man.

Take the Mulberry exit off of I-40 (exit #24) and head north on Hwy. 215 to Fern (past the turnoff to Devils Canyon). Continue another three miles and TURN LEFT onto FR#1505/CR#75/Shores Lake Road (paved). Continue past Shores Lake (pavement ends, road is called Bliss Ridge Road) another four miles up the hill and TURN LEFT onto White Rock Mountain Road (FR#1003). Follow it 2.2 miles and TURN RIGHT, go .5 mile and TURN LEFT (a side trip to the lookout on White Rock Mountain just up the road to the right is a must—plan to rent a cabin too!). Go 2.2 miles (Bear Hollow Road goes to the left here) and PARK on the RIGHT side of the road **(35.72437, -93.94653).** You can also get to the White Rock area from Hwy. 16 at Patrick (follow signs), or from Cass on Hwy. 23.

A four-wheeler trail takes off down the hill and to the right from the parking spot—follow this for 2.0 and then TURN LEFT onto another four-wheeler trail. This one will go steeply down the hill and then level out a bit—TURN LEFT onto another little four-wheeler trail and this will take you over to a creek and the top of the waterfall.

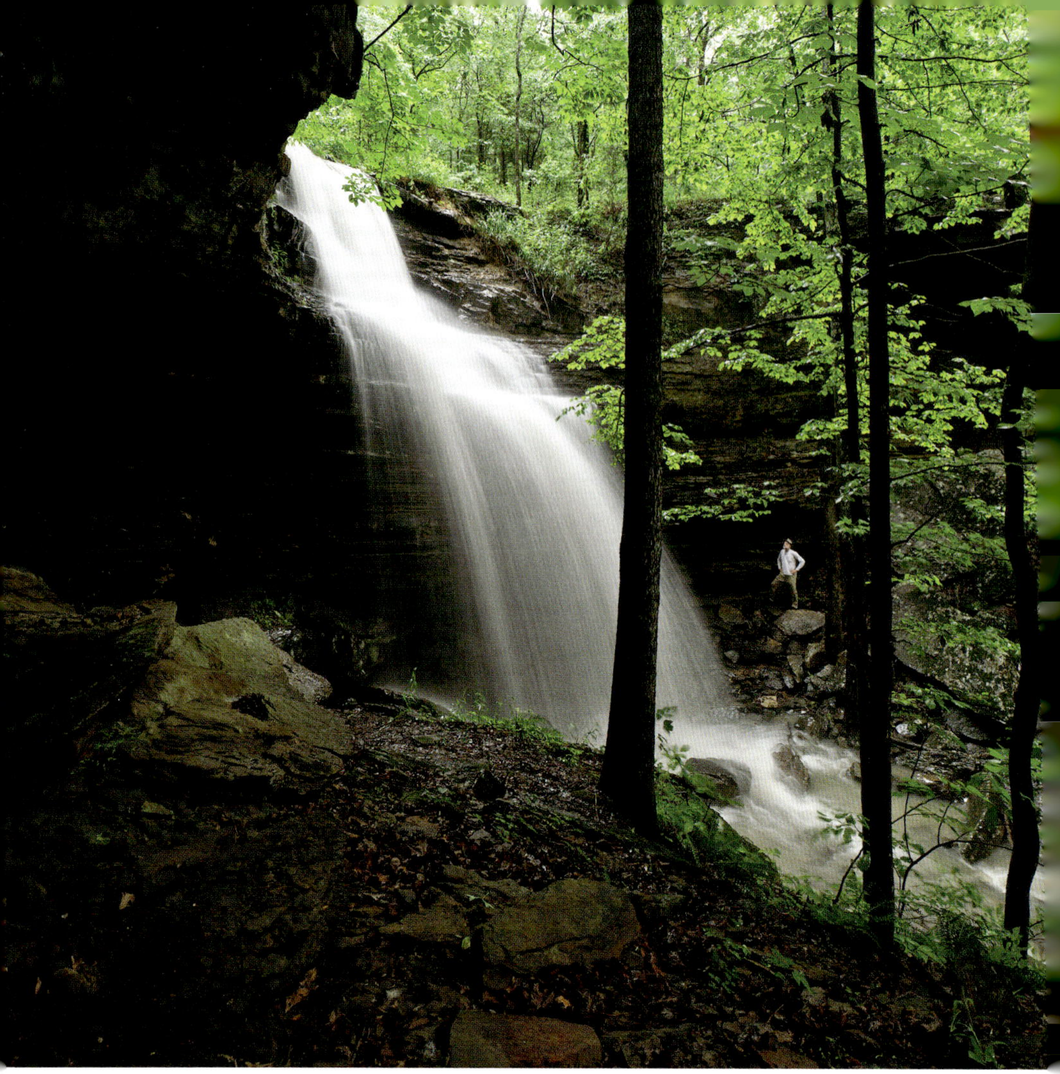

Jack White Falls (during high water)

PHIPPS BRANCH FALLS. This one is right next to the road and easy to find. I don't know who Phipps was but now he has a waterfall named after him!

From Jack White Falls parking spot head north on FR#1505/White Rock Mountain Road for 1.7 miles and TURN RIGHT onto FR#1007/Bidville Road. Go 2.5 miles and TURN RIGHT onto FR#1506/West Fly Gap Road /Potato Knob Road. Go .5 mile and TURN LEFT on FR#1506/West Fly Gap Road. Go 2.3 miles until you come to an intersection (five roads meet) that we used to call "The Summit" during deer camp. A historical note here—the old railroad that ran from Combs to Cass passed through this intersection, which was the highest point along that spur line (the Summit). You can still find the old railroad bed if you hunt around. From that intersection TURN RIGHT and then TURN LEFT 100 feet later onto FR#1520/Fane Creek Rd. Go 1.3 miles and PARK at a little pulloff beside the road on the right—the waterfall will be within sight next to the road down on your right. OR take FR#1520/Fane Creek Rd. from Cass on Hwy. 23, zero your odometer when you cross Fane Creek, then go 5.2 miles and PARK on the left **35.70584, -93.88002**).

Emergency contact: Franklin County Sheriff, 479–667–4127 Dogs are OK

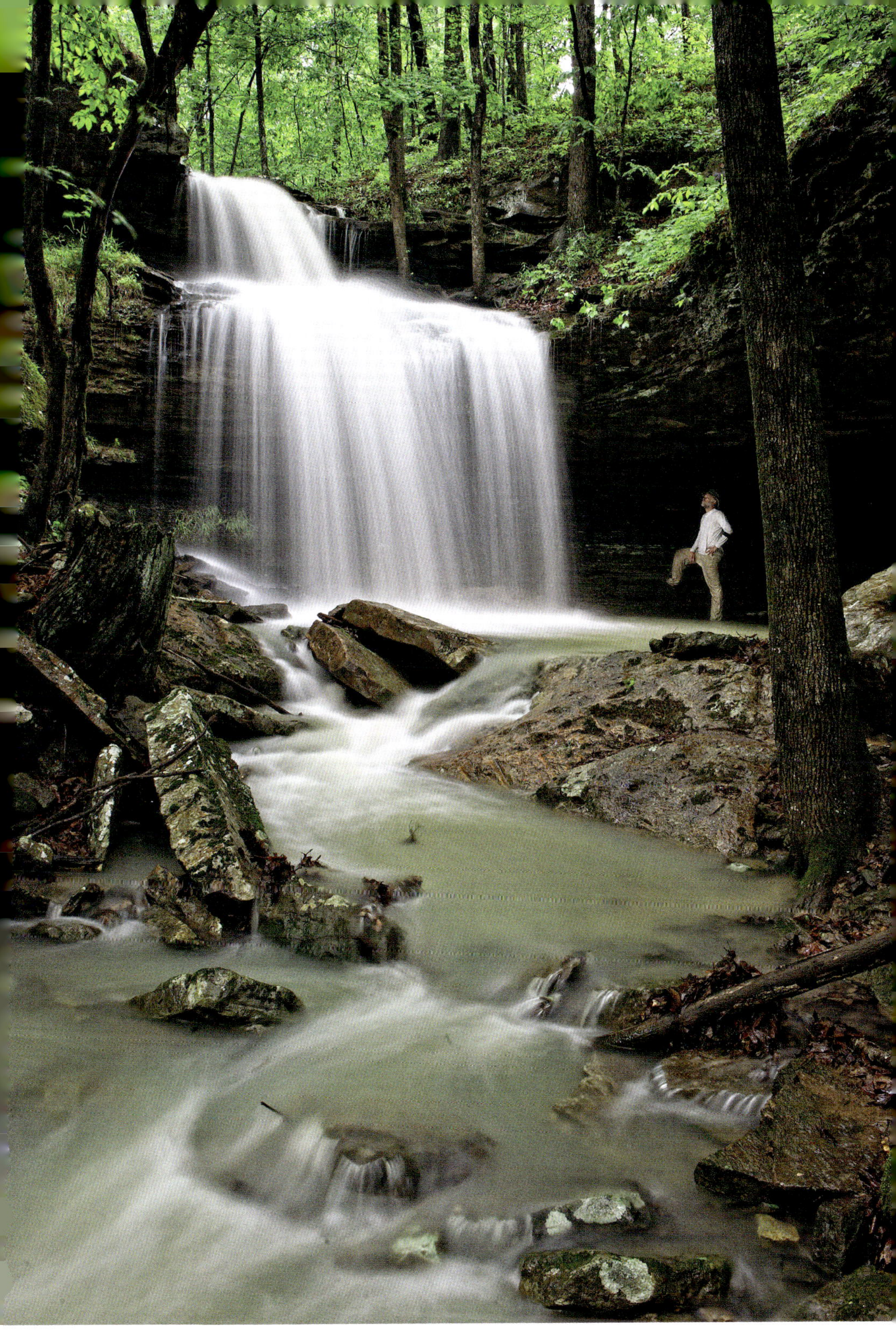

Phipps Branch Falls (during high water)

Tom Kennon Falls –42′

1.0 roundtrip (300' elevation drop), medium bushwhack, steep

GPS **35.64061, -94.00058**

Keefe Grotto – 21′

1.7 mi. roundtrip (500' elevation drop), medium bushwhack, steep

GPS **35.64390, -94.00415**

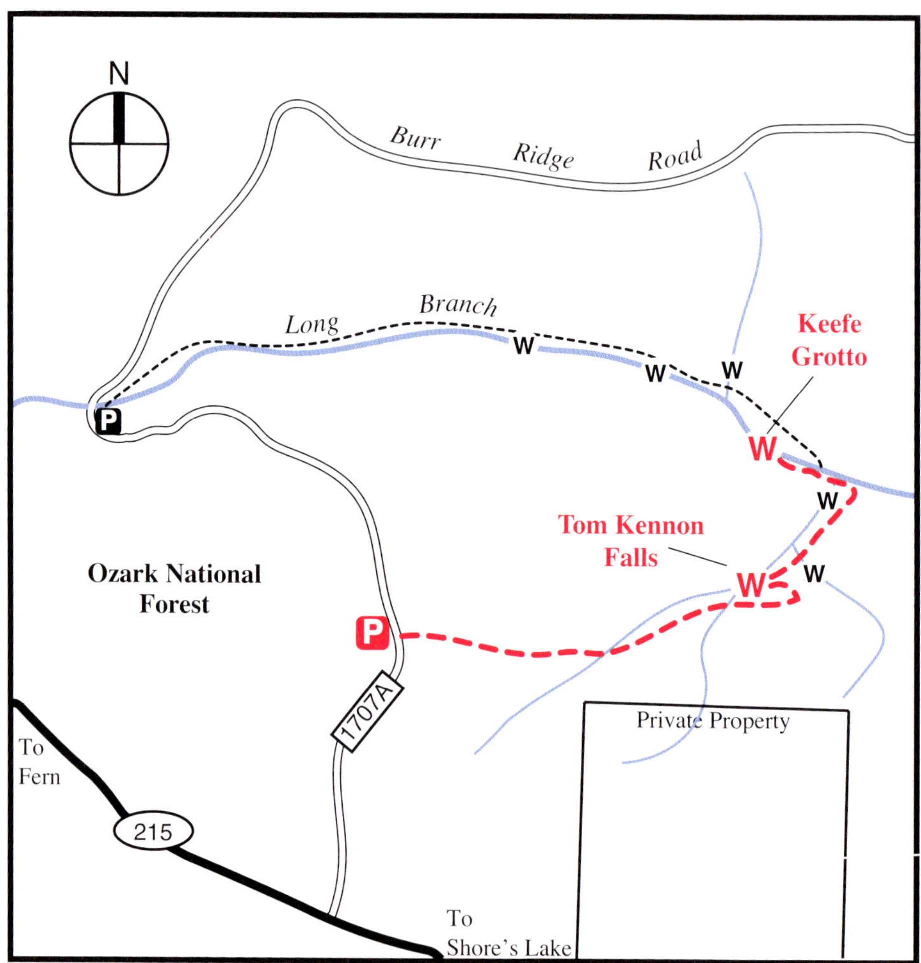

TOM KENNON FALLS/KEEFE GROTTO. Tom Kennon, expert whitewater guru and author of the best selling *Ozark Whitewater Guidebook* (and recent inductee to the Arkansas Outdoor Hall of Fame), and a terrific nature photographer (thanks to a very special lens he got from ME!). Tom helped me a great deal decades ago when I was working on the first edition of this guidebook, telling me about many nice waterfalls located in the middle of nowhere—that crazy kayakers would run during floods.

Terry Keefe (see page 143 for **Keefe Falls**), longtime special friend to me and thousands of others, led me to countless waterfalls over the years. He called one night excited about this new waterfall area, insisted that I promise to go visit. It would be the last phone call he ever made—early the next morning he died tragically while hiking with his wife near

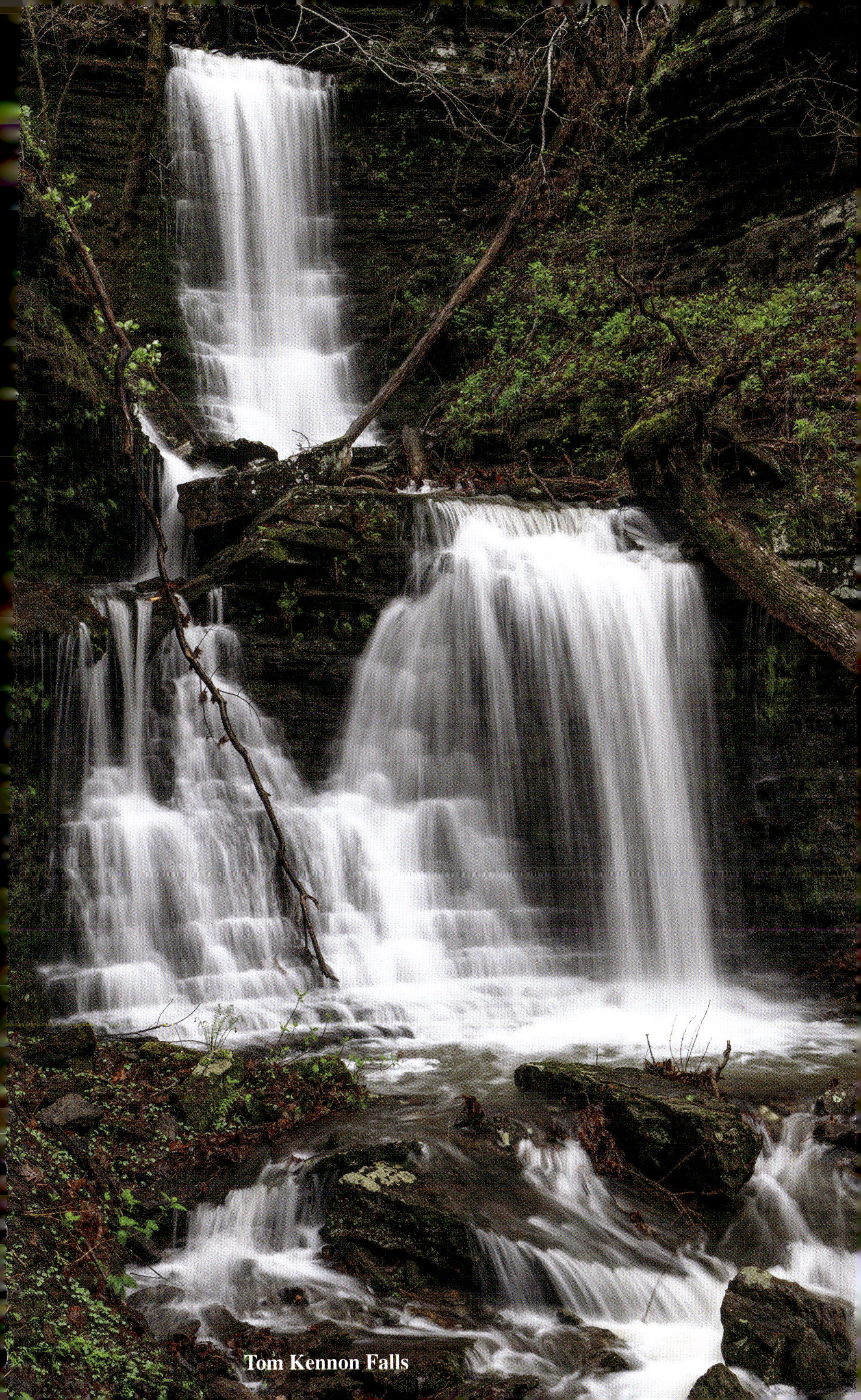

Tom Kennon Falls

their home. Rest In Peace my friend—your waterfalls will flow in our hearts and minds forever...

DIRECTIONS: Take exit #24 on I-40, take Hwy. 215 9.1 miles north to Fern then TURN RIGHT (towards Shores Lake and White Rock), go .5 mile and TURN LEFT onto FR 1707A, go .3 and PARK **(35.64035, -94.00636)**. (Alternate parking spot—continue .4 along the road to the bottom of the hill at Long Branch **(35.64291, -94.01150)**.

Head east/right away from the road and slightly downhill, soon the hill gets steeper and you drop down to the creek—cross the creek and stay on the RIGHT side as you go down. Eventually you'll be up on a very rocky hillside above the creek and will hike past the double-tiered falls down on your left—that's the first one we are after! But STAY up above the creek and continue downstream until you can find a break in the bluff, then TURN LEFT and back down to the base of **Tom Kennon Falls** at .5, an SSS for sure!

From Tom's falls, continue downstream along this rugged creek, passing a nice waterfall on the right. There's another really nice falls at the bottom of this creek where it intersects with Long Branch at .75. TURN LEFT and follow the creek upstream a couple hundred yards to **Keefe Grotto**, of course an SSS!

There are other waterfalls upstream (PARK at the top of Long Branch and follow it a mile downstream), including a BONUS 71' tall unnamed beauty at 1.1 **(35.64345, -94.00075)** This is on a north side drainage and would take a major flood to look really great (Long Branch would probably be flooded but you can park on the forest road up above this side drainage and hike down).

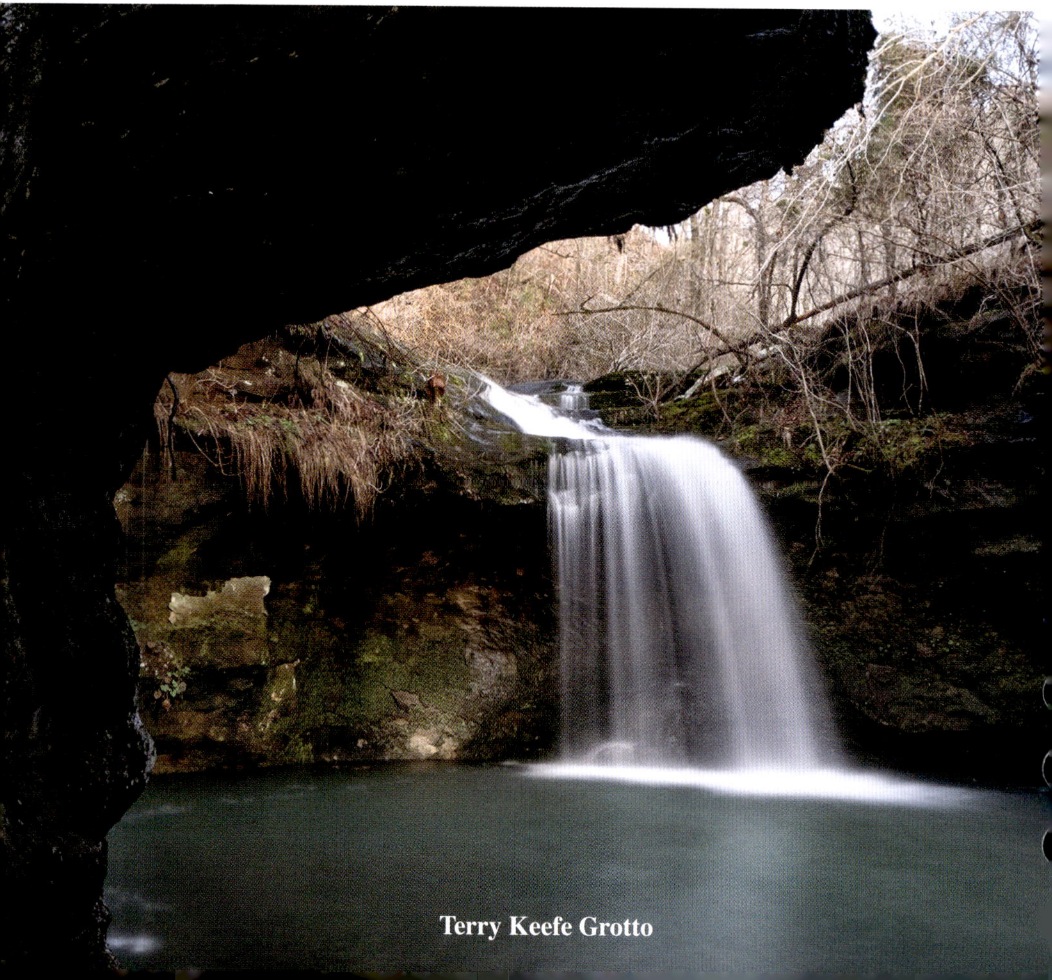

Terry Keefe Grotto

Devils Canyon Falls – 63′

2.0 miles roundtrip, difficult bushwhack, GPS recommended

GPS **35.63758, -94.03488**

Devils Canyon Jr. Falls –18′

2.0 miles roundtrip, medium bushwhack, GPS recommended

GPS **35.63470, -94.03095**

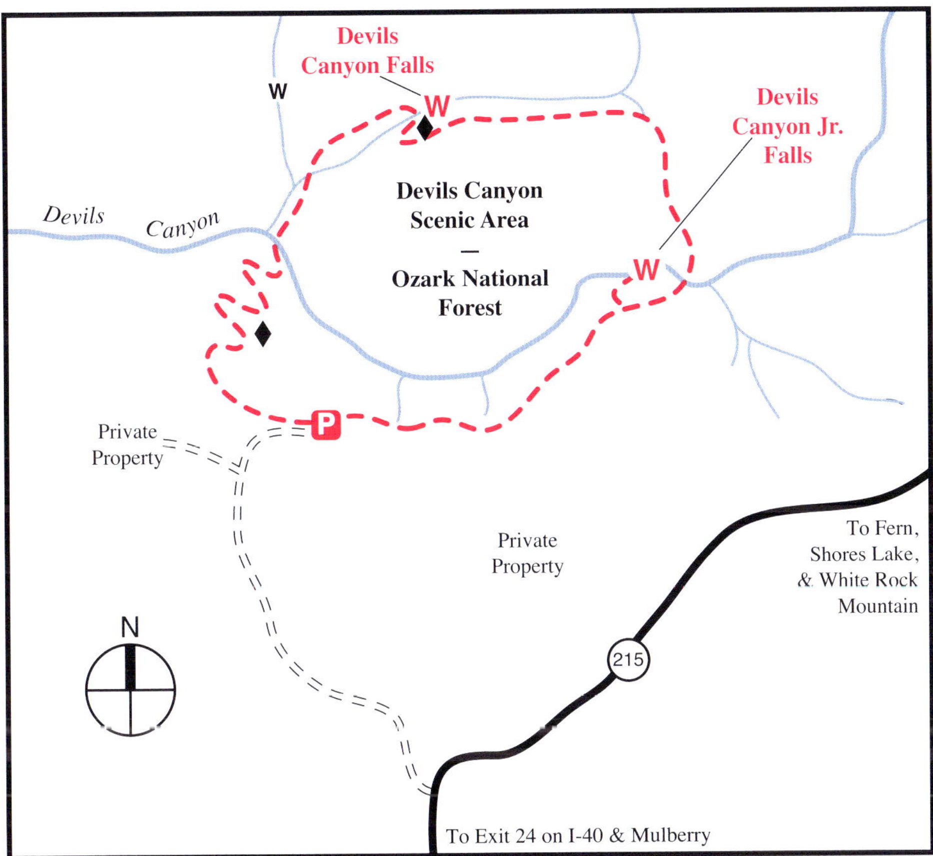

DEVILS CANYON & JR. FALLS. (photos are on the following pages) This seldom-visited scenic area is quite rugged, but is located right off the highway and is easy to get to—at least to get to the edge of it. Hiking around inside the area is another matter—there are no trails, and the terrain can be brutal. But the rewards are plenty, and the waterfall is really spectacular.

Take the Mulberry/Hwy. 215 exit (#24) off I-40 east of Ft. Smith and head north on Hwy. 215 to the tiny community of Fern. Zero your odometer there and head back south of Fern on Hwy. 215—go 1.4 miles and TURN RIGHT (west) onto an unmarked dirt road. A truck or 4wd vehicle helps as this road gets a little bit rough. Follow the road up and over a small hill—STAY STRAIGHT at the intersection (the left fork goes into private property)—and PARK once you come to the edge of the canyon .6 mile from the highway (**35.63160, -94.03873** —ish).

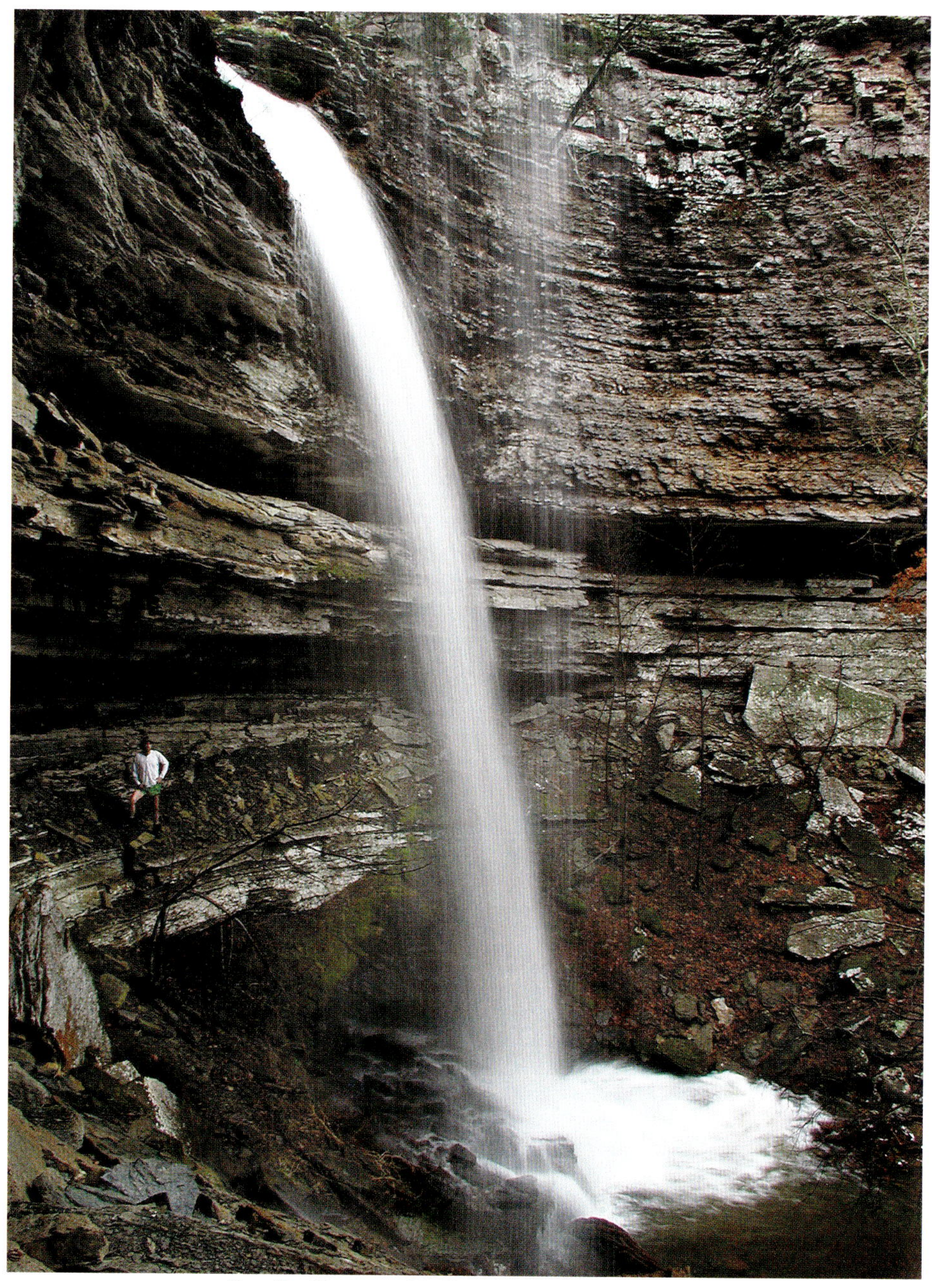

Devils Canyon Falls (during high water)

Once again there are no trails, but here is the route I normally take. Continue on the jeep road to the east from the parking spot—you'll be hiking right along the edge of the canyon, which is off to your left. The farther you go the worse this little road gets. Follow it around the edge of the canyon until you drop down a bit and come to a creek.

A little ways before you reach this creek crossing while you are still on top, look for a small trail to the LEFT that goes down through some giant boulders and eventually to the creek below—it comes out right on top of **Devils Canyon Jr. Falls** and is a beautiful little spot—see photo below. If you miss the little trail you can also bushwhack down the creek to the top of the falls from the creek crossing ahead.

OK, back to regular programming. Wade the creek and head up the hill and a little bit to your left, and away from that road trace—hike towards a low spot in the ridge if you can see one (a GPS helps a lot!). Bushwhack up into the "saddle," then continue down the other side, veering to the left as you go. Once you hit the creek TURN LEFT and follow it downstream until you come to the top of the falls. It is ***extremely dangerous*** ♦ at this point! You might be able to make it down to the base of the falls, but it is pretty tough.

To get back to the parking area, either return the way you came in, or loop around the other side of the hill (it's about a mile either way). To loop back, head downstream from the falls. Once you reach the main stream, find a way across it, then bushwhack *up* the hillside ♦ and back to the parking area—it is *very steep!*

Emergency contact: Franklin County Sheriff, 479–667–4127 Dogs are OK

Devils Canyon Jr. Falls

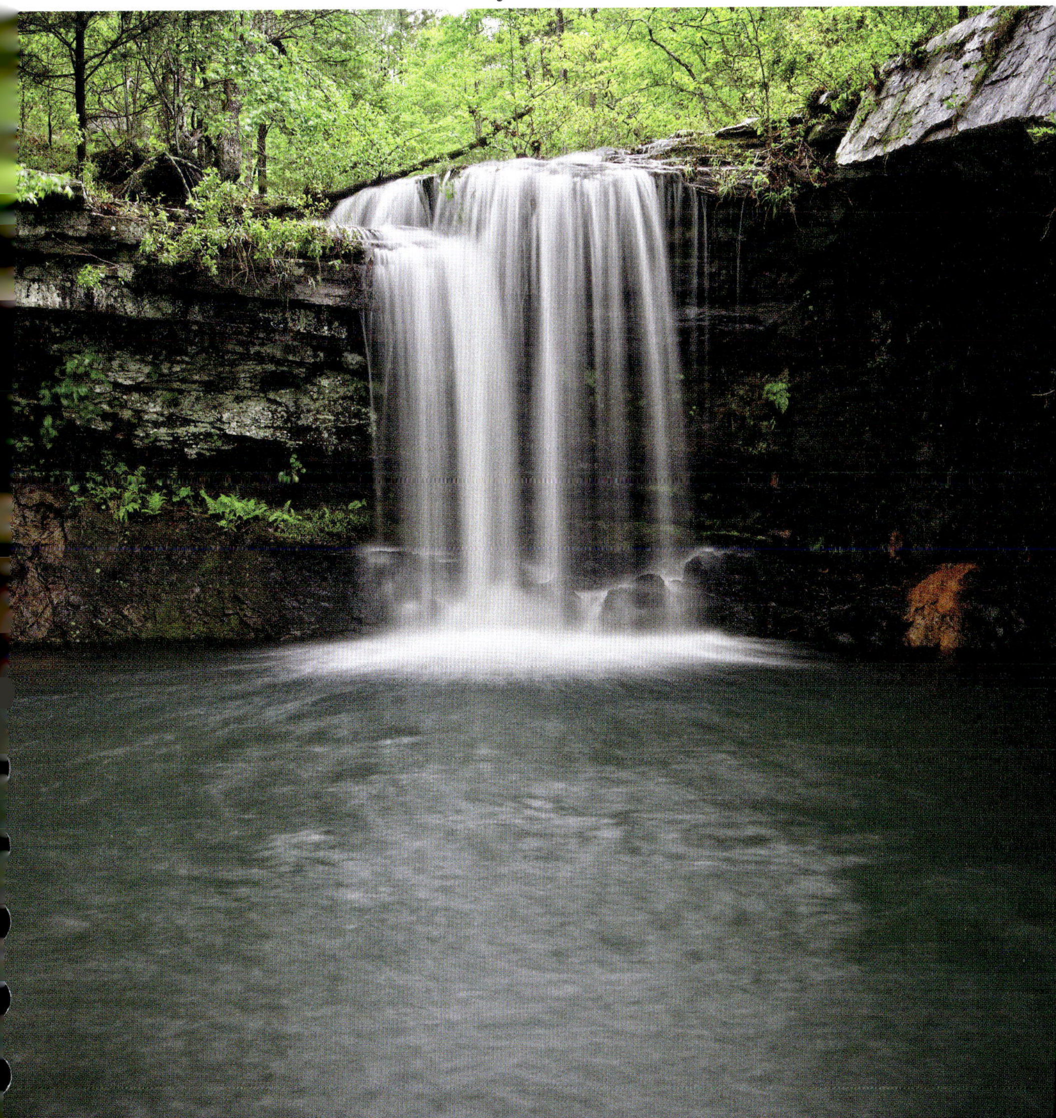

Rattlesnake Falls – 29′

.25 mile roundtrip, easy bushwhack, GPS not needed

GPS **35.69340, -94.02877**

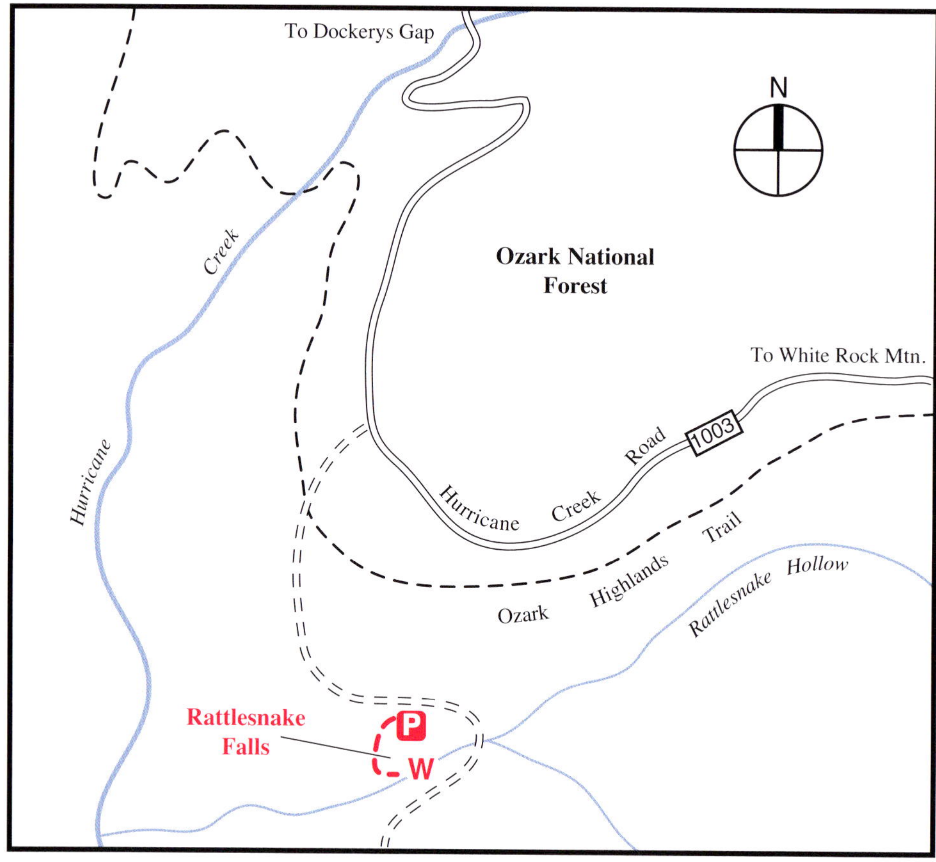

RATTLESNAKE FALLS. Here is a nice little out-of-the-way waterfall that is easy to get to and few people have visited. It's a short, easy bushwhack to get to it, and not too far off the Ozark Highlands Trail. I found out about this falls when friend Bill Herring e-mailed me a photo of him going over it in a kayak!

OK, try to follow these directions: Take the Mulberry exit off of I-40 (exit #24) and head north on Hwy. 215 to Fern (past the turnoff to Devils Canyon). Continue another three miles on the highway and TURN LEFT onto FR#1505/CR#75 (paved). Continue past Shores Lake (pavement ends, road is called Bliss Ridge Road) another four miles up the hill and TURN LEFT onto White Rock Mtn. Road (FR#1003). Follow it 2.2 miles and TURN LEFT onto Hurricane Creek Road (turn right to go to White Rock Mtn.). Go 4.7 miles and TURN LEFT onto an unmarked dirt road, and finally go .7 mile and PARK on the right just before you cross the creek (**35.69386, -94.02900**—ish). From Mountainburg—see directions to Dockery Gap Falls—then continue on past Hurricane Creek .7 mile up the hill, then TURN RIGHT on the unmarked dirt road, go .7 mile and PARK on the right.

From the parking area you can either continue along the road until you get to the creek, then follow it downstream to the top of the falls (very slick there!), or simply head

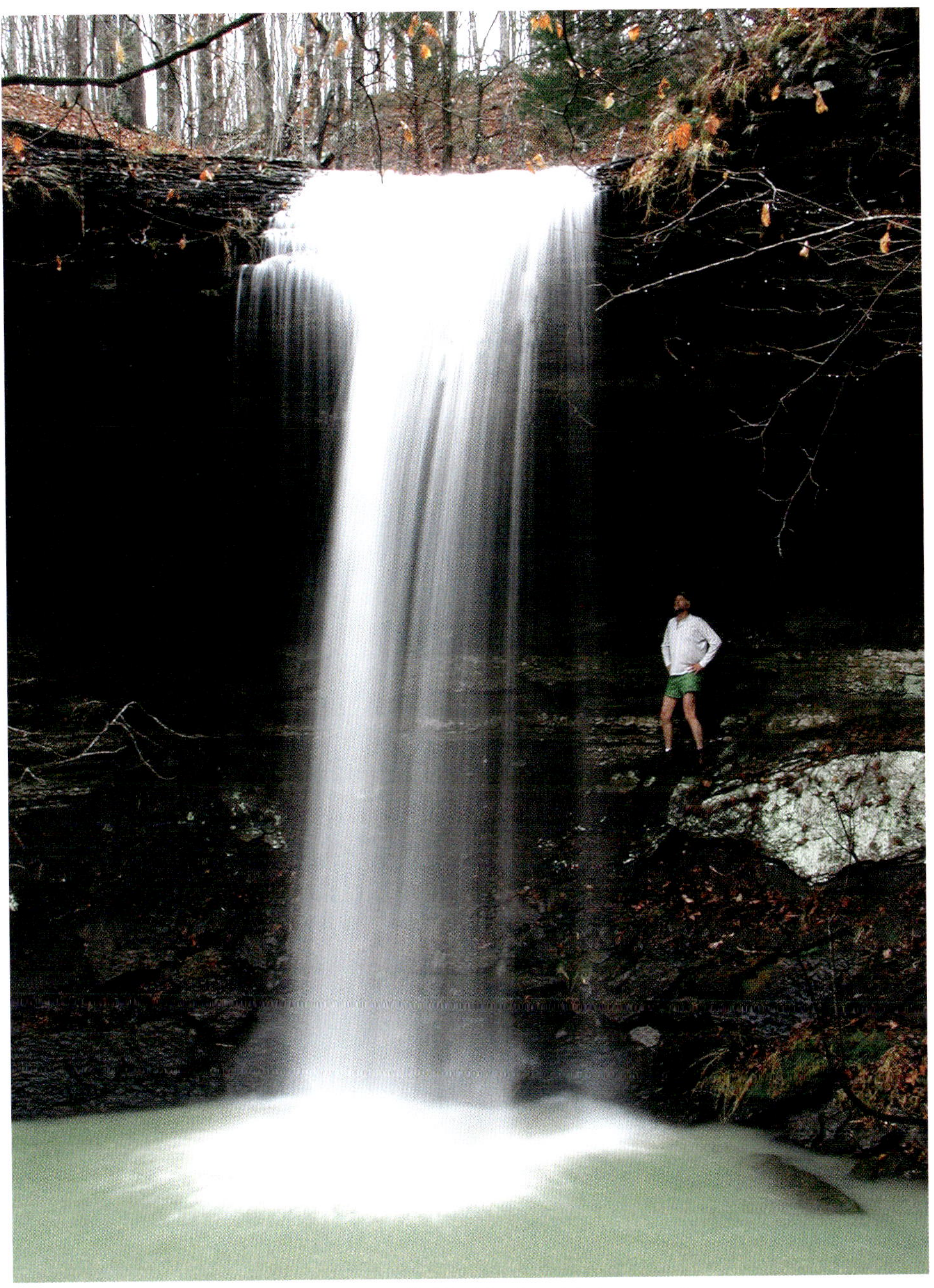

Rattlesnake Falls (during high water)

out into the woods to the south until you come to the stream and waterfall—it's not very far to the falls. If you hike downstream a ways there is access down through the bluffline and then you can come back upstream to the base of the falls. If you get down to the base, gaze on up to the top of the falls and just imagine a guy going over that in a *kayak!*

Emergency contact: Crawford County Sheriff, 479-474-2261 Dogs are OK

Dockery Gap Falls – 36′

3.0 miles roundtrip, difficult bushwhack, GPS recommended

GPS **35.72052, -94.01717**

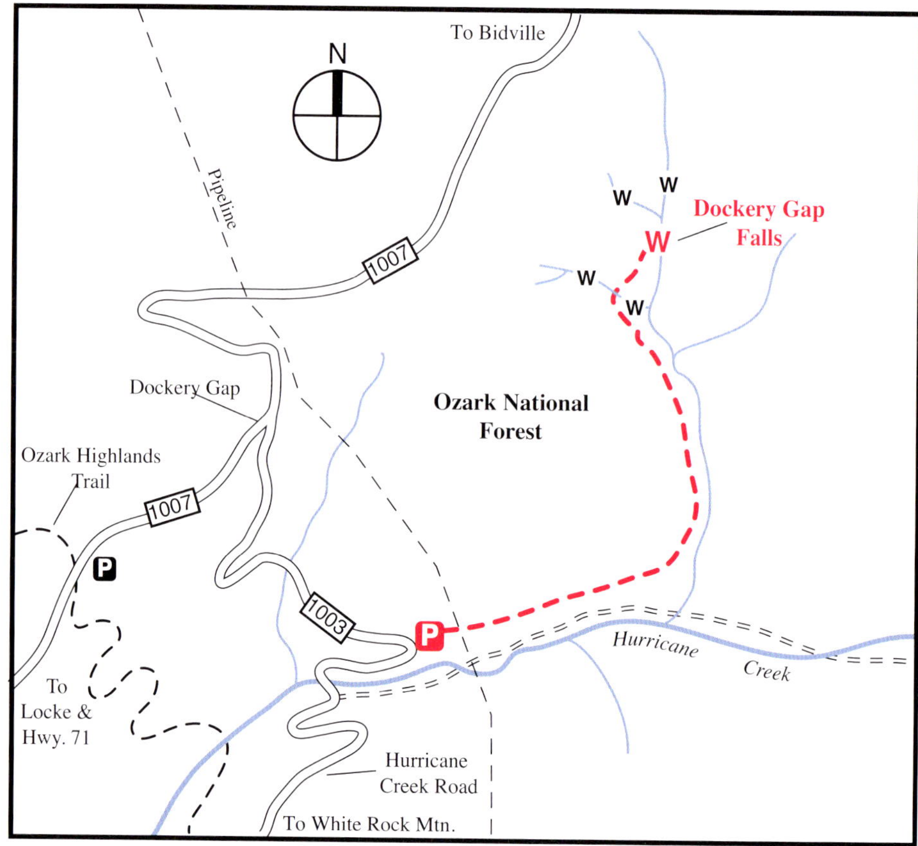

DOCKERY GAP FALLS. If you come to this spot during really high water, you will see more waterfalls than you can count! This grotto is tucked away back up in a side canyon of Hurricane Creek, and it takes a good bit of bushwhacking to reach it (no trail). Be sure to visit the nearby Rattlesnake Falls while you are in the area.

From Mountainburg, take Hwy. 71 south 2.6 miles to the top of the hill. TURN LEFT onto CR#348 (paved). Go 14.1 miles to Dockery Gap (the road will turn to dirt and to FR#1007 near Locke) and TURN RIGHT onto FR#1003 (Hurricane Creek Rd.). Then go .9 mile down the hill and PARK on the left side of the road at a hairpin curve (**35.70744, -94.02498** about .25 mile before you cross Hurricane Creek). You will be able to look over the edge and see Hurricane Creek below. You can also get to this spot from the White Rock Mountain area—just take FR#1003 (Hurricane Creek Rd.) to the west 5.4 miles to the bridge across Hurricane Creek, then continue on to the second sharp curve and PARK on the right.

Leave the road and head across the hillside along a bench. You'll soon cross a pipeline right of way, then back into the woods again. Stay on the level as best you can, just bushwhacking generally straight ahead. When you begin to come to a large drainage in front of you, follow the contour of the hillside around to the left, and up into that drainage.

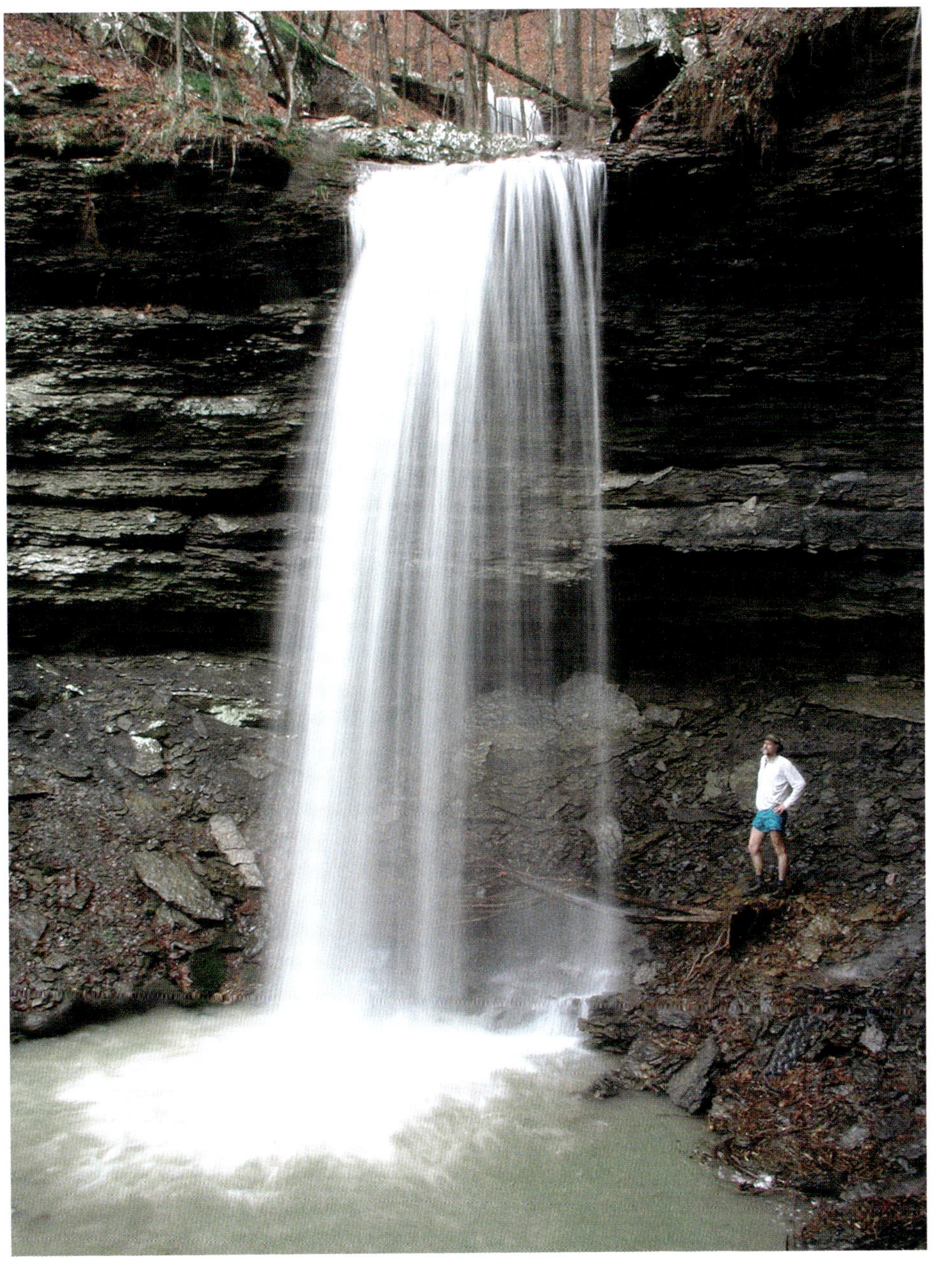

Dockery Gap Falls (during high water)

As you work your way up into this drainage you can either stay a bench or two above the creek, or simply go down and follow the creek upsteam—there will be some steep and rugged terrain either way. You will eventually come to a waterfall near the creek that enters from a side drainage on your left—there is also a larger one up that same little drainage. Continue on the main creek past these, and you will come to the big falls. It is quite a place when the water is running high! It's about 1.5 miles back to the road—the best way is simply to go back the same way you came in.

Emergency contact: Crawford County Sheriff, 479–474–2261 Dogs are OK

Twin Falls at Devil's Den – 47′/56′

1.5 miles roundtrip, easy hike, GPS not needed

GPS **35.78214, -94.24263**

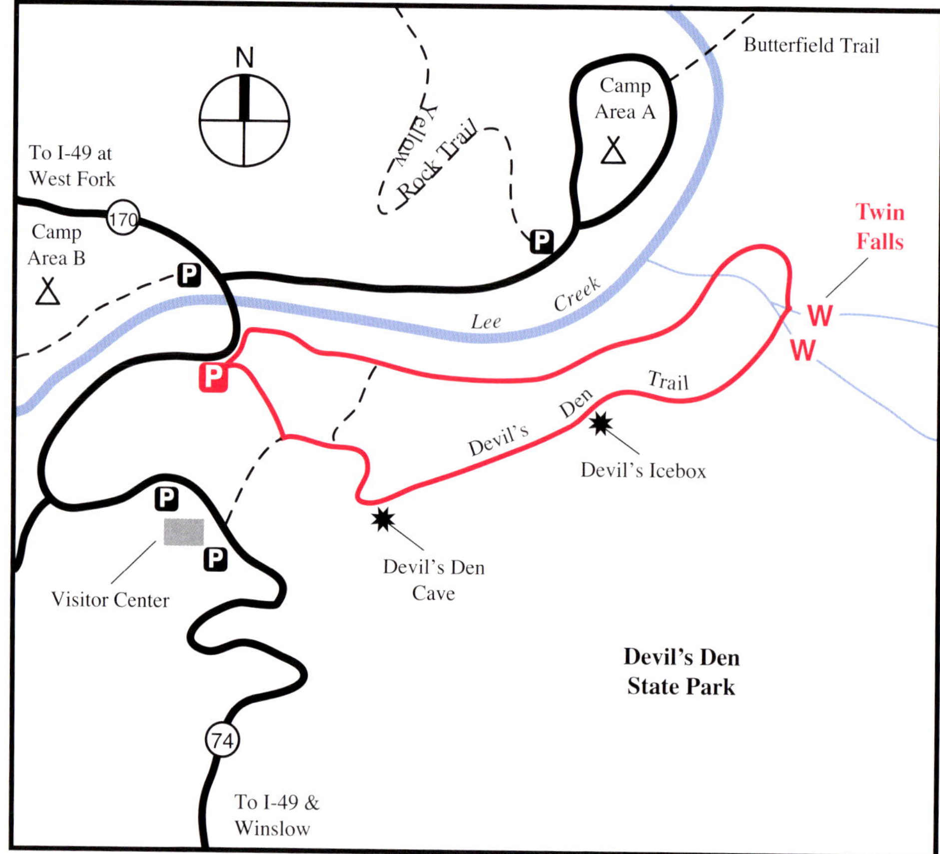

TWIN FALLS AT DEVIL'S DEN. This is one of the most popular hiking trails in the state. Most folks come to explore the little Devil's Den Cave, but I particularly love the waterfall because it is about the only one around I know of that has a bridge crossing the middle of it—reminds me of the giant waterfalls in the Columbia River Gorge in Oregon. You will also want to go see the spillway at the small lake—a beautiful cascade hand crafted by the Civilian Conservation Corps in the 1930's.

Devil's Den State Park is a longtime family favorite destination and has campsites, rental cabins, a swimming pool, picnic area, and many trails including the Butterfield Backpacking Trail, horse and mountain biking trails. To get there from I-49 between Fayetteville and Ft. Smith, either take the Winslow exit (#45) and follow Hwy. 74 to the park, or take the West Fork exit (#53) and follow Hwy. 170 to the park. The trailhead is located on the south side of the bridge that spans Lee Creek **(35.78132, -94.24989)**.

The trail is well marked, and there are interpretive stops along the way that are keyed to a brochure that you can pick up at the visitor center. From the main parking area the trail heads up the hill just a little bit, then swings around up to Devil's Den Cave (it's a crevice that goes 550 feet back into the hillside—be sure to bring a flashlight). The trail levels out some and passes through lots of broken bluffs and interesting geological formations, past the Devil's Icebox crevice, and finally comes to **Twin Falls** at about the one mile point.

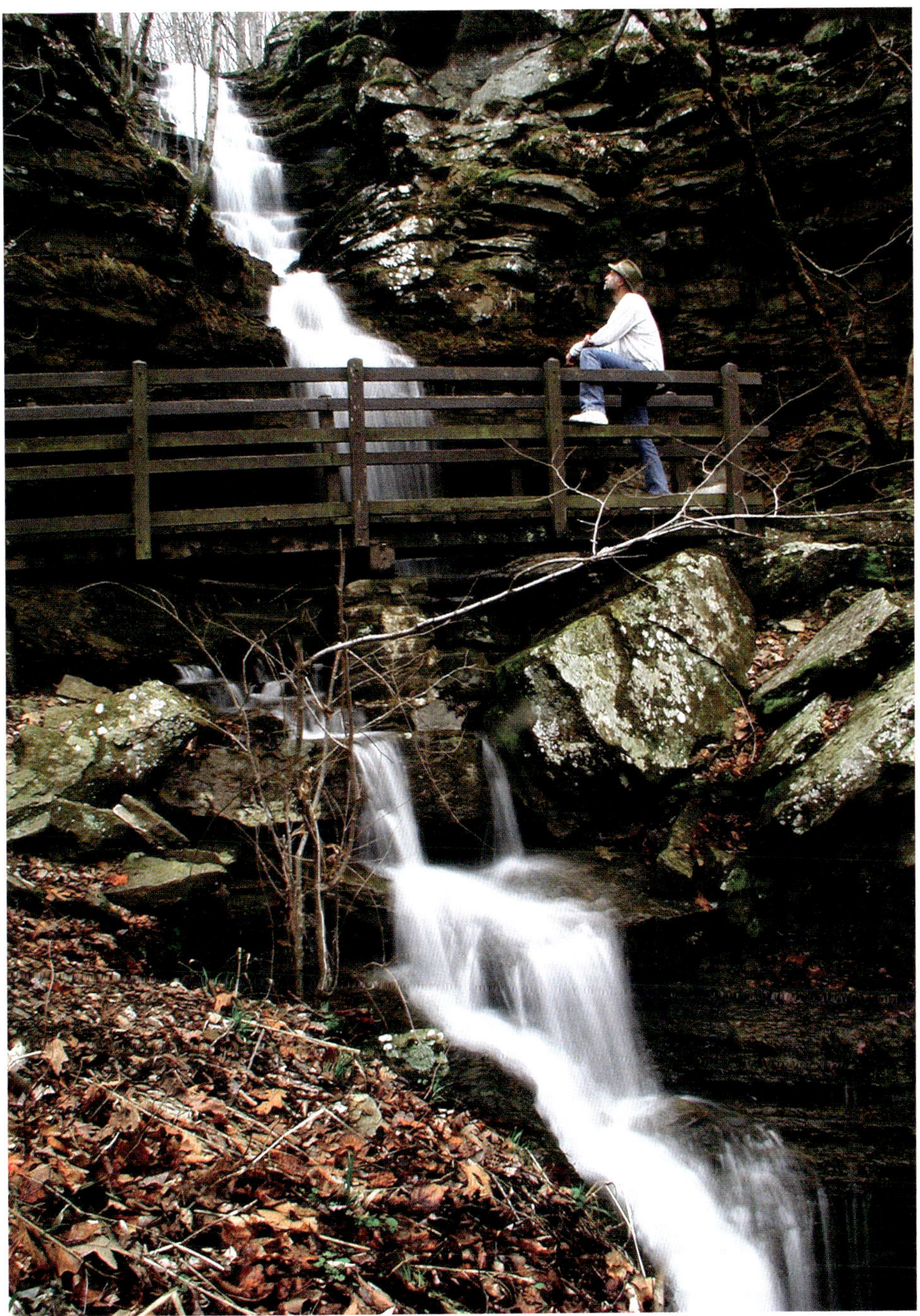

Twin Falls at Devil's Den
(this is a portion of the left falls of the twin)

The trail actually goes under the first of the two falls, and then crosses the middle of the second one via a wooden bridge (pictured above). From the falls the trail drops down the hill and follows alongside Lee Creek all the way back to the trailhead. Dogs are OK
Emergency: Washington County Sheriff, 479–444–1850; Park office 479–761–3325

Natural Dam – 8′ x 187′ GPS **35.64997, -94.39758**

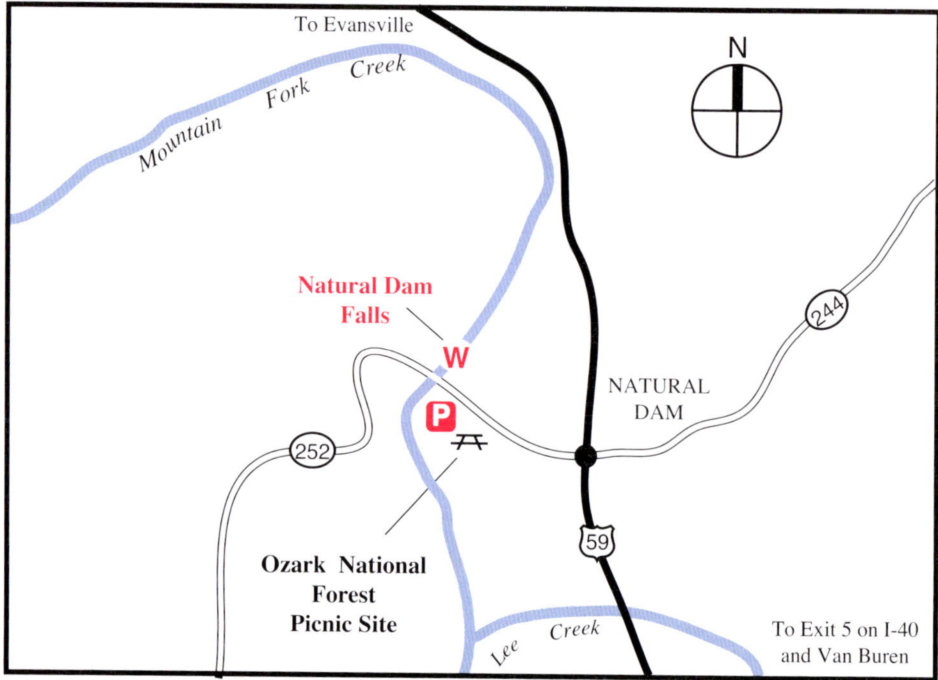

NATURAL DAM. How about a waterfall nearly 200 feet wide, and you don't even have to get out of your car to see it! That's the case with Natural Dam, which is, just like the name suggests, a natural wall of rock that spans the entire width of Mountain Fork Creek, creating a dam of sorts, and a great waterfall. It's a great spot to stop and have a picnic lunch while on a tour through the Ozarks.

To get to Natural Dam, take Exit #5 on I–40 at Van Buren and head north on Hwy. 59, then TURN LEFT at the community of Natural Dam—the picnic area and falls are within sight of the turn.

Emergency contact: Crawford County Sheriff, 479–474–2261

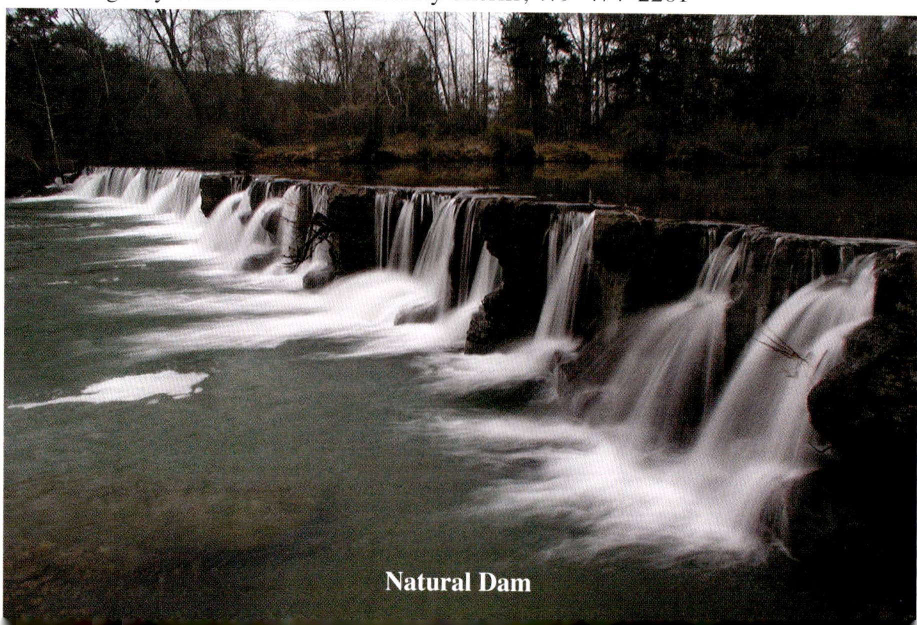

Natural Dam

Tanyard Creek Falls – 12′

.8 mile roundtrip, easy hike, GPS not needed

GPS **36.46772, -94.25848**

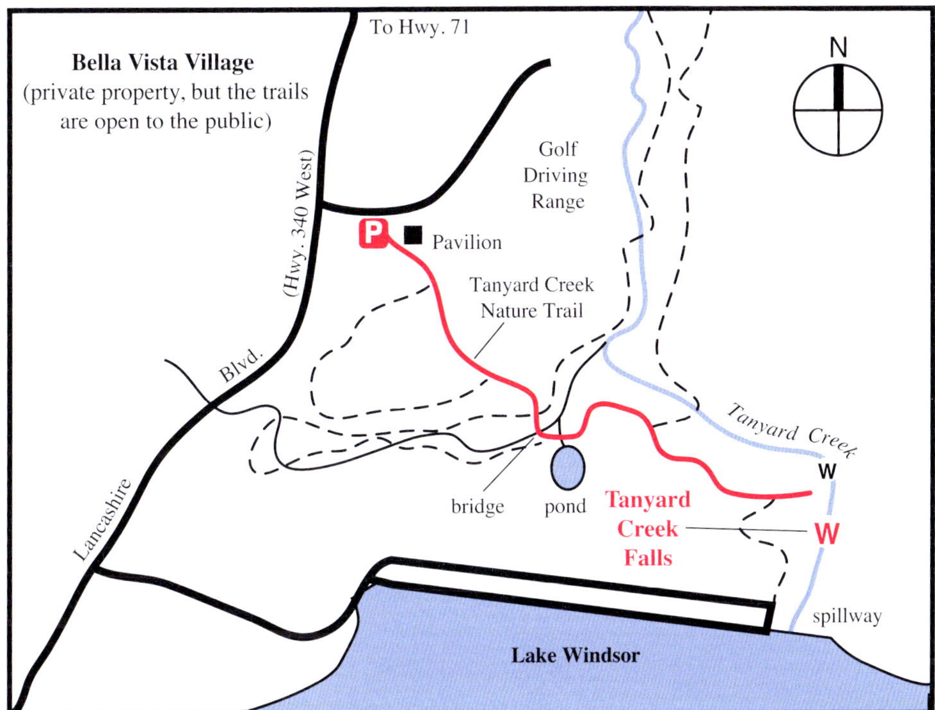

TANYARD CREEK FALLS. This one almost qualifies as an "urban" waterfall, at least that is what I thought when I heard about it and went up to hike to it. But much to my great surprise what I found was not only an interesting little waterfall and cascade, but a first class nature trail, all of that right in the middle of a busy community. It is located within the community of Bella Vista, nestled in between a couple of lakes, a golf course, and a driving range. The waterfall actually comes off the end of the spillway for a man-made lake (even runs in the summertime), but I decided to include it in this book because the nature trail is so very nice, and there really aren't many waterfalls in this extreme northwest part of the state. All of the property around this waterfall and trail is private, and unless you are a Bella Vista property owner you are not welcome (that includes the road on top of the dam that goes very near to the waterfall). But the trail is open to the public.

And what a great trail it is—built and maintained by volunteers, there must be 100 or more interpretive signs all over the place, benches, plus a number of bridges that cross two different creeks. And it is all mostly level so anyone can hike it, even smaller kids. The entire trail system is more than three miles long, but the hike directly to the waterfall is less than a mile roundtrip. Oh yea—there is a water faucet there with a stainless steel bowl attached that is specifically for watering your dog—being a dog owner I find that a really nice touch.

To get to the trailhead, head north on Hwy. 71 and take the Hwy. 340/Town Center exit, then TURN LEFT. Go just about a mile on Hwy. 340/Lancashire Blvd. and TURN LEFT—it is signed as "Tanyard Creek Recreation." Then TURN RIGHT into the parking lot. There is an open pavilion there, and restrooms.

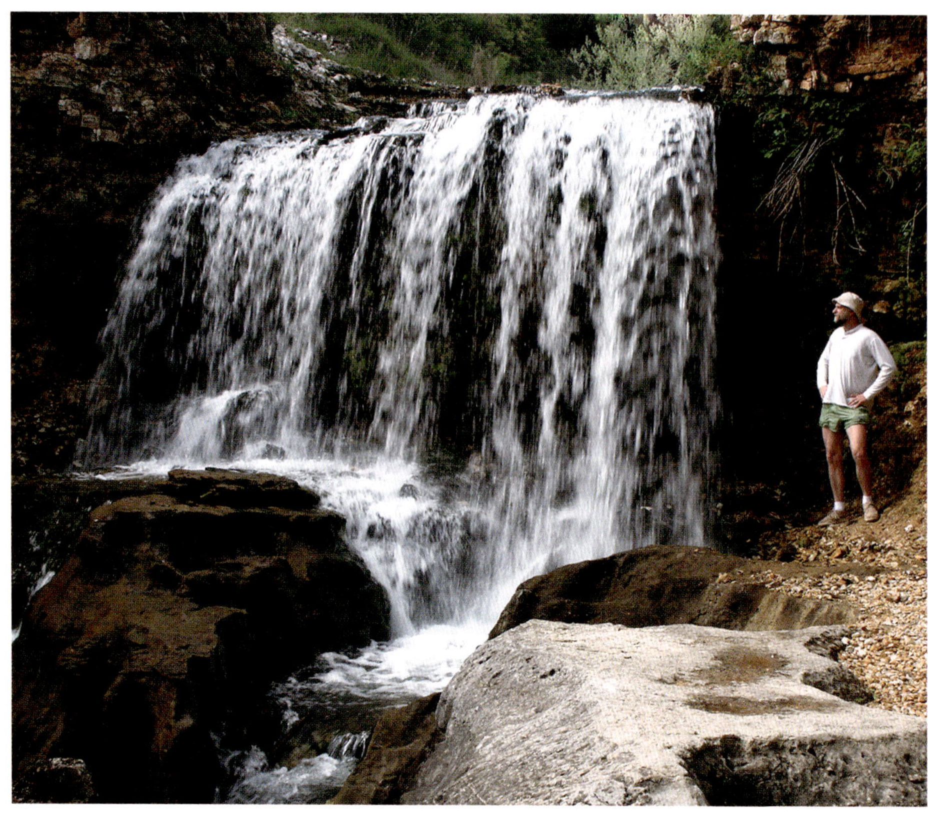

Tanyard Creek Falls

The trail begins next to the pavilion—TURN RIGHT and follow the paved trail out across an open field. You will pass two intersections with a paved trail that loops out through the field to the right, but you stay STRAIGHT AHEAD. There is a golf driving range off to your left. At the far end of the field you will pass under a powerline, come to the end of the pavement, then into the woods to a large signboard. GO STRAIGHT AHEAD past this sign to the bridge across the creek (there are trails to the right and to the left at the sign).

TURN LEFT after you cross the bridge and follow the trail past a little pond. The trail curves to the left over near the creek, then back to the right along a line of trees, and comes to an intersection after 100 yards or so—TURN RIGHT (the other trail crosses the stream over to the left and continues on downstream). Head on up the hill and into a beautiful stand of large trees—you can hear and see some cascades over on the creek. CONTINUE STRAIGHT at the next intersection, and you will come to the waterfall overlook at .4.

You can easily hike to this falls and back in 30 minutes, but allow plenty of time to read the little signs, and hike some of the rest of the trail if you can—at the very least hike the trail that is to the left of the pond on your way back—very nice indeed!

Emergency contact: Benton County Sheriff, 501–271–1008 Dogs are OK

Eagle's Nest Falls – 41′

.5 mile roundtrip, easy hike/bushwhack, GPS helpful

GPS **36.22403, -93.65342**

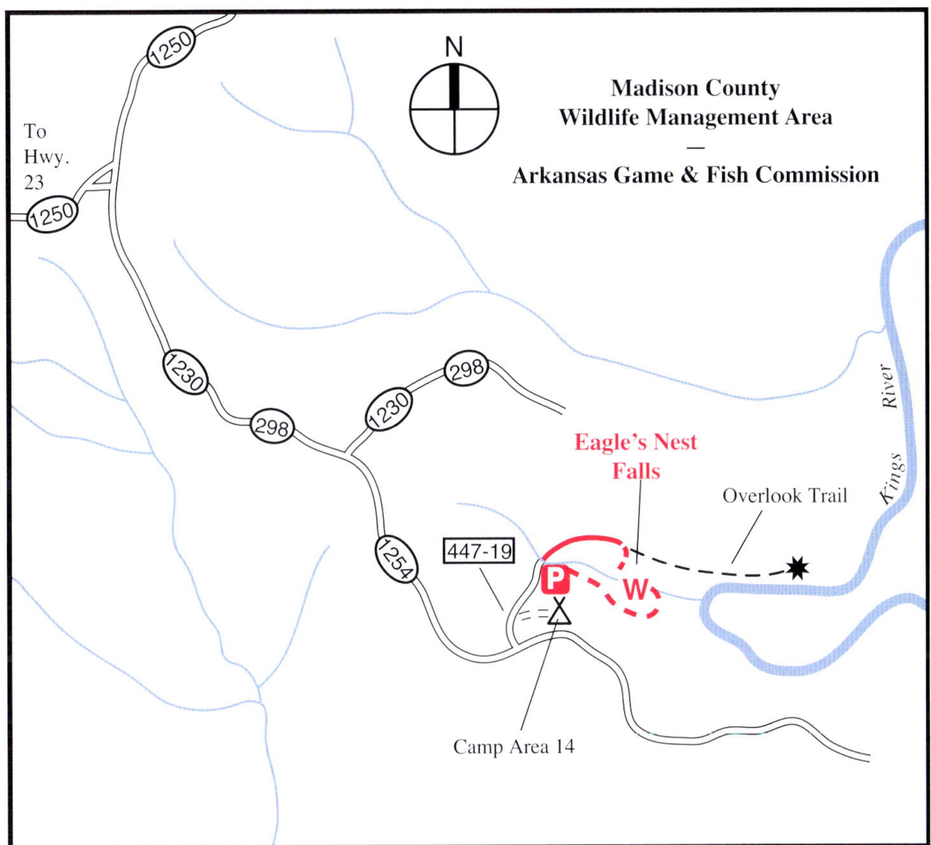

EAGLE'S NEST FALLS. This waterfall pours off into a narrow grotto that is not too far from the Kings River. It is located along the Kings River Overlook Trail, and there is now a nice big parking area, and directional signs to get there. Be sure to visit the other waterfalls nearby too.

The Madison County Wildlife Management Area is located between Huntsville and Eureka Springs, to the east of Hwy. 23. To get to the turnoff, go north out of Huntsville on Hwy. 23 to Forum. Go 3.5 miles and TURN RIGHT onto CR#1235 (gravel) at the management area sign. Go another .2 mile where you will meet with CR#1250 at the management area headquarters trailer—zero there. **OR** from Eureka Springs, head south on Hwy. 23 for 4.2 miles past the Hwy. 12 intersection and TURN LEFT onto CR#1250 (gravel) at the management area sign. Go .1 mile to the headquarters trailer—zero there. From that intersection go 3.1 miles and TURN RIGHT onto CR#1230/298. Go 1.0 miles and CONTINUE STRAIGHT onto CR#1254–Private Road (CR#1230 turns to the left there). Go another .7 miles and TURN LEFT onto management area road #447–19. Continue down the hill—***go past*** Camp Area #14 which is on the right—for .3 and PARK at the big trailhead **(36.22401, -93.65563)**. See map for red bushwhack route to bottom of falls...

From the parking area hike on the old jeep road behind the big sign and across a small stream—this is the stream that forms the waterfall downstream. The wide trail curves to the

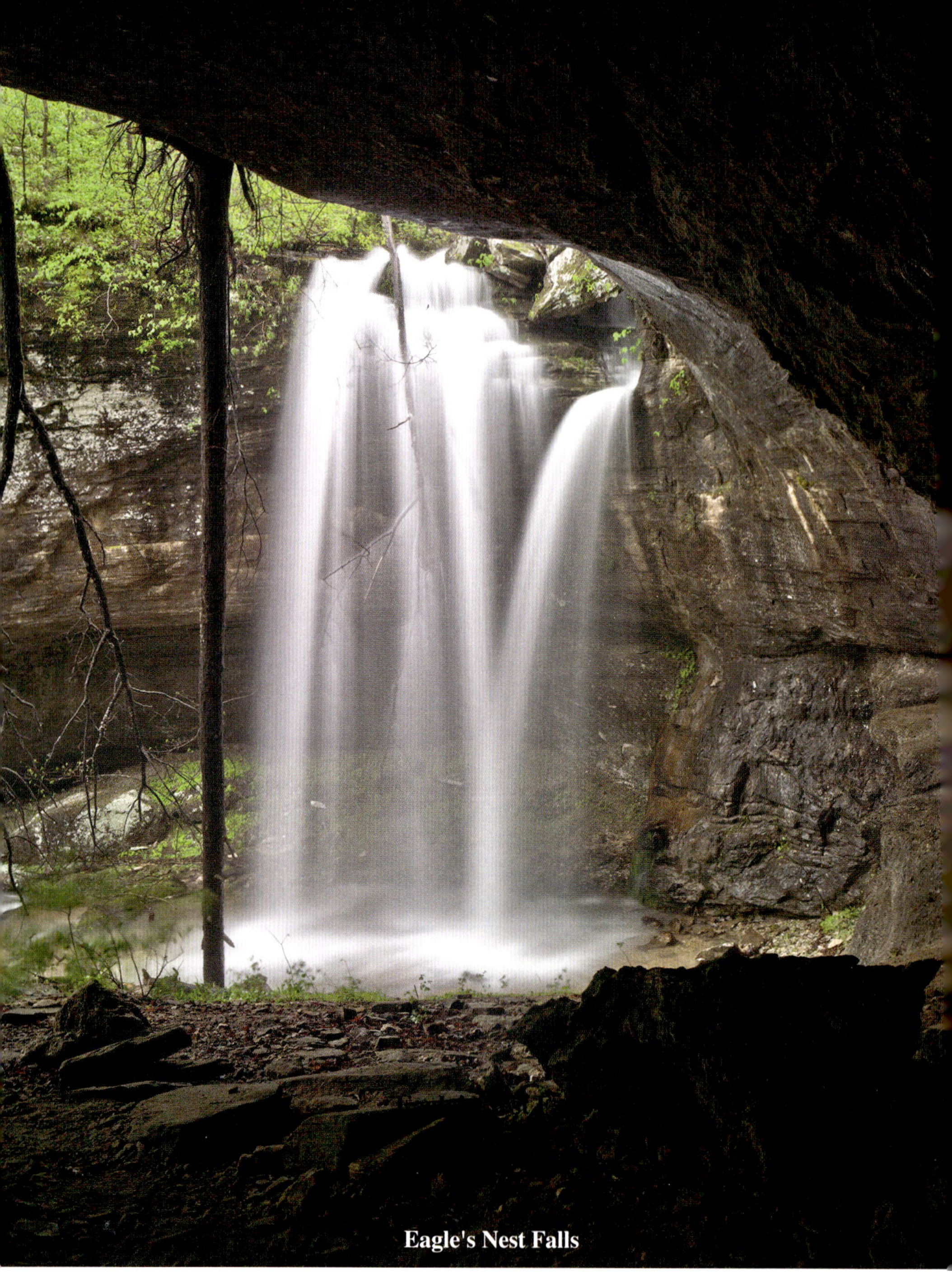
Eagle's Nest Falls

right and remains level—stay on it a couple of hundred yards (across a tiny stream) until you come to an open area on the left just after you cross a third small stream (neat area up in the woods to the left). TURN RIGHT and bushwhack down into the woods a couple hundred feet to the creek—you should be at or near the top of the falls. (If you continue along the trail it will take you to the great overlook of the Kings River.)

Emergency contact: Madison County Sheriff, 479–738–2320

Tea Kettle Falls – 46′

3.0 miles roundtrip, medium bushwhack, GPS helpful

GPS **36.26633, -93.71487**

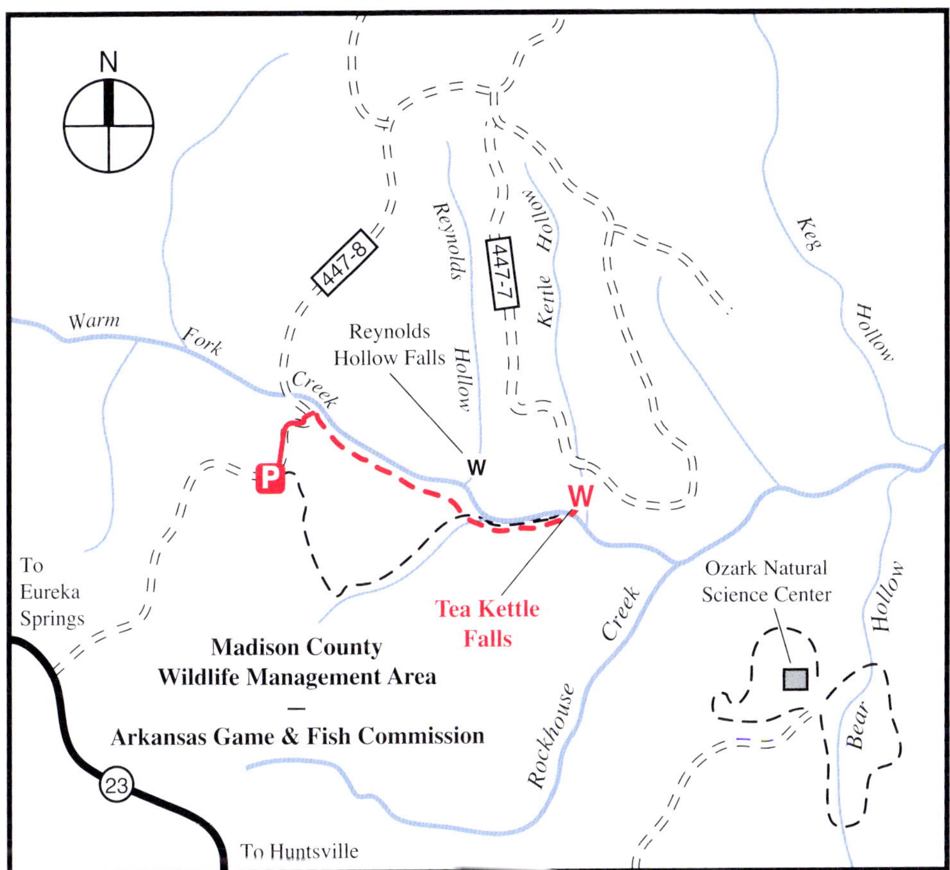

TEA KETTLE FALLS. This is one of the most unique waterfalls in Arkansas. The water has not only drilled a hole down into the top of an overhanging bluff, but before it got all the way through, the water turned 90 degrees and bored a horizontal hole out the front of the bluff! The water actually drops down into a small cave and then exits the bluff. It takes a good bit of water to get this one rolling—and a good bit of luck!

To get to the turnoff, go north out of Huntsville on Hwy. 23 to Forum, then 6.5 miles and TURN RIGHT onto management area road #447–8 (gravel, and may not be marked, but there is a management area sign on the left just after you turn onto the road). OR from Eureka Springs, head south on Hwy. 23, go 1.4 miles past the Hwy. 12 intersection and TURN LEFT onto management area road #447–8. Go 1.4 miles from the highway and PARK where the road is blocked off (**36.26764, -93.73286**—ish).

There are at least two different routes to the falls, both with social trails. I prefer the original route, which begins by hiking down the road past the barricades to a field on the right, just before the old road crosses Warm Fork.

Go across the field to the creek and head downstream. There is an old road that follows the creek but it gets pretty grown up and you may not be able to follow it. If you stay on the road or follow the creek you will have to cross the creek either way, so plan to get your

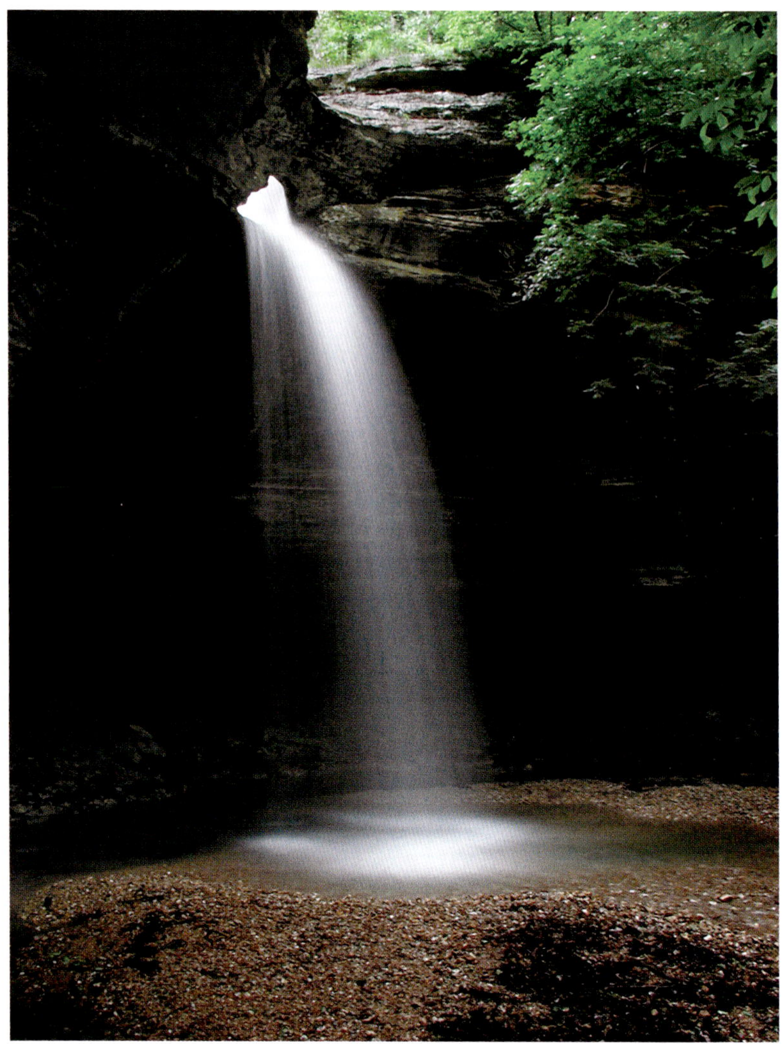

Tea Kettle Falls (during high water)

feet wet! At about the one mile point you will pass Reynolds Hollow coming in from the left—nice little waterfall there, Reynolds Hollow Falls (**36.267500, -93.721700** - I don't have a photo of it)—and there will be lots of interesting bluffs along the way from that point on. Once you get to the next stream that comes in from the left at 1.5, you should be able to hear and/or see the falls—TURN LEFT and follow the stream 100 yards to the base of the falls.

The Ozark Natural Science Center is located about a mile away—up and over the ridge. They have terrific outdoor educational facilities and programs for kids of all ages.

Emergency: Madison County Sheriff, 479–738–2320; Game & Fish, 479–789–5262

Road 299 Falls – 21′

100 yards from the road, easy bushwhack, GPS helpful

GPS **36.25670, -93.65675**

Glory B Falls – 16′

100 feet from the road, GPS helpful

GPS **36.19691, -93.69014**

Madison County Wildlife Management Area

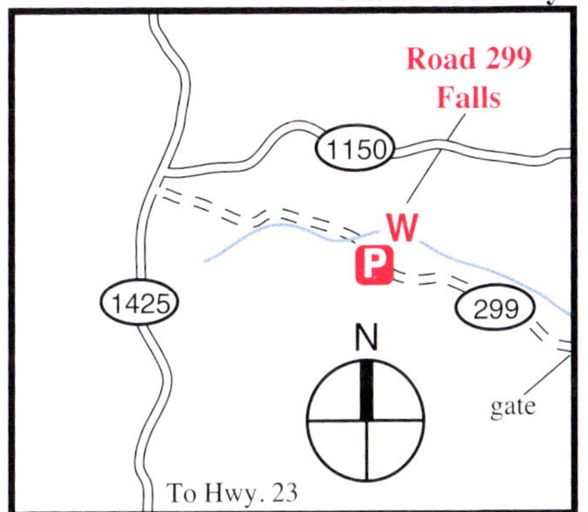

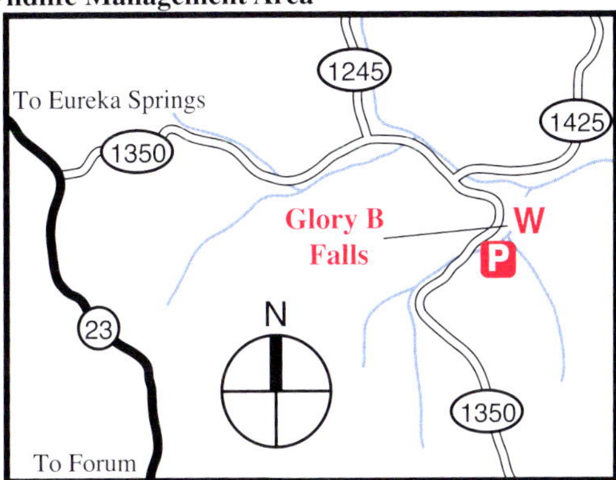

ROAD 299 FALLS. This is one of four waterfalls in this guidebook in the Madison County Wildlife Management Area that is located between Huntsville and Eureka Springs. To get to the turnoff, go north out of Huntsville on Hwy. 23 to Forum. Go 3.5 miles and TURN RIGHT onto CR#1235 (gravel) at the management area sign. Go another .2 mile where you will meet with CR#1250 at the management area headquarters trailer—zero there. **OR** from Eureka Springs, head south on Hwy. 23 for 4.2 miles past the Hwy. 12 intersection and TURN LEFT onto CR#1250 (gravel) at the management area sign. Go .1 mile to the headquarters trailer—zero there. From that intersection go 4.7 miles (the road becomes CR#1425) and TURN RIGHT onto CR#299. Follow this narrow road .5 miles and PARK on the left **(36.256421,-93.657374)**. The waterfall is just out of sight and down to your left.

GLORY B FALLS. This is another neat waterfall in the wildlife management area and it is right next to the road. From Forum take Hwy. 23 north 1.4 miles and TURN RIGHT onto CR#1350. Go 1.2 miles and BEAR RIGHT at the fork, then continue another .5 miles (still on CR#1350) and the waterfall will be just off the left side of the road. You may be able to park there, or continue ahead another .1 mile to a fork in the road where you can park at the wildlife management area sign **(36.196011,-93.691862)**. *Glory B!*

Emergency: Madison County Sheriff, 479–738–2320; Game & Fish, 479–789–5262

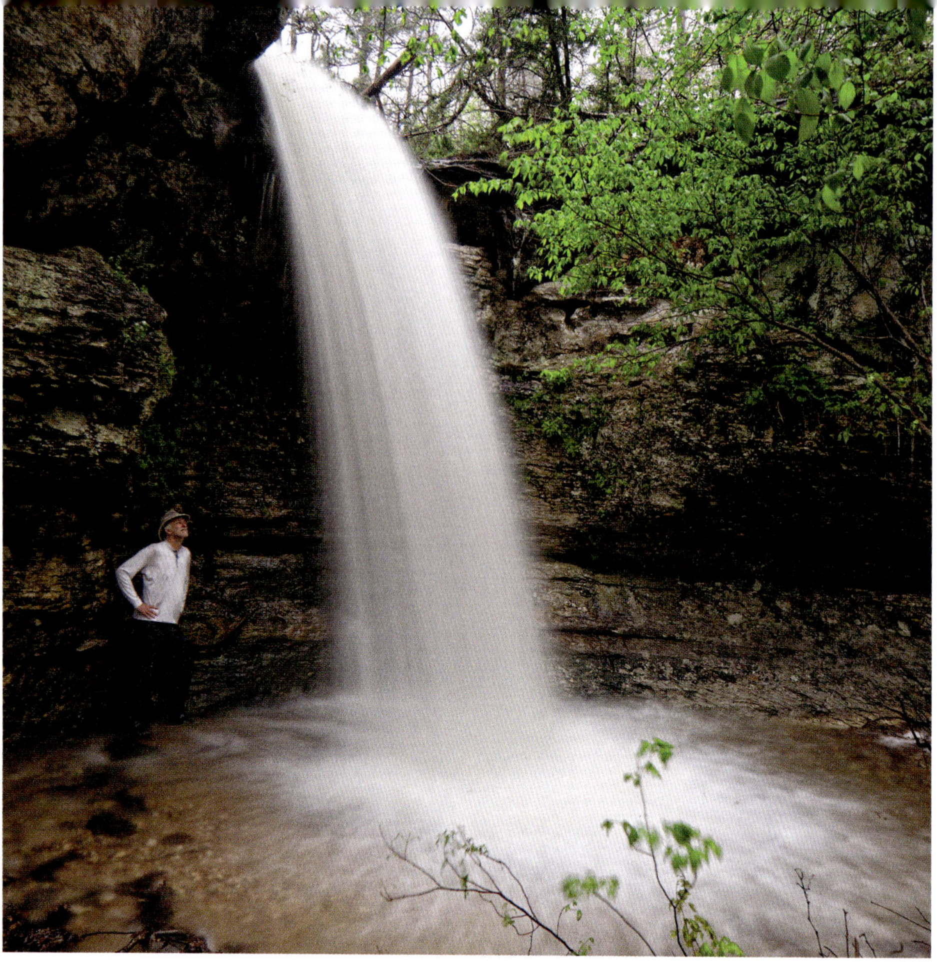

Road 299 Falls (above, during high water), **Glory B Falls** (below, high water)

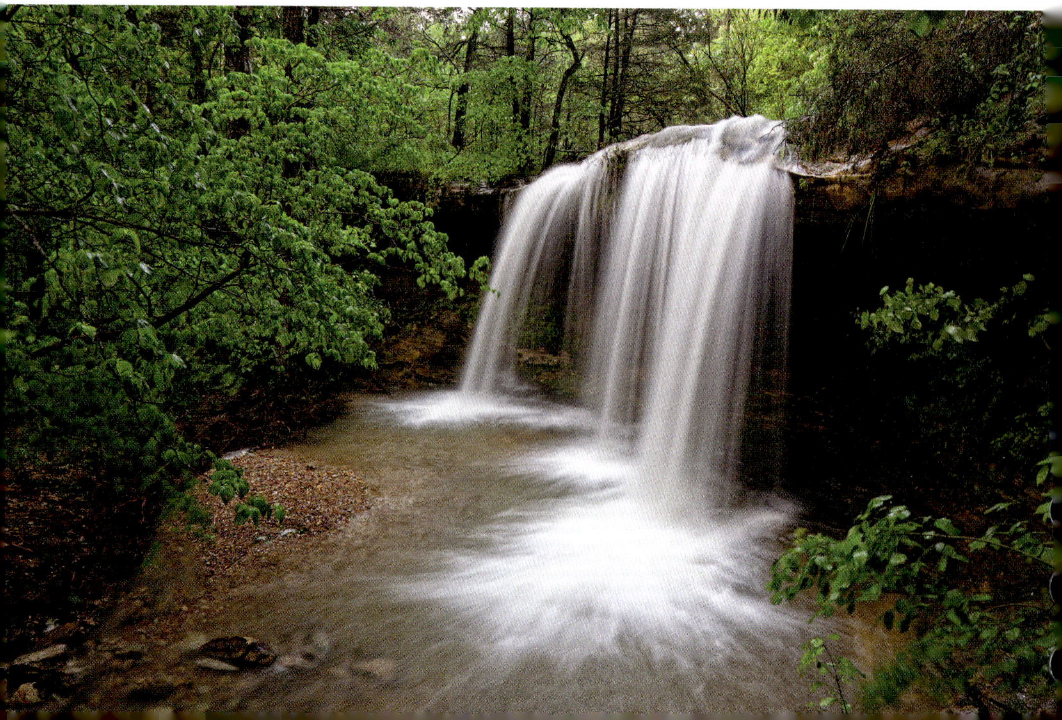

Arkansas River Valley Waterfalls

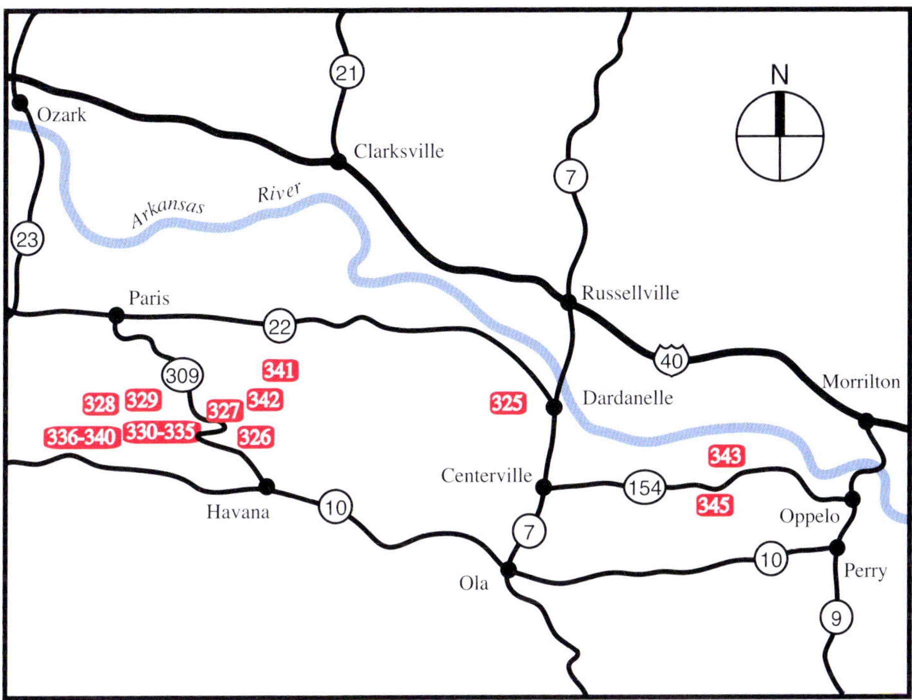

You don't expect to find waterfalls *down in the valley,* and you seldom ever do. In Arkansas there is a line of mountains that rise up from the floor of the Arkansas River Valley and are not a part of either the Ouachita or Ozark mountain ranges. They are anything but valley mountains, and in fact one of them is the tallest mountain in Arkansas—Mt. Magazine. The combination of moisture from the big river below and the relatively high elevations produce a lot of rain, which pours off of the mountains as waterfalls. I've selected some of the best here, including one of the most magnificent waterfalls in the state, Cedar Falls. Each of these waterfalls is located in a rather scenic park to begin with, so your trips to go visit them will be especially rewarding.

Fall #	Name	Height	Hike Difficulty	Page #
325	Mt. Nebo Falls	32	Easy	**419**
326	Hardy Falls	8	Easy	**420**
327	*Fringe Falls #2	75+	Easy	**422**
328	Mt. Magazine Cascade	100+	Easy	**424**
329	Mt. Magazine Falls	28	Medium	**424**
330	*Mag. Upper Clear Creek.	73	♦	**426**
331	*Mag. Middle Clear Creek	27	♦	**426**
332	*Wheeler Homestead Cas	51+	♦	**426**
333	*Chocolate Possum Pie	75+	♦	**426**
334	*Jungle Slate Falls	55	♦	**426**
335	*Flat Rock Falls	41	♦	**426**
336	*Pryor Falls	41	Medium	**432**
337	*Sycamore Root Falls	17	Easy	**432**
338	*Candi Wright Falls	28	Difficult	**432**
339	Lacey Creek Falls	45	Medium	**436**
340	*Rock Creek Quads	82 & 93	♦	**436**
341	Wildman Twin Falls	43	Medium	**440**
342	Big Shoal Cascade	8	Easy	**440**
343	Cedar Falls	95	Medium	**442**
345	Seven Hollows Grotto	18	Medium	**444**

* New waterfalls in this edition

Mt. Nebo Falls – 32′

Short hike from parking area, GPS not needed

GPS **35.21693, -93.25886**

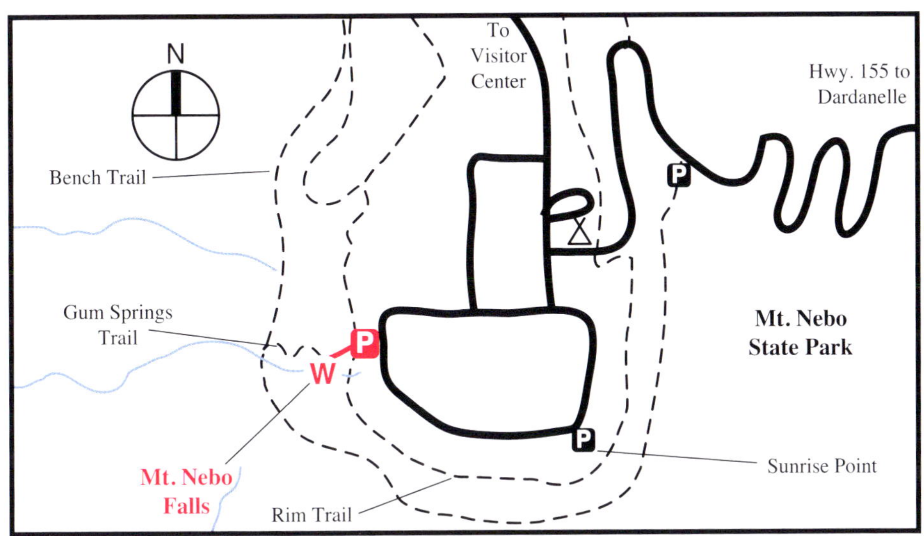

MT. NEBO FALLS. This is a neat waterfall on top of scenic Mt. Nebo that is right below the parking area—best viewed right after prolonged rains (**35.21693, -93.25886**). From Dardanelle take Hwy. 22 West, then TURN LEFT onto Hwy. 155 and climb to the top of Mt. Nebo. TURN LEFT at the stop sign on top, then RIGHT at the next stop sign, and park in the Gum Springs Trail parking area. The waterfall is located about 100 yards ***down*** this trail. In fact there is a cascade tumbling next to the trail most of the way down (one portion shown here) that ends with the big waterfall. Lots of other trails to explore in this park, plus sunrise and sunset views too!

Visitor Center—
479–963–8502

Dogs are OK

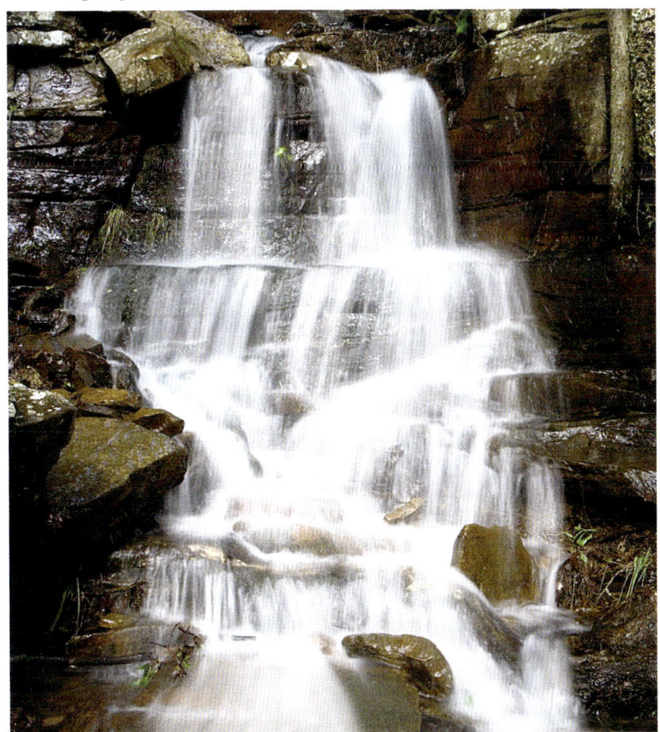

Mt. Nebo Falls Cascade

Hardy Falls – 8′

Short hike or view from your car, GPS not needed

GPS **35.15178, -93.56320**

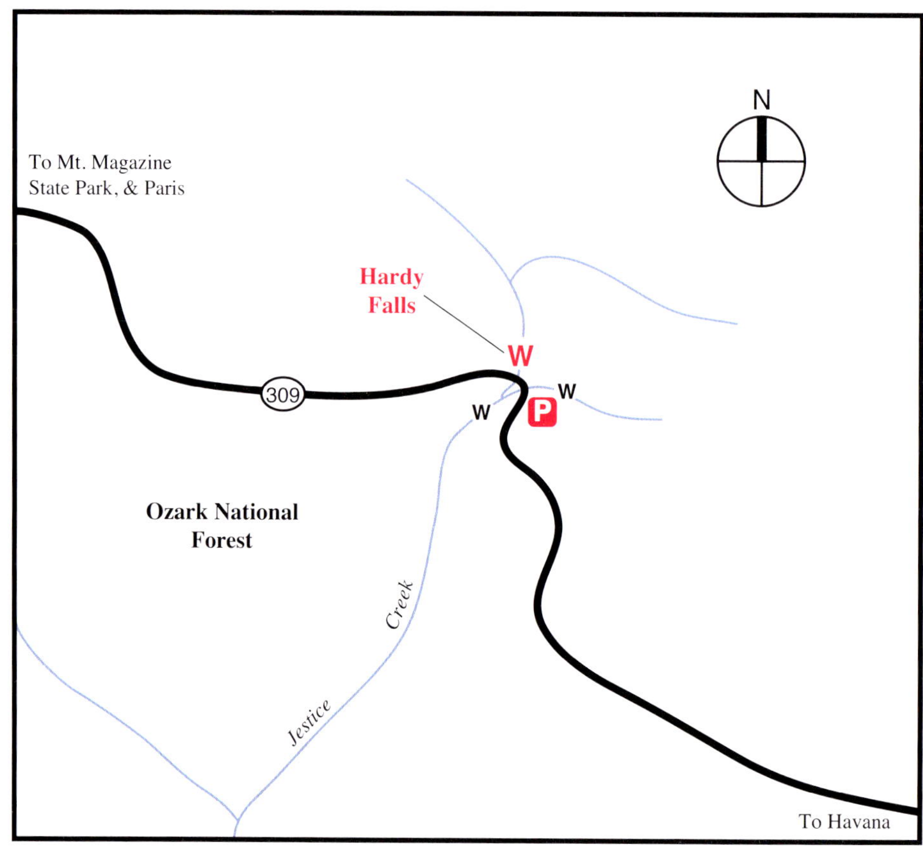

HARDY FALLS. The main attraction of this falls is not really the waterfall itself, but rather the unique rock work right in front of it. When the difficult job of designing a road up to the top of the highest mountain in Arkansas was being considered back in the 1930's, they brought in an expert named James W. Hardy. His craftsmanship in stone remains today in the form of culverts that are, well, beautiful. You can see these works of art at Hardy Falls. As you can see from the photo here the culverts line right up with the waterfall, showing both off to their fullest. While I don't recommend standing in one of the culverts during periods of high water, most of the time you can climb down into them and get this great view. Besides the waterfall at the upper end of the culverts, there are also some nice cascades down below, although they require a bit of a scramble to reach.

To get to Hardy Falls from Paris, take Hwy. 309 south about 17 miles to the state park visitor center located right on the highway. Continue on Hwy. 309 another 6.0 miles from there and you will find the falls just off to the left in a sharp curve—PARK just beyond on the left side of the road **(35.15095, -93.56329)**. You can also get to the falls by going north on Hwy. 309 from Havana.

While you are up this high, be sure to go hike the short Signal Hill Trail at Mt. Magazine State Park up to the highest point in Arkansas (2,753 feet), visit other waterfalls at the

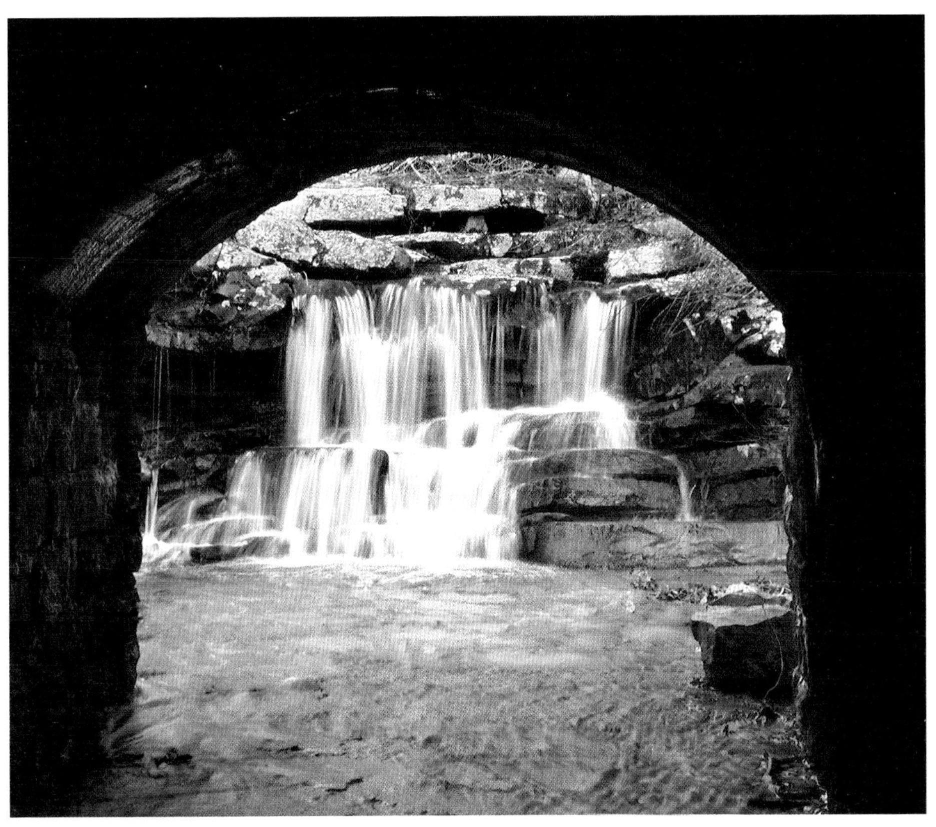

James W. Hardy Falls

park, and stop by the visitor center for the complete story of Mt. Magazine with some really nice exhibits and programs. Oh yes, and be sure to spend a night or two at the incredible lodge on top of the mountain—you'll have some of the very best views in the state for sure! Dogs are OK

Emergency: Logan County Sheriff, 479–963–3271; Visitor Center, 479–963–8502

Fringe Falls #2 – 75′+

1.3 miles roundtrip, easy hike but steep slope at the end

GPS **35.16785, -93.61000**

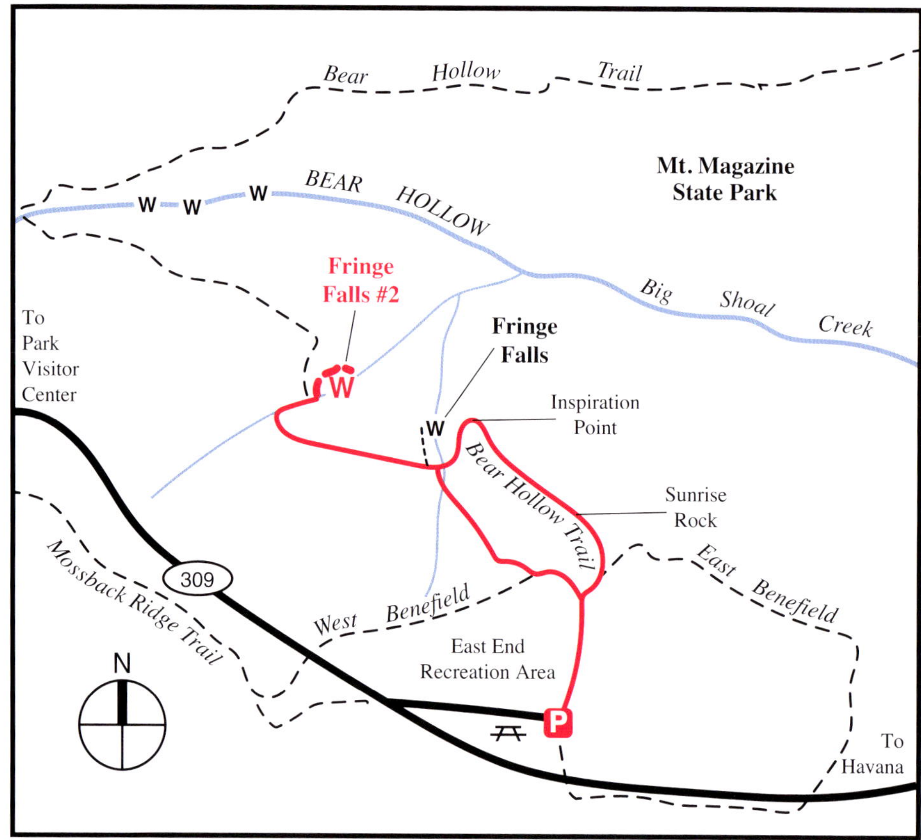

FRINGE FALLS #2. (named by Troy Garner for the surrounding fringe trees that have beautiful white blooms in May) This is one of many waterfall cascades that pour off the mountain within Mt. Magazine State Park. Some are more than 100' tall. Easy hike of 1.3 roundtrip (STEEP, ROCKY trip to the bottom though)—this really needs a LOT of water to look nice.

PARK at the East End Picnic Area Trailhead at the state park **(35.16297, -93.60593)** and take the Benefield West Loop Trail (easy, wide trail at first, built in the 1930's), and TURN LEFT at the first intersection (a right turn takes you on a detour out to a couple of great scenic views, and you can take that route and stay left at the fork, then rejoin at the Bear Hollow Trail—I am bypassing this trail in this description—this side trail may be listed as Bear Hollow Trail).

TURN RIGHT at the next trail intersection towards the Bear Hollow Trail. It drops down the hill a little and alongside a small creek on the left, then comes to a trail intersection at .4—TURN LEFT and continue along the Bear Hollow Trail.

(NOTE—this intersection is where you would rejoin my hike from the right if you took the detour for the scenic views. THIS intersection is also where you would begin your trek to the BONUS WATERFALL* below)

OK, continue along the Bear Hollow Trail as it drops down the hill alongside a creek that it crosses at .6. LEAVE the trail and follow the creek downstream to **Fringe Falls #2**.

CAUTION—the rocks along the bluff and waterfall area are ESPECIALLY HOLLOW! (Please don't ask me how I know this!)

If you continue along the trail to Bear Hollow there are three smaller waterfalls on the main creek. Dogs are OK

Emergency: Logan County Sheriff, 479–963–3271; Visitor Center, 479–963–8502

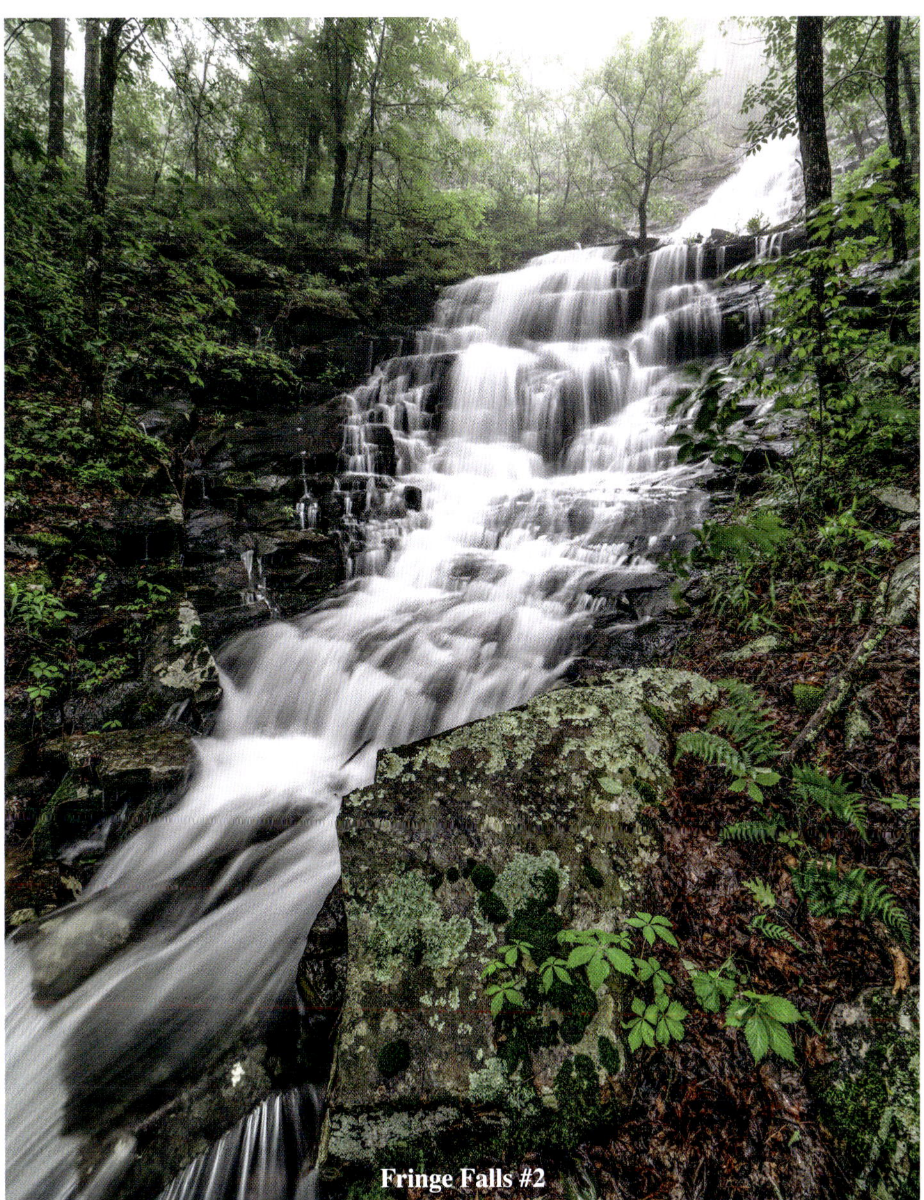

Fringe Falls #2

*BONUS WATERFALL, Fringe Falls (the original): If the water is high and you need an extra challenge, return to the trail intersection at .4 and follow that creek STEEPLY downstream to Fringe Falls (**35.16718, -93.60820**—measured by Troy Garner at 55', named for the surrounding Fringe Trees that have beautiful white blooms in May.) I don't have a photo of this one—maybe you can get a great one!

Mt. Magazine Cascade – 100+′

1.0 mile roundtrip, easy hike, GPS not needed

GPS **35.17185, -93.65567**

Mt. Magazine Falls – 28′

.7 mile roundtrip, easy/medium bushwhack, GPS not needed

GPS **35.16913, -93.63762**

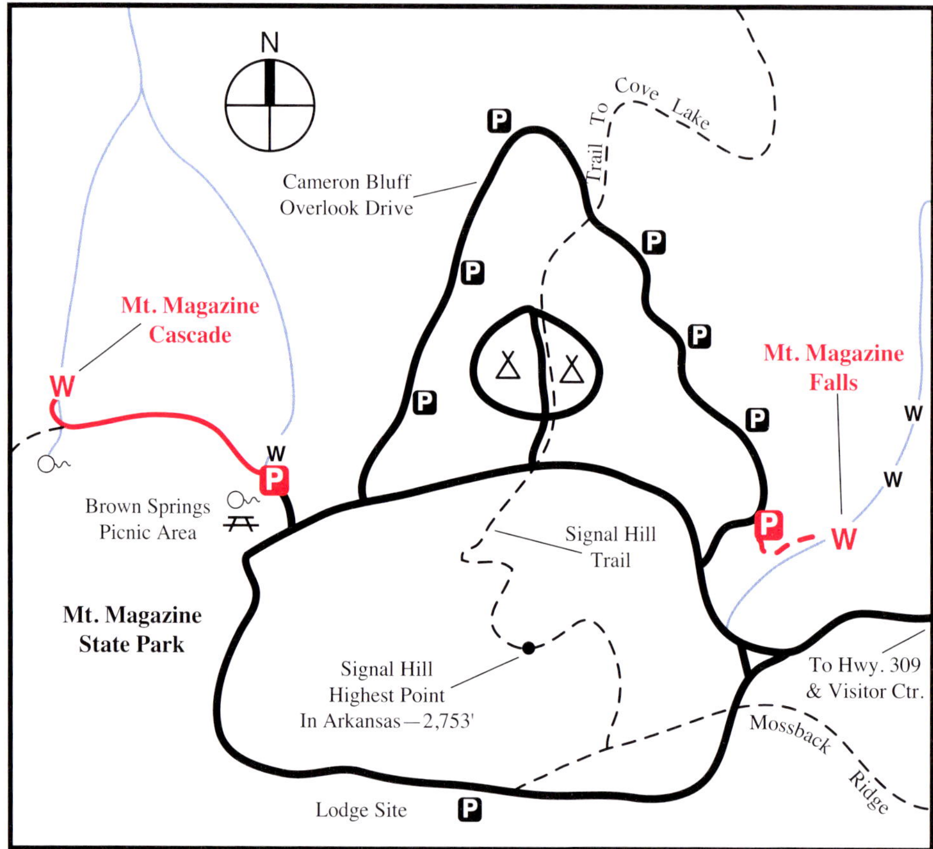

MT. MAGAZINE CASCADE/FALLS. How in the world did waterfalls get all the way up here? Sure enough, there are a couple of surprisingly scenic waterfalls within spitting distance of the tallest point in Arkansas.

To get to Mt. Magazine State Park, take Hwy. 309 south out of Paris 17 miles to the visitor center—TURN RIGHT there and drive to the far end of the park and PARK at the Brown Springs Picnic Area **(35.16985, -93.65059)**. Take the level trail out the back of the picnic area and follow it until you come to a creek about .5 mile in—**Mt. Magazine Cascade** is just down to the right, and the waters tumble out of sight and far down the mountain. To get to the **Mt. Magazine Falls** go back and drive around the Cameron Bluff Overlook Drive and PARK at the very last pulloff (**35.16996, -93.63919** it is a one-way road). There is no real trail—you simply head down the steep hillside to the right into the woods, under a bluff known as Barn Cave, until you come to the creek, then simply follow it downstream 100 yards to the falls. Dogs are OK

Emergency: Logan County Sheriff, 479–963–3271; Visitor Center, 479–963–8502

Mt. Magazine Cascade
(right)

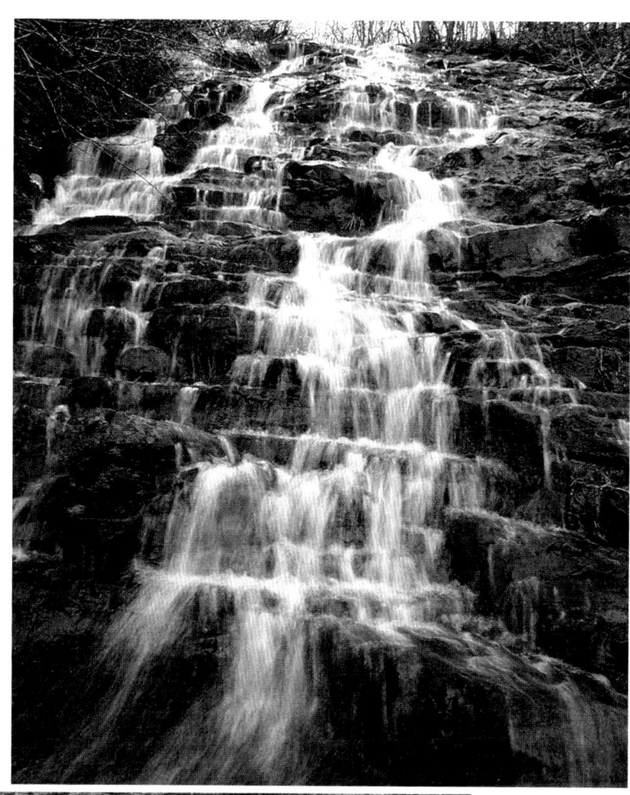

Mt. Magazine Falls
(below)

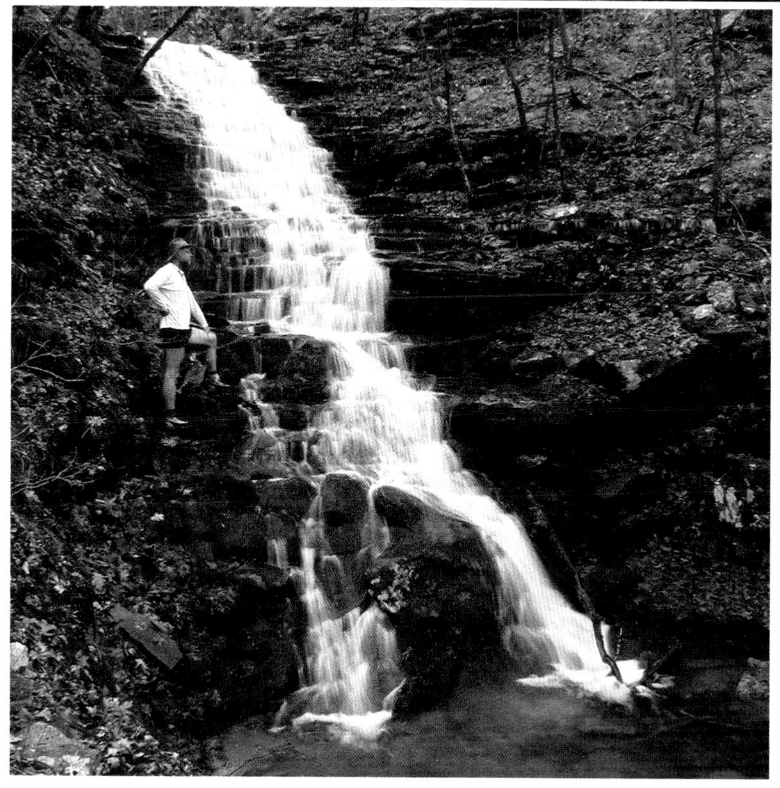

Magazine Upper Clear Creek Falls – 73′

.4 easy road then ♦ GPS **35.15928, -93.60976**

Magazine Middle Clear Creek Falls – 27′

.6 easy road then ♦ GPS **35.15724, -93.61011**

Wheeler Homestead Cascade – 51′+

1.0 easy road then ♦ GPS **35.15928, -93.61992**

Chocolate Possum Pie Falls – 75′+

1.5 (easy road to the top edge) GPS **35.15952, -93.62729**

Jungle Slate Falls – 55′

1.7 easy road then ♦ GPS **35.15980, -93.62915**

Flat Rock Falls – 41′

1.9 easy road then ♦ GPS **35.15832, -93.62906**

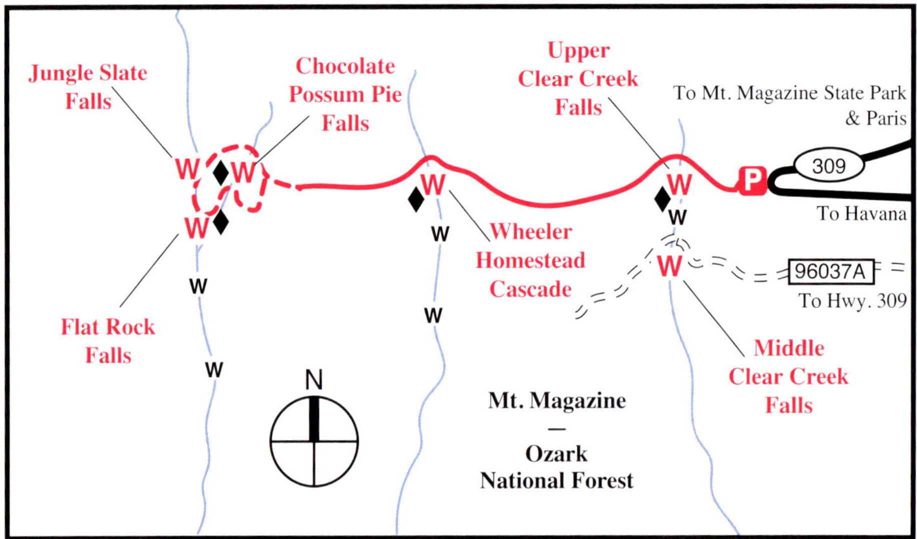

SOUTH SIDE MT. MAGAZINE UPPER FALLS. There is old historic bench road that runs just above one of the upper blufflines on the south side of Mt. Magazine below the state park (it's all national forest). Several drainages provide large waterfalls and hiking the road is easy access (although it's getting very grown up and jungle-like—hoping a social trail develops). BUT, once you drop over the side it is all black diamond ♦ slopes to any of the upper waterfalls.

Each drainage contains many more waterfalls on the way down the mountain to the Petit Jean River far below, but for this trek we'll stick near the top. Looking back through my notes and files from previous years I counted 91 waterfalls I've documented (photographed, measured the height of, logged GPS info), and I still have not made it to all the drainages yet (probably won't ever). I'm presenting a handful of these more challenging upper falls here, and also several from the lower flanks in the following pages. (Danny Hale has more in his guides.). Like so many Arkansas waterfalls, I advise to avoid the summer jungle and enjoy the spectacular leaf-off winter views! And one tiny personal note, this particular trek has been one of my most favorites of all time, and my last trip to document this (for new photos) was the week after my 70th B-day—watch out for a geezer in the JUNGLE!

DIRECTIONS. From Hwy 10 in Havana take Hwy. 309 north 7.1 miles and PARK on the left at the switchback **(35.15894, -93.60612)**.OR from the Mt. Magazine State Park Visitor Center go south on Hwy. 309 3.2 miles and park on the right at the switchback.

Follow the old bench road west downhill a little bit and across some small creeks and then across a larger creek to .3 and TURN LEFT **(35.15965, -93.61011)** and head into the woods DOWNHILL. Continue down this BLACK DIAMOND ♦ rocky slope, keeping to the left a little bit until you can hear the falls, then LEFT on down to the base of **Upper Clear Creek Falls** at .5.

Continue downstream above the creek a bit and you will pass an unnamed falls ♦, then keep going downstream until you land on a bench road at about .5 (this jeep road goes back left/east 1.75 miles to the highway). Continue downstream to the top of **Middle Clear Creek Falls** at .6—turn right to go around the bluff down to the base of the falls. Now all you gotta do is climb UP 300' back to the top road.

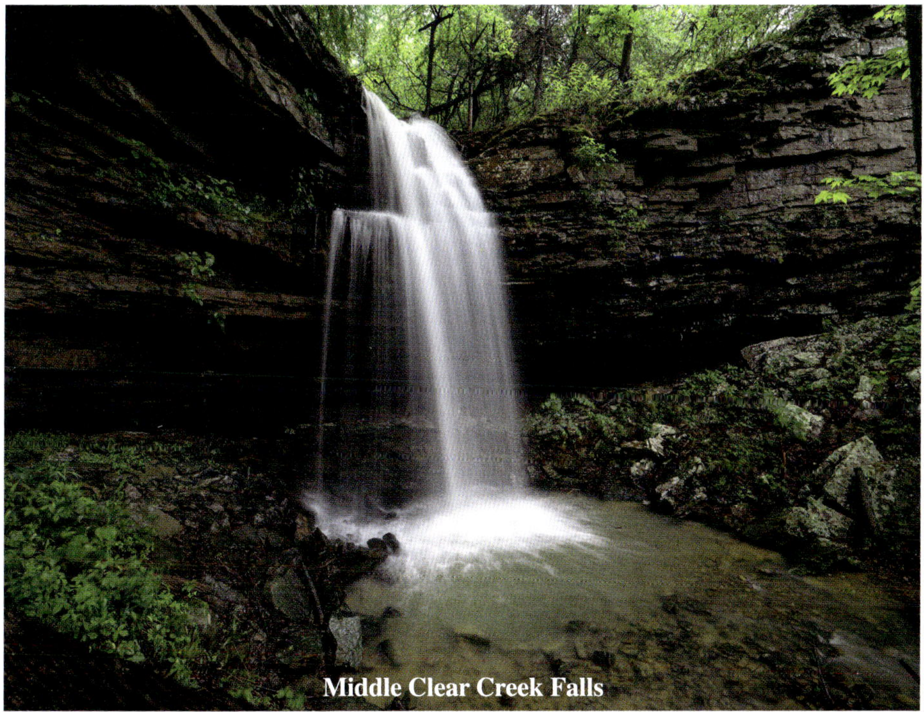

Middle Clear Creek Falls

Once back on top continue along the bench road (to the left)—it's pretty easy hiking and hopefully by the time you read this there will be a nice social trail all the way! At .5 there is an old road that joins in from below on the left—CONTINUE STRAIGHT along the bench road, to the Wheeler Homestead on the left at .9 (**35.15942, -93.61937**). Not much remains except the chimney base. Stop and look around a moment—imagine how amazing the VIEW was from this homesite!!!

Just beyond the ruins you cross a creek (their water supply), then TURN LEFT and

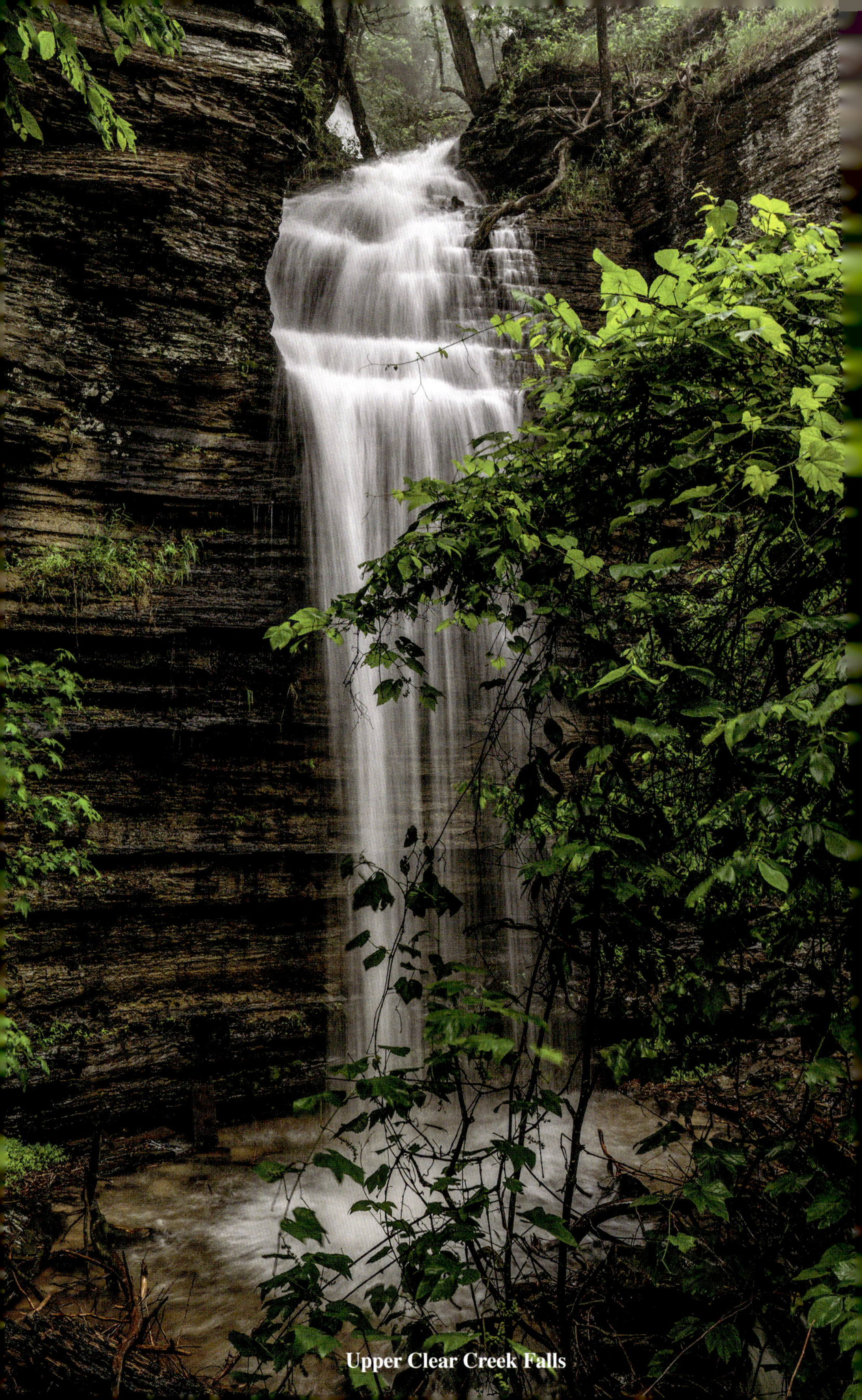
Upper Clear Creek Falls

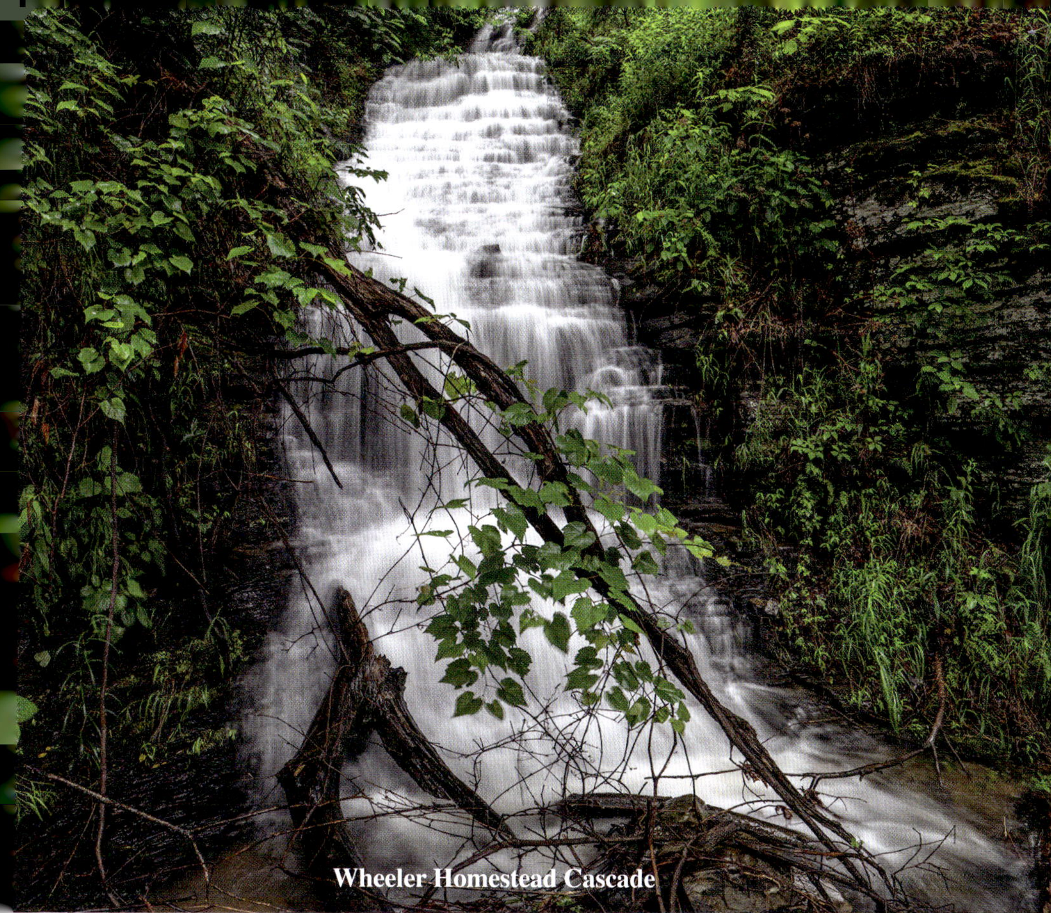
Wheeler Homestead Cascade

head down a BLACK DIAMOND slope ♦ until you reach **Wheeler Homestead Cascade** a short distance below. When running this is a spectacular SSS! This cascade is just the beginning of a series of waterfalls and cascades that continue down the mountain and out of sight far below.

Back on top, continue along the bench road through a rocky, thick jungle-like forest, to a small pond (the road trace may disappear)—just keep going along the bench until about 1.3 **(35.15896, -93.62659)**—the bench will curve around to the RIGHT, but there is a nice overlook to the LEFT, out to an open VISTA at the edge of a canyon—SSS view.

There are three named waterfalls in the canyon below/right, and there is no good way to any of them—pick and choose your own route, but here's the way I go as an example—your route and mileage may vary.

Return to the bench that you were following and continue on it and head into the side canyon to the RIGHT and then it curves back LEFT to cross a creek (it SHOULD be flowing, if not, maybe turn around and go home). Once across the creek curve back to the LEFT and down a few yards to where you can get a view of the top of **Chocolate Possum Pie Falls** at 1.5 (see photo—CAUTION—BLACK DIAMOND SPOT ♦!).

The little country store on the corner down in the valley on Hwy. 10 at Havana sometimes serves a yummy slice of Chocolate Possum Pie. I figured that anyone who has made it to this waterfall deserves to buy and enjoy a slice for themselves!

This may be the only view of the waterfall that you get—it disappears into the brush and hillside and where it emerges below you can't really see up to the top (but I'll tell you how to get there in a minute).

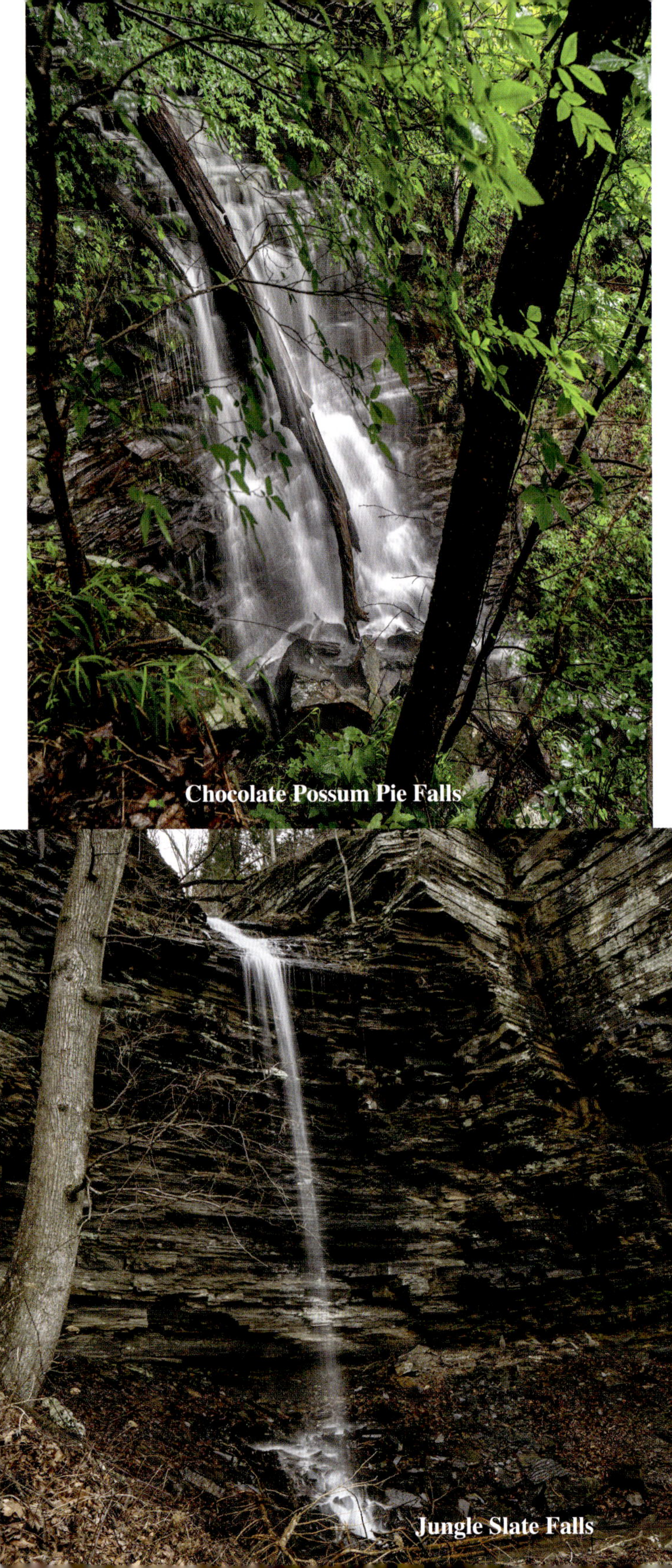
Chocolate Possum Pie Falls

Jungle Slate Falls

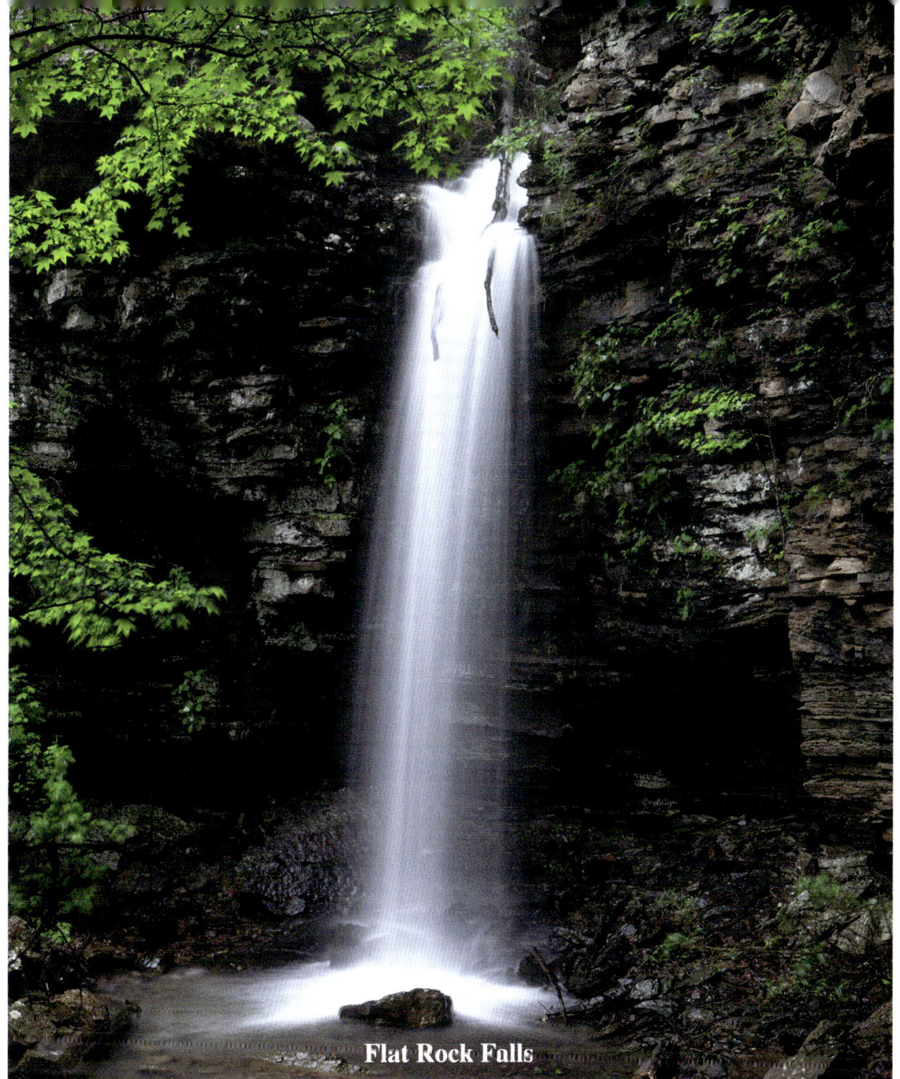
Flat Rock Falls

CONTINUE along the top for a couple hundred yards until the hill below gets less steep and you can find a spot to head down the black diamond slope ♦ on the LEFT **(35.15988, -93.62849)**. (I usually slide on my behind.) As you go down there will be a canyon on your right and one on your left. Wait until you get to the **bottom** of the steep slope before you attempt either side*. I prefer to go to the RIGHT, down to the creek, and follow it upstream to the base of **Jungle Slate Falls** at 1.7, an SSS! The slabs of slate here are numerous and just beautiful—and it's really a jungle to get there! (*You could also go LEFT to the base of Opossum Falls—an equal jungle to fight through, but not as good of a waterfall view.)

To continue, follow the creek DOWNSTREAM ♦ as best you can until you come to **Flat Rock Falls** at about 1.9, another SSS for sure!

RETURN the way you came for a total roundtrip of 3.8—4.8 (depending on which falls you visit). OR cut across the hillside back up to the VISTA and then back on the bench road. Or climb back up and work your way over to the base of Opossum Falls—it's a JUNGLE, and remember—you can't see very far up the falls.

Emergency: Logan County Sheriff, 479-963-3271 Dogs are OK

Pryor Falls – 41′

1.6 mi roundtrip, moderate bushwhack

GPS **35.15282, -93.64041**

Sycamore Root Falls – 17′

1.2 mile roundtrip, easy bushwhack

GPS **35.15282, -93.64041**

Candi Wright Falls – 28′

3.5 mile roundtrip, difficult bushwhack

GPS **35.152028°, -93.654403**

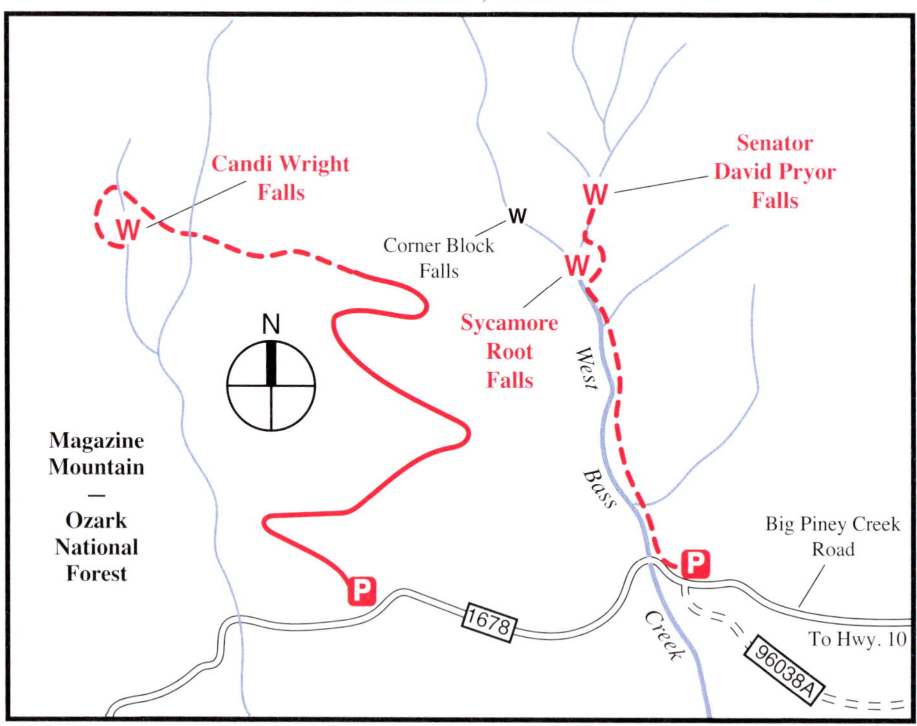

SYCAMORE ROOT FALLS. Going East on Hwy 10. from Blue Mountain, TURN LEFT onto "Falling Rock" Rd. (just before getting to Mountain View store at Waveland.) You will go under the old Rock Island RR bridge. Continue on Falling Rock Rd (#503) 1.7 miles. When you get to the intersection with Piney (#33) go STRAIGHT a couple hundred yards and TURN LEFT onto FR#1678/Big Piney Creek Road. (or come 3.5 miles on West Cedar/Piney Road from Hwy. 309 north of Havana) Follow this road 2.8 miles and PARK at FR96038A **(35.14333, -93.63780)**

Hike west along the main road until you come to the creek in the curve (West Bass Creek), then TURN RIGHT and head upstream. Continue upstream past a small falls and then to a very interesting **Sycamore Root Falls** and pool at .6. I've never seen anything like this before! A root from the giant sycamore tree has grown over the bluff and into the pool as a fireman's pole.

SENATOR DAVID PRYOR FALLS Continue on above Root Falls then TURN RIGHT and follow an intersecting creek upstream to **Senator David Pryor Falls** at .8, a wonderful

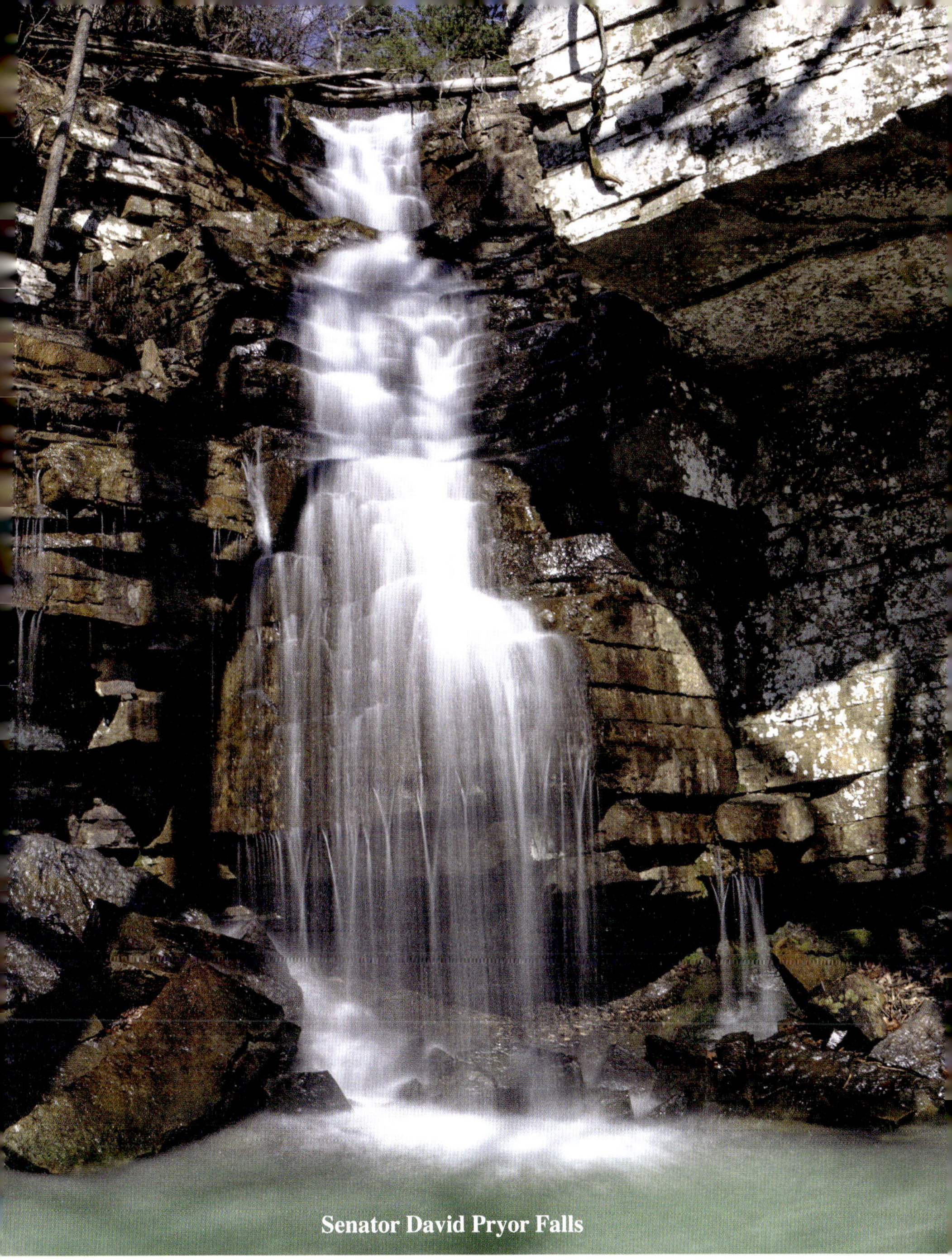

Senator David Pryor Falls

SSS. Named to honor one of the greatest statesman Arkansas has ever had! Pryor served as state legislative Representative and U.S. Congressman, Arkansas Governor, and United States Senator. Why *this* waterfall? Over on the right side of the pool and up at the base of the bluff is a giant rock slab in the shape of Arkansas (photo on page 435). Fit for a solid-as-a-rock statesman!

The bluff in this area is really nice too, and if you have time, follow it back to the LEFT a couple hundred yards to the main creek to Corner Block Falls at .9 (40'). Then follow the creek downstream back to the road where you parked.

CANDI WRIGHT FALLS. See directions to PARK for **Pryor Falls** on previous pages, then continue another .7 miles on the same road and you will come to a power line right-of-way and a pump station. Just past this point and on the right is a locked gate to FS#1678G. PARK here **(35.142825 -93.646922)** and please do not block the gate.

Candi was an avid waterfall lover and her spirit and laughter will forever live among the waterfalls of Magazine Mountain.

(The following info was provided by Alan Wagoner.) Hike up this road as it zig-zags uphill to another pump station approx.. 1.25 miles at: **(35.150806 N -93.647201)** W. From just above this pump station bushwhack west a half mile to: **(35.152409 N -93.654531)** W, where you will be in an old roadway and see a natural sandstone bridge over a little creek. Follow the creek down to the bluff to look off. There is a cute little waterfall between the bridge and **Candi Wright falls**. To get below go back up to the natural sandstone bridge and follow the old road trace that runs southwest and it will take you below the bluffs. It's the only easy way down below the bluffs that I have found. Once below the bluffs make your way back east to the waterfall. Due to the large amount of rocks that have fallen off the cliffs, it is easier to go a 100 yards below the bluffs to make your way east to the creek and falls. (waterfall photo by Jimmy Wright)

Emergency: Logan County Sheriff, 479–963–3271. Dogs are OK

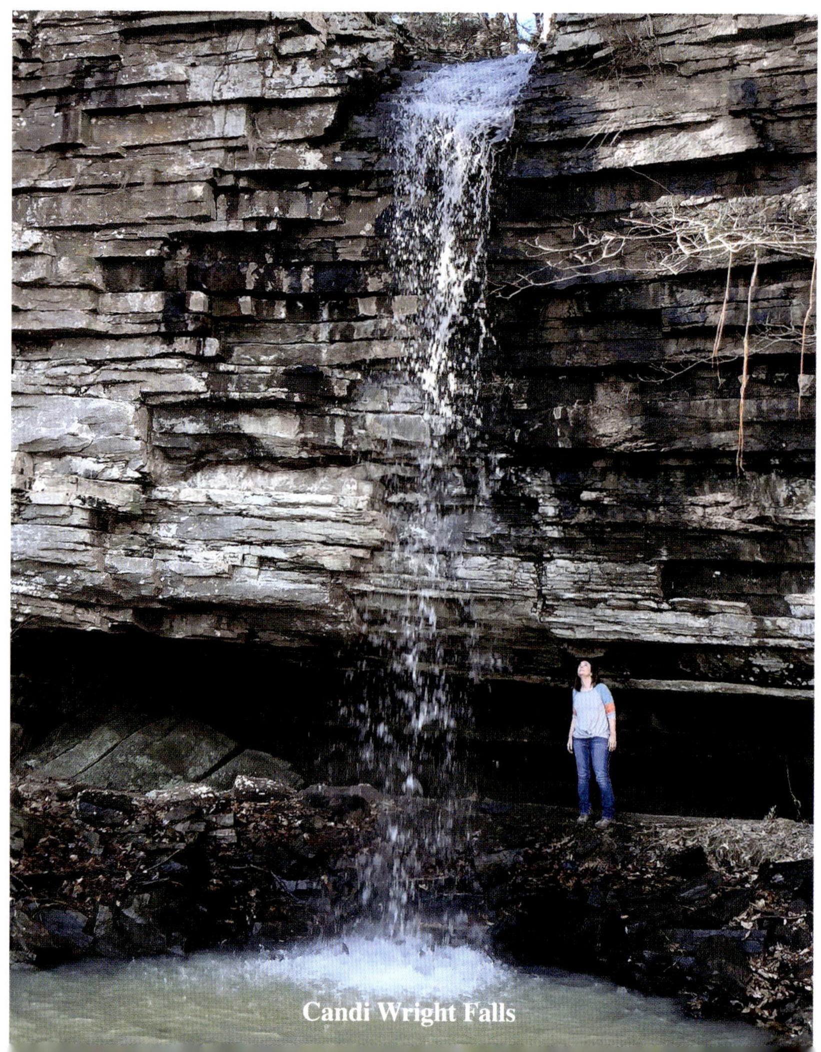

Candi Wright Falls

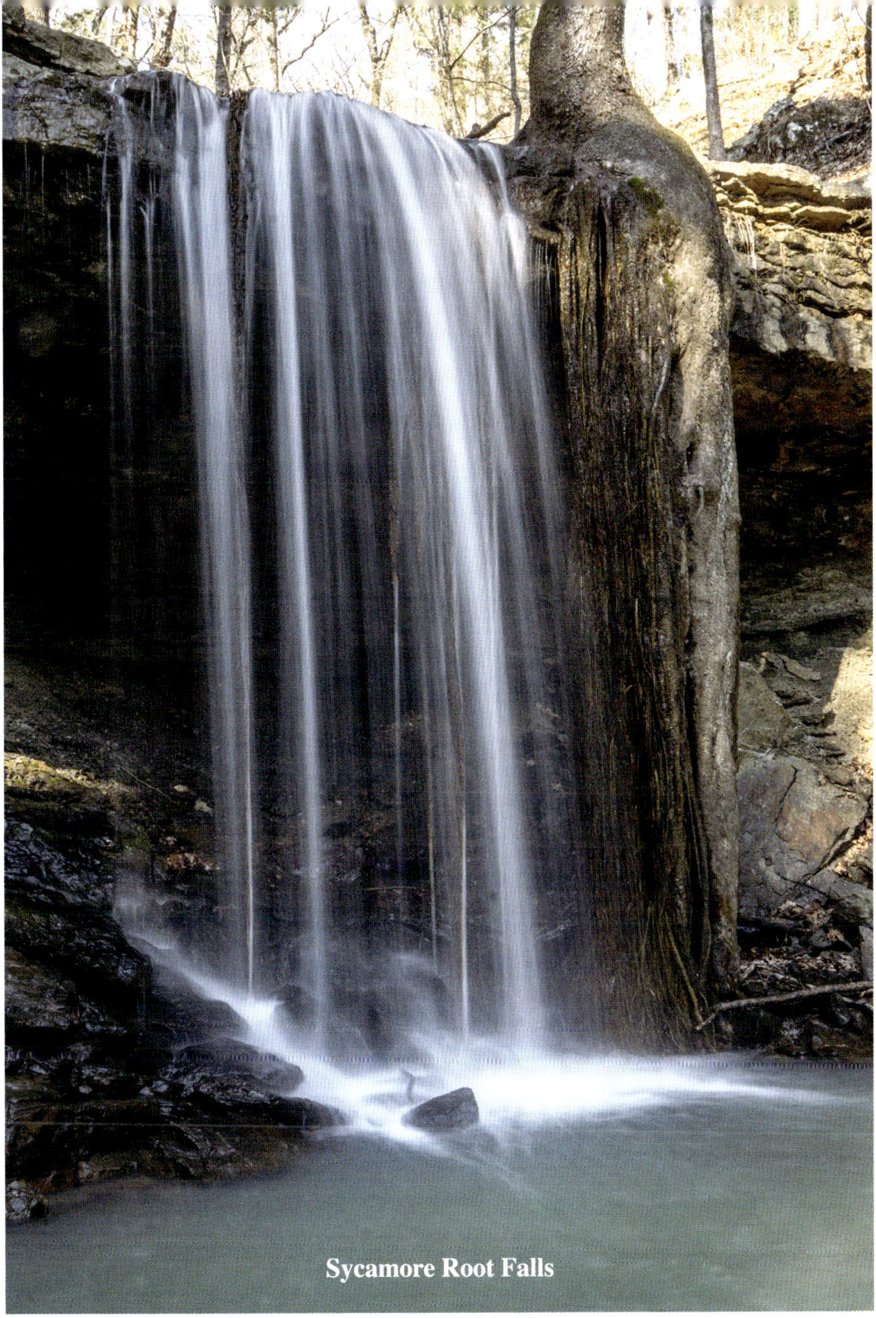

Sycamore Root Falls

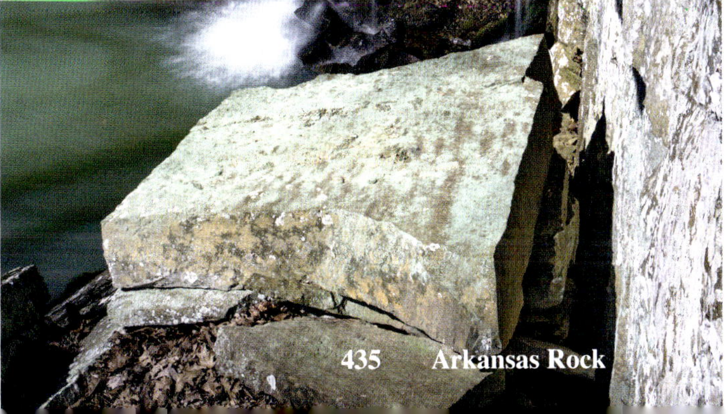

Arkansas Rock

Lacey Creek Falls – 45′

.8 mile roundtrip, medium bushwhack, GPS recommended

GPS **35.15067, -93.68587**

Rock Creek Quads – 82′ & 93′

1.6 or 2.5 mile roundtrip, difficult bushwhack at end ♦

GPS **35.14872, -93.68013**

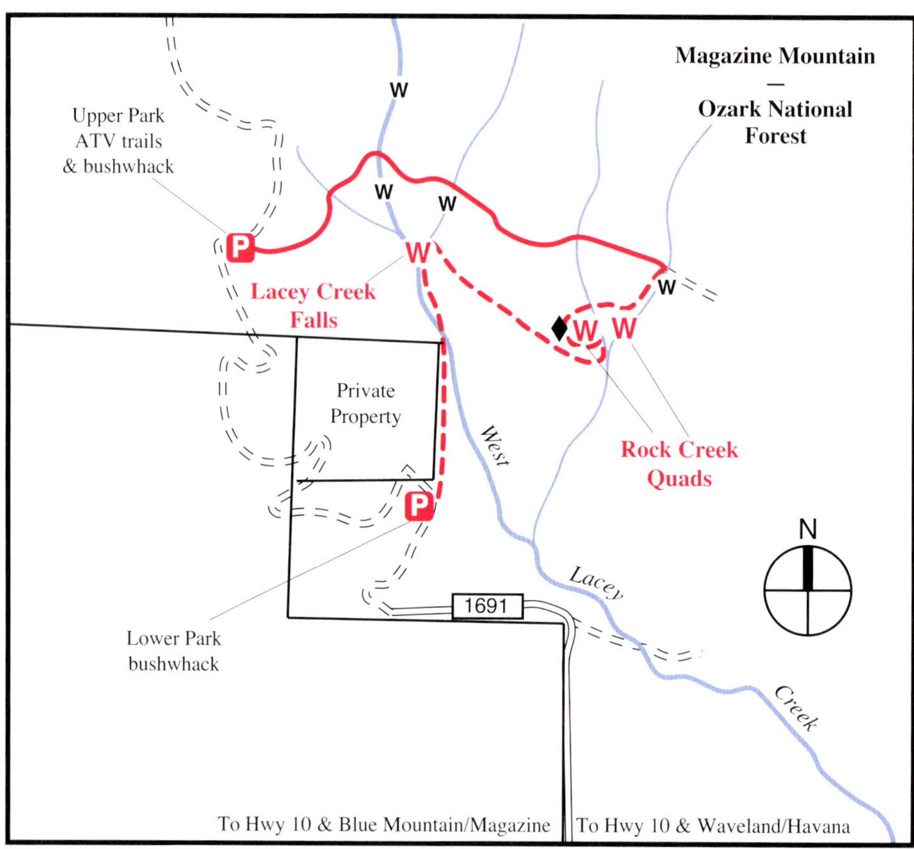

LACEY CREEK FALLS/ROCK CREEK QUADS. You can see these waterfalls from the highway far below on the south slope of Mt. Magazine in the winter with high water, but they look much better when you get up close.

The turnoff is located along Hwy. 10 between Blue Mountain and Havana, 3.0 miles west of Waveland (**35.13180, -93.68060).** TURN RIGHT/north onto FR1691 (can be a very bad road, turn left at the T intersection) and go 1.4 miles and PARK along the road for the lower parking area (**35.14442, -93.68512**).

Head straight into the woods (north, towards the mountain) and bushwhack mostly level, keeping to the RIGHT of private property until you get to West Lacey Creek. Follow the creek upstream to the base of **Lacey Creek Falls** at .4 (200' elevation gain).

If the road is too rough for your vehicle, park back near the T intersection, hike north into the woods to West Lacey Creek, then follow it upstream and to the left at the fork to **Lacey Creek Falls** at .7. (450' elevation gain) Or take the right fork up to **Rock Creek Quads**—turn RIGHT where the creek forks..

Rock Creek Quads It's not a bad bushwhack from the top of **Lacy Creek Falls** on over to these BIG waterfalls less than a half mile away—just contour your way around the hillside and eventually into the creekbed, then work your way UP to the base of the falls from below at .8. The last part up to the falls is pretty rough (♦). These are two double-drop falls side-by-side, or "Quads."

If you can drive all the way to the upper parking spot **(35.15084, -93.69105)**, it's an easier hike to the Quads. Hike along the old road you parked on for about a mile (waterfalls above and below the road along the way, then TURN RIGHT at .9 (**35.15044, -93.67791**—at a waterfall, of course!), and follow the creek down to the top of the **Rock Creek Quads** at 1.1. I go down below the waterfalls on the RIGHT side of them—BLACK DIAMOND ♦ and *rocky* though. When flowing well this is an incredible SSS!

Emergency: Logan County Sheriff, 479–963–3271 Dogs are OK

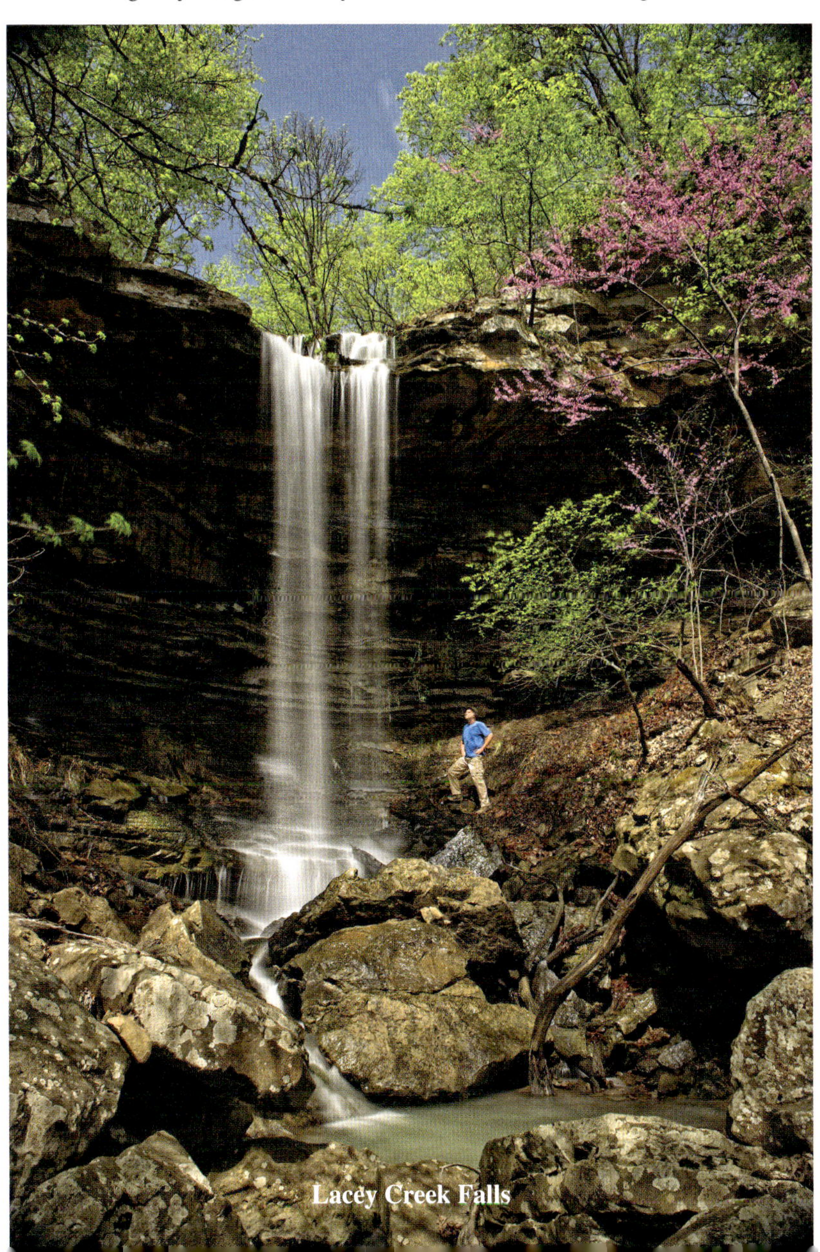
Lacey Creek Falls

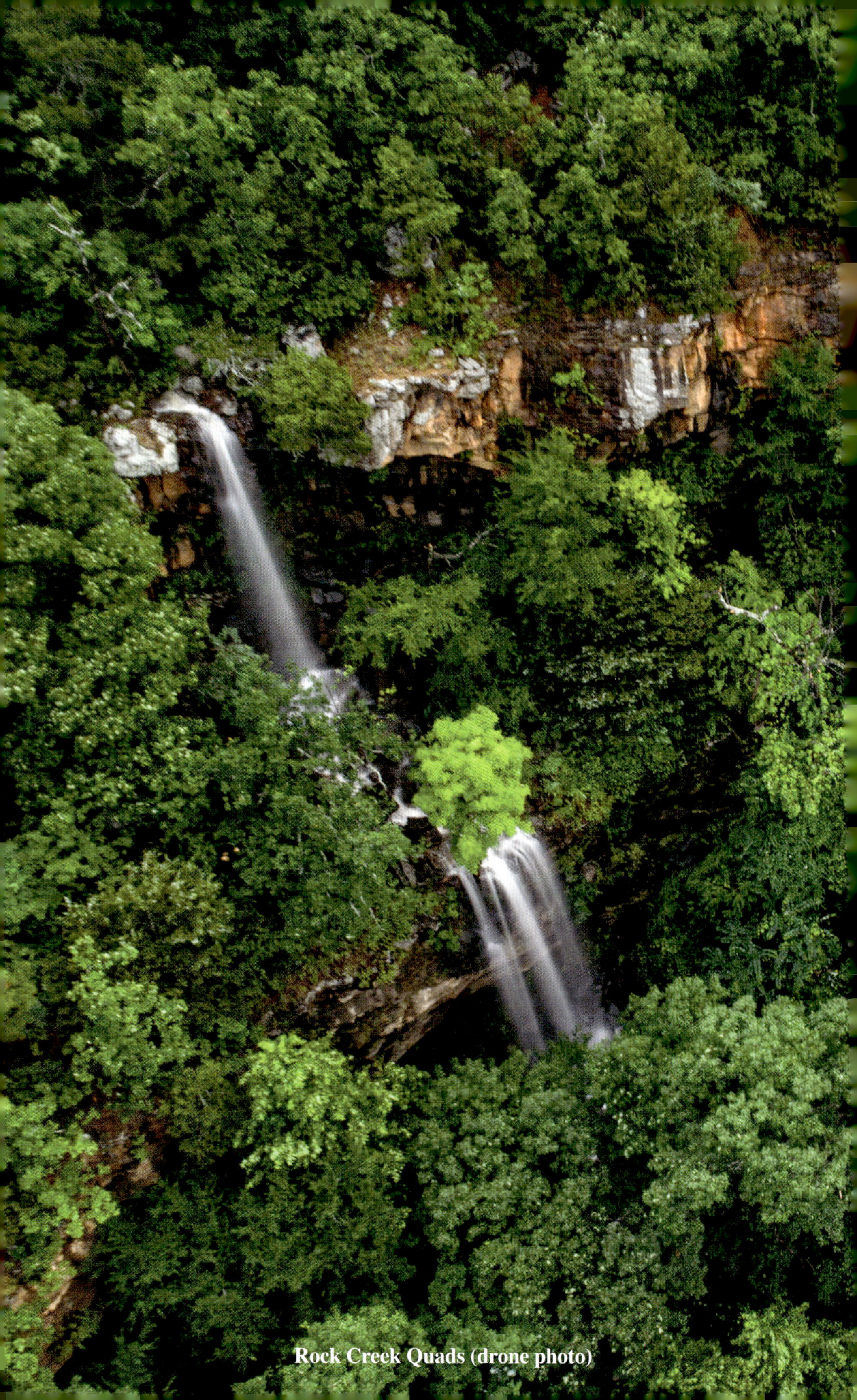

Rock Creek Quads (drone photo)

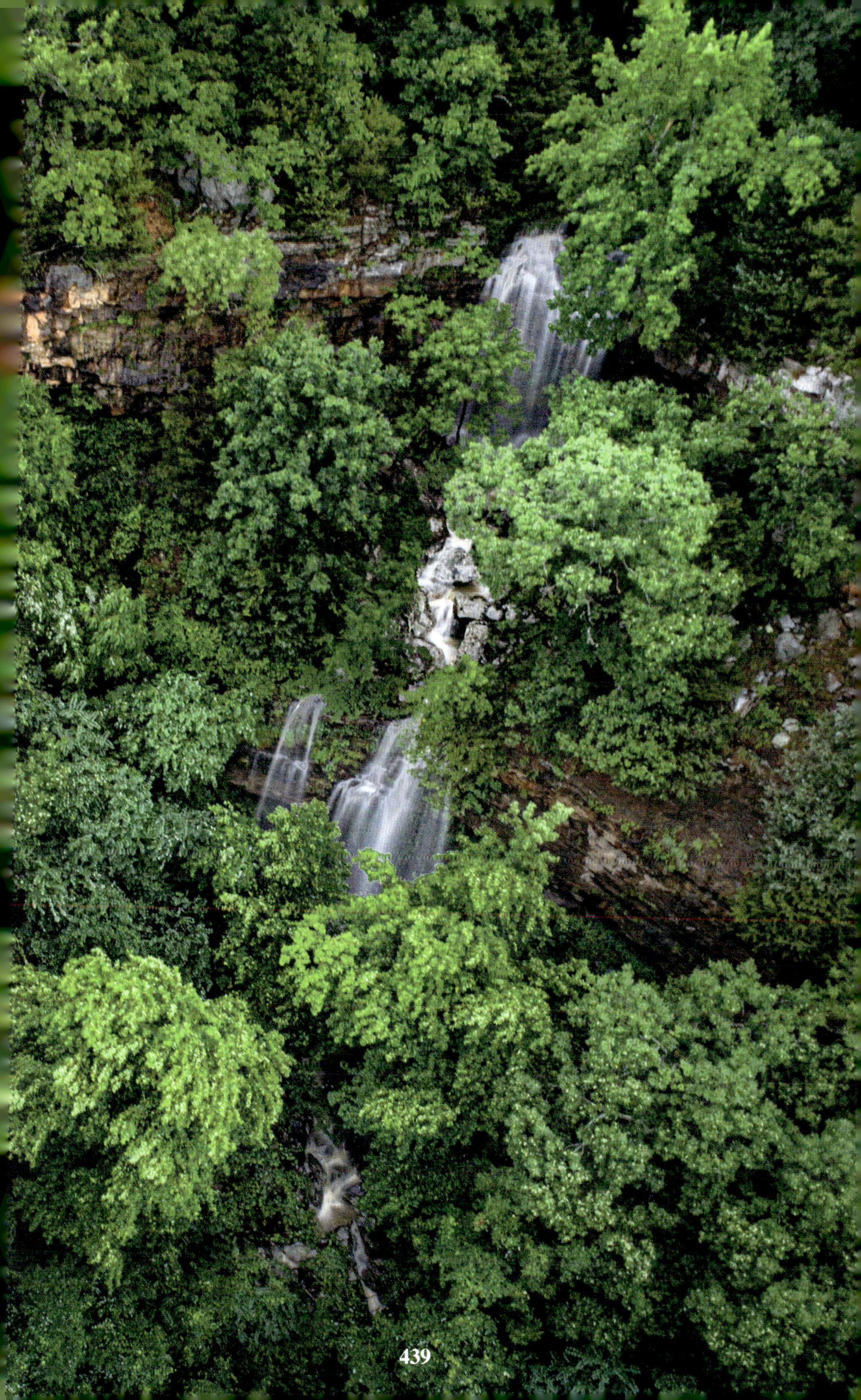

Wildman Twin Falls – 43′

1.0 mile roundtrip, easy hike/steep bushwhack, GPS helpful

GPS **35.22450, -93.55069**

Big Shoal Cascade – 8′

Park at falls, GPS not needed

GPS **35.19493, -93.54451**

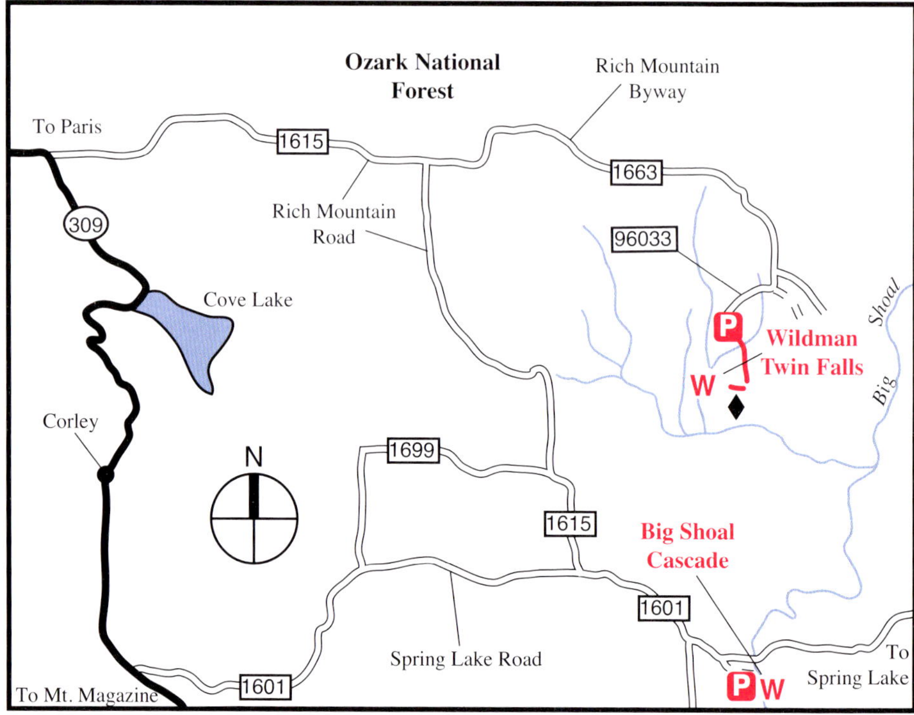

WILDMAN TWIN FALLS. There was only one Carl "Wildman" Ownbey, but no single waterfall was good enough for him so I have named this twin in honor of my great friend and fellow wilderness explorer who we lost in 2011. He always followed his bliss!

From Paris take Hwy. 309 south towards Cove Lake and Mt. Magazine (bear LEFT a mile from town). Go 7.3 miles and TURN LEFT onto FR#1615/Rich Mtn. Road (1.2 miles north of Cove Lake). Go 3.2 miles then GO STRAIGHT on FR#1663/Rich Mtn. Byway (Rich Mtn. Road goes on to the right at this intersection, towards Big Shoal Cascade). Continue 3.4 miles on Rich Mtn. Byway to a sharp curve to the left and GO STRAIGHT onto a lessor road FR#1685 (may be unmarked—the main road continues left). Take this little road just a couple hundred yards to a field and then TURN RIGHT onto road 96033. Follow this road .6 mile to the edge of a gas well opening and PARK on the left (**35.22847, -93.54926**). There will be a jeep road to your LEFT heading out into the woods. Hike along that jeep road across a small stream, then the road will curve back to the right and pass a gated food plot on the left. LEAVE the jeep road to the RIGHT just past that point and bushwhack down the steep slope ♦ until you hit the creek (may be a rope to hang onto)—the falls will be upstream to your right.

BIG SHOAL CASCADE. This is a beautiful cascade in the shadows of Mt. Magazine and you can drive right up to it. If coming from Wildman Twin Falls, when you drive back

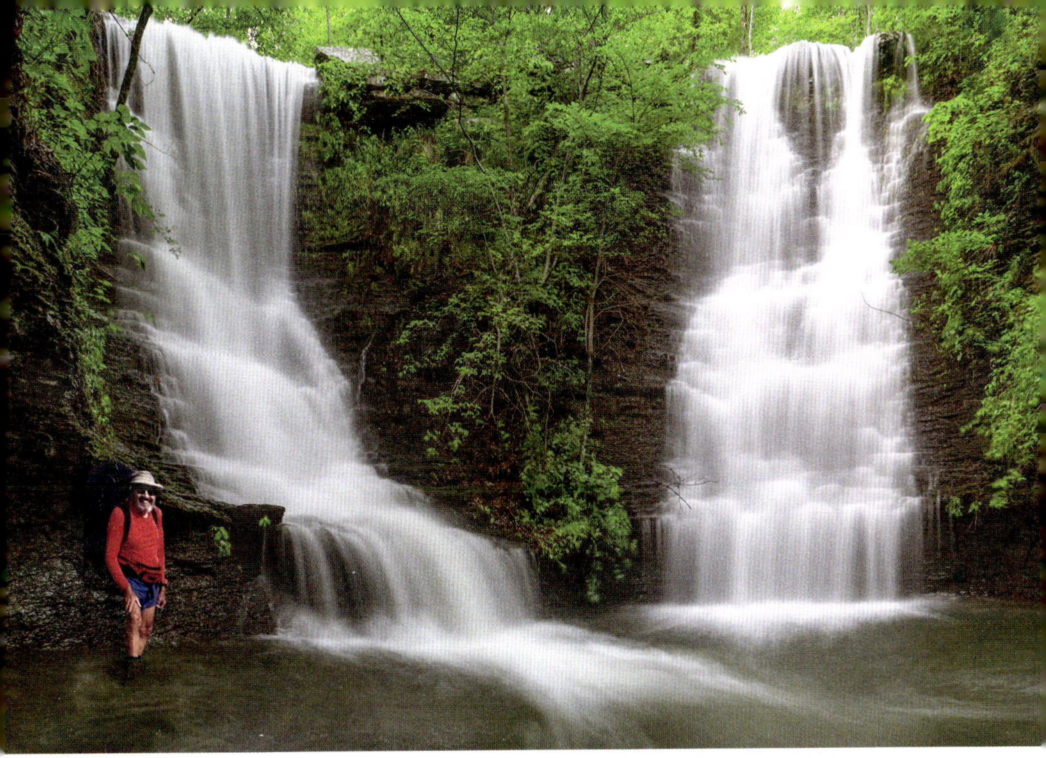

Wildman Twin Falls (himself, above), **Big Shoal Cascade** (below)

out TURN LEFT onto Rich Mtn. Road and follow it 3.6 miles and TURN LEFT onto FR#1601/Spring Lake Road. Go 1.5 miles and TURN RIGHT just before you cross Big Shoal Creek and the old road will take you right to the cascade. If coming off of Hwy. 309 take FR#1601/Spring Lake Road just south of the store at Corley and go 5.6 miles and TURN RIGHT just before you cross Big Shoal Creek and you will arrive!

Emergency: Logan County Sheriff, 479–963–3271 Dogs are OK

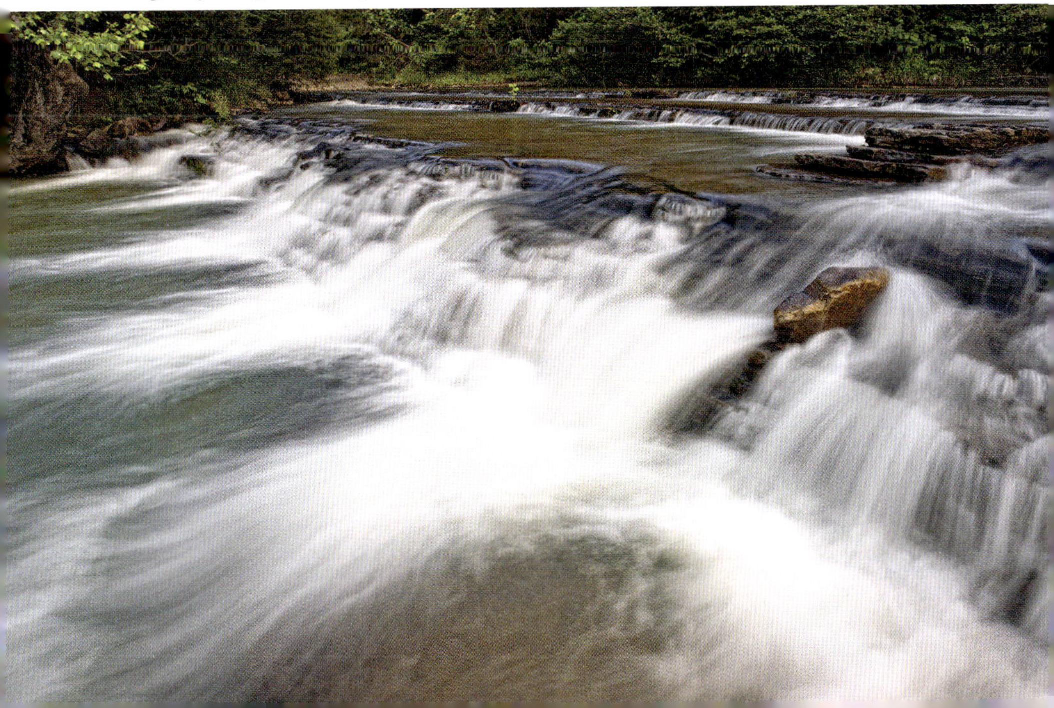

Cedar Falls – 95′

2.0 miles roundtrip, medium hike, GPS not needed

GPS **35.12148, -92.93410**

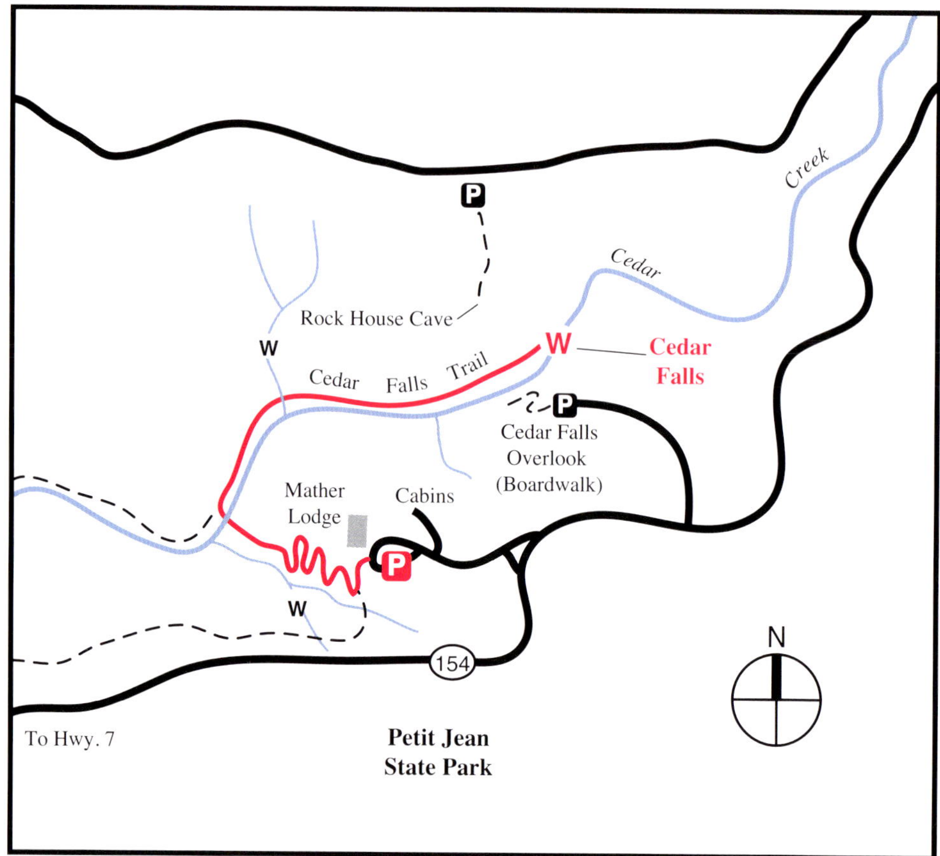

CEDAR FALLS. This is one of the most visited, photographed, powerful, and beautiful waterfalls in Arkansas. You will remember it for a long time. There are two ways to view this falls–via a wheelchair-accessible boardwalk from above, or by taking the Cedar Falls Trail down to the base of the falls. The hike back up from the base is a steep one, although I see tons of kids and folks of all ages making the trek all the time. Be sure to bring along plenty of water and allow some extra time for the hike out. We did not measure this falls, and were told by park staff that the height was estimated at 95 feet.

Petit Jean State Park is one of the finest examples of the craftsmanship done by the Civilian Conservation Corps back in the 1930's, and you will see many examples of their stone work throughout the park. To get to Petit Jean from Russellville, take Hwy. 7 south to Centerville, then TURN LEFT onto Hwy. 154 and follow it to the top of the mountain. Or from Morrilton take Hwy. 9 south to Oppelo and TURN RIGHT onto Hwy. 154 and take it up to the mountain. There is a sign for the overlook turnoff, and you will park at Mather Lodge for the Cedar Falls Trail, which begins right at the lodge (**35.11753, -92.93785**).

The trail begins its drop down the steep hillside almost immediately, switchbacking back and forth, back and forth (be sure *not* to shortcut any of the switchbacks!). If the water is running well you might see a nice waterfall out to your left as you go down. You

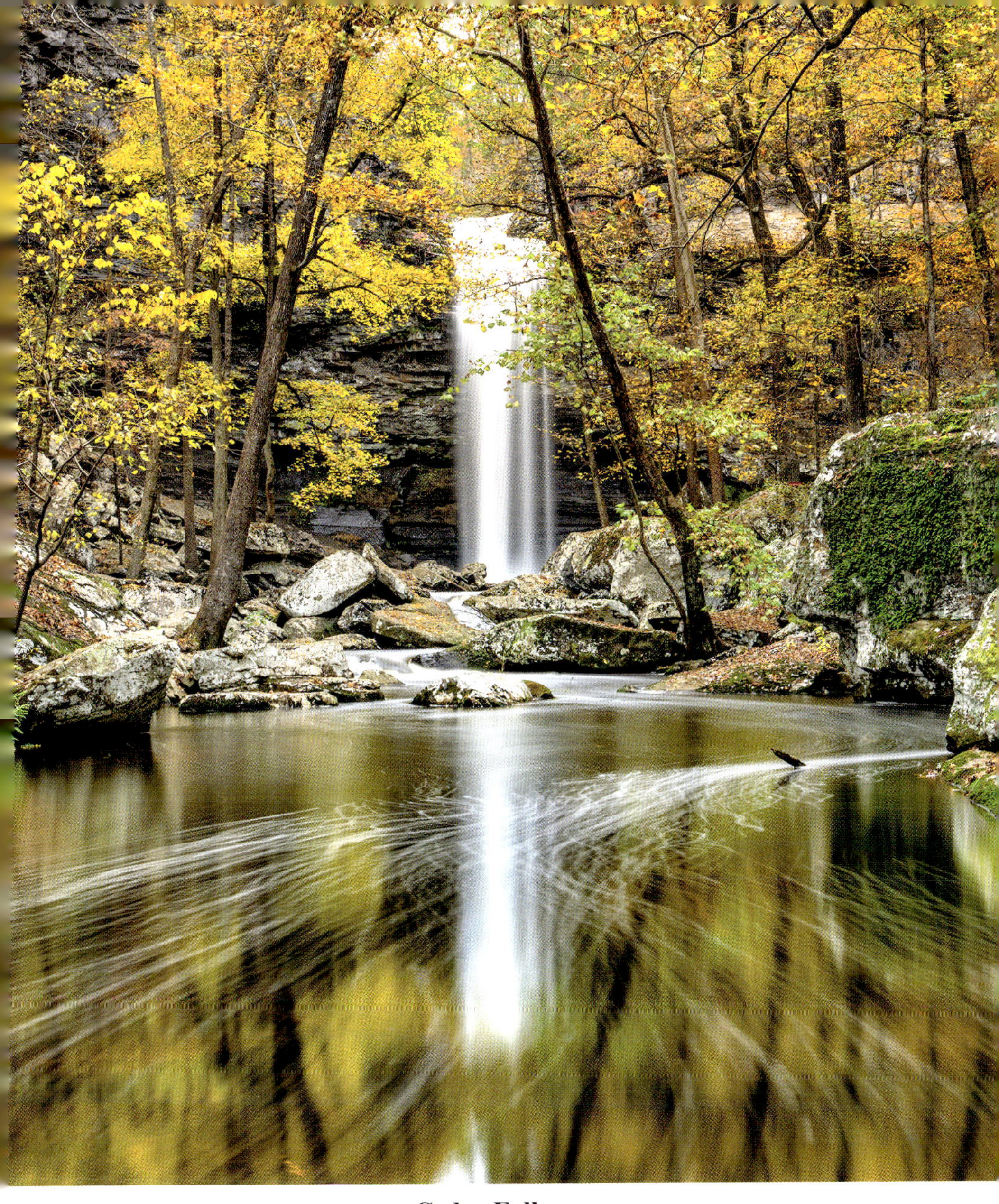

Cedar Falls

will also have some time to look at it on the way back up—while you are standing there resting and about to die from the climb! When the trail finally hits bottom it crosses Cedar Creek on a tall, narrow bridge—TURN RIGHT when you get to the other side. This trail will follow the creek upstream all the way to the falls. You will cross a side creek part way up, and there is a nice waterfall up to your left that can sometimes be seen and heard from the trail. The trail ends at **Cedar Falls** at the 1.0 mile point (no swimming in the pool). To return to the parking area you have to go back out the same way that you came in—up that nice little hill with all of those switchbacks! Take it slow and easy and enjoy the scenery on the way up. Be sure to visit the Seven Hollows Grotto Falls too (see next page).

Emergency contact: Yell County Sheriff, 479–495–2811; Park Office, 501–727–5441

Seven Hollows Grotto – 18′

4.5 miles roundtrip, medium hike, GPS not needed

GPS **35.09795, -92.94873**

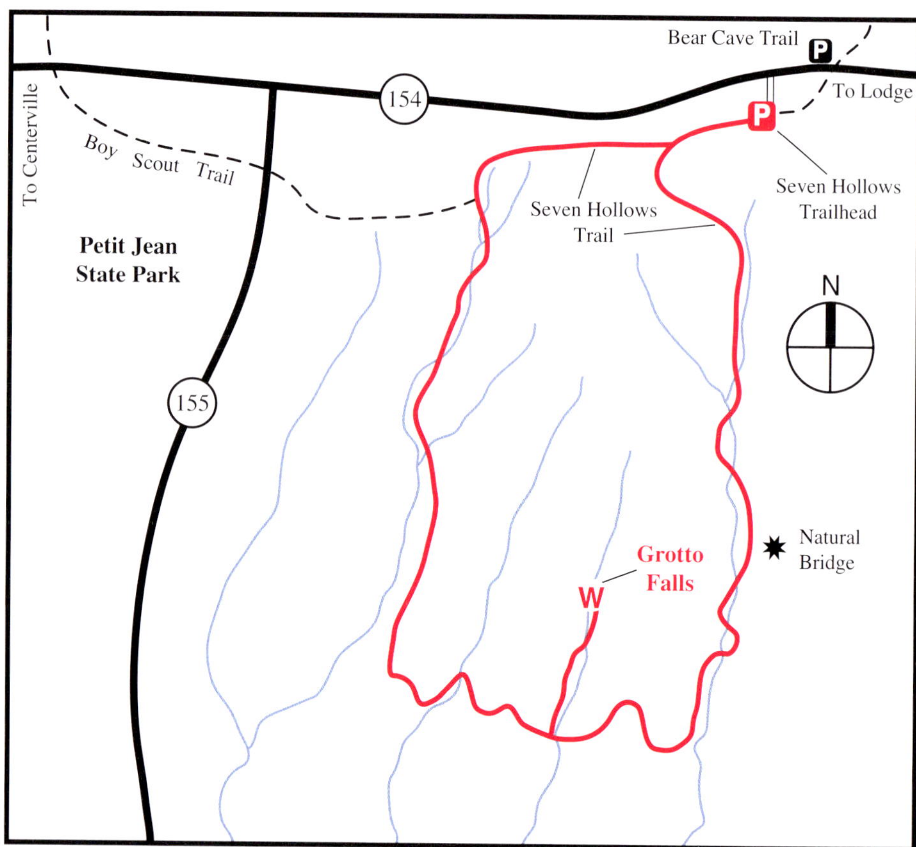

SEVEN HOLLOWS GROTTO. This waterfall is located halfway around the loop of one of the best hiking trails in the state. Each of the many hollows the trail visits is lined with bluffs on both sides, and you are actually winding in and out of canyons of stone. Tucked away in one of the canyons is a "grotto" where the creek spills down over the bluff—a really neat spot! It's not the tallest waterfall around, but is certainly one of the most scenic.

Petit Jean State Park is one of our most popular parks and gets a great deal of traffic, as does this hiking trail. To get to the trailhead at Petit Jean State Park, take Hwy. 7 south out of Russellville to Centerville, turn left onto Hwy. 154 and go 14.1 miles, then turn right into the trailhead parking area soon after you enter the park. From Morrilton, take Hwy. 9 south a few miles to Oppelo and turn right onto Hwy. 154, then turn left into the trailhead at the far end of the park **(35.11444, -92.94532)**. Everything is signed really well. In fact, there are even mile-point signs every half mile along the trail.

The Seven Hollows area was burned by a major fire in August of 2000, and you may see some evidence of this. It is all recovering well, and the new forest is thriving. The trail heads out into the burned area and comes to an intersection right away. The sign says the Grotto is to the right, but I prefer to hike this trail clockwise. Since the waterfall is located about halfway around the loop, it really doesn't matter which way you go, and I highly

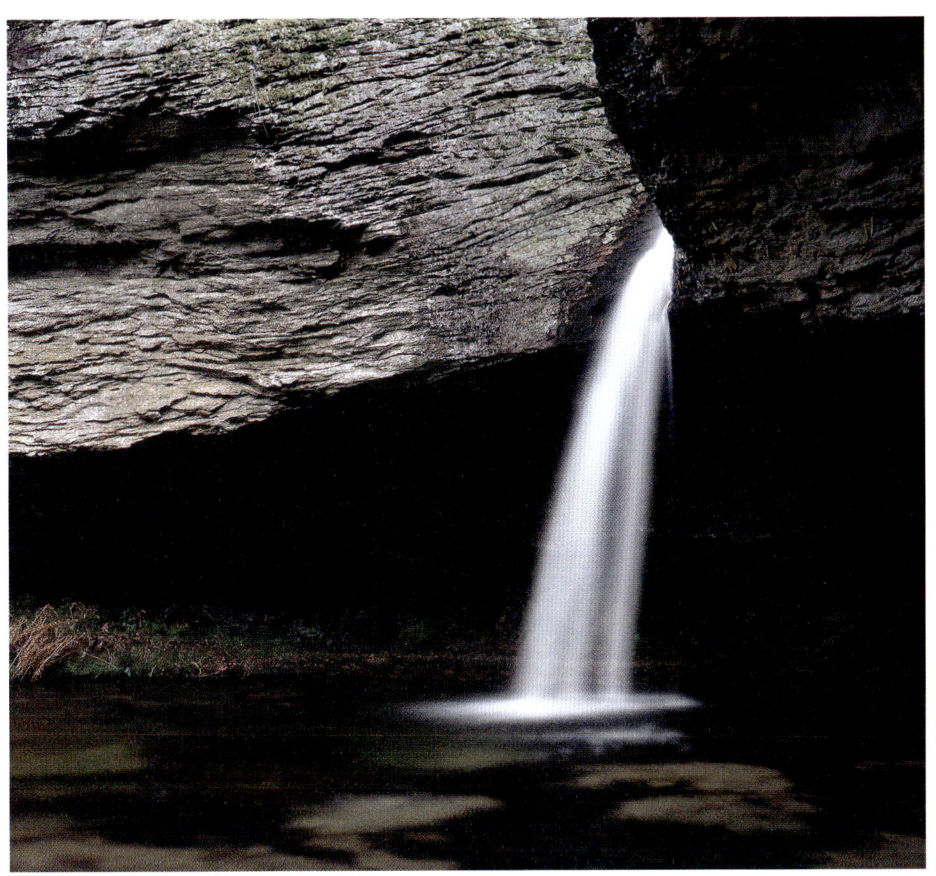

Seven Hollows Grotto

recommend that you hike the entire loop. So TURN LEFT at the intersection.

The trail gradually heads downhill and enters the first of many bluff-lined canyons, following a little stream. There are many inviting places to explore. At 1.3 you will find a large natural bridge of stone that is worth some extra time. The trail crosses the creek a few times, then leaves the canyon to the right and climbs out and up on top of a ridgetop, where you will visit a wonderful wildflower-filled glade. Lots of collared lizards running around up there, too. At 2.1 the trail drops down to another creek and to a trail intersection—TURN RIGHT here and follow the spur trail up into the "Grotto" to the falls.

For the rest of your hike simply return to the main trail and continue on. The trail climbs up onto the next little ridgetop—more wildflowers and lizards—then drops back down into another hollow. It works its way back uphill some, then back down into yet another hollow. Here you will begin a gradual rise back up to the trailhead, past many towering bluffs and interesting rock features. It is all quite beautiful! At 3.8 there is an intersection with the Boy Scout Trail (blazed a different color) that takes off to the left—stay STRAIGHT AHEAD. Eventually you will top out and pass through a couple more wildflower glades and back to the trail intersection—go STRAIGHT AHEAD to get back to the trailhead. If you have the time, be sure and visit the Bear Cave Trail just across the highway—a short excursion through very interesting rock formations.

Emergency contact: Yell County Sheriff, 479–495–2811 Dogs are OK

Ouachita Region Waterfalls

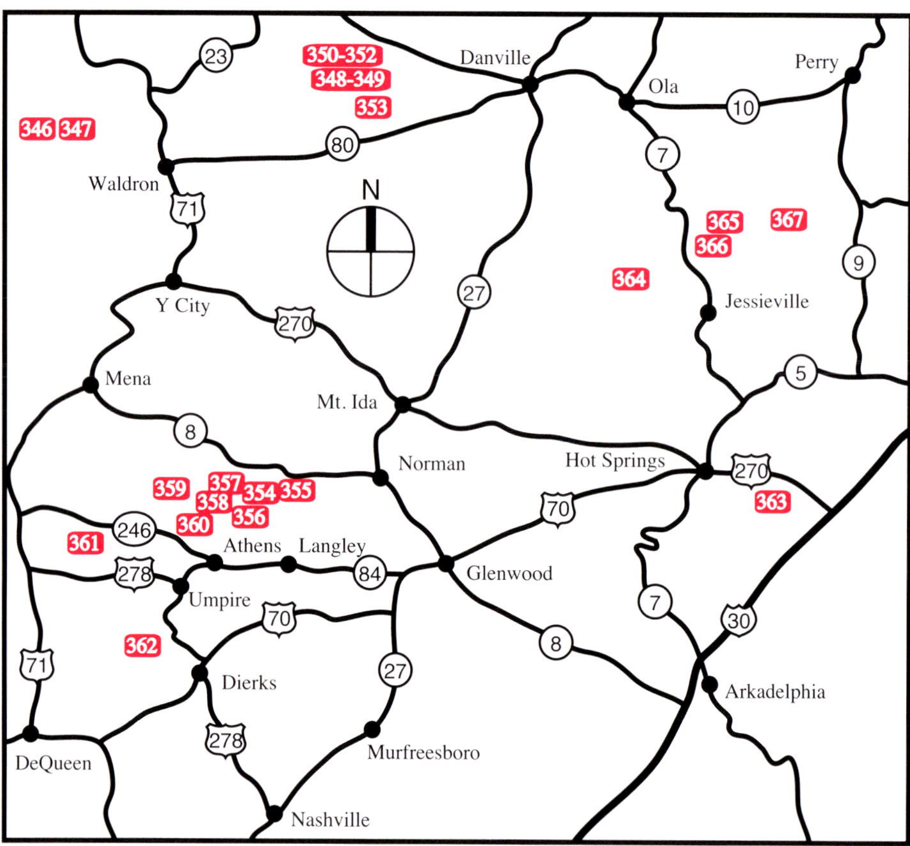

The Ouachitas are not known for their waterfalls, but there are a couple of really spectacular ones there, plus a number of others that are easy to get to and view. I'm not sure why waterfalls don't grow well in this land of rugged mountains—there is plenty of water and lots of height in the hills. I suspect it is because the rock layers that were pushed up millions of years ago now live at odd angles and don't provide the nice flat blufflines for streams to pour off to create waterfalls like the rock layers in the Ozarks do. Still, there is some great scenery to be had in our southern forest. You will see many more pine trees than in the Ozarks—that means a lot more color in the wintertime. I especially like the salt-and-pepper look of the mixed forest in the spring, when the new green growth of the hardwoods contrasts with the darker greens of the pines. If you are new to the waterfall-hunting game, I recommend that you begin with the waterfalls in the Ouachitas, then work your way up north.

Fall #	Name	Height	Hike Difficulty	Page #
346	Slate Falls	54	Med.	**448**
347	Belle Starr Cave Falls	27	Med.	**450**
348	*Jill Pickett Falls	27	♦	**452**
349	*Fireman Jeff Falls	53	♦	**452**
350	*Middle Flood Spgs Fall	31	♦	**452**
351	*Flood Springs Fall	91	♦	**452**
352	*Boulder Falls	37	♦	**452**
353	Mitchell Branch Falls	39	Med.	**457**
354	Little Missouri Falls	15	Easy	**459**
355	Crooked Creek Falls	16	Easy	**459**
356	Blaylock Creek Falls	31	Easy	**461**
357	*Bard Springs Falls		Easy	**461**
358	Trailhead Falls	21	Easy	**461**
359	Katy Falls	12	Difficult	**464**
360	Shady Lake Cascade	27	Easy	**466**
361	Cossatot Falls	33	Med.	**468**
362	Panther Bluff Falls	31	Easy	**470**
363	Falls Creek Falls	12	Easy	**472**
364	Blocker Creek Cascade	17	Med.	**474**
365	Forked Mountain Falls	10	Easy	**476**
366	Twist Cascade	12	Med.	**476**
367	Brown Creek Cascade	8	Easy	**478**

* New waterfalls in this edition

Slate Falls – 54′

4.6 miles roundtrip, medium hike/bushwhack, GPS recommended

GPS **34.98330, -94.27174**

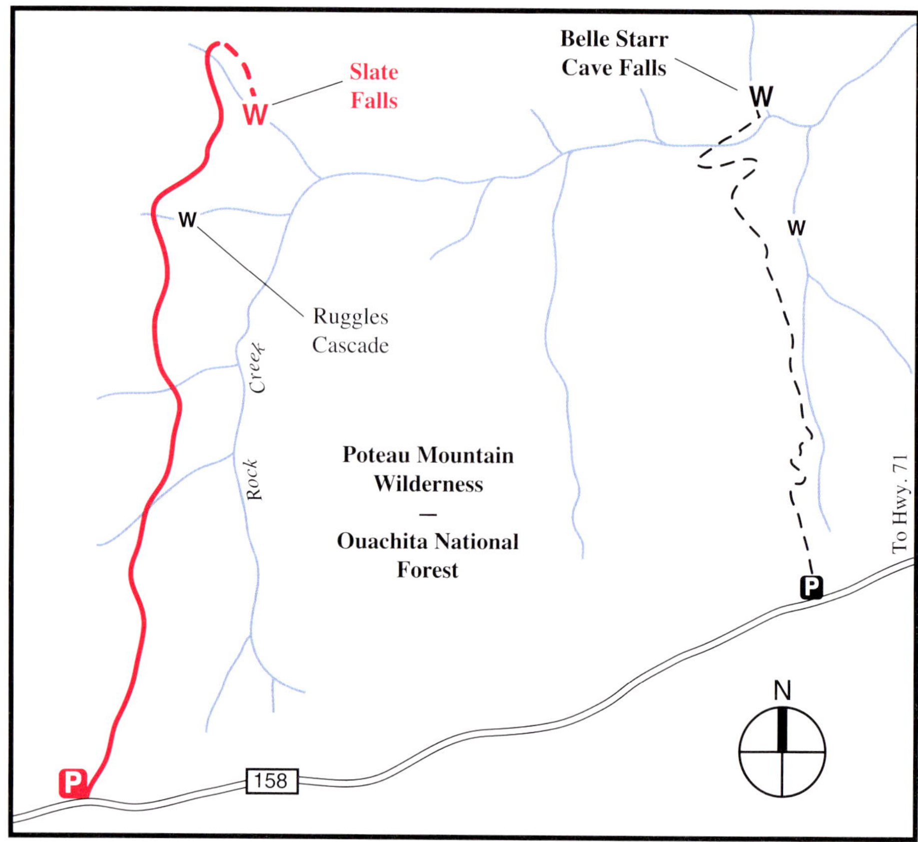

SLATE FALLS. This is a pretty tall waterfall for the Ouachita Mountains. An easy hike along an old logging road takes you most of the way, but the last couple hundred yards is a bushwhack down *steep* and rocky terrain. The old road is not maintained and may be blocked with numerous downed trees. Danny Ruggles grew up in these hills and said that they used to shower under this falls, and had to use a piece of slate rock to hold over their heads to keep from being pounded to death—hence the name (the cascade nearby is named after him). There is a really neat stone structure at the base of the falls that reminds me of the Indian dwellings at Mesa Verde in Colorado. The roof caved in long ago as pieces of the bluff crumbled away.

To get to the parking area from Waldron, take Hwy. 71 north—TURN LEFT onto FR#158/CR#70/Poteau Mtn. Road and zero your odometer there (this will be 2.9 miles north of the Hwy. 71 & Hwy. 28 intersection, and 4.7 miles south of the Hwy. 71 & Hwy. 23 intersection). Take the RIGHT fork after .3 mile (gravel) and continue through a residential area and then into the national forest. This road will climb *up* the southern spine of the Poteau Mountains, and you will have many terrific long views. There is a picnic table or two along the way, but keep your eye on the road because it gets a little hairy. The Poteau Mountain Wilderness will be on your right. PARK at 11.7—there is an open area on both sides of the road with a great view to the south **(34.95693, -94.27887)**.

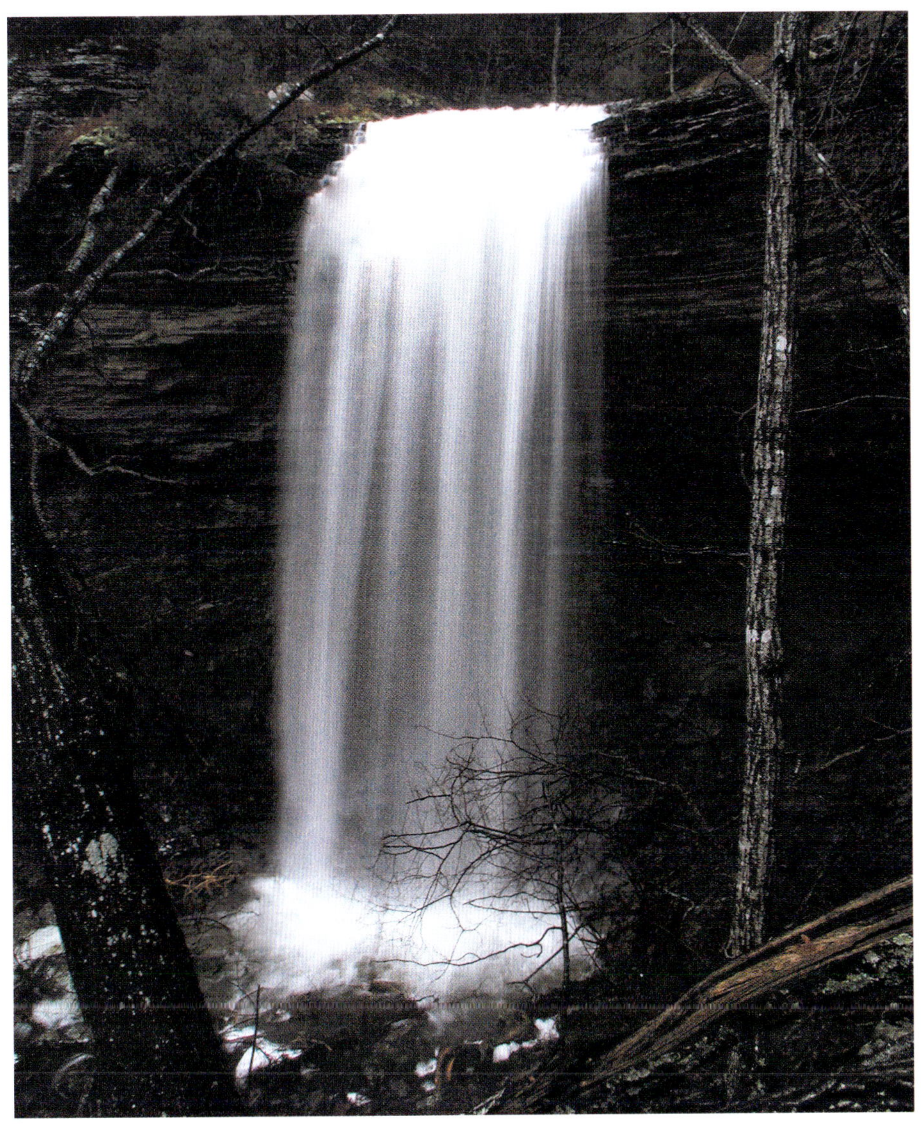

Slate Falls (high water—photo taken during downpour!)

An old road takes off to the north (right side of the road) at the back of a deer camp there—you will follow this old road all the way to near the top of the waterfall. The road eases down the hill just a little, winds around a bit, levels out, and crosses several small creeks. At about 1.7 you will come to a creek, and will be in an area where the forest is mostly pine trees. (If you want a side trip leave the road here (**34.97891, -94.27591**), and bushwhack down the stream a couple of hundred *steep* yards to Ruggles Cascade, a neat area of tumbling water (**34.97836, -94.27267**) Continue on the old road as it curves around to the left, and at about 2.2 you will come to another creek that should be flowing well. There will be lots of cedar trees mixed in with the pines here, and you will be in an obvious drainage. *Cross* the creek and LEAVE THE ROAD to the right and bushwhack down alongside the creek until you come to the falls. There is an easy way down to the base of the falls on that side, and you can go take a look at the old stone homesite.

Emergency contact: Sebastian County Sheriff, 479–783–1051 Dogs are OK

Belle Starr Cave Falls – 27′

4.4 miles roundtrip, medium hike/steep, GPS recommended

GPS **34.98264, -94.24743**

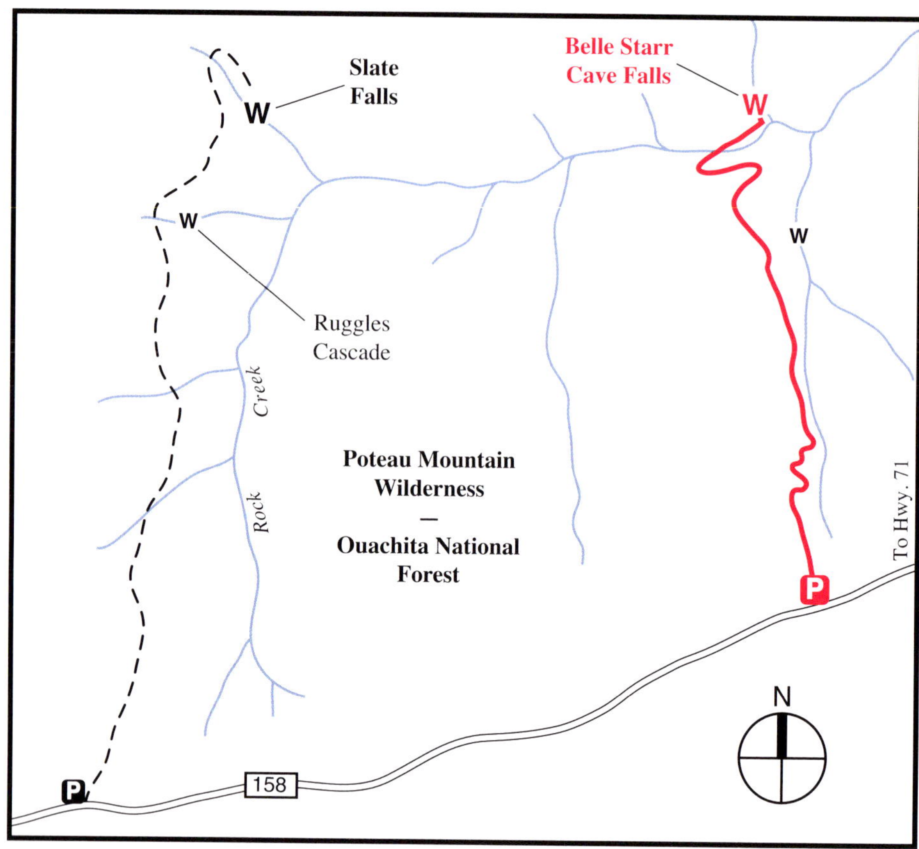

BELLE STARR CAVE FALLS. This is a wild and rugged wilderness area befitting a notorious outlaw like Belle Starr. They say she hid out in these hills, often staying hidden behind this waterfall. There is a stone structure half-buried there where she would have lived.

To get to the parking area from Waldron, take Hwy. 71 north—TURN LEFT onto FR#158/CR#70/Poteau Mtn. Road (this is 2.9 miles north of the Hwy. 71 & Hwy. 28 intersection, and 4.7 miles south of the Hwy. 71 & Hwy. 23 intersection). Go 9.5 miles and PARK on the right next to the wilderness area sign **(34.96462, -94.24476).**

Follow the four-wheeler trail north and down the hill (it gets pretty rocky in spots) until it gets near the bottom near the river, then it swings back to the left and upstream. (There are some nice falls/cascades in the drainage just to the east of the trail that are worth a look—you can hear them from the trail during high water.) Soon the trail turns back to the right and goes down through a small bluffline and comes to Rock Creek—cross the creek and continue on the trail downstream to your right until you come to the waterfall up on the bluff to your left (there may be a sign).

If you love to bushwhack and don't mind difficult terrain, you might think about going to Slate Falls first (see previous pages and map above), then bushwhacking down the hillside to Rock Creek and this falls, then looping back to your car via this trail and road.

Emergency contact: Sebastian County Sheriff, 479–783–1051 Dogs are OK

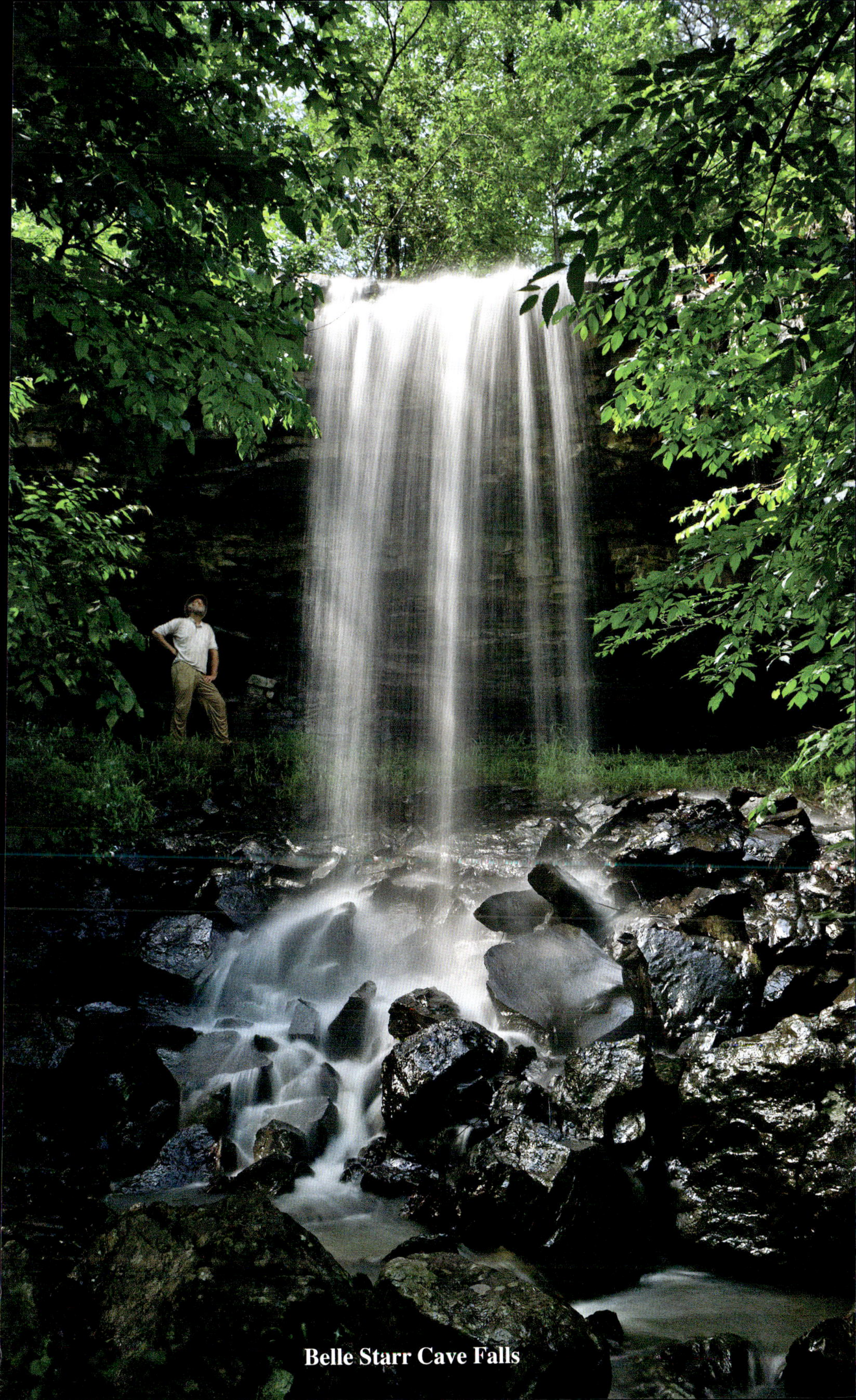
Belle Starr Cave Falls

Jill Pickett Falls – 27′

.8 mi. roundtrip to both falls difficult bushwhack ♦

GPS **35.02352, -93.69067**

Fireman Jeff Falls – 53′

GPS **35.02268, -93.6919**

Middle Flood Springs Fall – 31′

1.1 mile roundtrip for all three falls, difficult bushwhack ♦

35.03432, -93.69432

Flood Springs Fall – 91′

GPS **35.03427, -93.69348**

Boulder Falls – 37′

GPS **35.03434, -93.69292**

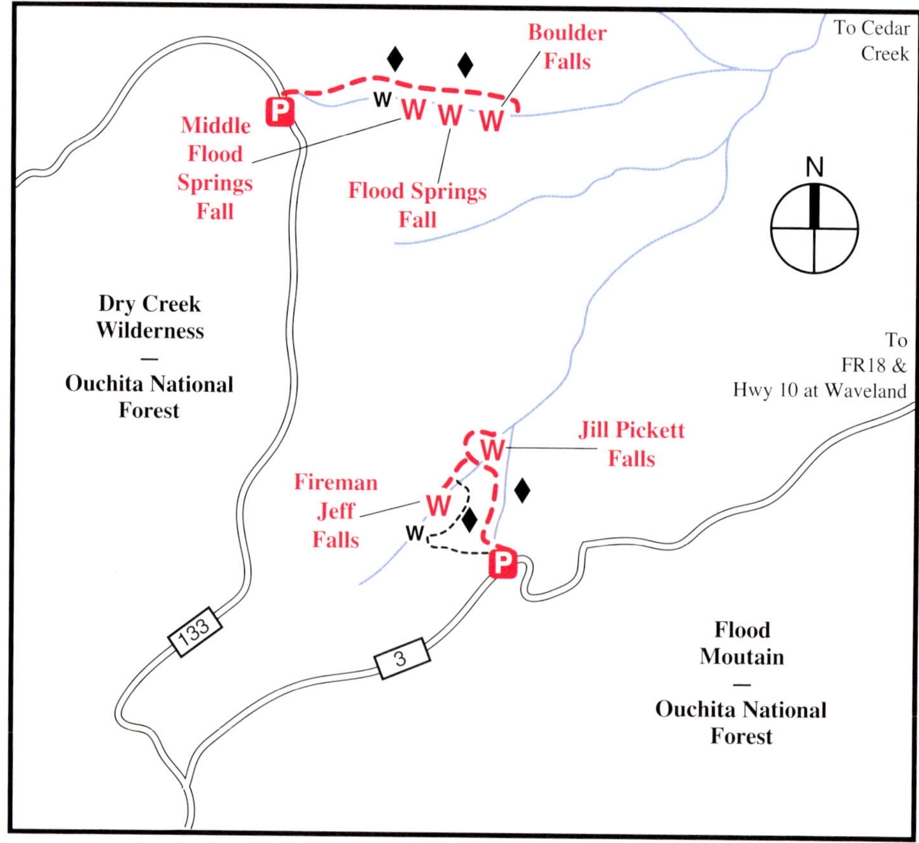

JILL PICKET FALLS/FIREMAN JEFF FALLS. From Havana, go 6.1 miles on Hwy. 10 to Waveland. Turn LEFT on Hwy. 309. Go 5.1 miles—the pavement ends, turns to the left, and becomes Mountain Road. Go 1.1 miles and continue straight on FR18. Go 2.6 miles and turn RIGHT on FR3. Go 2.6 miles and PARK just past a hairpin turn. (**35.02038, -93.69002**)

This is a short but very steep BLACK DIAMOND ♦ slope almost all the way. Head northwest and follow the level terrain a little ways to a drainage and then TURN RIGHT and head steeply downhill following the drainage. It soon becomes BLACK DIAMOND slope ♦. Follow this drainage all the way down to the main creek and **Jill Pickett Falls** at .25. From there head UPSTREAM past cascades and waterfalls to **Fireman Jeff Falls** at .34—it's all an SSS!

There's a long cascade above this waterfall that's worth a close look if the water is running well. You'll have to find a spot to climb up and out of the canyon and then around to the cascade. Then it will be an easy hike back to the road.

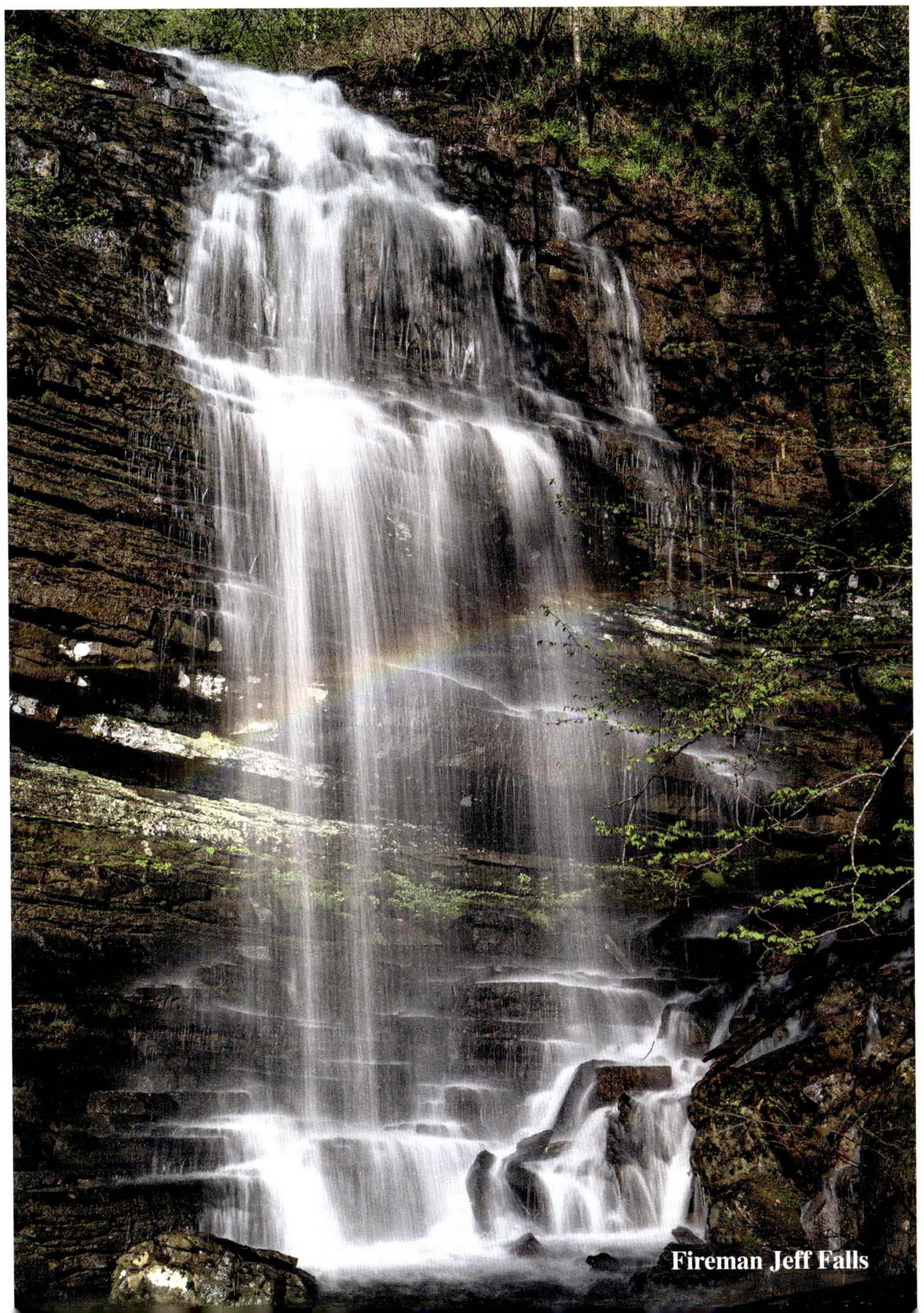

Fireman Jeff Falls

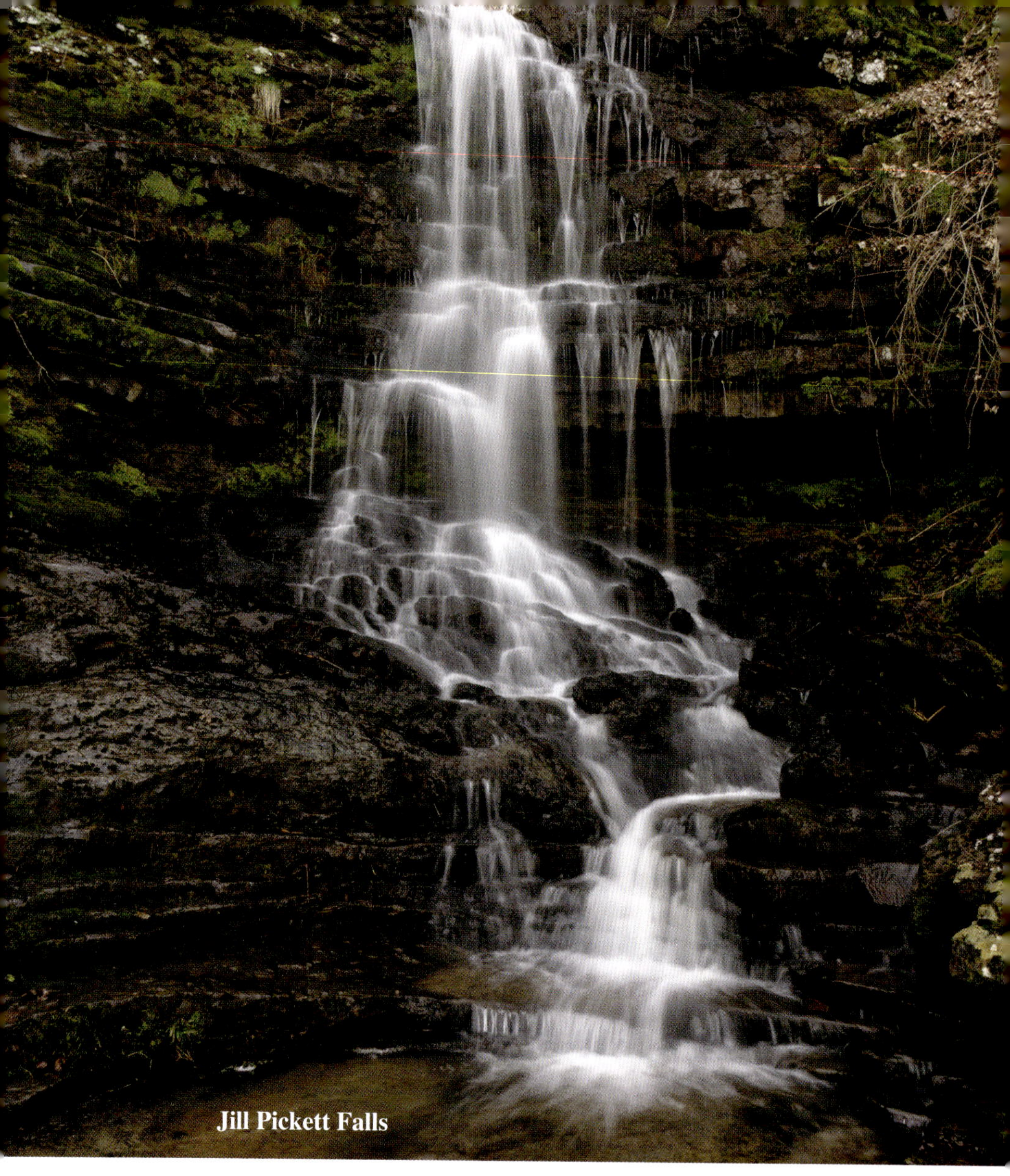
Jill Pickett Falls

FLOOD SPRINGS FALLS/BOULDER FALLS. From Havana: go 6.1 miles to Waveland. Turn LEFT on Hwy. 309. Go 5.1 miles—the pavement ends, turns to the left, and becomes Mountain Road. Go 1.1 miles and continue straight on FR18. Go 2.6 miles and turn RIGHT on FR3.. Go 3.4 miles and turn RIGHT on FR133. Go 1.6 miles and PARK where you can **(35.03450, -93.69808)**. See map to continue from FiremanJeff/Pickett parking.

The Flood Homestead and Springs are on the uphill/west side of the road on the left. Look for a small pond on the right/downhill side of the road—that's where you want to begin your hike—follow the water! This is the water that creates the tallest measured waterfall in the Ouachita Mountains at 91'.

It gets steep pretty soon, and then BLACK DIAMOND ♦ slope steep. I usually go down the left side of the creek at first, then farther down cross over and stay on the right side. There are several waterfalls and many cascades on the way down—including **Middle**

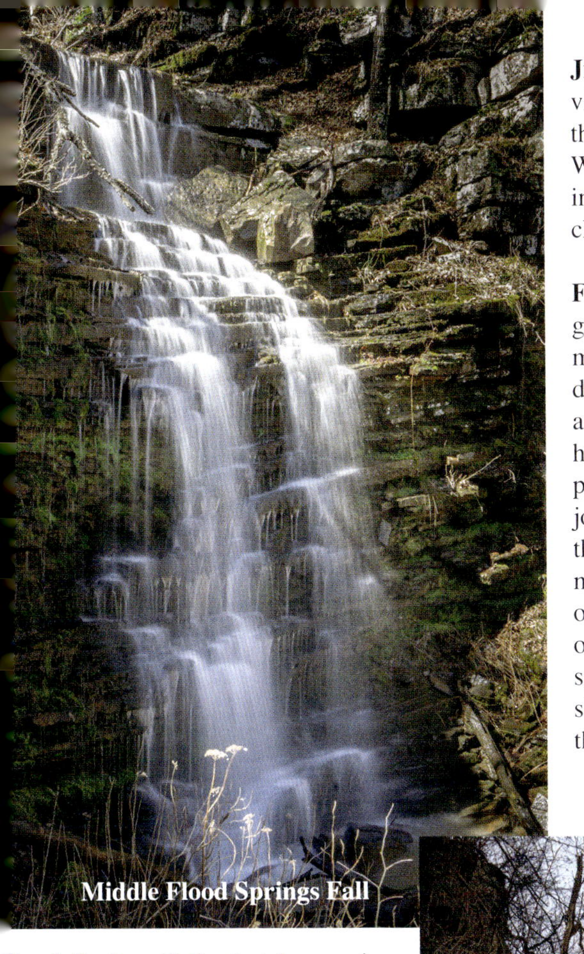
Middle Flood Springs Fall

Jill Pickett was the very first person to visit and record ALL 200^+ waterfalls in the Second Edition of this guidebook—WAY to GO GIRL! Jill has been an inspiration to many would-be waterfall chasers.

Fireman Jeff Davis has inspired ME to get out and discover new waterfalls for more than a decade, going on the most difficult adventures to find, photograph, and measure them. (Getting an accurate height measurement with a 200' tape is perhaps the most difficult and dangerous job of all—and who better than to do this than a FIREMAN!).He has saved my bacon many time in the middle of nowhere. He has an uncanny skill of looking at a Google map view and spotting a potential waterfall by a certain shadow pattern, which is how we found these two waterfalls.

'lood Springs Fall—just keep going)OWN—when you reach the bottom f **Flood Springs Fall** at .45 you will now it! All an SSS of course!

Continue on downstream just a ittle bit more to **Boulder Falls** not far elow—a most interesting falls! It's bout a 500' climb back UP to the road sorry...).

Emergency contact: Yell County Sheriff, 479–495–4881 Dogs are OK

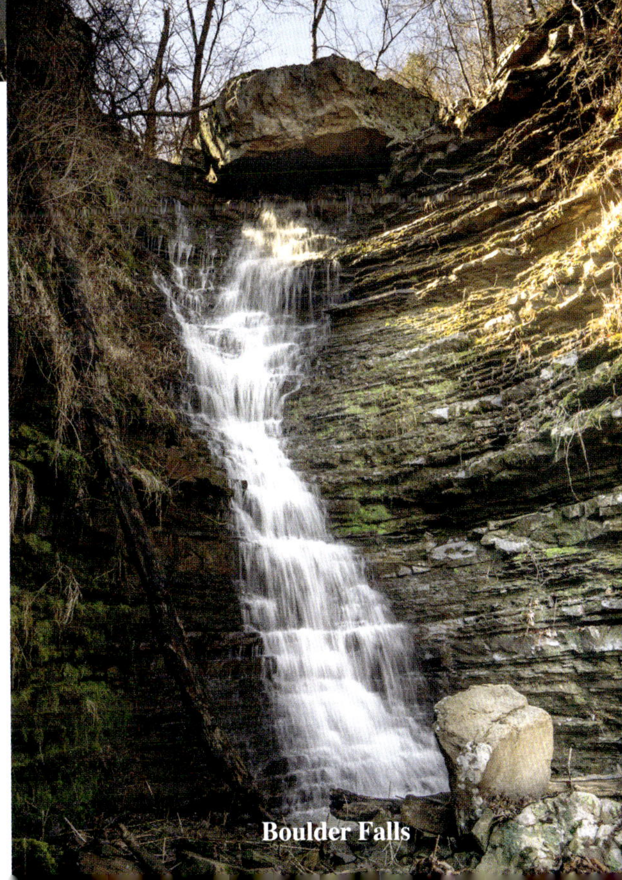
Boulder Falls

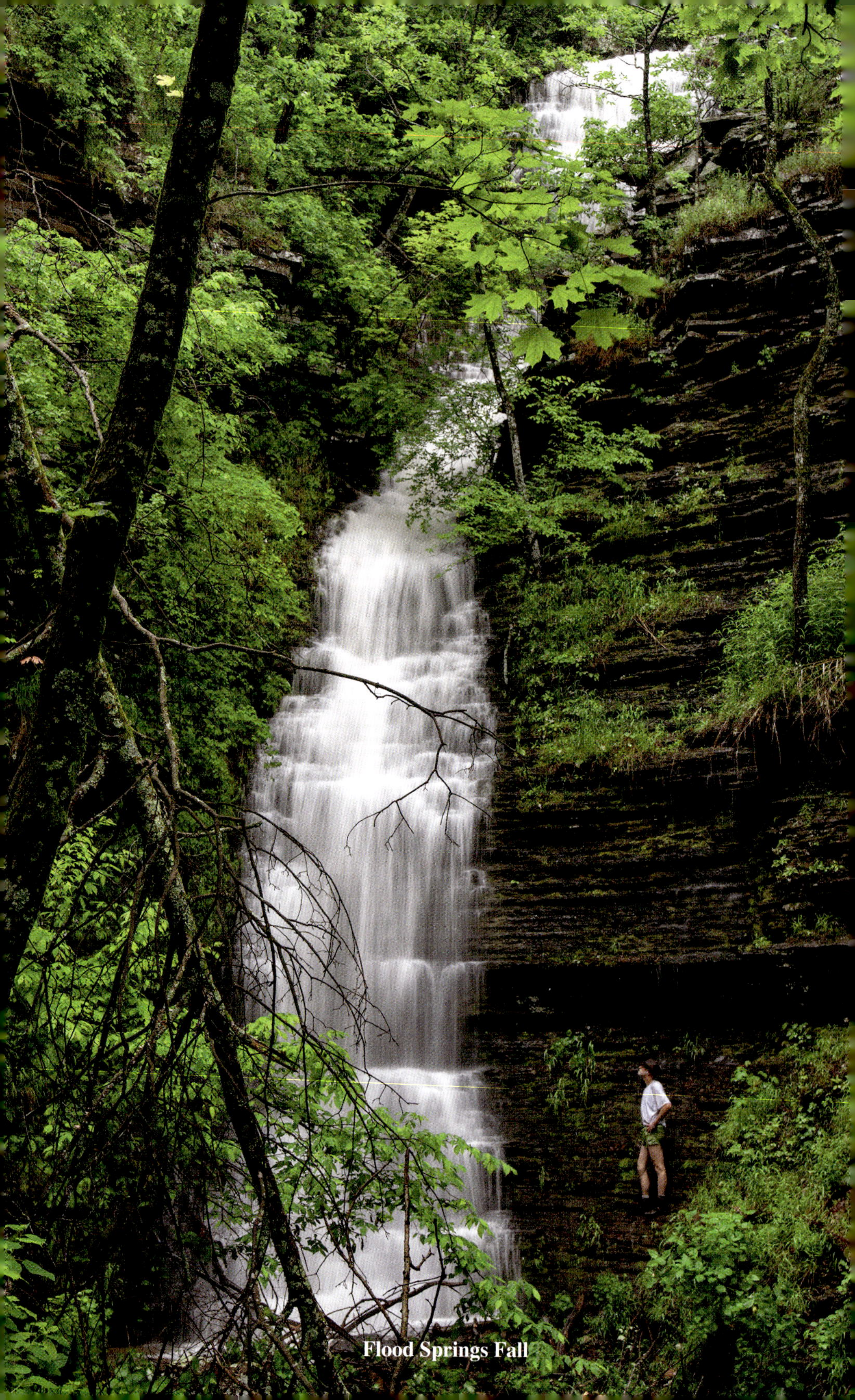

Flood Springs Fall

Mitchell Branch Falls – 39′

.6 mile roundtrip, medium bushwhack, GPS helpful

GPS **35.02353, -93.64114**

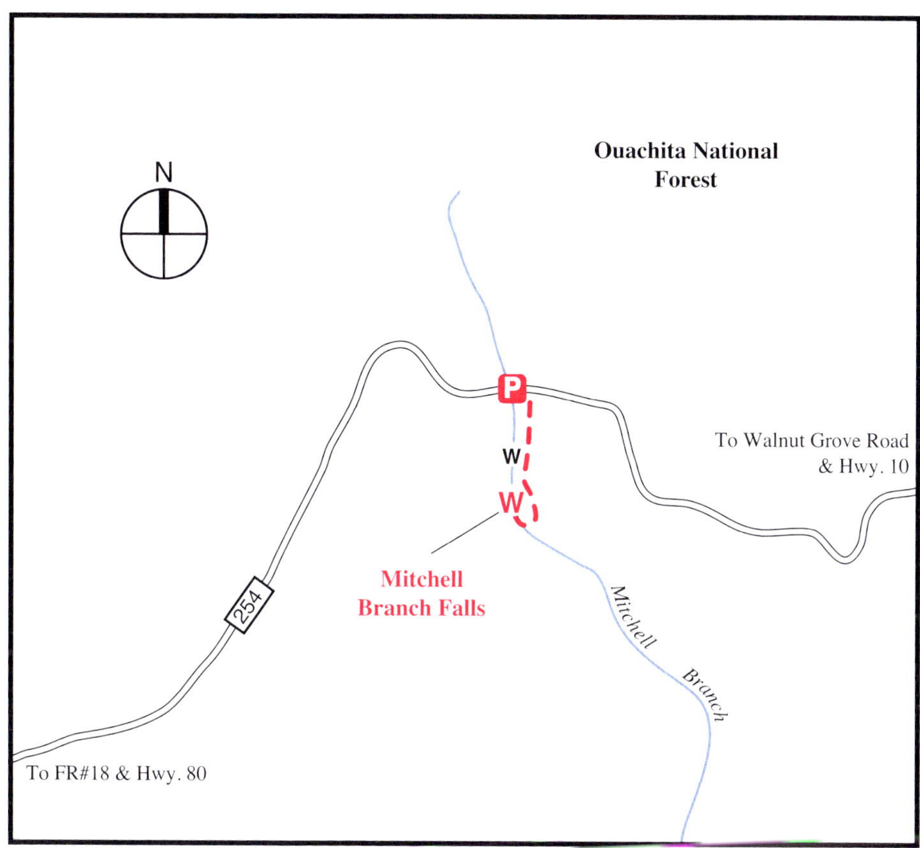

MITCHELL BRANCH FALLS. This is one of the more beautiful waterfalls in the Ouachitas and it is just a short bushwhack from the road. I love how it is a straight drop in the top half, forms a cascade in the middle, and then becomes a fan shape for the bottom half before pouring into an emerald pool—it has it all! It is located in the northern Ouachitas just south of Mt. Magazine.

The turnoff is located on Hwy. 80 between Waldron and Danville, 2.3 miles east of Amber's Cafe in Blue Ball*. From Hwy. 80 go NORTH on FR#18 up the mountain 3.7 miles and TURN RIGHT onto FR#254. Go 2.1 miles and PARK beside the road where it crosses the creek (**35.02556, -93.64114).**

Bushwhack downhill along the creek, past a nice smaller waterfall, and finally to the big falls below. You can get around it to the bottom down a steep slope just downstream. There is an interesting canyon just downstream as well.

* You can also get to this waterfall from the north: From the intersection of Hwy. 10 and 309 at Waveland, go south on Hwy. 309 for 2.3 miles then TURN LEFT onto Walnut Grove Road, go 2.5 miles and TURN RIGHT onto Jack Creek Road (which turns into FR#254 just past the ranch house complex), then stay on this road for 7.7 miles and PARK.

Emergency contact: Yell County Sheriff, 479–495–4881 Dogs are OK

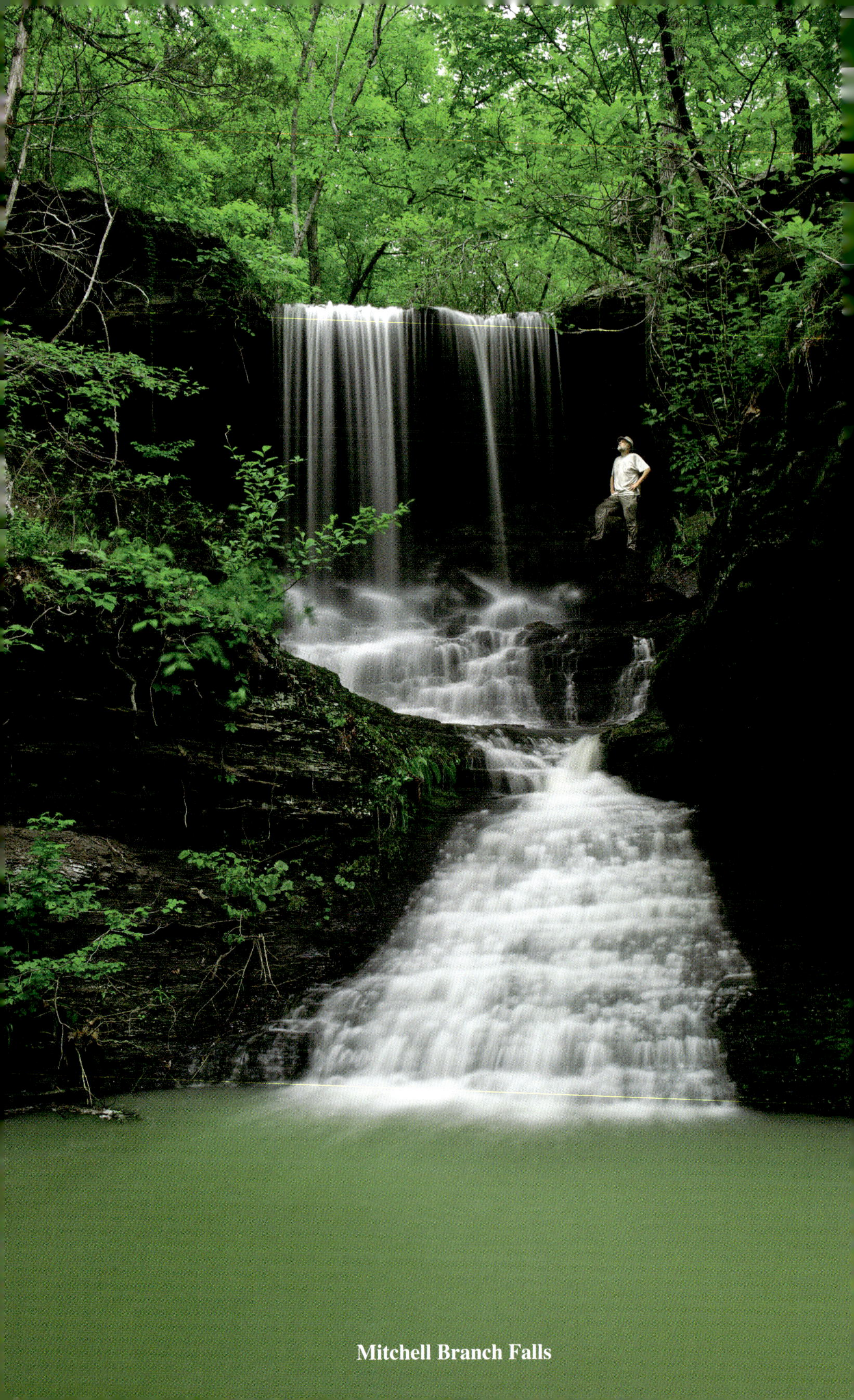

Mitchell Branch Falls

Little Missouri Falls – 15′

.25 mile roundtrip, easy short hike, GPS not needed

GPS **34.42162, -93.91875**

Crooked Creek Falls – 16′

Located next to the road, no hike, GPS not needed

GPS **34.42700, -93.88558**

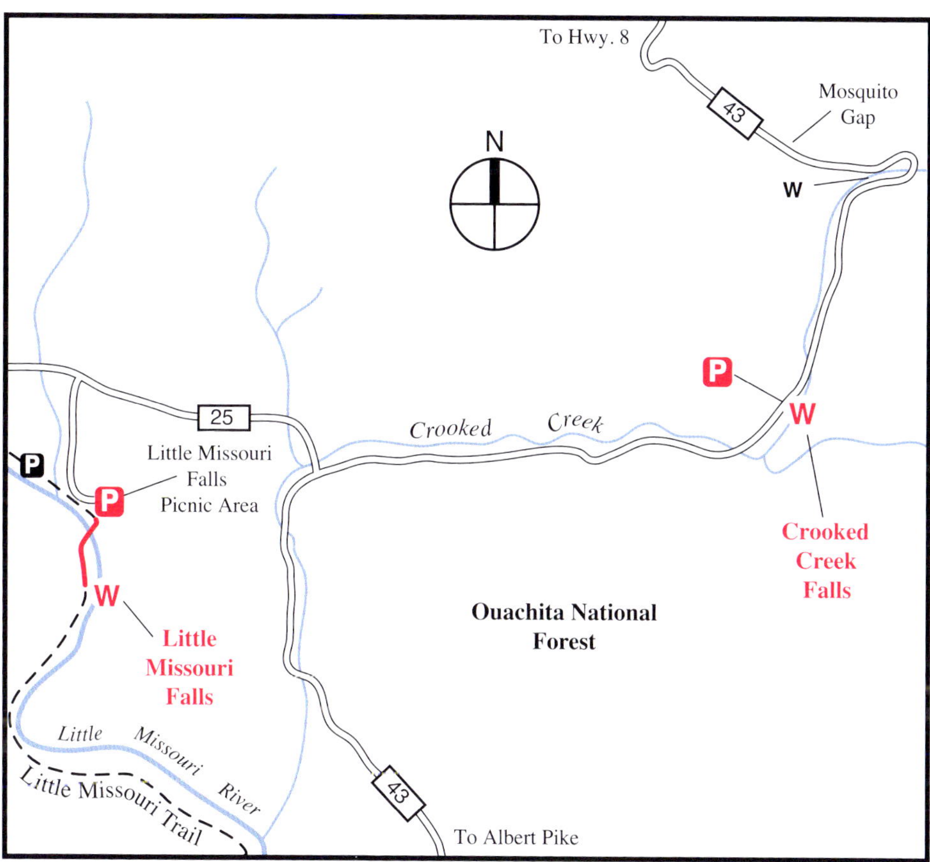

LITTLE MISSOURI FALLS/CROOKED CREEK FALLS. There are many different ways to get to this area—both falls are close to each other and require little or no hiking to view.

From Langley (west from Glenwood on Hwy. 70 and then west on Hwy. 84) take Hwy. 369 six miles to Albert Pike Recreation Area. Continue straight through the campground as the road turns to FR#73 (gravel), and follow it about three miles and TURN LEFT onto FR#43. Go 4.3 miles to the intersection with FR#25 (you will have been driving through the Crooked Creek Gorge for the past .5 mile—lots of nice cascades!). To get to Crooked Creek Falls continue STRAIGHT AHEAD 1.4 miles and PARK along the road—the falls will be just down to the right (**34.42700, -93.88558**). To get to Little Missouri Falls from the intersection above, TURN LEFT onto FR#25 and go .7 mile and TURN LEFT at the big sign, which will take you down into the picnic area & trailhead where you park (**34.42306, -93.92053**). The paved trail takes off there and crosses the creek on an accessible bridge (great view!) and goes to a pair of overlooks with good views of the cascade area.

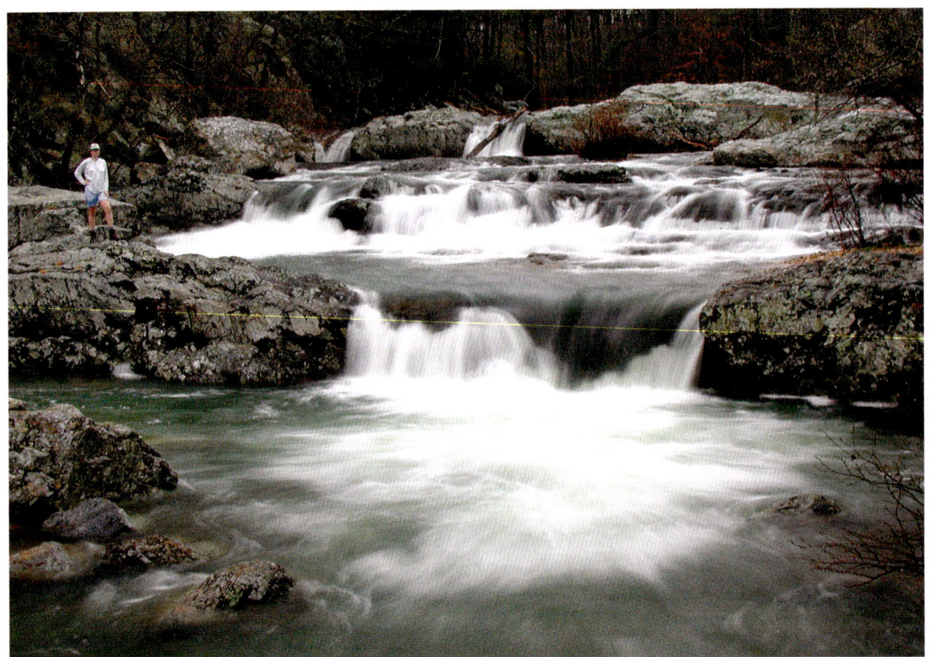

Little Missouri Falls (above), **Crooked Creek Falls** (below, during high water)

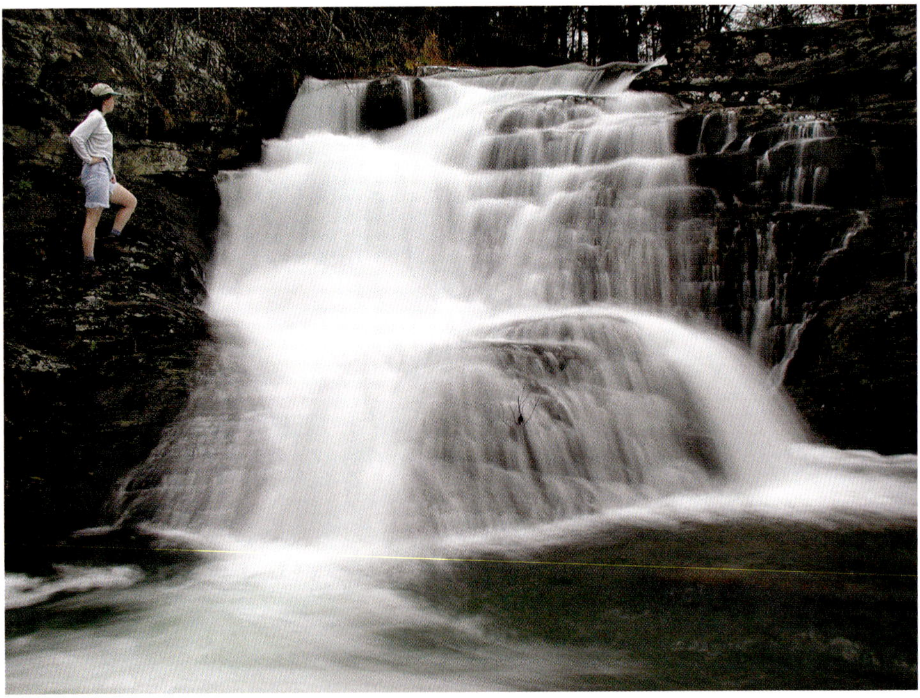

From Norman take Hwy. 8 west 12.7 miles and TURN LEFT onto FR#43. Go 3.3 miles and PARK—Crooked Creek Falls will be down on your left. Continue on another 1.4 miles and TURN RIGHT on FR#25, then TURN LEFT after .7 mile to get to Little Missouri Falls (**34.42306, -93.92053**).

Emergency contact: Montgomery County Sheriff, 870–867–3151 Dogs are OK

Blaylock Creek Falls – 31′

Next to the road, no hike GPS **34.37091, -93.92258**

Bard Springs Falls

100 yards from vehicle GPS **34.39083, -94.01011**

Trailhead Falls – 21′

Next to the road GPS **34.39593, -94.02123**

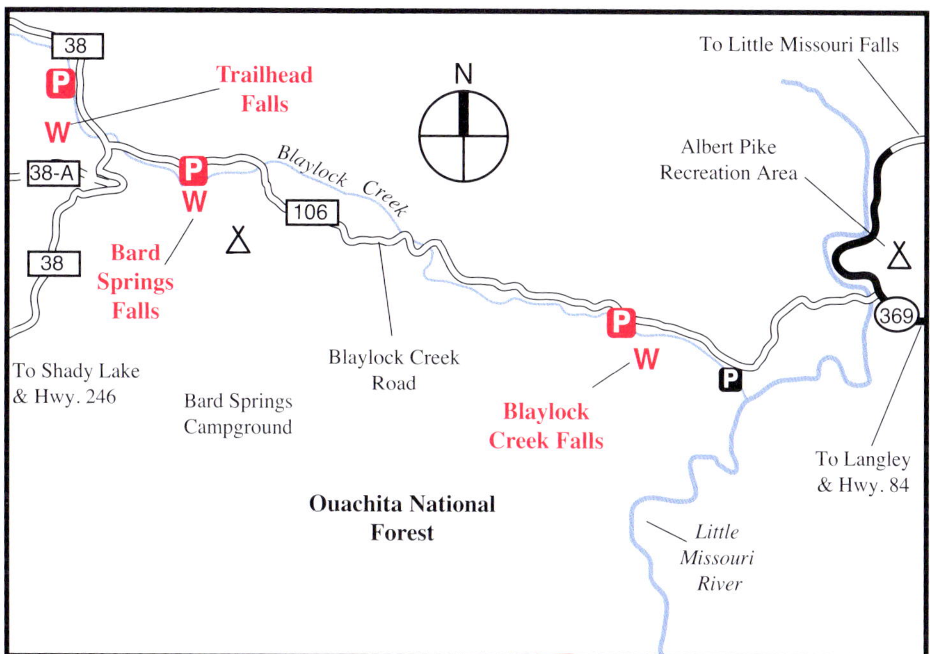

BLAYLOCK CREEK FALLS. This is the first of three waterfalls that pour into Blaylock Creek many miles apart. All are easy to get to.

From Langley (west from Glenwood on Hwy. 70 and then west on Hwy. 84) take Hwy. 369 six miles to Albert Pike Recreation Area. TURN LEFT onto FR#106/Blaylock Creek Road and go 3.2 miles then TURN LEFT and PARK (**34.37190, -93.92337**). Follow the road back to the left/downstream along the creek just about a hundred yards and the waterfall will be just across the creek.

Emergency contact: Montgomery County Sheriff, 870–867–3151 Dogs are OK

BARD SPRINGS FALLS. Continue another 6.4 miles and turn LEFT into the Bard Springs Recreation Area (**34.39095, -94.01083**). This is one of two dams and four structures here that remain from a Civilian Conservation Corps project in 1936—AMAZING rock work as usual! This dam is on the east end of the picnic area near the bathhouse (the other dam is upstream to the west).

TRAILHEAD FALLS. This is the third waterfall that pours into Blaylock Creek and takes its name from the wilderness trailhead nearby. It is beautiful and lush in the springtime with tons of wildflowers all around.

From Bard Springs, continue on FR#106 for another half mile and TURN RIGHT

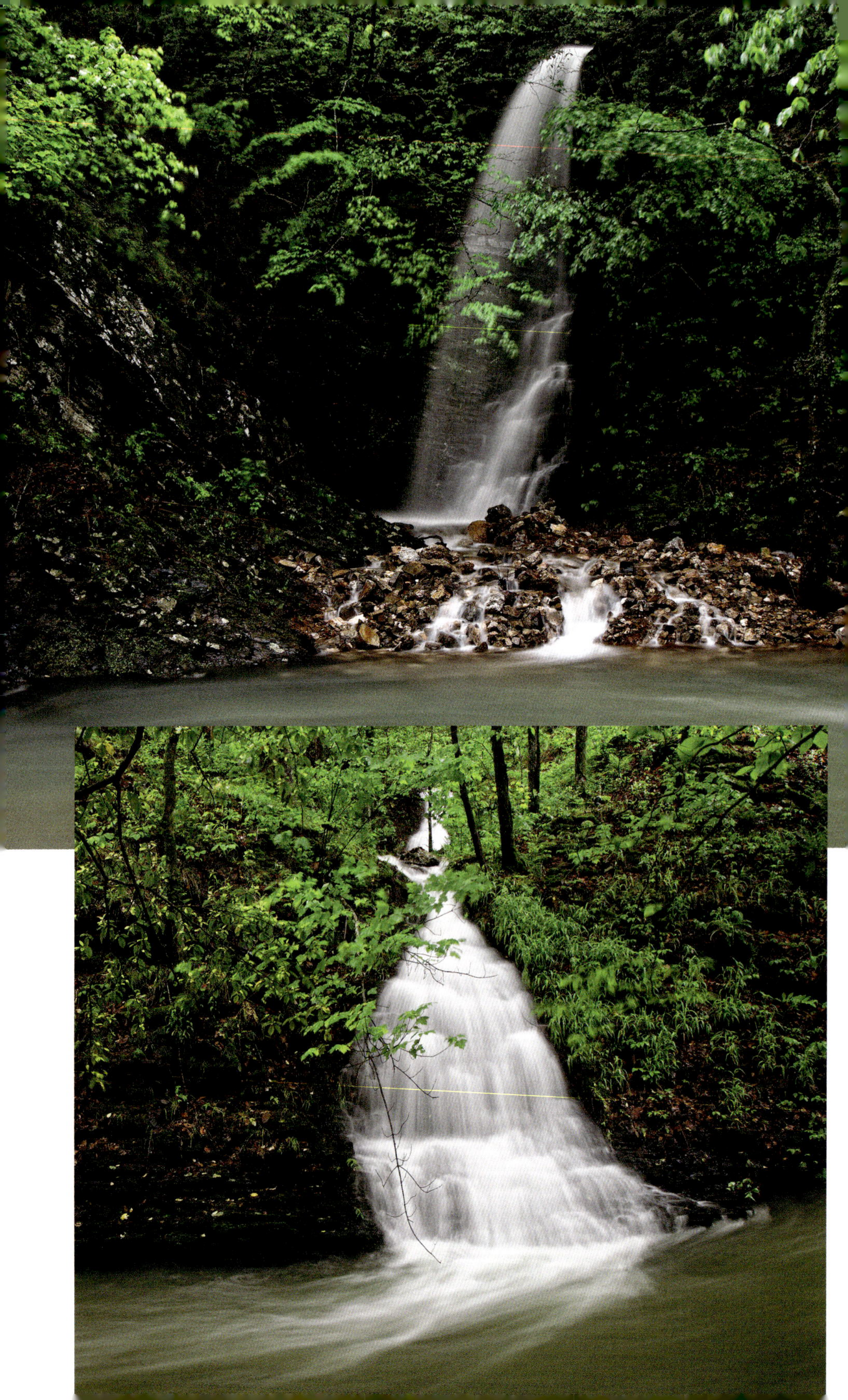

onto FR#38. Go less than a quarter mile and you should see the waterfall on the left, just across the creek. Either PARK there along the road or drive on just a little ways to the Caney Creek Wilderness Trailhead and park **(34.39685, -94.02243)**.

Emergency contact: Polk County Sheriff, 479–394–2511 Dogs are OK

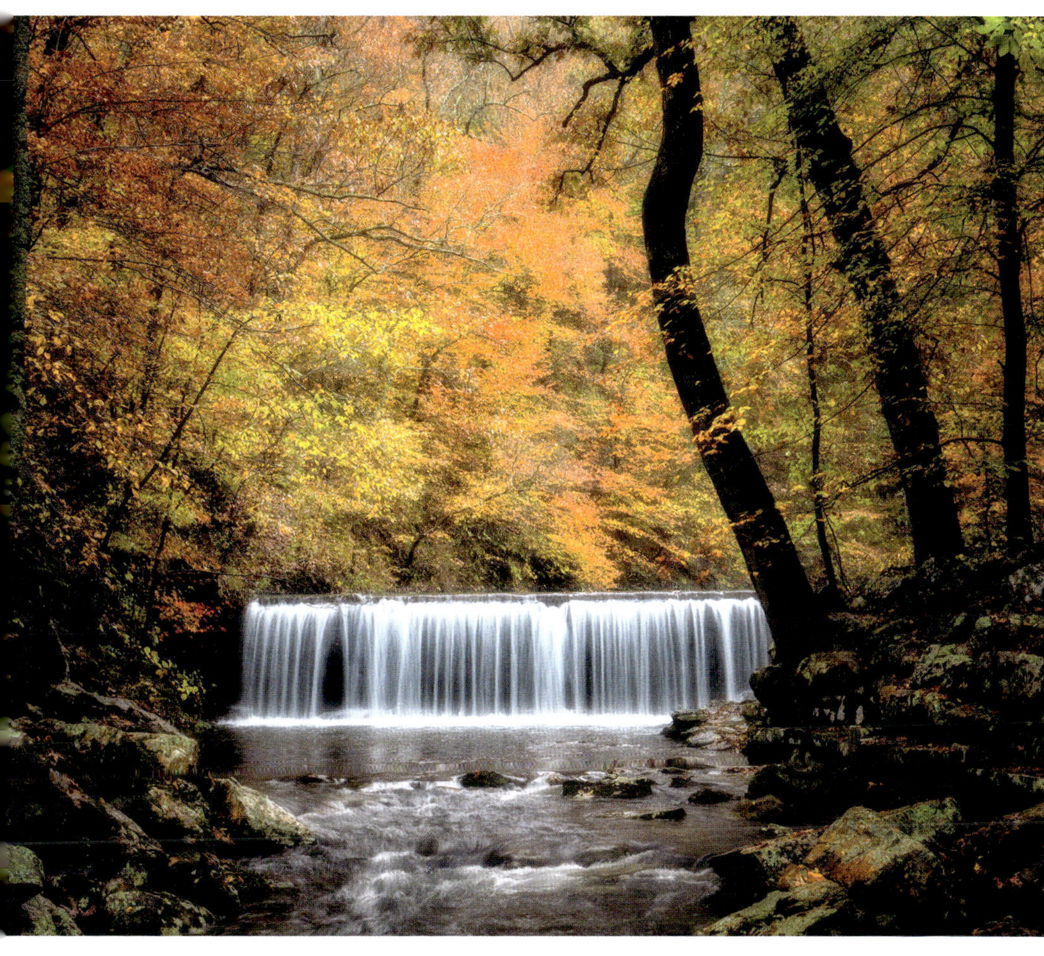

d Springs Falls (above), **Blaylock Creek Falls** (above left), **Trailhead Falls** (lower left)

Katy Falls – 12′

9.6 mile loop, medium backpack or difficult dayhike, GPS helpful

GPS **34.39692, -94.08030**

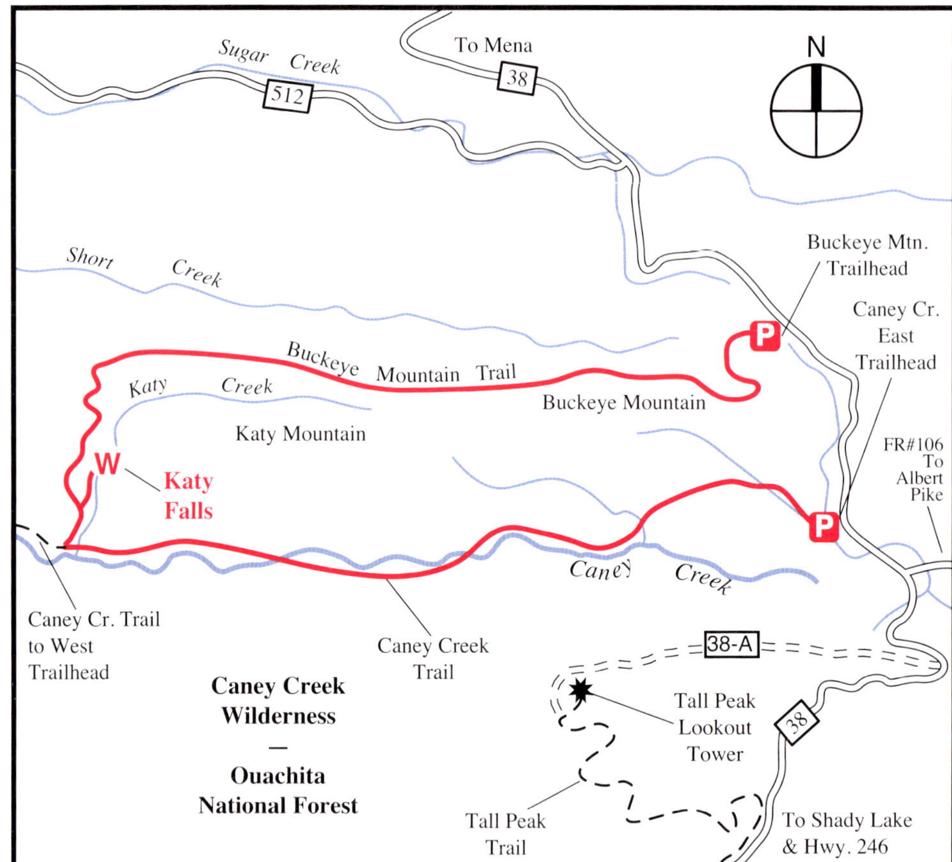

KATY FALLS. The 14,433-acre Caney Creek Wilderness area is the oldest one in Arkansas, and contains the first backpacking trail built in the state. When I taught backpacking 101 at the University of Arkansas back in the mid-1970's we used to come to Caney Creek for our weekend hikes, and Katy Falls was always one of the highlights. It is a pretty small falls, but well worth the side trip if you are hiking Caney. My favorite trip here now is to make a loop, starting with the Buckeye Mountain Trail, which has some terrific views, and coming out via the Caney Creek Trail. It's a great overnight trip, or a very long dayhike. The alternate route is shorter, but less scenic. It starts/ends at the East Caney Creek Trailhead and follows the Caney Creek Trail to the falls and back out via the same route.

To get to the Buckeye Mountain Trailhead for the big loop, take Hwy. 246 west from Athens a couple miles and TURN RIGHT onto FR#38 towards Shady Lake. Continue past Shady Lake, past the turnoff up to Tall Peak, past the turnoff to Bard Springs/Albert Pike, past the East Caney Creek Trailhead (park here for the alternate route), and continue on up to the top of the hill and PARK on the left at the Buckeye Mountain Trailhead after about eight or nine miles from Hwy. 246 **(34.40884, -94.02818)**.

The Buckeye Mountain Trail heads out into the woods and climbs gradually up and around Buckeye Mountain. It enters a high land of rocky outcrops, giant trees, and some

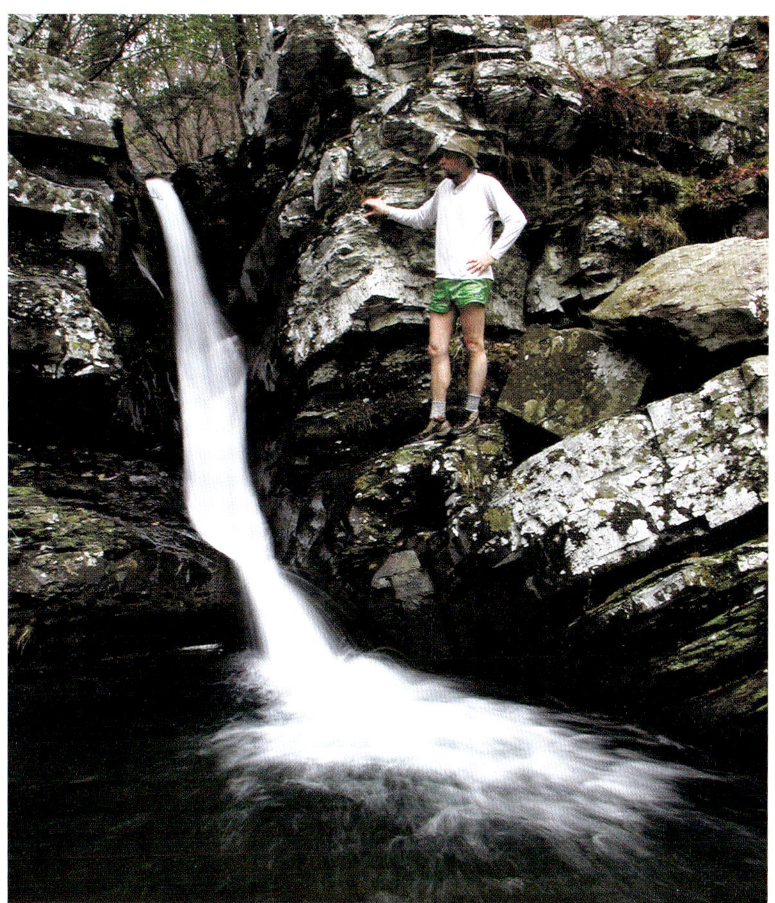

Katy Falls (it looks bigger in real life!)

terrific views. The trail does a lot of up-and-downing as it follows along near the top of a long ridge, dodging those many rock outcrops, knobs, and various other geological features. You'll find a lot of wildflowers in the open areas here in the spring and early summer. And did I say great views? The hills just seem to go on forever.

At 3.4 the trail TURNS LEFT, leaves the ridgetop, and begins a rapid descent down into the Katy and Caney Creek drainages. Just before you hit bottom at 4.5, TURN LEFT on a little spur trail. This runs alongside Katy Creek a couple hundred yards to the falls. There are a number of good campsites along Caney Creek, which is just down the main trail at 4.6, but this area really gets pounded with campers and many great sites have been closed.

To continue with the loop, TURN LEFT at the bottom of the hill at 4.6 when you hit the Caney Creek Trail. That hike out to the trailhead is 3.9 miles and follows along Caney Creek upstream most of the way, crossing it a couple of times. There is one good climb along the north side of the creek, and one last climb out of the drainage, and then you drop on down to the East Caney Creek Trailhead at 8.5. TURN LEFT and follow the forest road 1.1 miles back up the hill to complete the loop.

To do the alternate route (7.8 miles total), PARK at the East Caney Creek Trailhead **(34.39685, -94.02243)** and hike the Caney Creek Trail 3.9 miles to the falls and back out the same way. You will cross the creek several times each way, so plan on wet feet.

Emergency contact: Polk County Sheriff, 479–394–2511 Dogs are OK

Shady Lake Cascade – 27′

View from your car, GPS not needed

GPS **34.35960, -94.02810**

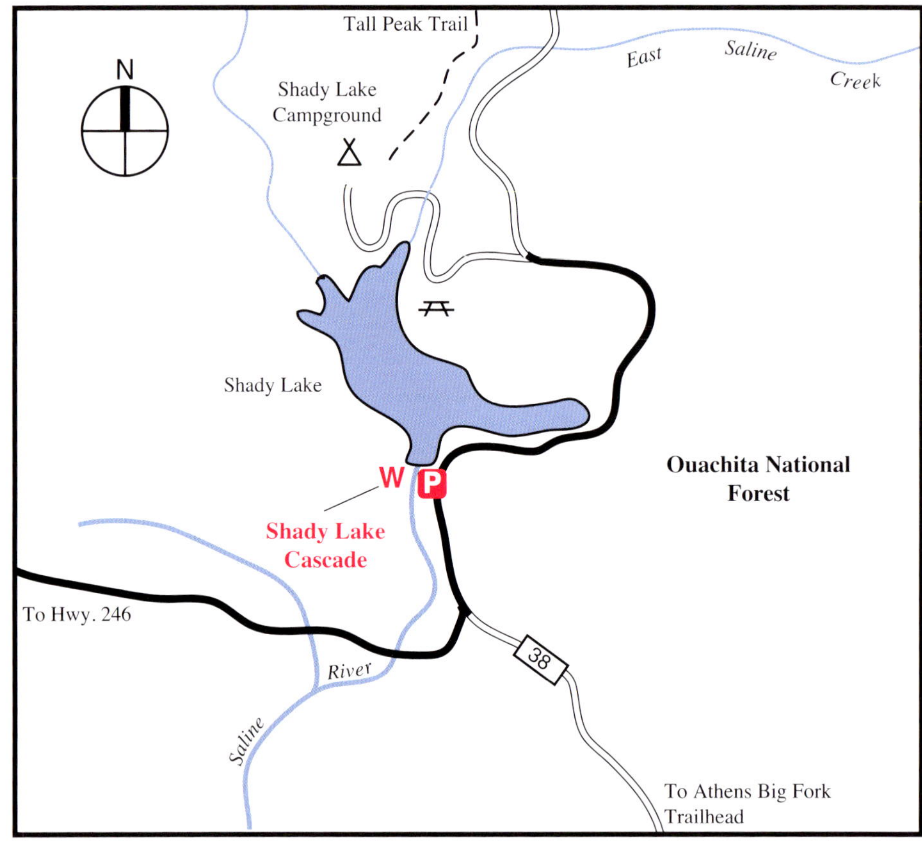

SHADY LAKE CASCADE. This really neat cascade is located just off to the side of the Shady Lake dam and spillway. There is a small pulloff that overlooks the spot, so no need to even hike in order to see it. Lots of campsites at the lake, plus a picnic area, swimming area, and a trailhead for the Tall Peak Trail.

To get to Shady Lake take Hwy. 246 west out of Athens 5.0 miles and TURN RIGHT onto CR694 (paved). Go 1.4 miles to Shady Lake (bear left at FR38) and pull off and PARK on the left at the overlook **(34.35981, -94.02754)**. You can see the cascade, the spillway, and the emerald creek below from there.

While you are in the area you might want to take the drive up to Tall Peak (or hike the trail up to it that begins in the campground)—just continue on FR#38 for several miles and turn left when you get to the top of the hill. There is an old historic lookout tower there. This little hilltop is absolutely *covered* with spiderworts in the spring!

Emergency contact: Polk County Sheriff, 479–394–2511 Dogs are OK

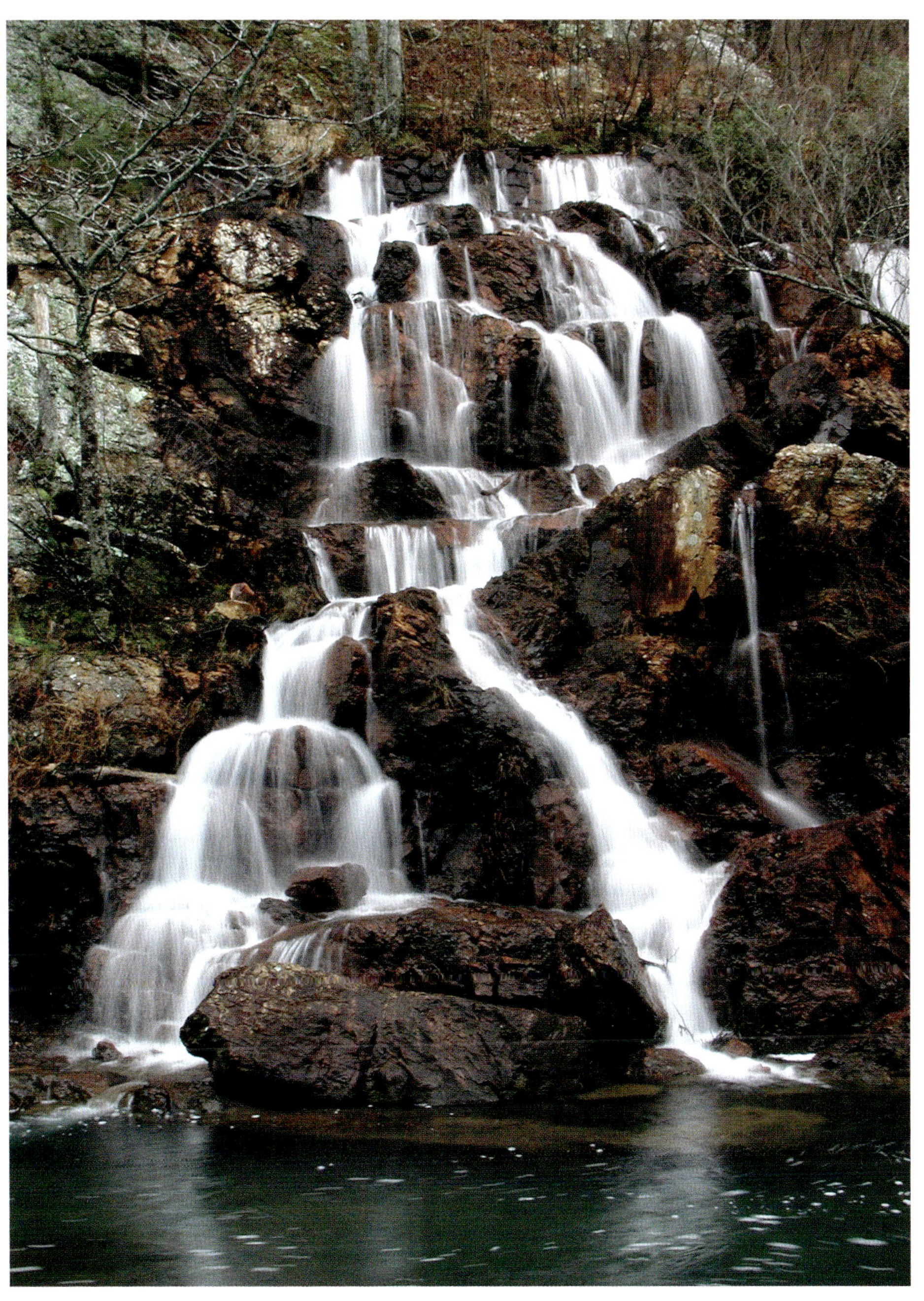

Shady Lake Cascade

Cossatot Falls – 33′

Up to 1.0 mile roundtrip, easy/medium hike, GPS not needed

GPS **34.31947, -94.22677**

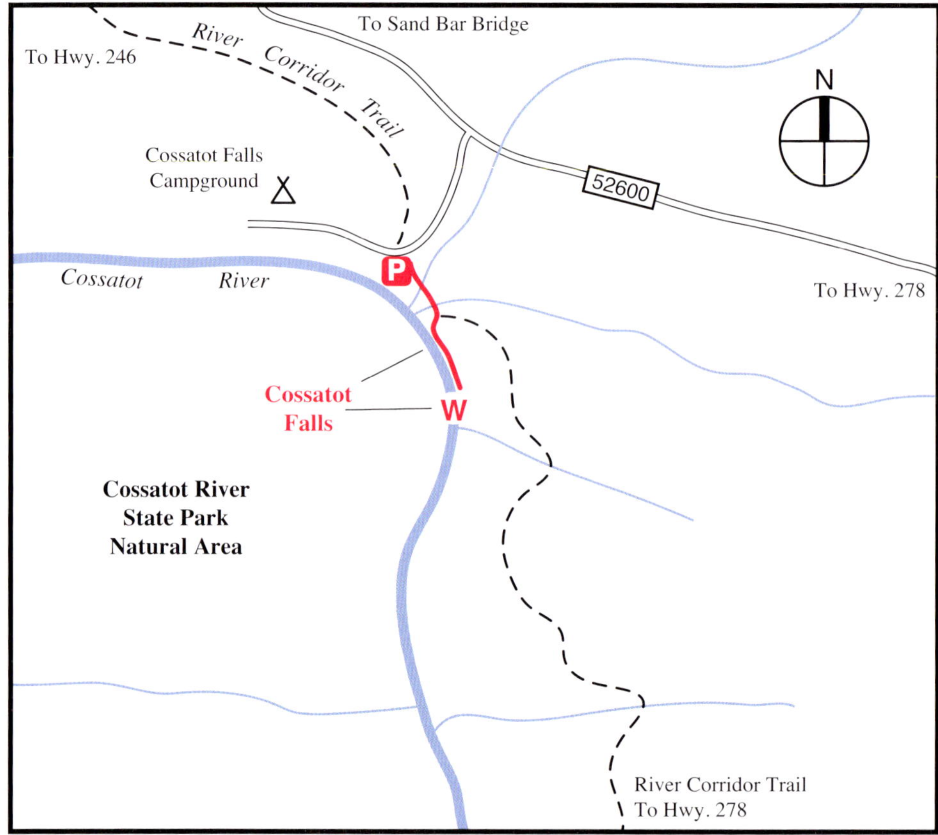

COSSATOT FALLS. Wow, this is one incredible spot that you must see! It has been long known as one of the best kayak playgrounds around, but more and more folks are discovering it for the pure scenic beauty it possesses. It is not really a waterfall, but rather a quarter-mile long series of cascades that roar and splash through many boulders that have been polished smooth by the powerful action of the Cossatot River (the name means "skull crusher," and it lives up to that name quite well). This area is terrific to visit even when the water is low—the sculptured rocks are really something to see, plus there is a great swimming hole or two downstream. The park is jointly managed by Arkansas State Parks and Arkansas Natural Heritage Commission, and contains 11 miles of the river and more than 5,000 acres. All of this is surrounded by paper company land, so you will see lots of tree farms being clearcut as you come and go, but you won't see any of this from the river itself. There will be future development at the park, including more hiking trails and a nice Visitor/Education Center. For now there is primitive camping available at several sites, including where we park to visit the falls, and a 14-mile long hiking trail.

To get to the parking area from Glenwood, take Hwy. 70 west and TURN RIGHT onto Hwy. 84 to Langley, Athens and Umpire, then TURN RIGHT onto Hwy. 278 at Umpire. Go 6.6 miles and TURN RIGHT onto paper company road #52600 (gravel—watch for log

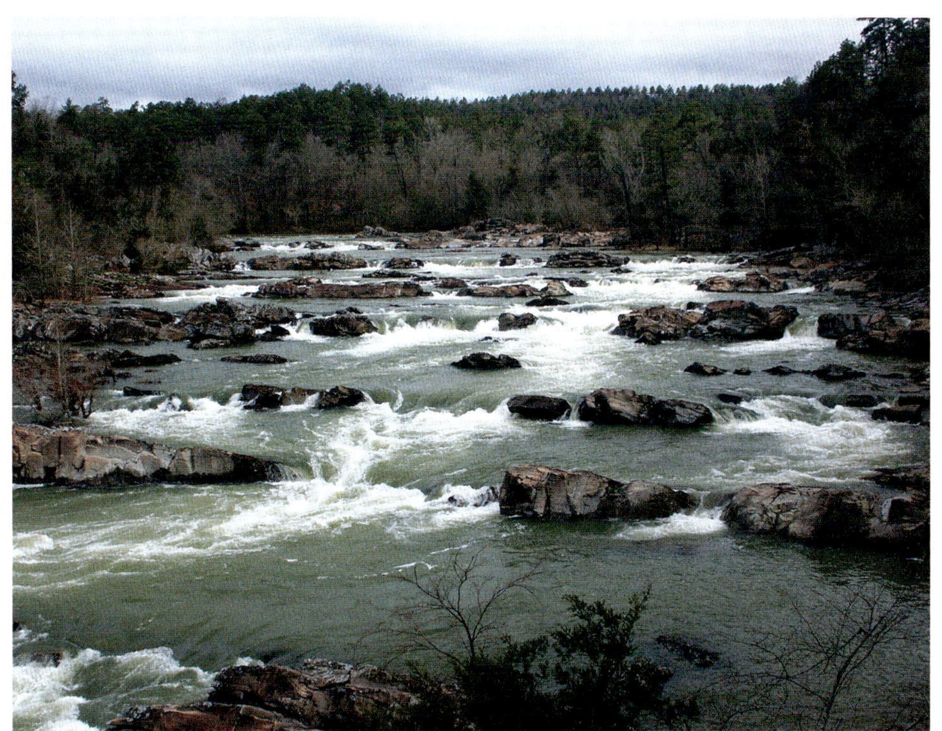

Cossatot Falls

trucks!). Go 4.6 miles and TURN LEFT into the Cossatot Falls Recreation Area and park at the restroom **(34.32139, -94.22768)** . By the way, as you drive along please remember that we are all consumers of trees every single day of our lives (they make toilet paper and houses from them you know), and tree farming is one of the best ways to produce enough to keep up with our demand! You can also get to the falls area via Hwy. 246 to the north, but the road is longer and rougher—the turnoff is located between Athens and Vandervoort.

NOTE: If the water levels are high, you may need to take a different road off of the highway. Instead of turning right onto road #52600 from Hwy. 278, CONTINUE south on the highway, across a bridge over Baker Creek, to the next road, which will be #52200 (both roads are signed for Cossatot River interior access). TURN RIGHT on this road and follow it for about 3.5 miles and then TURN LEFT onto #52600, then LEFT into the campground. This route will take you around a ford of Baker Creek that might be flooded.

There isn't a good way to construct an actual trail along the river to see the falls area, but there is a path of sorts that you can follow from the parking area. How difficult/safe this route will be depends a great deal on the level of the river. There is also a hiking trail that leaves the parking area and climbs the hills above the river, and you can get some views of the falls area from the trail during leaf-off periods. This is the river-length trail in the park that goes upstream from Hwy. 246 and downstream to Hwy. 278.

To view the falls up close, take the trail from the parking area across the two monster trail bridges. At the far end of the second bridge the hiking trail goes to the left and immediately climbs up the hill. You want to stay on the level and GO STRAIGHT ahead to the banks of the river. From that point on it is a scramble to find your way. At some point downstream your route will be blocked by a wall of rock and you will have to turn back.

Emergency contact: Howard County Sheriff, 479–845–2626 Dogs are OK

Panther Bluff Falls – 31′

Short hike from car, GPS not needed

GPS **34.19573, -94.08400**

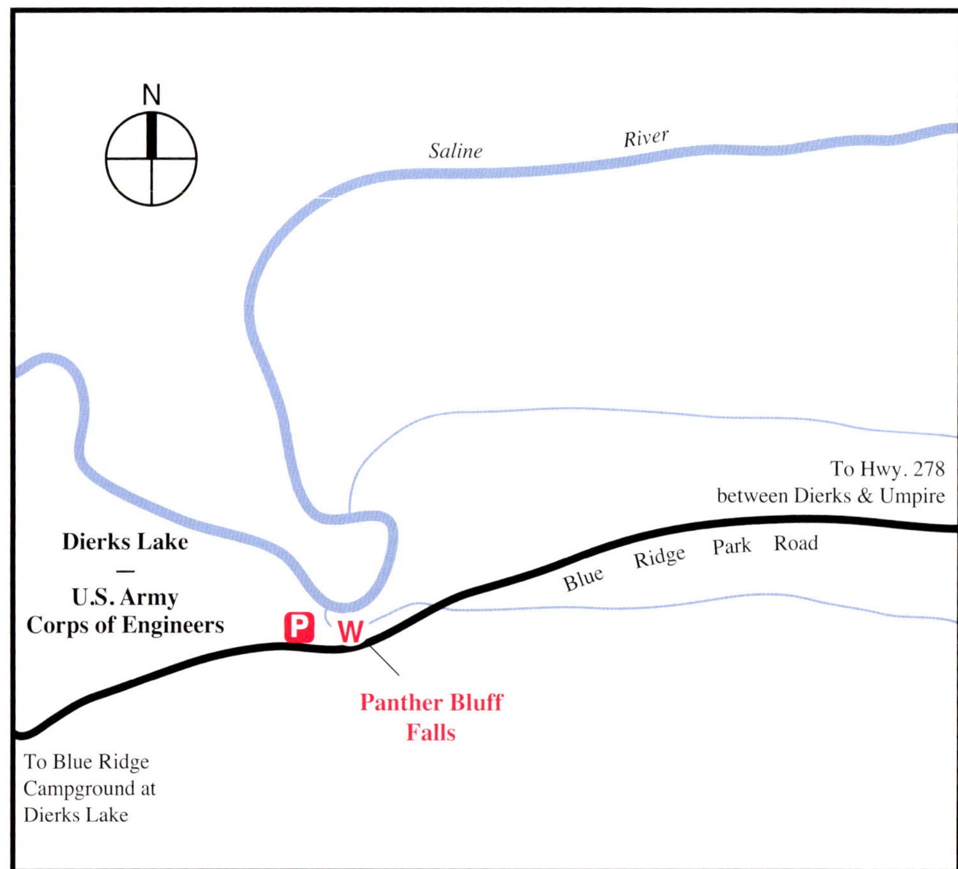

PANTHER BLUFF FALLS. I was somewhat surprised the day I pulled over to see this waterfall for the first time—it's a very nice little waterfall right there next to the road! And it is taller than most waterfalls in the Ouachitas. There is also a smaller falls just below this one, but the scramble down to see it is kind of dangerous, and you might end up in the Saline River if you slip. (I can speak from personal experience on that one—just before I took the photo at right I slipped and fell over the lower bluff!)

From Athens take Hwy. 84 six miles to Umpire and TURN LEFT onto Hwy. 278. Go 7.0 miles and TURN RIGHT onto Blue Ridge Park Road (this will be just after you cross over the Saline River bridge). Go 2.2 miles and PARK on the right. The waterfall is located just down the hill to the right. There is a small creek there running alongside the highway that spills over Panther Bluff, which is made up of many thin layers of shale. Right down below is the Saline River (it is actually considered the upper end of Dierks Lake at this point).

From Dierks go east on Hwy. 70 about three miles and TURN LEFT onto Hwy. 278. After four miles or so and just before you cross the Saline River Bridge, TURN LEFT onto Blue Ridge Park Road, then go 2.2 miles and PARK (**34.19573, -94.08400**).

Emergency contact: Howard County Sheriff, 479–845–2626 Dogs are OK

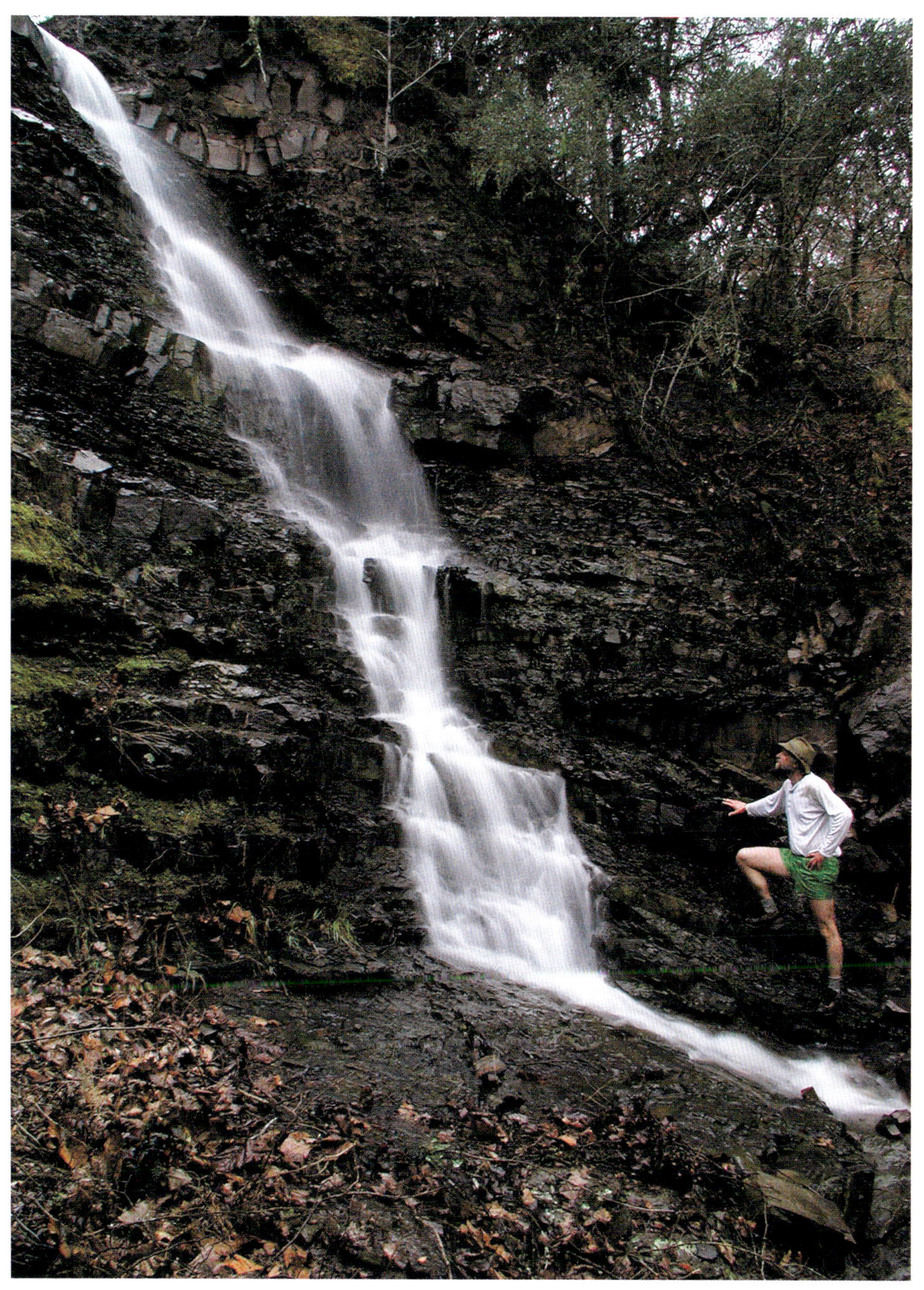

Panther Bluff Falls

Falls Creek Falls –12′

1.4 miles roundtrip, easy hike, GPS not needed

GPS **34.42532, -92.91137**

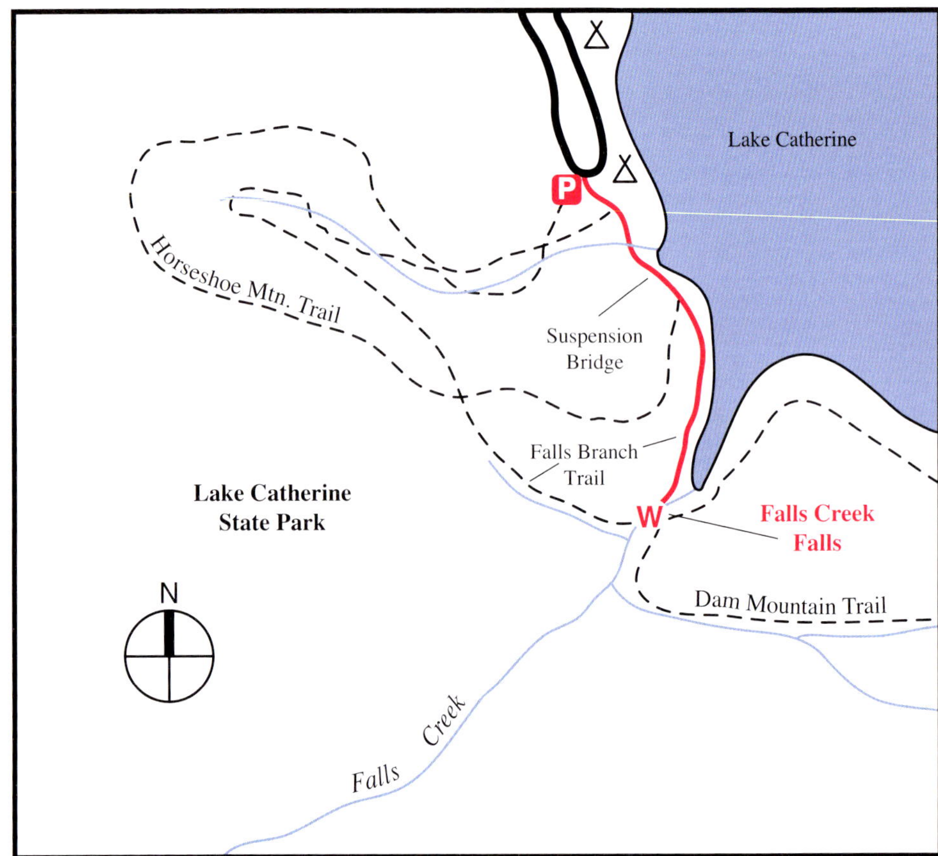

FALLS CREEK FALLS. You've probably seen this waterfall in dozens of photographs—it is one of the favorite falls used to advertise Arkansas State Parks. The hike to the falls is an easy stroll along the lake shore. If you are feeling energetic, you can hike several different loop trails that connect with this one for a total hike of 6.3 miles. But we'll just stick with the short hike to the base of the falls and back. By the way, the name of the creek is Falls "Creek" and the waterfall is Falls "Creek" Falls, but the name of the trail is Falls "Branch" Trail. Also, they tell me another name for the waterfall is Devil's Bathtub. I don't know what the fascination with the term "Devil" is in relation to waterfalls, but we have several with that reference in Arkansas (Devil's Den, Devils Canyon, Devils Fork). I suspect some of it may be that the watercourses that go along with the falls are very tough.

From Hot Springs, take Hwy. 270 east and TURN RIGHT onto Carpenter Dam Road (Hwy. 28), then LEFT on Hwy. 290, then LEFT again on Hwy. 171 and follow it all the way into the park. From Little Rock, take I–30 south to exit 97 near Malvern, then go north on Hwy. 171 until you reach the park. The trailhead is located at the back of the park, just past the amphitheater (**34.43145, -92.91356**). This is a fully-equipped campground with plenty of sites here, but you may find the constant drone of the powerhouse across the lake a bit annoying.

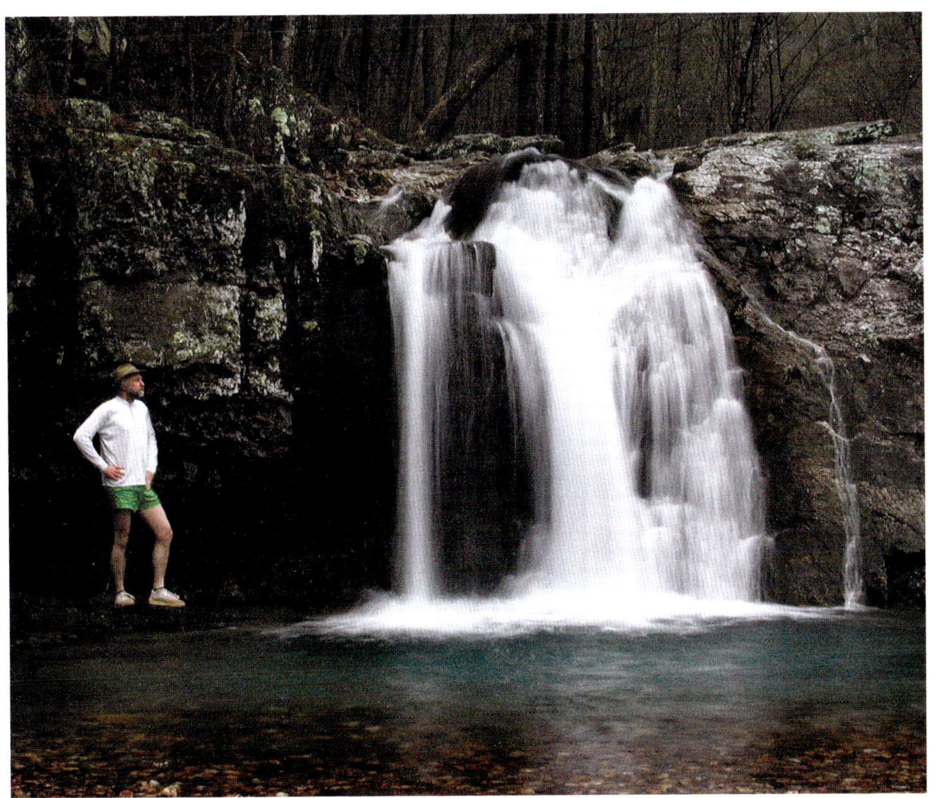

Falls Creek Falls

There are several trails that take off from the trailhead, but the one you want is the Falls Creek Trail that goes down near the lake shore. It heads out through some nice big trees, crosses a road near the camping area, and goes over a foot bridge—we are following the white blazes. (There are actually three different trails that share the first part of this route, so you will see different colored blazes on the trees). The trail begins to follow the lake shore, then at .4 crosses a nice suspension bridge. Just beyond it we come to an intersection— continue STRAIGHT AHEAD and along the lake.

Soon the trail curves around to the right and heads up into a small cove, and to the waterfall at .7. The trails continue from this point, one crossing the creek above the falls and looping around a hill and back to the same point, another trail follows a little stream (or "branch") uphill and then eventually back to the trailhead. You can take your pick of them all and spend a good part of your day hiking here, or simply head back the way you came and go find another waterfall! Dogs are OK

Emergency: Hot Spring County Sheriff, 501–332–3671; Park office, 501–844–4176.

Blocker Creek Cascade –17′

1.0 mile roundtrip, easy hike plus medium bushwhack, GPS helpful

GPS **34.73222, -93.21183**

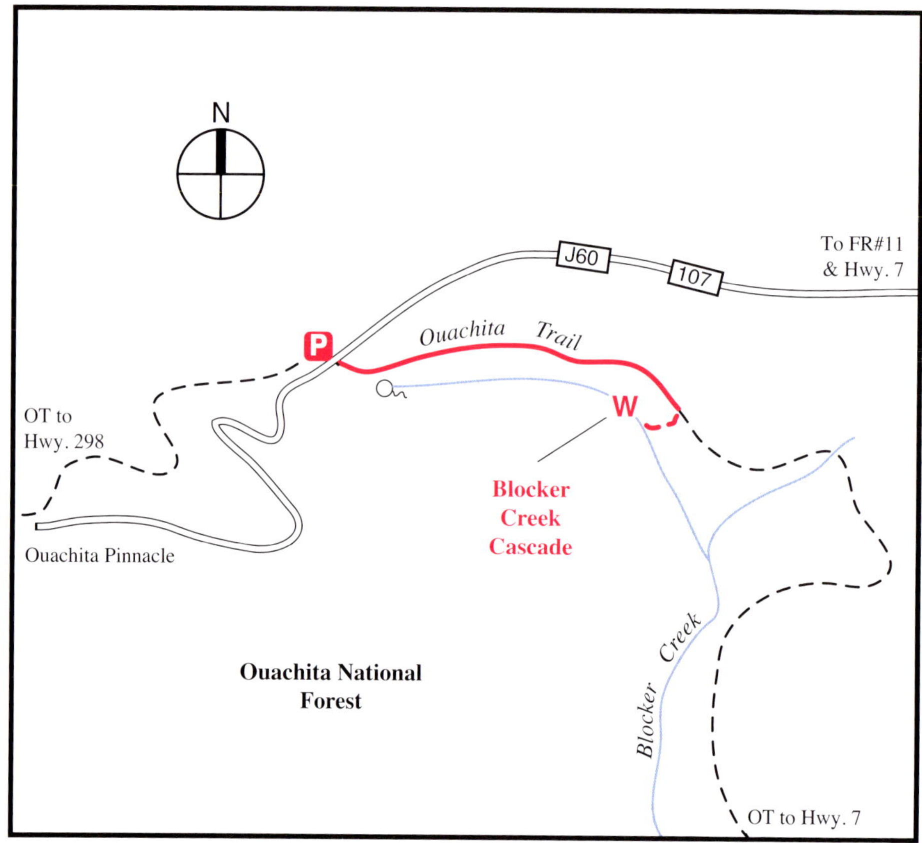

BLOCKER CREEK CASCADE. There aren't many waterfalls high in the Ouachitas, but this is a nice treat tucked away in the extreme headwaters of Blocker Creek. And once you make the drive up to Blue Ouachita Mountain to get to it, you can drive just a little bit farther and take in the view from Ouachita Pinnacle.

To get to the parking area from Jessieville, take Hwy. 7 north about seven miles, past the Iron Springs Recreation Area, and about .5 mile past the big parking lot to the Ouachita Trail, then TURN LEFT onto FR#11 (gravel). This turnoff is located just across the highway from the Winona Forest Drive (FR#132) that heads back to the east and is a beautiful drive along the southern boundary of the Flatside Wilderness area and connects to Hwy. 9.

From Hwy. 7 go about 6.5 miles to FR#154 (just before the pipeline crossing on FR#11). TURN LEFT on FR#154 for .3 miles, then after crossing a low water bridge you will come to a T intersection. TURN RIGHT on FR#779 for .5 miles, then TURN LEFT on #J60. Follow this road 3.6 miles up the hill (it becomes FR#107) and PARK where the Ouachita Trail crosses the road **(34.73306, -93.21900)**. NOTE: parts of FR#107 may be closed.

Get on the Ouachita Trail (which is an old roadbed at this point) and head south (to the left). You will be dropping gradually down the hillside and should see and hear a small

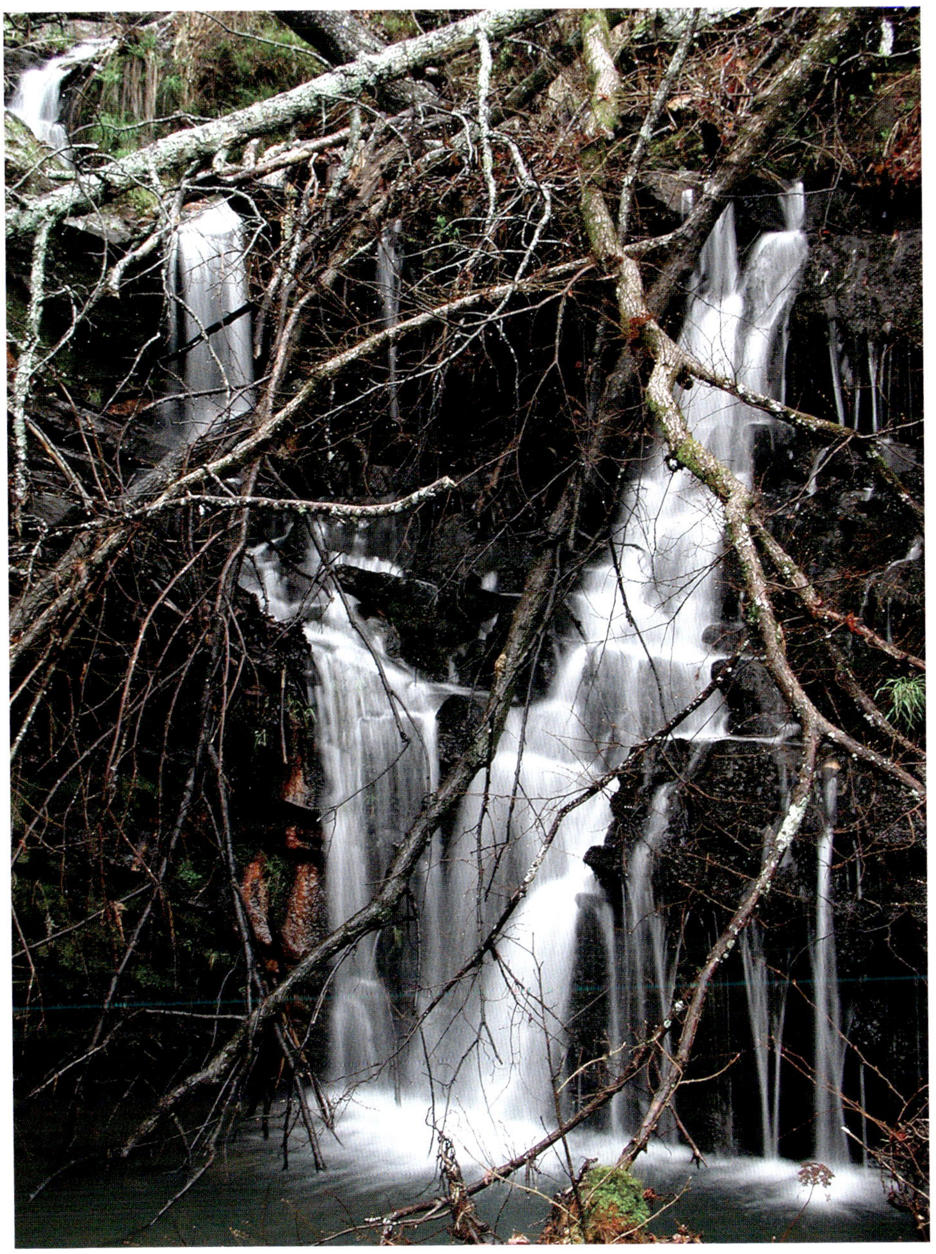

Blocker Creek Cascade

(This photo was taken in 2002 and shows the extreme damage from recent ice storms—the view should be better in the future!)

stream down the hill on your right—the waterfall is located on that stream. If you don't have a GPS, your best bet is to simply leave the trail after a couple hundred yards, get down to the stream, and follow it until you come to the waterfall—only about .25 mile from where you parked. If you have a GPS, stay on the trail until you come above the falls, then bushwhack down to it. The hillside is very steep!

Emergency contact: Garland County Sheriff, 501–622–3690 Dogs are OK

Forked Mountain Falls –10′

1.6 miles roundtrip, easy hike, GPS helpful

GPS **34.85497, -93.03075**

Twist Cascade –12′

Add 1.6 miles to above distance, medium bushwhack, GPS helpful

GPS **34.84935, -93.03567**

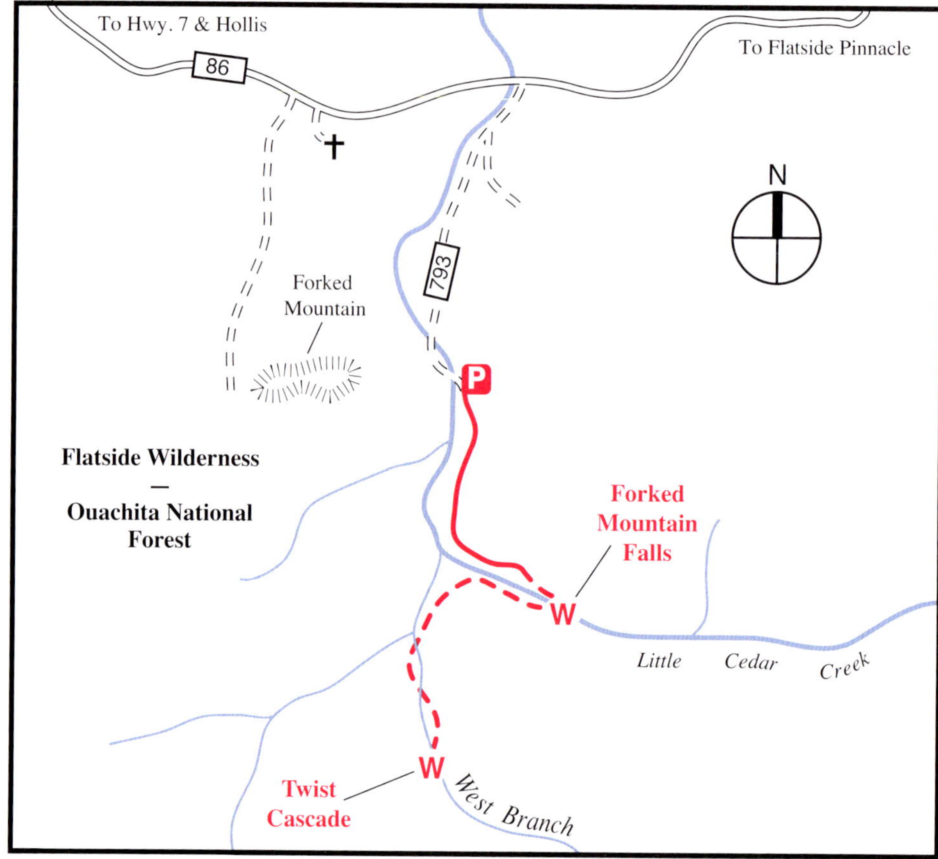

FORKED MOUNTAIN FALLS/TWIST CASCADE. Here are a couple of nice little falls in the shadow of Forked Mountain, which is my favorite mountain in Arkansas.

To get to the parking area, take FR#86 (gravel) east from Hwy. 7 (the turn is located just south of Hollis, and north of Jessieville). Go 4.7 miles and TURN RIGHT onto FR#793. Go .9 mile (cross the creek twice) and PARK at a locked gate at the wilderness boundary (**34.86251, -93.03323**).

Hike along the closed road, up and over a couple of humps, then veer off to the RIGHT on an old road trace at about .7—this old trace will take you over to **Forked Mountain Falls.** There is a nice pool of water there—hum, perhaps a quick dip?

To get to the cascade, either cross the stream or go downstream and cross on an old road trace that has become really grown up. Follow this trace across level ground until it comes to a small creek—cross there and stay on the old trace as it curves back to the left, then cross the stream again. The trace swings back to the right and uphill a little and comes alongside **Twist Cascade** which you will be able to see and hear below to the right.

Emergency contact: Saline County Sheriff, 501–303–5603 Dogs are OK

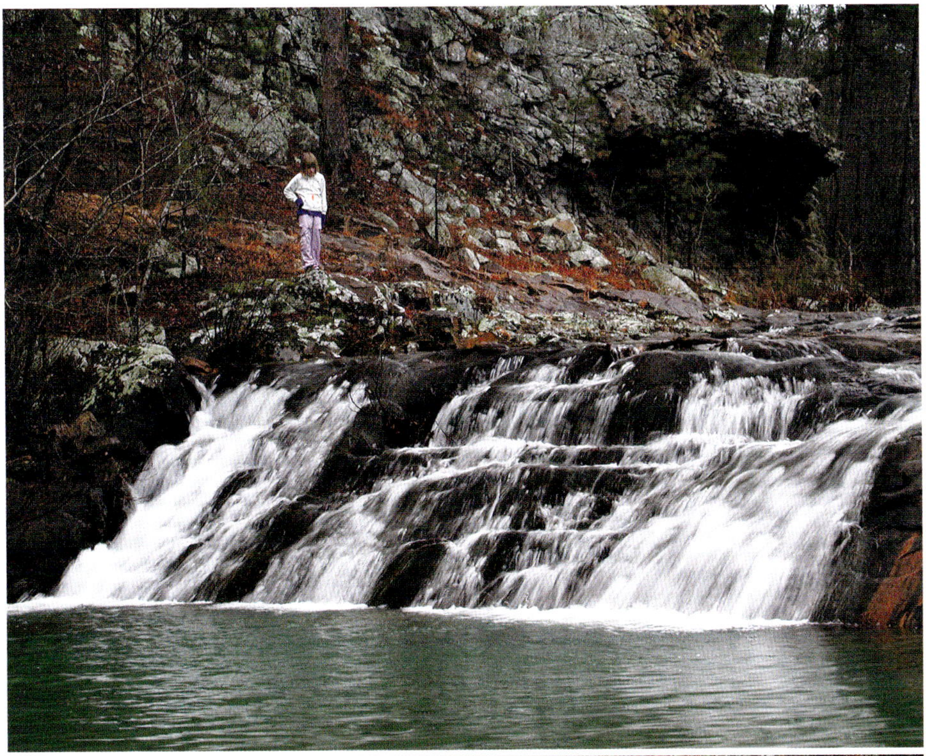

Forked Mountain Falls
(above, with our
daughter, Amber)

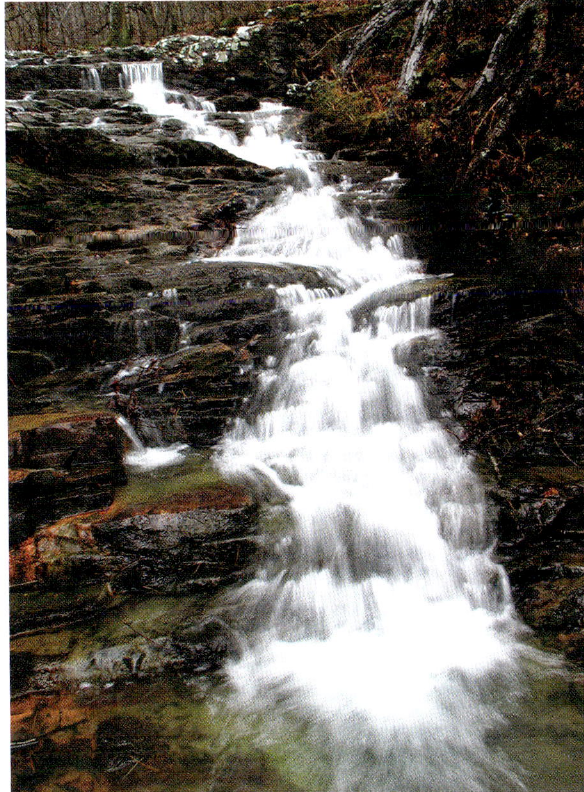

Twist Cascade (right)

Brown Creek Cascade – 8′

.5 mile roundtrip, easy hike, GPS not needed

GPS **34.86535, -92.88921**

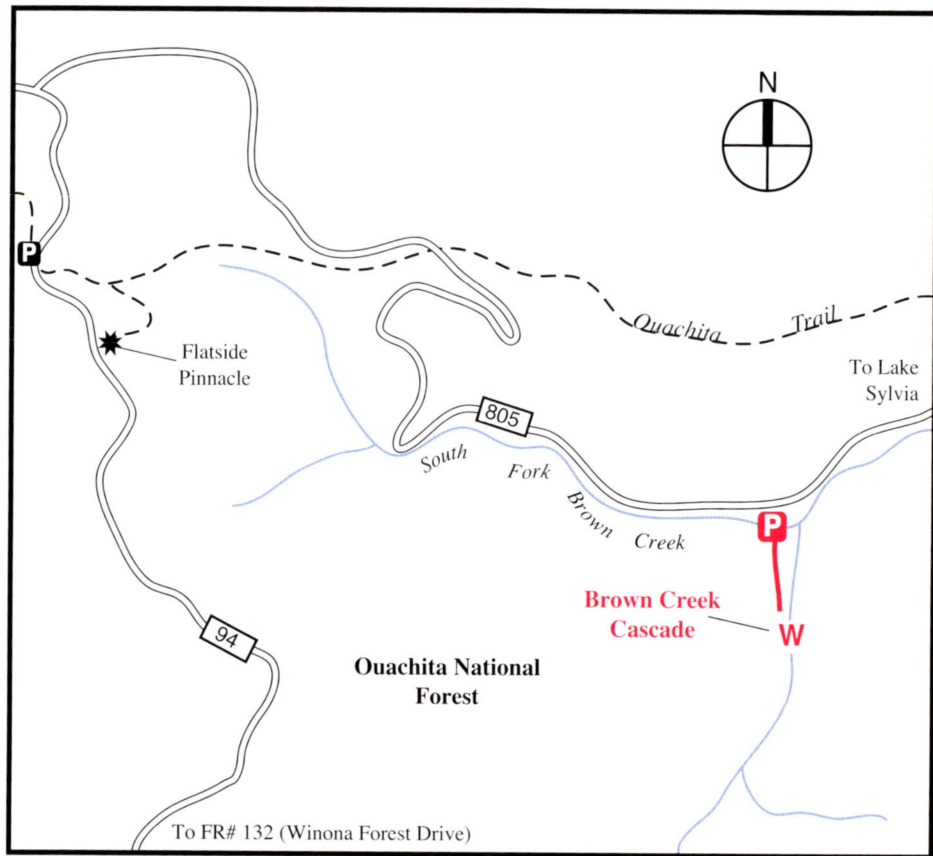

BROWN CREEK CASCADE. There are hundreds of little cascades like this one in the Ozarks, but not many of them in the Ouachitas. I decided to include this one in the guide because it is so easy to get to, and is close to Little Rock. It will be a big disappointment to most waterfall chasers, but it is actually a nice little cascade and a great destination for first-time waterfall hunters. It is especially great for kids as the hike to it is easy, and the cascade is "just their size." It's also a nice stop on the way to Flatside Pinnacle to view the sunset. Look for lots of wildflowers along the way in April and May.

To get to the parking spot TURN WEST onto Hwy. 324 (paved) from Hwy. 9 towards Lake Sylvia (this turn is just north of Williams Junction of Hwys 9 & 10, and south of Perryville). Go 1.7 miles and TURN RIGHT onto FR#805/Brown Creek Road (gravel). Go 5.3 miles and PARK in a little camp area on the left **(34.86850, -92.89002)**.

There is an old road trace (closed) that takes off from this camp area and immediately crosses Brown Creek. Stay on this road trace just a couple of hundred yards and you will come to the little cascade on the left.

If you want a quick hike up to one of the best sunset views in Arkansas, continue along FR#805 another 2.8 miles then TURN LEFT on FR#94 and take it on up to a big parking area at the base of Flatside Pinnacle. Park there and take the Ouachita Trail to the east,

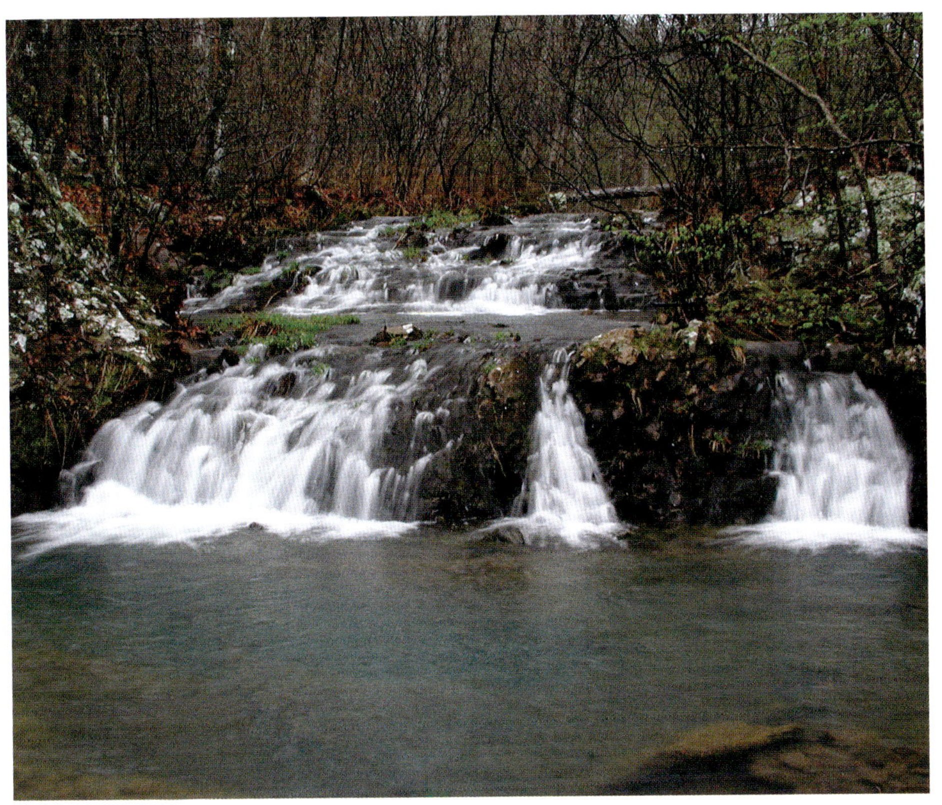

Brown Creek Cascade

up the hill a quarter mile, to an intersection with a spur trail that swings on up to the right and ends at the top edge of Flatside Pinnacle. There isn't too much room up there and the footing can be tricky, but the view to the west is wonderful!

Emergency contact: Perry County Sheriff, 501–889–2333 Dogs are OK

WATERFALL INDEX

NOTES 1

NOTES 2

NOTES 3

NOTES 4

Legend For All Maps (distance scale varies)

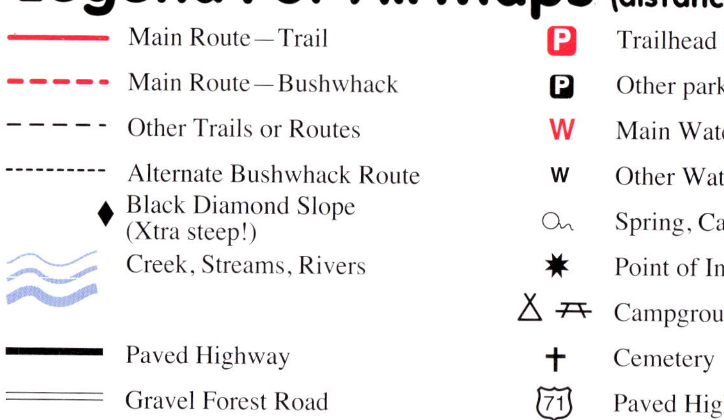

Main Route—Trail
Main Route—Bushwhack
Other Trails or Routes
Alternate Bushwhack Route
Black Diamond Slope (Xtra steep!)
Creek, Streams, Rivers
Paved Highway
Gravel Forest Road
Jeep Road
COMMUNITY/City, Building

P Trailhead Parking
P Other parking
W Main Waterfall
W Other Waterfall
Spring, Cave
Point of Interest
Campground, Picnic Area
Cemetery
71 Paved Highway
23 341 State/County Road-Paved/Gravel
1003 Gravel Forest Road

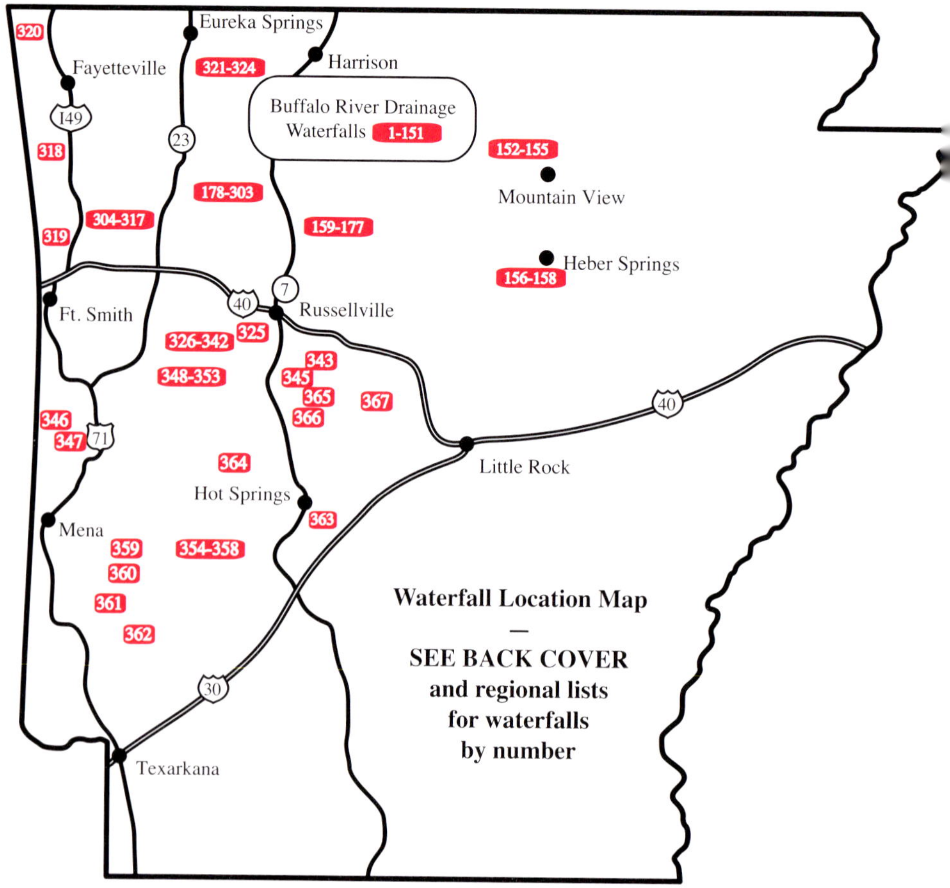

Eureka Springs
Harrison
Fayetteville
321-324
320
149
23
Buffalo River Drainage Waterfalls 1-151
152-155
318
Mountain View
178-303
304-317
159-177
319
Heber Springs
156-158
40
7
Ft. Smith
Russellville
325
326-342
343
348-353
345
365
367
366
346
347
71
40
Little Rock
364
Hot Springs
363
Mena
359
354-358
360
361
362
30
Texarkana

Waterfall Location Map

—

SEE BACK COVER and regional lists for waterfalls by number